(ATM) Automatid Teller machine

Discovering Computers 2005

A Gateway to Information

Web Enhanced

Complete

ch 9 = 502
ch 10 = 550
ch 11 = 610

Read Chapter: 10

516 - 525

Discovering Computers 2005

A Gateway to Information
Web Enhanced

Complete

Gary B. Shelly
Thomas J. Cashman
Misty E. Vermaat

Contributing Authors
Jeffrey J. Quasney
Susan L. Sebok
Timothy J. Walker
Jeffrey J. Webb

THOMSON
COURSE TECHNOLOGY

COURSE TECHNOLOGY
25 THOMSON PLACE
BOSTON MA 02210

SHELLY CASHMAN SERIES®

Australia • Canada • Denmark • Japan • Mexico • New Zealand • Philippines • Puerto Rico • Singapore
South Africa • Spain • United Kingdom • United States

THOMSON
COURSE TECHNOLOGY

Discovering Computers 2005: A Gateway to Information, Web Enhanced

Gary B. Shelly
Thomas J. Cashman
Misty E. Vermaat

Executive Editor:
Cheryl Costantini

Senior Acquisitions Editor:
Dana Merk

Senior Product Manager:
Alexandra Arnold

Product Manager:
Reed Cotter

Editorial Assistant:
Selena Coppock

Print Buyer:
Laura Burns

Signing Representative:
Cheryl Costantini

Series Consulting Editor:
Jim Quasney

Director of Production:
Becky Herrington

Production Editor:
Deb Massi

Production Assistant:
Jennifer Quiambao

Development Editor:
Ginny Harvey

Copy Editor:
Ginny Harvey

Proofreaders:
Nancy Lamm
Kim Kosmatka

Interior Designer:
Hector Arvizu

Cover Designers:
Richard Herrera
Kenny Tran

Illustrators:
Hector Arvizu
Richard Herrera
Andrew Bartel
Ken Russo
Kenny Tran

Compositors:
Hector Arvizu
Andrew Bartel
Kellee LaVars
Kenny Tran
Jeanne Black

Indexer:
Nancy Lamm

Printer:
Banta Menasha

Printed in the United States of America

2 3 4 5 6 7 8 9 10
BM 08 07 06 05 04

For more information, contact
Course Technology
25 Thomson Place
Boston, Massachusetts 02210

Or find us on the World Wide Web at:
www.course.com

ISBN 0-619-25525-0

Discovering Computers 2005

A Gateway to Information
Web Enhanced
Complete

Contents

SPECIAL FEATURE

CHAPTER 3
Application Software

CHAPTER 4
The Components of the System Unit

CHAPTER 5
Input

GPS - Global positioning system

GPS- Global-positioning-system

CHAPTER 10
Database Management

SPECIAL FEATURE

CHAPTER 11
Computers and Society, Security, Privacy, and Ethics

CHAPTER 12
Information System Development

CHAPTER 13
Programming Languages and Program Development

CHAPTER 14
Enterprise Computing

CHAPTER 15
Computer Careers and Certification

SPECIAL FEATURE

APPENDIX A
Making Use of the Web

APPENDIX B
Coding Schemes and Number Systems

APPENDIX C
Computer Acronyms

Preface

The Shelly Cashman Series® offers the finest textbooks in computer education. We are proud of the fact that the previous nine editions of this textbook have been the most widely used in computer education. With each new edition of the book, we have implemented significant improvements based on current computer trends and comments made by instructors and students. *Discovering Computers 2005* continues with the innovation, quality, and reliability you have come to expect from the Shelly Cashman Series.

In *Discovering Computers 2005: A Gateway to Information*, you will find an educationally sound, highly visual, and easy-to-follow pedagogy that presents an in-depth treatment of introductory computer subjects. Students will finish the course with a solid understanding of computers, how to use computers, and how to access information on the World Wide Web.

OBJECTIVES OF THIS TEXTBOOK

Discovering Computers 2005: A Gateway to Information is intended for use as a stand-alone textbook or in combination with an applications, Internet, or programming textbook in a one-quarter or one-semester introductory computer course. No experience with computers is assumed. The objectives of this book are to:

- Present the most-up-to-date technology in an ever-changing discipline
- Give students an in-depth understanding of why computers are essential components in business and society
- Teach the fundamentals of computers and computer nomenclature, particularly with respect to personal computer hardware and software, the World Wide Web, and enterprise computing
- Present the material in a visually appealing and exciting manner that motivates students to learn
- Assist students in planning a career and getting certified in the computer field
- Provide exercises and lab assignments that allow students to interact with a computer and learn by actually using the computer and the World Wide Web
- Present strategies for purchasing, installing, and maintaining a desktop computer, a notebook computer, a Tablet PC, and a PDA
- Offer alternative learning techniques and reinforcement via the Web
- Offer distance-education providers a textbook with a meaningful and exercise-rich companion Web site

DISTINGUISHING FEATURES

To date, more than 6 million students have learned about computers using a *Discovering Computers* textbook. With the additional World Wide Web integration and interactivity, streaming up-to-date audio and video, extraordinary step-by-step visual drawings and photographs, unparalleled currency, and the Shelly and Cashman touch, this book will make your computer concepts course exciting and dynamic. Distinguishing features of the Shelly Cashman Series *Discovering Computers* books include the following.

A Proven Pedagogy

Careful explanations of complex concepts, educationally-sound elements, and reinforcement highlight this proven method of presentation. A pictorial arrangement of the pedagogy can be found beginning on page 4.

A Visually Appealing Book that Maintains Student Interest

The latest technology, pictures, drawings, and text are combined artfully to produce a visually appealing and easy-to-understand book. Many of the figures include a step-by-step presentation (see item 6 on page xix), which simplifies the more complex computer concepts. Pictures and drawings reflect the latest trends in computer technology. Finally, the text is set in two columns, which instructors and reviewers say their students prefer. This combination of pictures, step-by-step drawings, and easy-to-read text layout sets a new standard for computer textbook design.

Latest Technologies and Terms

The technologies and terms your students see in this book are those they will encounter when they start using computers. Only the latest application software packages are shown throughout the book. New topics and terms include Internet receiver, hot spots, cyber cars, voice and video instant messaging, note taking software, Microsoft Office 2003, Microsoft Office System, Pentium M processor, IBM processor, terabyte (TB), magnetoresistive RAM (MRAM), text messaging, multimedia messaging, bar code reader, mobile printer, USB flash drive, keychain drive, RHD, DVD-RW, DVD-RW drive, xD Picture Card, card reader/writer, Windows XP Media Center Edition, Windows XP 64-bit Edition, Windows Small Business Server 2003, Windows Mobile 2003, XML, text messaging, picture messaging, MMS (multimedia message service), RFID, radio frequency identification, Children's Internet Protection Act (CIPA), fault-tolerant computer, Visual C++ .NET 2003, Visual C# .NET 2003, Visual J# .NET 2003, RSS, Dreamweaver MX, Flash MX, FrontPage 2003, Microsoft Certified Desktop Support Technician (MCDST), IBM Certified Specialist, and Certified Software Development Professional (CSDP).

World Wide Web Enhanced

This book uses the World Wide Web as a major supplement. The purpose of integrating the World Wide Web into the book is to (1) offer students additional information and currency on important topics; (2) use its interactive capabilities to offer creative reinforcement and online quizzes; (3) make available alternative learning techniques with Web-based learning games, practice tests, and interactive labs; (4) underscore the relevance of the World Wide Web as a basic information tool that can be used in all facets of society; (5) introduce students to doing research on the Web; and (6) offer instructors the opportunity to organize and administer their traditional campus-based or distance-education-based courses on the Web using WebCT, Blackboard, or MyCourse 2.1. This textbook, however, does not depend on Web access to be used successfully. The Web access adds to the already complete treatment of topics within the book.

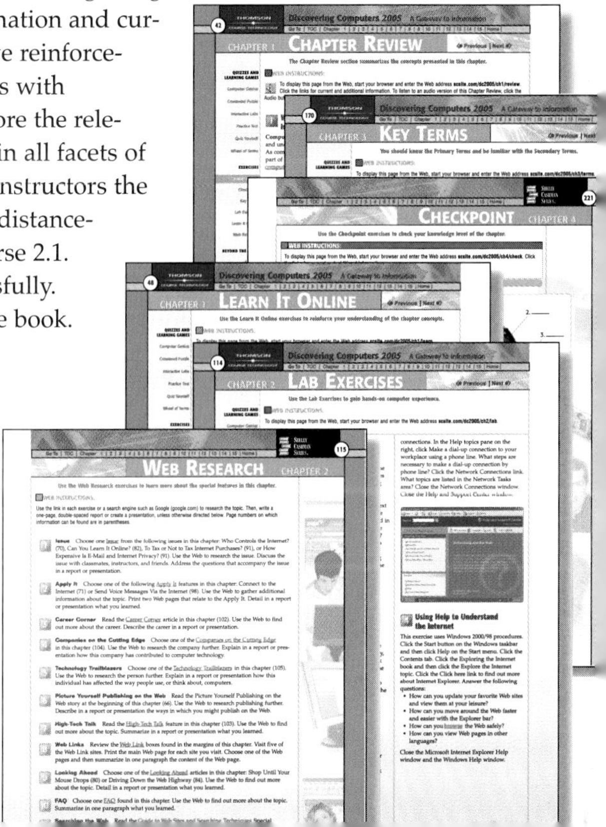

Extensive End-of-Chapter Materials

A notable strength of the *Discovering Computers* textbooks is the extensive student activities at the end of each chapter. Well-structured student activities can make the difference between students merely participating in a class and students retaining the information they learn. The activity in the *Discovering Computers 2005* books include: Chapter Review, Key Terms, Checkpoint, Learn It Online, Lab Exercises, and Web Research. A pictorial presentation of each end-of-chapter activity can be found beginning on page xviii.

ORGANIZATION OF THIS TEXTBOOK

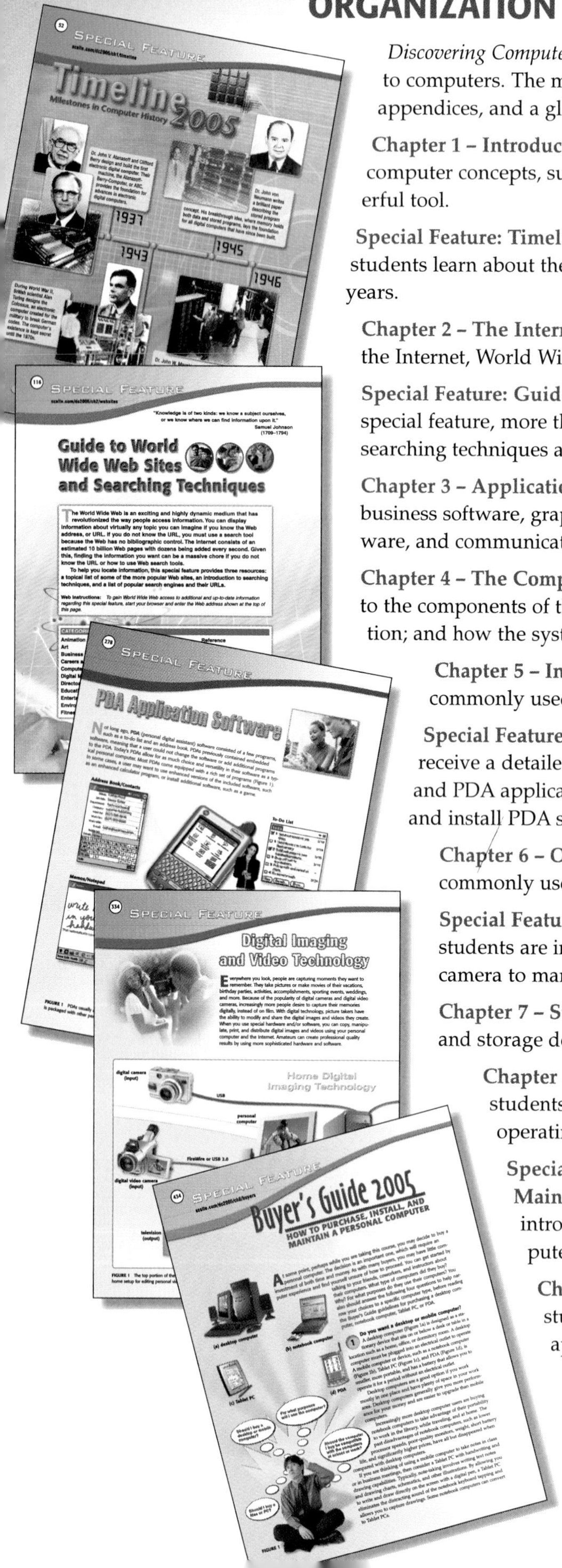

Discovering Computers 2005: A Gateway to Information provides a thorough introduction to computers. The material is divided into fifteen chapters, eight special features, three appendices, and a glossary/index.

Chapter 1 – Introduction to Computers In Chapter 1, students are introduced to basic computer concepts, such as what a computer is, how it works, and what makes it a powerful tool.

Special Feature: Timeline 2005 Milestones in Computer History In this special feature, students learn about the major computer technology developments during the past 65 years.

Chapter 2 – The Internet and the World Wide Web In Chapter 2, students learn about the Internet, World Wide Web, browsers, e-mail, FTP, and instant messaging.

Special Feature: Guide to World Wide Web Sites and Searching Techniques In this special feature, more than 150 popular up-to-date Web sites are listed and described. Basic searching techniques also are introduced.

Chapter 3 – Application Software In Chapter 3, students are introduced to a variety of business software, graphics and multimedia software, home/personal/educational software, and communications software.

Chapter 4 – The Components of the System Unit In Chapter 4, students are introduced to the components of the system unit; how memory stores data, instructions, and information; and how the system unit executes an instruction.

Chapter 5 – Input Chapter 5 describes the various techniques of input and commonly used input devices.

Special Feature: PDA Application Software In this special feature, students receive a detailed presentation of PDA operating systems, built-in PDA software, and PDA application software. Also included is a discussion about how to obtain and install PDA software.

Chapter 6 – Output Chapter 6 describes the various methods of output and commonly used output devices.

Special Feature: Digital Imaging and Video Technology In this special feature, students are introduced to using a personal computer, digital camera, and video camera to manipulate photographs and video.

Chapter 7 – Storage In Chapter 7, students learn about various storage media and storage devices.

Chapter 8 – Operating Systems and Utility Programs In Chapter 8, students learn about a variety of stand-alone operating systems, network operating systems, and embedded operating systems.

Special Feature: Buyer's Guide 2005: How to Purchase, Install, and Maintain a Personal Computer In this special feature, students are introduced to purchasing, installing, and maintaining a desktop computer, notebook computer, Tablet PC, and PDA.

Chapter 9 – Communications and Networks Chapter 9 provides students with an overview of communications technology and applications.

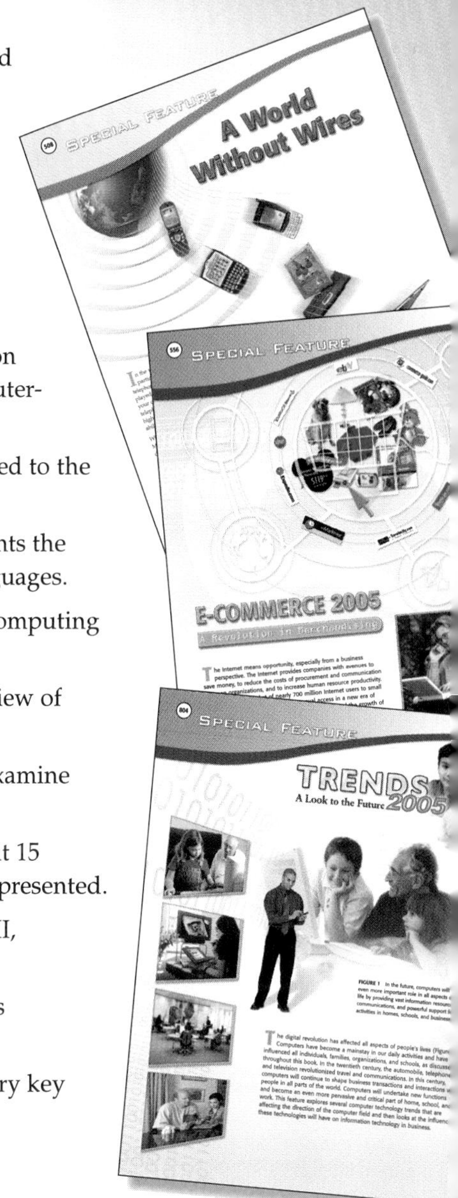

Special Feature: A World Without Wires In this special feature, students are presented with the latest in wireless hardware and wireless applications.

Chapter 10 – Database Management Chapter 10 presents students with the advantages of organizing data in a database and describes various types of data.

Special Feature: E-Commerce 2005: A Revolution in Merchandising This special feature introduces students to e-commerce basics, e-commerce business models, e-commerce revenue streams, and how to become an e-commerce merchant.

Chapter 11 – Computers and Society, Security, Privacy, and Ethics In Chapter 11, students learn about computer and Internet risks, ethical issues surrounding information accuracy, intellectual property rights, codes of conduct, information privacy, and computer-related health issues.

Chapter 12 – Information System Development In Chapter 12, students are introduced to the system development cycle and guidelines for system development.

Chapter 13 – Programming Languages and Program Development Chapter 13 presents the program development cycle, program design methods, and popular programming languages.

Chapter 14 – Enterprise Computing In Chapter 14, students learn about the special computing requirements used in an enterprise-sized organization.

Chapter 15 – Computer Careers and Certification Chapter 15 presents a broad overview of computer-related careers, career development, and certification.

Special Feature: Trends: A Look to the Future 2005 In this special feature, students examine several long-term trends that will influence the direction of the computer field.

Appendix A – Making Use of the Web Appendix A presents useful information about 15 categories of Web sites, tables of Web addresses, and exercises to reinforce the material presented.

Appendix B – Coding Schemes and Number Systems Appendix B presents the ASCII, EBCDIC, and Unicode coding schemes.

Appendix C – Computer Acronyms Appendix C summarizes the computer acronyms discussed in the book.

Glossary/Index The Glossary/Index includes a definition and page references for every key term presented in the book.

SHELLY CASHMAN SERIES INSTRUCTOR RESOURCES

The Shelly Cashman Series is dedicated to providing you with all of the tools you need to make your class a success. Information on all supplementary materials is available through your Course Technology representative or by calling one of the following telephone numbers: Colleges and Universities, 1-800-648-7450; High Schools, 1-800-824-5179; Private Career Colleges, 1-800-347-7707; Canada, 1-800-268-2222; Corporations with IT Training Centers, 1-800-648-7450; and Government Agencies, Health-Care Organizations, and Correctional Facilities, 1-800-477-3692.

Instructor Resources CD-ROM

The Instructor Resources CD-ROM includes both teaching and testing aids. The contents of each item on the Instructor Resources CD-ROM (ISBN 0-619-25530-7) are described below.

- **Instructors Manual** The Instructor's Manual is made up of Microsoft Word files, which include detailed lesson plans with page number references, lecture notes, classroom activities, discussion topics, and projects to assign.
- **Syllabus** Sample syllabi, which can be customized easily to a course, are included. The syllabi cover policies, class and lab assignments and exams, and procedural information.

- **Figure Files** Illustrations for every figure in the textbook are available in electronic form. Use this ancillary to present a slide show in lecture or to print transparencies for use in lecture with an overhead projector. If you have a personal computer and LCD device, this ancillary can be an effective tool for presenting lectures.
- **Solutions to Exercises** Solutions are included for all end-of-chapter exercises.
- **Test Bank & Test Engine** The ExamView test bank includes 220 questions for every chapter (50 multiple-choice, 100 true/false, and 70 completion) with page number references, and when appropriate, figure references. Each question also is identified by objective and type of term (primary or secondary). The test bank comes with a copy of the test engine, ExamView, the ultimate tool for your objective-based testing needs.
- **Printed Test Bank** A Microsoft Word version of the test bank you can print also is included.
- **Test Out/Final Exam** Use this objective-based test to test students out of your course, or use it as a final examination. A master answer sheet is included.
- **Pretest/Posttest** Use these carefully prepared tests at the beginning and the end of the semester to measure student progress. A master answer sheet is included.
- **Data Files for Students** All the files that are required by students to complete the exercises are included. You can distribute the files on the Instructor Resources CD-ROM to your students over a network, or you can have them follow the instructions on the inside back cover of this book to obtain a copy of the Data Disk.

Course Presenter

Course Presenter (ISBN (0-619-25531-5) is a one-click-per-slide presentation system on CD-ROM that provides PowerPoint slides for every subject in each chapter. Use this presentation system to give interesting, well-organized, and knowledge-based lectures. More than 30 two- to three-minute, up-to-date CNN computer-related video clips are available for optional presentation. Course Presenter provides consistent coverage for multiple lecturers.

Student Edition Labs

Thirty new Web-based interactive labs will help your students master hundreds of computer concepts including input and output devices, file management and desktop applications, computer privacy, virus protection, and much more. Featuring up-to-the-minute content, eye-popping graphics, and rich animation, the highly interactive Student Edition Labs offer students an alternative way to learn through dynamic observation, step-by-step practice, and challenging review questions. Access the free Student Edition Labs from the *Discovering Computers 2005* Web site at scsite.com/dc2005 or see the Student Edition Lab exercises on the Learn It Online pages at the end of each chapter.

Online Content

Course Technology offers textbook-based content for Blackboard, WebCT, and MyCourse 2.1.

- **BlackBoard and WebCT** As the leading provider of IT content for the Blackboard and WebCT platforms, Course Technology delivers rich content that enhances your textbook to give your students a unique learning experience.
- **MyCoure 2.1** MyCourse 2.1 is Course Technology's powerful online course management and content delivery system. MyCourse 2.1 allows nontechnical users to create, customize, and deliver Web-based courses; post content and assignments; manage student enrollment; administer exams; track results in the online grade book; and more.

SUPPLEMENTS

Two supplements can be used in combination with this textbook.

SAM Computer Concepts

You can add more vigor and flexibility to your Student Edition Labs with SAM (Skills Assessment Manager) Computer Concepts. SAM Computer Concepts adds the power of skill-based assessment and the award-winning SAM classroom administration system to your Student Edition Labs, putting you in control of how you deliver exams and training in your course. By adding SAM Computer Concepts to your curriculum, you can:

- Reinforce your students' knowledge of key computer concepts with hands-on application exercises.
- Allow your students to learn by listening, with access to rich audio in their Student Edition Labs.
- Build hands-on computer concepts exams from a test bank of more than 200 skill-based concepts tasks.
- Schedule your students' concepts training and testing exercises with powerful administrative tools.
- Track student exam grades and training progress using more than one dozen student and classroom reports.

Study Guide

This highly popular *Study Guide* (ISBN 0-619-20221-1) includes a variety of activities that help students recall, review, and master introductory computer concepts. The *Study Guide* complements the end-of-chapter material with a guided chapter outline; a self-test consisting of true/false, multiple-choice, short answer, fill-in, and matching questions; an entertaining puzzle; and other challenging exercises.

ACKNOWLEDGMENTS

The Shelly Cashman Series would not be the leading computer education series without the contributions of outstanding publishing professionals. First, and foremost, among them is Becky Herrington, director of production and book designer. She is the heart and soul of the Shelly Cashman Series, and it is only through her leadership, dedication, and tireless efforts that superior products are made possible.

Under Becky's direction, the following individuals made significant contributions to these books: Deb Masi, production editor; Jennifer Quiambao, production assistant; Ken Russo, senior Web and graphic designer; Richard Herrera, cover designer; Hector Arvizu, interior designer; Kellee LaVars, Andrew Bartel, Phillip Hajjar, and Kenny Tran, graphic artists; Andrew Bartel, Kenny Tran, Jeanne Black, and Kellee LaVars, QuarkXPress compositors; Ginny Harvey, Nancy Lamm, Kim Kosmatka, and Ellana Russo, copy editors and proofreaders; and Nancy Lamm, indexer.

We also would like to thank Kristen Duerr, executive vice president and publisher; Cheryl Costantini, executive editor; Dana Merk, senior acquisitions editor; Jim Quasney, series consulting editor; Alexandra Arnold, senior product manager; Reed Cotter, product manager; Marc Ouellette and Heather McKinstry, online product managers; and Selena Coppock, editorial assistant.

Gary B. Shelly
Thomas J. Cashman
Misty E. Vermaat

TO THE STUDENT...Getting the Most Out of Your Book

Welcome to *Discovering Computers 2005: A Gateway to Information, Web Enhanced*. You can save yourself a lot of time and gain a better understanding of the computer concepts presented in this book if you spend a few minutes reviewing this section.

1 Companion Web Site

Use the companion Web site at scsite.com/dc2005, which includes additional information about important topics and provides unparalleled currency; and make use of online learning games, practice tests, and additional reinforcement.

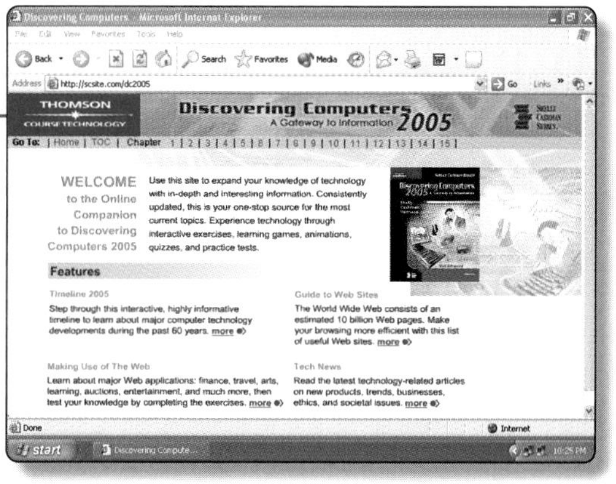

2 Picture Yourself

Picture yourself using the concepts presented in the chapter you are about to read. This section at the beginning of each chapter is intended to help you see how the specific material might apply to your everyday life using computers.

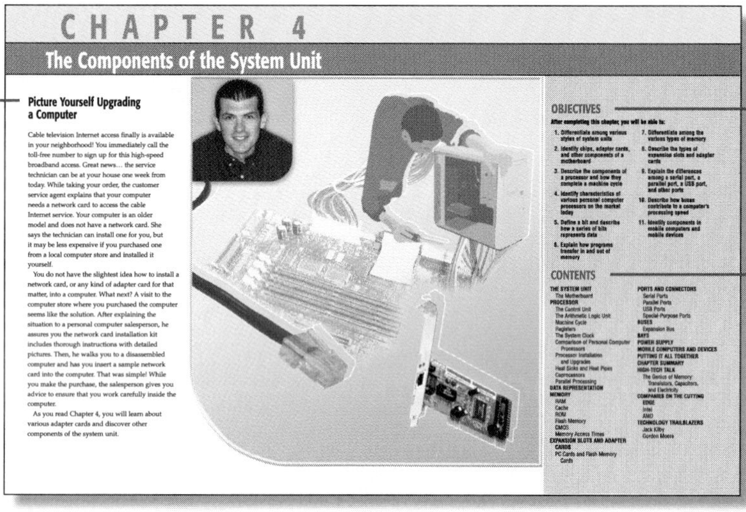

3 Chapter Objectives and Table of Contents

Before you read the chapter, carefully read through the Objectives and Contents so that you know what you should learn from the chapter.

4 Initial Chapter Figure

Carefully study the first figure in each chapter because it will give you an easy-to-follow overview of the major purpose of the chapter.

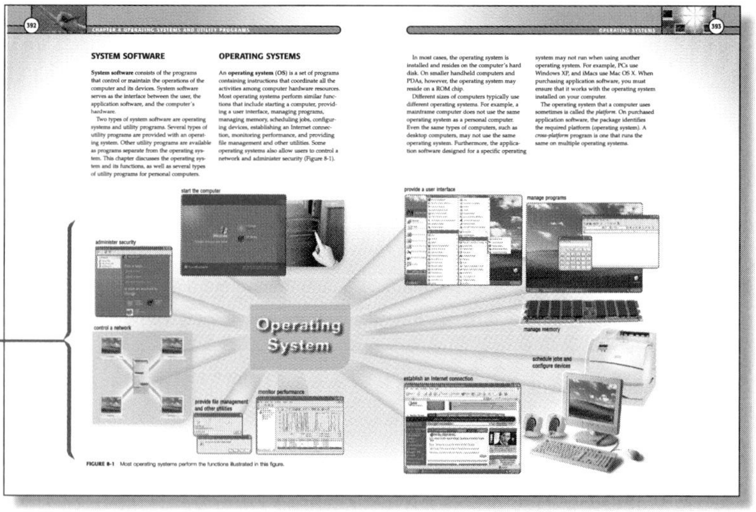

5 Web Link

Obtain current information and a different perspective about key terms and concepts by visiting the Web addresses in the Web Links found in the margins throughout the book.

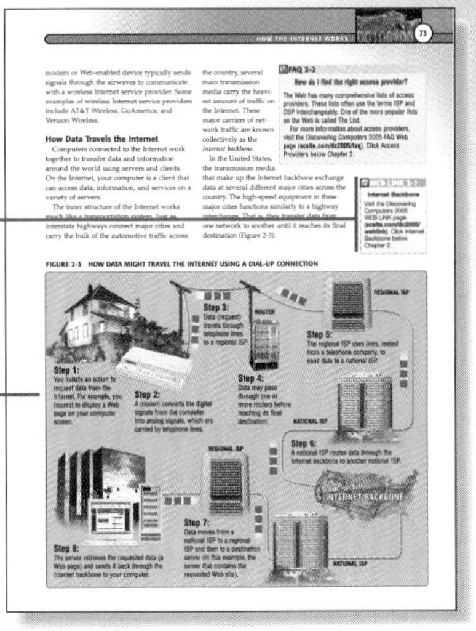

6 Step Figures

Each chapter includes numerous step figures that present the more complex computer concepts using a step-by-step pedagogy.

7 Apply It

The Apply It boxes illustrate how the material presented in the chapter can be applied to everyday life.

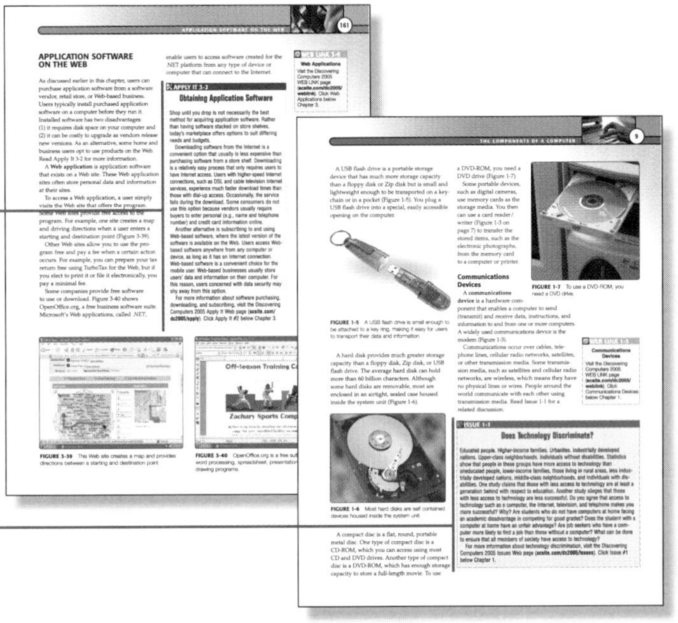

8 Issue

Issue boxes provide you with computer-related controversial topics of the day and stimulating questions that offer insight into the general concerns of computers in society.

9 Looking Ahead

The Looking Ahead boxes offer you a glimpse at the latest advances in computer technology that will be available, usually within five years.

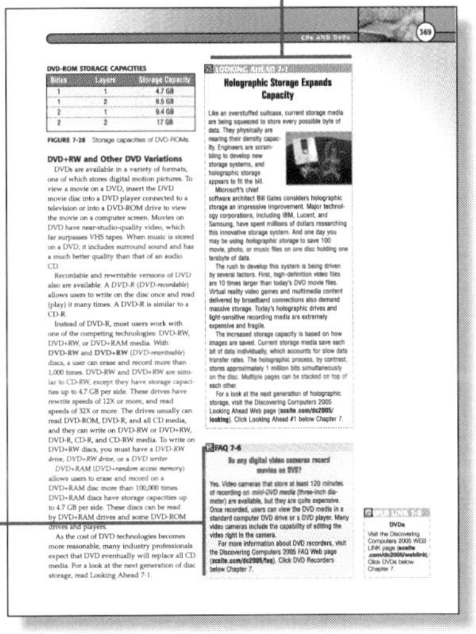

10 FAQ

FAQ (frequently asked questions) boxes offer common questions and answers about subjects related to the topic at hand.

11 Quiz Yourself

Three Quiz Yourself boxes per chapter help ensure that you know the material you just read and are ready to move on in the chapter. You take these quizzes on the Web for interactivity and easy use.

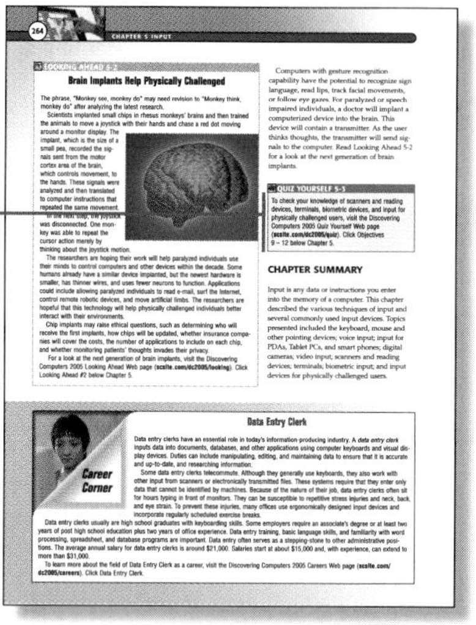

12 Career Corner

Each chapter ends with a Career Corner feature that introduces you to a computer-career opportunity relating to a topic covered in the chapter.

13 High-Tech Talk

If you are technically inclined, you will enjoy the High-Tech Talk article at the end of each chapter. These presentations expand on a topic covered in the chapter and present a more technical discussion.

14 Companies on the Cutting Edge

Each chapter includes a profile about two key computer-related companies of which you should be aware, especially if you plan to major in the computer field.

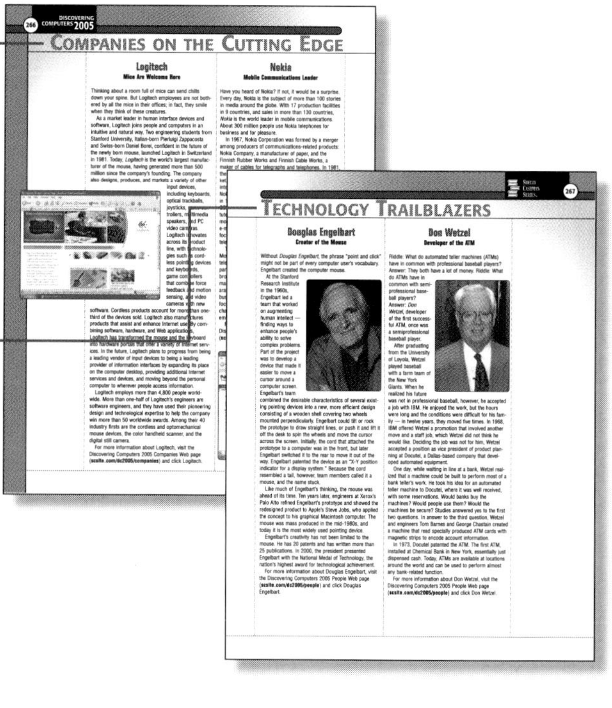

15 Technology Trailblazers

The Technology Trailblazers page in each chapter offers a glimpse into the life and times of the more famous leaders of the computer industry.

16 Chapter Review

Use the two-page Chapter Review before you take an examination to ensure that you are familiar with the computer concepts presented. This section includes each objective, followed by a one- or two-paragraph summary. Visit a Chapter Review page on the Web, and click the Audio button to listen to the Chapter Review.

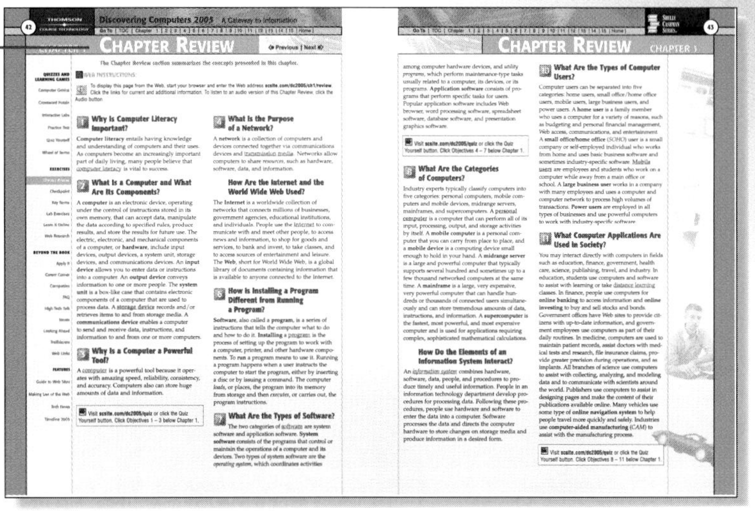

17 Primary and Secondary Key Terms

Before you take a test, use the Key Terms page as a checklist of terms you should know. In the text, primary key terms appear in bold font and secondary key terms appear in italic font. Ask your instructor whether you are responsible for knowing only the primary key terms or all the key terms. Visit a Key Terms page on the Web and click any term for additional information.

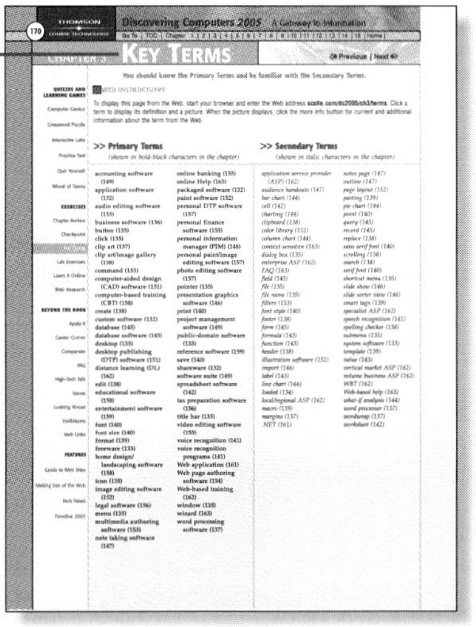

18 Checkpoint

Use these three pages of exercises to reinforce your understanding of the topics presented in the chapter.

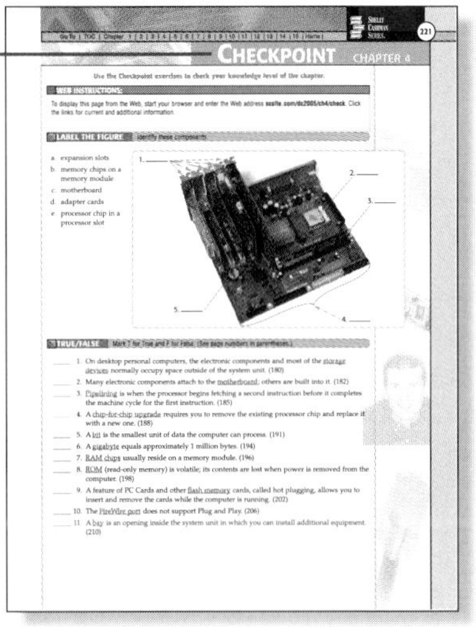

19 Learn It Online

If you prefer online reinforcement, then the Learn It Online exercises are for you. The exercises include online videos, practice tests, interactive labs, learning games, and Web-based activities.

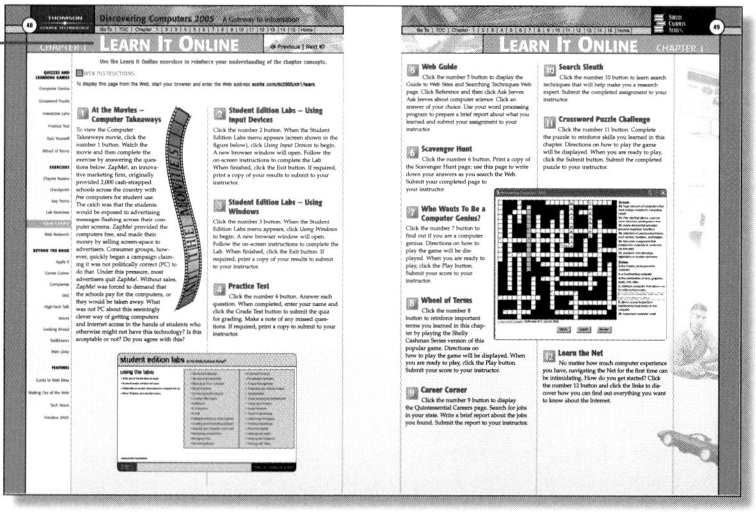

20 Lab Exercises

If you want to become proficient with the Windows operating system while you are taking your computer concepts course, then you should step through these carefully designed Windows exercises. Many of them take only a few minutes to complete.

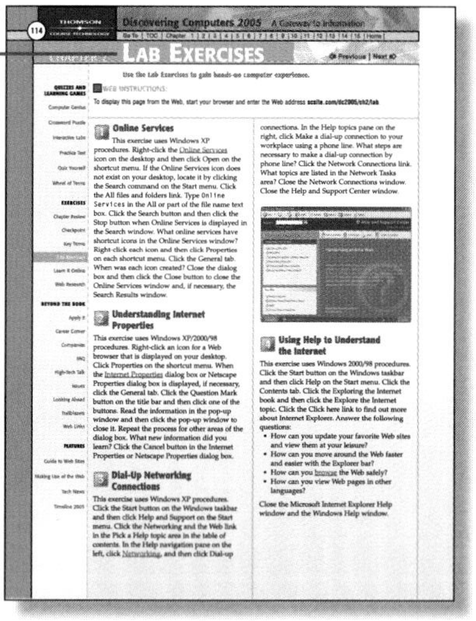

21 Web Research

If you enjoy doing research on the Web, then you will like the Web Research exercises. Each exercise in this section references an element in the book and suggests you write a short article or do a class presentation on your findings.

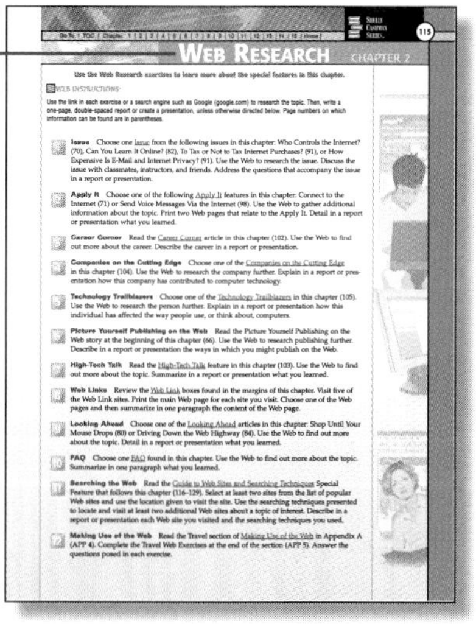

Shelly Cashman Series – Traditionally Bound Textbooks

The Shelly Cashman Series presents the following computer subjects in a variety of traditionally bound textbooks. For more information, see your Course Technology representative or call 1-800-648-7450. For Shelly Cashman Series information, visit Shelly Cashman Online at **scseries.com**

COMPUTERS	
Computers	Discovering Computers 2005: A Gateway to Information, Web Enhanced, Complete Edition Discovering Computers 2005: A Gateway to Information, Web Enhanced, Introductory Edition Discovering Computers 2005: A Gateway to Information, Web Enhanced, Brief Edition Discovering Computers: Fundamentals Edition Teachers Discovering Computers: Integrating Technology in the Classroom 3e Exploring Computers: A Record of Discovery 4e Study Guide for Discovering Computers 2005: A Gateway to Information, Web Enhanced Essential Introduction to Computers 5e (40-page)
WINDOWS APPLICATIONS	
Microsoft Office	Microsoft Office 2003: Essential Concepts and Techniques (5 projects) Microsoft Office 2003: Brief Concepts and Techniques (9 projects) Microsoft Office 2003: Introductory Concepts and Techniques (15 projects) Microsoft Office 2003: Advanced Concepts and Techniques (12 projects) Microsoft Office 2003: Post Advanced Concepts and Techniques (11 projects) Microsoft Office XP: Essential Concepts and Techniques (5 projects) Microsoft Office XP: Brief Concepts and Techniques (9 projects) Microsoft Office XP: Introductory Concepts and Techniques, Enhanced Edition (15 projects)[1] Microsoft Office XP: Advanced Concepts and Techniques (11 projects) Microsoft Office XP: Post Advanced Concepts and Techniques (11 projects)
Integration	Integrating Microsoft Office XP Applications and the World Wide Web: Essential Concepts and Techniques
PIM	Microsoft Office Outlook 2003: Introductory Concepts and Techniques • Microsoft Outlook 2002: Essential Concepts and Techniques
Microsoft Works	Microsoft Works 6: Complete Concepts and Techniques[2] • Microsoft Works 2000: Complete Concepts and Techniques[2]
Microsoft Windows	Microsoft Windows XP: Complete Concepts and Techniques[3] Microsoft Windows XP: Brief Concepts and Techniques Microsoft Windows 2000: Complete Concepts and Techniques (6 projects)[3] Microsoft Windows 2000: Brief Concepts and Techniques (2 projects) Microsoft Windows 98: Essential Concepts and Techniques (2 projects) Microsoft Windows 98: Complete Concepts and Techniques (6 projects)[3] Introduction to Microsoft Windows NT Workstation 4
Word Processing	Microsoft Office Word 2003[3] • Microsoft Word 2002[3]
Spreadsheets	Microsoft Office Excel 2003[3] • Microsoft Excel 2002[3]
Database	Microsoft Office Access 2003[3] • Microsoft Access 2002[3]
Presentation Graphics	Microsoft Office PowerPoint 2003[3] • Microsoft PowerPoint 2002[3]
Desktop Publishing	Microsoft Office Publisher 2003[2] • Microsoft Publisher 2002[2]
PROGRAMMING	
Programming	Microsoft Visual Basic.NET: Complete Concepts and Techniques[3] • Microsoft Visual Basic 6: Complete Concepts and Techniques[2] Programming in QBasic • Java Programming 2e: Complete Concepts and Techniques[3] • Structured COBOL Programming 2e
INTERNET	
Concepts	Discovering the Internet: Complete Concepts & Techniques[2]
Browser	Microsoft Internet Explorer 6: Introductory Concepts and Techniques • Microsoft Internet Explorer 5: An Introduction • Netscape Navigator 6: An Introduction
Web Page Creation and Design	Web Design: Introductory Concepts and Techniques • HTML: Complete Concepts and Techniques 2e[3] Microsoft Office FrontPage 2003[3] • Microsoft FrontPage 2002[3] • Microsoft FrontPage 2002: Essential Concepts and Techniques Java Programming: Complete Concepts and Techniques 2e[3] • JavaScript: Complete Concepts and Techniques 2e[2] • Macromedia Dreamweaver MX: Complete Concepts and Techniques[3]
SYSTEMS ANALYSIS	
Systems Analysis	Systems Analysis and Design 5e
DATA COMMUNICATIONS	
Data Communications	Business Data Communications: Introductory Concepts and Techniques 4e

[1]Available running under Windows XP or running under Windows 2000.
[2]Also available as an Introductory Edition, which is a shortened version of the complete book.
[3]Also available as an Introductory Edition, which is a shortened version of the complete book and also as a Comprehensive Edition, which is an extended version of the complete book.

Discovering Computers 2005

A Gateway to Information

CHAPTER 1

Introduction to Computers

Picture Yourself Using Computers

After thanking the loan officer for her time, you leave the bank and imagine driving down the highway in a black Corvette. When your friend bought the car ten years ago, you were first to ride in it. Just last week, he told you it is for sale. You want that car!

This is your lucky day. Your local bank is offering a zero percent interest, no money down, five-year car loan to students with at least a 3.0 grade point average. After dropping off the application, you anxiously await the results. The loan officer said she would place a message on the Internet letting you know if the loan is approved.

The next morning, you access the Internet from your home computer … no message about the loan. Later, when you meet your brother for lunch, he takes a small computer from his briefcase and uses it to access the Internet. Still no message. While visiting a friend that afternoon, you ask if he has Internet access. He pulls a cellular telephone out of his coat pocket and uses it to connect to the Internet. Your account has a message from the bank. You cross your fingers and then slowly read the message. Yes! You are going to own an awesome black Corvette. Life is good.

As you read Chapter 1, you will learn about Internet access and discover other practical uses of computers.

OBJECTIVES

After completing this chapter, you will be able to:

1. Recognize the importance of computer literacy
2. Define the term computer and identify its components
3. Explain why a computer is a powerful tool
4. Recognize the purpose of a network
5. Discuss the uses of the Internet and World Wide Web
6. Distinguish between installing and running a program
7. Identify the types of software
8. Describe the categories of computers
9. Determine how the elements of an information system interact
10. Identify the types of computer users
11. Discuss various computer applications in society

CONTENTS

A WORLD OF COMPUTERS

Computers are everywhere: at home, at work, and at school. Many daily activities either involve the use of or depend on information from a computer. As shown in Figure 1-1, people use all types and sizes of computers for numerous reasons and in various places. Some computers sit on top of a desk or on the floor; others are small enough to carry. Many are wireless.

Computers are a primary means of communications for all types of people. Employees correspond with clients, students with teachers, and family with friends and other family members. In addition to corresponding via text messages, people send each other pictures, diagrams, drawings, music, and videos. Today's technology provides the ability to see or hear others personally while you chat with them.

Through computers, society has instant access to information from around the globe. Local and national news, weather reports, sports scores, airline schedules, job listings, your credit report, and countless forms of educational material always are accessible. From the computer, you can meet new friends, shop, fill prescriptions, file taxes, or take a course.

At home or while on the road, people use computers to manage schedules, balance a checkbook, pay bills, track personal income and expenses, transfer funds, and buy or sell stocks. Banks place automated teller machines (ATMs) all over the world, making it easy to deposit or withdraw funds at anytime with a small plastic card. At the grocery store, a computer tracks purchases, calculates the amount of money due, and often generates

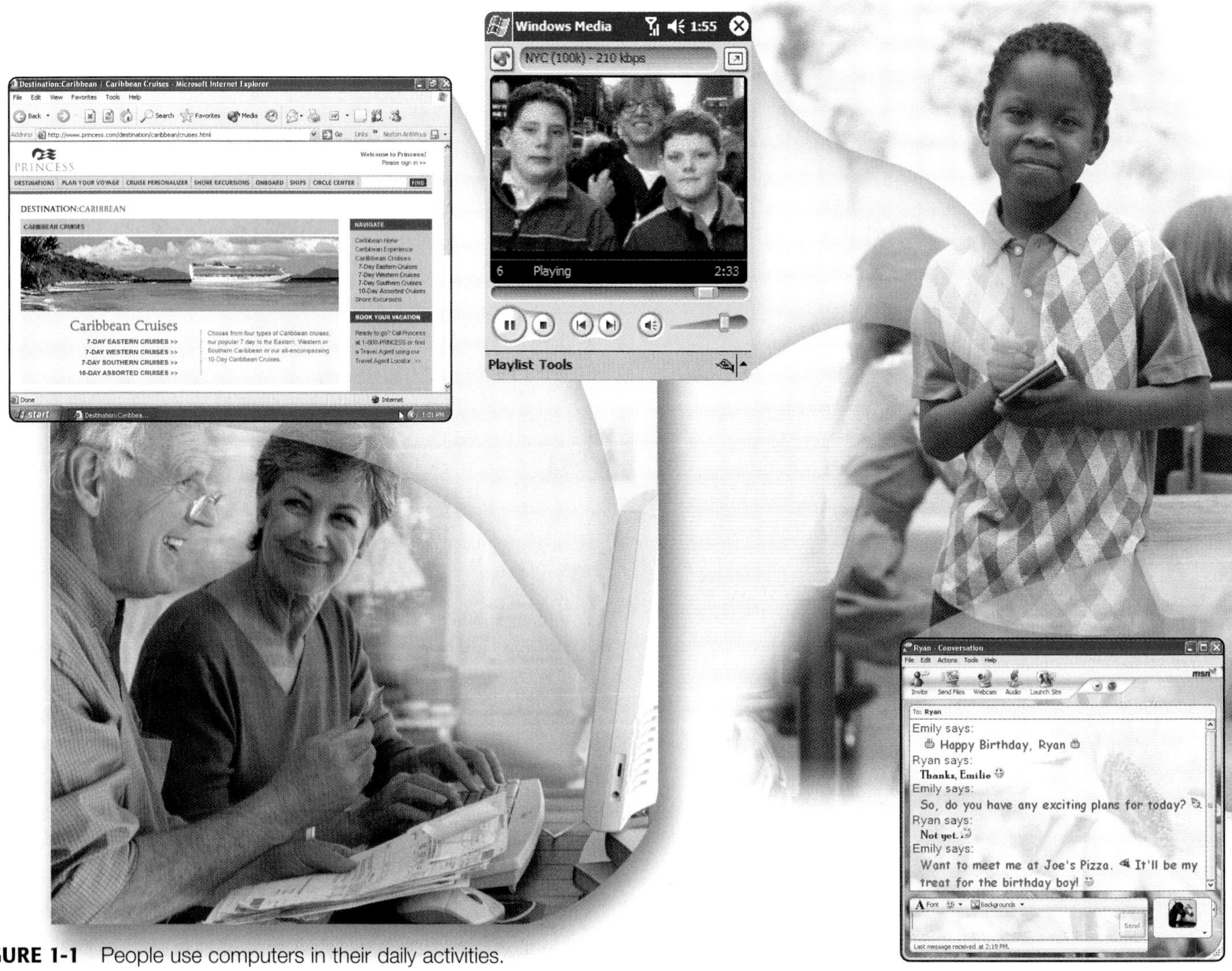

FIGURE 1-1 People use computers in their daily activities.

coupons customized to buying patterns. Vehicles include onboard navigation systems that provide directions, call for emergency services, and track the vehicle if it is stolen.

In the workplace, employees use computers to create correspondence such as memos and letters, calculate payroll, track inventory, and generate invoices. Some applications such as automotive design and weather forecasting use computers to perform complex mathematical calculations. At school, teachers use computers to assist with classroom instruction. Students complete assignments and do research on computers in lab rooms and at home.

People also spend hours of leisure time on the computer. They play games, listen to music, watch videos and movies, read books and magazines, research geneology, compose music and videos, retouch photographs, make reservations, and plan vacations.

As technology continues to advance, computers are becoming more a part of daily living. Thus, many people believe that computer literacy is vital to success. **Computer literacy** entails having knowledge and understanding of computers and their uses.

This book presents the knowledge you need to be computer literate. As you read this first chapter, keep in mind it is an overview. Many of the terms and concepts introduced in this chapter will be discussed in more depth later in the book.

WHAT IS A COMPUTER?

A **computer** is an electronic device, operating under the control of instructions stored in its own memory, that can accept data, manipulate the data according to specified rules, produce results, and store the results for future use.

Data and Information

Data is a collection of unprocessed items, which can include text, numbers, images, audio, and video. **Information** conveys meaning and is useful to one or more people. For example, when data such as course codes, course credit hours, and grades are arranged in the form of a grade report, a student has information.

Computers process data into information. In a grocery store, computers process several data items to print information in the form of a grocery receipt (Figure 1-2). To produce a paycheck (information), a computer processes the employee's name, number of hours worked, and the hourly rate of pay (data).

FAQ 1-1

Is data a singular or plural word?

With respect to computers, it is accepted and common practice to use the word data in both the singular and plural context.

For more information about data, visit the Discovering Computers 2005 FAQ Web page (**scsite.com/dc2005/faq**). Click Data below Chapter 1.

An **FAQ** (frequently asked questions) list helps you find answers to commonly asked questions. Web sites often post an FAQ section, and each chapter in this book includes FAQ boxes related to topics in the text.

Information Processing Cycle

Computers process input (data) into output (information). A computer often holds data, information, and instructions in storage for future use. *Instructions* are the steps that tell the computer how to perform a particular task. Some people refer to the series of input, process, output, and storage activities as the *information processing cycle*.

Most computers today can communicate with other computers. As a result, communications also has become an essential element of the information processing cycle.

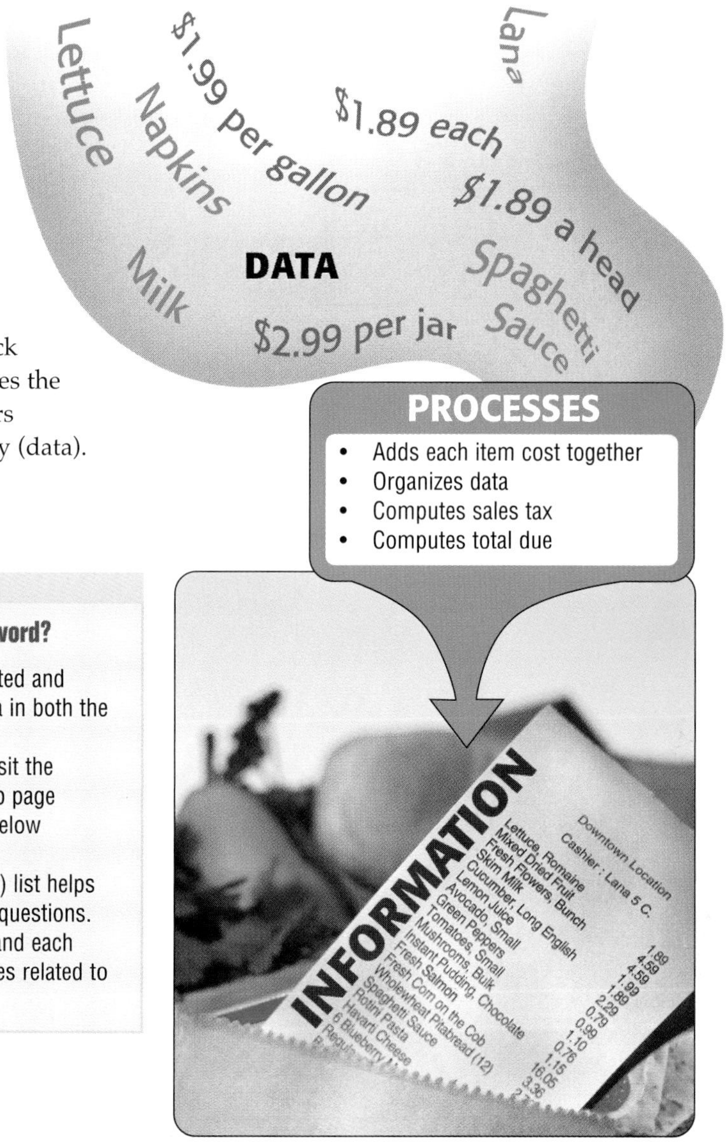

FIGURE 1-2 A computer processes data into information. In this example, the cashier name, grocery item, and cost per unit each represent data. The computer processes the data to produce the grocery receipt (information).

THE COMPONENTS OF A COMPUTER

A computer contains many electric, electronic, and mechanical components known as **hardware**. These components include input devices, output devices, a system unit, storage devices, and communications devices. Figure 1-3 shows some common computer hardware components.

Input Devices

An **input device** is any hardware component that allows you to enter data or instructions into a computer. Six widely used input devices are the keyboard, mouse, microphone, scanner, digital camera, and PC video camera (Figure 1-3). A computer keyboard contains keys you press to enter data into the computer. A mouse is a small handheld device. With the mouse, you control movement of a small symbol on the screen, called the pointer, and you make selections from the screen.

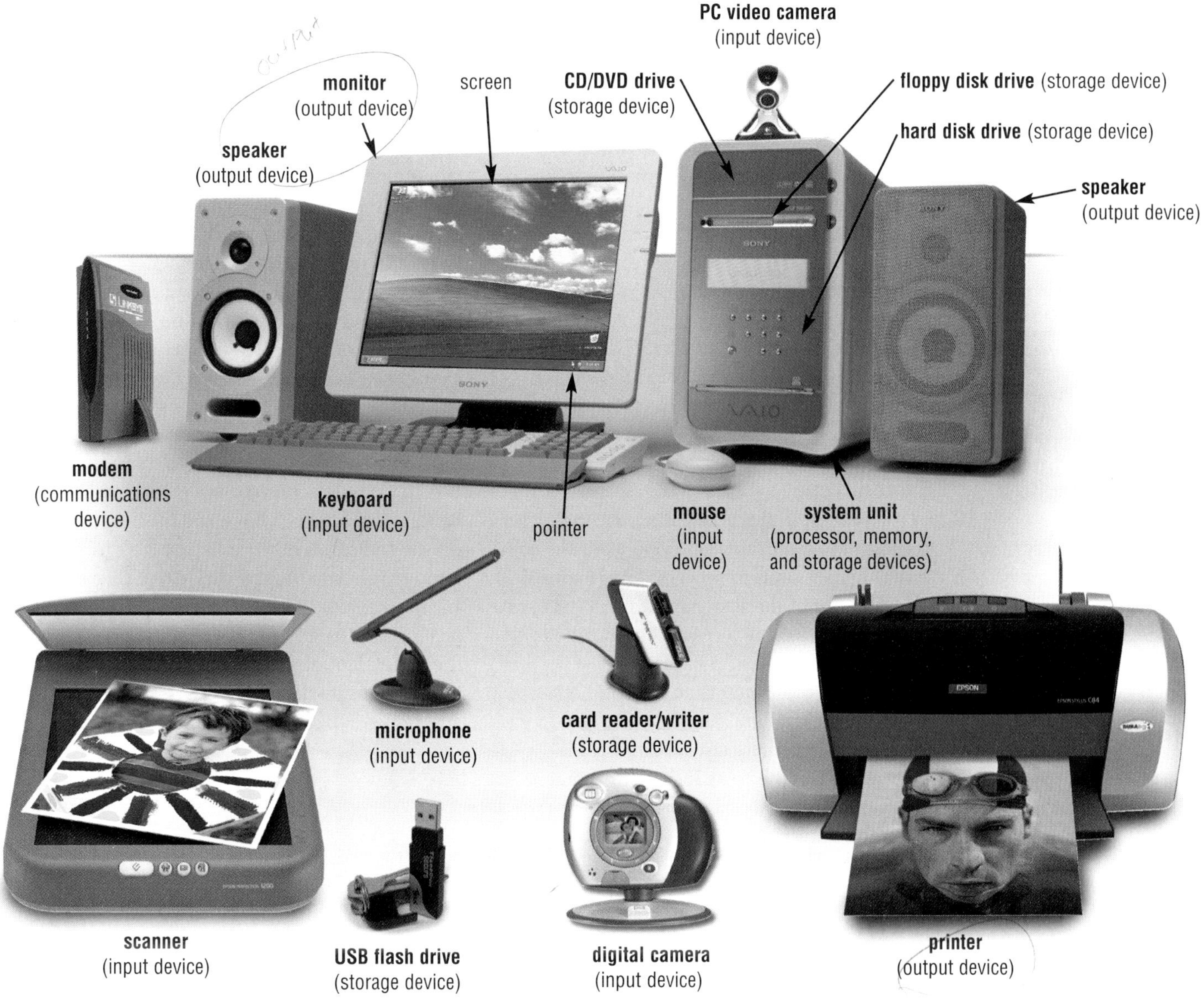

FIGURE 1-3 Common computer hardware components include the keyboard, mouse, microphone, scanner, digital camera, PC video camera, printer, monitor, speakers, system unit, disk drives, USB flash drives, card reader/writer, and modem.

A microphone allows a user to speak into the computer to enter data and instructions.

A scanner converts printed material (such as text and pictures) into a form the computer can use. For example, you can scan a picture and then include the picture in invitations you create on the computer.

With a digital camera, you take pictures and then transfer the photographed images to the computer or printer instead of storing the images on traditional film. A PC video camera is a digital video camera that allows users to create a movie or take still photographs electronically. With the PC video camera attached to the computer, users can see each other as they communicate via the computer.

WEB LINK 1-1

Input Devices

Visit the Discovering Computers 2005 WEB LINK page (**scsite.com/dc2005/weblink**). Click Input Devices below Chapter 1.

Output Devices

An **output device** is any hardware component that conveys information to one or more people. Three commonly used output devices are a printer, a monitor, and speakers (Figure 1-3 on the previous page).

A printer produces text and graphics on a physical medium such as paper. A monitor displays text, graphics, and videos on a screen. Many monitors look similar to a television. Speakers allow you to hear music, voice, and other audio (sounds).

WEB LINK 1-2

Output Devices

Visit the Discovering Computers 2005 WEB LINK page (**scsite.com/dc2005/weblink**). Click Output Devices below Chapter 1.

System Unit

The **system unit** is a box-like case that contains the electronic components of the computer that are used to process data (Figure 1-3). The circuitry of the system unit usually is part of or is connected to a circuit board called the motherboard.

Two main components on the motherboard are the processor and memory. The *processor* is the electronic component that interprets and carries out the basic instructions that operate the computer. *Memory* consists of electronic components that store instructions waiting to be executed and data needed by those instructions. Most memory keeps data and instructions temporarily, although some forms of memory are permanent.

FAQ 1-2

What is a CPU?

The processor. Most people in the computer industry use the terms *CPU* (*central processing unit*) and processor to mean the same.

For more information about processors, visit the Discovering Computers 2005 FAQ Web page (**scsite.com/dc2005/faq**). Click Processor below Chapter 1.

Storage Devices

Storage holds data, instructions, and information for future use. For example, computers can store hundreds or millions of customer names and addresses. Storage holds these items permanently.

A computer keeps data, instructions, and information on **storage media**. Examples of storage media are floppy disks, Zip disks, USB flash drives, hard disks, CDs, DVDs, and memory cards. A **storage device** records (writes) and/or retrieves (reads) items to and from storage media. Drives and readers/writers, which are types of storage devices, accept a certain kind of storage media. For example, a CD drive (storage device) accepts a CD (storage media). Storage devices often function as a source of input because they transfer items from storage into memory.

A floppy disk consists of a thin, circular, flexible disk enclosed in a square-shaped plastic shell. You insert a floppy disk in and remove it from a floppy disk drive (Figure 1-4). A Zip disk looks similar to a floppy disk but has much greater storage capabilities — up to the equivalent of 170 standard floppy disks. As with floppy disks, you insert Zip disks in and remove them from Zip drives.

FIGURE 1-4 A floppy disk is inserted in and removed from a floppy disk drive.

A USB flash drive is a portable storage device that has much more storage capacity than a floppy disk or Zip disk but is small and lightweight enough to be transported on a keychain or in a pocket (Figure 1-5). You plug a USB flash drive into a special, easily accessible opening on the computer.

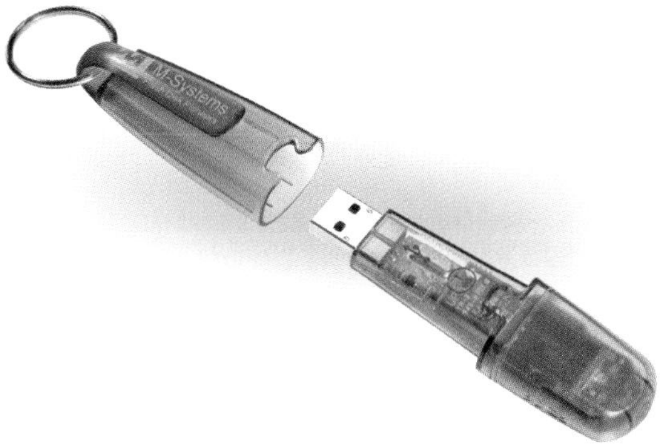

FIGURE 1-5 A USB flash drive is small enough to be attached to a key ring, making it easy for users to transport their data and information.

A hard disk provides much greater storage capacity than a floppy disk, Zip disk, or USB flash drive. The average hard disk can hold more than 60 billion characters. Although some hard disks are removable, most are enclosed in an airtight, sealed case housed inside the system unit (Figure 1-6).

FIGURE 1-6 Most hard disks are self contained devices housed inside the system unit.

A compact disc is a flat, round, portable metal disc. One type of compact disc is a CD-ROM, which you can access using most CD and DVD drives. Another type of compact disc is a DVD-ROM, which has enough storage capacity to store a full-length movie. To use a DVD-ROM, you need a DVD drive (Figure 1-7).

Some portable devices, such as digital cameras, use memory cards as the storage media. You then can use a card reader/writer (Figure 1-3 on page 7) to transfer the stored items, such as the electronic photographs, from the memory card to a computer or printer.

FIGURE 1-7 To use a DVD-ROM, you need a DVD drive.

Communications Devices

A **communications device** is a hardware component that enables a computer to send (transmit) and receive data, instructions, and information to and from one or more computers. A widely used communications device is the modem (Figure 1-3).

Communications occur over cables, telephone lines, cellular radio networks, satellites, or other transmission media. Some transmission media, such as satellites and cellular radio networks, are wireless, which means they have no physical lines or wires. People around the world communicate with each other using transmission media. Read Issue 1-1 for a related discussion.

WEB LINK 1-3

Communications Devices

Visit the Discovering Computers 2005 WEB LINK page (**scsite.com/dc2005/weblink**). Click Communications Devices below Chapter 1.

ISSUE 1-1

Does Technology Discriminate?

Educated people. Higher-income families. Urbanites. Industrially developed nations. Upper-class neighborhoods. Individuals without disabilities. Statistics show that people in these groups have more access to technology than uneducated people, lower-income families, those living in rural areas, less industrially developed nations, middle-class neighborhoods, and individuals with disabilities. One study claims that those with less access to technology are at least a generation behind with respect to education. Another study alleges that those with less access to technology are less successful. Do you agree that access to technology such as a computer, the Internet, television, and telephone makes you more successful? Why? Are students who do not have computers at home facing an academic disadvantage in competing for good grades? Does the student with a computer at home have an unfair advantage? Are job seekers who have a computer more likely to find a job than those without a computer? What can be done to ensure that all members of society have access to technology?

For more information about technology discrimination, visit the Discovering Computers 2005 Issues Web page (**scsite.com/dc2005/issues**). Click Issue #1 below Chapter 1.

WHY IS A COMPUTER SO POWERFUL?

Computers are powerful for a variety of reasons. They operate with amazing speed, reliability, consistency, and accuracy. Computers can store huge amounts of data and information. Also, computers allow users to communicate with other users or computers. A **user** is anyone who communicates with a computer or utilizes the information it generates.

Speed

In the system unit, operations occur through electronic circuits. When data, instructions, and information flow along these circuits, they travel at incredibly fast speeds. Most computers carry out billions of operations in a single second. The world's fastest computer can perform trillions of operations in one second.

Reliability and Consistency

The electronic components in modern computers are dependable because they have a low failure rate. The high reliability of components enables the computer to produce consistent results.

Accuracy

Computers process large amounts of data and generate error-free results, provided the data is input correctly and the instructions work properly. If data is inaccurate, the resulting output will be incorrect. A computing phrase — known as *garbage in, garbage out* — points out that the accuracy of a computer's output depends on the accuracy of the input.

Storage

With current storage devices, the computer can transfer data quickly from storage to memory, process it, and then store it again for future use. Many computers store enormous amounts of data and make this data available for processing anytime it is needed.

Communications

Most computers today can communicate with other computers, often wirelessly. Computers with this capability can share any of the four information processing cycle operations — input, process, output, and storage — with another computer. For example, two computers connected by a communications device, such as a modem, can share stored data, instructions, and information. These two computers can be located in the same room or thousands of miles away from each other in two different countries. For a more technical discussion about how data transfers among computers and devices, read the High-Tech Talk article on page 39.

QUIZ YOURSELF 1-1

To check your knowledge of computer literacy, computers and their components, and why a computer is powerful, visit the Discovering Computers 2005 Quiz Yourself Web page (**scsite.com/dc2005/quiz**). Click Objectives 1 – 3 below Chapter 1.

NETWORKS AND THE INTERNET

A **network** is a collection of computers and devices connected together via communications devices and transmission media. Networks allow computers to share *resources*, such as hardware, software, data, and information. Sharing resources saves time and money. For example, instead of purchasing one printer for every computer in a business, school, or home, you can connect all computers to a single printer via a network. The computers can be connected to the printer with wires or wirelessly. When a computer connects to a network, it is **online**.

In many networks, one or more computers act as a server. The *server* controls access to the resources on a network. The other computers on the network, each called a *client* or workstation, request resources from the server (Figure 1-8). The major differences between the server and client computers are that the server ordinarily has more power, more storage space, and is more reliable.

Many homes and most businesses and schools network their computers together. Home networks usually are small, existing within a single structure and often are wireless. Business and school networks can be small or quite widespread. A network can connect computers in a school laboratory, an office building, a group of buildings, or across a city, country, or the globe. The world's largest network is the Internet.

The Internet

The **Internet** is a worldwide collection of networks that connects millions of businesses, government agencies, educational institutions, and individuals (Figure 1-9).

Users can make well-informed decisions because they have instant access to information stored all over the world (read Apply It 1-1 for more information).

FIGURE 1-8 A server manages the resources on a network, Internet-ready portable computers and devices and clients access the resources on the server. This network enables three separate computers to share the same printer.

APPLY IT 1-1

Wireless Internet Access Anywhere

You can read messages and search the Internet in the cafeteria, on the bus, or in your backyard with wireless devices or with a portable computer equipped with wireless capability.

As the number of Internet-ready portable computers and devices proliferates, as many as 200,000 restaurants, hotels, airports, and other public-access areas worldwide are expected to install Internet access points, or hot spots, by 2008.

For more information about wireless Internet access, visit the Discovering Computers 2005 Apply It Web page (**scsite.com/dc2005/apply**). Click Apply It #1 below Chapter 1.

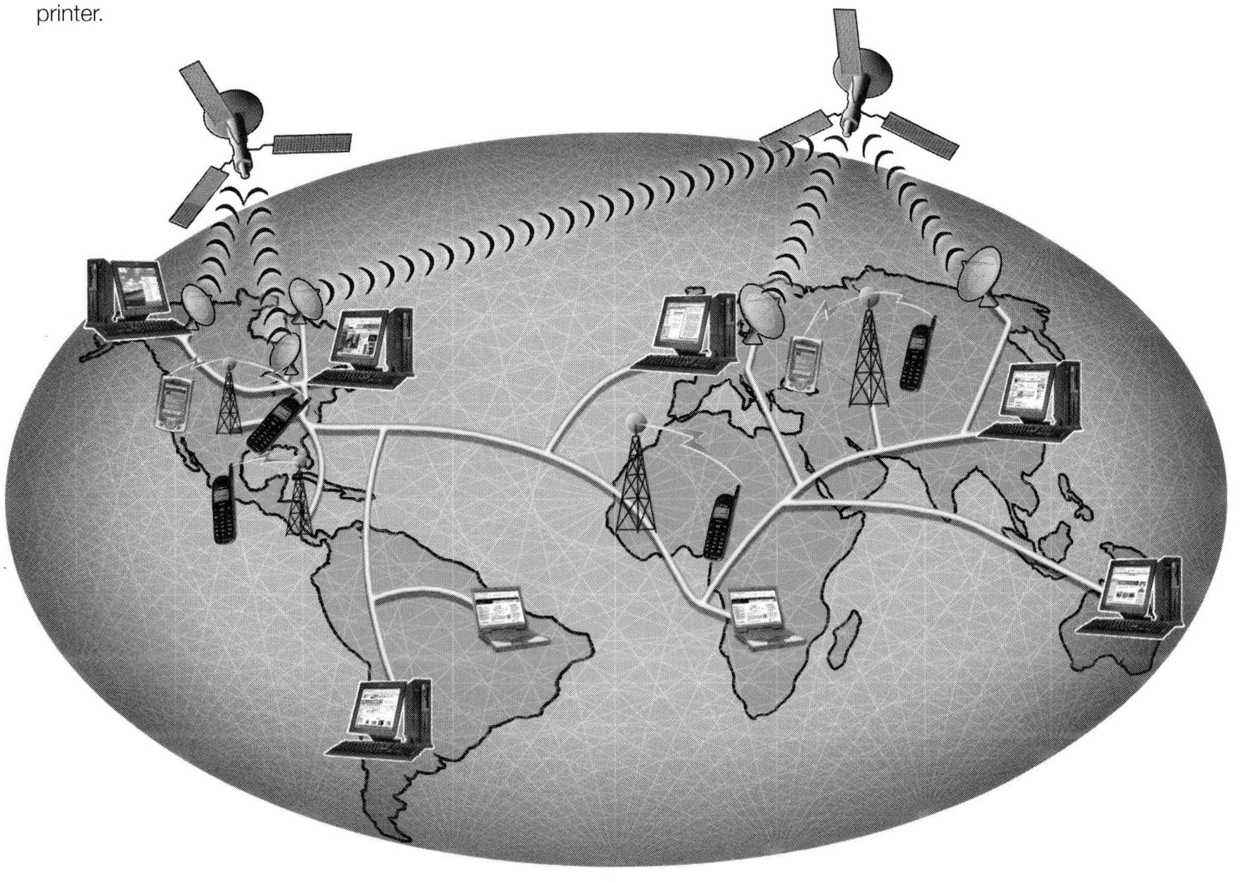

FIGURE 1-9 The Internet is the largest network, connecting millions of computers around the world.

More than one-half billion people around the world use the Internet daily for a variety of reasons, including the following purposes:

- Communicate with and meet other people around the world
- Access a wealth of information, news, and research findings
- Shop for goods and services
- Bank and invest
- Take a class
- Access sources of entertainment and leisure, such as online games, music, videos, books, and magazines

Figure 1-10 shows examples in each of these areas.

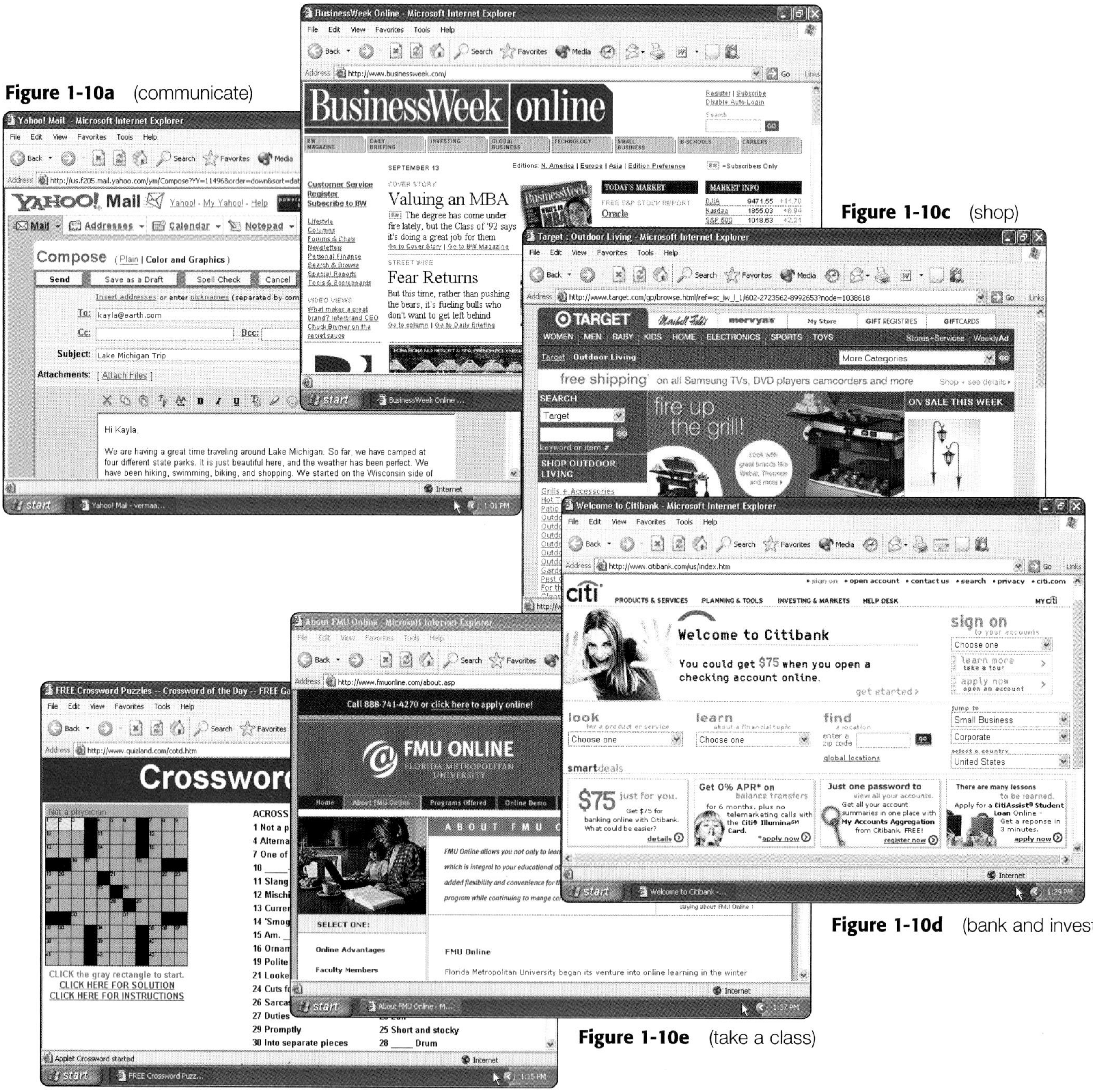

Figure 1-10a (communicate)

Figure 1-10b (access information)

Figure 1-10c (shop)

Figure 1-10d (bank and invest)

Figure 1-10e (take a class)

Figure 1-10f (access sources of entertainment)

FIGURE 1-10 Users access the Internet for a variety of reasons: to communicate with others, to access a wealth of information, to shop for goods and services, to bank and invest, to take a class, and for entertainment.

The **Web**, short for World Wide Web, is one of the more popular services on the Internet. Think of the Web as a global library of information available to anyone connected to the Internet. The Web contains billions of documents called Web pages. A **Web page** can contain text, graphics, audio, and video. The six screens shown in Figure 1-10 are examples of Web pages.

Web pages often have built-in connections, or links, to other documents, graphics, other Web pages, or Web sites. A Web site is a collection of related Web pages. For example, Target has a Web site that contains many Web pages. Some of the Web pages at the Target Web site display products for sale, other pages allow you to shop the Target store, and yet other pages provide information about Target.

People also connect to the Internet to exchange information with others around the world. E-mail allows you to send messages to other users. With instant messaging, you can have a live conversation with another connected user. In a chat room, you can communicate with multiple users at the same time — much like a group discussion. Some Web sites offer online calendars and address books so you can share appointments and contacts with others.

In addition to accessing and using information on the Web, many people use the Web as a means to share personal information, photographs, videos, or artwork with the world. Anyone can create a Web page and then make it available, or *publish* it, on the Internet for others to see (read Issue 1-2 for a related discussion). As an alternative, some Web sites provide publishing services free. At a **photo community** Web site, for example, users can create an online photo album and store their electronic photographs free (Figure 1-11).

Several companies offer access to the Internet. By paying a small monthly fee to this type of company, you can use your computer and a modem to connect to the many services of the Internet.

For more information about using the Web, read Making Use of the Web in Appendix A at the back of the book.

ISSUE 1-2

Is Everything You Read True?

It is against the law for Americans to contact space aliens. An ingredient in many popular shampoos has been proven to cause cancer. Chicken feet were discovered in the nuggets meal of a national fast-food chain. None of these statements is true, but each has appeared on a World Wide Web page. In today's society, many people think that anything in print is true. Yet, authors with a wide range of expertise, authority, and biases create Web pages. Web pages can be as accurate as the most scholarly journal, or no truer than the most disreputable supermarket tabloid. The Web makes it easy to obtain information, but Web page readers must make an extra effort to determine the quality of that information. In evaluating a Web page, experts suggest that you consider such factors as the purpose, scope, sponsor, timeliness, presentation, author, and permanence of the page. Ultimately, who is responsible for the accuracy of information on the Web? Why? What factors are most important in evaluating the accuracy of a Web page? Why?

For more information about Web page accuracy, visit the Discovering Computers 2005 Issues Web page (**scsite.com/dc2005/issues**). Click Issue #2 below Chapter 1.

WEB LINK 1-4

The Internet

Visit the Discovering Computers 2005 WEB LINK page (**scsite.com/dc2005/weblink**). Click The Internet below Chapter 1.

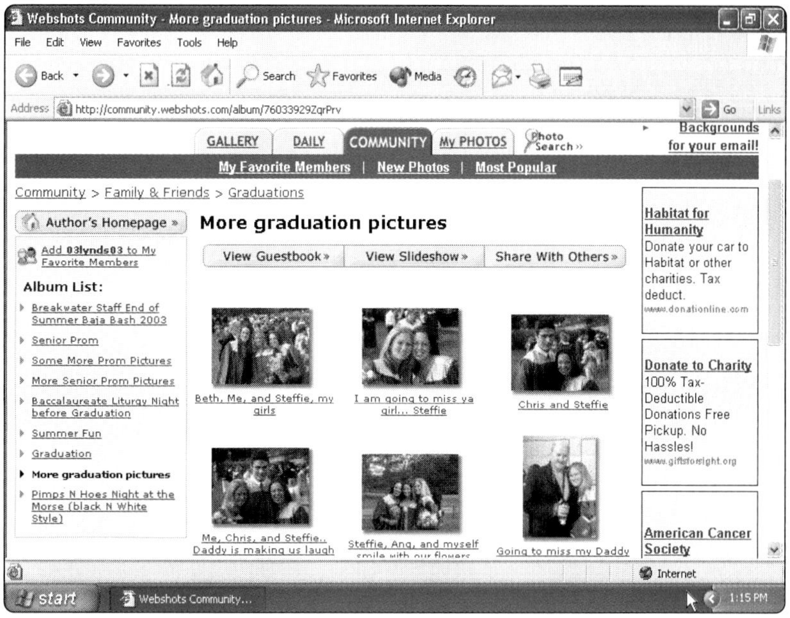

FIGURE 1-11 A happy student posted graduation pictures at a photo community.

COMPUTER SOFTWARE

Software, also called a **program**, is a series of instructions that tells the computer what to do and how to do it. A program exists on storage media such as a compact disc. When purchasing software from a computer store or on the Web, you typically receive a box that includes a CD(s) or DVD(s) that contains the program (Figure 1-12). You also may receive a manual or printed instructions explaining how to install, execute, and use the software.

Installing is the process of setting up the software to work with the computer, printer, and other hardware components. To begin installing the software from a CD or DVD, a user inserts the program disc in a CD or DVD drive. The computer then copies all or part of the program from the disc to the computer's hard disk.

During installation, the program may ask you to register or activate the software online. If your computer has an Internet connection, this online procedure saves the time of telephoning the vendor or completing a paper registration card and mailing it. If requested, it is important to register and/or activate software. Some vendors make the software so it does not function or has limited functionality until you register or activate it.

WEB LINK 1-5

Computer Programs

Visit the Discovering Computers 2005 WEB LINK page (**scsite.com/dc2005/weblink**). Click Computer Programs below Chapter 1.

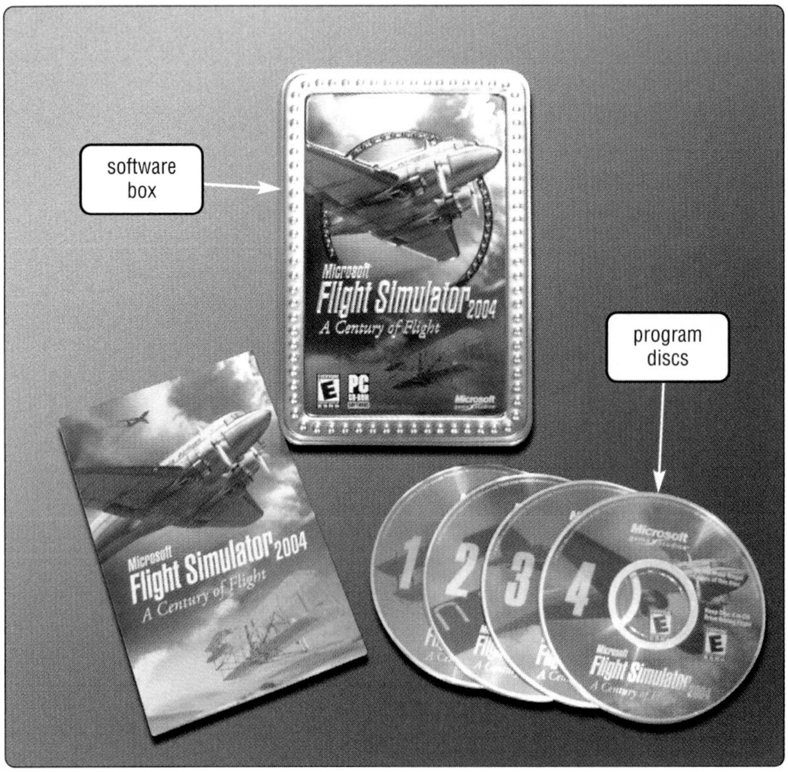

FIGURE 1-12 When buying software, you receive media such as a CD(s) or DVD(s) that contains the program.

When you buy a computer, it usually has some software preinstalled on its hard disk. This enables you to use the computer the first time you turn it on.

Once software is installed, you can use it. Some software requires you to insert the program disc into the drive while you use, or **run**, the software. Others do not, because the installation process copies the entire program to the hard disk. When a user tells the computer to start the program, the computer places, or *loads*, the program into its memory from storage (either the hard disk or the program disc). Once in memory, the computer can carry out, or *execute*, the instructions in a program. Figure 1-13 illustrates the steps that occur when a user installs and runs an encyclopedia program.

You interact with a program through its user interface. The user interface controls how you enter data and instructions and how information is displayed on the screen. Software today often has a graphical user interface. With a **graphical user interface** (**GUI** pronounced gooey), you interact with the software using text, graphics, and visual images such as icons (Figure 1-14). An *icon* is a small image that represents a program, an instruction, or some other object. You can use the mouse to select icons that perform operations such as starting a program.

Software is the key to productive use of computers. With the proper software, a computer can be a valuable tool. The two categories of software are system software and application software. The following sections describe these categories of software.

FAQ 1-3

Which spelling is correct, disk or disc?

Both are correct, depending on usage. When referring to CD, DVD, and other *optical* (laser) storage, computer professionals typically use the term disc. Floppy disks, Zip disks, hard disks, and other nonoptical storage media normally use the term disk.

For more information about disks and discs, visit the Discovering Computers 2005 FAQ Web page (**scsite.com/dc2005/faq**). Click Disk or Disc below Chapter 1.

FIGURE 1-13 INSTALLING AND RUNNING A COMPUTER PROGRAM

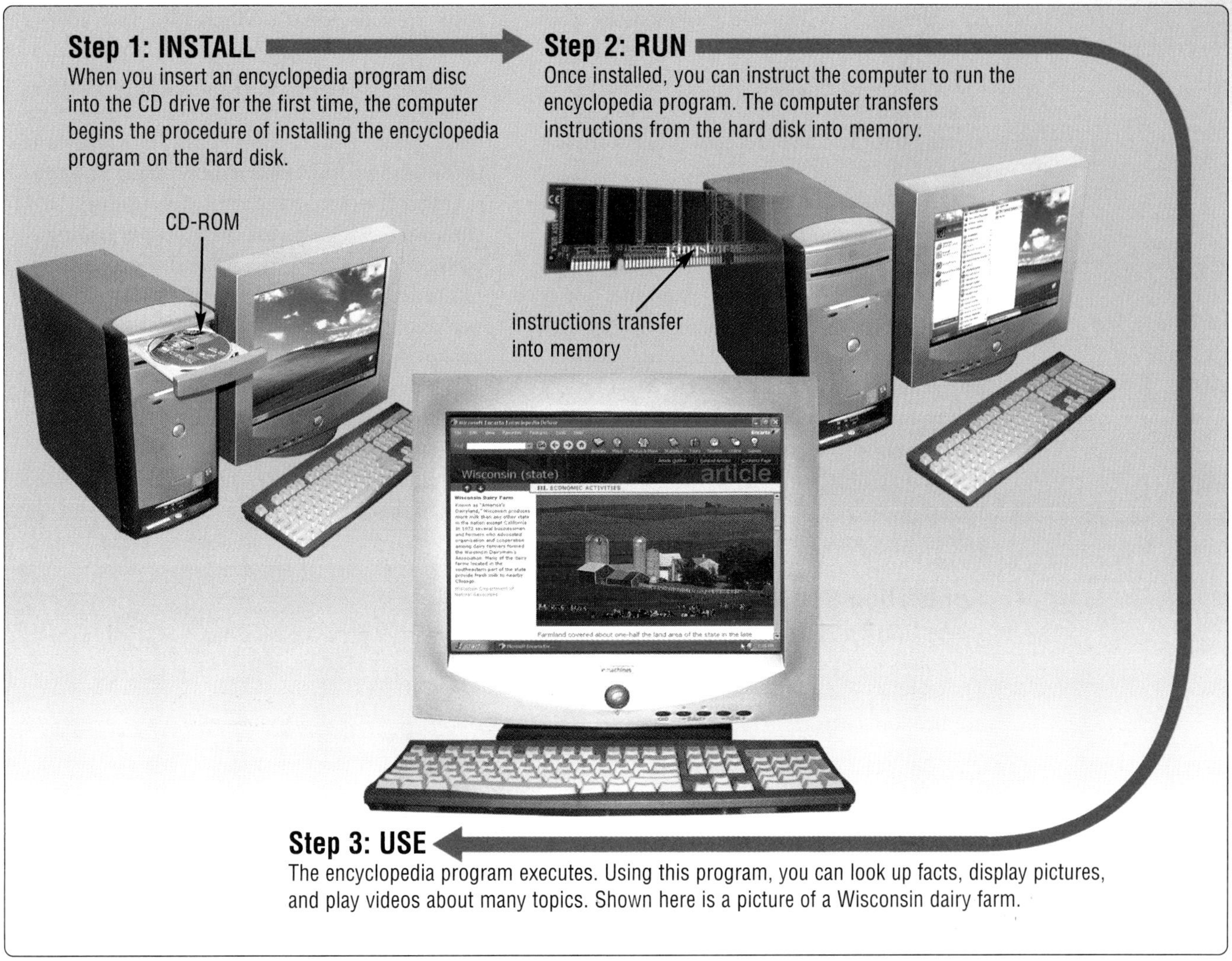

System Software

System software consists of the programs that control or maintain the operations of the computer and its devices. System software serves as the interface between the user, the application software, and the computer's hardware.

Two types of system software are the operating system and utility programs.

OPERATING SYSTEM An *operating system* is a set of programs that coordinates all the activities among computer hardware devices. The operating system also contains instructions that allow users to run application software. Many of today's computers use Microsoft's operating system, called Windows XP (Figure 1-14).

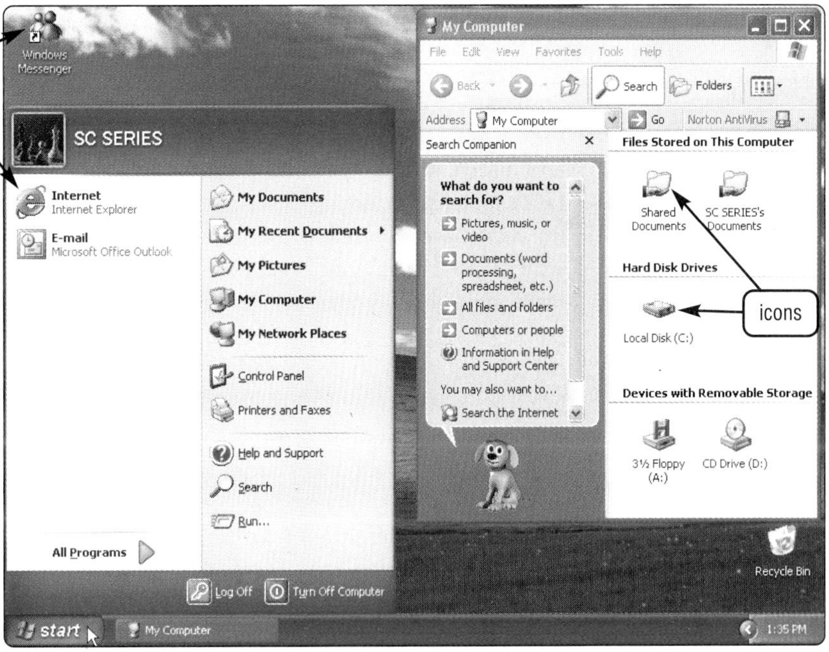

FIGURE 1-14 The graphical user interface of Windows XP.

When a user starts a computer, portions of the operating system load into memory from the computer's hard disk. It remains in memory while the computer is on. The operating system provides a means for users to communicate with the computer and other software.

UTILITY PROGRAMS A *utility program* allows a user to perform maintenance-type tasks usually related to managing a computer, its devices, or its programs. For example, one type of utility program can examine a floppy disk or hard disk to determine if it contains any physical flaws such as a scratch. Most operating systems include several utility programs for managing disk drives, printers, and other devices. You also can buy utility programs, which allow you to perform additional computer management functions.

Application Software

Application software consists of programs that perform specific tasks for users. A widely used type of application software related to communications is a Web browser, which allows users with an Internet connection to access and view Web pages. Other popular application software includes word processing software, spreadsheet software, database software, and presentation graphics software.

Word processing software allows users to create documents such as letters, memos, and brochures. Spreadsheet software calculates numbers arranged in rows and columns and allows users to perform financial tasks such as budgeting and forecasting. Database software provides a way to store data in an organized fashion, as well as retrieve, manipulate, and display that data in a variety of formats. With presentation graphics software, users create visual aids for a presentation.

Software vendors often bundle and sell word processing, spreadsheet, database, and presentation graphics application software together as a single unit. This bundle costs much less than if you purchased the application software individually. Microsoft Office 2003 is a very popular example.

Many other types of application software exist that enable users to perform a variety of tasks. Some widely used application software includes personal information manager, note taking, project management, accounting, computer-aided design, desktop publishing, paint/image editing, audio and video editing, multimedia authoring, Web page authoring, personal finance, legal, tax preparation, home design/landscaping, educational, reference, and entertainment (games, simulations, etc.). As shown in Figure 1-15, you often purchase application software from a store that sells computer products. Read Issue 1-3 for a related discussion.

FIGURE 1-15 Stores that sell computer products have shelves stocked with software for sale.

WEB LINK 1-6

Application Software

Visit the Discovering Computers 2005 WEB LINK page (**scsite.com/dc2005/weblink**). Click Application Software below Chapter 1.

ISSUE 1-3

Does Software Promote Violence?

One of today's more popular computer games is Grand Theft Auto. In the game, players advance through the mafia by conveying secret packages, following alleged snitches, and other similar activities. Since its release, buyers have purchased more than three million copies of Grand Theft Auto. Proponents praise the game's vivid graphics, edgy characters, and wide range of allowable behaviors. Critics condemn the game's explicit violence and the rewards it gives players for partaking in illegal acts. Grand Theft Auto is rated M (for Mature, meaning it is suitable for ages 17 and older), but children as young as 12 are familiar with it. Even worse, opponents fear that the game's popularity may influence future developers of computer games aimed at younger children. What impact do violent computer games or games that promote unacceptable acts have on individual behavior? Do these games desensitize players to violence or increase aggression? Why or why not? Should restrictions be placed on sales of computer games?

For more information about computer entertainment and video games, visit the Discovering Computers 2005 Issues Web page (**scsite.com/dc2005/issues**). Click Issue #3 below Chapter 1.

Software Development

A *programmer* is someone who develops application or system software. Programmers develop programs or write the instructions that direct the computer to process data into information. When writing instructions, a programmer must be sure the program works properly so the computer generates the desired results. Complex programs can require thousands to millions of instructions.

Programmers use a programming language or program development tool to create computer programs. Popular programming languages include C++, C#, Visual Basic .NET 2003, and JavaScript. Figure 1-16 shows some of the instructions a programmer may write to create an Internet application.

QUIZ YOURSELF 1-2

To check your knowledge of networks, the Internet and Web, installing and running programs, and types of software, visit the Discovering Computers 2005 Quiz Yourself Web page (**scsite.com/dc2005/quiz**). Click Objectives 4 – 7 below Chapter 1.

Figure 1-16a (JavaScript program)

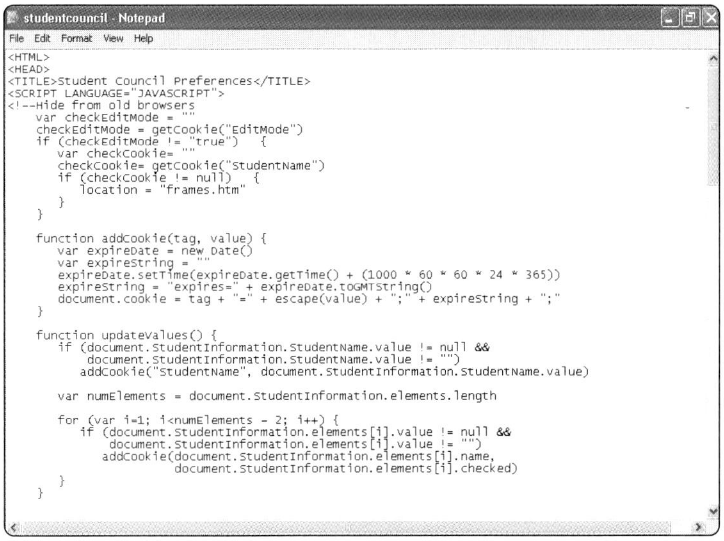

Figure 1-16b (resulting Internet application)

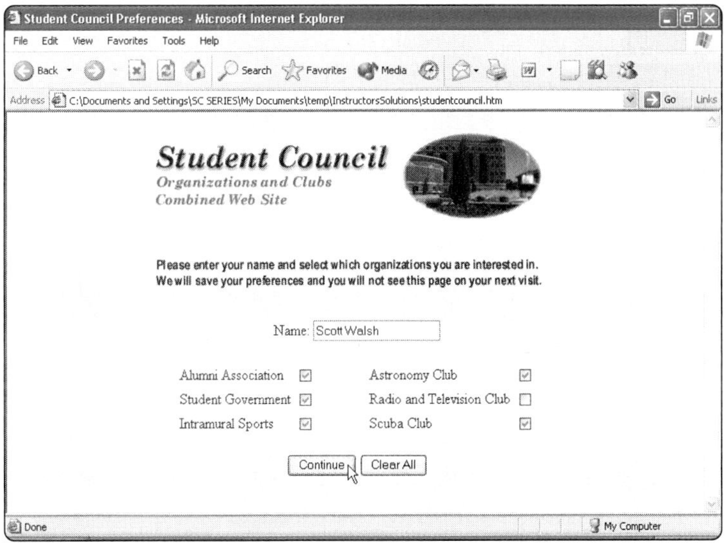

FIGURE 1-16 The top figure illustrates some of the instructions a programmer writes in JavaScript to create the application that runs on the Internet, shown in the bottom figure.

CATEGORIES OF COMPUTERS

Industry experts typically classify computers in five categories: personal computers, mobile computers and mobile devices, midrange servers, mainframes, and supercomputers. A computer's size, speed, processing power, and price typically determine the category it best fits. Due to rapidly changing technology, however, the distinction among categories is not always clear-cut. For example, the speed that defines a mainframe computer today may define a midrange server next year. Some characteristics may overlap categories. Still, many people refer to these categories when discussing computers.

Figure 1-17 summarizes the five categories of computers (read Looking Ahead 1-1 for a look at the next generation of computers). The following pages discuss computers and devices that fall into each category.

PERSONAL COMPUTERS

A **personal computer** is a computer that can perform all of its input, processing, output, and storage activities by itself. A personal computer contains a processor, memory, and one or more input, output, and storage devices.

CATEGORIES OF COMPUTERS

Category	Physical Size	Number of Simultaneously Connected Users	General Price Range
Personal computers (desktop)	Fits on a desk	Usually one (can be more if networked)	Several hundred to several thousand dollars
Mobile computers and mobile devices	Fits on your lap or in your hand	Usually one	Several thousand dollars or less
Midrange servers	Small cabinet	Two to thousands	$5,000 to $850,000
Mainframe computers	Partial room to a full room of equipment	Hundreds to thousands	$300,000 to several million dollars
Supercomputers	Full room of equipment	Hundreds to thousands	$500,000 to more than $85 million dollars

FIGURE 1-17 This table summarizes some of the differences among the categories of computers. These should be considered general guidelines only because of rapid changes in technology.

LOOKING AHEAD 1-1

Wearable Computers Serve Practical Purposes

When FedEx aircraft mechanics access detailed schematics, they consult their new wearable computers. People with disabilities wear head-mounted displays, speech interfaces, and pointing devices to help them function. Indeed, wearable computers are finding a home in classrooms, power plants, and manufacturing facilities.

Experts predict that this hardware will be a trillion-dollar business in the next few years. Hundreds of companies currently are testing devices that use headsets and eyeglasses for input and output.

For a look at the next generation of wearable computers, visit the Discovering Computers 2005 Looking Ahead Web page (**scsite.com/dc2005/looking**). Click Looking Ahead #1 below Chapter 1.

Two popular types of personal computers are the PC (Figure 1-18) and the Apple (Figure 1-19). The term, *PC-compatible*, refers to any personal computer based on the original IBM personal computer design. Companies such as Dell, Gateway, and Toshiba sell PC-compatible computers. PC and PC-compatible computers have processors with different architectures than processors in Apple computers. These two types of computers also use different operating systems. PC and PC-compatible computers use the Windows operating system. Apple computers use the Macintosh operating system (Mac OS).

Two types of personal computers are desktop computers and notebook computers. The next section discusses desktop personal computers. Notebook computers are discussed in the mobile computers section.

Desktop Computers

A **desktop computer** is designed so the system unit, input devices, output devices, and any other devices fit entirely on or under a desk or table. In many models, the system unit is a tall and narrow *tower,* which can sit on the floor vertically — if desktop space is limited. Towers are available in a variety of heights. A tower is at least 24 inches tall, a mid-tower is about 16 inches tall, and a minitower is usually 13 inches tall.

Some desktop computers are powerful enough to function as a server on a network. These high-end computers cost much more than the basic desktop computer.

Another expensive, powerful desktop computer is the workstation, which is geared for work that requires intense calculations and graphics capabilities. Fields such as engineering, desktop publishing, and graphic art require the power of a workstation. An architect uses a workstation to view and create maps. A graphic artist uses a workstation to create computer-animated special effects for full-length motion pictures and video games.

FAQ 1-4

Does the term workstation have two meanings?

Yes. In the computer industry, a *workstation* can be a high-powered computer or a client computer.

For more information about workstations, visit the Discovering Computers 2005 FAQ Web page (**scsite.com/dc2005/faq**). Click Workstation below Chapter 1.

WEB LINK 1-7

Personal Computers

Visit the Discovering Computers 2005 WEB LINK page (**scsite.com/dc2005/weblink**). Click Personal Computers below Chapter 1.

FIGURE 1-18 The PC and compatible computers use the Windows operating system.

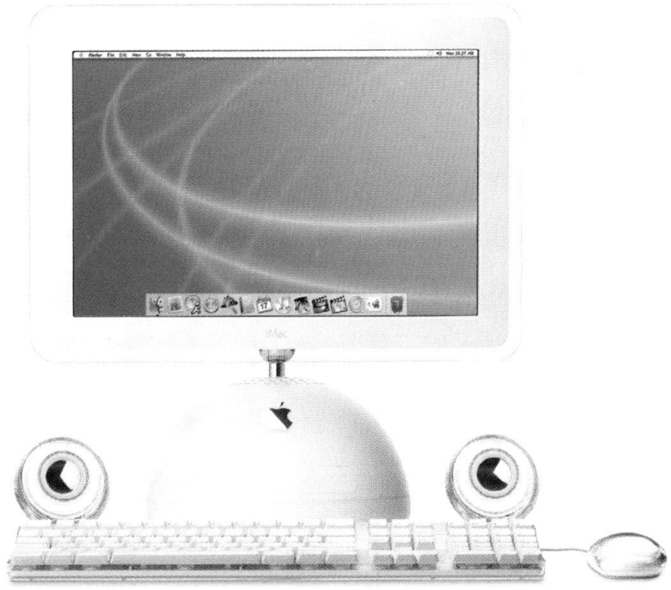

FIGURE 1-19 Apple computers, such as the iMac, use the Macintosh operating system.

MOBILE COMPUTERS AND MOBILE DEVICES

A **mobile computer** is a personal computer that you can carry from place to place. Similarly, a **mobile device** is a computing device small enough to hold in your hand.

The most popular type of mobile computer is the notebook computer. The following sections discuss the notebook computer and widely used mobile devices.

Notebook Computers

A **notebook computer**, also called a **laptop computer**, is a portable, personal computer small enough to fit on your lap. Today's notebook computers are thin and lightweight, yet they can be as powerful as the average desktop computer. Notebook computers generally are more expensive than desktop computers with equal capabilities.

On a typical notebook computer, the keyboard is on top of the system unit and the monitor attaches to the system unit with hinges (Figure 1-20). These computers weigh on average between 2.5 and 8 pounds, which allows users easily to transport the computers from place to place. Most notebook computers can operate on batteries or a power supply or both.

WEB LINK 1-8

Notebook Computers

Visit the Discovering Computers 2005 WEB LINK page (**scsite.com/dc2005/weblink**). Click Notebook Computers below Chapter 1.

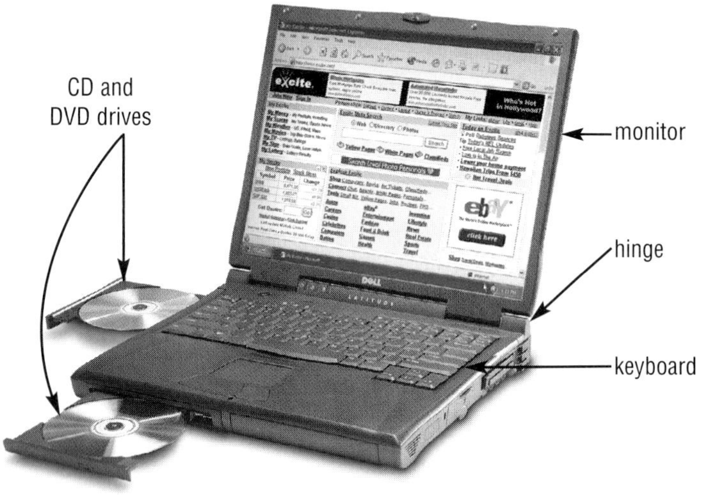

FIGURE 1-20 On a typical notebook computer, the keyboard is on top of the system unit, and the monitor attaches to the system unit with hinges.

TABLET PC Resembling a letter-sized slate, the **Tablet PC** is a special type of notebook computer that allows you to write or draw on the screen using a digital pen (Figure 1-21). With a *digital pen*, users write or draw on the screen or issue instructions to the Tablet PC, for example, by tapping on the screen. For users who prefer typing instead of handwriting, you can attach a keyboard to Tablet PCs that do not include one already. Most Tablet PC applications run with or without a keyboard. Tablet PCs also support voice input so users can enter text and issue instructions by speaking into the computer.

Tablet PCs are useful especially for taking notes in lectures, at meetings, conferences, and other forums where the standard notebook computer is not practical. With a cost of about only $2,000, some users may find Tablet PCs more appropriate for their needs than traditional notebook computers.

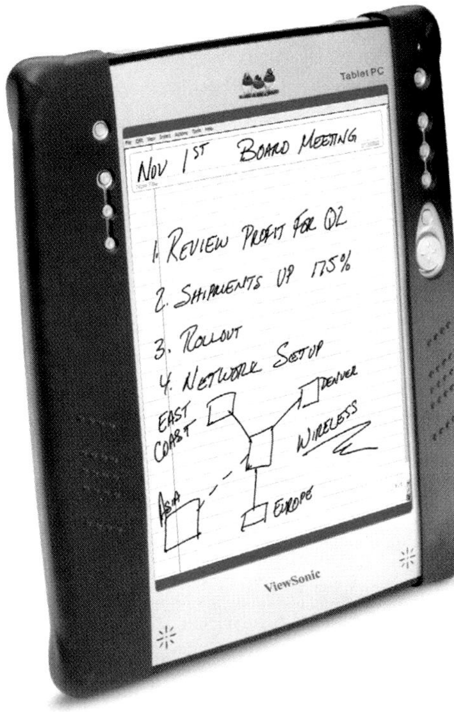

FIGURE 1-21 The Tablet PC combines the features of a traditional notebook computer with the simplicity of pencil and paper.

Mobile Devices

Some mobile devices are **Web-enabled**, meaning they can connect to the Internet wirelessly. Mobile devices usually do not have disk drives. Instead, these devices store programs and data permanently on memory inside the system unit or on small storage media such as memory cards. You typically connect a mobile device to a personal computer to exchange information between the computer and the mobile device.

Three popular types of mobile devices are handheld computers, PDAs, and smart phones. Some combination mobile devices also are available, for example, a PDA/smart phone.

HANDHELD COMPUTER A **handheld computer** is a computer small enough to fit in one hand while you operate it with the other hand. Because of their reduced size, the screens on handheld computers are quite small. The primary input device on a handheld computer is a small keyboard. A business traveler might prefer this type of handheld computer to a notebook computer.

Some handheld computers have a specialized keyboard. These industry-specific computers serve mobile employees, such as meter readers and parcel delivery people (Figure 1-22), whose jobs require them to move from place to place.

PDA The PDA is one of the more popular lightweight mobile devices in use today. A **PDA** (*personal digital assistant*) provides personal organizer functions such as a calendar, appointment book, address book, calculator, and notepad (Figure 1-23). Most PDAs also offer a variety of other application software such as word processing, spreadsheet, personal finance, and games. Some even include software that enables users to read a book on the device's screen.

The primary input device of a PDA is the stylus. A *stylus* looks like a small ballpoint pen, but uses pressure instead of ink to write and draw. If you prefer to type, you can insert PDAs without keyboards into a special keyboard. Some PDAs also support voice input.

FIGURE 1-22 UPS package delivery personnel use a handheld computer, called a DIAD (Delivery Information Acquisition Device), to collect shipment data, capture customer signatures, and transmit information wirelessly.

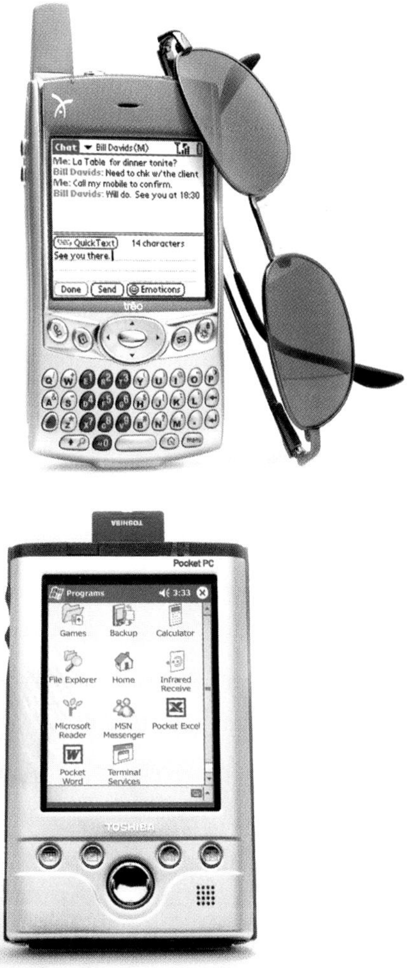

FIGURE 1-23 PDAs are a widely used mobile device, providing personal information management functions as well as Internet access and telephone capabilities. Shown here are two different styles of PDAs.

Many PDAs are Web-enabled so users can check e-mail and access the Internet. Some also provide telephone capabilities. Because of all the added features, increasingly more people are replacing their pocket-sized appointment books with PDAs (read Apply It 1-2 for more information).

APPLY IT 1-2

Prescription for Saving Doctors' Time

In doctors' hectic schedules, time is precious. Locating lab test reports, prescribed medications, and medical notes quickly at patients' bedsides during rounds can be challenging.

This task has been simplified with a wireless system that allows doctors to obtain patients' records on a PDA. The doctors can have this data available at their fingertips anywhere in the hospital or at their offices. This wireless PDA system helps reduce errors and paper and increase patient satisfaction.

For more information about PDAs, visit the Discovering Computers 2005 Apply It Web page (**scsite.com/dc2005/apply**). Click Apply It #2 below Chapter 1.

SMART PHONE Offering the convenience of one-handed operation, a **smart phone** is a Web-enabled telephone (Figure 1-24). In addition to basic telephone capabilities, a smart phone allows you to send and receive e-mail and access the Internet. Some higher-priced models have color screens, play music, and include built-in cameras so you immediately can share photographs or videos with others.

FIGURE 1-24 In addition to basic telephone functionality, smart phones allow you to check e-mail, access the Internet, and share photos.

MIDRANGE SERVERS

A **midrange server** is more powerful and larger than a workstation computer (Figure 1-25). Midrange servers typically support several hundred and sometimes up to a few thousand connected computers at the same time. In the past, midrange servers were known as *minicomputers*.

Midrange servers store data and programs. In many cases, one server accesses data on another server. In other cases, people use personal computers or terminals to access programs on a server. A terminal is a device with a monitor, keyboard, and memory. Some terminals have no processing power and must connect to a server to operate. Others have the capability of functioning when not connected to the server.

FIGURE 1-25 A midrange server is more powerful than a workstation, but less powerful than a mainframe.

MAINFRAMES

A **mainframe** is a large, expensive, very powerful computer that can handle hundreds or thousands of connected users simultaneously (Figure 1-26). Mainframes store tremendous amounts of data, instructions, and information. Large companies such as banks, airlines, and insurance companies use mainframes.

FIGURE 1-26 Mainframe computers are large, expensive, powerful computers that can handle thousands of connected computers and process millions of instructions per second.

Mainframes also can act as servers on a network environment. Midrange servers and other mainframes can access data and information from a mainframe. People also can access programs on the mainframe with terminals or personal computers.

SUPERCOMPUTERS

A **supercomputer** is the fastest, most powerful computer — and the most expensive (Figure 1-27). The fastest supercomputers are capable of processing more than 100 trillion instructions in a single second. With weights that exceed 100 tons, these computers can store more than 16,000 times the data and information of an average desktop computer. Supercomputers often are built using thousands of personal computer processors.

Applications requiring complex, sophisticated mathematical calculations use supercomputers. For example, applications in medicine, aerospace, automotive design, online banking, weather forecasting, nuclear energy research, and petroleum exploration use a supercomputer.

FIGURE 1-27 This IBM supercomputer requires an area the size of two basketball courts to house its more than 2,000 miles of wiring (enough wiring to connect Washington, D.C., to Phoenix, Arizona).

WEB LINK 1-9

Women in Technology

Visit the Discovering Computers 2005 WEB LINK page (**scsite.com/dc2005/weblink**). Click Women in Technology below Chapter 1.

WEB LINK 1-10

Minorities in Technology

Visit the Discovering Computers 2005 WEB LINK page (**scsite.com/dc2005/weblink**). Click Minorities in Technology below Chapter 1.

ELEMENTS OF AN INFORMATION SYSTEM

Obtaining timely and useful information from a computer requires more than the hardware and software discussed thus far. Other elements include accurate data, trained information technology staff and knowledgeable users (people), and documented procedures. Together, these elements (hardware, software, data, people, and procedures) comprise an *information system*. Figure 1-28 shows how each of the elements of an information system might interact.

The hardware must be reliable and capable of handling the expected workload. The software must be developed carefully and tested thoroughly. The data input into the computer must be accurate. Incorrect data generates incorrect information.

Most companies with mid-sized and large computers have an IT (information technology) department. Staff in the IT department should be highly skilled and up-to-date on the latest technology. IT staff also should train users so they understand how to use the computer properly. Today's users also work closely with IT staff in the development of computer applications that relate to their areas of work.

Finally, all the IT applications should have readily available documented procedures. These procedures should address starting, operating, and using the computer.

FIGURE 1-28 HOW THE ELEMENTS OF AN INFORMATION SYSTEM MIGHT INTERACT

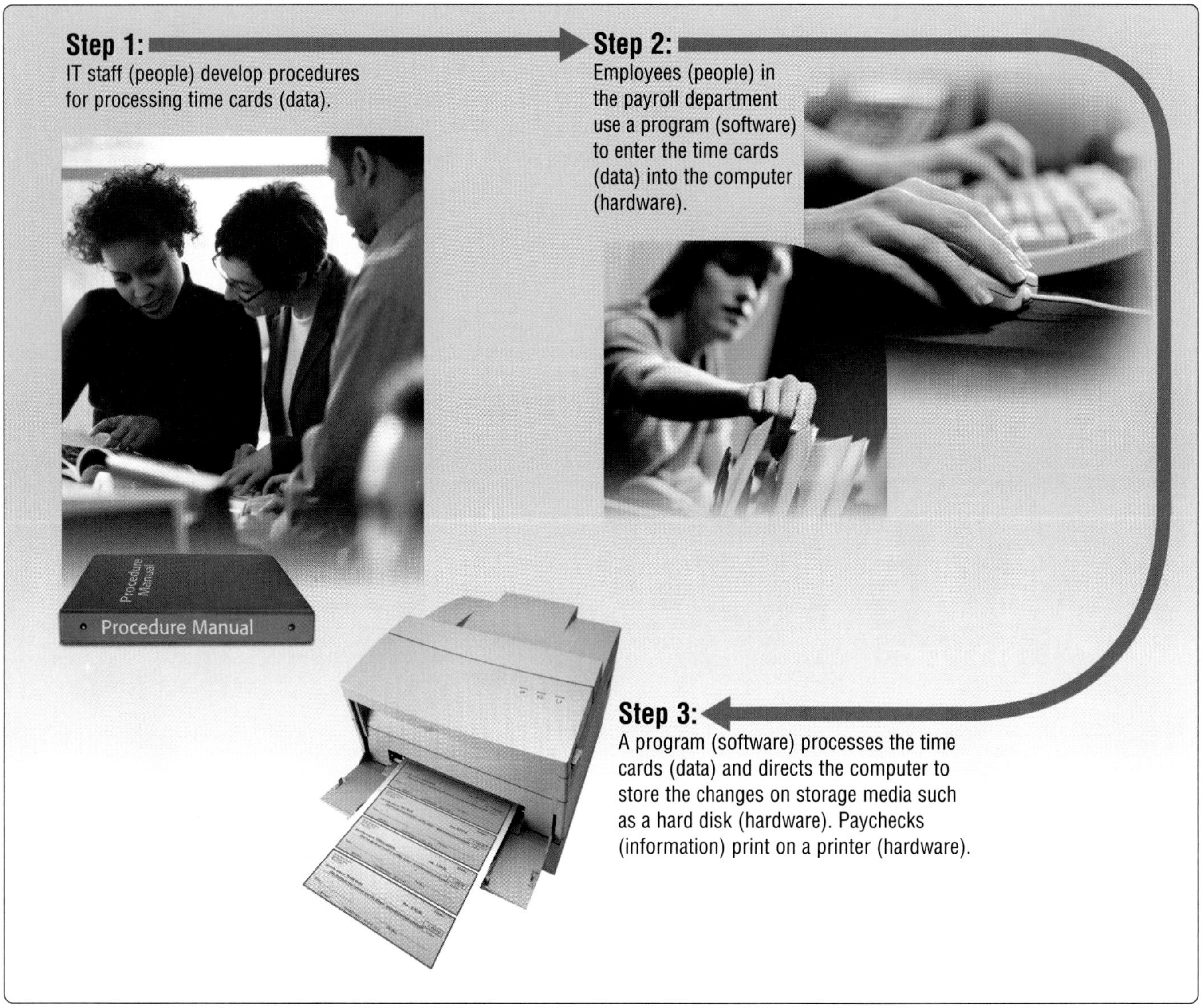

EXAMPLES OF COMPUTER USAGE

Every day, numerous users rely on different types of computers for a variety of applications. To illustrate the range of uses for computers, this section takes you on a visual and narrative tour of five categories of users: a home user, a small office/home office (SOHO) user, a mobile user, a large business user, and a power user.

The table in Figure 1-29 identifies some hardware and software that each user may require. The following pages discuss the items listed in the table. For a history of hardware and software developments, read the Timeline 2005 that follows this chapter.

CATEGORIES OF USERS

User	Hardware	Software
Home 	• Desktop computer • PDA • Smart phone	• Business (e.g., word processing) • Personal information manager • Personal finance, online banking, tax preparation • Web browser • E-mail, instant messaging, and chat rooms • Reference (e.g., encyclopedias, medical dictionaries, road atlas) • Entertainment (e.g., games, music composition, greeting cards) • Educational (e.g., tutorials, children's math and reading software)
Small Office/Home Office 	• Desktop computer • PDA • Shared network printer	• Business (e.g., word processing, spreadsheet, database) • Personal information manager • Company specific (e.g., accounting, legal reference) • Network management • Web browser • E-mail
Mobile 	• Notebook computer equipped with a modem, or a Tablet PC • Video projector • Web-enabled PDA/smart phone	• Business (e.g., word processing, spreadsheet, note taking, presentation graphics) • Personal information manager • Web browser • E-mail
Large Business 	• Midrange server or mainframe • Desktop or notebook computer • Industry-specific handheld computer • PDA • Kiosk	• Business (e.g., word processing, spreadsheet, database, presentation graphics) • Personal information manager • Accounting • Network management • Web browser • E-mail
Power 	• Workstation or other powerful computer with multimedia capabilities • PDA	• Desktop publishing • Multimedia authoring • Computer-aided design • Photo, audio, and video editing • Personal information manager • Web browser • E-mail

FIGURE 1-29 Today, computers are used by millions of people to support work tasks, school assignments, and leisure activities. Different computer users require different kinds of hardware and software to meet their needs effectively.

Home User

In an increasing number of homes, the computer no longer is a convenience. Instead, it is a basic necessity. Each family member, or **home user**, spends time on the computer for different reasons. These include budgeting and personal financial management, Web access, communications, and entertainment (Figure 1-30).

On the Internet, home users access a huge amount of information, take college classes, pay bills, manage investments, shop, listen to the radio, watch movies, read books, play games, file taxes, and make airline reservations. They also communicate with others around the world through e-mail, instant messaging, and chat rooms. Their communications are not limited to text. Today's technology provides users with the means to send graphics, audio, and video. With a digital camera, you can take a photograph and then send the electronic image to anyone. Using a

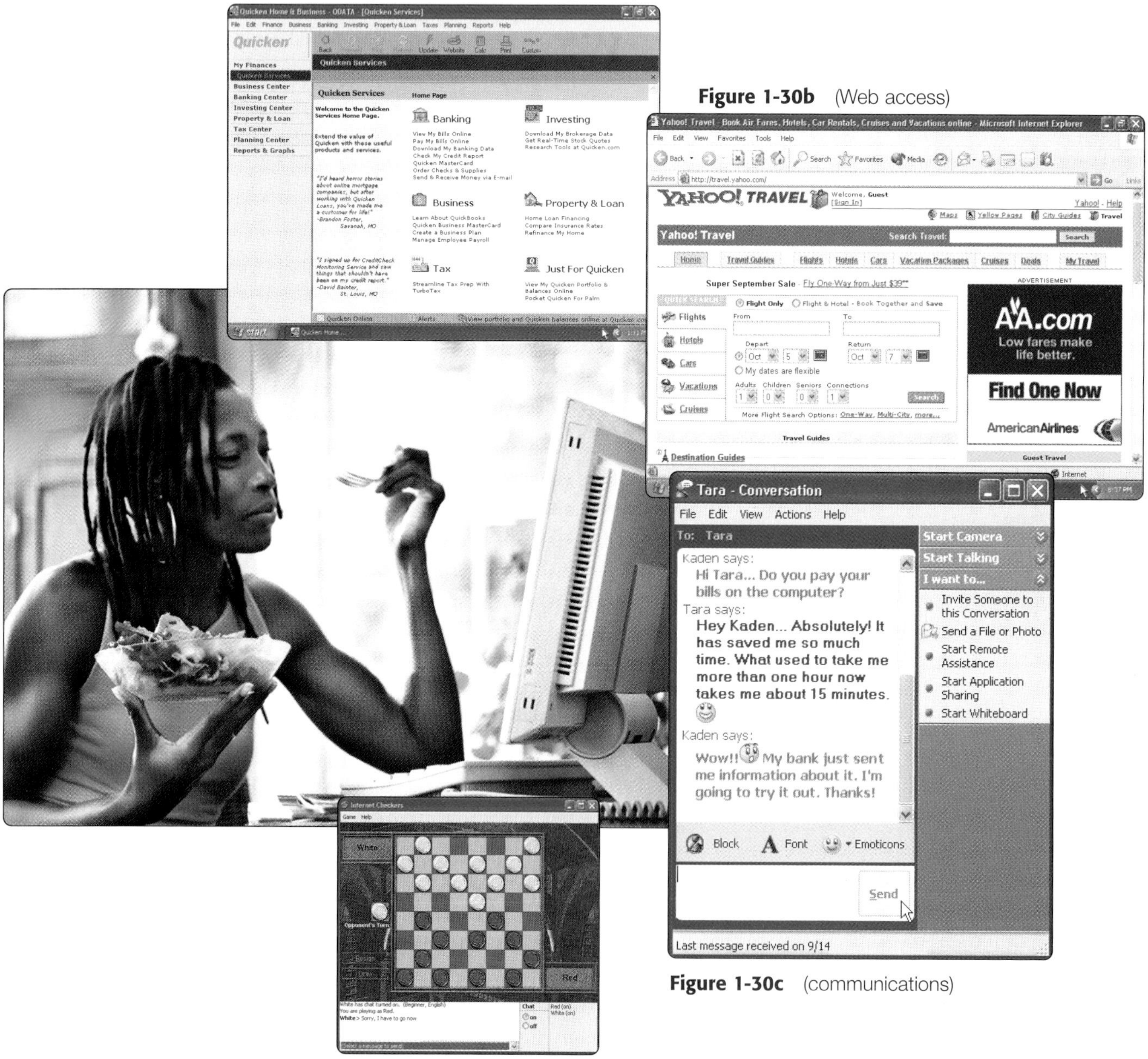

Figure 1-30a (personal financial management)

Figure 1-30b (Web access)

Figure 1-30c (communications)

Figure 1-30d (entertainment)

FIGURE 1-30 The home user spends time on a computer for a variety of reasons.

smart phone or PC video camera, which costs less than $100, home users easily have live video calls with friends and family members (Figure 1-31).

Today's homes typically have one or more desktop computers. Many are available in a variety of stylish colors and sleek designs, so the computer complements a room décor and the user's lifestyle. Some home users network multiple desktop computers throughout the house, often wirelessly. These small networks allow family members to access each other's data, information, programs, printers, and other devices.

Home users sometimes have PDAs to maintain daily schedules and address lists. Special-purpose handheld computers can manage and monitor the health condition of a family member.

Some families have an *Internet receiver*, which is a special type of computer that sits on top of or next to a television and allows the home user to access the Internet and navigate Web pages with a device that resembles a remote control or a wireless keyboard (Figure 1-32).

To meet their needs, home users have a variety of software. They type letters, homework assignments, and other documents with word processing software. Personal finance software helps the home user with personal finances, investments, and family budgets. Other software assists with preparing taxes, keeping a household inventory, and setting up maintenance schedules.

Reference software, such as encyclopedias, medical dictionaries, or a road atlas, provides valuable information for everyone in the family. With entertainment software, the home user can play games such as solitaire, chess, and Monopoly; compose music; research geneology; or create greeting cards. Educational software helps adults learn to speak a foreign language and youngsters to read, write, count, and spell. These forms of software are available on CD, DVD, and also on the Web.

FAQ 1-5

Can I listen to an audio CD on my computer?

Yes, in most cases. Simply insert the CD into the computer's CD or DVD drive. Within a few seconds, you should hear music from the computer's speakers or in your headset. If no music plays, it is possible the music company configured the CD so it will not play on a computer.

For more information about listening to music on the computer, visit the Discovering Computers 2005 FAQ Web page (**scsite.com/dc2005/faq**). Click Listen to Music below Chapter 1.

FIGURE 1-31 A dad uses a PC video camera to talk to and see his daughter on the family home computer.

FIGURE 1-32 With an Internet receiver and a wireless keyboard, home users can access the Internet from the comfort of their family room or any other room that has television access.

Small Office/Home Office User

Computers assist small business and home office users in managing their resources effectively. A **small office/home office** (*SOHO*) includes any company with fewer than 50 employees, as well as the self-employed who work from home. Small offices include local law practices, accounting firms, travel agencies, and florists. SOHO users typically have a desktop computer to perform some or all of their duties (Figure 1-33). Many also have PDAs to manage appointments and contact information.

Figure 1-33a (Web access)

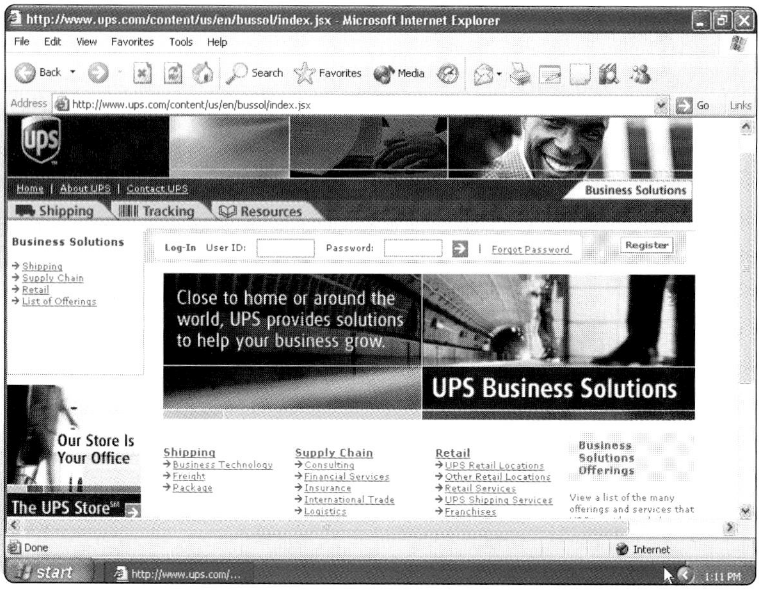

Figure 1-33b (spreadsheet)

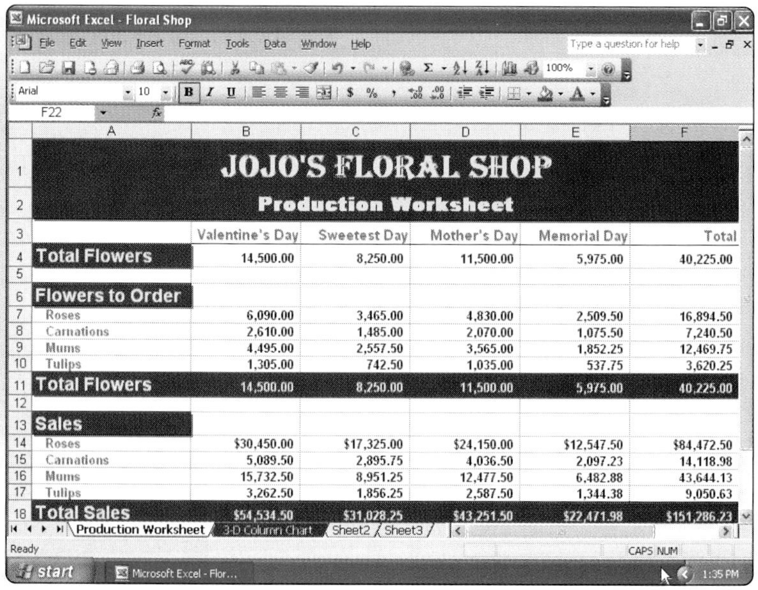

FIGURE 1-33 People with a home office and employees in small offices typically use a desktop personal computer for some or all of their duties.

SOHO users access the Web — often wirelessly — to look up information such as addresses, postal codes, flights, and package shipping rates. Nearly all SOHO users communicate with others through e-mail. Many are entering the *e-commerce* arena and conduct business on the Web (Figure 1-34). Their Web sites advertise products and services and may provide a means for taking orders. Small business Web sites sometimes use a *Web cam*, which is a video camera that displays its output on a Web page. A Web cam allows SOHO users to show the world a live view of some aspect of their business.

To save money on hardware and software, small offices often network their computers. For example, the small office connects one printer to a network for all employees to share. Many companies also purchase network versions of their software. A network version usually costs less than purchasing a separate software package for each desktop or notebook computer. Employees then access the software on a server, as needed.

SOHO users often have basic business software such as word processing and spreadsheet software to assist with document preparation and finances. They are likely to use other industry-specific types of software. A florist, for example, will have software that allows for taking orders, updating inventory, billing customers, and paying vendors.

Mobile User

Today, businesses and schools are expanding to serve people across the country and around the world. Thus, increasingly more employees and students are **mobile users**, who work on a computer while away from a main office or school (Figure 1-35). Examples of mobile users are sales representatives, real estate agents, insurance agents, meter readers, package delivery people, journalists, consultants, and students.

Mobile users often have a notebook computer, Web-enabled PDA, or smart phone. With these computers and devices, the mobile user connects to other computers — usually wirelessly — on a network or the Internet. Often, mobile users transfer information between their mobile device and another computer, such as one at the main office or school.

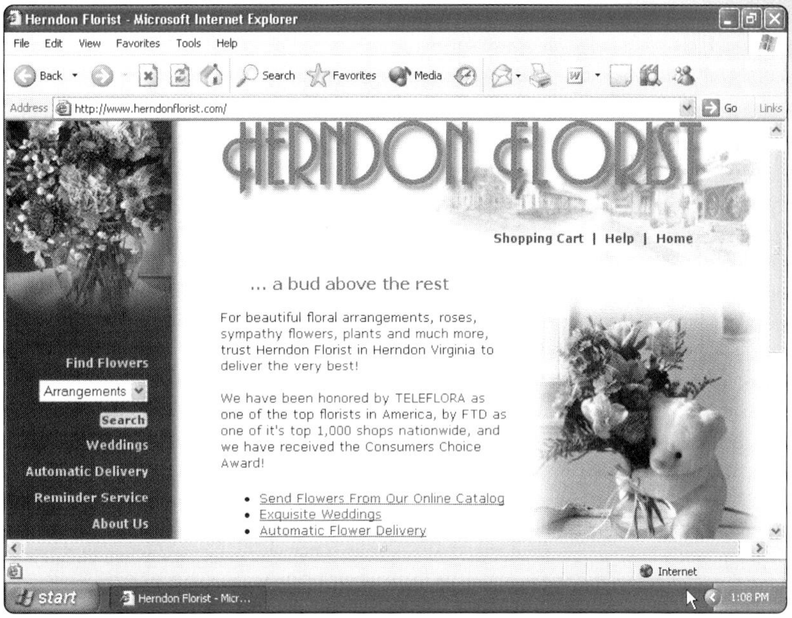

FIGURE 1-34 Many small businesses, such as this local florist, have a Web site to promote their products and services.

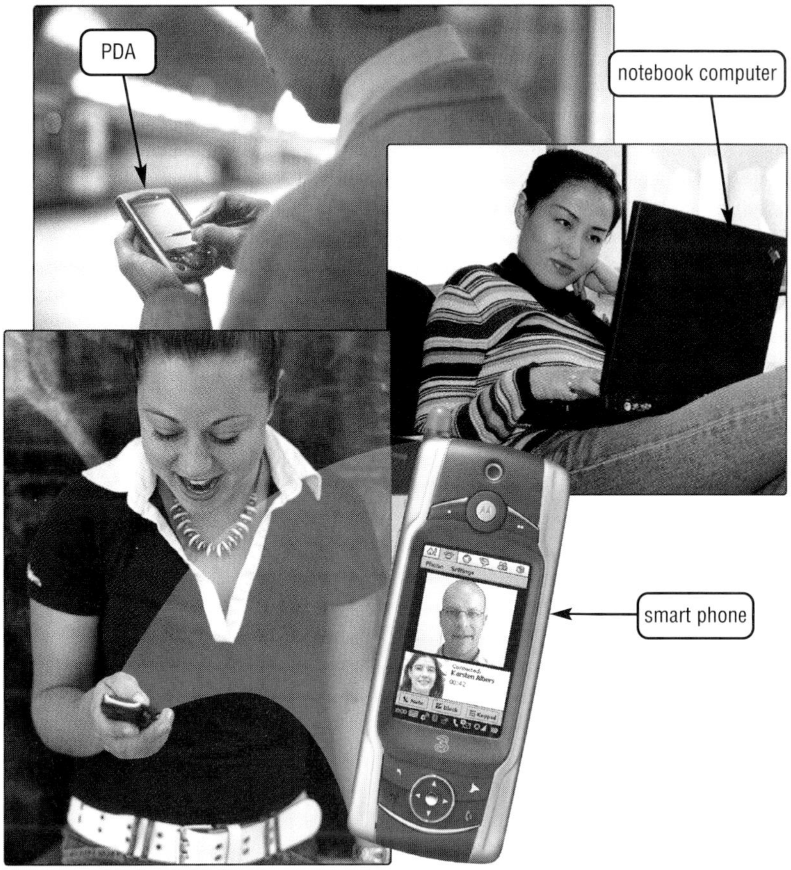

FIGURE 1-35 Mobile users have notebook computers, PDAs, and smart phones so they can work, do homework, send messages, or access the Internet while away from the office, home, or school.

The mobile user works with basic business software such as word processing and spreadsheet software. With presentation graphics software, the mobile user can create and deliver presentations to a large audience by connecting a mobile computer or device to a video projector that displays the presentation on a full screen (Figure 1-36). Many scaled-down programs are available for mobile devices such as PDAs and smart phones.

FIGURE 1-36 A mobile user often connects a notebook computer to a video projector to make a presentation.

Large Business User

A large business has hundreds or thousands of employees in offices across a region, the country, or around the world. Each employee who uses a computer in the large business is a **large business user** (Figure 1-37).

Many large companies use the words, *enterprise computing*, to refer to the huge network of computers that meets their diverse computing needs. The network facilitates communications among employees at all locations. Users access the network through desktop computers, mobile computers, and PDAs. Mainframes often act as servers in the large business network.

Large businesses use computers and the computer network to process high volumes of transactions in a single day. Although they may differ in size and in the products or services offered, all generally use computers for basic business activities. For example, they bill millions of customers, prepare payroll for thousands of employees, and manage thousands of items in inventory. Read Issue 1-4 for a related discussion.

In a large business, an automated telephone system routes telephone calls to the proper department or person. By telephone, fax, or

FIGURE 1-37 A large business can have hundreds or thousands of users in offices across a region, the country, or the world. Throughout the business, computers help employees perform a variety of job-related tasks.

ISSUE 1-4

Are You Ready for Automatic Checkout?

Move over bar codes, make way for RFID. *RFID* (*radio frequency identification*) uses a tiny computer chip that is mounted on a tag attached to a product or sewn into an article of clothing. The computer chip sends identifying information to a reader via radio waves. Unlike bar codes, RFID does not require line-of-sight transmission and can identify unique items, not just a category. For merchants, RFID can help to locate items in a warehouse, identify items that need to be replenished, and track items that have been removed from store shelves. For consumers, RFID can supply detailed product information, reduce costs associated with inventory management, and someday let buyers by-pass checkout lines and take purchases directly from the store, with the item's cost charged to their card.

Privacy advocates worry, however, that RFID could obliterate a buyer's anonymity. They fear that with an RFID reader, any individual or organization could track a purchaser's movements and make that information available to marketers or government agencies. Privacy advocates insist that merchants should be forced to disable RFID transmitters as soon as buyers leave a store. Would you be comfortable purchasing a product using RFID? Why or why not? Should buyers be allowed to request that RFID transmitters be disabled after they make a purchase, or should merchants be required to render transmitters inoperative when the product leaves the store? Why?

For more information about RFID, visit the Discovering Computers 2005 Issues Web page (**scsite.com/dc2005/issues**) and click Issue #4 below Chapter 1.

e-mail, order-entry clerks process millions of customer orders daily using a desktop computer. Some companies have inside sales representatives who handle customer telephone orders. Outside sales representatives — the mobile users in the firm — conduct business while on the road with mobile computers or devices.

Large businesses typically have e-commerce Web sites, allowing customers and vendors to make transactions online. The Web site showcases products, services, and other company information (Figure 1-38). Thousands of customers, vendors, and any other interested parties can access this information on the Web. Once an order is placed, computers update inventory records to reflect goods sold and goods purchased.

The marketing department in the large business uses desktop publishing software to prepare marketing literature such as newsletters, product brochures, and advertising material. The accounting department uses software for accounts receivable, accounts payable, billing, general ledger, and payroll activities. Computers process thousands of customer payments, generate checks to pay vendors, print invoices to send to customers, and balance all book records. Additionally, computers handle the payroll and taxes, ensuring that thousands of employees receive paychecks on time.

The employees in the *information technology (IT) department* keep the computers and the network running. They also determine when and if the company requires new hardware or software. Large business users access networked versions of word processing, spreadsheet, database, and presentation graphics software. They also may use calendar programs to post their schedules on the network. And, they might use PDAs to maintain contact information. E-mail and Web browsers enable communications among employees, vendors, and customers. Many large businesses have *customer relationship management* (*CRM*) software, which allows the company to provide a personalized touch and customized service to its customers.

Some large businesses place kiosks in public locations. A *kiosk* is a freestanding computer, usually with a touch screen (Figure 1-39). Certain kiosks simply provide information to the public. More advanced kiosks allow customers to place orders, make payments, and access the Web. Some stores, for example, have Web kiosks to save a sale, allowing a customer to purchase items not in stock in the store.

WEB LINK 1-11

Enterprise Computing

Visit the Discovering Computers 2005 WEB LINK page (**scsite.com/dc2005/weblink**). Click Enterprise Computing below Chapter 1.

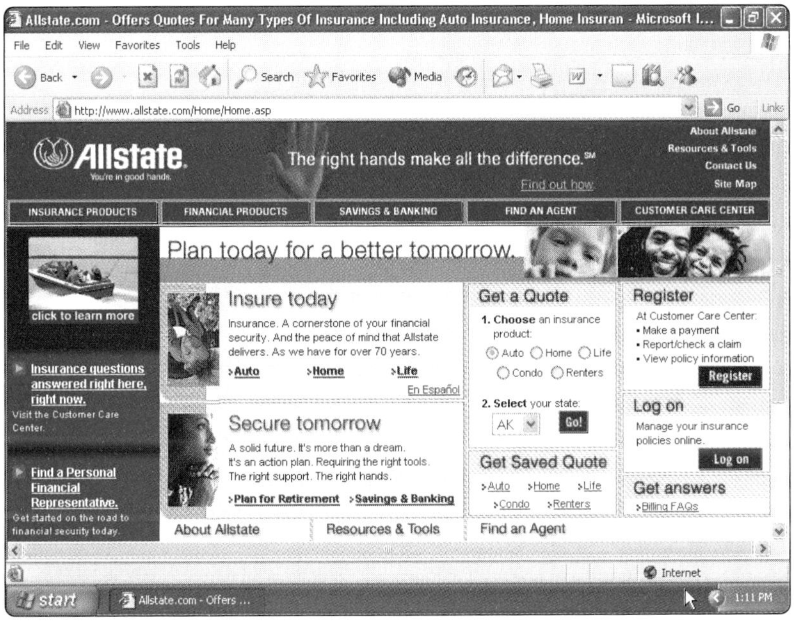

FIGURE 1-38 Large businesses, such as Allstate Insurance Company, usually have their own Web sites to showcase products, services, and company information.

FIGURE 1-39 A kiosk is a freestanding computer that often has a touch screen.

Many employees of large businesses today telecommute (Figure 1-40). **Telecommuting** is a work arrangement in which employees work away from a company's standard workplace and often communicate with the office through the computer. Employees who telecommute have flexible work schedules so they can combine work and personal responsibilities, such as child care. For those individuals with disabilities or those recovering from injury or illness, telecommuting provides a convenient, comfortable work environment.

FIGURE 1-40 Many employees of large businesses often telecommute, which allows them to combine work and other responsibilities such as child care.

Power User

Another category of user, called a **power user**, requires the capabilities of a workstation or other powerful computer (Figure 1-41). Examples of power users include engineers, scientists, architects, desktop publishers, and graphic artists. Power users typically work with *multimedia*, combining text, graphics, audio, and video into one application. These users need computers with extremely fast processors because of the nature of their work.

The power user's workstation contains industry-specific software. For example, engineers and architects use software to draft and design floor plans, mechanical assemblies, or vehicles. A desktop publisher uses software to prepare marketing literature such as newsletters, brochures, and annual reports. A geologist uses software to study the earth's surface. This software usually is quite expensive because of its specialized design.

Power users exist in all types of businesses, both large and small. Some also work at home. Depending on where they work, power users might fit into one of the previously discussed categories, as well. Their computers typically have network connections and Internet access.

FIGURE 1-41 Power users require the capabilities of a powerful computer.

COMPUTER APPLICATIONS IN SOCIETY

The computer has changed society today as much as the industrial revolution changed society in the eighteenth and nineteenth centuries. In a recent report, the United States government attributed one-third of the country's economic growth to digital technologies, resulting in tremendous increases in productivity.

People interact directly with computers in fields such as education, finance, government, health care, science, publishing, travel, and industry. In addition, they can reap the benefits from breakthroughs and advances in these fields. The following pages describe how computers have made a difference in people's interactions with these disciplines. Read Looking Ahead 1-2 for a look at the next generation of computer applications in society.

LOOKING AHEAD 1-2

Robots Perform Real-World Tasks

Cleaning your house may become less of a chore when your new robot arrives. So will guarding hazardous production plants, teaching children new vocabulary words, and performing daily inventory checks.

Robotic pets also may serve as companions for nursing home residents, although they are not replacing the relationship between families and the elderly.

Sophisticated robots soon will be commonplace as these products become easier and less expensive to manufacture. Robot developer kits include controls for mobility, speech recognition and synthesis, decision making, and vision. Some even include emotions and personalities. The robots can be trained to detect specific colors and search for objects.

For a look at the next generation of robots, visit the Discovering Computers 2005 Looking Ahead Web page (**scsite.com/dc2005/looking**). Click Looking Ahead #2 below Chapter 1.

Education

Education is the process of acquiring knowledge. In the traditional model, people learn from other people such as parents, teachers, and employers. Many forms of printed material such as books and manuals are used as learning tools. Today, educators also are turning to computers to assist with education.

As the cost of computers drops, many schools and companies can afford to equip labs and classrooms with computers (Figure 1-42). Some schools even require students to have a notebook computer or PDA, along with textbooks and other supplies.

Students use software to assist with learning or to complete assignments. To promote education by computer, many vendors offer substantial student discounts on software.

Sometimes, the delivery of education occurs at one place while the learning occurs at other locations. For example, students can take a class on the Web. Some classes are blended, that is, part of the learning occurs in a classroom and the other part occurs on the Web. More than 70 percent of colleges offer some type of distance learning classes. A few even offer entire degrees online.

A concern of society is the digital divide. The *digital divide* is the idea that you can split people of the world into two distinct groups: (1) those who have access to technology and (2) those who do not. In this definition, technology includes telephones, television, computers, and the Internet. The concern is that some of the less fortunate people in the world may not be able to take advantage of the technology that makes much of society prosper and grow. For example, a recent study shows that the 20 largest cities in the United States receive 86 percent of Internet delivery.

FIGURE 1-42 Many schools and businesses have computer labs to provide an environment conducive for students and employees to learn.

To help close the gap in the digital divide, the United States government and many organizations have efforts in progress. They are setting up community training centers and supplying teachers and students with necessary technology. For example, Microsoft and hardware partners such as Toshiba and IBM are part of the *Anytime Anywhere Learning program* that provides teachers and students with notebook computers or Tablet PCs ready with Microsoft applications and Internet access.

Finance

Many people and companies use computers to help manage their finances. Some use finance software to balance checkbooks, pay bills, track personal income and expenses, manage investments, and evaluate financial plans. This software usually includes a variety of online services. For example, computer users can track investments, compare insurance rates from leading insurance companies, and do online banking. With **online banking**, users access account balances, pay bills, and copy monthly transactions from the bank's computer right into their computers.

Many financial institutions' Web sites also offer online banking (Figure 1-43). When using a Web site instead of finance software on your computer, all your account information is stored on the bank's computer. The advantage is you can access your financial records from anywhere in the world. Web-based financial institutions often allow you to transfer cash from a credit card, debit card, or checking account to another person's credit card or bank account. Some people use this service for monetary gifts. Companies use it for rebates and refunds.

Investors often use **online investing** to buy and sell stocks and bonds — without using a broker. With online investing, the transaction fee for each trade usually is much less than when trading through a broker.

Government

A government provides society with direction by making and administering policies. Many people associate government with executive, judicial, and legislative offices. The United States government also includes areas such as law enforcement, employment, military, national security, taxes, and state and local agencies. To provide citizens with up-to-date information, most government offices have Web sites (Figure 1-44). A recent survey estimated that about 62 percent of people in the United States access government Web sites. They file taxes, apply for permits and licenses, pay parking tickets, buy stamps, report crimes, apply for financial aid, and renew vehicle registrations and driver's licenses.

Employees of government agencies use computers as part of their daily routine. North American 911 call centers use computers to dispatch calls for fire, police, and medical

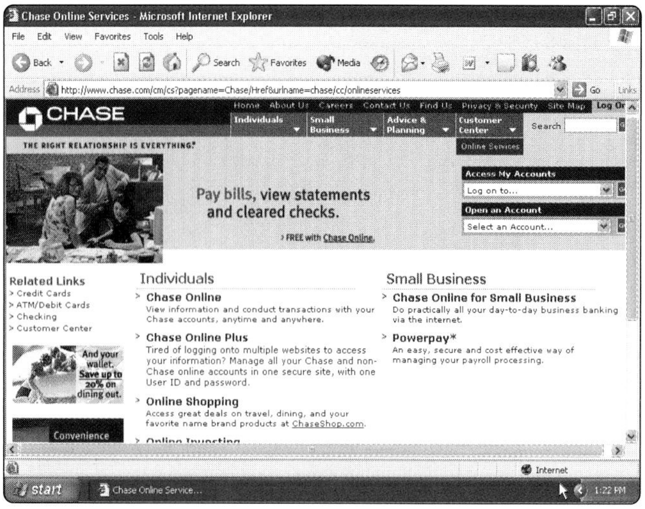

FIGURE 1-43 Many financial institutions' Web sites offer online banking.

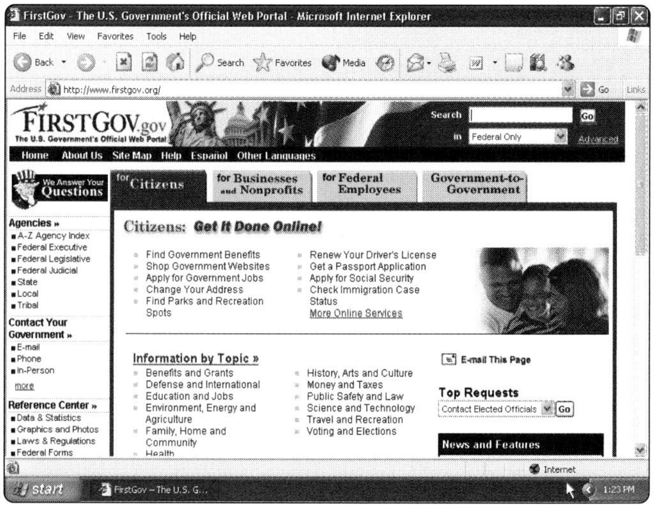

FIGURE 1-44 The United States government has many Web sites that provide official information.

assistance. Law enforcement officers have online access to the FBI's National Crime Information Center (NCIC) in police cars that have computers and fingerprint scanners. The NCIC contains more than 39 million criminal records, including names, fingerprints, parole/probation records, mug shots, and other information.

Health Care

Nearly every area of health care uses computers. Whether you are visiting a family doctor for a regular checkup, having lab work or an outpatient test, or being rushed in for emergency surgery, the medical staff around you will be using computers for various purposes:

- Hospitals and doctors use computers to maintain patient records.
- Computers monitor patients' vital signs in hospital rooms and at home.
- Computers and computerized devices assist doctors, nurses, and technicians with medical tests (Figure 1-45).
- Doctors use the Web and medical software to assist with researching and diagnosing health conditions.
- Doctors use e-mail to correspond with patients.
- Pharmacists use computers to file insurance claims.
- Surgeons implant computerized devices, such as pacemakers, that allow patients to live longer.
- Surgeons use computer-controlled devices to provide them with greater precision during operations, such as for laser eye surgery and robot-assisted heart surgery.

Many times, you leave a doctor's office or hospital with a diagnosis and a prescription in hand. On the way home, you stop at the pharmacy to fill the prescription. For more information about your diagnosis, you could read a medical dictionary or attend a seminar. You might find it preferable to use the Web. Many Web sites provide up-to-date medical, fitness, nutrition, or exercise information. These Web sites also maintain lists of doctors and dentists to help you find the one that suits your needs. They have chat rooms, so you can talk to others diagnosed with similar conditions. Some Web sites even allow you to order prescriptions online.

Much of society today is fitness conscious. Diet and exercise are a part of daily life. Doctors often recommend some type of physical activity along with proper nutrition to maintain a healthy lifestyle. Whether you exercise at the local health club or at home in your basement, the equipment often has a computer built into it to track your progress. These computers monitor physical conditions, such as heart rate and pulse, to be sure you are exercising within safe limits.

An exciting development in health care is telemedicine, which is a form of long-distance health care. Through *telemedicine*, health-care professionals in separate locations have live conferences on the computer. For example, a doctor at one location can have a conference with a doctor at another location to discuss a bone X-ray. Live images of each doctor, along with the X-ray, are displayed on each doctor's computer.

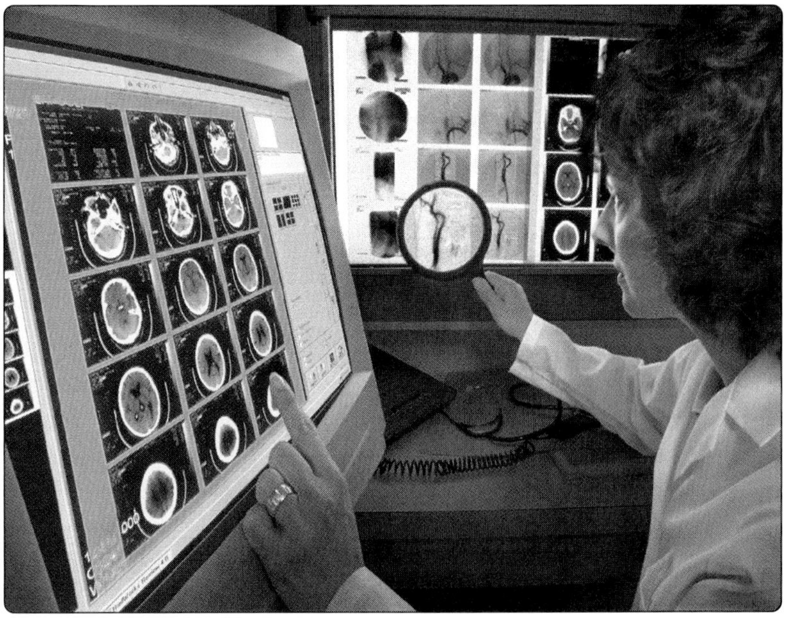

FIGURE 1-45 Dentists, doctors, nurses, technicians, and other medical staff use computers to perform tests on patients and analyze test results.

Science

All branches of science, from biology to astronomy to meteorology, use computers to assist them with collecting, analyzing, and modeling data. Scientists also use the Internet to communicate with colleagues around the world.

Breakthroughs in surgery, medicine, and treatments often result from scientists' use of computers. Tiny computers now imitate functions of the central nervous system, retina of the eye, and cochlea of the ear. A cochlear implant allows a deaf person to listen. Electrodes implanted in the brain stop tremors associated with Parkinson's disease. Cameras small enough to swallow take pictures inside your body to detect polyps, cancer, and other abnormalities (Figure 1-46).

The capability of the computer to recognize spoken words is a result of scientific experimentation with neural networks. A *neural network* is a system that attempts to imitate the behavior of the human brain. Scientists create neural networks by connecting thousands of processors together much like the neurons in the brain are connected.

Publishing

Publishing is the process of making works available to the public. These works include books, magazines, and newspapers. Special software assists publishers in designing pages that include text, graphics, and photographs. Journalists carry notebook computers, mobile devices, and digital cameras to capture and record news as it occurs.

In addition to printing materials, many publishers make the content of magazines and newspapers available online (Figure 1-47). Some Web sites allow you to copy an entire book to your desktop computer, handheld computer, or PDA. Handheld devices specially designed for reading electronic books also are available.

FIGURE 1-47 Many magazine and newspaper publishers make the content of their publications available online.

FIGURE 1-46 HOW A CAMERA PILL WORKS

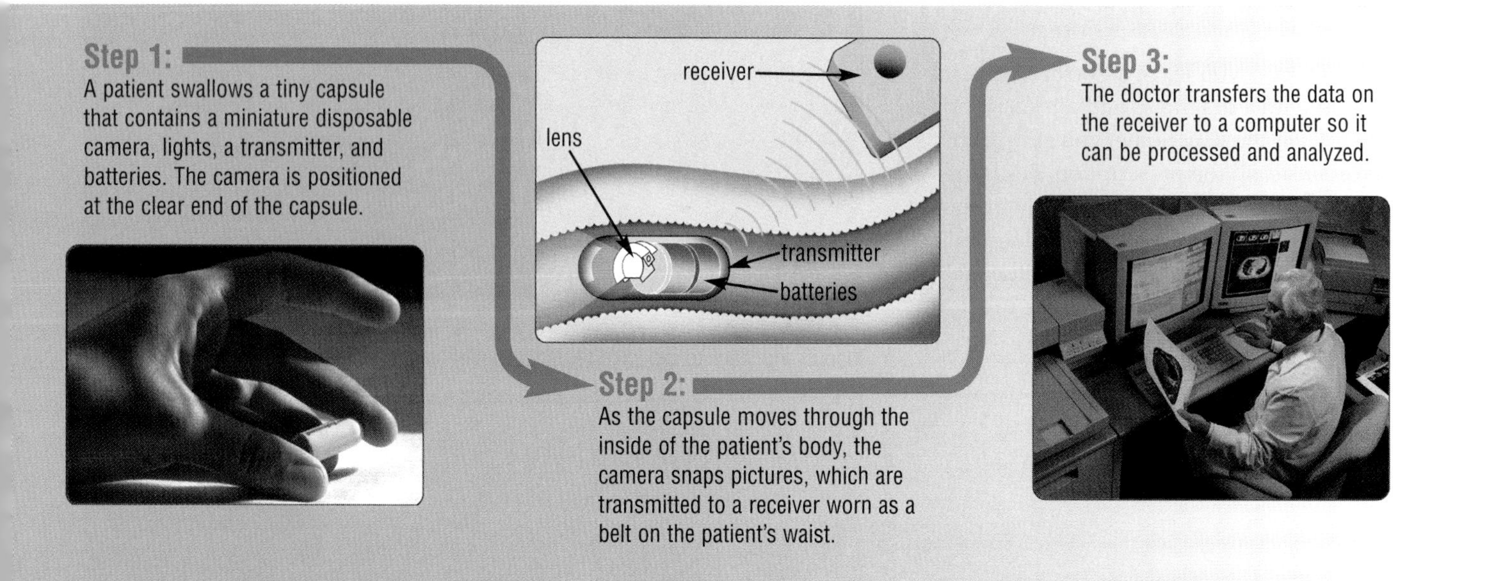

Travel

Whether traveling by car or airplane, your goal is to arrive safely at your destination. As you make the journey, you may interact with some of the latest technology.

Many vehicles manufactured today include some type of **onboard navigation system** (Figure 1-48). Depending on the one you choose, these communications systems offer the consumer many worthwhile features:

- Provide directions
- Automatically call for help if the airbag deploys and you do not respond to voice contact
- Provide emergency services as soon as you press the emergency button
- Dispatch roadside assistance
- Perform remote diagnostics if a warning light appears on the dashboard
- Unlock the driver's side door if you lock the keys in the car
- Track the vehicle if it is stolen
- Honk the horn to help you locate the car in a parking lot

Many vehicles today also include options such as screens with e-mail and Internet access, printers, and fax capability. Airlines also provide online access. Airplanes equipped with Internet connections allow passengers to connect their mobile computer or device to the Web. Some airlines even provide passengers with Web-enabled devices during flights.

In preparing for a trip, you may need to reserve a car, hotel, or flight. Many Web sites offer these services to the public. For example, you can order airline tickets on the Web and have the tickets waiting for you at the airport or delivered directly to your door. If you plan to drive somewhere and are unsure of the road to take to your destination, you can print directions and a map from the Web. By entering the starting address and ending address, the Web site generates the best route for your trip.

FIGURE 1-48 Many vehicles made by General Motors are equipped with an onboard navigation system called OnStar. By pushing the OnStar button, you immediately connect to an OnStar advisor who provides verbal assistance.

Industry

Industries that manufacture products usually have large numbers of employees and high capital expenditures. Capital includes factories, warehouses, machinery, and computers. **Computer-aided manufacturing** (*CAM*) refers to the use of computers to assist with manufacturing processes such as fabrication and assembly. Industries use CAM to reduce product development costs, shorten a product's time to market, and stay ahead of the competition.

Often, robots carry out processes in a CAM environment. CAM is used by a variety of industries, including oil drilling, power generation, food production, and automobile manufacturing. Automobile plants, for example, have an entire line of industrial robots that assemble a car (Figure 1-49).

Special computers on the shop floor record actual labor, material, machine, and computer time used to manufacture a particular product. The computers process this data and automatically update inventory, production, payroll, and accounting records on the company's network.

QUIZ YOURSELF 1-3

To check your knowledge of categories of computers, elements of an information system, types of computer users, and computer applications in society, visit the Discovering Computers 2005 Quiz Yourself Web page (**scsite.com/dc2005/quiz**). Click Objectives 8 – 11 below Chapter 1.

FIGURE 1-49 Automotive factories use industrial robots to weld car bodies.

CHAPTER SUMMARY

Chapter 1 introduced you to basic computer concepts such as what a computer is, how it works, and what makes it a powerful tool. You learned about the components of a computer. Next, the chapter discussed networks, the Internet, and computer software. The many different categories of computers, computer users, and computer applications in society also were presented. This chapter is an overview. Many of the terms and concepts introduced will be discussed further in later chapters.

Personal Computer Salesperson

When you decide to buy or upgrade a personal computer, the most important person with whom you interact probably will be a personal computer salesperson. This individual will be a valuable resource to you in providing the information and expertise you need to select a computer that meets your requirements.

Computer manufacturers, and retailers that sell several types of personal computers, need competent salespeople. A *personal computer salesperson* must be computer literate and have a specific knowledge of the computers he or she sells. In addition, a successful salesperson has a friendly, outgoing personality that helps customers feel comfortable. Through open-ended questions, the salesperson can determine a customer's needs and level of experience. With this information, the salesperson can choose the best computer for the customer and explain the features of the computer in language the customer will understand.

Most computer salespeople have at least a high school diploma. Before reaching the sales floor, however, salespeople usually complete extensive company training programs. These programs often consist of self-directed, self-paced Web-training classes. Most salespeople also participate in training updates, often on a monthly basis.

Personal computer salespeople generally earn a guaranteed amount plus a commission for each sale. A computer salesperson can earn about $40,000 a year. Top salespeople can be among a company's most highly compensated employees, earning more than $70,000.

To learn more about the field of personal computer salesperson as a career, visit the Discovering Computers 2005 Careers Web page (**scsite.com/dc2005/careers**). Click Personal Computer Salesperson.

HIGH-TECH TALK

Analog versus Digital: Making the Conversion

Data is processed in one of two ways: analog or digital. People generally process *analog* data — that is, continuous wave patterns. The sight and sound of a traveling subway car transmits to your eyes and ears as light and sound waves, or smooth up-and-down patterns (Figure 1-50a). A computer, by contrast, is *digital*, which means computers process data in two discrete states: positive (on or 1) and nonpositive (off or 0) as shown in Figure 1-50b. The 1 and 0 represent the two digits used by the binary number system. While this system is at the heart of digital computing, binary digital impulses appear as long strings of 1s and 0s and are difficult for most people to understand.

If sound and light waves are analog and a computer is digital, how does a computer record audio clips, play music, or show a movie? How can a digital computer use an analog telephone line to dial up to access the Internet?

The key lies in analog-to-digital and digital-to-analog conversions. The computer's sound card, for example, performs these conversions to record a digital audio clip of your analog voice. The sound card connects to the microphone, which is an analog input source. The diaphragm in the microphone converts the analog sound waves into an electrical signal. This signal flows to the sound card's *analog-to-digital converter* (*ADC*), which converts the signal into digital data. The digital data flows to the *digital signal processor* (*DSP*), compressing the data to save space. Finally, the DSP sends the compressed data to the processor, which stores the data in an audio file format.

To play a recorded sound, the computer reverses the process. The processor retrieves and sends the digital data to the DSP to be decompressed. The DSP sends the decompressed digital data to the sound card's *digital-to-analog converter* (*DAC*), which converts the digital data back to an analog voltage for output via a speaker or headset. In other words, a DAC takes that long binary number string of 1s and 0s and turns it into something meaningful.

Similarly, a video card allows you to record a video or play a movie on a DVD. A camera and microphone capture and send the analog picture and sound signals to a video card. The video card's ADC converts the signals into digital data. The digital data is compressed and saved in a file format such as AVI (audio/video interleave) or MPEG. When playing a movie, the computer decompresses and separates the video and audio data. It then sends the signals to the video card's DAC. The DAC translates the digital data into analog signals and sends them to the monitor and speakers, where they are displayed as your movie.

The modem in a computer also links the analog and digital worlds. When using a dial-up modem, the computer does not transmit digital data directly across analog telephone lines. Instead, the modem converts the computer's digital signals to analog signals (called *modulation*) to be sent over telephone lines. When the analog signal reaches its destination, another modem recreates the original digital signal (*demodulation*). This allows the receiving computer to process the data. The next time you dial up using a modem, pick up the telephone. The loud, screeching noise you hear is the sound of digital data after being converted to analog sound waves.

For more information about analog versus digital, visit the Discovering Computers 2005 High-Tech Talk Web page (**scsite.com/dc2005/tech**) and click Analog versus Digital.

Figure 1-50a (analog signal)

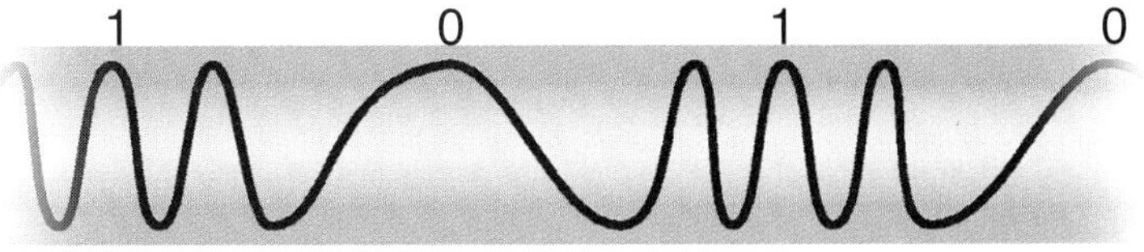

Figure 1-50b (digital signal)

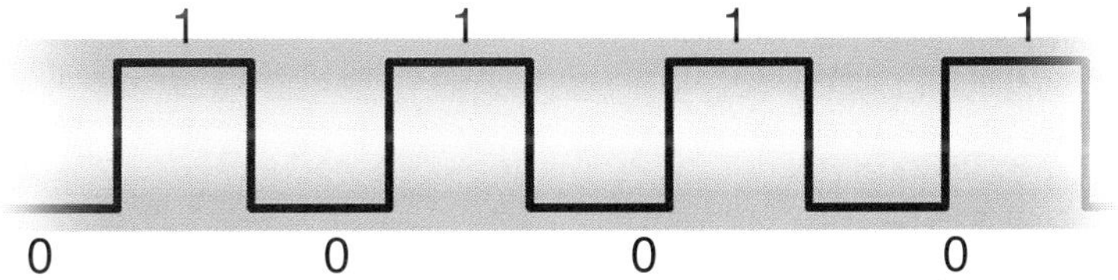

FIGURE 1-50 Analog versus digital signals.

COMPANIES ON THE CUTTING EDGE

Dell

Computers Your Way

"Easy as Dell". With this euphoric phrase, Dell tells potential buyers that they can acquire one of the world's favorite computers quickly and efficiently. Last year, Dell Inc. earned revenues exceeding $38 billion.

Founded by Michael Dell in 1984, the largest corporate employer in Austin, Texas, has millions of square feet of office and manufacturing space at its corporate headquarters. Along with its other U.S. location in Nashville, Tennessee, Dell has offices in Japan, Malaysia, Ireland, China, and Brazil.

Dell Inc. prides itself on its direct approach to sales. The company deals openly with customers, one at a time. The direct approach allows Dell to build every computer to order and offer complete systems at competitive prices. The approach also eliminates retailers that add time and cost, increases awareness of customer expectations, and allows faster introduction of new technologies.

Dell uses the Internet to enhance the advantages of direct marketing. In 1997, Dell became the first company to reach $1 million a day in online sales. Today, Dell hosts one of the world's largest volume e-commerce Web sites, where customers can configure and price computers, order systems, and track their orders.

Dell employs more than 24,000 people worldwide. Employees work in an environment that recognizes their diversity and skills. The Dell corporate philosophy fosters the creativity generated by a workforce composed of individuals with varied backgrounds and experiences. Workers have the opportunity to contribute fully to corporate goals and can achieve their professional goals through the company's virtual university, The Dell Learning Center. Dell also takes pride in its community involvement. Through The Dell Foundation, the company offers targeted grant programs with a focus on technology education.

For more information about Dell Inc., visit the Discovering Computers 2005 Companies Web page (**scsite.com/dc2005/companies**) and click Dell Inc.

palmOne

Ubiquitous PDAs Are a Phenomenon

The comforts of home beckon many college students as they look forward to being with friends and family. For Jeff Hawkins, Donna Dubinsky and Ed Colligan, home means being with friends and corporate family at palmOne. They cofounded Palm Computing in 1992, but left the company more than six years later to form a new company, JD Technology, which then became Handspring, Inc. In 2003, however, they returned to Palm, which had been renamed palmOne, when palmOne acquired Handspring.

palmOne is a leading provider of PDAs and a pioneer in the field of mobile and wireless Internet communications. PDAs manufactured by palmOne command nearly 70 percent of the PDA market worldwide. More than 13,000 types of application software are available for this versatile and stylish product. Currently, software for Palm PDAs enables users to perform a multitude of tasks, including read e-books, record golf scores, and play games.

palmOne emphasizes that PDAs are different from notebook or desktop computers. PDAs are designed to manage and access information, rather than create and edit documents. With this in mind, Palm PDAs are intended to be simple so that you easily can retrieve information, wearable so that you can carry it anywhere, expandable so that you can add functionality, and mobile so that you can access information anywhere.

Palm was acquired by U.S. Robotics in 1995. One year later, the company introduced the Pilot 1000 and 5000 products, which blazed a trail for the PDA market. In 1997, 3Com acquired U.S. Robotics and made Palm a subsidiary of the corporation. Two years later, 3Com made Palm an independent, publicly traded company. In 2002, Palm formed a subsidiary, called PalmSource, Inc., to separate the company's device and operating systems businesses.

For more information about palmOne, visit the Discovering Computers 2005 Companies Web page (**scsite.com/dc2005/companies**) and click palmOne.

TECHNOLOGY TRAILBLAZERS

Bill Gates

Microsoft's Founder

What advice does one of the richest men in the world have for students? Get the best education you can. Take advantage of high school and college. Learn how to learn.

As Microsoft's founder and former CEO, *Bill Gates* receives hundreds of e-mail messages from students asking for insight on education. He emphasizes that college graduates know about a multitude of subjects and group dynamics. Gates dropped out of Harvard during his junior year, but he stresses that students should not quit going to school unless they are facing extraordinary prospects.

Gates began programming computers when he was 13. Early in his career, he developed the BASIC programming language for the MITS Altair, one of the first microcomputers. He founded Microsoft in 1975 with Paul Allen, and five years later they provided the first operating system for the IBM PC, called MS-DOS. Under Gates's leadership, Microsoft continued to update MS-DOS and then develop Windows, Internet Explorer, and the MSNBC cable television news network and corresponding Web site. Today, Bill Gates's official title at Microsoft is chief software architect, which allows him a greater role in program design and development. He still is regarded as the most powerful person in the computer industry.

Gates has written two books: *Business @ The Speed of Thought* and *The Road Ahead*. All proceeds have been donated to nonprofit organizations. Bill Gates is a devoted father and claims that his children "make things fun all the time." The feeling for children has spilled over into his charitable contributions. Together with his wife, Gates has endowed the Bill & Melinda Gates Foundation, which supports global health and learning, with more than $24 billion.

For more information about Bill Gates, visit the Discovering Computers 2005 People Web page (**scsite.com/dc2005/people**) and click Bill Gates.

Carly Fiorina

CEO of Hewlett-Packard

Although seemingly improbable that a shipping department secretary someday would return to become the company's chairman of the board and chief executive officer, it is a true story for *Carly Fiorina*. As Hewlett-Packard's leader, she is focusing on improving profitability, innovation, customer service, and Internet applications.

Fiorina credits her liberal arts undergraduate studies at Stanford University, where she majored in philosophy and medieval history, with helping her learn how to think and make choices. She urges college graduates to love what they do and not to make decisions based on the desires of others.

After a brief stint in law school, she became a sales representative for AT&T. That short-term job eventually grew into leading and guiding the AT&T spin-off, Lucent Technologies, Inc., to one of the more successful initial public offering (IPO) stock offerings. Fiorina says leadership involves influencing others and mastering change. It also empowers people to reach their full potential and make decisions.

In 1999, Fiorina became CEO of Hewlett-Packard, one of the oldest companies in Silicon Valley. Many people felt that the company, once known for its innovations, had become stagnant and slow to embrace new ideas. To combat this, Fiorina engineered a merger between Hewlett-Packard and inventive, but struggling, Compaq Computer Corporation. Certain employees and retirees, and even children of Hewlett-Packard's founders, opposed the merger. But, after a nine-month struggle that included court appearances and some personal animosity, the merger was completed. "There's no question that there were a lot of unfortunate consequences…" Fiorina admits, "but I think it's also true that employees are ready to move on." In fact, the theme of the meeting that finally announced the merger was, "We are ready." And so is Fiorina, promising that Hewlett-Packard again will compete with the giants in technology.

For more information about Carly Fiorina, visit the Discovering Computers 2005 People Web page (**scsite.com/dc2005/people**) and click Carly Fiorina.

CHAPTER 1 CHAPTER REVIEW

The Chapter Review section summarizes the concepts presented in this chapter.

WEB INSTRUCTIONS:

To display this page from the Web, start your browser and enter the Web address **scsite.com/dc2005/ch1/review**. Click the links for current and additional information. To listen to an audio version of this Chapter Review, click the Audio button.

1 Why Is Computer Literacy Important?

Computer literacy entails having knowledge and understanding of computers and their uses. As computers become an increasingly important part of daily living, many people believe that computer literacy is vital to success.

2 What Is a Computer and What Are Its Components?

A **computer** is an electronic device, operating under the control of instructions stored in its own memory, that can accept data, manipulate the data according to specified rules, produce results, and store the results for future use. The electric, electronic, and mechanical components of a computer, or **hardware**, include input devices, output devices, a system unit, storage devices, and communications devices. An **input device** allows you to enter data or instructions into a computer. An **output device** conveys information to one or more people. The **system unit** is a box-like case that contains electronic components of a computer that are used to process data. A **storage device** records and/or retrieves items to and from storage media. A **communications device** enables a computer to send and receive data, instructions, and information to and from one or more computers.

3 Why Is a Computer a Powerful Tool?

A computer is a powerful tool because it operates with amazing speed, reliability, consistency, and accuracy. Computers also can store huge amounts of data and information.

Visit **scsite.com/dc2005/quiz** or click the Quiz Yourself button. Click Objectives 1 – 3 below Chapter 1.

4 What Is the Purpose of a Network?

A **network** is a collection of computers and devices connected together via communications devices and transmission media. Networks allow computers to share *resources*, such as hardware, software, data, and information.

5 How Are the Internet and the World Wide Web Used?

The **Internet** is a worldwide collection of networks that connects millions of businesses, government agencies, educational institutions, and individuals. People use the Internet to communicate with and meet other people, to access news and information, to shop for goods and services, to bank and invest, to take classes, and to access sources of entertainment and leisure. The **Web**, short for World Wide Web, is a global library of documents containing information that is available to anyone connected to the Internet.

6 How Is Installing a Program Different from Running a Program?

Software, also called a **program**, is a series of instructions that tells the computer what to do and how to do it. **Installing** a program is the process of setting up the program to work with a computer, printer, and other hardware components. To **run** a program means to use it. Running a program happens when a user instructs the computer to start the program, either by inserting a disc or by issuing a command. The computer *loads*, or places, the program into its memory from storage and then *executes*, or carries out, the program instructions.

7 What Are the Types of Software?

The two categories of software are system software and application software. **System software** consists of the programs that control or maintain the operations of a computer and its devices. Two types of system software are the *operating system*, which coordinates activities among computer hardware devices, and *utility programs,* which perform maintenance-type tasks usually related to a computer, its devices, or its programs. **Application software** consists of programs that perform specific tasks for users. Popular application software includes Web browser, word processing software, spreadsheet software, database software, and presentation graphics software.

Visit **scsite.com/dc2005/quiz** or click the Quiz Yourself button. Click Objectives 4 – 7 below Chapter 1.

8 What Are the Categories of Computers?

Industry experts typically classify computers into five categories: personal computers, mobile computers and mobile devices, midrange servers, mainframes, and supercomputers. A personal computer is a computer that can perform all of its input, processing, output, and storage activities by itself. A **mobile computer** is a personal computer that you can carry from place to place, and a **mobile device** is a computing device small enough to hold in your hand. A **midrange server** is a large and powerful computer that typically supports several hundred and sometimes up to a few thousand networked computers at the same time. A **mainframe** is a large, very expensive, very powerful computer that can handle hundreds or thousands of connected users simultaneously and can store tremendous amounts of data, instructions, and information. A **supercomputer** is the fastest, most powerful, and most expensive computer and is used for applications requiring complex, sophisticated mathematical calculations.

9 How Do the Elements of an Information System Interact?

An *information system* combines hardware, software, data, people, and procedures to produce timely and useful information. People in an information technology department develop procedures for processing data. Following these procedures, people use hardware and software to enter the data into a computer. Software processes the data and directs the computer hardware to store changes on storage media and produce information in a desired form.

10 What Are the Types of Computer Users?

Computer users can be separated into five categories: home users, small office/home office users, mobile users, large business users, and power users. A **home user** is a family member who uses a computer for a variety of reasons, such as budgeting and personal financial management, Web access, communications, and entertainment. A **small office/home office** (*SOHO*) user is a small company or self-employed individual who works from home and uses basic business software and sometimes industry-specific software. Mobile users are employees and students who work on a computer while away from a main office or school. A **large business user** works in a company with many employees and uses a computer and computer network to process high volumes of transactions. **Power users** are employed in all types of businesses and use powerful computers to work with industry-specific software.

11 What Computer Applications Are Used in Society?

You may interact directly with computers in fields such as education, finance, government, health care, science, publishing, travel, and industry. In education, students use computers and software to assist with learning or take distance learning classes. In finance, people use computers for **online banking** to access information and **online investing** to buy and sell stocks and bonds. Government offices have Web sites to provide citizens with up-to-date information, and government employees use computers as part of their daily routines. In medicine, computers are used to maintain patient records, assist doctors with medical tests and research, file insurance claims, provide greater precision during operations, and as implants. All branches of science use computers to assist with collecting, analyzing, and modeling data and to communicate with scientists around the world. Publishers use computers to assist in designing pages and make the content of their publications available online. Many vehicles use some type of **online navigation system** to help people travel more quickly and safely. Industries use **computer-aided manufacturing** (*CAM*) to assist with the manufacturing process.

Visit **scsite.com/dc2005/quiz** or click the Quiz Yourself button. Click Objectives 8 – 11 below Chapter 1.

CHAPTER 1 KEY TERMS

You should know the Primary Terms and be familiar with the Secondary Terms.

WEB INSTRUCTIONS:

To display this page from the Web, start your browser and enter the Web address **scsite.com/dc2005/ch1/terms**. Click a term to display its definition and a picture. When the picture appears, click the more info button for current and additional information about the term from the Web.

>> Primary Terms

(shown in bold-black characters in the chapter)

application software (16)
communications device (9)
computer (6)
computer literacy (5)
computer-aided manufacturing (38)
data (6)
desktop computer (19)
FAQ (6)
graphical user interface (GUI) (14)
handheld computer (21)
hardware (7)
home user (26)
information (6)
input device (7)
installing (14)
Internet (11)
laptop computer (20)
large business user (30)
mainframe (23)
midrange server (22)
mobile computer (20)
mobile device (20)
mobile users (29)
network (10)
notebook computer (20)
onboard navigation system (37)
online (10)
online banking (34)
online investing (34)
output device (8)
PDA (21)
personal computer (18)
photo community (13)
power user (32)
program (14)
run (14)
small office/home office (28)
smart phone (22)
software (14)
storage device (8)
storage media (8)
supercomputer (23)
system software (15)
system unit (8)
Tablet PC (20)
telecommuting (32)
user (10)
Web (13)
Web-enabled (21)
Web page (13)

>> Secondary Terms

(shown in italic characters in the chapter)

Anytime Anywhere Learning program (34)
CAM (38)
client (10)
customer relationship management (CRM) (31)
digital divide (33)
digital pen (20)
e-commerce (29)
enterprise computing (30)
execute (14)
garbage in, garbage out (10)
icon (14)
information processing cycle (6)
information system (24)
information technology (IT) department (31)
instructions (6)
Internet receiver (27)
kiosk (31)
loads (14)
memory (8)
minicomputers (22)
multimedia (32)
neural network (36)
operating system (15)
PC-compatible (19)
personal digital assistant (21)
processor (8)
programmer (17)
publish (13)
resources (10)
server (10)
SOHO (28)
stylus (21)
telemedicine (35)
tower (19)
utility program (16)
Web cam (29)

CHECKPOINT CHAPTER 1

Use the Checkpoint exercises to check your knowledge level of the chapter.

WEB INSTRUCTIONS:

To display this page from the Web, start your browser and enter the Web address **scsite.com/dc2005/ch1/check**. Click the links for current and additional information.

LABEL THE FIGURE

Identify these common computer hardware components.

a. card reader (storage) 8
b. CD/DVD drive (storage) 1
c. digital camera (input) 9
d. floppy disk drive (storage) 2
e. hard disk drive (storage) 3
f. keyboard (input) 12
g. microphone (input) 11
h. modem (communications) 5
i. monitor (output) 15
j. mouse (input) 14
k. PC video camera (input) 16
l. printer (output) 13
m. scanner (input) 7
n. speaker (output) 4
o. system unit (processor, memory, storage) 6
p. USB flash drive (storage) 10

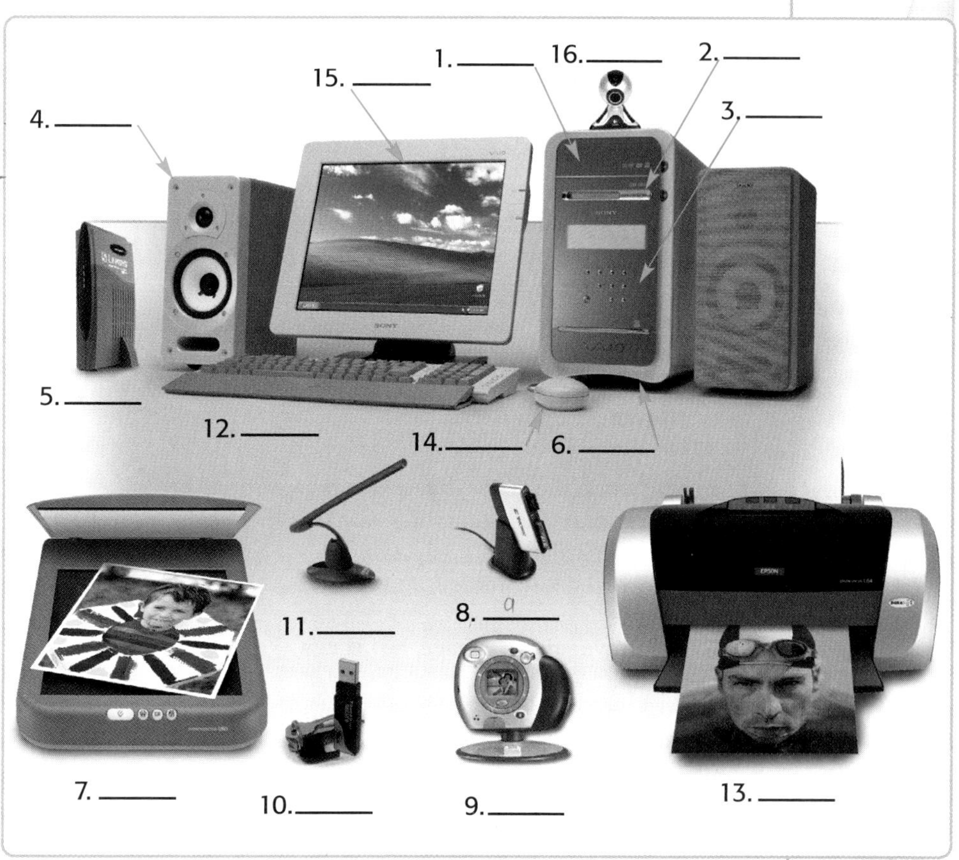

TRUE/FALSE

Mark T for True and F for False. (See page numbers in parentheses.)

T 1. Information conveys meaning and is useful to one or more people. (6)
____ 2. Computers process information (output) into data (input). (6) F
T 3. A user is anyone who communicates with a computer. (10)
F 4. When a computer connects to a network, it is offline. (10)
F 5. The Internet is a worldwide collection of ~~servers~~ network. (11)
T 6. Software is a series of instructions that tells the computer what to do. (14)
____ 7. System software is a set of programs that coordinates all the activities among computer hardware devices. (15)
T 8. A notebook computer is a portable, personal computer small enough to fit on your lap. (20)
____ 9. A power user requires the capabilities of a workstation or other powerful computer. (32)
____ 10. With online investing, the transaction fee for each trade usually is much more than when trading through a broker. (34)

CHAPTER 1 CHECKPOINT

MULTIPLE CHOICE

Select the best answer. (See page numbers in parentheses.)

1. Data is a collection of unprocessed items, which can include ______. (6)
   a. text and numbers
   b. images
   c. audio and video
   d. all of the above
2. A widely used ______ is a modem. (9)
   a. input device
   b. output device
   c. communications device
   d. storage device
3. A computing phrase known as garbage in, garbage out points out that the ______ of a computer's output depends on the accuracy of the input. (10)
   a. speed
   b. accuracy
   c. storage
   d. consistency
4. In a network, the major differences between the server and client computers are that the server ordinarily has ______. (10)
   a. less power, less storage, and is less reliable
   b. less power, more storage, but is less reliable
   c. more power, less storage, but is more reliable
   d. more power, more storage, and is more reliable
5. ______ allows people connected to the Internet to communicate with multiple users at the same time — much like a group discussion. (13)
   a. A chat room
   b. E-mail
   c. A Web paged.
   d. Instant messaging
6. During ______, a program may ask you to register or activate the software online. (14)
   a. execution
   b. loading
   c. installation
   d. running
7. Some widely used ______ include(s) personal information manager, desktop publishing, and Web page authoring. (16)
   a. system software
   b. operating systems
   c. application software
   d. utility programs
8. The term, PC-compatible, refers to any personal computer ______. (19)
   a. with processors having the same architecture as processors in Apple computers
   b. based on the original IBM personal computer design
   c. that uses the Macintosh operating system (Mac OS)
   d. all of the above
9. Two types of ______ are desktop computers and notebook computers. (19)
   a. personal computers
   b. midrange servers
   c. mainframe computers
   d. supercomputers
10. Three popular types of ______ are handheld computers, PDAs, and smart phones. (21)
    a. mobile devices
    b. notebook computers
    c. desktop computers
    d. tower computers
11. In addition to hardware and software, an information system includes ______. (24)
    a. accurate data
    b. trained information technology staff and knowledgeable users
    c. document procedures
    d. all of the above
12. In a large business, the employees in the ______ keep the computers and the network running. (31)
    a. product development department
    b. marketing department
    c. information technology (IT) department
    d. accounting department
13. ______ is the idea that you can split people of the world into two distinct groups: those who have access to technology and those who do not. (33)
    a. Computer-aided manufacturing
    b. The digital divide
    c. E-commerce
    d. Anytime Anywhere Learning
14. Many vehicles today include some type of onboard navigation system that can do all of the following except ______. (37)
    a. provide directions
    b. drive the vehicle
    c. dispatch roadside assistance
    d. track the vehicle if it is stolen

CHECKPOINT CHAPTER 1

MATCHING — Match the terms with their definitions. (See page numbers in parentheses.)

L 1. instructions (6)
b 2. hardware (7)
g 3. network (10)
c 4. server (10)
i 5. publish (13)
k 6. software (14)
f 7. icon (14)
h 8. digital pen (20)
a 9. Web-enabled (21)
e 10. kiosk (31)

a. mobile devices that can connect to the Internet wirelessly
b. computer's electric, electronic, and mechanical components
c. computer that controls access to network resources
d. someone who develops application or system programs
e. freestanding computer usually with a touch screen
f. small image that represents a program, an instruction, or some other object
g. collection of computers connected together that allows sharing of resources
h. used to write on the screen or issue instructions to a Tablet PC that fits in the palm of your hand
i. make a Web page available on the Internet for others to see
j. system that attempts to illustrate the behavior of the human brain
k. series of instructions that tells a computer what to do and how to do it
l. steps that tell a computer how to perform a particular task

SHORT ANSWER — Write a brief answer to each of the following questions.

1. What are some ways people use computers in the home, at work, and at school? laptop What does it mean to be computer literate? ______
2. How is hardware different from software? ______ What is installing software? ______
3. How is an input device different from an output device? ______ What are commonly used input and output devices? ______
4. What are six common storage devices? ______ How are they different? ______
5. Why do people use the Internet? ______ How do users access the Internet? ______

WORKING TOGETHER — Working with a group of your classmates, complete the following team exercises.

1. Six commonly used input devices are listed in this chapter. These devices include a keyboard, mouse, microphone, scanner, PC video camera, and digital camera. Using the Internet or other resources, prepare a report about each one of these devices. Discuss how and when you would use one device instead of another. What are some of the different features available in each device? How would you determine which keyboard, mouse, and so on is the best for your particular needs? Share your reports with the class.

2. Choose one Issue from the following issues in this chapter: Does Technology Discriminate? (9), Is Everything You Read True? (13), Does Software Promote Violence? (17), or Are You Ready for Automatic Checkout? (30). Use the Web and/or print media to research the issue. Then, present a debate for the class, with different members of your team supporting different responses to the questions that accompany the issue.

3. Computers are everywhere. Watching television, driving a car, using a charge card, ordering fast food, and the more obvious activity of typing a term paper on a personal computer, all involve interaction with computers. For one day, have each member of your team make a list of every computer he or she encounters (be careful not to limit yourselves just to the computers you *see*). Meet with the members of your team and combine your lists. Consider how each computer is used. How were the tasks the computers perform done before computers? Use PowerPoint to create a group presentation and share your findings with the class.

CHAPTER 1 LEARN IT ONLINE

Previous | Next

QUIZZES AND LEARNING GAMES
Computer Genius
Crossword Puzzle
Interactive Labs
Practice Test
Quiz Yourself
Wheel of Terms

EXERCISES
Chapter Review
Checkpoint
Key Terms
Lab Exercises
Learn It Online
Web Research

BEYOND THE BOOK
Apply It
Career Corner
Companies
FAQ
High-Tech Talk
Issues
Looking Ahead
Trailblazers
Web Links

FEATURES
Guide to Web Sites
Making Use of the Web
Tech News
Timeline 2005

Use the Learn It Online exercises to reinforce your understanding of the chapter concepts.

WEB INSTRUCTIONS:

To display this page from the Web, start your browser and enter the Web address **scsite.com/dc2005/ch1/learn**.

1 At the Movies – Computer Takeaways

To view the Computer Takeaways movie, click the number 1 button. Watch the movie and then complete the exercise by answering the questions below. ZapMe!, an innovative marketing firm, originally provided 2,000 cash-strapped schools across the country with *free* computers for student use. The catch was that the students would be exposed to advertising messages flashing across their computer screens. ZapMe! provided the computers free, and made their money by selling screen-space to advertisers. Consumer groups, however, quickly began a campaign claiming it was not politically correct (PC) to do that. Under this pressure, most advertisers quit ZapMe!. Without sales, ZapMe! was forced to demand that the schools pay for the computers, or they would be taken away. What was not PC about this seemingly clever way of getting computers and Internet access in the hands of students who otherwise might not have this technology? Is this acceptable or not? Do you agree with this?

2 Student Edition Labs – Using Input Devices

Click the number 2 button. When the Student Edition Labs menu appears (screen shown in the figure below), click *Using Input Devices* to begin. A new browser window will open. Follow the on-screen instructions to complete the Lab. When finished, click the Exit button. If required, print a copy of your results to submit to your instructor.

3 Student Edition Labs – Using Windows

Click the number 3 button. When the Student Edition Labs menu appears, click *Using Windows* to begin. A new browser window will open. Follow the on-screen instructions to complete the Lab. When finished, click the Exit button. If required, print a copy of your results to submit to your instructor.

4 Practice Test

Click the number 4 button. Answer each question. When completed, enter your name and click the Grade Test button to submit the quiz for grading. Make a note of any missed questions. If required, print a copy to submit to your instructor.

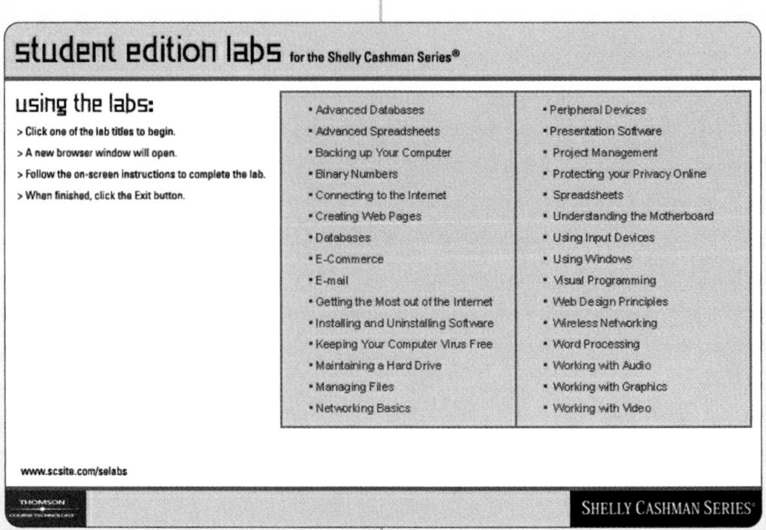

5 Web Guide

Click the number 5 button to display the Guide to Web Sites and Searching Techniques Web page. Click Reference and then click Ask Jeeves. Ask Jeeves about computer science. Click an answer of your choice. Use your word processing program to prepare a brief report about what you learned and submit your assignment to your instructor.

6 Scavenger Hunt

Click the number 6 button. Print a copy of the Scavenger Hunt page; use this page to write down your answers as you search the Web. Submit your completed page to your instructor.

7 Who Wants To Be a Computer Genius?

Click the number 7 button to find out if you are a computer genius. Directions on how to play the game will be displayed. When you are ready to play, click the Play button. Submit your score to your instructor.

8 Wheel of Terms

Click the number 8 button to reinforce important terms you learned in this chapter by playing the Shelly Cashman Series version of this popular game. Directions on how to play the game will be displayed. When you are ready to play, click the Play button. Submit your score to your instructor.

9 Career Corner

Click the number 9 button to display the Quintessential Careers page. Search for jobs in your state. Write a brief report about the jobs you found. Submit the report to your instructor.

10 Search Sleuth

Click the number 10 button to learn search techniques that will help make you a research expert. Submit the completed assignment to your instructor.

11 Crossword Puzzle Challenge

Click the number 11 button. Complete the puzzle to reinforce skills you learned in this chapter. Directions on how to play the game will be displayed. When you are ready to play, click the Submit button. Submit the completed puzzle to your instructor.

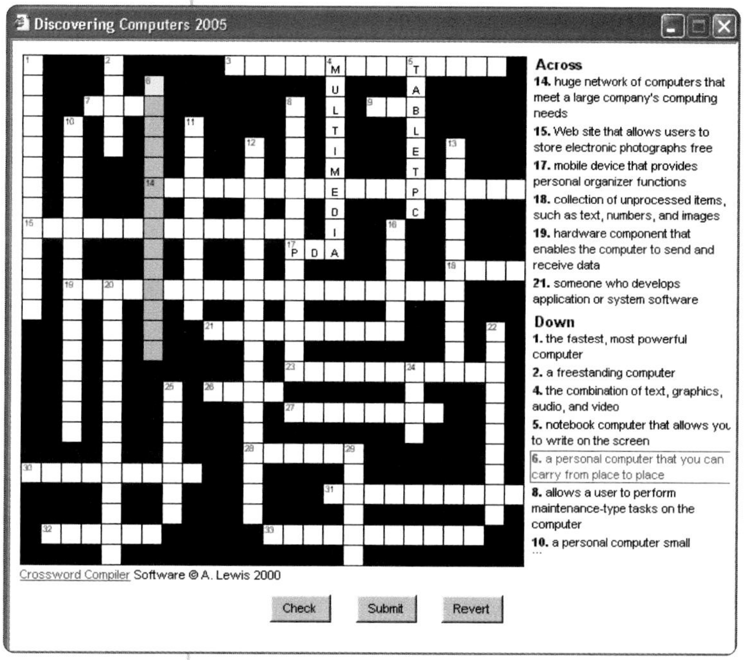

12 Learn the Net

No matter how much computer experience you have, navigating the Net for the first time can be intimidating. How do you get started? Click the number 12 button and click the links to discover how you can find out everything you want to know about the Internet.

CHAPTER 1 LAB EXERCISES

Use the Lab Exercises to gain hands-on computer experience.

QUIZZES AND LEARNING GAMES
Computer Genius
Crossword Puzzle
Interactive Labs
Practice Test
Quiz Yourself
Wheel of Terms

EXERCISES
Chapter Review
Checkpoint
Key Terms
Lab Exercises
Learn It Online
Web Research

BEYOND THE BOOK
Apply It
Career Corner
Companies
FAQ
High-Tech Talk
Issues
Looking Ahead
Trailblazers
Web Links

FEATURES
Guide to Web Sites
Making Use of the Web
Tech News
Timeline 2005

WEB INSTRUCTIONS:

To display this page from the Web, start your browser and enter the Web address **scsite.com/dc2005/ch1/lab**.

1 Using Windows XP Help and Support

Windows XP Help and Support brings together the Help features that were available in previous versions of Windows (Search, Index, and Favorites) with the online Help features found on the Microsoft Web site. Help and Support also allows you to see the differences among Windows XP and earlier versions of Windows. Click the Start button on the Windows taskbar and then click Help and Support on the Start menu. Click the What's new in Windows XP link and then click the What's new topics link. Click a topic in which you are interested. If necessary, scroll through and read the information. How is this version of Windows better than previous versions of Windows? Will the improvement make your work more efficient? Why or why not? What improvement, if any, would you still like to see? The Help and Support Center includes a Search text box below the Help toolbar. When would you use the Search text box to find Help? Click the Index button on the Help toolbar. What do you see? When would you use the Index sheet to find Help? Click the Favorites button on the Help toolbar. What do you see? When would you use the Favorites sheet to find Help? Close the Help and Support Center window.

2 Using Windows 2000/98 Help

In the past, when you purchased computer software, you also received large printed manuals that attempted to answer any questions you might have. Today, Help usually is offered directly on the computer. To make it easy to find exactly the Help you need, Windows Help is arranged on three sheets: Contents, Index, and Search. Windows 2000 includes a fourth sheet, Favorites. Click the Start button on the Windows taskbar and then click Help on the Start menu. Click the Contents tab in the Windows Help window. What do you see? When would you use the Contents sheet to find Help? Click the Index tab. What do you see? When would you use the Index sheet to find Help? Click the Search tab. What do you see? When would you use the Search sheet to find Help? If you are using Windows 2000, click the Favorites tab. What do you see? When would you use the Favorites sheet to find Help? Close the Windows Help window.

3 Improving Mouse Skills

This exercise uses Windows XP procedures. Click the Start button on the Windows taskbar. Point to All Programs on the Start menu, point to Games on the All Programs submenu, and then click Solitaire on the Games submenu. When the Solitaire window appears, click the Maximize button. Click Help on the Solitaire menu bar, and then click Contents. Click the Contents tab. Click the Solitaire overview topic and read the information. Click the Play Solitaire topic. Read and print the information by clicking the Solitaire Help window's Options button, clicking Print, and then clicking the OK button. Click the Close button in the Solitaire Help window. Play the game of Solitaire. Close the Solitaire window.

4 Learning About Your Computer

This exercise uses Windows XP/2000/98 procedures. You can learn some important information about your computer by studying the system properties. Click the Start button on the Windows taskbar. Click Control Panel on the Start menu. If necessary, click the Switch to Classic View link in the Control Panel area in the left pane of the Control Panel window. In Windows 2000/98, point to Settings on the Start menu, and then click Control Panel on the Settings submenu. Double-click the System icon in the Control Panel window. Click the General tab in the System Properties dialog box. Use the General sheet to find the answers to these questions:

- What operating system does your computer use?
- To whom is your computer registered?
- What type of processor does your computer have?
- How much memory (RAM) does your computer have?

Close the System Properties dialog box. Close the Control Panel window.

WEB RESEARCH CHAPTER 1

Use the Web Research exercises to learn more about the special features in this chapter.

WEB INSTRUCTIONS:

Use the link in each exercise or a search engine such as Google (google.com) to research the topic. Then, write a one-page, double-spaced report or create a presentation, unless otherwise directed below. Page numbers on which information can be found are in parentheses.

1 **Issue** Choose one Issue from the following issues in this chapter: Does Technology Discriminate? (9), Is Everything You Read True? (13), Does Software Promote Violence? (17), or Are You Ready for Automatic Checkout? (30). Use the Web to research the issue. Discuss the issue with classmates, instructors, and friends. Address the questions that accompany the issue in a report or presentation.

2 **Apply It** Choose one of the following Apply It features in this chapter: Wireless Internet Access Anywhere (11) or Prescription for Saving Doctors' Time (22). Use the Web to gather additional information about the topic. Print two Web pages that relate to the Apply It. Detail in a report or presentation what you learned.

3 **Career Corner** Read the Career Corner article in this chapter (38). Use the Web to find out more about the career. Describe the career in a report or presentation.

4 **Companies on the Cutting Edge** Choose one of the Companies on the Cutting Edge in this chapter (40). Use the Web to research the company further. Explain in a report or presentation how this company has contributed to computer technology.

5 **Technology Trailblazers** Choose one of the Technology Trailblazers in this chapter (41). Use the Web to research the person further. Explain in a report or presentation how this individual has affected the way people use, or think about, computers.

6 **Picture Yourself Using Computers** Read the Picture Yourself Using Computers story at the beginning of this chapter (2). Use the Web to research the uses of computers further. Describe in a report or presentation the ways in which you might use a computer.

7 **High-Tech Talk** Read the High-Tech Talk feature in this chapter (39). Use the Web to find out more about the topic. Summarize in a report or presentation what you learned.

8 **Web Link** Review the Web Link boxes found in the margins of this chapter. Visit five of the Web Link sites. Print the main Web page for each site you visit. Choose one of the Web pages and then summarize in one paragraph the content of the Web page.

9 **Looking Ahead** Choose one of the Looking Ahead articles in this chapter: Wearable Computers Serve Practical Purposes (18) or Robots Perform Real-World Tasks (33). Use the Web to find out more about the topic. Detail in a report or presentation what you learned.

10 **FAQ** Choose one FAQ found in this chapter. Use the Web to find out more about the topic. Summarize in one paragraph what you learned.

11 **History of Computers** Read the Timeline 2005 Special Feature that follows this chapter (52–65). Select an individual, product, or event presented in the Timeline 2005. Use the Web to learn more about your selection. Explain in a report or presentation why your selection is a milestone in computer history.

12 **Making Use of the Web** Read the Fun and Entertainment section of Making Use of the Web in Appendix A (APP 2). Complete the Fun and Entertainment Web Exercises at the end of the section (APP 3). Answer the questions posed in each exercise.

scsite.com/dc2005/ch1/timeline

Timeline 2005

Milestones in Computer History

Dr. John V. Atanasoff and Clifford Berry design and build the first electronic digital computer. Their machine, the Atanasoff-Berry-Computer, or ABC, provides the foundation for advances in electronic digital computers.

1937

Dr. John von Neumann writes a brilliant paper describing the stored program concept. His breakthrough idea, where memory holds both data and stored programs, lays the foundation for all digital computers that have since been built.

1945

1943

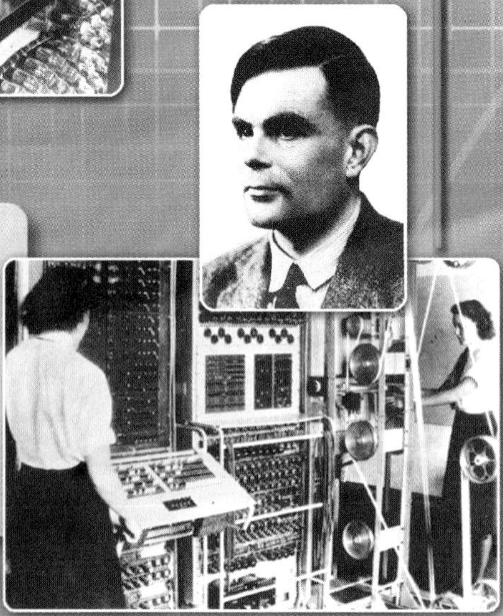

During World War II, British scientist Alan Turing designs the Colossus, an electronic computer created for the military to break German codes. The computer's existence is kept secret until the 1970s.

1946

Dr. John W. Mauchly and J. Presper Eckert, Jr. complete work on the first large-scale electronic, general-purpose digital computer. The ENIAC (Electronic Numerical Integrator And Computer) weighs thirty tons, contains 18,000 vacuum tubes, occupies a thirty-by-fifty-foot space, and consumes 160 kilowatts of power. The first time it is turned on, lights dim in an entire section of Philadelphia.

1947

William Shockley, John Bardeen, and Walter Brattain invent the transfer resistance device, eventually called the transistor. The transistor would revolutionize computers, proving much more reliable than vacuum tubes.

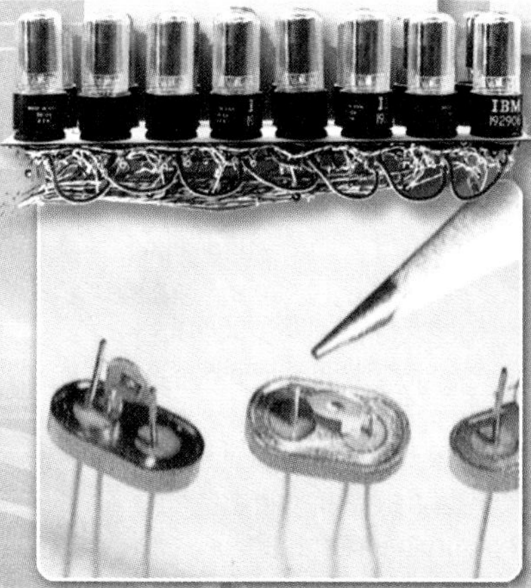

1951

The first commercially available electronic digital computer, the UNIVAC I (UNIVersal Automatic Computer), is introduced by Remington Rand. Public awareness of computers increases when the UNIVAC I, after analyzing only five percent of the popular vote, correctly predicts that Dwight D. Eisenhower will win the presidential election.

1952

Dr. Grace Hopper considers the concept of reusable software in her paper, "The Education of a Computer." The paper describes how to program a computer with symbolic notation instead of the detailed machine language that had been used.

1953

The IBM model 650 is one of the first widely used computers. Originally planning to produce only 50 machines, the system is so successful that eventually IBM manufactures more than 1,000. With the IBM 700 series of machines, the company will dominate the mainframe market for the next decade.

Core memory, developed in the early 1950s, provides much larger storage capacity than vacuum tube memory.

1957

The IBM 305 RAMAC system is the first to use magnetic disk for external storage. The system provides storage capacity similar to magnetic tape that previously was used, but offers the advantage of semi-random access capability.

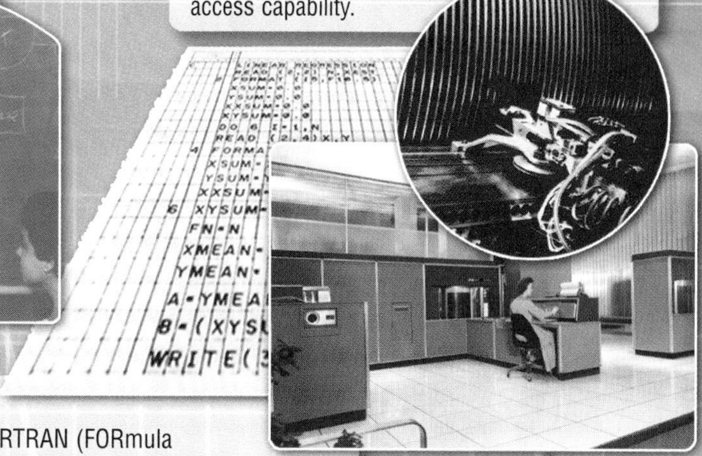

FORTRAN (FORmula TRANslation), an efficient, easy-to-use programming language, is introduced by John Backus.

1958

Jack Kilby of Texas Instruments invents the integrated circuit, which lays the foundation for high-speed computers and large-capacity memories. Computers built with transistors mark the beginning of the second generation of computer hardware.

1959

More than 200 programming languages have been created.

IBM introduces two smaller, desk-sized computers: the IBM 1401 for business and the IBM 1620 for scientists. The IBM 1620 initially is called the CADET, but IBM drops the name when campus wags claim it is an acronym for, Can't Add, Doesn't Even Try.

1960

COBOL, a high-level business application language, is developed by a committee headed by Dr. Grace Hopper. COBOL uses English-like phrases and runs on most business computers, making it one of the more widely used programming languages.

1964

Dr. John Kemeny of Dartmouth leads the development of the BASIC programming language. BASIC will be widely used on personal computers.

The number of computers has grown to 18,000.

Third-generation computers, with their controlling circuitry stored on chips, are introduced. The IBM System/360 computer is the first family of compatible machines, merging science and business lines.

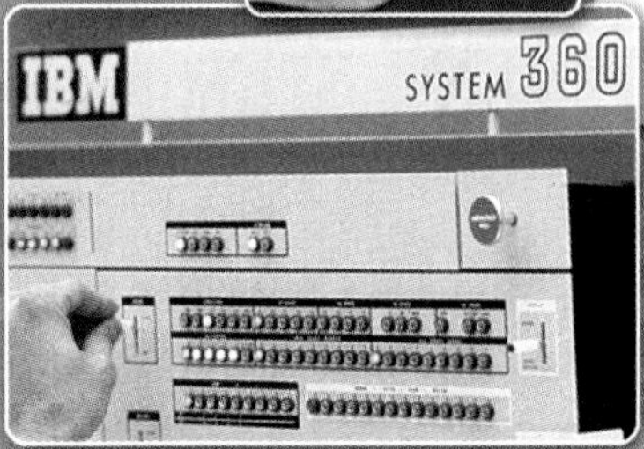

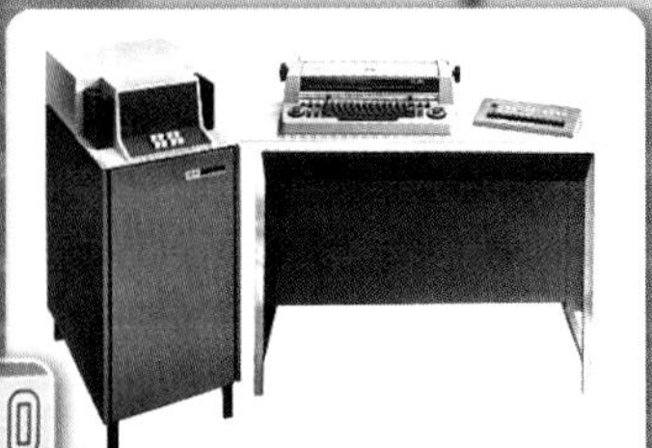

IBM introduces the term word processing for the first time with its Magnetic Tape/Selectric Typewriter (MT/ST). The MT/ST was the first reusable storage medium that allowed typed material to be edited without having to retype the document.

1965

Digital Equipment Corporation (DEC) introduces the first minicomputer, the PDP-8. The machine is used extensively as an interface for time-sharing systems.

1968

Computer Science Corporation becomes the first software company listed on the New York Stock Exchange.

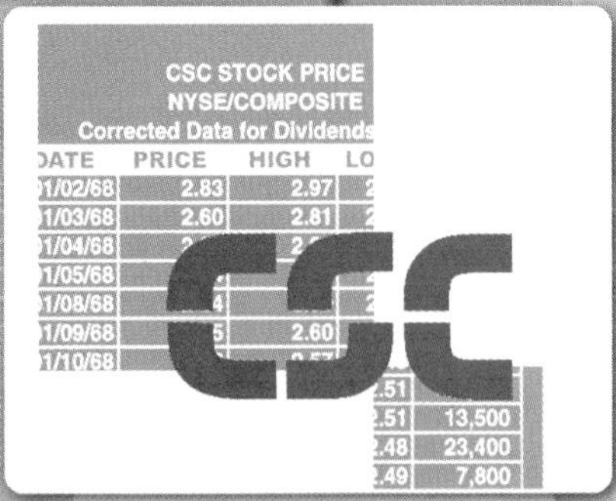

In a letter to the editor titled, "GO TO Statements Considered Harmful," Dr. Edsger Dijsktra introduces the concept of structured programming, developing standards for constructing computer programs.

Alan Shugart at IBM demonstrates the first regular use of an 8-inch floppy (magnetic storage) disk.

1969

IBM

Under pressure from the industry, IBM announces that some of its software will be priced separately from the computer hardware. This unbundling allows software firms to emerge in the industry.

ARPANET

The ARPANET network, a predecessor of the Internet, is established.

1970

Fourth-generation computers, built with chips that use LSI (large-scale integration) arrive. While the chips used in 1965 contained as many as 1,000 circuits, the LSI chip contains as many as 15,000.

1971

Dr. Ted Hoff of Intel Corporation develops a microprocessor, or microprogrammable computer chip, the Intel 4004.

1975

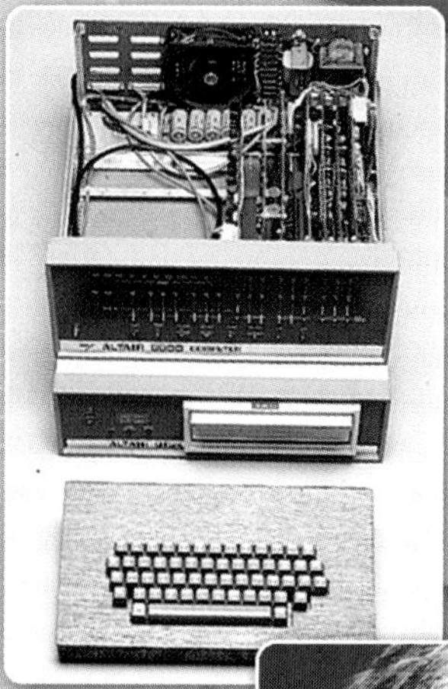

MITS, Inc. advertises one of the first microcomputers, the Altair. Named for the destination in an episode of *Star Trek*, the Altair is sold in kits for less than $400. Although initially it has no keyboard, no monitor, no permanent memory, and no software, 4,000 orders are taken within the first three months.

Ethernet, the first local area network (LAN), is developed at Xerox PARC (Palo Alto Research Center) by Robert Metcalf. The LAN allows computers to communicate and share software, data, and peripherals. Initially designed to link minicomputers, Ethernet will be extended to personal computers.

1976

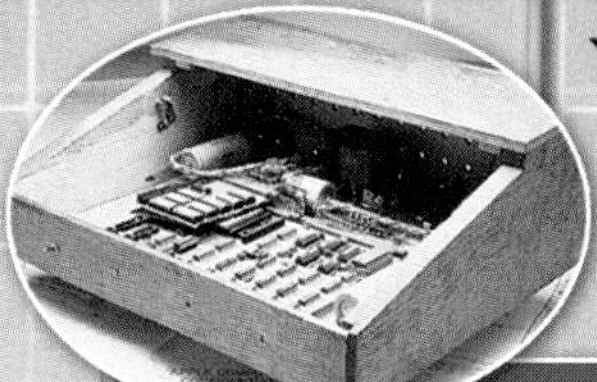

Steve Jobs and Steve Wozniak build the first Apple computer. A subsequent version, the Apple II, is an immediate success. Adopted by elementary schools, high schools, and colleges, for many students, the Apple II is their first contact with the world of computers.

1979

VisiCalc, a spreadsheet program written by Bob Frankston and Dan Bricklin, is introduced. Originally written to run on Apple II computers, VisiCalc will be seen as the most important reason for the acceptance of personal computers in the business world.

The first public online information services, CompuServe and the Source, are founded.

1980

IBM offers Microsoft Corporation cofounder, Bill Gates, the opportunity to develop the operating system for the soon-to-be announced IBM personal computer. With the development of MS-DOS, Microsoft achieves tremendous growth and success.

Alan Shugart presents the Winchester hard drive, revolutionizing storage for personal computers.

1981

The IBM PC is introduced, signaling IBM's entrance into the personal computer marketplace. The IBM PC quickly garners the largest share of the personal computer market and becomes the personal computer of choice in business.

1982

3,275,000 personal computers are sold, almost 3,000,000 more than in 1981.

COMPAQ

Compaq, Inc. is founded to develop and market IBM-compatible PCs.

Hayes introduces the 300 bps smart modem. The modem is an immediate success.

Instead of choosing a person for its annual award, *TIME* magazine names the computer Machine of the Year for 1982, acknowledging the impact of computers on society.

1983

Lotus Development Corporation is founded. Its spreadsheet software, Lotus 1-2-3, which combines spreadsheet, graphics, and database programs in one package, becomes the best-selling program for IBM personal computers.

1984

Apple introduces the Macintosh computer, which incorporates a unique, easy-to-learn, graphical user interface.

Hewlett-Packard announces the first LaserJet printer for personal computers.

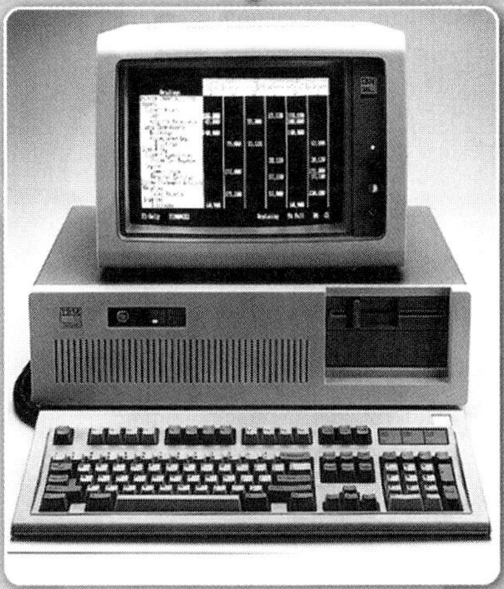

IBM introduces a personal computer, called the PC AT, that uses the Intel 80286 microprocessor.

1987

Several personal computers utilizing the powerful Intel 80386 microprocessor are introduced. These machines perform processing that once only large systems could handle.

1988

Microsoft surpasses Lotus Development Corporation to become the world's top software vendor.

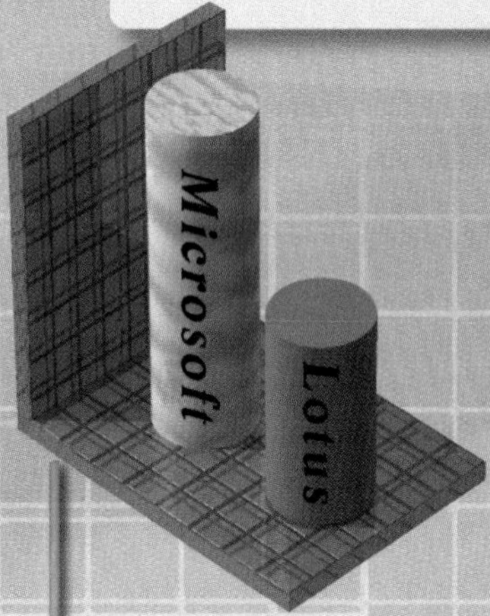

1989

The Intel 486 becomes the world's first 1,000,000 transistor microprocessor. It crams 1.2 million transistors on a .4" × .6" sliver of silicon and executes 15,000,000 instructions per second — four times as fast as its predecessor, the 80386 chip.

While working at CERN, Switzerland, Tim Berners-Lee invents an Internet-based hypermedia enterprise for information sharing. Berners-Lee will call this innovation the World Wide Web.

1991

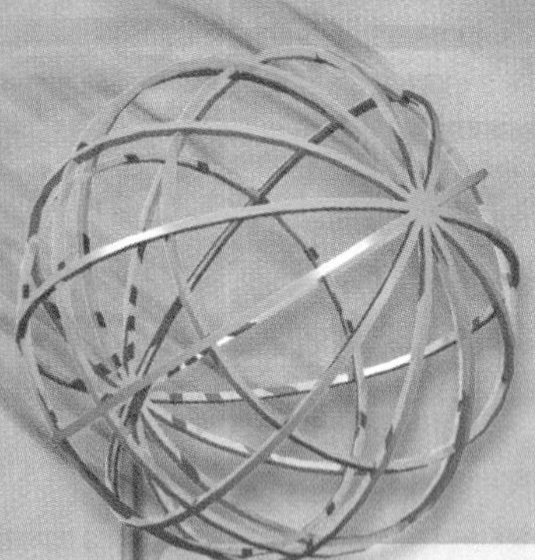

World Wide Web Consortium releases standards that describe a framework for linking documents on different computers.

1992

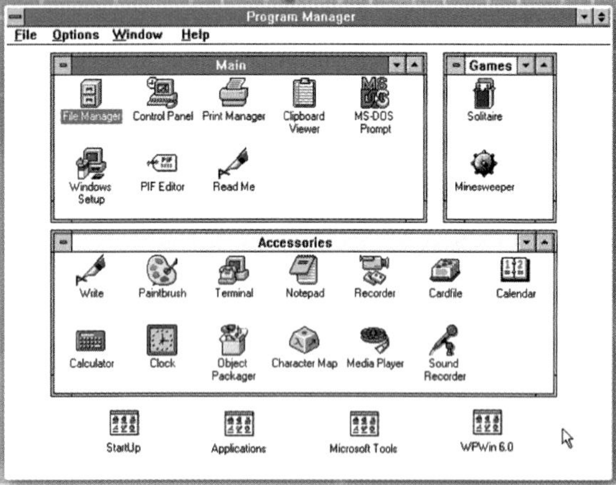

Microsoft releases Windows 3.1, the latest version of its Windows operating system. Windows 3.1 offers improvements such as TrueType fonts, multimedia capability, and object linking and embedding (OLE). In two months, 3,000,000 copies of Windows 3.1 are sold.

1993

Several companies introduce computers using the Pentium processor from Intel. The Pentium chip is the successor to the Intel 486 processor. It contains 3.1 million transistors and is capable of performing 112,000,000 instructions per second.

Microsoft releases Microsoft Office 3 Professional, the first version of Microsoft Office.

Marc Andreessen creates a graphical Web browser called Mosaic. This success leads to the organization of Netscape Communications Corporation.

The White House launches its Web site, which includes an interactive citizens' handbook and White House history and tours.

1994

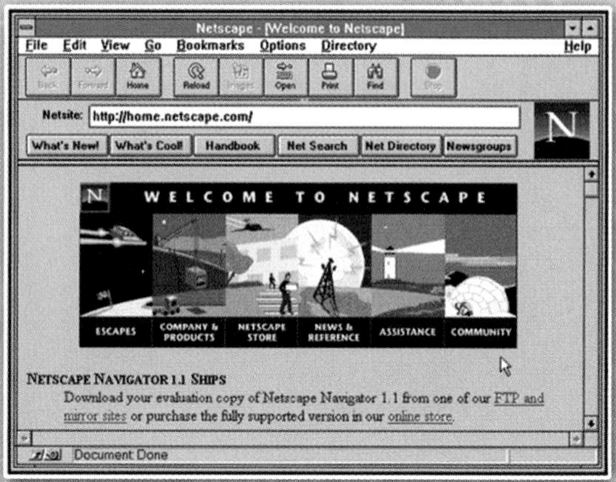

Jim Clark and Marc Andreessen found Netscape and launch Netscape Navigator 1.0, a browser for the World Wide Web.

Linus Torvalds creates the Linux kernel, a UNIX-like operating system that he releases free across the Internet for further enhancement by other programmers.

Sun Microsystems launches Java, an object-oriented programming language that allows users to write one application for a variety of computer platforms. Java becomes one of the hotter Internet technologies.

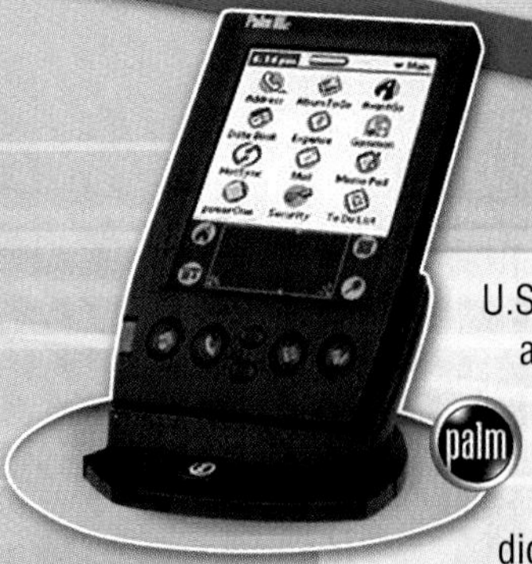

U.S. Robotics introduces PalmPilot, a handheld personal organizer. The PalmPilot's user friendliness and low price make it a standout next to more expensive personal digital assistants (PDAs).

The Summer Olympics in Atlanta makes extensive use of computer technology, using an IBM network of 7,000 personal computers, 2,000 pagers and wireless devices, and 90 industrial-strength computers to share information with more than 150,000 athletes, coaches, journalists, and Olympics staff members, and millions of Web users.

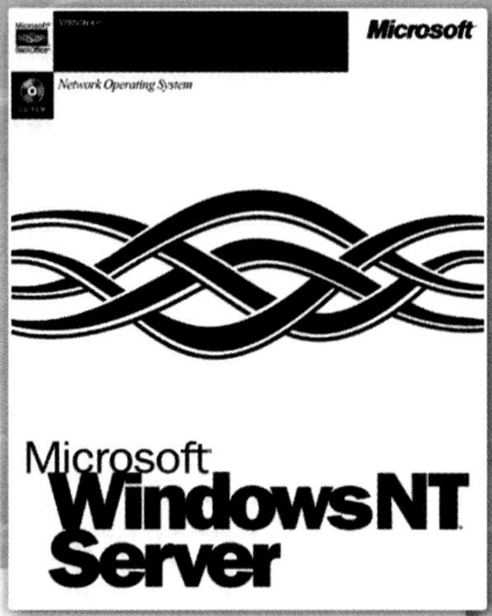

Microsoft releases Windows NT 4.0, an operating system for client-server networks. Windows NT's management tools and wizards make it easier for developers to build and deploy business applications.

1995

Microsoft releases Windows 95, a major upgrade to its Windows operating system. Windows 95 consists of more than 10,000,000 lines of computer instructions developed by 300 person-years of effort. More than 50,000 individuals and companies test the software before it is released.

1996

An innovative technology called webtv combines television and the Internet by providing viewers with tools to navigate the Web.

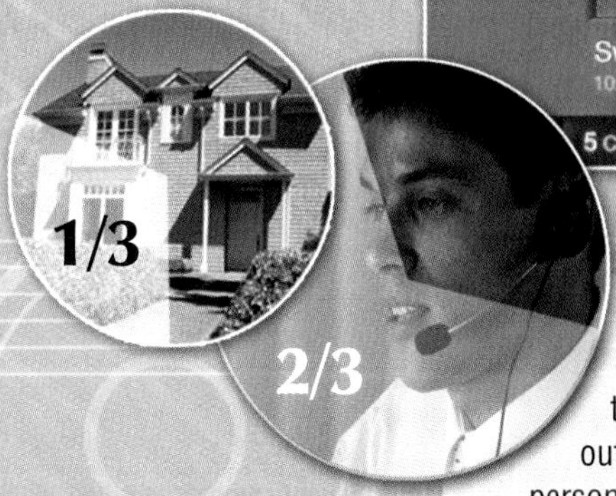

Two out of three employees in the United States have access to a personal computer, and one out of every three homes has a personal computer. Fifty million personal computers are sold worldwide and more than 250,000,000 are in use.

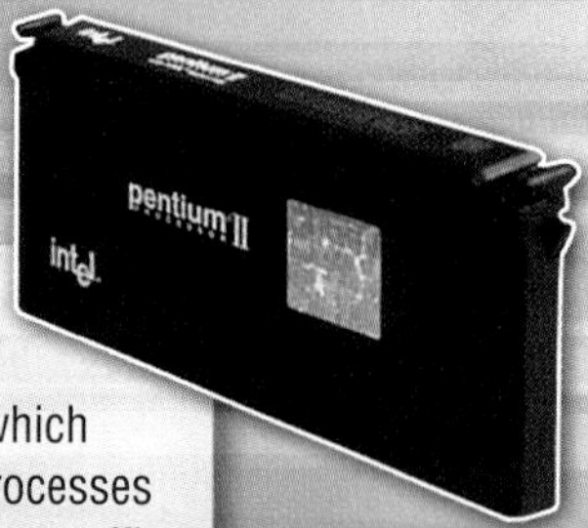

Intel introduces the Pentium II processor with 7.5 million transistors. The new processor, which incorporates MMX technology, processes video, audio, and graphics data more efficiently and supports applications such as movie editing, gaming, and more.

Microsoft releases Internet Explorer 4.0 and seizes a key place in the Internet arena. This new Web browser is greeted with tremendous customer demand.

Fifty million users are connected to the Internet and World Wide Web.

1997

Apple and Microsoft sign a joint technology development agreement. Microsoft buys $150,000,000 of Apple stock.

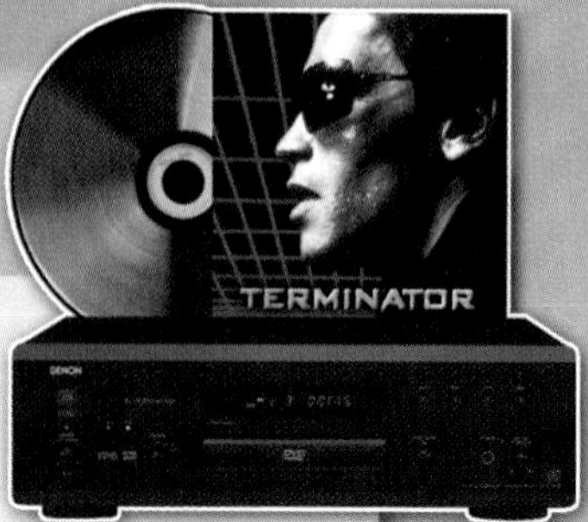

DVD, the next generation of optical disc storage technology, is introduced. DVD can store computer, audio, and video data in a single format, with the capability of producing near-studio quality. By year's end, 500,000 DVD players are shipped worldwide.

1998

More than 10,000,000 people take up telecommuting, which is the capability of working at home and communicating with an office via computer. Increasingly more firms embrace telecommuting to help increase productivity, reduce absenteeism, and provide greater job satisfaction.

E-commerce, or electronic commerce — the marketing of goods and services over the Internet — booms. Companies such as Dell, E*TRADE, and Amazon.com spur online shopping, allowing buyers to obtain everything from hardware and software to financial and travel services, insurance, automobiles, books, and more.

Microsoft ships Windows 98, an upgrade to Windows 95. Windows 98 offers improved Internet access, better system performance, and support for a new generation of hardware and software. In six months, more than 10,000,000 copies of Windows 98 are sold worldwide.

The Department of Justice's broad antitrust lawsuit asks that Microsoft offer Windows 98 without the Internet Explorer browser or that it bundle the competing Netscape Navigator browser with the operating system.

U.S. District Judge Thomas Penfield Jackson rules in the antitrust lawsuit brought by the Department of Justice and 19 states that Microsoft used its monopoly power to stifle competition.

Governments and businesses frantically work to make their computers Y2K (Year 2000) compliant, spending more than $500 billion worldwide. Y2K non-compliant computers cannot distinguish whether 01/01/00 refers to 1900 or 2000, and thus may operate using a wrong date. This Y2K bug can affect any application that relies on computer chips, such as ATMs, airplanes, energy companies, and the telephone system.

1998

1999

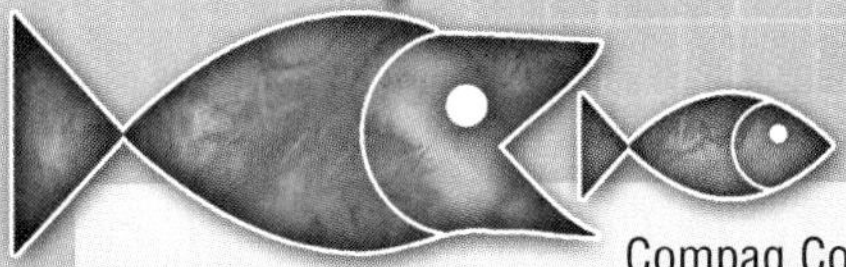

Compaq Computer, the United States' leading personal computer manufacturer, buys Digital Equipment Corporation in the biggest take-over in the history of the computer industry. Compaq becomes the world's second largest computer firm, behind IBM.

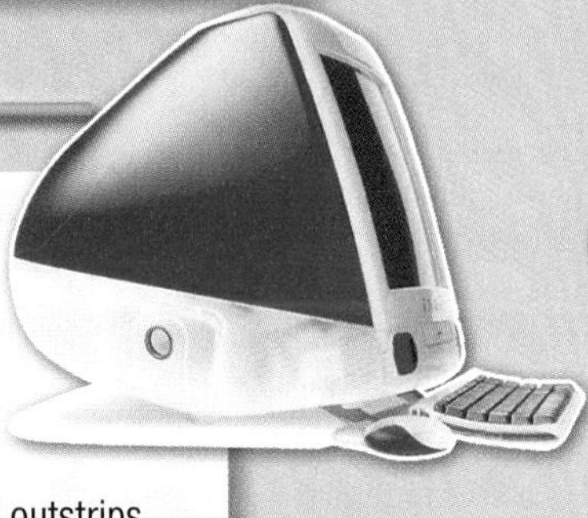

Apple Computer introduces the iMac, the next version of its popular Macintosh computer. The iMac abandons such conventional features as a floppy disk drive but wins customers with its futuristic design, see-through case, and easy setup. Consumer demand outstrips Apple's production capabilities, and some vendors are forced to begin waiting lists.

Microsoft introduces Office 2000, its premier productivity suite, offering new tools for users to create content and save it directly to a Web site without any file conversion or special steps.

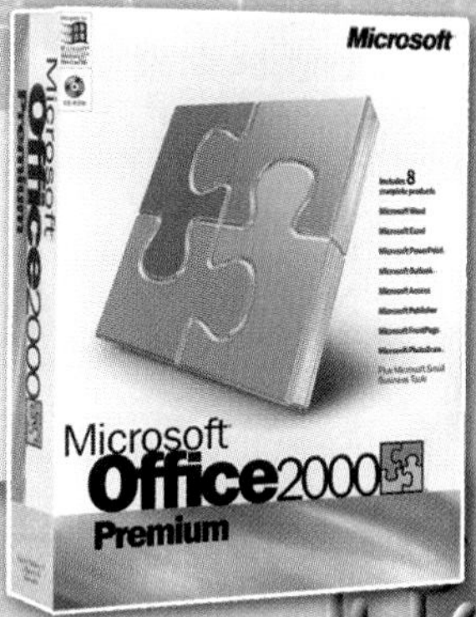

Open Source Code software, such as the Linux operating system and the Apache Web server created by unpaid volunteers, begin to gain wide acceptance among computer users.

scsite.com/dc2005/ch1/timeline

Microsoft ships Windows 2000 and Windows Me. Windows 2000 offers improved behind-the-scene security and reliability. Windows Me is designed for home users and lets them edit home movies, share digital photos, index music, and create a home network.

According to the U.S. Department of Commerce, Internet traffic is doubling every 100 days, resulting in an annual growth rate of more than 700 percent. It has taken radio and television 30 years and 15 years, respectively, to reach 60 million people. The Internet has achieved the same audience base in three years.

Shawn Fanning, 19, and his company, Napster, turn the music industry upside down by developing software that allows computer users to swap music files with one another without going through a centralized file server. The Recording Industry of America, on behalf of five media companies, sues Napster for copyright infringement.

Intel unveils its Pentium 4 chip with clock speeds starting at 1.4 GHz. The Pentium 4 includes 42 million transistors, nearly twice as many contained on its predecessor, the Pentium III.

2000

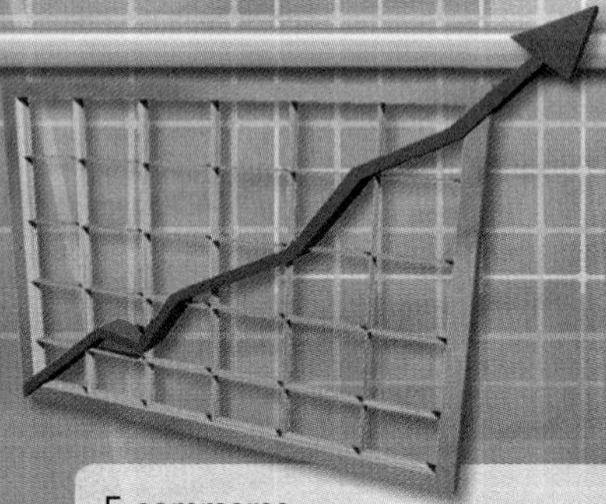

E-commerce achieves mainstream acceptance. Annual e-commerce sales exceed $100 billion, and Internet advertising expenditures reach more than $5 billion.

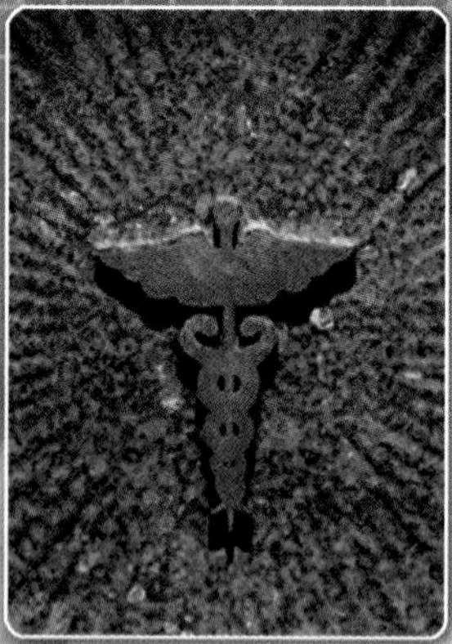

Telemedicine uses satellite technology and videoconferencing to broadcast consultations and to perform distant surgeries. Robots are used for complex and precise tasks. Computer-aided surgery uses virtual reality to assist with training and planning procedures.

Dot-com companies (Internet based) go out of business at a record pace — nearly one per day — as financial investors withhold funding due to the companies' unprofitability.

2001

Microsoft introduces Office XP, the next version of the world's leading suite of productivity software. Features include speech and handwriting recognition, smart tags, and task panes.

Microsoft releases major operating system updates with Windows XP for the desktop and servers, and Pocket PC 2002 for handheld computers. Windows XP is significantly more reliable than previous versions, features a 32-bit computing architecture, and offers a new look and feel. Pocket PC 2002 offers the handheld computer user a familiar Windows interface and consistent functionality.

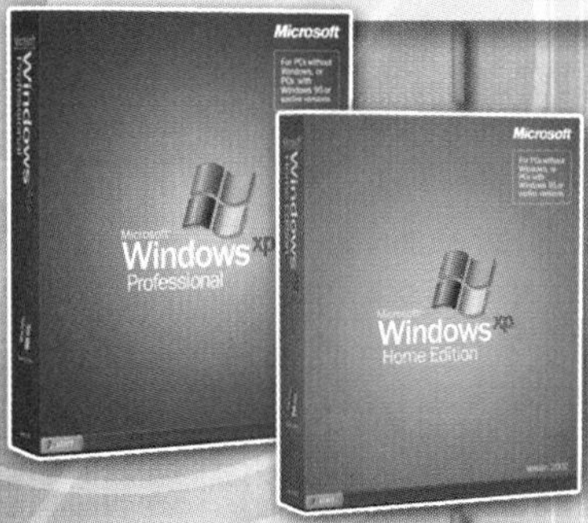

DVD writers (DVD+RW) begin to replace CD writers (CD-RW). DVDs can store up to eight times as much data as CDs. Uses include storing home movies, music, photos, and backups. Digital cameras and video editors help the average user develop quality video to store on DVDs.

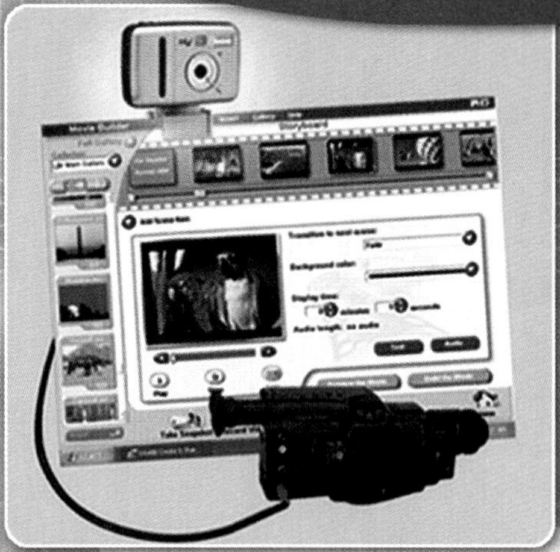

Digital video cameras, DVD writers, easy-to-use video editing software, and improvements in storage capabilities allow the average computer user to create Hollywood-like videos with introductions, conclusions, scenes rearranged, music, and voice-over.

2001

2002

Microsoft.net

Microsoft launches its .NET strategy, which is a new environment for developing and running software applications featuring ease of development of Web-based services. Users of applications immediately see the benefit of .NET as instant access to data and services in the context of their current task.

Handspring begins shipping the Treo communicator, a handheld computer with cellular telephone, e-mail, text messaging, and wireless Web capabilities.

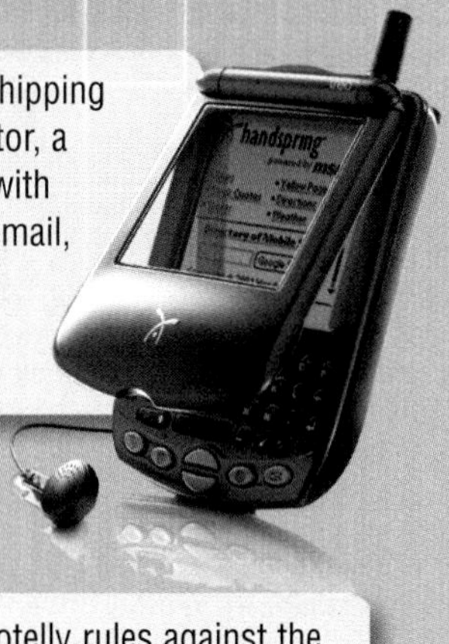

Avid readers enjoy e-books, which are digital texts read on compact computer screens. E-books can hold the equivalent of 10 traditional books containing text and graphics. Readers can search, highlight text, and add notes.

Intel ships its revamped Pentium 4 chip with the 0.13 micron processor and Hyper-Threading (HT) Technology, operating at speeds of 3.06 GHz. This new development eventually will enable processors with a billion transistors to operate at 20 GHz.

U.S. District Judge Colleen Kollar-Kotelly rules against the nine states appealing the antitrust settlement reached between Microsoft and the Justice Department. The nine states were seeking tougher sanctions against the software giant for abusing its monopoly power. Two of the nine states, Massachusetts and West Virginia, plan to appeal the latest ruling to the U.S. District Court of Appeals.

scsite.com/dc2005/ch1/timeline

After several years of negligible sales, the Tablet PC is reintroduced as the next-generation mobile PC. The lightweight device, the size of a three-ring notebook, is ideal for people on the go. It runs Windows XP Tablet PC Edition, has wireless capabilities, and features natural input capabilities including pen and speech technologies.

Computer manufacturers and software companies integrate high-end PCs and entertainment devices. The result is PCs with great entertainment functions that let you watch and record TV, burn CDs and DVDs, play games, and more.

Wireless computers and devices, such as keyboards, mouse devices, home networks, and public Internet access points become commonplace. Latest operating systems include support for both the Wi-Fi (wireless fidelity) and Bluetooth standards. Wireless capabilities are standard on many PDAs and Tablet PCs.

2003

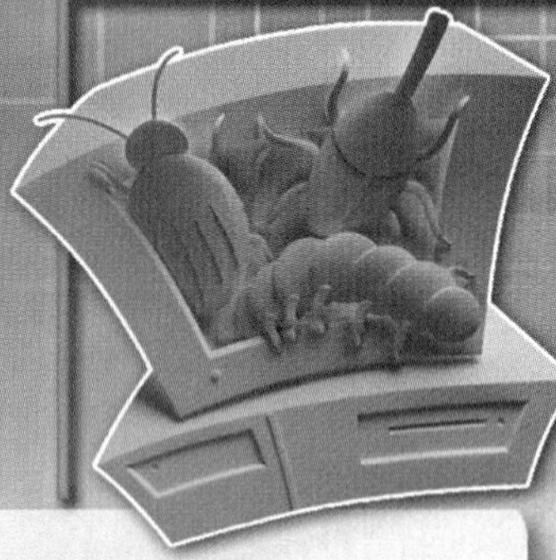

MSBlast worm and SoBig virus plague Microsoft Windows users. Microsoft Corporation responds by creating the Anti-Virus Reward Program, initially funded with $5 million, to help law enforcement agencies identify and bring to justice those who illegally release damaging worms, viruses and other types of malicious code on the Internet.

IBM puts its weight behind On Demand computing. Its intention is to invest up to $10 billion in hardware and software, and then sell computing time and the use of applications to businesses in a manner similar to an electric utility company.

In an attempt to maintain their current business model of selling songs, the Recording Industry Association of American (RIAA) files over 250 lawsuits against individual computer users who offer copyrighted music over peer-to-peer networks.

Microsoft ships Office 2003, the latest version of its flagship Office suite. New features include a consistent user interface, an overhauled Outlook, increased emphasis on task panes, improved collaboration, enhanced XML functionality, and a new application called OneNote for organizing your notes.

Companies such as RealNetworks, Microsoft, Sony, and Wal-Mart race to stake out turf in the online music store business started by Apple Computer. In the previous year, Apple's iTunes Music Store Web site sold nearly 20 million songs for 99 cents each.

Flat-panel LCD monitors overtake bulky CRT monitors as the popular choice of computer users. Although flat-panel LCD monitors cost more, they offer several advantages including physical size, weight, true display size, better power consumption, and no radiation emission.

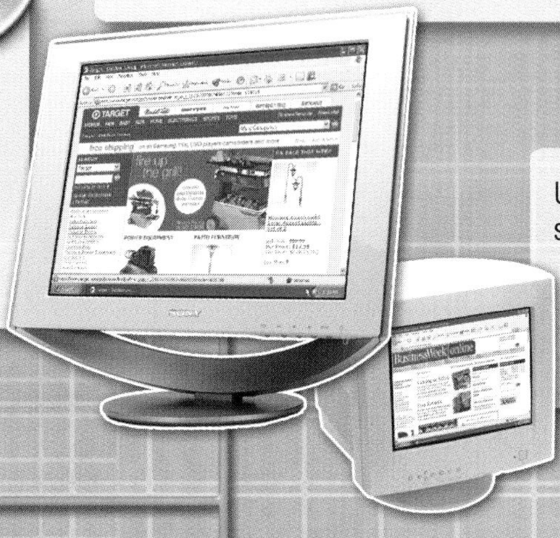

USB Flash Drives, which are small enough to fit on a key chain but can store up to 2 billion characters, become a cost-effective way to transport data and information from one computer to another.

2004

Linux, the open-source operating system, makes major inroads into the server market as a viable alternative to Microsoft Windows, Sun's Solaris, and the UNIX operating systems.

Major retailers begin requiring suppliers to include Radio Frequency Identification (RFID) tags or microchips with antennas, which can be as small as 1/3 of a millimeter across, in the goods they sell. When a transponder receives a certain radio query, it responds by transmitting its unique ID code. Besides carrying out the functions of the bar code, RFIDs may eventually eliminate long checkout lines.

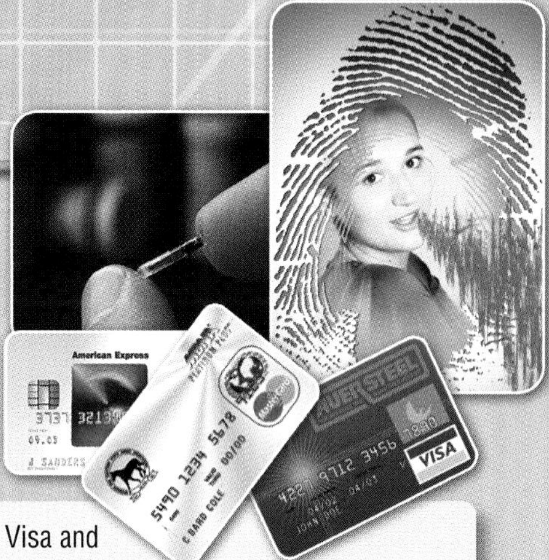

Visa and MasterCard aggressively test plastic card replacements, such as your fingerprint or a chip embedded under your skin, as a means of reducing credit card fraud and linking the charges directly to the person, rather than to the plastic card.

CHAPTER 2

The Internet and World Wide Web

Picture Yourself Publishing on the Web

Anticipating the end of your sophomore year means a respite from all the hard work. After finals, you and a friend from school are driving to Wisconsin Lake for a relaxing weekend with no thought of homework or studying! Before the semester ends, though, you plan to line up a summer job that starts as soon as you return from the trip.

Today, you meet with an adviser in the Career Placement Office. The adviser informs you that the office maintains a Resume Forwarding system. She shows you how to enter your resume into the system, and then automatically, it sends yours and all current resumes on file to potential employers. In addition, the adviser tells you that many companies look for employees over the Internet, so to be successful in your job search, you need to create a personal Web page with a resume. She recommends that you attend the Online Job Search seminar the week before the semester ends. Topics include finding out about available internships, getting information about various organizations and positions, and how to publish a resume on the Web.

While Computer Information Systems is not your major, after attending the seminar, you feel confident that you will be able to publish your resume on the Web and look forward to having summer employment plans lined up before your weekend getaway.

As you read Chapter 2, you will learn about Web publishing and discover other features of the Internet.

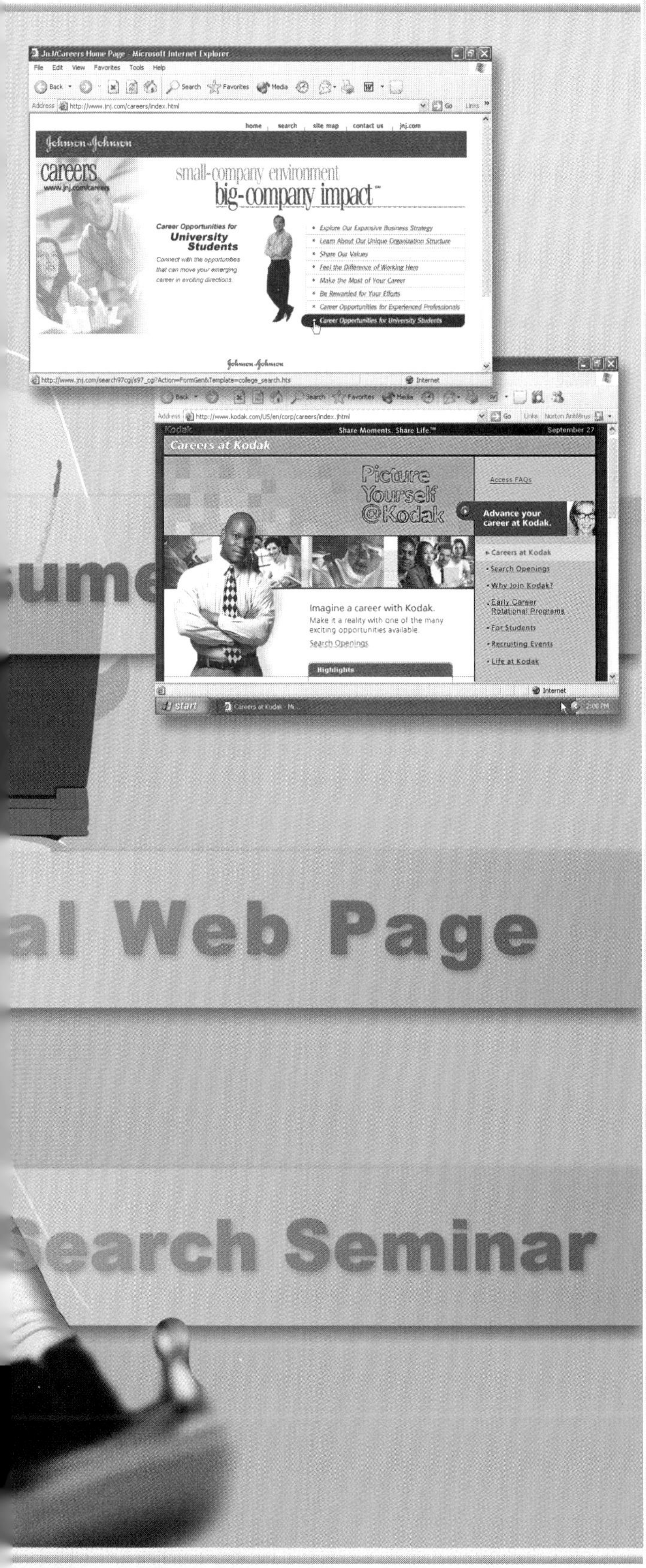

OBJECTIVES

After completing this chapter, you will be able to:

1. **Discuss the history of the Internet**
2. **Explain how to access and connect to the Internet**
3. **Analyze an IP address**
4. **Identify the components of a Web address**
5. **Explain the purpose of a Web browser**
6. **Search for information on the Web**
7. **Describe the types of Web sites**
8. **Recognize how Web pages use graphics, animation, audio, video, virtual reality, and plug-ins**
9. **Describe the types of e-commerce**
10. **Explain how e-mail, FTP, newsgroups and message boards, mailing lists, chat rooms, and instant messaging work**
11. **Identify the rules of netiquette**
12. **Identify the steps and tools required for Web publishing**

CONTENTS

THE INTERNET

One of the major reasons business, home, and other users purchase computers is for Internet access. Through the Internet, society has access to global information and instant communications. Further, access to the Internet can occur anytime from a computer anywhere: at home, at work, at school, in a restaurant, on an airplane, and even at the beach.

The **Internet**, also called the *Net*, is a worldwide collection of networks that links millions of businesses, government agencies, educational institutions, and individuals. Each of the networks on the Internet provides resources that add to the abundance of goods, services, and information accessible via the Internet.

Today, more than one-half billion users around the world connect to the Internet for a variety of reasons, some of which are shown in Figure 2-1. The World Wide Web and e-mail are two of the more widely accessed Internet services. Other services include FTP (File Transfer Protocol), newsgroups and message boards, mailing lists, chat rooms, and instant messaging. This chapter explains each of these services. To enhance understanding of these services, the chapter begins by discussing the history of the Internet and how the Internet works.

HISTORY OF THE INTERNET

The Internet has its roots in a networking project started by the Pentagon's *Advanced Research Projects Agency* (*ARPA*), an agency of the U.S. Department of Defense. ARPA's goal was to build a network that (1) allowed

Figure 2-1b (e-mail)

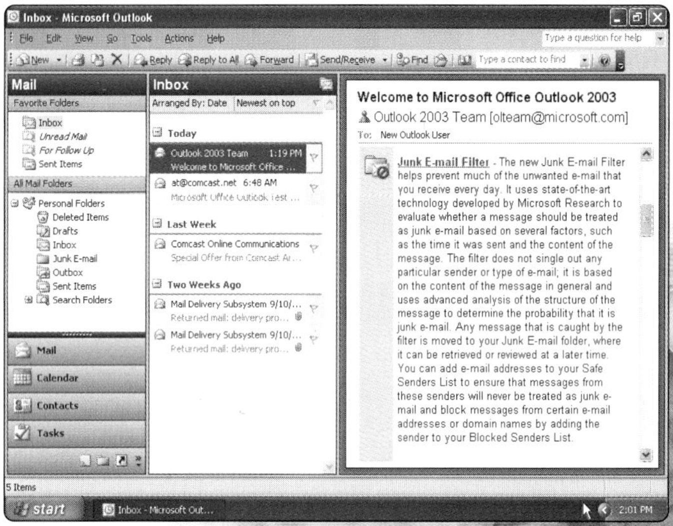

Figure 2-1a (Web)

Figure 2-1c (FTP - File Transfer Protocol)

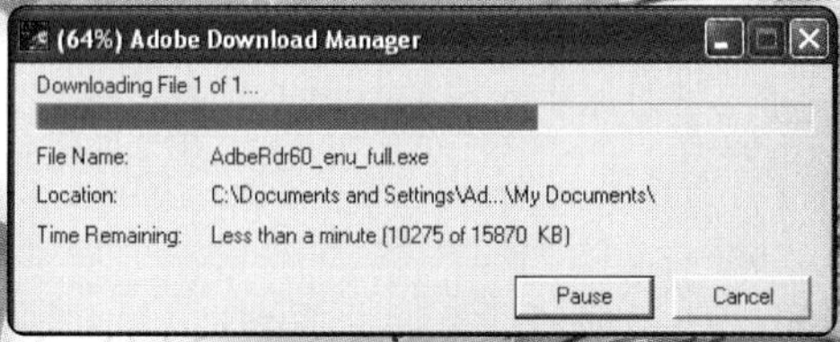

FIGURE 2-1 Users around the world connect to the Internet to access the Web, send e-mail messages, transfer documents and photographs, post messages, chat with a group, or have a private conversation with an online friend or family member.

scientists at different physical locations to share information and work together on military and scientific projects and (2) could function even if part of the network were disabled or destroyed by a disaster such as a nuclear attack. That network, called *ARPANET*, became functional in September 1969, linking scientific and academic researchers across the United States.

The original ARPANET consisted of four main computers, one each located at the University of California at Los Angeles, the University of California at Santa Barbara, the Stanford Research Institute, and the University of Utah. Each computer served as a host on the network. A *host* is any computer that provides services to other computers on a network. Hosts typically use high-speed communications to transfer data and messages over a network. They also provide network connections for other computers.

As researchers and others realized the great benefit of using ARPANET's e-mail to share data and information, ARPANET underwent phenomenal growth. By 1984, ARPANET had more than 1,000 individual computers linked as hosts. (Today, more than 150 million hosts connect to the Internet.)

Some organizations connected entire networks to ARPANET to take advantage of the high-speed communications it offered. In 1986, the National Science Foundation (NSF) connected its huge network of five supercomputer centers, called *NSFnet*, to ARPANET. This configuration of complex networks and hosts became known as the Internet.

Until 1995, NSFnet handled the bulk of the communications activity, or **traffic**, on the Internet. In 1995, NSFnet terminated its network on the Internet and returned its status to a research network.

Figure 2-1d (newsgroup)

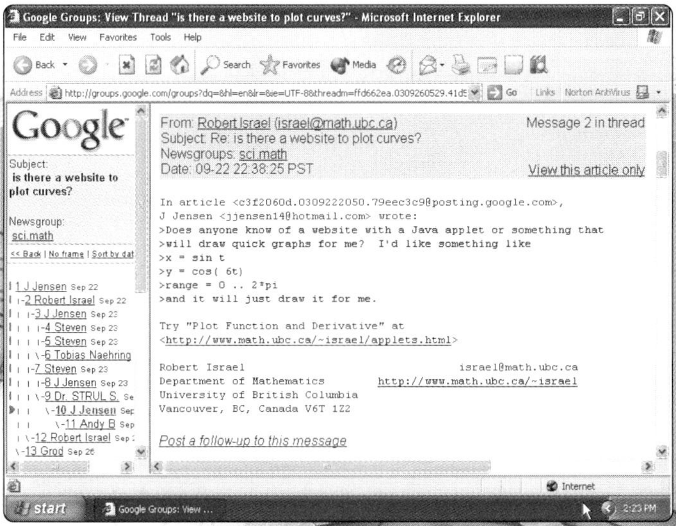

Figure 2-1e (chat)

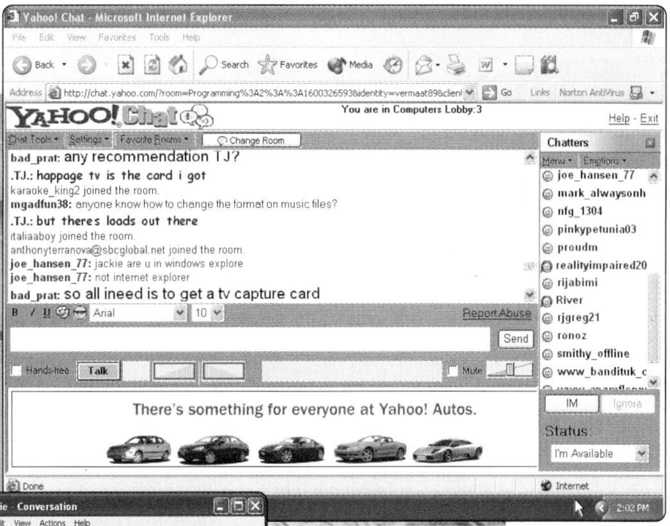

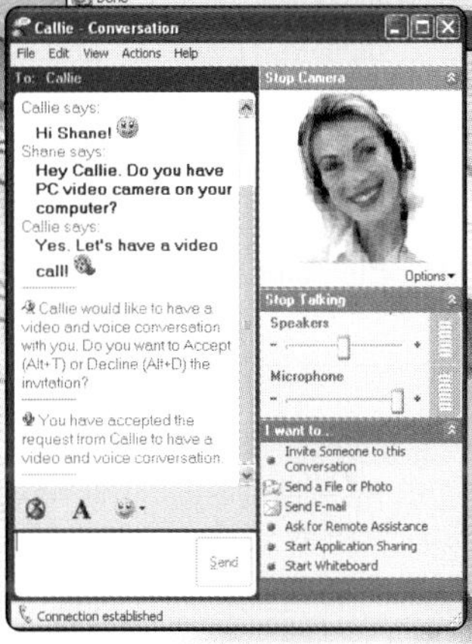

Figure 2-1f (instant messaging)

Today, the Internet consists of many local, regional, national, and international networks. Numerous corporations, commercial firms, and other companies provide networks to handle the Internet traffic. Both public and private organizations own networks on the Internet. These networks, along with telephone companies, cable and satellite companies, and the government, all contribute toward the internal structure of the Internet.

Even as the Internet grows, it remains a public, cooperative, and independent network. Each organization on the Internet is responsible only for maintaining its own network. No single person, company, institution, or government agency controls or owns the Internet (read Issue 2-1 for a related discussion). The *World Wide Web Consortium* (W3C), however, oversees research and sets standards and guidelines for many areas of the Internet. The mission of the W3C is to contribute to the growth of the Web. More than 500 organizations from around the world are members of the W3C. They advise, define standards, and address other issues.

ISSUE 2-1

Who Controls the Internet?

Who owns and controls the Internet? No one? Everyone? Ownership of the Internet is a complicated issue. In theory, everyone who uses the Internet owns it. Before 1995, the National Science Foundation primarily financed and controlled the Internet. Today, large corporations and political organizations wield the most influence over regulation of the Internet. Media conglomerates, for example, control most of the heavily accessed news and political Web sites. Because of its worldwide scope, many people maintain that the Internet simply is too massive for regulation. If the Internet is not restricted, however, it also may be a forum for covert and illegal activities. Modern terrorist organizations have established sophisticated communications by creating Web sites, using e-mail, and secretly coding pictures on Web pages. Should the Internet be regulated? If so, by whom or what entity? Does the public have the power to maintain control of the Internet? Why or why not?

For more information about Internet control and Internet access, visit the Discovering Computers 2005 Issues Web page (**scsite.com/dc2005/issues**). Click Issue #1 below Chapter 2.

Internet2

Internet2 is a not-for-profit Internet-related research and development project. The focus is to improve on the inefficiencies of the Internet, such as relieving bottlenecks in the current architecture. Thus, the intent of Internet2 is not to replace the current Internet but to enhance tomorrow's Internet with advanced technologies and capabilities. Members of Internet2 include more than 190 universities in the United States, along with more than 60 companies and the U.S. government. Various companies have invested more than $200 million in Internet2 technology.

Internet2 develops and tests advanced Internet technologies for research, teaching, and learning. These applications require an extremely high speed network that exceeds the capabilities of today's Internet. A current Internet2 project that will benefit a large number of Internet users in the future involves digital video applications, such as video conferencing and remote control of microscopes and other instruments.

Once this Internet2 technology reaches the mainstream Internet, many applications will reap its benefits. In the operating room, surgeons will consult other surgeons thousands of miles away over the Internet — during an operation. A professional musician, while on a concert tour, will check a student's finger position during an online lesson. Those working with Internet2 expect this type of high-quality video conferencing to be available on the current Internet within the next few years.

HOW THE INTERNET WORKS

Data sent over the Internet travels via networks and communications media owned and operated by many companies. The following sections present various ways to connect to these networks on the Internet.

Connecting to the Internet

Employees and students often connect to the Internet through a business or school network. In this case, the computers usually are part of a network that connects to an access provider through a high-speed connection line leased from the local telephone company.

Many homes and some small businesses use dial-up access to connect to the Internet. **Dial-up access** takes place when the modem in your computer uses a standard telephone line to connect to the Internet. This type of access is an easy and inexpensive way for users to connect to the Internet. A dial-up connection, however, is slow-speed technology.

As an alternative, some home and small business users are opting for higher-speed connections such as DSL, ISDN, or cable television Internet services. **DSL** (*digital subscriber line*) and **ISDN** (*Integrated Services Digital Network*) are technologies that provide higher-speed Internet connections using regular copper telephone lines. Some experts predict DSL eventually will replace ISDN because it is much easier to install and can provide faster data transfer speeds than ISDN. A **cable modem** provides high-speed Internet connections through the cable television network. These services cost about twice as much as dial-up access.

In most cases, higher-speed Internet access, such as through DSL, ISDN, and cable television, is always on. That is, it is connected to the Internet the entire time the computer is running. With a dial-up access, by contrast, you must establish the connection to the Internet. Usually a modem dials the telephone number to the access provider.

Many hotels and airports provide dial-up or broadband Internet connections for mobile users, which allows them to connect to the Internet while on the road. Some mobile users access the Internet without wires. Wireless Internet access technologies enable mobile users to connect easily to the Internet with notebook computers, Tablet PCs, PDAs, and smart phones while away from a telephone, cable, or other wired connection. A variety of wireless Internet technologies exists, including satellite connections and cellular radio network connections. Most wireless Internet connections transfer data at speeds comparable to dial-up access, but some are much faster.

Read Apply It 2-1 for more information about Internet access.

APPLY IT 2-1

Connect to the Internet

If you want a high-speed Internet connection, then DSL and cable television (CATV) Internet services are two feasible options. Referred to as *broadband* Internet connections, both DSL and CATV Internet services offer constant connections, so you can be online 24 hours a day.

If both are available in your area, consider these factors. CATV Internet connections are shared with other users in the neighborhood, whereas DSL is a dedicated line that is not shared. DSL transfers data at slightly faster speeds, but CATV Internet connections are a little less costly.

Nearly all new notebook computers are equipped for wireless Internet access. All you need to do is get near a Wi-Fi hot spot, which is an area that sends a two-way radio signal to any connected computer within its range. Many coffee shops, automobile dealerships, and fast-food restaurants are adding hot spots.

For more information about Internet access, visit the Discovering Computers 2005 Apply It Web page (**scsite.com/dc2005/apply**). Click Apply It #1 below Chapter 2.

FAQ 2-1

What does bandwidth have to do with Internet access?

Bandwidth is a measure of how fast data and information travel over transmission media. Thus, higher-speed broadband Internet connections have a higher bandwidth than dial-up connections.

For more information about bandwidth, visit the Discovering Computers 2005 FAQ Web page (**scsite.com/dc2005/faq**). Click Bandwidth below Chapter 2.

Access Providers

An **access provider** is a business that provides individuals and companies access to the Internet free or for a fee. The most common fee arrangement for an individual account is a fixed amount, usually about $10 to $25 per month for dial-up access and $40 to $55 for higher-speed access. For this fee, many providers offer unlimited Internet access. Others specify a set number of access hours per month. With the latter arrangement, the provider charges extra for each hour of connection time that exceeds an allotted number of access hours. To attract more customers, some access providers also offer Web publishing services. Web publishing is discussed later in this chapter.

With dial-up Internet access, the telephone number you dial connects you to an access point on the Internet, called a *point of presence* (*POP*). When selecting an access provider, ensure it provides at least one local POP telephone number. Otherwise, long-distance telephone charges will apply for the time you connect to the Internet.

Users access the Internet through regional or national ISPs, online service providers, and wireless Internet service providers (Figure 2-2). An **ISP (Internet service provider)** is a regional or national access provider. A *regional ISP* usually provides Internet access to a specific geographic area. A *national ISP* is a larger business that provides Internet access in several major cities and towns nationwide. For dial-up access, some national ISPs provide both local and toll-free telephone numbers. Due to their larger size, national ISPs usually offer more services and have a larger technical support staff than regional ISPs. Examples of national ISPs are AT&T Worldnet and EarthLink.

In addition to providing Internet access, an **online service provider** (**OSP**) also has many members-only features. These features include special content and services such as news, weather, legal information, financial data, hardware and software guides, games, travel guides, e-mail, photo communities, online calendars, and instant messaging. Some even have their own built-in Web browser. The fees for using an OSP sometimes are slightly higher than fees for an ISP. The two more popular OSPs are AOL (America Online) and MSN (Microsoft Network). AOL differs from many OSPs in that it provides gateway functionality to the Internet, meaning it regulates the Internet services to which members have access.

A **wireless Internet service provider** (*WISP*) is a company that provides wireless Internet access to users with wireless modems or Web-enabled mobile devices. Notebook computers, for example, can use wireless modems. Web-enabled mobile devices include PDAs, smart phones, and hands-free (voice activated) Internet devices in automobiles. An antenna on the wireless

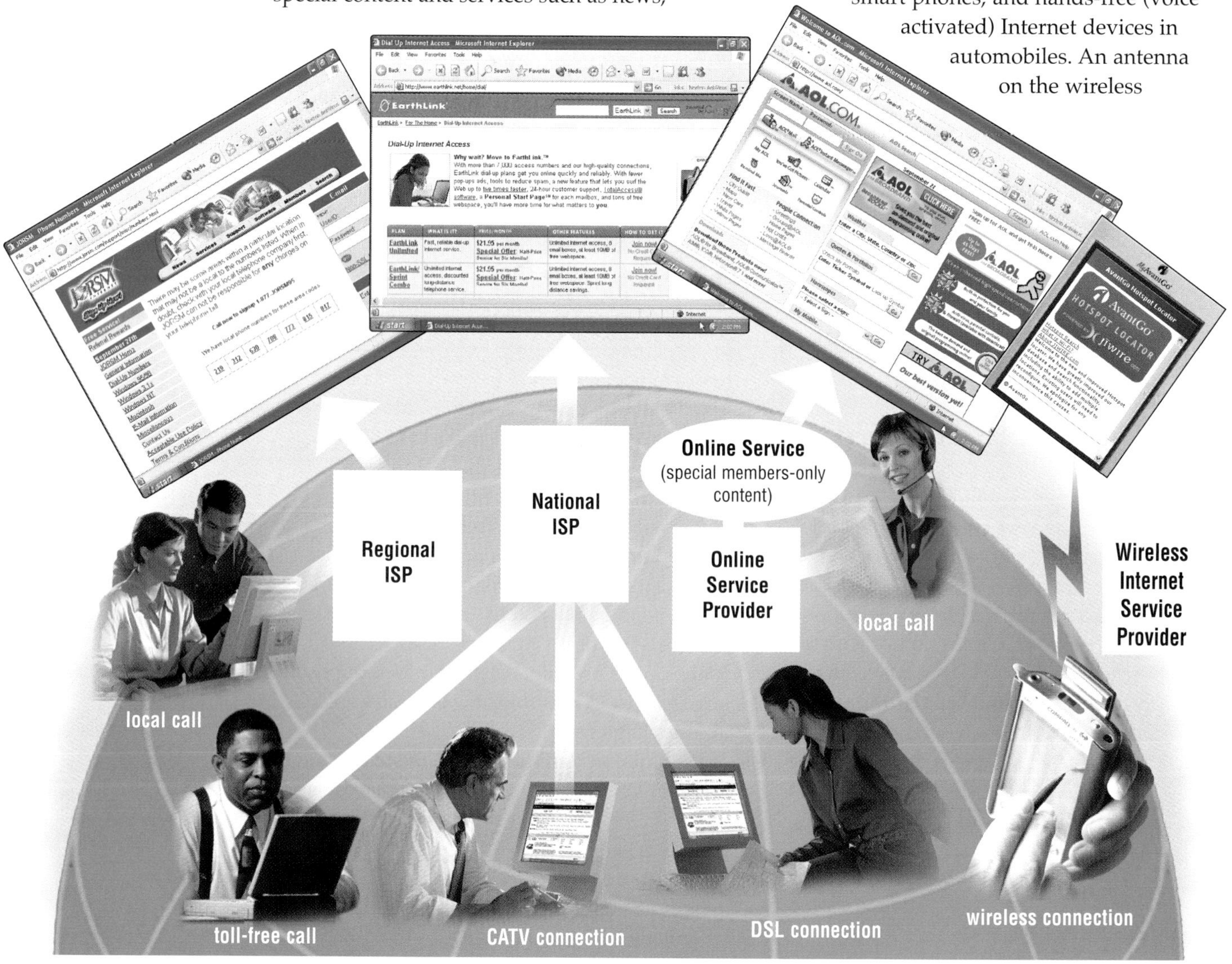

FIGURE 2-2 Common ways to access the Internet are through a regional or national Internet service provider, an online service provider, or a wireless Internet service provider.

modem or Web-enabled device typically sends signals through the airwaves to communicate with a wireless Internet service provider. Some examples of wireless Internet service providers include AT&T Wireless, GoAmerica, and Verizon Wireless.

How Data Travels the Internet

Computers connected to the Internet work together to transfer data and information around the world using servers and clients. On the Internet, your computer is a client that can access data, information, and services on a variety of servers.

The inner structure of the Internet works much like a transportation system. Just as interstate highways connect major cities and carry the bulk of the automotive traffic across the country, several main transmission media carry the heaviest amount of traffic on the Internet. These major carriers of network traffic are known collectively as the *Internet backbone.*

In the United States, the transmission media that make up the Internet backbone exchange data at several different major cities across the country. The high-speed equipment in these major cities functions similarly to a highway interchange. That is, they transfer data from one network to another until it reaches its final destination (Figure 2-3).

FAQ 2-2

How do I find the right access provider?

The Web has many comprehensive lists of access providers. These lists often use the terms ISP and OSP interchangeably. One of the more popular lists on the Web is called The List.

For more information about access providers, visit the Discovering Computers 2005 FAQ Web page (**scsite.com/dc2005/faq**). Click Access Providers below Chapter 2.

WEB LINK 2-1

Internet Backbone

Visit the Discovering Computers 2005 WEB LINK page (**scsite.com/dc2005/weblink**). Click Internet Backbone below Chapter 2.

FIGURE 2-3 HOW DATA MIGHT TRAVEL THE INTERNET USING A DIAL-UP CONNECTION

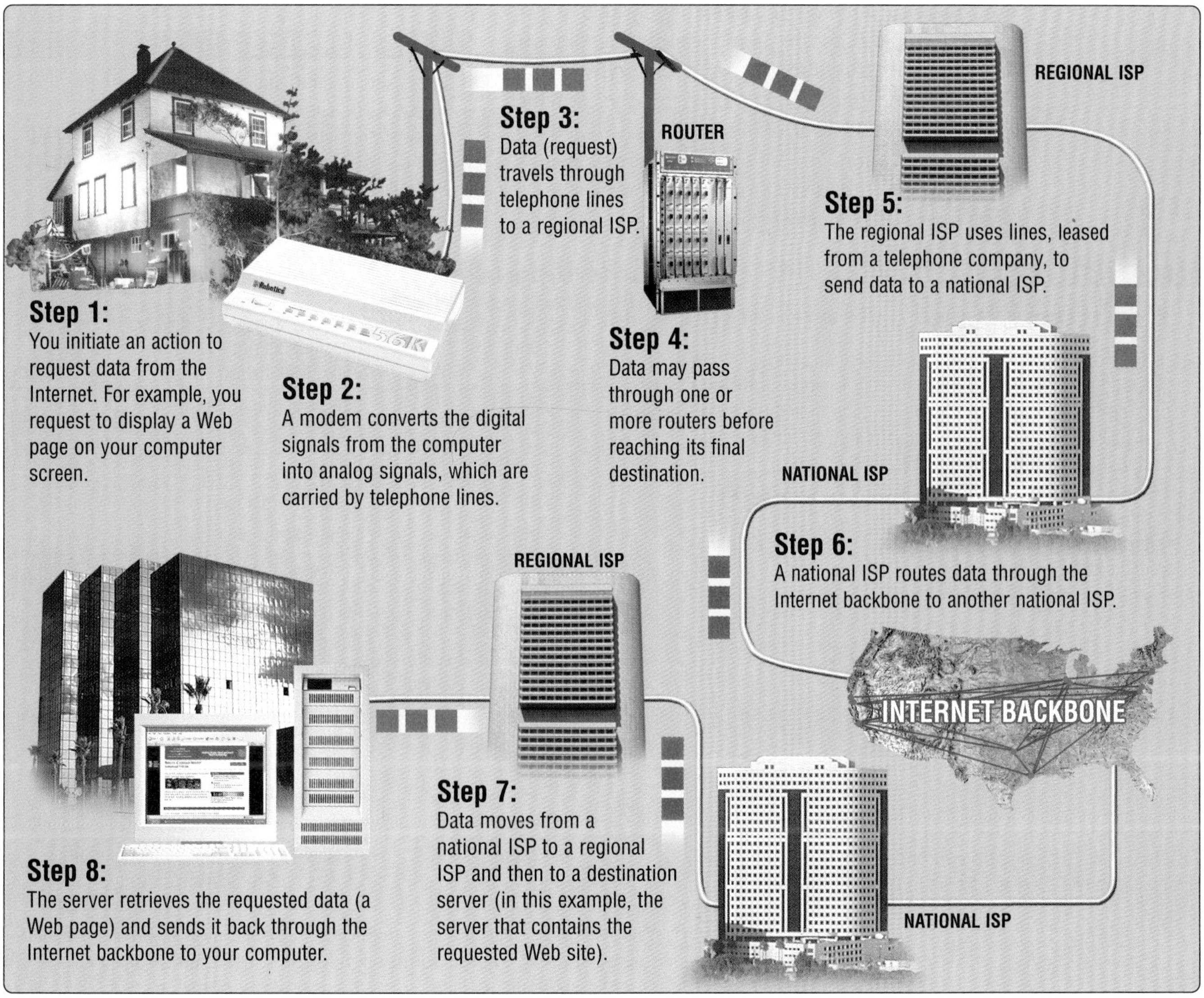

Internet Addresses

The Internet relies on an addressing system much like the postal service to send data to a computer at a specific destination. An **IP address**, short for *Internet Protocol address*, is a number that uniquely identifies each computer or device connected to the Internet. The IP address usually consists of four groups of numbers, each separated by a period. The number in each group is between 0 and 255. For example, the numbers 63.123.44.192 are an IP address. In general, the first portion of each IP address identifies the network and the last portion identifies the specific computer.

These all-numeric IP addresses are difficult to remember and use. Thus, the Internet supports the use of a text name that represents one or more IP addresses. A **domain name** is the text version of an IP address. Figure 2-4 shows an IP address and its associated domain name. As with an IP address, the components of a domain name are separated by periods.

In Figure 2-4, the com portion of the domain name is called the top-level domain. Every domain name contains a *top-level domain*, which identifies the type of organization associated with the domain. *Dot-com* is the term sometimes used to describe organizations with a top-level domain of com.

The group that assigns and controls top-level domains is the *Internet Corporation for Assigned Names and Numbers (ICANN* pronounced EYE-can). Figure 2-5 lists current top-level domains. For international Web sites outside the United States, the domain name also includes a country code. In these cases, the domain name ends with the country code, such as au for Australia or fr for France.

The *domain name system (DNS)* is the method that the Internet uses to store domain names and their corresponding IP addresses. When you specify a domain name, a *DNS server* translates the domain name into its associated IP address so data can route to the correct computer. A DNS server is an Internet server that usually is associated with an Internet access provider.

For a more technical discussion about Internet addresses, read the High-Tech Talk article on page 103.

QUIZ YOURSELF 2-1

To check your knowledge of Internet history, accessing and connecting to the Internet, and Internet addresses, visit the Discovering Computers 2005 Quiz Yourself Web page (**scsite.com/dc2005/quiz**). Click Objectives 1 – 3 below Chapter 2.

FAQ 2-3

How does a person or company get a domain name?

You register for a domain name from a *registrar*, which is an organization that maintains a master list of names for a particular top-level domain. In addition to determining prices and policies for a domain name registration, a registrar may offer additional services such as Web site hosting.

For more information about registering domain names, visit the Discovering Computers 2005 FAQ Web page (**scsite.com/dc2005/faq**). Click Registering Domain Names below Chapter 2.

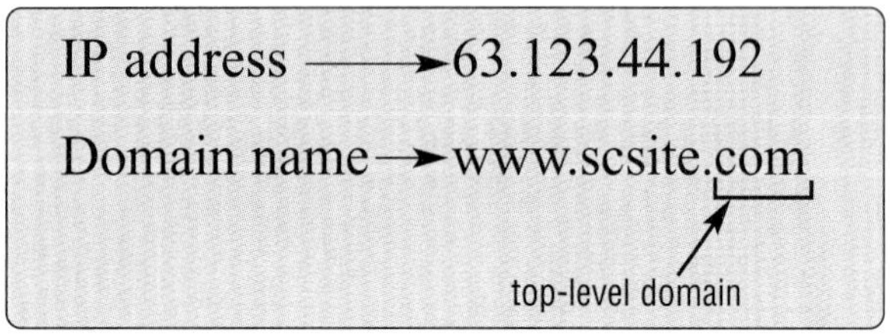

FIGURE 2-4 The IP address and domain name for the Shelly Cashman Series Instructional Web site.

TOP-LEVEL DOMAINS

Original Top-Level Domains	Type of Domain
com	Commercial organizations, businesses, and companies
edu	Educational institutions
gov	Government agencies
mil	Military organizations
net	Network providers
org	Nonprofit organizations
Newer Top-Level Domains	**Type of Domain**
museum	Accredited museums
biz	Businesses of all sizes
info	Businesses, organizations, or individuals providing general information
name	Individuals or families
pro	Certified professionals such as doctors, lawyers, and accountants
aero	Aviation community members
coop	Business cooperatives such as credit unions and rural electric co-ops

FIGURE 2-5 With the dramatic growth of the Internet during the last few years, the Internet Corporation for Assigned Names and Numbers (ICANN) recently adopted seven new top-level domains.

THE WORLD WIDE WEB

Although many people use the terms World Wide Web and Internet interchangeably, the World Wide Web actually is a newer service of the Internet. While the Internet was developed in the late 1960s, the World Wide Web emerged three decades later — in the early 1990s. Since then, however, it has grown phenomenally to become one of the more widely used services on the Internet.

The **World Wide Web** (*WWW*), or **Web**, consists of a worldwide collection of electronic documents. Each electronic document on the Web is called a **Web page**, which can contain text, graphics, audio (sound), and video. Additionally, Web pages usually have built-in connections to other documents. A **Web site** is a collection of related Web pages and associated items, such as documents and pictures, stored on a Web server.

The following pages discuss how to browse the Web, use a Web address, search for information on the Web, and recognize types of Web sites. Also discussed are multimedia on the Web and e-commerce (business on the Web).

Browsing the Web

A **Web browser**, or **browser**, is application software that allows users to access and view Web pages. To browse the Web, you need a computer that is connected to the Internet and that has a Web browser.

With the Internet connection established, you can use the mouse to start a Web browser. The browser retrieves and displays a starting Web page, sometimes called the browser's home page. The initial home page that is displayed is one selected by your Web browser. You can change your browser's home page at anytime.

The more widely used Web browsers for personal computers are Microsoft Internet Explorer, Netscape, and Mozilla. Figure 2-6 shows the steps a user may follow to start the Internet Explorer Web browser.

FIGURE 2-6 ONE METHOD OF STARTING A WEB BROWSER

Step 1:
Click the Web browser program name.

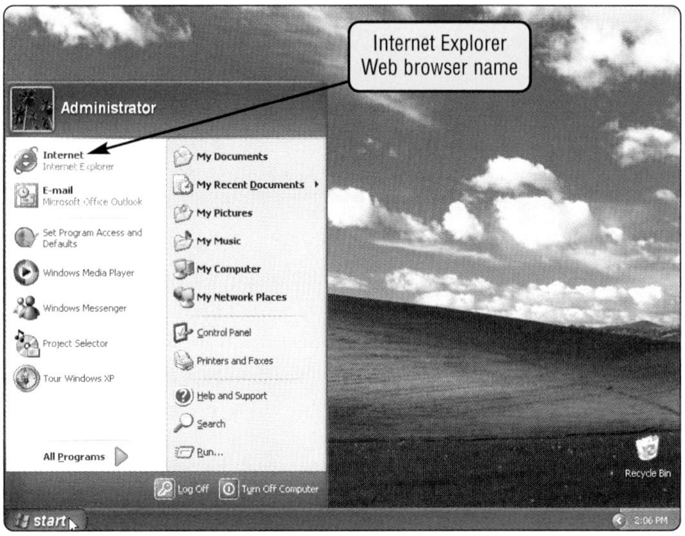

Step 2:
If you use dial-up Internet access and are not connected to the Internet already, your computer attempts to establish a connection with your access provider. In this case, click the Dial button.

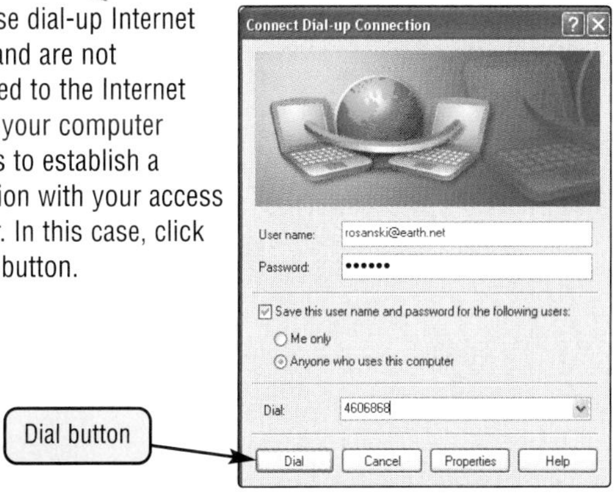

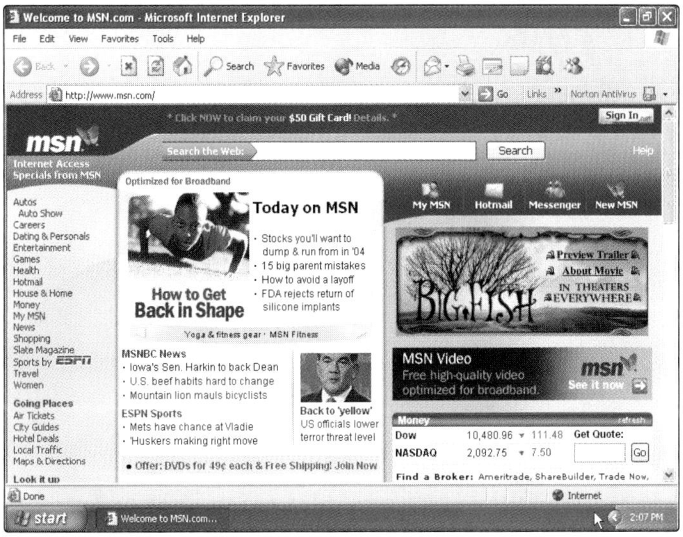

Step 3:
The Internet Explorer Web browser starts and displays its home page. Shown here is the MSN Home page. In your browser, you can customize (change) the home page that is displayed.

The more common usage of the term, **home page**, refers to the first page that a Web site displays (see Figure 2-9 on page 78 for an example). Similar to a book cover or a table of contents for a Web site, the home page provides information about the Web site's purpose and content. Often it provides connections to other documents, Web pages, or Web sites. Many Web sites allow you to personalize the home page so it contains areas of interest to you.

Web-enabled mobile devices such as PDAs and smart phones use a special type of browser, called a *microbrowser,* which is designed for their small screens and limited computing power. Many Web sites design Web pages specifically for display on a microbrowser (Figure 2-7).

Figure 2-7a
(microbrowser for a Web-enabled PDA)

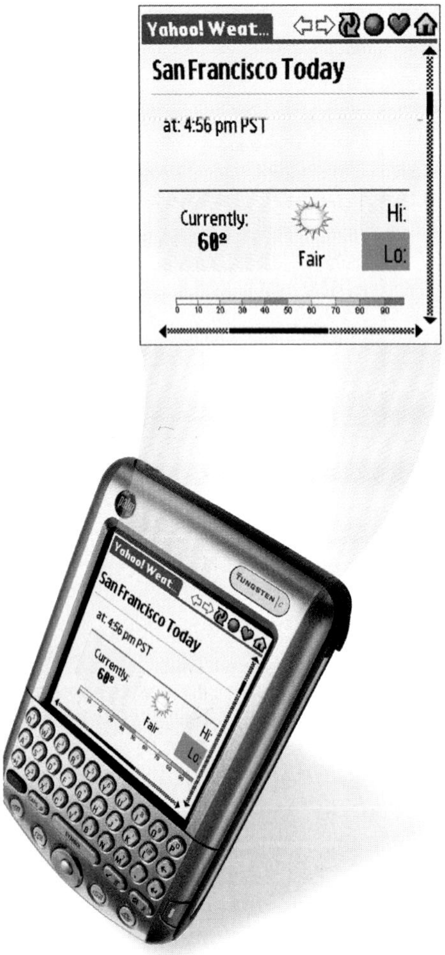

Figure 2-7b
(microbrowser for a smart phone)

FIGURE 2-7 Sample microbrowser screens.

Downloading is the process of a computer receiving information, such as a Web page, from a server on the Internet. While a browser downloads a Web page, it typically displays an animated logo or icon in the top-right corner of the browser window. The animation stops when the download is complete.

Depending on the speed of your Internet connection and the amount of graphics involved, a Web page download can take from a few seconds to several minutes. To speed up the display of Web pages, most Web browsers allow users to turn off the graphics and display only text.

FAQ 2-4

How do I change my Web browser's home page and graphics settings?

To change the home page in Internet Explorer, click Tools on the menu bar, click Internet Options, click the General tab, type the desired Web address, and then click the OK button. To turn off pictures from displaying, click the Advanced tab and remove the check mark from the Show pictures check box.

For more information about Internet Explorer, visit the Discovering Computers 2005 FAQ Web page (**scsite.com/dc2005/faq**). Click Internet Explorer below Chapter 2.

Web Addresses

A Web page has a unique address, called a **URL** (*Uniform Resource Locator*) or **Web address**. For example, the home page for the Eastman Kodak Company Web site has a Web address of http://www.kodak.com. A Web browser retrieves a Web page, such as Kodak's home page, using its Web address.

Many companies and organizations use the Web as an alternate or supplemental means of advertising or publicizing information. They assume the public is familiar with Web addresses. Television, radio broadcasts, printed newspapers, and magazines, for example, often refer viewers or readers to Web addresses for additional information.

If you know the Web address of a Web page, you can type it in the Address box at the top of the browser window. If you type the Web address http://www.kodak.com/US/en/corp/careers/index.jhtml in the Address box and then press the ENTER key, the browser downloads and displays a Web page about careers at Kodak (Figure 2-8).

As shown in Figure 2-8, a Web address consists of a protocol, domain name, and sometimes the path to a specific Web page or location on a Web page. Many Web page addresses begin with http://. The *http*, which stands for *Hypertext Transfer Protocol*, is a set of rules that defines how pages transfer on the Web.

If you do not enter a Web address correctly, your browser will not locate the Web site or Web page you want to visit (view). To help minimize errors, most current browsers and Web sites do not require the http://and www portions of the Web address. For example, typing kodak.com/US/en/corp/careers/index.jhtml instead of the entire address http://www.kodak.com/US/en/corp/careers/index.jhtml still accesses the Web site. If you enter an incorrect Web address, a list of similar addresses from which you can select may be displayed in the browser window. Many Web sites also allow users to eliminate the .htm, .html, or .jhtml from the Web page name.

A **Web server** is a computer that delivers requested Web pages to your computer. For example, when you enter the Web address, kodak.com/US/en/corp/careers/index.jhtml in the Web browser, it sends a request to the server that contains the www.kodak.com Web site. The server then retrieves the Web page named index.jhtml in the US/en/corp/careers path and delivers it to your browser.

The same Web server can store multiple Web sites. For example, many Internet service providers grant their subscribers free storage space on a Web server for personal or company Web sites.

When you enter a Web address, you request, or *pull*, information from a Web server. Some Web servers also can *push* content to your computer at regular intervals or whenever updates are made to the site. For example, some Web servers provide the capability of displaying current sporting event scores or weather reports on your computer screen.

For a list of widely used Web sites and their associated Web addresses, read the Guide to Web Sites and Searching Techniques feature that follows this chapter and Making Use of the Web in Appendix A at the back of the book.

WEB LINK 2-2

Web Addresses

Visit the Discovering Computers 2005 WEB LINK page (**scsite.com/dc2005/weblink**). Click Web Addresses below Chapter 2.

Navigating Web Pages

Most Web pages contain links. A **link**, short for *hyperlink*, is a built-in connection to another related Web page or part of a Web page. Links allow you to obtain information in a nonlinear way. That is, instead of accessing topics in a specified order, you move directly to a topic of interest. Reading a book from cover to cover is a linear way of learning. Branching off and researching related topics as you encounter them can be a different and very effective nonlinear way of learning.

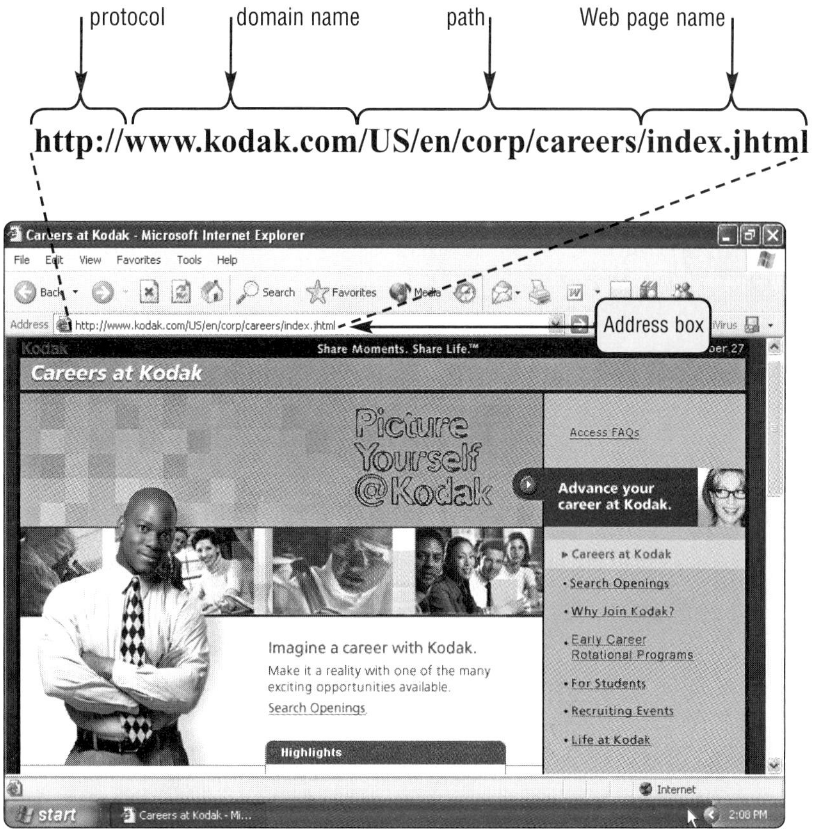

FIGURE 2-8 After entering the Web address www.kodak.com/US/en/corp/careers/index.jhtml in the Address box, this Kodak careers Web page is displayed.

While reading an article on the Web about nutrition, you might want to learn more about counting calories. Having linked to and read information about counting calories, you might want to find low-fat, low-calorie recipes. Reading these might inspire you to learn about a chef who specializes in healthy but tasty food preparation. Branching from one related topic to another in a nonlinear fashion is what makes links so powerful. Some people use the phrase, **surfing the Web**, to refer to the activity of using links to explore the Web.

On the Web, a link can be text or an image. You often identify text links by looking at the Web page. Text links usually are underlined and are in a color different from other text on the Web page. Pointing to, or positioning the pointer on, a link on the screen, typically changes the shape of the pointer to a small hand with a pointing index finger. The Web page shown in Figure 2-9 contains a variety of link types, with the pointer on one of the links.

Each link on a Web page corresponds to another Web address. To activate a link, you *click* it, that is, point to the link and then press the left mouse button. Clicking a link causes the Web page associated with the link to be displayed on the screen. The linked object might be on the same Web page, a different Web page at the same Web site, or a separate Web page at a different Web site in another city or country. To remind you visually that you have clicked a link, a text link often changes color after you click it.

Searching for Information on the Web

No single organization controls additions, deletions, and changes to Web sites. This means no central menu or catalog of Web site content and addresses exists. Several companies, however, maintain organized directories of Web sites to help people find information about specific topics.

A **search engine** is a program that finds Web sites and Web pages. Search engines are particularly helpful in locating Web pages about certain topics or in locating specific Web pages for which you do not know the exact Web address. Thousands of search engines are available. Some search about any topic and others are restricted to certain subjects, such as finding people, job hunting, or locating real estate. The table in Figure 2-10 lists the Web addresses of several popular general-purpose Internet search engines. For example, to use the Google search engine, you enter google.com in the Address box in the browser window.

FIGURE 2-9 This Web page contains various types of links: text that is underlined, text in a different color, and images.

WIDELY USED SEARCH ENGINES

Search Engine	Web Address
AlltheWeb	alltheweb.com
AltaVista	altavista.com
AOL Search	search.aol.com
Ask Jeeves	askjeeves.com
Excite	excite.com
Google	google.com
HotBot	hotbot.com
LookSmart	looksmart.com
Lycos	lycos.com
MSN Search	search.msn.com
Overture	overture.com
Teoma	teoma.com
WebCrawler	webcrawler.com
Yahoo!	yahoo.com

FIGURE 2-10 Many widely used search engines allow searching about any topic on the Web.

From a search engine, you easily can find Web pages. Simply enter a word or phrase, called **search text** or *keywords*, in the search engine's text box. For example, to display information about gift cards for Marcus movie theatres in the city of Sheboygan, you could enter Marcus Theatres gift cards Sheboygan as your search text. The search engine displays a list of *hits*, or Web page names, that contain the search text (Figure 2-11). Each hit in the list has a link that, when clicked, displays the associated Web site or Web page.

FIGURE 2-11 HOW TO DISPLAY WEB PAGES USING A SEARCH ENGINE

When you enter search text that contains multiple keywords, the search engine usually locates Web sites that contain all or most of the words. For example, a search with the search text, Marcus Theatres, displays more than 22,000 hits that contain the word Marcus and the word Theatres. To reduce the number of hits, be more specific in the search. The more specific search text, Marcus Theatres gift cards Sheboygan, reduces the number of hits to about 20.

Many search engines use a program, called a *spider*, to build and maintain lists of words found on Web sites. When you enter search text, the search engine scans this prebuilt list for hits. The more sophisticated the search engine combined with sophisticated search criteria, the more rapid the response and effective the search.

Most search engines also have subject directories of Web sites. On the Web, a **subject directory** classifies Web pages into an organized set of categories, such as sports or shopping, and related subcategories (Figure 2-12). If you want to find information about television programs, you could use a directory to click the subcategory television in the arts category.

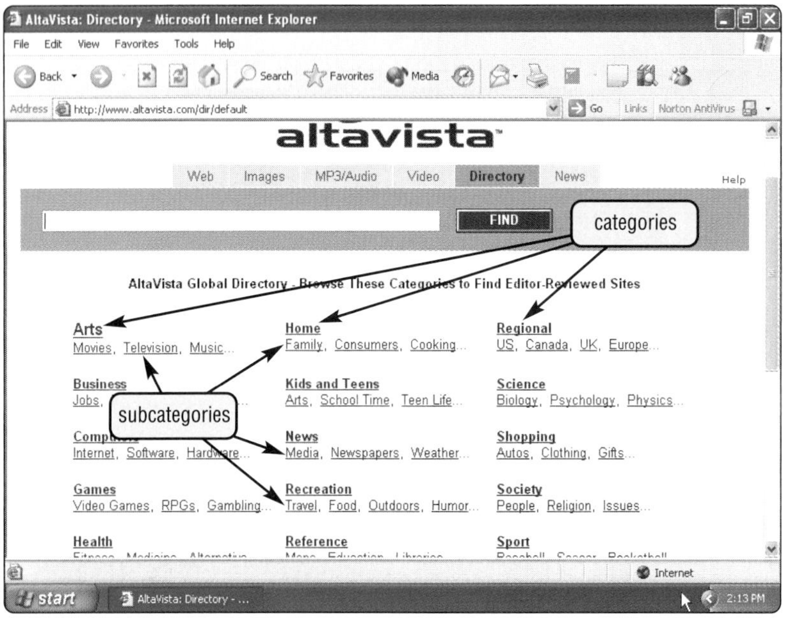

FIGURE 2-12 An example of a directory Web page.

Read Looking Ahead 2-1 for a look at the next generation of searching techniques. For more information about search engines, subject directories, and searching techniques, read the Guide to Web Sites and Searching Techniques feature that follows this chapter.

> **LOOKING AHEAD 2-1**
>
> ## Shop Until Your Mouse Drops
>
> 
>
> Driving from store to store in search of the perfect gift within a particular price range can be a daunting task. This chore can be simplified, however, by turning to the Internet. The World Wide Web has changed consumer's shopping behavior: nearly 80 percent of people shopping for big-ticket items, such as automobiles and appliances, consult Web sites for product information, reviews, and the lowest prices.
>
> Customers who currently search the Web for products have two major complaints: the sites are difficult to navigate, and customer service often is poor or nonexistent. As a result, market analysts forecast that computer shopping will become easier as online retailers streamline their Web pages by eliminating clutter. Also, the merchants will make searching for products easier by enlarging the search boxes and placing them in a more prominent location on the pages. In addition, many online retailers are planning to add live customer support, so a shopper can click a button to chat with a representative.
>
> For a look at the next generation of online shopping, visit the Discovering Computers 2005 Looking Ahead Web page (**scsite.com/dc2005/looking**). Click Looking Ahead #1 below Chapter 2.

Types of Web Sites

Eight types of Web sites are portal, news, informational, business/marketing, educational, entertainment, advocacy, and personal (Figure 2-13). Many Web sites fall into more than one of these categories. The following pages discuss each of these types of Web sites.

Figure 2-13a (portal)

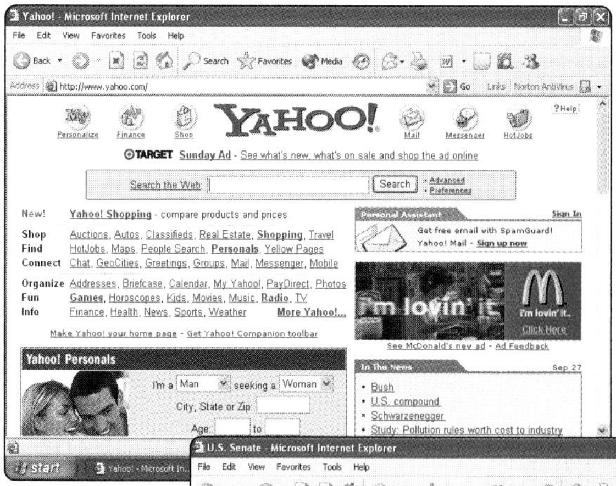

Figure 2-13b (news)

Figure 2-13c (informational)

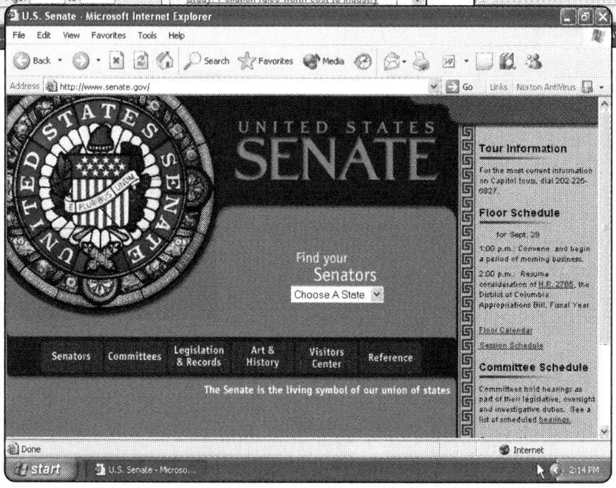

Figure 2-13d (business/ marketing)

Figure 2-13e (educational)

Figure 2-13f (entertainment)

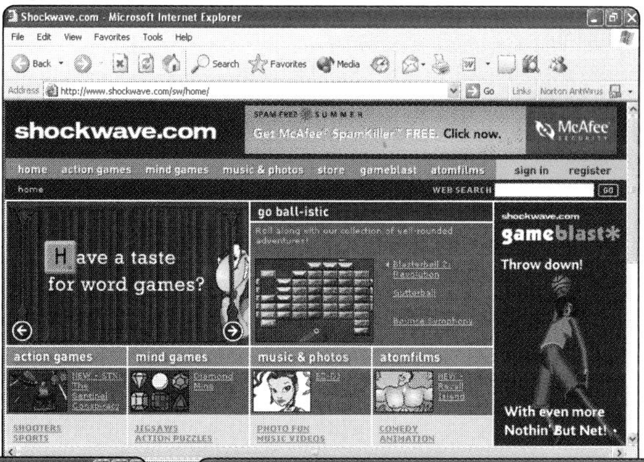

Figure 2-13g (advocacy)

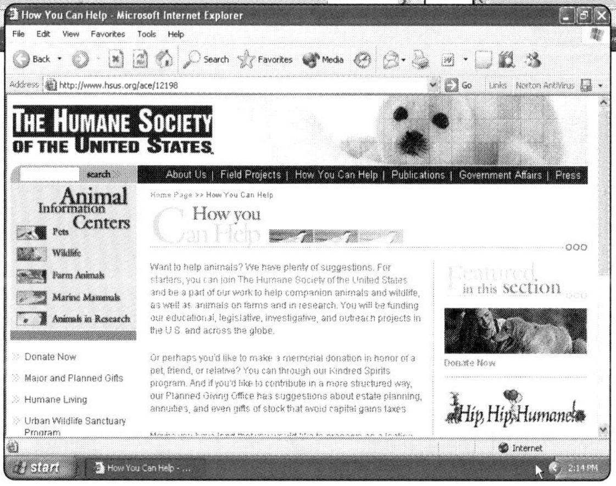

Figure 2-13h (personal)

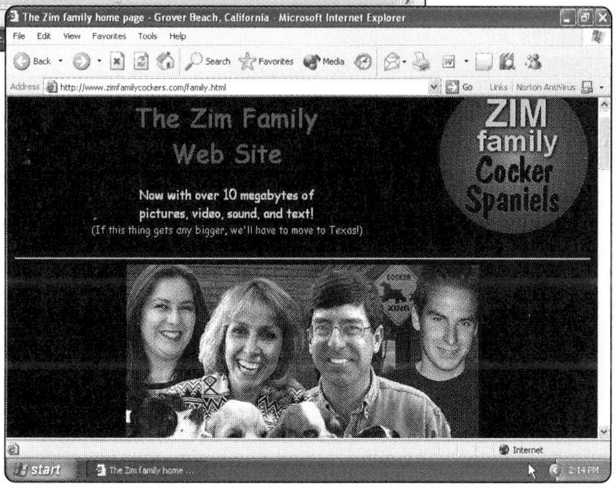

FIGURE 2-13 Types of Web sites.

PORTAL A **portal** is a Web site that offers a variety of Internet services from a single, convenient location (Figure 2-13a on the previous page). Most portals offer the following free services: search engine and/or subject directory; news; sports and weather; free Web publishing services; reference tools such as yellow pages, stock quotes, and maps; shopping malls and auctions; and e-mail and other forms of online communications. Some portals are for the general population, while others focus on a particular audience, such as gardeners or investors. Companies often create their own portals for use by employees, vendors, and customers.

Many portals have Web communities. A **Web community** is a Web site that joins a specific group of people with similar interests or relationships. These communities may offer online photo albums, chat rooms, and other services to facilitate communications among members.

When you connect to the Internet, the first Web page that is displayed often is a portal. Popular portals include AltaVista, America Online, Excite, GO.com, HotBot, LookSmart, Lycos, Microsoft Network, Netscape, and Yahoo!. You may notice that many of these portals are popular search engines or subject directories. Some also are Internet access providers.

A *wireless portal* is a portal specifically designed for Web-enabled mobile devices. Wireless portals attempt to provide all information a wireless user might require. These portals offer services geared to the mobile user such as search engines, news, stock quotes, weather, maps, e-mail, calendar, instant messaging, and shopping.

NEWS A news Web site contains newsworthy material including stories and articles relating to current events, life, money, sports, and the weather (Figure 2-13b). Many magazines and newspapers sponsor Web sites that provide summaries of printed articles, as well as articles not included in the printed versions. Newspapers and television and radio stations are some of the media that maintain news Web sites.

INFORMATIONAL An informational Web site contains factual information (Figure 2-13c). Many United States government agencies have informational Web sites providing information such as census data, tax codes, and the congressional budget. Other organizations provide information such as public transportation schedules and published research findings.

BUSINESS/MARKETING A business/marketing Web site contains content that promotes or sells products or services (Figure 2-13d). Nearly every business has a business/marketing Web site. Allstate Insurance Company, Dell Inc., General Motors Corporation, Kraft Foods Inc., and Walt Disney Company all have business/marketing Web sites. Many of these companies also allow you to purchase their products or services online.

EDUCATIONAL An educational Web site offers exciting, challenging avenues for formal and informal teaching and learning (Figure 2-13e). On the Web, you can learn how airplanes fly or how to cook a meal. For a more structured learning experience, companies provide online training to employees; colleges offer online classes and degrees (read Issue 2-2 for a related discussion). Instructors often use the Web to

ISSUE 2-2

Can You Learn It Online?

College can be a rewarding experience, both personally and professionally. Some people, however, do not have the opportunity, time, or money needed to attend a traditional college. Today, many schools address this obstacle with online learning. Online learning allows students to learn whenever and wherever they can access a course's Web page, often more economically than traditional tuitions. A student might be able to complete an entire degree program without ever physically attending a class. Many online classes present material using captivating simulations, real-life case studies, and interactive tools. Yet, even the best online classes lack some of the most important features of the campus experience, such as casual talks with professors, informal study groups in the dorm or library, or enthusiastic discussions in the campus coffee shop. What are the more important advantages and disadvantages of online classes? Why? What type of student is best, and least, suited for online classes? Why? Would you be interested in taking a class online? Why or why not? Should it be possible to obtain a four-year college degree without attending a single class on a college campus? Why?

For more information about online learning, visit the Discovering Computers 2005 Issues Web page (**scsite.com/dc2005/issues**). Click Issue #2 below Chapter 2.

enhance classroom teaching by publishing course materials, grades, and other pertinent class information.

ENTERTAINMENT An entertainment Web site offers an interactive and engaging environment (Figure 2-13f). Popular entertainment Web sites offer music, videos, sports, games, ongoing Web episodes, sweepstakes, chats, and more. Sophisticated entertainment Web sites often partner with other technologies. For example, you can cast your vote about a topic on a television show.

ADVOCACY An advocacy Web site contains content that describes a cause, opinion, or idea (Figure 2-13g). The purpose of an advocacy Web site is to convince the reader of the validity of the cause, opinion, or idea. These Web sites usually present views of a particular group or association. Sponsors of advocacy Web sites include the Democratic National Committee, the Republican National Committee, the Society for the Prevention of Cruelty to Animals, and the Society to Protect Human Rights.

PERSONAL A private individual or family not usually associated with any organization may maintain a personal Web site or just a single Web page (Figure 2-13h). People publish personal Web pages for a variety of reasons. Some are job hunting. Others simply want to share life experiences with the world. Publishing Web pages is discussed in more depth at the end of this chapter.

EVALUATING A WEB SITE Do not assume that information presented on the Web is correct or accurate. Any person, company, or organization can publish a Web page on the Internet. No one oversees the content of these Web pages. Figure 2-14 lists guidelines for assessing the value of a Web site or Web page before relying on its content.

Multimedia on the Web

Most Web pages include more than just formatted text and links. In fact, some of the more exciting Web pages use multimedia. **Multimedia** refers to any application that combines text with graphics, animation, audio, video, and/or virtual reality. A Web page that uses multimedia has much more appeal than one with only text on a gray background. Multimedia brings a Web page to life, increases the types of information available on the Web, expands the Web's potential uses, and makes the Internet a more entertaining place to explore. Multimedia Web pages often require proper hardware and software and take more time to download because they contain large graphics files and video or audio clips.

FAQ 2-5

What is a file?

A *file* is a unit of storage. When you want the computer to store items (e.g., data, information, programs, graphics, an audio clip, or a video clip), it places them into files on storage media such as a hard disk. File sizes vary depending on items being stored. For example, graphics files usually consume more storage space than data files.

For more information about files, visit the Discovering Computers 2005 FAQ Web page (**scsite.com/dc2005/faq**). Click Files below Chapter 2.

GUIDELINES FOR EVALUATING THE VALUE OF A WEB SITE

Evaluation Criteria	Reliable Web Sites
Affiliation	A reputable institution should support the Web site without bias in the information.
Audience	The Web site should be written at an appropriate level.
Authority	The Web site should list the author and the appropriate credentials.
Content	The Web site should be well organized and the links should work.
Currency	The information on the Web page should be current.
Design	The pages at the Web site should download quickly and be visually pleasing and easy to navigate.
Objectivity	The Web site should contain little advertising and be free of preconceptions.

FIGURE 2-14 Criteria for evaluating a Web site's content.

Read Looking Ahead 2-2 for a look at the next generation of Web Access. The sections that follow discuss how the Web uses graphics, animation, audio, video, and virtual reality.

LOOKING AHEAD 2-2

Driving Down the Web Highway

Analysts predict you will access the Internet from practically everywhere: home, office, airport, grocery store, and the local coffee shop. Why not from your car?

As your car sits in your garage, a computer in your car could connect to your home computer and then relay information about fluid levels and the amount of gas in the tank. It could notify you when the oil needs to be changed and when the tires should be rotated. You even could start the car remotely on chilly days by pressing a button on your notebook computer as you eat your breakfast cereal at the kitchen table.

Automobile manufacturers are touting their cyber cars of the future equipped with Internet access. They are planning in-dash screens with continuous information about traffic, weather forecasts, and restaurant guides. Their plans also call for having the Internet access disconnect when the vehicle is in motion so that drivers do not attempt to drive and surf the Web simultaneously.

For a look at the future of Internet access in your car, visit the Discovering Computers 2005 Looking Ahead Web page (**scsite.com/dc2005/looking**). Click Looking Ahead #2 below Chapter 2.

GRAPHICS A **graphic**, or *graphical image*, is a digital representation of nontext information such as a drawing, chart, or photograph. Graphics were the first media used to enhance the text-based Internet. The introduction of graphical Web browsers allowed Web page developers to incorporate illustrations, logos, and other images into Web pages. Today, many Web pages use colorful graphical designs and images to convey messages (Figure 2-15).

The Web contains countless images about a variety of subjects. You can download many of these images at no cost and use them for noncommercial purposes. Recall that downloading is the process of transferring an object from the Web to your computer. For example, you can incorporate images into greeting cards, announcements, and other documents.

Of the graphics formats that exist on the Web (Figure 2-16), the two more common are JPEG and GIF formats. *JPEG* is a format that compresses graphics to reduce their file size, which means the file takes up less storage space. Smaller file sizes result in faster downloading of Web pages because small files transmit faster than large files. The more compressed the file, the smaller the image, but the lower the quality. The goal with JPEG graphics is to reach a balance between image quality and file size.

GRAPHICS FORMATS USED ON THE WEB

Acronym	Name
BMP	Bit Map
GIF (pronounced JIFF)	Graphics Interchange Format
JPEG (pronounced JAY-peg)	Joint Photographic Experts Group
PCX	PC Paintbrush
PNG (pronounced ping)	Portable Network Graphics
TIFF	Tagged Image File Format

FIGURE 2-16 The Web uses graphics file formats for images.

FIGURE 2-15 This Disney Online Web page uses colorful graphical designs and images to convey its messages.

GIF graphics also use compression techniques to reduce file sizes. The GIF format works best for images that have only a few distinct colors, such as line drawings, single-color borders, and simple cartoons. The newer *PNG format* improves upon the GIF format, and thus is expected eventually to replace the GIF format.

The BMP, PCX, and TIFF formats listed in Figure 2-16 have larger file sizes, may require special viewer software, and thus are not used on the Web as frequently as JPEG and GIF.

Some Web sites use thumbnails on their pages because graphics can be time-consuming to display. A **thumbnail** is a small version of a larger graphic. You usually click a thumbnail to display a larger image (Figure 2-17).

ANIMATION Many Web pages use **animation**, which is the appearance of motion created by displaying a series of still images in sequence. Animation can make Web pages more visually interesting or draw attention to important information or links. For example, text that animates by scrolling across the screen can serve as a ticker to display stock updates, news, sports scores, weather, or other information. Web-based games often use animation. Some animations even contain links to a different Web page.

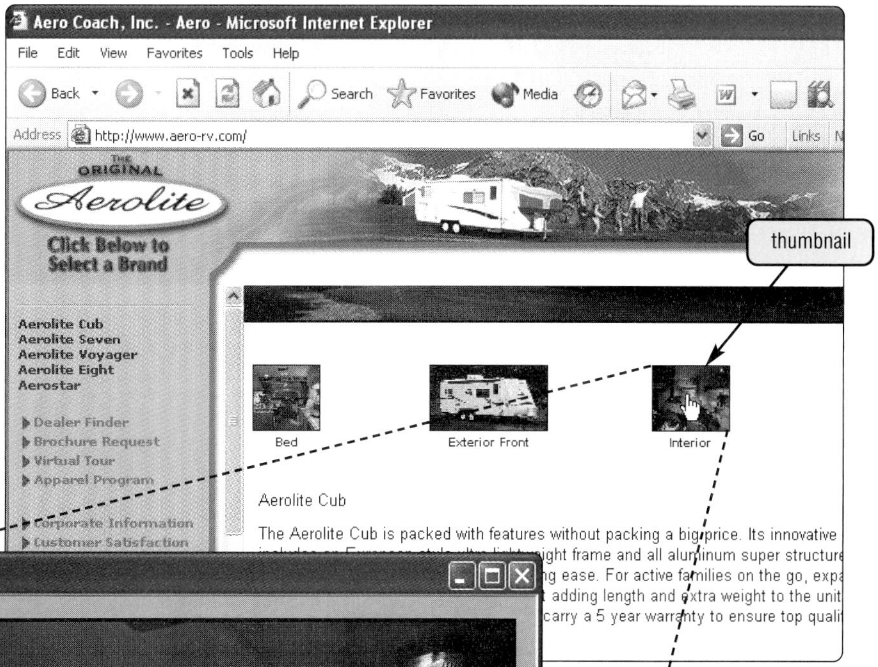

FIGURE 2-17 Clicking the thumbnail of the trailer interior in the top screen displays a larger image in a separate window.

A popular type of animation, called an *animated GIF*, uses computer animation and graphics software to combine several images into a single GIF file. Web page developers often find animated GIFs easier to create than using a programming language to create animations.

AUDIO On the Web, you can listen to audio clips and live audio. **Audio** includes music, speech, or any other sound.

Simple audio applications on the Web consist of individual sound files available for downloading to a computer. Once downloaded, you can play (listen to) the contents of these files. As with graphics files, audio files exist in a variety of formats. Some common Web audio file formats are MP3, WAV, WMA (Windows Media Audio), MPEG, RealAudio, and QuickTime. Audio files are compressed to reduce their file sizes. For example, the **MP3** format reduces an audio file to about one-tenth its original size, while preserving much of the original quality of the sound.

Some music publishers have Web sites that allow users to download sample tracks free to persuade them to buy the entire CD. Other Web sites allow a user to purchase and download an entire CD of music tracks to the hard disk (Figure 2-18). Keep in mind that it is legal

FIGURE 2-18 HOW TO PURCHASE AND DOWNLOAD MUSIC

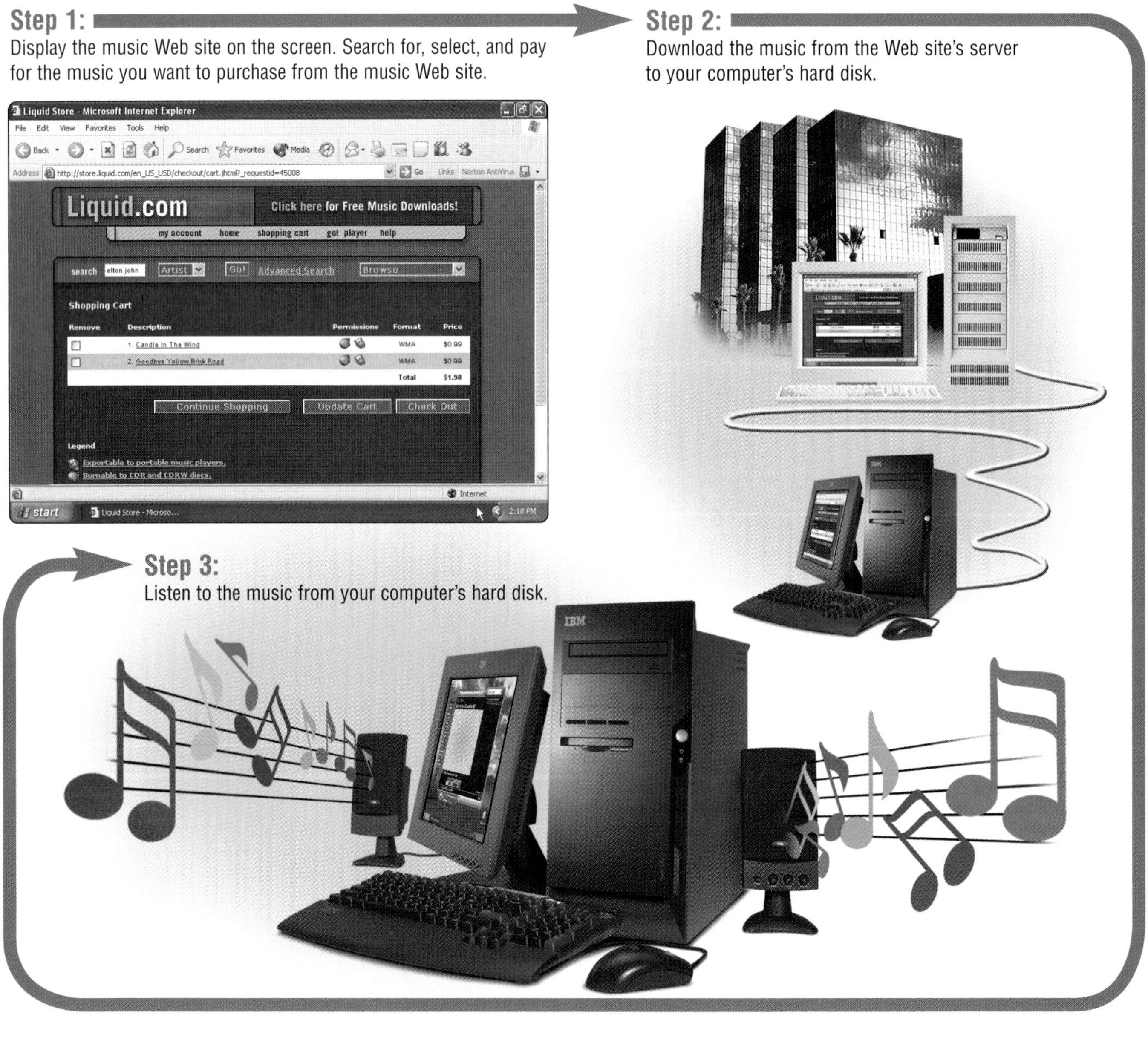

to download copyrighted music only if the song's copyright holder has granted permission for users to download and play the song.

To listen to an audio file on your computer, you need special software called a **player**. Most current operating systems contain a player. Windows Media Player and RealOne Player are two popular players. If your player will not play a particular audio format, you can download the necessary player free from the Web.

Some applications on the Web use streaming audio. **Streaming** is the process of transferring data in a continuous and even flow. Streaming allows users to access and use a file while it is transmitting. For example, *streaming audio* enables you to listen to music as it downloads to your computer. Many radio and television stations use streaming audio to broadcast music, interviews, talk shows, sporting events, music videos, news, live concerts, and other segments (Figure 2-19).

Accepted standards supported by most Web browsers for transmitting streaming audio data on the Internet are MP3, QuickTime, Windows Media Format, and RealAudio. RealAudio is a component of RealOne Player.

FAQ 2-6

How long does it take to download a single song from a music Web site?

Depending on the speed of your Internet connection and the size of the file, a single song can take from one to eight minutes to download.

For more information about downloading audio files, visit the Discovering Computers 2005 FAQ Web page (**scsite.com/dc2005/faq**). Click Downloading Audio Files below Chapter 2.

WEB LINK 2-3

Streaming Media

Visit the Discovering Computers 2005 WEB LINK page (**scsite.com/dc2005/weblink**). Click Streaming Media below Chapter 2.

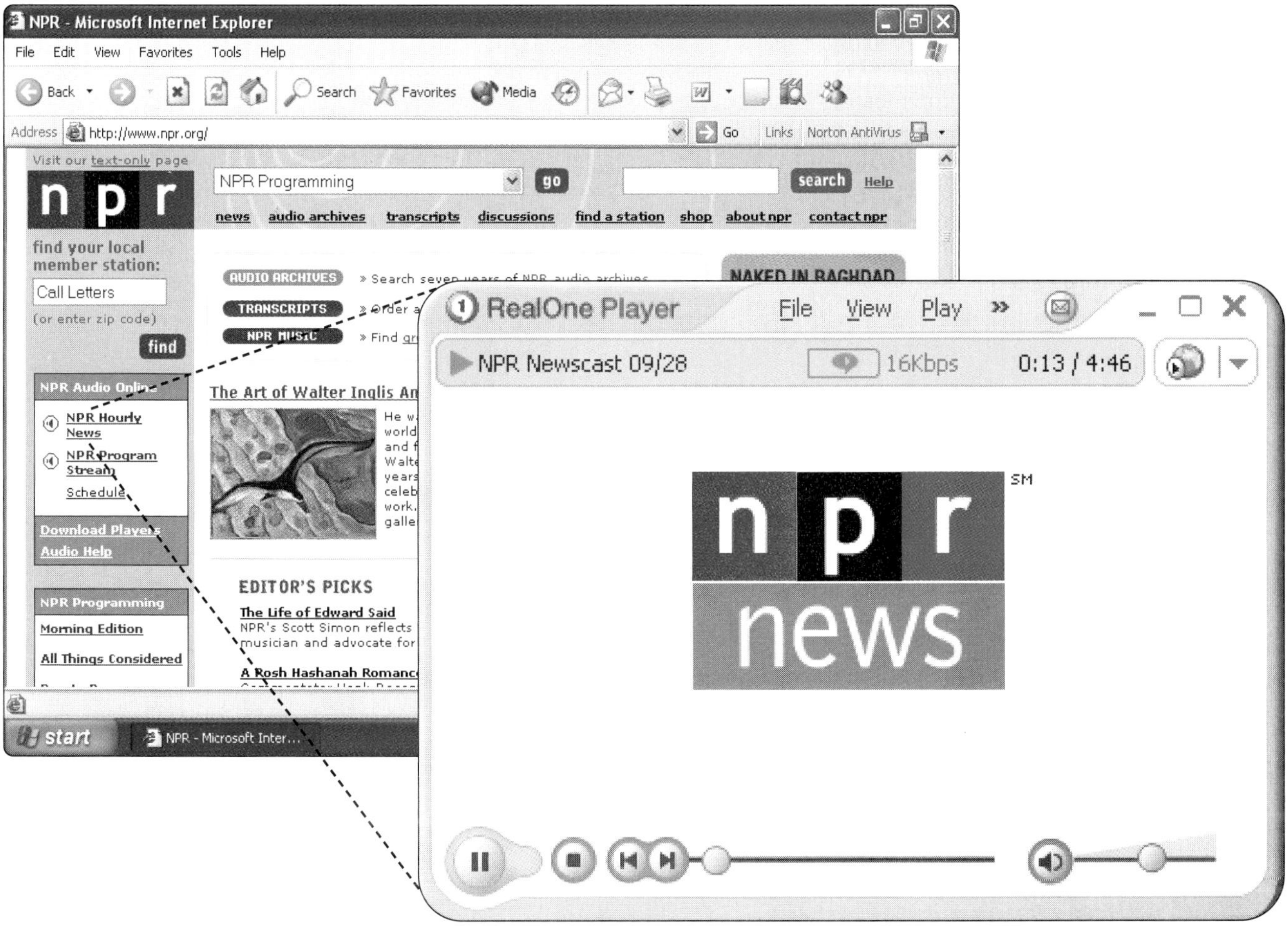

FIGURE 2-19 Many radio and television stations use streaming audio. An NPR (National Public Radio) news report is broadcast in RealOne Player in this illustration.

VIDEO **Video** consists of full-motion images that are played back at various speeds. Most video also has accompanying audio. As with audio, many Web sites include video to enhance your understanding or for entertainment purposes. Instead of turning on the television, you can watch live and prerecorded coverage of your favorite programs (Figure 2-20) or enjoy a live performance of your favorite vocalist right on the computer.

Like audio, simple video applications on the Web consist of individual video files, such as movie or television clips, that you must download completely before you can play them on the computer. Video files often are compressed because they are quite large in size. These clips also are quite short in length, usually less than 10 minutes, because they can take a long time to download. The *Moving Pictures Experts Group (MPEG)* defines a popular video compression standard, the current one being called *MPEG-4*.

As with streaming audio, *streaming video* allows you to view longer or live video images as they download to your computer. Widely used standards supported by most Web browsers for transmitting streaming video data on the Internet are AVI (Audio Video Interleaved), QuickTime, Windows Media Format, and RealVideo. Like RealAudio, RealVideo is a component of RealOne Player.

VIRTUAL REALITY **Virtual reality (VR)** is the use of computers to simulate a real or imagined environment that appears as a three-dimensional (3-D) space. On the Web, VR involves the display of 3-D images that users explore and manipulate interactively.

Using special VR software, a Web developer creates an entire 3-D Web site that contains infinite space and depth, called a *VR world*. A VR world, for example, might show a room with furniture. Users walk through such a VR room by moving an input device forward, backward, or to the side.

Games often use VR. Many practical applications of VR also exist. Science educators create VR models of molecules, organisms, and other structures for students to examine (Figure 2-21). Companies use VR to showcase products or create advertisements. Architects create VR models of buildings and rooms so clients can see how a completed construction project will look before it is built.

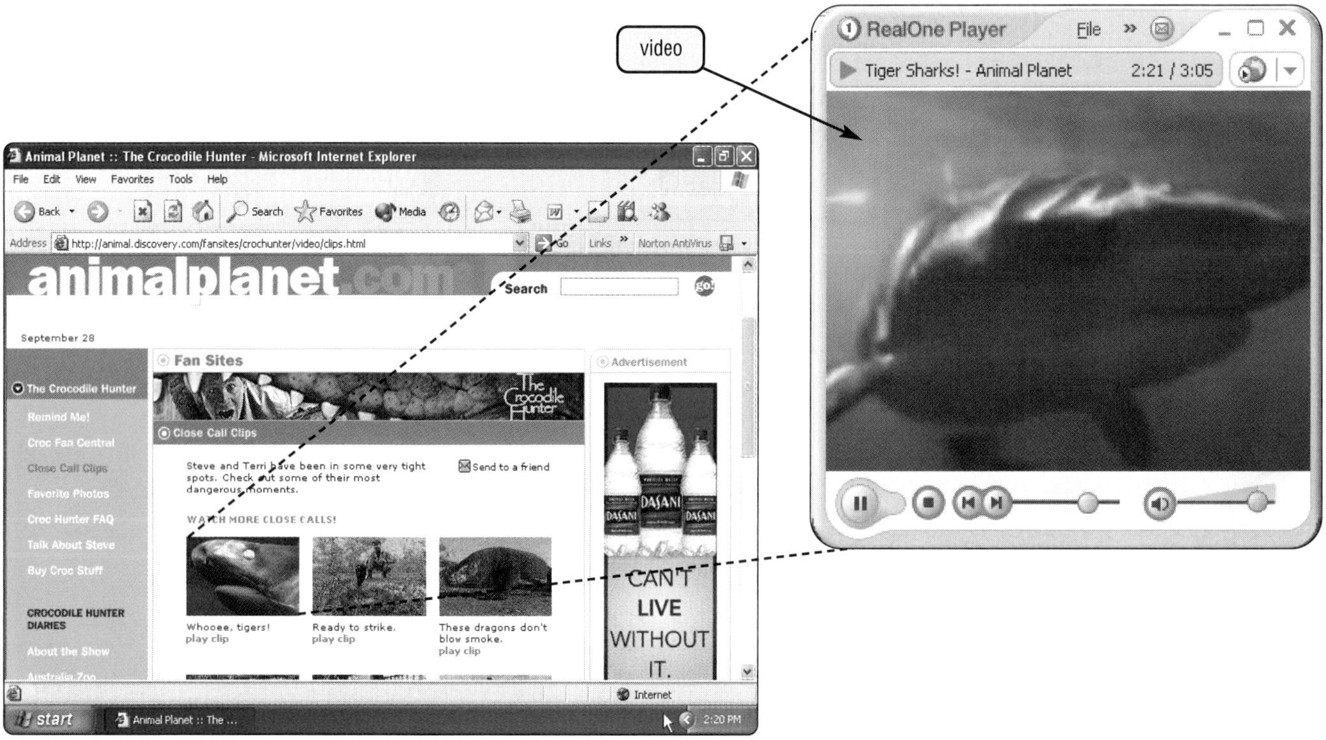

FIGURE 2-20 A video broadcast from the Animal Planet television channel Web site.

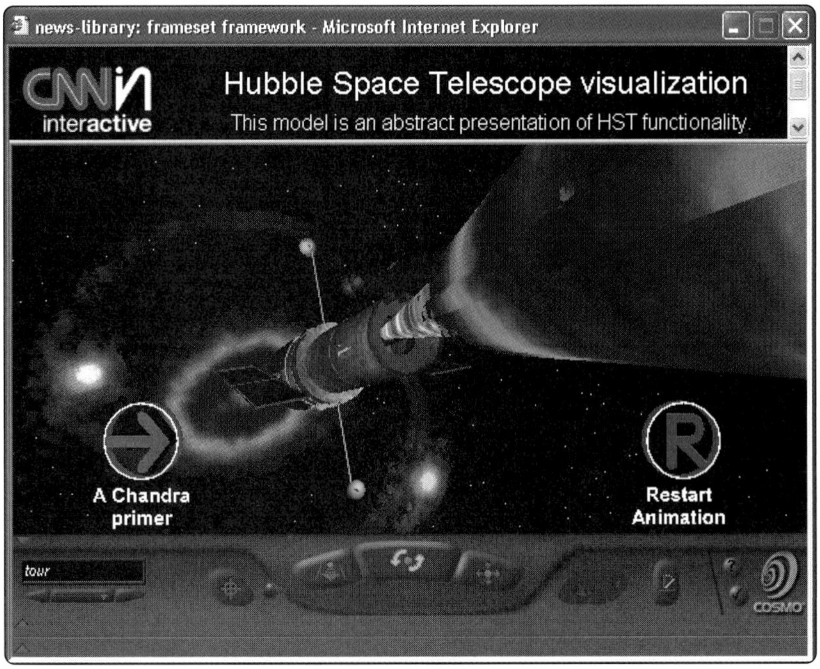

FIGURE 2-21 This Web site uses VR to illustrate the functionality of the Hubble Space Telescope.

PLUG-INS Most Web browsers have the capability of displaying basic multimedia elements on a Web page. Sometimes, a browser might need an additional program, called a plug-in. A **plug-in** is a program that extends the capability of a browser. You can download many plug-ins at no cost from various Web sites (Figure 2-22). Some plug-ins run on all sizes of personal computers and mobile devices. Others have special versions for mobile devices.

WEB LINK 2-4

Plug-Ins

Visit the Discovering Computers 2005 WEB LINK page (**scsite.com/dc2005/weblink**). Click Plug-Ins below Chapter 2.

POPULAR PLUG-IN APPLICATIONS

Plug-In Application		Description	Web Address
Get Adobe Reader	**Acrobat Reader**	View, navigate, and print Portable Document Format (PDF) files — documents formatted to look just as they look in print	adobe.com
INSTALL NOW	**Flash Player**	View dazzling graphics and animation, hear outstanding sound and music, display Web pages across an entire screen	macromedia.com
	QuickTime	View animation, music, audio, video, and VR panoramas and objects directly in a Web page	apple.com
realONE PLAYER	**RealOne Player**	Listen to live and on-demand near-CD-quality audio and newscast-quality video; stream audio and video content for faster viewing; play MP3 files; create music CDs	real.com
INSTALL NOW	**Shockwave Player**	Experience dynamic interactive multimedia, 3-D graphics, and streaming audio	macromedia.com
WindowsMedia Player 9 Series FREE	**Windows Media Player**	Listen to live and on-demand audio; play or edit WMA and MP3 files; burn CDs; watch DVD movies	microsoft.com

FIGURE 2-22 Most plug-ins can be downloaded free from the Web.

E-Commerce

E-commerce, short for *electronic commerce*, is a business transaction that occurs over an electronic network such as the Internet. Anyone with access to a computer, an Internet connection, and a means to pay for purchased goods or services can participate in e-commerce (Figure 2-23).

FIGURE 2-23 E-commerce activities include shopping for goods at an online auction.

In the past, e-commerce transactions were conducted primarily using desktop computers. Today, many mobile computers and devices, such as PDAs and smart phones, also access the Web wirelessly. Some people use the term *m-commerce* (mobile commerce) to identify e-commerce that takes place using mobile devices.

E-commerce has changed the way people conduct business. It virtually eliminates the barriers of time and distance that slow traditional transactions. Now, with e-commerce, transactions occur instantaneously and globally. This saves time for participants on both ends.

Popular uses of e-commerce by consumers include shopping, investing, and banking. Users can purchase just about any product or service on the Web. Some examples include flowers, books, computers, prescription drugs, music, movies, cars, airline tickets, and concert tickets. Through online investing, individuals buy and sell stocks or bonds without using a broker.

Three types of e-commerce are business-to-consumer, consumer-to-consumer, and business-to-business. *Business-to-consumer (B2C) e-commerce* consists of the sale of goods and services to the general public. For example, Dell has a B2C Web site. Instead of visiting a computer store to purchase a computer, customers can order one that meets their specifications directly from the Dell Web site.

A customer (consumer) visits an online business through an **electronic storefront**, which contains product descriptions, graphics, and a shopping cart. The **shopping cart** allows the customer to collect purchases. When ready to complete the sale, the customer enters personal data and the method of payment, preferably through a secure Internet connection (read Issue 2-3 for a related discussion).

ISSUE 2-3

To Tax or Not to Tax Internet Purchases?

The Supreme Court has ruled that buyers must pay state and local sales taxes only when merchants have a physical presence, such as a store or office building, in the buyer's state. Many Internet purchases usually are sales-tax free because the Internet merchants do not have a physical presence in a buyer's state. Some believe this tax-free status has a negative impact on local businesses that must charge sales tax and lower-income families who are less likely to buy online. A new study predicts that by 2011, online sales will cost state and local governments more than $54 billion in sales tax revenues, forcing governments either to raise taxes or cut services. Yet, many feel any tax on e-commerce would be unmanageable (forcing vendors to adjust to varying sales tax rates) and unjustified. Should a sales tax be applied to Internet purchases? Why or why not? How can the problems of taxing, or not taxing, Internet purchases be addressed?

For more information about e-commerce and taxing issues, visit the Discovering Computers 2005 Issues Web page (**scsite.com/dc2005/issues**). Click Issue #3 below Chapter 2.

Often, merchants ship goods to a specified location such as your house. As an alternative, merchants potentially can deliver some items directly to your mobile computer or device. For example, you could purchase a movie ticket on the Web and store the ticket on your PDA. When you want to see the movie, a device at the movie theater wirelessly collects the ticket from your PDA.

Instead of purchasing from a business, consumers can purchase from each other. For example, with an **online auction**, users bid on an item being sold by someone else. The highest bidder at the end of the bidding period purchases the item. *Consumer-to-consumer (C2C) e-commerce* occurs when one consumer sells directly to another, such as in an online auction. eBay is one of the more popular Web sites that provide a means for C2C e-commerce through online auctions (Figure 2-23).

Most e-commerce, though, actually takes place between businesses, which is called *business-to-business (B2B) e-commerce*. Businesses often provide goods and services to other businesses, such as online advertising, recruiting, credit, sales, market research, technical support, and training. For example, some MasterCard and Visa credit card companies provide corporations with Web-based purchasing, tracking, and transaction downloading capabilities.

QUIZ YOURSELF 2-2

To check your knowledge of Web addresses, Web browsers, searching, types of Web sites, elements of a Web page, and e-commerce, visit the Discovering Computers 2005 Quiz Yourself Web page (**scsite.com/dc2005/quiz**). Click Objectives 4 – 9 below Chapter 2.

WEB LINK 2-5

E-Commerce

Visit the Discovering Computers 2005 WEB LINK page (**scsite.com/dc2005/weblink**). Click E-Commerce below Chapter 2.

OTHER INTERNET SERVICES

The World Wide Web is only one of the many services on the Internet. Other Internet services include e-mail, FTP (File Transfer Protocol), newsgroups and message boards, mailing lists, chat rooms, and instant messaging. The following pages discuss each of these services.

E-Mail

E-mail (short for *electronic mail*) is the transmission of messages and files via a computer network. E-mail was one of the original services on the Internet, enabling scientists and researchers working on government-sponsored projects to communicate with colleagues at other locations. Today, e-mail is a primary communications method for both personal and business use. Read Issue 2-4 for a related discussion.

ISSUE 2-4

How Expensive Is E-Mail and Internet Privacy?

With security a major concern in the aftermath of terrorist attacks, law enforcement agencies have sought greater leeway in monitoring a suspect's computer activities such as e-mail communications. Investigators would like to expand their use of software that can be set up on an Internet service provider or local area network. The surveillance software can track e-mail exchanges, reconstruct e-mail messages, or recreate downloaded files and Web pages visited from a suspect's computer. Law enforcement agencies insist that this program is a valuable weapon in the fight for national security. Yet, privacy advocates maintain that no evidence exists proving that surveillance software increases national security, and it may provide access to information outside the limit of legitimate surveillance. Should government be allowed to use surveillance software to monitor computer use? Why or why not? Some analysts maintain that, to combat terrorism justifiably, surveillance tools must be restricted to terrorism investigations and be established for a limited period. Are these legitimate restrictions? Why or why not?

For more information about government monitoring, visit the Discovering Computers 2005 Issues Web page (**scsite.com/dc2005/issues**). Click Issue #4 below Chapter 2.

You use an **e-mail program** to create, send, receive, forward, store, print, and delete e-mail messages. Outlook and Outlook Express are two popular e-mail programs. The steps in Figure 2-24 illustrate how to send an e-mail message using Outlook. The message can be simple text or can include an attachment such as a word processing document, a graphic, an audio clip, or a video clip.

FIGURE 2-24 HOW TO SEND AN E-MAIL MESSAGE

Step 1:
Start an e-mail program and point to the New Mail Message button.

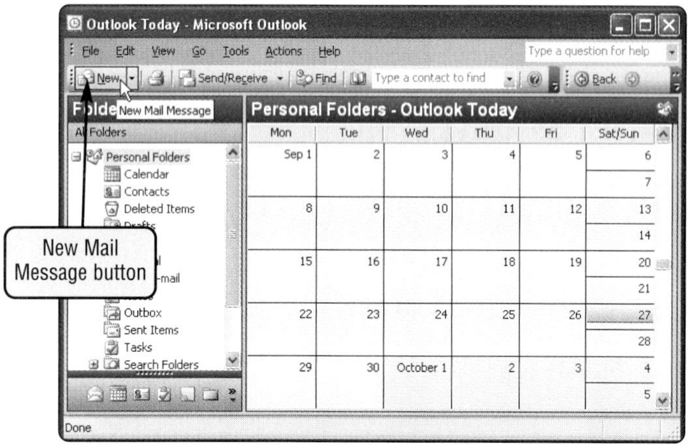

Step 2:
Click the New Mail Message button to display the Message window.

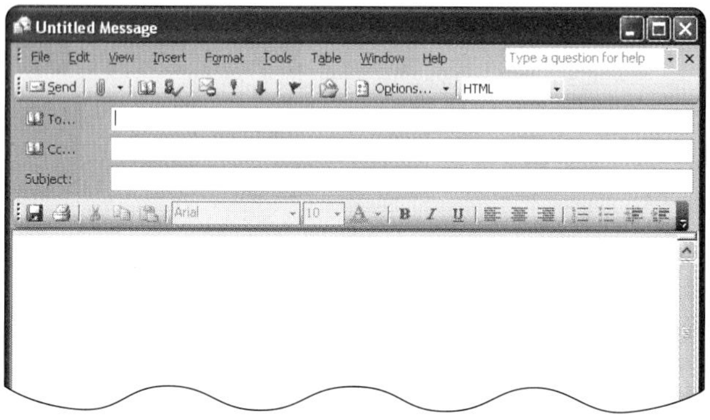

Step 3:
Enter the recipient's e-mail address, the subject, and the message in the Message window.

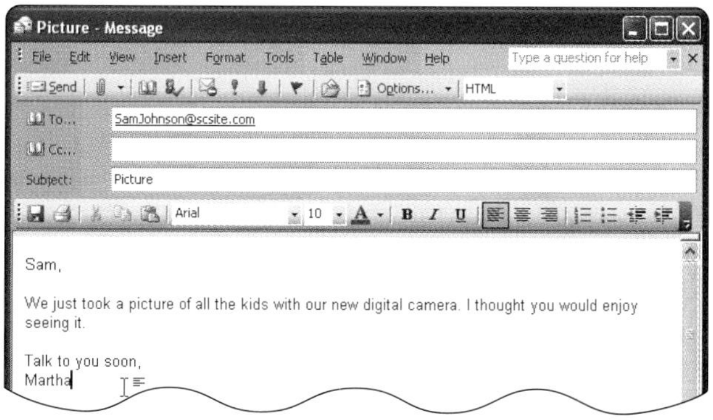

Step 4:
Click the Insert File button to attach a JPEG file containing a picture to the message. Click the Send button to send the message.

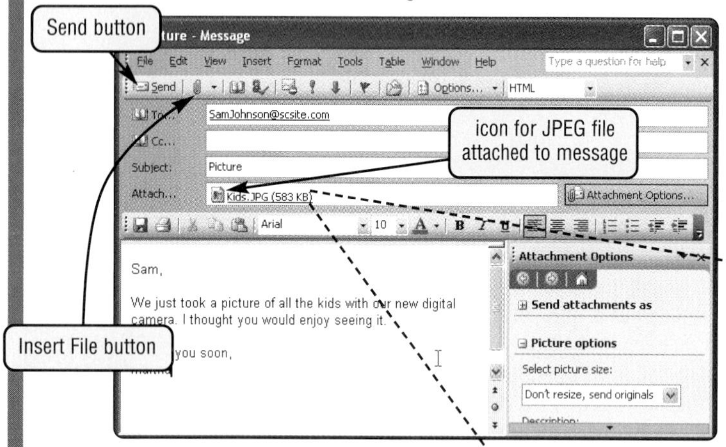

Step 5:
When Sam receives the e-mail message, he opens the JPEG file to view the picture.

Just as you address a letter when using the postal system, you must address an e-mail message with the e-mail address of your intended recipient. To receive messages, you need to have an e-mail address. Likewise, when someone sends you a message, they must have your e-mail address. An **e-mail address** is a combination of a user name and a domain name that identifies a user so he or she can receive Internet e-mail (Figure 2-25).

Internet access providers typically supply an e-mail program as a standard part of their Internet access services. Some Web sites, such as MSN Hotmail and Yahoo!, provide free e-mail services. To use these Web-based e-mail programs, you connect to the Web site and set up an e-mail account, which typically includes an e-mail address and a password.

A **user name** is a unique combination of characters, such as letters of the alphabet and/or numbers, that identifies a specific user. Your user name must be different from the other user names in the same domain. For example, a user named Sam Johnson whose server has a domain name of scsite.com might select SJohnson as his user name. If scsite.com already has an SJohnson (for Sheila Johnson), Sam will have to select a different user name, such as SamJohnson or Sam_Johnson.

Sometimes, companies decide user names for employees. In many cases, however, users select their own user names, often selecting a nickname or any other combination of characters for their user name. Many users select a combination of their first and last names so others can remember it easily.

In an Internet e-mail address, an @ (pronounced at) symbol separates the user name from the domain name. Your service provider supplies the domain name. Using the example in Figure 2-25, a possible e-mail address for Sam Johnson would be SamJohnson@scsite.com, which would be read as follows: Sam Johnson at s c site dot com. Most e-mail programs allow you to create an **address book**, which contains a list of names and e-mail addresses.

Although no complete listing of Internet e-mail addresses exists, several Web sites such as Yahoo! and Switchboard.com list addresses collected from public sources. Some of these Web sites allow you to list your e-mail address voluntarily so others can find it. The Web site also might ask for other information, such as your high school or college so others can determine if you are the person they want to reach.

When you send an e-mail message, an outgoing mail server that is operated by your Internet access provider determines how to route the message through the Internet and then sends the message. *SMTP (simple mail transfer protocol)* is a communications technology used by some outgoing mail servers.

As you receive e-mail messages, an incoming mail server — also operated by your Internet access provider — holds the messages in your mailbox until you use your e-mail program to retrieve them. *POP3* is the latest version of POP (*Post Office Protocol*), which is a communications technology used by some incoming mail servers.

FIGURE 2-25 An e-mail address is a combination of a user name and a domain name.

WEB LINK 2-6

E-Mail

Visit the Discovering Computers 2005 WEB LINK page (**scsite.com/dc2005/weblink**). Click E-Mail below Chapter 2.

Most e-mail programs have a mail notification alert that informs you via a message or sound when you receive new mail, even if you are working in another application. Figure 2-26 illustrates how an e-mail message may travel from a sender to a receiver.

FAQ 2-7

Can my computer get a virus through e-mail?

Yes. A *virus* is a potentially damaging computer program. Once in your computer, a virus can damage files and the operating system. One way that virus authors attempt to spread a virus is by sending virus-infected e-mail attachments. If you receive an e-mail attachment, you should use an antivirus program to verify that it is virus free.

For more information about viruses and antivirus programs, read the High-Tech Talk page at the end of Chapter 3, the section on viruses and antivirus programs in Chapter 8, and visit the Discovering Computers 2005 FAQ Web page (**scsite.com/dc2005/faq**). Click Viruses below Chapter 2.

FIGURE 2-26 HOW AN E-MAIL MESSAGE MAY TRAVEL FROM A SENDER TO A RECEIVER

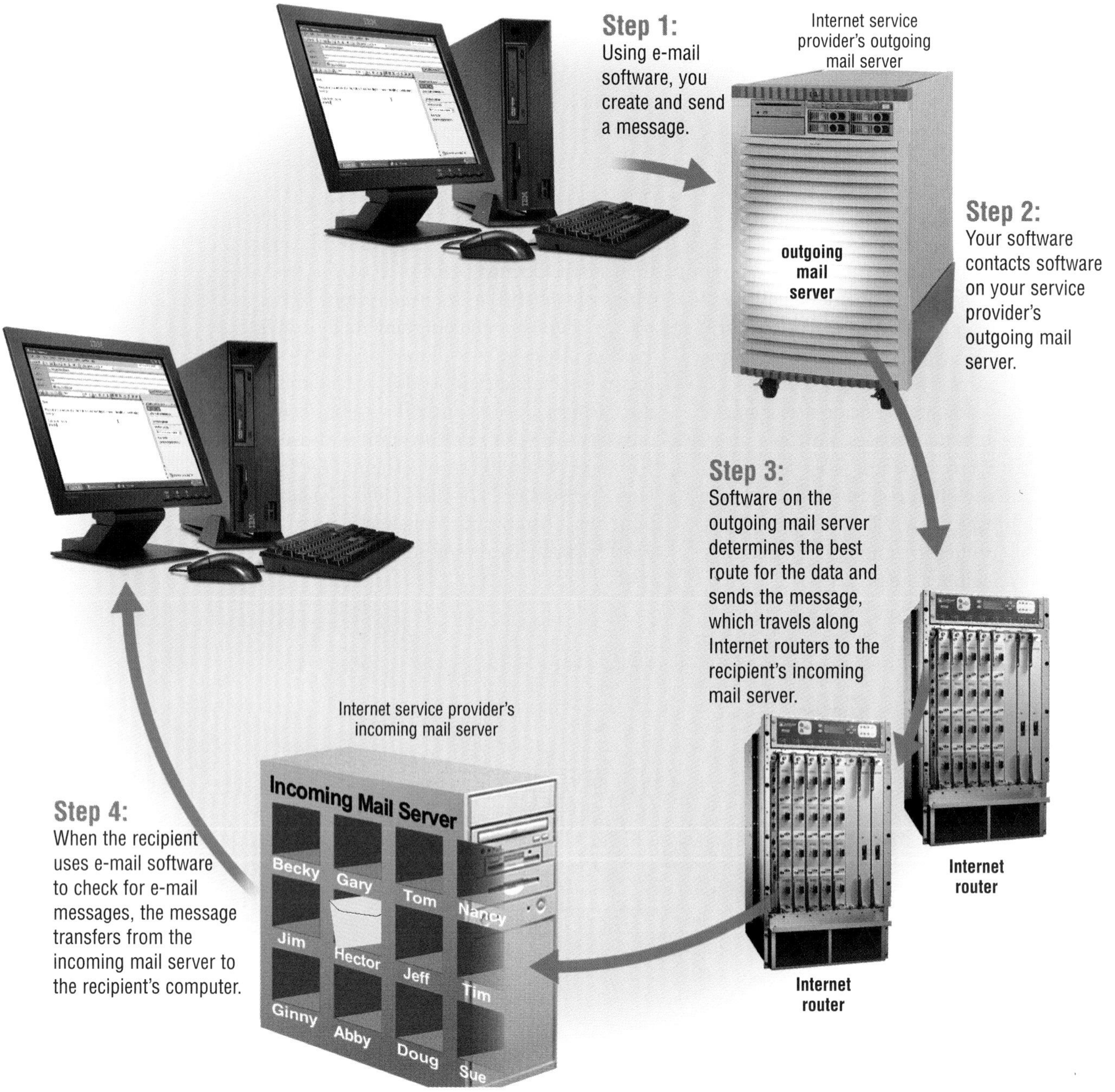

FTP

FTP (*File Transfer Protocol*) is an Internet standard that permits file uploading and downloading (transferring) with other computers on the Internet. Uploading is the opposite of downloading; that is, **uploading** is the process of transferring documents, graphics, and other objects from your computer to a server on the Internet.

Many operating systems include FTP capabilities (Figure 2-27). If yours does not, you can download FTP programs from the Web, usually for a small fee.

An *FTP server* is a computer that allows users to upload and download files using FTP. An FTP site is a collection of files including text, graphics, audio clips, video clips, and program files that reside on an FTP server. Many FTP sites have *anonymous FTP*, whereby anyone can transfer some, if not all, available files. Some FTP sites restrict file transfers to those who have authorized accounts (user names and passwords) on the FTP server.

Large files on FTP sites often are compressed to reduce storage space and download time. Before you can use a compressed (zipped) file, you must uncompress (unzip) it. Chapter 8 discusses utilities that zip and unzip files.

Newsgroups and Message Boards

A **newsgroup** is an online area in which users have written discussions about a particular subject. To participate in a discussion, a user sends a message to the newsgroup, and other users in the newsgroup read and reply to the message. The entire collection of Internet newsgroups is called *Usenet*, which contains thousands of newsgroups on a multitude of topics. Some major topic areas include news, recreation, society, business, science, and computers.

A computer that stores and distributes newsgroup messages is called a *news server*. Many universities, corporations, Internet access providers, and other large organizations have a news server. Some newsgroups require you to enter a user name and password to participate in the discussion. Only authorized members can use this type of newsgroup. For example, a newsgroup for students taking a college course may require a user name and password to access the newsgroup. This ensures that only students in the course participate in the discussion.

WEB LINK 2-7

FTP

Visit the Discovering Computers 2005 WEB LINK page (**scsite.com/dc2005/weblink**). Click FTP below Chapter 2.

FIGURE 2-27a (FTP site being added to My Network Places folder)

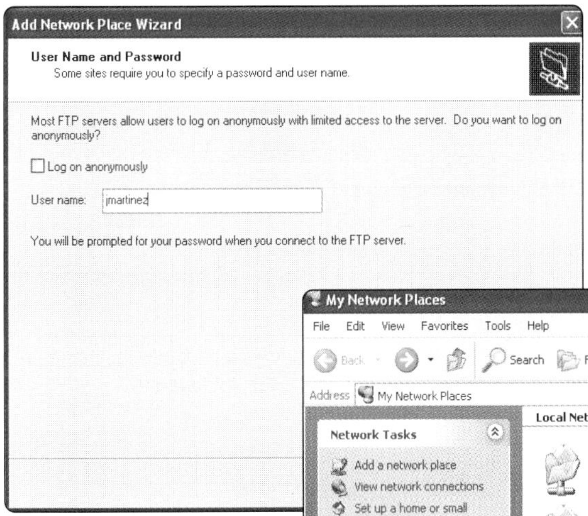

FIGURE 2-27b (FTP site link is displayed in My Network Places folder)

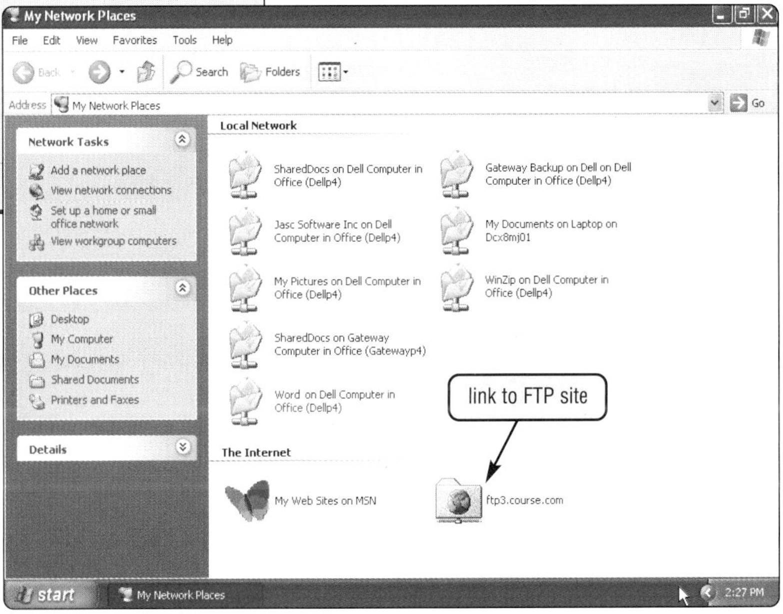

FIGURE 2-27 Many operating systems, such as Windows XP, have built-in FTP capabilities.

To participate in a newsgroup, typically you use a program called a *newsreader*. Most browsers have newsreaders. Instead of using your own newsreader, some Web sites that sponsor newsgroups have a built-in newsreader. A newsreader enables you to access a newsgroup to read previously entered messages, called *articles*. You can *post*, or add, articles of your own. The newsreader also keeps track of which articles you have and have not read.

Newsgroup members frequently post articles as a reply to another article — either to answer a question or to comment on material in the original article. These replies may cause the author of the original article, or others, to post additional articles related to the original article. A *thread* or *threaded discussion* consists of the original article and all subsequent related replies. A thread can be short-lived or continue for some time, depending on the nature of the topic and the interest of the participants.

WEB LINK 2-8

Newsgroups and Message Boards

Visit the Discovering Computers 2005 WEB LINK page (**scsite.com/dc2005/weblink**). Click Newsgroups and Message Boards below Chapter 2.

Using a newsreader, you can search for newsgroups discussing a particular subject such as a type of musical instrument, brand of sports equipment, or employment opportunities. If you like the discussion in a particular newsgroup, you can *subscribe* to it, which means its location is saved in your newsreader for easy future access.

In some newsgroups, posted articles are sent to a moderator instead of immediately displaying on the newsgroup. The *moderator* reviews the contents of the article and then posts it, if appropriate. With a *moderated newsgroup*, the moderator decides if the article is relevant to the discussion. The moderator may choose to edit or discard inappropriate articles. For this reason, the content of a moderated newsgroup is considered more valuable.

A popular Web-based type of discussion group that does not require a newsreader is a **message board** (Figure 2-28). Many Web sites use message boards instead of newsgroups because they are easier to use.

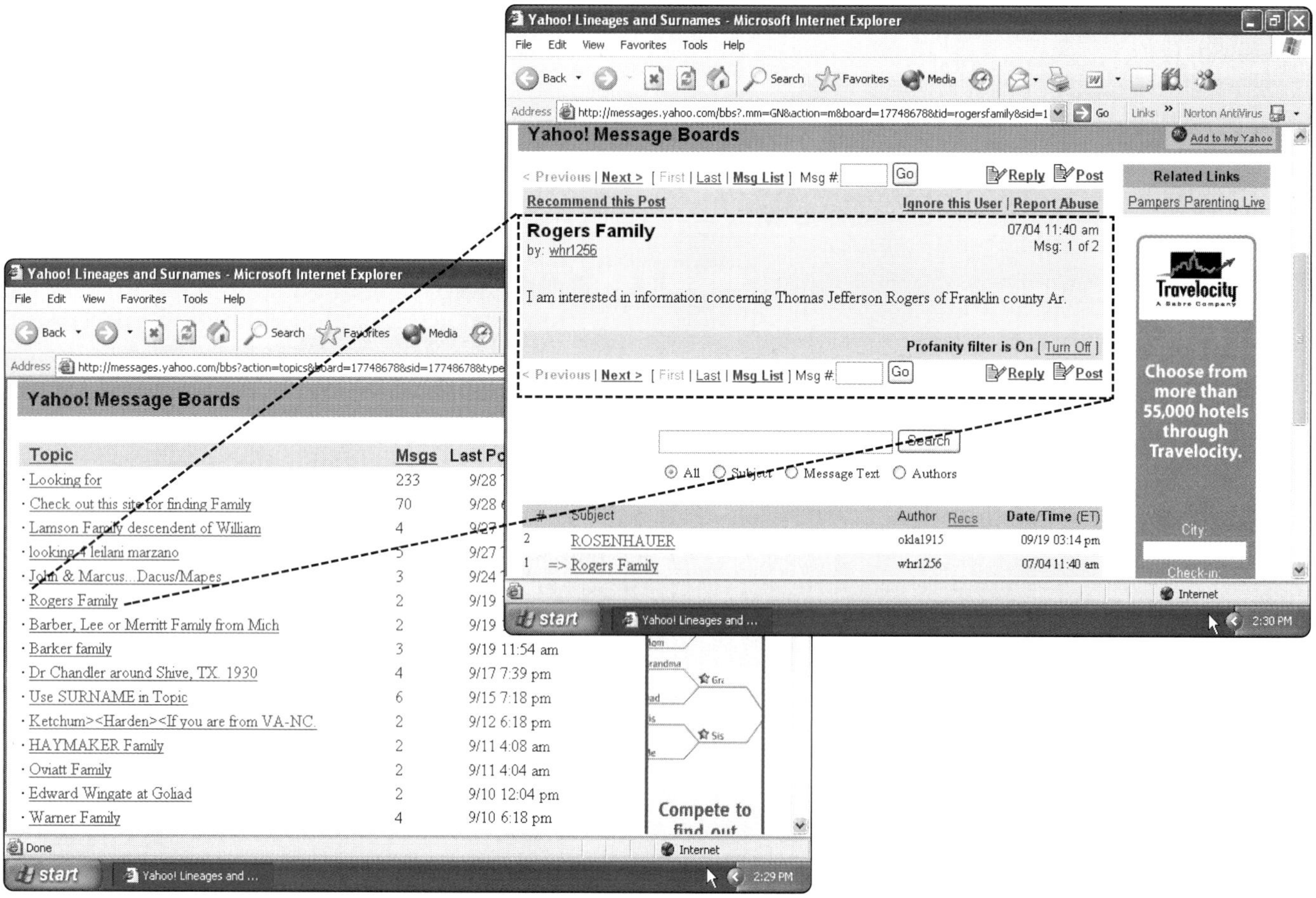

FIGURE 2-28 On this message board, users discuss genealogy.

Mailing Lists

A **mailing list** is a group of e-mail names and addresses given a single name. When a message is sent to a mailing list, every person on the list receives a copy of the message in his or her mailbox. To add your e-mail name and address to a mailing list, you **subscribe** to it (Figure 2-29). To remove your name, you **unsubscribe** from the mailing list. Some mailing lists are called *LISTSERVs*, named after a popular mailing list software product.

Thousands of mailing lists exist about a variety of topics in areas of entertainment, business, computers, society, culture, health, recreation, and education. To locate a mailing list dealing with a particular topic, search for the keywords, mailing list or LISTSERV, in a search engine. Many vendors use mailing lists to communicate with their customer base.

WEB LINK 2-9

Mailing Lists

Visit the Discovering Computers 2005 WEB LINK page (**scsite.com/dc2005/weblink**). Click Mailing Lists below Chapter 2.

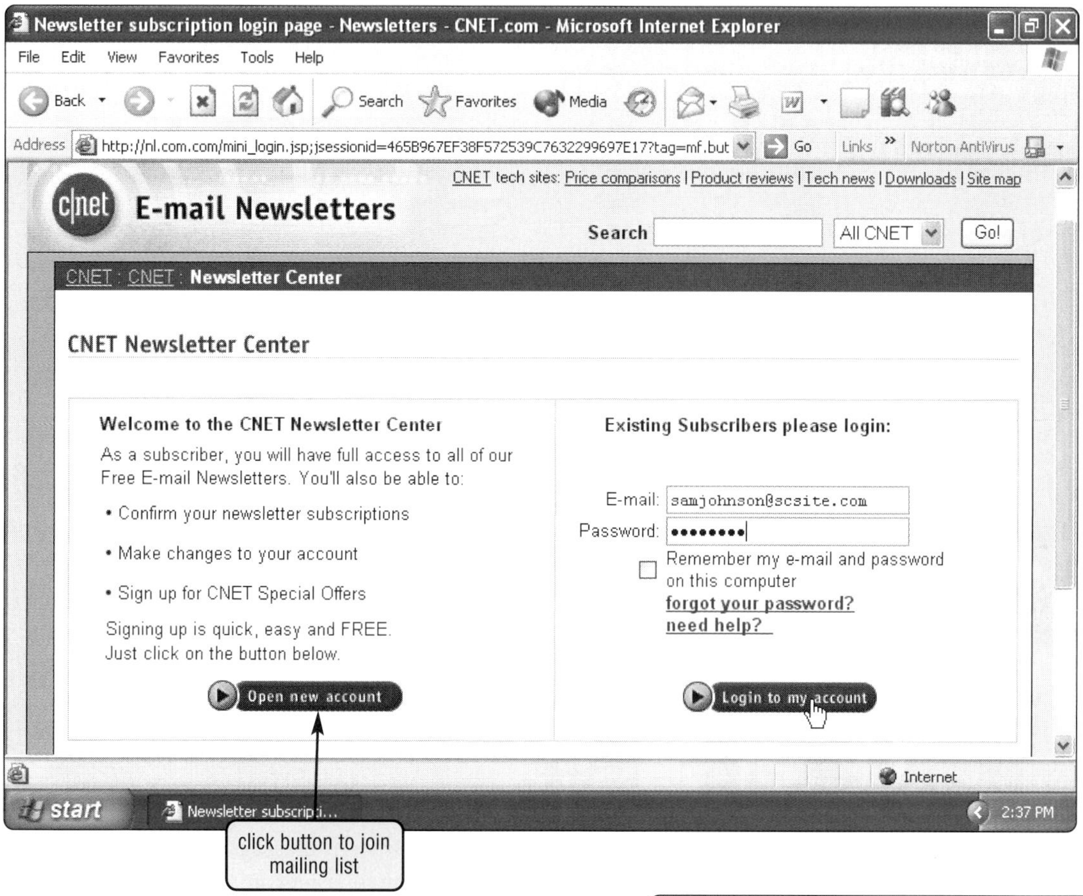

FIGURE 2-29 When you join a mailing list, you and all others on the mailing list receive e-mail messages from the Web site.

Chat Rooms

A **chat** is a real-time typed conversation that takes place on a computer. **Real time** means that you and the people with whom you are conversing are online at the same time. A **chat room** is a location on an Internet server that permits users to chat with each other. Anyone in the chat room can participate in the conversation, which usually is specific to a particular topic.

As you type on your keyboard, a line of characters and symbols is displayed on the computer screen. Others connected to the same chat room server also see what you have typed. In many chat rooms, you can click a button to see a profile of someone in the chat room.

Some chat rooms support voice chats and video chats, in which people hear or see each other as they chat (Figure 2-30). Read Apply It 2-2 for more information about voice communications.

WEB LINK 2-10

Chat Rooms

Visit the Discovering Computers 2005 WEB LINK page (**scsite.com/dc2005/weblink**). Click Chat Rooms below Chapter 2.

APPLY IT 2-2

Send Voice Messages Via the Internet

Talk is cheap, according to an old saying. It is particularly cheap — and effective — when using Internet services. You can add voice message attachments to e-mail messages, talk in chat rooms, and send voice instant messages. You also can make relatively inexpensive online calls to another computer or to a telephone, although the audio quality generally is no match for a home telephone line.

To accomplish this task, you need a computer with a sound card, speakers, and a microphone, and you must install the appropriate software. Many of these programs are free, and they offer volume control and compression, which reduces the size of the speech files.

For more information about voice messages, visit the Discovering Computers 2005 Apply It Web page (**scsite.com/dc2005/apply**). Click Apply It #2 below Chapter 2.

To start a chat session, you connect to a chat server through a chat client. A chat client is a program on your computer. Today's browsers usually include a chat client. If yours does not, you can download a chat client from the Web.

Once you have installed a *chat client*, you can create or join a conversation on the chat server to which you are connected. The chat room should indicate the discussion topic. The person who creates a chat room acts as the operator and has responsibility for monitoring the conversation and disconnecting anyone who becomes disruptive. Operator status can be shared or transferred to someone else.

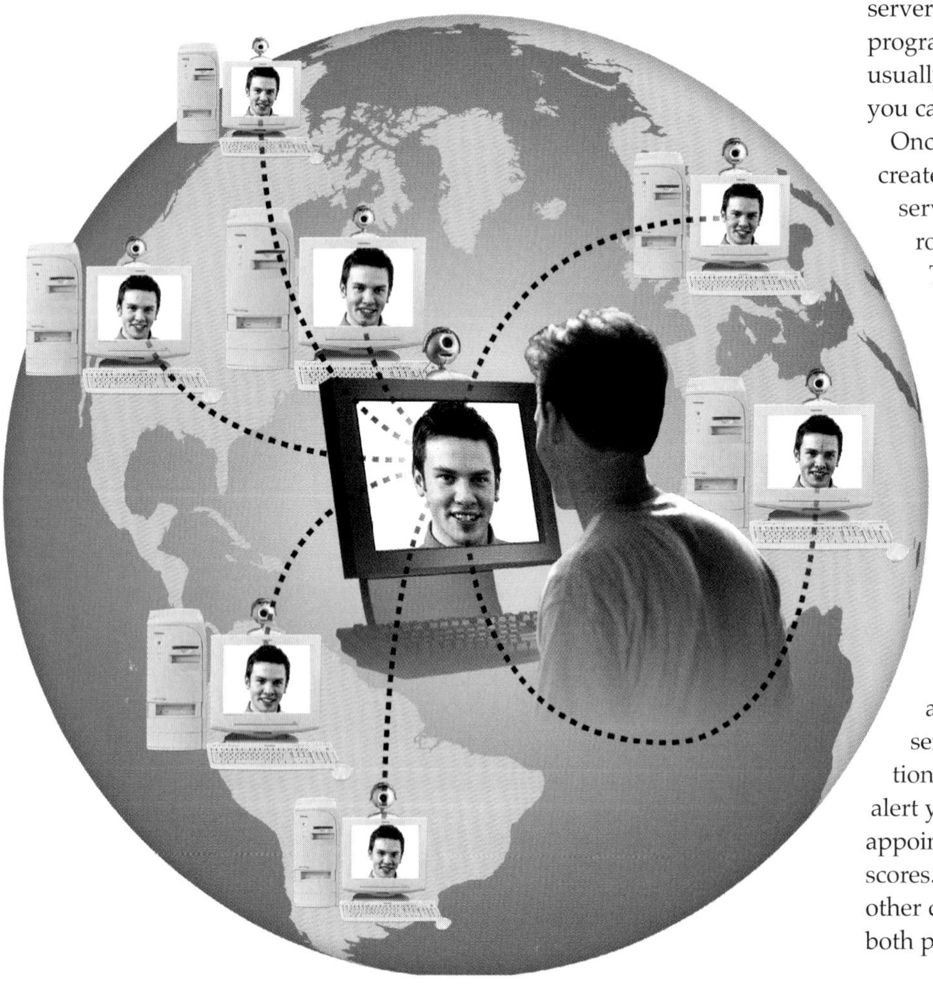

FIGURE 2-30 As you type, the words and symbols you enter are displayed on the computer screens of others in the same chat room. Some chat rooms allow people to see and hear each other as they chat.

Instant Messaging

Instant messaging (IM) is a real-time Internet communications service that notifies you when one or more people are online and then allows you to exchange messages or files or join a private chat room with them. Some IM services support voice and video conversations (Figure 2-31). Many IM services also can alert you to information such as calendar appointments, stock quotes, weather, or sports scores. They also allow you to send pictures or other documents to a recipient. For IM to work, both parties must be online at the same time.

Also, the receiver of a message must be willing to accept messages. Many businesses have found IM preferable to telephone tag for interoffice communications.

People use IM on all types of computers, including desktop computers and mobile computers and devices. To use IM, you may have to install *instant messenger* software onto the computer or device you plan to use IM. Some operating systems, such as Windows XP, include an instant messenger. No standards currently exist for IM. To ensure successful communications, all individuals on the notification list need to use the same or a compatible instant messenger.

WEB LINK 2-11

Instant Messaging

Visit the Discovering Computers 2005 WEB LINK page (**scsite.com/dc2005/weblink**). Click Instant Messaging below Chapter 2.

FIGURE 2-31 AN EXAMPLE OF INSTANT MESSAGING

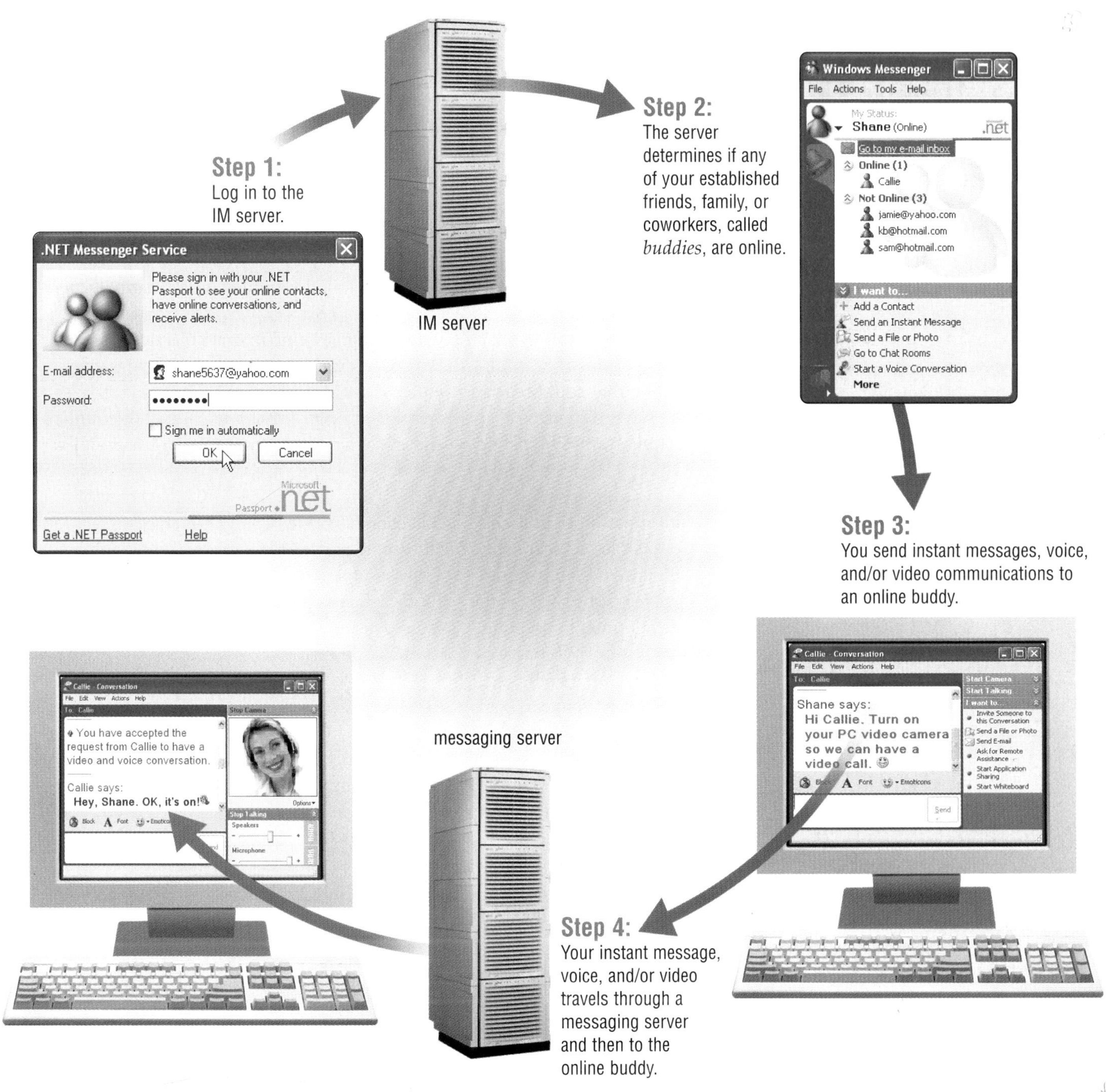

NETIQUETTE

Netiquette, which is short for Internet etiquette, is the code of acceptable behaviors users should follow while on the Internet; that is, it is the conduct expected of individuals while online. Netiquette includes rules for all aspects of the Internet, including the World Wide Web, e-mail, FTP, newsgroups and message boards, chat rooms, and instant messaging. Figure 2-32 outlines some of the rules of netiquette.

Netiquette

Golden Rule: Treat others as you would like them to treat you.

1. In e-mail, newsgroups, and chat rooms:
   - Keep messages brief and use proper grammar and spelling.
   - Be careful when using sarcasm and humor, as it might be misinterpreted.
   - Be polite. Avoid offensive language.
   - Avoid sending or posting *flames*, which are abusive or insulting messages. Do not participate in *flame wars*, which are exchanges of flames.
   - Avoid sending spam, which is the Internet's version of junk mail. *Spam* is an unsolicited e-mail message or newsgroup posting sent to many recipients or newsgroups at once.
   - Do not use all capital letters, which is the equivalent of SHOUTING!
   - Use **emoticons** to express emotion. Popular emoticons include
     :) Smile   :\ Undecided
     :(Frown   :o Surprised
     :| Indifference
   - Use abbreviations and acronyms for phrases:
     BTW by the way
     FYI for your information
     FWIW for what it's worth
     IMHO in my humble opinion
     TTFN ta ta for now
     TYVM thank you very much
   - Clearly identify a *spoiler*, which is a message that reveals a solution to a game or ending to a movie or program.
2. Read the *FAQ* (frequently asked questions), if one exists. Many newsgroups and Web pages have an FAQ.
3. Do not assume material is accurate or up-to-date. Be forgiving of others' mistakes.
4. Never read someone's private e-mail.

FIGURE 2-32 Some of the rules of netiquette.

WEB PUBLISHING

Before the World Wide Web, the means to share opinions and ideas with others easily and inexpensively was limited to the media, classroom, work, or social environments. Generating an advertisement or publication that could reach a massive audience required much expense. Today, businesses and individuals convey information to millions of people by creating their own Web pages.

Web publishing is the development and maintenance of Web pages. To develop a Web page, you do not have to be a computer programmer. For the small business or home user, Web publishing is fairly easy as long as you have the proper tools.

The five major steps to Web publishing are as follows:

1. Plan a Web site
2. Analyze and design a Web site
3. Create a Web site
4. Deploy a Web site
5. Maintain a Web site

Figure 2-33 illustrates these steps with respect to a personal Web site. The following paragraphs describe these steps in more depth.

Plan a Web Site

Planning a personal Web site involves thinking about issues that could affect the design of the Web site. Identify the purpose of the Web site and the characteristics of the people whom you want to visit the Web site. Determine ways to differentiate your Web site from similar ones.

Analyze and Design a Web Site

A Web site can be simple or complex. In this step, determine specific ways to meet the goals identified in the previous step. Design the layout of elements of the Web site such as text, graphics, audio, video, and virtual reality. Decide if you have the means to include all the elements of the design into the Web site.

Required hardware may include a digital camera, scanner, sound card, microphone, and PC video camera. To incorporate pictures in your Web pages, you can take digital photographs with a digital camera, have pictures developed on a CD or DVD, or scan existing photographs and other graphics into a digital format with a scanner. You also can download images from the Web or purchase a CD or DVD that contains a collection of images. With a sound card, you can add sounds to your Web pages. A microphone allows you to include your voice in a Web page. To incorporate videos, you could use a PC video camera or purchase special hardware that captures still photographs from videos.

Create a Web Site

Creating a Web site, sometimes called *Web page authoring*, involves working on the computer to compose the Web site. Many current word processing programs include Web page authoring features so you can create basic Web pages that contain text and graphics.

To create more sophisticated Web pages that include video, sound, animation, and other special effects, you can use *Web page authoring software*, which is software specifically designed to help you create Web pages. Both new and experienced users can create fascinating Web sites with this software. Popular Web page authoring programs include Microsoft FrontPage, Adobe GoLive, Macromedia Dreamweaver, and Macromedia Flash.

FIGURE 2-33 HOW TO PUBLISH YOUR RESUME ON THE WEB

Step 1:
Plan a Web site.
Think about issues that could affect the design of the Web site.

Step 2:
Analyze and design a Web site.
Design the layout of the elements of the Web site.

Step 3:
Create a Web site.
Use word processing or Web page authoring software to create the Web site.

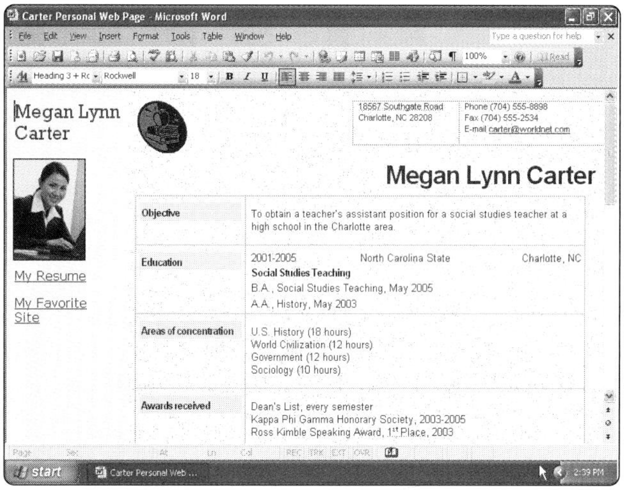

Step 4:
Deploy a Web site.
Save the Web site to a Web server.

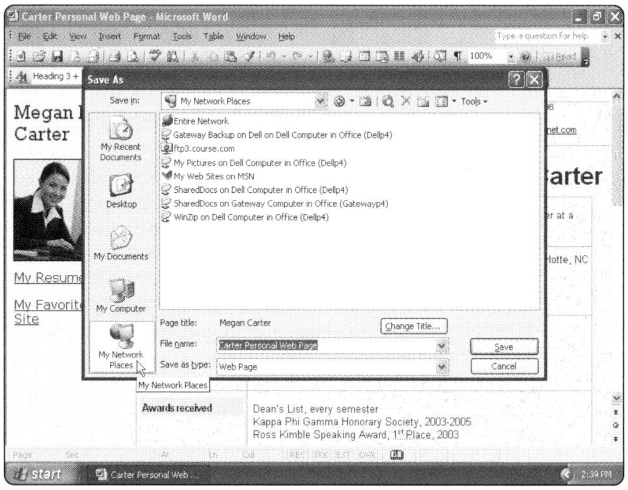

Step 5:
Maintain a Web site.
Visit your Web site regularly to be sure it is working and current.

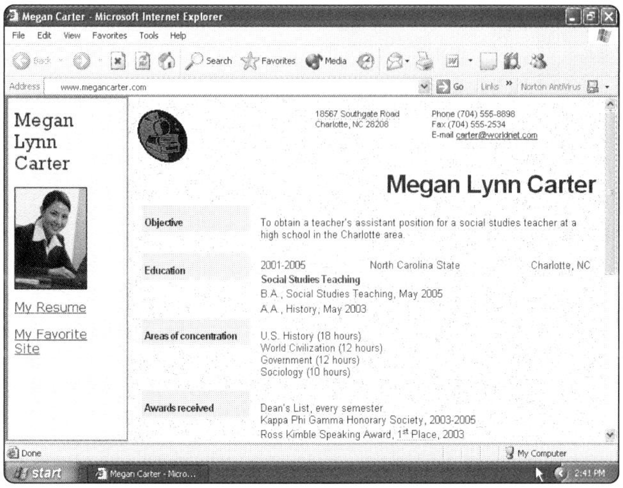

Deploy a Web Site

After the Web pages are created, you store them on a Web server. Many Internet access providers offer their customers storage space on a Web server for a personal Web site at no additional cost. If your access provider does not include this service, companies called *Web hosting services* provide storage for your Web pages for a reasonable monthly fee.

If your access provider does not supply a Web address or if you want to obtain a different domain name, you apply to an official registrar for a specific domain name. You then pay a small annual fee to continue using the domain name.

Once you have created a Web site and located a Web server to store it, you need to upload the Web site from your computer to the Web server. One way to upload files is with FTP.

To help others locate your Web site, you should register it with various search engines. Doing so ensures your site will appear in the hit lists for searches on related keywords. Many search engines allow you to register your Web address and keywords at no cost. Registering your site with the various search engines, however, can be an extremely time-consuming task. Instead, you can use a *submission service*, which is a Web-based business that registers your Web site with hundreds of search engines for a fee.

Maintain a Web Site

A successful Web site's contents must be up-to-date and its links must work properly at all times. Ensure currency and suitability by reviewing and updating the Web site frequently.

A **Webmaster** is the individual responsible for maintaining a Web site and developing Web pages. Webmasters and other Web developers maintain Web sites using software products. Most Web page authoring software provides basic Web site management tools, allowing you to add and modify Web pages within the Web site. For more advanced features such as managing users, passwords, chat rooms, and e-mail, you need to purchase specialized Web site management software, if your Internet access provider does not provide the software.

QUIZ YOURSELF 2-3

To check your knowledge of e-mail, FTP, newsgroups and message boards, mailing lists, chat rooms, instant messaging, netiquette, and Web publishing, visit the Discovering Computers 2005 Quiz Yourself Web page (**scsite.com/dc2005/quiz**). Click Objectives 10 – 12 below Chapter 2.

CHAPTER SUMMARY

This chapter presented the history and structure of the Internet. It discussed the World Wide Web at length, including topics such as browsing, navigating, searching, and e-commerce. It also introduced other services available on the Internet, such as e-mail, FTP, newsgroups and message boards, chat rooms, and instant messaging. Finally, the chapter listed rules of netiquette and discussed Web publishing.

Web Developer

If you are looking for a job working with the latest Internet technology, then Web developer could be the career for you. A *Web developer* analyzes, designs, develops, implements, and supports Web applications and functionality. Specialized programming skills required include HTML, JavaScript, Java, Perl, C++, and VBScript. Developers also may need multimedia knowledge, including Adobe Photoshop and Macromedia Flash and Macromedia Director. Developers must be aware of emerging technologies and know how they can be used to enhance a Web presence.

A Web developer must be able to appreciate a client's needs, recognize the technologies involved to meet those needs, and explain those technologies to the client. For example, if the client is a large corporation seeking to set up an online store, a Web developer must understand e-commerce and be able to explain what is required, probable costs, and possible outcomes in a way that the client can understand.

Educational requirements vary from company to company and can range from a high school education to a four-year degree. Many companies place heavy emphasis on certifications. Two of the more popular certifications are available through the International Webmasters Association (IWA) and the World Organization of Webmasters (WOW). A wide salary range exists — from $25,000 to $65,000 — depending on educational background and location.

To learn more about the field of Web Developer as a career, visit the Discovering Computers 2005 Careers Web page (**scsite.com/dc2005/careers**). Click Web Developer.

You Are One in a Few Billion (IP Addresses)

Every computer on the Internet has a unique address, called an IP address, that distinguishes it from other computers on the Internet. An IP address has two parts that identify a specific computer: one part to identify the network where that computer resides and a second part to pinpoint the specific computer or host within that network.

A typical IP address — such as 207.46.197.113 — has four groups of numbers that range from 0 through 255. This form of the IP address is sometimes called a *dotted decimal number* or *dotted quad*. The four groups of numbers in the dotted quad are called octets, because they each have 8 bits when viewed in binary form for a total of 32 bits in the IP address. For instance, the binary form of 207.46.197.113 is 11001111.00101110.11000101.01110001 (Figure 2-34). For more information about how the binary system works, see Appendix B.

Because each of the 8 bits can be 1 or 0, the total possible combinations per octet are 2^8, or 256. Combining the four octets of an IP address provides a possible 2^{32} or 4,294,967,296 unique values. The actual number of available addresses is about 3 billion, because some values are reserved for special use or are off limits.

To request data such as a Web page from a computer on the Internet, you really need only an IP address. For instance, if you type the Web address, http://207.46.197.113, your browser will display the home page on the machine hosting the Microsoft Web site. Of course, remembering one IP address out of billions is a little overwhelming — so you probably would just type the domain name, www.microsoft.com, into your browser. Your browser then contacts a domain name server (DNS) to resolve the human-readable domain name into a machine-readable IP address. Each domain name server houses a simple database that maps domain names to IP addresses. The DNS would resolve the human-readable domain name, www.microsoft.com, into a machine-readable IP address, 207.46.197.113.

Domain names are helpful because they are easier for people to remember than IP addresses. You can learn more about a domain using the whois form at the Network Solutions Web site (www.netsol.com and then click the whois link). If you type in a domain name, such as scsite.com, the form displays the registration information for that domain, including its IP address.

Like all others, your computer must have an IP address to connect to the Internet or another computer that has an IP address. Servers generally have *static IP addresses*, because they usually are connected to the Internet and their IP addresses do not change often. When you dial up to the Internet using your home computer, you most likely are using a temporary or *dynamic IP address*. Your access provider uses the *Dynamic Host Configuration Protocol (DHCP)* to assign your computer a temporary dynamic IP address from a pool of IP addresses. The dynamic IP address is unique only for that session. Once you disconnect, the DHCP server puts that IP address back into the IP address pool so it can assign it to the next requesting computer. Even if you immediately reconnect, the DHCP server might not assign you the same IP address. Using DHCP and dynamic IP addresses means an Internet service provider needs only one IP address for each modem it supports, rather than one for each of its millions of customers.

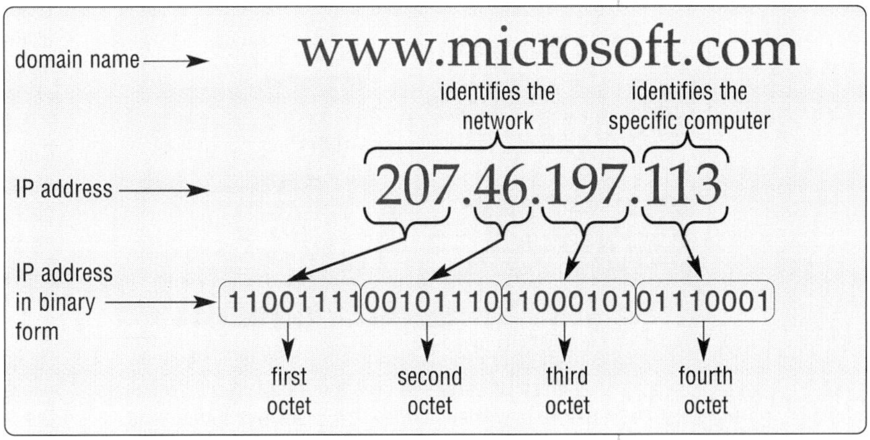

FIGURE 2-34 Components of an IP address.

Billions of IP addresses sounds like a lot. But, because so many computers connected to the Internet need unique IP addresses, a growing shortage of IP addresses exists. A new IP addressing scheme, called *IPv6* or *IPng (IP Next Generation)* will lengthen IP addresses from 32 bits to 128 bits and increase the number of available IP addresses to a whopping 3.4×10^{38}, or 340,000,000,000,000,000,000,000,000,000,000,000,000.

Do you want to know the IP address currently assigned to your computer?

- With Windows 2000/XP, click the Start button on the taskbar and then click Run. Type `cmd` to display the MS-DOS window. Type `ipconfig` and then press the ENTER key.
- With Windows 98, click the Start button on the taskbar and then click Run. Type `winipcfg` and then press the ENTER key.

If you are using an older version of AOL, the IP address might read 0.0.0.0 because AOL uses a proprietary method to assign IP addresses.

For more information about IP addresses, visit the Discovering Computers 2005 High-Tech Talk Web page (**scsite.com/dc2005/tech**) and click IP Addresses.

COMPANIES ON THE CUTTING EDGE

Yahoo!

Indexing the World Wide Web

One of the more popular sites on the World Wide Web has one of the more unusual names. *Yahoo!*, an online navigational guide, is visited by millions of people every day. Yahoo!'s cofounders, Jerry Yang and David Filo, claim they named their creation Yahoo! because they considered themselves two tough guys, or yahoos. For millions of grateful users, however, the name is the cry of joy they utter when Yahoo! guides them to an elusive Web site.

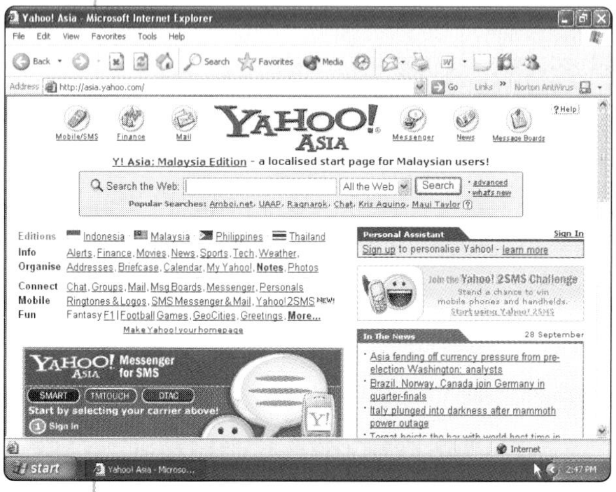

Yang and Filo started creating lists in 1994 at Stanford University to organize their favorite Web sites. Before they knew it, they had developed a tree-style database and a method of searching for specific Web pages. Yang maintained the lists on his student workstation, and Filo kept the search engine on his computer. The machines were dubbed "Akebono" and "Konishiki" in honor of two celebrated sumo wrestlers. Grappling with the Web went from part-time pursuit to full-time fixation. Yang and Filo shared their creation with thousands of information seekers and continued to add new categories and sites.

What makes Yahoo! unique is that people build the directory. Every Web site is visited and evaluated by a Yahoo! staff member. Site creators suggest the category under which a site belongs, but Yahoo! staff members ultimately decide where each site is placed by assuming the role of a typical user.

At Yahoo!, more than 237 million visitors access 1.62 billion pages daily, including the network's e-mail, chat rooms, shopping site, and personal Web pages. These services, which are supported by more advertisers than any other Web service, are free to users.

For more information about Yahoo!, visit the Discovering Computers 2005 Companies Web page (**scsite.com/dc2005/companies**) and click Yahoo!.

AOL

Interacting Anywhere

Meg Ryan and Tom Hanks fostered an online relationship in their hit movie, *You've Got Mail*. Worldwide, more than 34 million users likewise cultivate associations by using *America Online (AOL)*, a division of Time Warner, for their interactive requirements.

AOL's corporate mission is "to build a global medium as central to people's lives as the telephone or television …and even more valuable." With a strategy of AOL Anywhere, the company is the world's leading online service provider, with features such as e-mail, software, computer support services, and access to many other Internet services. Members use AOL more than 1 billion hours each month. Every day members send 390 million e-mail messages, seek 245 million stock quotes, and send 2.1 billion instant messages. At any given time, nearly 2.5 million users can be online simultaneously. AOL International operates in 17 countries and 8 different languages.

Stephen M. Case founded the company in 1985 as Quantum Computer Services Corporation with a vision of simplifying the Internet for people other than computer scholars and specialists. He partnered with a series of companies, including Commodore International, Ltd., Tandy Corporation, and Apple Computer. Case changed the company name to America Online in 1991.

AOL is renowned for providing a convenient and easy-to-use interactive service. The company pioneered technologies such as Keywords to simplify navigation and the Buddy List feature to enable instant messaging by displaying contacts who are online. Throughout the 1990s, AOL experienced tremendous growth, partly due to its aggressive marketing campaign using direct mail, membership kits, and magazine inserts. It acquired Netscape Communications in 1998 and, in a $172 billion pact, merged with Time Warner, one of the world's leading media conglomerates, in 2001.

For more information about America Online, visit the Discovering Computers 2005 Companies Web page (**scsite.com/dc2005/companies**) and click AOL.

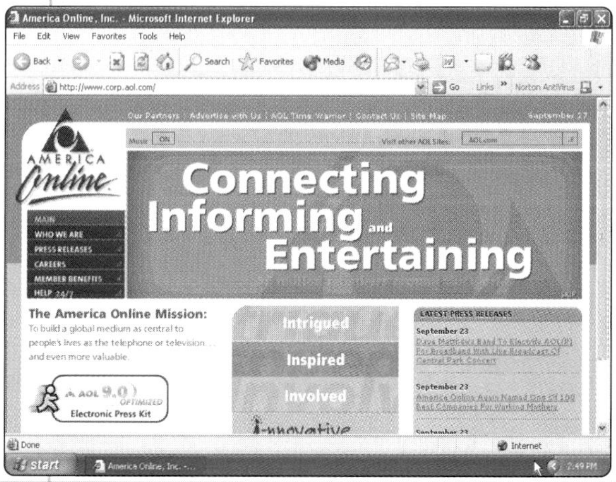

TECHNOLOGY TRAILBLAZERS

Tim Berners-Lee
Creator of the World Wide Web

WWW: three simple letters that have transformed the way people use computers and obtain information. Thanks to the innovation of *Tim Berners-Lee,* the World Wide Web has become the most popular service on the Internet. Many wonder why Berners-Lee refuses to step into the limelight to profit from his invention. In his words, commercializing his brainchild would suggest that people would be respecting him "as a function of [my] net worth. That's not an assumption I was brought up with."

Berners-Lee's parents, who met while working with one of the first commercially sold computers, instilled his values and sparked his interest in electronics and mathematics. After graduating from Queen's College at Oxford University with a degree in physics, Berners-Lee worked with various types of computer programs. He found that although computers could store and process information, "one of the things computers have not done… [is] store random associations between disparate things, although this is something the brain has always done relatively well." So, Berners-Lee developed a program called Enquire that stored both information and random associations in the form of links that pointed to related documents. Enquire's associations were limited, but Berners-Lee suggested a universal system using links that could point to any document — primitive or polished, personal or public, everyday or exotic. As a name for the project, the World Wide Web (WWW) was chosen as both descriptive and memorable. The World Wide Web debuted on the Internet in 1991, and its popularity exploded.

Today, Berners-Lee works quietly in academia as director of the World Wide Web Consortium (W3C) at the Massachusetts Institute of Technology. This organization consists of hundreds of representatives from the world's leading Internet companies, including IBM, Microsoft, and Hewlett-Packard. W3C considers issues in the Web's evolution and hopes to realize the Web's full potential and ensure its reliability.

For more information about Tim Berners-Lee, visit the Discovering Computers 2005 People Web page (**scsite.com/dc2005/people**) and click Tim Berners-Lee.

Anita Brown
Miss DC

She is known affectionately as Miss DC among the Internet community. As founder and chair of the Washington, D.C.-based Black Geeks Online, *Anita Brown* is guiding online participation among the African-American community.

Black Geeks Online is not just a Web site. "We are a network that HAS a website." Brown writes that, "Our objective has been to connect people of color from around the world — both on and off-line — to share our talents and time to make others aware of the potential and pitfalls of information technology."

Originally having 18 members in 1995, today more than 30,000 technical professionals, teachers, students, parents, and community leaders belong to Anita Brown's nonprofit virtual community. These volunteers impart their talents by educating others about the Internet, promoting computer literacy, and providing information regarding professional opportunities in the information technology field.

For more than 30 years, Brown has been developing a variety of businesses, including running a desktop publishing service and a T-shirt company and managing a help desk on America Online. She uses her experiences to tap resources and bring computers and professionals into the city's neighborhoods. At AOL, Brown served as "SistahGeek," translating confusing terms into language people could understand and supporting African-Americans, especially women, who were cautious of or puzzled by the growth of information technology.

Brown's honors include being named one of the 50 Most Important African-Americans in Technology and voted one of the Top 25 Women on the Web by the San Francisco Women on the Web. THE CONDUIT *the definitive technological guide for the African in America* voted Black Geeks Online seventh on its list of Top 20 Black Tech Companies.

For more information about Anita Brown, visit the Discovering Computers 2005 People Web page (**scsite.com/dc2005/people**) and click Anita Brown.

CHAPTER 2 CHAPTER REVIEW

Previous | Next

The Chapter Review section summarizes the concepts presented in this chapter.

QUIZZES AND LEARNING GAMES
Computer Genius
Crossword Puzzle
Interactive Labs
Practice Test
Quiz Yourself
Wheel of Terms

EXERCISES
Chapter Review
Checkpoint
Key Terms
Lab Exercises
Learn It Online
Web Research

BEYOND THE BOOK
Apply It
Career Corner
Companies
FAQ
High-Tech Talk
Issues
Looking Ahead
Trailblazers
Web Links

FEATURES
Guide to Web Sites
Making Use of the Web
Tech News
Timeline 2005

WEB INSTRUCTIONS:

To display this page from the Web, start your browser and enter the Web address **scsite.com/dc2005/ch2/review**. Click the links for current and additional information. To listen to an audio version of this Chapter Review, click the Audio button.

1 What Is the History of the Internet?

The **Internet** is a worldwide collection of networks that links millions of businesses, government agencies, educational institutions, and individuals. The Internet has its roots in *ARPANET*, a network started in 1969 by an agency of the U.S. Department of Defense to link scientific and academic researchers across the United States. In 1986, the National Science Foundation (NSF) connected its huge network, called *NSFnet*, to ARPANET, creating a configuration of complex networks and hosts that became known as the Internet. Today, the Internet consists of many local, regional, national, and international networks.

2 How Can You Access and Connect to the Internet?

Employees and students often connect to the Internet through a business or school network. The networks usually use a high-speed line leased from a local telephone company to connect to an access provider. Many home and small businesses connect to the Internet with **dial-up access**, which uses a modem in the computer and a standard telephone line. Some home and small business users opt for higher-speed connections, such as DSL, ISDN, or cable television Internet services. **DSL** and **ISDN** are technologies that provide Internet connections using regular copper telephone lines. A **cable modem** provides high-speed Internet connections through the cable television network. An **access provider** is a business that provides access to the Internet free or for a fee. An **ISP** (**Internet service provider**) is a regional or national access provider. An **online service provider** (**OSP**) provides Internet access in addition to members-only features. A **wireless Internet service provider** (*WISP*) is a company that provides wireless Internet access to users with wireless modems or Web-enabled mobile devices.

3 What Is an IP Address?

An **IP address** (*Internet Protocol address*) is a number that uniquely identifies each computer or device connected to the Internet. The Internet relies on IP addresses to send data to computers at specific locations. A **domain name** is the text version of an IP address. As with an IP address, the components of a domain name are separated by periods. A **DNS** (*domain name system*) **server** translates a domain name into its associated IP address so data can route to the correct computer.

Visit **scsite.com/dc2005/quiz** or click the Quiz Yourself button. Click Objectives 1 – 3 below Chapter 2.

4 What Are the Components of a Web Address?

The **World Wide Web** (*WWW*), or **Web**, consists of a worldwide collection of electronic documents. Each document is called a **Web page**. A **Web address**, or **URL** (*Uniform Resource Locator*), is a unique address for a Web page. A Web address consists of a protocol that defines how the page transfers on the Web, a domain name, and sometimes the path to a specific Web page or location on a Web page and the Web page name.

5 What Is the Purpose of a Web Browser?

A **Web browser**, or **browser**, is application software that allows users to access and view Web pages. When you type a Web address in the Address box at the top of the browser window, a computer called a **Web server** delivers the requested Web page to your computer. Most Web pages contain links. A **link** is a built-in connection to a related Web page or part of a Web page.

6 How Can You Search for Information on the Web?

A **search engine** is a program that finds Web pages and Web sites. A **Web site** is a collection of related Web pages and associated items. To display a search engine, enter the search engine Web address into your Web browser. From the search engine, enter a word or phrase, called **search text**, or *keywords*, in the search engine's text box. The search engine displays a list of *hits*, or Web page names, that contain the search text. Click the desired link to display the Web page.

7 What Are the Types of Web Sites?

A **portal** is a Web site that offers a variety of Internet services from a single location. A news Web site contains newsworthy material. An informational Web site contains factual information. A business/marketing Web site contains content that promotes or sells products or services. An educational Web site offers avenues for formal and informal teaching and learning. An entertainment Web site offers an interactive and engaging environment. An advocacy Web site contains content that describes a cause, opinion, or idea. A personal Web site is maintained by a private individual or family.

8 How Do Web Pages Use Graphics, Animation, Audio, Video, Virtual Reality, and Plug-Ins?

Some Web pages use **multimedia**, which combines text with graphics, animation, audio, video, and/or virtual reality. A **graphic** is a digital representation of nontext information such as a drawing, chart, or photograph. **Animation** is the appearance of motion created by displaying a series of still images in sequence. **Audio** includes music, speech, or any other sound. **Video** consists of full-motion images that are played back at various speeds. **Virtual reality** (**VR**) is the use of computers to simulate a real or imagined environment that appears as three-dimensional space.

9 What Are the Types of E-Commerce?

E-commerce, short for *electronic commerce*, is a business transaction that occurs over an electronic network such as the Internet. *Business-to-consumer (B2C) e-commerce* consists of the sale of goods and services to the general public. *Consumer-to-consumer* (C2C) *e-commerce* occurs when one consumer sells directly to another, such as an online auction. *Business-to-business* (B2B) *e-commerce*, which is the most common form of e-commerce, takes place between businesses that exchange goods and services.

Visit **scsite.com/dc2005/quiz** or click the Quiz Yourself button. Click Objectives 4 – 9 below Chapter 2.

10 How Do E-Mail, FTP, Newsgroups and Message Boards, Mailing Lists, Chat Rooms, and Instant Messaging Work?

E-mail (short for *electronic mail*) is the transmission of messages and files via a computer network. **FTP** (*File Transfer Protocol*) is an Internet standard that permits file uploading and downloading with other computers on the Internet. A **newsgroup** is an online area in which users have written about a particular subject. A **message board** is a popular Web-based type of discussion group that is easier to use than a newsgroup. A **mailing list** is a group of e-mail names and addresses given a single name, so that everyone on the list receives a message sent to the list. A **chat room** is a location on an Internet server that permits users to **chat**, or conduct real-time typed conversations. **Instant messaging** (**IM**) is a real-time Internet communications service that notifies you when one or more people are online.

11 What Are the Rules of Netiquette?

Netiquette, which is short for Internet etiquette, is the code of acceptable behaviors users should follow while on the Internet. Keep messages short. Be polite. Read the FAQ if one exists. Do not assume material is accurate or up-to-date, and never read someone's private e-mail.

12 What Are the Steps and Tools Required for Web Publishing?

Web publishing is the development and maintenance of Web pages. The five major steps to Web publishing are: (1) plan a Web site, (2) analyze and design a Web site, (3) create a Web site, (4) deploy a Web site, and (5) maintain a Web site. You can use *Web page authoring software* to create sophisticated Web pages with special effects. A **Webmaster** or Web developer maintains a Web site using software products.

Visit **scsite.com/dc2005/quiz** or click the Quiz Yourself button. Click Objectives 10 – 12 below Chapter 2.

CHAPTER 2 KEY TERMS

QUIZZES AND LEARNING GAMES

Computer Genius

Crossword Puzzle

Interactive Labs

Practice Test

Quiz Yourself

Wheel of Terms

EXERCISES

Chapter Review

Checkpoint

Key Terms

Lab Exercises

Learn It Online

Web Research

BEYOND THE BOOK

Apply It

Career Corner

Companies

FAQ

High-Tech Talk

Issues

Looking Ahead

Trailblazers

Web Links

FEATURES

Guide to Web Sites

Making Use of the Web

Tech News

Timeline 2005

You should know the Primary Terms and be familiar with the Secondary Terms.

WEB INSTRUCTIONS:

To display this page from the Web, start your browser and enter the Web address **scsite.com/dc2005/ch2/terms**. Click a term to display its definition and a picture. When the picture appears, click the more info button for current and additional information about the term from the Web.

>> Primary Terms

(shown in bold-black characters in the chapter)

access provider (71)
address book (93)
animation (85)
audio (86)
browser (75)
cable modem (71)
chat (98)
chat room (98)
dial-up access (71)
domain name (74)
downloading (76)
DSL (71)
e-commerce (90)
e-mail (91)
e-mail address (93)
e-mail program (92)
electronic storefront (90)
emoticons (100)
FTP (95)
graphic (84)
home page (76)
instant messaging (IM) (98)
Internet (68)
IP address (74)
ISDN (71)
ISP (Internet service provider) (72)
link (77)
mailing list (97)
message board (96)
MP3 (86)
multimedia (83)
netiquette (100)
newsgroup (95)
online auction (91)
online service provider (OSP) (72)
player (87)
plug-in (89)
portal (82)
real time (98)
search engine (78)
search text (79)
shopping cart (90)
streaming (87)
subject directory (80)
subscribe (mailing list) **(97)**
surfing the Web (78)
thumbnail (85)
traffic (69)
unsubscribe (97)
uploading (95)
URL (76)
user name (93)
video (88)
virtual reality (VR) (88)
Web (75)
Web address (76)
Web browser (75)
Web community (82)
Web page (75)
Web publishing (100)
Web server (77)
Web site (75)
Webmaster (102)
wireless Internet service provider (72)
World Wide Web (75)

>> Secondary Terms

(shown in italic characters in the chapter)

Advanced Research Projects Agency (ARPA) (68)
animated GIF (86)
anonymous FTP (95)
ARPANET (69)
articles (96)
buddies (99)
business-to-business (B2B) e-commerce (91)
business-to-consumer (B2C) e-commerce (90)
chat client (98)
click (78)
consumer-to-consumer (C2C) e-commerce (91)
digital subscriber line (71)
DNS server (74)
domain name system (DNS) (74)
dot-com (74)
electronic commerce (90)
electronic mail (91)
FAQ (100)
File Transfer Protocol (95)
flame wars (100)
flames (100)
FTP server (95)
GIF (85)
graphical image (84)
hits (79)
host (69)
http (77)
hyperlink (77)
Hypertext Transfer Protocol (77)
instant messenger (99)
Integrated Services Digital Network (71)
Internet backbone (73)
Internet Corporation for Assigned Names and Numbers (ICANN) (74)
Internet Protocol address (74)
Internet2 (70)
JPEG (84)
keywords (79)
LISTSERVs (97)
m-commerce (90)
microbrowser (76)
moderated newsgroup (96)
moderator (96)
Moving Pictures Experts Group (MPEG) (88)
MPEG-4 (88)
national ISP (72)
Net (68)
newsreader (96)
news server (95)
NSFnet (69)
PNG format (85)
point of presence (POP) (71)
POP3 (93)
post (96)
Post Office Protocol (93)
pull (77)
push (77)
regional ISP (72)
SMTP (simple mail transfer protocol) (93)
spam (100)
spider (80)
spoiler (100)
streaming audio (87)
streaming video (88)
submission service (102)
subscribe (newsgroup) *(96)*
thread (96)
threaded discussion (96)
top-level domain (74)
Uniform Resource Locator (76)
Usenet (95)
VR world (88)
Web hosting services (102)
Web page authoring (100)
Web page authoring software (100)
wireless portal (82)
World Wide Web Consortium (W3C) (70)
WISP (72)
WWW (75)

CHECKPOINT CHAPTER 2

Use the Checkpoint exercises to check your knowledge level of the chapter.

WEB INSTRUCTIONS:

To display this page from the Web, start your browser and enter the Web address **scsite.com/dc2005/ch2/check**. Click the links for current and additional information.

LABEL THE FIGURE

Identify each part of the Web address and e-mail address.

a. domain name
b. path
c. protocol
d. user name
e. Web page name
f. domain name

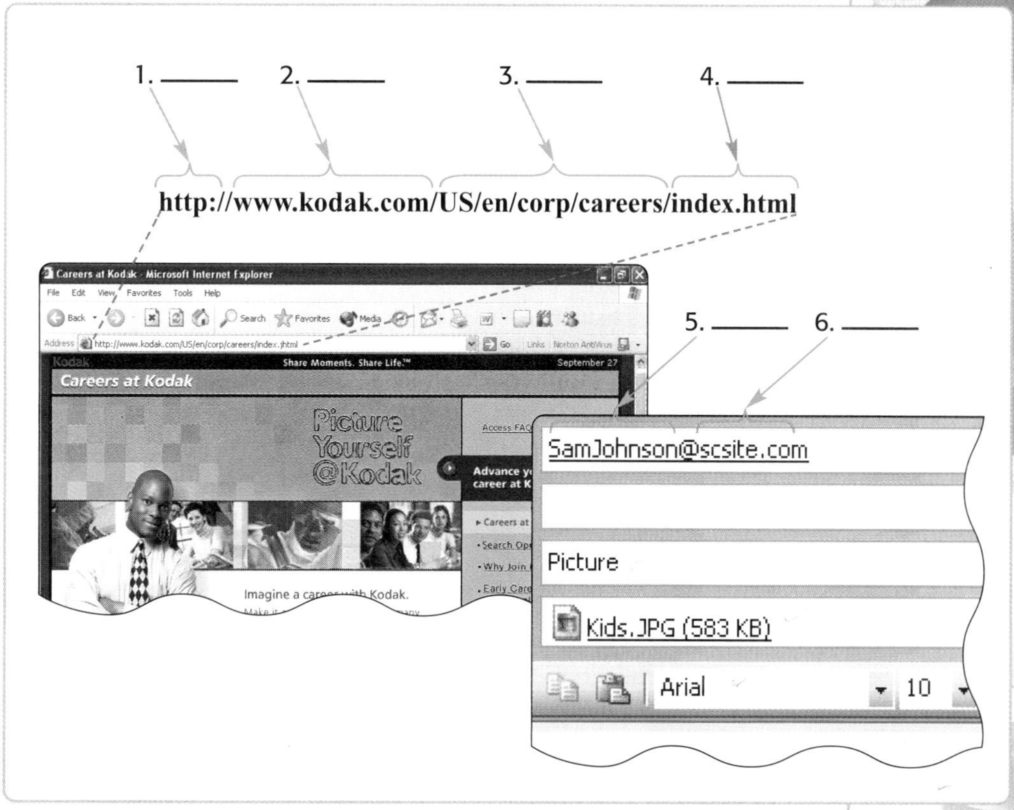

TRUE/FALSE

Mark T for True and F for False. (See page numbers in parentheses.)

T 1. The focus of Internet2 is to improve on the inefficiencies of the Internet, such as relieving bottlenecks in the current architecture. (70)

F 2. An access provider is a business that provides access to the Internet for a fee. (71)

T 3. The components of a domain name are separated by periods. (74)

F 4. Each electronic document on the Web is called a Web site. (75) web page

F 5. Downloading is the process of sending (receiving) information to a server on the Internet. (76)

T 6. A search engine is a software program that finds Web sites and Web pages. (78)

? F 7. A news Web site contains content that promotes or sells products or services. (82)

T 8. Streaming is the process of transferring data in a continuous and even flow. (87)

F 9. Consumer-to-consumer (C2C) e-commerce consists of the sale of goods and services to the general public. (91)

F 10. A chat room is a group of e-mail names and addresses given a single name. (98)

CHAPTER 2 CHECKPOINT

Previous | Next

QUIZZES AND LEARNING GAMES
Computer Genius
Crossword Puzzle
Interactive Labs
Practice Test
Quiz Yourself
Wheel of Terms

EXERCISES
Chapter Review
Checkpoint
Key Terms
Lab Exercises
Learn It Online
Web Research

BEYOND THE BOOK
Apply It
Career Corner
Companies
FAQ
High-Tech Talk
Issues
Looking Ahead
Trailblazers
Web Links

FEATURES
Guide to Web Sites
Making Use of the Web
Tech News
Timeline 2005

MULTIPLE CHOICE

Select the best answer. (See page numbers in parentheses.)

1. ______ oversees research and sets standards and guidelines for many areas of the Internet. (70)
   a. The World Wide Web Consortium (W3C)
   b. Internet2
   c. The National Science Foundation (NSF)
   d. The Advanced Research Projects Agency (ARPA)
2. As an alternative to dial-up access, some home and small business users are opting for a higher-speed connection such as _____. (71)
   a. DSL (digital subscriber line)
   b. ISDN (Integrated Services Digital Network)
   c. cable television Internet services
   d. all of the above
3. An IP address usually consists of ______. (74)
   a. two groups of numbers separated by commas
   b. two groups of numbers separated by periods
   c. four groups of numbers separated by commas
   d. four groups of numbers separated by periods
4. Web-enabled mobile devices use a ______, which is designed for small screens and limited computing power. (76)
   a. unibrowser
   b. microbrowser
   c. demibrowser
   d. minibrowser
5. Many Web addresses begin with http, which is the ______. (77)
   a. path
   b. domain name
   c. protocol
   d. page name
6. On the Web, a _____ classifies Web pages into an organized set of categories. (80)
   a. home page
   b. mailing list
   c. subject directory
   d. message board
7. Many ______ have Web communities that join a specific group of people with similar interests or relationships. (82)
   a. portals
   b. news Web sites
   c. informational Web sites
   d. entertainment Web sites
8. The purpose of an advocacy Web site is to ______. (83)
   a. present newsworthy material related to current events
   b. contain factual information of public interest
   c. promote or sell products or services
   d. convince the reader of the validity of the cause, opinion, or idea
9. The _____ format, which reduces the size of graphic files, improves on the GIF format and is expected eventually to replace it. (85)
   a. PCX
   b. BMP
   c. PNG
   d. all of the above
10. In ______ e-commerce, a customer visits an online business through an electronic storefront. (90)
    a. consumer-to-consumer
    b. business-to-business
    c. consumer-to-business
    d. business-to-consumer
11. A computer that stores and distributes newsgroup messages is called a(n) ______. (95)
    a. news server
    b. moderator
    c. newsreader
    d. article
12. In a newsgroup, a thread or threaded discussion consists of the original article and all ______. (96)
    a. previous related antecedents
    b. previous unrelated antecedents
    c. subsequent related replies
    d. subsequent unrelated replies
13. ______ is a rule of netiquette. (100)
    a. Use all capital letters
    b. Avoid offensive language
    c. Participate in flame wars
    d. Assume material is accurate
14. Web page authoring involves _____. (100)
    a. registering a Web site with search engines
    b. building a list of words on a Web site
    c. working on a computer to compose a Web site
    d. delivering requested Web pages to a computer

CHECKPOINT CHAPTER 2

MATCHING
Match the terms with their definitions. (See page numbers in parentheses.)

a 1. traffic (69)
f 2. home page (76)
h 3. downloading (76)
J 4. thumbnail (85)
b 5. player (87)
d 6. streaming (87)
g 7. shopping cart (90)
K 8. e-mail program (92)
C 9. e-mail address (93)
L 10. uploading (95)

a. communications activity on the Internet
b. special software needed to listen to an audio file on a computer
c. combination of a user name and a domain name that identifies an Internet user
d. process of transferring data in a continuous and even flow
e. built-in connection to a related Web page or part of a Web page
f. first page that a Web site displays
g. allows an e-commerce customer to collect purchases
h. process of a computer receiving information from a server on the Internet
i. software that extends the multimedia capabilities of a browser
j. small version of a larger graphic
k. software used to create, send, receive, forward, store, print, and delete e-mail messages
l. process of transferring documents, graphics, and other objects from your computer to an Internet server

SHORT ANSWER
Write a brief answer to each of the following questions.

1. How is a regional ISP different from a national ISP? __________ How are an ISP, OSP, and WISP different? __________
2. How is a Web page different from a Web site? __________ How can you use a Web address to display a Web page? __________
3. What is a search engine? __________ How can you reduce the number of hits a search engine returns? __________
4. What is an FTP server? __________ What is anonymous FTP? __________
5. What happens when you subscribe to, or unsubscribe from, a mailing list? __________ How can you locate a mailing list about a particular topic? __________

WORKING TOGETHER
Working with a group of your classmates, complete the following team exercises.

1. This chapter lists eight types of Web sites: portal, news, informational, business/marketing, educational, entertainment, advocacy, and personal. Working as a team, use the Internet to find at least two examples of each type of Web site. For each Web site, identify the Web address, the multimedia elements used, the purpose of the Web site, and the type of Web site. Explain why you classified each site as you did. Then, keeping in mind the purpose of each Web site, rank the sites in terms of their effectiveness. Share your findings in a report and/or a PowerPoint presentation with the class.

2. Choose one Issue from the following issues in this chapter: Who Controls the Internet? (70), Can You Learn It Online? (82), To Tax or Not to Tax Internet Purchases? (91), or How Expensive Is E-Mail and Internet Privacy? (91). Use the Web and/or print media to research the issue. Then, present a debate for the class, with different members of your team supporting different responses to the questions that accompany the issue.

3. The Internet has had a tremendous impact on business. For some businesses, that influence has not been positive. For example, surveys suggest that as a growing number of people make their own travel plans online, travel agents are seeing fewer customers. Have each member of your team interview a businessperson who is or has been affected negatively by the Internet. What effect has the Internet had? How has the Internet changed business in positive ways? How can the business compete with the Internet? Meet with your team to discuss the results of your interviews. Create a group PowerPoint presentation and share your findings with the class.

LEARN IT ONLINE

QUIZZES AND LEARNING GAMES
Computer Genius
Crossword Puzzle
Interactive Labs
Practice Test
Quiz Yourself
Wheel of Terms
EXERCISES
Chapter Review
Checkpoint
Key Terms
Lab Exercises
Learn It Online
Web Research
BEYOND THE BOOK
Apply It
Career Corner
Companies
FAQ
High-Tech Talk
Issues
Looking Ahead
Trailblazers
Web Links
FEATURES
Guide to Web Sites
Making Use of the Web
Tech News
Timeline 2005

Use the Learn It Online exercises to reinforce your understanding of the chapter concepts.

WEB INSTRUCTIONS:

To display this page from the Web, start your browser and enter the Web address **scsite.com/dc2005/ch2/learn**.

1 At the Movies – Small Town Tech

To view the Small Town Tech movie, click the number 1 button. Hartwell, Georgia, population 5,000, is the test-site for a new technology delivering telephone service, high-speed Internet access, and cable television all through existing telephone lines. Today, most telephone companies also provide DSL high-speed Internet access, but not television signals. Cable TV companies also provide high-speed access, but not phone service. The technology being tested in Hartwell can provide all three services together (a process called convergence) over one, standard telephone line. If you were an investor in this new technology, would you be wary of cellular and "wireless" technologies? Why or why not? Can you name three types of businesses that would benefit greatly from this technology convergence?

2 Student Edition Labs – Connecting to the Internet

Click the number 2 button. When the Student Edition Labs menu appears, click *Connecting to the Internet* to begin. A new browser window will open. Follow the on-screen instructions to complete the Lab. When finished, click the Exit button. If required, print a copy of your results to submit to your instructor.

3 Student Edition Labs – Getting the Most Out of the Internet

Click the number 3 button. When the Student Edition Labs menu appears, click *Getting the Most Out of the Internet* to begin. A new browser window will open. Follow the on-screen instructions to complete the Lab. When finished, click the Exit button. If required, print a copy of your results to submit to your instructor.

4 Student Edition Labs – E-mail

Click the number 4 button. When the Student Edition Labs menu appears, click *E-mail* to begin. A new browser window will open. Follow the on-screen instructions to complete the Lab. When finished, click the Exit button. If required, print a copy of your results to submit to your instructor.

5 Practice Test

Click the number 5 button. Answer each question. When completed, enter your name and click the Grade Test button to submit the quiz for grading. Make a note of any missed questions. If required, print a copy to submit to your instructor.

6 Web Guide

Click the number 6 button to display the Guide to Web Sites and Searching Techniques Web page. Click Reference and then click AskERIC. Click ERIC Database and search for Internet History. Click the search results link of your choice. Use your word processing program to prepare a brief report about what you learned and submit your assignment to your instructor.

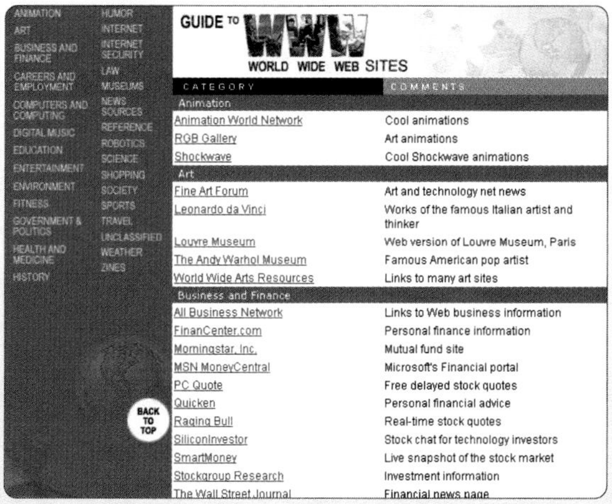

7 Scavenger Hunt

Click the number 7 button. Print a copy of the Scavenger Hunt page; use this page to write down your answers as you search the Web. Submit your completed page to your instructor.

8 Who Wants To Be a Computer Genius?

Click the number 8 button to find out if you are a computer genius. Directions on how to play the game will be displayed. When you are ready to play, click the Play button. Submit your score to your instructor.

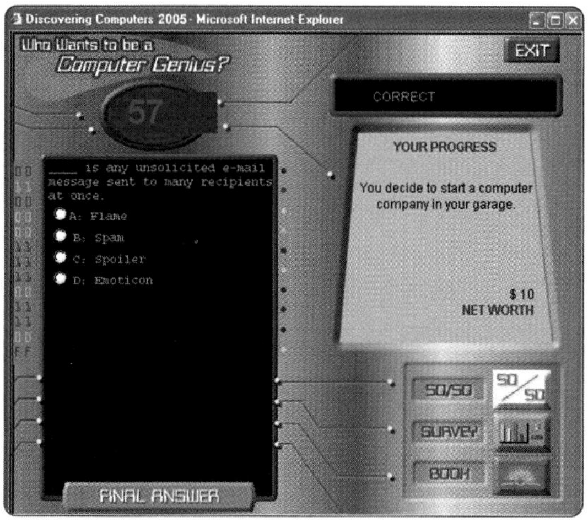

9 Wheel of Terms

Click the number 9 button to reinforce important terms you learned in this chapter by playing the Shelly Cashman Series version of this popular game. Directions on how to play the game will be displayed. When you are ready to play, click the Play button. Submit your score to your instructor.

10 Career Corner

Click the number 10 button to display the Quintessential Careers page. Search for jobs in your state. Write a brief report about the jobs you found. Submit the report to your instructor.

11 Search Sleuth

Click the number 11 button to learn search techniques that will help make you a research expert. Submit the completed assignment to your instructor.

12 Crossword Puzzle Challenge

Click the number 12 button. Complete the puzzle to reinforce skills you learned in this chapter. Directions on how to play the game will be displayed. When you are ready to play, click the Submit button. Submit the completed puzzle to your instructor.

13 Internet Newsgroups

One of the more popular topics for Internet newsgroups is the Internet. Click the number 13 button for a list of newsgroups. Find one or more newsgroups that discuss something about the Internet. Read the newsgroup postings and briefly summarize the topic under discussion. If you like, post a reply to a message.

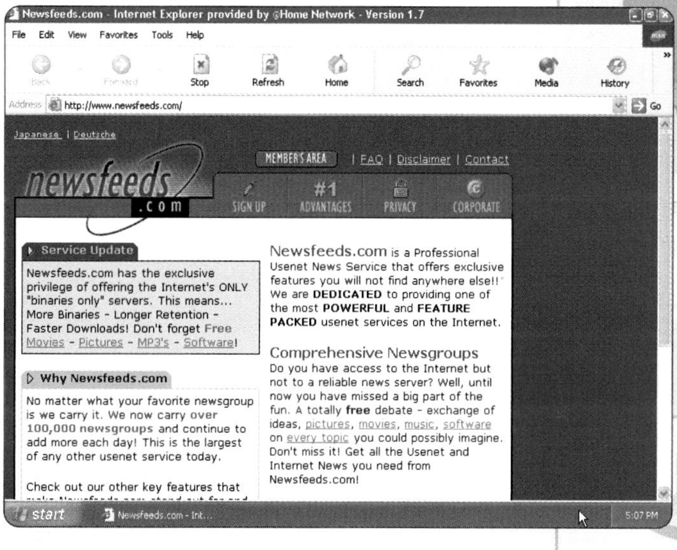

14 In the News

In her book, *Caught in the Net*, Kimberly S. Young contends that the Internet can be addictive. Young's methodology and conclusions have been questioned by several critics, but Young remains resolute. She points out that at one time, no one admitted to the existence of alcoholism. Click the number 14 button and read a news article about the impact of Internet use on human behavior. What effect did the Internet have? Why? In your opinion, is the Internet's influence positive or negative? Why?

CHAPTER 2 LAB EXERCISES

QUIZZES AND LEARNING GAMES
Computer Genius
Crossword Puzzle
Interactive Labs
Practice Test
Quiz Yourself
Wheel of Terms
EXERCISES
Chapter Review
Checkpoint
Key Terms
Lab Exercises
Learn It Online
Web Research
BEYOND THE BOOK
Apply It
Career Corner
Companies
FAQ
High-Tech Talk
Issues
Looking Ahead
Trailblazers
Web Links
FEATURES
Guide to Web Sites
Making Use of the Web
Tech News
Timeline 2005

Use the Lab Exercises to gain hands-on computer experience.

WEB INSTRUCTIONS:

To display this page from the Web, start your browser and enter the Web address **scsite.com/dc2005/ch2/lab**.

1 Online Services

This exercise uses Windows XP procedures. Right-click the Online Services icon on the desktop and then click Open on the shortcut menu. If the Online Services icon does not exist on your desktop, locate it by clicking the Search command on the Start menu. Click the All files and folders link. Type `Online Services` in the All or part of the file name text box. Click the Search button and then click the Stop button when Online Services is displayed in the Search window. What online services have shortcut icons in the Online Services window? Right-click each icon and then click Properties on each shortcut menu. Click the General tab. When was each icon created? Close the dialog box and then click the Close button to close the Online Services window and, if necessary, the Search Results window.

2 Understanding Internet Properties

This exercise uses Windows XP/2000/98 procedures. Right-click an icon for a Web browser that is displayed on your desktop. Click Properties on the shortcut menu. When the Internet Properties dialog box or Netscape Properties dialog box is displayed, if necessary, click the General tab. Click the Question Mark button on the title bar and then click one of the buttons. Read the information in the pop-up window and then click the pop-up window to close it. Repeat the process for other areas of the dialog box. What new information did you learn? Click the Cancel button in the Internet Properties or Netscape Properties dialog box.

3 Dial-Up Networking Connections

This exercise uses Windows XP procedures. Click the Start button on the Windows taskbar and then click Help and Support on the Start menu. Click the Networking and the Web link in the Pick a Help topic area in the table of contents. In the Help navigation pane on the left, click Networking, and then click Dial-up connections. In the Help topics pane on the right, click Make a dial-up connection to your workplace using a phone line. What steps are necessary to make a dial-up connection by phone line? Click the Network Connections link. What topics are listed in the Network Tasks area? Close the Network Connections window. Close the Help and Support Center window.

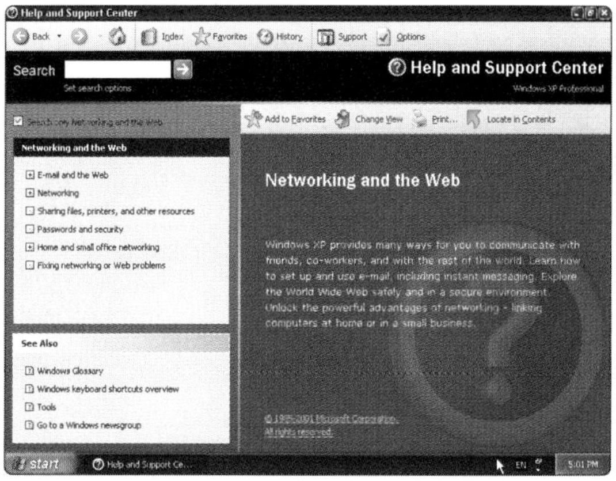

4 Using Help to Understand the Internet

This exercise uses Windows 2000/98 procedures. Click the Start button on the Windows taskbar and then click Help on the Start menu. Click the Contents tab. Click the Exploring the Internet book and then click the Explore the Internet topic. Click the Click here link to find out more about Internet Explorer. Answer the following questions:

- How can you update your favorite Web sites and view them at your leisure?
- How can you move around the Web faster and easier with the Explorer bar?
- How can you browse the Web safely?
- How can you view Web pages in other languages?

Close the Microsoft Internet Explorer Help window and the Windows Help window.

WEB RESEARCH

CHAPTER 2

Use the Web Research exercises to learn more about the special features in this chapter.

WEB INSTRUCTIONS:

Use the link in each exercise or a search engine such as Google (google.com) to research the topic. Then, write a one-page, double-spaced report or create a presentation, unless otherwise directed below. Page numbers on which information can be found are in parentheses.

1 **Issue** Choose one Issue from the following issues in this chapter: Who Controls the Internet? (70), Can You Learn It Online? (82), To Tax or Not to Tax Internet Purchases? (91), or How Expensive Is E-Mail and Internet Privacy? (91). Use the Web to research the issue. Discuss the issue with classmates, instructors, and friends. Address the questions that accompany the issue in a report or presentation.

2 **Apply It** Choose one of the following Apply It features in this chapter: Connect to the Internet (71) or Send Voice Messages Via the Internet (98). Use the Web to gather additional information about the topic. Print two Web pages that relate to the Apply It. Detail in a report or presentation what you learned.

3 **Career Corner** Read the Career Corner article in this chapter (102). Use the Web to find out more about the career. Describe the career in a report or presentation.

4 **Companies on the Cutting Edge** Choose one of the Companies on the Cutting Edge in this chapter (104). Use the Web to research the company further. Explain in a report or presentation how this company has contributed to computer technology.

5 **Technology Trailblazers** Choose one of the Technology Trailblazers in this chapter (105). Use the Web to research the person further. Explain in a report or presentation how this individual has affected the way people use, or think about, computers.

6 **Picture Yourself Publishing on the Web** Read the Picture Yourself Publishing on the Web story at the beginning of this chapter (66). Use the Web to research publishing further. Describe in a report or presentation the ways in which you might publish on the Web.

7 **High-Tech Talk** Read the High-Tech Talk feature in this chapter (103). Use the Web to find out more about the topic. Summarize in a report or presentation what you learned.

8 **Web Links** Review the Web Link boxes found in the margins of this chapter. Visit five of the Web Link sites. Print the main Web page for each site you visit. Choose one of the Web pages and then summarize in one paragraph the content of the Web page.

9 **Looking Ahead** Choose one of the Looking Ahead articles in this chapter: Shop Until Your Mouse Drops (80) or Driving Down the Web Highway (84). Use the Web to find out more about the topic. Detail in a report or presentation what you learned.

10 **FAQ** Choose one FAQ found in this chapter. Use the Web to find out more about the topic. Summarize in one paragraph what you learned.

11 **Searching the Web** Read the Guide to Web Sites and Searching Techniques Special Feature that follows this chapter (116–129). Select at least two sites from the list of popular Web sites and use the location given to visit the site. Use the searching techniques presented to locate and visit at least two additional Web sites about a topic of interest. Describe in a report or presentation each Web site you visited and the searching techniques you used.

12 **Making Use of the Web** Read the Travel section of Making Use of the Web in Appendix A (APP 4). Complete the Travel Web Exercises at the end of the section (APP 5). Answer the questions posed in each exercise.

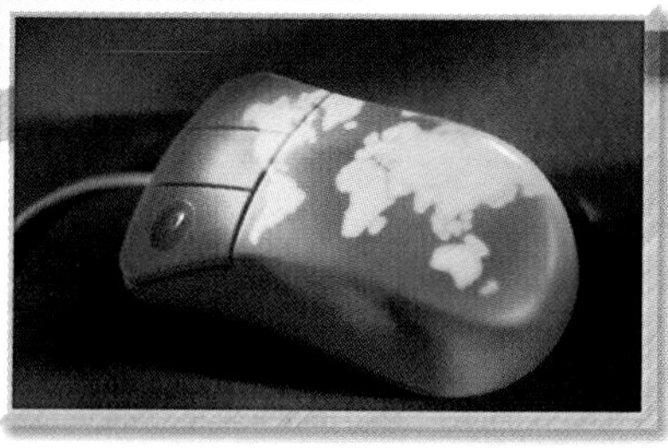

CATEGORY/SITE NAME	LOCATION	COMMENT
Computers and Computing		
Computer companies	Insert name or initials of most computer companies before .com to find their Web sites. Examples: ibm.com, microsoft.com, dell.com	
Computer History Museum	computerhistory.org	Exhibits and history of computing
Expertcity	expertcity.com	Live experts offer technical support
Internet.com	internet.com	E-business and technology network
MIT Media Lab	www.media.mit.edu	Information on computer trends
The Apple Museum	theapplemuseum.com	The history of the Apple computer
The PC Guide	pcguide.com	PC reference information
The Virtual Museum of Computing	vlmp.museophile.com/computing	History of computing and online computer-based exhibits
Virtual Computer Library	www.utexas.edu/computer/vcl	Information on computers and computing
ZDNet	zdnet.com	Downloads and product reviews
Digital Music		
Digital Music Network	www.dmn.com/	Free plug-in to leading media players
MP3.com	mp3.com	Music files
Sonique	sonique.com	MP3 player and media products
This American Life	thislife.org	Public radio program
Directories		
555-1212.com	555-1212.com	Online directory information service
InfoSpace	infospace.com	Directory and search engine
SuperPages.com	superpages.com	Verizon Information Services
Switchboard.com	switchboard.com	Variety of directories
WhoWhere?	whowhere.lycos.com	Lycos directory
Yahoo! People Search	people.yahoo.com	Yahoo! directory
Education		
CollegeNET	www.collegenet.com	Searchable database of thousands of colleges and universities
EdLinks	webpages.marshall.edu/~jmullens/edlinks.html	Links to many educational Web sites
The Open University	www.open.ac.uk	Independent study courses from the U.K.
UMUC Distance Education	umuc.edu/distance	University of Maryland distance education
WiredScholar	www.wiredscholar.com	Information on financing an education

*For an updated list: **scsite.com/dc2005/ch2/websites***

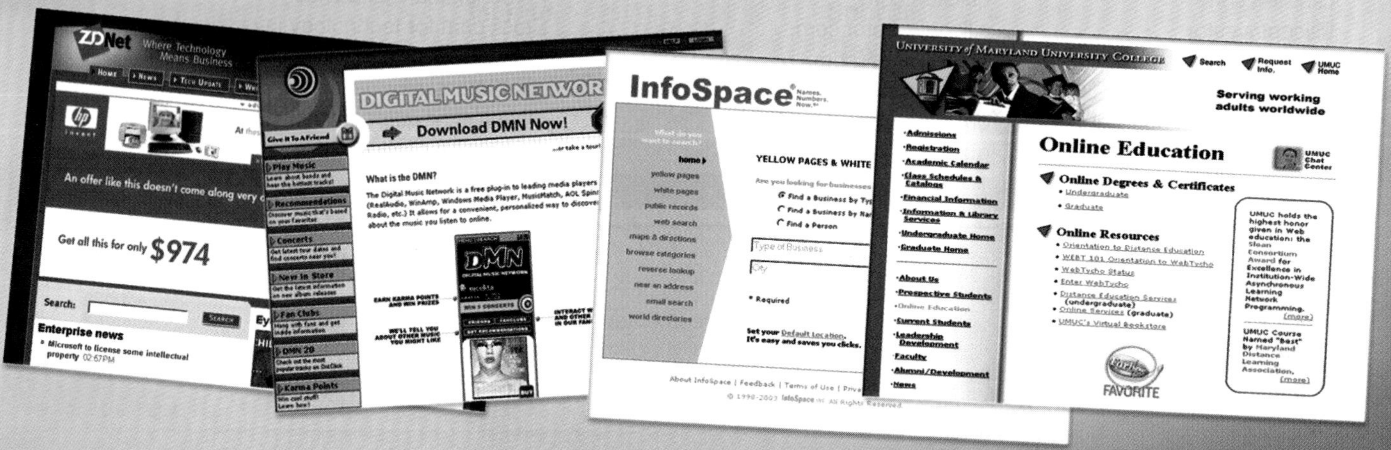

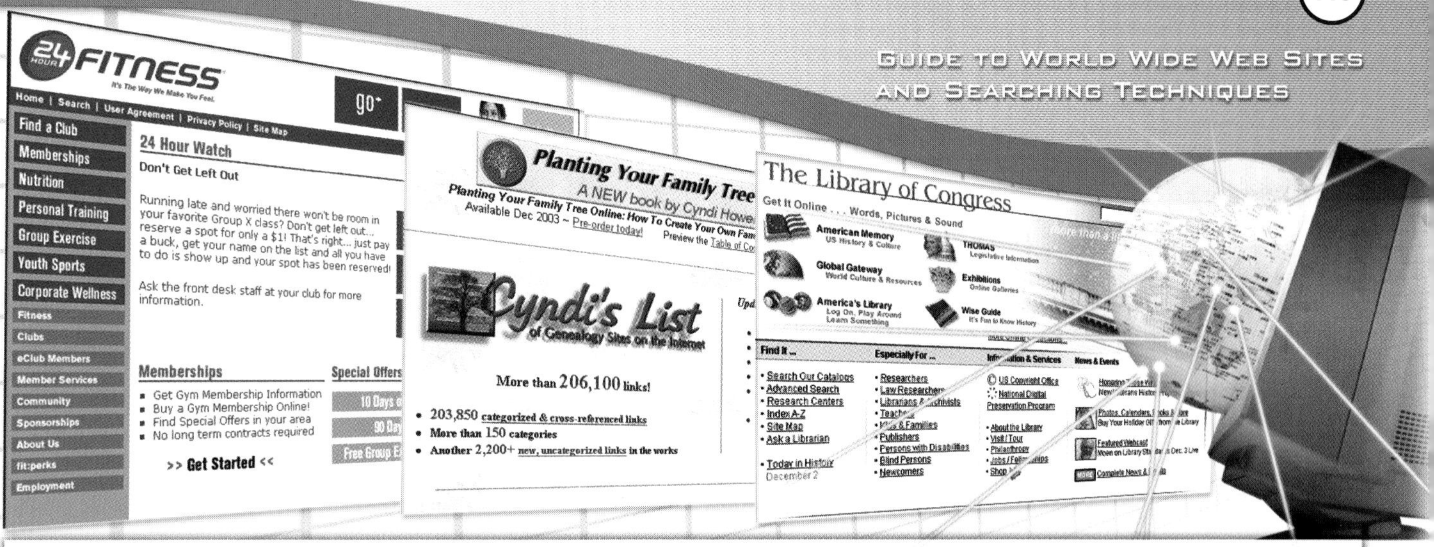

CATEGORY/SITE NAME	LOCATION	COMMENT
Entertainment		
CDNOW	cdnow.com	Search for and buy all types of music
Internet Movie Database (IMDb)	imdb.com	Movies
IUMA (Music Archive)	iuma.com	Underground music database
Online Classics	www.onlineclassics.com	Classical music information
Playbill On-Line	playbill.com	Theater news
Rock and Roll Hall of Fame	rockhall.com	Cleveland museum Web site
Yahoo! Directory Entertainment	dir.yahoo.com/Entertainment/	Yahoo's entertainment directory
Environment		
EnviroLink Network	envirolink.com	Environmental information
Greenpeace	greenpeace.org	Environmental activism
EPA	epa.gov	U.S. government environmental news
Fitness		
24 Hour Fitness	24hourfitness.com	A health and fitness community
GlobalFitness.com	global-fitness.com	Health and fitness
Genealogy		
Cyndi's List	cyndislist.com	List of genealogy sites
Mormon Church	familysearch.org	Renowned Internet genealogy service
National Genealogical Society	ngsgenealogy.org	Genealogical information
Government and Politics		
CIA	cia.gov	International information about countries
Democratic National Committee	democrats.org	Democratic party news
FedWorld	www.fedworld.gov	Links to U.S. government Web sites
Political Science Resources	www.lib.umich.edu/govdocs/polisci.html	Political science resources on the Web
Republican National Committee	rnc.org	GOP party news
The Library of Congress	www.loc.gov	Variety of U.S. government information
The White House	www.whitehouse.gov	Take a tour and learn about the occupants
U.S. Census Bureau	www.census.gov	Population and other statistics
United Nations	www.un.org	Latest UN projects and information
Health and Medicine		
Centers for Disease Control and Prevention (CDC)	www.cdc.gov	How to prevent and control disease
Cornucopia of Disability Information (CODI)	codi.buffalo.edu	Resource for disability products and services
Health Topics for Women's Health	www.amwa-doc.org/healthtopics /healthlist.html	American Medical Women's Association health topics
Mayo Clinic	wwww.mayoclinic.com	Diseases and conditions reference

For an updated list: scsite.com/dc2005/ch2/websites

CATEGORY/SITE NAME	LOCATION	COMMENT
History		
American Memory	memory.loc.gov/	American history
The History Channel	historychannel.com	Search any topic in history
Virtual Library History	www.ku.edu/history/VL	Organized links to history Web sites
World History Archives	www.hartford-hwp.com/archives	Links to history Web sites
Humor		
Comedy Central	comcentral.com	Comedy TV network online
Late Show with David Letterman	cbs.com/latenight/lateshow/	Letterman's nightly show including archived Top 10 lists
Dilbert.com	dilbert.com	Humorous insights about the workplace
Ucomics.com	ucomics.com	Comic strip gallery
Internet		
Beginners' Central	northernwebs.com/bc	Beginners' guide to the Internet
Glossary of Internet Terms	matisse.net/files/glossary.html	Matisse Enzer's definitions of Internet terms
WWW Frequently Asked Questions	www.boutell.com/faq/oldfaq/index.html	Common Web questions and answers
Internet Security		
F-Secure Security Information Center	f-secure.com/virus-info/	Industry standard information source for new virus hoaxes and false alerts
Internet Security Alliance	www.isalliance.org	A Public-Private Partnership for Information Sharing and E-Security Issues
Kid-Safe Sites		
CartoonNetwork.com	cartoonnetwork.com	Interactive site for the cable network
Disney Online	disney.com	Disney's interactive site
FoxKids	foxkids.com	The Fox network's interactive site for children
Nick.com	nick.com	Nickelodeon's site for fun and games
Law		
American Bar Association	www.abanet.org	Source for legal information
Copyright Website	benedict.com	Provides copyright information
FindLaw	findlaw.com	Law resource portal
KuesterLaw	kuesterlaw.com	Technology law resource
Legal Information Institute	www.law.cornell.edu	Cornell Law School legal information

For an updated list: scsite.com/dc2005/ch2/websites

CATEGORY/SITE NAME	LOCATION	COMMENT
Museums		
Smithsonian Institution	www.si.edu	Information and links to Smithsonian museums
The National Gallery of Art, Washington, D.C.	nga.gov	Plan a visit or take an online tour
U.S. Holocaust Memorial Museum	ushmm.org	Dedicated to World War II victims
University of California Museum of Paleontology	www.ucmp.berkeley.edu	Information about dinosaurs and other exhibits
News Sources		
Cable News Network	cnn.com	CNN all-news network
CNET	cnet.com	Technology news
Newsday.com	newsday.com	All the latest information
TIME.com	time.com	Excerpts from Time-Warner magazines
USA TODAY	usatoday.com	Latest U.S. and international news
Wired News	wired.com	Wired magazine online and HotWired network
Reference		
AskERIC Virtual Library	askeric.org/Virtual	Educational resources
Ask Jeeves	askjeeves.com	Search engine
Bartleby	bartleby.com	Reference books online
Internet Public Library	ipl.org	Literature and reference works
The New York Public Library	www.nypl.org	Extensive reference and research material
Webopedia	webopedia.com	Online dictionary and search engine
What You Need to Know About	about.com	Search engine and portal
Robotics		
Remotebot.net	remotebot.net	Control a robot with your Netscape Web browser; interactive Robotic Museum
Robotics and Intelligent Machines Laboratory	robotics.eecs.berkeley.edu	Robotics and mechanical and electrical engineering
University of Massachusetts Robotics Information	www-robotics.cs.umass.edu	Robotics resource index page
Science		
American Institute of Physics	www.aip.org	Physics research information
Exploratorium	exploratorium.edu	Interactive science exhibits
Chemistry Information Service	chemie.de	List of chemistry information Web sites
Molecular Expressions: Science, Optics and You	www.micro.magnet.fsu.edu/primer/java/scienceopticsu/powersof10/index.html	Examine the Milky Way at 10 million light years from Earth; travel space and more
National Institute for Discovery Science (NIDS)	www.nidsci.org	Research of anomalous phenomena
Solar System Simulator	space.jpl.nasa.gov	JPL's spyglass on the cosmos
The NASA Homepage	www.nasa.gov	Information about U.S. space program
The Nine Planets	www.nineplanets.org	Tour the solar system's nine planets

For an updated list: scsite.com/dc2005/ch2/websites

CATEGORY/SITE NAME	LOCATION	COMMENT
Shopping		
ActivePlaza	activeplaza.com	Online shopping mall
Amazon.com	amazon.com	Books and gifts
Barnes & Noble	bn.com	Online bookstore
BizRate	bizrate.com	Rates e-commerce Web sites
BizWeb	bizweb.com	Search for products from more than 46,000 companies
CNET Shopper	shopper.cnet.com	Computer and electronic products
CommerceNet	www.commerce.net	Nonprofit with focus on B2B e-commerce
Consumer World	consumerworld.org	Consumer information
Ebay	ebay.com	Online auctions
CarsDirect.com	www.carsdirect.com/home	Automobile buying Web site
Internet Bookshop	www.bookshop.co.uk	1.4 million titles about more than 2,000 subjects
Lands' End	landsend.com	Classic clothing for the family
Society		
Association for Computing Machinery (ACM)	acm.org	World's first educational and scientific computing society
Center for Computing and Social Responsibility	www.ccsr.cse.dmu.ac.uk/index.html	Social and ethical impacts of information and communications technologies
Computer Ethics Resources	www.ethicsweb.ca/resources/computer/index.html	Links to topics on computer ethics
Computer Professionals for Social Responsibility	cpsr.org	A public-interest alliance of computer scientists and others concerned about the impact of computer technology on society
Computers and Society	acm.org/sigcas	Special interest group within Association for Computing Machinery (ACM)
Electronic Frontier Foundation	eff.org	Protecting rights and promoting freedom
Electronic Privacy Information Center	epic.org	Links to latest news regarding privacy issues
International Center for Information Ethics (ICIE)	icie.zkm.de	An academic Web site about information ethics
International Federation for Information Processing (IFIP)	www.ifip.or.at/	Computers and social accountability
ISWorld Net Professional Ethics	http://www.iscityu.edu.hk/Research/Resources/isword/ethics/index.htm	Practice of ethics in the information systems profession
Privacy.Org	privacy.org	Current privacy issues

For an updated list: scsite.com/dc2005/ch2/websites

CATEGORY/SITE NAME	LOCATION	COMMENT
Sports		
ESPN SportsZone	msn.espn.go.com/main.html	Latest sports news
NBA Basketball	nba.com	Information and links to team Web sites
NFL Football	nfl.com	Information and links to team Web sites
Sports Illustrated	sportsillustrated.cnn.com	Leading sports magazine
Travel		
CitySearch	citysearch.com	United States and international city guides
InfoHub Specialty Travel Guide	infohub.com	Worldwide travel information
Lonely Planet Online	www.lonelyplanet.com	Budget travel guides and stories
Expedia.com	expedia.com	Complete travel resource
Travelocity.com	www.travelocity.com	Online travel agency
TravelWebSM	travelweb.com	Places to stay
Unclassified		
American Singles.com	americansingles.com	Links to dating resources
Cool Site of the Day	cool.infi.net	Different Web site each day
Famous Name Changes	www.famousnamechanges.com	Names of stars before they were stars
WebPhotos	webphotos.com	Online photo community
Where's George?	wheresgeorge.com	The Great American Dollar Bill Locator
Weather		
Intellicast	intellicast.com	International weather and skiing information
The Weather Channel	weather.com	National and local forecasts
Weather Underground	wunderground.com	Weather maps
Zines		
Rock School	rockschool.com	Everything you need to know about being in a rock band
The AFU & Urban Legends Archive	urbanlegends.com	Urban legends
TruthOrFiction.com	truthorfiction.com	Check out the latest rumors circulating on the Web

For an updated list: scsite.com/dc2005/ch2/websites

World Wide Web Search Tools

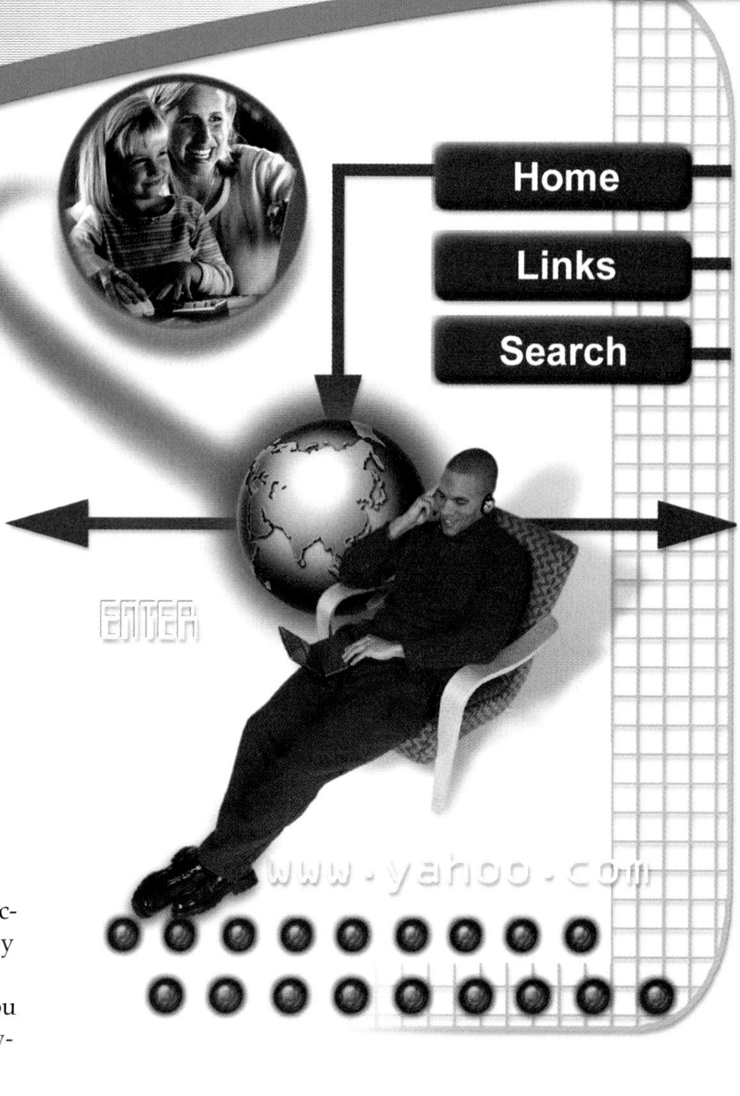

Successful Searching

Successful searching of the Web involves two key steps:

1. Briefly describe the information you are seeking. Start by identifying the main idea or concept in your topic and determine any synonyms, alternate spellings, or variant word forms for the concept.
2. Use the brief description with a search tool to display links to pages containing the desired information.

The two most common search tools are subject directories and search engines. You use a **subject directory** by clicking through its collection of categories and subcategories until you reach the information you want. You use a **search engine** to search for a keyword. The following sections describe how to use a subject directory and a search engine.

Using a Subject Directory

A subject directory provides categorized lists of links. These categorized lists are arranged by subject and then displayed in a series of menus. Using this type of search tool, you can locate a particular topic by starting from the top and clicking links through the different levels, going from the general to the specific. Each time you click a category link, the search tool displays a page of subcategory links from which you again choose. You continue in this fashion until the search tool displays a list of Web pages on the desired topic. Browsing a subject directory requires that you make assumptions about the topic's hierarchical placement within the categorized list.

For the following example, assume you have been assigned the task of writing a research paper about Stephen King's background. The assignment requires that you include at least one Web page citation. This example uses the Yahoo! (yahoo.com) directory to locate information about Stephen King's background.

1 Start your browser and enter the URL yahoo.com in the Address box. When the Yahoo! home page is displayed, point to the scroll box on the right side of the screen as shown in Figure 1.

FIGURE 1 Yahoo! home page.

2 Scroll down to display the Web Site Directory. Point to the Literature link below Arts & Humanities as shown in Figure 2. You point to Literature because that is the category in which Stephen King made his contributions.

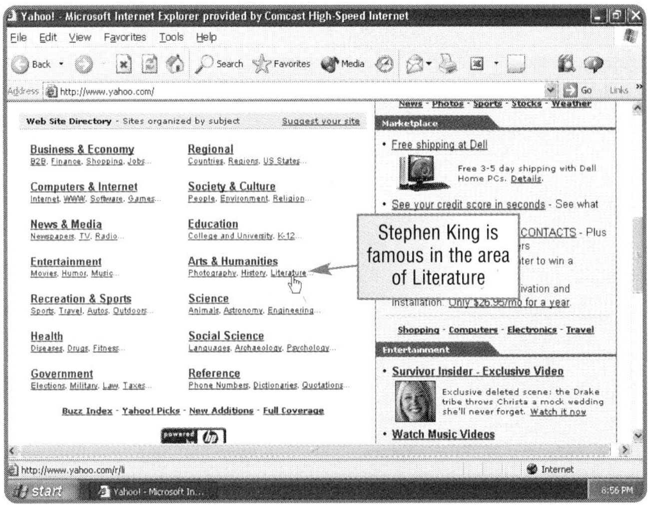

FIGURE 2 Web site directory.

3 Click the Literature link. When the Literature page is displayed, scroll down and point to the Authors link as shown in Figure 3. You point to Authors because Stephen King is an author. Each time you click a category link, you move closer to the topic.

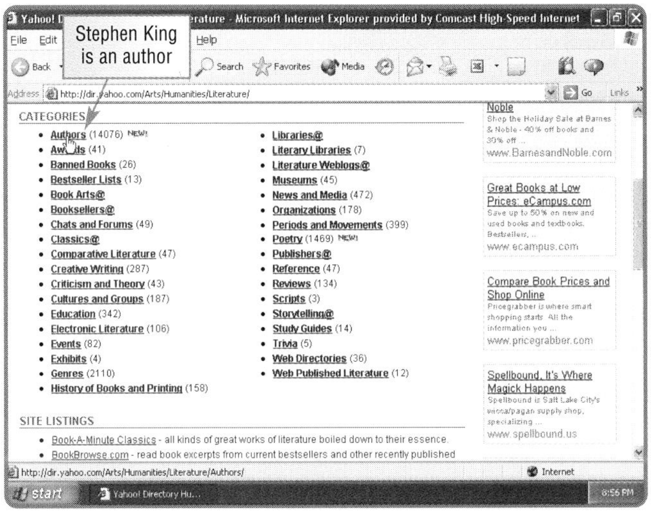

FIGURE 3 Literature categories.

4 Click the Authors link. When the Authors page is displayed, scroll down and point to the Horror link as shown in Figure 4. You point to Horror because that is the area of literature in which Stephen King specializes.

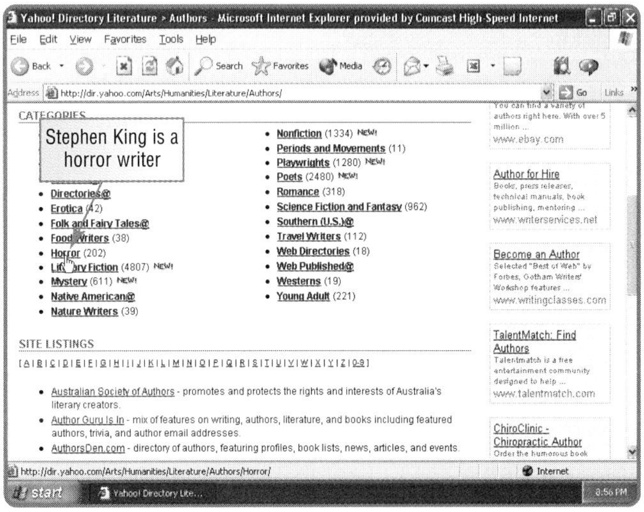

FIGURE 4 Authors categories.

5 Click the Horror link. Scroll down and point to the King, Stephen link as shown in Figure 5.

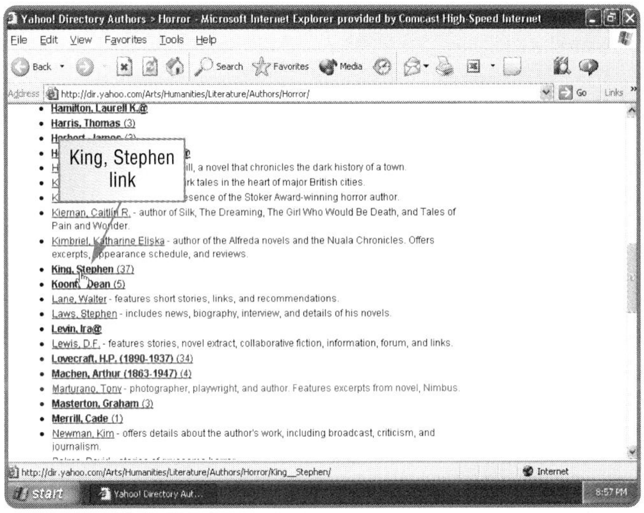

FIGURE 5 Alphabetical listing.

6 Click the King, Stephen link. When the King, Stephen page is displayed, scroll down to the alphabetical listings, and then point to the Official Stephen King Web Presence, The link as shown in Figure 6.

FIGURE 6 King, Stephen categories.

7 Click the Official Stephen King Web Presence, The link. When The Official Stephen King Web Presence page is displayed (Figure 7), one at a time, click the links. Use the browser's Back button to return to The Official Stephen King Web Presence page after viewing each page associated with a link.

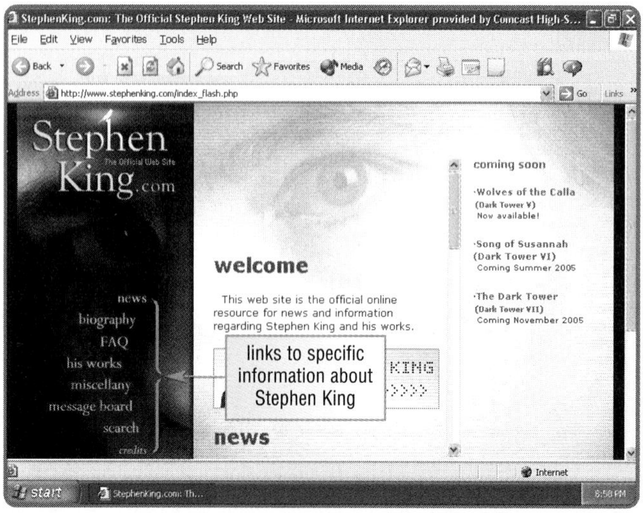

FIGURE 7 The Official Stephen King Web Site.

With just a few clicks, the Yahoo! subject directory displays information about Stephen King's background. The Stephen King page in Figure 7 shows several links to pages describing his life.

The major problem with a subject directory is deciding which categories to choose as you work through the menus of links presented. For additional information about how to use the Yahoo! subject directory, click the Help link in the upper-right corner of its home page (Figure 1 on page 124).

Using a Search Engine

Search engines require that you enter search text or keywords (single word, words, or phrase) that define what you are looking for, rather than clicking through menus of links. Search engines often respond with results that include thousands of links to Web pages, many of which have little or no bearing on the information you are seeking. You can eliminate the superfluous pages by carefully crafting a keyword that limits the search. The following example uses the Google search engine to search for the phrase, Stephen King quotations.

1 Start your browser and enter the URL `google.com` in the Address box. When the Google home page is displayed, type `stephen king quotations` in the Search text box and then point to the Google Search button as shown in Figure 8.

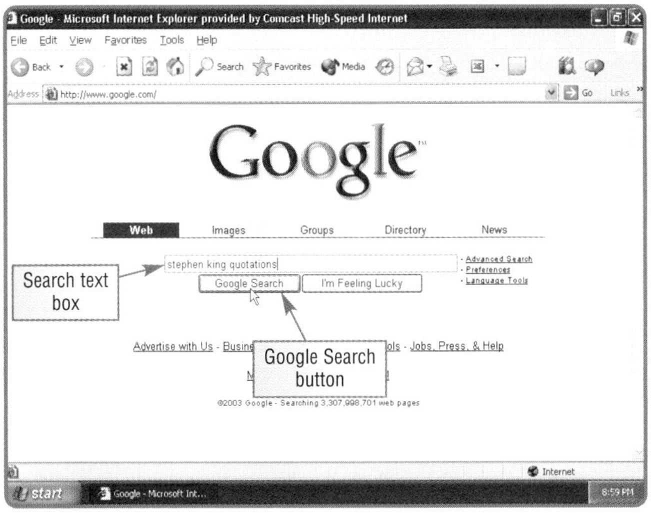

FIGURE 8 Google home page.

2 Click the Google Search button. When the results of the search are displayed, scroll through the links and read the descriptions. Point to the Stephen King quotes and quotations link as shown in Figure 9.

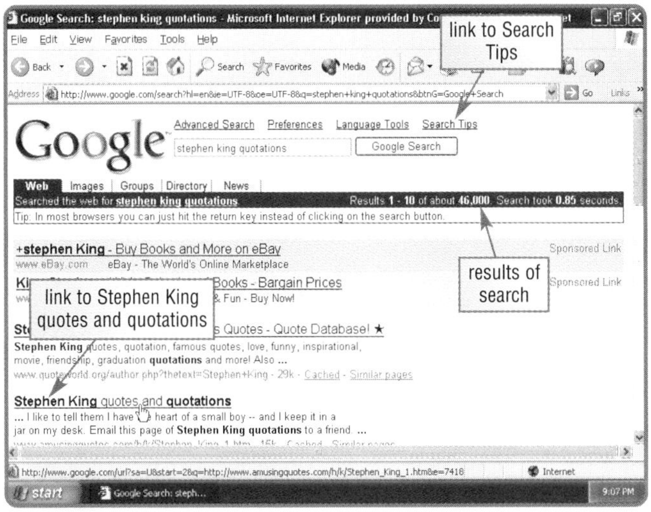

FIGURE 9 Google search results.

3 Click the Stephen King quotes and quotations link. A Web page is displayed containing links to quotations, special features awards, and other resources about Stephen King (Figure 10).

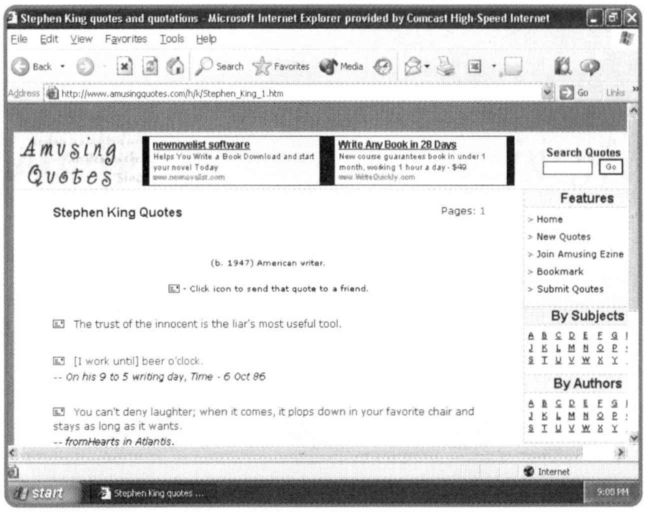

FIGURE 10 Web page containing quotes from Stephen King.

The results shown in Figure 9 include about 24,600 links to Web pages that reference Stephen King's quotations. Most search engines sequence the results based on how close the words in the keyword are to one another in the Web page titles and their descriptions. Thus, the first few links probably contain more relevant information. For additional information about how to use the Google search engine, click the Search Tips link in the upper-right corner of the results page (Figure 9).

Limiting the Search

If you enter a phrase with spaces between the keywords, most search engines return links to pages that include all of the words. Figure 11 lists some common operators, commands, and special characters you can use to refine your search.

Guidelines to Successful Searching

You can improve your Web searches by following these guidelines.

1. Use nouns as keywords, and put the most important terms first in your keyword.
2. Use the asterisk (*) to find plurals of words. For example: retriev* returns retrieves, retrieval, retriever, and any other variation.
3. Type keywords in lowercase to find both lowercase and uppercase variations.
4. Use quotation marks to create phrases so the search engine finds the exact sequence of words.
5. Use a hyphen alternative. For example, use email, e-mail.
6. Limit the search by language.
7. Use uppercase characters for Boolean operators in your search statements to differentiate between the words and operators.
8. Before you use a search engine, read its Help.
9. The Internet contains many search engines. If your search is unsuccessful with one search engine, try another.

CATEGORY OF OPERATOR	OPERATOR	KEYWORD EXAMPLES	DESCRIPTION
Boolean	AND (+)	art AND music smoking health hazards fish +pollutants +runoff	Requires both words to be in the page. No operator between words or the plus sign (+) are shortcuts for the Boolean operator AND.
	OR	mental illness OR insane canine OR dog OR puppy flight attendant OR stewardess OR steward	Requires only one of the words to be in the page.
	AND NOT (–)	auto AND NOT SUV AND NOT convertible computers–programming shakespeare–hamlet	Excludes page with the word following AND NOT. The minus sign (–) is a shortcut for the Boolean operator AND NOT.
Parentheses	( )	physics AND (relativity OR einstein) –(romeo+juliet)	Parentheses group portions of Boolean operators together.
Phrase Searching	" "	"harry potter" "19th century literature"	Requires the exact phrase within quotation marks to be in the page.
Wildcard	*	writ* clou*	The asterisk (*) at the end of words substitutes for any combination of characters.

FIGURE 11 Search engine keyword operators, commands, and special characters.

Popular Search Sites

Figure 12 contains a list of popular search sites, their URLs, and their usage in a recent study. Most of these search sites have both a search engine and subject directory. For additional information on search sites, visit searchenginewatch.com.

SEARCH ENGINE	URL	USAGE
Google	google.com	29.5%
Yahoo!	yahoo.com	28.9%
MSN Search	search.msn.com	27.6%
AOL Search	search.aol.com	18.4%
Ask Jeeves	askjeeves.com	9.9%
Overture	overture.com	4.8%
InfoSpace	Infospace.com	4.5%
Netscape Search	search.netscape.com	4.4%
AltaVista	altavista.com	4.0%
Lycos	lycos.com	2.4%
EarthLink	earthlink.com	2.0%
LookSmart	looksmart.com	1.7%

Source: NetRatings for SearchEngineWatch.com (choice of 60,000 users during January 2003)

FIGURE 12 Popular search sites, their URLs, and a summary of their usage in a recent study. Because a Web surfer may visit more than one service, the combined totals in the search site usage study exceed 100 percent. Also, several of the search engines listed use other search engines in the list for some or all searches.

CHAPTER 3

Application Software

Picture Yourself Using Software

With the morning coffee brewing, you start the computer and check e-mail. As you begin deleting the unwanted junk e-mail messages, you notice a message from your bank. This one could be important — probably related to your online banking. As you open the message, you think back when it took hours to balance a bank statement.

Today, checkbook registers are a thing of the past. Once a week, you connect to the bank and copy your personal account transactions from the bank's computer to your computer. Your computerized checkbook balance always is up-to-date. It shows cleared checks, ATM withdrawals, debit card transactions, and automatic payments. Bank statement reconciliations literally take minutes. The online payment feature also saves you time. Your bank automatically transfers the specified funds on a specified date from your checking account to the payees' accounts.

This e-mail message from your bank is offering an opportunity to prepare and file your taxes online. Having just received your W2, you immediately click the link in the message and sign up for the service. Next, you complete an online tax preparation form and answer some tax-related questions. As soon as you click the File Taxes button, a message appears indicating that the refund will be in your checking account within two weeks!

As you read Chapter 3, you will learn about personal finance and Web-based tax preparation software and discover other types of application software.

OBJECTIVES

After completing this chapter, you will be able to:

1. **Identify the categories of application software**
2. **Explain ways software is distributed**
3. **Explain how to start and interact with application software**
4. **Identify the key features of widely used business programs**
5. **Identify the key features of widely used graphics and multimedia programs**
6. **Identify the key features of widely used home, personal, and educational programs**
7. **Identify the types of application software used in communications**
8. **Discuss the advantages of using application software on the Web**
9. **Describe the learning aids available for application software**

CONTENTS

APPLICATION SOFTWARE

Application software consists of programs that perform specific tasks for users. Application software is used for a variety of reasons:

1. As a business tool
2. To assist with graphics and multimedia projects
3. To support home, personal, and educational activities
4. To facilitate communications

The table in Figure 3-1 categorizes popular types of application software by their general use. Although many types of communications software exist, the ones listed in Figure 3-1 are application software oriented. Many of these communications software are included as a part of other application or system software.

As you become proficient in your understanding of application software, it is likely that you will find yourself using software from more than one of the categories in Figure 3-1. The four categories are not mutually exclusive. That is, software listed in one category may be used in other categories. For example, software suites (business) often include e-mail (communications) and Web page authoring software (graphics and multimedia). Although home users have educational and reference software, businesses also may use this type of software.

Application software is available in a variety of forms: packaged, custom, shareware, freeware, and public domain.

- **Packaged software** is mass produced, copyrighted retail software that meets the needs of a wide variety of users, not just a single user or company. Word processing and spreadsheet software are examples of packaged software. Packaged software is available in retail stores or on the Web. Figure 3-2 shows packaged software for purchase at one online retailer.
- **Custom software** performs functions specific to a business or industry. Sometimes a company cannot find packaged software that meets its unique requirements. In this case, the company may use a programmer to develop tailor-made custom software, which usually costs more than packaged software.
- **Shareware** is copyrighted software that is distributed free for a trial period. To use a shareware program beyond that period, you

CATEGORIES OF APPLICATION SOFTWARE

1 Business	2 Graphics and Multimedia	3 Home/Personal/Educational
• Word Processing	• Computer-Aided Design (CAD)	• Software Suite (for Personal Use) (e.g., word processing, spreadsheet, database)
• Spreadsheet	• Desktop Publishing (for the Professional)	• Personal Finance
• Database	• Paint/Image Editing (for the Professional)	• Legal
• Presentation Graphics	• Video and Audio Editing	• Tax Preparation
• Note Taking	• Multimedia Authoring	• Desktop Publishing (for Personal Use)
• Personal Information Manager (PIM)	• Web Page Authoring	• Paint/Image Editing (for Personal Use)
• PDA Business Software		• Clip Art/Image Gallery
• Software Suite (e.g., word processing, spreadsheet, presentation graphics, PIM)		• Home Design/Landscaping
• Project Management		• Educational
• Accounting		• Reference

4 Communications			
• E-Mail	• FTP	• Web Browser	• Newsgroup/Message Board
• Chat Room	• Instant Messaging	• Video Conferencing/Telephone Calls	

FIGURE 3-1 The four major categories of popular application software are outlined in this table. Many types of communications software are application software oriented. The communications software usually is bundled with other application or system software.

send a payment to the person or company who developed the program. Developers of shareware rely on the honor system, trusting users to send payment if software use extends beyond the stated trial period. In some cases, the shareware is a scaled-down version of the software, and payment entitles the user to a fully functional product.

- **Freeware** is software provided at no cost to a user by an individual or a company. Freeware is copyrighted. Thus, programmers cannot incorporate freeware into applications they intend to sell.
- **Public-domain software** also is free software, but it has been donated for public use and has no copyright restrictions. Anyone can copy or distribute public-domain software to others.

Thousands of shareware, freeware, and public-domain programs are available on the Web for users to download. Other ways to obtain copies of these programs are from the developer, a coworker, or a friend. Shareware, freeware, and public-domain programs usually have fewer capabilities than retail programs. Examples of shareware, freeware, and public-domain programs include communications programs, graphics programs, and games.

The Role of System Software

System software serves as the interface between the user, the application software, and the computer's hardware (Figure 3-3). To use application software, such as a word processing program, your computer must be running system software, specifically, an operating system. Two popular personal computer operating systems are Microsoft's Windows XP and Apple's Mac OS X.

FIGURE 3-2 Many online retailers, such as Buy.com, have packaged software available for sale.

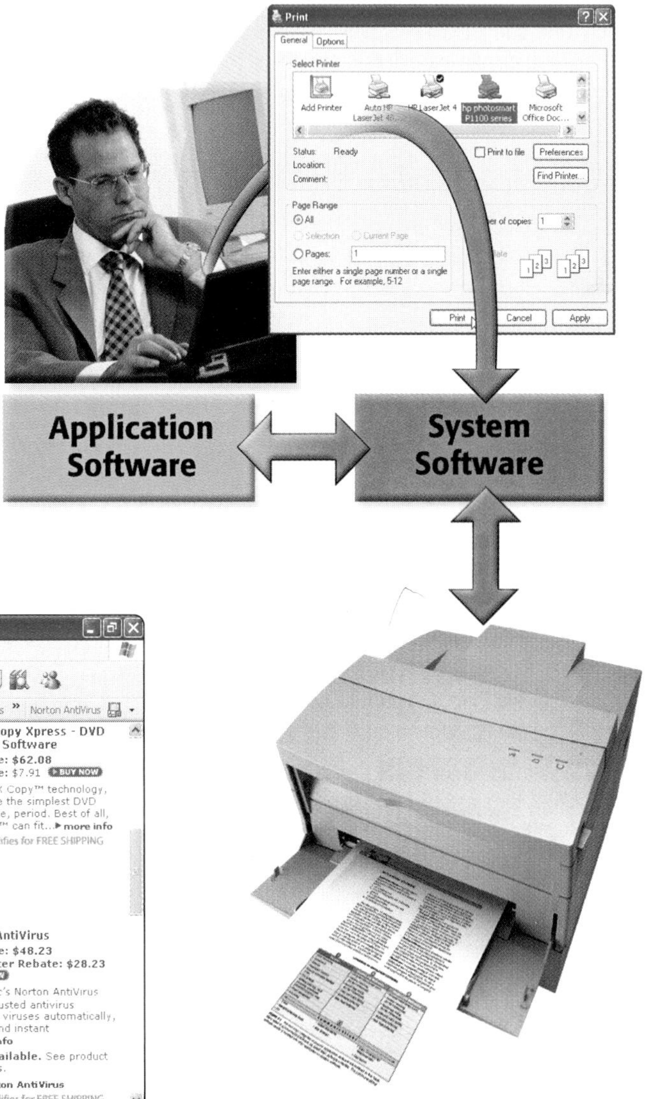

FIGURE 3-3 A user does not communicate directly with the computer hardware. Instead, system software is the interface between the user, the application software, and the hardware. For example, when a user instructs the application software to print, the application software sends the print instruction to the system software, which in turn sends the print instruction to the hardware.

Each time you start a computer, the operating system is *loaded* (copied) from the computer's hard disk into memory. Once the operating system is loaded, it coordinates all the activities of the computer. This includes starting application programs and transferring data among input and output devices and memory. While the computer is running, the operating system remains in memory.

Starting and Interacting with Application Software

To use application software, you must instruct the operating system to start the program. The steps in Figure 3-4 illustrate how to start and interact with the Paint program. The following paragraphs explain the steps in Figure 3-4.

FIGURE 3-4 HOW TO START AN APPLICATION

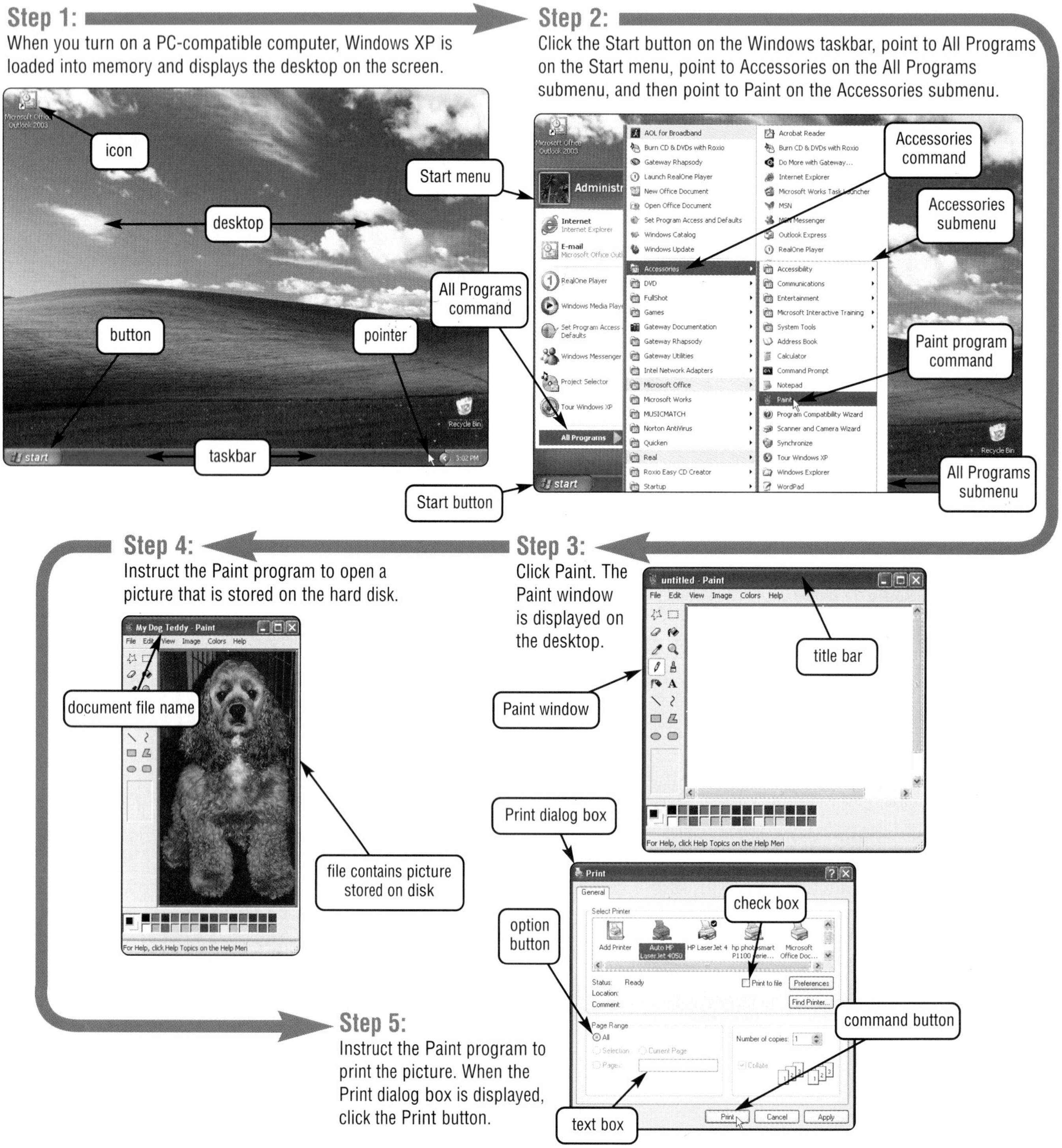

Both the Windows XP and the Mac OS X operating systems use the concept of a desktop to make the computer easier to use. The **desktop** is an on-screen work area that has a graphical user interface. Step 1 of Figure 3-4 shows icons, a button, and a pointer on the Windows XP desktop. An **icon** is a small image displayed on the screen that represents a program, a document, or some other object. A **button** is a graphical element that you activate to cause a specific action to take place. For example, activating a button may cause a program to start. Buttons usually are rectangular or square shapes.

One way to activate a button is to click it. To **click** a button on the screen requires moving the pointer to the button and then pressing and releasing a button on the mouse (usually the left mouse button). The **pointer** is a small symbol displayed on the screen that moves as you move the mouse. Common pointer shapes are an I-beam (I), a block arrow ( ), and a pointing hand ( ).

The Windows XP desktop contains a Start button in its lower-left corner. Using the Start button starts an application. When you click the Start button, the Start menu is displayed on the desktop. A **menu** contains a list of commands from which you make selections. A **command** is an instruction that causes a program to perform a specific action.

The arrowhead symbol at the right edge of some menu commands indicates a submenu of additional commands is available. A *submenu* is a menu that is displayed when you point to a command on a previous menu. As illustrated in Step 2 of Figure 3-4, when you click the Start button and point to the All Programs command on the Start menu, the All Programs submenu is displayed. Pointing to the Accessories command on the All Programs submenu displays the Accessories submenu. Notice that the Accessories submenu contains several programs such as Calculator, Paint, and WordPad.

Programs sometimes display shortcut menus. A *shortcut menu* is a list of commonly used commands for completing a task related to the current activity or selected item. To display a shortcut menu in Windows applications, for example, you click the right mouse button.

To start a program, you can click its program name on a menu or submenu. This action instructs the operating system to start the application, which means the program's instructions load from a storage medium (such as a hard disk) into memory. For example, when you click Paint on the Accessories submenu, Windows loads the Paint program instructions from the computer's hard disk into memory.

Once loaded in memory, a program is displayed in a window on the desktop (Step 3 of Figure 3-4). A **window** is a rectangular area of the screen that displays a program, data, and/or information. The top of a window has a **title bar**, which is a horizontal space that contains the window's name.

With the program loaded, you can create a new file or open an existing one. A *file* is a named collection of stored data, instructions, or information. A file can contain text, images, audio, and video. To distinguish among various files, each file has a file name. A *file name* is a unique combination of letters of the alphabet, numbers, and other characters that identifies a file. For example, a picture of your dog may have the file name My Dog Teddy. The title bar of the document window usually displays a document's file name. Step 4 of Figure 3-4 shows the contents of the file, My Dog Teddy, displaying in the Paint window. The file contains an image photographed with a digital camera.

In some cases, when you instruct a program to perform an activity such as printing, the program displays a dialog box. A *dialog box* is a special window that provides information, presents available options, or requests a response. For example, a Print dialog box includes many printing options such as specifying a different printer, printing all or part of a document, or printing multiple copies. Dialog boxes, such as the one shown in Step 5 of Figure 3-4, often contain option buttons, text boxes, check boxes, and command buttons. Clicking the Print button, for example, instructs the computer to print the picture.

FAQ 3-1

Will a document print like it looks on a screen?

Yes, because most current application software is *WYSIWYG* (*what you see is what you get*). The application software embeds invisible codes around the text and graphics, which instructs the computer how to present the information.

For more information about WYSIWYG, visit the Discovering Computers 2005 FAQ Web page (**scsite.com/dc2005/faq**). Click WYSIWYG below Chapter 3.

QUIZ YOURSELF 3-1

To check your knowledge of application software categories, ways software is distributed, and starting and interacting with application software, visit the Discovering Computers 2005 Quiz Yourself Web page (**scsite.com/dc2005/quiz**). Click Objectives 1 – 3 below Chapter 3.

BUSINESS SOFTWARE

Business software is application software that assists people in becoming more effective and efficient while performing their daily business activities. Business software includes programs such as word processing, spreadsheet, database, presentation graphics, note taking, personal information manager, PDA business software, software suite, project management, and accounting. Figure 3-5 lists popular programs for each of these categories. Read Issue 3-1 for a related discussion.

The following sections discuss the features and functions of business software. Word processing and spreadsheet software have a heavier emphasis because of their predominant use.

ISSUE 3-1

Is It Ethical to Copy Software?

With purchased software, users typically are allowed to install the program on one computer and legally make one copy of the software for backup purposes. Despite the law, many people make several copies, either to share or to sell. In a recent survey, more than 50 percent of respondents admitted that they had illegally copied, or would illegally copy, software. Microsoft, a leading software manufacturer, estimates that almost 25 percent of software in the United States has been copied illegally. Illegally copied software costs the software industry more than $10 billion a year in lost revenues. Some of the reasons that people give for copying software illegally include: software prices are too high, copying software harms no one, software often is copied for educational or other altruistic purposes, you can do whatever you want with software you have purchased, and everyone copies software. Do you think it is ethical to copy purchased software and install it on your computer and also a friend's computer? Why or why not? Can you counter the reasons people give for copying software illegally? How? Would you copy software illegally? Why or why not?

For more information about illegally copying software, visit the Discovering Computers 2005 Issues Web page (**scsite.com/dc2005/issues**). Click Issue #1 below Chapter 3.

WEB LINK 3-1

Sun StarOffice

Visit the Discovering Computers 2005 WEB LINK page (**scsite.com/dc2005/weblink**). Click Sun StarOffice below Chapter 3.

BUSINESS SOFTWARE

Application Software	Popular Programs
Word Processing	• Microsoft Office Word 2003 • Sun StarOffice Writer • Corel WordPerfect
Spreadsheet	• Microsoft Office Excel 2003 • Sun StarOffice Calc • Corel Quattro Pro
Database	• Microsoft Office Access 2003 • Sun StarOffice Base • Corel Paradox • Microsoft Visual FoxPro • Oracle • MySQL
Presentation Graphics	• Microsoft Office PowerPoint 2003 • Sun StarOffice Impress • Corel Presentations
Note Taking	• Microsoft Office OneNote 2003
Personal Information Manager (PIM)	• Microsoft Office Outlook 2003 • Lotus Organizer • Microsoft Pocket Outlook • Palm Desktop
PDA Business Software	• CNetX Pocket SlideShow • Microsoft Pocket Word • Microsoft Pocket Excel • Microsoft Pocket Outlook • Ultrasoft Money Pocket Edition
Software Suite (for the Professional)	• Microsoft Office 2003 • Microsoft Office 2004 for Mac • Sun StarOffice Suite • OpenOffice.org • Corel WordPerfect Office • IBM Lotus SmartSuite
Project Management	• Microsoft Office Project 2003 • Primavera SureTrak Project Manager
Accounting	• Intuit QuickBooks • Peachtree Complete Accounting

FIGURE 3-5 Popular business programs.

Word Processing Software

Word processing software is one of the more widely used types of application software. **Word processing software**, sometimes called a *word processor*, allows users to create and manipulate documents containing mostly text and sometimes graphics (Figure 3-6). Millions of people use word processing software every day to develop documents such as letters, memos, reports, fax cover sheets, mailing labels, newsletters, and Web pages.

Word processing software has many features to make documents look professional and visually appealing. Some of these features include the capability of changing the shape and size of characters in headlines and headings, changing the color of characters, and organizing text into newspaper-style columns. When using colors for characters, however, they will print as black or gray unless you have a color printer.

Most word processing software allows users to incorporate many types of graphical images in documents. One popular type of graphical image is clip art. **Clip art** is a collection of drawings, diagrams, maps, and photographs that you can insert in documents. In Figure 3-6, a user inserted clip art images of baseball players in the document. Word processing software usually includes public-domain clip art. You can find additional public-domain and proprietary images on the Web or purchase them on CD or DVD.

All word processing software provides at least some basic capabilities to help users create and modify documents. Defining the size of the paper on which to print and specifying the *margins*, that is, the portion of the page outside the main body of text, including the top, the bottom, and both sides of the paper, are examples of some of these capabilities. If you type text that extends beyond the right page margin, the word processing software automatically positions text at the beginning of the next line. This feature, called *wordwrap*, allows users to type words in a paragraph continually without pressing the ENTER key at the end of each line. When you modify paper size or margins, the word processing software automatically re-wraps text so it fits within the adjusted paper size and margins.

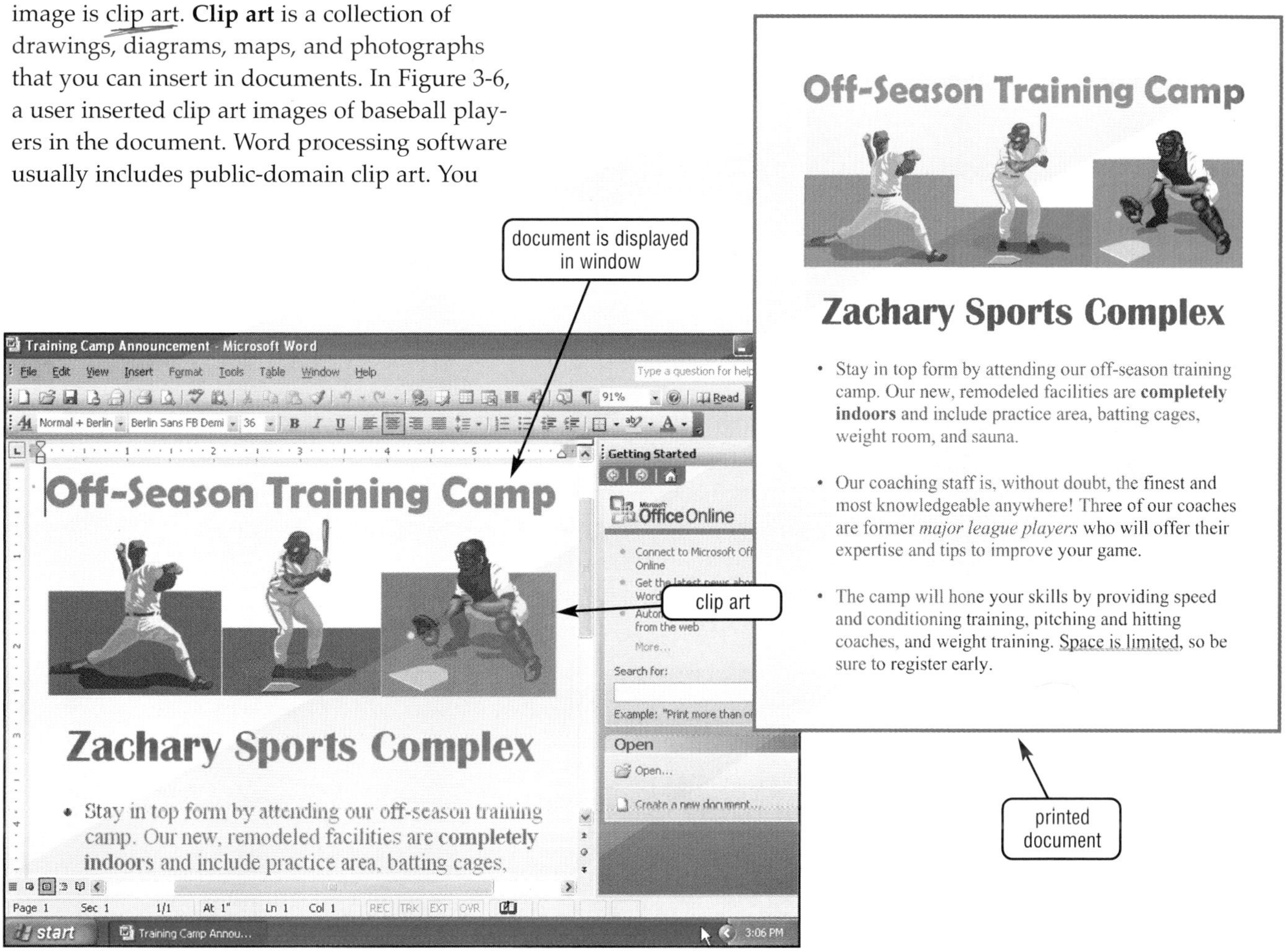

FIGURE 3-6 Word processing software enables users to create professional and visually appealing documents.

As you type more lines of text than can be displayed on the screen, the top portion of the document moves upward, or scrolls, off the screen. *Scrolling* is the process of moving different portions of the document on the screen into view.

A major advantage of using word processing software is that users easily can change what they have written. For example, a user can insert, delete, or rearrange words, sentences, paragraphs, or entire sections. The find or *search* feature allows you to locate all occurrences of a certain character, word, or phrase. This feature in combination with the *replace* feature allows you to substitute existing characters or words with new ones. For example, the word processing software can locate the word, finest, in an announcement and replace it with the word, best.

Current word processing programs also have a feature that automatically corrects errors and makes word substitutions as users type text. For instance, when you type the abbreviation asap, the word processing software replaces the abbreviation with the phrase, as soon as possible.

Word processing software includes a *spelling checker*, which reviews the spelling of individual words, sections of a document, or the entire document. The spelling checker compares the words in the document with an electronic dictionary that is part of the word processing software. You can customize the electronic dictionary by adding words such as companies, streets, cities, and personal names, so the software can check the spelling of those words too. Many word processing programs allow you to check the spelling of a whole document at one time, or to check the spelling of individual words as you type them.

Another benefit of word processing software is the ability to insert headers and footers into a document. A *header* is text that appears at the top of each page, and a *footer* is text that appears at the bottom of each page. Page numbers, company names, report titles, and dates are examples of items often included in headers and footers.

In addition to these basic features, most current word processing programs provide numerous additional features. The table in Figure 3-7 lists these additional features. Read Issue 3-2 for a related discussion.

ISSUE 3-2

Personal or Processed?

Two schools of thought exist when it comes to composing and editing documents on the computer. Many people believe word processing software greatly improves the quality of written material by making it easier to create, modify, and print documents. Some word processing software even provides templates — patterns or blueprints for a document — that produce reports, memos, cover letters, resumes, legal pleadings, and even personal letters. Yet, other people argue word processing software has become a crutch, making it unnecessary for students to learn the rudiments and nuances of languages. These people feel that much of the work produced with word processing software is processed, lacking the beauty, artistry, and individuality of great literature. What effect do you think word processing software has on written communications? Does it result in better work or simply more correct mediocre work? What word processing features, if any, do you feel are particularly valuable to an author?

For more information about word processing and the writing process, visit the Discovering Computers 2005 Issues Web page (**scsite.com/dc2005/issues**). Click Issue #2 below Chapter 3.

Developing a Document

With application software, such as word processing, users create, edit, format, print, and save documents. During the process of developing a document, users likely will switch back and forth among all of these activities.

When you **create** a document, you enter text or numbers, insert graphical images, and perform other tasks using an input device such as a keyboard, mouse, microphone or digital pen. If you are using Microsoft Office Word 2003 to design an announcement, for example, you are creating a document.

To **edit** a document means to make changes to its existing content. Common editing tasks include inserting, deleting, cutting, copying, and pasting. In Microsoft Word, inserting text indicates that you are adding text to a document, such as listing a facility's hours of operation. Deleting text means that you are removing text or other content.

ADDITIONAL WORD PROCESSING FEATURES

AutoCorrect	As you type words, the AutoCorrect feature corrects common spelling errors. AutoCorrect also corrects capitalization mistakes.
AutoFormat	As you type, the AutoFormat feature automatically applies formatting to the text. For example, it automatically numbers a list or converts a Web address to a hyperlink.
Collaboration	Collaboration includes discussions and online meetings. Discussions allow multiple users to enter comments in a document and read and reply to each other's comments. Through an online meeting, users share documents with others in real time and view changes as they are being made.
Columns	Most word processing software can arrange text in two or more columns to look like a newspaper or magazine. The text from the bottom of one column automatically flows to the top of the next column.
Grammar Checker	The grammar checker proofreads documents for grammar, writing style, sentence structure errors, and reading statistics.
Ink Input	Supports input from a digital pen. Word processing software that supports ink input incorporates user's handwritten text and drawings in a word processing document. Ink input is popular on Tablet PCs.
Macros	A *macro* is a sequence of keystrokes and instructions that a user records and saves. When you want to execute the same series of instructions, execute the macro instead.
Mail Merge	Creates form letters, mailing labels, and envelopes.
Reading Layout	For those users who prefer reading on the screen, reading layout increases the readability and legibility of an on-screen document by hiding unnecessary toolbars, increasing the size of displayed characters, and providing navigation tools.
Research	Some word processing software allows you to search through various forms of online and Internet reference information — based on selected text in a document. Research services available include a thesaurus, English and bilingual dictionaries, encyclopedias, and Web sites that provide information such as stock quotes, news articles, and company profiles.
Smart Tags	*Smart tags* automatically appear on the screen when you perform a certain action. For example, typing an address causes a smart tag to appear. Clicking this smart tag provides options to display a map of the address or driving directions to or from the address.
Tables	Tables organize information into rows and columns. In addition to evenly spaced rows and columns, some word processing programs allow you to draw tables of any size or shape.
Templates	A *template* is a document that contains the formatting necessary for a specific document type. Templates usually exist for memos, fax cover sheets, and letters. In addition to templates provided with the software, users have access to many online templates through the manufacturer's Web site.
Thesaurus	With a thesaurus, a user looks up a synonym (word with the same meaning) for a word in a document.
Tracking Changes	If multiple users work with a document, the word processing software highlights or color-codes changes made by various users.
Voice Recognition	With some word processing programs, users can speak into the computer's microphone and watch the spoken words appear on the screen as they talk. With these programs, users edit and format the document by speaking or spelling an instruction.
Web Page Development	Most word processing software allows users to create, edit, format, and convert documents to be displayed on the World Wide Web.

FIGURE 3-7 Many additional features are included with word processing software.

To cut involves removing a portion of the document and storing it in a temporary storage location, sometimes called a *clipboard*. A clipboard also contains items that you copy (duplicate) in a document. *Pasting* is the process of transferring an item from a clipboard to a specific location in a document.

When users **format** a document, they change its appearance. Formatting is important because the overall look of a document significantly can affect its ability to communicate clearly. Examples of formatting tasks are changing the font, font size, or font style of text.

A **font** is a name assigned to a specific design of characters. Two basic types of fonts are serif and sans serif. A *serif font* has short decorative lines at the upper and lower ends of the characters. Sans means without. Thus, a *sans serif font* does not have the short decorative lines at the upper and lower ends of the characters. Times New Roman is an example of a serif font. Arial is an example of a sans serif font.

Font size indicates the size of the characters in a particular font. Font size is gauged by a measurement system called points. A single *point* is about 1/72 of an inch in height. The text you are reading in this book is 10 point. Thus, each character is about 5/36 (10/72) of an inch in height. A *font style* adds emphasis to a font. Bold, italic, and underline are examples of font styles. Figure 3-8 illustrates fonts, font sizes, and font styles.

During the process of creating, editing, and formatting a document, the computer holds it in memory. To keep the document for future use requires that you save it. When you **save** a document, the computer transfers the document from memory to a storage medium such as a floppy disk, USB flash drive, hard disk, or CD. Once saved, a document is stored permanently as a file on the storage medium.

It is a good practice to save frequently while working on documents. Saving at regular intervals ensures that the majority of your work will not be lost in case a power failure or other system failure occurs. Many programs have an optional AutoSave feature that automatically saves open documents at specified time intervals.

When you **print** a document, the computer sends a copy of the document to a medium such as paper. One of the benefits of word processing software is the ability to print the same document many times, with each copy looking just like the first. Instead of printing a document and physically distributing it, some users e-mail the document to others on a network such as the Internet. Either they include the document as part of an e-mail message, or they attach the electronic document (file) to an e-mail message.

FAQ 3-2

How does the computer know which application software was used to save a file?

When the computer saves a file, it often appends an extension to the file name. The *extension* indicates the file type. For example, files saved in Word have an extension of .doc and files saved in Paint have an extension of .bmp.

For more information about file types and extensions, visit the Discovering Computers 2005 FAQ Web page (**scsite.com/dc2005/faq**). Click File Types and Extensions below Chapter 3.

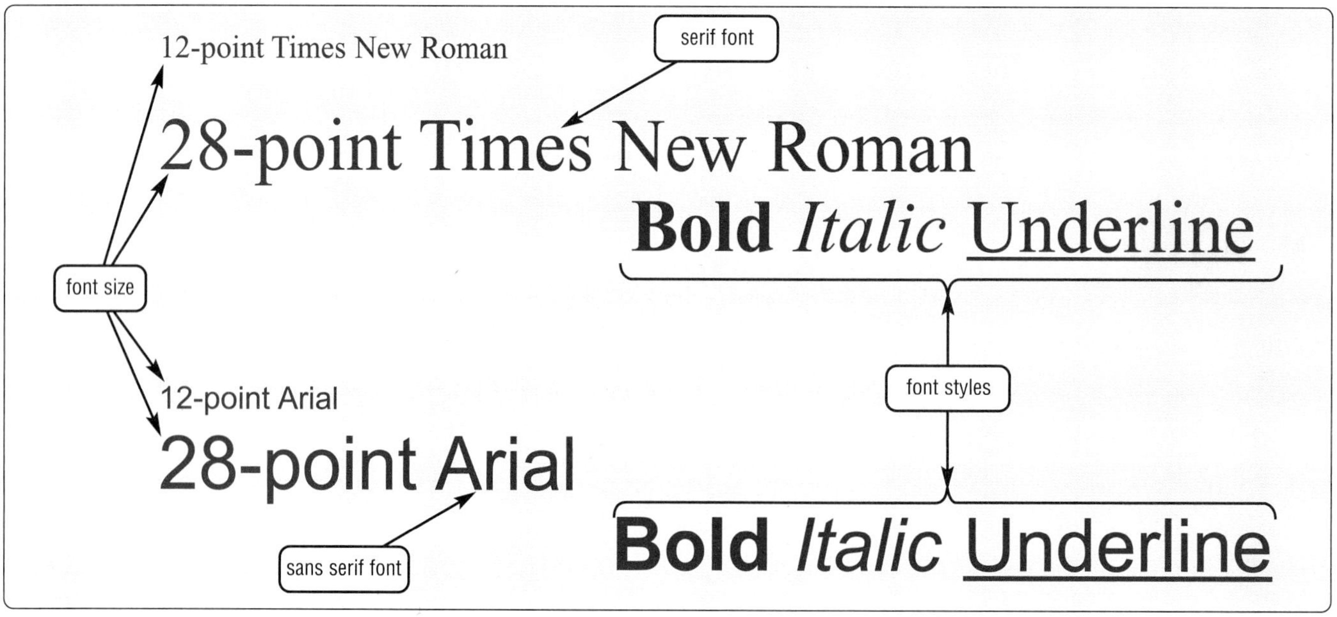

FIGURE 3-8 The Times New Roman and Arial fonts are shown in two font sizes and a variety of font styles.

VOICE RECOGNITION Many programs support **voice recognition**, which is the computer's capability of distinguishing spoken words. Users can speak into the computer's microphone or into a headset attached to the computer and watch the spoken words appear on the screen as they talk. This feature, also called *speech recognition*, allows users to edit and format a document by speaking or spelling instructions. Figure 3-9 illustrates how Word recognizes dictated words and voice commands.

Voice recognition programs available for purchase allow users to speak into their existing application software. Popular voice recognition programs include IBM ViaVoice and Dragon NaturallySpeaking. Chapter 5 discusses voice recognition in more depth.

WEB LINK 3-2

Voice Recognition Software

Visit the Discovering Computers 2005 WEB LINK page (**scsite.com/dc2005/weblink**). Click Voice Recognition below Chapter 3.

FIGURE 3-9 HOW TO DICTATE WORDS AND COMMANDS

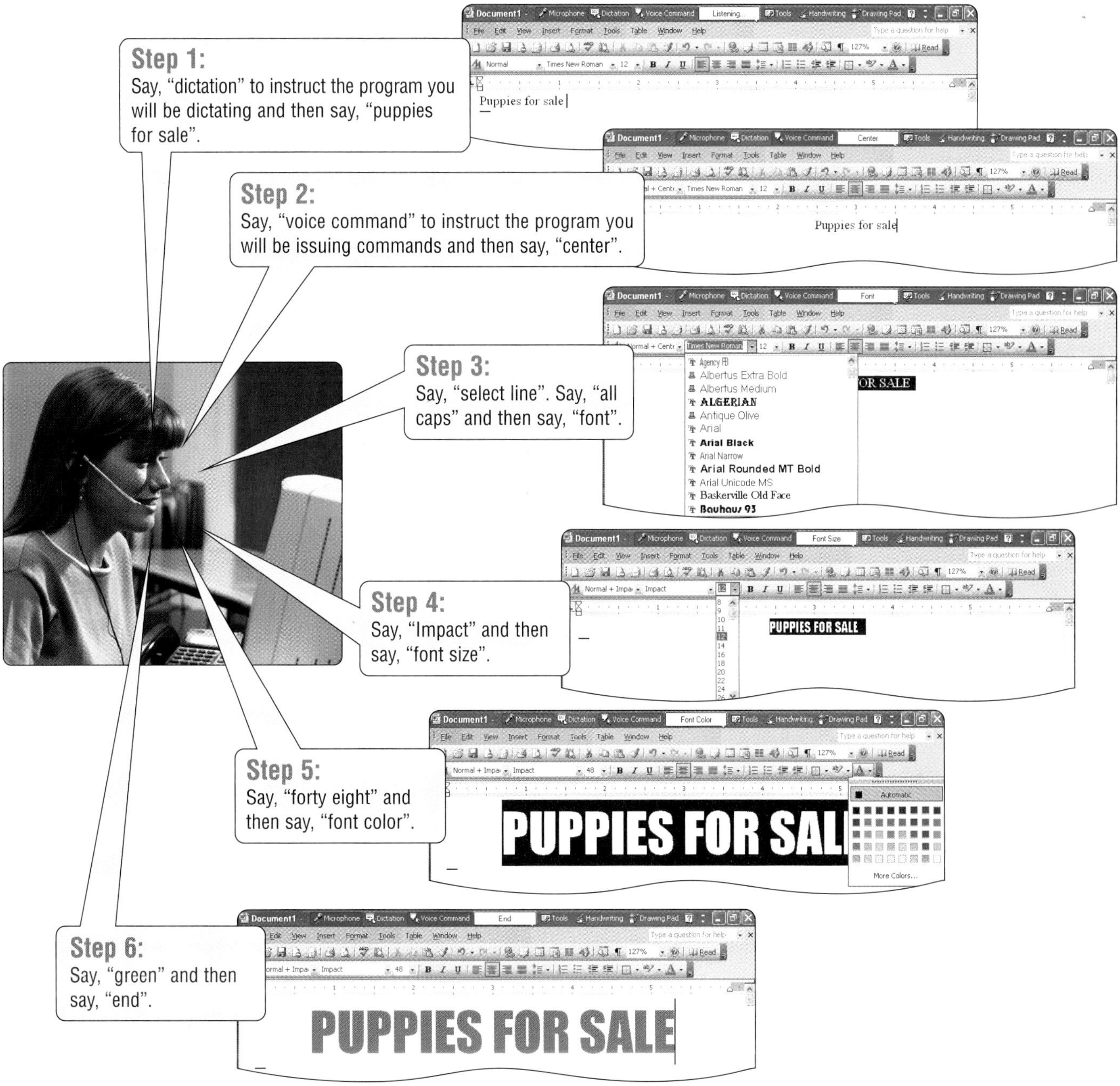

Spreadsheet Software

Spreadsheet software is another widely used type of application software. **Spreadsheet software** allows users to organize data in rows and columns and perform calculations on the data. These rows and columns collectively are called a *worksheet*. For years, people used pencil and gridded accounting paper to organize data and do calculations by hand. In an electronic worksheet, you organize data in the same manner, and the computer does the calculations more quickly and accurately (Figure 3-10). Because of the logical approach that spreadsheet software has for organizing data, many people use this software to organize and present non-financial data, as well as financial data.

As with word processing software, most spreadsheet software has basic features to help users create, edit, and format worksheets. Spreadsheet software also incorporates many of the features found in word processing software such as macros, checking spelling, changing fonts and font sizes, adding colors, tracking changes, recognizing voice input, inserting audio and video clips, research, ink input, and converting an existing spreadsheet document into a format for the World Wide Web.

The following sections describe the features unique to most spreadsheet programs.

SPREADSHEET ORGANIZATION A spreadsheet file is similar to a notebook with up to 255 related individual worksheets. Data is organized vertically in columns and horizontally in rows on each worksheet. Each worksheet typically has 256 columns and 65,536 rows. One or more letters identify each column, and a number identifies each row. The column letters begin with A and end with IV. The row numbers begin with 1 and end with 65,536. Only a small fraction of these columns and rows are displayed on the screen at one time. As with word processing software, scrolling through the worksheet displays different parts of it on the screen.

A *cell* is the intersection of a column and row. Each worksheet has more than 16 million (256 ◊ 65,536) cells in which you can enter data. The spreadsheet software identifies cells by the column and row in which they are located. For example, the intersection of column B and row 6 is referred to as cell B6. As shown in Figure 3-10, cell B6 contains the number, $72,631,781, which represents the electricity revenue for the first quarter.

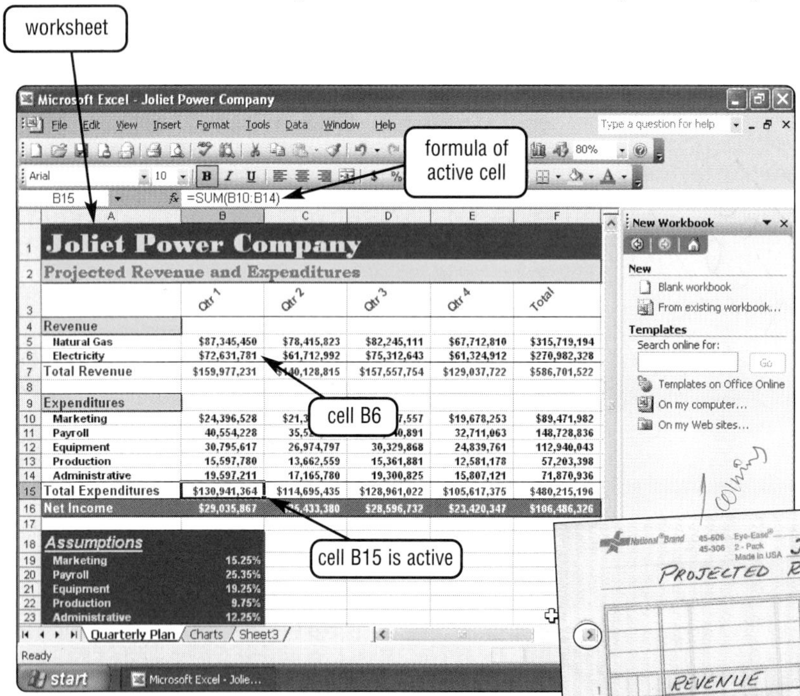

FIGURE 3-10 With spreadsheet software, you create worksheets that contain data arranged in rows and columns, and you perform calculations on the data in the worksheets.

Cells may contain three types of data: labels, values, and formulas. The text, or *label*, entered in a cell identifies the worksheet data and helps organize the worksheet. Using descriptive labels, such as Total Revenue and Total Expenditures, helps make a worksheet more meaningful.

CALCULATIONS Many of the worksheet cells shown in Figure 3-10 contain a number that can be used in a calculation, called a *value*. Other cells, however, contain formulas that generate values. A *formula* performs calculations on the data in the worksheet and displays the resulting value in a cell, usually the cell containing the formula. When creating a worksheet, you can enter your own formulas. In Figure 3-10, for example, cell B15 could contain the formula =B10+B11+B12+B13+B14 to calculate the projected total expenditures for the first quarter. A much more efficient way to sum the contents of cells, however, is to use a function, which is built into the spreadsheet software.

A *function* is a predefined formula that performs common calculations such as adding the values in a group of cells or generating a value such as the time or date. For example, instead of using the formula =B10+B11+B12+B13+B14 to calculate the projected total expenditures for the first quarter, using the function =SUM(B10:B14) totals the contents of cells B10 through B14. Figure 3-11 lists functions commonly included in spreadsheet programs.

RECALCULATION One of the more powerful features of spreadsheet software is its capability of recalculating the rest of the worksheet when data in a worksheet changes. To appreciate this capability, consider what happens each time you change a value in a manual worksheet. You must erase the old value, write in a new value, erase any totals that contain calculations based on the changed value, and then recalculate these totals and enter the new results. When working with a manual worksheet, accurately making changes and updating the affected values can be time-consuming and may result in new errors.

Making changes in an electronic worksheet is much easier and faster. When you enter a new value to change data in a cell, any value affected

SPREADSHEET FUNCTIONS

Financial	
FV (rate, number of periods, payment)	Calculates the future value of an investment
NPV (rate, range)	Calculates the net present value of an investment
PMT (rate, number of periods, present value)	Calculates the periodic payment for an annuity
PV (rate, number of periods, payment)	Calculates the present value of an investment
RATE (number of periods, payment, present value)	Calculates the periodic interest rate of an annuity
Date and Time	
DATE	Returns the current date
NOW	Returns the current date and time
TIME	Returns the current time
Mathematical	
ABS (number)	Returns the absolute value of a number
INT (number)	Rounds a number down to the nearest integer
LN (number)	Calculates the natural logarithm of a number
LOG (number, base)	Calculates the logarithm of a number to a specified base
ROUND (number, number of digits)	Rounds a number to a specified number of digits
SQRT (number)	Calculates the square root of a number
SUM (range)	Calculates the total of a range of numbers
Statistical	
AVERAGE (range)	Calculates the average value of a range of numbers
COUNT (range)	Counts how many cells in the range have numeric entries
MAX (range)	Returns the maximum value in a range
MIN (range)	Returns the minimum value in a range
STDEV (range)	Calculates the standard deviation of a range of numbers
Logical	
IF (logical test, value if true, value if false)	Performs a test and returns one value if the result of the test is true and another value if the result is false

FIGURE 3-11 Functions typically found in spreadsheet software.

by the change is updated automatically and instantaneously. In Figure 3-10 on page 142, for example, if you change the electricity revenue for the first quarter from $72,631,781 to $77,631,781, the total revenue in cell B7 automatically changes from $159,977,231 to $164,977,231.

Spreadsheet software's capability of recalculating data also makes it a valuable budgeting, forecasting, and decision making tool. Most spreadsheet software includes a *what-if analysis* feature, where you change certain values in a spreadsheet to reveal the effects of those changes.

WEB LINK 3-3

Spreadsheet Software

Visit the Discovering Computers 2005 WEB LINK page (**scsite.com/dc2005/weblink**). Click Spreadsheet Software below Chapter 3.

CHARTING Another standard feature of spreadsheet software is *charting*, which depicts the data in graphical form. A visual representation of data through charts often makes it easier for users to see at a glance the relationship among the numbers.

Three popular chart types are line charts, column charts, and pie charts. Figure 3-12 shows examples of these charts that were plotted from the data in Figure 3-10 on page 142. A *line chart* shows a trend during a period of time, as indicated by a rising or falling line. For example, a line chart could show the expenditures for the four quarters. A *column chart*, also called a *bar chart*, displays bars of various lengths to show the relationship of data. The bars can be horizontal, vertical, or stacked on top of one another. For example, a column chart might show the expenditure breakdown by quarter, with each bar representing a different expenditure. A *pie chart*, which has the shape of a round pie cut into slices, shows the relationship of parts to a whole. For example, you might use a pie chart to show the percentage each expenditure category contributed to the total expenditure.

Charts, as well as any other part of a workbook, can be linked to or embedded in a word processing document.

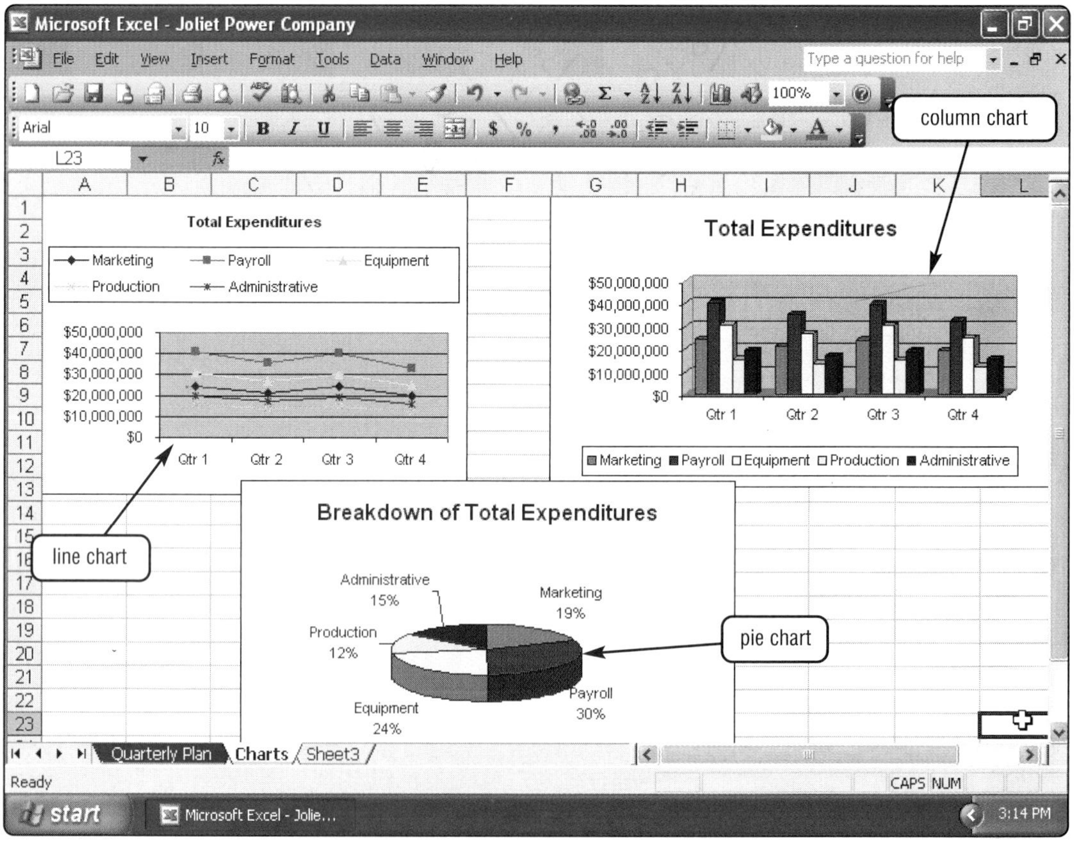

FIGURE 3-12 Three basic types of charts provided with spreadsheet software are line charts, column charts, and pie charts. The line chart, column chart, and pie chart shown here were created from the data in the worksheet in Figure 3-10 on page 142.

Database Software

A **database** is a collection of data organized in a manner that allows access, retrieval, and use of that data. In a manual database, you might record data on paper and store it in a filing cabinet. With a computerized database, such as the one shown in Figure 3-13, the computer stores the data in an electronic format on a storage medium such as a floppy disk or hard disk.

Database software is application software that allows users to create, access, and manage a database. Using database software, you can add, change, and delete data in a database; sort and retrieve data from the database; and create forms and reports using the data in the database.

With most popular personal computer database programs, a database consists of a collection of tables, organized in rows and columns. Each row, called a *record*, contains data about a given person, product, object, or event. Each column, called a *field*, contains a specific category of data within a record.

The Restaurant Supply database shown in Figure 3-13 consists of two tables: a Customer table and a Sales Rep table. The Customer table contains ten records (rows), each storing data about one customer. The customer data is grouped into seven fields (columns): customer number, name, address, telephone, balance, amount paid, and sales rep num. The balance field, for instance, contains the customer's balance due. The Customer and Sales Rep tables relate to one another through a common field, Sales Rep Num.

Users run queries to retrieve data. A *query* is a request for specific data from the database. For example, a query might request a list of customers that have a balance due. Database software can take the results of a query and present it in a window on the screen, called a *form*, or send it as a report to the printer.

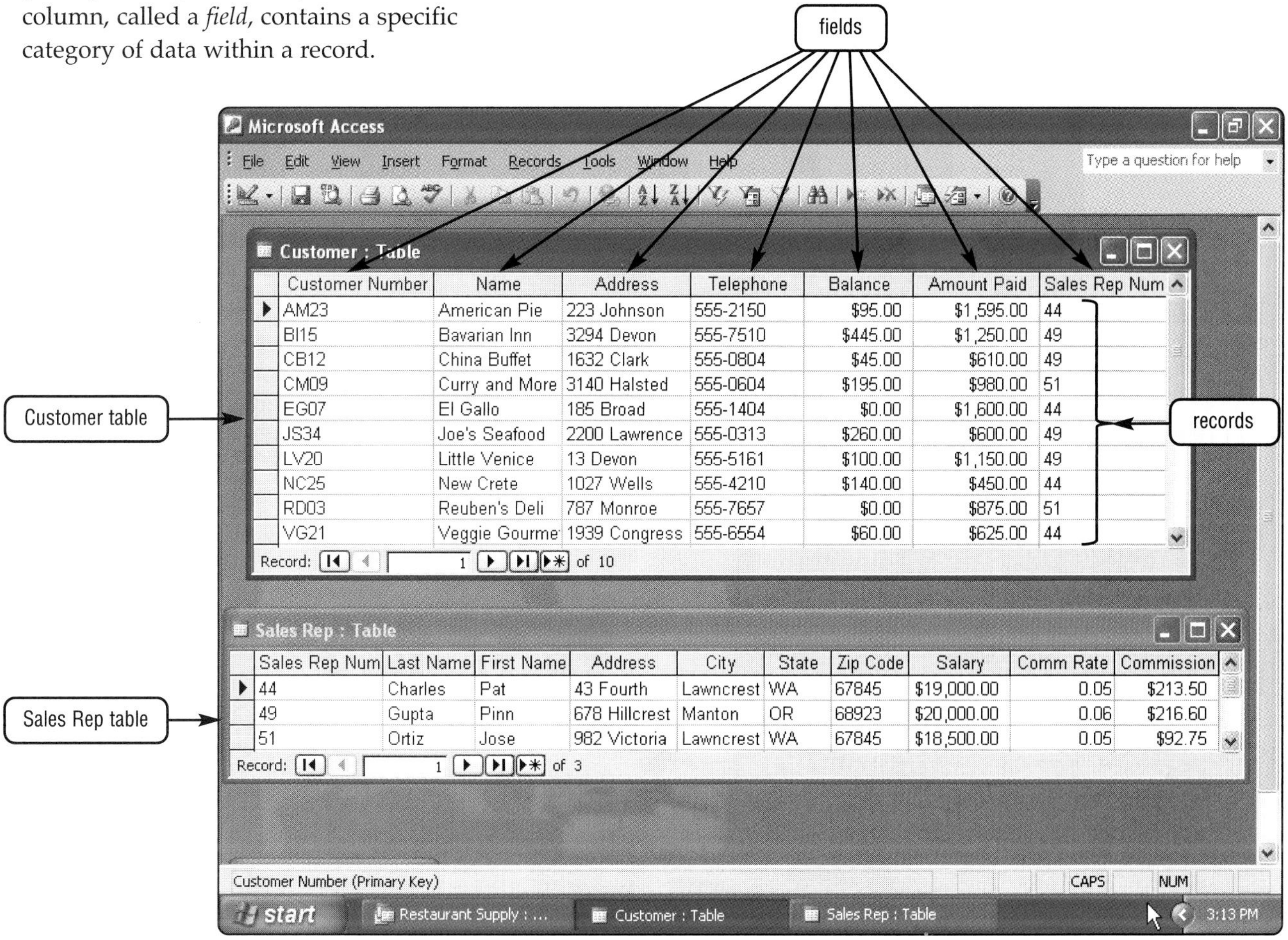

Customer Number	Name	Address	Telephone	Balance	Amount Paid	Sales Rep Num
AM23	American Pie	223 Johnson	555-2150	$95.00	$1,595.00	44
BI15	Bavarian Inn	3294 Devon	555-7510	$445.00	$1,250.00	49
CB12	China Buffet	1632 Clark	555-0804	$45.00	$610.00	49
CM09	Curry and More	3140 Halsted	555-0604	$195.00	$980.00	51
EG07	El Gallo	185 Broad	555-1404	$0.00	$1,600.00	44
JS34	Joe's Seafood	2200 Lawrence	555-0313	$260.00	$600.00	49
LV20	Little Venice	13 Devon	555-5161	$100.00	$1,150.00	49
NC25	New Crete	1027 Wells	555-4210	$140.00	$450.00	44
RD03	Reuben's Deli	787 Monroe	555-7657	$0.00	$875.00	51
VG21	Veggie Gourme	1939 Congress	555-6554	$60.00	$625.00	44

Sales Rep Num	Last Name	First Name	Address	City	State	Zip Code	Salary	Comm Rate	Commission
44	Charles	Pat	43 Fourth	Lawncrest	WA	67845	$19,000.00	0.05	$213.50
49	Gupta	Pinn	678 Hillcrest	Manton	OR	68923	$20,000.00	0.06	$216.60
51	Ortiz	Jose	982 Victoria	Lawncrest	WA	67845	$18,500.00	0.05	$92.75

FIGURE 3-13 This database contains two tables: one for Customer and one for Sales Rep. The Customer table has 10 records and 7 fields; the Sales Rep table has 3 records and 10 fields.

Presentation Graphics Software

Presentation graphics software is application software that allows users to create visual aids for presentations to communicate ideas, messages, and other information to a group. The presentations can be viewed as slides, sometimes called a *slide show*, that are displayed on a large monitor or on a projection screen (Figure 3-14).

Presentation graphics software typically provides a variety of predefined presentation formats that define complementary colors for backgrounds, text, and graphical accents on the slides. This software also provides a variety of layouts for each individual slide such as a title slide (Figure 3-15), a two-column slide, and a slide with clip art, a chart, a table, or animation. In addition, you can enhance any text, charts, and graphical images on a slide with 3-D and other special effects such as shading, shadows, and textures.

When building a presentation, users can set the slide timing so the presentation automatically displays the next slide after a preset delay. Presentation graphics software allows you to apply special effects to the transition between each slide. One slide, for example, might fade away slowly as the next slide is displayed.

To help organize the presentation, you can view thumbnail versions of all the slides in slide sorter view. *Slide sorter view* presents a screen view similar to how 35mm slides look on a photographer's light table. The slide sorter allows users to arrange the slides in any order.

Presentation graphics software typically includes a clip gallery that provides images, pictures, video clips, and audio clips to enhance multimedia presentations. Users with an artistic ability can create their own graphics using paint/image editing software (discussed later in the chapter) and then *import* (bring in) the graphics into the slide. Users also can insert their own video, music, and audio commentary in a presentation.

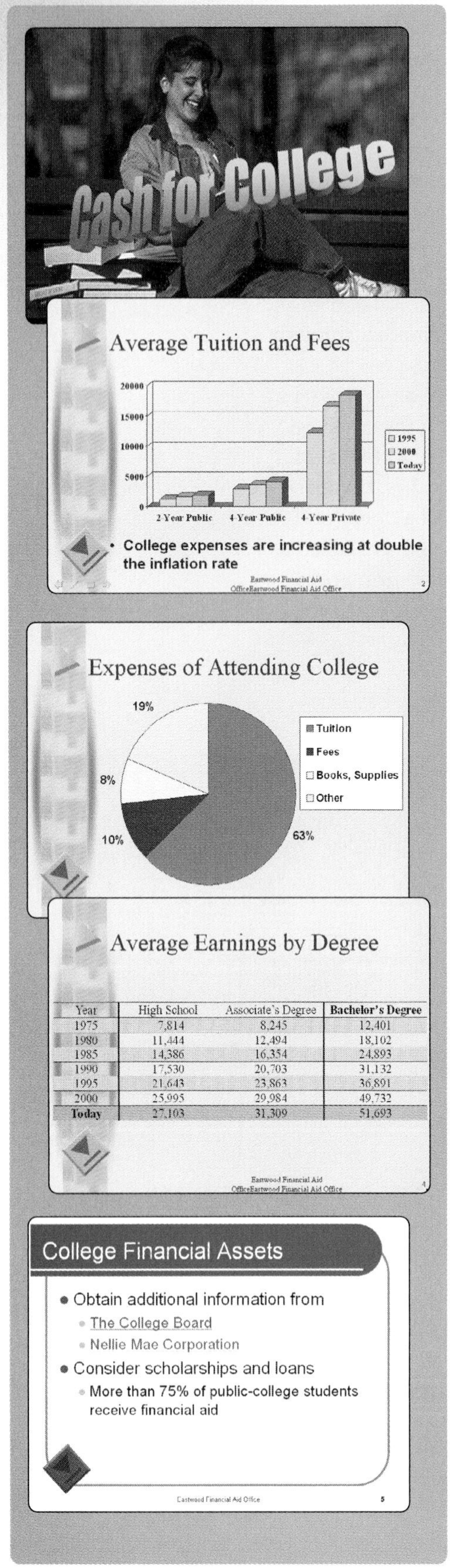

FIGURE 3-14 This presentation created with presentation graphics software consists of five slides.

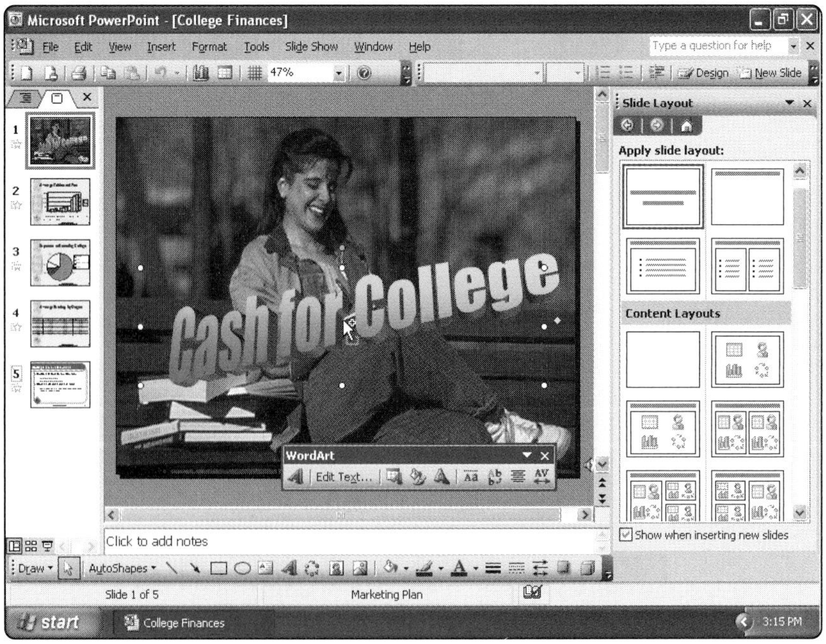

FIGURE 3-15 In presentation graphics software, users can change the design and layout of any slide in a presentation.

You can view or print a finished presentation in a variety of formats. An *outline* includes only the text from each slide such as the slide title and the key points. *Audience handouts* include images of two or more slides on a page, for distribution to audience members (Figure 3-16a). Speakers sometimes print a notes page to help them deliver the presentation. A *notes page* shows an image of the slide along with any additional notes a presenter wants to see while discussing a topic or slide (Figure 3-16b).

Presentation graphics software incorporates some of the features found in word processing software such as checking spelling, formatting, recognizing voice input, research, ink input, and converting an existing slide show into a format for the World Wide Web.

Figure 3-16a (audience handout)

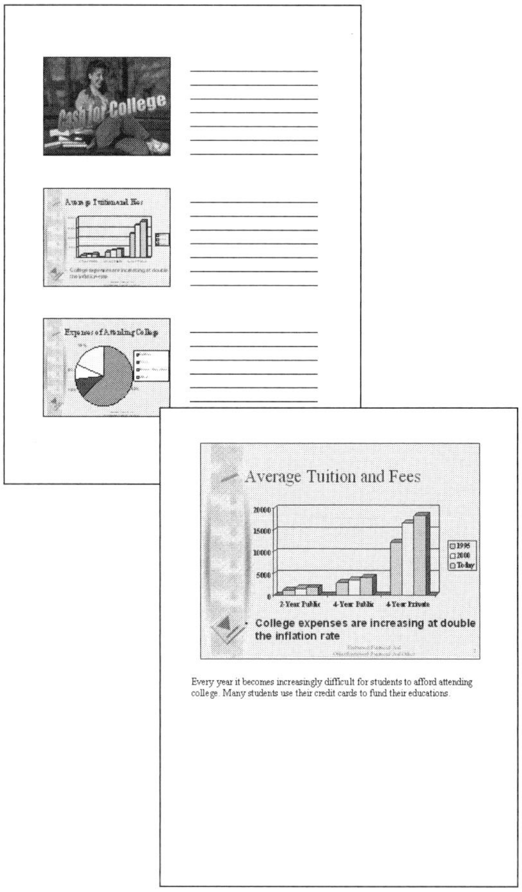

Figure 3-16b (notes page)

FIGURE 3-16 An example of an audience handout and a notes page.

Note Taking Software

Note taking software is application software that enables users to enter typed text, handwritten comments, drawings, or sketches anywhere on a page (Figure 3-17) and then save the page as part of a notebook. Users also can include audio recordings as part of their notes.

Once the notes are captured (entered and saved), users easily can organize them, reuse them, and share them. This software allows users to search through saved notes for specific text. It even can search through an entire notebook. Users also can flag important notes with color, highlights, and shapes.

On a desktop or notebook computer, users enter notes primarily via the keyboard or microphone. On a Tablet PC, however, the primary input device is the digital pen. Users find note taking software convenient during meetings, lectures, conferences, in libraries, and other settings that previously required a pencil and tablet of paper for recording thoughts and discussions.

Note taking software incorporates many of the features found in word processing software such as checking spelling, changing fonts and font sizes, adding colors, recognizing voice input, inserting audio and video clips, research, and ink input.

WEB LINK 3-4

Presentation Graphics Software

Visit the Discovering Computers 2005 WEB LINK page (**scsite.com/dc2005/weblink**). Click Presentation Graphics Software below Chapter 3.

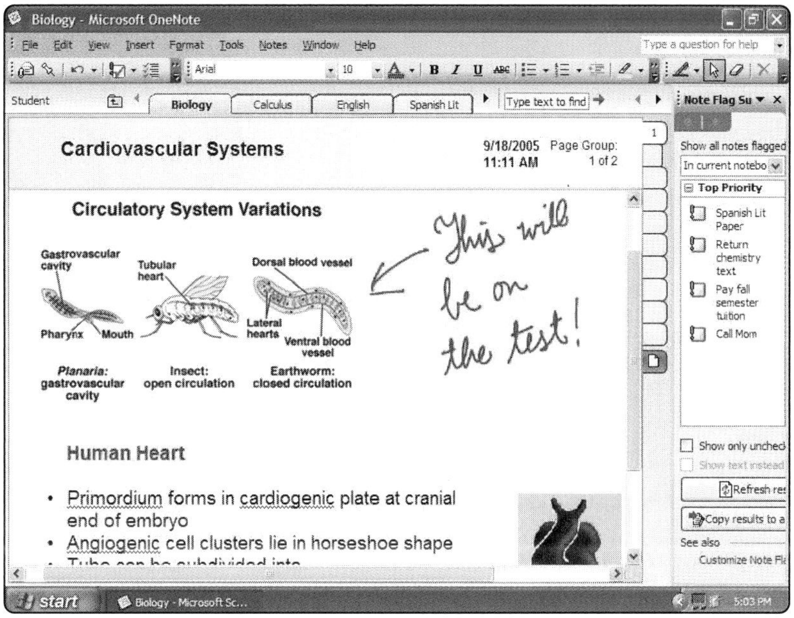

FIGURE 3-17 With note taking software, users can handwrite notes, draw sketches, or type text.

Personal Information Managers

A **personal information manager** (**PIM**) is application software that includes an appointment calendar, address book, notepad, and other features to help users organize personal information. The appointment calendar allows you to schedule activities for a particular day and time. With the address book, you can enter and maintain names, addresses, telephone numbers, and e-mail addresses of customers, coworkers, family members, and friends. Instead of writing notes on a piece of paper, you can use the notepad to record ideas, reminders, and other important information. With a PIM, you can take information previously tracked in a weekly or daily calendar, and organize and store it on your computer.

Most PDAs today include, among many other features, PIM functionality. Using a PDA, you can synchronize, or coordinate, information so that both the PDA and the computer have the latest version of the information. Some PDAs synchronize with the computer wirelessly. With others, you connect the PDA to the computer with a cable, or you insert the PDA into a cradle, which has a cable that plugs into the computer (Figure 3-18).

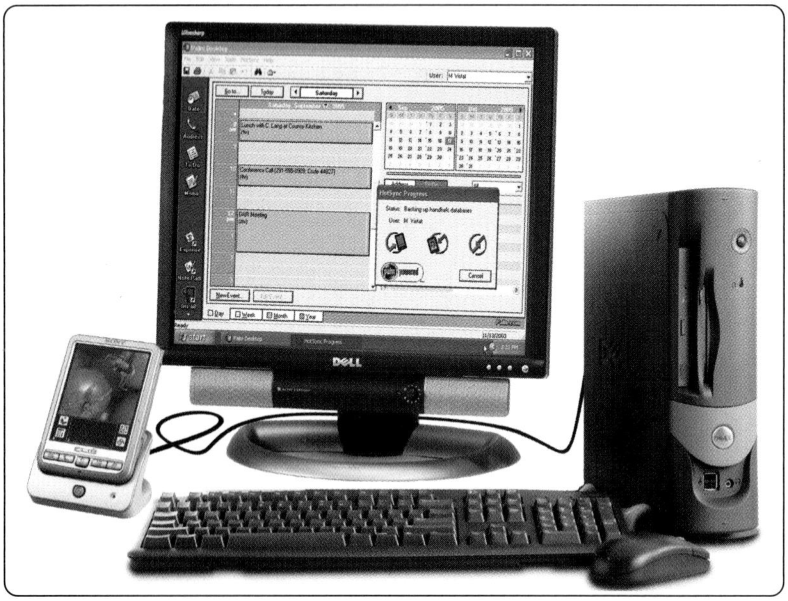

FIGURE 3-18 With most PDAs, you can synchronize or transfer PIM information from the PDA to a personal computer, so the updated list of appointments, addresses, and other important information always is available.

PDA Business Software

In addition to PIM software, a huge variety of business software is available for PDAs. Although some PDAs have software built in, most have the capability of accessing software on miniature storage media such as memory cards. The software on memory cards allows PDA users to create documents, take notes, manage budgets and finances, create slide shows, view and edit photographs, read electronic books, plan travel routes, and play games. For additional information about available software for PDAs, read the PDA Software feature that follows Chapter 5. Read Looking Ahead 3-1 for a look at the next generation of accessing software on PDAs and other mobile devices.

LOOKING AHEAD 3-1

3G Wireless Service Developing

Mobile communications service in the United States is undergoing a series of upgrades. The third-generation (*3G*) standard is available in Asia and parts of Europe, but U.S. service has been developing slowly.

3G service features enhanced data transfer capability so files download more quickly to handheld computers and PDAs. In Japan, consumers eagerly use 3G service to download songs and video clips, shop, bank, and share digital images.

In the United States, Verizon and AT&T Wireless are developing 3G networks and increasing their coverage. As hardware supporting the 3G standard is manufactured, demand for this service is expected to grow as an alternative method of remotely accessing the Internet and computer networks.

For a look at the next generation of accessing software on PDAs and other mobile devices, visit the Discovering Computers 2005 Looking Ahead Web page (**scsite.com/dc2005/looking**). Click Looking Ahead #1 below Chapter 3.

Software Suite

A **software suite** is a collection of individual programs sold as a single package. When installing the software suite, you install the entire collection of programs at once instead of installing each one individually. Business software suites typically include the following programs: word processing, spreadsheet, e-mail, and presentation graphics. Two of the more widely used software suites are Microsoft Office 2003 and Sun StarOffice.

Software suites offer two major advantages: lower cost and ease of use. Buying a collection of programs in a software suite usually costs significantly less than purchasing them individually. Software suites provide ease of use because the programs within a software suite normally use a similar interface and share features such as clip art and spelling checker. Once you learn how to use one program in the software suite, you are familiar with the interface of the other programs in the software suite. For example, once you learn how to print using the software suite's word processing program, you can apply the same skill to the spreadsheet and presentation graphics programs in the software suite.

Project Management Software

Project management software allows a user to plan, schedule, track, and analyze the events, resources, and costs of a project (Figure 3-19). Project management software helps users track, control, and manage project variables, allowing them to complete a project on time and within budget. A general contractor, for example, might use project management software to manage a home-remodeling job to schedule carpenters, electricians, painters, and other subcontractors. A publisher might use it to coordinate the production of a textbook.

Accounting Software

Accounting software helps companies record and report their financial transactions (Figure 3-20). With accounting software, business users perform accounting activities related to the general ledger, accounts receivable, accounts payable, purchasing, invoicing, and payroll functions. Accounting software also enables users to write and print checks, track checking account activity, and update and reconcile balances on demand.

FAQ 3-3

What is the difference between Microsoft Office 2003 and Microsoft Office System?

Microsoft Office 2003 is a suite of core desktop business programs. Office 2003 is available in a variety of editions, each of which includes at least Word, Excel, and Outlook. *Microsoft Office System* is a portfolio of programs and services that are tightly integrated yet available for purchase as separate entities. In addition to Microsoft Office 2003, other products in the Microsoft Office System include OneNote, InfoPath, Visio, FrontPage, and Project.

For more information about Microsoft Office 2003 and Microsoft Office System, visit the Discovering Computers 2005 FAQ Web page (**scsite.com/dc2005/faq**). Click Microsoft Office 2003 and Microsoft Office System below Chapter 3.

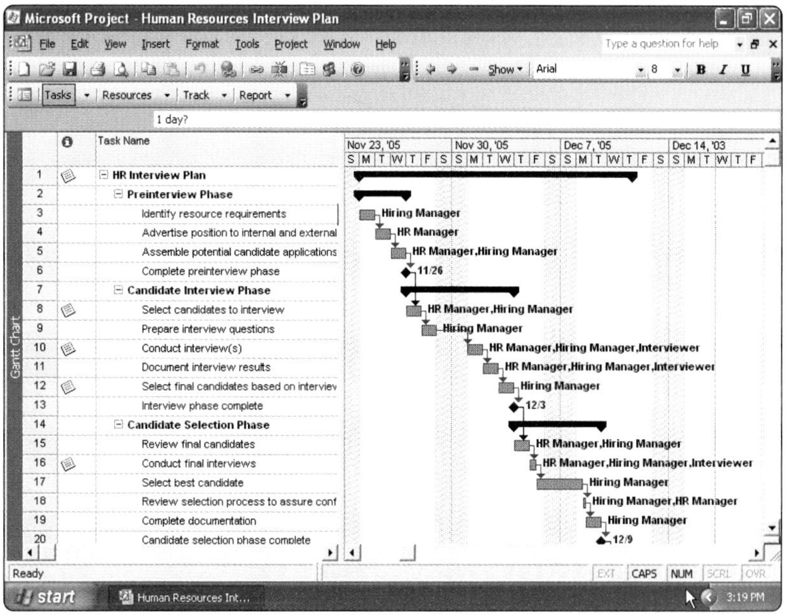

FIGURE 3-19 Project management software allows users to track, control, and manage the events, resources, and costs of a project.

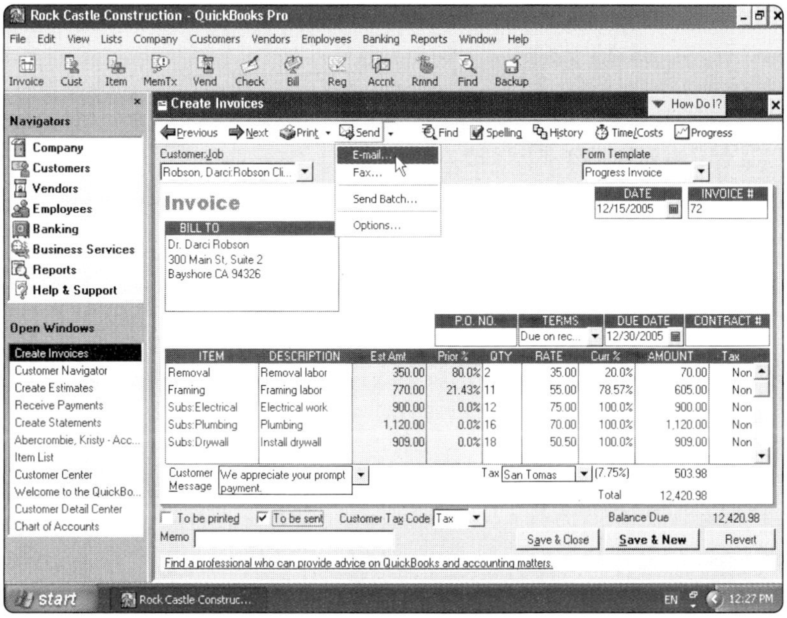

FIGURE 3-20 Accounting software helps companies record and report their financial transactions.

Newer accounting software supports online credit checks, billing, direct deposit, and payroll services. For example, a company can deposit paychecks directly into employees' checking accounts and pay employee taxes electronically.

Some accounting software offers more complex features such as job costing and estimating, time tracking, multiple company reporting, foreign currency reporting, and forecasting the amount of raw materials needed for products. The cost of accounting software for small businesses ranges from less than one hundred to several thousand dollars. Accounting software for large businesses can cost several hundred thousand dollars.

GRAPHICS AND MULTIMEDIA SOFTWARE

In addition to business software, many people work with software designed specifically for their field of work. Power users such as engineers, architects, desktop publishers, and graphic artists often use sophisticated software that allows them to work with graphics and multimedia. This software includes computer-aided design, desktop publishing, paint/image editing, video and audio editing, animation, multimedia authoring, and Web page authoring. Figure 3-21 lists the more popular programs for each of these categories. Some of these programs incorporate user-friendly interfaces, or scaled-down versions, making it possible for the home and small business users to create documents in these programs. The following sections discuss the features and functions of this application software.

GRAPHICS AND MULTIMEDIA SOFTWARE

Application Software	Popular Programs
Computer-Aided Design (CAD)	• Autodesk AutoCAD • Quality Plans Chief Architect • Microsoft Office Visio 2003
Desktop Publishing (for the Professional)	• Adobe InDesign • Adobe PageMaker • Corel VENTURA • Quark QuarkXPress
Paint/Image Editing (for the Professional)	• Adobe Illustrator • Adobe Photoshop • Corel CorelDRAW • Macromedia FreeHand • Corel Painter
Video and Audio Editing	• Adobe Audition • Adobe Encore DVD • Adobe Premiere Pro • Cakewalk SONAR • Macromedia SoundEdit • Pinnacle Systems Studio DV • Ulead MediaStudio Pro
Multimedia Authoring	• click2learn.com ToolBook Instructor • Macromedia Authorware • Macromedia Director
Web Page Authoring	• Adobe GoLive • Adobe LiveMotion • Macromedia Dreamweaver • Macromedia Fireworks • Macromedia Flash • Microsoft FrontPage

FIGURE 3-21 Popular graphics and multimedia programs.

Computer-Aided Design

Computer-aided design (CAD) software is a sophisticated type of application software that assists a professional user in creating engineering, architectural, and scientific designs. For example, engineers create design plans for airplanes and security systems. Architects design building structures and floor plans (Figure 3-22). Scientists design drawings of molecular structures.

FIGURE 3-22 CAD software is sophisticated software that assists engineers, architects, and scientists in creating designs.

CAD software eliminates the laborious manual drafting that design processes can require. Using CAD software, designers make changes to a drawing or design and immediately view the results. Three-dimensional CAD programs allow designers to rotate designs of 3-D objects to view them from any angle. Some CAD software even can generate material lists for building designs.

Some manufacturers of CAD software sell a scaled-down product, designed specifically for the home user or small business user.

Desktop Publishing Software (for the Professional)

Desktop publishing (DTP) software enables professional designers to create sophisticated documents that contain text, graphics, and many colors. Professional DTP software is ideal for the production of high-quality color documents such as textbooks, corporate newsletters, marketing literature (Figure 3-23), product catalogs, and annual reports. In the past, documents of this type were created by slower, more expensive traditional publishing methods such as typesetting. Today's DTP software also allows designers to convert a color document into a format for use on the World Wide Web.

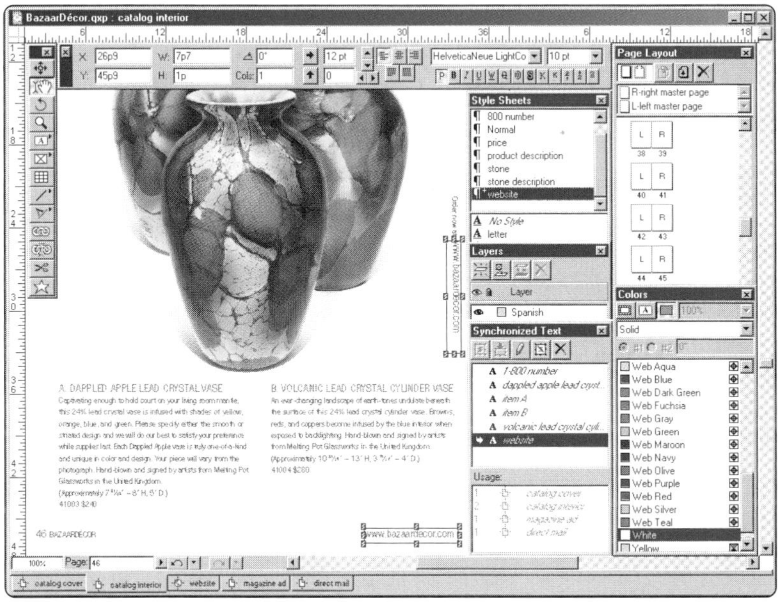

FIGURE 3-23 Professional designers and graphic artists use DTP software to produce sophisticated publications such as marketing literature.

FAQ 3-4

What prevents me from opening some files on the Web that contain company literature and brochures?

Although some companies require a password to view documents, in many other cases, you simply need Adobe Acrobat Reader software. This is because some companies save documents on the Web, such as brochures, using the Adobe PDF format. To view and print a PDF file, simply download the free Adobe Acrobat Reader software from Adobe's Web site.

For more information about Adobe Acrobat Reader, visit the Discovering Computers 2005 FAQ Web page (**scsite.com/dc2005/faq**). Click Adobe Acrobat Reader below Chapter 3.

Although many word processing programs have some of the capabilities of DTP software, professional designers and graphic artists use DTP software because it supports page layout. *Page layout* is the process of arranging text and graphics in a document on a page-by-page basis. DTP software includes color libraries to assist in color selections for text and graphics. A *color library* is a standard set of colors used by designers and printers to ensure that colors will print exactly as specified. Designers and graphic artists can print finished publications on a color printer, take them to a professional printer, or post them on the Web.

Paint/Image Editing Software (for the Professional)

Graphic artists, multimedia professionals, technical illustrators, and desktop publishers use paint software and image editing software to create and modify graphical images such as those used in DTP documents and Web pages. **Paint software**, also called *illustration software*, allows users to draw pictures, shapes, and other graphical images with various on-screen tools such as a pen, brush, eyedropper, and paint bucket. **Image editing software** provides the capabilities of paint software and also includes the ability to modify existing images (Figure 3-24). Modifications can include adjusting or enhancing image colors, and adding special effects such as shadows and glows. This software often has photo editing tools, allowing users to retouch photographs. Read Issue 3-3 for a related discussion.

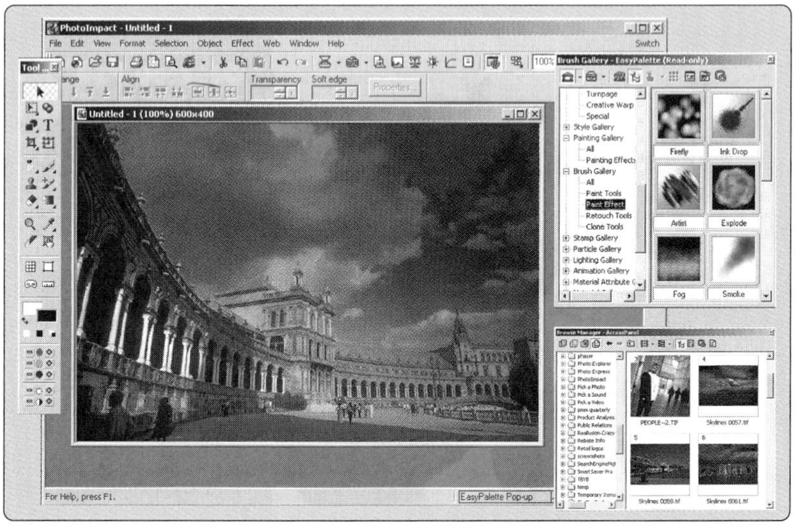

FIGURE 3-24 With image editing software, artists create and modify any type of graphical image.

ISSUE 3-3

Should What We See Be What We Get?

Today, many commercial artists, photojournalists, and creators of cartoons, book covers, and billboards use paint and image editing software. With this software, artists can convert photographs to a digital form that can be colorized, stretched, squeezed, texturized, or otherwise altered. They can import graphics files and manipulate the images in ways that previously were unachievable. For example, you can add clouds to a blue sky, manipulate a picture of a group of people so that it looks like they are standing in front of the Great Pyramids of Egypt, or even remove a person from a picture altogether. The National Press Photographers Association endorses the following: "As [photo] journalists we believe the guiding principle of our profession is accuracy; therefore, we believe it is wrong to alter the content of a photograph in any way, electronically or in the darkroom, that deceives the public." Do you agree with this guideline? Should professional graphic artists be able to alter photographs or other existing illustrations with paint and image editing software? Is it ethical? Is altering someone else's photograph a copyright issue?

For more information about paint and image editing software and photograph altering, visit the Discovering Computers 2005 Issues Web page (**scsite.com/dc2005/issues**). Click Issue #3 below Chapter 3.

Video and Audio Editing Software

Video editing software (Figure 3-25) allows users to modify a segment of a video, called a clip. For example, you can reduce the length of a video clip, reorder a series of clips, or add special effects such as words that move horizontally across the screen. Video editing software typically includes audio editing capabilities.

FIGURE 3-25 With video editing software, users modify video images.

Audio editing software lets users modify audio clips and produce studio-quality soundtracks. Audio editing software usually includes *filters*, which are designed to enhance audio quality. For example, a filter might remove a distracting background noise from the audio clip.

Some operating systems include audio editing and video editing capabilities. These operating systems give the home user the ability to edit home movies and share clips on the Web.

Multimedia Authoring Software

Multimedia authoring software allows users to combine text, graphics, audio, video, and animation into an interactive application (Figure 3-26). With this software, users control the placement of text and images and the duration of sounds, video, and animation. Once created, multimedia presentations often take the form of interactive computer-based presentations or Web-based presentations designed to facilitate learning, demonstrate product functionality, and elicit direct-user participation. Training centers, educational

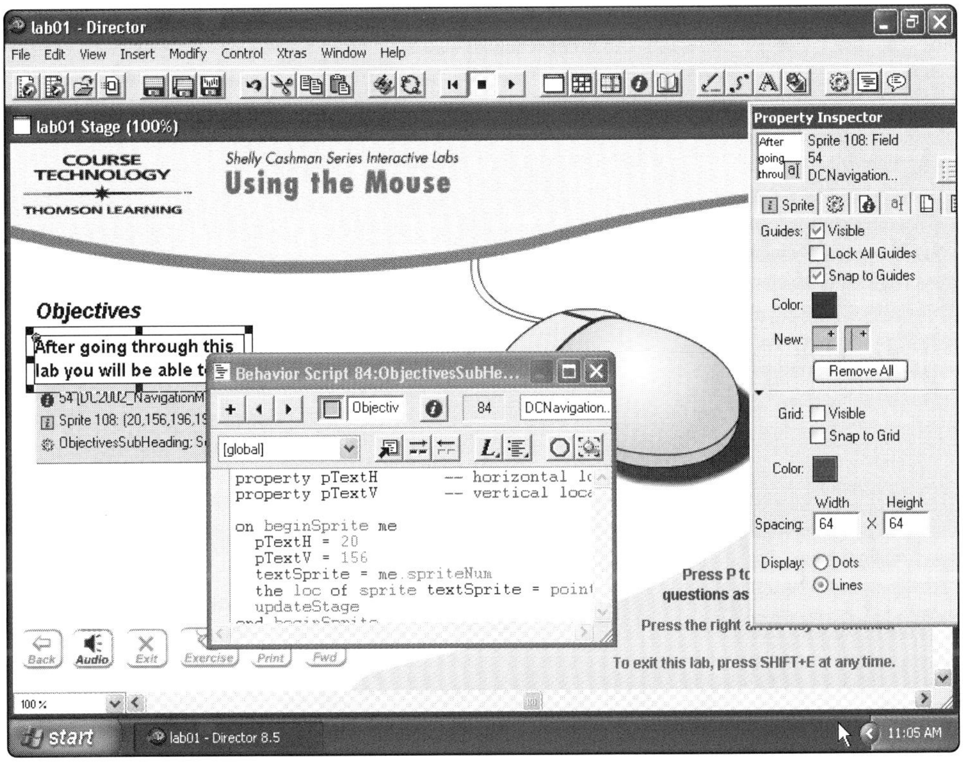

FIGURE 3-26 Multimedia authoring software allows you to create dynamic presentations that include text, graphics, video, sound, and animation.

institutions, and online magazine publishers all use multimedia authoring software to develop interactive applications. These applications may be available on a CD or DVD, over a local area network, or via the Internet.

Web Page Authoring Software

Web page authoring software helps users of all skill levels create Web pages that include graphical images, video, audio, animation, and other special effects. In addition, many Web page authoring programs allow users to organize, manage, and maintain Web sites.

Application software programs, such as Word and Excel, often include Web page authoring features. This allows home users to create basic Web pages using application software they already own. For more sophisticated Web pages, users work with Web page authoring software. Many Web page developers also use multimedia authoring software along with, or instead of, Web page authoring software for Web page development.

FAQ 3-5

How do I know which program to buy?

Many companies offer downloadable *trial versions* of their software that allow you to use the software free for a limited time. Try a few. Read computer magazines and Web sites for reviews of various products.

For more information about trial versions, visit the Discovering Computers 2005 FAQ Web page (**scsite.com/dc2005/faq**). Click Trial Versions below Chapter 3.

QUIZ YOURSELF 3-2

To check your knowledge of the types and features of business programs and graphics/multimedia programs, visit the Discovering Computers 2005 Quiz Yourself Web page (**scsite.com/dc2005/quiz**). Click Objectives 4 – 5 below Chapter 3.

SOFTWARE FOR HOME, PERSONAL, AND EDUCATIONAL USE

A large amount of application software is designed specifically for home, personal, and educational use. Most of the programs in this category are relatively inexpensive, often priced less than $100. Figure 3-27 lists popular programs for many of these categories. The following sections discuss the features and functions of this application software.

PROGRAMS FOR HOME/PERSONAL/EDUCATIONAL USE

Application Software	Popular Programs
Software Suite (for Personal Use)	• Microsoft Works
Personal Finance	• Intuit Quicken • Microsoft Money
Legal	• Broderbund Family Lawyer • Cosmi Perfect Attorney • Kiplinger's Home & Business Attorney • Kiplinger's WILLPower • Quicken Lawyer
Tax Preparation	• H&R Block Kiplinger TaxCut • Quicken TurboTax
Desktop Publishing (for Personal Use)	• Broderbund The Print Shop • Microsoft Office Publisher 2003
Paint/Image Editing (for Personal Use)	• Adobe Photoshop Elements • Broderbund PrintMaster • Broderbund The Print Shop • Corel Photobook • Jasc Paint Shop Pro • Microsoft Picture It! Photo • Sun StarOffice Draw • Ulead PhotoImpact
Clip Art/Image Gallery	• Broadband ClickArt • Nova Development Art Explosion
Home Design/Landscaping	• Broderbund 3D Home Design Suite • Broderbund 3D Home Architect • Broderbund 3D Home Landscape Designer • Quality Plans 3D Home Architect • ValuSoft Complete LandDesigner
Reference	• American Heritage Talking Dictionary Classic • Microsoft Encarta • Microsoft Streets & Trips • Rand McNally Road Atlas • Rand McNally StreetFinder • Rand McNally TripMaker

FIGURE 3-27 Many popular programs are available for home, personal, and educational use.

Software Suite (for Personal Use)

A software suite (for personal use) combines application software such as word processing, spreadsheet, and database into a single, easy-to-use package. Many computer vendors install Microsoft Works on new computers sold to home users.

As mentioned earlier, the programs within a software suite use a similar interface and share some common features. Once you learn how to use one program in the software, you are familiar with the interface in the other programs.

The programs in software suites for personal use usually are available only through the software suite; that is, you cannot purchase them individually. These programs typically do not have all the capabilities of business application software such as Word and Excel. These software suites thus are less expensive than a more powerful software suite. For many home users, however, the capabilities of software suites for personal use more than meet their needs. Word processing typically is the most widely used program in this software.

Personal Finance Software

Personal finance software is a simplified accounting program that helps home users and small office/home office users balance their checkbooks, pay bills, track personal income and expenses, track investments, and evaluate financial plans (Figure 3-28). Personal finance software helps determine where, and for what purpose, you are spending money so you can manage your finances. Reports can summarize transactions by category (such as dining), by payee (such as the electric company), or by time (such as the last two months).

Most of these programs also offer a variety of online services, which require access to the Internet. For example, users can track investments online, compare insurance rates from leading insurance companies, and bank online. **Online banking** offers access to account balances, provides bill paying services, and includes copies of monthly transactions from the bank's computer into your computer. Additionally, you can download monthly transactions and statements from the Web directly into your computer.

Most personal finance software includes financial planning features, such as analyzing home and personal loans, preparing income taxes, and managing retirement savings. Other features include managing home inventory and setting up budgets.

WEB LINK 3-5

Personal Finance Software

Visit the Discovering Computers 2005 WEB LINK page (**scsite.com/dc2005/weblink**). Click Personal Finance Software below Chapter 3.

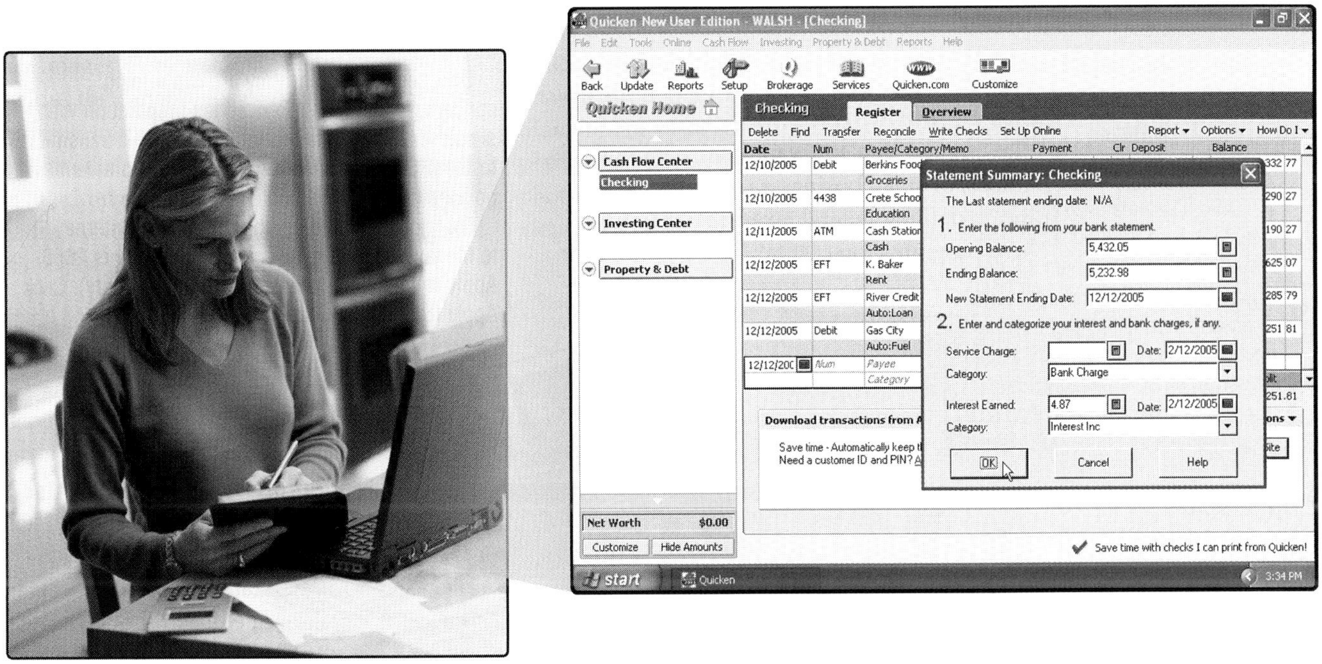

FIGURE 3-28 Personal finance software assists home users with balancing their checkbooks and paying bills.

WEB LINK 3-7

Microsoft Design Gallery Live

Visit the Discovering Computers 2005 WEB LINK page (**scsite.com/dc2005/weblink**). Click Microsoft Design Gallery Live below Chapter 3.

Clip Art/Image Gallery

Application software often includes a **clip art/image gallery**, which is a collection of clip art and photographs. Some applications have links to additional clips available on the Web (Figure 3-33). You also can purchase clip art/image gallery software that contains thousands of images.

In addition to clip art, many clip art/image galleries provide fonts, animations, sounds, video clips, and audio clips. You can use the images, fonts, and other items from the clip art/image gallery in all types of documents, including word processing, desktop publishing, spreadsheet, and presentation graphics.

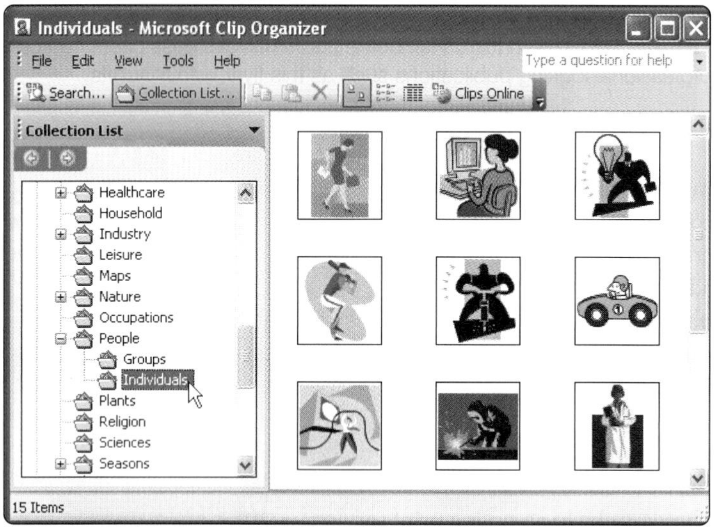

FIGURE 3-33 Application software often includes a built-in clip art/image gallery that has links to the Web for additional images.

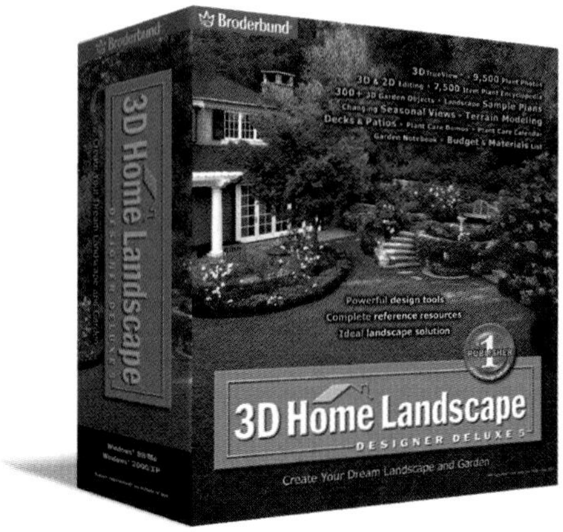

FIGURE 3-34 Home design/landscaping software helps users design or remodel a home, deck, or landscape.

Home Design/Landscaping Software

Homeowners or potential homeowners can use **home design/landscaping software** to assist them with the design, remodeling, or improvement of a home, deck, or landscape (Figure 3-34). Home design/landscaping software includes hundreds of predrawn plans that you can customize to meet your needs. Once designed, many home design/landscaping programs print a materials list outlining costs and quantities for the entire project.

Educational and Reference Software

Educational software is software that teaches a particular skill. Educational software exists for just about any subject, from learning how to type to learning how to cook. Preschool to high school learners use educational software to assist them with subjects such as reading and math or to prepare them for class or college entry exams. Educational software often includes games and contents to make the learning experience more fun.

Many educational programs use a computer-based training approach. **Computer-based training** (**CBT**), also called computer-aided instruction (CAI), is a type of education in which students learn by using and completing exercises with instructional software. CBT typically consists of self-directed, self-paced instruction about a topic. Athletes, for example use CBT programs to learn the intricacies of baseball, football, soccer, tennis, and golf. The military uses CBT simulations to train pilots to fly in various conditions and environments (Figure 3-35). Schools use CBT to teach students math, language, and software skills.

FIGURE 3-35 A soldier practices flight patterns using a CBT flight simulation program.

Reference software provides valuable and thorough information for all individuals (Figure 3-36). Popular reference software includes encyclopedias, dictionaries, health/medical guides, and travel directories. Read Looking Ahead 3-2 for a look at software for teachers.

LOOKING AHEAD 3-2

Plagiarism Software Detects Cheating

Term paper Web sites provide complete papers on a vast number of topics. Instructors, however, have tools to help them detect these plagiarized papers easily and quickly.

A variety of Web sites, such as turnitin.com, have databases of papers found on the term paper Web sites.

Instructors upload suspected papers to these Web sites, at which computers attempt to match the phrases and paragraphs with text in the database documents. The Web sites then return an originality report highlighting text that may have been copied.

As the plagiarism services become easier to use and less expensive, many instructors are expected to submit every paper their students write to these Web services. The objective and reliable results ultimately are expected to help deter plagiarism.

For a look at the next generation of plagiarism-detection software, visit the Discovering Computers 2005 Looking Ahead Web page (**scsite.com/dc2005/looking**). Click Looking Ahead #2 below Chapter 3.

Entertainment Software

Entertainment software for personal computers includes interactive games, videos, and other programs designed to support a hobby or provide amusement and enjoyment. For example, you might use entertainment software to play games, make a family tree, compose music, or fly an aircraft (Figure 3-37).

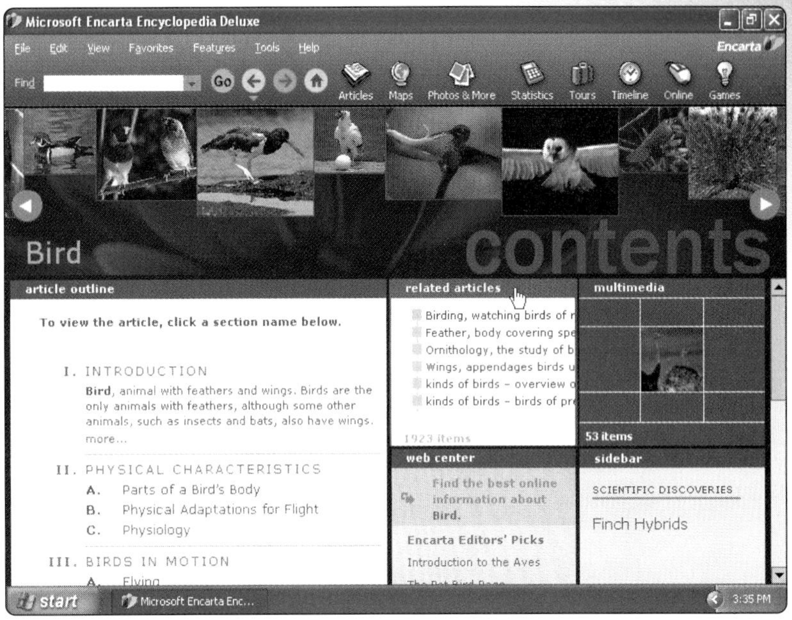

FIGURE 3-36 Reference software provides valuable and thorough information for all types of users. This reference software shows text you can read about birds and includes a variety of pictures, videos, and links to the Web.

WEB LINK 3-8

Entertainment Software

Visit the Discovering Computers 2005 WEB LINK page (**scsite.com/dc2005/weblink**). Click Entertainment Software below Chapter 3.

FIGURE 3-37 Entertainment software, such as this flight simulator, can provide hours of recreation.

APPLICATION SOFTWARE FOR COMMUNICATIONS

One of the main reasons people use computers is to communicate and share information with others. Some communications software is considered system software because it works with hardware and transmission media. Other communications software performs specific tasks for users, and thus, is considered application software. Chapter 2 presented a variety of application software for communications, which are summarized in the table in Figure 3-38. Read Issue 3-4 for a related discussion.

ISSUE 3-4

Is Someone Watching You?

A recent survey indicates that more than 75 percent of Fortune 500 companies routinely monitor employees' e-mail and Web browsing habits. About one company in four has fired an employee based on its discoveries. Some companies even use automated software that searches e-mail messages for derogatory language. One unidentified woman, for example, was fired for using her office e-mail to complain about her boss. Although she felt her e-mail conversations were private and would not be monitored, she learned, to her chagrin, that she was wrong. Do you think that employers have the right to monitor e-mail? Why or why not? If you knew that a fellow employee criticized the company through the e-mail system, would you tell your boss? What if you heard the same employee planning a theft of company products? At what point do you refuse to get involved?

For more information about employee monitoring, visit the Discovering Computers 2005 Issues Web page (**scsite.com/dc2005/issues**). Click Issue #4 below Chapter 3.

APPLICATION SOFTWARE FOR COMMUNICATIONS

E-Mail
- Transmission of messages and files via a network such as the Internet
- Requires an e-mail program
  - Integrated in many software suites and operating systems
  - Available free at portals on the Web
  - Included with paid Internet access service
  - Can be purchased separately from retailers

FTP
- Method of uploading and downloading files with other computers on the Internet
- Download may require an FTP program; upload usually requires an FTP program
  - Integrated in some operating systems
  - Available for download on the Web for a small fee
  - Can be purchased separately from retailers

Web Browser
- Allows users to access and view Web pages on the Internet
- Requires a Web browser program
  - Integrated in some operating systems
  - Available for download on the Web free or for a fee
  - Included with paid Internet access service

Newsgroup/Message Board
- Online area where users have written discussions
- Newsgroup may require a newsreader program
  - Integrated in some operating systems, e-mail programs, and Web browsers
  - Available for download on the Web, usually at no cost
  - Included with some paid Internet access services
  - Built into some Web sites

Chat Room
- Real-time, online typed conversation
- Requires chat client software
  - Integrated in some operating systems, e-mail programs, and Web browsers
  - Available for download on the Web, usually at no cost
  - Included with some paid Internet access services
  - Built into some Web sites

Instant Messaging
- Real-time exchange of messages, files, audio, and/or video with another online user
- Requires instant messenger software
  - Integrated in some operating systems
  - Available for download on the Web, usually at no cost
  - Included with some paid Internet access services

Video Conferencing/Telephone Calls
- Meeting/conversation between geographically separated people who use a network such as the Internet to transmit audio and video
- Requires a microphone, speakers, and a video camera attached to your computer
- Requires video conferencing software, which is included with some digital video cameras

FIGURE 3-38 A summary of application software for home and business communications.

APPLICATION SOFTWARE ON THE WEB

As discussed earlier in this chapter, users can purchase application software from a software vendor, retail store, or Web-based business. Users typically install purchased application software on a computer before they run it. Installed software has two disadvantages: (1) it requires disk space on your computer and (2) it can be costly to upgrade as vendors release new versions. As an alternative, some home and business users opt to use products on the Web. Read Apply It 3-2 for more information.

A **Web application** is application software that exists on a Web site. These Web application sites often store personal data and information at their sites.

To access a Web application, a user simply visits the Web site that offers the program. Some Web sites provide free access to the program. For example, one site creates a map and driving directions when a user enters a starting and destination point (Figure 3-39).

Other Web sites allow you to use the program free and pay a fee when a certain action occurs. For example, you can prepare your tax return free using TurboTax for the Web, but if you elect to print it or file it electronically, you pay a minimal fee.

Some companies provide free software to use or download. Figure 3-40 shows OpenOffice.org, a free business software suite. Microsoft's Web applications, called *.NET*, enable users to access software created for the .NET platform from any type of device or computer that can connect to the Internet.

APPLY IT 3-2

Obtaining Application Software

Shop until you drop is not necessarily the best method for acquiring application software. Rather than having software stacked on store shelves, today's marketplace offers options to suit differing needs and budgets.

Downloading software from the Internet is a convenient option that usually is less expensive than purchasing software from a store shelf. Downloading is a relatively easy process that only requires users to have Internet access. Users with higher-speed Internet connections, such as DSL and cable television Internet services, experience much faster download times than those with dial-up access. Occasionally, the service fails during the download. Some consumers do not use this option because vendors usually require buyers to enter personal (e.g., name and telephone number) and credit card information online.

Another alternative is subscribing to and using Web-based software, where the latest version of the software is available on the Web. Users access Web-based software anywhere from any computer or device, as long as it has an Internet connection. Web-based software is a convenient choice for the mobile user. Web-based businesses usually store users' data and information on their computer. For this reason, users concerned with data security may shy away from this option.

For more information about software purchasing, downloading, and subscribing, visit the Discovering Computers 2005 Apply It Web page (**scsite.com/dc2005/apply**). Click Apply It #2 below Chapter 3.

WEB LINK 3-9

Web Applications

Visit the Discovering Computers 2005 WEB LINK page (**scsite.com/dc2005/weblink**). Click Web Applications below Chapter 3.

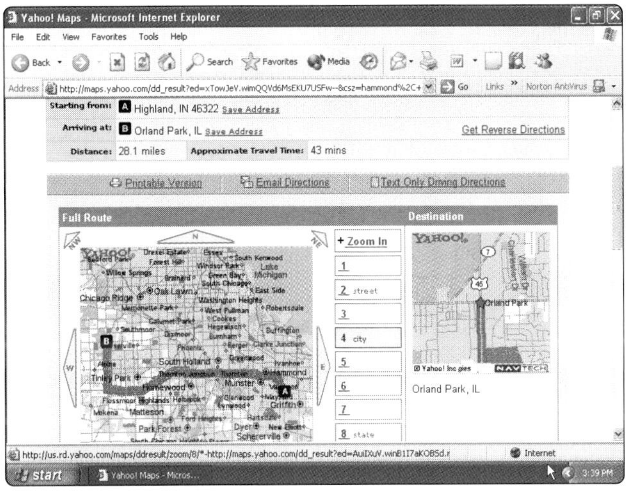

FIGURE 3-39 This Web site creates a map and provides directions between a starting and destination point.

FIGURE 3-40 OpenOffice.org is a free suite that consists of word processing, spreadsheet, presentation graphics, and drawing programs.

Application Service Providers

Storing and maintaining programs can be a costly investment for businesses. Thus, some have elected to outsource one or more facets of their information technology (IT) needs to an application service provider. An *application service provider* (*ASP*) is a third-party organization that manages and distributes software and services on the Web. That is, instead of installing the software on your computer, you run the programs from the Internet.

The five categories of ASPs are:

1. *Enterprise ASP*: customizes and delivers high-end business applications, such as finance and database
2. *Local/Regional ASP*: offers a variety of software applications to a specific geographic region
3. *Specialist ASP*: delivers applications to meet a specific business need, such as human resources or project management
4. *Vertical Market ASP*: provides applications for a particular industry, such as construction, health care, or retail
5. *Volume Business ASP*: supplies prepackaged applications, such as accounting, to businesses

Despite the advantages, companies may wait to outsource to an ASP until they have faster Internet connections. A variety of payment schemes exist. Some rent use of the application on a monthly basis or charge based on the number of user accesses. Others charge a one-time fee.

Web-Based Training

Web-based training (*WBT*) is a type of CBT (computer-based training) that uses Internet technology and consists of application software on the Web. Similar to CBT, WBT typically consists of self-directed, self-paced instruction about a topic. WBT is popular in business, industry, and schools for teaching new skills or enhancing existing skills of employees, teachers, or students. When using a WBT product, students actively become involved in the learning process instead of passive recipients of information.

WEB LINK 3-10

Web-Based Training

Visit the Discovering Computers 2005 WEB LINK page (**scsite.com/dc2005/weblink**). Click Web-Based Training below Chapter 3.

Many Web sites offer WBT to the general public. Such training covers a wide range of topics, from how to change a flat tire to creating documents in Word (Figure 3-41). Many of these Web sites are free. Others require registration and payment to take the complete Web-based course.

WBT often is combined with other materials for distance learning courses. **Distance learning** (**DL**) is the delivery of education at one location while the learning takes place at other locations. DL courses provide time, distance, and place advantages for students who live far from a college campus or work full time. These courses enable students to attend class from anywhere in the world and at times that fit their schedules. Many national and international companies offer DL training. These training courses eliminate the costs of airfare, hotels, and meals for centralized training sessions.

WBT companies often specialize in providing instructors with the tools for preparation, distribution, and management of DL courses. These tools enable instructors to create rich, educational Web-based training sites and allow the students to interact with a powerful Web learning environment. Through the training site, students can check their progress, take practice tests, search for topics, send e-mail, and participate in discussions and chats. The appeal of these products is they generally are quite easy to learn and use for both the instructors and the students.

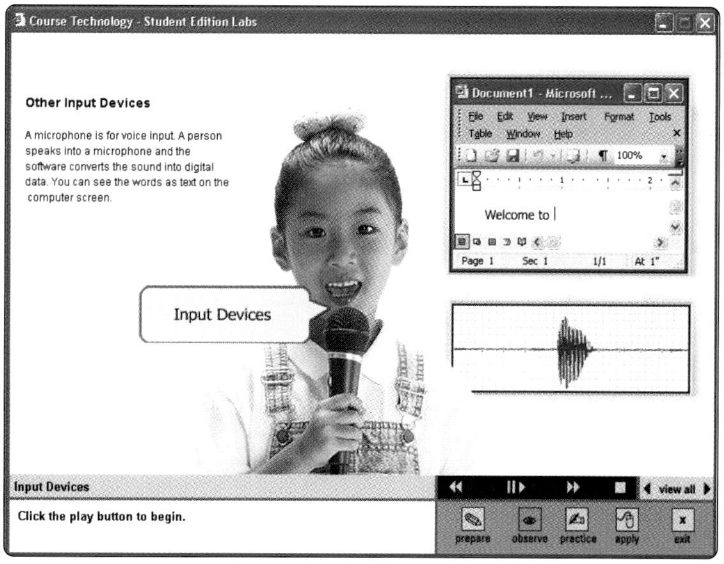

FIGURE 3-41 Web-based training, such as SAM Computer Concepts, is designed so students can choose learning activities that complement their learning styles.

LEARNING AIDS AND SUPPORT TOOLS FOR APPLICATION SOFTWARE

Learning how to use application software effectively involves time and practice. To assist in the learning process, many programs provide online Help, Web-based Help, and wizards.

Online Help is the electronic equivalent of a user manual (Figure 3-42a). It usually is integrated into a program. Online Help provides assistance that help users increase productivity and reduce frustrations by minimizing the time spent learning how to use application software.

In most programs, a function key or a button on the screen starts the Help feature. When using a program, you can use the Help feature to ask a question or access the Help topics in subject or alphabetical order. Often the Help is *context-sensitive,* meaning that the Help information relates to the current task being attempted.

Most online Help also links to Web sites that offer *Web-based help,* which provides updates and more comprehensive resources to respond to technical issues about software (Figure 3-42b). These Web sites often have an *FAQ* (frequently asked questions) list to help you find answers to common questions. Some Web sites contain chat rooms, in which a user can talk directly with a technical support person or join a conversation with other users who may be able to answer questions or solve problems.

A **wizard** is an automated assistant that helps a user complete a task by asking questions and then automatically performing actions based on the responses (Figure 3-42c). Many software applications include wizards.

Figure 3-42a (online Help)

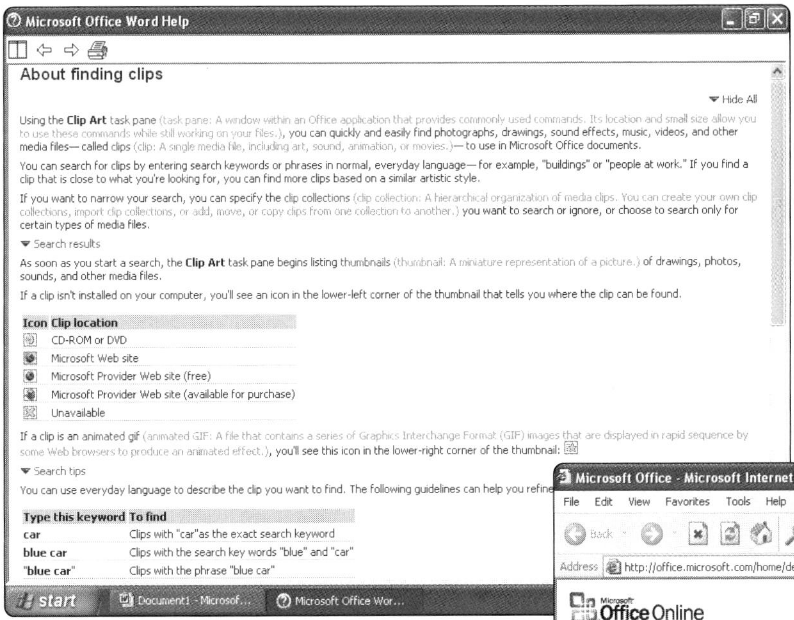

Figure 3-42b (Web-based help)

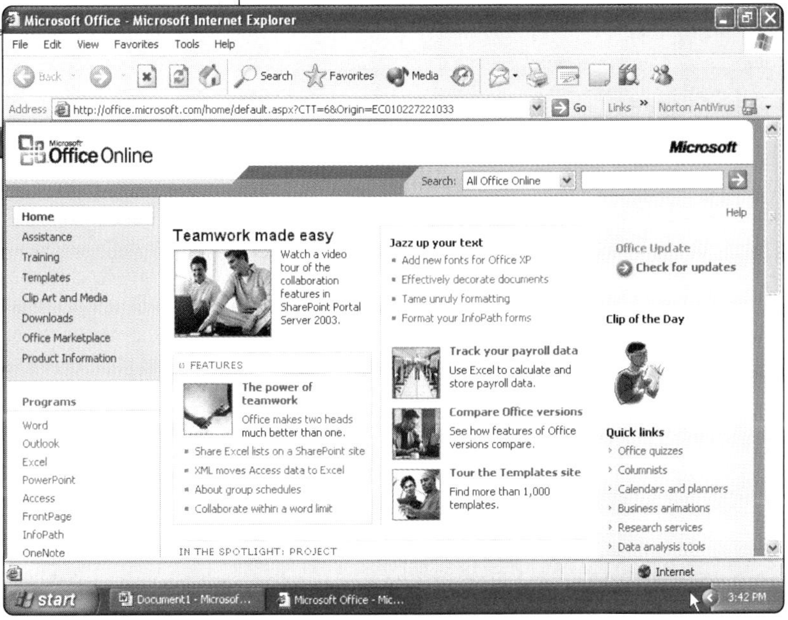

Figure 3-42c (wizard)

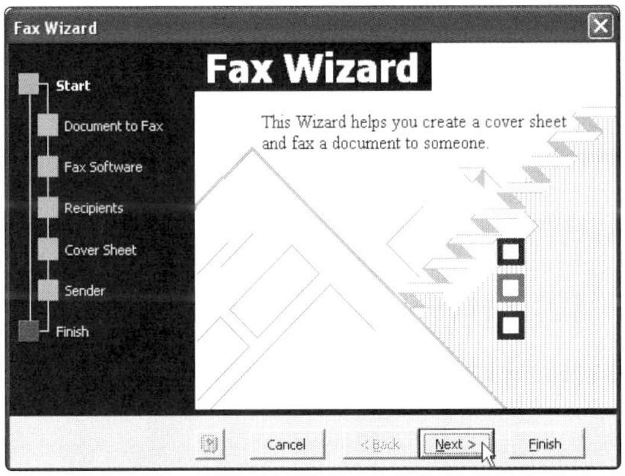

FIGURE 3-42 Many programs include online Help, Web-based help, and wizards.

For example, word processing software uses wizards to help you create memorandums, meeting agendas, fax cover sheets, flyers, letters, and resumes. Spreadsheet software includes chart and function wizards. Database software has form and report wizards.

In many cases, online Help has replaced the user manual altogether. Most software developers no longer include user manuals with the software. If you want to learn more about a particular program from a printed manual, however, many books are available to help you learn to use the features of personal computer programs. These books typically are available in bookstores and software stores (Figure 3-43).

Many colleges and schools provide training on several of the applications discussed in this chapter. If you would like more direction than is provided in online Help, Web-based Help, wizards, and trade books, contact your local school for a list of class offerings.

FIGURE 3-43 Bookstores often sell trade books to help you learn to use the features of personal computer application software.

QUIZ YOURSELF 3-3

To check your knowledge of the types and features of home, personal, educational, and communications programs, Web applications, and software learning aids, visit the Discovering Computers 2005 Quiz Yourself Web page (**scsite.com/dc2005/quiz**). Click Objectives 6 – 9 below Chapter 3.

CHAPTER SUMMARY

This chapter illustrated how to start and use application software. It then presented an overview of a variety of business software, graphics and multimedia software, home/personal/educational software, and communications software. The chapter identified various Web applications. Finally, learning aids and support tools for application software were presented.

Help Desk Specialist

A Help Desk specialist position is an entryway into the information technology (IT) field. A *Help Desk specialist* deals with problems in hardware, software, or communications systems. Job requirements may include the following:

- Solve procedural and software questions both in person and over the telephone
- Develop and maintain Help Desk operations manuals
- Assist in training new Help Desk personnel

Usually, a Help Desk specialist must be knowledgeable about the major programs in use. Entry-level positions primarily answer calls from people with questions. Other positions provide additional assistance and assume further responsibilities, often demanding greater knowledge and problem-solving skills that can lead to more advanced positions in the IT field. Help Desk specialist is an ideal position for people who must work irregular hours, because many companies need support people to work evenings, weekends, or part-time.

Educational requirements are less stringent than they are for other jobs in the computer field. In some cases, a high school diploma is sufficient. Advancement requires a minimum of a two-year degree, while management generally requires a bachelor's degree in IT or a related field. Certification is another way Help Desk specialists can increase their attractiveness in the marketplace. Entry-level salaries average $30,000 per year. Managers average between $42,000 and $50,000.

To learn more about the field of Help Desk specialist as a career, visit the Discovering Computers 2005 Careers Web page (**scsite.com/dc2005/careers**). Click Help Desk Specialist.

Infection and Delivery: How Computer Viruses Work

Blaster. Sobig. Melissa. Nachi. Like the common cold, tons of variations of computer viruses exist. A *virus* is a potentially damaging program that affects a computer negatively by altering the way the computer works without a user's knowledge or permission. Unlike the biological viruses that cause the common cold, people create computer viruses. To create a virus, an unscrupulous programmer must code and then test the virus code to ensure the virus can replicate itself, conceal itself, monitor for certain events, and then deliver its *payload* — the destructive event or prank the virus was created to deliver. Despite the many variations of viruses, most have two phases to their execution: infection and delivery.

To start the infection phase, the virus must be activated. Today, the most common way viruses spread is by people running infected programs disguised as e-mail attachments. During the infection phase, viruses typically perform three actions:

1. First, a virus replicates by attaching itself to program files. A *macro virus* hides in the macro language of an application, such as Word. A *boot sector virus* targets the master boot record and executes when the computer boots up. A *file virus* attaches itself to program files. The file virus, Win32.Hatred, for example, replicates by first infecting Windows executable files for the Calculator, Notepad, Help, and other applications on the hard disk. The virus then scans the computer to locate .exe files on other drives and stores this information in the system registry. The next time an infected file is run, the virus reads the registry and continues infecting another drive.
2. Viruses also conceal themselves to avoid detection. A *stealth virus* disguises itself by hiding in fake code sections, which it inserts within working code in a file. A *polymorphic virus* actually changes its code as it infects computers. Win32.Hatred uses both concealment techniques. The virus writes itself to the last file section, while modifying the file header to hide the increased file size. It also uses a polymorphic engine to scramble and encrypt the virus code as it infects files.
3. Finally, viruses watch for a certain condition or event and activate when that condition or event occurs. The event might be booting up the computer or hitting a date on the system clock. A *logic bomb* activates when it detects a specific condition (say, a name deleted from the employee list). A *time bomb* is a logic bomb that activates on a particular date or time. Win32.Hatred, for instance, unleashes its destruction when the computer clock hits the seventh day of any month. If the triggering condition does not exist, the virus simply replicates.

During the delivery phase, the virus unleashes its payload, which might be a harmless prank that displays a silly message — or it might be destructive, corrupting or deleting data and files. When Win32.Hatred triggers, it displays the author's message and then covers the screen with black dots. The virus also deletes several antivirus files as it infects the system. The most dangerous viruses do not have an obvious payload, instead they quietly modify files. A virus, for example, could randomly change numbers in an inventory program or introduce delays to slow a computer.

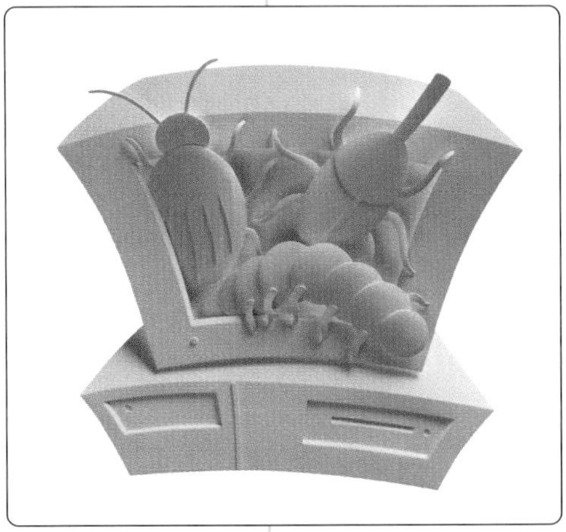

Other kinds of electronic annoyances exist, in addition to viruses. While often called viruses, worms and Trojan horse applications actually are part of a broader category called *malicious-logic programs*.

- A *worm*, such as the CodeRed or Sircam worm, resides in active memory and replicates itself over a network to infect machines, using up the system resources and possibly shutting the system down.
- A *Trojan horse* is a destructive program disguised as a real application, such as a screen saver. When a user runs a seemingly innocent program, a Trojan horse hiding inside can capture information, such as user names and passwords, from your system or open up a backdoor that allows a hacker remotely to control your computer. Unlike viruses, Trojan horses do not replicate themselves.

As with the common cold, every computer user is susceptible to a computer virus. In 1995, the chance that a virus would infect your computer was 1 in 1,000; by 2002, the odds were only 1 in 9. Even with better antivirus software, viruses are tough to avoid, as deceitful programmers craft new electronic maladies to infect your computer.

For more information about computer viruses, visit the Discovering Computers 2005 High-Tech Talk Web page (**scsite.com/dc2005/tech**) and click Computer Viruses.

COMPANIES ON THE CUTTING EDGE

Microsoft

Realizing Potential with Business Software

In 1975, *Microsoft* had three programmers, one product, and revenues of $16,000. Less than 30 years later, the software giant is one of the larger corporations in the world, employs nearly 55,000 people, offers scores of software titles, has offices in 60 countries, and has annual earnings of more than $32.1 billion. Microsoft's rapid ascent is an achievement unparalleled in the history of American business.

In 1980, Microsoft got its big break when IBM, a $30 billion dollar behemoth, asked Microsoft to provide an operating system for its new personal computer. Fortunately, Bill Gates, founder of Microsoft, was able to purchase and modify an operating system he later called MS-DOS. By 1984, Microsoft's sales rocketed to $97 million.

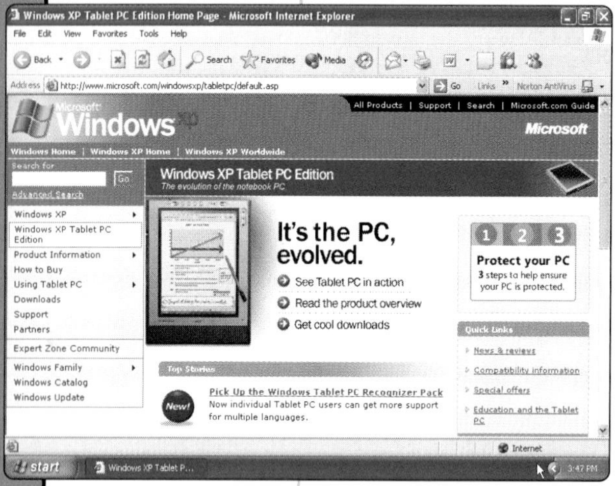

Microsoft did not rest. It began to develop and sell mouse units and keyboards that eventually sold by the millions. While updating its MS-DOS operating system, it worked on its successor, Windows. Originally released in 1985, Windows did not take hold until Windows 3.0 was released in 1990. From that point on, Windows replaced MS-DOS as the standard operating system on personal computers. During this same period, Microsoft developed its Office suite, which today dominates the application software market.

Considered to have a lock on the software industry, the company reinvented itself in 1995 in response to the growing Internet craze when it incorporated its newly created browser, Internet Explorer, in the Windows 95 operating system. Microsoft also invested heavily in the telecommunications area and an online service, called MSN. In less than two years, Microsoft moved from the peripheral to the vanguard of the information revolution.

Microsoft's recent efforts have focused on server operating systems for large companies, .NET software technologies for connectivity, and scaling down Windows to run on PDAs and Tablet PCs. The company's Trustworthy Computing initiative focuses on ensuring security, privacy, reliabilty, and business integrity.

For more information about Microsoft, visit the Discovering Computers 2005 Companies Web page (**scsite.com/dc2005/companies**) and click Microsoft.

Apple Computer

Introducing Innovative Technologies

Apple Computer users share a fervent kind of loyalty. With a passion usually reserved for fans of musical groups or sports teams, millions of users in more than 120 countries extol the virtues of Apple's hardware and software.

Steven Jobs and Stephen Wozniak founded Apple in 1976 when they decided to market the Apple I, a circuit board they had developed in Jobs's garage. Jobs suggested the name Apple, but no one is sure why. "He doesn't always let on where ideas come from," Wozniak says, "or how they come into his head." Whatever the origin, Wozniak maintains that other names "all sounded boring compared to Apple." The company's logo is easier to explain — an apple with a bite (a play on byte) taken out of it. In 1977, Apple Computer incorporated and introduced the Apple II, the first mass-marketed personal computer. The machine helped generate more than $1 billion in annual sales and became a school standard. Apple's Macintosh computer and operating system, released in 1984, was one of the first commercially successful GUIs.

Apple discontinued the Apple II product line in 1993, and the following year introduced the high-performance Power Macintosh line. The Macintosh had a larger processor and more memory, but its greatest strengths were its stability, flexibility, creative capabilities, and user-friendliness. Advertised as "the computer for the rest of us," buyers enthusiastically embraced the Macintosh. Apple then licensed its Macintosh computer and operating system to other computer manufacturers. This decision was reversed later, however, as other manufacturers reduced Apple's market share and revenues dropped. After a series of personnel changes, Jobs became Apple's CEO. Under his direction, *Apple Computer* introduced the iMac, the iPod, the iBook, the Power Mac G5, and Mac OS X, which includes applications that let users create desktop movies, rip MP3s, and burn CDs and DVDs.

For more information about Apple Computer, visit the Discovering Computers 2005 Companies Web page (**scsite.com/dc2005/companies**) and click Apple Computer.

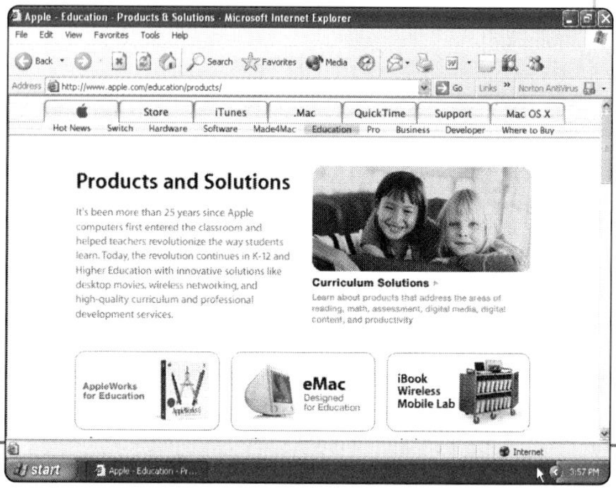

TECHNOLOGY TRAILBLAZERS

Dan Bricklin

Developer of VisiCalc

The next time you use your calculator to balance your checkbook, think about *Dan Bricklin*. He used his Texas Instruments calculator constantly in the late 1970s and recognized a need to develop VisiCalc (Visible Calculator), the first electronic spreadsheet, in graduate school. He still owns that calculator, along with the original VisiCalc code.

Bricklin got the idea for VisiCalc at Harvard Business School. There, classes often asked students to calculate the effect of changing one value on a business balance or account sheet. "Creating VisiCalc involved figuring out how to make a calculating tool that was easier than the back of an envelope so people would do their first calculation on a computer spreadsheet so that their second one could be automatic." Bricklin and his friend, Bob Frankston, formed a company called Software Arts and programmed the VisiCalc prototype using Apple Basic on an Apple II computer. The small program included many of the features found in today's spreadsheet software. VisiCalc did not make Bricklin a great deal of money (the final version sold for $100), but it had an immediate impact, increasing computer sales and reducing business costs. "I'm not rich because of VisiCalc," Bricklin says, "but I feel that I've made a change in the world. That's a satisfaction money can't buy." VisiCalc still runs on personal computers, and Bricklin includes the program on his personal Web site.

Lotus Software purchased Software Arts in 1985. After serving as a consultant to Lotus, Bricklin turned his attention to starting a new company, Software Garden, Inc., and developing new software that focuses on pen-based computing and interactive video conferencing. His current venture, Trellix, lets people turn everyday documents into Web pages with colors, graphics, and links.

For more information about Dan Bricklin, visit the Discovering Computers 2005 People Web page (**scsite.com/dc2005/people**) and click Dan Bricklin.

Masayoshi Son

Japan's Bill Gates

Often called "the Bill Gates of Japan," *Masayoshi Son* has helped bring that country to the forefront of the digital age.

When he was 16 years old, the second-generation Korean-Japanese moved from Japan to California to learn English. At the University of California, Berkeley, Son majored in economics and also took some computer courses. He recalls being fascinated by a picture of a microchip in a magazine, realizing the microchip would change people's lives. Other students carried pictures of Elvis Presley, but in his book bag Son kept the picture of the microchip.

While in school, Son earned his first million dollars by importing arcade games from Japan for the campus, developing computer games, and selling a patent for a multilingual pocket translator to Sharp Corporation. In 1981, at age 23 he founded Softbank Corporation, a software distribution operation. Son predicted that the company would be worth $400 million in five years and $1 billion in ten. His first employees were less optimistic — both left after two weeks — but Son's forecasts proved uncannily accurate. By 1995, Softbank Corporation controlled one-half of the personal computer software in Japan. Profits from this company formed the basis for other profitable investments, including Yahoo!, Kingston Technology, Ziff Davis Media, and E*TRADE. Besides these software investments, Son has holdings in more than 50 international technology companies, including publishing, electronic banking, and broadcasting.

Son is a leading member of Japan's Prime Minister's IT Strategy Council. Though criticized for heavy investment in U.S. Internet companies, Son sees such alliances as helpful to both countries' economies. Today, Son is one of the world's wealthiest entrepreneurs, but that is not enough. "Some people make money just to make money...My satisfaction comes when I see people smile."

For more information about Masayoshi Son, visit the Discovering Computers 2005 People Web page (**scsite.com/dc2005/people**) and click Masayoshi Son.

CHAPTER 3 CHAPTER REVIEW

Previous | Next

QUIZZES AND LEARNING GAMES
Computer Genius
Crossword Puzzle
Interactive Labs
Practice Test
Quiz Yourself
Wheel of Terms

EXERCISES
Chapter Review
Checkpoint
Key Terms
Lab Exercises
Learn It Online
Web Research

BEYOND THE BOOK
Apply It
Career Corner
Companies
FAQ
High-Tech Talk
Issues
Looking Ahead
Trailblazers
Web Links

FEATURES
Guide to Web Sites
Making Use of the Web
Tech News
Timeline 2005

The Chapter Review section summarizes the concepts presented in this chapter.

WEB INSTRUCTIONS:

To display this page from the Web, start your browser and enter the Web address **scsite.com/dc2005/ch3/review**. Click the links for current and additional information.

1 What Are the Categories of Application Software?

Application software consists of programs that perform specific tasks for users. The four major categories of popular application software are business software; graphics and multimedia software; software for home, personal, and educational use; and software for communications.

2 How Is Software Distributed?

Application software is available in a variety of forms. **Packaged software** is mass produced, copyrighted retail software that meets the needs of a variety of users. **Custom software** performs functions specific to a business or industry. **Shareware** is copyrighted software that is distributed free for a trial period. **Freeware** is copyrighted software provided at no cost to a user by an individual or a company. Public-domain software is free software that has been donated for public use and has no copyright restrictions.

3 How Do You Start and Interact with Application Software?

The Windows XP operating system uses the concept of a desktop, which is an on-screen work area that has a graphical user interface. On the Windows desktop are a Start button and a pointer. A **button** is a graphical element you activate to cause a specific action to take place. The **pointer** is a small symbol displayed on the screen that moves as you move the mouse. To start an application, move the pointer to the Start button on the Windows taskbar and then **click** the Start button by pressing and releasing a button on the mouse. Windows displays the Start menu. A **menu** contains a series of commands from which you make selections. Click the program name on the menu or on the *submenu* that is displayed when you point to a command. Once loaded in memory, the program is displayed in a **window**.

Visit **scsite.com/dc2005/quiz** or click the Quiz Yourself button. Click Objectives 1 – 3 below Chapter 3.

4 What Are the Key Features of Widely Used Business Programs?

Business software is application software that assists people in becoming more effective and efficient while performing business activities. Business software includes the following programs. **Word processing software** allows users to **create** a document by entering text and inserting graphical images, **edit** the document by making changes, and **format** the document by altering its appearance. **Spreadsheet software** allows users to organize data in rows and columns (called a *worksheet*), perform calculations, recalculate when data changes, and chart the data. **Database software** allows users to create a **database**, which is a collection of data organized in a manner that allows access, retrieval, and use of that data. **Presentation graphics software** allows users to create a *slide show* that is displayed on a large monitor or on a projection screen and print an *outline* with text from each slide. **Note taking software** enables users to enter typed text, handwritten comments or sketches on a page and then save the page as part of a notebook. A **personal information manager** (**PIM**) is software that includes an appointment calendar, address book, notepad, and other features to help users organize personal information. A **software suite** is a collection of individual programs sold as a single package. **Project management software** allows users to plan, schedule, track, and analyze a project. **Accounting software** helps companies record and report their financial transactions.

5 What Are the Key Features of Widely Used Graphics and Multimedia Programs?

Graphics and multimedia software includes the following. **Computer-aided design** (**CAD**) **software** assists a professional user in creating engineering, architectural, and scientific designs. Desktop publishing (DTP) software enables professional designers to create sophisticated documents that contain text, graphics, and brilliant colors. **Paint software**, also called *illustration software*, allows users to draw pictures, shapes, and other graphical images with various on-screen tools. **Image editing software** provides the capabilities of paint software and also includes the ability to modify existing images. **Video editing software** allows users to modify a segment of a video, called a clip. **Audio editing software** lets users modify audio clips and produce studio-quality soundtracks. **Multimedia authoring software** allows users to combine text, graphics, audio, video, and animation into an interactive application. **Web page authoring software** helps users of all skill levels create Web pages that include graphical images, video, audio, animation, and other special effects.

Visit **scsite.com/dc2005/quiz** or click the Quiz Yourself button. Click Objectives 4 – 5 below Chapter 3.

6 What Are the Key Features of Widely Used Home, Personal, and Educational Programs?

Software for home, personal, and educational use includes the following. A **software suite** (for personal use) combines application software such as word processing, spreadsheet, and database into a single, easy-to-use package. **Personal finance software** is a simplified accounting program that helps users balance their checkbooks, pay bills, track personal income and expenses, track investments, and evaluate financial plans. **Legal software** assists in the preparation of legal documents and provides legal information. **Tax preparation software** guides users through the process of filing federal taxes. **Personal DTP software** helps users create newsletters, brochures, advertisements, postcards, greeting cards, letterhead, business cards, banners, calendars, logos, and Web pages. **Paint/image editing software** for personal use provides an easy-to-use interface, usually with more simplified capabilities than its professional counterpart, including functions tailored to meet the needs of the home and small business users. Application software often includes a **clip art/image gallery**, which is a collection of clip art and photographs. **Home design/landscaping software** assists users with the design, remodeling, or improvement of a home, deck, or landscape. **Educational software** teaches a particular skill. **Reference software** provides valuable and thorough information for all individuals. **Entertainment software** for personal computers includes interactive games, videos, and other programs to support hobbies or provide amusement and enjoyment.

7 What Are the Types of Application Software Used in Communications?

Application software for communications includes e-mail programs to transmit messages via a network, FTP programs to upload and download files on the Internet, Web browser programs to access and view Web pages, newsreader/message board programs that allow online written discussions with other users, chat room software to have real-time, online typed conversations, instant messaging software for real-time exchange of messages or files, and video conferencing/telephone call software for meetings or conversations on a network between geographically separated people.

8 What Are the Advantages of Using Application Software on the Web?

A **Web application** is application software that exists on a Web site. It requires less disk space on your computer than installed software and is less expensive to upgrade as vendors release new versions. An *application service provider (ASP)* is a third-party organization that manages and distributes software and services on the Web.

9 What Learning Aids Are Available for Application Software?

To assist in the learning process, many programs provide a variety of Help features. **Online Help** is the electronic equivalent of a user manual. Most online Help also links to *Web-based help*, which provides updates and more comprehensive resources to respond to technical issues about software. A **wizard** is an automated assistant that helps a user complete a task by asking questions and then automatically performing actions based on the responses.

Visit **scsite.com/dc2005/quiz** or click the Quiz Yourself button. Click Objectives 6 – 9 below Chapter 3.

CHAPTER 3 KEY TERMS

You should know the Primary Terms and be familiar with the Secondary Terms.

WEB INSTRUCTIONS:

To display this page from the Web, start your browser and enter the Web address **scsite.com/dc2005/ch3/terms**. Click a term to display its definition and a picture. When the picture displays, click the more info button for current and additional information about the term from the Web.

>> Primary Terms

(shown in bold-black characters in the chapter)

accounting software (149)
application software (132)
audio editing software (153)
business software (136)
button (135)
click (135)
clip art (137)
clip art/image gallery (158)
command (135)
computer-aided design (CAD) software (151)
computer-based training (CBT) (158)
create (138)
custom software (132)
database (145)
database software (145)
desktop (135)
desktop publishing (DTP) software (151)
distance learning (DL) (162)
edit (138)
educational software (158)
entertainment software (159)
font (140)
font size (140)
format (139)
freeware (133)
home design/landscaping software (158)
icon (135)
image editing software (152)
legal software (156)
menu (135)
multimedia authoring software (153)
note taking software (147)
online banking (155)
online Help (163)
packaged software (132)
paint software (152)
personal DTP software (157)
personal finance software (155)
personal information manager (PIM) (148)
personal paint/image editing software (157)
photo editing software (157)
pointer (135)
presentation graphics software (146)
print (140)
project management software (149)
public-domain software (133)
reference software (159)
save (140)
shareware (132)
software suite (149)
spreadsheet software (142)
tax preparation software (156)
title bar (135)
video editing software (153)
voice recognition (141)
voice recognition programs (141)
Web application (161)
Web page authoring software (154)
Web-based training (162)
window (135)
wizard (163)
word processing software (137)

>> Secondary Terms

(shown in italic characters in the chapter)

application service provider (ASP) (162)
audience handouts (147)
bar chart (144)
cell (142)
charting (144)
clipboard (138)
color library (152)
column chart (144)
context-sensitive (163)
dialog box (135)
enterprise ASP (162)
FAQ (163)
field (145)
file (135)
file name (135)
filters (153)
font style (140)
footer (138)
form (145)
formula (143)
function (143)
header (138)
illustration software (152)
import (146)
label (143)
line chart (144)
loaded (134)
local/regional ASP (162)
macro (139)
margins (137)
.NET (161)
notes page (147)
outline (147)
page layout (152)
pasting (139)
pie chart (144)
point (140)
query (145)
record (145)
replace (138)
sans serif font (140)
scrolling (138)
search (138)
serif font (140)
shortcut menu (135)
slide show (146)
slide sorter view (146)
smart tags (139)
specialist ASP (162)
speech recognition (141)
spelling checker (138)
submenu (135)
system software (133)
template (139)
value (143)
vertical market ASP (162)
volume business ASP (162)
WBT (162)
Web-based help (163)
what-if analysis (144)
word processor (137)
wordwrap (137)
worksheet (142)

CHECKPOINT CHAPTER 3

Use the Checkpoint exercises to check your knowledge level of the chapter.

WEB INSTRUCTIONS:

To display this page from the Web, start your browser and enter the Web address **scsite.com/dc2005/ch3/check**. Click the links for current and additional information.

LABEL THE FIGURE

Identify these elements in the Windows XP graphical user interface.

a. All Programs command
b. All Programs submenu
c. Accessories command
d. Accessories submenu
e. Paint program command
f. Start menu
g. Start button

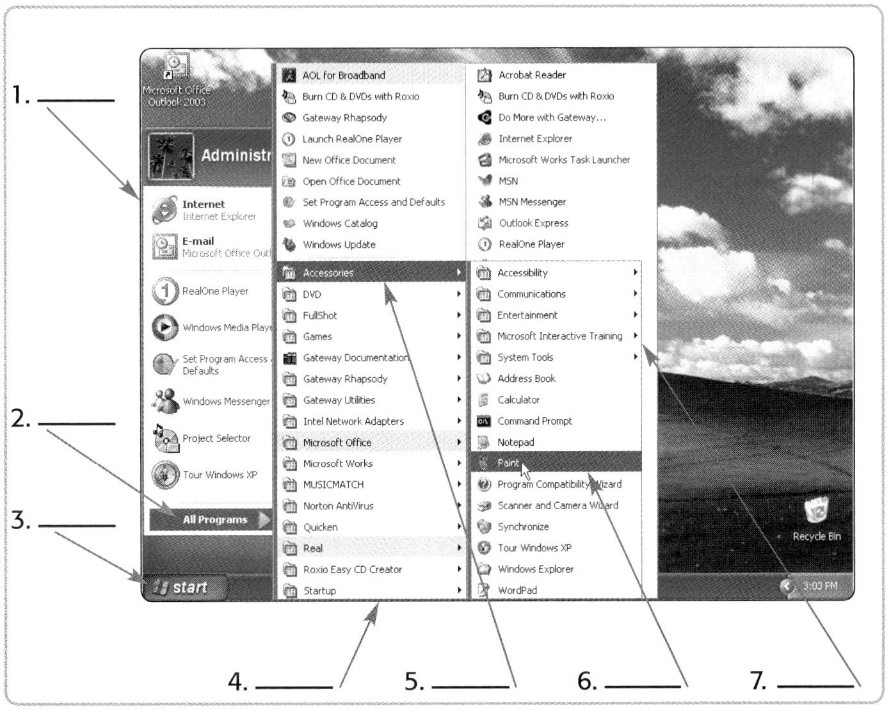

TRUE/FALSE

Mark T for True and F for False. (See page numbers in parentheses.)

F 1. Freeware is copyrighted software that is distributed free for a trial period. (133)

F 2. Shareware, freeware, and public-domain programs are not usually available on the Web for users to download. (133)

T 3. The desktop is an on-screen work area that has a graphical user interface. (135)

F 4. An icon is a rectangular area on the screen that displays a program, data, and/or other information. (135)

T 5. Business software includes programs such as word processing, spreadsheet, and presentation graphics. (136)

HW

T 6. A font is a name assigned to a specific design of characters. (140)

T 7. The programs within a software suite use a similar interface and share common features. (155)

F 8. Educational software is software that assists instructors in planning a course. (158)

F 9. A Web application is application software that helps you design a Web site. (161)

T 10. A wizard is an automated assistant that helps a user complete a task by asking questions and then automatically performing actions based on the responses. (163)

CHAPTER 3 CHECKPOINT

MULTIPLE CHOICE

Select the best answer. (See page numbers in parentheses.)

1. Computer-aided design (CAD), video and audio editing, and Web page authoring are examples of _____ software. (132)
   a. business
   b. home, person, and educational
   c. communications
   d. graphics and multimedia
2. If a company cannot find software to meet its unique requirements, the company may use a programmer to develop tailor-made ______. (132)
   a. freeware
   b. custom software
   c. shareware
   d. packaged software
3. In Windows applications, you click the right mouse button to display a _____, which lists commonly used commands related to the current activity. (135)
   a. desktop
   b. submenu
   c. title bar
   d. shortcut menu
4. The title bar of a document window usually displays the document's ______. (135)
   a. file name
   b. file size
   c. file path
   d. all of the above
5. A feature, called ______, allows users of word processing software to type words continually without pressing the ENTER key at the end of each line. (137)
   a. AutoCorrect
   b. wordwrap
   c. AutoFormat
   d. clipboard
6. When using spreadsheet software, a function ______. (143)
   a. depicts data in graphical form
   b. changes certain values to reveal the effects of the changes
   c. is a predefined formula that performs common calculations
   d. contains the formatting necessary for a specific worksheet type
7. With database software, users can run a ______ to request specific data from the database. (145)
   a. query
   b. record
   c. field
   d. form
8. Page layout, which is a feature of DTP software, is the process of ______. (152)
   a. drawing pictures, shapes, and other images with various on-screen tools
   b. modifying a segment of a video, called a page
   c. arranging text and graphics in a document on a page-by-page basis
   d. standardizing the colors on a page used by designers and printers
9. Training centers, educational institutions, and online magazine publishers all use ______ software to develop interactive applications. (154)
   a. multimedia authoring
   b. desktop publishing
   c. computer-aided design
   d. image editing
10. A software suite (for personal use) _____. (155)
    a. usually offers programs that can be purchased individually
    b. typically has all the capabilities of business application software
    c. has capabilities that more than meet the needs of many home users
    d. all of the above
11. ______ typically consists of self-directed, self-paced instruction about a topic. (158)
    a. CBT (computer-based training)
    b. DTP (desktop publishing)
    c. CAD (computer-aided design)
    d. PIM (personal information manager)
12. A(n) ______ program, which allows messages and files to be transmitted via a network, is integrated in many software suites and operating systems. (160)
    a. FTP
    b. instant messenger
    c. Web browser
    d. e-mail
13. An enterprise ASP _____. (162)
    a. provides applications for a particular industry
    b. customizes and delivers high-end business applications
    c. offers a variety of applications to a specific geographic region
    d. supplies prepackaged applications to business
14. Online Help often is context-sensitive, meaning that the Help information ______. (163)
    a. is available only to certain users
    b. lists answers to common questions
    c. provides updates and more comprehensive resources
    d. relates to the current task being attempted

CHECKPOINT CHAPTER 3

MATCHING Match the terms with their definitions. (See page numbers in parentheses.)

______ 1. clip art (137)
______ 2. clipboard (138)
______ 3. voice recognition (141)
______ 4. cell (142)
______ 5. record (145)
______ 6. slide sorter view (146)
______ 7. filters (153)
______ 8. online banking (155)
______ 9. specialist ASP (162)
______ 10. distance learning (162)

a. column in a database table that contains a specific category of data
b. row in a database table that contains data about a given item
c. capability of a computer to distinguish spoken words
d. usually included in audio editing software to enhance audio quality
e. collection of drawings, diagrams, maps, and photographs
f. intersection of a row and column in a worksheet
g. offers access to account balances and provides bill paying services
h. delivers applications to meet a specific business need
i. temporary storage location that contains items cut from a document
j. indicates the size of characters in a particular font
k. presents a screen view that helps to organize presentations
l. delivery of education at one location while learning takes place at another

SHORT ANSWER Write a brief answer to each of the following questions.

1. How is a serif font different from a sans serif font? __________ How is font size measured? __________
2. In a spreadsheet, how are labels, values, and formulas different? __________ What is what-if analysis? __________
3. Why do professional designers and graphic artists use DTP software instead of word processing packages? __________ What is a color library? __________
4. What are two disadvantages of using installed software? __________ How can you access a Web application? __________
5. What is online Help? __________ How do FAQs and wizards help software users? __________

WORKING TOGETHER Working with a group of your classmates, complete the following team exercises.

1. A Web application is a software application that exists on a Web site. With your group, develop a report describing at least three Web applications and explaining how an individual could use these various applications effectively. Include in your report a description of each application, a short overview of any online Help or FAQs, and the Web address for each application within your report. Share your findings with your class.

2. Choose one Issue from the following issues in this chapter: Is It Ethical to Copy Software? (136), Personal or Processed? (138), Should What We See Be What We Get? (152), or Is Someone Watching You? (160). Use the Web and/or print media to research the issue. Then, present a debate for the class, with different members of your team supporting different responses to the questions that accompany the issue.

3. In any software application, each program is not exactly the same. Different spreadsheet programs, for example, may have different methods to enter formulas, use functions, and draw charts. Have each member of your team interview someone who works with an application described in this chapter. What specific program is used? Why? For what purpose is the program used? What does the interviewee like, or dislike, about the program? Would the interviewee recommend this program? Why? Meet with the members of your team to discuss the results of your interviews. Then, use PowerPoint to create a group presentation and share your findings with the class.

CHAPTER 3 LEARN IT ONLINE

QUIZZES AND LEARNING GAMES
Computer Genius
Crossword Puzzle
Interactive Labs
Practice Test
Quiz Yourself
Wheel of Terms
EXERCISES
Chapter Review
Checkpoint
Key Terms
Lab Exercises
Learn It Online
Web Research
BEYOND THE BOOK
Apply It
Career Corner
Companies
FAQ
High-Tech Talk
Issues
Looking Ahead
Trailblazers
Web Links
FEATURES
Guide to Web Sites
Making Use of the Web
Tech News
Timeline 2005

Use the Learn It Online exercises to reinforce your understanding of the chapter concepts.

WEB INSTRUCTIONS:

To display this page from the Web, start your browser and enter the Web address **scsite.com/dc2005/ch3/learn**.

1 At the Movies – China Voice Recognition

To view the China Voice Recognition movie, click the number 1 button. Because it takes up to five keystrokes to make a single Chinese letter, the drive to develop voice recognition technology is perhaps strongest in China. IBM, Intel, and others are collaborating with the Chinese to make communicating easier for the 20 million people a day using computers in that country. And if they succeed with Chinese, there is no doubt the rest of the world's languages will follow easily. What factors make China such a good laboratory for development of voice recognition software? What are some of the first applications you can envision for accessing information from the Internet via voice? How would this technology impact cellular telephones? Thinking about convergence, what other technologies could be incorporated?

2 Student Edition Labs – Word Processing

Click the number 2 button. When the Student Edition Labs menu appears, click *Word Processing* to begin. A new browser window will open. Follow the on-screen instructions to complete the Lab. When finished, click the Exit button. If required, print a copy of your results to submit to your instructor.

3 Student Edition Labs – Spreadsheets

Click the number 3 button. When the Student Edition Labs menu appears, click *Spreadsheets* to begin. A new browser window will open. Follow the on-screen instructions to complete the Lab. When finished, click the Exit button. If required, print a copy of your results to submit to your instructor.

4 Student Edition Labs – Databases

Click the number 4 button. When the Student Edition Labs menu appears, click *Databases* to begin. A new browser window will open. Follow the on-screen instructions to complete the Lab. When finished, click the Exit button. If required, print a copy of your results to submit to your instructor.

5 Student Edition Labs – Presentation Software

Click the number 5 button. When the Student Edition Labs menu appears, click *Presentation Software* to begin. A new browser window will open. Follow the on-screen instructions to complete the Lab. When finished, click the Exit button. If required, print a copy of your results to submit to your instructor.

6 Practice Test

Click the number 6 button. Answer each question. When completed, enter your name and click the Grade Test button to submit the quiz for grading. Make a note of any missed questions. If required, print a copy to submit to your instructor.

7 Web Guide

Click the number 7 button to display the Guide to Web Sites and Searching Techniques Web page. Click Shopping and then click eBay. Search for Software. Use your word processing program to prepare a brief report about the software you found. Submit your assignment to your instructor.

LEARN IT ONLINE CHAPTER 3

8 Scavenger Hunt

Click the number 8 button. Print a copy of the Scavenger Hunt page; use this page to write down your answers as you search the Web. Submit your completed page to your instructor.

9 Who Wants To Be a Computer Genius?

Click the number 9 button to find out if you are a computer genius. Directions on how to play the game will be displayed. When you are ready to play, click the Play button. Submit your score to your instructor.

10 Wheel of Terms

Click the number 10 button to reinforce important terms you learned in this chapter by playing the Shelly Cashman Series version of this popular game. Directions on how to play the game will be displayed. When you are ready to play, click the Play button. Submit your score to your instructor.

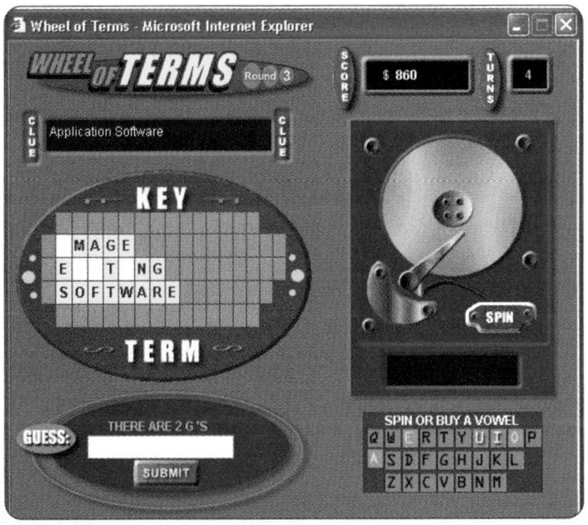

11 Career Corner

Click the number 11 button to display the Penn State's Career Services Web page. Click a link of your choice. Write a brief report about the information you found. Submit the report to your instructor.

12 Search Sleuth

Click the number 12 button to learn search techniques that will help make you a research expert. Submit the completed assignment to your instructor.

13 Crossword Puzzle Challenge

Click the number 13 button. Complete the puzzle to reinforce skills you learned in this chapter. Directions on how to play the game will be displayed. When you are ready to play, click the Submit button. Submit the completed puzzle to your instructor.

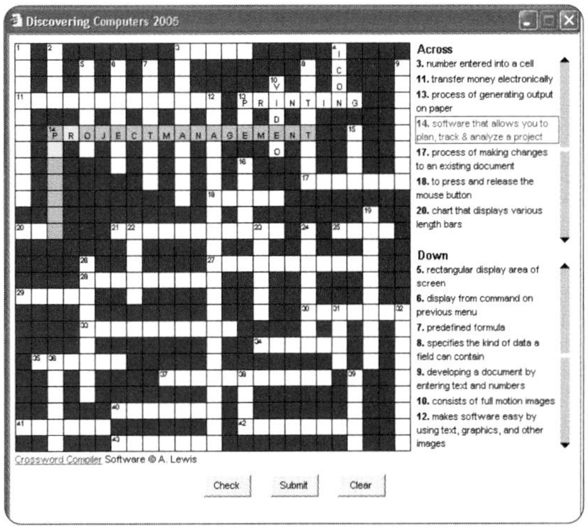

14 Setting Up an E-Mail Account

E-mail has become one of the more widespread ways of communication in today's society. Based on various 1999 estimates, 610 billion to 1,100 billion messages are sent each year. To set up a free e-mail account, click the number 14 button. Follow the online procedures to establish an e-mail account. When you are finished, send yourself an e-mail message.

15 In the News

It is a computer user's worst fear — he or she opens an unfamiliar e-mail message or uses a disk of unknown origin and a computer virus is released that damages and/or deletes files. Fortunately, specialized software prevents such things from happening to your computer. Click the number 15 button and read a news article about antivirus programs. Which program does the article recommend? What does it do? Who will benefit from using this software? Why? Where can the software be obtained? Would you be interested in this software? Why or why not?

CHAPTER 3 LAB EXERCISES

Use the Lab Exercises to gain hands-on computer experience.

WEB INSTRUCTIONS:

To display this page from the Web, start your browser and enter the Web address **scsite.com/dc2005/ch3/lab**.

1 Working with Application Programs

This exercise uses Windows XP procedures. Windows is a multitasking operating system, meaning you can work on two or more applications that reside in memory at the same time. To find out how to work with multiple application programs, click the Start button on the Windows taskbar and then click Help and Support on the Start menu. Click the Windows basics link in the Pick a Help topic area. Click the plus sign to the left of Core Windows tasks and then click the Working with programs link. Click an appropriate topic to answer each of the following questions:

- How do you start a program?
- How do you switch between running programs?
- How do you add a program to your computer?
- How do you quit a program?

Close the Windows Help and Support Center window.

2 Creating a Word Processing Document

This exercise uses Windows XP/2000/98 procedures. WordPad is a simple word processing program included with the Windows operating system. To create a document with WordPad, click the Start button on the Windows taskbar, point to All Programs (Programs in Windows 2000/98) on the Start menu, point to Accessories on the All Programs submenu (Programs submenu in Windows 2000/98), and then click WordPad on the Accessories submenu. If necessary, when the WordPad window is displayed, click its Maximize button. Click View on the WordPad menu bar. If a check mark is not displayed to the left of the Toolbar command, click the Toolbar command. Type two paragraphs summarizing the features of one of the software programs in Figure 3-5 on page 136. Press the TAB key to indent the first line of each paragraph and the ENTER key to begin a new paragraph. To correct errors, press the BACKSPACE key to erase to the left of the insertion point or press the DELETE key to erase to the right. To insert text, position the I-beam mouse pointer at the location where the text is to be inserted and then begin typing. At the end of the document, press the ENTER key twice and then type your name. When the document is complete, save it on a floppy disk inserted into drive A. Click the Save button on the WordPad toolbar, type `a:\lab3-2` in the File name text box and then click the Save button in the Save As dialog box. Click the Print button on the WordPad toolbar to print the document. Close the WordPad window.

3 Using WordPad Help

This exercise uses Windows XP procedures. Start WordPad as described in exercise 2 on this page. Click Help on the WordPad menu bar and then click Help Topics. When the WordPad Help window is displayed, if necessary, click the Index tab. Type `documents saving` in the Type in the keywords to find text box and then press the ENTER key. If necessary, click Create, open, or save a WordPad document in the Topics Found dialog box and then click the Display button.

- How can you save changes to a document?
- How can you save an existing document with a new name?

Close the WordPad Help window and quit WordPad.

4 Business Software Products

This exercise uses Windows XP/2000/98 procedures. What business software packages are on your computer? Click the Start button on the Windows taskbar and then point to All Programs (Programs in Windows 2000/98) on the Start menu. Scan the All Programs submenu (Programs submenu in Windows 2000/98) for the names of popular productivity programs (if necessary, point to the arrow at the top or bottom of the submenu to scroll the submenu up or down). Write the program name and type of application software (refer to Figure 3-5 on page 136). When you are finished, click an empty area of the desktop.

WEB RESEARCH

Use the Web Research exercises to learn more about the special features in this chapter.

WEB INSTRUCTIONS:

Use the link in each exercise or a search engine such as Google (google.com) to research the topic. Then, write a one-page, double-spaced report or create a presentation, unless otherwise directed below. Page numbers on which information can be found are in parentheses.

1. **Issue** Choose one Issue from the following issues in this chapter: Is It Ethical to Copy Software? (136), Personal or Processed? (138), Should What We See Be What We Get? (152), or Is Someone Watching You? (160). Use the Web to research the issue. Discuss the issue with classmates, instructors, and friends. Address the questions that accompany the issue in a report or presentation.

2. **Apply It** Choose one of the following Apply It features in this chapter: Easing a Taxing Part of Life (156) or Obtaining Application Software (161). Use the Web to gather additional information about the topic. Print two Web pages that relate to the Apply It. Detail in a report or presentation what you learned.

3. **Career Corner** Read the Career Corner article in this chapter (164). Use the Web to find out more about the career. Describe the career in a report or presentation.

4. **Companies on the Cutting Edge** Choose one of the Companies on the Cutting Edge in this chapter (166). Use the Web to research the company further. Explain in a report or presentation how this company has contributed to computer technology.

5. **Technology Trailblazers** Choose one of the Technology Trailblazers in this chapter (167). Use the Web to research the person further. Explain in a report or presentation how this individual has affected the way people use, or think about, computers.

6. **Picture Yourself Using Software** Read the Picture Yourself Using Software story at the beginning of this chapter (130). Use the Web to research software further. Describe in a report or presentation the ways in which you might use software.

7. **High-Tech Talk** Read the High-Tech Talk feature in this chapter (165). Use the Web to find out more about the topic. Summarize in a report or presentation what you learned.

8. **Web Links** Review the Web Link boxes found in the margins of this chapter. Visit five of the Web Link sites. Print the main Web page for each site you visit. Choose one of the Web pages and then summarize in one paragraph the content of the Web page.

9. **Looking Ahead** Choose one of the Looking Ahead articles in this chapter: 3G Wireless Service Developing (148) or Plagiarism Software Detects Cheating (159). Use the Web to find out more about the topic. Detail in a report or presentation what you learned.

10. **FAQ** Choose one FAQ found in this chapter. Use the Web to find out more about the topic. Summarize in one paragraph what you learned.

11. **Making Use of the Web** Read the Finance section of Making Use of the Web in Appendix A (APP 6). Complete the Finance Web Exercises at the end of the section (APP 7). Answer the questions posed in each exercise.

CHAPTER 4

The Components of the System Unit

Picture Yourself Upgrading a Computer

Cable television Internet access finally is available in your neighborhood! You immediately call the toll-free number to sign up for this high-speed broadband access. Great news... the service technician can be at your house one week from today. While taking your order, the customer service agent explains that your computer needs a network card to access the cable Internet service. Your computer is an older model and does not have a network card. She says the technician can install one for you, but it may be less expensive if you purchased one from a local computer store and installed it yourself.

You do not have the slightest idea how to install a network card, or any kind of adapter card for that matter, into a computer. What next? A visit to the computer store where you purchased the computer seems like the solution. After explaining the situation to a personal computer salesperson, he assures you the network card installation kit includes thorough instructions with detailed pictures. Then, he walks you to a disassembled computer and has you insert a sample network card into the computer. That was simple! While you make the purchase, the salesperson gives you advice to ensure that you work carefully inside the computer.

As you read Chapter 4, you will learn about various adapter cards and discover other components of the system unit.

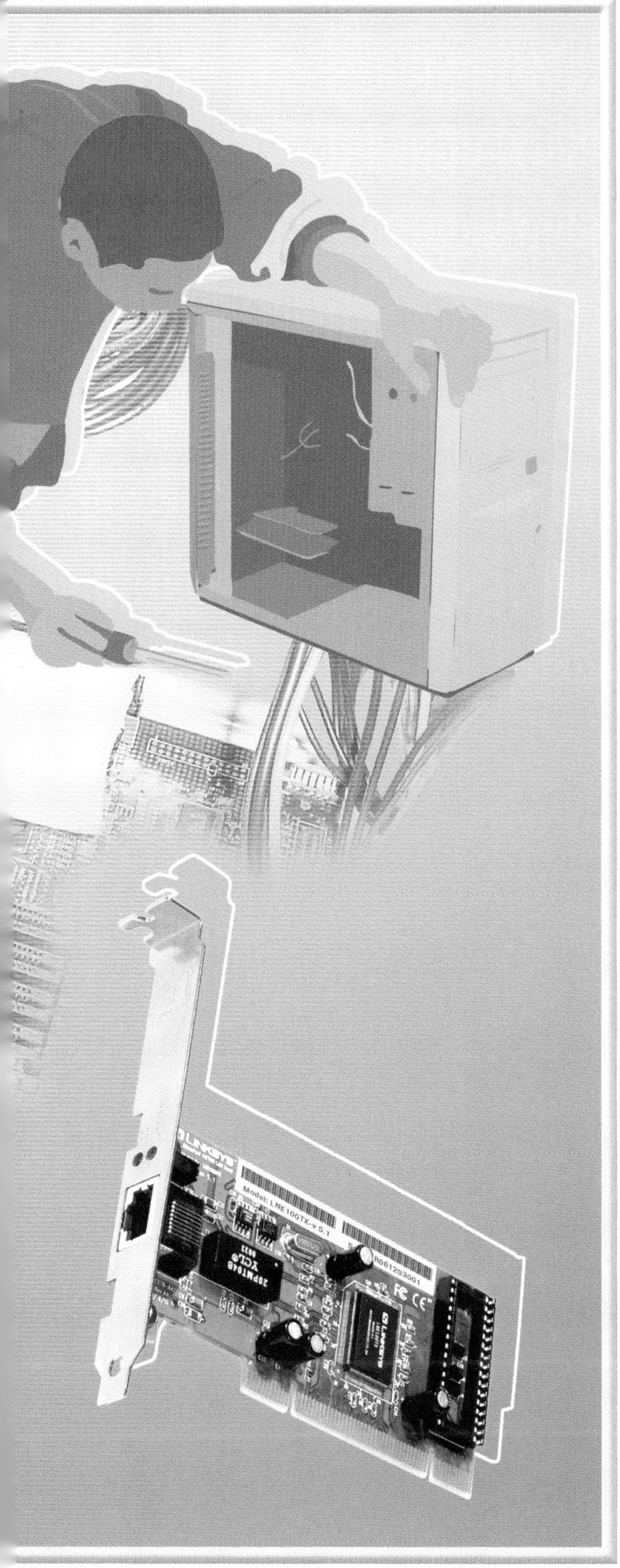

OBJECTIVES

After completing this chapter, you will be able to:

1. Differentiate among various styles of system units
2. Identify chips, adapter cards, and other components of a motherboard
3. Describe the components of a processor and how they complete a machine cycle
4. Identify characteristics of various personal computer processors on the market today
5. Define a bit and describe how a series of bits represents data
6. Explain how programs transfer in and out of memory
7. Differentiate among the various types of memory
8. Describe the types of expansion slots and adapter cards
9. Explain the differences among a serial port, a parallel port, a USB port, and other ports
10. Describe how buses contribute to a computer's processing speed
11. Identify components in mobile computers and mobile devices

CONTENTS

THE SYSTEM UNIT

Whether you are a home user or a business user, you most likely will make the decision to purchase a new computer or upgrade an existing computer within the next several years. Thus, you should understand the purpose of each component in a computer. As Chapter 1 discussed, a computer includes devices used for input, processing, output, storage, and communications. Many of these components are part of the system unit.

The **system unit** is a case that contains electronic components of the computer used to process data. Although many system units resemble a box, they are available in many shapes and sizes. The case of the system unit, sometimes called the *chassis*, is made of metal or plastic and protects the internal electronic components from damage. All computers have a system unit (Figure 4-1).

On desktop personal computers, the electronic components and most storage devices are part of the system unit. Other devices, such as the keyboard, mouse, microphone, monitor, printer, scanner, PC video camera, and speakers, normally occupy space outside the system unit. On notebook computers, the keyboard and pointing device often occupy the area on the top of the system unit, and the display attaches to the system unit by hinges. The location of the system unit on a Tablet PC varies, depending on the design of the Tablet PC. Some models position the system unit behind the keyboard, while others build the system unit into the back of the display. The system unit on a PDA usually consumes the entire device. On these mobile devices, the display often is part of the system unit.

FIGURE 4-1 All sizes of computers have a system unit.

At some point, you might have to open the system unit on a desktop personal computer to replace or install a new electronic component. For this reason, you should be familiar with the electronic components of a system unit. Figure 4-2 identifies some of these components, which include the processor, memory, adapter cards, ports, drive bays, and the power supply.

The processor interprets and carries out the basic instructions that operate a computer. Memory typically holds data waiting to be processed and instructions waiting to be executed. The electronic components and circuitry of the system unit, such as the processor and memory, usually are part of or are connected to a circuit board called the motherboard.

Adapter cards are circuit boards that provide connections and functions not built into the motherboard. Four adapter cards found in some desktop personal computers today are a sound card, a video card, a modem card, and a network card. Devices outside the system unit often attach to ports on the system unit by a connector on a cable. These devices may include a keyboard, mouse, microphone, monitor, printer, scanner, card reader/writer, digital camera, PC video camera, and speakers. A drive bay holds a disk drive. The power supply allows electricity to travel through a power cord from a wall outlet into a computer.

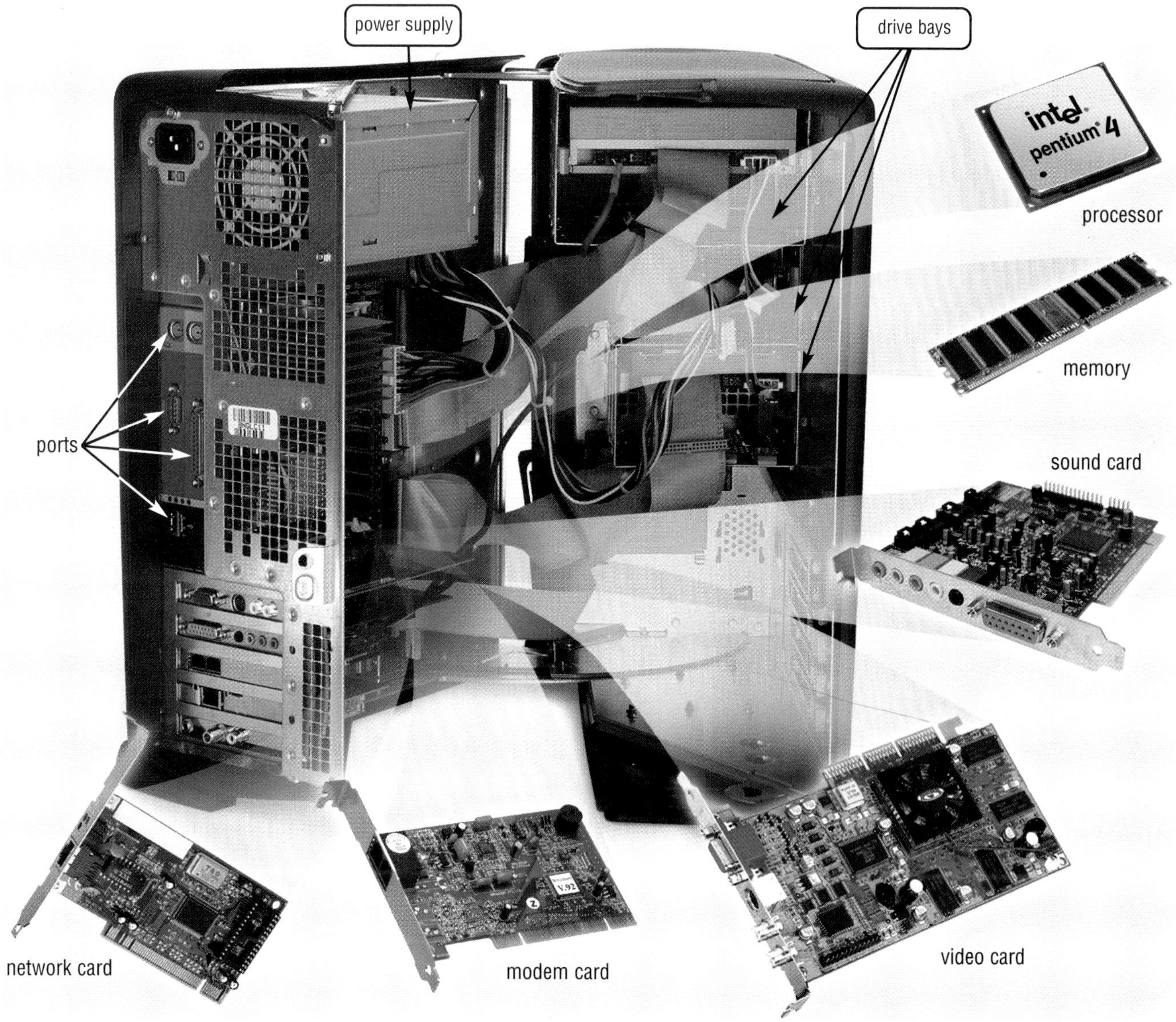

FIGURE 4-2 The system unit on a typical personal computer consists of numerous electronic components, some of which are shown in this figure. The sound card, video card, modem card, and network card are four types of adapter cards.

The Motherboard

The **motherboard**, sometimes called a *system board*, is the main circuit board of the system unit. Many electronic components attach to the motherboard; others are built into it. Figure 4-3 shows a photograph of a desktop personal computer motherboard and identifies components that attach to it, including adapter cards, the processor, and memory. The processor, memory, and other components on the motherboard consist of one or more computer chips.

A computer **chip** is a small piece of semiconducting material, usually silicon, on which integrated circuits are etched. An *integrated circuit* contains many microscopic pathways capable of carrying electrical current. Each integrated circuit can contain millions of elements such as resistors, capacitors, and transistors. A *transistor*, for example, can act as an electronic switch that opens or closes the circuit for electrical charges. Most chips are no bigger than one-half-inch square. Read Apply It 4-1 for information about a use of chips.

WEB LINK 4-1

Motherboards

Visit the Discovering Computers 2005 WEB LINK page (**scsite.com/dc2005/weblink**). Click Motherboards below Chapter 4.

FIGURE 4-3 Many electronic components attach to the motherboard in a desktop personal computer, including a processor, memory, and expansion slots. A processor slot holds the processor chip. Memory slots hold memory cards (modules), which contain memory chips. Expansion slots hold adapter cards.

APPLY IT 4-1

Chip Identifies Pets and Valuables

The next time a beloved pet runs away from home, it can be traced back to its owner if it has been implanted with a tiny, permanent chip.

Veterinarians and animal breeders inject this programmed chip under the animal's skin. It contains a unique identification number that cannot be lost, intentionally removed, or altered. If the animal needs to be identified, a small, handheld scanning device is held close to the implant site and sends a radio signal to the chip. The chip transmits its number to the scanner, and then the breeder or veterinarian can telephone a central office to determine the pet owner's identity. The animal does not feel the chip, which has a useful life of more than 25 years. It does not require any care and does not move in or through the body.

The chip has many other uses, including protecting and studying grizzly bears, ferrets, tortoises, whales, elephants, birds, and snakes. Wildlife research communities implant the chips in endangered animals to guard and observe these animals humanely in their natural habitats. The technology also is used to identify valuable works of art and other priceless possessions.

For more information about injectable identification chips, visit the Discovering Computers 2005 Apply It Web page (**scsite.com/dc2005/apply**). Click Apply It #1 below Chapter 4.

Manufacturers package chips so the chips can be attached to a circuit board, such as a motherboard or an adapter card. Two types of packaging for processor and memory chips in desktop personal computers are the DIP and PGA (Figure 4-4). A *DIP* (*dual inline package*) consists of two parallel rows of downward-pointing thin metal feet (pins) that attach to the circuit board. A *PGA* (*pin grid array*) holds a larger number of pins because the pins are mounted on the surface of the package. A variation of the PGA, called the *flip chip-PGA* (*FC-PGA*), places the chip on the opposite side (flip side) of the pins.

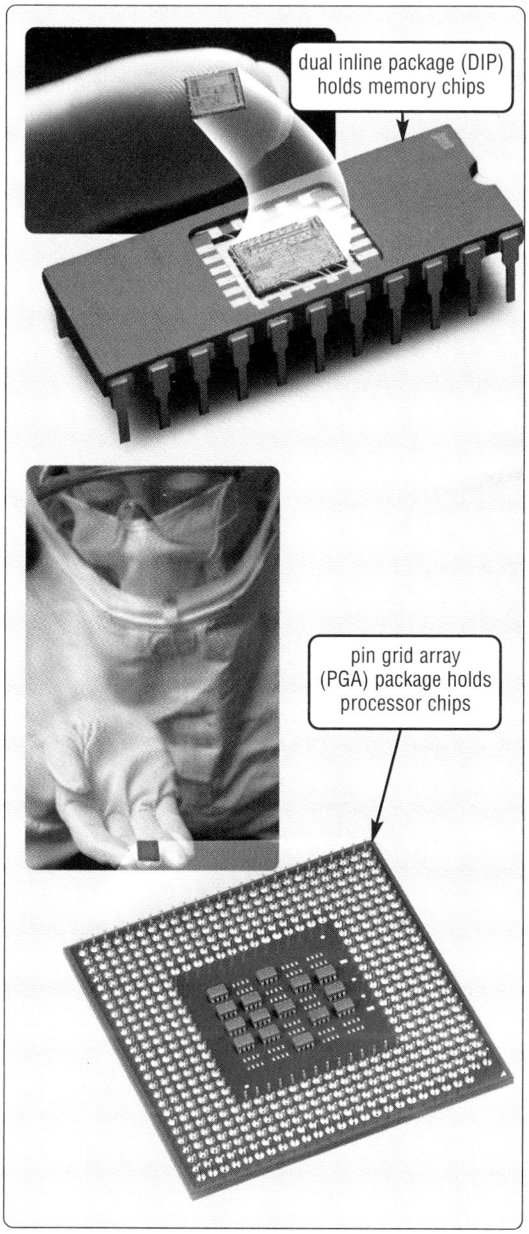

FIGURE 4-4 Chips are packaged so they can be attached to a circuit board.

PROCESSOR

The **processor**, also called the **central processing unit** (**CPU**), interprets and carries out the basic instructions that operate a computer. The processor significantly impacts overall computing power and manages most of a computer's operations. On larger computers, such as mainframes and supercomputers, the various functions performed by the processor extend over many separate chips and often multiple circuit boards. On a personal computer, all functions of the processor usually are on a single chip. Some computer and chip manufacturers use the term *microprocessor* to refer to a personal computer processor chip.

Processors contain a control unit and an arithmetic logic unit (ALU). These two components work together to perform processing operations. Figure 4-5 illustrates how other devices connected to the computer communicate with the processor to carry out a task.

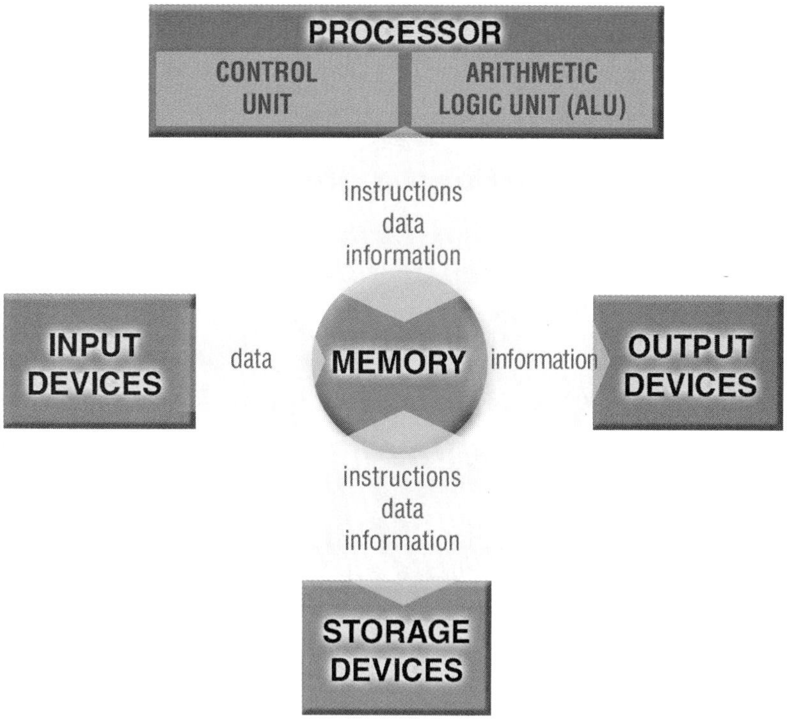

FIGURE 4-5 Most devices connected to the computer communicate with the processor to carry out a task. When a user starts a program, for example, its instructions transfer from a storage device to memory. Data needed by programs enters memory from either an input device or a storage device. The control unit interprets and executes instructions in memory and the ALU performs calculations on the data in memory. Resulting information is stored in memory, from which it can be sent to an output device or a storage device for future access, as needed.

The Control Unit

The **control unit** is the component of the processor that directs and coordinates most of the operations in the computer. The control unit has a role much like a traffic cop: it interprets each instruction issued by a program and then initiates the appropriate action to carry out the instruction.

The Arithmetic Logic Unit

The **arithmetic logic unit** (*ALU*), another component of the processor, performs arithmetic, comparison, and logical operations. *Arithmetic operations* include basic calculations such as addition, subtraction, multiplication, and division. *Comparison operations* involve comparing one data item with another to determine whether the first item is greater than, equal to, or less than the other item. Depending on the result of the comparison, different actions may occur. For example, to determine if an employee should receive overtime pay, the software instructs the ALU to compare the number of hours an employee worked during the week with the regular time hours allowed (e.g., 40 hours). If the hours worked are greater than 40, the ALU calculates an overtime wage. If the hours worked are not greater than 40, the ALU does not calculate an overtime wage.

Logical operations include conditions along with logical operators such as AND, OR, and NOT. For example, if only employees paid hourly can receive overtime pay, the ALU must verify two conditions before computing an overtime wage: (1) the employee is paid hourly AND (2) the employee worked more than 40 hours.

Machine Cycle

For every instruction, a processor repeats a set of four basic operations: (1) fetching, (2) decoding, (3) executing, and, if necessary, (4) storing. *Fetching* is the process of obtaining a program instruction or data item from memory. The term *decoding* refers to the process of translating the instruction into signals the computer can execute. *Executing* is the process of carrying out the commands. *Storing*, in this context, means writing the result to memory (not to a storage medium). Together, these four operations (fetching, decoding, executing, and storing) comprise a *machine cycle* (Figure 4-6). Read Issue 4-1 for a related discussion.

FIGURE 4-6 THE STEPS IN A MACHINE CYCLE

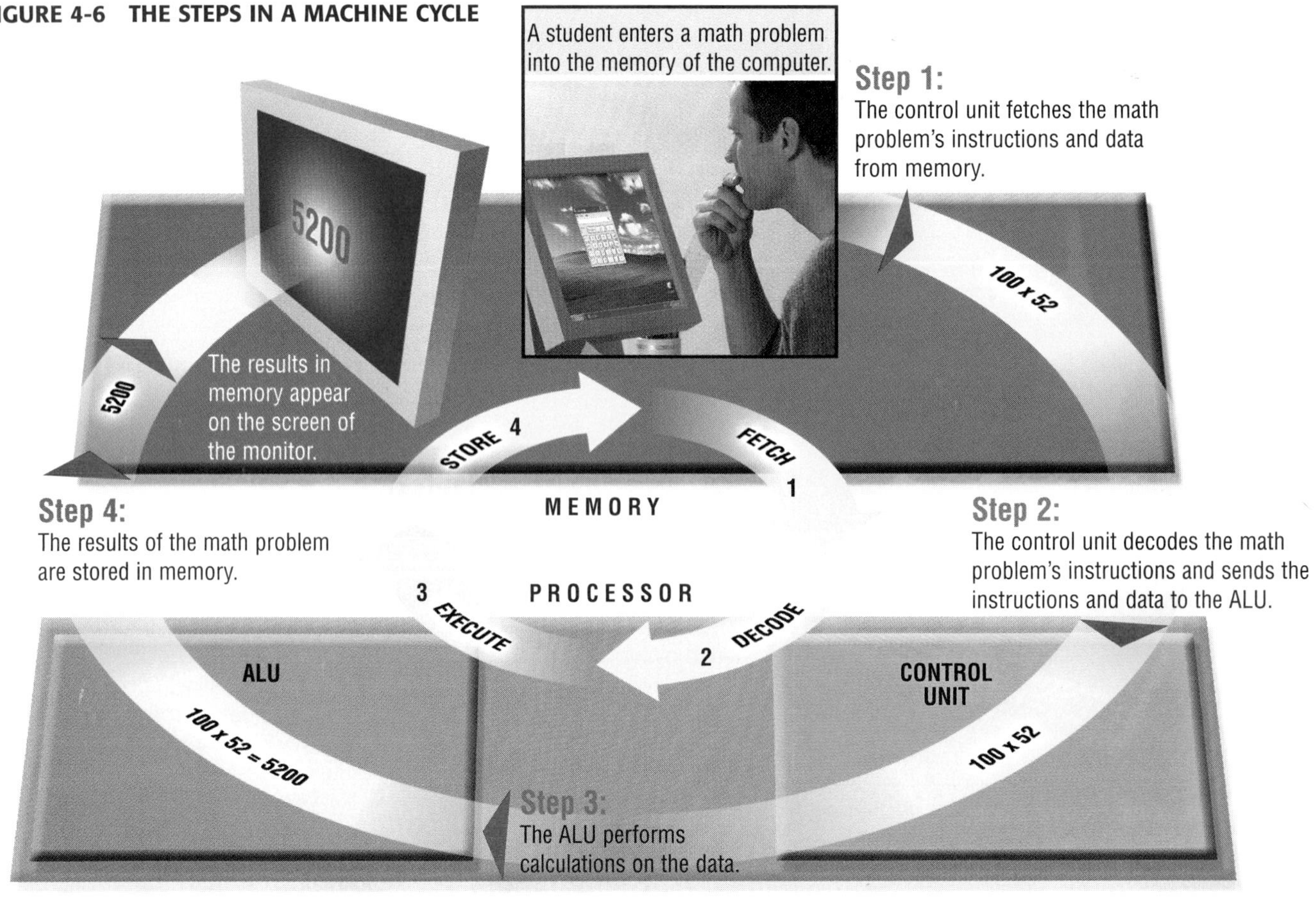

In some computers, the processor fetches, decodes, executes, and stores only one instruction at a time. In these computers, the processor waits until an instruction completes all four stages of the machine cycle (fetch, decode, execute, and store) before beginning work on the next instruction.

Most of today's personal computers support a concept called pipelining. With *pipelining*, the processor begins fetching a second instruction before it completes the machine cycle for the first instruction. Processors that use pipelining are faster because they do not have to wait for one instruction to complete the machine cycle before fetching the next. Think of a pipeline as an assembly line. By the time the first instruction is in the last stage of the machine cycle, three other instructions could have been fetched and started through the machine cycle (Figure 4-7).

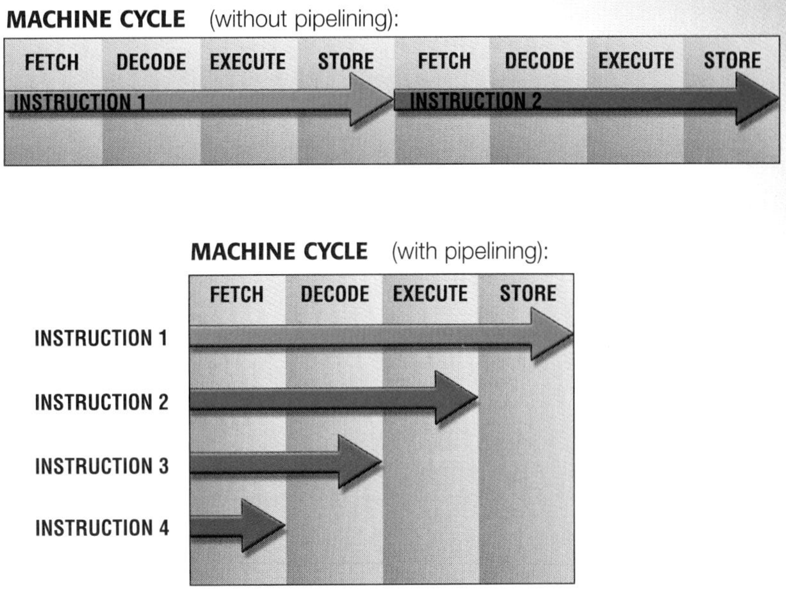

FIGURE 4-7 Most modern personal computers support pipelining. With pipelining, the processor fetches a second instruction before the first instruction is completed. The result is faster processing.

ISSUE 4-1

Does Your Brain Use Machine Cycles?

The control unit's function is to direct and coordinate most of the operations in the computer. To do this, the control unit performs the machine cycle. For each instruction, the processor repeats a set of four operations: fetching, decoding, executing, and storing. These four operations may seem new to you, but in a sense you carry out these same operations each time you complete certain ordinary tasks. Through one of your five senses, you input data, you decode this data and change it into information, you execute the task in some way, and then you store this information for later retrieval. Do people solve all problems in the same way that a computer solves a problem? Why or why not? Describe a simple task in which you perform operations such as those in the machine cycle. What is different and why? If the human brain can perform all of these functions, are computers really necessary? Why?

For more information about the control unit versus the human brain, visit the Discovering Computers 2005 Issues Web page (**scsite.com/dc2005/issues**). Click Issue #1 below Chapter 4.

Registers

A processor contains small high-speed storage locations, called *registers*, that temporarily hold data and instructions. Registers are part of the processor, not part of memory or a storage device. Processors have many different types of registers, each with a specific storage function. Register functions include storing the location from where an instruction was fetched, storing an instruction while the control unit decodes it, storing data while the ALU computes it, and storing the results of a calculation.

The System Clock

The processor relies on a small quartz crystal circuit called the **system clock** to control the timing of all computer operations. Just as your heart beats at a regular rate to keep your body functioning, the system clock generates regular electronic pulses, or ticks, that set the operating pace of components of the system unit.

Each tick equates to a *clock cycle*. In the past, processors used one or more clock cycles to execute each instruction. Processors today often are *superscalar*, which means they can execute more than one instruction per clock cycle.

The pace of the system clock, called the **clock speed**, is measured by the number of ticks per second. Current personal computer processors have clock speeds in the gigahertz range. Giga is a prefix that stands for billion, and a *hertz* is one cycle per second. Thus, one **gigahertz (GHz)** equals one billion ticks of the system clock per second. A computer that operates at 2.8 GHz has 2.8 billion (giga) clock cycles in one second (hertz).

The system clock is one of the major factors that influence a computer's speed. The faster the clock speed, the more instructions the processor can execute per second. Given two otherwise equal processors, the one with a higher clock speed will process more instructions per second. For example, a 3.2 GHz processor is faster than a 2.4 GHz processor. The speed of the system clock has no effect on devices such as a printer or disk drive.

Some computer professionals measure a processor's speed according to the number of *MIPS* (*millions of instructions per second*) it can process. Current desktop personal computers, for example, can process more than 300 MIPS. No real standard for measuring MIPS exists, however, because different instructions require varying amounts of processing time.

FAQ 4-1

Does the system clock also keep track of the current day and time?

No, a separate battery-backed chip, called the *real-time clock*, keeps track of the date and time in a computer. The battery continues to run the real-time clock even when the computer is off.

For more information about the system and real-time clocks, visit the Discovering Computers 2005 FAQ Web page (**scsite.com/dc2005/faq**). Click Computer Clocks below Chapter 4.

WEB LINK 4-2

Clock Speed

Visit the Discovering Computers 2005 WEB LINK page (**scsite.com/dc2005/weblink**). Click Clock Speed below Chapter 4.

Comparison of Personal Computer Processors

The leading processor chip manufacturers for personal computers are Intel, AMD (Advanced Micro Devices), IBM, and Motorola. These manufacturers often identify their processor chips by a model name or model number. Figure 4-8 summarizes the historical development of the personal computer processor and documents the increases in clock speed and number of transistors in chips since 1982. The greater the number of transistors, the more complex and powerful the chip.

With its earlier processors, Intel used a model number to identify the various chips. After learning that processor model numbers could not be trademarked and protected from use by competitors, Intel began identifying its processors with names — thus emerged the series of processors known as the Pentium. Most high-performance PCs use some type of **Pentium** processor. Notebook computers and Tablet PCs use a **Pentium M** processor. Less expensive, basic PCs use a brand of Intel processor called the **Celeron**. Two more brands, called the **Xeon** and **Itanium** processors, are ideal for workstations and low-end servers. Read Issue 4-2 for a related discussion.

ISSUE 4-2

Perfection at What Price?

A glitch within a single computer chip can cause untold problems. A design flaw in Intel's Pentium processor chip caused a rounding error once in nine billion division operations. For most users, this would result in a mistake only once in every 27,000 years, so Intel initially ignored the problem. After an unexpected public outcry, however, Intel eventually supplied replacements to anyone who wanted one, at a cost of almost $500 million to the company. (Intel's costs were equivalent to half a year's research and development budget.) In 2000 and 2001, overheating, processing delays, and microcode problems affected Intel's Pentium III chips, resulting in a recall of the defective chips. Do people overreact to chip issues? Why? How much perfection do consumers have a right to expect? How serious should the problem be before a chip is recalled? Should the company be responsible for notifying all customers who have purchased defective chips?

For more information about processors and flaw issues, visit the Discovering Computers 2005 Issues Web page (**scsite.com/dc2005/issues**). Click Issue #2 below Chapter 4.

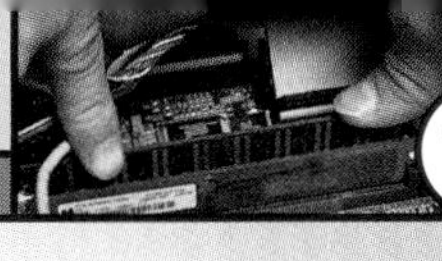

COMPARISON OF WIDELY USED PERSONAL COMPUTER PROCESSORS

Name	Date Introduced	Manufacturer	Clock Speed	Number of Transistors
Xeon MP	2002	Intel	1.4–2.8 GHz	108 million
Itanium 2	2002	Intel	1.3–1.5 GHz	221 million
Xeon	2001	Intel	1.4–3.06 GHz	140 million
Itanium	2001	Intel	733–800 MHz	25.4–60 million
Pentium 4	2000	Intel	1.4–3.2 GHz	42–55 million
Pentium III Xeon	1999	Intel	500–900 MHz	9.5–28 million
Pentium III	1999	Intel	400 MHz–1.4 GHz	9.5–44 million
Celeron	1998	Intel	266 MHz–2.6 GHz	7.5–44 million
Pentium II Xeon	1998	Intel	400–450 MHz	7.5–27 million
Pentium II	1997	Intel	234–450 MHz	7.5 million
Pentium with MMX technology	1997	Intel	166–233 MHz	4.5 million
Pentium Pro	1995	Intel	150–200 MHz	5.5 million
Pentium	1993	Intel	75–200 MHz	3.3 million
80486DX	1989	Intel	25–100 MHz	1.2 million
80386DX	1985	Intel	16–33 MHz	275,000
80286	1982	Intel	6–12 MHz	134,000
AMD64	2003	AMD	2–2.4 GHz	100 million
Opteron	2003	AMD	2–2.4 GHz	100 million
Athlon MP	2002	AMD	1.53–2.25 GHz	54.3 million
Athlon XP	2001	AMD	1.33–2.26 GHz	54.3 million
Athlon	1999	AMD	500 MHz–1.4 GHz	22–38 million
Duron	1999	AMD	600 MHz–1.3 GHz	25 million
AMD–K6 III	1999	AMD	400–450 MHz	21.3 million
AMD–K6–2	1998	AMD	366–550 MHz	9.3 million
AMD–K6	1998	AMD	300 MHz	8.8 million
PowerPC	1994	Motorola/IBM	50 MHz–1.25 GHz	Up to 50 million
68040	1989	Motorola	25–40 MHz	1.2 million
68030	1987	Motorola	16–50 MHz	270,000
68020	1984	Motorola	16–33 MHz	190,000

FIGURE 4-8 A comparison of some of the more widely used personal computer and server processors.

AMD is the leading manufacturer of **Intel-compatible processors**, which have a similar internal design as Intel processors and perform the same functions and can be as powerful, but often are less expensive. Intel and Intel-compatible processors are used in PCs.

Apple computers use an *IBM processor* or a *Motorola processor*, which has a design different from the Intel-style processor. The PowerPC processor has a new architecture that increased the speed of the latest Apple computers.

Many of Intel's latest processor chips contain *Hyper-Threading (HT) Technology*, which improves processing power and time by allowing the processor chip to mimic the power of two processors. Intel, AMD, and Motorola processors have built-in instructions to improve the performance of multimedia, the Web, and 3-D graphics. Their processors for notebook computers also include technology to integrate wireless capabilities and optimize and extend battery life.

A new type of processor, called *system on a chip*, integrates the functions of a processor, memory, and a video card on a single chip. Lower priced personal computers, Tablet PCs, Internet receivers, networking devices, and consumer electronics such as music players and game consoles sometimes have a system-on-a-chip processor. The goal of system-on-a-chip manufacturers is to create processors that have faster clock speeds, consume less power, are small, and are cost effective.

If you are ready to buy a new computer, the processor you select should depend on how you plan to use the computer. If you purchase an IBM-compatible PC, you will choose an Intel processor or an Intel-compatible processor. Apple Macintosh and Power Macintosh users will choose a Motorola or IBM processor. Current models include the PowerPC G4 and PowerPC G5.

Your intended use also will determine the clock speed you need. A home user surfing the Web, for example, will not need as fast a processor as an artist working with graphics or applications requiring multimedia capabilities such as full-motion video. Figure 4-9 outlines guidelines for selecting an Intel processor. Remember, the higher the clock speed, the faster the processor, and the more expensive the computer.

Processor Installation and Upgrades

Instead of buying an entirely new computer, you might be able to upgrade your processor to increase the computer's performance. Be certain the processor you buy is compatible with your computer's motherboard; otherwise, you will have to replace the motherboard, too. Replacing a processor is a fairly simple process, whereas replacing a motherboard is much more complicated.

Processor upgrades fall into one of three types: chip for chip, piggyback, or daughterboard. A *chip-for-chip upgrade* requires you to remove the existing processor chip and replace it with a new one. With a *piggyback upgrade,* you stack the new processor chip on top of the old one. In a *daughterboard upgrade,* the new

GUIDELINES FOR SELECTING AN INTEL PROCESSOR

Intel Processor	Desired Clock Speed	Use
Itanium or **Xeon MP**  	1.3 GHz and up	Power users with workstations; low-end servers on a network
Pentium family 	3.0 GHz and up	Power users or users who design professional drawings; produce and edit videos; record and edit music; participate in video conferences; create professional Web sites; play graphic-intensive multiplayer Internet games
	2.4 GHz to 3.0 GHz	Users who design professional documents containing graphics such as newsletters or number-intensive spreadsheets; produce multimedia presentations; use the Web as an intensive research tool; send documents and graphics via the Web; watch videos; play graphic-intensive games on CD or DVD; create personal Web sites
	Up to 2.4 GHz	Home users who manage personal finances; create basic documents with word processing and spreadsheet software; edit photographs; communicate with others on the Web via e-mail, chat rooms, and discussions; shop on the Web; create basic Web pages
Celeron 	2.2 GHz and up	Home users who manage personal finances; create basic documents with word processing and spreadsheet software; edit photographs; make greeting cards and calendars; use educational or entertainment CDs; communicate with others on the Web via e-mail, chat rooms, and discussions

FIGURE 4-9 Determining which processor to obtain when you purchase a computer depends on computer usage.

processor chip is physically on an adapter card that plugs into the motherboard.

With some chip-for-chip upgrades, you insert the new processor chip into an opening, or *socket*, on the motherboard. Many PGA (pin grid array) chips use a zero-insertion force socket. A *zero-insertion force* (*ZIF*) socket has a small lever or screw that allows users to install and remove processor chips with no force (Figure 4-10). Some motherboards have a second ZIF socket that holds an upgrade chip. In this case, the existing processor chip remains on the motherboard, and you install the upgrade chip into the second ZIF socket.

FIGURE 4-10 HOW TO INSTALL A PROCESSOR CHIP IN A ZERO-INSERTION FORCE SOCKET

Step 1:
Lift the lever on the socket.

Step 2:
Insert the chip.

Step 3:
Push the lever down.

FAQ 4-2

Do I need to take any special precautions when I am working inside the computer case?

Turn off and unplug the computer before opening the case. For less than $10 from an electronics or computer store, buy an *antistatic wristband* to prevent static electricity from damaging the computer's circuitry while you replace components. Do not twist, bend, or force components into place. Gently work around existing cables.

For more information about replacing components in the system unit, visit the Discovering Computers 2005 FAQ Web page (**scsite.com/dc2005/faq**). Click Replacing Components below Chapter 4.

Heat Sinks and Heat Pipes

Newer processor chips generate a lot of heat, which could cause the chip to burn up. Although the computer's main fan generates airflow, today's processors require additional cooling. A *heat sink* is a small ceramic or metal component with fins on its surface that absorbs and ventilates heat produced by electrical components such as a processor (Figure 4-11). Some heat sinks are packaged as part of a processor chip. Others are installed on top or the side of the chip. Because a heat sink consumes a lot of space, a smaller device called a *heat pipe* cools processors in notebook computers.

FIGURE 4-11 A heat sink, which is attached to the top of a processor below the fan, prevents the chip from overheating. The heat sink fan helps distribute air dissipated by the heat sink.

Coprocessors

A *coprocessor* is a special additional processor chip or circuit board that assists the processor in performing specific tasks and increases the performance of the computer. Users running engineering or scientific programs, for instance, will notice a dramatic increase in speed in applications that take advantage of a *floating-point coprocessor*. Floating-point coprocessors sometimes are called math or numeric coprocessors. Processors for personal computers today usually include floating-point processing capabilities.

Parallel Processing

Some computers use more than one processor to speed processing times. Known as *parallel processing*, this method uses multiple processors simultaneously to execute a program (Figure 4-12). Parallel processing divides up a problem so that multiple processors work on their assigned portion of the problem at the same time. As you might expect, parallel processing requires special software that recognizes how to divide up the problem and then bring the results back together again. Supercomputers use parallel processing for applications such as weather forecasting. Some applications draw on the idle time of home users' personal computers to achieve parallel processing. Read Apply It 4-2 for more information.

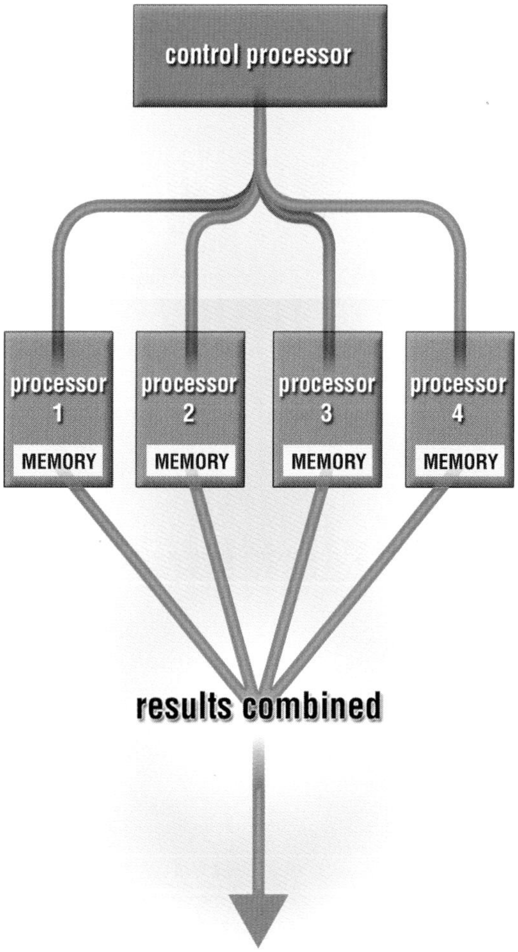

FIGURE 4-12 Parallel processing divides up a problem so that multiple processors work on their assigned portion of a problem at the same time. In this illustration, one processor, called the control processor, is managing the operations of four other processors.

APPLY IT 4-2

Computers at Work While You Sleep

When you are napping, studying for a test, or going to class, your computer can be working to cure life-threatening diseases, thanks to a special Intel-sponsored PC philanthropy program.

The *Intel Philanthropic Peer-to-Peer Program* researches cures and medicines for cancer, Alzheimer's disease, Type II diabetes, Mad Cow disease, and other medical conditions. The company has recorded more than 3 million users and is networking thousands of computers to perform complex calculations and run intricate programs during the computers' idle time, which has amounted to more than 1 million years of processing time.

The research expenses are reduced for these researchers because they are obtaining unlimited computational power for practically no cost. Instead of needing expensive supercomputers to perform these operations, they use this peer-to-peer computing network to process up to 1 zettaflop (10 followed by 21 zeros) per second, which is the largest computation ever performed. Intel estimates it has saved $500 million during the past 10 years utilizing this networking technology to develop new chips.

Medical science is not the only peer-to-peer application, however. The *SETI@home* screensaver program searches for extraterrestrial communications by processing radio telescope signals. Other applications have searched for unique prime numbers, mapped hydrogen gas in the Milky Way, looked for disappearing black holes, and investigated global climate changes.

A few companies pay home users to donate their spare computer time based on the computers' productivity, which usually amounts to a sum that defrays Internet access charges.

For more information about peer-to-peer philanthropy, visit the Discovering Computers 2005 Apply It Web page (**scsite.com/dc2005/apply**). Click Apply It #2 below Chapter 4.

QUIZ YOURSELF 4-1

To check your knowledge of the system unit styles, motherboards, processor components and machine cycles, and characteristics of personal computer processors, visit the Discovering Computers 2005 Quiz Yourself Web page (**scsite.com/dc2005/quiz**). Click Objectives 1 – 4 below Chapter 4.

DATA REPRESENTATION

To understand fully the way a computer processes data, you should know how a computer represents data. People communicate through speech by combining words into sentences. Human speech is **analog** because it uses continuous (wave form) signals that vary in strength and quality. Most computers are **digital**. They recognize only two discrete states: on and off. This is because computers are electronic devices powered by electricity, which also has only two states: on and off.

The two digits, 0 and 1, easily can represent these two states (Figure 4-13). The digit 0 represents the electronic state of off (absence of an electronic charge). The digit 1 represents the electronic state of on (presence of an electronic charge).

When people count, they use the digits in the decimal system (0 through 9). The computer, by contrast, uses a binary system because it recognizes only two states. The **binary system** is a number system that has just two unique digits, 0 and 1, called bits. A **bit** (short for *binary digit*) is the smallest unit of data the computer can process. By itself, a bit is not very informative.

When 8 bits are grouped together as a unit, they form a **byte**. A byte is informative because it provides enough different combinations of 0s and 1s to represent 256 individual characters. These characters include numbers, uppercase and lowercase letters of the alphabet, punctuation marks, and others, such as the letters of the Greek alphabet.

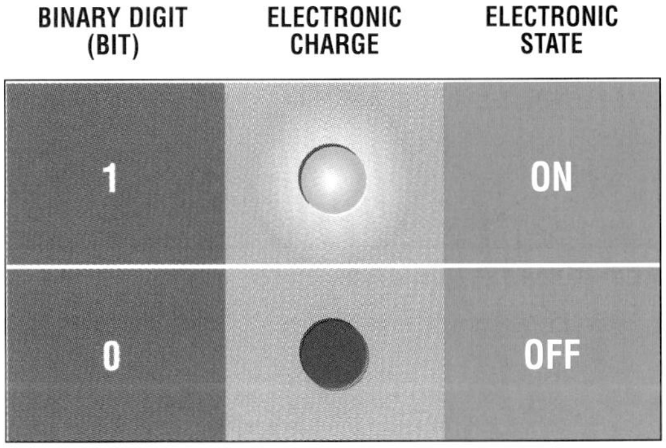

FIGURE 4-13 A computer circuit represents the 0 or the 1 electronically by the presence or absence of an electronic charge.

The combinations of 0s and 1s that represent characters are defined by patterns called a coding scheme. In one coding scheme, the number 3 is represented as 00110011, the number 5 as 00110101, and the capital letter D as 01000100 (Figure 4-14). Two popular coding schemes are ASCII and EBCDIC (Figure 4-15). The *American Standard Code for Information Interchange* (*ASCII* pronounced ASK-ee) scheme is the most widely used coding system to represent data. Most personal computers and midrange servers use the ASCII coding scheme. The *Extended Binary Coded Decimal Interchange Code* (*EBCDIC* pronounced EB-see-dik) scheme is used primarily on mainframe computers and high-end servers.

The ASCII and EBCDIC coding schemes are sufficient for English and Western European languages but are not large enough for Asian and other languages that use different alphabets. *Unicode* is a 16-bit coding scheme that has the capacity of representing more than 65,000 characters and symbols. The Unicode coding scheme is capable of representing almost all the world's current written languages, as well as classic and historical languages. To allow for expansion, Unicode reserves 30,000 codes for future use and 6,000 codes for private use. Unicode is implemented in several operating systems, including Windows XP, Mac OS X, and Linux. Unicode-enabled programming languages and software products include Java, XML, Microsoft Office 2003, and Oracle.

Appendix B at the back of this book discusses the ASCII, EBCDIC, and Unicode schemes in more depth, along with the parity bit and number systems.

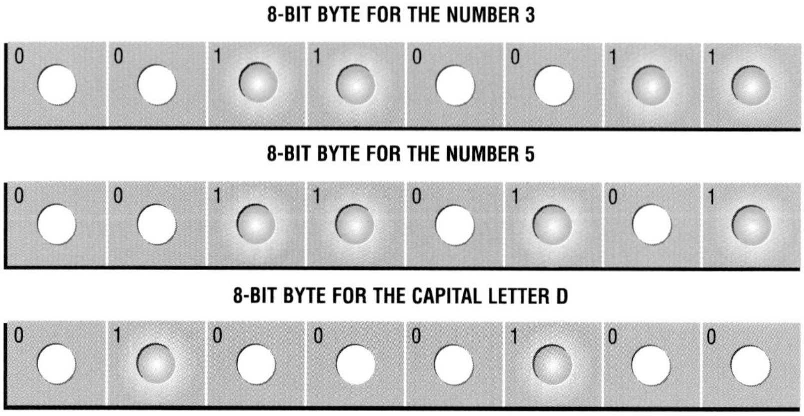

FIGURE 4-14 Eight bits grouped together as a unit are called a byte. A byte represents a single character in the computer.

ASCII	SYMBOL	EBCDIC
00110000	0	11110000
00110001	1	11110001
00110010	2	11110010
00110011	3	11110011
00110100	4	11110100
00110101	5	11110101
00110110	6	11110110
00110111	7	11110111
00111000	8	11111000
00111001	9	11111001
01000001	A	11000001
01000010	B	11000010
01000011	C	11000011
01000100	D	11000100
01000101	E	11000101
01000110	F	11000110
01000111	G	11000111
01001000	H	11001000
01001001	I	11001001
01001010	J	11010001
01001011	K	11010010
01001100	L	11010011
01001101	M	11010100
01001110	N	11010101
01001111	O	11010110
01010000	P	11010111
01010001	Q	11011000
01010010	R	11011001
01010011	S	11100010
01010100	T	11100011
01010101	U	11100100
01010110	V	11100101
01010111	W	11100110
01011000	X	11100111
01011001	Y	11101000
01011010	Z	11101001
00100001	!	01011010
00100010	"	01111111
00100011	#	01111011
00100100	$	01011011
00100101	%	01101100
00100110	&	01010000
00101000	(	01001101
00101001	)	01011101
00101010	*	01011100
00101011	+	01001110

FIGURE 4-15 Two popular coding schemes are ASCII and EBCDIC.

Coding schemes such as ASCII make it possible for humans to interact with a digital computer that processes only bits. When you press a key on a keyboard, a chip in the keyboard converts the key's electronic signal into a scan code that is sent to the system unit. Then, the system unit converts the scan code into a binary form the computer can process and stores it in memory. Every character is converted to its corresponding byte. The computer then processes the data as bytes, which actually is a series of on/off electrical states. When processing is finished, software converts the byte into a human-recognizable number, letter of the alphabet, or special character that is displayed on a screen or is printed (Figure 4-16). All of these conversions take place so quickly that you do not realize they are occurring.

Standards, such as those defined by ASCII, EBCDIC, and Unicode, also make it possible for components within computers to communicate with each other successfully. By following these and other standards, manufacturers can produce a component and be assured that it will operate correctly in a computer. Standards also enable consumers to purchase components that are compatible with their computer configurations.

MEMORY

Memory consists of electronic components that store instructions waiting to be executed by the processor, data needed by those instructions, and the results of processed data (information). Memory usually consists of one or more chips on the motherboard or some other circuit board in the computer.

FIGURE 4-16 HOW A LETTER IS CONVERTED TO BINARY FORM AND BACK

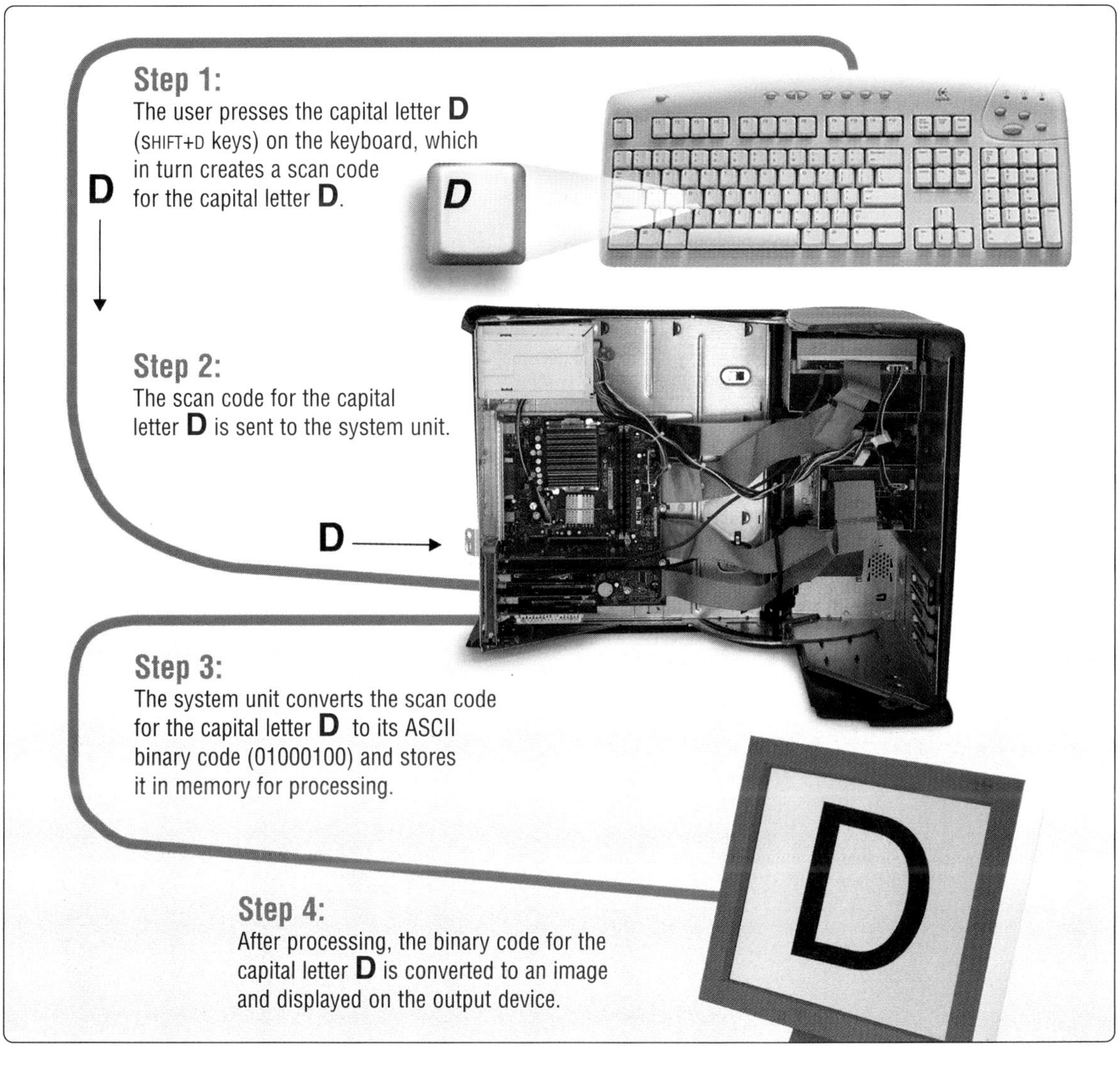

Memory stores three basic categories of items: (1) the operating system and other system software that control or maintain the computer and its devices; (2) application programs that carry out a specific task such as word processing; and (3) the data being processed by the application programs and resulting information. This role of memory to store both data and programs is known as the *stored program concept*.

A byte (character) is the basic storage unit in memory. When application program instructions and data transfer into memory from storage devices, the instructions and data exist as bytes. Each byte resides temporarily in a location in memory, called an *address*. An address simply is a unique number that identifies the location of the byte in memory. The illustration in Figure 4-17 shows how seats on a long-distance passenger train are similar to addresses in memory: (1) a seat holds one person at a time and an address in memory holds a single byte; (2) both a seat and an address can be empty; and (3) a seat has a unique identifier and so does a memory address. To access data or instructions in memory, the computer references the addresses that contain bytes of data.

FIGURE 4-17 Seats in a long-distance passenger train are similar to addresses in memory in several ways: (1) a seat holds one person at a time and an address in memory holds a single byte; (2) both a seat and an address can be empty; and (3) a seat has a unique identifier and so does a memory address.

Manufacturers state the size of memory chips and storage devices in terms of the number of bytes the chip or device has available for storage (Figure 4-18). Recall that storage devices hold data, instructions, and information for future use, while most memory holds these items temporarily. A **kilobyte** (**KB** or **K**) is equal to exactly 1,024 bytes. To simplify memory and storage definitions, computer users often round a kilobyte down to 1,000 bytes. For example, if a memory chip can store 100 KB, it can hold approximately 100,000 bytes (characters). A **megabyte** (**MB**) is equal to approximately 1 million bytes. A **gigabyte** (**GB**) equals approximately 1 billion bytes. A **terabyte** (**TB**) is equal to approximately 1 trillion bytes.

The system unit contains two types of memory: volatile and nonvolatile. When the computer's power is turned off, *volatile memory* loses its contents. *Nonvolatile memory*, by contrast, does not lose its contents when power is removed from the computer; for example, when the computer is turned off or in case of a power failure or other loss of electricity to the computer. Thus, volatile memory is temporary and nonvolatile memory is permanent. RAM is the most common type of volatile memory. Examples of nonvolatile memory include ROM, flash memory, and CMOS. The following sections discuss these types of memory.

MEMORY AND STORAGE SIZES

Term	Abbreviation	Approximate Size	Exact Amount	Approximate Number of Pages of Text
Kilobyte	KB or K	1 thousand bytes	1,024 bytes	1/2
Megabyte	MB	1 million bytes	1,048,576 bytes	500
Gigabyte	GB	1 billion bytes	1,073,741,824 bytes	500,000
Terabyte	TB	1 trillion bytes	1,099,511,627,776 bytes	500,000,000

FIGURE 4-18 Terms commonly used to define memory and storage sizes.

RAM

Users typically are referring to RAM when discussing computer memory. **RAM** (*random access memory*), also called *main memory* or *primary storage*, consists of memory chips that can be read from and written to by the processor and other devices. When the computer is powered on, certain operating system files (such as the files that determine how the Windows XP desktop is displayed) load into RAM from a storage device such as a hard disk. These files remain in RAM as long as the computer has continuous power. As additional programs and data are requested, they also load into RAM from storage.

The processor interprets and executes a program's instructions while the program is in RAM. During this time, the contents of RAM may change (Figure 4-19). RAM can hold multiple programs simultaneously, provided the computer has enough RAM to accommodate all the programs. The program with which you are working usually is displayed on the screen.

FIGURE 4-19 HOW PROGRAM INSTRUCTIONS TRANSFER IN AND OUT OF RAM

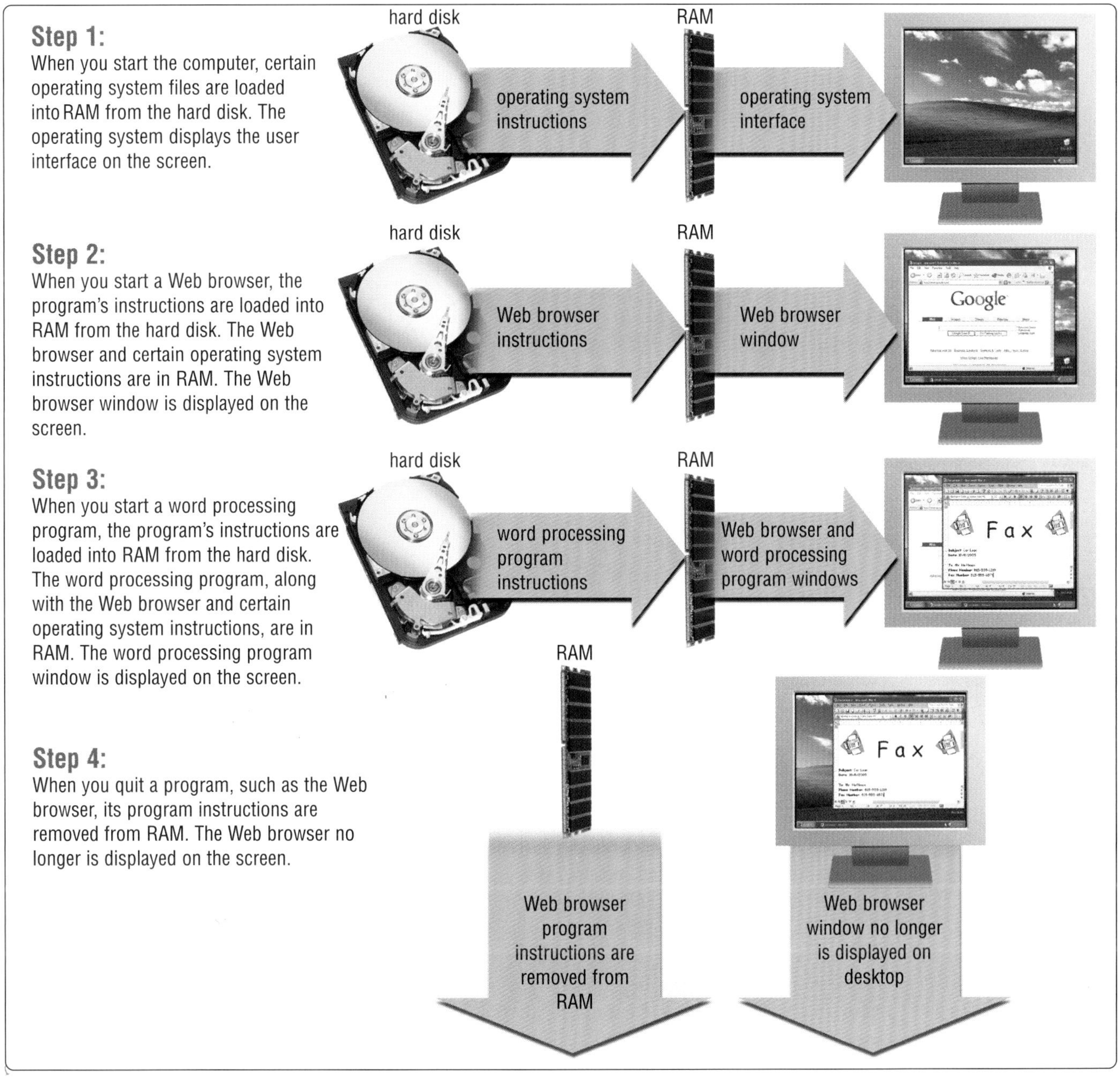

WEB LINK 4-3

RAM

Visit the Discovering Computers 2005 WEB LINK page (**scsite.com/dc2005/weblink**). Click RAM below Chapter 4.

Most RAM is volatile, which means it loses its contents when the power is removed from the computer. For this reason, you must save any items you may need in the future. Saving is the process of copying items from RAM to a storage device such as a hard disk.

Three basic types of RAM chips exist: dynamic RAM, static RAM, and magnetoresistive RAM.

- *Dynamic RAM* (*DRAM* pronounced DEE-ram) chips must be re-energized constantly or they lose their contents. Many variations of DRAM chips exist, most of which are faster than the basic DRAM. *Synchronous DRAM* (*SDRAM*) chips are much faster than DRAM chips because they are synchronized to the system clock. *Double Data Rate SDRAM* (*DDR SDRAM*) chips are even faster than SDRAM chips because they transfer data twice for each clock cycle, instead of just once, and DDR 2 is even faster than DDR. *Rambus DRAM* (*RDRAM*) chips are yet another type of DRAM chips that are much faster than SDRAM chips because they use pipelining techniques. Most personal computers today use some form of SDRAM chips or RDRAM chips.
- *Static RAM* (*SRAM* pronounced ESS-ram) chips are faster and more reliable than any variation of DRAM chips. These chips do not have to be re-energized as often as DRAM chips, thus, the term static. SRAM chips, however, are much more expensive than DRAM chips. Special applications such as cache use SRAM chips. A later section in this chapter discusses cache.
- A newer type of RAM, called *magnetoresistive RAM* (*MRAM* pronounced EM-ram), stores data using magnetic charges instead of electrical charges. Manufacturers claim that MRAM has greater storage capacity, consumes less power, and has faster access times than electronic RAM. Also, MRAM retains its contents after power is removed from the computer, which could prevent loss of data for users. As the cost of MRAM declines, experts predict MRAM could replace both DRAM and SRAM.

RAM chips often are smaller in size than processor chips. RAM chips usually reside on a **memory module**, which is a small circuit board. **Memory slots** on the motherboard hold memory modules (Figure 4-20). Three types of memory modules are SIMMs, DIMMs, and RIMMs. A *SIMM* (*single inline memory module*) has pins on opposite sides of the circuit board that connect together to form a single set of contacts. With a *DIMM* (*dual inline memory module*), by contrast, the pins on opposite sides of the circuit board do not connect and thus form two sets of contacts. SIMMs and DIMMs typically hold SDRAM chips. A *RIMM* (*Rambus inline memory module*) houses RDRAM chips. For a more technical discussion about RAM, read the High-Tech Talk article on page 215 at the end of this chapter.

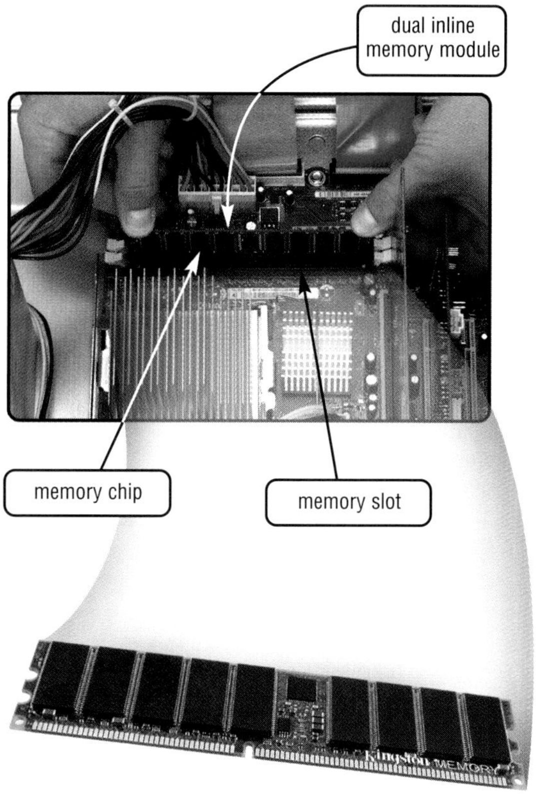

FIGURE 4-20 This photo shows a memory module being inserted into a motherboard.

RAM CONFIGURATIONS The amount of RAM necessary in a computer often depends on the types of software you plan to use. A computer executes programs that are in RAM. Think of RAM as the workspace on the top of your desk. Just as the top of your desk needs a certain amount of space to hold papers, a computer needs a certain amount of memory to store programs, data, and information. The more RAM a computer has, the faster the computer will respond.

A software package typically indicates the minimum amount of RAM it requires (Figure 4-21). If you want the application to perform optimally, usually you need more than the minimum specifications on the software package.

Generally, home users running Windows XP and using basic application software such as word processing should have at least 256 MB of RAM. Most business users who work with accounting, financial, or spreadsheet programs, voice recognition, and programs requiring multimedia capabilities should have a minimum of 512 MB of RAM. Users creating professional Web sites or using graphics-intensive applications will want at least 2 GB of RAM.

Figure 4-22a provides guidelines for the amount of RAM for various types of users. Figure 4-22b shows advertisements that match to each user requirement. Advertisements normally list the type of processor, the clock speed of the processor, and the amount of RAM in the computer. The amount of RAM in computers purchased today ranges from 256 MB to 2 GB.

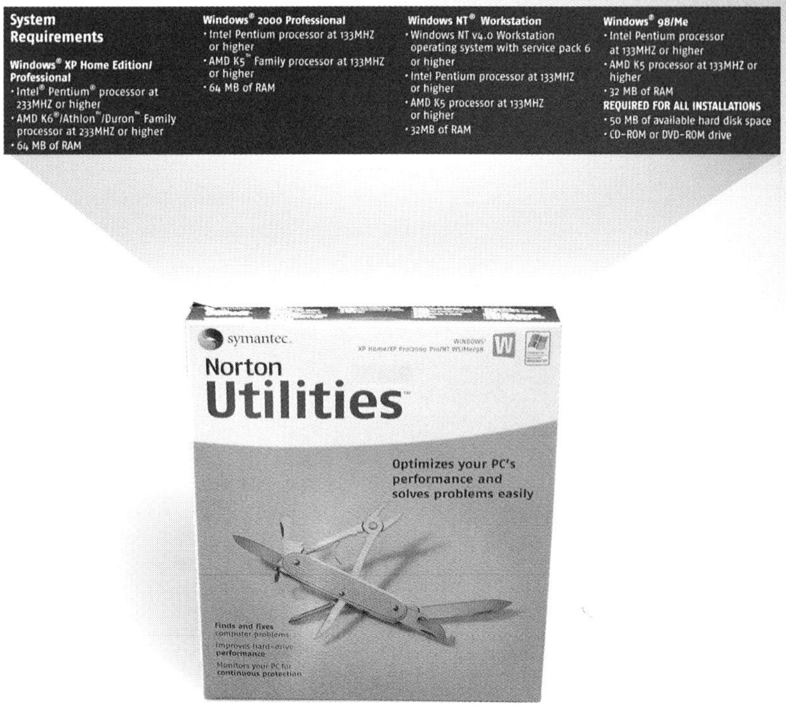

FIGURE 4-21 The minimum system requirements for a software product usually are printed on the box.

FAQ 4-3

Can I add more RAM to my computer?

Check your computer documentation to see how much RAM you can add. RAM modules are relatively inexpensive and usually include easy-to-follow installation instructions. Be sure to purchase RAM compatible with your brand and model of computer.

For more information about upgrading RAM, visit the Discovering Computers 2005 FAQ Web page (**scsite.com/dc2005/faq**). Click Upgrading RAM below Chapter 4.

Figure 4-22a (RAM guidelines)

RAM	256 MB	256 to 1 GB	1 GB and up
Use	Home and business users managing personal finances; using standard application software such as word processing; using educational or entertainment CD-ROMs; communicating with others on the Web	Users requiring more advanced multimedia capabilities; running number-intensive accounting, financial, or spreadsheet programs; using voice recognition; working with videos, music, and digital imaging; creating Web sites; participating in video conferences; playing Internet games	Power users creating professional Web sites; running sophisticated CAD, 3-D design, or other graphics-intensive software

Figure 4-22b (computers for sale)

Model	C220	A226	P3.2G	A225M	P253R
Processor	2.2 GHz Celeron processor	2.26 GHz Athlon XP processor	3.2 GHz Pentium 4 processor	2.25 Athlon MP processor	2.8 GHz Xeon MP processor
Memory	256 MB SDRAM	512 MB SDRAM	512 MB SDRAM	1 GB SDRAM	2 GB RDRAM

FIGURE 4-22 Determining how much RAM you need depends on the applications you intend to run on your computer. Advertisements for computers normally list the type of processor, the speed of the processor, and the amount of RAM installed.

Cache

Most of today's computers improve processing times with **cache** (pronounced cash). Two types of cache are memory cache and disk cache. This chapter discusses memory cache. Chapter 7 discusses disk cache.

Memory cache helps speed the processes of the computer because it stores frequently used instructions and data. Most personal computers today have two types of memory cache: L1 cache and L2 cache. Servers also may have L3 cache.

- *L1 cache* is built directly into the processor chip. L1 cache usually has a very small capacity, ranging from 8 KB to 128 KB. The most common size is 8 KB.
- *L2 cache* is slightly slower than L1 cache but has a much larger capacity, ranging from 64 KB to 4 MB. When discussing cache, most users are referring to L2 cache. On older computers, L2 cache consisted of high-speed SRAM chips on the motherboard or an adapter card of chips inserted into the motherboard. Current processors include *advanced transfer cache*, a type of L2 cache built directly on the processor chip. Processors that use advanced transfer cache perform at much faster rates than those that do not use it.
- *L3 cache* is a cache separate from the processor chip on the motherboard. L3 cache exists only on computers that use L2 advanced transfer cache.

Cache speeds up processing time because it stores frequently used instructions and data. When the processor needs an instruction or data, it searches memory in this order: L1 cache, then L2 cache, then L3 cache (if it exists), then RAM — with a greater delay in processing for each level of memory it must search. If the instruction or data is not found in memory, then it must search a slower speed storage medium such as a hard disk, CD, or DVD.

A computer with L2 cache usually performs at speeds 10- to 40-percent faster than those without cache. To realize the largest increase in performance, a personal computer should have at least 256 KB of L2 advanced transfer cache (Figure 4-23). Servers and workstations can have at least 2 MB of L2 or L3 cache.

WEB LINK 4-4

Cache

Visit the Discovering Computers 2005 WEB LINK page (**scsite.com/dc2005/weblink**). Click Cache below Chapter 4.

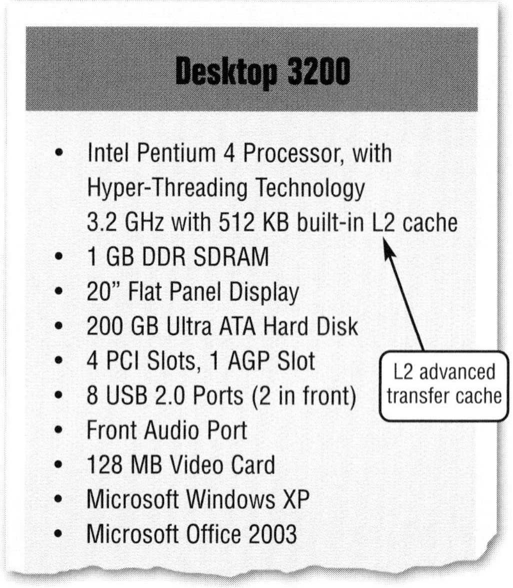

FIGURE 4-23 This computer advertisement shows that new computers often have 512 KB of L2 advanced transfer cache.

ROM

Read-only memory (**ROM** pronounced rahm) refers to memory chips storing permanent data and instructions. The data on most ROM chips cannot be modified — hence, the name read-only. ROM is nonvolatile. Its contents are not lost when power is removed from the computer. In addition to the computer, many devices contain ROM chips. For example, ROM chips in printers contain data for fonts.

Manufacturers of ROM chips often record data, instructions, or information on the chips when they manufacture the chip. These ROM chips, called **firmware**, contain permanently written data, instructions, or information. One type of firmware, for example, contains the computer's startup instructions.

A *PROM* (*programmable read-only memory*) chip is a blank ROM chip onto which a programmer can write permanently. Programmers use *microcode* instructions to program a PROM chip. Once a programmer writes the microcode onto the PROM chip, it functions like a regular ROM chip and cannot be erased or changed.

A variation of the PROM chip, called an *EEPROM* (*electrically erasable programmable read-only memory*) chip, allows a programmer to erase the microcode with an electric signal.

Flash Memory

Flash memory is a type of nonvolatile memory that can be erased electronically and rewritten, similar to EEPROM. Most computers use flash memory to hold their startup instructions because it allows the computer easily to update its contents. For example, when the computer changes from standard time to daylight savings time, the contents of a flash memory chip (and the real-time clock chip) change to reflect the new time. When you add new hardware devices to the computer, the flash memory chip changes the configuration information about the computer.

Flash memory chips also store data and programs on many mobile computers and devices, such as PDAs, digital cellular telephones, printers, Internet receivers, digital cameras, automotive devices, music players, digital voice recorders, and pagers. When you enter names and addresses into a PDA, a flash memory chip stores the data. The flash memory chip in a digital cellular telephone stores names and telephone numbers. Current MP3 players can play more than one hour of music stored on a flash memory chip (Figure 4-24). Read Looking Ahead 4-1 for a look at the next generation of computers and chips.

Another type of flash memory is the flash memory card. A later section in this chapter discusses flash memory cards, which store flash memory on a removable device instead of a chip.

WEB LINK 4-5

Flash Memory

Visit the Discovering Computers 2005 WEB LINK page (**scsite.com/dc2005/weblink**). Click Flash Memory below Chapter 4.

FIGURE 4-24 HOW AN MP3 MUSIC PLAYER MIGHT STORE MUSIC

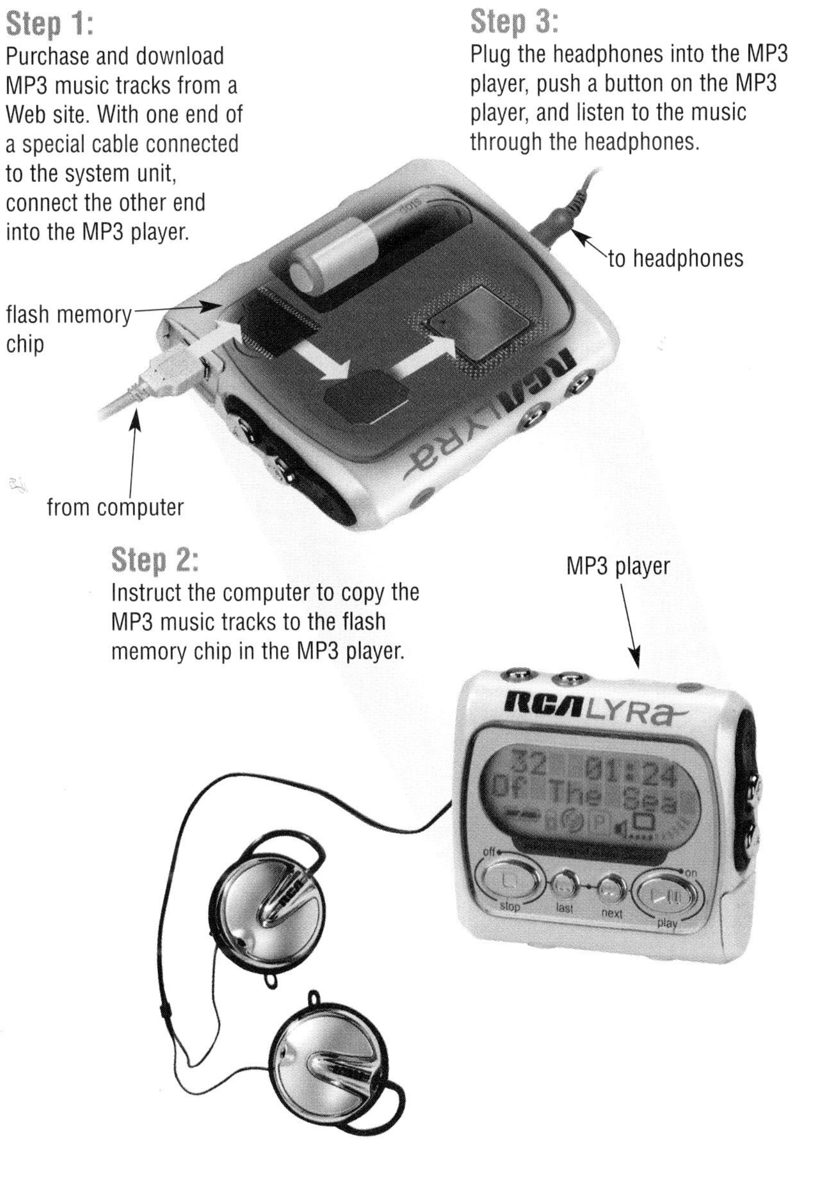

LOOKING AHEAD 4-1

Next-Generation Computers and Chips: Faster and Smaller

When Intel cofounder Gordon Moore predicted in 1965 that the number of transistors and resistors placed on computer chips would double every year, he realized that the computer industry was in store for incredible growth and technological advances. Although he changed his prediction in 1975 to doubling every two years, the computer industry has continued to develop at breakneck speed.

Researchers and engineers have a variety of predictions for the next generation of computers. For example, *ovonic memory* chips store data virtually forever and are expected eventually to replace flash memory chips, which wear out over time. Scientists at Newcastle University in England are developing clock-free systems, called *asynchronous computers*, that would reduce heat and further shrink hardware sizes. These computers would be useful in complex systems demanding speedy performance, such as in global air traffic control.

Ovonic Memory Diagram

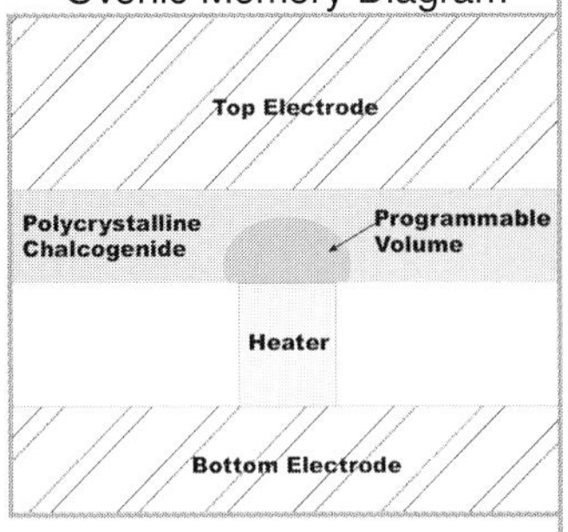

For a look at next-generation computers and chips, visit the Discovering Computers 2005 Looking Ahead Web page (**scsite.com/dc2005/looking**). Click Looking Ahead #1 below Chapter 4.

CMOS

Some RAM chips, flash memory chips, and other types of memory chips use **complementary metal-oxide semiconductor** (**CMOS** pronounced SEE-moss) technology because it provides high speeds and consumes little power. CMOS technology uses battery power to retain information even when the power to the computer is off. Battery-backed CMOS memory chips, for example, can keep the calendar, date, and time current even when the computer is off. The flash memory chips that store a computer's startup information often use CMOS technology.

FAQ 4-4

What should I do if my computer's date and time are wrong?

First, try resetting the date and time. To do this in Windows XP, double-click the time at the right edge of the taskbar. If the computer continues to lose time or display an incorrect date, you may need to replace the CMOS battery on the motherboard that powers the system clock.

For more information about the CMOS battery, visit the Discovering Computers 2005 FAQ Web page (**scsite.com/dc2005/faq**). Click CMOS Battery below Chapter 4.

Memory Access Times

Access time is the amount of time it takes the processor to read data, instructions, and information from memory. A computer's access time directly affects how fast the computer processes data. Today's manufacturers use a variety of terminology to state access times (Figure 4-25). Some use fractions of a second, which for memory occurs in nanoseconds. A **nanosecond** (abbreviated *ns*) is one billionth of a second. A nanosecond is extremely fast (Figure 4-26). In fact, electricity travels about one foot in a nanosecond.

Other manufacturers state access times in MHz; for example, 83 MHz SDRAM. If a manufacturer states access time in megahertz, you can convert it to nanoseconds by dividing the megahertz number into 1 billion ns. For example, 133 MHz equals approximately 7.5 ns (1,000,000,000 / 133,000,000).

The access time (speed) of memory contributes to the overall performance of the computer. Standard SDRAM chips can have access times up to 133 MHz (about 7.5 ns), and access times of the DDR SDRAM chips reach 333 MHz (about 3 ns). The faster RDRAM chips can have access times up to 800 MHz (about 1.25 ns). ROM access times range from 25 to 250 ns. Accessing data in memory can be more than 200,000 times faster than accessing data on a hard disk because of the mechanical motion of the hard disk.

While access times of memory greatly affect overall computer performance, manufacturers and retailers usually list a computer's memory in terms of its size, not its access time. Thus, an advertisement might describe a computer as having 128 MB of SDRAM expandable to 512 MB.

QUIZ YOURSELF 4-2

To check your knowledge of bits, bytes, data representation, and types of memory, visit the Discovering Computers 2005 Quiz Yourself Web page (**scsite.com/dc2005/quiz**). Click Objectives 5 – 7 below Chapter 4.

ACCESS TIME TERMINOLOGY

Term	Abbreviation	Speed
Millisecond	ms	One-thousandth of a second
Microsecond	μs	One-millionth of a second
Nanosecond	ns	One-billionth of a second
Picosecond	ps	One-trillionth of a second

FIGURE 4-25 Access times are measured in fractions of a second. This table lists the terms used to define access times.

10 million operations = 1 blink

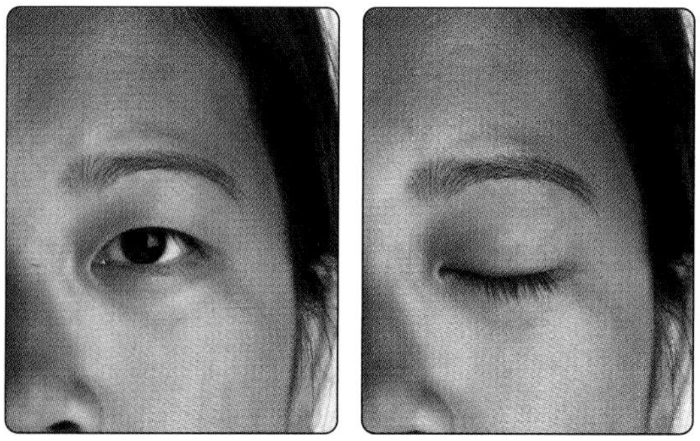

FIGURE 4-26 It takes about one-tenth of a second to blink your eye, which is the equivalent of 100 million nanoseconds. A computer can perform some operations in as few as 10 nanoseconds. In the time it takes to blink your eye, a computer can perform some operations 10 million times.

EXPANSION SLOTS AND ADAPTER CARDS

An **expansion slot** is a socket on the motherboard that can hold an adapter card. An **adapter card**, sometimes called an *expansion card*, is a circuit board that enhances functions of a component of the system unit and/or provides connections to peripherals. A **peripheral** is a device that connects to the system unit and is controlled by the processor in the computer. Examples of peripherals are modems, disk drives, printers, scanners, and keyboards.

Figure 4-27 lists a variety of types of adapter cards. Sometimes, all functionality is built into the adapter card. With others, a cable connects the adapter card to a peripheral, such as a scanner, outside the system unit. Figure 4-28 shows an adapter card being inserted into an expansion slot on a personal computer motherboard.

TYPES OF ADAPTER CARDS

Adapter Card	Purpose
Accelerator	Increases the speed of the processor
Disk controller	Connects disk drives
Game	Connects a joystick
I/O	Connects input and output devices such as a printer or mouse; being phased out because newer motherboards support these connections
Interface	Connects other peripherals such as a mouse, CD, DVD, or scanner
MIDI	Connects musical instruments
Modem	Connects other computers through telephone or cable television lines
Network	Connects other computers and peripherals
PCtoTV converter	Connects a television
Sound	Connects speakers or a microphone
TV tuner	Allows viewing of television channels on the monitor
USB 2.0	Connects USB 2.0 devices
Video	Connects a monitor
Video capture	Connects a camcorder

FIGURE 4-27 Various types of adapter cards and their functions.

FIGURE 4-28 Illustrated is an adapter card being inserted into an expansion slot on the motherboard of a personal computer.

Some motherboards include all necessary capabilities and do not require adapter cards. For example, sound and video functions may be built into a newer motherboard. Other motherboards may require adapter cards to provide sound, video, modem, and network capabilities. A **sound card** enhances the sound-generating capabilities of a personal computer by allowing sound to be input through a microphone and output through external speakers or headset. A **video card**, also called a *graphics card*, converts computer output into a video signal that travels through a cable to the monitor, which displays an image on the screen. A **modem card**, also called an *internal modem*, is a communications device that enables computers to communicate via telephone lines, cable television lines, or other media. A **network card** is a communications device that allows the computer to access a network. Read Issue 4-3 for a related discussion.

ISSUE 4-3

Does Lower Price Mean Less Value?

Today, you can buy a personal computer for less than $1,000 that can do more than one nearly twice its cost two years ago. Part of the plunge in prices is lower-cost components, but another factor is a growing demand for less expensive machines. Many consumers are looking for inexpensive computers that are adequate for basic tasks, such as word processing and Internet access. They feel that paying higher prices for faster processors, more memory, 3-D video cards, higher-quality sound cards, more hard disk space, and other extras is an unnecessary, frivolous expense. As one industry analyst asks, "Why buy a Porsche when you are going to drive only 55 miles per hour?" How might a greater availability of lower-priced personal computers change the way people, schools, and businesses buy and use them? With respect to computers, does a higher price always mean greater usefulness? Why or why not? Who might be satisfied with less than the latest computer technology? Why?

For more information about personal computer prices, visit the Discovering Computers 2005 Issues Web page (**scsite.com/dc2005/issues**). Click Issue #3 below Chapter 4.

In the past, installing a card was not easy and required you to set switches and other elements on the motherboard. Many of today's computers support **Plug and Play**, which means the computer automatically can configure adapter cards and other peripherals as you install them. Having Plug and Play support means you can plug in a device, turn on the computer, and then immediately begin using the device.

WEB LINK 4-6

Adapter Cards

Visit the Discovering Computers 2005 WEB LINK page (**scsite.com/dc2005/weblink**). Click Adapter Cards below Chapter 4.

PC Cards and Flash Memory Cards

Notebook and other mobile computers have at least one **PC Card slot**, which is a special type of expansion slot that holds PC Cards. A **PC Card** is a thin, credit card-sized device that adds memory, storage, sound, fax/modem, communications, and other capabilities to mobile computers (Figure 4-29). Because of their small size and versatility, some consumer electronics products such as digital cameras and automobiles use PC Cards.

All PC Cards conform to standards developed by the *Personal Computer Memory Card International Association* (these cards originally were called *PCMCIA cards*). These standards help to ensure the interchangeability of PC Cards among mobile computers.

WEB LINK 4-7

PC Cards

Visit the Discovering Computers 2005 WEB LINK page (**scsite.com/dc2005/weblink**). Click PC Cards below Chapter 4.

PC Cards are one type of **flash memory card**, or removable flash memory device, that allows users to transfer data and information conveniently from mobile devices to their desktop computers. Figure 4-30 shows a variety of flash memory cards. Many mobile and consumer devices, such as PDAs, digital cameras, digital music players, and cellular telephones, use these memory cards. Some printers and computers have built-in card readers/writers or slots. In addition, you can purchase an external card reader/writer that attaches to any computer. The type of flash memory card you have will determine the type of card reader/writer you need.

Unlike adapter cards that require you to open the system unit and install the card onto the motherboard, you can change a flash memory card, such as a PC Card, without having to open the system unit or restart the computer. For example, if you need to connect to the Internet, simply insert the modem card in the PC Card slot of your notebook computer while the computer is running. The operating system automatically recognizes the new PC Card and allows you to connect to the Internet, often wirelessly.

This feature of PC Cards and other flash memory cards, called *hot plugging*, allows you to insert and remove the cards while the computer is running. Chapter 7 discusses flash memory cards in more depth.

FIGURE 4-29 Shown here is a PC Card sticking out of a PC Card slot on a notebook computer.

FIGURE 4-30 Flash memory cards are available in a wide range of sizes.

PORTS AND CONNECTORS

A **port** is the point at which a peripheral attaches to a system unit so it can send data or receive information from the computer. An external device, such as a keyboard, monitor, printer, mouse, and microphone, often attaches by a cable to a port on the system unit. Instead of port, the term *jack* sometimes is used to identify audio and video ports. The back of the system unit contains many ports; some newer personal computers also have ports on the front of the system unit (Figure 4-31).

Ports have different types of connectors. A **connector** joins a cable to a peripheral (Figure 4-32). One end of a cable attaches to the connector on the system unit and the other end of the cable attaches to a connector on the peripheral. Most connectors are available in one of two genders: male or female. *Male connectors* have one or more exposed pins, like the end of an electrical cord you plug into the wall. *Female connectors* have matching holes to accept the pins on a male connector, like an electrical wall outlet.

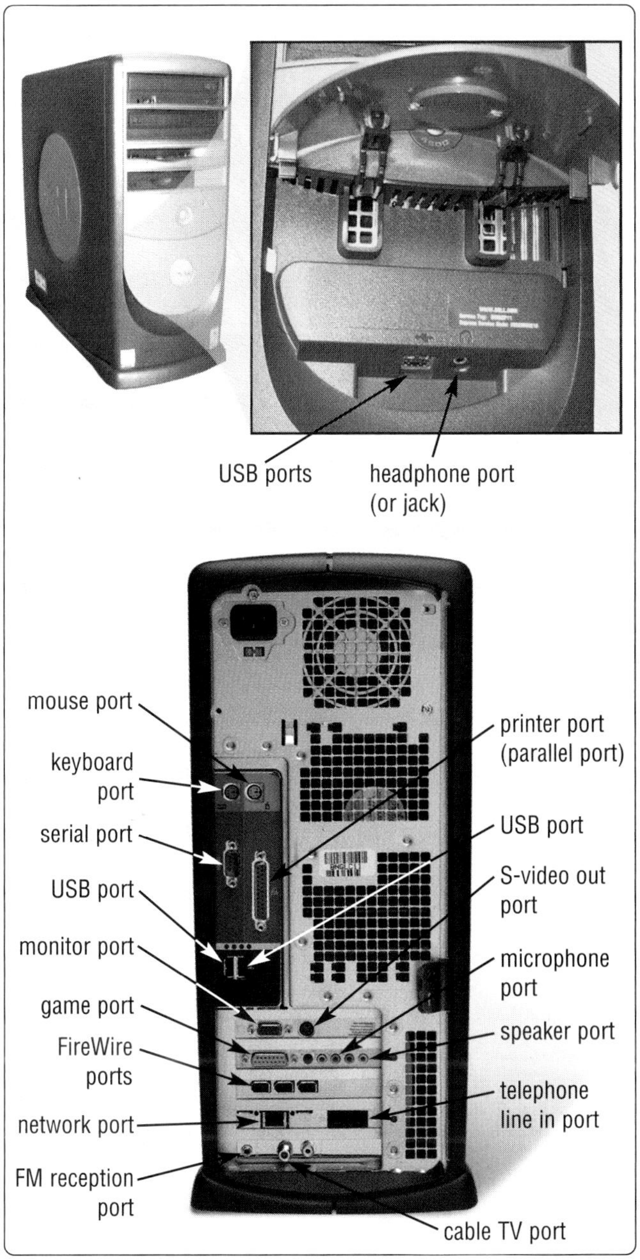

FIGURE 4-31 The back of a system unit has many ports. Some computers have ports on the front of the system unit, also.

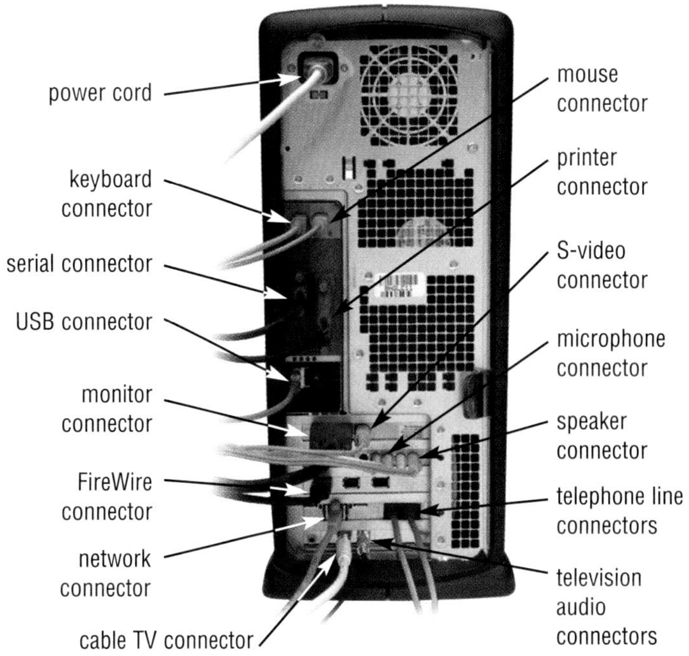

FIGURE 4-32 A connector attaches an external peripheral to the system unit.

WEB LINK 4-8

Ports and Connectors

Visit the Discovering Computers 2005 WEB LINK page (**scsite.com/dc2005/weblink**). Click Ports and Connectors below Chapter 4.

Sometimes, attaching a new peripheral to the computer is not possible because the connector on the system unit is the same gender as the connector on the cable. In this case, purchasing a gender changer solves this problem. A *gender changer* is a device that enables you to join two connectors that are both female or both male.

Manufacturers often identify the cables by their connector types to assist you with purchasing a cable to connect a computer to a peripheral. For example, a printer port might use any one of these connectors: 25-pin female, 36-pin female, 36-pin Centronics female, or USB. Thus, you should understand the differences among connector types.

Figure 4-33 shows the different types of connectors on a system unit. Some system units include these connectors when you buy the computer. You add other connectors by inserting adapter cards onto the motherboard. Certain adapter cards have ports that allow you to attach a peripheral to the adapter card.

Most personal computers have at least one serial port, one parallel port, and four USB ports. The next section discusses these and other ports.

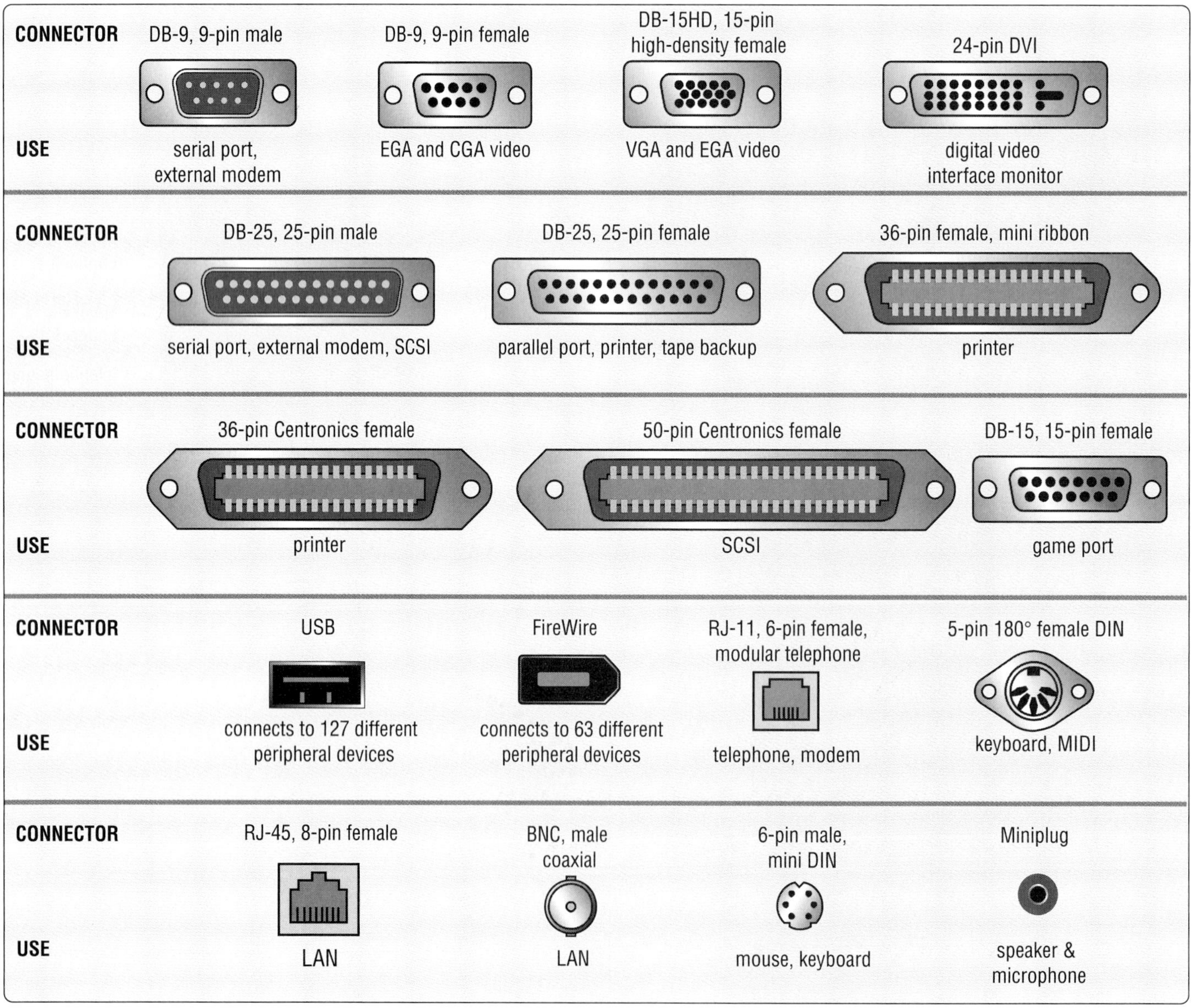

FIGURE 4-33 Examples of different types of connectors on a system unit.

Serial Ports

A **serial port** is a type of interface that connects a device to the system unit by transmitting data 1 bit at a time (Figure 4-34). Serial ports usually connect devices that do not require fast data transmission rates, such as a mouse, keyboard, or modem. The *COM port* (short for communications port) on the system unit is one type of serial port.

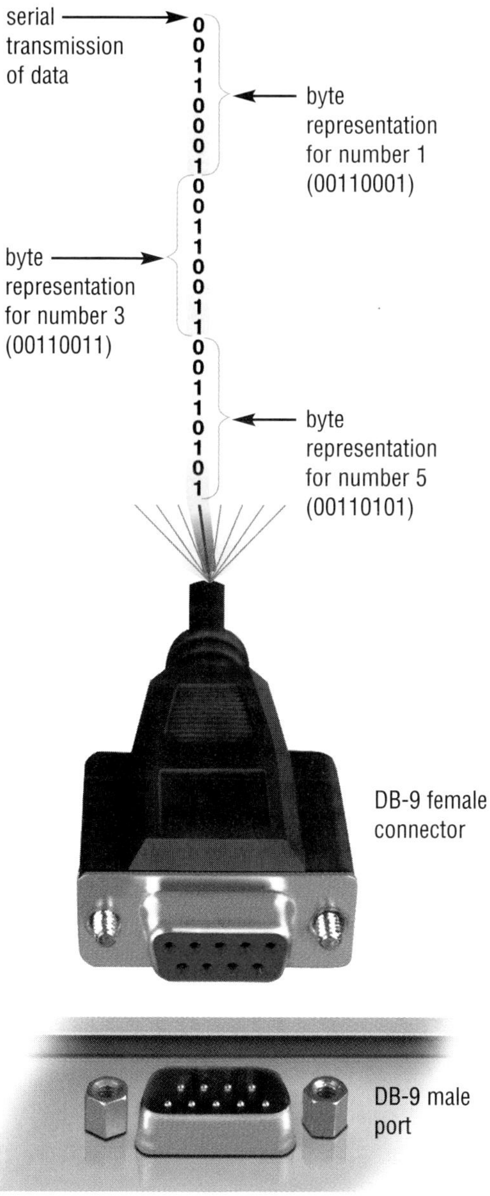

FIGURE 4-34 A serial port transmits data 1 bit at a time. One wire sends data, another receives data, and the remaining wires are used for other communications operations.

Some modems that connect the system unit to a telephone line use a serial port because the telephone line expects the data in a specific frequency. Serial ports conform to either the RS-232 or RS-422 standard, which specifies the number of pins used on the port's connector. Two common connectors for serial ports are a male 25-pin connector and a male 9-pin connector.

Parallel Ports

Unlike a serial port, a **parallel port** is an interface that connects devices by transferring more than 1 bit at a time (Figure 4-35). Originally, parallel ports were developed as an alternative to the slower speed serial ports.

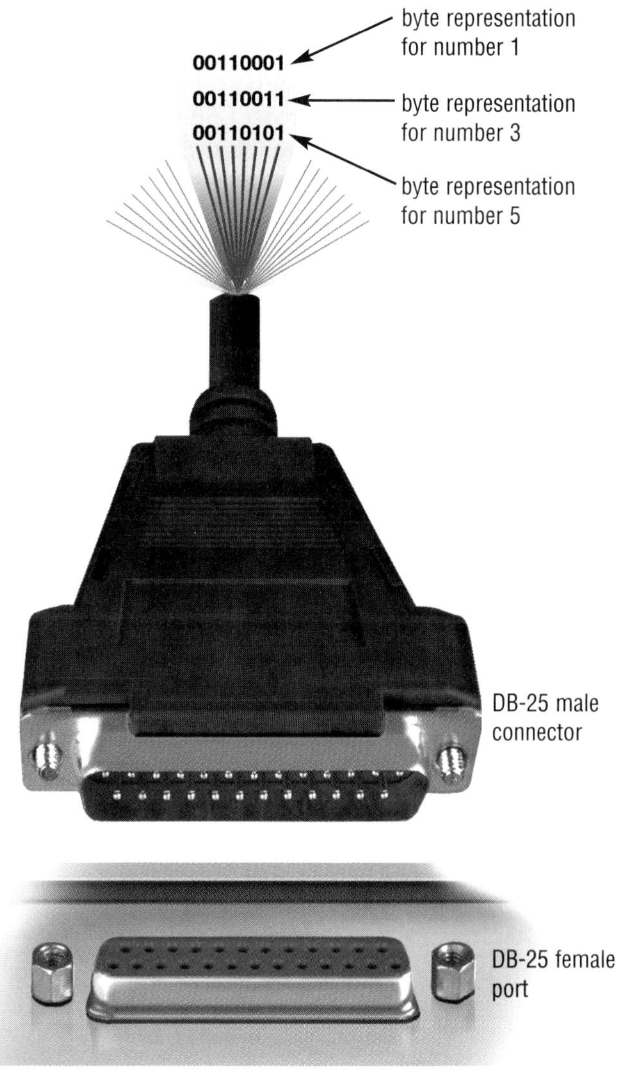

FIGURE 4-35 A parallel port is capable of transmitting more than 1 bit at a time. The port shown in this figure has eight wires that transmit data; the remaining wires are used for other communications operations.

Many printers connect to the system unit using a parallel port with a 25-pin female connector. This parallel port can transfer 8 bits of data (one byte) simultaneously through eight separate lines in a single cable. A parallel port sometimes is called a *Centronics interface*, after the company that first defined the standard for communications between the system unit and a printer.

USB Ports

A **USB port**, short for *universal serial bus port*, can connect up to 127 different peripherals together with a single connector type. Personal computers typically have four to eight USB ports either on the front or back of the system unit (Figure 4-31 on page 203).

The latest version of USB, called *USB 2.0*, is a more advanced and faster USB, with speeds 40 times higher than that of its predecessor. A USB 2.0 port supports higher-powered devices than those of older USB ports. The USB 2.0 port is designed for devices that transfer a lot of data, such as MP3 music players, CDs, DVDs, and removable hard disks.

To attach multiple peripherals using a single port, you can daisy chain the devices together outside the system unit. *Daisy chain* means the first USB device connects to the USB port on the computer, the second USB device connects to the first USB device, the third USB device connects to the second USB device, and so on. An alternative to daisy chaining is to use a USB hub. A **USB hub** is a device that plugs into a USB port on the system unit and contains multiple USB ports into which you plug cables from USB devices.

Some newer peripherals may attach only to a USB port. Others attach to either a serial or parallel port, as well as a USB port. When you connect a device to a USB port, you do not need to install an adapter card in the computer. Simply plug one end of the cable into the USB port and the other end into the device. Having a standard port and connector greatly simplifies the process of attaching devices to a personal computer.

USB also supports hot plugging and Plug and Play, which means you can attach peripherals while the computer is running. With serial and parallel port connections, by contrast, you often must restart the computer after attaching the peripheral.

FAQ 4-5

Can older USB devices plug into a USB 2.0 port?

Yes. USB 2.0 is *backward compatible*, which means that it supports older USB devices as well as new USB 2.0 devices. Keep in mind, though, that older USB devices do not run any faster in a USB 2.0 port.

For more information about USB 2.0, visit the Discovering Computers 2005 FAQ Web page (**scsite.com/dc2005/faq**). Click USB 2.0 below Chapter 4.

Special-Purpose Ports

Five special-purpose ports are FireWire, MIDI, SCSI, IrDA, and Bluetooth. The following sections discuss each of these ports.

FIREWIRE PORT Previously called an *IEEE 1394 port*, a **FireWire port** is similar to a USB port in that it can connect multiple types of devices that require faster data transmission speeds, such as digital video cameras, digital VCRs, color printers, scanners, digital cameras, and DVD drives, to a single connector. Using a FireWire port allows you to connect up to 63 devices together. The FireWire port also supports Plug and Play.

Many computer professionals believe that ports such as USB and FireWire someday will replace all other types of ports (Figure 4-36).

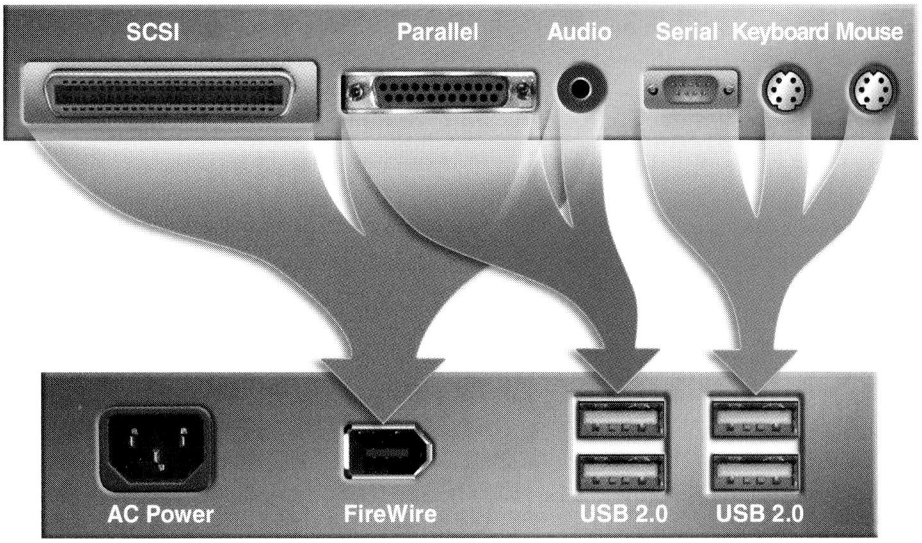

FIGURE 4-36 Many computer professionals believe that ports such as USB and FireWire someday will replace all other ports completely.

MIDI PORT A special type of serial port that connects the system unit to a musical instrument, such as an electronic keyboard, is called a **MIDI port**. Short for *Musical Instrument Digital Interface*, MIDI (pronounced MID-dee) is the electronic music industry's standard that defines how devices, such as sound cards and synthesizers, represent sounds electronically. A *synthesizer*, which can be a peripheral or a chip, creates sound from digital instructions.

A system unit with a MIDI port has the capability of recording sounds that have been created by a synthesizer and then processing the sounds (the data) to create new sounds. Just about every sound card supports the MIDI standard, so you can play and manipulate sounds on a computer that were created originally on another computer.

SCSI PORT A special high-speed parallel port, called a **SCSI port**, allows you to attach SCSI (pronounced skuzzy) peripherals such as disk drives and printers. Depending on the type of *SCSI*, which stands for *small computer system interface*, you can daisy chain either up to 7 or 15 devices together. Some computers include a SCSI port. Others have a slot that supports a SCSI card.

IrDA PORT Some devices can transmit data via infrared light waves. For these wireless devices to transmit signals to a computer, both the computer and the device must have an **IrDA port** (Figure 4-37). These ports conform to standards developed by the *IrDA* (*Infrared Data Association*).

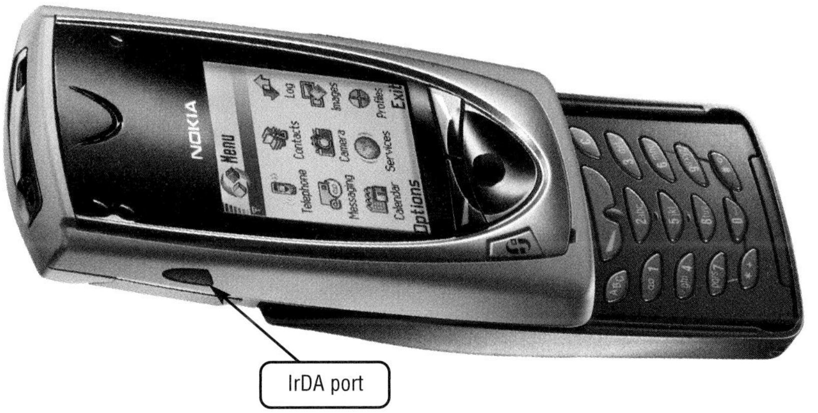

FIGURE 4-37 Smart phones and other mobile devices have IrDA ports, allowing the device to communicate wirelessly with other devices and computers.

To ensure nothing obstructs the path of the infrared light wave, you must align the IrDA port on the device with the IrDA port on the computer, similarly to the way you operate a television remote control. Devices that use IrDA ports include a PDA, keyboard, mouse, printer, cellular telephone, and pager. Several of these devices use a high-speed IrDA port, sometimes called a *fast infrared port*.

BLUETOOTH PORTS An alternative to IrDA, **Bluetooth** technology uses radio waves to transmit data between two devices. Unlike IrDA, the Bluetooth devices do not have to be aligned with each other. Many computers, peripherals, PDAs, cellular telephones, cars, and other consumer electronics are Bluetooth-enabled, which means they contain a small chip that allows them to communicate with other Bluetooth-enabled computers and devices. If you have a computer that is not Bluetooth enabled, you can purchase a Bluetooth wireless port adapter that will convert an existing USB port or serial port into a Bluetooth port. Also available are Bluetooth PC Cards for notebook computers and Bluetooth cards for PDAs and cellular telephones.

BUSES

As explained earlier in this chapter, a computer processes and stores data as a series of electronic bits. These bits transfer internally within the circuitry of the computer along electrical channels. Each channel, called a **bus**, allows the various devices both inside and attached to the system unit to communicate with each other. Just as vehicles travel on a highway to move from one destination to another, bits travel on a bus (Figure 4-38).

Buses transfer bits from input devices to memory, from memory to the processor, from the processor to memory, and from memory to output or storage devices. Buses consist of two parts: a data bus and an address bus. The *data bus* transfers actual data and the *address bus* transfers information about where the data should reside in memory.

The size of a bus, called the *bus width*, determines the number of bits that the computer can transmit at one time. For example, a 32-bit bus can transmit 32 bits (4 bytes) at a time. On a 64-bit bus, bits transmit from one location to another 64 bits (8 bytes) at a time. The larger the number of bits handled by the bus, the faster the computer transfers data. Using the highway analogy again, assume that one lane on a highway can carry 1 bit. A 32-bit bus is like a 32-lane highway. A 64-bit bus is like a 64-lane highway.

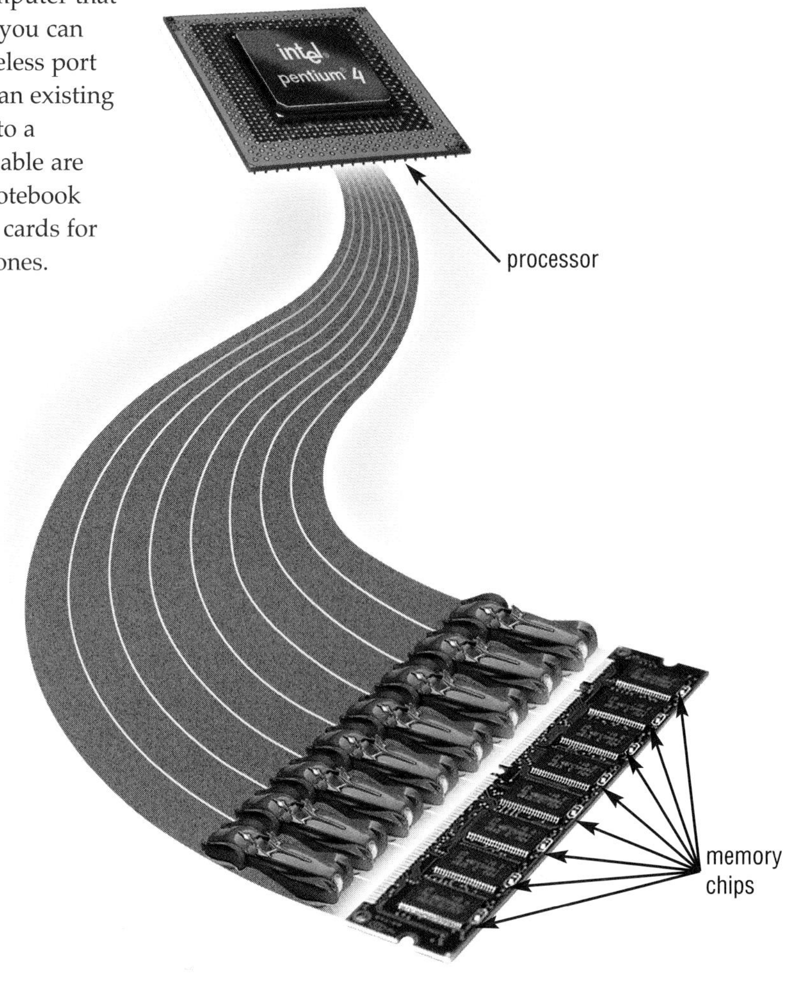

FIGURE 4-38 Just as vehicles travel on a highway to move from one destination to another, bits travel on a bus. Buses transfer bits from input devices to memory, from memory to the processor, from the processor to memory, and from memory to output or storage devices.

If a number in memory occupies 8 bytes, or 64 bits, the computer must transmit it in two separate steps when using a 32-bit bus: once for the first 32 bits and once for the second 32 bits. Using a 64-bit bus, the computer can transmit the number in a single step, transferring all 64 bits at once. The wider the bus, the fewer number of transfer steps required and the faster the transfer of data. Most personal computers today use a 64-bit bus.

In conjunction with the bus width, many computer professionals refer to a computer's word size. **Word size** is the number of bits the processor can interpret and execute at a given time. That is, a 64-bit processor can manipulate 64 bits at a time. Computers with a larger word size can process more data in the same amount of time than computers with a smaller word size. In most computers, the word size is the same as the bus width.

Every bus also has a clock speed. Just like the processor, manufacturers state the clock speed for a bus in hertz. Recall that one megahertz (MHz) is equal to one million ticks per second. Most of today's processors have a bus clock speed of 400, 533, or 800 MHz. The higher the bus clock speed, the faster the transmission of data, which results in applications running faster.

A computer has two basic types of buses: a system bus and an expansion bus. A *system bus* is part of the motherboard and connects the processor to main memory. An *expansion bus* allows the processor to communicate with peripherals. When computer professionals use the term bus by itself, they usually are referring to the system bus.

WEB LINK 4-9

Buses

Visit the Discovering Computers 2005 WEB LINK page (**scsite.com/dc2005/weblink**). Click Buses below Chapter 4.

Expansion Bus

Some peripherals outside the system unit connect to a port on an adapter card, which is inserted into an expansion slot on the motherboard. This expansion slot connects to the expansion bus, which allows the processor to communicate with the peripheral attached to the adapter card. Data transmitted to memory or the processor travels from the expansion bus via the expansion bus and the system bus (Figure 4-39).

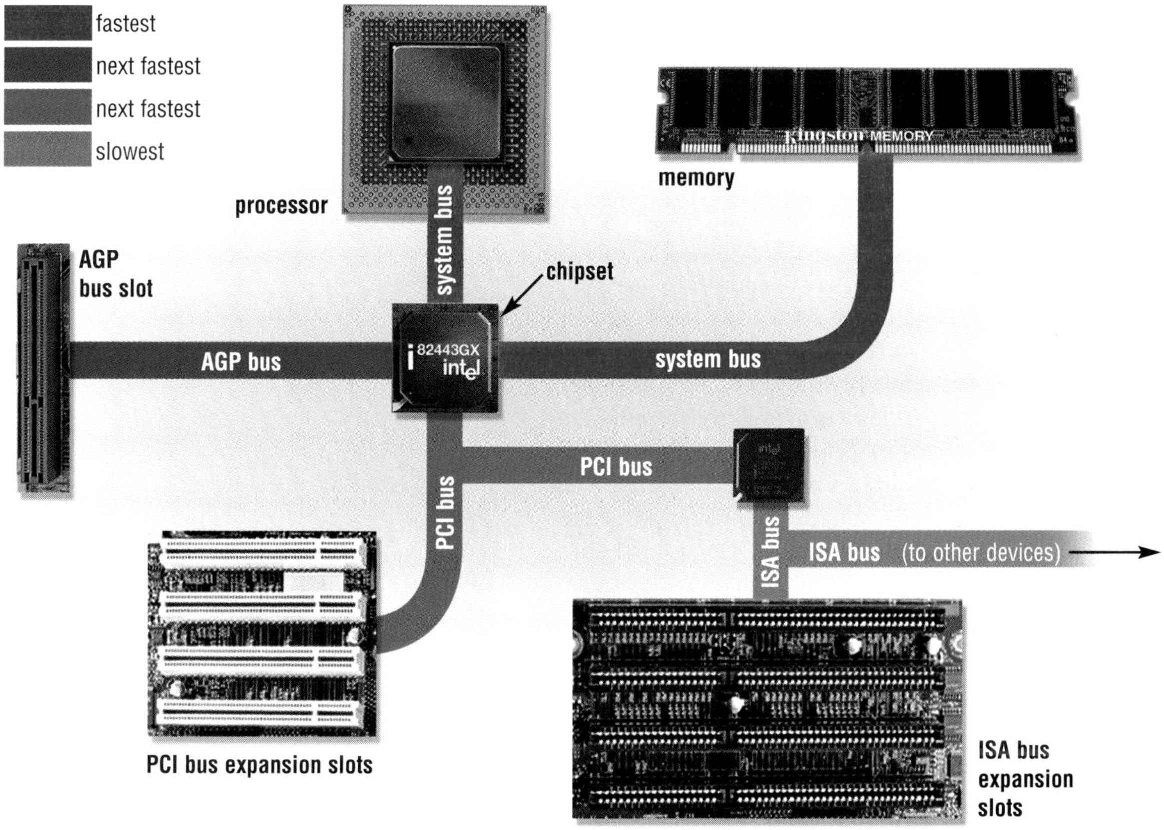

FIGURE 4-39 Buses allow the various devices both inside and attached to the system unit to communicate with each other. The buses in order of speed from fastest to slowest are the system bus, the AGP bus, the PCI bus, and the ISA bus.

FAQ 4-6

What is the chipset shown in Figure 4-39 on the previous page?

A *chipset* is a set of integrated circuits. These circuits work together to perform a common task. In this case, the chipset is a bus controller.

For more information about chipsets, visit the Discovering Computers 2005 FAQ Web page (**scsite.com/dc2005/faq**). Click Chipsets below Chapter 4.

The types of expansion buses on a motherboard determine the types of cards you can add to the computer. Thus, you should understand the following types of expansion buses: ISA bus, PCI bus, AGP bus, USB, FireWire bus, and PC Card bus.

- The most common and slowest expansion bus is the *ISA bus* (*Industry Standard Architecture bus*). A mouse, modem card, sound card, and low-speed network card are examples of devices that connect to the ISA bus directly or through an ISA bus expansion slot.
- A *local bus* is a high-speed expansion bus that connects higher speed devices such as hard disks. The first standard local bus was the *VESA local bus* (*Video Electronics Standards Association local bus*), which was used primarily for video cards. The current local bus standard is the *PCI bus* (*Peripheral Component Interconnect bus*) because it is more versatile than the VESA local bus. Types of cards you can insert into a PCI bus expansion slot include video cards, sound cards, SCSI cards, and high-speed network cards. The PCI bus transfers data about four times faster than the ISA bus. Most current personal computers have a PCI bus as well as an ISA bus.
- The *Accelerated Graphics Port* (*AGP*) is a bus designed by Intel to improve the speed with which 3-D graphics and video transmit. With an AGP video card in an AGP bus slot, the AGP bus provides a faster, dedicated interface between the video card and memory. Newer processors support AGP technology.
- The USB (universal serial bus) and *FireWire bus* are buses that eliminate the need to install cards into expansion slots. In a computer with a USB, for example, USB devices connect to each other outside the system unit and then a single cable attaches to the USB port. The USB port then connects to the USB, which connects to the PCI bus on the motherboard. The FireWire bus works in a similar fashion. With these buses, expansion slots are available for devices not compatible with USB or FireWire.
- The expansion bus for a PC Card is the *PC Card bus*. With a PC Card inserted into a PC Card slot, data travels on the PC Card bus to the PCI bus.

BAYS

After you purchase a computer, you may want to install an additional storage device such as a disk drive into the system unit. A **bay** is an opening inside the system unit in which you can install additional equipment. A bay is different from a slot, which is used for the installation of adapter cards. Rectangular openings, called **drive bays**, typically hold disk drives.

Two types of drive bays exist: internal and external. An *external drive bay* allows a user to access the drive from outside the system unit. Floppy disk drives, CD drives, DVD drives, Zip drives (Figure 4-40), and tape drives are examples of devices installed in external drive bays. An *internal drive bay* is concealed entirely within the system unit. Hard disk drives are installed in internal bays.

FIGURE 4-40 External drive bays usually are located beside or on top of one another.

POWER SUPPLY

Many personal computers plug into standard wall outlets, which supply an alternating current (AC) of 115 to 120 volts. This type of power is unsuitable for use with a computer, which requires a direct current (DC) ranging from 5 to 12 volts. The **power supply** is the component of the system unit that converts the wall outlet AC power into DC power.

Near the power supply is a fan that keeps components of the system unit cool. This fan dissipates heat generated by the processor and other components of the system unit. Many newer computers have additional fans near certain components in the system unit such as the processor, hard disk, and ports.

Some external peripherals such as an external modem, speakers, or a tape drive have an **AC adapter**, which is an external power supply. One end of the AC adapter plugs into the wall outlet and the other end attaches to the peripheral. The AC adapter converts the AC power into DC power that the peripheral requires.

FAQ 4-7

Can I disable the computer fan?

No. Without the fan, the electronics could overheat. For optimum performance, be sure the vents on the computer case are not blocked and keep the area around the system unit dust free. To reduce noise level, purchase a utility program that slows or stops the fan until the temperature reaches a certain level.

For more information about the computer fan, visit the Discovering Computers 2005 FAQ Web page (**scsite.com/dc2005/faq**). Click Computer Fan below Chapter 4.

MOBILE COMPUTERS AND DEVICES

As businesses and schools expand to serve people across the country and around the world, increasingly more people need to use a computer while traveling to and from a main office or school to conduct business, communicate, or do homework. As Chapter 1 discussed, users with such mobile computing needs — known as mobile users — often have a mobile computer, such as a notebook computer or Tablet PC, or a mobile device such as a PDA (Figure 4-41).

Weighing on average between 2.5 and 8 pounds, notebook computers can run either using batteries or using a standard power supply. Smaller PDAs run strictly on batteries.

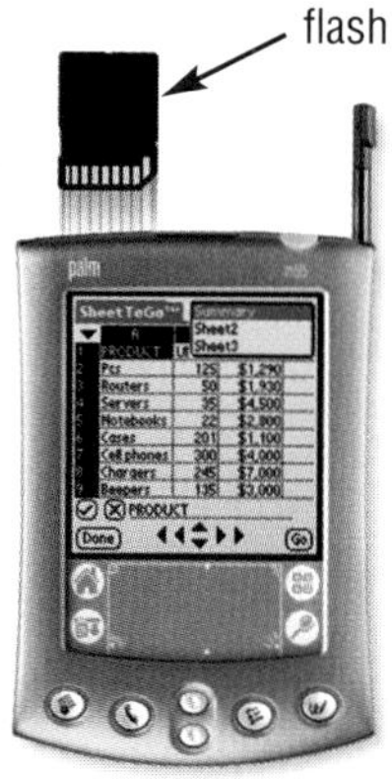

Figure 4-41b (PDA)

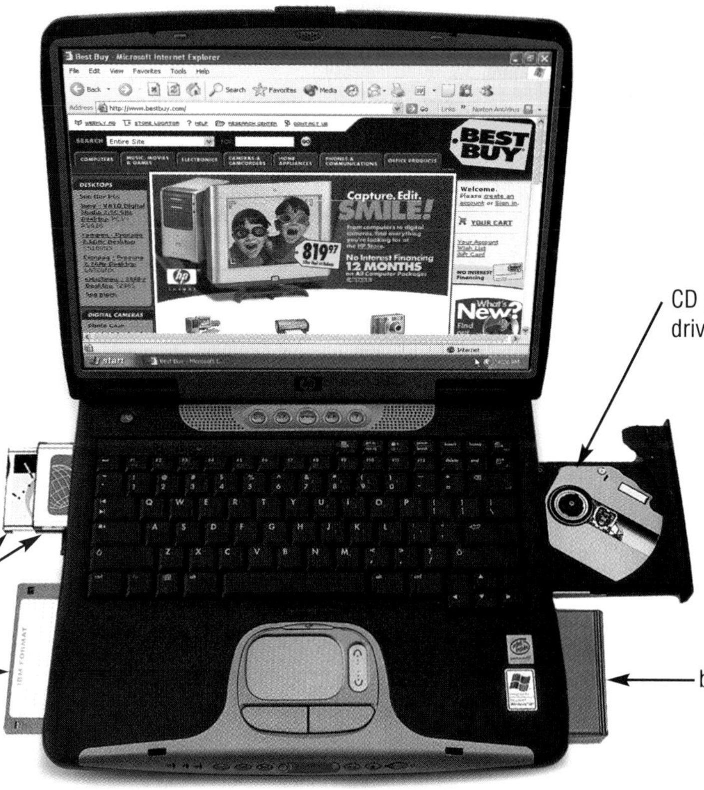

Figure 4-41a (notebook computer)

FIGURE 4-41 Users with mobile computing needs often have a notebook computer and/or PDA.

Like their desktop counterparts, mobile computers and devices have a motherboard that contains electronic components that process data (Figure 4-42). The difference is many other devices also are part of the system unit. In addition to the motherboard, processor, memory, sound card, PC Card slot, and drive bay, the system unit also houses devices such as the keyboard, pointing device, speakers, and display.

A notebook computer usually is more expensive than a desktop computer with the same capabilities because it is more costly to miniaturize the components. The typical notebook computer often has parallel, serial, video, USB, speaker, microphone, and keyboard/mouse ports (Figure 4-43).

Two basic designs of Tablet PC are available: slate and convertible. With the slate Tablet PC (shown in Figure 4-1 on page 180), all the hardware is behind the display — much like a PDA. Users can attach a removable keyboard to the slate Tablet PC. The display on the convertible Tablet PC, which is attached to a keyboard, can be rotated 180 degrees and folded down over the keyboard. Thus, the convertible Tablet PC can be repositioned to look like either a notebook computer or a slate Tablet PC. Tablet PCs usually include several slots and ports (Figure 4-44).

PDAs are quite affordable, usually priced at a few hundred dollars or less. PDAs often have an IrDA port or are Bluetooth enabled so users can communicate wirelessly with other computers or devices such as a printer. Many also include a serial port. Read Issue 4-4 for a discussion about another type of mobile computer.

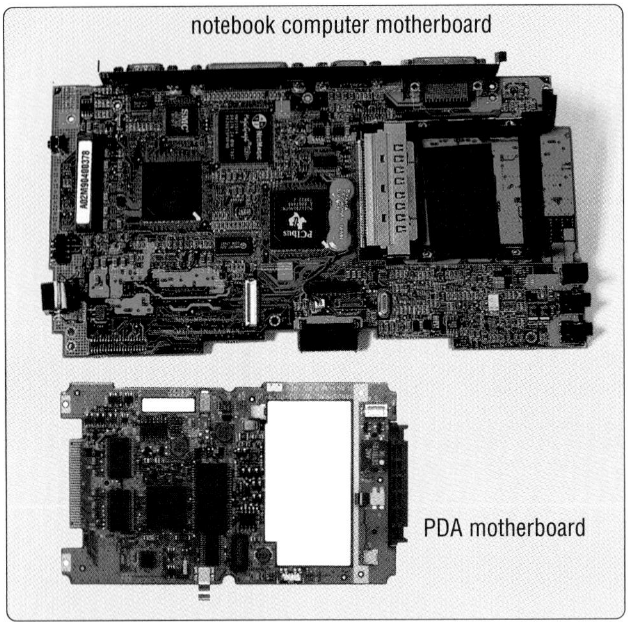

FIGURE 4-42 The motherboard in notebook computers and PDAs contains electronic components that process data.

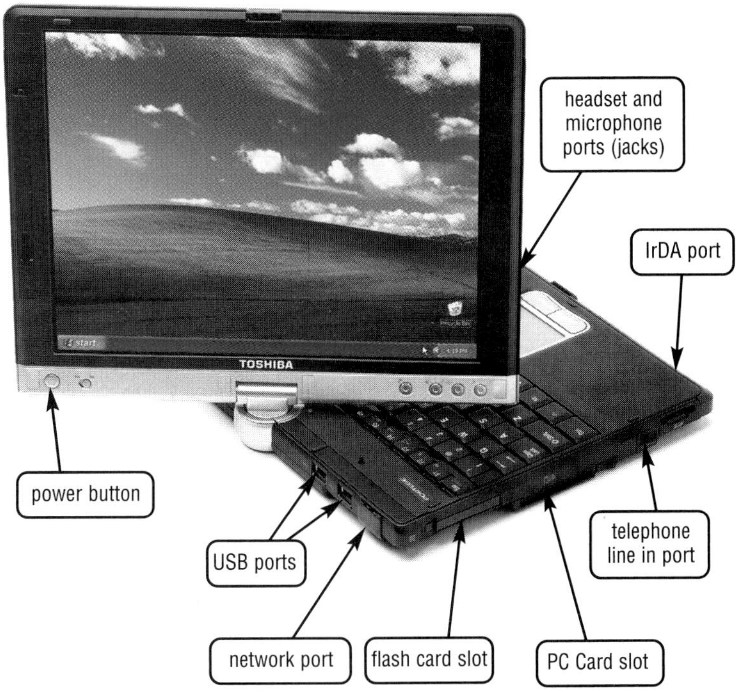

FIGURE 4-44 Slots and ports on a Tablet PC.

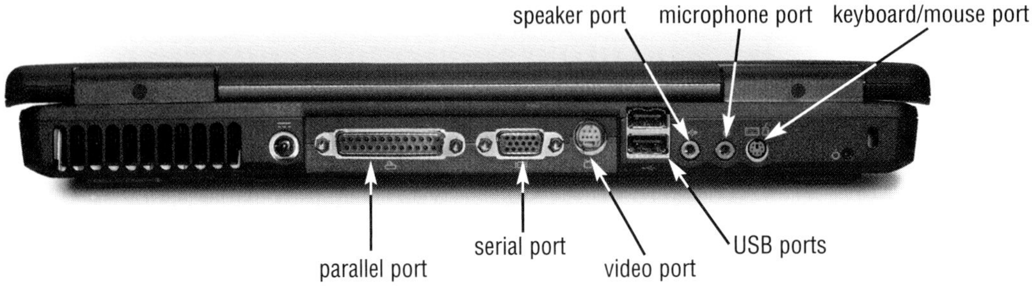

FIGURE 4-43 Ports on a typical notebook computer.

ISSUE 4-4

Do You Want Air Conditioning? Power Windows? A Car Computer?

About five years ago, Citroen unveiled the first car equipped with an onboard computer. Today, a number of automobiles incorporate a car computer that allows drivers to access e-mail, receive weather and traffic data, obtain navigation information, and even allow passengers to watch movies on DVD. Developing and producing car computers is expensive. Because of their special environment, they must be more durable than desktop computers and provide a simpler interface. Some manufacturers wonder if car computers offer buyers enough to justify the cost. Would you be interested in a car computer and, if so, how much would you be willing to spend for one? The state of New York recently passed a law mandating that automobile drivers not hold and talk on portable telephones while in motion. Should a similar law be enacted regarding the use of car computers? Why or why not? What activities performed on a car computer could, and could not, endanger drivers? Why?

For more information about car computers, visit the Discovering Computers 2005 Issues Web page (**scsite.com/dc2005/issues**). Click Issue #4 below Chapter 4.

PUTTING IT ALL TOGETHER

When you purchase a computer, it is important to understand how the components of the system unit work. Many components of the system unit influence the speed and power of a computer. These include the type of processor, the clock speed of the processor, the amount of RAM, and the clock speed of the bus. The configuration you require depends on your intended use.

The table in Figure 4-45 lists the suggested minimum processor, clock speed, and RAM requirements based on the needs of various types of computer users.

SUGGESTED MINIMUM CONFIGURATIONS BY USER

User	Processor and Clock Speed
Home 	Pentium 4 or Athlon XP 2.4 GHz or higher or Celeron 2.2 GHz or higher Minimum RAM: 256 MB
Small Office/Home Office 	Pentium 4 or Athlon XP 3 GHz or higher Minimum RAM: 512 MB
Mobile 	Pentium M or Athlon XP-M 2.4 GHz or higher Minimum RAM: 512 MB
Large Business 	Pentium 4 or Athlon XP 3 GHz or higher Minimum RAM: 1 GB
Power 	Xeon MP or Itanium 2 or AMD64 2.8 GHz or higher Minimum RAM: 2 GB

FIGURE 4-45 Suggested processor, clock speed, and RAM configurations by user.

For more detailed computer purchasing guidelines, read the Buyer's Guide 2005 feature that follows Chapter 8. Read Looking Ahead 4-2 for a look at the next generation of computers.

QUIZ YOURSELF 4-3

To check your knowledge of expansion slots, adapter cards, ports, buses, and components of mobile computers and devices, visit the Discovering Computers 2005 Quiz Yourself Web page (**scsite.com/dc2005/quiz**). Click Objectives 8 – 11 below Chapter 4.

CHAPTER SUMMARY

Chapter 4 presented the components of the system unit, described how memory stores data, instructions, and information, and discussed the sequence of operations that occur when a computer executes an instruction. The chapter included a comparison of various personal computer processors on the market today.

LOOKING AHEAD 4-2

Robotic Rats May Perform Rescue Missions

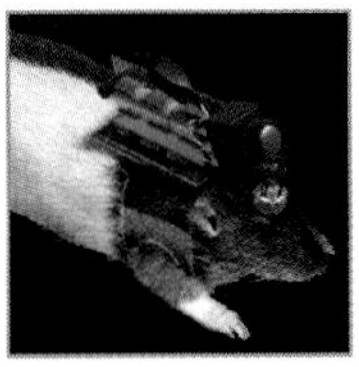

When people are trapped under piles of rubble from a collapsed building, emergency teams may have a new tool for their rescue operations: rats.

Researchers at the State University of New York Downstate Medical Center at Brooklyn have attached electrodes and battery-powered backpacks to five rats and have trained these rodents to dash in precise locations in response to radio signals sent from the scientists' computers. For example, signals to the left-whisker neurons command the rats to turn left. The researchers then send another signal to the rats' pleasure center in the brain when the assigned task is complete. The scientists hope their research will be used in search-and-rescue missions.

Research from these experiments has the potential for other uses, including helping paralyzed individuals use their brain signals to control artificial limbs. Electrodes implanted in the brain receive signals generated when paralyzed people think about moving their hands, tongue, or eyes; the electrodes then send feedback to the artificial hands or arms to perform such actions as hold a pencil or a cup or grasp a barbell.

For a look at the next generation of remotely controlled rodents, visit the Discovering Computers 2005 Looking Ahead Web page (**scsite.com/dc2005/looking**). Click Looking Ahead #2 below Chapter 4.

Computer Engineer

A *computer engineer* designs and develops the electronic components found in computers and peripheral devices. Computer engineers work as researchers, theorists, and inventors. Computer engineers can work as part of a company's permanent staff or as consultants, with jobs that extend from a few months to a few years, depending on the project. Engineers in research and development often work on projects that will not be released to the general public for two years.

Responsibilities vary from company to company. All computer engineering work, however, demands problem-solving skills and the ability to create and use new technologies. Computer engineers also must be able to handle multiple tasks and concentrate on detail. Computer engineers often function as part of a team. Therefore, computer engineers must be able to communicate clearly with both computer personnel and computer users, who may have little technical knowledge.

Before taking in-depth computer engineering design and development classes, students usually take mathematics, physics, and basic engineering. Computer engineering degrees include B.S., M.S., and Ph.D. Because computer engineers employed in private industry often advance into managerial positions, many computer engineering graduates obtain a master's degree in business administration (M.B.A.). Most computer engineers earn between $35,000 and $90,000 annually, depending on their experience and employer, but salaries can approach $115,000.

To learn more about the field of Computer Engineer as a career, visit the Discovering Computers 2005 Careers Web page (**scsite.com/dc2005/careers**). Click Computer Engineer.

The Genius of Memory: Transistors, Capacitors, and Electricity

Inside your computer, RAM takes the form of separate microchip modules that plug into slots in the computer's motherboard. These slots connect through a line (bus) or set of electrical paths to the computer's processor. Before you turn on a computer, its RAM is a blank slate. As you start and use your computer, the operating system files, applications, and any data currently being used by the processor are written to and stored in RAM so the processor can access them quickly.

How is this data written to and stored in RAM? In the most common form of RAM, dynamic random access memory (DRAM), *transistors* (in this case, acting as switches) and a *capacitor* (as a data storage element) create a *memory cell*, which represents a single bit of data.

Memory cells are etched onto a silicon wafer in a series of columns (bitlines) and rows (wordlines), known as an *array*. The intersection of a column and row constitutes the *address* of the memory cell (Figure 4-46). Each memory cell has a unique address that can be found by counting across columns and then counting down by row. The address of a character consists of a series of memory cell addresses put together. Most DRAM chips actually have arrays that are 16 rows deep.

To write data to RAM, the processor sends the memory controller the address of a memory cell in which to store data. The *memory controller* organizes the request and sends the column and row address in an electrical charge along the appropriate address lines, which are very thin electrical lines etched into the RAM chip. This causes the transistors along those address lines to close.

These transistors act as a switch to control the flow of electrical current in an either closed or open circuit. While the transistors are closed, the software sends bursts of electricity along selected data lines. When the electrical charge traveling down the data line reaches an address line where a transistor is closed, the charge flows through the closed transistor and charges the capacitor.

A capacitor works as electronic storage that holds an electrical charge. Each charged capacitor along the address line represents a 1 bit. An uncharged capacitor represents a 0 bit. The combination of 1s and 0s from eight data lines forms a single byte of data.

The capacitors used in dynamic RAM, however, lose their electrical charge. The processor or memory controller continuously has to recharge all of the capacitors holding a charge (a 1 bit) before the capacitor discharges. During this *refresh operation*, which happens automatically thousands of times per second, the memory controller reads memory and then immediately rewrites it. This refresh operation is what gives dynamic RAM its name. Dynamic RAM has to be refreshed continually, or it loses the charges that represent bits of data. A specialized circuit called a counter tracks the refresh sequence to ensure that all of the rows are refreshed.

The process of reading data from RAM uses a similar, but reverse, series of steps. When the processor gets the next instruction it is to perform, the instruction may contain the address of a memory cell from which to read data. This address is sent to the memory controller. To locate the memory cell, the memory controller sends the column and row address in an electrical charge down the appropriate address lines.

This electrical charge causes the transistors along the address line to close. At every point along the address line where a capacitor is holding a charge, the capacitor discharges through the circuit created by the closed transistors, sending electrical charges along the data lines.

A specialized circuit called a *sense amplifier* determines and amplifies the level of charge in the capacitor. A capacitor charge over a certain voltage level represents the binary value 1; a capacitor charge below that level represents a 0. The sensed and amplified value is sent back down the address line to the processor.

As long as a computer is running, data continuously is being written to and read from RAM. As soon as you shut down a computer, RAM loses its data. The next time you turn on a computer, operating system files and other data are again loaded into RAM and the read/write process starts all over.

For more information about memory, visit the Discovering Computers 2005 High-Tech Talk Web page (**scsite.com/dc2005/tech**) and click Memory.

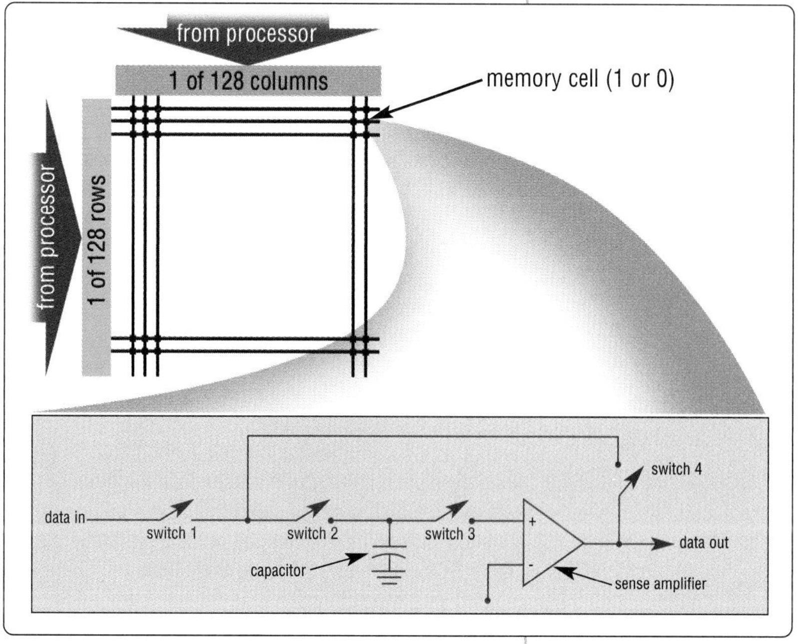

FIGURE 4-46 An illustration of one type of DRAM. When writing data, switches 1 and 2 in the circuit are closed and switches 3 and 4 are open. When reading data, switches 2, 3, and 4 in the circuit are closed and switch 1 is open.

COMPANIES ON THE CUTTING EDGE

Intel

Chip Maker Dominates the Computer Market

On an August day in 1968, Robert Noyce was mowing his lawn when Gordon Moore, a coworker at Fairchild Semiconductor, stopped by to talk. The two shared gripes about work and, in a moment of inspiration, decided to start their own company. Noyce typed a one-page business plan, and a company called "Moore Noyce" was born. The name, unfortunately, sounded a lot like "More Noise" — hardly suitable for an electronics firm — so they incorporated as NM Electronics. Later, after they purchased rights from a motel chain, they adopted a new name — *Intel* (for integrated electronics).

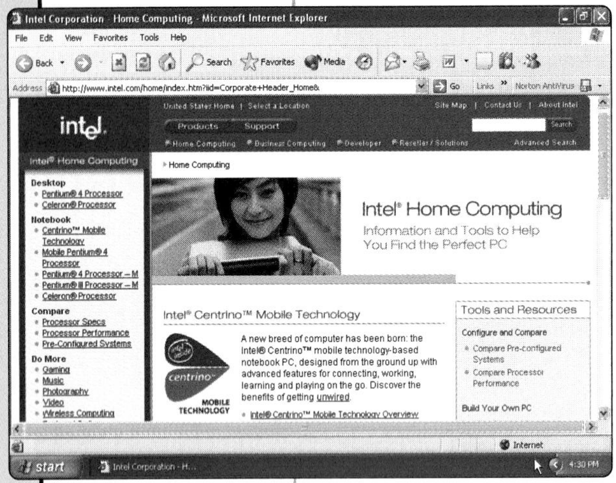

From such humble beginnings came a company that today is the world's largest maker of computer chips. When Moore and Noyce started Intel, their goal was to build semiconductor memory to replace magnetic core memory. Critics maintained that even if semiconductors could be used for memory storage, they would cost too much to manufacture. Undismayed, Noyce and Moore, together with Andy Grove, another Fairchild expatriate, struggled to reduce production costs. They refined the process of placing thousands of tiny electronic devices on a silicon chip and, in 1970, successfully introduced the 1103, the first DRAM chip. One year later, this product became the world's best-selling semiconductor device. In 1971, Intel developed the 4004, the world's first processor. In 1980, when IBM chose the Intel 8088 chip for its new personal computer, Intel chips became standard for all IBM-compatible personal computers.

Today, Intel's chips are the building blocks in countless personal computers, servers, networks, and communications devices. In 2003, Intel developed its Centrino mobile technology, which integrates wireless capabilities and extends battery life in notebook computers and Tablet PCs. Currently, Intel has more than 78,000 employees in more than 50 countries.

For more information about Intel, visit the Discovering Computers 2005 Companies Web page (**scsite.com/dc2005/companies**) and click Intel.

AMD

Intel-Compatible Processor Leader

In the eighteenth century, philosophers spoke of The Age of Enlightenment. Could today be The Age of Asparagus? In the early 1980s, *Advanced Micro Devices* (*AMD*) adopted the phrase to characterize its commitment to develop increasing numbers of proprietary products for the computer industry. Executives identified this goal with asparagus farming because the crop grows slowly, but it is very lucrative once it takes hold.

AMD's seeds sprouted and grew into the world's second-largest manufacturer of processors for Microsoft Windows-compatible personal computers. Along with the AMD-K6-2 and Athlon processors, AMD also produces flash memory devices, embedded processors, and support circuitry for communications and networking applications. Among the company's most recent products are the AMD Opteron processor for servers and workstations and the AMD Athlon 64 processor for desktop and personal computers.

A Fortune 500 company, AMD develops advanced process technologies at its Submicron Development Center (SDC) in Sunnyvale, California. The technologies are put into production at manufacturing facilities in the United States, Europe, Asia, and Japan. Today, AMD employs more than 12,000 people worldwide. More than one-half of the approximately $2.7 billion in annual company revenues is generated from sales outside the United States.

Cofounders Jerry Sanders and John Carey laid the foundation for AMD in Carey's living room in 1968. From the beginning, AMD guaranteed its microchips for every customer would meet or exceed stringent standards. More than three decades later, the company continues this commitment to "parametric superiority." A central tenet of AMD's corporate philosophy is that people are the ultimate source of its competitive advantage. "Our customer's success is our success."

For more information about AMD, visit the Discovering Computers 2005 Companies Web page (**scsite.com/dc2005/companies**) and click AMD.

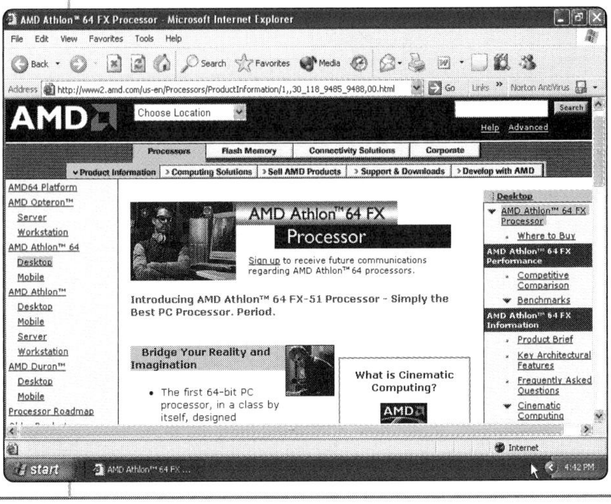

TECHNOLOGY TRAILBLAZERS

Jack Kilby

Inventor of the Integrated Circuit

The National Inventors Hall of Fame honors inventors whose innovations have made progress possible. In 1982, *Jack Kilby* took his place in this elite group. His invention, the integrated circuit, is an essential part of the high-speed computers that form the foundation of today's information age.

Kilby started his work with miniature electrical components at Centralab, where he developed transistors for hearing aids. The transistors were made from germanium, but scientists at Bell Laboratories convinced Kilby that silicon was a better choice. Because Centralab seemed committed to germanium, Kilby went to Texas Instruments where he could be at the forefront of the effort to connect electrical components.

When he arrived in the summer of 1958, most of the staff was on vacation. Almost alone in the lab, Kilby examined prototypes that used wires to join stacks of components. He theorized that if the circuit elements were made from the same material (silicon) they could be placed on a single chip, eliminating the need for wire connections. With this thought in mind, Kilby developed a working model of the first integrated circuit, which was patented in 1959. Coincidentally, at about the same time, Robert Noyce of Fairchild Semiconductor filed for a patent on a similar integrated circuit produced with a different manufacturing process. Both Kilby and Noyce are given credit for inventing the integrated circuit.

Today, retired from Texas Instruments, Kilby works as a consultant and teacher and holds more than 60 patents. In 2000, Kilby was awarded the Nobel Prize in Physics for his invention of the integrated circuit, an innovation he believes will continue to change the world. "Every day [new crops of engineers are] pushing the limits of integrated circuits and making practical what was once considered impossible."

For more information about Jack Kilby, visit the Discovering Computers 2005 People Web page (**scsite.com/dc2005/people**) and click Jack Kilby.

Gordon Moore

Intel Cofounder

The name Intel has become synonymous with processors. From its inception, the name *Gordon Moore* has been synonymous with Intel.

Moore's lifelong interest in technology was kindled at an early age by a neighbor's chemistry set. Even then, he displayed the passion for practical outcomes that has typified his work as a scientist and engineer. "With the chemistry set," he says, "I had to get a good explosion at the end or I wasn't happy." Yet, Moore was hardly a science geek. In high school, he devoted more time to athletics than to homework, lettering in four different sports. Moore was the first member of his family to attend college, graduating from the California Institute of Technology with a Ph.D. in chemistry and physics.

Moore worked with Bill Shockley, inventor of the transistor, at Shockley Semiconductor. There, he met Robert Noyce, and eventually the two left to join Fairchild Semiconductor. At Fairchild in 1965, in an article for *Electronics* magazine, Moore made a startling prediction. The number of transistors and resistors placed on computer chips, he claimed, would double every year, with a proportional increase in computing power and decrease in cost. This bold forecast, now known as Moore's law, proved amazingly accurate for 10 years (when Moore revised the estimate to doubling every two years). Convinced of the future of silicon chips, and frustrated by the company's response to their work, in 1968 Moore founded Intel.

Moore's career illustrates a key characteristic: the willingness to make a commitment even when results are unknown. Although all decisions involve some risk, they should not be feared. After all, Moore says, "If everything you try works, then you are not trying hard enough."

For more information about Gordon Moore, visit the Discovering Computers 2005 People Web page (**scsite.com/dc2005/people**) and click Gordon Moore.

CHAPTER 4 CHECKPOINT

MULTIPLE CHOICE

Select the best answer. (See page numbers in parentheses.)

1. On _____, the display often is part of the system unit. (180)
   a. desktop personal computers
   b. notebook computers
   c. mobile devices
   d. all of the above
2. A transistor _____. (182)
   a. can act as an electronic switch that opens or closes the circuit for electrical charges
   b. speeds the processes of a computer by storing frequently used instructions
   c. is where a peripheral attaches to the system unit so it can send or retrieve data
   d. converts a wall outlet's AC power into the DC power a computer needs
3. _____ include conditions along with operators such as AND, OR, and NOT. (184)
   a. Arithmetic operations
   b. Logical operations
   c. Comparison operations
   d. all of the above
4. Processors that use _____ are faster because they do not have to wait for one instruction to complete the machine cycle before fetching the next. (185)
   a. registering
   b. hot plugging
   c. pipelining
   d. daisy chaining
5. The higher the clock speed, the _____ the computer. (186)
   a. slower the processor, and more expensive
   b. faster the processor, and more expensive
   c. slower the processor, and less expensive
   d. faster the processor, and less expensive
6. _____ is a 16-bit coding scheme that is capable of representing more than 65,000 characters and symbols, enough for almost all the world's current written languages. (192)
   a. Unicode
   b. ASCII
   c. Microcode
   d. EBCDIC
7. Memory stores _____. (194)
   a. the operating system and other system software
   b. application programs that carry out specific tasks
   c. the data being processed by the application programs
   d. all of the above
8. A _____ of memory is equal to exactly 1,024 bytes, but often is rounded down to 1,000 bytes. (194)
   a. kilobyte (KB)
   b. megabyte (MB)
   c. gigabyte (GB)
   d. terabyte (TB)
9. A _____ is a type of memory module with pins on opposite sides of the circuit board that do not connect, and thus form two sets of contacts. (196)
   a. RIMM (Rambus inline memory module)
   b. DIMM (dual inline memory module)
   c. ROMM (Rambus online memory module)
   d. SIMM (single inline memory module)
10. Many of today's computers support _____, which means the computer automatically can configure adapter cards and other peripherals as you install them. (202)
    a. Pack and Go
    b. Park and Ride
    c. Pick and Choose
    d. Plug and Play
11. Personal computers typically have four to eight _____ either on the front or back of the system unit. (206)
    a. MIDI ports
    b. serial ports
    c. USB ports
    d. parallel ports
12. Word size is the _____. (209)
    a. pace of the system clock
    b. size of the bus
    c. amount of time it takes the processor to read instructions from memory
    d. number of bits the processor can interpret and execute at a given time
13. The most common and slowest expansion bus is the _____. (210)
    a. ISA bus
    b. VESA local bus
    c. PCI bus
    d. FireWire bus
14. _____ usually are installed in internal bays. (210)
    a. Floppy disk drives
    b. DVD drives
    c. Zip drives
    d. Hard disk drives

CHECKPOINT CHAPTER 4

MATCHING
Match the terms with their definitions. (See page numbers in parentheses.)

_____ 1. chassis (180)
_____ 2. microprocessor (183)
_____ 3. superscalar (185)
_____ 4. coprocessor (190)
_____ 5. address (194)
_____ 6. memory module (196)
_____ 7. microcode (198)
_____ 8. synthesizer (207)
_____ 9. expansion bus (209)
_____ 10. bay (210)

a. small circuit board on which RAM chips usually reside
b. integrates the functions of a processor, memory, and video card on a single chip
c. processors that can execute more than one instruction per clock cycle
d. metal or plastic case that protects the internal components of the system unit
e. additional processor chip or circuit board that assists in performing specific tasks
f. allows the processor to communicate with peripherals
g. type of instructions used to program a PROM chip
h. term used by some manufacturers to refer to a personal computer processor chip
i. peripheral or chip that creates sound from digital instructions
j. unique number that identifies the location of a byte in memory
k. opening inside the system unit in which additional equipment can be installed
l. small ceramic or metal component that absorbs and ventilates heat

SHORT ANSWER
Write a brief answer to each of the following questions.

1. What is the system clock? _________ How does clock speed affect a computer's speed? _________
2. How are a chip-for-chip upgrade, a piggyback upgrade, and a daughterboard upgrade different? ___________ What is a zero-insertion force (ZIF) socket? ___________
3. How is dynamic RAM different from static RAM? ___________ Why are synchronous DRAM, Double Data Rate SDRAM, and Rambus DRAM chips faster than basic DRAM? ___________
4. What is memory cache? ___________ How are the three types of cache (L1 cache, L2 cache, and L3 cache) different? ___________
5. How are male connectors different from female connectors? ___________ What is a gender changer and when would it be used? ___________

WORKING TOGETHER
Working with a group of your classmates, complete the following team exercises.

1. Prepare a report on the different types of ports and the way you connect peripheral devices to a computer. As part of your report, include the following subheadings and an overview of each subheading topic: (1) What is a port? (2) What is a connector? (3) What is a serial port and how does it work? (4) What is a parallel port and how does it work? (5) What is a USB port and how does it work? Expand your report so that it includes information beyond that in your textbook. Create a PowerPoint presentation from your report. Share your presentation with your class.
2. Choose one Issue in this chapter from page 185, 186, 201, or 213. Use the Web and/or print media to research the issue. Then, present a debate for the class, with different members of your team supporting different responses to the questions that accompany the issue.
3. Notebook computers comprise almost 40 percent of personal computer sales. How do notebook computers compare with desktop models? Have each member of your team use a catalogue, access a manufacturer's Web site, or visit a retailer and find a notebook computer and a desktop computer with comparable system units. What is the price of each computer? How are the system units similar? How are they different? Contrast the peripheral devices (displays, keyboards, and so on) and the software included. Meet with the members of your team to discuss results of your investigations. Which computer is the better buy? Why? Use PowerPoint to create a group presentation and share your findings with the class.

CHAPTER 4 LEARN IT ONLINE

Use the Learn It Online exercises to reinforce your understanding of the chapter concepts.

WEB INSTRUCTIONS:

To display this page from the Web, start your browser and enter the Web address **scsite.com/dc2005/ch4/learn**.

1 At the Movies – Biz/Intel Pentium 4

To view the Biz/Intel Pentium 4 movie, click the number 1 button. Watch the movie and then complete the exercise by answering the question below. According to most analysts, the power and speed of Intel's Pentium 4 chip will not have much of an impact on the company's profits. The reasons are two-fold: (1) though faster, they are not significantly faster than older, less expensive chips; and (2) the market for these faster, very powerful chips is only about five percent of the total market. For the market to expand and the demand for these higher priced/higher profit chips to increase, more sophisticated applications —- such as MP3, graphics-intensive games, high-end video, and interactive Internet programs — would need to become more popular. Thinking about wireless technology and technology convergence, what are some developing applications that could spur consumer demand for more computer speed and power?

2 Student Edition Labs – Understanding the Motherboard

Click the number 2 button. When the Student Edition Labs menu appears, click *Understanding the Motherboard* to begin. A new browser window will open. Follow the on-screen instructions to complete the Lab. When finished, click the Exit button. If required, print a copy of your results to submit to your instructor.

3 Student Edition Labs – Binary Numbers

Click the number 3 button. When the Student Edition Labs menu appears, click *Binary Numbers* to begin. A new browser window will open. Follow the on-screen instructions to complete the Lab. When finished, click the Exit button. If required, print a copy of your results to submit to your instructor.

4 How a Processor Works

After reading about what a processor does and the way it interacts with other system unit components, it still can be difficult to understand how a processor performs even a simple task such as adding two plus three. Click the number 4 button, and complete this exercise to learn what a processor does to find the answer.

5 Practice Test

Click the number 5 button. Answer each question. When completed, enter your name and click the Grade Test button to submit the quiz for grading. Make a note of any missed questions. If required, print a copy to submit to your instructor.

6 Web Guide

Click the number 6 button to display the Guide to Web Sites and Searching Techniques Web page. Click Computers and Computing and then click Virtual Museum of Computing. Scroll down the page, locate and click On-line exhibits and information. Click a link of your choice. Use your word processing program to prepare a brief report about your selection and submit the assignment to your instructor.

7 Scavenger Hunt

Click the number 7 button. Print a copy of the Scavenger Hunt page; use this page to write down your answers as you search the Web. Submit your completed page to your instructor.

8 Who Wants To Be a Computer Genius?

Click the number 8 button to find out if you are a computer genius. Directions on how to play the game will be displayed. When you are ready to play, click the Play button. Submit your score to your instructor.

9 Wheel of Terms

Click the number 9 button to reinforce important terms you learned in this chapter by playing the Shelly Cashman Series version of this popular game. Directions on how to play the game will be displayed. When you are ready to play, click the Play button. Submit your score to your instructor.

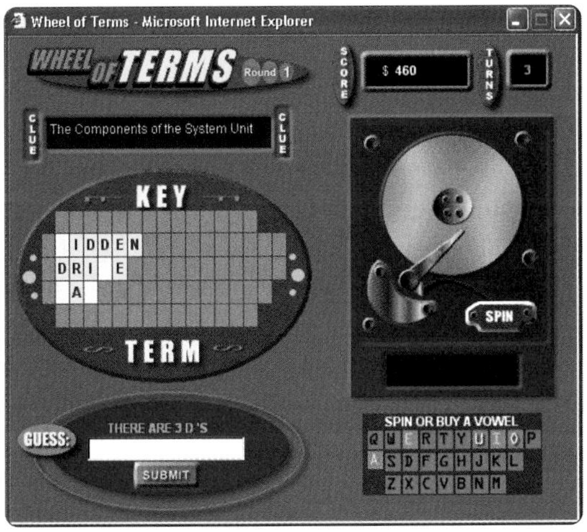

10 Career Corner

Click the number 10 button to display the Penn State's Career Services Web page. Click a link of your choice. Write a brief report about the information you found. Submit the report to your instructor.

11 Search Sleuth

Click the number 11 button to learn search techniques that will help make you a research expert. Submit the completed assignment to your instructor.

12 Crossword Puzzle Challenge

Click the number 12 button. Complete the puzzle to reinforce skills you learned in this chapter. Directions on how to play the game will be displayed. When you are ready to play, click the Play button. Submit the completed puzzle to your instructor.

13 Newsgroups

Would you like more information about a special interest? Maybe you would like to share opinions and advice with people who have the same interests. If so, you might be interested in newsgroups, also called discussion groups or forums. A newsgroup offers the opportunity to read articles about a specific subject, respond to the articles, and even post your own articles. Click the number 13 button to find out more about newsgroups. What is lurking? What is Usenet? Click the how do I find a newsgroup? link at the bottom of the page. Read and print the how do I find a newsgroup? Web page. How can you locate a newsgroup on a particular topic?

14 In the News

In February 2006, the forerunner of the modern computer will have its 60th anniversary. By today's standards for electronic computers, the ENIAC (Electronic Numerical Integrator And Computer) was a grotesque monster. It had 30 separate units, plus a power supply and forced-air cooling, and it weighed more than 30 tons. Its 19,000 vacuum tubes, 1,500 relays, and hundreds of thousands of resistors, capacitors, and inductors consumed almost 200 kilowatts of electrical power. The ENIAC performed fewer than 1,000 calculations per minute; today, personal computers can process more than 300 million instructions per second. The rapid development of computing power and capabilities is astonishing, and the rate of that development is accelerating. Click the number 14 button and read a news article about the introduction of a new or improved computer component. What is the component? Who is introducing it? Will the component change the way people use computers? If so, how?

CHAPTER 4 LAB EXERCISES

Use the Lab Exercises to gain hands-on computer experience.

WEB INSTRUCTIONS:

To display this page from the Web, start your browser and enter the Web address **scsite.com/dc2005/ch4/lab**.

1 Installing New Hardware

This exercise uses Windows XP procedures. Plug and Play technology allows users to install new devices without having to reconfigure the system manually. To learn how to install a new device with Plug and Play technology, click the Start button on the taskbar, and then click Help and Support on the Start menu. When the Help and Support Center window displays, click the Hardware link in the Pick a Help topic list. Click Installing and configuring new hardware. Click the Install a device link in the Pick a task list.

- What are the two steps in installing a Plug and Play device?
- When would Windows not detect a Plug and Play device?
- How is a device that is not Plug and Play installed?

Close the Help and Support Center window.

2 Setting the System Clock

This exercise uses Windows XP procedures. Click the Start button on the taskbar and then click Control Panel on the Start menu. If necessary, switch to Category view. Click the Date, Time, Language, and Regional Options link in the Pick a category list. Click the Date and Time icon. Click the Question Mark button on the title bar of the Date and Time Properties dialog box, and then click the picture of the calendar. Read the information in the pop-up window and then click it to close it. Repeat this process for other areas of the dialog box. Answer these questions:

- What is the purpose of the calendar?
- How do you change the time zone?
- What is the difference between the OK and the Apply buttons?

Close the Date and Time Properties dialog box. Close the Date, Time, Language, and Regional Options window.

3 Using Calculator to Perform Number System Conversion

This exercise uses Windows XP/2000/98 procedures. Instead of the decimal (base 10) number system that people use, computers use the binary (base 2) or hexadecimal (base 16) number systems. It is not necessary to understand these number systems to use a computer, but it is interesting to see how decimal numbers look when in binary or hexadecimal form. Click the Start button on the taskbar, point to All Programs (Programs in Windows 2000/98) on the Start menu, point to Accessories on the All Programs submenu (Programs submenu in Windows 2000/98), and then click Calculator. Click Scientific on the View menu to display the scientific calculator. Perform the following tasks:

- Click Dec (decimal). Enter 35 by clicking the numeric buttons or using the numeric keypad. Click Bin (binary). What number displays? Click Hex (hexadecimal). What number displays? Click the C (Clear) button.
- Convert the following decimal numbers to binary and hexadecimal: 7,256 and 3,421.
- What decimal number is equal to 10010 in the binary system? What decimal number is equal to 2DA9 in the hexadecimal system?

Close the Calculator window.

4 Power Management

This exercise uses Windows XP procedures. Environmental and financial considerations make it important to manage the amount of power a computer uses. Click the Start button on the taskbar, click Control Panel on the Start menu. Click the Performance and Maintenance icon in the Control Panel window. Click the Power Options icon in the Performance and Maintenance window. If necessary, click the Power Schemes tab in the Power Options Properties dialog box.

- What is a power scheme?
- What power scheme currently is being used on your computer?
- After how many minutes of inactivity is the monitor turned off?
- After how many minutes of inactivity are the hard disks turned off?

Close the Power Options Properties dialog box and the Performance and Maintenance window.

WEB RESEARCH

Use the Web Research exercises to learn more about the special features in this chapter.

WEB INSTRUCTIONS:

Use the link in each exercise or a search engine such as Google (google.com) to research the topic. Then, write a one-page, double-spaced report or create a presentation, unless otherwise directed below. Page numbers on which information can be found are in parentheses.

1. **Issue** Choose one Issue from the following issues in this chapter: Does Your Brain Use Machine Cycles? (185), Perfection at What Price? (186), Does Lower Price Mean Less Value? (201), or Do You Want Air Conditioning? Power Windows? A Car Computer? (213). Use the Web to research the issue. Discuss the issue with classmates, instructors, and friends. Address the questions that accompany the issue in a report or presentation.

2. **Apply It** Choose one of the following Apply It features in this chapter: Chip Identifies Pets and Valuables (182) or Computers at Work While You Sleep (191). Use the Web to gather additional information about the topic. Print two Web pages that relate to the Apply It. Detail in a report or presentation what you learned.

3. **Career Corner** Read the Career Corner article in this chapter (214). Use the Web to find out more about the career. Describe the career in a report or presentation.

4. **Companies on the Cutting Edge** Choose one of the Companies on the Cutting Edge in this chapter (216). Use the Web to research the company further. Explain in a report or presentation how this company has contributed to computer technology.

5. **Technology Trailblazers** Choose one of the Technology Trailblazers in this chapter (217). Use the Web to research the person further. Explain in a report or presentation how this individual has affected the way people use, or think about, computers.

6. **Picture Yourself Upgrading a Computer** Read the Picture Yourself Upgrading a Computer story at the beginning of this chapter (178). Use the Web to research upgrading your computer further. Describe in a report or presentation the ways in which you might upgrade your computer.

7. **High-Tech Talk** Read the High-Tech Talk feature in this chapter (215). Use the Web to find out more about the topic. Summarize in a report or presentation what you learned.

8. **Web Links** Review the Web Link boxes found in the margins of this chapter. Visit five of the Web Link sites. Print the main Web page for each site you visit. Choose one of the Web pages and then summarize in one paragraph the content of the Web page.

9. **Looking Ahead** Choose one of the Looking Ahead articles in this chapter: Next-Generation Computers and Chips: Faster and Smaller (199) or Robotic Rats May Perform Rescue Missions (214). Use the Web to find out more about the topic. Detail in a report or presentation what you learned.

10. **FAQ** Choose one FAQ found in this chapter. Use the Web to find out more about the topic. Summarize in one paragraph what you learned.

11. **Making Use of the Web** Read the Resources section of Making Use of the Web in Appendix A (APP 8). Complete the Resources Web Exercises at the end of the section (APP 9). Answer the questions posed in each exercise.

CHAPTER 5

Input

Picture Yourself Using a PDA

What a great birthday! Everyone pitched in and bought you a color Web-enabled PDA. No more writing class notes on paper. You will be taking notes by writing with a stylus onto the PDA's screen. Even more convenient, all your appointments and addresses always will be just a tap away.

Your second present is a gift certificate for a full-sized keyboard and two of the following accessories: a combination stylus/writing pen, a mini keyboard, a snap-on digital camera, a specialized pen and data reader, or a scanner. Which accessories are the most important?

The only easy decision is which full-sized keyboard to choose — you would like the wireless keyboard. Choosing the two other accessories is a much more difficult decision. The combination pen/stylus would be handy. The smaller-sized mini keyboard would be a lot easier to carry at school than a full-sized keyboard. Taking digital pictures of friends and family and saving them on the PDA would be real cool. Automatically transferring notes from a regular pad of paper as you write them is a neat idea. Scanning friends' business cards would save time of entering addresses manually. You have many viable options. You want them all!

You opt to be practical and select the mini keyboard. Then, you decide to have fun and choose the digital camera as the second accessory.

As you read Chapter 5, you will learn about input devices for PDAs and discover other types of input.

OBJECTIVES

After completing this chapter, you will be able to:

1. Define input
2. List the characteristics of a keyboard
3. Describe different mouse types and how they work
4. Summarize how pointing devices work
5. Explain how voice recognition works
6. Describe various input devices for PDAs, Tablet PCs, and smart phones
7. Explain how a digital camera works
8. Describe the uses of PC video cameras, Web cams, and video conferencing
9. Discuss various scanners and reading devices and how they work
10. Explain the types of terminals
11. Summarize the various biometric devices
12. Identify alternative input devices for physically challenged users

CONTENTS

WHAT IS INPUT?

Input is any data or instructions entered into the memory of a computer. People have a variety of options available to input data and instructions into a computer. As shown in Figure 5-1, users can type characters on a keyboard; click a button or roll a wheel on a mouse; press a finger on a touch screen; write, draw on, or tap a device's screen with a stylus or digital pen; speak into a microphone; send images from a digital camera; transmit live images with a PC video camera; or scan an image.

As discussed in Chapter 1, *data* is a collection of unprocessed text, numbers, images, audio, and video. Once data is in memory, the computer interprets and executes instructions to process the data into information. *Instructions* are the steps that tell the computer how to perform a particular task.

Input to a computer consists of either data or instructions (Figure 5-2). Instructions entered into the computer can be in the form of programs, commands, and user responses.

- A *program* is a series of instructions that tells a computer what to do and how to do it. When a programmer writes a program, he or

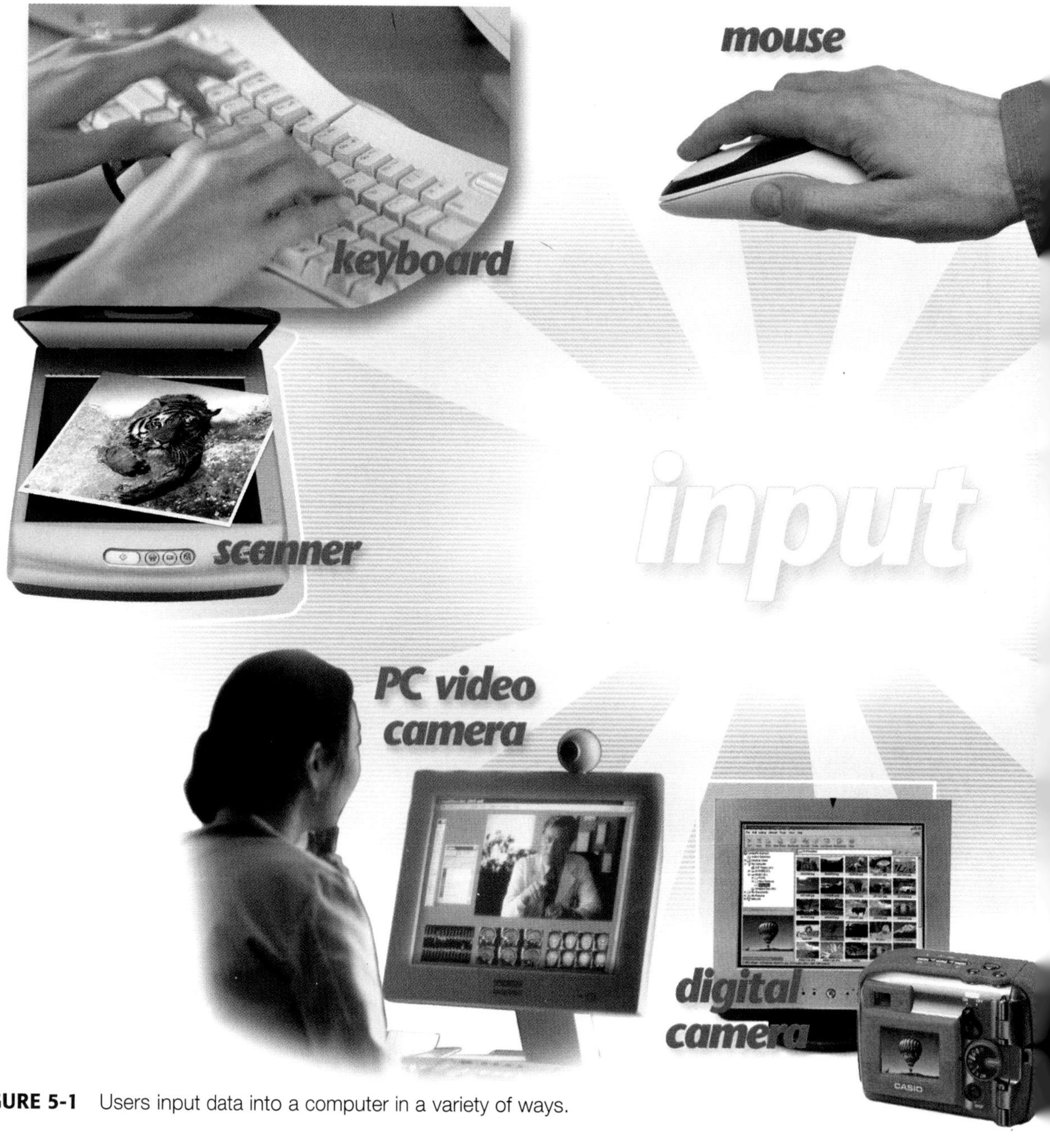

FIGURE 5-1 Users input data into a computer in a variety of ways.

she inputs the program into the computer by using a keyboard, mouse, or other input device. The programmer then stores the program in a file that a user can execute (run). When a user runs a program, the computer loads the program from a storage medium to memory. Thus, a program is input into a computer's memory.

- Programs respond to commands that a user issues. A *command* is an instruction that causes a program to perform a specific action. Users issue commands by typing or pressing keys on the keyboard, clicking a mouse button, speaking into a microphone, or touching an area on a screen.
- A *user response* is an instruction a user issues by replying to a question displayed by a program. A response to the question instructs the program to perform certain actions. Assume the program asks the question, Is the time card correct? If you answer Yes, the program processes the time card. If you answer No, the program gives you the opportunity to modify the time card entries.

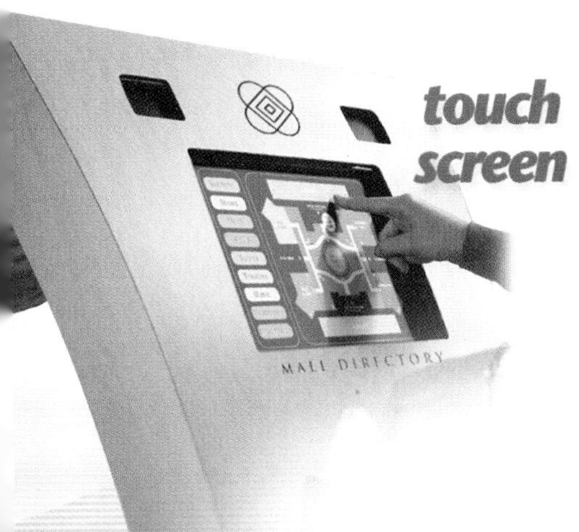

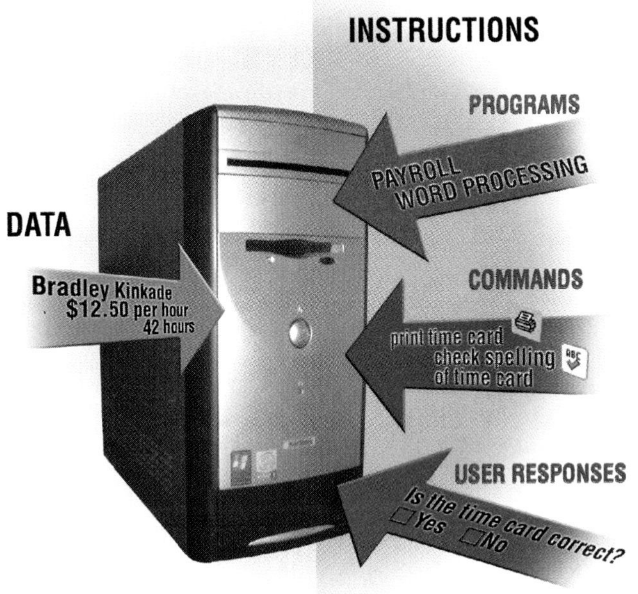

FIGURE 5-2 Two types of input are data and instructions. Instructions entered into the computer can be in the form of programs, commands, and user responses.

WHAT ARE INPUT DEVICES?

An **input device** is any hardware component that allows users to enter data or instructions (programs, commands, and user responses) into a computer. Depending on the application and your particular requirements, the input device selected may vary. Popular input devices include the keyboard, mouse, stylus, digital pen, microphone, digital camera, and scanner. The following pages discuss these and other input devices.

Storage devices, such as disk drives, serve as both input and output devices. Chapter 7 discusses storage devices.

THE KEYBOARD

Many people use a keyboard as one of their input devices. A **keyboard** is an input device that contains keys users press to enter data into a computer (Figure 5-3).

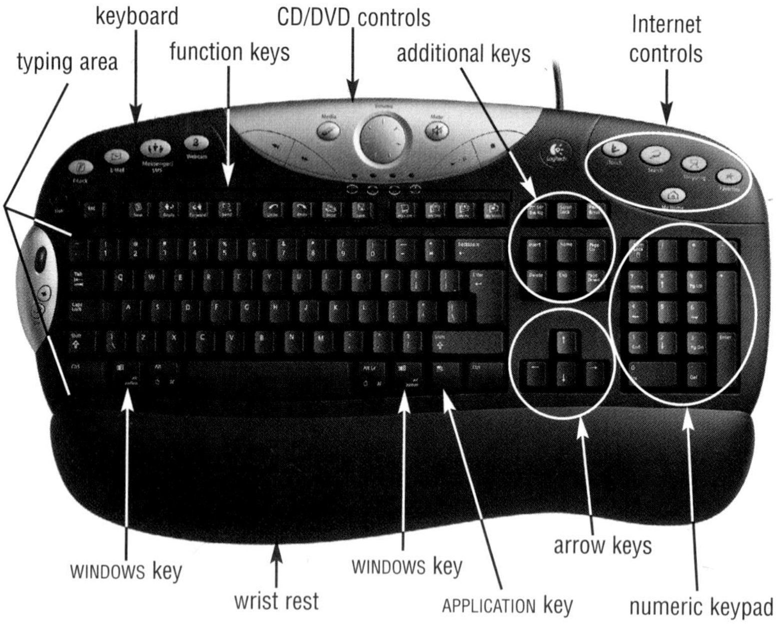

FIGURE 5-2 On a desktop computer keyboard, you type using keys in the typing area and on the numeric keypad.

Desktop computer keyboards typically have from 101 to 105 keys. Keyboards for smaller computers such as notebook computers contain fewer keys. All computer keyboards have a typing area that includes the letters of the alphabet, numbers, punctuation marks, and other basic keys. Many desktop computer keyboards also have a numeric keypad on the right side of the keyboard. A keyboard also contains other keys that allow users to enter data and instructions into the computer. Read Issue 5-1 for a related discussion.

ISSUE 5-1

What Is Happening on Your Computer?

Do you question your employees' work on company computers? Are you curious about your spouse's long e-mail messages? Do you have concerns about your teenager's conversations in Internet chat rooms? Keyboard monitoring software can dispel your doubts. When installed on a computer, *keyboard monitoring software* records every keystroke in a file, which you later access by supplying the correct password. With keyboard monitoring software, you see everything that was typed on the computer keyboard, including documents, e-mail, and other messages. You could catch a disgruntled employee preparing a resume on company time, discover that your spouse is e-mailing gardening tips to a distant friend, or keep your teenager from a potentially dangerous contact in a chat room. Many maintain, however, that keyboard monitoring software is an invasion of privacy. Should keyboard monitoring software ever be used? If so, when? Some marketers of keyboard monitoring software recommend that computer users should be informed that the software is installed. Is this a good idea? Why or why not?

For more information about keyboard monitoring, visit the Discovering Computers 2005 Issues Web page (**scsite.com/dc2005/issues**). Click Issue #1 below Chapter 5.

Across the top of most keyboards are function keys, which are labeled with the letter F followed by a number (Figure 5-3). *Function keys* are special keys programmed to issue commands to a computer. The command associated with a function key depends on the program. To issue commands, users often press a function key in combination with other special keys (SHIFT, CTRL, ALT, and others). Many programs enable users to press key combinations, select a menu command, or click a button to obtain the same result (Figure 5-4).

MICROSOFT OFFICE WORD 2003 KEY COMBINATION EQUIVALENTS

Command	Key Combination	Menu | Command	Button
Copy	SHIFT+F2 or CTRL+C	Edit | Copy	
Open	CTRL+F12	File | Open	
Paste	CTRL+V	Edit | Paste	

FIGURE 5-4 Many programs allow you to use key combinations, a menu, or a button on a toolbar to obtain the same result, as shown by these examples from Microsoft Office Word 2003.

Keyboards also contain keys that allow you to position the insertion point, also known as a *cursor* in some applications. The **insertion point** is a symbol on the screen, usually a blinking vertical bar, that indicates where the next character you type will be displayed (Figure 5-5). Users can move the insertion point left, right, up, or down by pressing the arrow keys and other keys on the keyboard.

Nearly all keyboards have toggle keys. A *toggle key* is a key that switches between two states each time a user presses the key. When you press the NUM LOCK key, for example, it locks the numeric keypad so you can use the keypad to type numbers. When you press the NUM LOCK key again, the numeric keypad unlocks so the same keys function as keys that move the insertion point. Many keyboards have status lights that light up when you activate a toggle key.

Most of today's desktop computer keyboards are enhanced keyboards. An *enhanced keyboard* has twelve function keys along the top, two CTRL keys, two ALT keys, and a set of arrow and additional keys between the typing area and the numeric keypad (Figure 5-3). Many keyboards also have a WINDOWS key(s) and an APPLICATION key. When pressed, the WINDOWS key displays the Start menu, and the APPLICATION key displays an item's shortcut menu.

Newer keyboards also include buttons that allow you to access the computer's CD/DVD drive, adjust speaker volume, open an e-mail program, start a Web browser, and search the Internet. Some keyboards even have USB ports so a user can plug a USB device directly into the keyboard instead of into the system unit.

FAQ 5-1

What is the rationale for the arrangement of keys in the typing area?

The keys are arranged to reduce the frequency of key jams in a mechanical typewriter. Called a *QWERTY keyboard*, the first letters on the top alphabetic line spell QWERTY. A *Dvorak keyboard*, by contrast, places frequently typed letters in the middle of the typing area. Despite the Dvorak keyboard's logical design, the QWERTY keyboard is more widely used with computer keyboards.

For more information about keyboards, visit the Discovering Computers 2005 FAQ Web page (**scsite.com/dc2005/faq**). Click Keyboards below Chapter 5.

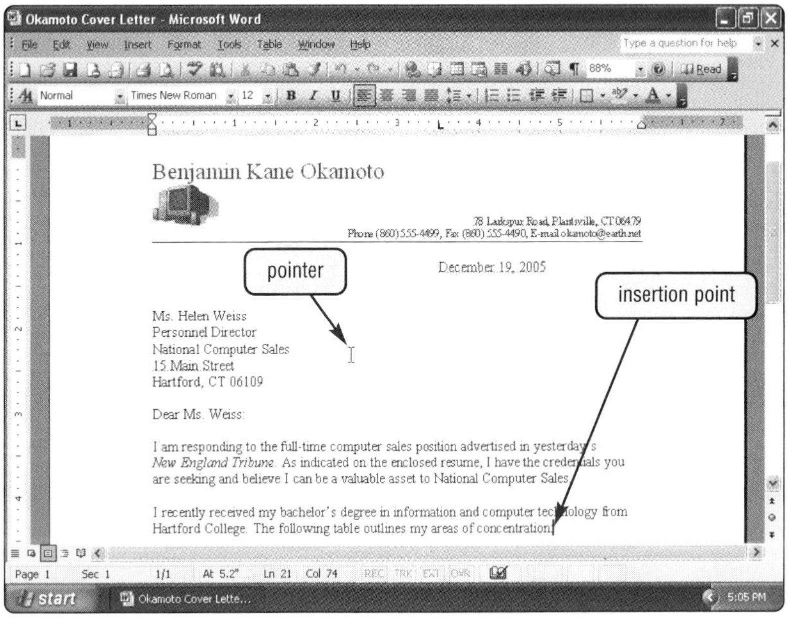

FIGURE 5-5 In most programs, such as Word, the insertion point is a blinking vertical bar. You use the keyboard or other input device to move the insertion point. The pointer, another symbol that is displayed on the screen, is controlled using a pointing device such as a mouse.

Keyboard Connections

Desktop computer keyboards often attach via a cable to a serial port, a keyboard port, or a USB port on the system unit. Some keyboards, however, do not use wires at all. A *cordless keyboard* is a battery-powered device that transmits data using wireless technology, such as radio waves or infrared light waves. Cordless keyboards communicate with a receiver attached to a port on the system unit (Figure 5-6). The port type varies depending on the type of wireless technology. For example, a Bluetooth-enabled keyboard communicates via radio waves with a Bluetooth receiver plugged into a serial, parallel, or USB port.

On notebook and many handheld computers, the keyboard is built into the top of the system unit (Figure 5-7). To fit in these smaller computers, the keyboards usually are smaller and have fewer keys. Most desktop computer keyboards have at least 101 keys. A typical notebook computer keyboard, by contrast, usually has about 85 keys. To provide all of the functionality of a desktop computer keyboard, manufacturers design many of the keys to serve two or three different purposes.

FIGURE 5-6 A cordless keyboard communicates with a receiver, which attaches to a port on the system unit.

Keyboard Ergonomics

Regardless of size, many keyboards have a rectangular shape with the keys aligned in straight, horizontal rows. Users who spend a lot of time typing on these keyboards sometimes experience repetitive strain injuries (RSI) of their wrists and hands. For this reason, some manufacturers offer ergonomic keyboards. An **ergonomic keyboard** has a design that reduces the chance of wrist and hand injuries. Even keyboards that are not ergonomically designed attempt to offer a user more comfort. For example, many keyboards today include a wrist rest or palm rest to reduce strain on the wrist while typing (Figure 5-3 on page 232).

The goal of **ergonomics** is to incorporate comfort, efficiency, and safety into the design of items in the workplace. Employees can be injured or develop disorders of the muscles, nerves, tendons, ligaments, and joints from working in an area that is not ergonomically designed.

FAQ 5-2

What can I do to reduce chances of experiencing repetitive strain injuries?

Do not rest your wrist on the edge of a desk; use a wrist rest. Keep your forearm and wrist level so your wrist does not bend. Do hand exercises every fifteen minutes. Keep your shoulders, arms, hands, and wrists relaxed while you work. Maintain good posture. Keep feet flat on the floor, with one foot slightly in front of the other.

For more information about repetitive strain injuries, visit the Discovering Computers 2005 FAQ Web page (**scsite.com/dc2005/faq**). Click Repetitive Strain Injuries below Chapter 5.

FIGURE 5-7 On notebook computers and many handheld computers, the keyboard is built into the top of the system unit.

POINTING DEVICES

A **pointing device** is an input device that allows a user to control a pointer on the screen. In a graphical user interface, a **pointer** is a small symbol on the screen (Figure 5-5 on page 233) whose location and shape change as a user moves a pointing device. For example, a pointing device can move the insertion point; select text, graphics, and other objects; and click buttons, icons, links, and menu commands. The following sections discuss the mouse and other pointing devices.

MOUSE

A **mouse** is a pointing device that fits comfortably under the palm of your hand. The mouse is the most widely used pointing device on desktop computers.

With a mouse, users control the movement of the pointer, often called a *mouse pointer* in this case. The top and sides of a mouse have one to four buttons; some also have a small wheel. The bottom of a mouse is flat and contains a mechanism that detects movement of the mouse.

Mouse Types

A *mechanical mouse* has a rubber or metal ball on its underside (Figure 5-8). When the ball rolls in a certain direction, electronic circuits in the mouse translate the movement of the mouse into signals the computer can process. You should place a mechanical mouse on a mouse pad. A **mouse pad** is a rectangular rubber or foam pad that provides better traction than the top of a desk. The mouse pad also protects the ball in the mouse from a build-up of dust and dirt, which could cause it to malfunction.

An optical mouse, by contrast, has no moving mechanical parts inside. Instead, an *optical mouse* uses devices that emit and sense light to detect the mouse's movement (Figure 5-9). Some use optical sensors, others use a laser. You can place an optical mouse that uses optical sensors on nearly all types of surfaces, eliminating the need for a mouse pad. An optical mouse that uses a laser usually requires a special mouse pad. An optical mouse is more precise than a mechanical mouse and does not require cleaning as does a mechanical mouse, but it also is more expensive.

A mouse connects to a computer in several ways. Many types connect with a cable that attaches to a serial port, mouse port, or USB port on the system unit. A *cordless mouse* is a battery-powered device that transmits data using wireless technology, such as radio waves or infrared light waves. The wireless technology used for a cordless mouse is very similar to that of a cordless keyboard discussed earlier. Some users prefer a cordless mouse because it frees up desk space and eliminates the clutter of a cord. For a more technical discussion about the wireless keyboard and mouse, read the High-Tech Talk article on page 265 at the end of this chapter.

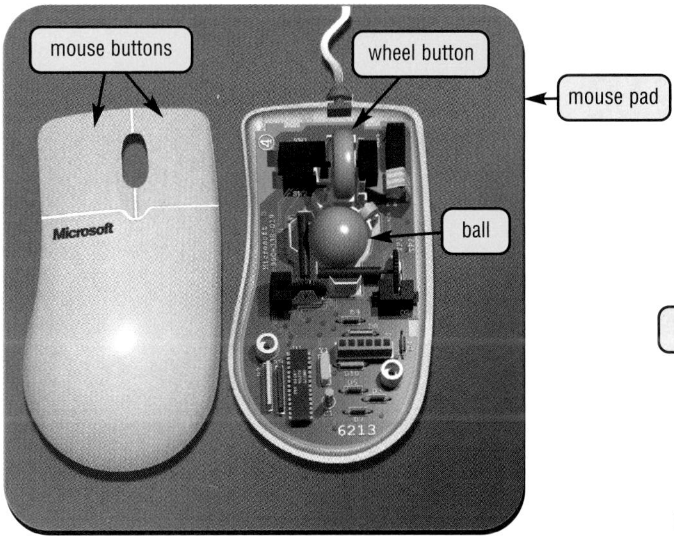

FIGURE 5-8 A mechanical mouse contains a small ball.

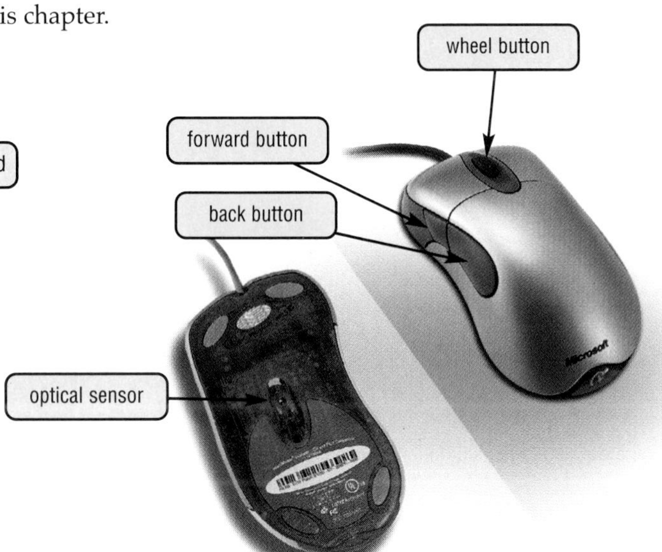

FIGURE 5-9 This optical mouse uses an optical sensor. It also includes buttons to push with your thumb that enable forward and backward navigation through Web pages.

Using a Mouse

As you move a mouse, the pointer on the screen also moves (Figure 5-10). If you have never worked with a mouse, you might find it awkward at first. With a little practice, however, you will discover that a mouse is quite easy to use. Read Issue 5-2 for a related discussion.

Generally, you use the mouse to move the pointer on the screen to an object such as a button, a menu, an icon, a link, or text. Then, you press a mouse button to perform a certain action associated with that object. Windows users work with a mouse that has at least two buttons. For a right-handed user, the left button usually is the primary mouse button and the right mouse button is the secondary mouse button. Left-handed people, however, can reverse the function of these buttons. Read Apply It 5-1 for more information.

FIGURE 5-10 HOW TO MOVE THE POINTER WITH A MOUSE

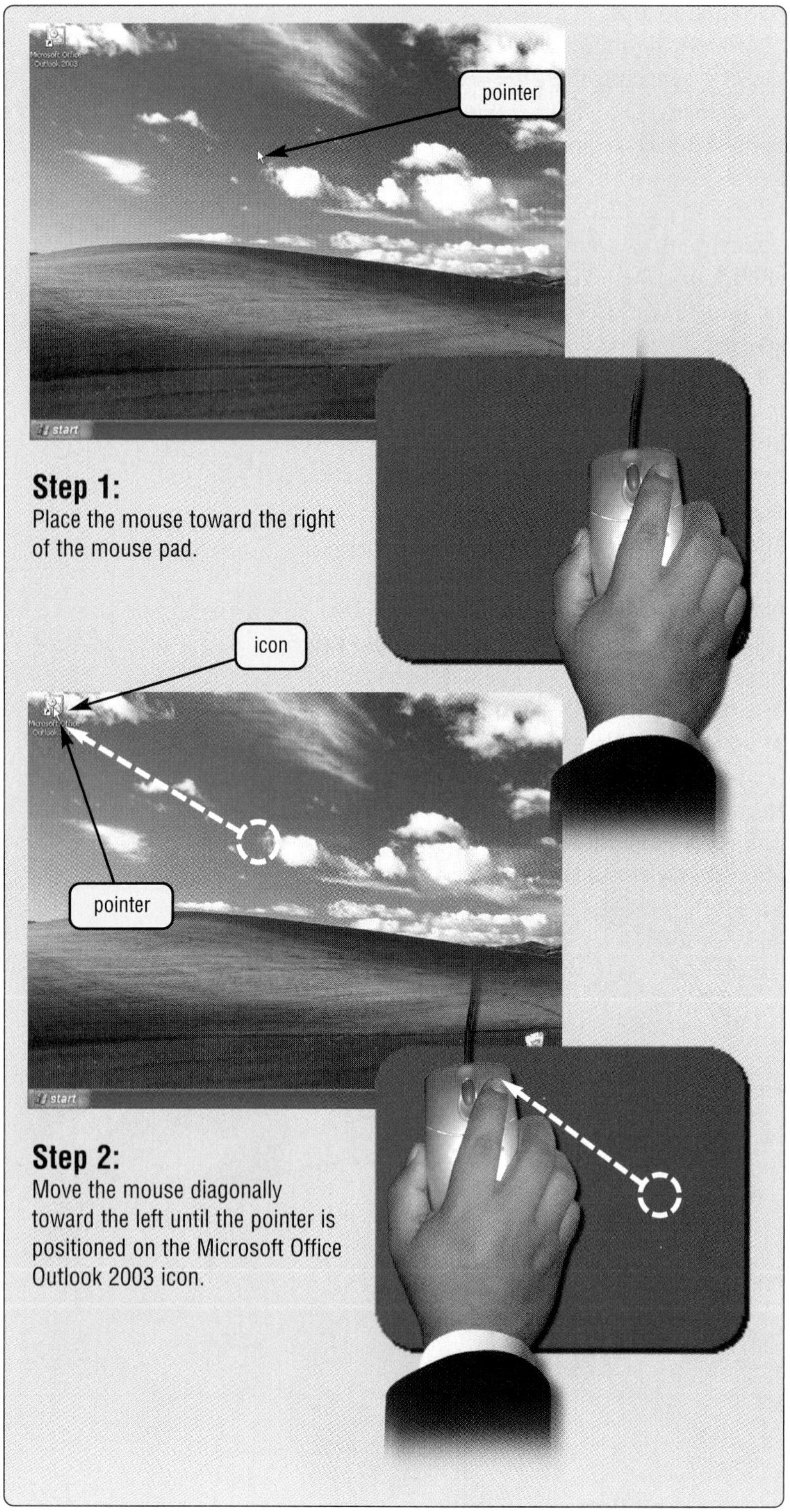

ISSUE 5-2

A Mouse Did What?

When you consider the causes of workplace injuries, you might not put clicking a mouse in the same category with lifting a bag of concrete, but perhaps you should. According to the chairman of a National Academy of Sciences panel that investigated workplace injuries, every year a million Americans lose workdays because of repetitive strain injuries. These injuries, which often result from prolonged use of a computer mouse and keyboard, are the largest job-related injury and illness problem in the United States today. OSHA proposed standards whereby employers would have to establish programs to prevent workplace injuries with respect to computer use. Yet, Congress rejected the standards, accepting the argument that the cost to employers would be prohibitive and unfair, because no proof exists that the injuries are caused exclusively by office work. Should standards for computer use be established by the government? Why or why not? Who is responsible for this type of workplace injury? Why?

For more information about workplace injuries, visit the Discovering Computers 2005 Issues Web page (**scsite.com/dc2005/issues**). Click Issue #2 below Chapter 5.

In addition to pointing, you can perform several operations using the mouse. These operations include click, right-click, double-click, triple-click, drag, right-drag, rotate wheel, and press wheel button. The table in Figure 5-11 explains how to perform these mouse operations. Some programs also use keys in combination with the mouse to perform certain actions. The function of the mouse buttons and the wheel varies depending on the program.

APPLY IT 5-1

Configuring the Mouse to Suit Your Preferences

Ten percent of the population is left-handed, according to some estimates. If they also are computer users, they may feel awkward using a mouse because this device is configured for a right-handed user. They can, however, configure the mouse to fit their needs. In fact, all mouse users can customize their mouse-usage preferences in a few simple steps.

Using Windows XP, click the Start button on the taskbar, click Control Panel, and then in Classic View double-click the Mouse icon in the Control Panel box. Windows displays the Mouse Properties dialog box, which contains a variety of options.

For example, on the Buttons tab you can configure the mouse for right- or left-handed use by choosing the primary and secondary buttons, adjust the double-click speed, and turn on ClickLock, which allows you to highlight or drag without holding down the mouse button.

On the Pointers tab, you can select a scheme of predefined mouse pointers, customize the pointers, and select whether you want a shadow to display under the pointer.

The Pointer Options tab includes options to select the pointer speed, automatically move the pointer to a default button in a dialog box, make the mouse pointer leave a trail, hide the mouse pointer while you type, and show the mouse pointer's location when the CTRL key is pressed.

If the Mouse Properties dialog box has a Wheel tab, you also can specify the number of lines the screen should scroll when you roll the wheel one notch.

For more information about configuring a mouse, visit the Discovering Computers 2005 Apply It Web page (**scsite.com/dc2005/apply**). Click Apply It #1 below Chapter 5.

FAQ 5-3

What is the purpose of a wheel on a mouse?

To scroll and zoom. Roll it forward or backward to scroll up or down. Hold down the CTRL key while rolling the wheel to make the text on the screen bigger or smaller. These scrolling and zooming functions work with most software and also on the Web.

For more information about using a mouse, visit the Discovering Computers 2005 FAQ Web page (**scsite.com/dc2005/faq**). Click Using a Mouse below Chapter 5.

WEB LINK 5-1

Mouse

Visit the Discovering Computers 2005 WEB LINK page (**scsite.com/dc2005/weblink**). Click Mouse below Chapter 5.

MOUSE OPERATIONS

Operation	Mouse Action	Example
Point	Move the mouse across a flat surface until the pointer on the desktop is positioned on the item of choice.	Position the pointer on the screen.
Click	Press and release the primary mouse button, which usually is the left mouse button.	Select or deselect items on the screen or start a program or program feature.
Right-click	Press and release the secondary mouse button, which usually is the right mouse button.	Display a shortcut menu.
Double-click	Quickly press and release the left mouse button twice without moving the mouse.	Start a program or program feature.
Triple-click	Quickly press and release the left mouse button three times without moving the mouse.	Select a paragraph.
Drag	Point to an item, hold down the left mouse button, move the item to the desired location on the screen, and then release the left mouse button.	Move an object from one location to another or draw pictures.
Right-drag	Point to an item, hold down the right mouse button, move the item to the desired location on the screen, and then release the right mouse button.	Display a shortcut menu after moving an object from one location to another.
Rotate wheel	Roll the wheel forward or backward.	Scroll up or down a few lines.
Press wheel button	Press the wheel button while moving the mouse on the desktop.	Scroll continuously.

FIGURE 5-11 The more common mouse operations.

OTHER POINTING DEVICES

The mouse is the most widely used pointing device today. Some users, however, work with other pointing devices. These include the trackball, touchpad, pointing stick, joystick, wheel, light pen, touch screen, stylus, and digital pen. The following sections discuss each of these pointing devices.

WEB LINK 5-2

Touchpad

Visit the Discovering Computers 2005 WEB LINK page (**scsite .com/dc2005/weblink**). Click Touchpad below Chapter 5.

Trackball

Similar to a mechanical mouse that has a ball on the bottom, a **trackball** is a stationary pointing device with a ball on its top (Figure 5-12). The ball in most trackballs is about the size of a Ping-Pong ball.

To move the pointer using a trackball, you rotate the ball with your thumb, fingers, or the palm of your hand. In addition to the ball, a trackball usually has one or more buttons that work just like mouse buttons.

A trackball requires frequent cleaning because it picks up oils from fingers and dust from the environment. For users who have limited desk space, however, a trackball is a good alternative to a mouse because the device is stationary.

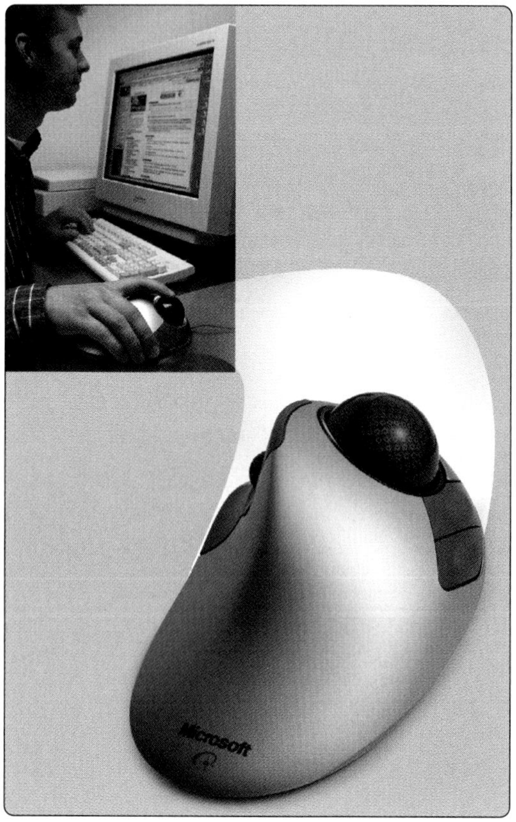

FIGURE 5-12 A trackball is like an upside-down mouse.

Touchpad

A **touchpad** is a small, flat, rectangular pointing device that is sensitive to pressure and motion (Figure 5-13). To move the pointer using a touchpad, slide your fingertip across the surface of the pad. Some touchpads have one or more buttons around the edge of the pad that work like mouse buttons. On many touchpads, you also can tap the pad's surface to imitate mouse operations such as clicking.

Although you can attach a stand-alone touchpad to any personal computer, touchpads are found most often on notebook computers.

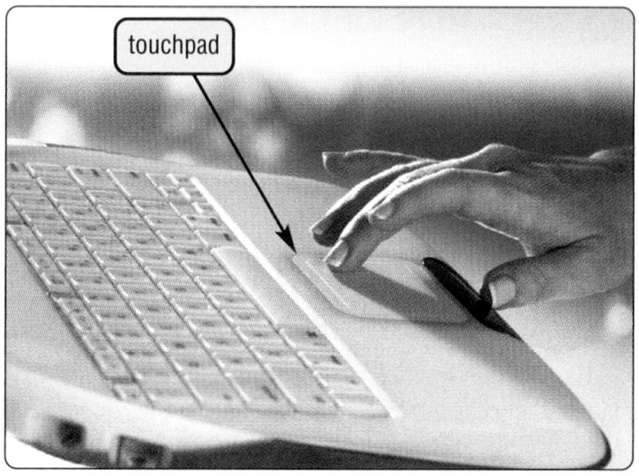

FIGURE 5-13 Many notebook computers have a touchpad that allows users to control the movement of the pointer.

Pointing Stick

A **pointing stick** is a pressure-sensitive pointing device shaped like a pencil eraser that is positioned between keys on a keyboard (Figure 5-14). To move the pointer using a pointing stick, you push the pointing stick

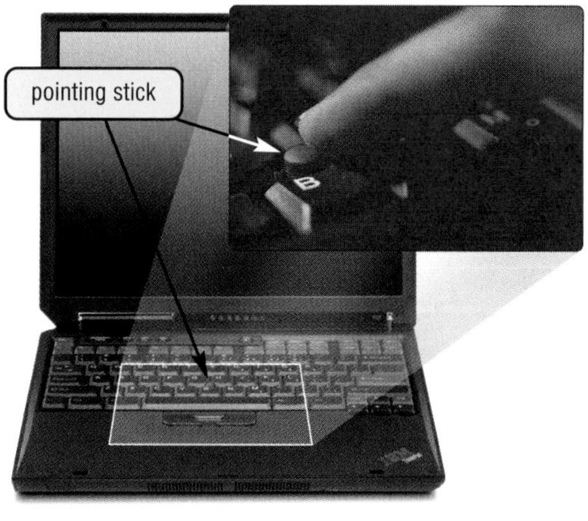

FIGURE 5-14 Some notebook computers include a pointing stick to allow a user to control the movement of the pointer.

WEB LINK 5-3

Pointing Stick

Visit the Discovering Computers 2005 WEB LINK page (**scsite .com/dc2005/weblink**). Click Pointing Stick below Chapter 5.

with a finger. The pointer on the screen moves in the direction you push the pointing stick. By pressing buttons below the keyboard, users can click and perform other mouse-type operations with a pointing stick.

A pointing stick does not require any additional desk space. In addition, it does not require cleaning like a mechanical mouse or trackball. IBM developed the pointing stick for its notebook computers.

Whether you select a notebook computer that has a touchpad or pointing stick is a matter of personal preference. Some notebook computers have both a touchpad and a pointing stick.

Joystick and Wheel

Users running game software or flight and driving simulation software often use a joystick or wheel as a pointing device (Figure 5-15). A **joystick** is a vertical lever mounted on a base. You move the lever in different directions to control the actions of the simulated vehicle or player. The lever usually includes buttons called triggers that you press to activate certain events. Some joysticks also have additional buttons you set to perform other actions.

A **wheel** is a steering-wheel-type input device. Users turn the wheel to simulate driving a car, truck, or other vehicle. Most wheels also include foot pedals for acceleration and braking actions. A joystick and wheel typically attach via a cable to the game port on a sound card or game card or to a USB port.

Light Pen

A **light pen** is a handheld input device that can detect the presence of light. Some light pens require a specially designed monitor, while others work with a standard monitor (Figure 5-16). To select objects on the screen, a user presses the light pen against the surface of the screen or points the light pen at the screen and then presses a button on the pen.

Health care professionals, such as doctors and dentists, use light pens because they can slide a protective sleeve over the pen — keeping their fingers free of contaminants. Light pens also are ideal for areas where employees' hands might contain food, dirt, grease, or other chemicals that could damage the computer. Applications with limited desktop space such as industrial or manufacturing environments find light pens convenient, as well.

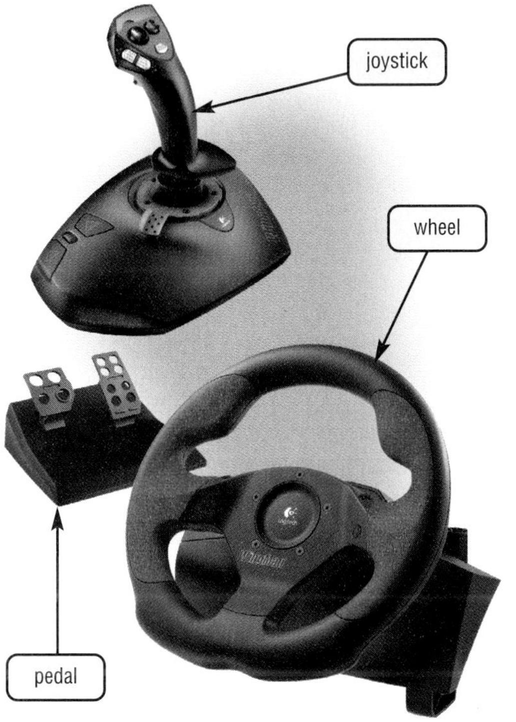

FIGURE 5-15 Joysticks and wheels help a user control the actions of players and vehicles in game and simulation software.

FIGURE 5-16 To make selections on the screen while processing an insurance claim, this insurance agent uses a light pen.

Touch Screen

A **touch screen** is a touch-sensitive display device. Users interact with these devices by touching areas of the screen with a finger or a stylus. Because touch screens require a lot of arm movements, you do not enter large amounts of data into touch screens. Instead, you touch words, pictures, numbers, or locations identified on the screen.

Kiosks often have touch screens. Travelers use kiosks in airports to print tickets ordered online, and they use kiosks in hotels for easy check in and check out. Store kiosks allow customers to order items not in stock at the store. Museum kiosks give visitors information. To allow easy access of your bank account from a car, many ATM machines have touch screens. Computers in restaurants (Figure 5-17), cafeterias, gift shops, and resorts also have touch screens. Most PDAs and Tablet PCs have touch screens, and some notebook computers even have touch screens.

WEB LINK 5-4

Touch Screen

Visit the Discovering Computers 2005 WEB LINK page (**scsite .com/dc2005/weblink**). Click Touch Screen below Chapter 5.

Stylus, Digital Pen, and Cursor

A **stylus** and a **digital pen** look like an ink pen, but use pressure, instead of ink, to write text and draw lines. Both allow a user to write, draw, and tap on a flat surface for input. A digital pen typically provides more functionality than a stylus. Originally called an electronic pen, this device was used primarily in professional graphical applications such as computer-aided design and drafting. Digital pens, often simply called pens, can be quite sophisticated, featuring electronic erasers and programmable buttons.

Architects, mapmakers, designers, and artists create drawings and sketches by using a pen or a cursor on a graphics tablet (Figure 5-18). A **graphics tablet** is a flat, rectangular, electronic plastic board. Large-scale applications sometimes refer to this device as a *digitizer*. A *cursor* looks similar to a mouse, except it has a window with crosshairs, so the

FIGURE 5-17 A customer uses a kiosk touch screen to place an order at a fast-food restaurant.

Figure 5-18a (artist using pen)

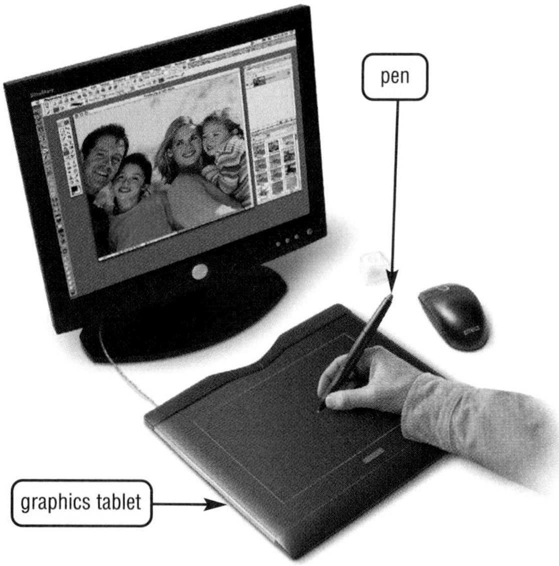

Figure 5-18b (civil engineer using cursor)

FIGURE 5-18 Artists, designers, and engineers use pens and cursors with graphics tablets or digitizers.

user can see through to the tablet. Each location on the graphics tablet corresponds to a specific location on the screen. When drawing on the tablet with a pen or cursor, the tablet detects and converts the movements into digital signals that are sent into the computer.

Some desktop computer monitors and many mobile computers and devices have touch screens that allow you to input data using a pen or stylus (Figure 5-19). Instead of using a keyboard, you write or make selections on the computer screen with the stylus or pen. PDAs use a stylus, and Tablet PCs typically use a digital pen. With a stylus or pen, users enter text, handwritten comments, drawings, and sketches. The computers or mobile devices then use *handwriting recognition software* that translates the handwritten letters and symbols into characters that the computer or device can process.

Mobile users often work with a stylus or pen as their primary input device. Read Looking Ahead 5-1 for a look at the next generation of pointing devices.

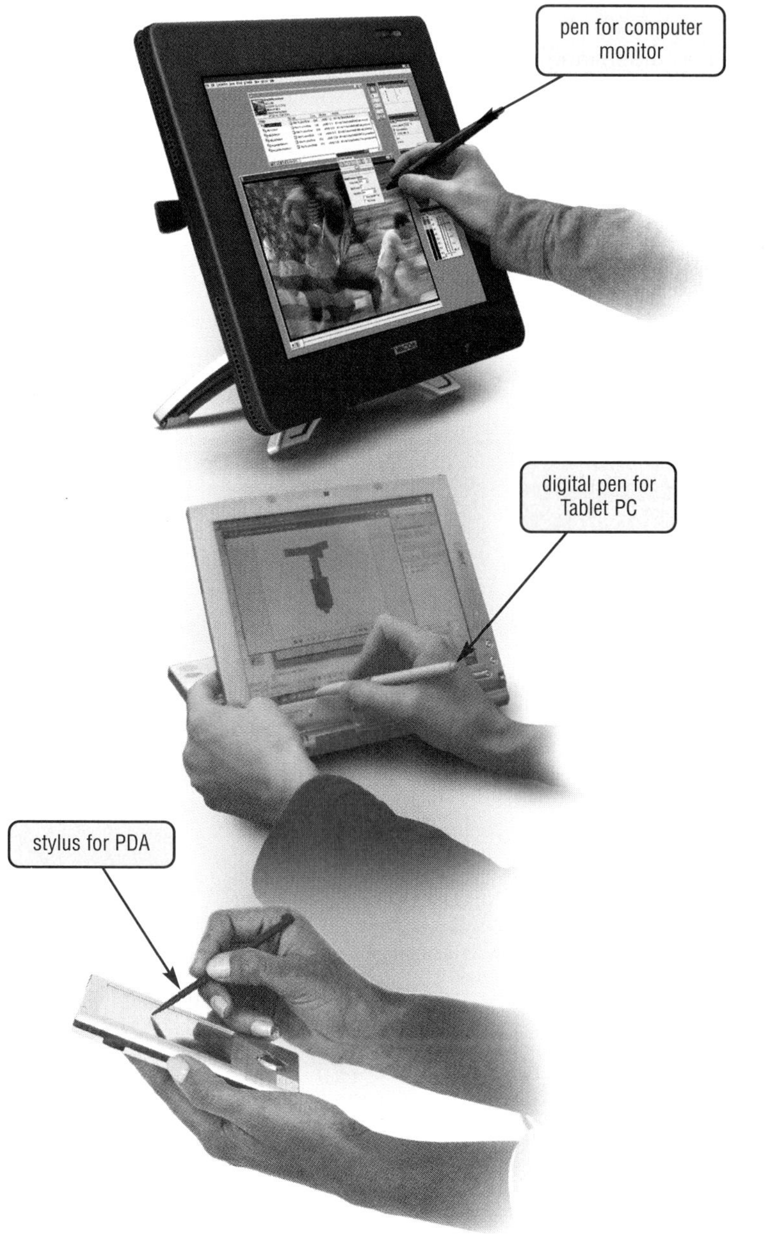

FIGURE 5-19 All sizes of computers and mobile devices support handwriting input through a pen or stylus.

WEB LINK 5-5

Stylus and Pen

Visit the Discovering Computers 2005 WEB LINK page (**scsite.com/dc2005/weblink**). Click Stylus and Pen below Chapter 5.

LOOKING AHEAD 5-1

Wireless Pens Revolutionize Input Devices

The typewriter is regarded as the first significant everyday business tool. Patented in 1868, it had one major flaw: the keys jammed easily. To solve this problem, the keyboard was redesigned to reduce the frequency of jammed keys.

Most computer users have learned to memorize this keyboard and use it, along with a mouse, to gather and edit text, play games, draw images, and research the Internet. But a new generation of input devices is gathering support to facilitate entering data.

Intel's Human Computer Interface Devices project is exploring new hardware to replace the keyboard and mouse. One of the key products from its Microcomputer Research Labs (MRL) is the digital wireless pen. A similar device, the VPen, is being developed at OTM Technologies to perform the same functions as a keyboard and mouse.

The digital pen resembles the stylus PDA owners use to enter and retrieve data. A tiny optical laser reader at the point interfaces with handwriting recognition software to convert handwriting to text. It also can be used as a joystick for games and to draw graphical images. The pen tip can be used on any surface, including the palm of a hand.

For a look at the next generation of pointing devices, visit the Discovering Computers 2005 Looking Ahead Web page (**scsite.com/dc2005/looking**). Click Looking Ahead #1 below Chapter 5.

QUIZ YOURSELF 5-1

To check your knowledge of input techniques, the keyboard, the mouse, and other pointing devices, visit the Discovering Computers 2005 Quiz Yourself Web page (**scsite.com/dc2005/quiz**). Click Objectives 1 – 4 below Chapter 5.

VOICE INPUT

As an alternative to using a keyboard to input data, some users are talking to their computers. **Voice input** is the process of entering data by speaking into a microphone. The microphone may be a stand-alone peripheral that sits on top of a desk, or is built into the computer or device, or is in a headset. Some external microphones have a cable that attaches to a port on the sound card on the computer. Others communicate using wireless technology such as IrDA or Bluetooth.

Voice recognition, also called *speech recognition*, is the computer's capability of distinguishing spoken words (Figure 5-20). Voice recognition programs do not understand speech. They recognize a vocabulary of preprogrammed words. The vocabulary of voice recognition programs can range from two words to millions of words. The automated telephone system at your bank may ask you to answer questions by speaking the words Yes or No into the telephone. A voice recognition program on your computer, by contrast, may recognize up to two million words.

In the past, voice recognition systems were found only in specialized applications in which a user's hands were occupied or disabled. Today, voice recognition applications are affordable and easy to use, providing all types of users with a convenient form of input. Users can search the Web, participate in chat rooms, and send and receive e-mail and instant messages — all by speaking into a microphone on a desktop computer, mobile computer, or mobile device. Some business software, such as word processing and spreadsheet, includes voice recognition as part of the program. For example, users can dictate memos and letters into a word processing program instead of typing them.

The first voice recognition programs were speaker dependent. Today, most are a combination of speaker dependent and speaker independent. With *speaker-dependent software*, the

WEB LINK 5-6

Voice Input

Visit the Discovering Computers 2005 WEB LINK page (**scsite.com/dc2005/weblink**). Click Voice Input below Chapter 5.

FIGURE 5-20 HOW VOICE RECOGNITION WORKS

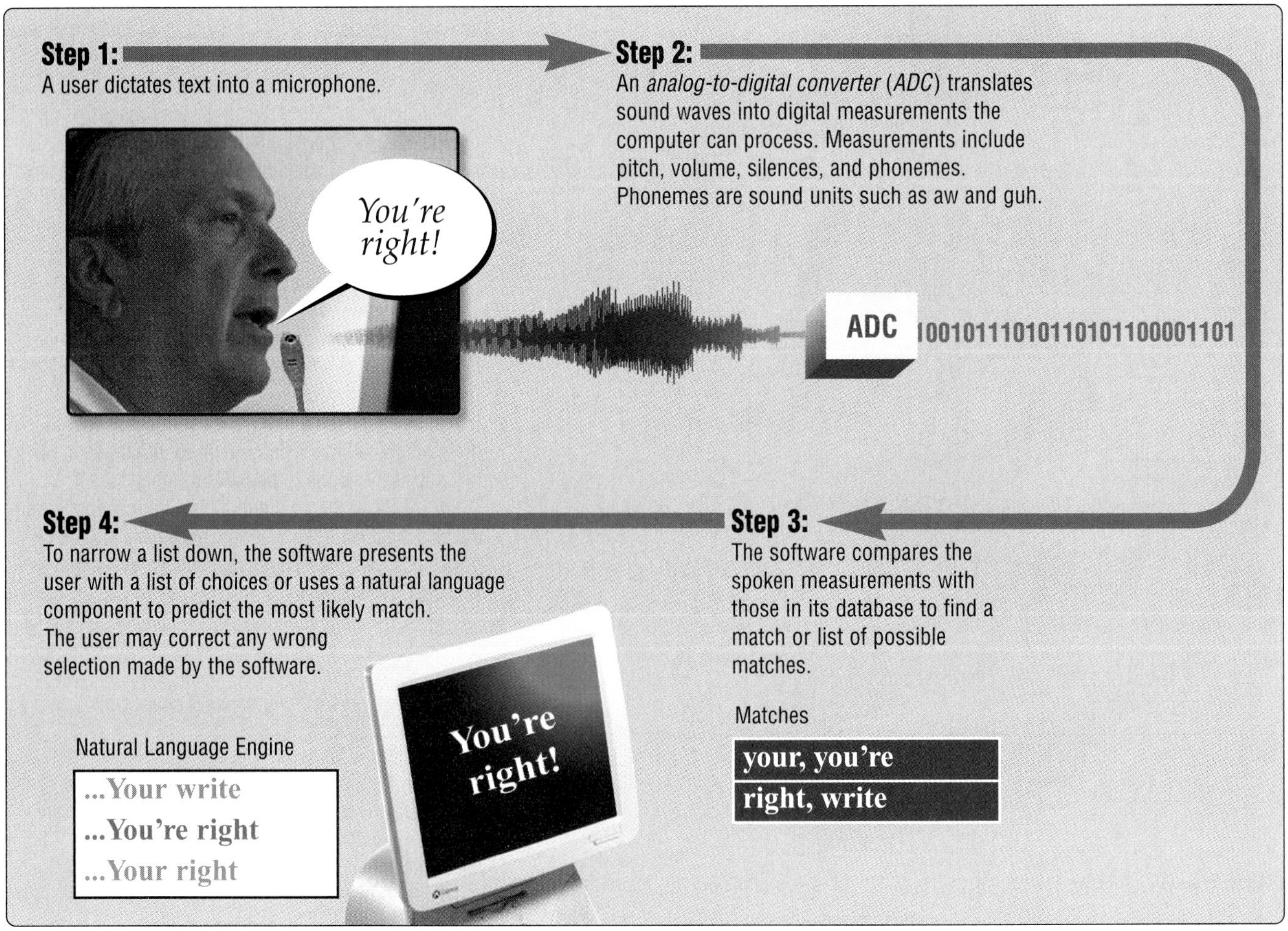

computer makes a profile of your voice, which means you have to train the computer to recognize your voice. To train the computer, you must speak each of the words in the vocabulary into the computer repeatedly. After hearing the spoken word repetitively, the program develops and stores a digital pattern for the word. When you later speak a word, the program compares the spoken word with those stored. *Speaker-independent software* has a built-in set of word patterns. That is, you do not have to train a computer to recognize your voice. Many products today include a built-in set of words that grows as the software learns your words.

Some voice recognition software requires *discrete speech,* which means you have to speak slowly and separate each word with a short pause. Most of today's products, however, allow you to speak in a flowing conversational tone, called *continuous speech.*

Keep in mind that the best voice recognition programs are 90 to 95 percent accurate, which means the software may interpret as many as one in ten words incorrectly. Experts agree voice recognition capability represents the future of software.

FAQ 5-4

Which type of microphone is best?

For voice recognition software, headsets that have a microphone provide the highest quality because they typically do not pick up background noises. For group discussions, however, where multiple people will use the same microphone at the same time, you need a stand-alone or built-in microphone.

For more information about microphones, visit the Discovering Computers 2005 FAQ Web page (**scsite.com/dc2005/faq**). Click Microphones below Chapter 5.

Audio Input

Voice input is part of a larger category of input called audio input. **Audio input** is the process of entering any sound into the computer such as speech, music, and sound effects. To input high-quality sound, a personal computer must have a sound card. Users input sound via devices such as microphones, tape players, CD/DVD players, or radios, each of which plugs into a port on the sound card.

Some users also input music and other sound effects using external MIDI devices such as an electronic piano keyboard (Figure 5-21). As discussed in the previous chapter, in addition to being a port, *MIDI* (*musical instrument digital interface*) is the electronic music industry's standard that defines how digital musical devices represent sounds electronically. These devices connect to the sound card on a computer. Software that conforms to the MIDI standard allows users to compose and edit music and many other sounds. For example, you can change the speed, add notes, or rearrange the score to produce an entirely new sound.

FIGURE 5-21 An electronic piano keyboard is an external MIDI device that allows users to record music, which can be stored in the computer.

INPUT FOR PDAs, TABLET PCs, AND SMART PHONES

Mobile devices, such as the PDA and smart phone, and mobile computers, such as the Tablet PC, offer convenience for the mobile user. A variety of input alternatives are available for these devices and computers.

PDAs

A user inputs data into a PDA in many ways (Figure 5-22). PDAs ship with a basic stylus, which is the primary input device.

Users often purchase a more elaborate stylus that has a ballpoint pen at one end and a stylus at the other. With the stylus, you enter data in two ways: using an on-screen keyboard or using handwriting recognition software. PDAs typically use their own handwriting recognition software. For example, palmOne PDAs include Graffiti that allows users to write characters on the device's screen. For example, drawing a straight vertical line in a downward motion displays the number 1 on the PDA. With a specialized pen and data reader, you can transfer notes as you write them on a pad of paper.

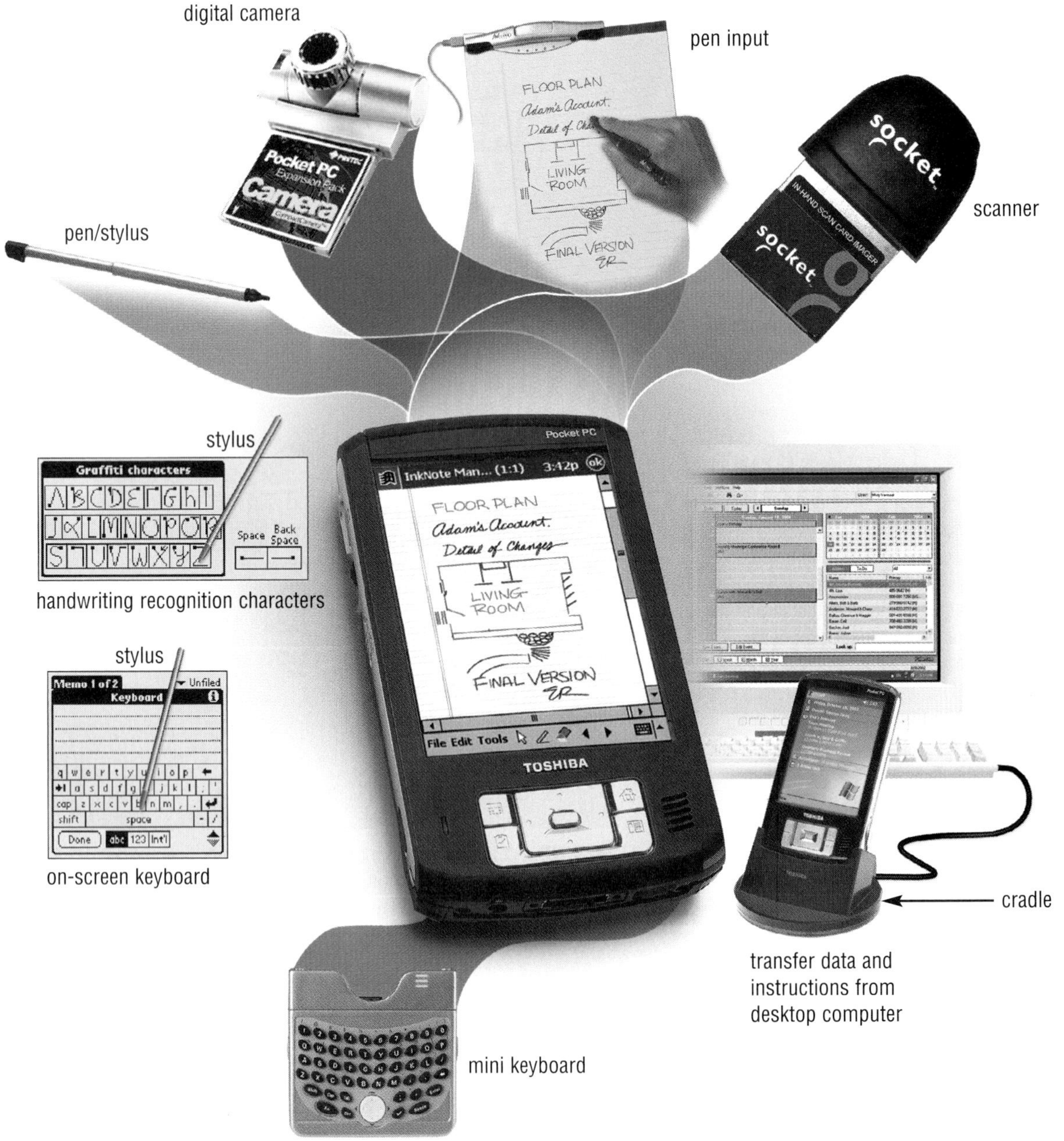

FIGURE 5-22 Users input data into a PDA using a variety of techniques.

For users who prefer typing to handwriting, some PDAs have a built-in keyboard. For PDAs without a keyboard, users can purchase a mini keyboard that snaps onto the bottom of the device. Other users type onto a desktop computer or notebook computer keyboard and transfer the data into the PDA. As an alternative to typing, some PDAs support voice input that allows users to speak data and instructions into the device. To take photographs and view them on a PDA, simply attach a digital camera directly to the PDA. Various types of scanners enable mobile users to use their PDA to scan small documents, such as business cards and product labels.

Instead of using a mini keyboard, some users prefer to enter data into a PDA using a portable keyboard. A *portable keyboard* is a full-sized keyboard you conveniently attach to and remove from a PDA. Figure 5-23 shows a pocket-sized portable keyboard that unfolds into a full-sized keyboard.

For information about software for PDAs, read the PDA feature that follows this chapter.

Tablet PCs

The primary input device for a Tablet PC is a digital pen, which allows users to write on the device's screen. A Tablet PC's handwriting recognition software works similarly to that of a PDA. The computer converts the handwriting into characters it can process.

Both the slate and convertible designs of Tablet PC provide a means for keyboard input for those users who prefer typing to handwriting. You can attach a removable keyboard to the slate Tablet PC. The convertible Tablet PC has an attached keyboard that can be rotated 180 degrees so the computer resembles a notebook computer.

To access peripherals at their home or office, users have the option to slide their Tablet PC into a docking station. A *docking station*, which is an external device that attaches to a mobile computer, contains a power connection, and provides connections to peripherals. In the docking station, Tablet PC users can work with a full-sized keyboard, mouse, and other desktop peripherals (Figure 5-24). The design of docking stations varies, depending on the type of mobile computer or the device to which they attach.

FIGURE 5-23 This convenient portable keyboard unfolds into a full-sized keyboard, to which you can attach a PDA.

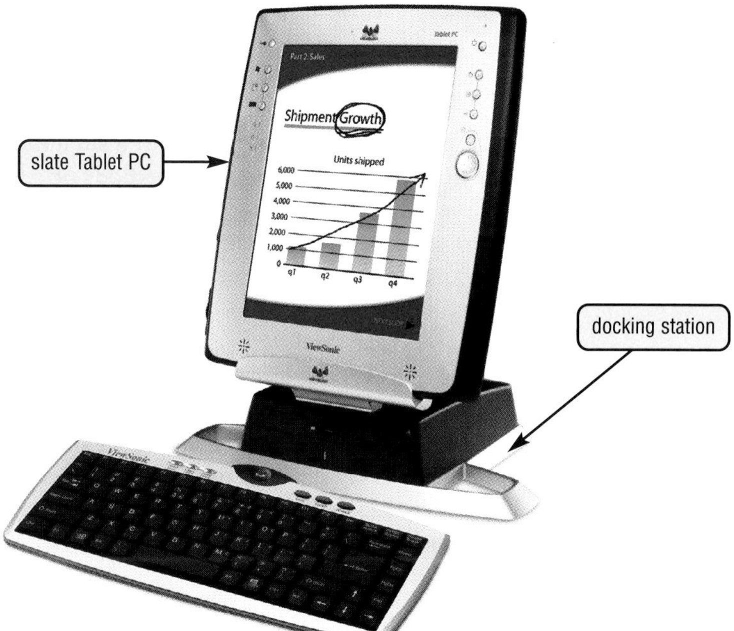

FIGURE 5-24 To use a slate Tablet PC while working at a desk, simply insert the Tablet PC into a docking station. Devices such as a keyboard and mouse attach to the docking station.

Read Issues 5-3 for a discussion related to Tablet PCs.

ISSUE 5-3

Can I Borrow Your Notes?

Bill Gates, cofounder of Microsoft, believes one of the next great innovations in the classroom will be the Tablet PC. The Tablet PC is a compact notebook computer that, according to Gates, combines "the simplicity of paper with the power of the PC." With a digital pen, students use the Tablet PC to run Windows-based applications. They also write notes on the Tablet PC screen and then sort, search, and save those notes and even convert them into typed documents. With wireless connectivity, students use a Tablet PC to access Web pages or communicate with classmates. The Tablet PC could enhance a classroom experience, but some fear that for most students it would be more of a distraction than a learning aid. How would the Tablet PC benefit students? What might be disadvantages of the Tablet PC in the classroom? With the benefits and disadvantages in mind, would you be better off in the classroom with a Tablet PC or with pencil and paper? Why?

For more information about the Tablet PC, visit the Discovering Computers 2005 Issues Web page (**scsite.com/dc2005/issues**). Click Issue #3 below Chapter 5.

Smart Phones

Voice is the traditional method of input for smart phones. That is, a user speaks into the phone. Today, however, short message service, multimedia message service, and instant messaging have become popular methods of inputting data.

Instead of calling someone's smart phone or cellular telephone, users can input and send text messages using *SMS* (*short message service*) also called *text messaging*. To send an SMS message, users type text messages, typically up to 160 characters, by pressing buttons on the telephone's keypad. As with chat rooms and instant messaging, SMS uses abbreviations and emoticons to minimize the amount of typing required. For example, instead of typing the text, I have just graduated, a user can type the emoticon, L:-), where the L stands for the tassel on the graduation cap.

Users can send graphics, pictures, video clips, and sound files, as well as short text messages, with MMS (*multimedia message service*), also called *multimedia messaging*, to another smart phone with MMS. Many smart phones today have a built-in or attachable camera so users easily can take pictures and videos and even incorporate short voice recordings in their multimedia messages (Figure 5-25).

Some wireless Internet services providers (WISPs) partner with instant messaging (IM) services so you can use your smart phone to communicate with other smart phone or computer users of the same IM service. For example, with AT&T Wireless service, users can send and receive instant messages with AOL Instant Messenger or Yahoo! Messenger.

FIGURE 5-25 Many smart phones include a digital camera so users can send pictures and videos to other smart phones.

FAQ 5-5

Can a mobile computer or device get a virus?

Yes. Mobile computers and devices can get a virus from downloading a Web page. A virus can transfer from a desktop computer to a mobile device when users connect the two together to synchronize data. Viruses also can transmit via wireless data transfer when two wireless devices communicate with one another, such as when receiving an SMS text message.

For more information about viruses and mobile devices, visit the Discovering Computers 2005 FAQ Web page (**scsite.com/dc2005/faq**). Click Viruses and Mobile Devices below Chapter 5.

DIGITAL CAMERAS

A **digital camera** allows users to take pictures and store the photographed images digitally, instead of on traditional film (Figure 5-26). While many digitial cameras look like a traditional camera, some models attach to or are built into PDAs and smart phones. Mobile users such as real estate agents, insurance agents, general contractors, and photojournalists use digital cameras so they immediately can view photographed images right on the camera. Home and business users have digital cameras to save the expense of film developing, duplication, and postage.

With photo editing software, users add dazzling special effects to digital images. Many users share their digital images with family, friends, coworkers, and clients by posting the photographs on a Web site, e-mailing them, or simply printing copies of the images from a home or office printer.

Digital cameras use a variety of miniature mobile storage media to store images, including a floppy disk, flash memory card, memory stick, and mini-disc. Chapter 7 discusses these and other storage media in depth. Generally, higher-capacity storage devices can hold more pictures.

Digital cameras typically allow users to review, and sometimes edit, images while they are in the camera. Some digital cameras connect directly to or communicate directly with a printer or television. This feature eliminates the need to copy images to a computer's hard disk. Instead, users print or view images entirely from the camera.

Often users prefer to *download*, or transfer a copy of, the images from the digital camera to the computer's hard disk. With some digital cameras, images download through a cable that connects between the digital camera and a USB port or a FireWire port on the system unit. For cameras that store images on miniature mobile storage media, simply insert the media into a reading/writing device that communicates wirelessly or attaches to a parallel port or USB port on the system unit. Copying images from the miniature media to the computer's hard disk is just like copying files from any other disk drive. Some cameras store images on a floppy disk. In this case, insert the floppy disk into the computer's disk drive and then copy the pictures to the computer's hard disk.

When you copy images to the hard disk in a computer, the images are available for editing with photo editing software, printing, faxing, sending via e-mail, including in another document, or posting to a Web site or photo community for everyone to see. Many users add pictures to greeting cards, a computerized photo album, a family newsletter, certificates, and awards.

FIGURE 5-26 With a digital camera, users can view photographed images immediately through a small screen on the camera to see if the picture is worth keeping.

Figure 5-27 illustrates how one type of digital camera transforms the captured image into a screen display and printout.

The three basic types of digital cameras are studio cameras, field cameras, and point-and-shoot cameras. The most expensive and highest quality of the three is a *studio camera*, which is a stationary camera used for professional studio work. Often used by photojournalists, a *field camera* is a portable camera that has many lenses and other attachments. As with the studio camera, a field camera can be quite expensive. A *point-and-shoot camera* is much more affordable and lightweight and provides acceptable quality photographic images for the home or small business user.

A point-and-shoot camera often features flash, zoom, automatic focus, and special effects. Some allow users to record short audio narrations for photographed images. Others even record short video clips in addition to still images. Point-and-shoot digital cameras

FIGURE 5-27 HOW A DIGITAL CAMERA MIGHT WORK

often have a built-in TV out port, allowing users to display photographed images or play recorded video clips directly on a television. Read Apply It 5-2 for more information.

For additional information about digital cameras, read the Digital Imaging and Video Technology feature that follows Chapter 6.

Digital Camera Quality

One factor that affects the quality of a digital camera is its resolution. **Resolution** describes the sharpness and clearness of an image. A digital camera's resolution is defined in pixels. A *pixel* (short for picture element) is the smallest element in an electronic image (Figure 5-28). The greater the number of pixels the camera uses to capture an image, the better the quality of the image. Thus, the higher the resolution, the better the image quality, but the more expensive the camera.

FIGURE 5-28 A pixel is a single point in an electronic image.

Digital camera resolutions range from approximately 1 million to more than 6 million pixels (*MP*). A camera with a 4.2-megapixel (4,200,000 pixels) resolution will provide a better quality than one with a 2.2-megapixel resolution. As a rule, a 1-megapixel camera is fine for screen displays such as photo communities, Web pages, and e-mail attachments. These low-end cameras cost less than $200. Users planning to print photographs larger than 5 x 7 inches should have at least a 2-megapixel camera. For images as good as film-based cameras, use a 3-megapixel or higher camera. High-end point-and-shoot cameras cost less than $1,000.

Manufacturers often use pixels per inch to represent a digital camera's resolution. *Pixels per inch* (*ppi*) is the number of pixels in one inch of screen display. For example, a 1600 x 1200 (pronounced 1600 by 1200) ppi camera has 1,600 pixels per vertical inch and 1,200 pixels per horizontal inch. Multiplying these two numbers together will give you an approximate number of megapixels. For example, 1600 times 1200 equals approximately 2 million, or 2 megapixels. If just one number is stated, such as 1200 ppi, then both the vertical and horizontal numbers are the same.

Digital cameras for the consumer range from 640 x 480 ppi to 2280 x 1720 ppi. Some digital cameras provide a means to adjust the ppi to the desired resolution. With a lower ppi, you can capture and store more images in the camera. For example, a camera set at 800 x 600 ppi might capture and store 61 images, if it has sufficient storage capacity. The number of

APPLY IT 5-2

Share Digital Photos with Friends and Family

If you have not made the switch to digital photography, it is likely you might think that the cameras are complicated and expensive. After all, the mere thought of setting shutter speeds and making aperture adjustments can be overwhelming. As digital cameras have become easier to use and less costly, however, more people are making the leap to this technology.

Taking photos with digital cameras now can be easy and fun. With prices for feature-rich cameras less than $200 and with many automatic settings, nearly everyone can capture the moment almost instantly after unpacking the camera.

When choosing a camera, consider the capacity of its storage media, resolution, and price. A higher resolution increases price, so choose the model that fits your budget and lifestyle. In addition, consider the type of lens. For example, if you take close-up shots of flowers, you will want a camera with macro capability or a macro lens. By contrast, if you take pictures of birds roosting in tall trees, you will need a camera with zoom capability or a zoom lens.

Sharing these photos with friends and family can be accomplished easily with features found on some cameras. With the push of a button, these cameras send the images to printers or to designated e-mail recipients when the camera connects to a computer or docking station. These individuals should use antivirus programs to safeguard their computers from viruses that may be imbedded in these picture files.

For more information about digital cameras, visit the Discovering Computers 2005 Apply It Web page (**scsite.com/dc2005/apply**). Click Apply It #2 below Chapter 5.

images may reduce to 24 on the same camera set at 1600 × 1200 ppi, because each image consumes more storage space.

The actual photographed resolution is known as the *optical resolution*. Some manufacturers state *enhanced resolution*, instead of, or in addition to, optical resolution. Optical resolution is different from enhanced resolution. The enhanced resolution usually is higher because it uses a special formula to add pixels between those generated by the optical resolution. Be aware that some manufacturers compute a digital camera's megapixels from the enhanced resolution, instead of optical resolution.

Another measure of a digital camera's quality is the number of bits it stores in a pixel. Each pixel consists of 1 or more bits of data. The more bits used to represent a pixel, the more colors and shades of gray that can be represented. One bit per pixel is enough for simple one-color images. For multiple colors and shades of gray, each pixel requires more than 1 bit of data. A point-and-shoot camera should be at least 24 bit.

FAQ 5-6

What is dpi?

Some advertisements incorrectly use dpi to mean the same as ppi. The acronym *dpi*, which stands for *dots per inch*, is a measure of a print resolution. For screen resolution, the proper measurement term is ppi (pixels per inch).

For more information about resolution, visit the Discovering Computers 2005 FAQ Web page (**scsite.com/dc2005/faq**). Click Resolution below Chapter 5.

VIDEO INPUT

Video input is the process of capturing full-motion images into a computer and storing them on a storage medium such as a hard disk or DVD. Some video devices use analog video signals. Computers, by contrast, use digital signals. To input video from an analog device, the analog signal must be converted to a digital signal. To do this, plug a video camera, VCR, or other analog video device into a video capture port on the system unit. One type of adapter card that has a video capture port is a **video capture card**, which converts an analog video signal into a digital signal that a computer can use. (Most new computers are not equipped with a video capture card because not all users have the need for this type of adapter card.)

The new generation of video camera (camcorder), called a **digital video (DV) camera**, records video as digital signals instead of analog signals. Many DV cameras can capture still frames, as well as motion. To transfer recorded images to a hard disk or CD or DVD, users connect DV cameras directly to a USB port or a FireWire port on the system unit. Thus, the computer does not need a video capture card. Simply connect the video device to the computer and begin transferring images. After saving the video on a storage medium, such as a hard disk or DVD, you can play it or edit it using video editing software on a computer (Figure 5-29).

FIGURE 5-29 This home user transfers video to her computer, where she can use video editing software to edit the video.

PC Video Cameras

A **PC video camera**, or **PC camera**, is a type of digital video camera that enables a home or small business user to capture video and still images, send e-mail messages with video attachments, add live images to instant messages, broadcast live images over the Internet, and make video telephone calls. During a **video telephone call**, both parties see each other as they talk over the Internet (Figure 5-30). The cost of PC video cameras usually is less than $100.

Attached to the computer's USB port or FireWire port, a PC video camera usually sits on top of your monitor. For more flexibility, some PC video cameras are portable. That is, you can detach them from the computer and use them anywhere.

FIGURE 5-30 Using a PC video camera, these business associates communicate via video telephone calls on the Internet.

Web Cams

A **Web cam** is a video camera that displays its output on a Web page. A Web cam attracts Web site visitors by showing images that change regularly. Home or small business users might use Web cams to show a work in progress, weather and traffic information, employees at work, photographs of a vacation, and countless other images.

Some Web sites have live Web cams that display still pictures and update the displayed image at a specified time or time intervals, such as 15 seconds. Another type of Web cam, called a *streaming cam*, has the illusion of moving images because it sends a continual stream of still images.

Video Conferencing

A **video conference** is a meeting between two or more geographically separated people who use a network or the Internet to transmit audio and video data (Figure 5-31). To participate in a video conference, you need video conferencing software along with a microphone, speakers, and a video camera attached to a computer.

As you speak, members of the meeting hear your voice on their speakers. Any image in front of the video camera, such as a person's face, appears in a window on each participant's screen. A *whiteboard* is another window on the screen that displays notes and drawings simultaneously on all participants' screens. This window provides multiple users with an area on which they can write or draw.

Users with higher-speed broadband Internet connections experience much better video performance. As the costs of video conferencing hardware and software decrease, increasingly more business meetings, corporate training, and educational classes will be conducted as video conferences.

FIGURE 5-31 To save on travel expenses, many large businesses are turning to video conferencing.

QUIZ YOURSELF 5-2

To check your knowledge of voice input; input for PDAs, Tablet PCs, and smart phones; digital cameras; and video input; visit the Discovering Computers 2005 Quiz Yourself Web page (**scsite.com/dc2005/quiz**). Click Objectives 5 – 8 below Chapter 5.

WEB LINK 5-7

PC Video Cameras

Visit the Discovering Computers 2005 WEB LINK page (**scsite.com/dc2005/weblink**). Click PC Video Cameras below Chapter 5.

SCANNERS AND READING DEVICES

Some input devices save users time by eliminating manual data entry. With these devices, users do not type, speak, or write into the computer. Instead, these devices capture data from a *source document*, which is the original form of the data. Examples of source documents are time cards, order forms, invoices, paychecks, advertisements, brochures, photographs, inventory tags, or any other document that contains data to be processed.

Devices that can capture data directly from a source document include optical scanners, optical readers, bar code readers, and magnetic-ink character recognition readers. The following pages discuss each of these devices.

Optical Scanner

An *optical scanner*, usually called a **scanner**, is a light-sensing input device that reads printed text and graphics and then translates the results into a form the computer can process. Four types of scanners are flatbed, pen, sheet-fed, and drum (Figure 5-32).

TYPES OF SCANNERS

Scanner	Method of Scanning and Use	Scannable Items
Flatbed 	• Similar to a copy machine • Scanning mechanism passes under the item to be scanned, which is placed on a glass surface	• Single-sheet documents • Bound material • Photographs • Some models include trays for slides, transparencies, and negatives
Pen or Handheld 	• Move pen over text to be scanned, then transfer data to computer • Ideal for mobile users, students, and researchers • Some connect to a PDA	• Any printed text
Sheet-fed 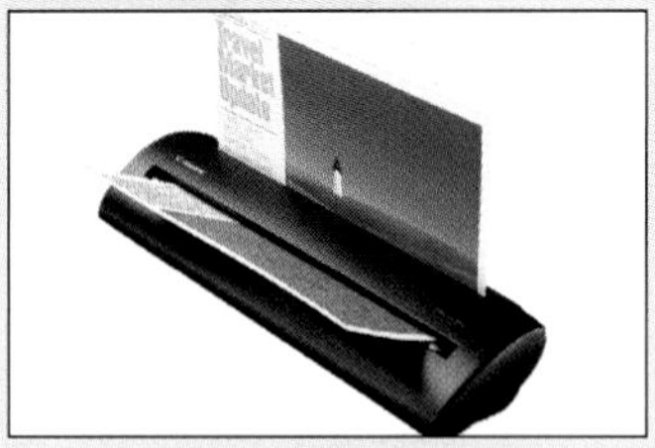	• Item to be scanned is pulled into a stationary scanning mechanism • Smaller than a flatbed scanner • Some models designed specifically for photographs are called a *photo scanner*	• Single-sheet documents • Photographs • Slides (with an adapter) • Negatives
Drum 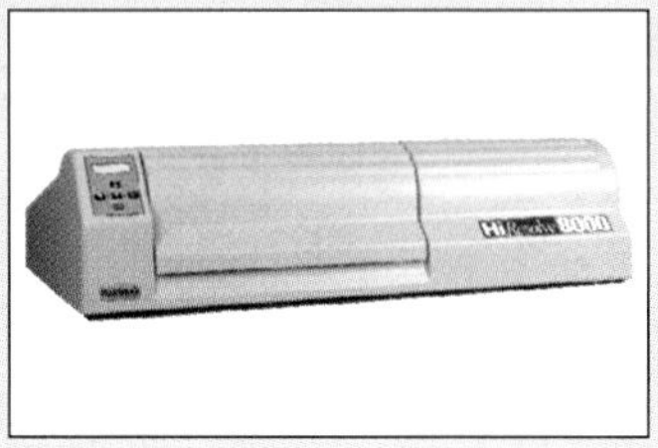	• Item to be scanned rotates around stationary scanning mechanism • Very expensive • Used in publishing industry	• Single-sheet documents • Photographs • Slides • Negatives

FIGURE 5-32 This table describes the various types of scanners.

A **flatbed scanner** works in a manner similar to a copy machine except it creates a file of the document in memory instead of a paper copy (Figure 5-33). For example, you scan a picture and then include the picture when creating a brochure. A user can display a scanned object on the screen, store it on a storage medium, print it, fax it, attach it to an e-mail message, include it in another document, or post it to a Web site or photo community for everyone to see.

FIGURE 5-33 HOW A FLATBED SCANNER WORKS

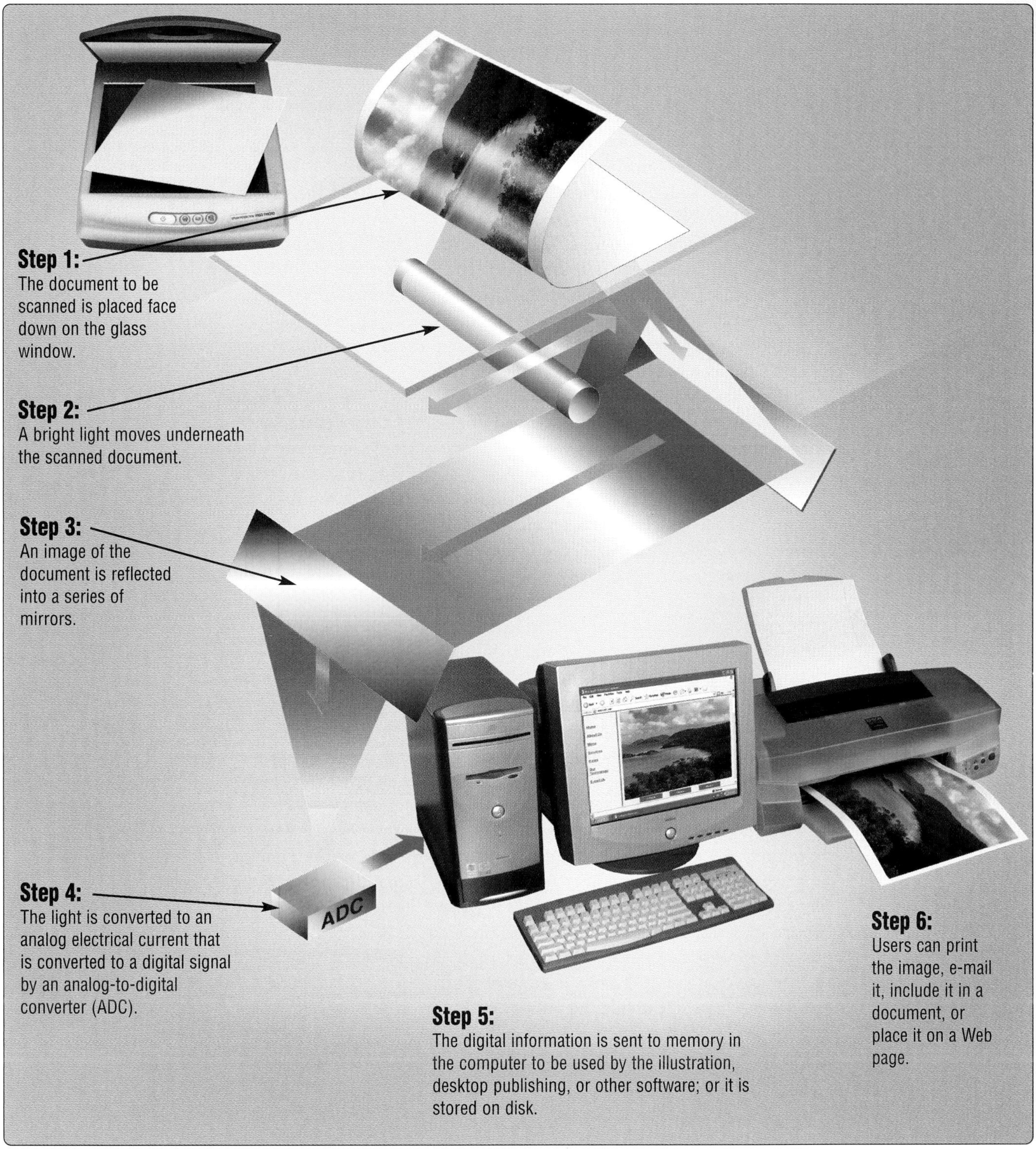

WEB LINK 5-8

Scanners

Visit the Discovering Computers 2005 WEB LINK page (**scsite.com/dc2005/weblink**). Click Scanners below Chapter 5.

As with a digital camera, the quality of a scanner is measured by the number of bits it stores in a pixel and the number of pixels per inch, or resolution. The higher each number, the better the quality, but the more expensive the scanner. Most of today's affordable color desktop scanners for the home or small business range from 30 to 48 bit and have an optical resolution ranging from 600 to 4800 ppi. Commercial scanners designed for power users range from 4800 to 14,000 ppi.

Many scanners include *OCR (optical character recognition) software*, which can read and convert text documents to electronic files. Suppose users need to modify a business report but do not have the original word processing file. If they scan the document with a flatbed scanner, they would not be able to edit the report. The scanner, which does not differentiate between text and graphics, saves the report as an image. OCR software converts a scanned image into a text file that can be edited, for example, with a word processing program. OCR software typically places any graphics in the scanned image into a separate file.

Current OCR software has a very high success rate and usually can identify more than 99 percent of scanned material. OCR software also marks text it cannot read, allowing users to make corrections easily.

Businesses often use scanners for *image processing*, which consists of capturing, storing, analyzing, displaying, printing, and manipulating images. Image processing allows users to convert paper documents such as reports, memos, and procedure manuals into electronic images. Users distribute and publish these electronic documents on networks and the Internet.

Business users typically store and index electronic documents with an image processing system. An *image processing system* is similar to an electronic filing cabinet that provides access to exact reproductions of the original documents. Local governments, for example, use image processing systems to store property deeds and titles to provide the public and professionals, such as lawyers and loan officers, quick access to electronic documents.

FAQ 5-7

How can I improve the quality of scanned documents?

Place a blank sheet of paper behind translucent papers, newspapers, and other see-through types of paper. If the original image is crooked, draw a line on the back at the bottom of the image. Use that mark to align the original on the scanner. Using photo editing software, editing the scanned image is easy.

For more information about scanning, visit the Discovering Computers 2005 FAQ Web page (**scsite.com/dc2005/faq**). Click Scanning below Chapter 5.

Optical Readers

An *optical reader* is a device that uses a light source to read characters, marks, and codes and then converts them into digital data that a computer can process. Two technologies used by optical readers are optical character recognition and optical mark recognition.

OPTICAL CHARACTER RECOGNITION

Optical character recognition (**OCR**) is a technology that involves reading typewritten, computer-printed, or hand-printed characters from ordinary documents and translating the images into a form that the computer can process. Most **OCR devices** include a small optical scanner for reading characters and sophisticated software to analyze what is read.

OCR devices range from large machines that can read thousands of documents per minute to handheld wands that read one document at a time. OCR devices read printed characters in an OCR font. A widely used OCR font is called OCR-A (Figure 5-34). During the scan of a document, an OCR device determines the shapes of characters by detecting patterns of light and dark. OCR software then compares these shapes with predefined shapes stored in memory and converts the shapes into characters the computer can process.

ABCDEFGHIJKLM
NOPQRSTUVWXYZ
1234567890-=■;',./

FIGURE 5-34 A portion of the characters in the OCR-A font. Notice how characters such as the number 0 and the letter O are shaped differently so the reading device easily can distinguish between them.

Many companies use OCR characters on turnaround documents. A **turnaround document** is a document that you return (turn around) to the company that creates and sends it. For example, when consumers receive a bill, they tear off a portion of the bill and send it back to the company with their payment (Figure 5-35). The portion of the bill they return usually has their payment amount, account number, and other information printed in OCR characters.

OPTICAL MARK RECOGNITION **Optical mark recognition (OMR)** is a technology that reads hand-drawn marks such as small circles or rectangles. A person places these marks on a form, such as a test, survey, or questionnaire answer sheet. With a test, the OMR device first scans the answer key sheet to record correct answers based on patterns of light. The OMR device then scans the remaining documents and matches their patterns of light against the answer key sheet.

FIGURE 5-35 OCR characters frequently are used with turnaround documents. With this bill, you tear off the bottom portion and return it with a payment.

Bar Code Reader

A **bar code reader**, also called a *bar code scanner*, is an optical reader that uses laser beams to read bar codes (Figure 5-36). A **bar code** is an identification code that consists of a set of vertical lines and spaces of different widths. The bar code represents data that identifies the manufacturer and the item.

Manufacturers print a bar code either on a product's package or on a label that is affixed to a product. A bar code reader reads a bar code by using light patterns that pass through the bar code lines.

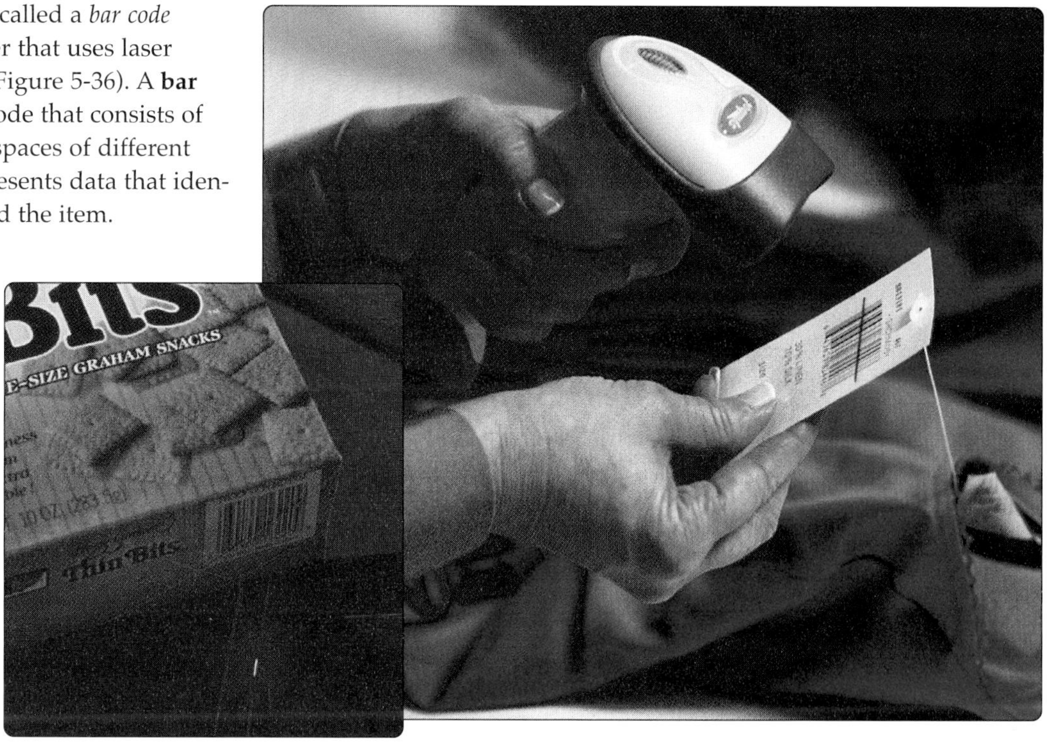

FIGURE 5-36 A bar code reader uses laser beams to read bar codes on products such as clothing, groceries, pharmacy supplies, vehicles, mail, books, and packages.

A variety of products such as groceries, pharmacy supplies, vehicles, mail, magazines, and books have bar codes. Each industry uses its own type of bar code. Retail and grocery stores use the *UPC* (*Universal Product Code*) bar code (Figure 5-37). Read Issue 5-4 for a related discussion. The United States Postal Service (USPS) uses a POSTNET bar code. The table in Figure 5-38 summarizes some of the more widely used bar codes.

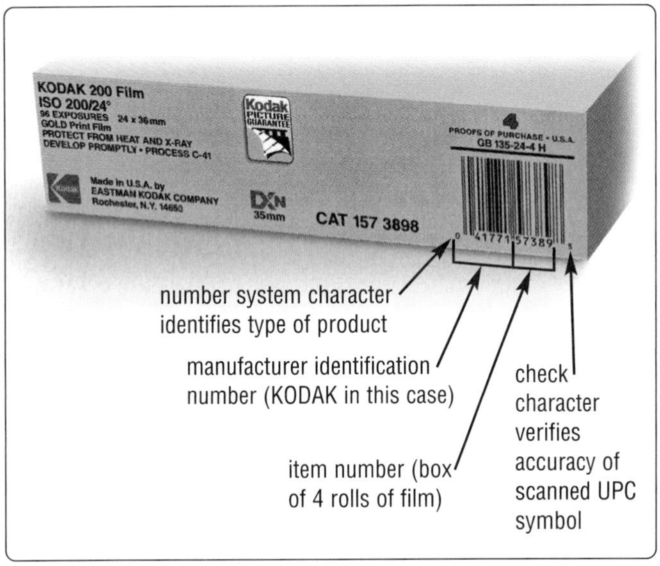

FIGURE 5-37 This UPC identifies a box of Kodak film.

Bar Code Name/Sample	Primary Market
Codabar A 1 2 3 4 5 6 7 8 9 0 1 2 A	Libraries, blood banks, and air parcel carriers
Code 39 C O D E 3 9	Nonretail applications such as manufacturing, inventory, military, and health applications requiring numbers and letters in the bar code
EAN – European Article Numbering 1 234567 890128	Similar to UPC, only used internationally except the U.S. and Canada; variation of EAN is used for bar codes on books
Interleaved 2 of 5 1 2 3 4 5 6 7 8 9 0 1 2	Nonretail applications, such as game tickets, requiring only numbers in the bar code
POSTNET – Postal Numeric Encoding Technique	United States Postal Service (USPS), used to represent a postal code or delivery point code
UPC – Universal Product Code 0 12345 67890 5	Supermarkets, convenience stores, and specialty stores use to identify manufacturers and products

FIGURE 5-38 Some of the more widely used types of bar codes.

ISSUE 5-4

What Is the Price of That Item?

Have you ever taken an item to a store's checkout counter and discovered that the price displayed when the item's bar code was scanned was different from the price shown on a shelf tag, sign, or advertisement? If you have, you are not alone. A government survey found that eight percent of the time, an item's scanned price is different from the price presented elsewhere. When an item is scanned at a store's checkout counter, a computer finds the item's price in the store's database. Store owners claim that discrepancies between the scanned price and a listed price are the result of human error, either failure to update the store's price database or incorrect shelf tags, signs, or advertisements. Yet, some consumer advocates insist that the discrepancy is intentional. They accuse stores of *scanner fraud*, insisting that some stores advertise one price and then charge another, hoping consumers will not recognize the difference. Who do you think is responsible for differences between scanned prices and posted costs? Why? Should stores be responsible for pricing errors? Why or why not?

For more information about bar code readers, visit the Discovering Computers 2005 Issues Web page (**scsite.com/dc2005/issues**). Click Issue #4 below Chapter 5.

MICR Reader

MICR (*magnetic-ink character recognition*) devices read text printed with magnetized ink. An **MICR reader** converts MICR characters into a form the computer can process. The banking industry almost exclusively uses MICR for check processing. Each check in your checkbook has precoded MICR characters beginning at the lower-left edge (Figure 5-39). The MICR characters represent the bank number, the customer account number, and the check number. These numbers may appear in a different order than the ones shown in the sample in Figure 5-39.

When a bank receives a check for payment, it uses an MICR inscriber to print the amount of the check in MICR characters in the lower-right corner. The check then is sorted or routed to the customer's bank, along with thousands of others. Each check is inserted into an MICR reader, which sends the check information — including the amount of the check — to a computer for processing. When you balance your checkbook, verify that the amount printed in the lower-right corner is the same as the amount written on the check; otherwise, your statement will not balance.

The banking industry has established an international standard not only for bank numbers, but also for the font of the MICR characters. This standardization makes it possible for people to write checks in other countries.

Data Collection Devices

Instead of reading or scanning data from a source document, a *data collection device* obtains data directly at the location where the transaction or event takes place. For example, employees use bar code readers, PDAs, handheld computers, or other mobile devices to collect data wirelessly (Figure 5-40). These types of data collection devices are used in factories, warehouses, the outdoors, or other locations where heat, humidity, and cleanliness are not easy to control.

Data collection devices and many mobile computers and devices such as PDAs and smart phones have the capability of wirelessly transmitting data over a network or the Internet. Increasingly more users today send data wirelessly to central office computers using these devices.

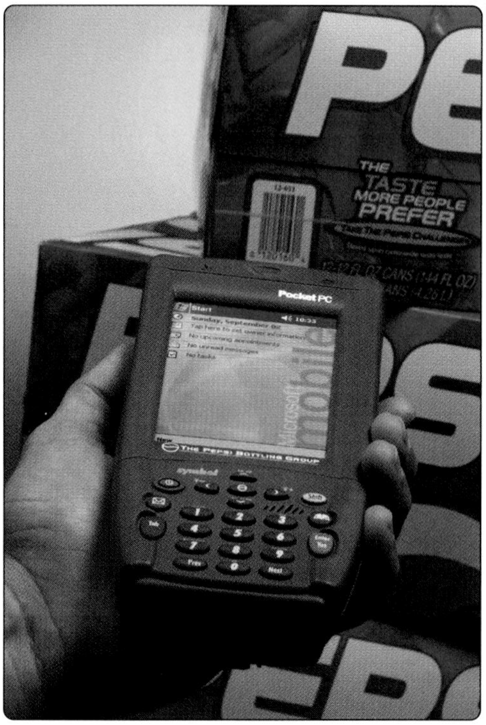

FIGURE 5-40 Sales representatives use this rugged mobile device to take on-site orders from customers. The device, which is a combination PDA/bar code reader, wirelessly transmits the orders to the company's order and routing system. Upon delivery to the customer, the route driver uses the mobile device to record deliveries and print customer receipts wirelessly. Then, the device wirelessly transmits route information and updates inventory in the company's system.

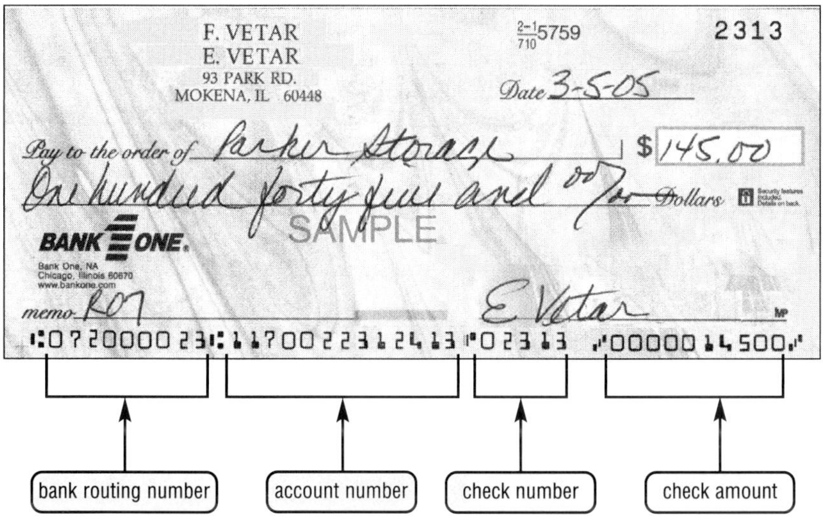

FIGURE 5-39 The MICR characters preprinted on the check represent the bank routing number, the customer account number, and the check number. The amount of the check in the lower-right corner is added after the check is cashed.

TERMINALS

A *terminal* consists of a keyboard, a monitor, a video card, and memory. Often, these components are housed in a single unit.

Terminals fall into three basic categories: dumb terminals, smart terminals, and special-purpose terminals. A *dumb terminal* has no processing power, thus, cannot function as an independent device. Users enter data into a dumb terminal and then transmit the data to a host computer over a network. The host computer processes the data and then, if necessary, sends information back to the dumb terminal. The host computer usually is a midrange server or mainframe. A *smart terminal* has a processor, giving it the capability of performing some functions independent of the host computer. In recent years, personal computers have replaced most smart terminals.

Special-purpose terminals perform specific tasks and contain features uniquely designed for use in a particular industry. Three special-purpose terminals are point-of-sale (POS) terminals, automated teller machines, and smart displays. The following sections discuss these types of terminals.

Point-of-Sale Terminals

The location in a retail or grocery store where a consumer pays for goods or services is the **point of sale** (**POS**). Most retail stores use a **POS terminal** to record purchases, process credit or debit cards, and update inventory.

In a grocery store, the POS terminal is a combination of an electronic cash register, bar code reader, and printer. When the checkout clerk scans the bar code on the food product, the computer uses the manufacturer and item numbers to look up the price of the item and the complete product name in a database. Then, the price of the item in the database shows on the display device, the name of the item and its price print on a receipt, and the item being sold is recorded so the inventory can be updated. Thus, the output from a POS terminal serves as input to other computers to maintain sales records, update inventory, verify credit, and perform other activities associated with the sales transactions that are critical to running the business. Some POS terminals are Web-enabled, allowing them to update inventory at geographically dispersed locations.

Many POS terminals handle credit card or debit card payments. Consumers simply swipe a credit or debit card through a **card reader**, which reads the customer's personal data from the magnetic strip on the card. Once the transaction is approved, the terminal prints a receipt for the customer.

A self-service POS terminal allows consumers to perform all checkout related activities (Figure 5-41). That is, they scan the items, bag the items, and pay for the items themselves. Consumers with small orders find the new self-service POS terminals very convenient because they often eliminate the hassle of waiting in long lines.

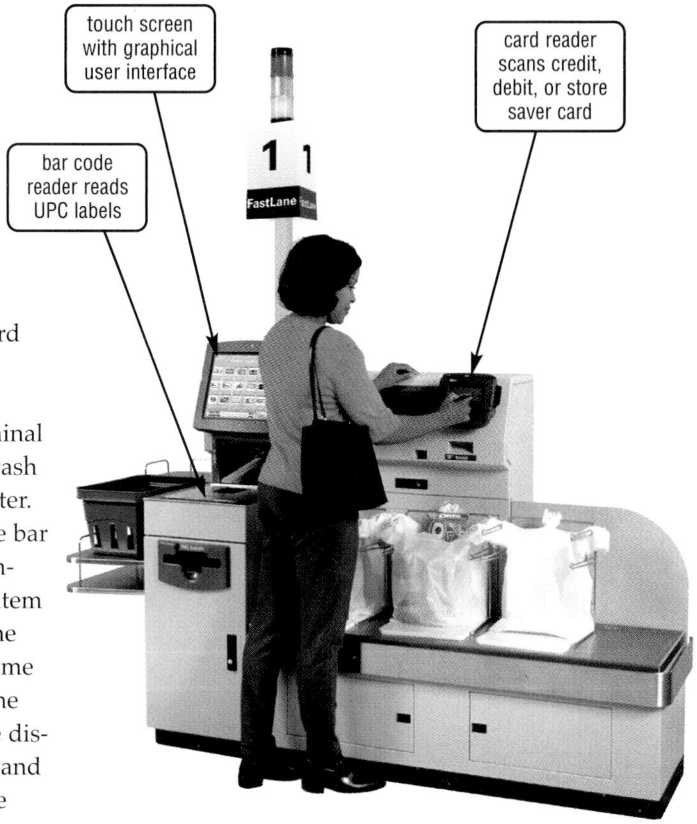

FIGURE 5-41 Some grocery stores offer self-serve checkouts, where the consumers themselves use the POS terminals to scan purchases, scan their store saver card and coupons, and then pay for the goods. This POS terminal prints a receipt for the customer.

Automated Teller Machines

An **automated teller machine (ATM)** is a self-service banking machine that connects to a host computer through a network (Figure 5-42). Banks place ATMs in convenient locations, including grocery stores, convenience stores, retail outlets, shopping malls, and gas stations, so customers conveniently can access their bank accounts.

Using an ATM, people withdraw cash, deposit money, transfer funds, or inquire about an account balance. Some ATMs have a touch screen; others have special buttons or keypads for input. To access a bank account, you insert a plastic bankcard into the ATM's card reader, which reads personal data on the bankcard's magnetic strip. The ATM asks you to enter a password, called a *personal identification number (PIN)*, which verifies that you are the holder of the bankcard. When your transaction is complete, the ATM prints a receipt for your records.

FIGURE 5-42 An ATM is a self-service banking terminal that allows customers to access their bank accounts.

Smart Displays

A **smart display** is a thin desktop monitor that detaches from the computer to function as a portable wireless touch screen, which can access the computer remotely (Figure 5-43). The intent of the smart display is to provide home users with the convenience of accessing their personal computers from anywhere in the house, using the portable monitor. For example, instead of writing down a home inventory list and then sitting down to enter the list into the computer, the smart display allows the home user to detach the monitor and walk from room to room — entering the items as he or she moves through the house.

As a user enters data into the smart display, it communicates with the computer through a wireless network. That is, from the wireless smart display, a user can access programs or data on his or her computer, browse the Web, send e-mail, and perform other functions, just as if he or she is sitting at the computer.

At the computer, a user interacts with the smart display using a standard keyboard, mouse, or any other personal computer input device. When detached from the computer, a user enters data and instructions into the smart display with a stylus or through an on-screen keyboard.

The outward appearance of a smart display resembles that of a Tablet PC. The cost of a smart display is about one-third that of the Tablet PC.

FIGURE 5-43 A smart display allows home users to access their computer wirelessly from anywhere in the house.

BIOMETRIC INPUT

Biometrics is the technology of authenticating a person's identity by verifying a personal characteristic. Biometric devices grant users access to programs, systems, or rooms by analyzing some biometric identifier. A *biometric identifier* is a physical or behavioral characteristic. Examples include fingerprints, hand geometry, facial features, voice, signatures, and eye patterns.

A *biometric device* translates a personal characteristic (the input) into a digital code that is compared with a digital code stored in the computer. If the digital code in the computer does not match the personal characteristic's code, the computer denies access to the individual.

The most widely used biometric device today is a fingerprint scanner. A **fingerprint scanner** captures curves and indentations of a fingerprint. With the cost of fingerprint scanners dropping to less than $100, many believe this technology will become the home user's authentication device for e-commerce transactions. To make a credit-card transaction, the Web site would require you to hold your finger on the scanner. Businesses use fingerprint scanners to authenticate users before they can access a personal computer. Grade schools use fingerprint scanners as an alternative to lunch money. Their account balance adjusts for each lunch purchased. External fingerprint scanners usually plug into a parallel or USB port. To save on desk space, some newer keyboards and notebook computers have a fingerprint scanner built into them (Figure 5-44).

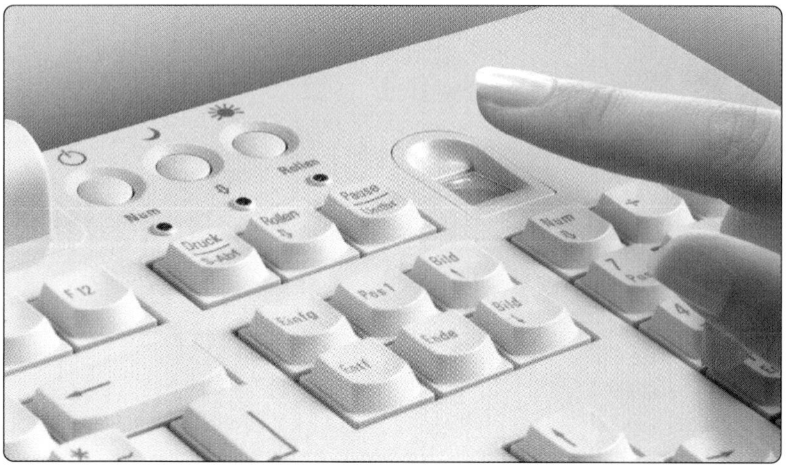

FIGURE 5-44 This user has access to a computer only if her fingerprint matches one in a database.

A *face recognition system* captures a live face image and compares it with a stored image to determine if the person is a legitimate user. Buildings secure rooms with face recognition systems. Law enforcement, surveillance systems, and airports use face recognition to protect the public. Some notebook computers use this security technique to safeguard a computer. The computer will not start unless the user is legitimate. These programs are becoming more sophisticated and can recognize people with or without glasses, makeup, or jewelry, and with new hairstyles. Read Issue 5-5 for a related discussion.

Biometric devices measure the shape and size of a person's hand using a *hand geometry system* (Figure 5-45). Because their cost is more than $1,000, larger companies typically use these systems as time and attendance devices or as security devices. One university cafeteria uses a hand geometry system to verify students when they use their meal card. A day-care center uses a hand geometry system to verify parents who pick up their children.

FIGURE 5-45 A hand geometry system verifies a pilot's identity before he is allowed access to the airplane.

A *voice verification system* compares a person's live speech with their stored voice pattern. Larger organizations sometimes use voice verification systems as time and attendance devices. Many companies also use this technology for access to sensitive files and networks. Some financial services use voice verification systems to secure telephone banking transactions. These systems use speaker-dependent voice recognition software. That is, users train the computer to recognize their inflection patterns.

A *signature verification system* recognizes the shape of your handwritten signature, as well as measuring the pressure exerted and the motion used to write the signature. Signature verification systems use a specialized pen and tablet.

Very high security areas use iris recognition systems. The camera in an *iris recognition system* uses iris recognition technology to read patterns in the iris of the eye (Figure 5-46). These patterns are as unique as a fingerprint. Iris recognition systems are very expensive and are used by government security organizations, the military, and financial institutions that deal with highly sensitive data.

FIGURE 5-46 An iris recognition system.

ISSUE 5-5

Have You Seen This Face Before?

In the wake of terrorist attacks, biometric security has become a prominent part of national security. According to the International Biometric Group, the biometric industry approached $930 million in sales in 2003. Face recognition systems represented 11 percent of the sales. These systems calculate up to 60 facial characteristics, such as the distance between the eyes or cheekbone height, and convert the measurements into a mathematical formula that is checked against a database. At a recent Super Bowl, ticket buyers were scanned as they passed security cameras coming through the turnstiles. Using face recognition technology, the images gathered were compared against a database of known criminals and militants. Advocates of facial scanners say these systems help identify potential terrorists, but opponents maintain that the systems represent an unnecessary invasion of privacy and sometimes produce false identifications. At what events, if any, should facial scanners be used? Why? Are opponents of facial scanners justified in saying that the technology represents an unjustified invasion of privacy? Why or why not?

For more information about facial scanners, visit the Discovering Computers 2005 Issues Web page (**scsite.com/dc2005/issues**). Click Issue #5 below Chapter 5.

Sometimes, fingerprint, iris, and other biometric data are stored on a smart card. A **smart card**, which is comparable in size to a credit card or ATM card, stores the personal data on a thin microprocessor embedded in the card (Figure 5-47). Smart cards add an extra layer of protection. For example, when a user places a smart card through a smart card reader, the computer compares a fingerprint stored on the card with the one read by the fingerprint scanner.

WEB LINK 5-9

Biometric Input

Visit the Discovering Computers 2005 WEB LINK page (**scsite .com/dc2005/weblink**). Click Biometric Input below Chapter 5.

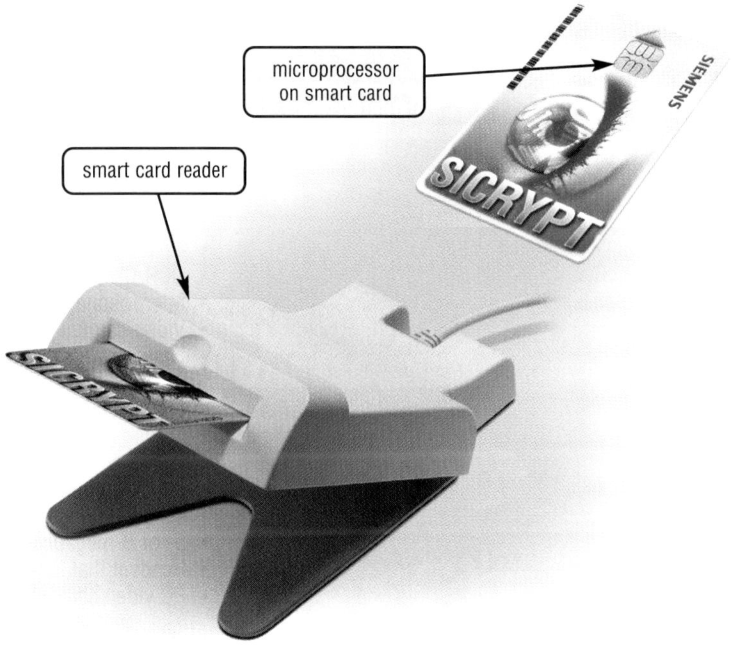

FIGURE 5-47 A smart card reader reads data stored on a smart card's microprocessor.

CHAPTER 5 CHAPTER REVIEW

The Chapter Review section summarizes the concepts presented in this chapter.

WEB INSTRUCTIONS:

To display this page from the Web, start your browser and enter the Web address **scsite.com/dc2005/ch5/review**. Click the links for current and additional information. To listen to an audio version of this Chapter Review, click the Audio button.

1 What Is Input?

Input is any *data* or *instructions* entered into the memory of a computer. An input device is any hardware component that allows users to enter data or instructions.

2 What Are the Characteristics of a Keyboard?

A **keyboard** is an input device that contains keys users press to enter data into a computer. Computer keyboards have a typing area that includes letters of the alphabet, numbers, punctuation marks, and other basic keys. Most keyboards also have *function keys* programmed to issue commands; keys used to move the **insertion point**, usually a blinking vertical bar, on the screen; and toggle keys that switch between two states when pressed.

3 What Are Different Mouse Types and How Do They Work?

A **pointing device** is an input device that allows users to control a small graphical symbol, called a **pointer**, on the computer screen. A **mouse** is a pointing device that fits under the palm of your hand. As you move a mouse, the pointer on the screen also moves. A *mechanical mouse* translates the movement of a ball on its underside into signals the computer can process. An *optical mouse* uses devices that emit and sense light to detect the mouse's movement. A *cordless mouse* transmits data using wireless technology.

4 How Do Pointing Devices Work?

A **trackball** is a stationary device with a ball that you rotate to move the pointer. A **touchpad** is a flat, pressure-sensitive device that you slide your finger across to move the pointer. A pointing stick is a device positioned on the keyboard that you push to move the pointer. A **joystick** is a vertical lever that you move to control a simulated vehicle or player. A **wheel** is a steering-wheel-type device that you turn to simulate driving a vehicle. A **light pen** is a light-sensitive device that you press against or point at the screen to select objects. A **touch screen** is a touch-sensitive display device that you interact with by touching areas of the screen. A **stylus** and a **digital pen** use pressure to write text and draw lines.

Visit **scsite.com/dc2005/quiz** or click the Quiz Yourself button. Click Objectives 1 – 4 below Chapter 5.

5 How Does Voice Recognition Work?

Voice recognition is the computer's capability of distinguishing spoken words. Voice recognition programs recognize a vocabulary of preprogrammed words. Most voice recognition programs are a combination of *speaker-dependent software*, which makes a profile of your voice, and *speaker-independent software*, which has a built-in set of word patterns.

6 What Are Input Devices for PDAs, Tablet PCs, and Smart Phones?

A primary input device for a PDA is a basic stylus. Some PDAs have a built-in keyboard or support voice input. You can attach a mini keyboard or a full-sized *portable keyboard* to a PDA. The primary input device for a Tablet PC is a digital pen, with which you can write on the device's screen. If you slide a Tablet PC into a *docking station*, you can use a full-sized keyboard and mouse. Voice is the traditional input method for smart phones. With *SMS (short message service)*, you can type and send text messages using the telephone's keypad. *MMS* (*multimedia message service*) allows smart phone users to send pictures, video, and sound files.

7 How Does a Digital Camera Work?

A **digital camera** allows users to take pictures and store the photographed images digitally.

CHAPTER REVIEW

When you take a picture, light passes into the camera lens, which focuses the image on a *charge-coupled device (CCD)*. The CCD generates an analog signal that represents the image. An analog-to-digital converter (ADC) converts the analog signal to a digital signal. A *digital signal processor (DSP)* stores the digital image on the camera's storage media. The image is downloaded to a computer's hard disk via cable or copied from the camera's storage media.

8 How Are PC Video Cameras, Web Cams, and Video Conferencing Used?

A **PC video camera** is a digital video camera that enables users to capture video and still images and then send or broadcast the images over the Internet. A **Web cam** is a video camera that displays its output on a Web page. A **video conference** is a meeting between geographically separated people who use a network or the Internet to transmit audio and video data.

> Visit **scsite.com/dc2005/quiz** or click the Quiz Yourself button. Click Objectives 5 – 8 below Chapter 5.

9 What Are Various Types of Scanners and Reading Devices and How Do They Work?

A **scanner** is a light-sensing input device that reads printed text and graphics and translates the results into a form the computer can process. A **flatbed scanner** works in a manner similar to a copy machine except it creates a file of the document. An *optical reader* uses a light source to read characters, marks, and codes and converts them into digital data. **Optical character recognition** (**OCR**) reads characters from ordinary documents. **Optical mark recognition** (**OMR**) reads hand-drawn marks such as small circles. A **bar code reader** is an optical reader that uses laser beams to read a **bar code**, or identification code. **MICR** (*magnetic-ink character recognition*) reads text printed with magnetized ink.

10 What Are Types of Terminals?

A *terminal* consists of a keyboard, a monitor, a video card, and memory. A *dumb terminal* has no processing power and relies on a host computer for processing. A *smart terminal* has a processor and can perform some functions independent of the host computer. POS terminals, ATMs, and smart displays are special-purpose terminals. A **POS** (**point-of-sale**) **terminal** records purchases, processes credit cards or debit cards, and updates delivery at a consumer's location. Many POS terminals have a **card reader**, which reads personal data from the magnetic strip on a credit or debit card. An **automated teller machine** (**ATM**) is a self-service banking machine that connects to a host computer. To access a bank account, you insert a bankcard into the ATM's card reader and enter a *personal identification number (PIN)*. A **smart display** is a thin monitor that detaches from a computer to function as a wireless touch screen.

11 What Are Various Biometric Devices?

A *biometric device* translates a personal characteristic into digital code that is compared with a digital code stored in the computer to identify an individual. A **fingerprint scanner** captures curves and indentations of a fingerprint. A *face recognition system* captures a live face image. A *hand geometry system* measures the shape and size of a hand. A *voice verification system* compares live speech with a stored voice pattern. A *signature verification system* recognizes the shape of a signature. An *iris recognition system* reads patterns in the iris of the eye.

12 What Are Alternative Input Devices for Physically Challenged Users?

Voice recognition is ideal for visually impaired users. A *keyguard* is a plate placed over the keyboard that allows users with limited hand mobility to rest their hands and press only one key at a time. Keyboards with larger keys or an *on-screen keyboard* displayed on a user's screen also are available. A small trackball or a *head-mounted pointer* helps users with limited hand movement to control the pointer. Two developments in the prototype stage are *gesture recognition* and computerized implant devices.

> Visit **scsite.com/dc2005/quiz** or click the Quiz Yourself button. Click Objectives 9 – 12 below Chapter 5.

CHAPTER 5 KEY TERMS

QUIZZES AND LEARNING GAMES
Computer Genius
Crossword Puzzle
Interactive Labs
Practice Test
Quiz Yourself
Wheel of Terms

EXERCISES
Chapter Review
Checkpoint
Key Terms
Lab Exercises
Learn It Online
Web Research

BEYOND THE BOOK
Apply It
Career Corner
Companies
FAQ
High-Tech Talk
Issues
Looking Ahead
Trailblazers
Web Links

FEATURES
Guide to Web Sites
Making Use of the Web
Tech News
Timeline 2005

You should know the Primary Terms and be familiar with the Secondary Terms.

WEB INSTRUCTIONS:

To display this page from the Web, start your browser and enter the Web address **scsite.com/dc2005/ch5/terms**. Click a term to display its definition and a picture. When the picture appears, click the more info button for current and additional information about the term from the Web.

>> Primary Terms

(shown in bold-black characters in the chapter)

Americans with Disabilities Act (ADA) (263)
audio input (243)
automated teller machine (ATM) (259)
bar code (255)
bar code reader (255)
card reader (258)
digital camera (247)
digital pen (240)
digital video (DV) camera (250)
ergonomic keyboard (234)
ergonomics (234)
fingerprint scanner (260)
flatbed scanner (253)
graphics tablet (240)
input (230)
input device (232)
insertion point (233)
joystick (239)
keyboard (232)
light pen (239)
MICR (257)
MICR reader (257)
mouse (235)
mouse pad (235)
OCR devices (254)
optical character recognition (OCR) (254)
optical mark recognition (OMR) (255)
PC camera (250)
PC video camera (250)
point of sale (POS) (258)
pointer (235)
pointing device (235)
pointing stick (238)
POS terminal (258)
resolution (249)
scanner (252)
smart card (261)
smart display (259)
stylus (240)
touch screen (240)
touchpad (238)
trackball (238)
turnaround document (255)
video capture card (250)
video conference (251)
video input (250)
video telephone call (250)
voice input (242)
voice recognition (242)
Web cam (251)
wheel (239)

>> Secondary Terms

(shown in italic characters in the chapter)

analog-to-digital converter (ADC) (242)
bar code scanner (255)
biometric device (260)
biometric identifier (260)
biometrics (260)
charge-coupled device (CCD) (248)
command (231)
continuous speech (243)
cordless keyboard (234)
cordless mouse (235)
cursor (application program) (233)
cursor (graphics tablet) (240)
data (230)
data collection device (257)
digital signal processor (DSP) (248)
digitizer (240)
discrete speech (243)
docking station (245)
download (247)
dumb terminal (258)
enhanced keyboard (233)
enhanced resolution (250)
face recognition system (260)
field camera (248)
function keys (233)
gesture recognition (263)
hand geometry system (260)
handwriting recognition software (241)
head-mounted pointer (263)
image processing (254)
image processing system (254)
instructions (230)
iris recognition system (261)
keyguard (263)
magnetic-ink character recognition (257)
mechanical mouse (235)
MIDI (musical instrument digital interface) (243)
mouse pointer (235)
MP (249)
multimedia message service (246)
multimedia messaging (246)
OCR (optical character recognition) software (254)
on-screen keyboard (263)
optical mouse (235)
optical reader (254)
optical resolution (250)
optical scanner (252)
personal identification number (PIN) (259)
pixel (249)
pixels per inch (ppi) (249)
point-and-shoot camera (248)
portable keyboard (245)
program (230)
signature verification system (261)
smart terminal (258)
SMS (short message service) (246)
source document (252)
speaker-dependent software (242)
speaker-independent software (243)
speech recognition (242)
streaming cam (251)
studio camera (248)
terminal (258)
text messaging (246)
toggle key (233)
UPC (Universal Product Code) (256)
user response (231)
voice verification system (261)
whiteboard (251)

CHECKPOINT CHAPTER 5

Use the Checkpoint exercises to check your knowledge level of the chapter.

WEB INSTRUCTIONS:

To display this page from the Web, start your browser and enter the Web address **scsite.com/dc2005/ch5/check**. Click the links for current and additional information.

LABEL THE FIGURE

Identify these areas and keys on a desktop computer keyboard.

a. additional keys
b. APPLICATION key
c. arrow keys
d. CD/DVD controls
e. function keys
f. Internet controls
g. numeric keypad
h. typing area
i. WINDOWS key
j. wrist rest

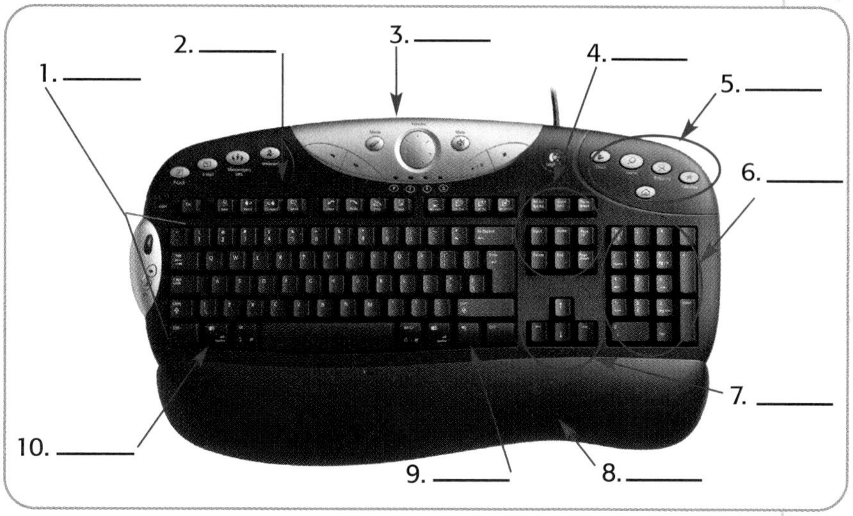

TRUE/FALSE

Mark T for True and F for False. (See page numbers in parentheses.)

H.W

T 1. Once data is in memory, a computer interprets and executes instructions to process the data into information. (230)

T 2. An input device is any hardware component that allows users to enter data or instructions into a computer. (232)

T 3. The goal of ergonomics is to incorporate comfort, efficiency, and safety into the design of items in the workplace. (234)

T 4. A trackball requires frequent cleaning because it picks up oils from fingers and dust from the environment. (238)

F 5. Audio input is the process of entering data by speaking into a microphone. (243) F

F 6. A portable keyboard is a miniature-sized keyboard you conveniently attach and remove from a PDA. (245)

T 7. Digital cameras typically allow users to review, and sometimes edit, images while they are in the camera. (247)

T 8. A video conference is a meeting between two or more geographically separated people who use a network or the Internet to transmit audio and video data. (251)

T 9. An optical reader is a device that uses a light source to read characters, marks, and codes and then converts them into digital data that a computer can process. (254)

F 10. Many companies use optical mark recognition (OMR) to read hand-printed characters on turnaround documents. (255)

T 11. A biometric identifier is a physical or behavioral characteristic, such as a fingerprint or facial feature. (260)

F 12. No pointing devices currently are available for users with motor limitations. (263)

CHAPTER 5 CHECKPOINT

MULTIPLE CHOICE

Select the best answer. (See page numbers in parentheses.)

1. _______ is a series of instructions that tells a computer what to do and how to do it. (230)
   a. Data b. A program or software
   c. A command d. A user response
2. _______ keys are special keys programmed to issue commands to a computer. (233)
   a. Toggle b. Arrow
   c. Function d. Numeric
3. A(n) _______ is a battery-powered device that transmits data using wireless technology, such as radio waves or infrared light waves. (234)
   a. enhanced keyboard
   b. ergonomic keyboard
   c. portable keyboard
   d. cordless keyboard
4. _______ is a common mouse operation in which you press and release the primary mouse button. (237)
   a. Point b. Click
   c. Drag d. Right-click
5. To allow easy access of your bank account from a car, many ATMs have _______. (240)
   a. touch screens b. joy sticks
   c. touchpads d. pointing sticks
6. Voice input is the process of _______. (242)
   a. entering data by speaking into a microphone
   b. entering any sound into the computer such as speech, music, and sound effects
   c. capturing full-motion images into a computer and storing them on a storage medium
   d. all of the above
7. A portable keyboard _______. (245)
   a. is an infrared image of a keyboard projected on a flat surface
   b. is built into the top of a handheld computer
   c. has a design that reduces the chance of wrist and hand injuries
   d. is a full-sized keyboard you conveniently attach and remove from a PDA
8. The most expensive and highest quality digital camera is a _______, which is a stationary camera used for professional work. (248)
   a. PC camera
   b. point-and-shoot camera
   c. studio camera
   d. field camera
9. A digital video (DV) camera _______. (250)
   a. records video as analog signals instead of digital signals
   b. is a stationary camera used for professional studio work
   c. records video as digital signals instead of analog signals
   d. is a mobile camera used for amateur studio work
10. Scanners capture data from a _______, which is the original form of the data. (252)
    a. duplicate document
    b. secondary document
    c. derivative document
    d. source document
11. The UPC (Universal Product Code) bar code is used by _______. (256)
    a. retail and grocery stores
    b. libraries, blood banks, and air parcel carriers
    c. the United States Postal Service (USPS)
    d. nonretail applications such as game tickets
12. Point-of-sale terminals, automated teller machines, and smart displays are types of _______ that perform specific tasks and contain features uniquely designed for use in a particular industry. (258)
    a. smart terminals
    b. dumb terminals
    c. general-purpose terminals
    d. special-purpose terminals
13. The most widely used biometric device is the _______. (260)
    a. face recognition system
    b. fingerprint scanner
    c. hand geometry system
    d. iris recognition system
14. A(n) _______ is a metal or plastic plate that allows users to wrest their hands on the keyboard without accidentally pressing any keys. (263)
    a. on-screen keyboard
    b. keyguard
    c. head-mounted pointer
    d. computerized implant

MATCHING

Match the terms with their definitions. (See page numbers in parentheses.)

b 1. insertion point (233)
a 2. ergonomic keyboard (234)
e 3. pointer (235)
g 4. mouse pad (235)
i 5. graphics tablet (240)
k 6. video capture card (250)
h 7. video telephone call (251)
f 8. bar code (255)
d 9. data collection device (257)
c 10. smart card (261)

a. designed to reduce the chance of wrist and hand injuries
b. symbol on the screen that indicates where the next character typed will display
c. stores personal data on a thin, embedded microprocessor
d. obtains data directly at the location where a transaction or event takes place
e. graphical symbol whose location changes with the movement of a pointing device
f. identification code that consists of vertical lines and spaces of different widths
g. rectangular pad that provides better traction than the top of a desk
h. allows both parties to see each other as they talk over the Internet
i. flat, rectangular, electronic plastic board sometimes called a digitizer
j. self-service banking machine that connects to a host computer
k. converts an analog video signal into a digital signal a computer can use
l. projects an infrared image of a keyboard on any flat surface

SHORT ANSWER

Write a brief answer to each of the following questions.

1. How does voice recognition work? __________ How is discrete speech different from continuous speech? ____________
2. What is a video capture card? __________ Why is a video capture card not needed with a digital video (DV) camera? __________
3. What is OCR (optical character recognition) software? ____________ What is an image processing system? ____________
4. What is optical character recognition (OCR), optical mark recognition (OMR), and MICR (magnetic-ink character recognition)? ____________ How is each technology used? ____________
5. What is the Americans with Disabilities Act (ADA)? ____________ How might gesture recognition and computerized implant devices help physically challenged users in the future? ____________

WORKING TOGETHER

Working with a group of your classmates, complete the following team exercises.

1. Carpal tunnel syndrome is the most well-known of a series of musculoskeletal disorders that fall under the umbrella of repetitive strain injuries (RSIs). Prepare a report and PowerPoint presentation about RSIs. Include information about RSI warning signs and risk factors and suggestions about proper workstation ergonomics. Share your report and presentation with your class.

2. Choose one Issue in this chapter: 232, 236, 246, 256, or 261. Use the Web and/or print media to research the issue. Then, present a debate for the class, with different members of your team supporting different responses to the questions that accompany the issue.

3. Stores, libraries, parcel carriers, and other organizations use optical codes. Some people mistakenly believe that an optical code contains the name of a product or its price, but the codes are only a link to a database in which this information, and more, is stored. Have each member of your team visit an organization that uses optical codes. How are the optical codes read? What information is obtained when the code is read? What information is recorded? How is the information used? Meet with the members of your team to discuss the results of your investigations. Then, use PowerPoint to create a group presentation and share your findings with the class.

CHAPTER 5 LEARN IT ONLINE

Previous | Next

QUIZZES AND LEARNING GAMES
Computer Genius
Crossword Puzzle
Interactive Labs
Practice Test
Quiz Yourself
Wheel of Terms

EXERCISES
Chapter Review
Checkpoint
Key Terms
Lab Exercises
Learn It Online
Web Research

BEYOND THE BOOK
Apply It
Career Corner
Companies
FAQ
High-Tech Talk
Issues
Looking Ahead
Trailblazers
Web Links

FEATURES
Guide to Web Sites
Making Use of the Web
Tech News
Timeline 2005

Use the Learn It Online exercises to reinforce your understanding of the chapter concepts.

WEB INSTRUCTIONS:

To display this page from the Web, start your browser and enter the Web address **scsite.com/dc2005/ch5/learn**.

1 At the Movies – Think In Ink

To view the Think In Ink movie, click the number 1 button. Watch the movie, and then complete the exercise by answering the questions below. Taking classroom notes with pen and paper may be a thing of the past if the Tablet PC continues its rise in popularity. This computer recognizes handwriting and stores it as notes that later can be searched and accessed. In spite of its advantages, some experts believe people are so accustomed to pen and paper that the Tablet PC will require a tremendous amount of effort and time if it is ever to catch on. What type of input device does a Tablet PC use, and how does it work? Why is note-taking using the Tablet PC preferable to writing notes using pen and paper? Why is the Tablet PC expected to be especially popular in Asia?

2 Student Edition Labs – Working with Audio

Click the number 2 button. When the Student Edition Labs menu appears, click *Working with Audio* to begin. A new browser window will open. Follow the on-screen instructions to complete the Lab. When finished, click the Exit button. If required, print a copy of your results to submit to your instructor.

3 Student Edition Labs – Working with Video

Click the number 3 button. When the Student Edition Labs menu appears, click *Working with Video* to begin. A new browser window will open. Follow the on-screen instructions to complete the Lab. When finished, click the Exit button. If required, print a copy of your results to submit to your instructor.

4 Sending E-Mail

It is estimated that 75 percent of all workers and 45 percent of all consumers, which represents a total of 58 percent of the U.S. population, use e-mail. E-mail allows you to send messages anywhere in the world. Use the e-mail account you set up in Learn It Online 14 in Chapter 3 on page 175 to send a message. Click the number 4 button to display your e-mail service. Log in to your e-mail service and then follow the instructions for composing a message. The subject of the message should be input devices. Type the e-mail address of one of your classmates. In the message itself, type something your classmate should know about input devices, and then send the message. Next, follow the instructions to read and reply to any messages you have received. When you are finished, quit your e-mail service.

5 Practice Test

Click the number 5 button. Answer each question. When completed, enter your name and click the Grade Test button to submit the quiz for grading. Make a note of any missed questions. If required, print a copy to submit to your instructor.

6 Web Guide

Click the number 6 button to display the Guide to Web Sites and Searching Techniques Web page. Click Computers and Computing and then click ZDNet. In the Search text box, type `Web camera`. Scroll through the results and then click a link of your choice. Use your word processing program to prepare a brief report about your findings and submit your assignment to your instructor.

7 Scavenger Hunt

Click the number 7 button. Print a copy of the Scavenger Hunt page; use this page to write down your answers as you search the Web. Submit your completed page to your instructor.

8 Who Wants To Be a Computer Genius?

Click the number 8 button to find out if you are a computer genius. Directions on how to play the game will be displayed. When you are ready to play, click the Play button. Submit your score to your instructor.

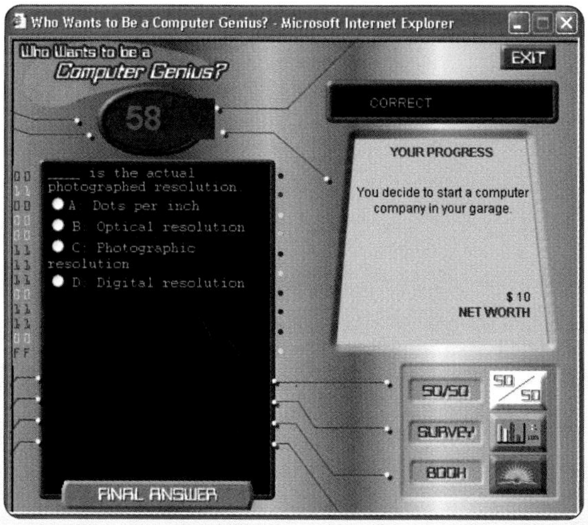

9 Wheel of Terms

Click the number 9 button to reinforce important terms you learned in this chapter by playing the Shelly Cashman Series version of this popular game. Directions on how to play the game will be displayed. When you are ready to play, click the Play button. Submit your score to your instructor.

10 Career Corner

Click the number 10 button to display the Penn State's Career Services Web page. Click a link of your choice. Write a brief report about the information you found. Submit the report to your instructor.

11 Search Sleuth

Click the number 11 button to learn search techniques that will help make you a research expert. Submit the completed assignment to your instructor.

12 Crossword Puzzle Challenge

Click the number 12 button. Complete the puzzle to reinforce skills you learned in this chapter. Directions on how to play the game will be displayed. When you are ready to play, click the Submit button. Submit the completed puzzle to your instructor.

13 In the News

Many people spend a lot of time jotting notes on scratch pads, napkins, or little yellow Post-it notes. This may be fine for the occasional thought; however, in a situation where you would rather concentrate on the substance of the ideas being expressed, you may need a more sophisticated method for taking notes. Tape recorders have long been the mainstay for recording lectures, interviews, or one's thoughts, but they are restricted by the fact that the tapes last only so long before they have to be flipped over or switched altogether. One new development is the voice pen, which is a flash-memory-based recording device. It records digitally, which offers higher quality over standard tapes, easy indexing, and instant erasure. It is approximately the size of a small cellular telephone or remote control unit, and can record up to 500 minutes on long play settings. Click the number 13 button and read a news article about a new or improved input device, an input device being used in a new way, or an input device being made more available. What is the device? Who is promoting it? How will it be used? Will the input device change the number, or effectiveness, of potential users? If so, why?

CHAPTER 5 LAB EXERCISES

◀ Previous | Next ▶

Use the Lab Exercises to gain hands-on computer experience.

QUIZZES AND LEARNING GAMES
Computer Genius
Crossword Puzzle
Interactive Labs
Practice Test
Quiz Yourself
Wheel of Terms

EXERCISES
Chapter Review
Checkpoint
Key Terms
Lab Exercises
Learn It Online
Web Research

BEYOND THE BOOK
Apply It
Career Corner
Companies
FAQ
High-Tech Talk
Issues
Looking Ahead
Trailblazers
Web Links

FEATURES
Guide to Web Sites
Making Use of the Web
Tech News
Timeline 2005

WEB INSTRUCTIONS:

To display this page from the Web, start your browser and enter the Web address **scsite.com/dc2005/ch5/lab**.

1 About Your Computer

This exercise uses Windows XP procedures. Your computer probably has more than one input device. To learn about the input devices on your computer, click the Start button on the Windows taskbar, and then right-click My Computer on the Start menu. Click Properties on the shortcut menu. When the System Properties dialog box displays, click the Hardware tab. Click the Device Manager button. If necessary, click the plus sign next to the label for your computer in the Device Manager window to display a list of hardware device categories. What input devices appear in the list? Click the plus sign next to each category that contains an input device. What specific input devices in each category are connected to your computer? Close the Device Manager window. Click the Cancel button in the System Properties dialog box.

2 Customizing the Keyboard

This exercise uses Windows XP procedures. The Windows operating system provides several ways to customize the keyboard for people with physical limitations. Some of these options are StickyKeys, FilterKeys, and ToggleKeys. To discover more about each option, click the Start button on the Windows taskbar, and then click Control Panel on the Start menu. If necessary, switch to Category View. Click the Accessibility Options icon in the Control Panel window. Click the Accessibility Options icon in the Accessibility Options window. If necessary, click the Keyboard tab in the Accessibility Options dialog box. Click the Question Mark button on the title bar, click the StickyKeys area, read the information in the pop-up window, and then click the pop-up window to close it. Repeat this process for FilterKeys and ToggleKeys. What is the purpose of each option? How might each option benefit someone with a physical limitation? Click the Cancel button in the Accessibility Options dialog box and then click the Close button in the Accessibility Options window.

3 Using the Mouse and Keyboard to Interact with an Online Program

This exercise uses Windows XP/2000/98 procedures. Insert the Discover Data Disk into drive A or see your instructor for the location of the Loan Payment Calculator program. Click the Start button on the Windows taskbar, and then click Run on the Start menu to display the Run dialog box. In the Open text box, type the path and file name of the program. For example, type `a:loancalc.exe` and then press the ENTER key to display the Loan Payment Calculator window. Type `12500` in the LOAN AMOUNT text box. Click the YEARS right scroll arrow or drag the scroll box until YEARS equals 15. Click the APR right scroll arrow or drag the scroll box until APR equals 8.5. Click the Calculate button. Write down the monthly payment and sum of payments. Click the Clear button. What are the monthly payment and sum of payments for each of these loan amounts, years, and APRs: (1) 28000, 5, 7.25; (2) 98750, 30, 9; (3) 6000, 3, 8.75; (4) 62500, 15, 9.25. Close the Loan Payment Calculator.

4 MouseKeys

This exercise uses Windows XP procedures. A graphical user interface allows you to perform many tasks simply by pointing the mouse and clicking a mouse button. Yet, what if you do not have, or cannot use, a mouse? The Windows XP operating system covers this possibility with an option called MouseKeys. When the MouseKeys option is turned on, you can use numeric keypad keys to move the mouse pointer, click, right-click, double-click, and drag. To find out how, click the Start button on the Windows taskbar and then click Help and Support on the Start menu. Type `MouseKeys` in the Search text box and then click the Start searching button. To answer each of the following questions, click an appropriate link in the Search Results box and then read the Help information. To display a different result in the right pane, click a different link in the Search Results box.

- How do you turn on MouseKeys?
- How do you change MouseKeys options?
- How do you click using MouseKeys?
- How do you drag using MouseKeys?

Click the Close button to close the Help and Support Center window.

WEB RESEARCH CHAPTER 5

Use the Web Research exercises to learn more about the special features in this chapter.

WEB INSTRUCTIONS:

Use the link in each exercise or a search engine such as Google (google.com) to research the topic. Then, write a one-page, double-spaced report or create a presentation, unless otherwise directed below. Page numbers on which information can be found are in parentheses.

1 **Issue** Choose one Issue from the following issues in this chapter: What Is Happening on Your Computer? (232), A Mouse Did What? (236), Can I Borrow Your Notes? (246), What Is the Price of That Item? (256), or Have You Seen This Face Before? (261). Use the Web to research the issue. Discuss the issue with classmates, instructors, and friends. Address the questions that accompany the issue in a report or presentation.

2 **Apply It** Choose one of the following Apply It features in this chapter: Configuring the Mouse to Suit Your Preferences (237) or Share Digital Photos with Friends and Family (249). Use the Web to gather additional information about the topic. Print two Web pages that relate to the Apply It. Detail in a report or presentation what you learned.

3 **Career Corner** Read the Career Corner article in this chapter (264). Use the Web to find out more about the career. Describe the career in a report or presentation.

4 **Companies on the Cutting Edge** Choose one of the Companies on the Cutting Edge in this chapter (266). Use the Web to research the company further. Explain in a report or presentation how this company has contributed to computer technology.

5 **Technology Trailblazers** Choose one of the Technology Trailblazers in this chapter (267). Use the Web to research the person further. Explain in a report or presentation how this individual has affected the way people use, or think about, computers.

6 **Picture Yourself Using a PDA** Read the Picture Yourself Using a PDA story at the beginning of this chapter (228). Use the Web to research PDAs further. Describe in a report or presentation the ways in which you might use a PDA.

7 **High-Tech Talk** Read the High-Tech Talk feature in this chapter (265). Use the Web to find out more about the topic. Summarize in a report or presentation what you learned.

8 **Web Links** Review the Web Link boxes found in the margins of this chapter. Visit five of the Web Link sites. Print the main Web page for each site you visit. Choose one of the Web pages and then summarize in one paragraph the content of the Web page.

9 **Looking Ahead** Choose one of the Looking Ahead articles in this chapter: Wireless Pens Revolutionize Input Devices (241) or Brain Implants Help Physically Challenged (264). Use the Web to find out more about the topic. Detail in a report or presentation what you learned.

10 **FAQ** Choose one FAQ found in this chapter. Use the Web to find out more about the topic. Summarize in one paragraph what you learned.

11 **PDA Application Software** Read the PDA Application Software Special Feature that follows this chapter (278–289). Select a field that uses PDA software. Use the Web to learn more about your selection. Describe in a report or presentation how PDA software is used in the field you selected.

12 **Making Use of the Web** Read the Auctions section of Making Use of the Web in Appendix A (APP 10). Complete the Auctions Web Exercises at the end of the section (APP 11). Answer the questions posed in each exercise.

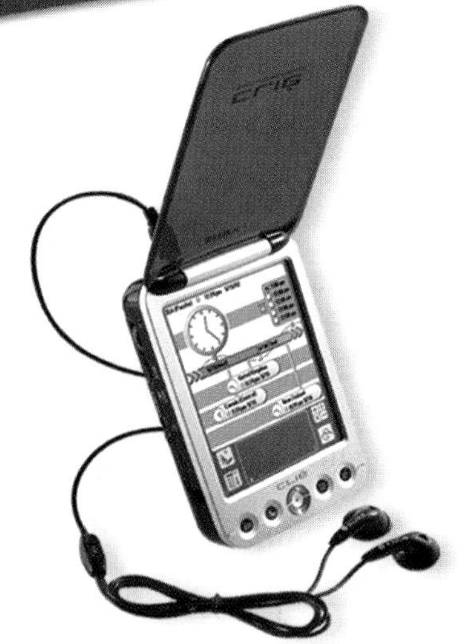

MULTIMEDIA SOFTWARE

Most PDAs include the capability of viewing images and some are powerful enough to view short video clips. Some PDAs also double as audio players, allowing the user to take his or her favorite music anywhere. PDAs that are more recent contain, or allow the user to attach, a camera or recording device to capture video or audio, and then download the captured media to a personal computer. Some image viewers allow the user to use a PDA as an electronic picture frame while the PDA rests in its cradle on the user's desk. Popular multimedia software for PDAs is listed in Figure 12.

MULTIMEDIA SOFTWARE FOR PDAS

Application	Description	Samples
Picture viewer	Allows a user to view images uploaded to the PDA using software on a personal computer. Some viewers have a slide show mode that rotates through a list of images automatically.	• SplashPhoto • PocketPhoto • Palbum Picture Viewer
Video player	Allows the user to watch video clips on a PDA.	• FireViewer • Windows Media Player for Pocket PC • PocketTV for Pocket PC
Audio player	Permits a user to listen to his or her favorite music or record and playback voice recordings for meetings or personal audio notes. Some PDAs are equipped with additional hardware such as microphones, headphones, or audio controls to enhance the audio experience.	• AudioPlus • Windows Media Player for Pocket PC • Replay Radio

FIGURE 12 Multimedia PDA software gives the user the ability to view images, watch video, and listen to audio.

ENTERTAINMENT SOFTWARE

While on the train ride into work or waiting at the airport, a PDA user can enjoy his or her favorite games on a PDA. The infrared port or wireless connectivity of a PDA allows a user to play some games against other players. Most PDAs include buttons to control games. Figure 13 lists popular entertainment software for PDAs.

ENTERTAINMENT SOFTWARE FOR PDAS

Application	Description	Samples
Strategy	Includes classic board games such as chess, backgammon, and Monopoly.	• PocketChess • ChessGenius • Handmark Monopoly • SimCity
Card	Includes casino games, solitaire games, and other card games.	• AcidSolitaire • BlackJack++ • Pocket Cribbage
Action	Games that require quickreflexes, including many arcade-style games.	• Tomb Raider • Bejeweled
Puzzle	Thought-provoking puzzles to pass time and sharpen the mind, such as crossword puzzles, mazes, and word games.	• Handmark SCRABBLE • Crossword

FIGURE 13 Entertainment software allows a user to relax with a PDA and enjoy his or her favorite games.

OBTAINING AND INSTALLING PDA SOFTWARE

PDA software often is available at a computer or electronics store. A significant number of programs are available as shareware, freeware, or trial editions at a number of Web sites. Most of the software listed in the previous figures are accessible on the Web sites listed in Figure 14. Because PDA software usually is smaller than the personal computer counterparts, downloading the software from the Web to your personal computer and then uploading it to your PDA often is the best alternative when you want to try something new. PDA software downloaded from the Web to a personal computer requires that the software be installed using the PDA's synchronization software. Additionally, some personal computer application software includes accompanying PDA software that corresponds with the personal computer software.

PDA software sold in a retail location usually is supplied on a CD-ROM. The CD-ROM first installs the PDA software on a personal computer. The PDA's synchronization software then is used to load the software onto the PDA while the PDA is connected to the personal computer. Depending on the type of software installed, this process may be automatic. Some PDA software is packaged as an add-on card that the user inserts into the PDA's expansion slot. Some Web sites allow the user to browse a software catalog from the PDA's Web browser and download the software directly to the PDA. When synchronizing a PDA on a corporate network, some companies automatically install software to the employees' PDAs with no interaction required from the employee.

WHERE TO GET PDA SOFTWARE

Application	Description	Samples
Web sites	Software publishers make their products available at their Web sites. Several Web sites also exist specifically to distribute PDA software. Tens of thousands of titles are available and most can be downloaded on a trial basis.	www.palmgear.com www.handandgo.com www.pdamd.com www.tucows.com
Retail	Many popular software titles can be purchased at electronic and computer stores. The most popular titles at these locations include productivity and entertainment software.	www.bestbuy.com
Develop in-house	Many corporations develop their own PDA software to use internally to meet specific needs. These programs usually tap into existing corporate databases of product and customer information. The companies that produce PDA operating systems often make the development tools for such software available at no cost or a minimal cost.	www.palmsource.com www.microsoft.com/mobile/developer

FIGURE 14 PDA software is available from a number of sources.

CHAPTER 6

Output

Picture Yourself Printing Pictures

A friend of yours, who is a computer guru and always has the latest digital equipment, just sold his *old* digital camera to you for $50. You know it was a great deal! What he considers old equipment actually still is state of the art. This one is a 2-megapixel digital camera that saves pictures on a memory card. You do not have a card reader/writer, so you purchase one for about $30 from a local electronics store. At the store, you also buy some high-gloss photo paper.

No more film to purchase or develop ever again! Now you have all the equipment and supplies necessary to take and print high-quality pictures. You immediately take photographs with the digital camera. As soon as the memory card is full, you remove it from the camera and insert it into the card reader/writer. After transferring images from the memory card to the computer's hard disk, you insert the photo paper in your ink-jet printer and print the pictures in a variety of sizes — wallet, 4 x 6, 5 x 7, and 8 x 10. Although the larger prints are a little grainy, the quality of the smaller sizes is great. In the future, you plan to invest in a photo printer so you can print high-quality enlargements, too.

As you read Chapter 6, you will learn about printers and discover other types of output.

OBJECTIVES

After completing this chapter, you will be able to:

1. Describe the four categories of output
2. Describe the characteristics of a CRT monitor and factors that affect its quality
3. Explain the relationship between a video card and CRT monitor
4. Summarize the characteristics of LCD monitors, LCD screens, gas plasma displays, and HDTVs
5. Differentiate between an impact printer and a nonimpact printer
6. Summarize the characteristics of ink-jet printers, photo printers, laser printers, thermal printers, mobile printers, label and postage printers, and plotters and large-format printers
7. Describe the methods used for wireless printing
8. Describe the uses of speakers and headsets
9. Identify the output characteristics of fax machines and fax modems, multifunction peripherals, data projectors, joysticks, and wheels
10. Identify output options for physically challenged users

CONTENTS

WHAT IS OUTPUT?

Output is data that has been processed into a useful form. That is, computers process input (data) into output (information). A computer generates several types of output, depending on the hardware and software being used and the requirements of the user.

Users view output on a screen, print it, or hear it though speakers or headsets. Monitors, notebook computers, Tablet PCs, PDAs, and smart phones have screens that allow users to view documents, Web sites, e-mail messages, and other types of output. Some printers produce black-and-white documents, and others produce brilliant colors, enabling users to print color documents, photographs, and transparencies. Through the computer's speakers or a headset, users listen to sounds, music, and voice messages.

While working with a computer, a user encounters four basic categories of output: text, graphics, audio, and video (Figure 6-1). Very often, a single form of output, such as a Web site, includes more than one of these categories.

- Text — Examples of text-based documents are memorandums, letters, announcements, press releases, reports, advertisements, newsletters, envelopes, and mailing labels. On the Web, users view and print many other types of text-based documents. These include newspapers, magazines, books, play or television show transcripts, stock quotes, famous speeches, and historical lectures.
- Graphics — Documents often include graphics to enhance their visual appeal and convey information. Business letters have logos. Reports include charts. Newsletters use drawings, clip art, and photographs. Users print high-quality photographs taken

FIGURE 6-1 Four categories of output are text, graphics, audio, and video.

with a digital camera, eliminating the need for film or film developers. Many Web sites use animated graphics, such as blinking icons, scrolling messages, or simulations.

- Audio — Users insert their favorite music CD in a CD or DVD drive and listen to the music while working on the computer. Software such as games, encyclopedias, and simulations often have musical accompaniments for entertainment and audio clips, such as narrations and speeches, to enhance understanding. On the Web, users tune into radio and television stations and listen to audio clips or live broadcasts of interviews, talk shows, sporting events, news, music, and concerts. They also use the Internet to have real-time conversations with friends, coworkers, or family members, just as if they were speaking on the telephone.
- Video — As with audio, software and Web sites often include video clips to enhance understanding. Users watch a live or prerecorded news report, view a movie, see a doctor perform a life-saving surgery, observe a hurricane in action, or enjoy a live performance of their favorite jazz band on the computer.

Attaching a video camera to the computer allows users to watch home movies on the computer. They also can attach a television's antenna or cable to the computer and watch a television program on the computer screen.

An **output device** is any type of hardware component that conveys information to one or more people. Commonly used output devices include display devices, printers, speakers and headsets, fax machines and fax modems, multifunction peripherals, data projectors, and force-feedback joysticks and wheels. This chapter discusses each of these output devices.

DISPLAY DEVICES

A **display device**, or simply *display*, is an output device that visually conveys text, graphics, and video information. Information on a display device, sometimes called *soft copy*, exists electronically and appears for a temporary period.

Display devices consist of a screen and the components that produce the information on the screen. Desktop computers typically use a monitor as their display device. A **monitor** is a plastic or metal case that houses a display device as a separate peripheral (Figure 6-2). Most mobile computers and devices, by contrast, integrate the display and other components into the same physical case. For example, the display on a notebook computer attaches with hinges. Some PDA displays also attach with a hinge to the device; with others, the display is part of the PDA case.

Most display devices show text, graphics, and video information in color. Some, however, are monochrome. *Monochrome* means the information appears in one color (such as white, amber, green, black, blue, or gray) on a different color background, for example, black or grayish-white. Some PDAs and other mobile devices use monochrome displays to save battery power. To enhance the quality of their graphics, monochrome displays often use gray scaling. *Gray scaling* involves using many shades of gray from white to black, which provides better contrast on the images.

FIGURE 6-2 Most desktop monitors have color displays.

Two types of display devices are CRT monitors and flat-panel displays. The following sections discuss each of these display devices.

CRT MONITORS

A **CRT monitor** is a desktop monitor that is similar to a standard television because it contains a cathode-ray tube (Figure 6-3). A *cathode-ray tube* (*CRT*) is a large, sealed glass tube. The front of the tube is the screen. Tiny dots of phosphor material coat the screen on a CRT. Each dot consists of a red, a green, and a blue phosphor. The three dots combine to make up each pixel. Recall from Chapter 5 that a *pixel* (short for picture element) is a single point in an electronic image. Inside the CRT, an electron beam moves back and forth across the back of the screen. This causes the dots on the front of the screen to glow, which produces an image on the screen.

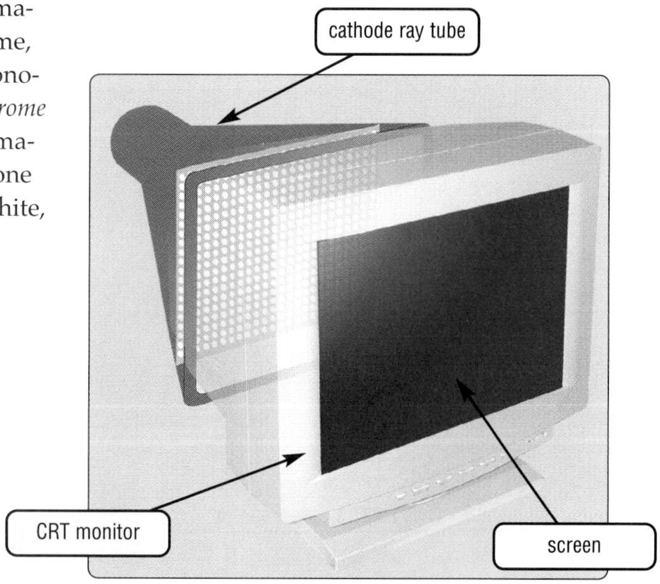

FIGURE 6-3 The core of most desktop monitors is a cathode-ray tube.

CRT monitors for desktop computers are available in various sizes, with the more common being 15, 17, 19, 21, and 22 inches. You measure a monitor the same way as you measure a television, that is, diagonally from one corner of the casing to the other. In addition to monitor size, advertisements also list a monitor's viewable size. The *viewable size* is the diagonal measurement of the actual viewing area provided by the screen in the monitor. A 21-inch monitor, for example, may have a viewable size of 20 inches.

Determining what size monitor to purchase depends on your intended use. A large monitor allows you to view more information on the screen at once, but usually is more expensive. You may want to invest in a 19-inch monitor if you use multiple applications at one time or do a lot of research on the Web. Users working with intense graphics applications, such as desktop publishing and engineering, typically have even larger monitors. Some use two monitors side by side at once — with one monitor showing the left half of a document and the other showing the right half.

CRT Monitor Ergonomics

CRT monitors usually include features to address ergonomic issues. Most monitors have a tilt-and-swivel base that allows users to adjust the angle of the screen to minimize neck strain and reduce glare from overhead lighting. Monitor controls permit users to adjust the brightness, contrast, positioning, height, and width of images. These controls usually are on the front of the monitor for easy access. Newer monitors have digital controls that allow fine-tuning of the display in small increments. An advantage of digital controls is that they allow users quickly to return to the default settings by pressing a reset button.

To help reduce the amount of electricity used by monitors and other computer components, the United States Department of Energy (DOE) and the United States Environmental Protection Agency (EPA) developed the **ENERGY STAR program**. This program encourages manufacturers to create energy-efficient devices that require little power when they are not in use. Monitors and devices that meet ENERGY STAR guidelines display an ENERGY STAR label (Figure 6-4).

FIGURE 6-4 Products with an ENERGY STAR label are energy efficient as defined by the Environmental Protection Agency (EPA).

In the past, CRT monitor screens were curved slightly. Many current models have flat screens. A flat screen reduces glare, reflection, and distortion of images. With a flat screen, users do not notice as much eyestrain and fatigue. Thus, a flat screen is an ergonomic screen.

FAQ 6-1

What can I do to ease eyestrain while using my computer?

Blink your eyes every five seconds. Use a glare screen. Adjust the room lighting. Use larger fonts or zoom a display. Take an eye break every 10 to 15 minutes: look into the distance and focus on an object for 20 to 30 seconds; roll your eyes in a complete circle; and then close your eyes for at least 30 seconds. If you wear glasses, ask your doctor about computer glasses.

For more information about computer eye strain, visit the Discovering Computers 2005 FAQ Web page (**scsite.com/dc2005/faq**). Click Eye Strain below Chapter 6.

Quality of a CRT Monitor

The quality of a CRT monitor depends largely on its resolution, dot pitch, and refresh rate. As mentioned in Chapter 5, **resolution** describes the sharpness and clearness of an image. Manufacturers state the resolution of a monitor in pixels. For example, a monitor set at an 800 x 600 resolution displays up to 800 pixels per horizontal inch and 600 pixels per vertical inch, for a total of 480,000 pixels to create a screen image.

Most monitors support a variety of screen resolutions. Standard CRT monitors today usually display up to a maximum of 1600 x 1200 pixels, with 800 x 600 often the norm. High-end CRT monitors (for the power user) can display 2048 x 1536 pixels or more.

WEB LINK 6-1

CRT Monitors

Visit the Discovering Computers 2005 WEB LINK page (**scsite .com/dc2005/weblink**). Click CRT Monitors below Chapter 6.

Setting a monitor to display a higher resolution uses a greater number of pixels and thus provides a smoother image. As the resolution increases, however, some items on the screen appear smaller, such as menu bars, toolbars, and rulers (Figure 6-5). For this reason, you would not use a high resolution on a small display, such as a 15-inch monitor, because the small characters would be difficult to read. The display resolution you choose is a matter of preference. Larger monitors typically look best at a higher resolution, and smaller monitors look best at a lower resolution. For example, a 21-inch monitor may be set at a 1600 x 1200 resolution, while a 17-inch monitor may be set at a resolution of 800 x 600. A higher resolution also is desirable for graphics applications. A lower resolution usually is satisfactory for business applications such as word processing.

Figure 6-5a (screen resolution at 800 x 600)

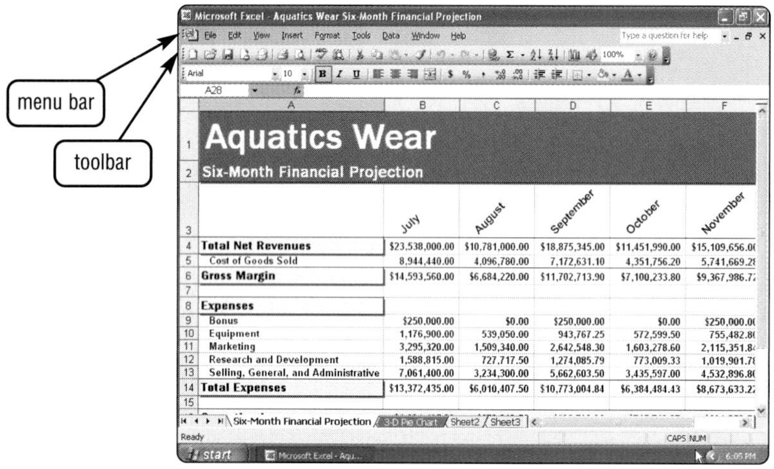

Figure 6-5b (screen resolution at 1600 x 1200)

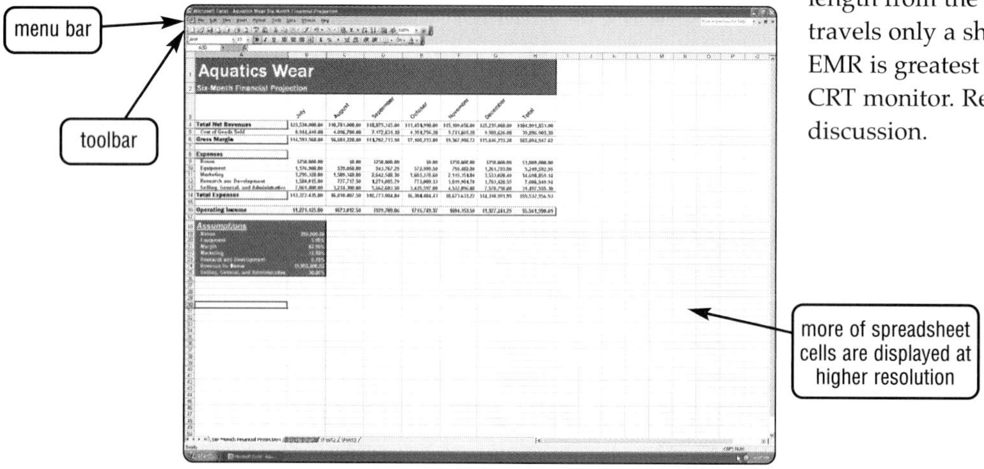

FIGURE 6-5 This comparison illustrates that some elements on the screen become smaller when the resolution is increased from 800 x 600 to 1600 x 1200. The higher resolution also displays more spreadsheet cells on the screen.

Dot pitch is another measurement of image clarity on a CRT monitor. *Dot pitch,* sometimes called *pixel pitch,* is the distance in millimeters between each like-colored pixel on a display. The smaller the distance between the pixels, the sharper the image. Text created with a smaller dot pitch is easier to read. To minimize eye fatigue, use a monitor with a dot pitch of .27 millimeters or lower. Advertisements normally specify a monitor's dot pitch.

Refresh rate is yet another measure of a CRT monitor's quality. *Refresh rate,* also called *scan rate,* is the speed that a monitor redraws the images on the screen. Ideally, a CRT monitor's refresh rate should be fast enough to maintain a constant, flicker-free image. A slower refresh rate causes the image to fade and then flicker as it is redrawn. This flicker can lead to eye fatigue and cause headaches for some users. Refresh rate is the number of times per second the screen is redrawn and is expressed in hertz (Hz). Although most people can tolerate a vertical refresh rate of 60 Hz, a high-quality CRT monitor will provide a vertical refresh rate of at least 75 Hz. This means the image on the screen redraws itself vertically 75 times in a second.

CRT monitors produce a small amount of electromagnetic radiation. *Electromagnetic radiation (EMR)* is a magnetic field that travels at the speed of light. Excessive amounts of EMR can pose a health risk. To be safe, all high-quality CRT monitors comply with MPR II standards. *MPR II* is a set of standards that defines acceptable levels of EMR for a monitor. To protect yourself even further, sit at arm's length from the CRT monitor because EMR travels only a short distance. In addition, EMR is greatest on the sides and back of the CRT monitor. Read Issue 6-1 for a related discussion.

ISSUE 6-1

Who Is Responsible for Disposing of an Old Monitor?

Studies conducted by the National Recycling Coalition forecast that by the year 2007, up to 500 million computers will become obsolete. According to environmentalists, disposing of old CRT monitors will be a major problem. CRT monitors can contain as much as eight pounds of lead, which protects users from radiation. When monitors are discarded in a landfill, however, the lead pollutes the environment and can cause developmental problems in children exposed to it. In the United States, several states already have proposed, or passed, laws prohibiting the dumping of old monitors in landfills. Other countries have taken a more extreme approach. In Germany, for example, because the computer makers are responsible for the eventual disposal of computer components, the price of every computer includes a fee for the cost of recycling. Should laws be enacted on the federal level barring the disposal of old monitors in landfills? Why or why not? Should manufacturers be made responsible for disposal of computer components? Why?

For more information about disposing of monitors, visit the Discovering Computers 2005 Issues Web page (**scsite.com/dc2005/issues**). Click Issue #1 below Chapter 6.

Video Cards and CRT Monitors

Many CRT monitors use an analog signal to produce an image. To display high-quality color on this type of CRT monitor, a desktop computer sends a signal through a video card on the motherboard. A cable on the CRT monitor plugs into a port on the video card. A **video card**, also called a *graphics card*, converts digital output from the computer into an analog video signal and sends the signal through the cable to the monitor, which displays output on the screen (Figure 6-6).

The number of colors a video card displays is determined by its bit depth. The video card's *bit depth*, also called the *color depth*, is the number of bits it uses to store information about each pixel. For example, an 8-bit video card (also called 8-bit color) uses 8 bits to store information about each pixel. Thus, this video card can display 256 different colors (computed as 2^8 or $2 \times 2 \times 2 \times 2 \times 2 \times 2 \times 2 \times 2$). A 24-bit video card uses 24 bits to store information about each pixel and can display 2^{24} or 16.7 million colors. The greater the number of bits, the better the resulting image.

FIGURE 6-6 HOW VIDEO TRAVELS FROM THE PROCESSOR TO A CRT MONITOR

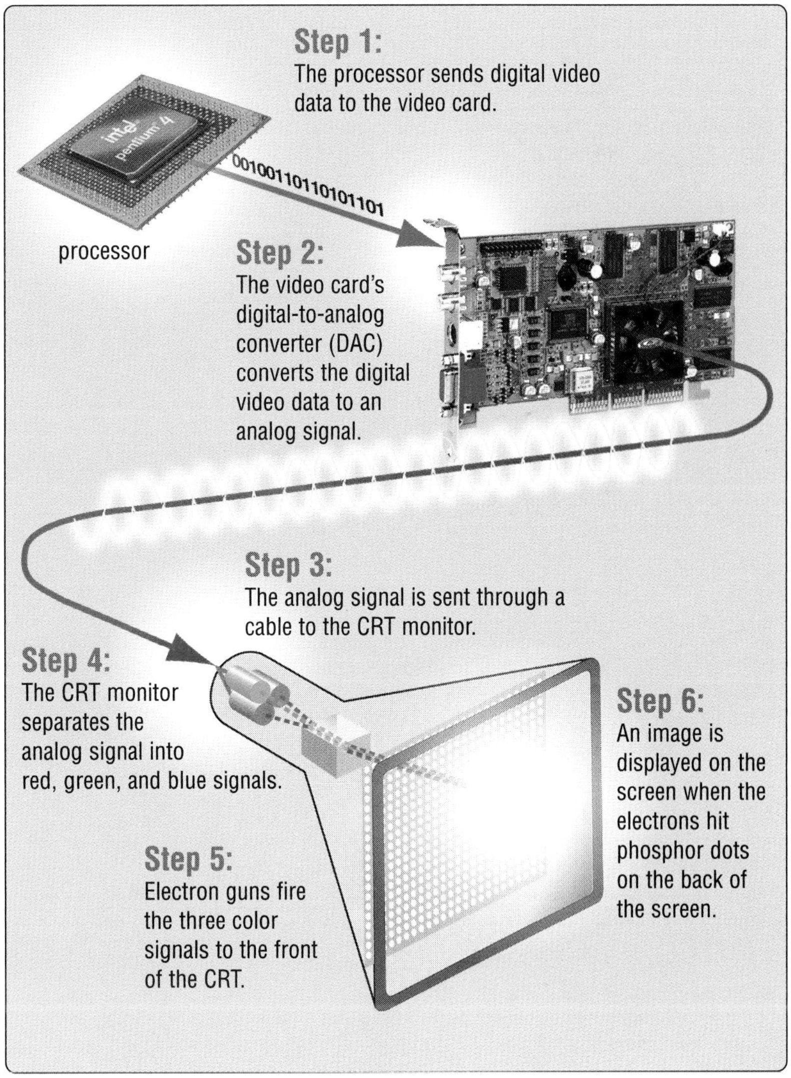

Over the years, several video standards have been developed to define the resolution, number of colors, and other display properties. Today, *VESA* (*Video Electronics Standards Association*), which consists of video card and monitor manufacturers, develops video standards. Most current video cards support the *SVGA* (*super video graphics array*) standard, which also supports resolutions and colors in the VGA standard. The table in Figure 6-7 outlines the suggested resolution and number of displayed colors in the MDA, VGA, XGA, SVGA, SXGA, UXGA, and beyond UXGA standards.

VIDEO STANDARDS

Standard	Suggested Resolution	Maximum Possible Colors
Monochrome Display Adapter (MDA)	720 x 350	1 for text
Video Graphics Array (VGA)	640 x 480	16
	320 x 200	256
Extended Graphics Array (XGA)	1024 x 768	256
	640 x 480	65,536
Super Video Graphics Array (SVGA)	800 x 600	16.7 million
Super Extended Graphics Array (SXGA)	1280 x 1024	16.7 million
Ultra Extended Graphics Array (UXGA)	1600 x 1200	16.7 million
Beyond UXGA	1920 x 1440	16.7 million
	2048 x 1536	16.7 million

FIGURE 6-7 Various video standards are available.

For a monitor to display images using the resolution and number of colors defined by a video standard, the monitor must support the same video standard, and the video card must be capable of communicating appropriate signals to the monitor. Both the video card and the monitor must support the video standard to generate the desired resolution and number of colors.

A video card also must have enough memory to generate the resolution and number of colors you want to display. The memory in a video card stores information about each pixel. Video cards use many types of video memory: VRAM (video RAM), WRAM (window RAM), SGRAM (synchronous graphics RAM), or SDRAM (synchronous DRAM).

Manufacturers state video memory in megabytes. The table in Figure 6-8 outlines the amount of video memory required for various screen resolutions and color depth configurations. For example, if you want a 1600 x 1200 resolution with 32-bit color, then your video card should have at least 8 MB of video memory. Most video cards have 16 MB to 128 MB of video memory.

In addition to memory chips, the video card contains a processor chip, sometimes called a *graphics processing unit* (*GPU*) because it performs calculations used to display images on the screen. A video card's processor and memory chips generate a lot of heat. Thus, video cards usually contain a fan or heat sink to keep the chips from overheating.

VARIOUS VIDEO CARD CONFIGURATIONS

Video Memory	Color Depth	Number of Colors	Maximum Resolution
1 MB	8-bit	256	1024 x 768
	16-bit	65,536	800 x 600
2 MB	8-bit	256	1024 x 768
	16-bit	65,536	1280 x 1024
	24-bit	16.7 million	800 x 600
4 MB	24-bit	16.7 million	1024 x 768
6 MB	24-bit	16.7 million	1280 x 1024
8 MB	32-bit	16.7 million	1600 x 1200
16 MB	32-bit	16.7 million	1920 x 1440
32 MB	32-bit	16.7 million	2048 x 1536
64 MB	32-bit	16.7 million	2048 x 1536
128 MB	32-bit	16.7 million	2048 x 1536
256 MB	32-bit	16.7 million	2048 x 1536

FIGURE 6-8 Video memory requirements vary for a range of screen resolutions.

WEB LINK 6-2

Video Memory

Visit the Discovering Computers 2005 WEB LINK page (**scsite.com/dc2005/weblink**). Click Video Memory below Chapter 6.

FLAT-PANEL DISPLAYS

A *flat-panel display* is a display device with a shallow depth that does not use CRT technology. LCD monitors, LCD screens, gas plasma monitors, and many HDTVs are types of flat-panel displays. The following sections discuss various types of flat-panel displays.

LCD Monitors and Screens

An **LCD monitor**, also called an *LCD flat panel monitor*, is a desktop monitor that uses a liquid crystal display instead of a cathode-ray tube to produce images (Figure 6-9). These monitors produce sharp, flicker-free images.

LCD monitors have a much smaller *footprint* than do CRT monitors; that is, they take up less desk space. For additional space savings, some LCD monitors are wall mountable. An LCD monitor also uses less than one-third the power consumed by a CRT monitor, produces less heat, and does not produce electromagnetic radiation. LCD monitors are available in a variety of sizes, with the more common being 15, 17, 18, 20, 21, and 23 inches. For an even wider screen area, some users position two or more monitors side by side or stacked (Figure 6-10). For example, one monitor can show the left side of a document, game, graphic design, or other item, with the other monitor showing the right side. This arrangement also is convenient if you want to run multiple applications simultaneously. Users of side-by-side monitors include music editors, video editors, network administrators, gamers, researchers, Web developers, graphic designers, and engineers. Read Issue 6-2 for a related discussion.

FIGURE 6-9 An LCD monitor is much thinner and weighs less than a CRT monitor.

FIGURE 6-10 Users sometimes have multiple LCD monitors stacked or side by side to increase their viewing area.

ISSUE 6-2

LCD or CRT?

Home and business users currently spend a substantial amount of time working on computers. To reduce eyestrain and other types of monitor-related health conditions, it is important users have high-quality monitors that produce crisp, bright images. Until recently, CRT (cathode-ray tube) technology dominated the monitor industry. Today, however, LCD monitors are transforming the way people look at their computers. The space-saving, brighter LCD monitor, that uses LCD technology, has emerged as a key competitor in the monitor market. Although the goal of the LCD monitor industry is to replace the CRT monitor as the dominant desktop monitor, some industry experts predict that LCD monitors will appear on only one-half of users' desktops in the coming years. Can LCD monitors compete against CRT monitors for desktop applications? Will price issues affect LCD monitor sales? If so, how? Will health-related concerns influence the sales of LCD monitors?

For more information about LCD monitors, visit the Discovering Computers 2005 Issues Web page (**scsite.com/dc2005/issues**). Click Issue #2 below Chapter 6.

Mobile computers, such as notebook computers and Tablet PCs, and mobile devices, such as PDAs and smart phones, often have LCD screens (Figure 6-11). Notebook computer screens are available in a variety of sizes, with the more common being 14.1, 15.4, and 16 inches. Tablet PC screens range from 8 inches to 15 inches. PDA screens average 3 inches wide by 4 inches tall. On smart phones, users see approximately five lines of text at a time on the screen.

E-books are another mobile device that use an LCD screen. An **e-book** (*electronic book*) is a small, book-sized computer that allows users to read, save, highlight, bookmark, and add notes to online text. You download new book content to an e-book, mobile device, or computer. To obtain the same functionality as an e-book device, some users install a program called *Microsoft Reader* onto a PDA or computer.

Microsoft developed a technology called *ClearType* to improve the quality of reading material on LCD screens, such as an e-book or notebook computer. ClearType changes the brightness and contrast of pixels surrounding each letter to give the letter more of a printed appearance.

LCD Technology

Similar to LCDs in watches and calculators, a **liquid crystal display** (**LCD**) uses a liquid compound to present information on a display. Computer LCDs typically have fluorescent tubes that emit light waves toward the liquid-crystal cells, which are sandwiched between two sheets of material (Figure 6-12). When an electrical charge passes through the cells, the cells twist. This twisting causes some light waves to be blocked and allows others to pass through, creating images on the display.

FIGURE 6-11 Notebook computers and Tablet PCs have color LCD screens. Many PDAs and smart phones also have color screens.

FIGURE 6-12 HOW LCD WORKS

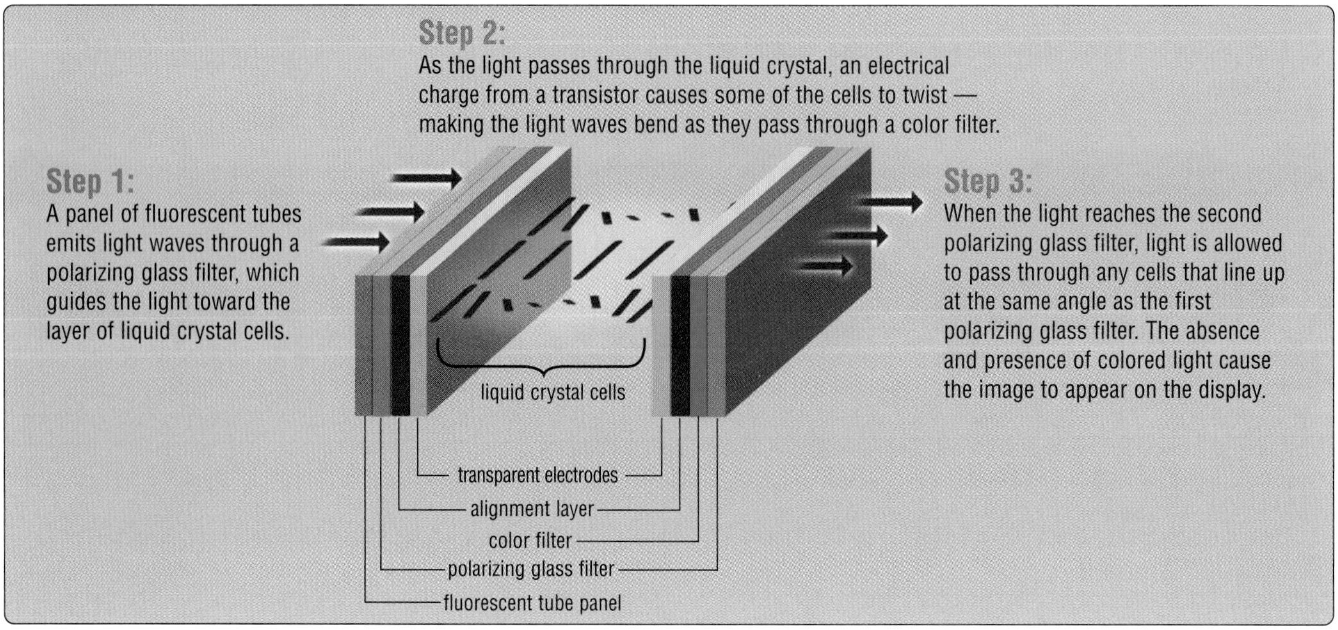

LCD monitors and LCD screens produce color using either passive-matrix or active-matrix technology. An *active-matrix display*, also known as a *TFT (thin-film transistor) display*, uses a separate transistor to apply changes to each liquid crystal cell and thus displays high-quality color that is viewable from all angles. A newer type of TFT, called *organic LED (OLED)*, uses organic molecules that produce an even brighter, easier-to-read display than standard TFT displays. Also, OLEDs are less expensive to produce, consume less power, and can be fabricated on flexible surfaces.

A *passive-matrix display* uses fewer transistors and requires less power than an active-matrix display. The color on a passive-matrix display often is not as bright as an active-matrix display. Users view images on a passive-matrix display best when working directly in front of it. The latest passive-matrix displays use *high-performance addressing (HPA)*, which provides image quality near that of TFT displays. Passive-matrix displays are less expensive than active-matrix displays.

LCD Quality

The quality of an LCD monitor or LCD screen depends primarily on its resolution, which generally is proportional to the size of a monitor or screen. That is, the resolution increases for larger monitors and screens. For example, a 15-inch LCD monitor typically has a resolution of 1024 x 768, while a 17-inch has a resolution of 1280 x 1024. Unlike CRT monitors that can display a variety of resolutions, LCDs usually are geared for a specific resolution. When set at other resolutions, the quality often is not as good as the manufacturer's original resolution.

For most business applications, refresh rates usually are not an issue with LCD monitors or LCD screens because the images either are on or off. If you intend to watch videos, movies, or play graphic-intensive games, however, slower refresh rates may be distracting. Thus, users of these applications often opt for a higher hertz or a CRT monitor.

An important measure of LCD monitors is the *response time*, which is the time in milliseconds (ms) that it takes to turn a pixel on or off. LCD monitors' response times average 25 ms. The lower the number, the faster the response time.

Brightness of an LCD monitor or LCD screen is measured in nits. A *nit* is a unit of visible light intensity equal to one candela (formerly called candlepower) per square meter. The *candela* is the standard unit of luminous intensity. LCD monitors today range from 200 to 350 nits. The higher the nits, the brighter the images.

Video Cards and LCD Monitors

LCD monitors use a digital signal to produce a picture. When you plug an LCD monitor into a video card that delivers analog signals, the LCD monitor converts the analog signal from the video card back to a digital signal. This is one reason why LCD monitors are more expensive than CRT monitors, sometimes costing two to three times as much as a comparable CRT monitor.

Ideally, an LCD monitor should plug into a *DVI (Digital Video Interface)* port on the computer. Developed by the *Digital Display Working Group (DDWG)*, a *DVI port* accepts digital signals directly, eliminating the need for the analog to digital conversion. Newer video cards have DVI ports, some of which send both digital and analog signals to a monitor (Figure 6-13). These video cards usually also have a standard monitor port and an *S-video port*, allowing users to connect external devices such as a television, DVD player, or video recorder, to the computer.

WEB LINK 6-3

LCD Technology

Visit the Discovering Computers 2005 WEB LINK page (**scsite .com/dc2005/weblink**). Click LCD Technology below Chapter 6.

FAQ 6-2

Is a flat display the same as a flat-panel display?

No. A *flat display* refers to a CRT monitor that has a flat screen. A flat-panel display, by contrast, has a shallow depth and uses LCD, gas plasma, or some technology other than CRT.

For more information about flat-panel displays, visit the Discovering Computers 2005 FAQ Web page (**scsite.com/dc2005/faq**). Click Flat-Panel Displays below Chapter 6.

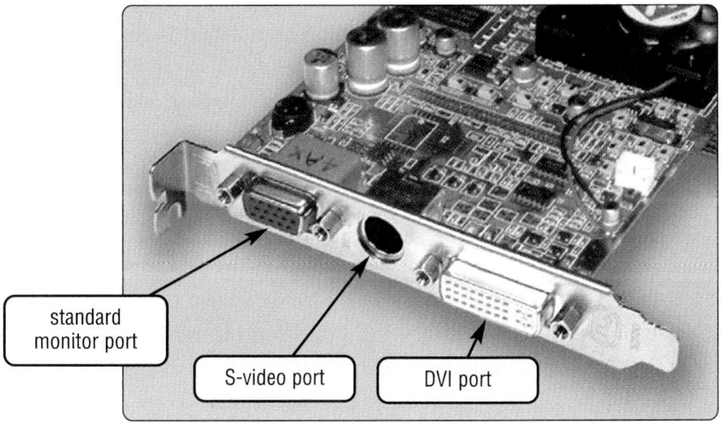

FIGURE 6-13 Ports on a video card.

Gas Plasma Monitors

Large business users or power users sometimes have gas plasma monitors, which often measure more than 50 inches wide (Figure 6-14). A **gas plasma monitor** is a display device that uses gas plasma technology, which substitutes a layer of gas for the liquid crystal material in an LCD monitor. When voltage is applied, the gas releases ultraviolet (UV) light. This UV light causes the pixels on the screen to glow and form an image.

Gas plasma monitors offer larger screen sizes and higher display quality than LCD monitors but are much more expensive. These monitors also can hang directly on a wall.

FIGURE 6-14 Large gas plasma monitors can measure more than 50 inches wide.

Televisions and HDTVs

Home users may have a television as a display device. Connecting a computer to an analog television requires an *NTSC converter*, which converts the digital signal from the computer into an analog signal that the television can display. NTSC stands for *National Television Standards Committee* and consists of industry members who have technical expertise about television-related issues. The best analog televisions have a resolution of only 520 x 400 pixels. Thus, users are turning to *digital television (DTV)* for crisper, higher-quality output.

Although televisions can use either CRT or LCD technology, the trend in newer digital models is LCD. Digital television signals provide two major advantages over analog signals. First, digital signals produce a higher-quality picture. Second, many programs can be broadcast on a single digital channel, whereas only one program can be broadcast on an analog channel. By 2006, all stations must be broadcasting digital signals, as mandated by the FCC.

HDTV (*high-definition television*) is the most advanced form of digital television, working with digital broadcast signals, transmitting digital sound, supporting wide screens, and providing resolutions up to 1920 x 1080 pixels. With HDTV, the broadcast signals are digitized when they are sent via over-the-air (OTA) broadcasts from local television networks, satellite, or cable. To receive the HDTV signals via OTA broadcasts, you need a VHF/UHF antenna; via satellite, you need an HDTV-compatible satellite receiver/tuner; and via cable, you need an HDTV-compatible cable box.

As the cost of HDTV becomes more reasonable, home users may begin to use it as their computer's display device. HDTV also is ideal for presenting material to a large group. HDTV technology makes the use of interactive TV more widespread. **Interactive TV** is a two-way communications technology in which users interact with television programming. HDTV works directly with interactive TV. Uses of interactive TV include selecting a movie from a central library of movies, voting or responding to network questionnaires, banking and shopping, playing games, and video conferencing.

FAQ 6-3

Can I watch digital television broadcasts on my analog television?

Yes, if you buy a device that converts the digital signal to an analog signal. The image on your analog television, however, will not have HDTV resolution.

For more information about HDTV, visit the Discovering Computers 2005 FAQ Web page (**scsite.com/dc2005/faq**). Click HDTV below Chapter 6.

QUIZ YOURSELF 6-1

To check your knowledge of categories of output, CRT monitors, and flat-panel displays, visit the Discovering Computers 2005 Quiz Yourself Web page (**scsite.com/dc2005/quiz**). Click Objectives 1 – 4 below Chapter 6.

PRINTERS

A **printer** is an output device that produces text and graphics on a physical medium such as paper or transparency film. Printed information, called *hard copy*, exists physically and is a more permanent form of output than that presented on a display device (soft copy).

A hard copy, also called a *printout*, is either in portrait or landscape orientation (Figure 6-15). A printout in *portrait orientation* is taller than it is wide, with information printed across the shorter width of the paper. A printout in *landscape orientation* is wider than it is tall, with information printed across the widest part of the paper. Letters, reports, and books typically use portrait orientation. Spreadsheets, slide shows, and graphics often use landscape orientation.

Home computer users might print less than a hundred pages a week. Small business computer users might print several hundred pages a day. Users of mainframe computers, such as large utility companies that send printed statements to hundreds of thousands of customers each month, require printers that are capable of printing thousands of pages per hour.

Figure 6-15a (portrait orientation)

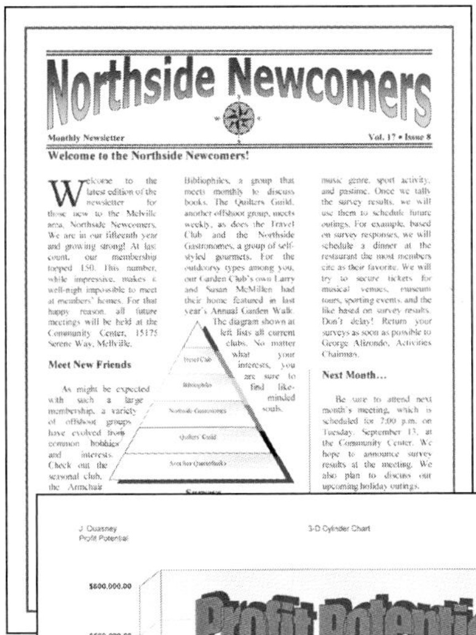

Figure 6-15b (landscape orientation)

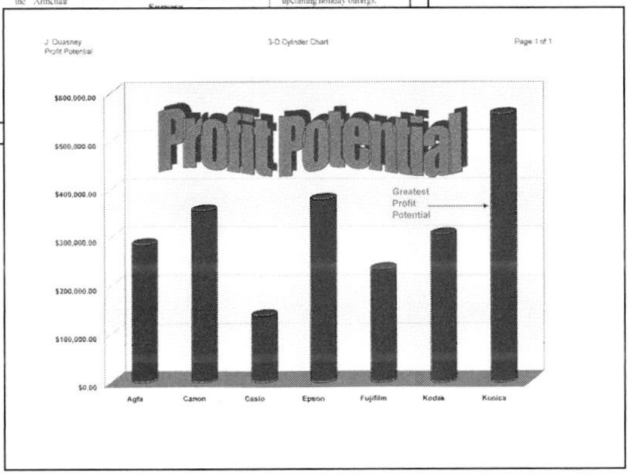

FIGURE 6-15 Portrait orientation is taller than it is wide. Landscape orientation is wider than it is tall.

To meet this range of printing needs, many different printers exist with varying speeds, capabilities, and printing methods. Figure 6-16 presents a list of questions to help you decide on the printer best suited to your needs. Read Looking Ahead 6-1 for a look at the next generation of paper.

1. What is my budget?
2. How fast must my printer print?
3. Do I need a color printer?
4. What is the cost per page for printing?
5. Do I need multiple copies of documents?
6. Will I print graphics?
7. Do I want to print photographs?
8. Do I want to print directly from a memory card or other type of miniature storage media?
9. What types of paper does the printer use?
10. What sizes of paper does the printer accept?
11. Do I want to print on both sides of the paper?
12. How much paper can the printer tray hold?
13. Will the printer work with my computer and software?
14. How much do supplies such as ink and paper cost?
15. Can the printer print on envelopes and transparencies?
16. How many envelopes can the printer print at a time?
17. How much printing do I print now, and what will I be printing in a year or two?
18. Will the printer be connected to a network?
19. Do I want wireless printing capability?

FIGURE 6-16 Questions to ask when purchasing a printer.

LOOKING AHEAD 6-1

Electronic Paper Writes a New Page

Magic wands often are found in fairy tales and in magicians' hands, but they may be finding the way to your home or office. The wands could be used to create images and text on electronic reusable paper.

Engineers at Xerox PARC (Palo Alto Research Center) and the Massachusetts Institute of Technology Media Laboratory are leaders in this technology. The Xerox inventors named their product Gyricon, which is the Greek word for rotating image. Each sheet has millions of beads randomly dispersed in oil between thin, transparent, plastic sheets. A bead is smaller than a grain of sand and has two contrasting colors, such as black and white or red and white; it rotates to display one of these colors when a voltage is applied to the sheet's surface. The various color patterns form letters and images that remain until a new voltage pattern changes the display.

The Xerox researchers envision waving a wand over the reusable paper, so the sheets can function as an all-in-one printer, copier, fax machine, and scanner. The technology also has possibilities in the advertising field, where in-store signs and prices can be updated regularly, and for electronic newspapers and magazines.

For a look at the next generation of electronic paper, visit the Discovering Computers 2005 Looking Ahead Web page (**scsite.com/dc2005/looking**). Click Looking Ahead #1 below Chapter 6.

A printer often connects by a cable to a parallel port or a USB port. Two categories of printers are impact and nonimpact. The following pages discuss various types of impact and nonimpact printers.

Impact Printers

An **impact printer** forms characters and graphics on a piece of paper by striking a mechanism against an inked ribbon that physically contacts the paper. Impact printers characteristically are noisy because of this striking activity. These printers commonly produce *near letter quality* (*NLQ*) output, which is print quality slightly less clear than what is acceptable for business letters.

Companies may use impact printers for routine jobs such as printing mailing labels, envelopes, and invoices. Impact printers also are ideal for printing multipart forms because they easily print through many layers of paper. Factories and retail counters use impact printers because these printers withstand dusty environments, vibrations, and extreme temperatures.

Two commonly used types of impact printers are dot-matrix printers and line printers. The following paragraphs discuss each of these printers.

DOT-MATRIX PRINTERS A **dot-matrix printer** is an impact printer that produces printed images when tiny wire pins on a print head mechanism strike an inked ribbon (Figure 6-17). When the ribbon presses against the paper, it creates dots that form characters and graphics.

Most dot-matrix printers use *continuous-form paper*, in which thousands of sheets of paper are connected together end to end. The pages have holes along the sides to help feed the paper through the printer. Perforations along the inside of the holes and at each fold allow users to separate the sheets into standard-sized sheets of paper, such as 8½-by-11 inches. Many dot-matrix printers can print pages in either portrait or landscape orientation.

The print head mechanism on a dot-matrix printer contains 9 to 24 pins, depending on the manufacturer and the printer model. A higher number of pins means the printer prints more dots per character, which results in higher print quality.

The speed of a dot-matrix printer is measured by the number of characters per second (cps) it can print. The speed of most dot-matrix printers ranges from 300 to 1100 characters per second (cps), depending on the desired print quality.

LINE PRINTERS A **line printer** is a high-speed impact printer that prints an entire line at a time (Figure 6-18). The speed of a line printer is measured by the number of lines per minute (lpm) it can print. Some line printers print as many as 3,000 lpm. Mainframes, midrange servers, or networked applications, such as manufacturing, distribution, or shipping, often use line printers. These printers typically use 11-by-17-inch continuous-form paper.

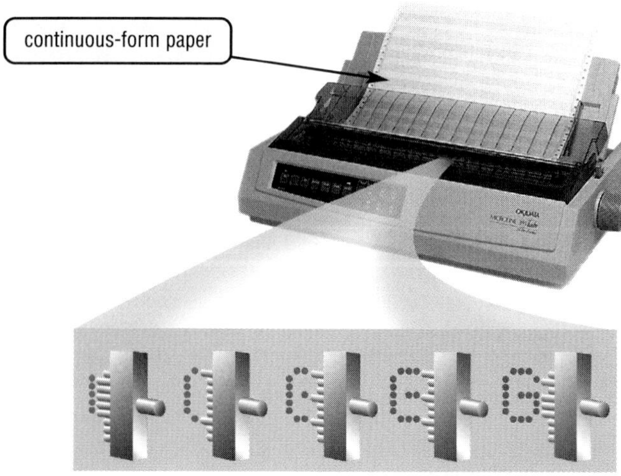

FIGURE 6-17 A dot-matrix printer produces printed images when tiny pins strike an inked ribbon.

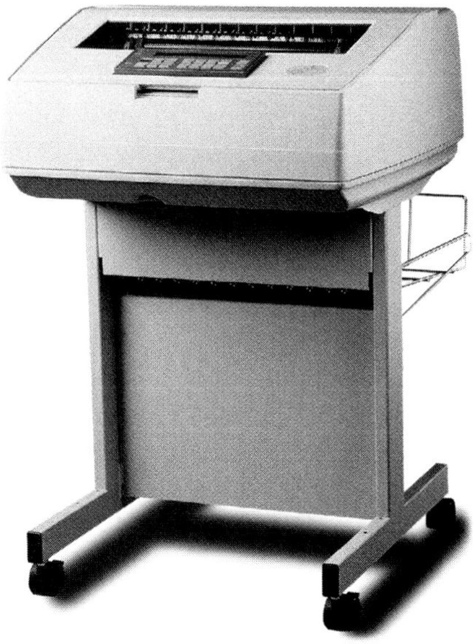

FIGURE 6-18 A line printer is a high-speed printer often connected to a mainframe, midrange server, or network.

Two popular types of line printers used for high-volume output are band and shuttle-matrix. A *band printer* prints fully formed characters when hammers strike a horizontal, rotating band that contains shapes of numbers, letters of the alphabet, and other characters. A *shuttle-matrix printer* functions more like a dot-matrix printer. The difference is the shuttle-matrix printer moves a series of print hammers back and forth horizontally at incredibly high speeds, as compared with standard line printers. Unlike a band printer, a shuttle-matrix printer prints characters in various fonts and font sizes.

Nonimpact Printers

A **nonimpact printer** forms characters and graphics on a piece of paper without actually striking the paper. Some spray ink, while others use heat or pressure to create images. These printers are much quieter than the previously discussed impact printers because nonimpact printers do not strike the paper.

Commonly used nonimpact printers are ink-jet printers, photo printers, laser printers, thermal printers, mobile printers, label and postage printers, plotters, and large-format printers. The following sections discuss each of these printers.

Ink-Jet Printers

An **ink-jet printer** is a type of nonimpact printer that forms characters and graphics by spraying tiny drops of liquid ink onto a piece of paper. Ink-jet printers have become the most popular type of color printer for use in the home because of their lower cost and *letter-quality* (*LQ*) print, which is an acceptable quality of print for business letters (Figure 6-19). A reasonable quality ink-jet printer costs less than $100.

Ink-jet printers produce text and graphics in both black-and-white and color on a variety of paper types. Ink-jet printers normally use individual sheets of paper stored in one or two removable or stationary trays. Available paper types include plain paper, ink-jet paper, photo paper, glossy paper, and perhaps banner paper. Some ink-jet printers can print photographic-quality images on any of these types of paper. Others require heavier weight ink-jet paper for better-looking color documents.

FIGURE 6-19 Ink-jet printers are the most popular type of color printer used in the home.

Ink-jet printers also print on other materials such as envelopes, labels, index cards, greeting card paper, transparencies, and iron-on T-shirt transfers. Many ink-jet printers include software for creating greeting cards, banners, business cards, letterheads, and transparencies. Read Issue 6-3 for a related discussion.

As with many other input and output devices, one factor that determines the quality of an ink-jet printer is its resolution, or sharpness and clarity. Printer resolution is measured by the number of *dots per inch (dpi)* a printer can output. With an ink-jet printer, a dot is a drop of ink. A higher dpi means the drops of ink are smaller. Most ink-jet printers range from 300 to 2400 dpi. Printers with a higher dpi usually are more expensive.

As shown in Figure 6-20, the higher the dpi, the better the print quality. The difference in quality becomes noticeable when the size of the printed image increases. That is, a wallet-sized image printed at 300 dpi may look similar in quality to one printed at 1200 dpi. When you increase the size of the image, to 5 x 7 for example, the printout of the 300 dpi resolution looks grainier than the one printed using a 1200 dpi resolution.

The speed of an ink-jet printer is measured by the number of pages per minute (ppm) it can print. Most ink-jet printers print from 3 to 21 ppm. Graphics and colors print at a slower rate. For example, an ink-jet printer may print 17 ppm for black text and only 13 ppm for color and/or graphics.

FIGURE 6-20 You will notice a higher quality output with printers that can print at a higher dpi.

The print head mechanism in an ink-jet printer contains ink-filled print cartridges. Each cartridge has fifty to several hundred small ink holes, or nozzles. The steps in Figure 6-21 illustrate how a drop of ink appears on a page. Each nozzle in the print cartridge is similar to an individual pin on a dot-matrix printer. Just as any combination of dot-matrix pins can be activated, the ink propels through any combination of the nozzles to form a character or image on the paper. A *bubble-jet printer* is a printer that uses a technology very similar to the ink-jet, that is, propelling ink through tiny nozzles.

When the print cartridge runs out of ink, you simply replace the cartridge. Most ink-jet printers have at least two print cartridges: one containing black ink and the other(s) containing colors. These cartridges cost approximately $30 each. The number of pages a single cartridge can print varies by manufacturer and the type of documents you print. In some cases, a single cartridge might print as many as 300 pages.

On average, it costs from $.03 to $.05 per page for black ink and $.10 to $.15 per page for color ink. When coupled with premium photo paper, the cost for a high-quality photograph increases to about $1.00 per page.

ISSUE 6-3

Short of Cash?

Some college students found a solution to their money problems: they made their own. With a scanner, personal computer, and color printer, they produced bogus bills and passed more than $1,000 in counterfeit currency before they were caught. As printer quality improves, an estimated $1 million in counterfeit currency is passed every week. Police have arrested counterfeiters ranging from high school students to senior citizens. Spotting fake money is not that difficult, but most people never look that closely. Counterfeiting does not stop with money. With templates for diplomas, degrees, transcripts, Social Security cards, driver's licenses, birth certificates, and Green Cards available on the Web, almost any document can be produced. As one federal agent points out, counterfeiting has gone from a high-skill, low-tech job to a high-tech, low-skill job. Should printer manufacturers take responsibility for this problem? Why or why not? What, if anything, could printer makers do? Can you offer any other possible solutions? What should be the penalty for selling counterfeit documents online?

For more information about counterfeit cash, visit the Discovering Computers 2005 Issues Web page (**scsite.com/dc2005/issues**). Click Issue #3 below Chapter 6.

FIGURE 6-21 HOW AN INK-JET PRINTER WORKS

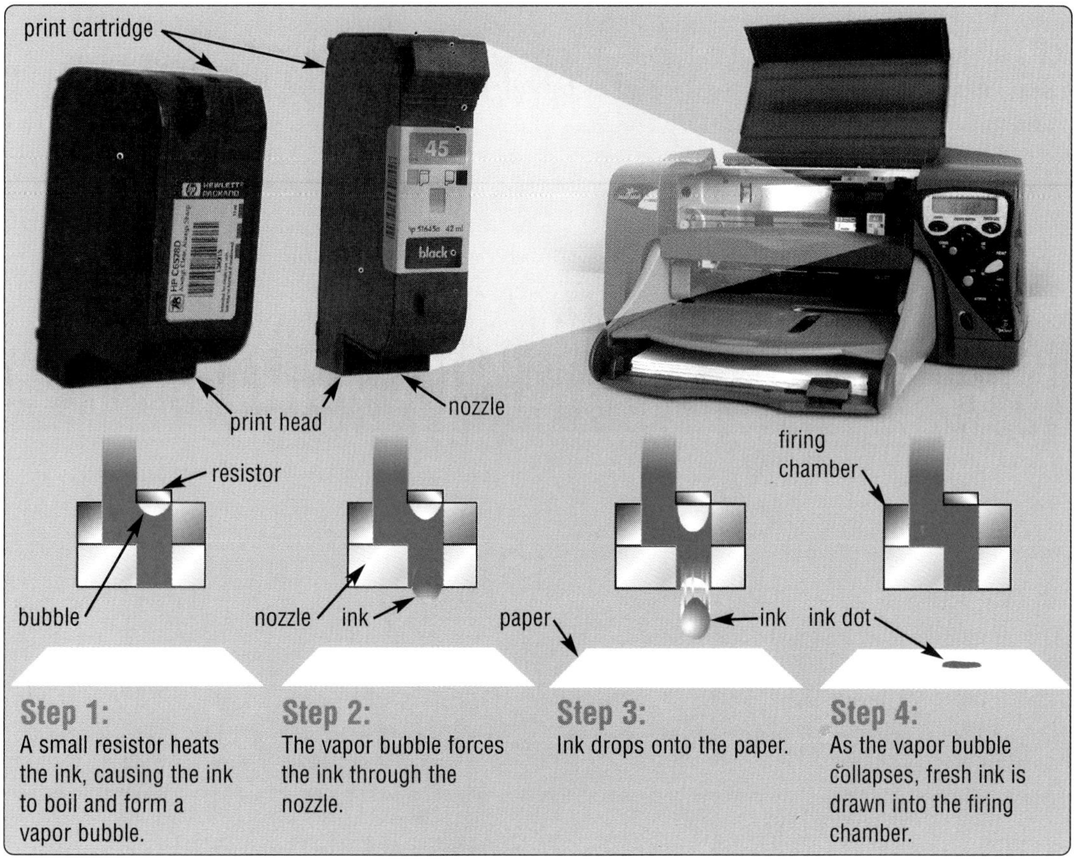

WEB LINK 6-4

Ink-Jet Printers

Visit the Discovering Computers 2005 WEB LINK page (**scsite .com/dc2005/weblink**). Click Ink-Jet Printers below Chapter 6.

FAQ 6-4

Can ink-jet cartridges be refilled?

Yes. An ink-jet refill kit costs about one-half the price of a new cartridge. Keep a spare refill kit on hand, so you can refill an empty cartridge immediately. Once an empty cartridge dries, its ink jets may clog. While refilling, wear the latex gloves supplied with the kit and be careful not to squeeze the cartridge — which may cause it to ooze ink onto hands, clothing, furniture, or equipment.

For more information about ink-jet refill kits, visit the Discovering Computers 2005 FAQ Web page (**scsite.com/dc2005/faq**). Click Ink-Jet Refill Kits below Chapter 6.

Photo Printers

A **photo printer** is a color printer that produces photo-lab-quality pictures. Some photo printers print just one or two sizes of images, for example, 3 x 5 inches and 4 x 6 inches. Others print up to letter size, legal size, or even as large as 13 x 19 inches. Some even print panoramic photographs. Read Apply It 6-1 for more information.

APPLY IT 6-1

Picture This: Printing Digital Photographs

Seeing is believing. When you are ready to share printed copies of images you took with your digital camera, the right paper can help you get the best results.

Many photo papers are available, so you need to look at the specifications printed on the cartons and then match the products to your needs and budget. To start, consider the surface finishes: high gloss, soft gloss, satin, or matte.

Next, look at the paper weight, which is measured in pounds. In the United States, the weight of paper is stated in pounds per 500 sheets of 17" × 22" paper, each sheet of which equals four letter-sized sheets. Professional papers have the highest quality and are the heaviest, with weights ranging from 44 to 58 pounds. Price per sheet is about 50 cents. Premium papers have weights from 24 to 32 pounds and cost about 15 cents per sheet. Everyday presentation and document papers are best for reports and generally weigh 20 to 24 pounds. Each sheet costs approximately 2 cents.

Another factor is paper brightness. The higher the brightness rating, the more brilliant the whiteness. Brightness ranges from 84 to 113+.

Acid-free paper will not crumble or yellow over time, so it is good to use for important photos that you will keep for a long time. Other considerations are using recycled paper and the option of two-sided printing.

For more information about photo papers, visit the Discovering Computers 2005 Apply It Web page (**scsite.com/dc2005/apply**). Click Apply It #1 below Chapter 6.

Many inexpensive photo printers use ink-jet technology. With models that can print letter-sized documents, users connect the photo printer to their computer and use it for all their printing needs. For a few hundred dollars, this type of photo printer is ideal for the home or small business user. Other photo printer technologies are discussed later in the chapter.

Many photo printers have a built-in card slot so the printer can print digital photographs directly from a media card (Figure 6-22). That is, you do not need to transfer the images from the media card to the computer to print them. Simply remove the media card from the digital camera and insert it into the printer's card slot. Then, push buttons on the printer to select the desired photo, specify the number of copies, and indicate the size of the printed image. Some photo printers have built-in LCD color screens, allowing users to view and enhance the pictures before printing them.

WEB LINK 6-5

Photo Printers

Visit the Discovering Computers 2005 WEB LINK page (**scsite .com/dc2005/weblink**). Click Photo Printers below Chapter 6.

FIGURE 6-22 HOW A PHOTO PRINTER PRINTS DIRECTLY FROM A MEDIA CARD

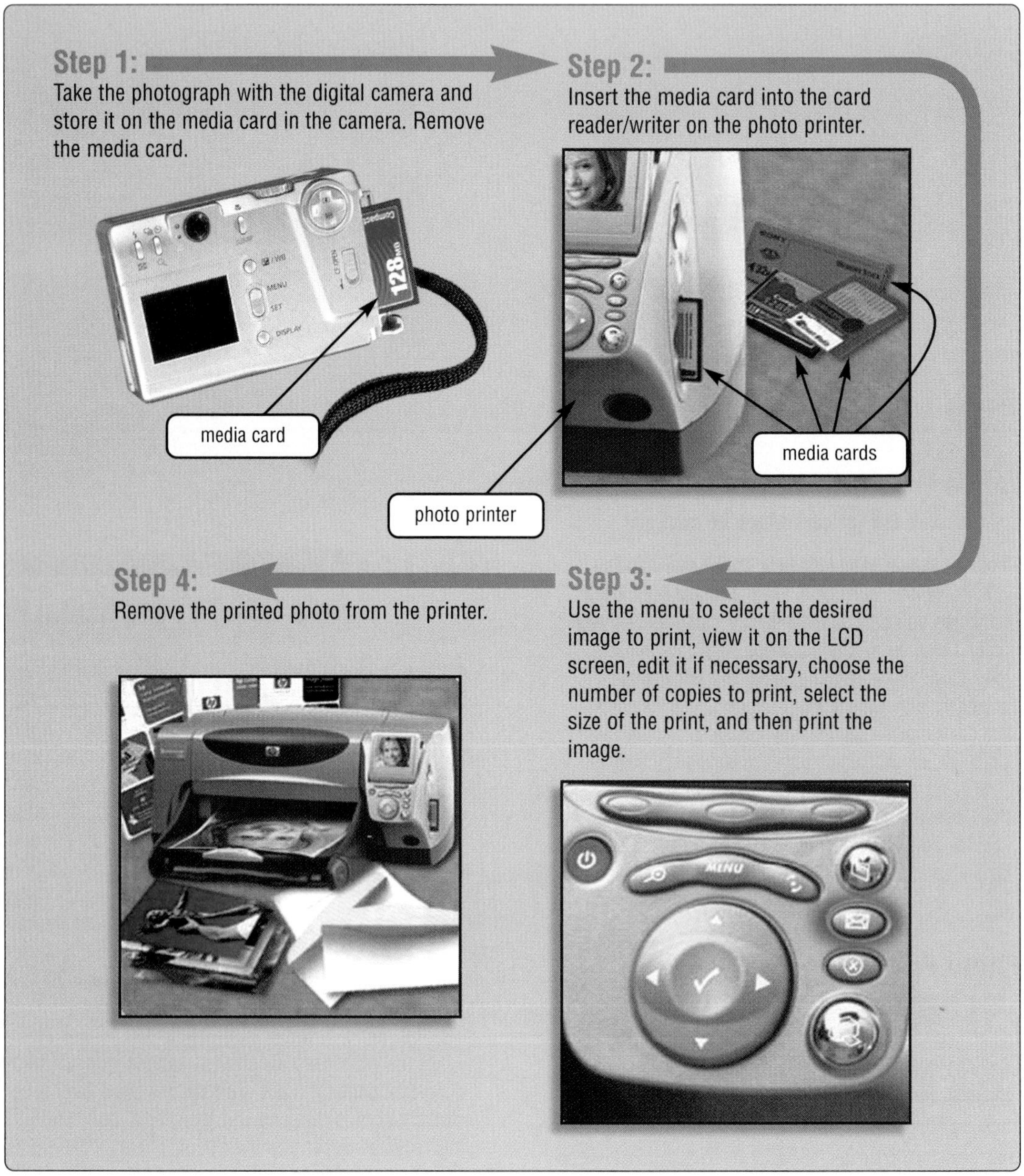

Laser Printers

A **laser printer** is a high-speed, high-quality nonimpact printer (Figure 6-23). Laser printers for personal computers ordinarily use individual sheets of paper stored in one or more removable trays that slide into the printer case. Some laser printers have built-in trays that accommodate different sizes of paper, while others require separate trays for letter- and legal-sized paper. Most laser printers have a manual feed slot where you can insert individual sheets and envelopes. You also can print transparencies on a laser printer.

Laser printers print text and graphics in very high quality resolutions, usually ranging from 600 to 2400 dpi. While laser printers usually cost more than ink-jet printers, they also are much faster. A laser printer for the home and small office user typically prints text at speeds of 9 to 50 ppm. Laser printers for large business users print more than 150 ppm.

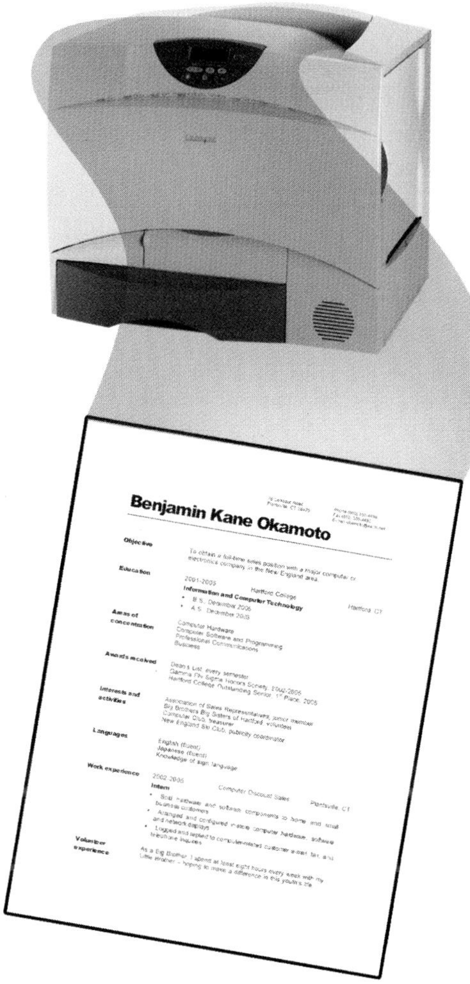

FIGURE 6-23 Laser printers are used with personal computers, as well as larger computers.

Depending on the quality and speed of the printer, the cost of a black-and-white laser printer ranges from a few hundred to several thousand dollars for the home and small office user, and several hundred thousand dollars for the large business user. The higher the resolution and speed, the more expensive the printer. Although color laser printers are available, they are relatively expensive, with prices for the home and small business user starting at about $700.

When printing a document, laser printers process and store the entire page before they actually print it. For this reason, laser printers sometimes are called page printers. Storing a page before printing requires that the laser printer has a certain amount of memory in the device.

Depending on the amount of graphics you intend to print, a laser printer for the home or small business user can have up to 384 MB of memory. To print a full-page 600-dpi picture, for instance, you might need 16 MB of memory in the printer. If the printer does not have enough memory to print the picture, either it will print as much of the picture as its memory will allow, or it will display an error message and not print any of the picture. If the printer memory is expandable, inserting a memory module into the printer's expansion slot(s) increases the memory.

Laser printers use software that enables them to interpret a *page description language (PDL)*, which tells the printer how to lay out the contents of a printed page. When you purchase a laser printer, it comes with at least one of two common page description languages: PCL or PostScript. Developed by Hewlett-Packard, a leading printer manufacturer, *PCL (Printer Control Language)* is a standard printer language that supports the fonts and layout used in standard office documents. Professionals in the desktop publishing and graphic art fields commonly use *PostScript* because it is designed for complex documents with intense graphics and colors.

WEB LINK 6-6

Laser Printers

Visit the Discovering Computers 2005 WEB LINK page (**scsite .com/dc2005/weblink**). Click Laser Printers below Chapter 6.

Operating in a manner similar to a copy machine, a laser printer creates images using a laser beam and powdered ink, called *toner*. The laser beam produces an image on a special drum inside the printer. The light of the laser alters the electrical charge on the drum wherever it hits. When this occurs, the toner sticks to the drum and then transfers to the paper through a combination of pressure and heat (Figure 6-24).

When the toner runs out, you replace the toner cartridge. Toner cartridge prices range from $50 to $100 for about 5,000 printed pages. On average, the cost per printed page on a black-and-white laser printer is $.02 to $.03.

FIGURE 6-24 HOW A LASER PRINTER WORKS

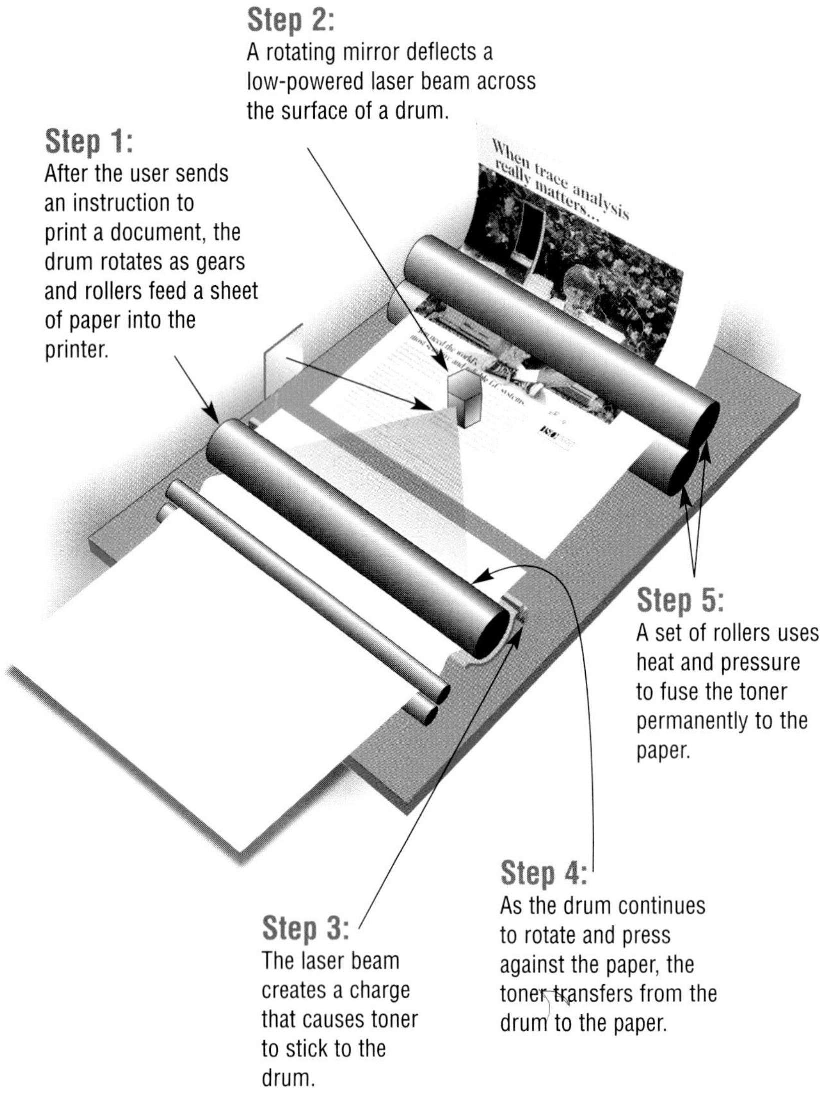

FAQ 6-5

How do I dispose of toner cartridges?

Do not throw them in the garbage. The housing contains iron, metal, and aluminum that is not biodegradable. The ink toner inside the cartridges contains toxic chemicals that pollute water and soil if disposed in dumps. Instead, recycle empty toner cartridges. Contact your printer manufacturer to see if it has a recycling program.

For more information about recycling toner cartridges, visit the Discovering Computers 2005 FAQ Web page (**scsite.com/dc2005/faq**). Click Recycling Toner Cartridges below Chapter 6.

Thermal Printers

A **thermal printer** generates images by pushing electrically heated pins against heat-sensitive paper. Basic thermal printers are inexpensive, but the print quality is low and the images tend to fade over time. Self-service gas pumps often print gas receipts using a built-in lower-quality thermal printer.

Two special types of thermal printers have very high print quality. A *thermal wax-transfer printer* generates rich, nonsmearing images by using heat to melt colored wax onto heat-sensitive paper. Thermal wax-transfer printers are more expensive than ink-jet printers, but less expensive than many color laser printers.

A *dye-sublimation printer*, sometimes called a *digital photo printer*, uses heat to transfer colored dye to specially coated paper. Most dye-sublimation printers create images that are of photographic quality (Figure 6-25). Professional applications requiring very high image quality, such as photography studios, medical labs, and security identification systems, use dye-sublimation printers. These high-end printers cost thousands of dollars and print images in a wide range of sizes. Most dye-sublimation printers for the home or small business user, by contrast, typically print images in only one or two sizes and are much slower than their professional counterparts. These lower-end dye-sublimation printers cost more than a photo printer based on ink-jet technology, but usually less than $1,000. Some are small enough for the mobile user to carry the printer in a briefcase.

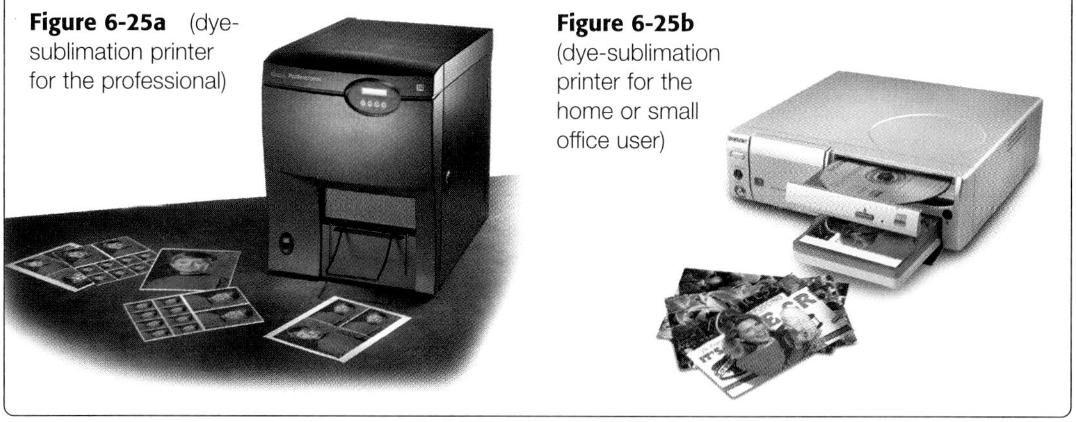

Figure 6-25a (dye-sublimation printer for the professional)

Figure 6-25b (dye-sublimation printer for the home or small office user)

FIGURE 6-25 The printers shown in this figure use dye-sublimation technology to create photographic-quality output.

Mobile Printers

A **mobile printer** is a small, lightweight, battery-powered printer that allows a mobile user to print from a notebook computer, Tablet PC, or PDA while traveling (Figure 6-26). Barely wider than the paper on which they print, mobile printers fit easily in a briefcase alongside a notebook computer.

Mobile printers mainly use ink-jet, thermal, thermal wax-transfer, or dye-sublimation technology. Many of these printers connect to a parallel port or USB port. Others have a built-in wireless port through which they communicate with the computer wirelessly. Wireless printing is discussed later in this chapter.

FIGURE 6-26 A mobile printer is a compact printer that allows the mobile user to print from a notebook computer or mobile device.

Label and Postage Printers

A **label printer** is a small printer that prints on an adhesive-type material (Figure 6-27) that can be placed on a variety of items such as envelopes, packages, floppy disks, CDs, DVDs, audio-cassettes, photographs, file folders, and toys. Most label printers also print bar codes.

A *postage printer* is a special type of label printer that has a built-in digital scale and prints postage stamps. Postage printers allow users to buy and print digital postage, called *Internet postage,* right from their personal computer. That is, you purchase an amount of postage from an authorized postal service Web site. As you need a stamp, you print it on the postage printer. Each time a postage stamp prints, your postage account is updated.

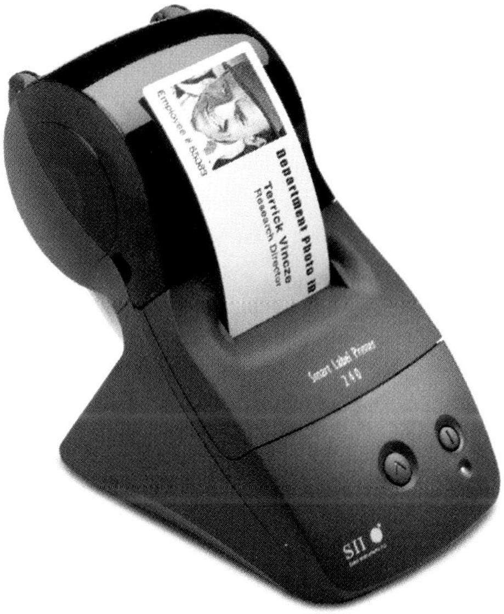

FIGURE 6-27 A label printer.

Plotters and Large-Format Printers

Plotters are sophisticated printers used to produce high-quality drawings such as blueprints, maps, and circuit diagrams. These printers are used in specialized fields such as engineering and drafting and usually are very costly. Current plotters use a row of charged wires (called styli) to draw an electrostatic pattern on specially coated paper and then fuse toner to the pattern. The printed image consists of a series of very small dots, which provides high-quality output.

Using ink-jet printer technology, but on a much larger scale, a **large-format printer** creates photo-realistic-quality color prints. Graphic artists use these high-cost, high-performance printers for signs, posters, and other professional quality displays (Figure 6-28).

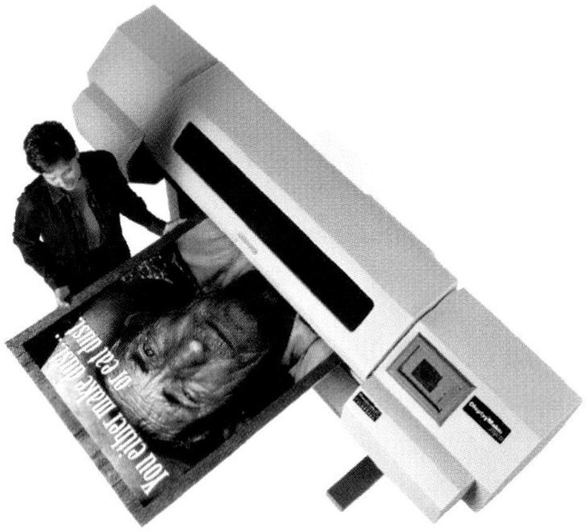

FIGURE 6-28 Graphic artists use large-format printers to print signs, posters, and other professional quality displays.

Plotters and large-format printers handle paper with widths up to 60 inches because blueprints, maps, signs, posters and other such drawings and displays can be quite large. Some plotters and large-format printers use individual sheets of paper, while others take large rolls.

Wireless Printing

Until a few years ago, users had to connect computers and devices to printers with a cable if they wanted to print. Today, wireless printing technology makes the task of printing from a notebook computer, Tablet PC, PDA, or digital camera much easier. As discussed in Chapter 4, two wireless technologies for printing are infrared and Bluetooth.

With *infrared printing*, a printer communicates with a device using infrared light waves. Each device must have an IrDA port. To print from a PDA, for example, a user lines up the IrDA port on the PDA with the IrDA port on the printer. With *Bluetooth printing*, a device transmits output to a printer via radio waves (Figure 6-29). Bluetooth printing is more convenient than infrared printing because Bluetooth devices do not have to be aligned with each other, rather, they need to be within an approximate 30-foot range. Users can convert existing printers and devices into Bluetooth devices with a Bluetooth wireless port adapter or a Bluetooth card, which plugs into a USB port or parallel port.

WEB LINK 6-7

Wireless Printing

Visit the Discovering Computers 2005 WEB LINK page (**scsite .com/dc2005/weblink**). Click Wireless Printing below Chapter 6.

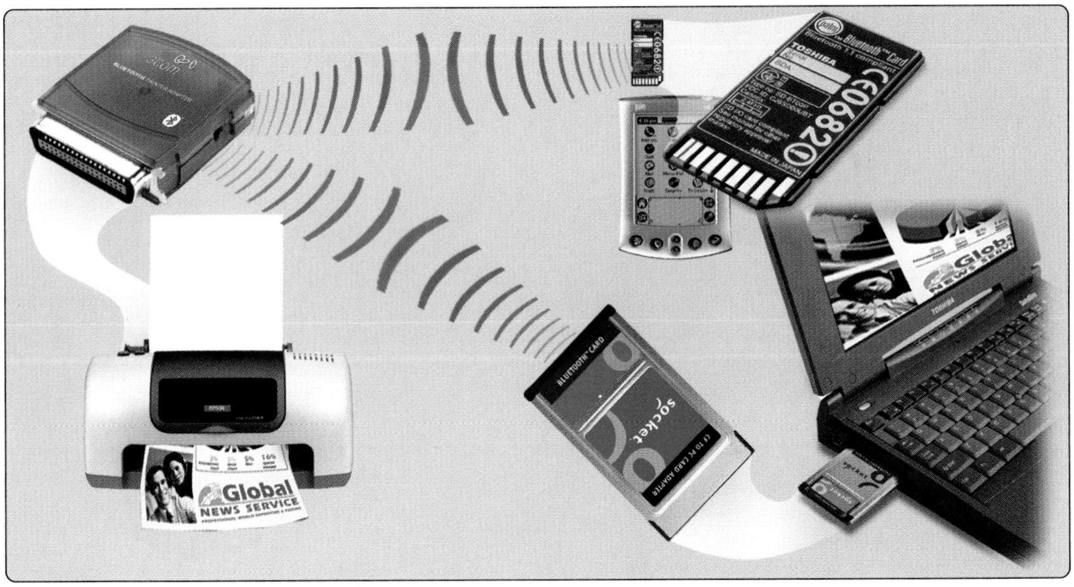

FIGURE 6-29 Bluetooth technology allows computers and devices to transmit to a printer wirelessly, as long as each is Bluetooth enabled or has a Bluetooth adapter or card.

FAQ 6-6

Where did the name Bluetooth originate?

Harald Blatand was king of Denmark circa 950. This king, whose last name they say roughly translates to blue tooth, was able to unite Denmark and Norway despite their differences. When Ericsson, Intel, IBM, Nokia, and Toshiba collectively were able to develop a new wireless communications standard, they named it Bluetooth — after the Danish leader.

For more information about Bluetooth, visit the Discovering Computers 2005 FAQ Web page (**scsite.com/dc2005/faq**). Click Bluetooth below Chapter 6.

QUIZ YOURSELF 6-2

To check your knowledge of various types of printers and wireless printing, visit the Discovering Computers 2005 Quiz Yourself Web page (**scsite.com/dc2005/quiz**). Click Objectives 5 – 7 below Chapter 6.

SPEAKERS AND HEADSETS

An **audio output device** is a component of a computer that produces music, speech, or other sounds, such as beeps. Two commonly used audio output devices are speakers and headsets.

Most personal computers have a small internal speaker that usually outputs only low-quality sound. Thus, many personal computer users add stereo **speakers** to their computers to generate a higher-quality sound (Figure 6-30). Some monitors even have larger speakers built into the sides of the monitor. Most speakers have tone and volume controls, allowing users to adjust settings. To boost the low bass sounds, some users add a *woofer* (also called a *subwoofer*). Users connect the stereo speakers and subwoofer to ports on the sound card. For a more technical discussion about how sound cards produce sound, read the High-Tech Talk article on page 321.

FIGURE 6-30 Most personal computer users add high-quality stereo speakers and a subwoofer to their computers.

When using speakers, anyone within listening distance can hear the output. In a computer laboratory or some other crowded environment, speakers might not be practical. Instead, users can plug a headset into a port on the sound card, into a speaker, or even into the front of the system unit. With the **headset**, only the individual wearing the headset hears the sound from the computer (Figure 6-31).

FIGURE 6-31 In a crowded environment where speakers are not practical, users wear a headset to hear audio output.

WEB LINK 6-8

Speakers and Headsets

Visit the Discovering Computers 2005 WEB LINK page (**scsite.com/dc2005/weblink**). Click Speakers and Headsets below Chapter 6.

Electronically produced voice output is growing in popularity. **Voice output** occurs when you hear a person's voice or when the computer talks to you through the speakers on the computer. In some software applications, the computer can speak the contents of a document through voice output. On the Web, you can listen to (or download and then listen to) interviews, talk shows, sporting events, news, recorded music, and live concerts from many radio and television stations (read Issue 6-4 for a related discussion). Some Web sites dedicate themselves to providing voice output, where you can hear songs, quotes, historical lectures, speeches, and books (Figure 6-32). Read Apply It 6-2 for more information.

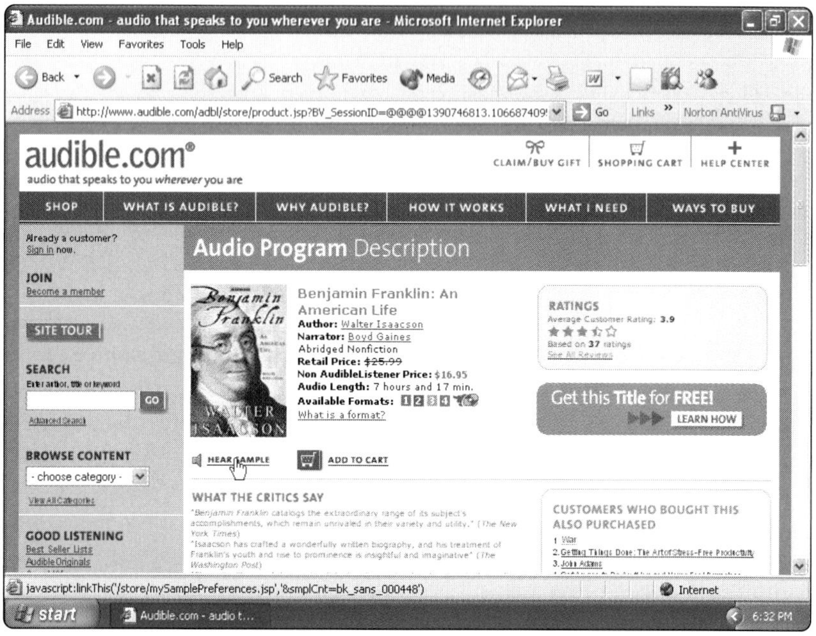

FIGURE 6-32 Users can listen to book contents from the Web. Shown here is a sample audio broadcast of the book titled *Benjamin Franklin: An American Life*. For users desiring to hear the entire book, they can purchase and download the entire audio file.

ISSUE 6-4

Wearing the Web?

A Hewlett-Packard executive predicts that someday the boundary between people and the Internet may disappear. The reason for its dissolution is a concept called "Internet wearables," which consist of portable, wireless output devices that people can wear to access the Web. On the surface, these devices may appear as innocuous as eyeglasses, a hearing aid, or a tooth filling. But, when a wearer speaks into a tiny microphone attached to the device, information from a remote computer or a Web site is seen on a lens of the eyeglasses or heard through a speaker in the hearing aid. Advocates say Internet wearables will make people more efficient by providing immediate material to those who need it. Critics argue, however, that people could become overly dependent on, or easily distracted by, the devices. Will Internet wearables help people be more productive? Why or why not? When would Internet wearables be a good idea? When would they not be a good idea? Why?

For more information about Internet wearables, visit the Discovering Computers 2005 Issues Web page (**scsite.com/dc2005/issues**). Click Issue #4 below Chapter 6.

APPLY IT 6-2

Audio Books Tell a Good Story

Many students' fondest memories are recalling their teachers and parents reading favorite books aloud. You can relive these times with audio books that you hear while relaxing at the end of a hectic day, while traveling in the car or on an airplane, or while exercising on a treadmill at the gym.

Audio books are available from several sources. You can purchase CD and cassette versions at retail stores or online. One newer method is downloading from a service called Audible.

This supplier has more than 18,000 selections in the fiction, nonfiction, business, history, science, and comedy categories. For less than $20 per month, you can make several selections, download the files, and then listen to the text using a headset or speakers and a PDA, MP3 player, or computer. File sizes range from a few to more than 100 megabytes; the greater the file size, the better the sound quality.

You can burn many of the files onto a CD and then listen conveniently in your car or on a portable CD player. While some people question the ethics of making copies of these files, others say the practice really is no different from lending books to friends. Another option is listening to the texts as audio streams over the Internet, but this technique works best with a high-speed Internet connection.

For more information about audio books, visit the Discovering Computers 2005 Apply It Web page (**scsite.com/dc2005/apply**). Click Apply It #2 below Chapter 6.

Very often, voice output works with voice input. For example, when you call an airline to check the status of gates, terminals, and arrival times, your voice interacts with a computer-generated voice output. *Internet telephony* allows users to have conversations over the Web, just as if they were on the telephone.

Sophisticated programs enable the computer to converse with you. Talk into the microphone and say, "I'd like today's weather report." The computer replies, "For which city?" You reply, "Chicago." The computer says, "Sunny and 80 degrees."

OTHER OUTPUT DEVICES

In addition to monitors, printers, and speakers, many other output devices are available for specific uses and applications. These devices include fax machines and fax modems, multi-function peripherals, data projectors, and force-feedback joysticks and wheels. The following pages discuss these devices.

Fax Machines and Fax Modems

A **fax machine**, short for *facsimile machine*, is a device that transmits and receives documents over telephone lines. The documents can contain text, drawings, or photographs, or can be handwritten. The term *fax* refers to a document that you send or receive via a fax machine.

A stand-alone fax machine scans an original document, converts the image into digitized data, and transmits the digitized image (Figure 6-33). A fax machine at the receiving end reads the incoming data, converts the digitized data back into an image, and prints or stores a copy of the original image.

Many computers include fax capability by using a fax modem. A *fax modem* is a modem that also allows you to send (and sometimes receive) electronic documents as faxes (Figure 6-34). A fax modem transmits computer-prepared documents, such as a word processing letter, or documents that have been digitized with a scanner or digital camera. A fax modem transmits these faxes to a fax machine or to another fax modem.

FIGURE 6-33 A stand-alone fax machine.

WEB LINK 6-9

Fax Modems

Visit the Discovering Computers 2005 WEB LINK page (**scsite.com/dc2005/weblink**). Click Fax Modems below Chapter 6.

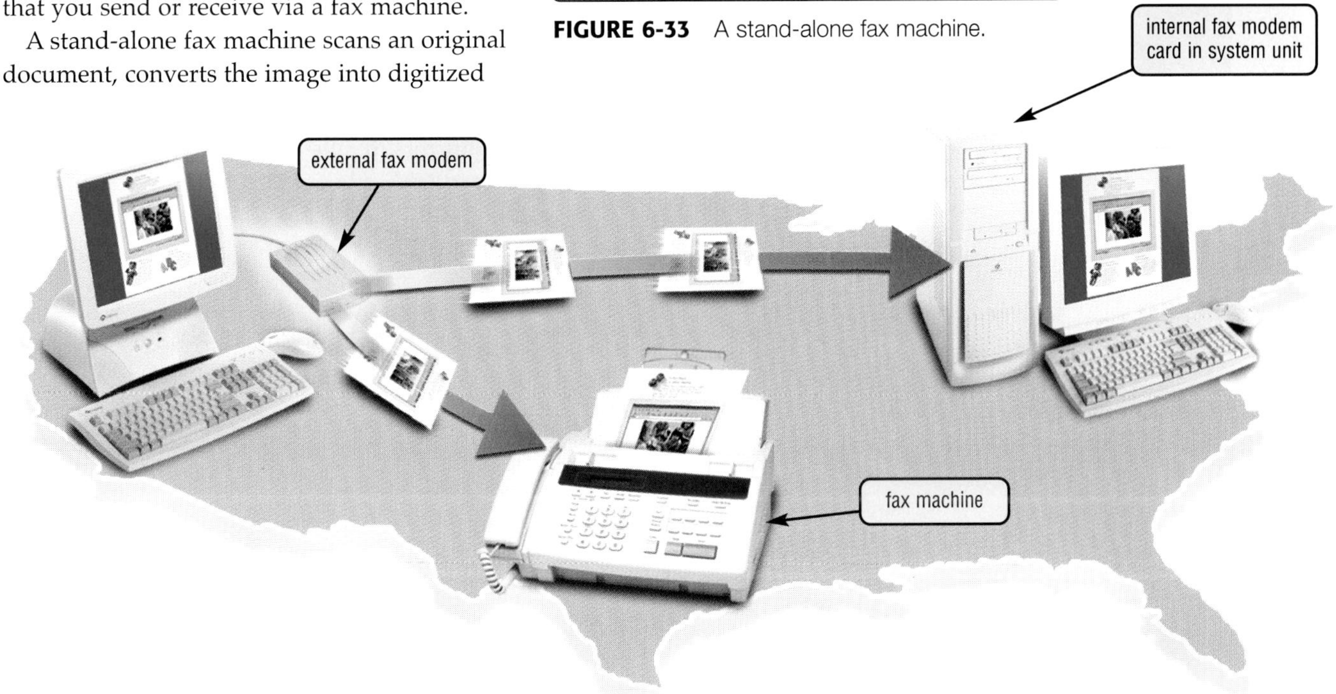

FIGURE 6-34 A fax modem allows users to send (and sometimes receive) electronic documents as faxes to a fax machine or another computer.

When a computer (instead of a fax machine) receives a fax, users can view the fax on the screen, saving the time and expense of printing it. If necessary, you also can print the fax using special fax software. The quality of a viewed or printed fax is less than that of a word processing document because the fax actually is an image. Optical character recognition (OCR) software, which was discussed in Chapter 5, enables you to convert the image to text and then edit it.

A fax modem can be an external device that plugs into a port on the back of the system unit or an internal adapter card inserted into an expansion slot on the motherboard.

Multifunction Peripherals

WEB LINK 6-10

Multifunction Peripherals

Visit the Discovering Computers 2005 WEB LINK page (**scsite.com/dc2005/weblink**). Click Multifunction Peripherals below Chapter 6.

A **multifunction peripheral** is a single device that looks like a copy machine but provides the functionality of a printer, scanner, copy machine, and perhaps a fax machine (Figure 6-35). The features of these devices, which sometimes are called *all-in-one devices*, vary widely. For example, some use color ink-jet printer technology, while others include a black-and-white laser printer.

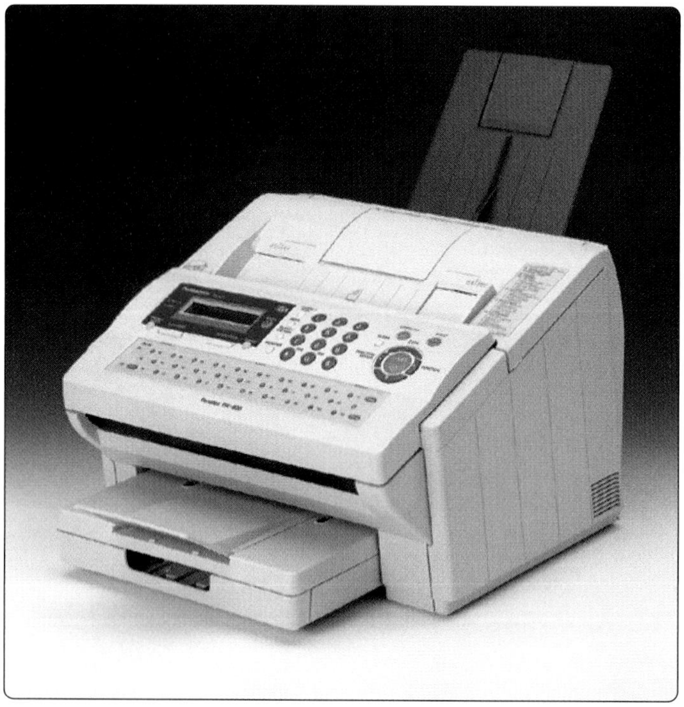

FIGURE 6-35 This multifunction peripheral is a color printer, scanner, copy machine, and fax machine all in one device.

Small offices and home offices (SOHOs) use multifunction peripherals because they require less space than having a separate printer, scanner, copy machine, and fax machine. Another advantage of these devices is that it is significantly less expensive than if you purchase each device separately. If the device breaks down, however, you lose all four functions, which is the primary disadvantage. Despite this disadvantage, increasingly more users are bringing multifunction peripherals into their offices and homes.

Data Projectors

A **data projector** is a device that takes the image from a computer screen and projects it onto a larger screen so an audience of people can see the image clearly. For example, many classrooms use data projectors so all students easily can see an instructor's presentation on the screen.

Some data projectors are large devices that attach to a ceiling or wall in an auditorium. Others are small portable devices. Two types of smaller, lower-cost units are LCD projectors and DLP projectors.

An *LCD projector*, which uses liquid crystal display technology, attaches directly to a computer, and uses its own light source to display the information shown on the computer screen. Because LCD projectors tend to produce lower-quality images, users often prefer DLP projectors for their sharper, brighter images.

A *digital light processing* (*DLP*) *projector* uses tiny mirrors to reflect light, which produces crisp, bright, colorful images that remain in focus and can be seen clearly even in a well-lit room (Figure 6-36). Read Looking Ahead 6-2 for a look at the next generation of movie projectors.

FIGURE 6-36 DLP projectors produce sharp, bright images.

Force-Feedback Joysticks and Wheels

As discussed in Chapter 5, joysticks and wheels are input devices used to control actions of a player or movements of a vehicle. Today's joysticks and wheels also include *force feedback,* which is a technology that sends resistance to the device in response to actions of the user (Figure 6-37). For example, as you use the simulation software to drive from a smooth road onto a gravel alley, the steering wheel jars itself — to make the driving experience as realistic as possible. In addition to games, these devices are used in practical training applications such as in the military and aviation.

WEB LINK 6-11

Force Feedback Devices

Visit the Discovering Computers 2005 WEB LINK page (**scsite.com/dc2005/weblink**). Click Force Feedback Devices below Chapter 6.

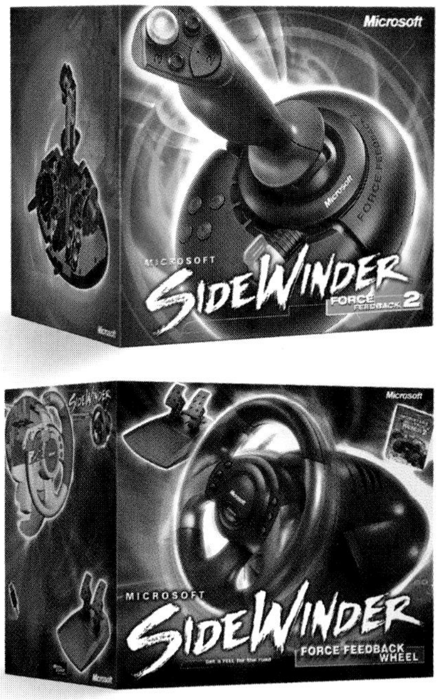

FIGURE 6-37 Joysticks, wheels, and other gaming devices often provide force feedback, giving the user a realistic experience.

LOOKING AHEAD 6-2

Digital Movies Project New Image

George Eastman experimented in his mother's kitchen and developed the flexible transparent base for film in the late 1800s. More than 100 years later, George Lucas experimented in a computer laboratory and developed the highest-profile movie entirely shot and shown in a digital format, *Star Wars, Episode 2: Attack of the Clones.*

Movie industry experts predict digital technology will replace film by 2007 with some of these individuals forecasting that the movie projector will be obsolete by 2005. Seven of the bigger Hollywood studios are collaborating to develop digital technical standards, and leading equipment manufacturers, including Kodak and Texas Instruments, are developing projection hardware.

The Boeing Company is one of the project's major investors. Being the largest satellite manufacturer, this corporation desires to help transmit full-length digital movies throughout the world and supply movie theaters with digital equipment.

While digital movies offer superior visual and sound clarity, they also are susceptible to piracy. Hundreds of thousands of copies of *Attack of the Clones* were downloaded from the Internet before the film's release. The Motion Picture Association of America predicts that more than 1 million movies will be downloaded illegally daily, resulting in billions of dollars of lost profits. This organization and other groups are wrestling with convincing the public that this piracy is unethical and ultimately leads to increased ticket prices at the box office.

For a look at the next generation of digital movies, visit the Discovering Computers 2005 Looking Ahead Web page (**scsite.com/dc2005/looking**). Click Looking Ahead #2 below Chapter 6.

PUTTING IT ALL TOGETHER

Many factors influence the type of output devices you should use: the type of output desired, the hardware and software in use, and the anticipated cost. Figure 6-38 outlines several suggested monitors, printers, and other output devices for various types of computer users.

SUGGESTED OUTPUT DEVICES BY USER

User	Monitor	Printer	Other
Home 	• 17- or 19-inch color CRT monitor or LCD monitor	• Ink-jet color printer • Photo printer	• Speakers • Headset • Force-feedback joystick and wheel
Small Office/Home Office 	• 19- or 21-inch color CRT monitor or LCD monitor • Color LCD screen on Tablet PC or PDA	• Multifunction peripheral; or • Ink-jet color printer; or • Laser printer, black and white • Label printer • Postage printer	• Fax machine • Speakers
Mobile 	• 15.7-inch color LCD screen on notebook computer • Color LCD screen on PDA	• Mobile color printer • Ink-jet color printer; or • Laser printer, black and white, for in-office use • Photo printer	• Fax modem • Headset • DLP data projector
Large Business 	• 19- or 21-inch color CRT monitor or LCD monitor • Color LCD screen on Tablet PC and PDA	• High-speed laser printer • Laser printer, color • Line printer (for large reports from a mainframe) • Label printer	• Fax machine or fax modem • Speakers • Headset • DLP data projector
Power 	• 23-inch color LCD monitor	• Laser printer, black and white • Plotter or large-format printer; or • Photo printer; or • Dye-sublimation printer	• Fax machine or fax modem • Speakers • Headset

FIGURE 6-38 This table recommends suggested output devices for various types of users.

OUTPUT DEVICES FOR PHYSICALLY CHALLENGED USERS

As discussed in Chapter 5, the growing presence of computers has generated an awareness of the need to address computing requirements for those with physical limitations. Read Issue 6-5 for a related discussion.

ISSUE 6-5

How Should Employers Accommodate Employees with Disabilities?

Section 508 of the Workforce Investment Act (Rehabilitation Act Amendments) requires that electronics and information technology in federal agencies accommodate the needs of all end users — including people with disabilities. Computers used in federal agencies must be compatible with assistive technologies, such as screen readers that translate what appears on a computer screen into audible output and refreshable Braille displays for people who are visually impaired. To date, Section 508 does not apply to the private sector. Some believe, however, that the same standards should apply to private companies and organizations. Opponents insist that applying such standards to private companies would place an undue burden on employers. Should private companies be forced to make their computers accessible to physically challenged employees? Why or why not? Should such regulations apply only to companies with a minimum number of employees? If so, how many? What relatively inexpensive measures could employers take to accommodate employees with disabilities?

For more information about accommodating employees with disabilities, visit the Discovering Computers 2005 Issues Web page (**scsite.com/dc2005/issues**). Click Issue #5 below Chapter 6.

For users with mobility, hearing, or vision disabilities, many different types of output devices are available. Hearing-impaired users, for example, can instruct programs to display words instead of sounds. With the Windows XP operating system, users also can set options to make programs easier to use. For example, the Magnifier command enlarges text and other items in a window on the screen (Figure 6-39).

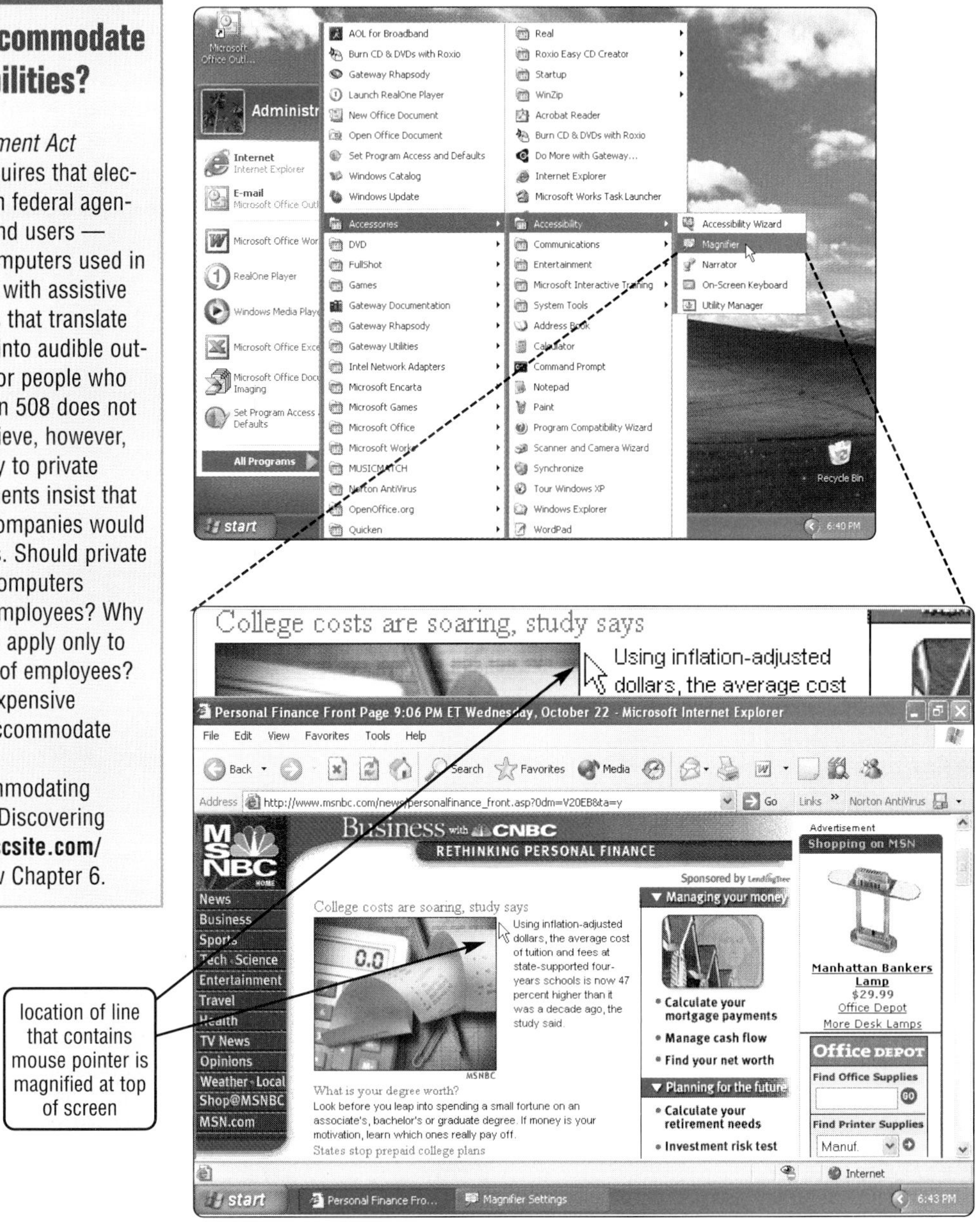

FIGURE 6-39 The Magnifier command in Windows XP enlarges text and other on-screen items for individuals with vision disabilities.

Visually impaired users can change Windows XP settings, such as increasing the size or changing the color of the text to make the words easier to read. Instead of using a monitor, blind users can work with voice output. That is, the computer reads the information that is displayed on the screen. Another alternative is a *Braille printer,* which outputs information in Braille onto paper (Figure 6-40).

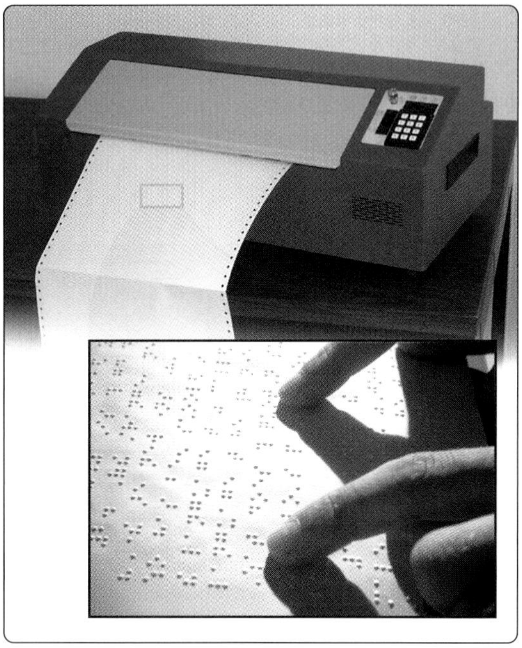

FIGURE 6-40 A Braille printer.

QUIZ YOURSELF 6-3

To check your knowledge of speakers and headsets, other output devices, and output for physically challenged users, visit the Discovering Computers 2005 Quiz Yourself Web page (**scsite.com/dc2005/quiz**). Click Objectives 8 – 10 below Chapter 6.

CHAPTER SUMMARY

Computers process and organize input into output. This chapter described the various methods of output and several commonly used output devices. Output devices presented included CRT monitors, flat-panel displays, printers, speakers and headsets, fax machines and fax modems, multifunction peripherals, data projectors, and force-feedback joysticks and wheels.

Graphic Designer/Illustrator

Graphic designers and *graphic illustrators* are artists, but many do not create original works. Instead, they portray visually the ideas of their clients. Illustrators create pictures for books and other publications and sometimes for commercial products, such as greeting cards. They work in fields such as fashion, technology, medicine, animation, or even cartoons. Illustrators often prepare their images on a computer. Designers combine practical skills with artistic talent to convert abstract concepts into designs for products and advertisements. Many use computer-aided design (CAD) tools to create, visualize, and modify designs. Designer careers usually are specialized in particular areas, such as:

- Graphic designers — book covers, stationery, and CD covers
- Commercial and industrial designers — products and equipment
- Costume and theater designers — costumes and settings for theater and television
- Interior designers — layout, decor, and furnishings of homes and buildings
- Merchandise displayers — commercial displays
- Fashion designers — clothing, shoes, and other fashion accessories

Certificate, two-year, four-year, and masters-level educational programs are available within design areas. About 30 percent of graphic illustrators/designers choose to freelance, while others work with advertising agencies, publishing companies, design studios, or specialized departments within large companies. Salaries range from $25,000 to $75,000-plus, based on experience and educational background.

To learn more about the field of Graphic Designer/Illustrator as a career, visit the Discovering Computers 2005 Careers Web page (**scsite.com/dc2005/careers**). Click Graphic Designer/Illustrator.

Sound Cards: Creating Music to Your Ears

Speakers, headsets, and other audio output devices rely on sound cards to produce sounds such as music, voice, beeps, and chimes. Sound cards contain the chips and circuitry to record and play back a wide range of sounds using analog-to-digital conversion and digital-to-analog conversion, as described in the Chapter 1 High-Tech Talk on page 39.

To record a sound, the sound card must be connected to an input device, such as a microphone or audio CD player. The input device sends the sound to the sound card as an analog signal. The analog signal flows to the sound card's analog-to-digital-converter (ADC). The ADC converts the signal into digital (binary) data of 1s and 0s by sampling the signal at set intervals.

The analog sound is a continuous waveform, with a range of frequencies and volumes. To represent the waveform in a recording, the computer would have to store the waveform's value at every instant in time. Because this is not possible, the sound is recorded using a sampling process. *Sampling* involves breaking up the waveform into set intervals and representing all values during that interval with a single value.

Several factors in the sampling process — sampling rate, audio resolution, and mono or stereo recording — affect the quality of the recorded sound during playback.

- *Sampling rate*, also called sampling frequency, refers to the number of times per second the sound is recorded (Figure 6-41). The more frequently a sound is recorded, the smaller the intervals and the better the quality. The sampling frequency used for audio CDs, for example, is 44,100 times per second, which is expressed in hertz (Hz) as 44,100 Hz. Cassette tape-quality multimedia files use a sampling rate of 22,050 Hz; and basic Windows sounds use a sampling rate of 11,025 Hz.
- *Audio resolution* — defined as a bit rate such as 8-bit, 16-bit, or 24-bit — refers to the number of bytes used to represent the sound at any one interval. A sound card using 8-bit resolution, for example, represents a sound with any 1 of 256 values (2^8). A 16-bit sound card uses any 1 of 65,536 values (2^{16}) for each interval. Using a higher resolution provides a finer measurement scale, which results in a more accurate representation of the value of each sample and better sound quality. With 8-bit resolution, the sound quality is like that of an AM radio; 16-bit resolution gives CD quality sound, and a 24-bit resolution is used for high-quality digital audio editing.
- Mono or stereo recording refers to the number of channels used during recording. *Mono* means that the same sound emits from both the left and right speaker during playback; *stereo* means that two separate channels exist in the recording: one each for the right and left speakers. Most sound cards support stereo recording for better playback.

After the ADC converts the analog sound through sampling, the digital data flows to the digital signal processor (DSP) on the sound card. The DSP then requests instructions from the sound card's memory chip on how to process the digital data. Typically, the DSP then compresses the digital data to save space. Finally, the DSP sends the compressed data to the computer's main processor, which stores the data in .WAV, .MP3, or other audio file format.

To play a recorded sound, such as a WAV, an MP3, or a CD track, the main processor retrieves the sound file from a hard disk, CD, or other storage device. The processor then sends the digital data to the DSP, which decompresses the data and looks to the memory chip to determine how to recreate the sound.

The DSP then sends the digital signals to the sound card's digital-to-analog converter (DAC), which converts the digital data back to an analog electrical voltage. An output device, such as a speaker, uses an amplifier to strengthen the electrical voltage. This causes the speaker's cone to vibrate, recreating the sound.

All of this happens in an instant. The next time your computer beeps or chirps, consider the complex process required to make that simple sound. Then, insert your favorite CD and enjoy the sweet music provided courtesy of the sound card.

For more information about sound cards, visit the Discovering Computers 2005 High-Tech Talk Web page (**scsite.com/dc2005/tech**) and click Sound Cards.

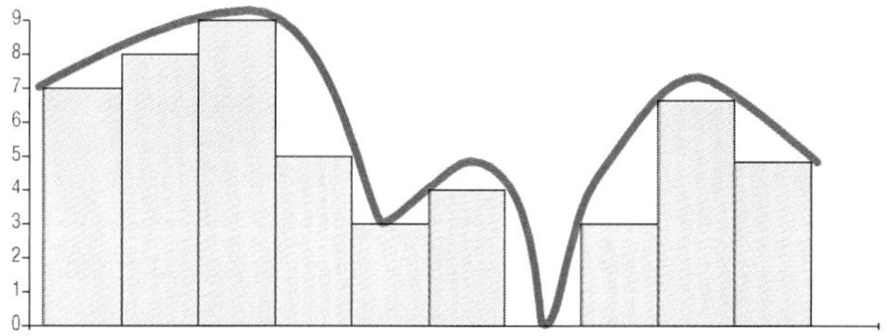

Figure 6-41a (recording made using low sampling rate and resolution causes significant sampling error; results in recorded sound with poor sound quality)

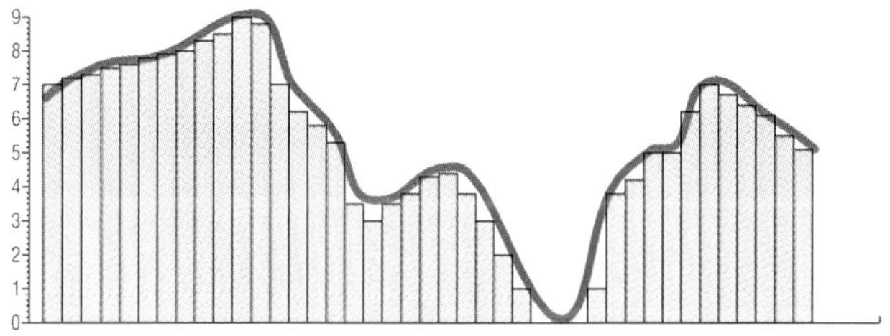

Figure 6-41b (recording made using higher sampling rate and resolution reduces sampling error; results in recorded sound with better sound quality)

FIGURE 6-41 Comparison of low versus high sampling rates.

COMPANIES ON THE CUTTING EDGE

Hewlett-Packard

Technology for Business and Life

In a one-car garage, two 26-year-old engineers started a company with a collection of simple tools and $538 in working capital. They decided to use their last names to identify the company, but whose name would be first? William Hewlett and David Packard tossed a coin, and Hewlett won. That one-car garage where *Hewlett-Packard* (*HP*) was born now is a California State Historical Landmark.

HP's first product was an audio oscillator, an instrument used to test sound equipment. In 1939, the Walt Disney Studios bought eight oscillators to use in developing sound effects for the movie, *Fantasia*. Soon after, HP constructed its first building, but the founders designed the new facility so it easily could be converted into a grocery store if the electronics business failed.

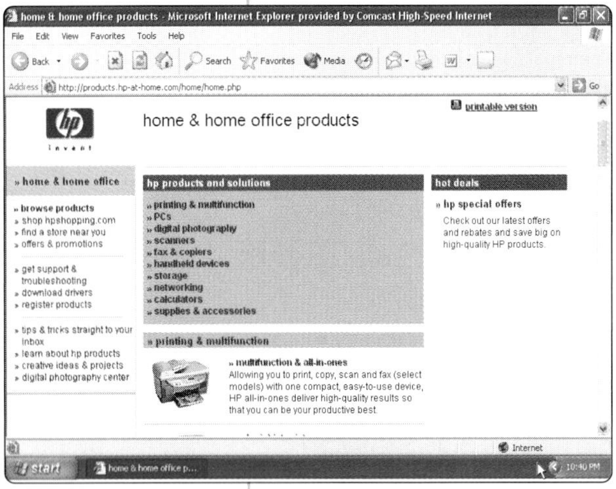

Instead of failing, HP grew. The company's initial products were test and measurement equipment, but in the 1960s, its product line expanded to include calculators. In the 1980s, HP turned toward the computer and printer markets. By 1993, HP had sold 20 million printers. Today, market analysts estimate that 60 percent of printers sold bear the HP logo. HP is noted for a range of high-quality, computer-related products including personal computers, notebook computers, scanners, and ink-jet and laser printers. In 2002, HP enlarged its presence in the computer market with a $25 billion buyout of Compaq Computer Corporation.

In addition to new products, HP spearheaded changes in corporate culture. In 1957, HP created the first set of corporate objectives, which became known as the HP Way. This philosophy embraced the free exchange of information, trust and respect, integrity, teamwork, and what HP calls Management by Walking Around.

For more information about HP, visit the Discovering Computers 2005 Companies Web page (**scsite.com/dc2005/companies**) and click Hewlett-Packard.

RealNetworks

Delivering Multimedia Content

Imagine having hundreds of thousands of new users visit your home page each day. That is the success RealNetworks has experienced with its RealOne Player (formerly RealPlayer), amounting to a 300 percent growth since 1998.

RealNetworks develops technology that allows people to create, send, and receive multimedia over the Internet. More than 85 percent of all streaming media-enabled Web pages rely on RealNetworks software to deliver audio, video, and multimedia services to personal computers and other electronic devices. RealNetworks technology is used to broadcast more than 350,000 hours of live music, sports, news, and entertainment every week.

One year after leaving Microsoft in 1994, RealNetworks founder Rob Glaser introduced the first version of RealAudio, and the company set the standard for sending multimedia content across the Internet. Today, the company's two more popular products are RealPlayer and RealJukebox. RealPlayer, the second most popular Internet-based software application, uses streaming-media technology to deliver a song when you click its title. According to RealNetworks, RealPlayer is installed on 90 percent of America's home computers. RealJukebox stores and plays downloadable files such as MP3s, a popular digital music format. RealOne Player integrates RealPlayer and RealJukebox functions and allows subscribers to download and stream premium digital music, sports, entertainment, and news. Its Rhapsody streaming audio service offers customers a broad variety of music to download at less than $1 per song.

For more information about RealNetworks, visit the Discovering Computers 2005 Companies Web page (**scsite.com/dc2005/companies**) and click RealNetworks.

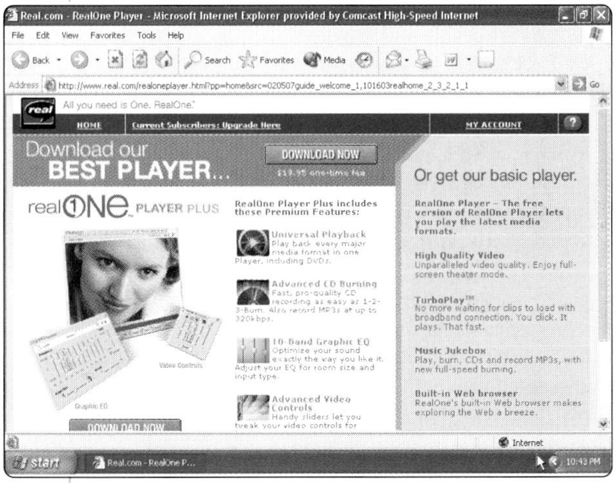

TECHNOLOGY TRAILBLAZERS

Donna Dubinsky

Cofounder of Handspring

For most people, being the president and CEO of 3Com's Palm Computing Division, the world's leading producer of PDAs, would be enough of a challenge. Yet, in 1998 Palm's CEO, *Donna Dubinsky*, left to found Handspring with Jeff Hawkins and revolutionize the PDA market.

In 2003, Palm divided into palmOne and PalmSource and acquired Handspring. Dubinsky always has been independent. After graduating from Harvard Business School, instead of following her classmates to high-paying jobs in established firms, Dubinsky took an unassuming position in customer service at Apple Computer. There, she worked her way up to director of distribution and international vice president at Claris, the company's software unit. When Apple failed to spin off Claris as a separate firm, Dubinsky left and traveled to Paris, where she learned French, studied painting, and taught school. When she returned to Silicon Valley, California, Dubinsky met Jeff Hawkins, an engineer who was developing a user-friendly electronic organizer. The pair introduced the PalmPilot in 1996, and sales of more than two million units made it the most-rapidly adopted new computing product ever manufactured. To learn how consumers actually used the PalmPilot, Dubinsky even took some technical support calls to hear the questions they asked.

When Dubinsky and Hawkins left 3Com to form Handspring, they introduced several innovative products: the Handspring Visor and the Treo. The Visor uses the same operating system as the PalmPilot and allows users to add modules for pagers, music players, and games. The Treo wireless smart phones have a built-in keyboard, organizer, Web connection, and e-mail functions.

For more information about Donna Dubinsky, visit the Discovering Computers 2005 People Web page (**scsite.com/dc2005/people**) and click Donna Dubinsky.

Heidi Van Arnem

Advocate for the Physically Challenged

In 1983, 16-year old *Heidi Van Arnem* accidentally was shot in the neck. The shooting left her paralyzed, but not defeated. As a law student at the University of Detroit, Van Arnem taught herself to type using the knuckle of her little finger. "That's when I realized," Van Arnem recalled, "I could have some value in my life, some control." Throughout her life, Van Arnem worked to enhance the lives of people with disabilities and help the individuals and organizations that support them.

For eight years, Van Arnem owned and operated a Birmingham travel agency, specializing in making arrangements for travelers with disabilities. In 1998, she sold the travel agency and started iCan!, Inc., a company that provides an online forum for the physically challenged community. The iCan! Web site is designed for people with disabilities and helps businesses better address their needs. As chairman and CEO of iCan!, Van Arnem brought together businesses, the medical industry, government-led efforts, and nonprofit organizations. To assist people with special needs, iCan! works in the travel industry, the automotive industry, and computer technology. "With this," Van Arnem once said, indicating her notebook computer, "I'm just as productive as the next person."

As a successful businesswoman, entrepreneur, and inventor, Van Arnem was recognized as one of the Top 25 Women on the Web. She was the first recipient of the Evan Kemp Entrepreneur of the Year award by the President's Committee on Employment of People with Disabilities and received numerous awards for her business achievements and community outreach by organizations such as the U.S. Chamber of Commerce. In addition, Van Arnem's Spend a Day in a Wheelchair program received national acclaim for helping sensitize students to the difficulties wheelchair users face.

For more information about Heidi Van Arnem, visit the Discovering Computers 2005 People Web page (**scsite.com/dc2005/people**) and click Heidi Van Arnem.

CHAPTER 6 CHAPTER REVIEW

The Chapter Review section summarizes the concepts presented in this chapter.

WEB INSTRUCTIONS:

To display this page from the Web, start your browser and enter the Web address **scsite.com/dc2005/ch6/review**. Click the links for current and additional information. To listen to an audio version of this Chapter Review, click the Audio button.

1 What Are the Four Categories of Output?

Output is data that has been processed into a useful form. Four categories of output are text, graphics, audio, and video. An **output device** is any hardware component that conveys information to one or more people.

2 What Is a CRT Monitor and What Factors Affect Its Quality?

A **CRT monitor** is a desktop monitor that is similar to a standard television set because it contains a *cathode ray tube (CRT)*. The screen on the front of the CRT is coated with tiny dots of red, green, and blue phosphor that combine to make up each *pixel*, which is a single element in an electronic image. As an electron beam inside the CRT moves back and forth across the back of the screen, the dots glow, which produces an image. The quality of a CRT monitor depends largely on its resolution, dot pitch, and refresh rate. **Resolution** describes the sharpness and clearness of an image. *Dot pitch*, sometimes called *pixel pitch*, is the distance in millimeters between each like-colored pixel on the screen. *Refresh rate* is the speed that a monitor redraws the images on the screen.

3 How Are a Video Card and CRT Monitor Related?

Many CRT monitors use an analog signal to produce an image. A **video card**, also called a *graphics card*, converts digital output from the computer into an analog video signal and sends the signal through a cable to the CRT monitor, which displays output on the screen.

4 What Are LCD Monitors, LCD Screens, Gas Plasma Monitors, and HDTVs?

LCD monitors, LCD screens, gas plasma monitors, and many HDTVs are types of flat-panel displays. A *flat-panel display* is a display with a shallow depth that does not use CRT technology. An **LCD monitor** is a desktop monitor that uses a liquid crystal display instead of a cathode-ray tube. A **liquid crystal display (LCD)** uses a liquid compound to present information on a display. A **gas plasma monitor** is a display device that uses gas plasma technology, which substitutes a layer of gas for the liquid crystal material in an LCD monitor. **HDTV** (*high-definition television*) is the most advanced form of digital television, working with digital broadcasting signals, transmitting digital sound, supporting wide screens, and providing resolutions up to 1920 ◊ 1080 pixels.

Visit **scsite.com/dc2005/quiz** or click the Quiz Yourself button. Click Objectives 1 – 4 below Chapter 6.

5 How Is an Impact Printer Different From a Nonimpact Printer?

A **printer** is an output device that produces text and graphics on a physical medium, such as paper or transparency film. An **impact printer** forms characters and graphics on a piece of paper by striking a mechanism against an inked ribbon that physically contacts the paper. Two commonly used types of impact printers are a **dot-matrix printer** and a **line printer**. A **nonimpact printer** forms characters and graphics on a piece of paper without actually striking the paper. Commonly used nonimpact printers are ink-jet printers, photo printers, laser printers, thermal printers, mobile printers, label and postage printers, plotters, and large-format printers.

6 What Are Ink-Jet Printers, Photo Printers, Laser Printers, Thermal Printers, Mobile Printers, Label and Postage Printers, and Plotters and Large-Format Printers?

An ink-jet printer is a type of nonimpact printer that forms characters and graphics by spraying tiny drops of liquid ink onto a piece of paper. A **photo printer** is a color printer that produces photo-lab-quality pictures. A **laser printer** is a high-speed, high-quality nonimpact printer that operates in a manner similar to a copy machine, creating images using a laser beam and powdered ink, called *toner*. A **thermal printer** generates images by pushing electronically heated pins against heat-sensitive paper. A **mobile printer** is a small, lightweight, battery-powered printer that allows a mobile user to print from a notebook computer. A **label printer** is a small printer that prints on an adhesive-type material that can be placed on a variety of items. A *postage printer* is a special type of label printer that has a built-in scale and prints postage stamps. **Plotters** are sophisticated printers used to produce high-quality drawings. A **large-format printer** uses ink-jet technology on a large scale to create photo-realistic-quality color prints.

7 What Methods Are Used for Wireless Printing?

Two wireless technologies for printing are infrared and Bluetooth. With *infrared printing*, a printer communicates with a device using infrared light waves. With *Bluetooth printing*, a device transmits output to a printer via radio waves.

Visit **scsite.com/dc2005/quiz** or click the Quiz Yourself button. Click Objectives 5 – 7 below Chapter 6.

8 How Are Speakers and Headsets Used?

Speakers and headsets are two commonly used audio output devices. An **audio output device** is a component of a computer that produces sound. Many personal computer users add stereo **speakers** to their computers to generate a higher-quality sound. With a **headset**, only the individual wearing the headset hears the sound from the computer.

9 What Are Fax Machines and Fax Modems, Multifunction Peripherals, Data Projectors, Joysticks, and Wheels?

A **fax machine**, short for *facsimile machine*, is a device that transmits and receives documents over telephone lines. A document sent or received via a fax machine is a *fax*. Many computers include fax capability using a *fax modem*, which is a modem that allows you to send (and sometimes receive) electronic documents as faxes. A **multifunction peripheral** is a single device that looks like a copy machine but provides the functionality of a printer, scanner, copy machine, and perhaps a fax machine. A **data projector** is a device that takes the image from a computer screen and projects it onto a larger screen so an audience of people can see the image clearly. Joysticks and wheels are input devices used to control actions of a player or vehicle. Today's joysticks and wheels also include *force feedback*, which is a technology that sends resistance to the device in response to actions of the user.

10 What Output Options Are Available for Physically Challenged Users?

Hearing-impaired users can instruct programs to display words instead of sound. With Windows XP, visually impaired users can enlarge items on the screen and change other settings, such as increasing the size or changing the color of text to make words easier to read. Blind users can work with voice output instead of a monitor. Another alternative is a *Braille printer*, which outputs information in Braille onto paper.

Visit **scsite.com/dc2005/quiz** or click the Quiz Yourself button. Click Objectives 8 – 10 below Chapter 6.

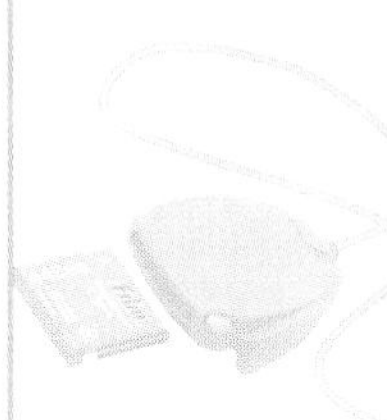

CHAPTER 6 KEY TERMS

You should know the Primary Terms and be familiar with the Secondary Terms.

QUIZZES AND LEARNING GAMES
Computer Genius
Crossword Puzzle
Interactive Labs
Practice Test
Quiz Yourself
Wheel of Terms

EXERCISES
Chapter Review
Checkpoint
Key Terms
Lab Exercises
Learn It Online
Web Research

BEYOND THE BOOK
Apply It
Career Corner
Companies
FAQ
High-Tech Talk
Issues
Looking Ahead
Trailblazers
Web Links

FEATURES
Guide to Web Sites
Making Use of the Web
Tech News
Timeline 2005

WEB INSTRUCTIONS:

To display this page from the Web, start your browser and enter the Web address **scsite.com/dc2005/ch6/terms**. Click a term to display its definition and a picture. When the picture appears, click the more info button for current and additional information about the term from the Web.

>> Primary Terms

(shown in bold-black characters in the chapter)

audio output device (313)
CRT monitor (294)
data projector (316)
display device (294)
dot-matrix printer (304)
e-book (300)
ENERGY STAR program (295)
fax machine (315)
gas plasma monitor (302)
HDTV (302)
headset (313)
impact printer (304)
ink-jet printer (305)
interactive TV (302)
label printer (311)
large-format printer (312)
laser printer (309)
LCD monitor (299)
line printer (304)
liquid crystal display (LCD) (300)
mobile printer (311)
monitor (294)
multifunction peripheral (316)
nonimpact printer (305)
output (292)
output device (294)
photo printer (307)
plotters (312)
printer (303)
resolution (295)
speakers (313)
thermal printer (310)
video card (297)
voice output (314)

>> Secondary Terms

(shown in italic characters in the chapter)

active-matrix display (301)
all-in-one devices (316)
band printer (305)
bit depth (297)
Bluetooth printing (312)
Braille printer (320)
bubble-jet printer (306)
candela (301)
cathode-ray tube (CRT) (294)
ClearType (300)
color depth (297)
continuous-form paper (304)
Digital Display Working Group (DDWG) (301)
digital light processing (DLP) projector (316)
digital photo printer (310)
digital television (DTV) (302)
display (294)
dot pitch (296)
dots per inch (dpi) (306)
DVI (Digital Video Interface) (301)
DVI port (301)
dye-sublimation printer (310)
electromagnetic radiation (EMR) (296)
electronic book (300)
facsimile machine (315)
fax (315)
fax modem (315)
flat-panel display (299)
footprint (299)
force feedback (317)
graphics card (297)
graphics processing unit (GPU) (298)
gray scaling (294)
hard copy (303)
high-definition television (302)
high-performance addressing (HPA) (301)
infrared printing (312)
Internet postage (311)
Internet telephony (315)
landscape orientation (303)
LCD flat panel monitor (299)
LCD projector (316)
letter-quality (LQ) (305)
Microsoft Reader (300)
monochrome (294)
MPR II (296)
National Television Standards Committee (302)
near letter quality (NLQ) (304)
nit (301)
NTSC converter (302)
organic LED (OLED) (301)
page description language (PDL) (309)
passive-matrix display (301)
PCL (Printer Control Language) (309)
pixel (294)
pixel pitch (296)
portrait orientation (303)
postage printer (311)
PostScript (309)
printout (303)
refresh rate (296)
response time (301)
scan rate (296)
shuttle-matrix printer (305)
soft copy (294)
subwoofer (313)
SVGA (super video graphics array) (298)
S-video port (301)
TFT (thin-film transistor) display (301)
thermal wax-transfer printer (310)
toner (310)
VESA (Video Electronics Standards Association) (298)
viewable size (295)
woofer (313)

CHECKPOINT CHAPTER 6

Use the Checkpoint exercises to check your knowledge level of the chapter.

WEB INSTRUCTIONS:

To display this page from the Web, start your browser and enter the Web address **scsite.com/dc2005/ch6/check**. Click the links for current and additional information.

LABEL THE FIGURE

Identify the ports on the video card.

a. DVI port
b. standard monitor port
c. S-video port

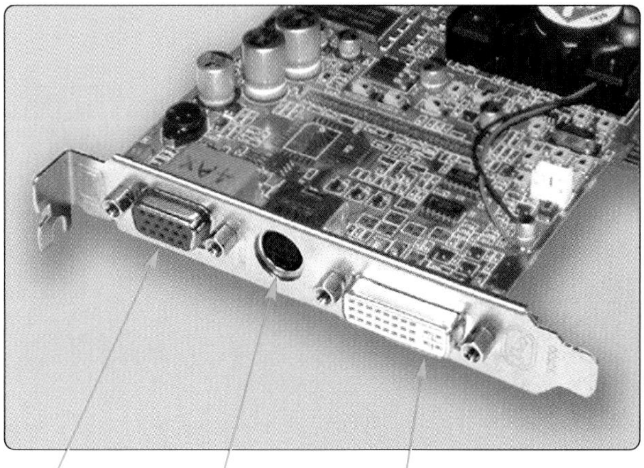

1._____ 2._____ 3._____

TRUE/FALSE

Mark T for True and F for False. (See page numbers in parentheses.)

____ 1. A computer generates several types of output, depending on the hardware and software being used and the requirements of the user. (292)

____ 2. Information on a display device is sometimes called hard copy. (294)

____ 3. A video card converts digital output from the computer into an analog video signal. (297)

____ 4. A flat-panel display is a display device with a shallow depth that uses CRT technology. (299)

____ 5. A pixel is a unit of visible light intensity equal to one candela per square meter. (301)

____ 6. The speed of a line printer is measured by the number of lines per minute (lpm) it can print. (304)

____ 7. A photo printer is a color printer that produces photo-lab-quality pictures. (307)

____ 8. A thermal printer is a high-speed, high-quality nonimpact printer. (310)

____ 9. With Bluetooth printing, a device transmits output to a printer via radio waves. (312)

____ 10. A fax modem is a modem that allows you to send (and sometimes receive) electronic documents as faxes. (315)

____ 11. A multifunction peripheral is a single device that looks like a copy machine but provides the functionality of a printer, scanner, copy machine, and perhaps a fax machine. (316)

____ 12. In addition to games, input devices with force feedback are used in practical training applications, such as in the military and aviation. (317)

CHAPTER 6 CHECKPOINT

MULTIPLE CHOICE

Select the best answer. (See page numbers in parentheses.)

1. Examples of text-based documents are _____. (292)
   a. drawings, clip art, and photographs
   b. letters, reports, and mailing labels
   c. music, narrations, and speeches
   d. home movies and live performances
2. The viewable size of a monitor is the _____ measurement of the actual viewing area provided by the screen in the monitor. (295)
   a. horizontal
   b. vertical
   c. diagonal
   d. three-dimensional
3. The number of colors a video card displays is determined by its _____. (297)
   a. dot pitch
   b. refresh rate
   c. bit depth
   d. viewable size
4. To generate the desired resolution and number of colors, both the video card and the monitor must _____. (298)
   a. be the same size
   b. contain a fan or heat sink
   c. use an analog signal
   d. support the same video standard
5. A passive matrix display _____ an active matrix display. (301)
   a. uses more transistors than
   b. requires more power than
   c. often is not as bright as
   d. is more expensive than
6. Gas plasma monitors offer larger screens _____. (302)
   a. but lower display quality than LCD monitors and are less expensive
   b. but lower display quality than LCD monitors and are more expensive
   c. and higher display quality than LCD monitors but are less expensive
   d. and higher display quality than LCD monitors but are more expensive
7. The speed of a(n) _____ is measured by the number of characters per second (cps) it can print. (304)
   a. dot-matrix printer
   b. laser printer
   c. ink-jet printer
   d. thermal printer
8. Printer resolution is measured by the number of _____ a printer can output. (306)
   a. pages per minute (ppm)
   b. dots per inch (dpi)
   c. lines per minute (lpm)
   d. pixels per inch (ppi)
9. Laser printers usually cost _____. (309)
   a. more than ink-jet printers and are faster
   b. less than ink-jet printers and are faster
   c. more than ink-jet printers and are slower
   d. less than ink-jet printers and are slower
10. Existing printers and devices can be converted into Bluetooth devices with a Bluetooth wireless port adaptor or a Bluetooth card, which plugs into a(n) _____. (312)
    a. IrDA port or serial port
    b. serial port or MIDI port
    c. MIDI port or parallel port
    d. parallel port or USB port
11. _____ allows users to have conversations over the Web. (315)
    a. An electronic book
    b. Internet postage
    c. Force feedback
    d. Internet telephony
12. When a computer receives a fax, _____ software enables the user to convert the image to text and then edit it. (316)
    a. optical character recognition (OCR)
    b. magnetic-ink character recognition (MICR)
    c. optical mark recognition (OMR)
    d. bar code recognition (BCR)
13. The disadvantage of multifunction peripherals is that _____. (316)
    a. they require more space than having separate devices
    b. they are significantly more expensive than purchasing each device separately
    c. if the multifunction peripheral breaks down, all functions are lost
    d. all of the above
14. The _____ command in Windows XP enlarges text and other on-screen items for individuals with vision disabilities. (319)
    a. Magnifier
    b. On-Screen Keyboard
    c. Narrator
    d. Utility Manager

CHECKPOINT CHAPTER 6

MATCHING

Match the terms with their definitions. (See page numbers in parentheses.)

______ 1. soft copy (294)	a. uses many shades of gray from white to black to enhance the quality of graphics
______ 2. monochrome (294)	b. printed information that exists physically and is a more permanent form of output
______ 3. gray scaling (294)	c. added to boost low bass sounds
______ 4. nit (301)	d. changes the brightness and contrast of pixels surrounding each letter
______ 5. hard copy (303)	e. acceptable print quality for business letters
______ 6. near letter quality (NLQ) (304)	f. unit of visible light intensity equal to one candela
______ 7. letter quality (LQ) (305)	g. uses tiny mirrors to reflect light, which produces crisp, bright, colorful images
______ 8. woofer (313)	h. information on a display device that exists electronically and appears for a temporary period
______ 9. LCD projector (316)	i. magnetic field that travels at the speed of light
______ 10. DLP projector (316)	j. print quality slightly less clear than what is acceptable for business letters
	k. information appears in one color on a different background color
	l. attaches directly to a computer and uses its own light source to display information

SHORT ANSWER

Write a brief answer to each of the following questions.

1. What features do CRT monitors usually include to address ergonomic issues? ______ What is the ENERGY STAR program? ______
2. What does the quality of an LCD monitor or LCD screen depend on? __________ When are refresh rates an issue with LCD monitors or LCD screens? __________
3. What advantages do digital television signals provide over analog signals? _______ What is interactive TV? _______
4. How is portrait orientation different from landscape orientation? ______ What is continuous-form paper? ______
5. What is a page description language? ______ How is PCL different from PostScript? ______

WORKING TOGETHER

Working with a group of your classmates, complete the following team exercises.

1. A group of business employees would like to set up a small accounting office, with 10 to 12 employees. They have hired your group as consultants to help with the setup. Your primary responsibility is to determine the type of output devices you think they will need within the office. Consider the types and number of printers, types and number of display devices, audio and video devices, and whether fax machines, fax modems, and/or multifunction peripherals are needed. Use the Internet to research information. Prepare a report to share with the class. Include a table listing the pros and cons of the various devices and a short explanation of why you selected each device.
2. Choose one Issue in this chapter from page 297, 299, 306, 314, 319. Use the Web and/or print media to research the issue. Present a debate for the class, with different members of your team supporting different responses to the questions that accompany the issue.
3. Plotters can draw on any part of a page at random, and then move on to any other part. This capability and their capacity to use large sheets of paper, make plotters invaluable to engineers, electrical contractors, architects, home builders, and city planners. Have each member of your team interview someone in an organization that uses plotters. What type of plotter is used? Why? For what purpose is the plotter used? What is the advantage (or disadvantage) of using a plotter compared with simply creating a drawing by hand? Discuss the results of your interviews in the group. Use PowerPoint to create a group presentation and share your findings with the class.

CHAPTER 6 LEARN IT ONLINE

QUIZZES AND LEARNING GAMES
Computer Genius
Crossword Puzzle
Interactive Labs
Practice Test
Quiz Yourself
Wheel of Terms

EXERCISES
Chapter Review
Checkpoint
Key Terms
Lab Exercises
Learn It Online
Web Research

BEYOND THE BOOK
Apply It
Career Corner
Companies
FAQ
High-Tech Talk
Issues
Looking Ahead
Trailblazers
Web Links

FEATURES
Guide to Web Sites
Making Use of the Web
Tech News
Timeline 2005

Use the Learn It Online exercises to reinforce your understanding of the chapter concepts.

WEB INSTRUCTIONS:

To display this page from the Web, start your browser and enter the Web address **scsite.com/dc2005/ch6/learn**.

1 At the Movies – E-Books

To view the E-Books movie, click the number 1 button. Watch the movie and then complete the exercise by answering the questions below. Electronic books are here. Holding half-a-dozen novels, a semester's worth of textbooks, or a library of sales and service manuals, they promise a new world of portability, access, and convenience. Book files can be downloaded easily from the Internet. Prices range from $150 to $500 for the e-book itself, with thousands of titles currently available for $5 to $25 each. The technology and the market for e-books continue to improve in parallel. Better screens and voice recognition already are in the works. What other features might you suggest? What, if anything, do you think inhibits consumer acceptance of this technology?

2 Student Edition Labs – Peripheral Devices

Click the number 2 button. When the Student Edition Labs menu appears, click *Peripheral Devices* to begin. A new browser window will open. Follow the on-screen instructions to complete the Lab. When finished, click the Exit button. If required, print a copy of your results to submit to your instructor.

3 Student Edition Labs – Working with Graphics

Click the number 3 button. When the Student Edition Labs menu appears, click *Working with Graphics* to begin. A new browser window will open. Follow the on-screen instructions to complete the Lab. When finished, click the Exit button. If required, print a copy of your results to submit to your instructor.

4 Practice Test

Click the number 4 button. Answer each question. When completed, enter your name and click the Grade Test button to submit the quiz for grading. Make a note of any missed questions. If required, print a copy to submit to your instructor.

5 Web Guide

Click the number 5 button to display the Guide to Web Sites and Searching Techniques Web page. Click Computers and Computing. Click ZDNet and then type `audio devices` in the Search text box. Click the Go button and then review the information. Use your word processing program to prepare a brief report about your findings and submit your assignment to your instructor.

6 Scavenger Hunt

Click the number 6 button. Print a copy of the Scavenger Hunt page; use this page to write down your answers as you search the Web. Submit your completed page to your instructor.

7 Who Wants To Be a Computer Genius?

Click the number 7 button to find out if you are a computer genius. Directions on how to play the game will be displayed. When you are ready to play, click the Play button. Submit your score to your instructor.

8 Wheel of Terms

Click the number 8 button to reinforce important terms you learned in this chapter by playing the Shelly Cashman Series version of this popular game. Directions on how to play the game will be displayed. When you are ready to play, click the Play button. Submit your score to your instructor.

9 Career Corner

Click the number 9 button to display the Penn State's Career Services Web page. Click a link of your choice. Write a brief report about the information you found. Submit the report to your instructor.

10 Search Sleuth

Click the number 10 button to learn search techniques that will help make you a research expert. Submit the completed assignment to your instructor.

11 Crossword Puzzle Challenge

Click the number 11 button. Complete the puzzle to reinforce skills you learned in this chapter. Directions on how to play the game will be displayed. When you are ready to play, click the Submit button. Submit the completed puzzle to your instructor.

12 Choosing a Printer

The printer is a key component of any new personal computer that you purchase. Whether you are printing black and white reports or producing photo-lab-quality pictures, determining which printer is best for your individual needs requires some research. Printers are available in a range of speeds and capabilities. Click the number 12 button for a tutorial on how to select the printer that is best for your particular requirements.

13 In the News

Display device technology continues to advance. Not long ago, computer users would have considered connecting their $1,000 computers to a color television instead of paying outrageous prices for a color monitor. Today, you can purchase a 20-inch monitor that is faster and sharper than that color television for less than $300. Yet, as prices fall, consumers surely will purchase the display devices for HDTV and crystal-clear Internet access. Click the number 13 button and then read a news article about a new or improved output device. What is the device? Who manufactures it? How is the output device better than, or different from, earlier devices? Who do you think is most likely to use the device? Why?

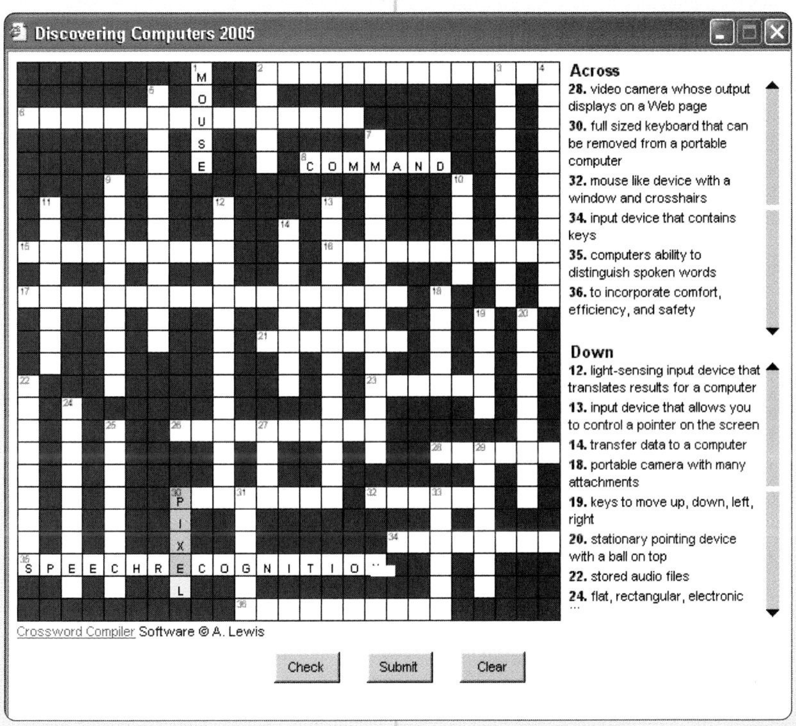

CHAPTER 6 LAB EXERCISES

Use the Lab Exercises to gain hands-on computer experience.

QUIZZES AND LEARNING GAMES
Computer Genius
Crossword Puzzle
Interactive Labs
Practice Test
Quiz Yourself
Wheel of Terms

EXERCISES
Chapter Review
Checkpoint
Key Terms
Lab Exercises
Learn It Online
Web Research

BEYOND THE BOOK
Apply It
Career Corner
Companies
FAQ
High-Tech Talk
Issues
Looking Ahead
Trailblazers
Web Links

FEATURES
Guide to Web Sites
Making Use of the Web
Tech News
Timeline 2005

WEB INSTRUCTIONS:

To display this page from the Web, start your browser and enter the Web address **scsite.com/dc2005/ch6/lab**.

1 About Your Computer

This exercise uses Windows XP procedures. To learn about the output devices on your computer, click the Start button on the taskbar, and then right-click the My Computer icon on the Start menu. Click Properties on the shortcut menu. When the System Properties dialog box is displayed, click the Hardware tab. Click the Device Manager button. Click the plus sign next to Computer. Below Computer, a list of hardware device categories appears. What output devices are listed? Click the plus sign next to each category. What specific output devices in each category are connected to your computer? Close the Device Manager window. Click the Cancel button in the System Properties dialog box.

2 Accessibility Options

This exercise uses Windows XP procedures. The Windows operating system offers several output options for people with hearing or visual impairments. Three of these options are SoundSentry, ShowSounds, and High Contrast. To find out more about each option, click the Start button on the taskbar and then click Control Panel on the Start menu. In Category View, click the Accessibility Options icon in the Control Panel window, and then click the Accessibility Options icon in the Accessibility Options window. Click the Sound tab in the Accessibility Options dialog box. Click the Question Mark button on the title bar, click SoundSentry, read the information in the pop-up window, and then click the pop-up window to close it. Repeat this process for ShowSounds. Click the Display tab. Click the Question Mark button on the title bar and then click High Contrast. Read the information in the pop-up window, and then click the pop-up window to close it. What is the purpose of each option? Click the Cancel button. Click the Close button to close the Accessibility Options window.

3 Self-Portrait

This exercise uses Windows XP/2000/98 procedures. Windows includes a drawing program called Paint. The quality of graphics produced with this program depends on a variety of factors, including the quality of your printer, your understanding of the software, and (to some extent) your artistic talent. In this exercise, you use Paint to create a self-portrait. To access Paint, click the Start button on the taskbar, point to All Programs (Programs in Windows 2000/98) on the Start menu, point to Accessories on the All Programs submenu (Programs submenu in Windows 2000/98), and then click Paint on the Accessories submenu. When the untitled - Paint window is displayed, you will see the Paint toolbar on the left side of the window. Point to a toolbar button to see a tool's name; click a button to use that tool. Use the tools and colors available in Paint to draw a picture of yourself. If you make a mistake, you can click Undo on the Edit menu to undo your most recent action, you can erase part of your picture using the Eraser/Color Eraser tool, or you can clear the entire picture by clicking Clear Image on the Image menu. When your self-portrait is finished, print it by clicking Print on the File menu. Close Paint. Do not save your changes.

4 Magnifier

This exercise uses Windows 2000 procedures. Magnifier is a Windows utility for the visually impaired. To find out about the Magnifier capabilities, click the Start button on the taskbar and then click Help on the Start menu. Click the Index tab in the Windows 2000 window and then type `magnifier` in the Type in the keyword to find text box. Click the overview subentry below the Magnifier entry in the list of topics and then click the Display button. Click Magnifier overview in the Topics Found dialog box and then click the Display button. Read the Help information in the right pane of the Windows 2000 window and answer the following questions:

- How does Magnifier make the screen more readable for the visually impaired?
- What viewing options does Magnifier have?
- What tracking options does Magnifier have?

Click the Close button to close the Windows 2000 window.

Web Research

Chapter 6

Use the Web Research exercises to learn more about the special features in this chapter.

Web Instructions:

Use the link in each exercise or a search engine such as Google (google.com) to research the topic. Then, write a one-page, double-spaced report or create a presentation, unless otherwise directed below. Page numbers on which information can be found are in parentheses.

1 **Issue** Choose one Issue from the following issues in this chapter: Who Is Responsible for Disposing of an Old Monitor? (297), LCD or CRT? (299), Short of Cash? (306), Wearing the Web? (314), or How Should Employers Accommodate Employees with Disabilities? (319). Use the Web to research the issue. Discuss the issue with classmates, instructors, and friends. Address the questions that accompany the issue in a report or presentation.

2 **Apply It** Choose one of the following Apply It features in this chapter: Picture This: Printing Digital Photographs (307) or Audio Books Tell a Good Story (314). Use the Web to gather additional information about the topic. Print two Web pages that relate to the Apply It. Detail in a report or presentation what you learned.

3 **Career Corner** Read the Career Corner article in this chapter (320). Use the Web to find out more about the career. Describe the career in a report or presentation.

4 **Companies on the Cutting Edge** Choose one of the Companies on the Cutting Edge in this chapter (322). Use the Web to research the company further. Explain in a report or presentation how this company has contributed to computer technology.

5 **Technology Trailblazers** Choose one of the Technology Trailblazers in this chapter (323). Use the Web to research the person further. Explain in a report or presentation how this individual has affected the way people use, or think about, computers.

6 **Picture Yourself Printing Pictures** Read the Picture Yourself Printing Pictures story at the beginning of this chapter (290). Use the Web to research printing pictures further. Describe in a report or presentation the ways in which you might print pictures.

7 **High-Tech Talk** Read the High-Tech Talk feature in this chapter (321). Use the Web to find out more about the topic. Summarize in a report or presentation what you learned.

8 **Web Links** Review the Web Link boxes found in the margins of this chapter. Visit five of the Web Link sites. Print the main Web page for each site you visit. Choose one of the Web pages and then summarize in one paragraph the content of the Web page.

9 **Looking Ahead** Choose one of the Looking Ahead articles in this chapter: Electronic Paper Writes a New Page (303) or Digital Movies Project New Image (317). Use the Web to find out more about the topic. Detail in a report or presentation what you learned.

10 **FAQ** Choose one FAQ found in this chapter. Use the Web to find out more about the topic. Summarize in one paragraph what you learned.

11 **Digital Imaging and Video Technology** Read the Digital Imaging and Video Technology Special Feature that follows this chapter (334–345). Select the technology in which you are most interested (digital imaging or video). Use the Web to learn more about your selection. Explain in a report or presentation the entire process, from capturing a digital image or video to distributing it.

12 **Making Use of the Web** Read the Government section of Making Use of the Web Appendix A (APP 12). Complete the Government Web Exercises at the end of the section (APP 13). Answer the questions posed in each exercise.

Digital Imaging and Video Technology

Everywhere you look, people are capturing moments they want to remember. They take pictures or make movies of their vacations, birthday parties, activities, accomplishments, sporting events, weddings, and more. Because of the popularity of digital cameras and digital video cameras, increasingly more people desire to capture their memories digitally, instead of on film. With digital technology, picture takers have the ability to modify and share the digital images and videos they create. When you use special hardware and/or software, you can copy, manipulate, print, and distribute digital images and videos using your personal computer and the Internet. Amateurs can create professional quality results by using more sophisticated hardware and software.

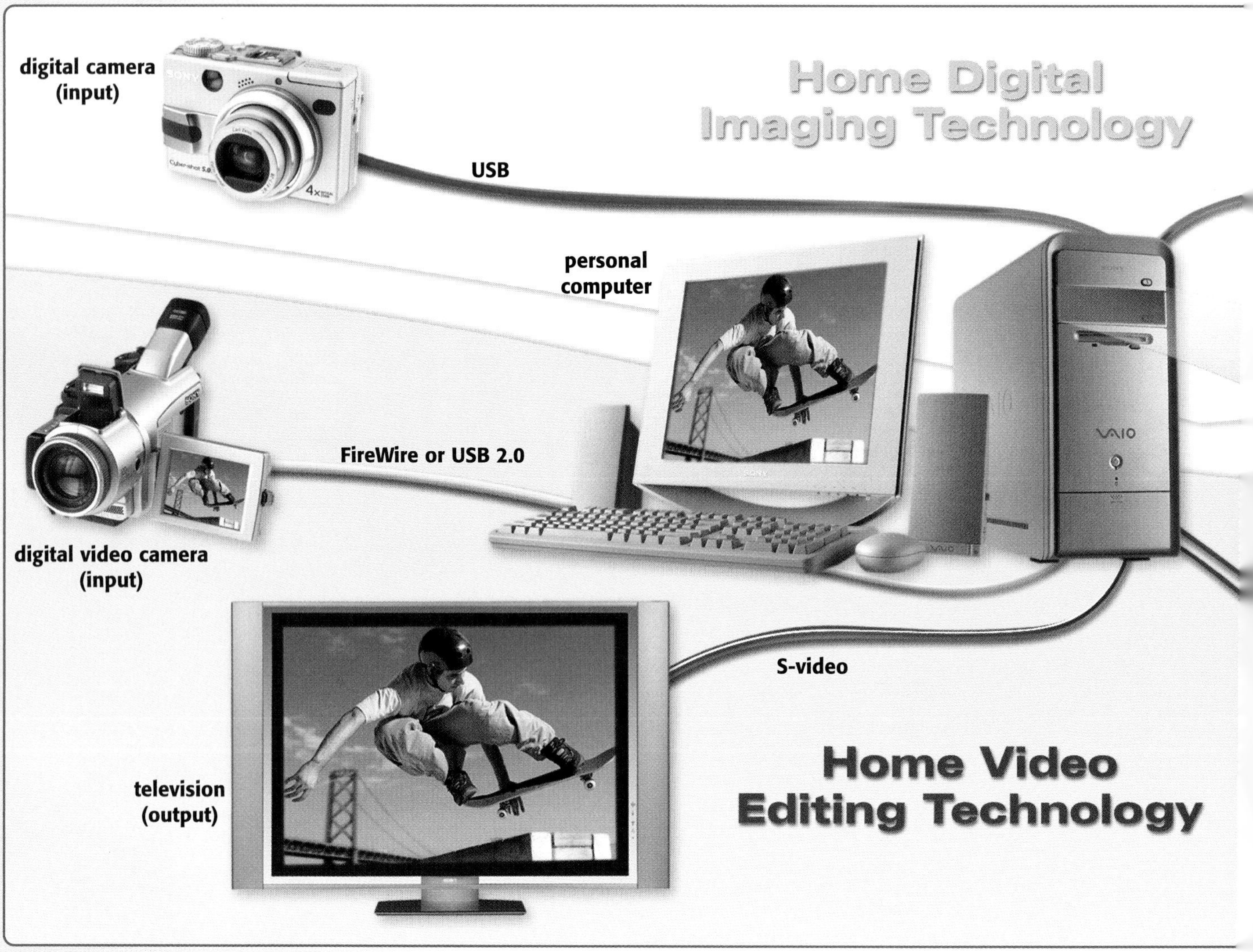

FIGURE 1 The top portion of the figure shows a typical home digital imaging setup and the lower portion of the figure shows a typical home setup for editing personal video.

Digital photography and recordings deliver significant benefits over film-based photography and movie making. With digital cameras, no developing is needed. Instead, the images reside on storage media such as a hard disk, DVD, or flash memory card. Unlike film, storage media can be reused, which reduces costs, saves time, and provides immediate results. Digital technology allows greater control over the creative process, both while taking pictures and video and in the editing process. You can check results immediately after capturing a picture or video to determine whether it meets your expectations. If you are dissatisfied with a picture or video, you can erase it and recapture it, again and again.

As shown in the top portion of Figure 1, a digital camera functions as an input device when it transmits pictures through a cable to a personal computer via a USB port or FireWire port. Using a digital camera in this way allows you to edit the pictures, save them on storage media, and print them on a photographic-quality printer via a parallel port or USB port.

The lower portion of Figure 1 illustrates how you might use a digital video camera with a personal computer. The process typically is the same for most digital video cameras. You capture the images or video with the video camera. Next, you connect the video camera to your personal computer using a FireWire or USB 2.0 port, or you place the storage media used on the camera in the computer. The video then is copied or downloaded to the computer's hard disk. Then, you can edit the video using video editing software. If desired, you can preview the video during the editing process on a television. Finally, you save the finished result to the desired media, such as a VHS tape or DVD+RW or, perhaps, e-mail the edited video. In this example, a VCR and a DVD player also can be used to input video from a VHS tape or a DVD.

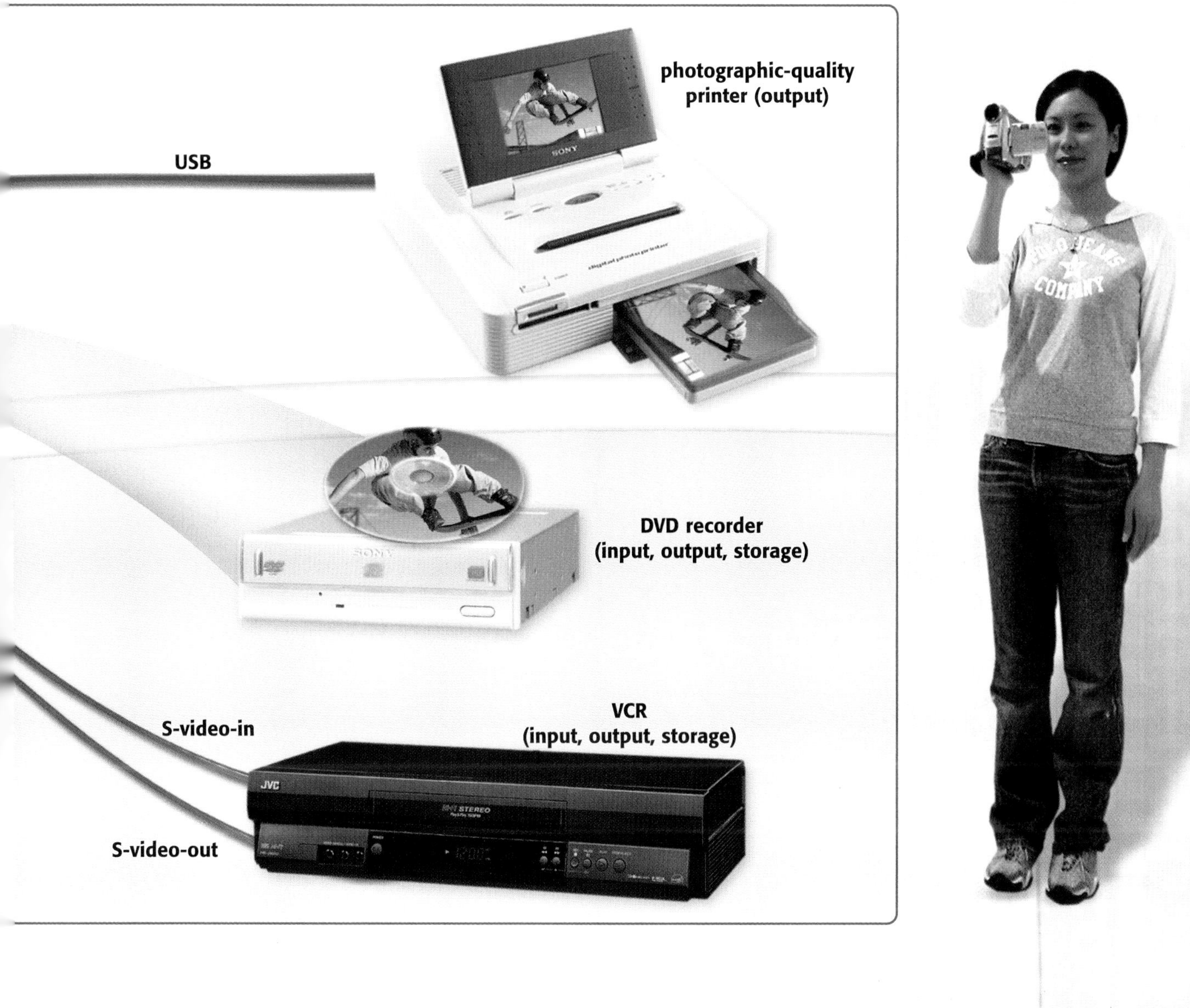

DIGITAL IMAGING TECHNOLOGY

Digital imaging technology involves capturing and manipulating still photographic images in an electronic format. The following sections outline the steps involved in the process of using digital imaging technology.

1 Select a Digital Camera

A **digital camera** is a type of camera that stores photographed images electronically instead of on traditional film. Digital cameras are divided into three categories (Figure 2) based mainly on image resolution, features, and of course, price. The image resolution is measured in pixels (short for picture element). The image quality increases with the number of pixels. The image resolution usually is measured in **megapixels** (million of pixels), often abbreviated as **MP**. Features of digital cameras include red-eye reduction, zoom, autofocus, flash, self-timer, and manual mode for fine-tuning settings. Figure 3 summarizes the three categories of digital cameras.

TYPES OF DIGITAL CAMERAS

Type	Maximum Resolution	Comment	Price
Low-end point and shoot	Less than 2 MP	Fully automatic; fits in your pocket; usually limited to 4-by-6-inch printed output; ideal for Web pages, e-mail attachments, and newsletters	Less than $200
High-end point and shoot	Greater than 2 MP and less than 5 MP	Includes more advanced features that allow for creative control of the camera's settings; makes up to 8-by-10-inch printed pictures; capable of taking pictures at lower resolutions	$200 to $1,000
Professional	Greater than 5 MP	Based on 35mm and APS SLR cameras; includes three image sensors for capturing great color and resolution; has much greater control over exposure and lenses	$1,000 and up

FIGURE 3 Digital cameras often are categorized by image resolution, features, and price.

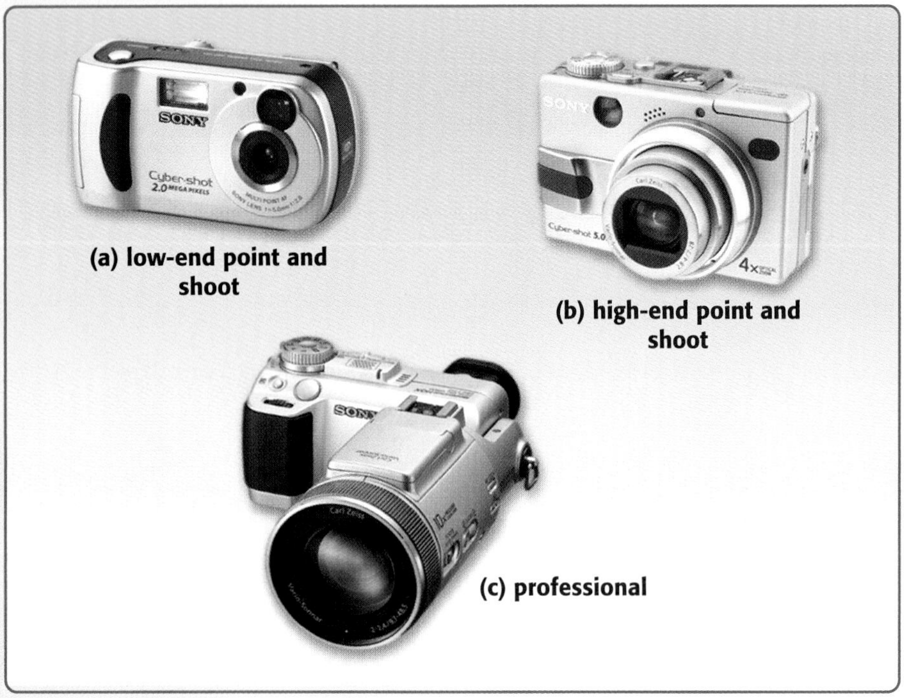

FIGURE 2 The low-end point and shoot digital camera (a) requires no adjustments before shooting. The high-end point and shoot digital camera (b) offers improved quality and features that allow you to make manual adjustments before shooting. The professional digital camera (c) offers better color and resolution and greater control over exposure and lenses.

2 Take Pictures

Digital cameras provide you with several options that are set before a picture is taken. Three of the more important options are the resolution, compression, and image file format in which the camera should save the picture. While a camera may allow for a very high resolution for a large print, you may choose to take a picture at a lower resolution if the image does not require great detail or must be a small size. For example, you may want to use the image on a Web page where smaller image file sizes are beneficial.

Compression results in smaller image file sizes. Figure 4 illustrates the image file sizes for varying resolutions and compressions under standard photographing conditions using a 4 megapixel digital camera. Figure 4 also shows the average picture size for a given resolution. The camera may take more time to save an image at lower compression, resulting in a longer delay before the camera is ready to take another picture. A higher compression, however, may result in loss of some image quality. If a camera has a 16 MB flash memory card, you can determine the number of pictures the card can hold by dividing 16 MB by the file size. Flash memory cards are available in sizes from 16 MB to 2 GB.

IMAGE FILE SIZE WITH A FOUR MEGAPIXEL DIGITAL CAMERA

	COMPRESSION			
Resolution in Pixels	Low	Medium	High	Picture Size in Inches
2272 x 1704	2 MB	1.1 MB	556 KB	11 by 17
1600 x 1200	1 MB	558 KB	278 KB	8 by 10
1024 x 768	570 KB	320 KB	170 KB	4 by 6
640 x 480	249 KB	150 KB	84 KB	3 by 5

FIGURE 4 Image file sizes for varying resolutions and compressions under standard shooting conditions using a 4 megapixel digital camera.

Most digital cameras also allow you to choose an image file format. Two popular file formats are TIFF and JPEG. The **TIFF** file format saves the image uncompressed. All of the image detail is captured and stored, but the file sizes can be large. The **JPEG** file format is compressed. The resolution of the image may be the same as a TIFF file, but some detail may be lost in the image.

Finally, before you take the photograph, you should choose the type of media on which to store the resulting image file. Some cameras allow for a choice of locations, such as a CompactFlash card or Memory Stick, while others allow for only one type of storage media. One major advantage of a digital camera is that you easily can erase pictures from its media, freeing up space for new pictures.

3 Transfer and Manage Image Files

The method of transferring images from the camera to the personal computer differs greatly depending on the capabilities of both. Digital cameras use a variety of storage media (Figure 5). If your camera uses a flash memory card such as a CompactFlash, SmartMedia, Secure Digital (SD), or Memory Stick, then, you can remove the media from the camera and place it in a slot on the personal computer or in a device connected to the personal computer for reading the cards. Your camera also may connect to the personal computer using a USB, USB 2.0 (Figure 6), or FireWire port. When you insert the memory card or connect the camera, software on the personal computer guides you through the process of transferring the images to the hard disk. Some operating systems and software recognize a memory card or camera as though it is another hard disk on the computer. This feature allows you to access the files, navigate them, and then copy, delete, or rename the files while the media still is in the camera.

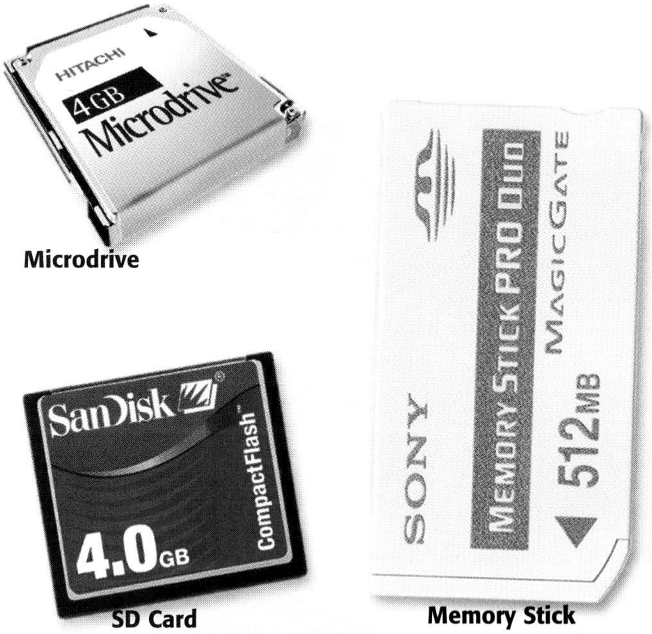

FIGURE 5 Microdrives, SD Cards, and Memory Sticks are popular storage devices for digital cameras.

FIGURE 6 Using a USB or FireWire connection, you can add a card reader to your personal computer.

After you transfer the files to the hard disk on your personal computer, you should organize the files by sorting them or renaming them so that information, such as the subject, date, time, and purpose, is saved along with the image. Finally, before altering the images digitally, or using the images for other purposes, you should back up the images to another location, such as a CD or DVD, so the original image is recoverable.

4 Edit Images

Image editing software allows you to edit digital images. The following list summarizes the more common image enhancements or alterations:

- Adjust the contrast and brightness; correct lighting problems; or help give the photograph a particular feeling; such as warm or stark.
- Remove red-eye.
- Crop an image to remove unnecessary elements and resize it.
- Rotate the image to change its orientation.
- Add elements to the image, such as descriptive text, a date, a logo, or decorative items; create collages or add missing elements.
- Replace individual colors with a new color.
- Add special effects, such as texture or motion blurring to enhance the image.

Figure 7 shows some of the effects available in Jasc's Paint Shop Pro on the Add/Remove Noise submenu.

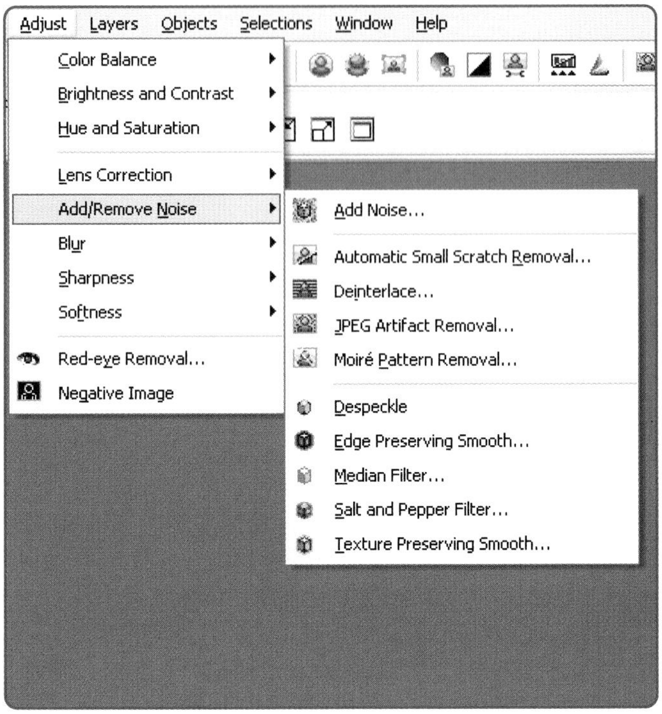

FIGURE 7 The ability to use effects separates digital photography from film photography.

5 Print Images

Once an image is digitally altered, it is ready to be printed. You can print images on a personal color printer, or send them to a professional service that specializes in digital photo printing.

When printing the images yourself, make sure that the resolution used to create the image was high enough for the size of the print you want to create. For example, if the camera used a resolution of 640 x 480 pixels, then the ideal print size is a wallet size. If you print such an image at a size of 8-by-10 inches, then the image will appear **pixilated**, or blurry. Use high-quality photo paper for the best results. A photo printer gives the best results when printing digital photography.

Many services print digital images, either over the Internet or through traditional photo developing locations and kiosks (Figure 8), such as those found in drug stores or shopping marts. Some services allow you to e-mail or upload the files to the service, specify the size, quality, and quantity of print, and then they send the prints to you via the postal service. Other services allow you to drop off flash memory cards, CD-ROMs, or floppy disks at a photo shop and allow you to pick up the prints, just as you do with traditional photo developing shops.

FIGURE 8 A Sony PictureStation kiosk allows you to print digital images in high resolution on photo paper.

Distribute Images Electronically

Rather than printing images, you often need to use the images electronically. Depending on the electronic use of the image, the image may require additional processing. If you use the images on a Web site or want to e-mail a photo, you probably want to send a lower-resolution image. Image editing software allows you to lower the resolution of the image, resulting in a smaller file size. You also should use standard file formats when distributing an electronic photo. The JPEG format is viewable using most personal computers or Web browsers.

You can store very high resolution photos on a DVD or a CD. **DVD and CD mastering software** (Figure 9) allows you to create slide show presentations on a recordable DVD or CD that can play in many home DVD players or personal computer DVD drives.

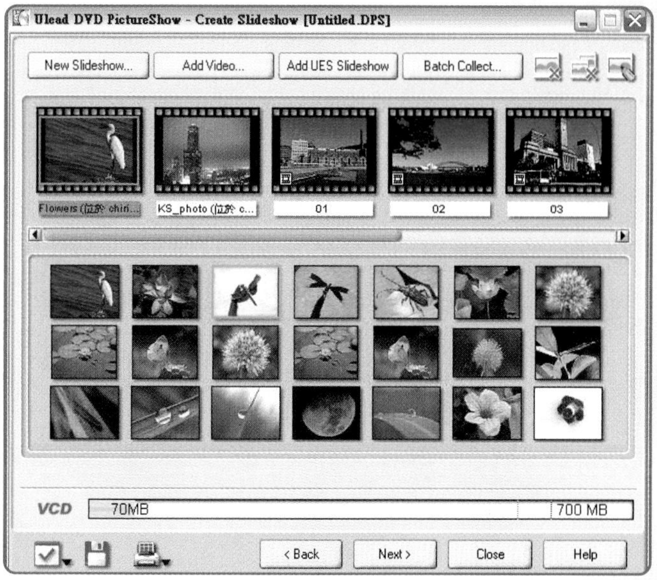

FIGURE 9 Ulead DVD PictureShow and similar software applications allow you to create your own photo slide shows on DVD or CD.

Finally, you should back up and store images that you distribute electronically with the same care as you store your traditional film negatives.

DIGITAL VIDEO TECHNOLOGY

Digital video technology allows you to input, edit, manage, publish, and share your videos using a personal computer. With digital video technology, you can transform home videos into Hollywood-style movies by enhancing the videos with scrolling titles and transitions, cutting out or adding scenes, and adding background music and voice-over narration. The following sections outline the steps involved in the process of using digital video technology.

1 Select a Video Camera

Video cameras record in either analog or digital format. **Analog formats** include 8mm, Hi8, VHS, VHS-C, and Super VHS-C. The latter three formats use the types of tapes similar to those used in a standard VCR. **Digital formats** include Mini-DV, MICROMV, Digital8, and DVD. Consumer digital video cameras are by far the most popular type among consumers. They fall into three general categories, high-end consumer, consumer, and webcasting and monitoring (Figure 10). Digital video cameras provide more features than analog video cameras, such as a higher level of zoom, better sound, or more control over color and lighting.

FIGURE 10 The high-end consumer digital video camera (a) can produce professional-grade results. The consumer digital video camera (b) produces amateur-grade results. The webcasting and monitoring digital video camera (c) is appropriate for webcasting and security monitoring.

2 Record a Video

Video cameras are easier to use than digital cameras. Video cameras, for example, do not require you to set the resolution, compression, or file format before recording. Most video cameras do, however, provide you with a choice of recording programs sometimes called automatic settings. Each recording program includes a different combination of camera settings, so you can adjust the exposure and other functions to match the recording environment. Usually, several different programs are available, such as point and shoot, point and shoot with manual adjustment, sports, portrait, spot lit scenes, and low light. You also have the ability to select special digital effects, such as fade, wipe, and black and white. If you are shooting outside on a windy day, then you can enable the wind screen to prevent wind noise. If you are shooting home videos, then the point-and-shoot recording program is sufficient.

3 Transfer and Manage Videos

After recording the video, the next step is to transfer the video to your personal computer. Most video cameras connect directly to a USB 2.0 or FireWire port on your personal computer (Figure 11). Transferring video with a digital camera is easy, because the video already is in a digital format that the computer can understand.

An analog camcorder or VCR requires additional hardware to convert the analog signals into a digital counterpart before the video can be manipulated on a personal computer. The additional hardware includes a special video capture card using a standard RCA video cable or an S-video cable (Figure 12). *S-video* cables provide greater quality. When you use video capture hardware with an analog video, be sure to close all open programs on your computer because capturing video requires a great deal of processing power.

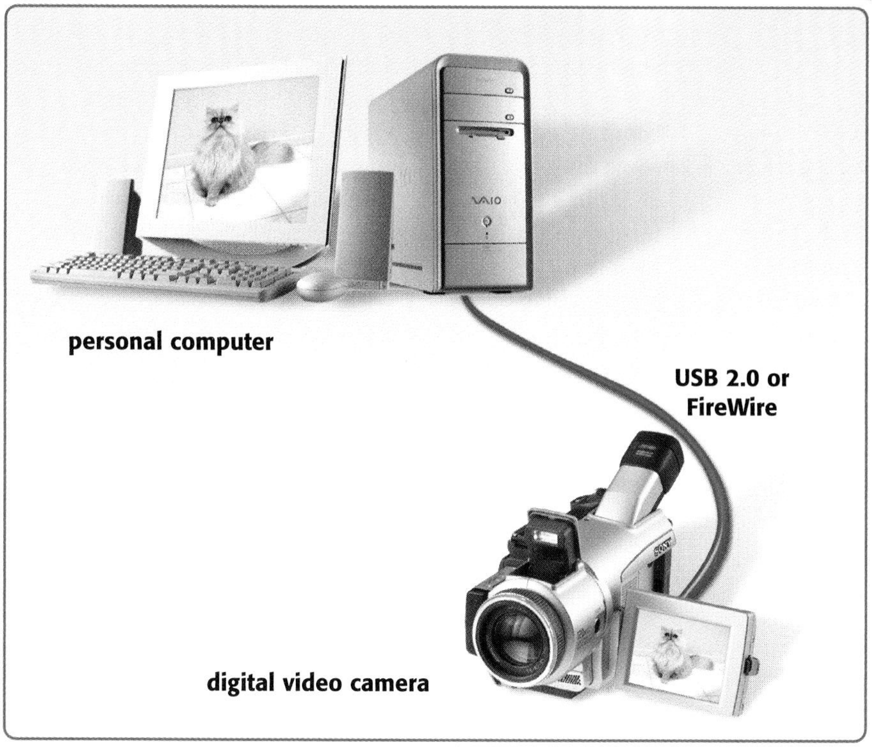

FIGURE 11 A digital video camera is connected to the personal computer via a FireWire or USB 2.0 port and the video. No additional hardware is needed.

When transferring video, plan to use approximately 15 to 30 gigabytes of hard disk storage space per hour of digital video. A typical video project requires about four times the amount of raw footage as the final product. Therefore, at the high end, a video that lasts an hour may require up to 120 gigabytes of storage for the raw footage, editing process, and final video. This storage requirement can vary depending on the software you use to copy the video from the video camera to the hard disk and the format you select to save the video. For example, Microsoft claims that the latest version of its Windows Movie Maker can save 15 hours of video in 10 gigabytes when creating video for playback on a computer but saves only 1 hour of video in 10 gigabytes when creating video for playback on a DVD or VCR.

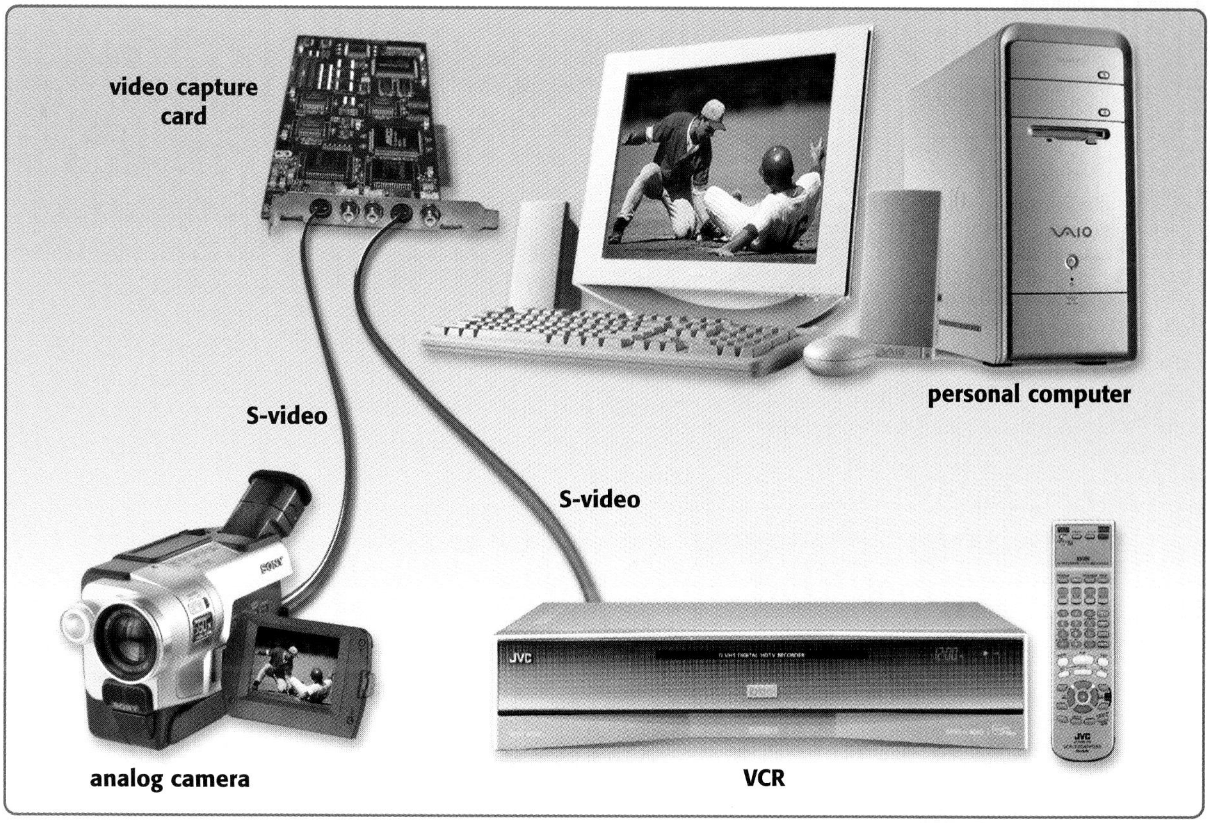

FIGURE 12 An analog camcorder or VCR is connected to the personal computer via an s-video port on a video capture card.

The video transfer requires application software on the personal computer. Windows XP includes the Windows Movie Maker software (Figure 13) that allows you to transfer the video from your video camera. Depending on the length of video and the type of connection used, the video may take a long time to download. Make certain that no other programs are running on your personal computer while transferring the video.

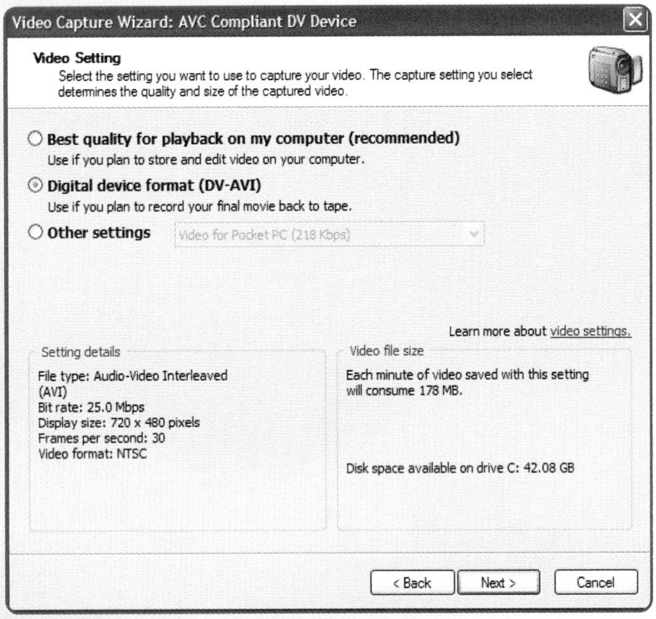

FIGURE 13 Some video editing software, such as Microsoft Windows Movie Maker, allows you to transfer your video from any video source to a hard disk.

When transferring video, the software may allow you to choose a file format and a codec to store the video. A video **file format** holds the video information in a manner specified by a vendor, such as Apple or Microsoft. Some of the more popular file formats are listed in Figure 14.

POPULAR VIDEO FILE FORMATS

File Format	File Extensions
Apple QuickTime	.MOV or .QT
Microsoft Windows Media Video	.WMV or .ASF
RealNetworks RealMedia	.RM or .RAM

FIGURE 14 Apple, Microsoft, and RealNetworks offer the more popular video file formats.

File formats support codecs to encode the audio and video into the file formats. A particular file format may be able to store audio and video in a number of different codecs. A **codec** specifies how the audio and video is compressed and stored within the file. Figure 15 shows some options available for specifying a file format and codec in the Microsoft Windows Movie Maker. The file format and codec you choose often is based on what you plan to do with the movie. For example, if you plan to stream video over the Web using RealNetworks software, the best choice for the file format is the RealMedia format, which uses the RealVideo codec.

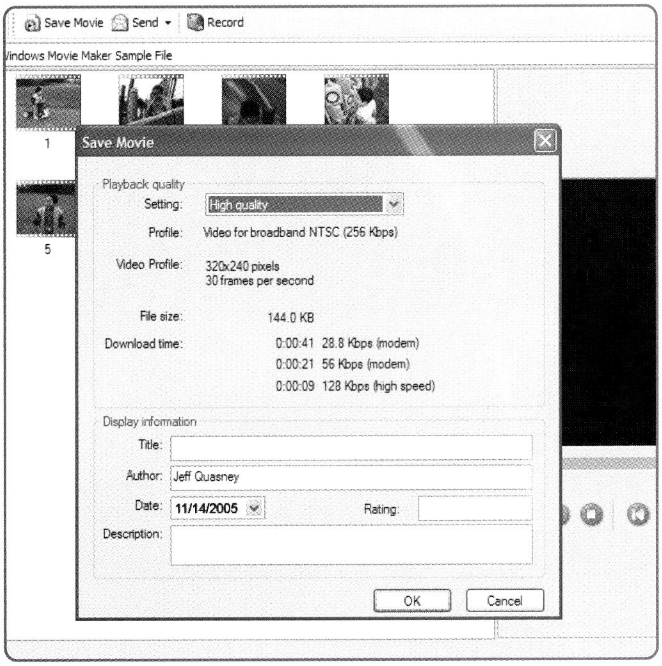

FIGURE 15 Video editing software applications allow you to specify a combination of file format and codec when saving a video.

After transferring the video to a personal computer, and before manipulating the video, you should store the video files in appropriate folders, named correctly, and backed up. Most video transfer application software helps manage these tasks.

4 Edit a Video

Once the video is stored on your hard disk, the next step is to edit, or manipulate, the video. If you used a video capture card to transfer analog video to your computer (Figure 12 on the previous page), the files may require extra initial processing. When you use a video capture card, some of the video frames may be lost in the transfer process. Some video editing programs allow you to fix this problem with **frame rate correction** tools.

The first step in the editing process is to split the video into smaller pieces, or *scenes*, that you can manipulate more easily. This process is called *splitting*. Most video software automatically splits the video into scenes, thus saving you the time. After splitting, you should cut out unwanted scenes or portions of scenes. This process is called *pruning*.

After you create the scenes you want to use in your final production, you edit each individual scene. You can *crop*, or change the size of, scenes. That is, you may want to cut out the top or a side of a scene that is irrelevant. You also can resize the scene. For example, you may be creating a video that will display in a Web browser. Making a smaller video, such as 320 x 200 pixels instead of 640 x 480 pixels, results in a smaller file that transmits faster over the Internet.

If video has been recorded over a long period, using different cameras or under different lighting conditions, the video may need color correction. *Color correction tools* (Figure 16) analyze your video and match brightness, colors, and other attributes of video clips to create a smooth look to the video.

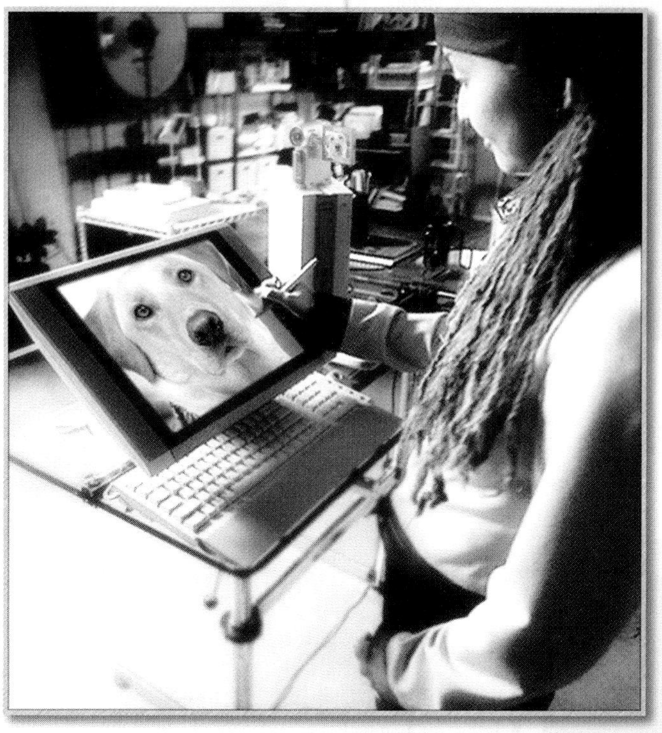

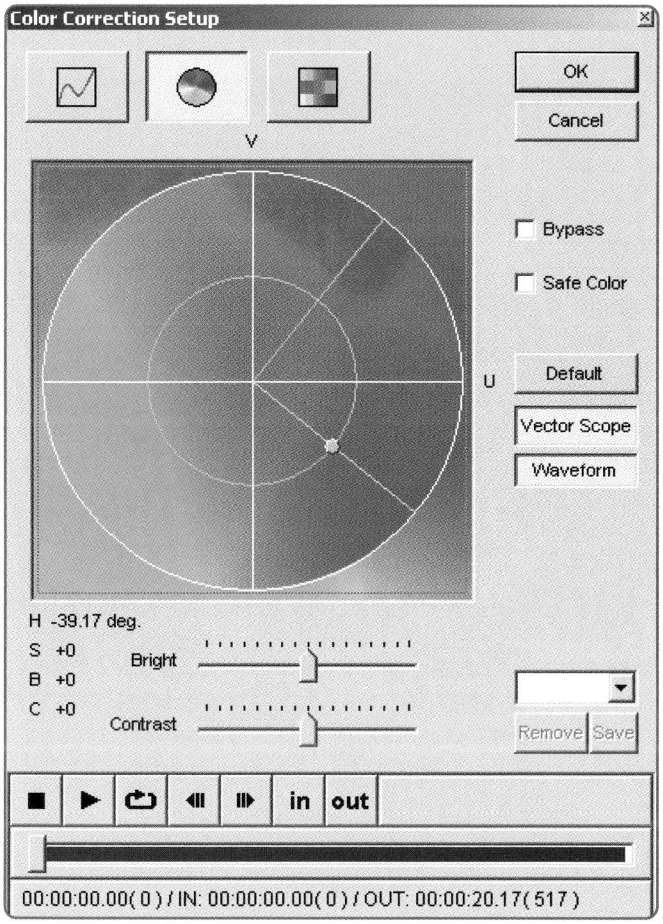

FIGURE 16 Color correction tools in video editing software allow a great deal of control over the mood of your video creation.

You can add logos, special effects, or titles to scenes. You can place a company logo or personal logo in a video to identify yourself or the company producing the video. Logos often are added on the lower-right corner of a video and remain for the duration of the video. Special effects include warping, changing from color to black and white, morphing, or zoom motion. *Morphing* is a special effect in which one video image is transformed into another image over the course of several frames of video, creating the illusion of metamorphosis. You usually add titles at the beginning and end of a video to give the video context. A training video may have titles throughout the video to label a particular scene, or each scene may begin with a title.

The next step in editing a video is to add audio effects, including voice-over narration and background music. Many video editing programs allow you to add additional tracks, or *layers*, of sound to a video in addition to the sound that was recorded on the video camera. You also can add special audio effects.

The final step in editing a video is to combine the scenes into a complete video (Figure 17). This process involves ordering scenes and adding transition effects between scenes (Figure 18). Video editing software allows you to combine scenes and separate each scene with a transition. *Transitions* include fading, wiping, blurry, bursts, ruptures, erosions, and more.

FIGURE 17 Scenes, shown on the right, are combined into a sequence on the bottom of the screen.

FIGURE 18 Smooth and dynamic transitions eliminate the hard cuts between scenes typically found in raw footage.

5 Distribute the Video

After editing the video, the final step is to distribute it or save it on a desired media. You can save video in a variety of formats. Using special hardware, you can save the video on standard video tape. *A digital-to-analog converter* is necessary to allow your personal computer to transmit video to a VCR. A digital-to-analog converter may be an external device that connects to both the computer and input device, or may be a video capture card inside the computer.

Video also can be stored in digital formats in any of several DVD formats, on CD-R, or on video CD (VCD). *DVD* or *CD creation software*, which often is packaged with video editing software, allows you to create, or *master*, DVDs and CDs. You can add interactivity to your DVDs. For example, you can allow viewers to jump to certain scenes using a menu (Figure 19). A *video CD* (*VCD*) is a CD format that stores video on a CD-R that can be played in many DVD players.

You also can save your video creation in electronic format, for distribution over the Web or via e-mail. Your video editing software must support the file format and codec you want to use. For example, RealNetworks's Helix media delivery system allows you to save media files in the RealVideo file formats.

FIGURE 19 DVD mastering software allows you to create interactive menus on your DVD.

Professionals use hardware and software that allow them to create a film version of digital video that can be played in movie theaters. This technology is becoming increasingly popular and has been used in such movies as the recent *Lord of the Rings* movies. Some Hollywood directors believe that eventually, all movies will be recorded and edited digitally.

After creating your final video for distribution or your personal video collection, you should backup the final video file. You can save your scenes for inclusion in other video creations or create new masters using different effects, transitions, and ordering of scenes.

CHAPTER 7

Storage

Picture Yourself Using a Picture CD

At your family reunion this weekend, you took several rolls of film. While filling out the film-processing envelope, you notice it has a check box for a Kodak Picture CD. "What's a Picture CD?" you ask the clerk. He explains that in addition to prints and negatives, you receive a CD that contains digital images of all your pictures. Picture CDs can last longer and take up less storage space than printed pictures. Some users also print additional pictures from the Picture CD.

You mention that you do not have a high-quality printer. He says you can print pictures on the Picture CD using the Kodak Picture Maker, which is an in-store kiosk that offers the capabilities of enlarging, cropping, eliminating red eye, and adding text to pictures before you print them. You also could e-mail the images from the Picture CD or post them on a photo community (usually without cost).

After thanking the clerk for his great explanation, you mark the Kodak Picture CD box on the film-processing envelope. With the Picture CD, you will be able to send images of the family reunion to everyone. Using the Kodak Picture Maker, you can make printed copies of the great pictures to hang on your wall.

As you read Chapter 7, you will learn about Picture CDs and discover other types of storage.

OBJECTIVES

After completing this chapter, you will be able to:

1. Discuss the various types of items that users store on computer media
2. Differentiate between storage devices and storage media
3. Describe the characteristics of a floppy disk drive
4. Identify the uses of Zip disks
5. Describe the characteristics of a hard disk
6. Identify the advantages of using an Internet hard drive
7. Describe the characteristics of CDs and DVDs
8. Differentiate among CD-ROMs, CD-RWs, DVD-ROMs, and DVD+RWs
9. Identify the uses of tape
10. Discuss PC Cards and the various types of miniature storage media
11. Identify uses of microfilm and microfiche

CONTENTS

STORAGE

Storage holds data, instructions, and information for future use. Every computer uses storage to hold software, specifically, system software and application software. To start up, a computer locates an operating system (system software) in storage and loads it into memory. When a user issues a command to start application software, such as word processing or a Web browser, the operating system locates the program in storage and loads it into memory.

In addition to programs, users store a variety of data and information on mainframe computers, servers, desktop computers, notebook computers, handheld computers, Tablet PCs, PDAs, and smart phones:

- The home user might store letters, budgets, bank statements, a household inventory, records of stock purchases, tax data, addresses of friends and relatives, daily schedules, e-mail messages, homework assignments, recipes, digital photographs, music, and videos.
- The small office/home office user often stores correspondence, faxes, business reports, financial records, tax data, travel records, appointments, contact information, e-mail messages, customer orders, payroll records, inventory records, and Web pages.
- The mobile user usually stores letters, faxes, presentations, appointments, travel records, contacts and addresses, homework assignments, quotations, e-mail messages, and digital photographs.
- The large business user accesses many stored items, including customer orders and invoices, vendor payments, payroll records, tax data, inventory records, presentations, contracts, marketing literature, contacts,

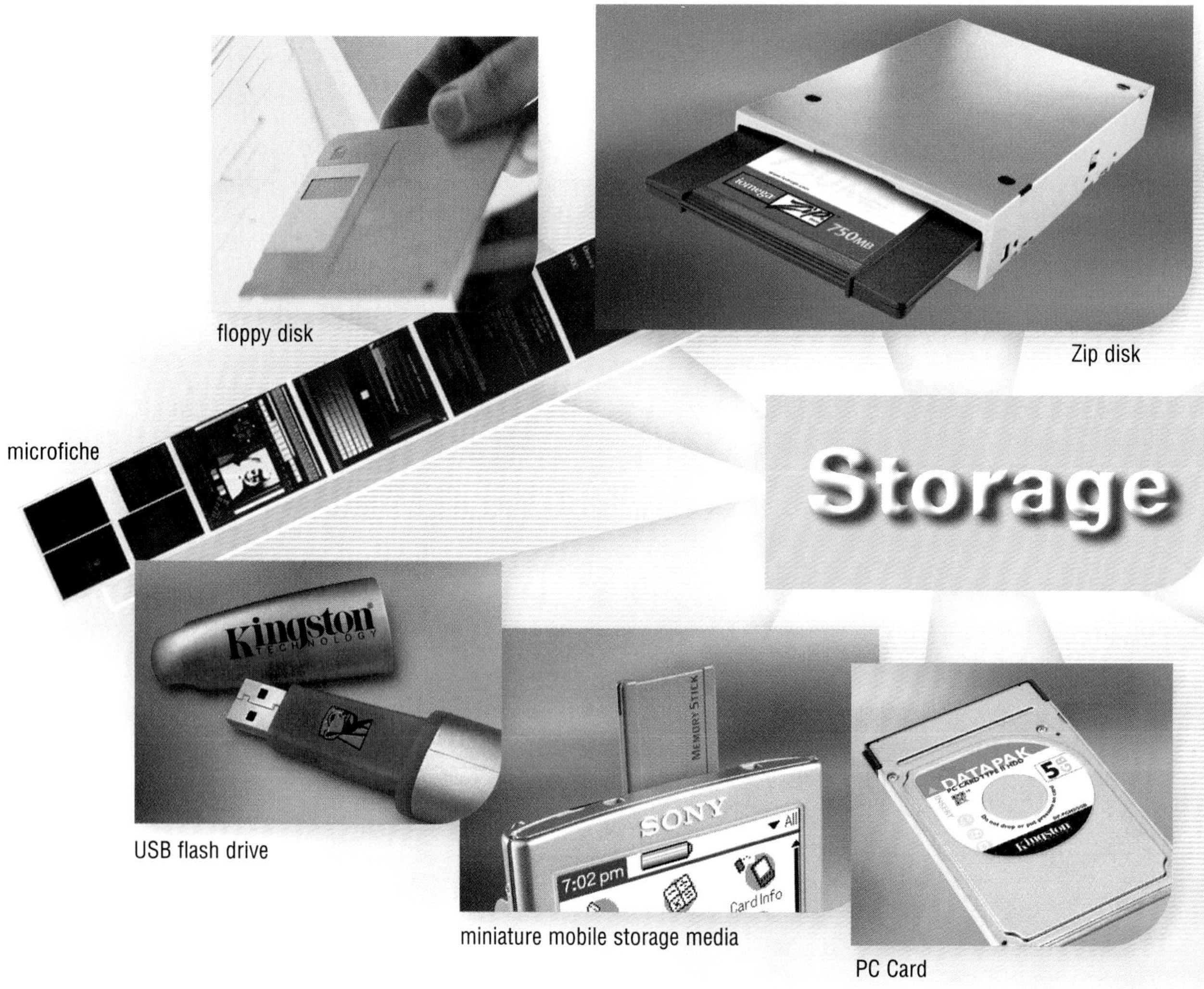

FIGURE 7-1 Data, instructions, and information are stored on a variety of storage media.

appointments, schedules, e-mail messages, and Web pages. The large business user accesses hundreds or thousands of employee, customer, and vendor records, whereas the small office/home office user may access less than one hundred of these types of records.
- The power user stores diagrams, drawings, blueprints, designs, marketing literature, corporate newsletters, product catalogs, videos, audio recordings, multimedia presentations, digital photographs, Web pages, letters, contacts, appointments, schedules, and e-mail messages.

Storage requirements among these users vary greatly. Home users, small office/home office users, and mobile users typically have much smaller storage requirements than the large business user or power user. For example, a home user may need 80 billion bytes of storage, while large businesses may require 50 trillion bytes of storage.

A **storage medium** (media is the plural), also called *secondary storage*, is the physical material on which a computer keeps data, instructions, and information. Examples of storage media are floppy disks, Zip disks, hard disks, CDs and DVDs, tape, PC Cards, miniature mobile storage media such as memory sticks or cards, USB flash drives, and microfiche (Figure 7-1). Memory, by contrast, typically consists of one or more chips on the motherboard or some other circuit board in the computer.

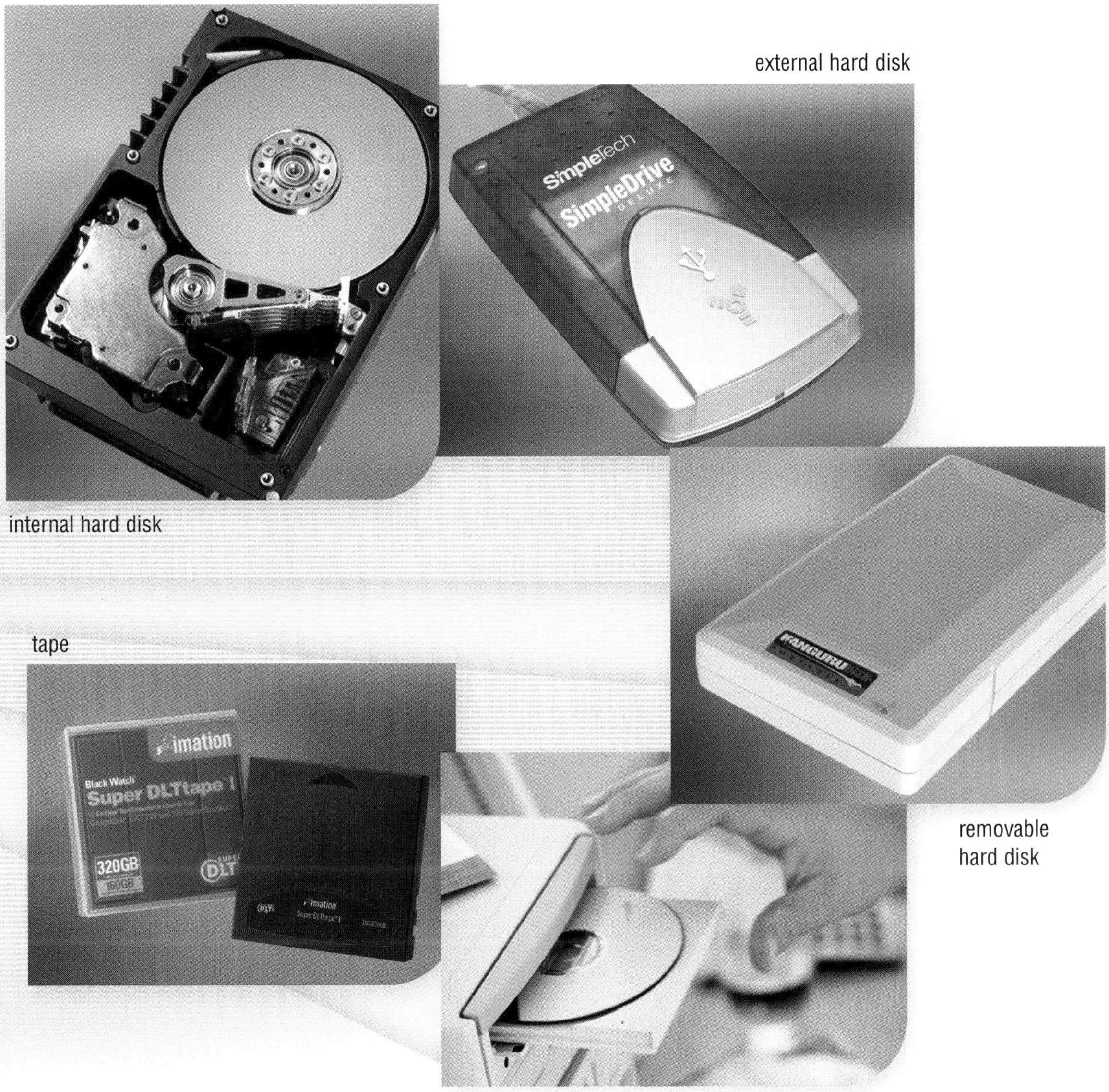

Capacity is the number of bytes (characters) a storage medium can hold. Figure 7-2 identifies the terms manufacturers use to define the capacity of storage media. For example, a typical floppy disk can store up to 1.44 MB of data (approximately 1.4 million bytes) and a typical hard disk has 80 GB (approximately 80 billion bytes) of storage capacity.

Items on a storage medium remain intact even when power is removed from the computer. Thus, a storage medium is nonvolatile. Most memory, by contrast, holds data and instructions temporarily and thus is volatile. Figure 7-3 illustrates the concept of volatility.

STORAGE TERMS

Storage Term	Approximate Number of Bytes	Exact Number of Bytes
Kilobyte (KB)	1 thousand	2^{10} or 1,024
Megabyte (MB)	1 million	2^{20} or 1,048,576
Gigabyte (GB)	1 billion	2^{30} or 1,073,741,824
Terabyte (TB)	1 trillion	2^{40} or 1,099,511,627,776
Petabyte (PB)	1 quadrillion	2^{50} or 1,125,899,906,842,624
Exabyte (EB)	1 quintillion	2^{60} or 1,152,921,504,606,846,976
Zettabyte (ZB)	1 sextillion	2^{70} or 1,180,591,620,717,411,303,424
Yottabyte (YB)	1 septillion	2^{80} or 1,208,925,819,614,629,174,706,176

FIGURE 7-2 The capacity of storage media is measured by the amount of bytes it can hold.

AN ILLUSTRATION OF VOLATILITY

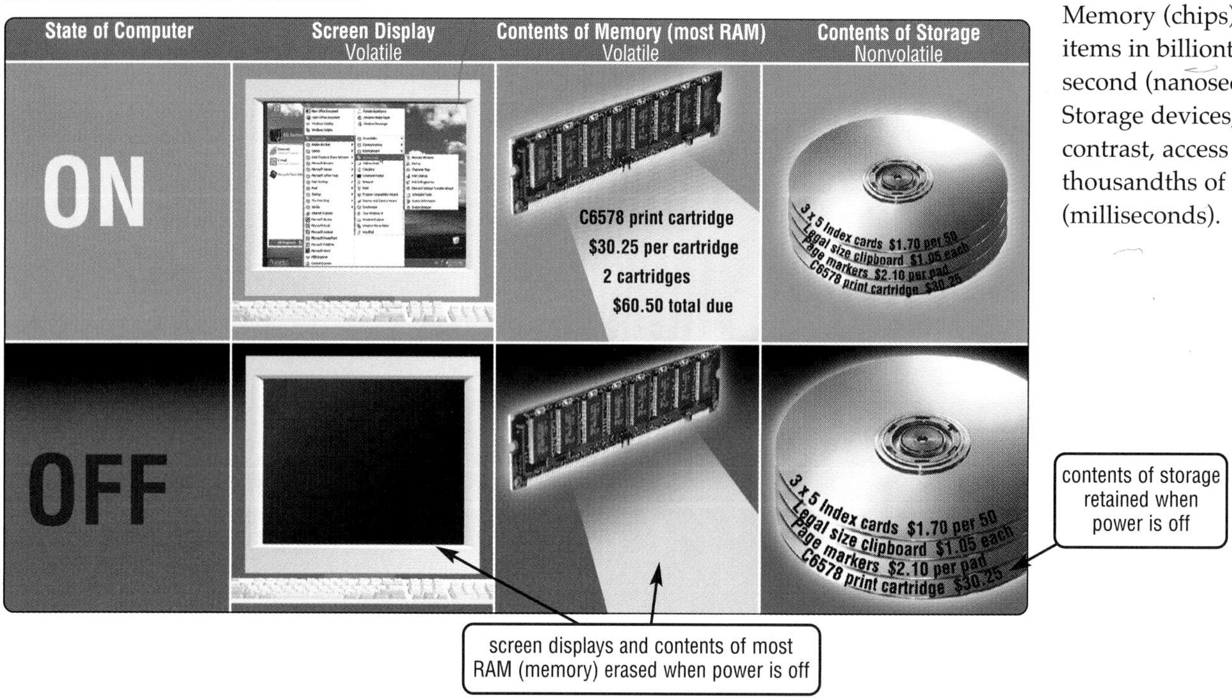

FIGURE 7-3 A screen display is considered volatile because its contents disappear when power is removed. Likewise, most RAM chips are volatile. That is, their contents are erased when power is removed from the computer. Storage, by contrast, is nonvolatile. Its contents remain when power is off.

For an analogy, think of a filing cabinet that holds file folders as a storage medium, and the top of your desk as memory. When you want to work with a file, you remove it from the filing cabinet (storage medium) and place it on your desk (memory). When you are finished with the file, you remove it from your desk (memory) and return it to the filing cabinet (storage medium).

A **storage device** is the computer hardware that records and/or retrieves items to and from storage media. **Writing** is the process of transferring data, instructions, and information from memory to a storage medium. **Reading** is the process of transferring these items from a storage medium into memory. When storage devices write data on storage media, they are creating output. Similarly, when storage devices read from storage media, they function as a source of input. Nevertheless, they are categorized as storage devices, not as input or output devices.

The speed of storage devices and memory is defined by access time. **Access time** measures (1) the amount of time it takes a storage device to locate an item on a storage medium or (2) the time required to deliver an item from memory to the processor. The access time of storage devices is slow, compared with the access time of memory. Memory (chips) accesses items in billionths of a second (nanoseconds). Storage devices, by contrast, access items in thousandths of a second (milliseconds).

Instead of, or in addition to access time, some manufacturers state a storage device's transfer rate because it affects access time. *Transfer rate* is the speed with which data, instructions, and information transfer to and from a device. Transfer rates for disks are stated in *KBps* (kilobytes per second) and *MBps* (megabytes per second).

Numerous types of storage media and storage devices exist to meet a variety of users' needs. Figure 7-4 shows how different types of storage media and memory compare in terms of transfer rates and uses. This chapter discusses these storage media, as well as other media.

faster transfer rates

		Stores...
Primary Storage	Memory (most RAM)	Items waiting to be interpreted and executed by the processor
Secondary Storage	Hard Disk	Operating system, application software, user data and information
	CDs and DVDs	Software, backups, movies, music
	Miniature Mobile Storage Media	Digital pictures or files to be transported
	Tape	Backups
	Floppy Disk	Small files to be transported

slower transfer rates

FIGURE 7-4 A comparison of different types of storage media and memory in terms of relative speed and uses. Memory is faster than storage, but is expensive and not practical for all storage requirements. Storage is less expensive but is slower than memory.

FLOPPY DISKS

A **floppy disk**, also called a *diskette*, is a portable, inexpensive storage medium that consists of a thin, circular, flexible plastic Mylar film with a magnetic coating enclosed in a square-shaped plastic shell (Figure 7-5).

A typical floppy disk can store up to 500 double-spaced pages of text, several digital photographs, or a small audio file. Floppy disks are not as widely used as they were ten years ago because of their low storage capacity. They are used, however, for specific applications. Some digital cameras store pictures on a floppy disk. Users work with floppy disks to transport small files to and from non-networked personal computers, such as from school or work to home. If your personal computer malfunctions, you could use a floppy disk to boot it up (or start it). Chapter 8 discusses booting up a computer.

When IBM first introduced the floppy disk as a new type of storage in the early 1970s, these 8-inch-wide disks were known as floppies because they had flexible plastic covers. The next generation of floppies looked much the same, but they were only 5.25 inches wide. Today, the standard floppy disk is 3.5 inches wide and has a rigid plastic outer cover. Although the exterior of the 3.5-inch disk is not floppy, users still refer to this storage medium as a floppy disk because of the flexible Mylar film inside the plastic outer cover.

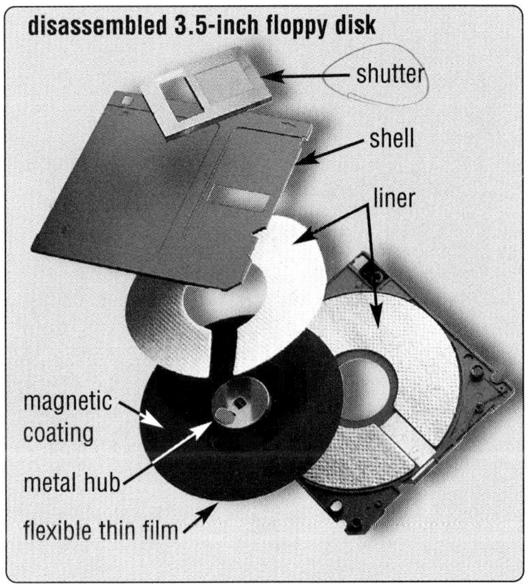

FIGURE 7-5 In a 3.5-inch floppy disk, a thin, circular, flexible Mylar film is enclosed between two liners. A piece of metal called a shutter covers an opening to the recording surface in the rigid plastic shell.

A floppy disk is a portable storage medium. With respect to a storage medium, the term *portable* means you can remove the medium from one computer and carry it to another computer.

Floppy Disk Drives

A **floppy disk drive** is a device that reads from and writes on a floppy disk. A user inserts a floppy disk into and removes it from a floppy disk drive. Desktop personal computers and notebook computers may have a floppy disk drive installed inside the system unit (Figure 7-6a). Some notebook computers allow you to remove the floppy disk drive and replace it with another type of drive.

Some computers use an *external floppy disk drive*, in which the drive is a separate device with a cable that plugs into a port on the system unit (Figure 7-6b). These external drives are attached to the computer only when the user needs to access items on a floppy disk. Users who seldom work with floppy disks purchase their computers without an internal floppy disk drive and opt for the external floppy disk drive instead. A mobile user who seldom uses floppy disks, for example, may purchase a notebook computer without an internal floppy disk drive to eliminate the extra weight.

If a personal computer has one floppy disk drive, it is named drive A. To read from or write on a floppy disk, a floppy disk drive must support that floppy disk's density. *Density* is the number of bits in an area on a storage medium. A disk with a higher density has more bits in an area and thus has a larger storage capacity. Most standard floppy disks today are high density (*HD*). To access a high-density floppy disk, you must have a high-density floppy disk drive.

Floppy disk drives usually are *downward compatible*, which means they recognize and can use earlier media. Floppy disk drives are not *upward compatible*, and thus cannot recognize newer media. For example, a lower-density floppy disk drive cannot read from or write on a high-density floppy disk.

When you insert a 3.5-inch floppy disk into a floppy disk drive, the drive slides a piece of metal on the disk called the *shutter* to the side, exposing a portion of both sides of the disk's recording surface. The *read/write head* in the drive is the mechanism that reads items or writes items as it barely touches the disk's recording surface. Most floppy disk drives have an external light emitting diode (LED) that lights up when the drive is accessing the floppy disk. You should not remove a floppy disk when the LED is lit.

Figure 7-7 illustrates how a floppy disk drive reads from and writes on a floppy disk. The average time it takes a current floppy disk drive to locate an item on a disk (access time) is 84 milliseconds, or approximately 1/12 of a second. The transfer rates range from 250 to 500 KBps.

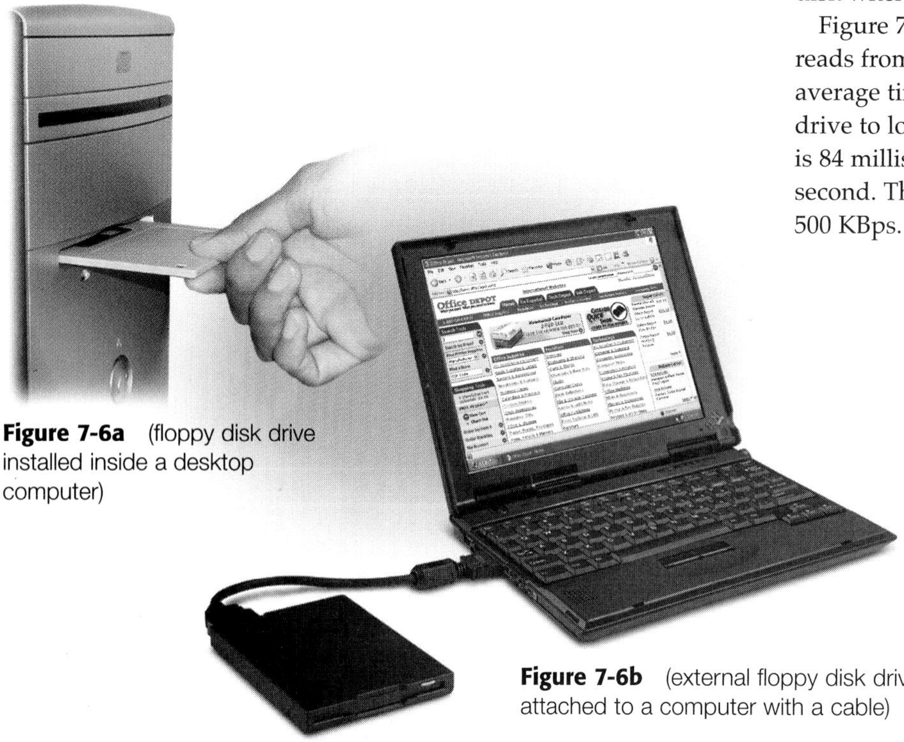

Figure 7-6a (floppy disk drive installed inside a desktop computer)

Figure 7-6b (external floppy disk drive attached to a computer with a cable)

FIGURE 7-6 On a personal computer, you insert and remove a floppy disk from a floppy disk drive.

FIGURE 7-7 HOW A FLOPPY DISK DRIVE WORKS

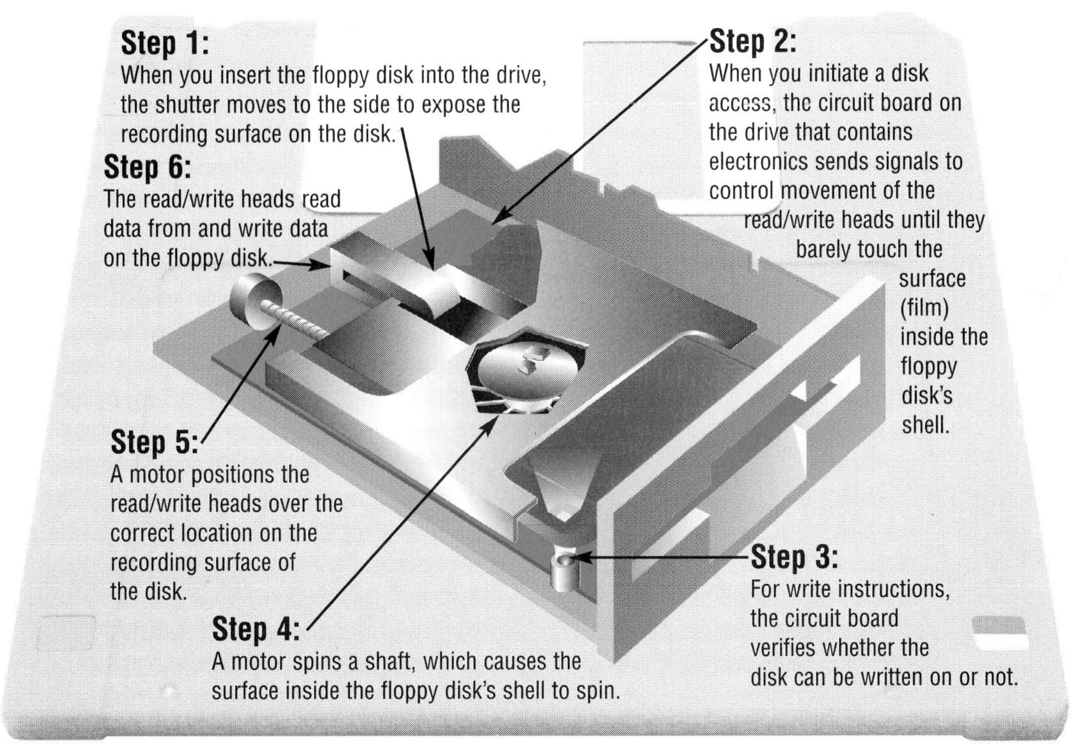

FAQ 7-1

What is the problem when the floppy disk drive will not read a disk?

The disk may be corrupt, which is why it is important to keep backup copies of all data. If the problem repeats with multiple floppy disks, the read/write heads in the floppy disk drive may have a buildup of dust or dirt. Try cleaning the read/write heads with a floppy disk cleaning kit. If the drive still malfunctions, you usually can replace it for less than $50.

For more information about floppy disk drives, visit the Discovering Computers 2005 FAQ Web page (**scsite.com/dc2005/faq**). Click Floppy Disk Drives below Chapter 7.

Characteristics of a Floppy Disk

A floppy disk is a type of magnetic media that allows users to read from and write on a disk any number of times. *Magnetic media* use magnetic particles to store items such as data, instructions, and information on a disk's surface. Depending on how the magnetic particles are aligned, they represent either a 0 bit or a 1 bit. Recall from Chapter 4 that a bit (binary digit) is the smallest unit of data a computer can process. Thus, the alignment of the magnetic particles represents the data.

A floppy disk stores data in tracks and sectors (Figure 7-8). A *track* is a narrow recording band that forms a full circle on the surface of the disk. The disk's storage locations consist of pie-shaped sections, which break the tracks into small arcs called *sectors*. A sector stores up to 512 bytes of data. A typical floppy disk stores data on both sides of the disk, has 80 tracks on each side of the recording surface, and has 18 sectors per track.

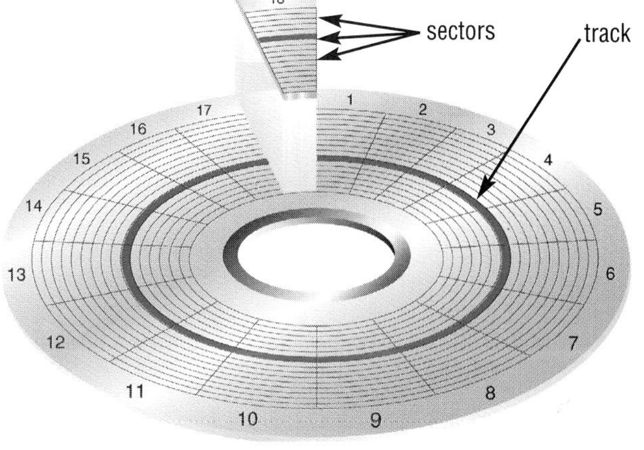

FIGURE 7-8 Tracks form circles on the surface of a disk. The disk's storage locations are divided into pie-shaped sections, which break the tracks into small arcs called sectors.

To compute a disk's storage capacity, you multiply the number of sides on the disk, the number of tracks on the disk, the number of sectors per track, and the number of bytes in a sector. For example, the following is the formula for a high-density 3.5-inch floppy disk: 2 (sides) x 80 (tracks) x 18 (sectors per track) x 512 (bytes per sector) = 1,474,560 bytes (Figure 7-9). Disks often store system files in some tracks, which means the available capacity on a disk may be less than the total possible capacity.

CHARACTERISTICS OF A 3.5-INCH HIGH-DENSITY FLOPPY DISK

Capacity	1.44 MB
Sides	2
Tracks	80
Sectors per track	18
Bytes per sector	512
Sectors per disk	2880

FIGURE 7-9 Most of today's personal computers use high-density disks.

The actual number of available bytes on a floppy disk is 1,474,560, yet manufacturers call them 1.44 MB disks. The 1.44 MB is not a rounding of the 1,474,560. Instead, it is a result of dividing the number of bytes in the disk (1,474,560) by the number of bytes in a kilobyte (1,024).

For reading and writing purposes, sectors are grouped into clusters. A *cluster* is the smallest unit of disk space that stores data. Each cluster, also called an *allocation unit*, consists of two to eight sectors (the number varies depending on the operating system). Even if a file consists of only a few bytes, it uses an entire cluster. Each cluster holds data from only one file. One file, however, can span many clusters.

WEB LINK 7-1

Floppy Disks

Visit the Discovering Computers 2005 WEB LINK page (**scsite .com/dc2005/weblink**). Click Floppy Disks below Chapter 7.

Sometimes, a sector has a flaw and cannot store data. When you format a disk, the operating system marks these bad sectors as unusable. **Formatting** is the process of preparing a disk for reading and writing. For a technical discussion about formatting, read the High-Tech Talk article on page 377.

Care of Floppy Disks

Disk manufacturers state that a floppy disk can last at least seven years, with reasonable care. In many cases, the disks do not have that long of a life span. A floppy disk drive may malfunction and ruin the disk. More commonly, the disk itself is damaged from improper care.

When you handle a floppy disk, avoid exposing it to heat, cold, magnetic fields, magnets, and contaminants such as dust, smoke, or salt air. Exposure to any of these elements could damage or destroy the data, instructions, and information stored on the floppy disk. Never open the disk's shutter and touch its recording surface. When you are not using disks, keep them in a storage tray or some other container that allows them to stand vertically.

To protect a floppy disk from accidentally being erased, the plastic outer shell on the disk contains a write-protect notch in its corner. A **write-protect notch** is a small opening that has a tab you slide to cover or expose the notch (Figure 7-10). The write-protect notch works much like the recording tab on a VHS tape: if you remove the recording tab, a VCR cannot record onto the VHS tape.

On a floppy disk, if the write-protect notch is open, the drive cannot write on the floppy disk. If the write-protect notch is covered, or closed, the drive can write on the floppy disk. A floppy disk drive can read from a floppy disk whether the write-protect notch is open or closed. On the opposite corner, some floppy disks have a second opening without a small tab. This opening identifies the disk as a high-density floppy disk (Figure 7-10).

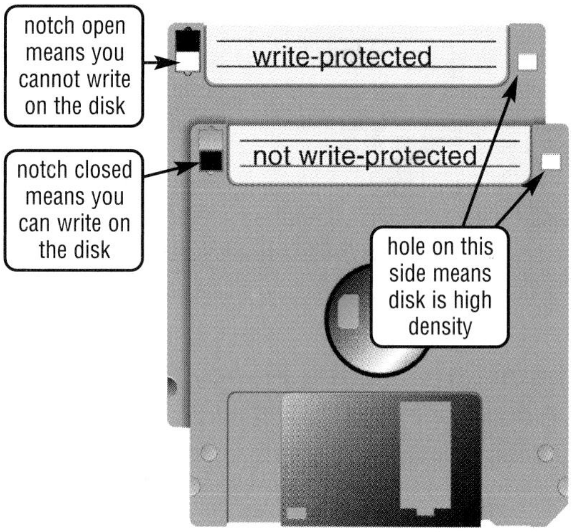

FIGURE 7-10 To protect data from being erased accidentally, floppy disks have a write-protect notch. By sliding a small tab, you either can cover or expose the notch.

ZIP DISKS

A **Zip disk** is a type of portable magnetic media that can store from 100 MB to 750 MB of data. The larger capacity Zip disks hold about 500 times more than a standard floppy disk. These large capacities make it easy to transport many files or large items such as graphics, audio, or video files. Another popular use of Zip disks is to back up important data and information. A **backup** is a duplicate of a file, program, or disk that you can use in case the original is lost, damaged, or destroyed. Chapter 8 discusses backup utilities.

Zip disks are slightly larger than and about twice as thick as a 3.5-inch floppy disk. A **Zip drive** is a high-capacity disk drive developed by Iomega Corporation that reads from and writes on a Zip disk (Figure 7-11). These drives cannot read standard 3.5-inch floppy disks.

Many users prefer to purchase an external Zip drive, which connects to a USB port, FireWire port, or parallel port on the system unit. The external Zip drive is convenient for users with multiple computers, because it allows them to move the drive from computer to computer as needed. As an alternative, some users prefer to order a computer with a built-in Zip drive.

FIGURE 7-11 An external Zip drive.

QUIZ YOURSELF 7-1

To check your knowledge of items users store, storage devices and storage media, floppy disks, and Zip disks, visit the Discovering Computers 2005 Quiz Yourself Web page (**scsite.com/dc2005/quiz**). Click Objectives 1 – 4 below Chapter 7.

WEB LINK 7-2

Zip Disks

Visit the Discovering Computers 2005 WEB LINK page (**scsite.com/dc2005/weblink**). Click Zip Disks below Chapter 7.

HARD DISKS

A **hard disk**, also called a *hard disk drive*, is a storage device that contains one or more inflexible, circular platters that store data, instructions, and information. Today's hard disks have enough storage capacity for the most complex multimedia software. People use hard disks to store all types of documents, spreadsheets, presentations, databases, e-mail messages, Web pages, digital photographs, music, videos, and software. Businesses use hard disks to store correspondence, reports, financial records, e-mail messages, customer orders and invoices, payroll records, inventory records, presentations, contracts, marketing literature, schedules, and Web sites.

The system unit on most desktop and notebook computers contains at least one hard disk. The hard disk inside the system unit sometimes is called a *fixed disk* because it is mounted in a drive bay and usually is not portable (Figure 7-12). The entire device is enclosed in an airtight, sealed case to protect it

FIGURE 7-12 The hard disk in a desktop computer is enclosed inside an airtight, sealed case inside the system unit.

from contamination. Two other types of hard disks, external and removable, are discussed later in this chapter.

Current personal computer hard disks have storage capacities from 40 to 250 GB and more. The storage capacity of the average hard disk is more than 40,000 times that of a standard floppy disk. Like floppy disks and Zip disks, hard disks store data magnetically. Hard disks also are read/write storage media. That is, you can read from and write on a hard disk any number of times. A recently developed hard disk, called an *optically assisted hard drive*, combines optic technologies with the magnetic media. These optically assisted hard drives have potential storage capacities up to 400 GB.

If the computer contains only one hard disk, the operating system designates it as drive C. Additional hard disks are assigned the next available drive letter. Read Issue 7-1 for a discussion about how some merchants use a hard disk.

ISSUE 7-1

Do You Use a Shoppers Card?

Grocery stores, pharmacies, hotel chains, and other merchants are offering shoppers cards to customers. With these cards, sometimes called names such as saver card, buyers card, or club card, consumers earn reduced prices when they make purchases. In return, sellers track consumer acquisitions, preferences, and buying habits and store the information on their computer's hard disk. Merchants claim that these cards reward loyal customers. Yet, not everyone agrees. One study found that, on average, shoppers card customers spent more money on each store visit than customers who do not use shoppers cards. CASPIAN (Consumers Against Supermarket Privacy Invasion and Numbering), a consumers group opposed to the use of club cards, argues that the shoppers cards give artificial discounts on inflated prices. Additionally, consumers have no guarantee that information gained by a merchant will remain private. In a recent divorce case, a lawyer used information from a merchant about an alcohol purchase against a spouse. Are shoppers cards a good idea? Why or why not? Should the buying information remain private? Would you or do you use a shoppers card? Why or why not?

For more information about shoppers cards, visit the Discovering Computers 2005 Issues Web page (**scsite.com/dc2005/issues**). Click Issue #1 below Chapter 7.

Characteristics of a Hard Disk

Characteristics of a hard disk include its capacity, platters, read/write heads, cylinders, sectors and tracks, revolutions per minute, transfer rate, and access time. Figure 7-13 shows sample characteristics of a 120 GB hard disk. The following paragraphs discuss each of these characteristics.

The capacity of a hard disk is determined from the number of platters it contains, together with composition of the magnetic coating on the platters. A *platter* is made of aluminum, glass, or ceramic and is coated with an alloy material that allows items to be recorded magnetically on its surface. The coating usually is three millionths of an inch thick.

SAMPLE HARD DISK CHARACTERISTICS

Advertised capacity	120 GB
Platters	3
Read/write heads	6
Cylinders	16,383
Bytes per sector	512
Sectors per track	63
Sectors per drive	234,441,648
Revolutions per minute	7,200
Transfer rate	133 MB per second
Access time	8.9 ms

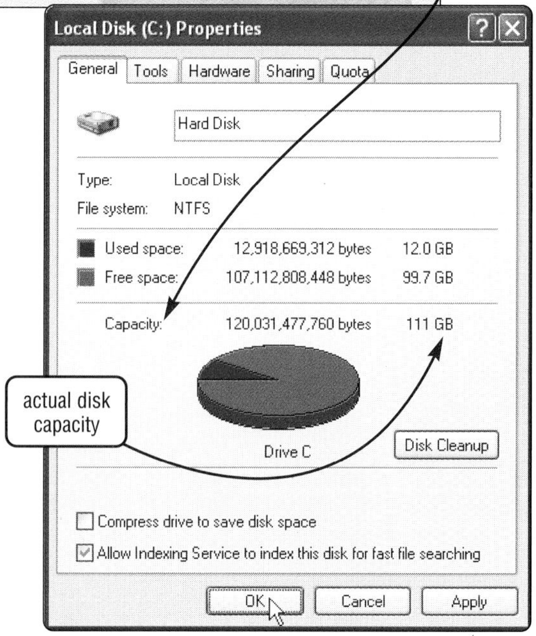

FIGURE 7-13 Characteristics of a sample 120 GB hard disk. The actual disk's capacity sometimes is different from the advertised capacity because of bad sectors on the disk.

On desktop computers, platters have a *form factor*, or size, of approximately 5.25 inches or more commonly 3.5 inches in diameter. A typical hard disk has multiple platters stacked on top of one another. Each platter has two read/write heads, one for each side. The hard disk has arms that move the read/write heads to the proper location on the platter (Figure 7-14).

The location of the read/write heads often is referred to by its cylinder. A *cylinder* is the vertical section of a track that passes through all platters (Figure 7-15). A single movement of the read/write head arms accesses all the platters in a cylinder. If a hard disk has two platters (four sides), each with 1,000 tracks, then it will have 1,000 cylinders with each cylinder consisting of 4 tracks (2 tracks for each platter).

While the computer is running, the platters in the hard disk rotate at a high rate of speed. This spinning, which usually is 5,400 to 7,200 *revolutions per minute* (*rpm*), allows nearly instant access to all tracks and sectors on the platters. The platters typically continue to spin until power is removed from the computer. (On some computers, the hard disk stops spinning after a specified time to save power.) The spinning motion creates a cushion of air between the platter and its read/write head. This cushion ensures that the read/write head floats above the platter instead of making direct contact with the platter surface. The distance between the read/write head and the platter is about two millionths of one inch.

FIGURE 7-14 HOW A HARD DISK WORKS

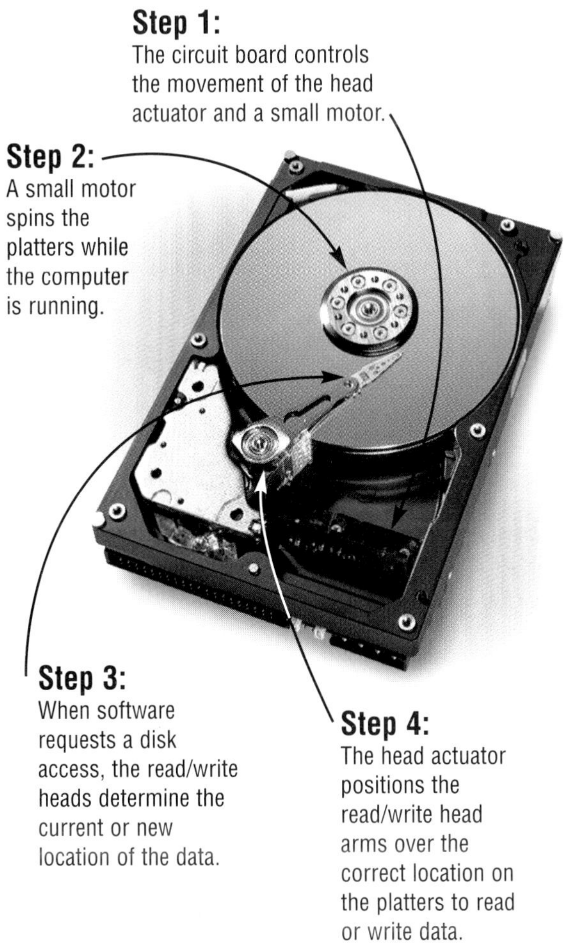

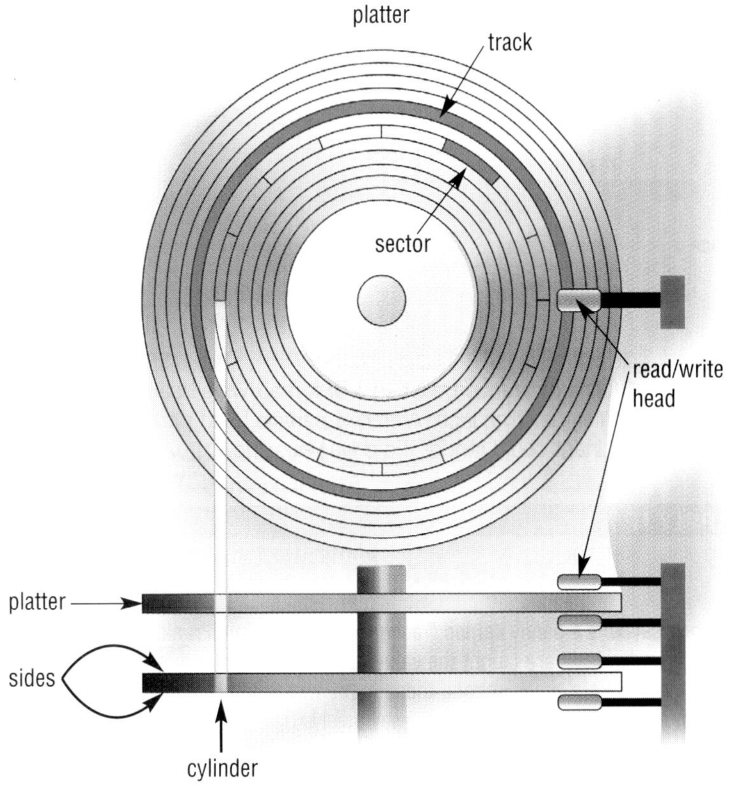

FIGURE 7-15 A cylinder is the vertical section of a track through all platters on a hard disk.

EIDE One of the more widely used controllers for hard disks is the *EIDE* (*Enhanced Integrated Drive Electronics*) controller. EIDE controllers can support up to four hard disks at 137 GB per disk. They transfer data, instructions, and information to and from the disk at rates up to 100 MBps. This interface also provides connections for CD and DVD drives and tape drives.

Some manufacturers market their EIDE controllers as Fast ATA or Ultra ATA. EIDE controllers are downward compatible with earlier IDE and ATA controllers.

SCSI Depending on the type of *SCSI controller*, it can support up to eight or fifteen peripheral devices, including hard disks, CD and DVD drives, tape drives, printers, scanners, network cards, and much more. Recall from Chapter 4 that SCSI is an acronym for Small Computer System Interface. Some computers have a built-in SCSI controller, while others use an adapter card to add a SCSI controller.

SCSI controllers are faster than EIDE controllers, providing up to 320 MBps transfer rates. Newer versions of SCSI controllers generally are downward compatible with earlier SCSI devices.

FAQ 7-2

What are the transfer rates of USB and FireWire?

USB 1.1 has a transfer rate of 12 *Mbps* (megabits per second). USB 2.0 is much faster with transfer rates up to 480 Mbps. FireWire is even faster, with transfer rates up to 3,200 Mbps. When performance has a higher priority than cost, choose FireWire. For example, FireWire is the better choice for high-quality video streaming.

For more information about USB and FireWire controllers, visit the Discovering Computers 2005 FAQ Web page (**scsite.com/dc2005/faq**). Click USB and FireWire Controllers below Chapter 7.

Maintaining Data Stored on a Hard Disk

Most manufacturers guarantee their hard disks to last approximately three to five years. Many last much longer with proper care. To prevent the loss of items stored on a hard disk, you regularly should perform preventive maintenance such as defragmenting or scanning the disk for errors. Chapter 8 discusses these and other utilities in depth.

Internet Hard Drives

Instead of storing data locally on a hard disk, some users choose to store data on an Internet hard drive. An **Internet hard drive**, sometimes called **online storage**, is a service on the Web that provides storage to computer users, usually for a minimal monthly fee (Figure 7-19). Fee arrangements vary. For example, one online storage service charge is as low as $4.99 per month for 100 MB of storage.

Users store data and information on an Internet hard drive for a variety of reasons:

- To access files on the Internet hard drive from any computer or device that has Internet access
- To save time by storing large audio, video, and graphics files on an Internet hard drive instantaneously, instead of downloading to a local hard disk
- To allow others to access files on your Internet hard drive to play an audio file, watch a video clip, or view a picture — instead of e-mailing the file to them
- To view time-critical data and images immediately while away from the main office or location. For example, doctors can view x-ray images from another hospital, home, or office, or while on vacation
- To store offsite backups of data. Chapter 8 presents this and other backup strategies

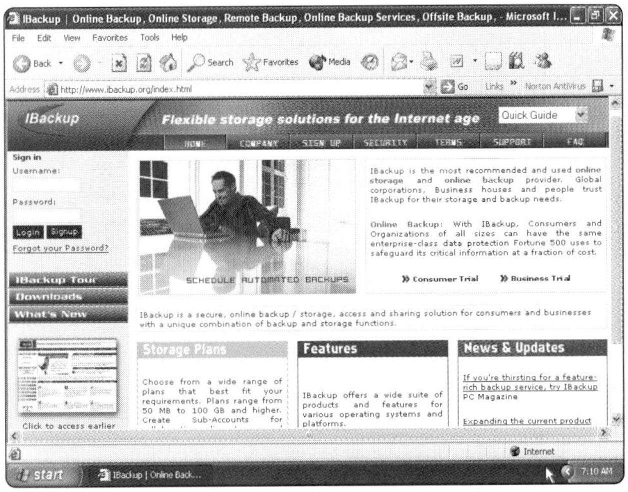

FIGURE 7-19 An example of one Web site advertising its Internet hard drive service.

In addition to storage space, these Web sites offer other services. These services often include e-mail, calendar, address book, and task list applications. As with other files on the Internet hard drive, you can share your calendars, address books, and tasks lists with others who have Web access.

Some operating systems support access to Internet hard drives. Once users subscribe to the Internet hard drive service, they can save on the Internet hard drive in the same manner they save on a floppy disk, their hard disk, or any other drive.

WEB LINK 7-4

Internet Hard Drives

Visit the Discovering Computers 2005 WEB LINK page (**scsite .com/dc2005/weblink**). Click Internet Hard Drives below Chapter 7.

CDs AND DVDs

CDs and DVDs are a type of optical storage media that consists of a flat, round, portable disc made of metal, plastic, and lacquer. These discs usually are 4.75 inches in diameter and less than one-twentieth of an inch thick. (Recall from Chapter 1 that the term disk is used for magnetic media, and disc is used for optical media.)

CDs and DVDs primarily store software, data, digital photographs, movies, and music. Some CD and DVD formats are read only, meaning you cannot write (save) on the media. Others are read/write, which allows users to save on the disc just as they save on a hard disk. The specifics of various CD and DVD formats are discussed later in this chapter.

Just about every personal computer today includes some type of CD or DVD drive installed in a drive bay. These drives read CDs and DVDs, and in many cases, will play audio CDs. On these drives, you push a button to slide out a tray, insert the disc with the label side up, and then push the same button to close the tray (Figure 7-20). Other convenient features on most of these drives include a volume control button and a headphone port (or jack) so you can use stereo headphones to listen to audio without disturbing others nearby.

FIGURE 7-20 On CD and DVD drives, you push a button to slide out a tray, insert the disc with the label side up, and then push the same button to close the tray.

Characteristics of CDs and DVDs

Recall that a floppy disk drive is designated as drive A. The drive designation of a CD or DVD drive usually follows alphabetically after that of all the hard disks and portable disks. For example, if the computer has one hard disk (drive C), a Zip disk drive (drive D), and an external hard disk (drive E), then the first CD or DVD drive is drive F. A second CD or DVD drive would be drive G.

CDs and DVDs are not magnetic media. Instead, they are optical media that store items such as data, instructions, and information by using microscopic pits (indentations) and lands (flat areas) that are in the middle layer of the disc (Figure 7-21). (Most manufacturers place a silk-screened label on the top layer of the disc so users can identify the disc.) A high-powered laser light creates the pits. A lower-powered laser light reads items from the disc by reflecting light through the bottom of the disc, which usually is either solid gold or silver in color. The reflected light is converted into a series of bits the computer can process. A land causes light to reflect, which is read as binary digit 1. Pits absorb the light; this absence of light is read as binary digit 0.

CDs and DVDs commonly store items in a single track that spirals from the center of the disc to the edge of the disc. As with a hard disk, this single track is divided into evenly sized sectors in which items are stored (Figure 7-22).

FIGURE 7-21 HOW A LASER READS DATA ON A CD OR DVD

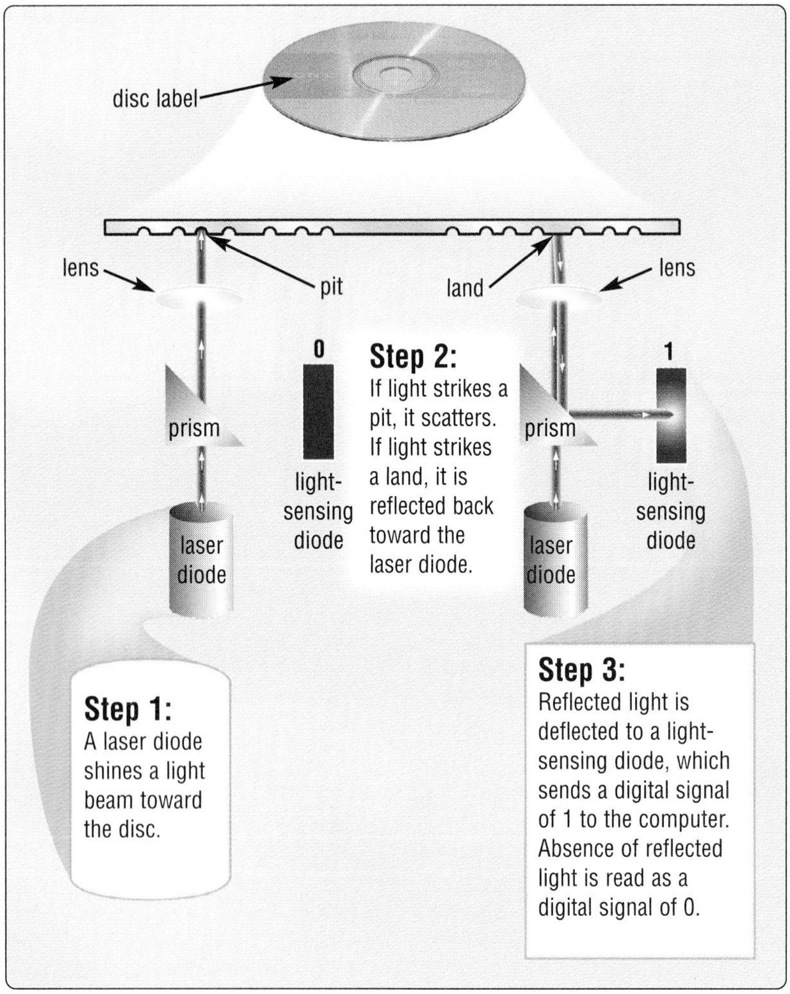

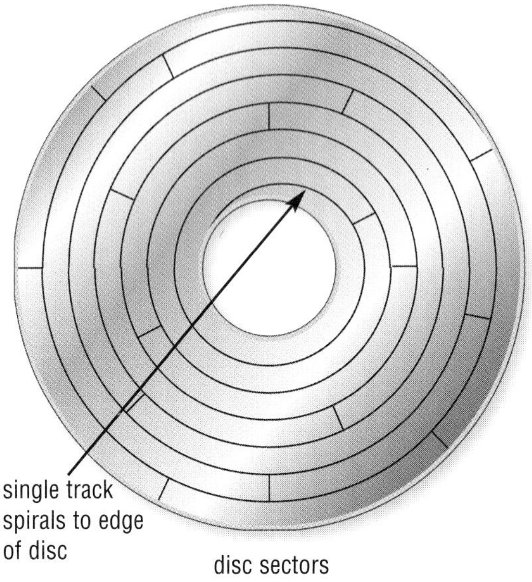

FIGURE 7-22 CDs and DVDs typically store data, instructions, and information in a single track that spirals from the center of the disc to the edge of the disc.

Care of CDs and DVDs

Manufacturers guarantee that a properly cared for CD or DVD will last 5 years, but could last up to 100 years. Figure 7-23 outlines some guidelines for the proper care of CDs and DVDs. Never bend a disc; it may break. If a disc becomes warped or if its surface is scratched, data on the disc may be unreadable. Exposing these discs to extreme temperatures or humidity could cause them to warp. The ideal temperature range for disc storage is 50 to 70 degrees Fahrenheit. Stacking discs, touching the underside of discs, or exposing them to any type of contaminant may scratch a disc. Thus, place a CD or DVD in its protective case, called a *jewel box*, when you are finished using it.

FIGURE 7-23 Some guidelines for the proper care of CDs and DVDs.

CD-ROMs

A **CD-ROM** (pronounced SEE-DEE-rom), or *compact disc read-only memory*, is a type of optical disc that uses laser technology to store data, instructions, and information. In addition to audio, a CD-ROM can contain text, graphics, and video.

Manufacturers write, or record, the contents of standard CD-ROMs. Users can read only the contents of these discs. That is, you cannot erase or modify their contents — hence, the name read-only. A standard CD-ROM is called a *single-session disc* because manufacturers write all items on the disc at one time.

To read items stored on a CD-ROM, insert the disc into a **CD-ROM drive** or a CD-ROM player. Because audio CDs and CD-ROMs use the same laser technology, you may be able to use a CD-ROM drive to listen to an audio CD while you are working on the computer. Some music companies, however, configure their CDs so the music will not play on a computer. They do this to protect themselves from customers illegally copying and sharing the music.

FAQ 7-3

Can I clean a CD or DVD?

Yes, you can remove dust, dirt, smudges, and fingerprints from the bottom surface of a CD or DVD. Moisten a soft cloth with warm water or window cleaner and then wipe the disc in straight lines from the center outward. You also can repair scratches on the bottom surface with a specialized disc repair kit.

For more information about cleaning and repairing CDs and DVDs, visit the Discovering Computers 2005 FAQ Web page (**scsite.com/dc2005/faq**). Click Cleaning and Repairing CDs and DVDs below Chapter 7.

QUIZ YOURSELF 7-2

To check your knowledge of hard disks, Internet hard drives, and CDs and DVDs, visit the Discovering Computers 2005 Quiz Yourself Web page (**scsite.com/dc2005/quiz**). Click Objectives 5 – 7 below Chapter 7.

WEB LINK 7-5

CD-ROMs

Visit the Discovering Computers 2005 WEB LINK page (**scsite .com/dc2005/weblink**). Click CD-ROMs below Chapter 7.

A typical CD-ROM holds from 650 MB to 1 GB of data, instructions, and information. This is equivalent to about 450 high-density 3.5-inch floppy disks. Manufacturers use CD-ROMs to store and distribute today's multimedia and other complex software because these discs have such high storage capacities (Figure 7-24). Read Issue 7-2 for a related discussion.

The speed of a CD-ROM drive determines how fast it installs programs and accesses the disc. Original CD-ROM drives were single-speed drives with transfer rates of 150 KBps (kilobytes per second). Manufacturers measure all CD-ROM drives relative to this original CD-ROM drive. They use an X to denote the original transfer rate of 150 KBps. For example, a 48X CD-ROM drive has a data transfer rate of 7,200 (48 x 150) KBps, or 7.2 MBps. Current CD-ROM drives have transfer rates, or speeds, ranging from 48X to 75X or faster. The higher the number, the faster the CD-ROM drive. Faster CD-ROM drives, however, are more expensive than slower drives.

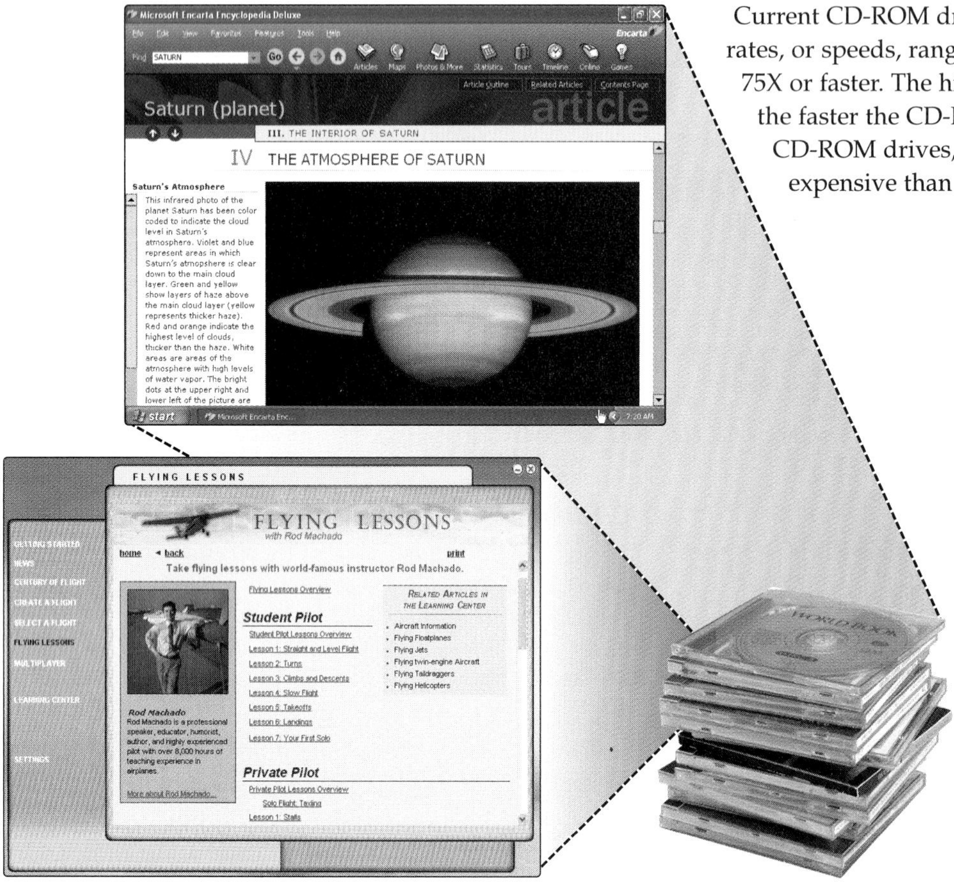

FIGURE 7-24 Encyclopedias, games, and many other programs are distributed on CD-ROM.

ISSUE 7-2

Promotions on CD-ROM?

Instead of printed brochures, many companies now offer marketing CD-ROMs to potential customers. CD-ROMs are more expensive than conventional advertisements, but companies feel that the storage medium's interactivity is worth the cost. Some automobile manufacturers, for example, offer a CD-ROM that introduces new vehicles to prospective buyers. The CD-ROM shows photographs, statistics, option packages, and pricing information. Using a mouse, automobile shoppers can "walk around and kick the tires" by viewing the car from different angles, seeing close-ups of special features, and even enjoying a simulated test drive. But, not everyone is convinced that marketing on CD-ROM is worthwhile. Despite their cost, some believe that consumers do not use most publicity CD-ROMs; they insist that potential customers are more likely to page through a brochure than to use a promotional CD-ROM. In general, is advertising on CD-ROM worth the cost? Why or why not? What products are best suited to promotion on CD-ROM? Why? What products are least suited? Why? Will marketing CD-ROMs ever replace printed advertising materials? Why or why not?

For more information about advertising on CD-ROM, visit the Discovering Computers 2005 Issues Web page (**scsite.com/dc2005/issues**). Click Issue #2 below Chapter 7.

Picture CDs and PhotoCDs

A Kodak **Picture CD** is a type of compact disc that stores digital versions of a single roll of film using a jpg file format. Many film developers offer Picture CD service for consumers when they drop off film to be developed. That is, in addition to printed photographs and negatives, you also receive a Picture CD containing the film's pictures. The resolution of images on a Picture CD usually is 1024 x 1536 pixels. The additional cost for a Picture CD is about $10 per roll of film.

A standard CD-ROM drive can read a Picture CD. Using photo editing software and the photographs on the Picture CD, you can remove red eye, crop the photograph, enhance colors, trim away edges, adjust the lighting, and edit just about any aspect of a photograph. In addition, a Picture CD allows you to print copies of the photographs on glossy paper with an ink-jet printer. If you do not have a printer to print the images, many stores have kiosks at which you can print pictures from a Picture CD (Figure 7-25).

Another type of compact disc that stores digital photographic images is the PhotoCD. A single *PhotoCD* stores images from multiple rolls of film using the Image Pac, or PCD, file format, which is a file format developed by Eastman Kodak. Designed for commercial and professional users, images on a PhotoCD are available in many resolutions, ranging from 128 x 192 to 4096 x 6144 pixels. Film developers and professional photography businesses store images from 35mm pictures, negatives, slides, and scanned items on PhotoCDs for users. Most professional desktop publishing software reads the PhotoCD format. PhotoCDs can be read by most standard CD-ROM drives.

A PhotoCD is a *multisession disc*, which means users can save additional photos on the disc at a later time. That is, as users capture more photographs, they can save them to the PhotoCD. The next section discusses recordable discs.

FAQ 7-4

How do I share my digital pictures with others?

You can send them as e-mail attachments or post them on an Internet hard drive, a personal Web page, or a photo community. At a *photo community*, users can create online photo albums and share their digital photographs on the Web. Some photo communities provide free, unlimited storage space; others charge a nominal fee.

For more information about photo communities, read Making Use of the Web in Appendix A at the back of the book or visit the Discovering Computers 2005 FAQ Web page (**scsite.com/dc2005/faq**). Click Photo Communities below Chapter 7.

WEB LINK 7-6

Picture CDs

Visit the Discovering Computers 2005 WEB LINK page (**scsite.com/dc2005/weblink**). Click Picture CDs below Chapter 7.

FIGURE 7-25 HOW A PICTURE CD WORKS

Step 1: Drop off the film to be developed. Mark the Picture CD box on the film-processing envelope.

Step 2: When you pick up prints and negatives, a Picture CD contains digital images of each photograph.

Step 3: At home, print images from the Picture CD on your ink-jet or photo printer. At a store, print images from the Picture CD at a kiosk.

CD-Rs and CD-RWs

Many personal computers today include either a CD-R or CD-RW drive as a standard feature. Others offer one or more of these drives as an option. Unlike standard CD-ROM drives, users record, or write, their own data onto a disc with a CD-R or CD-RW drive. The process of writing on an optical disc is called *burning*. Some operating systems, such as Windows XP, include the capability of burning discs.

A **CD-R** (*compact disc-recordable*) is a multisession CD onto which users record their own items such as text, graphics, and audio. With a CD-R, you can write on part of the disc at one time and another part at a later time. Once recorded, a CD-R can be read from as many times as necessary. Each part of a CD-R can be written on only one time, and the disc's contents cannot be erased. Most current CD-ROM drives can read a CD-R.

Writing on the CD-R requires a *CD recorder* or a **CD-R drive**. A CD-R drive usually can read both audio CDs and standard CD-ROMs. These drives read at speeds of 48X or more and write at speeds of 40X or more. Manufacturers often list the write speed first, for example, as 40/48. CD-R drives are slightly more expensive than standard CD-ROM drives.

Instead of using a CD-R drive, many users opt for a CD-RW drive. A **CD-RW** (*compact disc-rewritable*) is an erasable disc you can write on multiple times. Originally called an *erasable CD* (*CD-E*), a CD-RW overcomes the major disadvantage of CD-R disks, which is being able to write on them only once. With CD-RW, the disc acts like a floppy disk or hard disk, allowing users to write and rewrite data, instructions, and information onto it multiple times. Reliability of the disc tends to drop, however, with each successive rewrite.

To write on a CD-RW disc, you must have CD-RW software and a **CD-RW drive**. These drives have write speeds of 52X or more, rewrite speeds of 24X or more, and read speeds of 52X or more. Manufacturers state the speeds in this order; that is, write speed, rewrite speed, and read speed as 52/24/52.

Multiread CD drives are the only drives that can read CD-RW discs. A *multiread CD drive* is a drive that reads audio CDs, data CDs, CD-Rs, and CD-RWs. Most current CD drives are multiread.

Using a CD-RW disc, users easily back up large files from a hard disk. They also share data and information with other users who have a multiread CD drive.

A popular use of CD-RW and CD-R discs is to create audio CDs. For example, users can record their own music and save it on a CD, purchase and download MP3 songs from the Web, or rearrange tracks on a purchased music CD. The process of copying an individual song from a purchased audio CD and converting it to a digital format is called *ripping*. The steps in Figure 7-26 illustrate techniques for copying the song(s) from an existing audio CD or downloading the song(s) from the Web, in most cases for a fee. Read Issue 7-3 for a related discussion.

ISSUE 7-3

Is It Ethical to Copy CDs?

A musician's recent release quickly became the second most-played CD in computer CD drives — before the CD even appeared on store shelves. CD-R and CD-RW technology makes copying music easy and affordable. People use CD-R and CD-RW technology to copy CDs they have purchased, CDs they have borrowed, or CDs they have pirated on the Web. At some campuses, students use college servers to create music Web sites, download copyrighted music, and then record and distribute unauthorized copies. The recording industry claims this practice is unfair to the industry and, in essence, steals from the recording artists. Others, however, insist that bootlegged music actually is a marketing vehicle, influencing listeners who pay to attend concerts eventually to purchase the CD. Is it ethical to download and copy portions of a music CD, or an entire music CD, from the Web? Why? If you purchase a CD, is it ethical to make copies for yourself? For a friend? Why? Should recording or movie companies be able to use formatting techniques to keep people from copying CDs or DVDs?

For more information about copying music, visit the Discovering Computers 2005 Issues Web page (**scsite.com/dc2005/issues**). Click Issue #3 below Chapter 7.

WEB LINK 7-7

CD-Rs and CD-RWs

Visit the Discovering Computers 2005 WEB LINK page (**scsite .com/dc2005/weblink**). Click CD-Rs and CD-RWs below Chapter 7.

FIGURE 7-26 HOW TO CREATE AN AUDIO CD

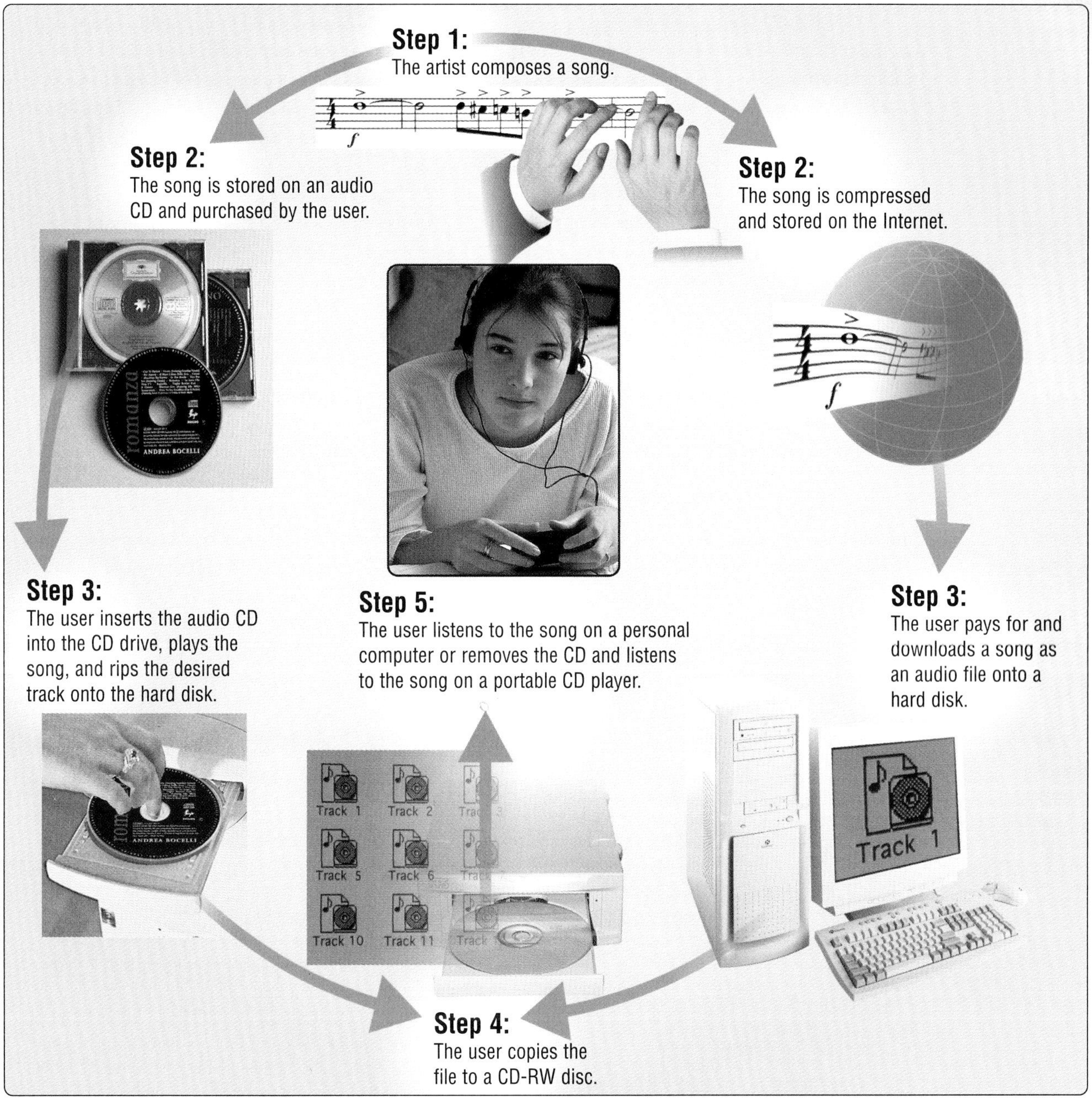

FAQ 7-5

Is it legal to copy songs onto a CD?

It is legal to copy songs from an audio CD that you obtained legally, if you use the copied music for your own personal use. If you share the copy with a friend, however, you are violating copyright law. It is legal to download copyrighted music if the song's copyright holder has granted permission for users to download and play the song. In most cases, you pay a fee for the song.

For more information about copying music, visit the Discovering Computers 2005 FAQ Web page (**scsite.com/dc2005/faq**). Click Copying Music below Chapter 7.

DVD-ROMs

A **DVD-ROM** (*digital versatile disc-ROM* or *digital video disc-ROM*) is an extremely high capacity optical disc capable of storing 4.7 GB to 17 GB (Figure 7-27). The storage capacity of a DVD-ROM is more than enough to hold a telephone book containing every resident in the United States. Not only is the storage capacity of a DVD-ROM greater than that of a CD-ROM, a DVD-ROM's quality also far surpasses that of a CD-ROM because images are stored at higher resolution.

The goal of DVD technology is to meet the needs of home entertainment, computer usage, and business data and information storage with a single medium (read Apply It 7-2 for more information). DVDs store huge databases, music, complex software, and movies. When you rent or buy a DVD movie, it uses the *DVD-video format* to store the motion picture digitally.

FIGURE 7-27 A DVD-ROM is an extremely high-capacity optical disc.

To read a DVD-ROM, you must have a **DVD-ROM drive** or DVD player. These drives can read at speeds of 48X or more. Newer DVD-ROM drives also can read audio CDs, CD-ROMs, CD-Rs, and CD-RWs. Manufacturers advertise this multifunctional drive as a *CD-RW/DVD*.

At a glance, a DVD-ROM looks like a CD-ROM. Although the size and shape are similar, a DVD-ROM stores data, instructions, and information in a slightly different manner and thus achieves a higher storage capacity.

A DVD-ROM uses one of three storage techniques. The first involves making the disc denser by packing the pits closer together. The second involves using two layers of pits. For this technique to work, the lower layer of pits is semitransparent so the laser can read through it to the upper layer. This technique doubles the capacity of the disc. Finally, some DVD-ROMs are double-sided, which means you must remove the DVD-ROM and turn it over to read the other side. The storage capacities of various types of DVD-ROMs are shown in the table in Figure 7-28.

APPLY IT 7-2

Turn Your Computer into a Home Theater System

Do you dream about the day when surround sound and an awesome entertainment system will be at your fingertips? That day can be today with a good set of speakers and a few inexpensive add-ons that turn your computer into a full-functioning home entertainment system.

Several companies have developed hardware priced at less than $300 that transforms a computer into a home theater with five- or six-speaker surround sound from DVDs and MP3s. Some of these products install in minutes and do not require opening the system unit because they plug into a computer's USB port. Other products require a bit more work by inserting sound cards into an expansion slot on the computer's motherboard.

Microsoft is collaborating with Hewlett-Packard, NEC, and Samsung to create the *e-Home initiative*, which is a system that will interface computers with televisions. Consumers will be able to download and store television programs on their computers and then play these files on their televisions. In addition, they will use their computers to control playing music and videos and also show digital photos on their big-screen televisions.

For more information about home entertainment system add-ons, visit the Discovering Computers 2005 Apply It Web page (**scsite.com/dc2005/apply**). Click Apply It #2 below Chapter 7.

DVD-ROM STORAGE CAPACITIES

Sides	Layers	Storage Capacity
1	1	4.7 GB
1	2	8.5 GB
2	1	9.4 GB
2	2	17 GB

FIGURE 7-28 Storage capacities of DVD-ROMs.

DVD+RW and Other DVD Variations

DVDs are available in a variety of formats, one of which stores digital motion pictures. To view a movie on a DVD, insert the DVD movie disc into a DVD player connected to a television or into a DVD-ROM drive to view the movie on a computer screen. Movies on DVD have near-studio-quality video, which far surpasses VHS tapes. When music is stored on a DVD, it includes surround sound and has a much better quality than that of an audio CD.

Recordable and rewritable versions of DVD also are available. A *DVD-R* (*DVD-recordable*) allows users to write on the disc once and read (play) it many times. A DVD-R is similar to a CD-R.

Instead of DVD-R, most users work with one of the competing technologies: DVD-RW, DVD+RW, or DVD+RAM media. With **DVD-RW** and **DVD+RW** (*DVD-rewriteable*) discs, a user can erase and record more than 1,000 times. DVD-RW and DVD+RW are similar to CD-RW, except they have storage capacities up to 4.7 GB per side. These drives have rewrite speeds of 12X or more, and read speeds of 32X or more. The drives usually can read DVD-ROM, DVD-R, and all CD media, and they can write on DVD-RW or DVD+RW, DVD-R, CD-R, and CD-RW media. To write on DVD+RW discs, you must have a *DVD-RW drive, DVD+RW drive,* or a *DVD writer*.

DVD+RAM (*DVD+random access memory*) allows users to erase and record on a DVD+RAM disc more than 100,000 times. DVD+RAM discs have storage capacities up to 4.7 GB per side. These discs can be read by DVD+RAM drives and some DVD-ROM drives and players.

As the cost of DVD technologies becomes more reasonable, many industry professionals expect that DVD eventually will replace all CD media. For a look at the next generation of disc storage, read Looking Ahead 7-1.

LOOKING AHEAD 7-1

Holographic Storage Expands Capacity

Like an overstuffed suitcase, current storage media are being squeezed to store every possible byte of data. They physically are nearing their density capacity. Engineers are scrambling to develop new storage systems, and holographic storage appears to fit the bill.

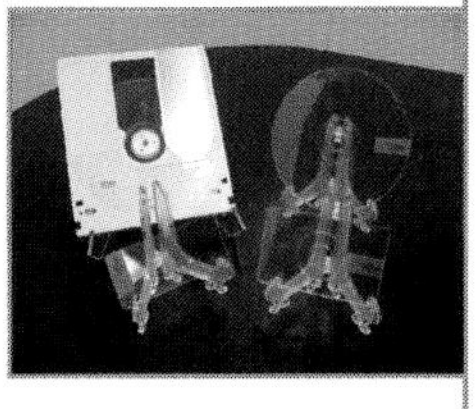

Microsoft's chief software architect Bill Gates considers holographic storage an impressive improvement. Major technology corporations, including IBM, Lucent, and Samsung, have spent millions of dollars researching this innovative storage system. And one day you may be using *holographic storage* to save 100 movie, photo, or music files on one disc holding one terabyte of data.

The rush to develop this system is being driven by several factors. First, high-definition video files are 10 times larger than today's DVD movie files. Virtual reality video games and multimedia content delivered by broadband connections also demand massive storage. Today's holographic drives and light-sensitive recording media are extremely expensive and fragile.

The increased storage capacity is based on how images are saved. Current storage media save each bit of data individually, which accounts for slow data transfer rates. The holographic process, by contrast, stores approximately 1 million bits simultaneously on the disc. Multiple pages can be stacked on top of each other.

For a look at the next generation of holographic storage, visit the Discovering Computers 2005 Looking Ahead Web page (**scsite.com/dc2005/looking**). Click Looking Ahead #1 below Chapter 7.

FAQ 7-6

Do any digital video cameras record movies on DVD?

Yes. Video cameras that store at least 120 minutes of recording on *mini-DVD media* (three-inch diameter) are available, but they are quite expensive. Once recorded, users can view the DVD media in a standard computer DVD drive or a DVD player. Many video cameras include the capability of editing the video right in the camera.

For more information about DVD recorders, visit the Discovering Computers 2005 FAQ Web page (**scsite.com/dc2005/faq**). Click DVD Recorders below Chapter 7.

WEB LINK 7-8

DVDs

Visit the Discovering Computers 2005 WEB LINK page (**scsite .com/dc2005/weblink**). Click DVDs below Chapter 7.

WEB LINK 7-9

Tape

Visit the Discovering Computers 2005 WEB LINK page (**scsite.com/dc2005/weblink**). Click Tape below Chapter 7.

TAPE

One of the first storage media used with mainframe computers was tape. **Tape** is a magnetically coated ribbon of plastic capable of storing large amounts of data and information at a low cost. Tape no longer is used as a primary method of storage. Instead, business and home users utilize tape most often for long-term storage and backup.

Comparable to a tape recorder, a **tape drive** reads and writes data and information on a tape. Although older computers used reel-to-reel tape drives, today's tape drives use tape cartridges. A *tape cartridge* is a small, rectangular, plastic housing for tape (Figure 7-29). Tape cartridges that contain quarter-inch-wide tape are slightly larger than audiocassette tapes. Business and home users sometimes back up personal computer hard disks onto tape.

FIGURE 7-29 A tape drive and a tape cartridge.

Some personal computers have external tape units. Others have the tape drive built into the system unit. On larger computers, tape cartridges are mounted in a separate cabinet called a *tape library*.

Common types of tape drives are digital audio tape (also called digital data storage), digital linear tape, linear tape-open, quarter-inch cartridge, and Travan. The table in Figure 7-30 compares the storage capacities of each of these types of tape. Transfer rates of tape drives range from 1.2 MBps to 6 MBps.

POPULAR TYPES OF TAPE

Name	Abbreviation	Storage Capacity
Digital audio tape (also called digital data storage)	DAT (also called DDS)	2 GB to 240 GB
Digital linear tape	DLT	20 GB to 220 GB
Linear tape-open	LTO	100 GB to 200 GB
Quarter-inch cartridge	QIC	40 MB to 50 GB
Travan	TR	8 GB to 50 GB

FIGURE 7-30 Common types of tape.

Tape storage requires *sequential access*, which refers to reading or writing data consecutively. As with a music tape, you must forward or rewind the tape to a specific point to access a specific piece of data. For example, to access item W requires passing through points A through V sequentially.

Floppy disks, Zip disks, hard disks, CDs and DVDs all use direct access. *Direct access*, also called *random access*, means that the device can locate a particular data item or file immediately, without having to move consecutively through items stored in front of the desired data item or file. When writing or reading specific data, direct access is much faster than sequential access.

PC CARDs

As discussed in Chapter 4, a **PC Card** is a thin, credit-card-sized device that fits into a PC Card slot. Different types and sizes of PC Cards add storage, additional memory, fax/modem, networking, sound, and other capabilities to a desktop or notebook computer. PC Cards commonly are used in notebook computers (Figure 7-31).

FIGURE 7-31 A PC Card in a notebook computer.

Originally, PC Cards were called PCMCIA cards. They are available in three kinds: Type I, Type II, and Type III (Figure 7-32). The only difference in size among the three types is their thickness. Some digital cameras use a Type II or Type III PC Card to store photographs. PC Cards that house a hard disk have storage capacities up to 5 GB. The advantage of a PC Card for storage is portability. You easily can transport large amounts of data, instructions, and information from one computer to another using a Type II or Type III PC Card.

PC CARDS

Category	Thickness	Use
Type I	3.3 mm	RAM, SRAM, flash memory
Type II	5.0 mm	Modem, LAN, SCSI, sound, TV tuner, hard disk, or other storage
Type III	10.5 mm	Rotating storage such as a hard disk

FIGURE 7-32 Various uses of PC Cards.

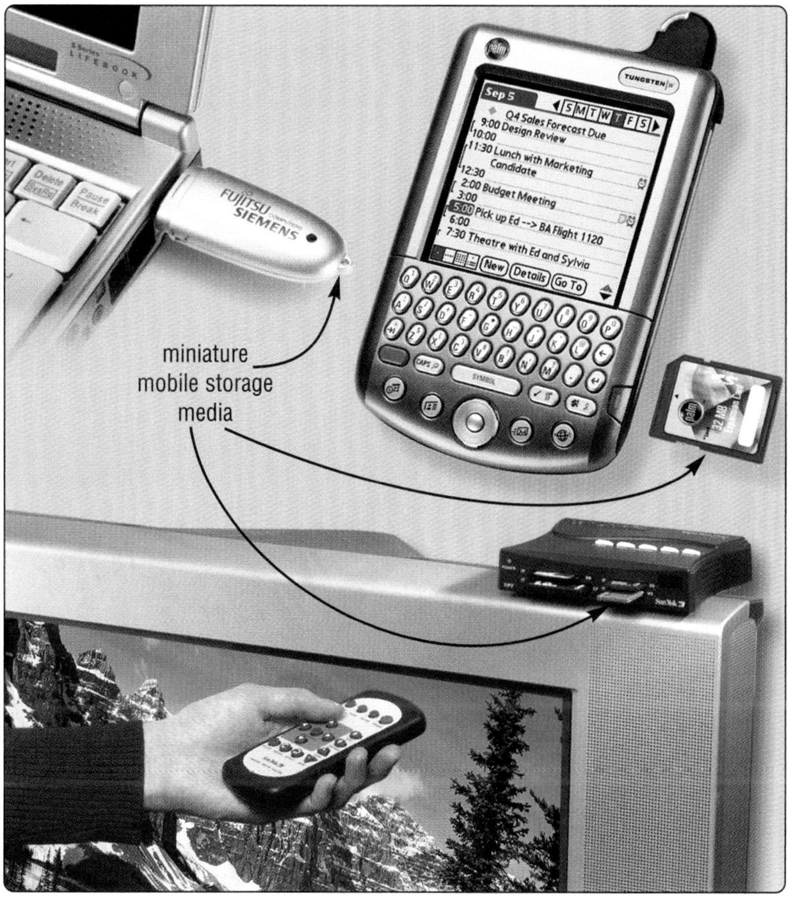

FIGURE 7-33 Digital photo viewers, PDAs, and notebook computers use miniature mobile storage media.

MINIATURE MOBILE STORAGE MEDIA

Miniature mobile storage media allow mobile users easily to transport digital images, music, or documents to and from computers and other devices (Figure 7-33). Today, many desktop computers, notebook computers, Tablet PCs, PDAs, digital cameras, music players, and smart phones have ports or slots to hold miniature mobile storage media.

Many types of miniature mobile storage media are available, with capacities ranging from 16 MB to 4 GB. Most miniature storage media are no bigger than a postage stamp. For a look at the next generation of miniature storage, read Looking Ahead 7-2.

LOOKING AHEAD 7-2

Millipede Reinvents Punched Card Storage Concept

In the 1880s, Herman Hollerith invented the punched card to store data gathered in the 1890 U.S. Census. Operators worked at keyboarding machines and punched holes in the dollar-bill-sized cards. Hollerith's company became International Business Machines (IBM) in 1923 and held a monopoly on using punch cards for storage.

Today, IBM has reinvented the punched card with *Millipede*, a postage-size storage device that can hold as much as 1 terabit of data per square inch. In fact, 3 billion bits of Millipede data will fit in an area the size of one hole punched in Hollerith's card. This capacity is the equivalent of 25 million printed textbook pages, which is more than 20 times larger than any of today's storage devices.

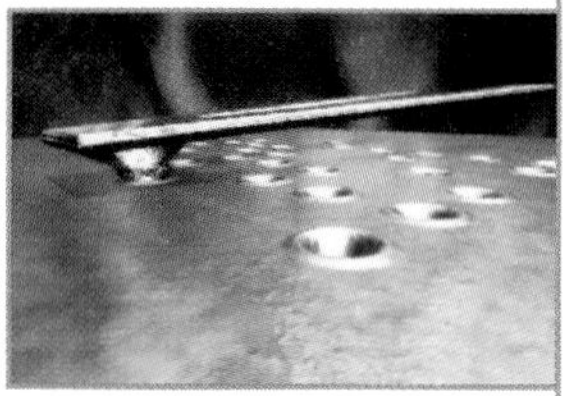

Unlike magnetic storage media, Millipede uses more than 4,000 sharp tips to indent a thin, reusable plastic film. The indentations are 10 nanometers apart.

Although IBM has no current plans to market its Millipede device, company engineers believe the prototype can be used as a basis for developing storage media to replace the flash memory cards currently used in digital cameras, PDAs, and cellular telephones.

For a look at the next generation of storage, visit the Discovering Computers 2005 Looking Ahead Web page (**scsite.com/dc2005/looking**). Click Looking Ahead #2 below Chapter 7.

Common types of miniature mobile storage media include *CompactFlash* (*CF*), *Smart Media*, *Secure Digital* (*SD*), *xD Picture Card*, *Memory Stick*, and *Microdrive*. The table in Figure 7-34 compares storage capacities and uses of these miniature storage media. The next section discusses USB flash drives, which are another type of miniature mobile storage media.

These miniature, rewritable media usually are in the form of flash memory cards or miniature hard disks. Flash memory cards are sometimes called *solid-state devices*, which means they consist entirely of electronics (chips, wires, etc.) and contain no moving parts. Miniature hard disks are magnetic media and operate like their desktop-sized counterparts — just on a smaller scale.

Depending on the device, manufacturers claim miniature mobile storage media can last from 10 to 100 years. Transfer rates range from

MINIATURE MOBILE STORAGE MEDIA

Media or Device Name	Storage Capacity	Type	Use
CompactFlash 	32 MB to 4 GB	Flash memory card	Digital cameras, PDAs, notebook computers, printers, music players, cellular telephones
Smart Media 	32 MB to 128 MB	Flash memory card	Digital cameras, PDAs, photo printers, cellular telephones
Secure Digital 	16 MB to 1 GB	Flash memory card	Digital cameras, PDAs, music players, cellular telephones, digital video cameras, car navigation systems, e-books
xD Picture Card 	64 MB to 512 MB	Flash memory card	Digital cameras
Memory Stick 	128 MB to 1 GB	Flash memory card	Digital cameras, notebook computers, photo printers
Microdrive 	1 GB to 4 GB	Magnetic media	Digital cameras, PDAs, music players, notebook computers, video cameras

FIGURE 7-34 A variety of miniature mobile storage media.

WEB LINK 7-10

Flash Memory Cards

Visit the Discovering Computers 2005 WEB LINK page (**scsite.com/dc2005/weblink**). Click Flash Memory Cards below Chapter 7.

about 1 MBps to 10 MBps or more, depending on the device. Miniature storage media are much smaller, lighter in weight, and more portable than other storage media such as hard disks. They are, however, much more expensive. For example, a 2 GB flash memory card costs more than twice that of a 80 GB hard disk.

To view, edit, or print images and information stored on miniature mobile storage media, you transfer the contents to your desktop computer or other device. Some printers also have slots to read PC Cards and other miniature mobile storage media. If your computer or printer does not have a built-in slot, card reader/writers are available. A **card reader/writer** is a device that reads and writes data, instructions, and information stored on PC Cards or memory cards (Figure 7-35). Card reader/writers usually connect to the USB port, FireWire port, or parallel port on the system unit. The type of card you have will determine the type of card reader/writer needed.

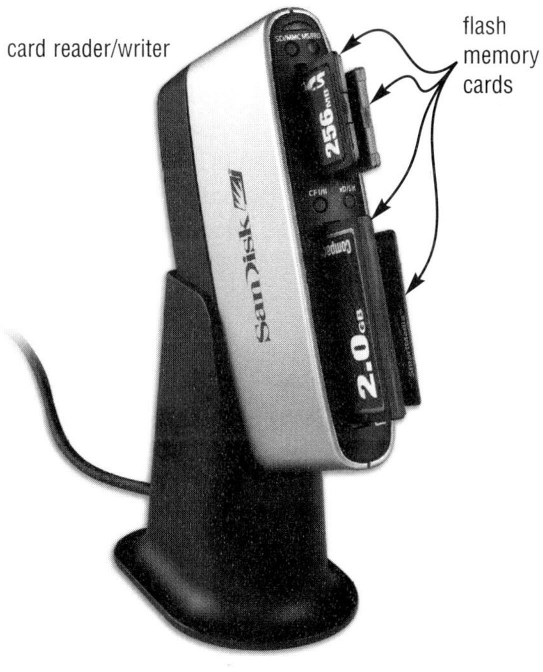

FIGURE 7-35 A card reader/writer.

USB Flash Drives

A **USB flash drive**, sometimes called a *keychain drive*, is a flash memory storage device that plugs into a USB port on a computer or portable device (Figure 7-36). USB flash drives are convenient for mobile users because they are small and lightweight enough to be transported on a keychain or in a pocket. Current USB flash drives have data transfer rates of about 8 MBps and storage capacities up to 2 GB.

Experts predict that USB flash drives will become the mobile user's primary storage device, eventually making the floppy disk obsolete because they have much greater storage capacities and are much more convenient to carry. Some desktop computers today ship without a floppy disk drive, and instead, include a USB flash drive.

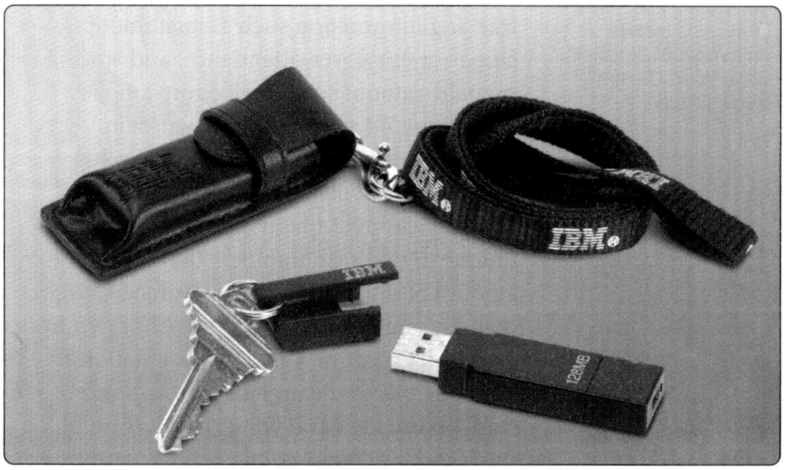

FIGURE 7-36 A USB flash drive.

Smart Cards

A **smart card**, which is similar in size to a credit card or ATM card (Figure 7-37), stores data on a thin microprocessor embedded in the card. Smart cards contain a processor and have input, process, output, and storage capabilities. Thus, some people refer to these cards as intelligent smart cards to differentiate them from a flash memory card, which has only storage capabilities.

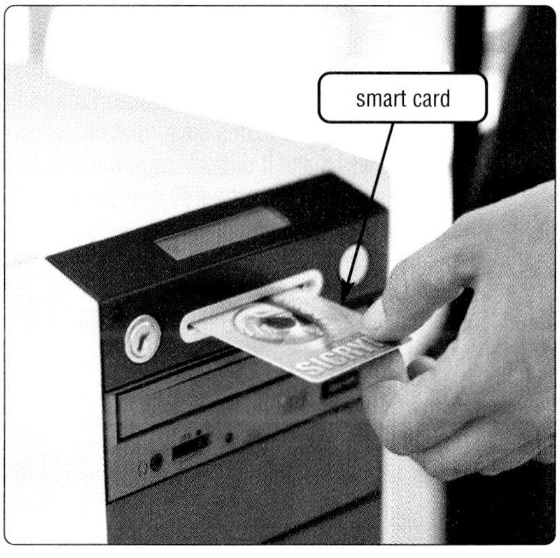

FIGURE 7-37 A sample smart card.

QUIZ YOURSELF 7-3

To check your knowledge of types of CDs and DVDs, tape, PC Cards, miniature mobile storage media, and microfilm and microfiche, visit the Discovering Computers 2005 Quiz Yourself Web page (**scsite.com/dc2005/quiz**). Click Objectives 8 – 11 below Chapter 7.

CHAPTER SUMMARY

Storage holds data, instructions, and information for future use. Users depend on storage devices to provide access to their storage media for years and decades to come. Read Issue 7-5 for a discussion about the future of storage.

This chapter identified and discussed various storage media and storage devices. Storage media covered included floppy disks, Zip disks, internal hard disks, external hard disks, removable hard disks, CD-ROMs, CD-RWs, DVD-ROMs, DVD+RWs, tape, PC Cards, flash memory cards, USB flash drives, and other miniature mobile storage media, and microfilm and microfiche.

ISSUE 7-5

Can You Read It Tomorrow?

Up to 75 percent of today's data is created digitally and has never existed on paper. Although written documents can be read hundreds of years after they are created, rapid changes in computer technology can make digital records almost inaccessible in just one decade. For most computer users, hardware changes have made data stored on once-popular 5-inch floppy disks, or on the 8-inch floppy disks used in the early '70s, unavailable today. Software changes also take a toll. One computer expert claims that trying to read material written with an obsolete word processing program is like trying to interpret Egyptian hieroglyphics without the Rosetta Stone. Pennsylvania State University recently admitted that almost 3,000 student and school files could not be accessed due to lost or outdated software. Is the potential unavailability of digital data a problem? Why or why not? What can be done to keep today's digital information available in the future?

For more information about digital data, visit the Discovering Computers 2005 Issues Web page (**scsite.com/dc2005/issues**). Click Issue #5 below Chapter 7.

Computer Technician

Computer technicians are in great demand in every organization and industry. For many, this is the entry point for a career in the computer/information technology field. The responsibilities of a *computer technician*, also called a computer service technician, include a variety of duties. Most companies that employ someone with this title expect the technician to have basic across-the-board knowledge of concepts in the computer electronics field. Some of the tasks are hardware repair and installation; software installation, upgrade, and configuration; and troubleshooting client and/or server problems. Because computers are a rapidly changing field, technicians must work to remain abreast of current technology and become aware of future developments. Computer technicians generally work with a variety of users, which requires expert people skills, especially the ability to work with groups of nontechnical users.

Most entry-level computer technicians possess the *A+ certification*. This certification attests that a computer technician has demonstrated knowledge of computer setup, maintenance, and software that meets industry standards and has at least six months of experience in the field. The Electronics Technicians Association also provides a Computer Service Technician (CST) certification program.

Because this is an entry-level position, the pay scale is not as high as other more demanding and skilled positions. Individuals can expect an average annual starting salary of around $25,000 to $35,000. Companies pay more for computer technicians with experience and certification.

To learn more about the field of computer technician as a career, visit the Discovering Computers 2005 Careers Web page (**scsite.com/dc2005/careers**). Click Computer Technician.

Disk Formatting and File Systems

Formatting a disk can be compared to starting a library. Before any books can be put in place, you must install the bookshelves and a catalog system. Similarly, a disk must have a file system set up to make it ready to receive data. This is true of many different storage media — including floppy disks, hard disks, removable hard disks, and CD-ROMs — all of which must be formatted, to allow a way to organize and find files saved on the disk.

This discussion focuses on the formatting process required to take a hard disk from its newly manufactured state to a fully functional storage medium. Three main steps are involved in the process of formatting a hard disk: (1) low-level (physical) formatting; (2) partitioning; and (3) high-level (logical) formatting.

A hard disk must be formatted physically before it can be formatted logically. A hard drive physically formats a hard disk by writing a pattern of 1s and 0s on the surface of the disk. The pattern of 1s and 0s serves as small electronic markers, which divide the hard disk platter into its basic physical elements: tracks, sectors, and cylinders.

These elements define the way data is written on and read from the disk physically. As the read/write head moves over the spinning disks, it reads the electronic markers that define the tracks, sectors, and cylinders to determine where it is in relation to the data on the disk's surface. The hard disk manufacturer usually performs a hard disk's physical, or *low-level, formatting.*

Once a hard disk has been formatted physically, it can be partitioned. *Partitioning* is the process of dividing the hard disk into regions called partitions. Each partition occupies a group of adjacent cylinders. Partitioning allows you to organize a hard disk into segments and lets you run multiple operating systems on a single computer. You also can keep the entire hard disk as one partition. After a disk partition has been formatted, it is referred to as a *volume.*

After a hard disk has been formatted physically and partitioned, it must be formatted logically. Logical, or *high-level, formatting* places a file system on the disk. A *file system* allows an operating system, such as DOS or Windows XP, to use the space available on a hard disk to store and retrieve files. The operating system uses the file system to store information about the disk's directory, or folder, structure.

The file system also defines the size of the clusters used to store data on the hard disk. A cluster, or *block,* is made up of two or more sectors on a single track on a hard disk. A cluster is the minimum unit the operating system uses to store information. Even if a file has a size of 1 byte, a cluster as large as 64 KB might be used to store the file on large drives. The number of sectors and tracks and, therefore, the number of clusters that a drive can create on a disk's surface, determine the capacity of the disk.

While creating the file system during logical formatting, the drive creates a special table in the disk's first sector, sector 0. This table stores entries that the operating system uses to locate files on a disk. Each entry in the table takes up a certain number of bits, which is why file systems often are referred to as 12-bit, 16-bit, or 32-bit. The content of each entry consists of a whole number, which identifies one or more clusters where the file is stored.

Depending on the operating system used to format the disk, the file system can be one of several types, as shown in the table in Figure 7-41. Whatever file system is used, the file system is the interface between the operating system and drives.

For more information about formatting a hard disk, visit the Discovering Computers 2005 High-Tech Talk Web page (**scsite.com/dc2005/tech**) and click Disk Formatting.

File System	Description	Key Features
FAT (also called FAT12 and FAT16)	The standard file system for DOS and Windows. Because of its widespread use, FAT also is accessible by most other operating systems.	• FAT12 is used for floppy disk drives and very small hard disks (up to 16 MB) • FAT16 is used for small to moderate-sized hard disk volumes (up to 2 GB)
VFAT (Virtual FAT)	A newer protected-mode version of the FAT file system, introduced with Windows 95.	• Supports long file names up to 255 characters long • Faster than FAT because the computer can read files at least 32 bits at a time
FAT32	A 32-bit version of FAT, introduced with Windows 95.	• Same key features as VFAT • Used for medium-sized to very large hard disk volumes (up to 2 terabytes)
NTFS (NT File System)	The 32-bit file system currently used for Windows NT, Windows 2000, and Windows XP.	• 32- or 64-bit entries in file system table • Fully recoverable file system, designed to restore consistency after a system crash • Used for medium-sized to very large hard disk volumes (up to 16 billion GB)

FIGURE 7-41 Comparison of various file systems.

COMPANIES ON THE CUTTING EDGE

Kingston

Memory in the Making

Have you ever sat down to take a test and have your mind go blank, and then wonder if you were losing your memory?

The computer industry also thought it was losing its memory in 1987. At that time, memory for personal computers was scarce. John Tu and David Sun knew they could help solve the problem. They founded *Kingston Technology* and designed a standard single inline memory module (SIMM) using a readily available alternative chip.

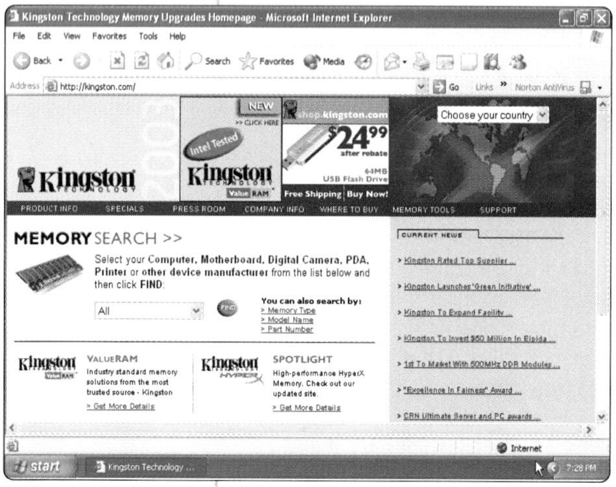

As the memory shortage problem eased a few years later, Kingston branched into manufacturing processor upgrades, storage subsystems, and networking solutions. Today, Kingston is the world's leading independent manufacturer of memory products for computers, servers, digital cameras, and other electronic devices. Headquartered in Fountain Valley, California, Kingston has manufacturing facilities in the United States, Taiwan, Malaysia, and China to meet memory market needs on a global scale. Kingston sells more than 2,000 products and enjoys annual sales of more than $1.4 billion.

Kingston's success results from an emphasis on reliability. This emphasis contributes to the trust between Kingston and its customers. Kingston uses some of the most rigorous testing procedures in the memory industry. The company exceeds industry standards for product quality and product dependability. To ensure memory reliability, Kingston screens components thoroughly and uses only the highest quality components. In addition, Kingston tests modules at all stages of production. Kingston's manufacturing process is so effective that the mean time between failure rating, a measure of product reliability, exceeds 500 years!

Fortune magazine has honored Kingston as one of the 100 Best Companies to Work for in the United States. Part of this honor is due to Kingston's company philosophy of treating all employees as family members and of displaying such traits as courtesy, honesty, and compassion.

For more information about Kingston Technology, visit the Discovering Computers 2005 Companies Web page (**scsite.com/dc2005/companies**) and click Kingston.

EMC

Big-Time Storage Solutions

When your closet gets too small for your wardrobe, one solution is to find a larger closet. When the world's larger corporations run out of space to store their data, they, too, can look for additional storage space. Chances are that when they do, they consider EMC Corporation, a provider of storage systems.

EMC Corporation supplies storage capabilities to large companies. EMC is a world leader in providing systems that store, safeguard, and control information resources, allowing companies to combine their information resources into a single asset. Richard Egan and Roger Marino (the "E" and "M" in EMC) founded EMC in 1979 to fill a demand for add-on memory boards in the minicomputer market. In 1981, EMC introduced its first computer product, a 64 KB chip memory board. By 1984, sales approached $20 million. In the late 1980s, EMC moved from a supplier of memory products to a provider of storage solutions. Soon, the company expanded to provide small disk drives for mainframe computers, which is the industry standard for storage systems today.

In 1990, EMC introduced Symmetrix, a 24 GB storage system with speeds significantly faster than other available products but using less than a quarter of the floor space. By 1993, EMC had abandoned its memory products to focus entirely on disk storage. EMC improved its Symmetrix systems with intelligent software programs and has received recognition as being the world's foremost provider of networked storage. General Motors has named EMC supplier of the year every year since 2000.

EMC recently was named by *Fortune* as one of the 100 Best Companies to Work for in America.

For more information about EMC Corporation, visit the Discovering Computers 2005 Companies Web page (**scsite.com/dc2005/companies**) and click EMC.

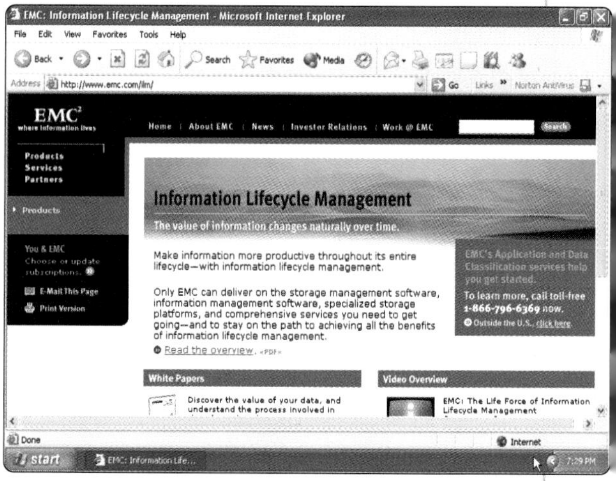

Technology Trailblazers

Al Shugart
Storage Expert

The day after receiving his Bachelor of Science degree in Engineering Physics from the University of Redlands in 1951, *Al Shugart* joined IBM as a customer engineer. He got into it because he liked fixing things and went to work for IBM as a broken machine repairman. He was intrigued with being faced with a problem and then having to fix it. When he felt he had fixed all the problems, he was going to quit, but instead IBM made him part of a product development program that would have a profound impact on the computer industry. Shugart supervised the development of a removable, portable data storage device, an effort that led to the construction of the first removable rigid read/write disk drive. Shugart left IBM in 1969 and went to work as vice president of product development for Memorex. In 1973, he started Shugart Associates, a pioneer in the manufacture of floppy disks. Because of internal problems, the following year Shugart left the company bearing his name. He spent the next few years as a bar-owner, a salmon fisherman, and a private consultant to the technology industry.

In 1979, Shugart and some associates founded Seagate Technology, Inc, which is a leader in the design and marketing of storage products. Seagate has more than 100,000 employees worldwide and the largest revenue share in the hard disk industry. Today he is serving as founder, president, CEO, and chairman of Al Shugart International, a venture capital firm in California.

Despite his success, Shugart feels that life has more important things to offer. He has said, "Your priority has to be on being nice, not on being successful. If you're a nice person and you're talented, then success will follow. If you're a nice person and you're not talented, success won't follow, but at least you're a nice person and you'll enjoy life."

For more information about Al Shugart, visit the Discovering Computers 2005 People Web page (**scsite.com/dc2005/people**) and click Al Shugart.

Mark Dean
Inventor

Not many first graders can handle algebra problems. But, Mark Dean was no ordinary first grader. Along with solving math equations in his first year of school, he also tutored older students, surprising some of his classmates with his scholastic ability.

As one of the few African-Americans in his high school, and a straight-A student and star athlete, Dean spent hours inventing new products. Together with his dad, he built a tractor from scratch. After graduating at the top of his class from the University of Tennessee in 1979, he joined IBM and helped design improvements in architecture that allow components, such as modems and printers, to communicate with personal computers. This technology is used in more than 40 million personal computers manufactured each year. Dean earned his Ph.D. degree at Stanford, and he headed a team at IBM that invented the first CMOS microprocessor chip to operate at 1 gigahertz (1,000 MHz). As an IBM idea man and Vice President of Systems in IBM Research, Dean is responsible today for developing future-generation hardware and software. Currently, he is developing an electronic tablet that functions as an e-book, DVD player, radio, wireless telephone, and Web-enabled device. "If you can talk about it," Dean says, "that means it's possible."

Dean is the first African-American to receive an IBM Fellowship, the company's highest technical ranking. He has received numerous awards including the National Society of Black Engineers Distinguished Engineer Award, the Black Engineer of the Year President's Award, and the Ronald H. Brown American Innovators Award. Dean was inducted into the National Inventor's Hall of Fame, an honor he shares with fewer than 150 other people. Dean has more than 30 patents or patents pending, three of which are for the internal architecture of the original personal computer.

For more information about Mark Dean, visit the Discovering Computers 2005 People Web page (**scsite.com/dc2005/people**) and click Mark Dean.

The Chapter Review section summarizes the concepts presented in this chapter.

QUIZZES AND LEARNING GAMES
Computer Genius
Crossword Puzzle
Interactive Labs
Practice Test
Quiz Yourself
Wheel of Terms

EXERCISES
Chapter Review
Checkpoint
Key Terms
Lab Exercises
Learn It Online
Web Research

BEYOND THE BOOK
Apply It
Career Corner
Companies
FAQ
High-Tech Talk
Issues
Looking Ahead
Trailblazers
Web Links

FEATURES
Guide to Web Sites
Making Use of the Web
Tech News
Timeline 2005

WEB INSTRUCTIONS:

To display this page from the Web, start your browser and enter the Web address **scsite.com/dc2005/ch7/review**. Click the links for current and additional information. To listen to an audio version of this Chapter Review, click the Audio button.

1 What Types of Items Do Users Store on Computer Media?

Storage holds data, instructions, and information for future use. Every computer uses storage to hold software. In addition to programs, users store a variety of data and information including correspondence, reports, records, digital photographs, music, video, Web pages, drawings, and multimedia presentations. Home users, small office/home office users, and mobile users typically have much smaller storage requirements than the large business or power user.

2 How Are Storage Devices Different from Storage Media?

A **storage medium** (media is the plural) is the physical material on which a computer keeps data, instructions, and information. The number of bytes (characters) a storage medium can hold is its capacity. A **storage device** is the computer hardware that records and/or retrieves items to and from storage media. **Writing** is the process of transferring items from memory to a storage medium, and **reading** is the process of transferring these items from a storage medium into memory.

3 What Are the Characteristics of a Floppy Disk Drive?

A **floppy disk** is a portable, inexpensive storage medium that consists of a thin, circular, flexible plastic Mylar film enclosed in a square-shaped plastic shell. Floppy disks are a *magnetic media* that uses magnetic particles to store items in tracks and sectors. A *track* is a narrow recording band that forms a full circle on the surface of the disk. Each track is broken into small, arc-shaped storage locations called *sectors*. A floppy disk drive is a device that reads from and writes on a floppy disk. A mechanism in the drive called the *read/write head* reads items or writes items as it barely touches the disk's recording surface.

4 How Are Zip Disks Used?

A **Zip disk** is a type of portable magnetic media that can store up to 500 times more than a standard floppy disk. These large capacities make it easy to transport many files or large items. Another popular use of Zip disks is to make a backup, or duplicate, of a file, program, or disk that you can use in case the original is lost, damaged, or destroyed.

Visit **scsite.com/dc2005/quiz** or click the Quiz Yourself button. Click Objectives 1 – 4 below Chapter 7.

5 What Are the Characteristics of a Hard Disk?

A **hard disk**, also called a *hard disk drive*, is a storage device that contains one or more inflexible, circular platters that store data, instructions, and information. A *platter* is made of aluminum, glass, or ceramic and is coated with a material that allows items to be recorded magnetically on its surface. Each platter has two read/write heads, one for each side. The location of a read/write head often is referred to by its cylinder. A *cylinder* is the vertical section of a track that passes through all platters. While the computer is running, the platters rotate at 5,400 to 7,200 *revolutions per minute* (*rpm*), which allows nearly instant access to all tracks and sectors on the platters. The spinning creates a cushion of air between the platters and the read/write heads. A *head crash* occurs when a read/write head touches the surface of a platter, usually resulting in a loss of data.

6 What Are the Advantages of Using an Internet Hard Drive?

An **Internet hard drive** is a service on the Web that provides storage to computer users, usually for a minimal fee. An Internet hard drive allows users to access files from any computer or device that has Internet access, save time by storing large files instantaneously instead of downloading them to a local hard disk, permit others to access files, view time-critical data and images immediately while away from the main computer location, and store offsite backups of data.

7 What Are the Characteristics of CDs and DVDs?

CDs and DVDs are a type of storage media that consist of a flat, round, portable disc made of metal, plastic, and lacquer. CDs and DVDs are optical media that store items by using microscopic pits (indentations) and lands (flat areas). A high-powered laser light creates the pits, and a lower-powered laser light reads items by reflecting light through the bottom of the disc. CDs and DVDs commonly store items in a single track that spirals from the center to the edge of the disc.

> Visit **scsite.com/dc2005/quiz** or click the Quiz Yourself button. Click Objectives 5 – 7 below Chapter 7.

8 How Are CD-ROMs, CD-RWs, DVD-ROMs, and DVD+RWs Different?

A **CD-ROM** is a type of optical disc that uses laser technology to store items. A typical CD-ROM holds from 650 MB to 1 GB of data, instructions, and information. Users can read the contents of standard CD-ROMs but cannot erase or modify their contents. A **CD-R** (*compact disc-recordable*) is a *multisession disc* onto which users record their own items. Each part of a CD-R can be written on only one time, and the disc's contents cannot be erased. A CD-RW (*compact disc-rewritable*) is an erasable disc that can be written on multiple times. A **DVD-ROM** (*digital versatile disc-ROM* or *digital video disc-ROM*) is an extremely high capacity optical disk capable of storing from 4.7 GB to 17 GB. Not only is the storage capacity of a DVD-ROM greater than that of a CD-ROM, a DVD-ROM's quality also far surpasses that of a CD-ROM. **DVD-RW** and **DVD+RW** discs are a recordable version of DVD that allows users to erase and record more than 1,000 times.

9 How Is Tape Used?

Tape is a magnetically coated ribbon of plastic capable of storing large amounts of data and information at a low cost. A tape drive reads and writes data and information on tape. Businesses and home users sometimes back up personal computer hard disks on tape.

10 What Are PC Cards and Other Types of Miniature Storage Media?

A PC Card is a thin, credit-card-sized device that fits into a PC Card slot to add storage or other capabilities to a desktop or notebook computer. PDAs, digital cameras, music players, and smart phones use some form of miniature storage media to store digital images, music, or documents. Common types of miniature mobile storage media include *CompactFlash* (*CF*), *Smart Media*, *Secure Digital* (*SD*), *xD Picture Card*, *Memory Stick*, and *Microdrive*. A **smart card**, which is similar in size to a credit card, stores data on a thin microprocessor embedded in the card.

11 How Are Microfilm and Microfiche Used?

Microfilm is a 100- to 215-foot roll of film. **Microfiche** is a small sheet of film, usually about 4 inches by 6 inches. Libraries use microfilm and microfiche to store back issues of newspapers, magazines, and records; large organizations use them to archive inactive files; banks use them to store transactions and canceled checks; and the U.S. Army uses them to store personnel records.

> Visit **scsite.com/dc2005/quiz** or click the Quiz Yourself button. Click Objectives 8 – 11 below Chapter 7.

CHAPTER 7 CHECKPOINT

MULTIPLE CHOICE

Select the best answer. (See page numbers in parentheses.)

1. Examples of storage media include all of the following, except _____. (349)
   a. monitors and printers
   b. floppy disks and hard disks
   c. CDs and DVDs
   d. tape and PC Cards
2. A _____ is a narrow recording band that forms a full circle on the surface of a floppy disk. (353)
   a. track
   b. cluster
   c. shutter
   d. sector
3. On a floppy disk, if the write-protect notch is closed, the floppy disk drive _____. (354)
   a. can write on but cannot read from the floppy disk
   b. can write on and read from the floppy disk
   c. can read from but cannot write on the floppy disk
   d. cannot read from or write on the floppy disk
4. A Zip disk can store from _____ of data. (355)
   a. 10 MB to 75 MB
   b. 100 MB to 750 MB
   c. 10 GB to 75 GB
   d. 100 GB to 750 GB
5. If a computer contains only one hard disk drive, the operating system designates it as drive _____. (356)
   a. A
   b. B
   c. C
   d. D
6. External hard disks and removable hard disks offer all of the following advantages over internal hard disks, except _____. (359)
   a. they can transport a large number of files
   b. they can add storage space to a notebook computer
   c. they can be shared with multiple computers
   d. they can transfer data at much faster rates
7. Users store data and information on an Internet hard drive to _____. (360)
   a. save time by storing large files instantaneously
   b. allow others to access files
   c. store offsite backups of data
   d. all of the above
8. When a laser light reads CDs or DVDs, a land _____. (362)
   a. causes light to reflect, which is read as binary digit 0
   b. causes light to reflect, which is read as binary digit 1
   c. absorbs the light, which is read as binary digit 0
   d. absorbs the light, which is read as binary digit 1
9. All of the following are guidelines for the proper care of optical discs except _____. (363)
   a. do not expose the disc to extreme temperatures
   b. do not stack discs
   c. do not hold a disc by its edges
   d. do not eat, smoke, or drink near a disc
10. The process of writing on an optical disc is called _____. (366)
    a. formatting
    b. ripping
    c. burning
    d. reading
11. A storage technique that a DVD-ROM uses to achieve a higher storage capacity than a CD-ROM is _____. (368)
    a. making the disc denser by packing the pits closer together
    b. using two layers of pits
    c. using both sides of the disc
    d. all of the above
12. _____ storage requires sequential access. (370)
    a. Hard disk
    b. Tape
    c. Floppy disk
    d. CD
13. _____ is a type of flash memory card used in digital cameras, PDAs, music players, digital video cameras, car navigation systems, and e-books. (372)
    a. Smart Media
    b. Memory Stick
    c. Secure Digital
    d. Microdrive
14. Microfilm and microfiche _____. (375)
    a. greatly increase the amount of paper firms must handle
    b. are expensive
    c. have the longest life of any storage media
    d. all of the above

CHECKPOINT CHAPTER 7

MATCHING

Match the terms with their definitions. (See page numbers in parentheses.)

_____ 1. transfer rate (351)
_____ 2. shutter (352)
_____ 3. formatting (354)
_____ 4. form factor (357)
_____ 5. disk cache (358)
_____ 6. disk controller (359)
_____ 7. Picture CD (365)
_____ 8. DVD-video format (368)
_____ 9. tape library (370)
_____ 10. e-money (374)

a. portion of memory that the processor uses to store frequently accessed items
b. speed with which data, instructions, and information move to and from a device
c. used to store a motion picture digitally
d. piece of metal on a floppy disk that slides to expose the surface of the disk
e. combines optic technologies with magnetic media
f. size of hard disk platters on desktop computers
g. compact disc that stores digital versions of a single roll of film
h. number of bytes a storage medium can hold
i. means of paying for goods and services over the Internet
j. separate cabinet on which tape cartridges are mounted on larger computers
k. special-purpose chip and electronic circuits that control the transfer of items to and from the system bus
l. process of preparing a disk for reading and writing

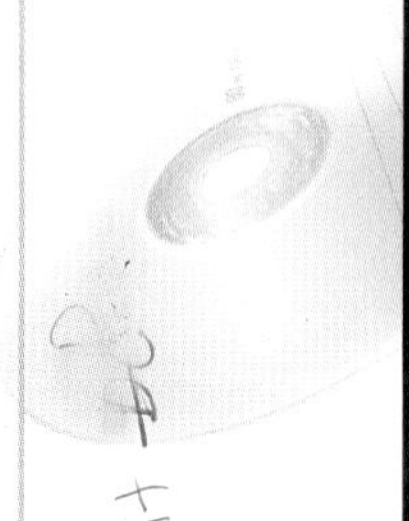

SHORT ANSWER

Write a brief answer to each of the following questions.

1. What is access time? ___________ Why is the average hard disk access time faster than the average floppy disk access time? ___________
2. What is density? ___________ What does it mean to say that floppy disk drives usually are downward compatible but not upward compatible? ___________
3. Why is a hard disk inside the system unit sometimes called a fixed disk? ___________ How is an external hard disk different from a removable hard disk? ___________
4. How is a single-session disc different from a multisession disc? ___________ What is a multiread CD drive? ___________
5. What are PC Cards and why are they used? _________ What is the advantage of a PC Card? _________

WORKING TOGETHER

Working with a group of your classmates, complete the following team exercises.

1. Data and information backup is as important for people with personal computers as it is for companies. Develop a report detailing what your group would consider to be the ideal backup system and required devices for the following scenarios: (1) a home computer for personal use, (2) a computer used in a home-based business, (3) a small business with 6 to 8 computers, (4) a business or organization with up to 100 computers, and (5) a business or organization with more than 100 computers. Include information that supports why you selected the particular options. Develop a PowerPoint presentation to share the information with your class.
2. Choose one Issue from the following issues in this chapter: Do You Use a Shoppers Card? (356), Promotions on CD-ROM? (364), Is It Ethical to Copy CDs? (366), Should the World Become a Cashless Society? (374), or Can You Read It Tomorrow? (376). Use the Web and/or print media to research the issue. Then, present a debate for the class, with different members of your team supporting different responses to the questions that accompany the issue.
3. Some organizations, such as insurance companies, banks, and libraries, are information intensive, meaning that they must keep track of and manipulate large amounts of data. For these organizations, choosing a suitable storage medium is a crucial decision. Have each member of your team visit an information intensive organization and interview someone responsible for maintaining data. What are the storage requirements? What type of storage medium is used? Why? What backup procedures are employed? Meet with the members of your team to discuss the results of your interviews. Then, use PowerPoint to create a group presentation and share your findings with the class.

CHAPTER 7 LEARN IT ONLINE

QUIZZES AND LEARNING GAMES
Computer Genius
Crossword Puzzle
Interactive Labs
Practice Test
Quiz Yourself
Wheel of Terms

EXERCISES
Chapter Review
Checkpoint
Key Terms
Lab Exercises
Learn It Online
Web Research

BEYOND THE BOOK
Apply It
Career Corner
Companies
FAQ
High-Tech Talk
Issues
Looking Ahead
Trailblazers
Web Links

FEATURES
Guide to Web Sites
Making Use of the Web
Tech News
Timeline 2005

Use the Learn It Online exercises to reinforce your understanding of the chapter concepts.

WEB INSTRUCTIONS:

To display this page from the Web, start your browser and enter the Web address **scsite.com/dc2005/ch7/learn**.

1 At the Movies – Super Bonus

To view the Super Bonus movie, click the number 1 button. Watch the movie and then complete the exercise by answering the questions below. Kingston Technology is the world's leading independent manufacturer of memory products for computers, servers, digital cameras, and other electronic devices. The company sells more than 2,000 products. Many companies of this size have difficulty finding talented employees, and frequently lose their best employees to other companies. Why is Kingston Technology flooded with resumes from job seekers, and why do they rarely have the need for new employees? What does founder John Tu mean when he says "business is about people"? What does he do to prove it?

2 Student Edition Labs – Maintaining a Hard Drive

Click the number 2 button. When the Student Edition Labs menu appears, click *Maintaining a Hard Drive* to begin. A new browser window will open. Follow the on-screen instructions to complete the Lab. When finished, click the Exit button. If required, print a copy of your results to submit to your instructor.

3 Student Edition Labs – Managing Files

Click the number 3 button. When the Student Edition Labs menu appears, click *Managing Files* to begin. A new browser window will open. Follow the on-screen instructions to complete the Lab. When finished, click the Exit button. If required, print a copy of your results to submit to your instructor.

4 DVD

A DVD can hold almost 25 times more data than a CD. This translates into richer sound and images than ever seen or heard before. The quality of DVD storage is having a major impact on the market. Some industry professionals expect that the sales of DVD drives soon will approach the $10 billion mark. Click the number 4 button and complete this exercise to learn more about DVDs.

5 Practice Test

Click the number 5 button. Answer each question. When completed, enter your name and click the Grade Test button to submit the quiz for grading. Make a note of any missed questions. If required, print a copy to submit to your instructor.

6 Web Guide

Click the number 6 button to display the Guide to Web Sites and Searching Techniques Web page. Click Reference and then click Webopedia. Search for DVD. Click one of the DVD links. Use your word processing program to prepare a brief report about your findings and submit your assignment to your instructor.

7 Scavenger Hunt

Click the number 7 button. Print a copy of the Scavenger Hunt page; use this page to write down your answers as you search the Web. Submit your completed page to your instructor.

8 Who Wants To Be a Computer Genius?

Click the number 8 button to find out if you are a computer genius. Directions on how to play the game will be displayed. When you are ready to play, click the Play button. Submit your score to your instructor.

9 Wheel of Terms

Click the number 9 button to reinforce important terms you learned in this chapter by playing the Shelly Cashman Series version of this popular game. Directions on how to play the game will be displayed. When you are ready to play, click the Play button. Submit your score to your instructor.

10 Career Corner

Click the number 10 button to display the Campus Career Center page. Click a link of an area of interest and review the information. Write a brief report describing what you discovered. Submit the report to your instructor.

11 Search Sleuth

Click the number 11 button to learn search techniques that will help make you a research expert. Submit the completed assignment to your instructor.

12 Crossword Puzzle Challenge

Click the number 12 button. Complete the puzzle to reinforce skills you learned in this chapter. Directions on how to play the game will be displayed. When you are ready to play, click the Submit button. Submit the completed puzzle to your instructor.

13 Personal Information Management

Are you tired of forgetting birthdays, missing meetings, overlooking appointments, or neglecting to complete important tasks? If so, then personal information management software may be perfect for you. Click the number 13 button to find out about a free, Internet-based calendar. How could this calendar help you organize your life? How might the calendar help you have more fun? After reading the information, you may sign up to create your own Internet-based calendar.

14 In the News

IBM sells a small disk drive, about the size of a quarter, which is capable of storing 1 GB of information, as much as 690 floppy disks. The drive will be used in devices such as digital cameras. What other storage devices are on the horizon? Click the number 14 button and read a news article about a new or improved storage device. What is the device? Who manufactures it? How is the storage device better than, or different from, earlier devices? How will the device be used? Why?

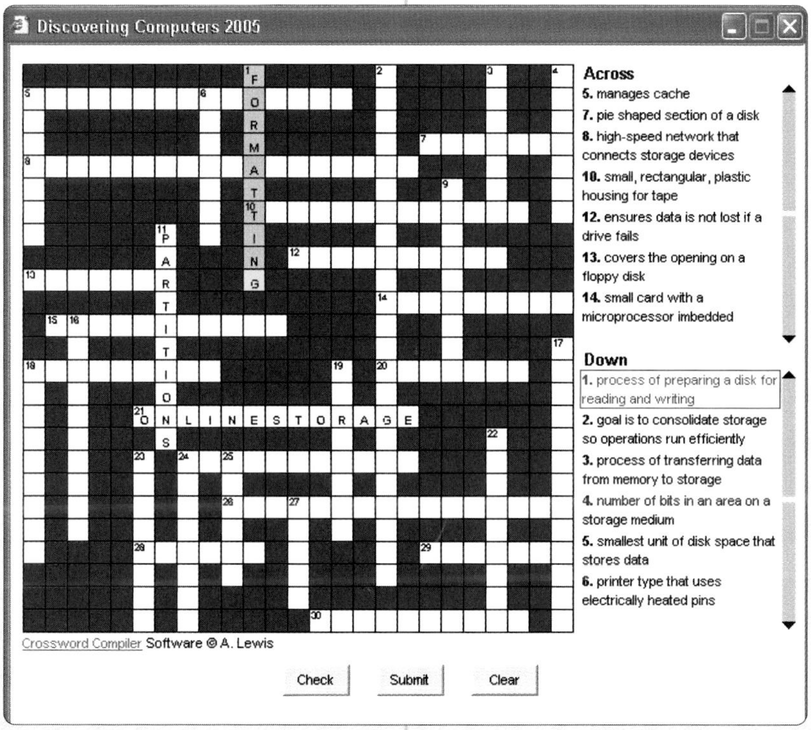

CHAPTER 7 LAB EXERCISES

Use the Lab Exercises to gain hands-on computer experience.

WEB INSTRUCTIONS:

To display this page from the Web, start your browser and enter the Web address **scsite.com/dc2005/ch7/lab**.

1 Recycle Bin

This exercise uses Windows XP procedures. The Recycle Bin, which is located on the desktop, provides a safety net when deleting files or folders. When you send an item to the Recycle Bin, it remains there until it is deleted permanently. Use the Recycle Bin to retrieve files you deleted in error, or empty the Recycle Bin to create more disk space. Windows XP provides one Recycle Bin for each hard disk. To find out more about the Recycle Bin, click the Start button on the taskbar and then click Help and Support on the Start menu. Type `recycle bin` in the Search text box and then click the Start searching button. To answer each of the following questions, click an appropriate result link in the Search Results box and then read the Help information. To display a different result, click another result link.

- How do you delete a file or folder?
- How do you restore a file?
- How can you change the storage capacity of the Recycle Bin?
- How do you empty the Recycle Bin?

Click the Close button to close the Help and Support Center window.

2 Working with Files

This exercise uses Windows XP/2000/98 procedures. To complete this exercise, you first must complete Lab Exercises 2 in Chapter 3 on page 176. Insert your floppy disk into drive A. Click the Start button on the taskbar. Click My Computer on the Start menu (double-click the My Computer icon on the desktop in Windows 2000/98). When the My Computer window is displayed, right-click the 3½ Floppy (A:) icon. Click Open on the shortcut menu. Click View on the menu bar and then click Icons (Large Icons in Windows 2000/98). Right-click the lab3-2 icon. Click Copy on the shortcut menu. Click Edit on the menu bar and then click Paste. How has the 3½ Floppy (A:) window changed? Right-click the new icon (Copy of lab3-2) and then click Rename on the shortcut menu. Type `lab7-2` and then press the ENTER key. Right-click the lab7-2 icon and then click Print on the shortcut menu. Close the 3½ Floppy (A:) window. Close the My Computer window.

3 Learning About the Hard Disk

This exercise uses Windows 2000/98 procedures. What are the characteristics of your hard disk? To find out, right-click the My Computer icon on the desktop. Click Open on the shortcut menu. Right-click the Hard disk (C:) icon in the My Computer window. Click Properties on the shortcut menu. If necessary, click the General tab and then answer the following questions:

- What Label is on the disk?
- What Type of disk is it?
- How much of the hard disk is Used space?
- How much of the hard disk is Free space?
- What is the total Capacity of the hard disk?

Close the Hard disk (C:) Properties dialog box and the My Computer window.

4 Disk Cleanup

This exercise uses Windows XP procedures. Just as people maintain they never can have too much money, computer users insist that you never can have too much hard disk space. Fortunately, Windows includes a utility program called Disk Cleanup that can increase available hard disk space. To find out more about Disk Cleanup, click the Start button on the taskbar and then click Help and Support on the Start menu. Type `disk cleanup` in the Search text box and then click the Start searching button. Click the Using Disk Cleanup link in the Search Results box. Read the information in the right pane of the Help and Support Center window and answer the following questions:

- How does Disk Cleanup help to free up space on the hard disk?
- How do you start Disk Cleanup using the Start button?

Click the Close button to close the Help and Support Center window.

WEB RESEARCH CHAPTER 7

Use the Web Research exercises to learn more about the special features in this chapter.

WEB INSTRUCTIONS:

Use the link in each exercise or a search engine such as Google (google.com) to research the topic. Then, write a one-page, double-spaced report or create a presentation, unless otherwise directed below. Page numbers on which information can be found are in parentheses.

1 **Issue** Choose one Issue from the following issues in this chapter: Do You Use a Shoppers Card? (356), Promotions on CD-ROM? (364), Is It Ethical to Copy CDs? (366), Should the World Become a Cashless Society? (374), or Can You Read It Tomorrow? (376). Use the Web to research the issue. Discuss the issue with classmates, instructors, and friends. Address the questions that accompany the issue in a report or presentation.

2 **Apply It** Choose one of the following Apply It features in this chapter: Save Data Now for Safekeeping (358) or Turn Your Computer into a Home Theater System (368). Use the Web to gather additional information about the topic. Print two Web pages that relate to the Apply It. Detail in a report or presentation what you learned.

3 **Career Corner** Read the Career Corner article in this chapter (376). Use the Web to find out more about the career. Describe the career in a report or presentation.

4 **Companies on the Cutting Edge** Choose one of the Companies on the Cutting Edge in this chapter (378). Use the Web to research the company further. Explain in a report or presentation how this company has contributed to computer technology.

5 **Technology Trailblazers** Choose one of the Technology Trailblazers in this chapter (379). Use the Web to research the person further. Explain in a report or presentation how this individual has affected the way people use, or think about, computers.

6 **Picture Yourself Using a Picture CD** Read the Picture Yourself Using a Picture CD story at the beginning of this chapter (346). Use the Web to research Picture CDs further. Describe in a report or presentation the ways in which you might use a Picture CD.

7 **High-Tech Talk** Read the High-Tech Talk feature in this chapter (377). Use the Web to find out more about the topic. Summarize in a report or presentation what you learned.

8 **Web Links** Review the Web Link boxes found in the margins of this chapter. Visit five of the Web Link sites. Print the main Web page for each site you visit. Choose one of the Web pages and then summarize in one paragraph the content of the Web page.

9 **Looking Ahead** Choose one of the Looking Ahead articles in this chapter: Holographic Storage Expands Capacity (369) or Millipede Reinvents Punched Card Storage Concept (371). Use the Web to find out more about the topic. Detail in a report or presentation what you learned.

10 **FAQ** Choose one FAQ found in this chapter. Use the Web to find out more about the topic. Summarize in one paragraph what you learned.

11 **Making Use of the Web** Read the Shopping section of Making Use of the Web in Appendix A (APP 14). Complete the Shopping Web Exercises at the end of the section (APP 15). Answer the questions posed in each exercise.

CHAPTER 8

Operating Systems and Utility Programs

Picture Yourself with a Virus-Infected Computer

While reading your new e-mail messages, you see one that congratulates you on winning a weekend getaway. As soon as you open the attachment in the message, the computer freezes and then displays the word, Gotcha. You click the mouse button. Nothing happens. You press a key on the keyboard. The computer beeps. You click the mouse again. Still no response. You restart the computer. By now, you expect to see the Windows XP desktop, but it does not appear. Something is wrong.

You call a friend of yours, who works as a computer technician, for help. After explaining the situation to her, she says the computer probably has a virus that was hidden in the attachment that you opened. She asks you several questions, and you answer: Did you have antivirus software installed on the computer? No. Did you have firewall software installed on the computer? No. Do you have a backup of the computer's hard disk? No. After explaining the importance of antivirus software, firewall software, and backups, she tells you the first step in solving this problem is to start the computer again — this time with the recovery disk in the floppy disk drive. Now you know you are in trouble… what's a recovery disk?

As you read Chapter 8, you will learn about recovery disks and antivirus, firewall, and backup utilities, and discover features common to most operating systems and utility programs.

OBJECTIVES

After completing this chapter, you will be able to:

1. Identify the types of system software
2. Summarize the startup process on a personal computer
3. Describe the functions of an operating system
4. Discuss ways that some operating systems help administrators control a network and administer security
5. Explain the purpose of the utilities included with most operating systems
6. Summarize the features of several stand-alone operating systems
7. Identify various network operating systems
8. Identify devices that use several embedded operating systems
9. Explain the purpose of several stand-alone utility programs

CONTENTS

SYSTEM SOFTWARE

System software consists of the programs that control or maintain the operations of the computer and its devices. System software serves as the interface between the user, the application software, and the computer's hardware.

Two types of system software are operating systems and utility programs. Several types of utility programs are provided with an operating system. Other utility programs are available as programs separate from the operating system. This chapter discusses the operating system and its functions, as well as several types of utility programs for personal computers.

OPERATING SYSTEMS

An **operating system** (**OS**) is a set of programs containing instructions that coordinate all the activities among computer hardware resources. Most operating systems perform similar functions that include starting a computer, providing a user interface, managing programs, managing memory, scheduling jobs, configuring devices, establishing an Internet connection, monitoring performance, and providing file management and other utilities. Some operating systems also allow users to control a network and administer security (Figure 8-1).

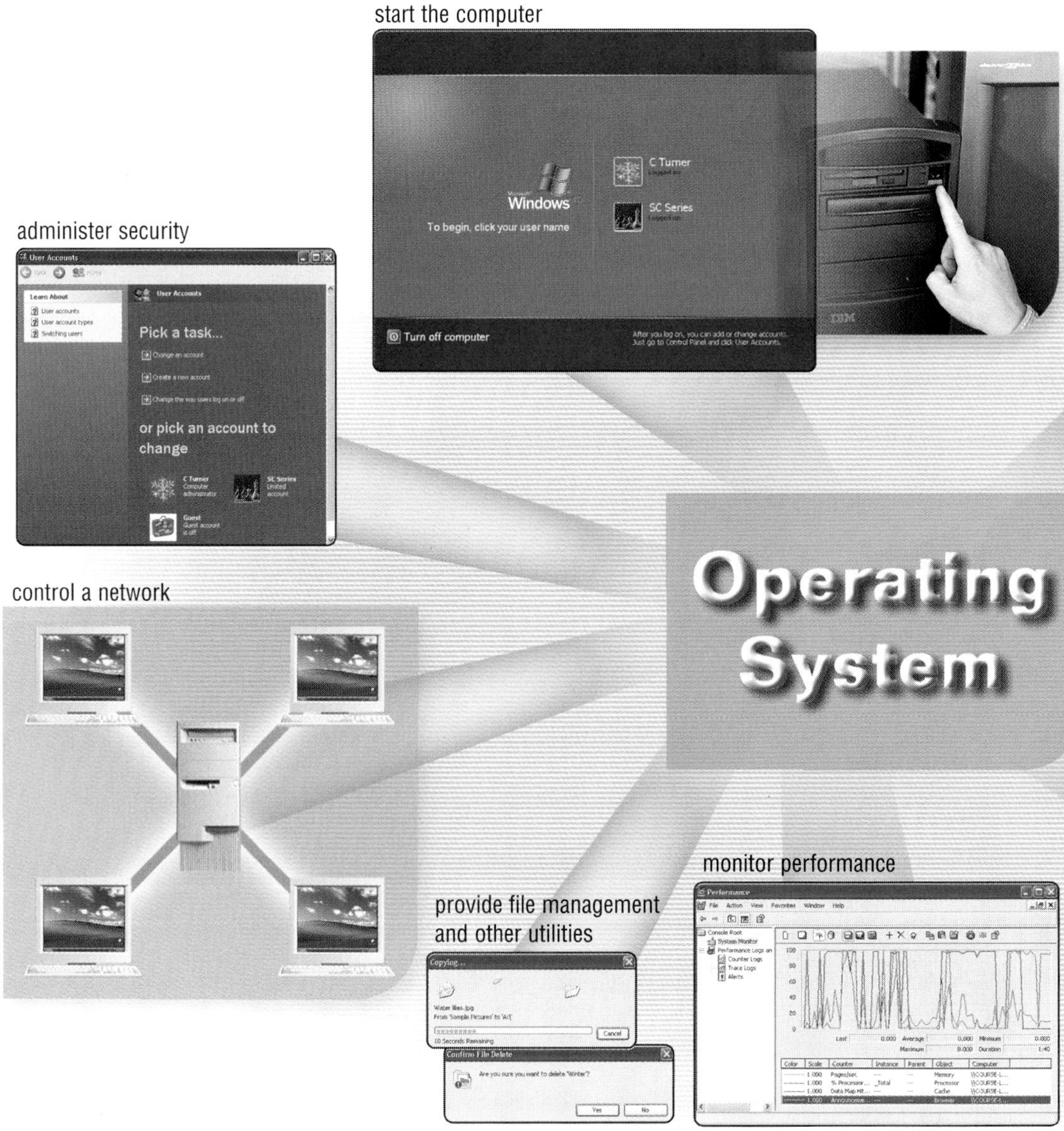

FIGURE 8-1 Most operating systems perform the functions illustrated in this figure.

In most cases, the operating system is installed and resides on the computer's hard disk. On smaller handheld computers and PDAs, however, the operating system may reside on a ROM chip.

Different sizes of computers typically use different operating systems. For example, a mainframe computer does not use the same operating system as a personal computer. Even the same types of computers, such as desktop computers, may not use the same operating system. Furthermore, the application software designed for a specific operating system may not run when using another operating system. For example, PCs use Windows XP, and iMacs use Mac OS X. When purchasing application software, you must ensure that it works with the operating system installed on your computer.

The operating system that a computer uses sometimes is called the *platform*. On purchased application software, the package identifies the required platform (operating system). A *cross-platform* program is one that runs the same on multiple operating systems.

provide a user interface

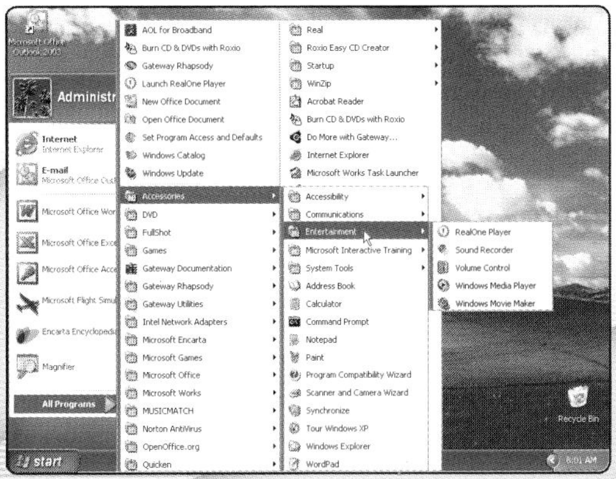

manage programs

manage memory

schedule jobs and configure devices

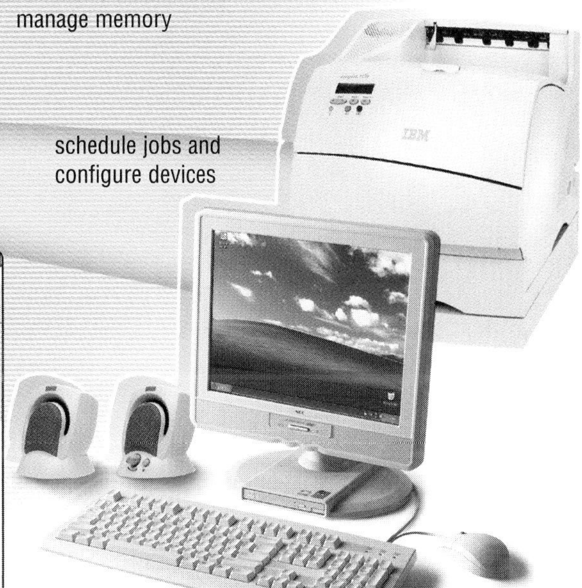

establish an Internet connection

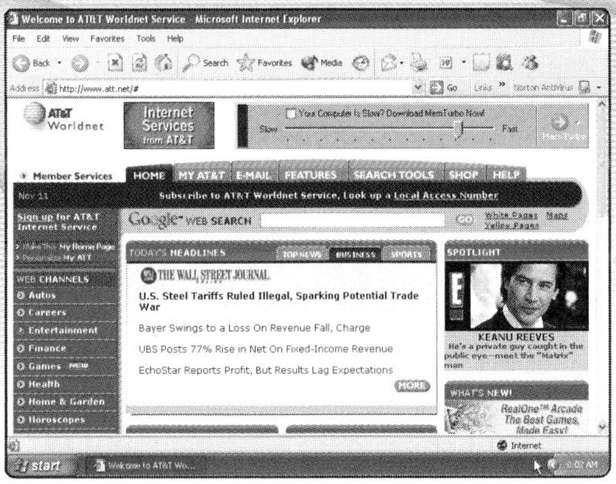

OPERATING SYSTEM FUNCTIONS

Many different operating systems exist, designed for all types of computers. Regardless of the size of the computer, however, most operating systems provide similar functions. The following sections discuss functions common to most operating systems. The operating system handles many of these functions automatically, without requiring any input from a user.

Starting a Computer

The process of starting or restarting a computer is called **booting**. When turning on a computer that has been powered off completely, you are performing a **cold boot**. A **warm boot**, by contrast, is the process of restarting a computer that already is powered on. With Windows XP, for example, you can perform a warm boot by pressing a combination of keyboard keys (CTRL+ALT+ DEL), selecting a button from a list in a dialog box (Figure 8-2a), or pressing the reset button on the computer (Figure 8-2b).

When you install new software, often an on-screen prompt instructs you to restart the computer. In this case, a warm boot is appropriate. If your computer stops responding, try to restart it with a warm boot first. If it does not respond to the warm boot, then restart the computer with a cold boot; that is, push the power button.

Each time you boot a computer, the kernel and other frequently used operating system instructions are loaded, or copied, from the hard disk (storage) to the computer's memory (RAM). The *kernel* is the core of an operating system that manages memory and devices, maintains the computer's clock, starts applications, and assigns the computer's resources, such as devices, programs, data, and information. The kernel is *memory resident*, which means it remains in memory while the computer is running. Other parts of the operating system are *nonresident*, that is, these instructions remain on the hard disk until they are needed.

When you boot a computer, a series of messages may be displayed on the screen (Figure 8-3). The actual information displayed varies depending on the make and type of the computer and the equipment installed. The boot process, however, is similar for large and small computers.

Figure 8-2a (warm boot from Windows desktop)

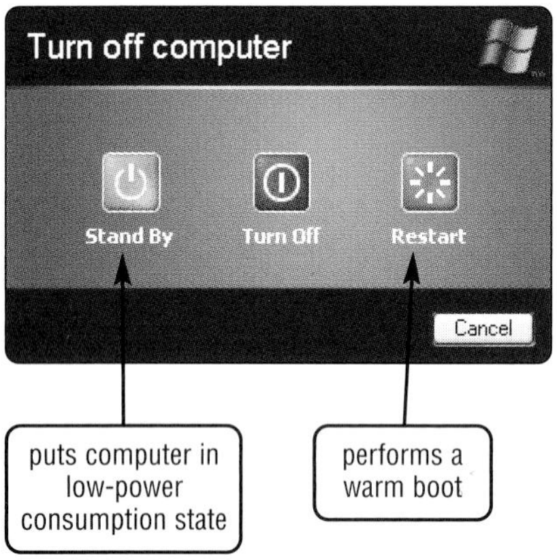

Figure 8-2b (warm boot from system unit)

FIGURE 8-2 To perform a warm boot, click the Restart button in the dialog box or press the reset button on the system unit.

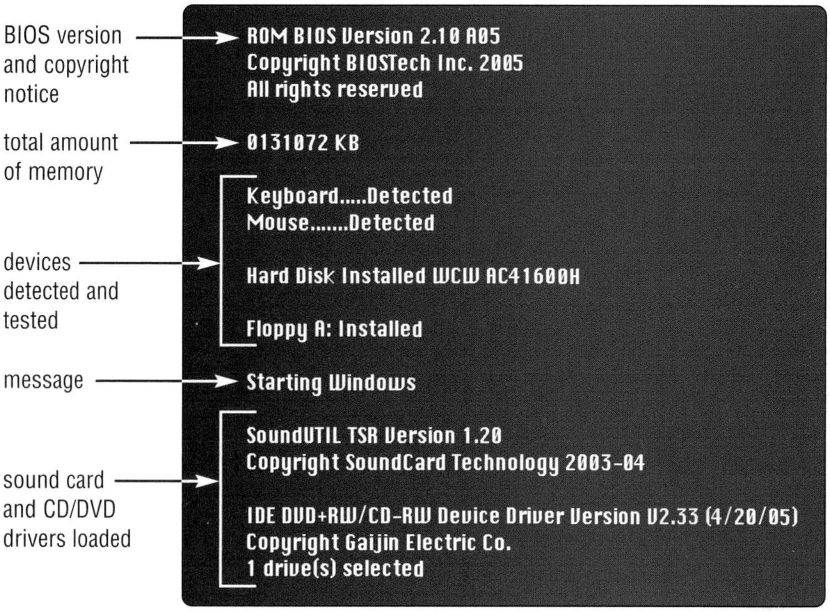

FIGURE 8-3 When you boot a computer, a set of messages may be displayed on the screen. The actual information displayed varies depending on the make of the computer and the devices installed.

The following steps explain what occurs during a cold boot on a personal computer using the Windows XP operating system. Figure 8-4 illustrates and briefly summarizes these steps.

1. When you turn on the computer, the power supply sends an electrical signal to the components in the system unit.
2. The charge of electricity causes the processor chip to reset itself and find the ROM chip(s) that contains the BIOS. The **BIOS** (pronounced BYE-ose), which stands for *basic input/output system*, is firmware that contains the computer's startup instructions.

FIGURE 8-4 HOW A PC BOOTS UP

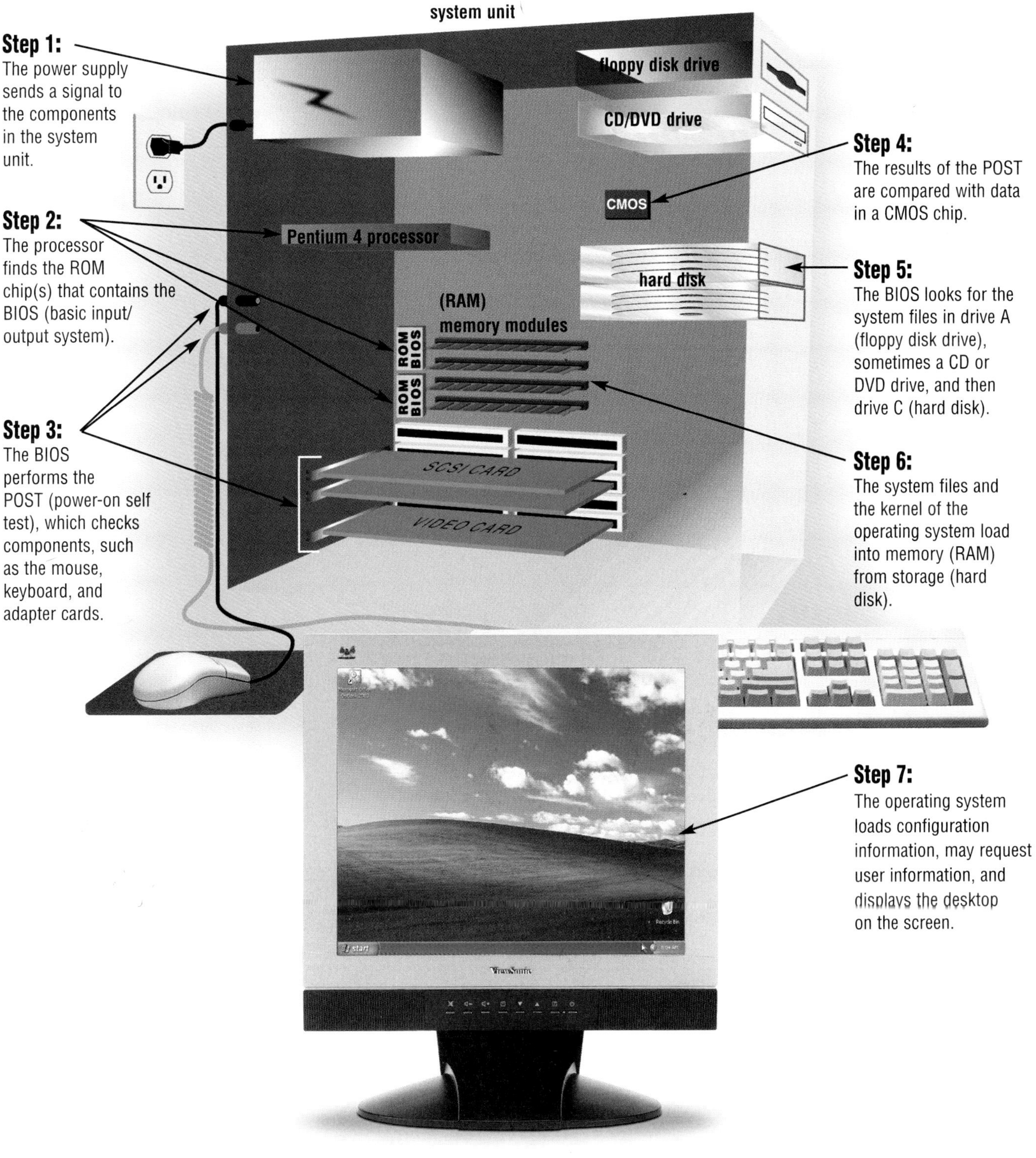

3. The BIOS executes a series of tests to make sure the computer hardware is connected properly and operating correctly. The tests, collectively called the *power-on self test* (*POST*), check the various system components including the buses, system clock, adapter cards, RAM chips, mouse, keyboard, and drives. As the POST executes, LEDs (tiny lights) flicker on devices such as the disk drives and keyboard. Several beeps also sound, and messages are displayed on the screen.
4. The POST results are compared with data in a CMOS chip. As discussed in Chapter 4, CMOS is a technology that uses battery power to retain information when the computer is off. The CMOS chip stores configuration information about the computer, such as the amount of memory; type of disk drives, keyboard, and monitor; the current date and time; and other startup information. It also detects any new devices connected to the computer. If any problems are identified, the computer may beep, display error messages, or cease operating — depending on the severity of the problem.
5. If the POST completes successfully, the BIOS searches for specific operating system files called *system files*. Usually, the operating system looks first to see if a disk is in drive A (the designation for a floppy disk drive). If drive A contains a disk, the BIOS checks the disk for system files. If drive A does not contain a disk or if the system files are not on a disk in drive A, the BIOS looks in drive C (the designation usually given to the first hard disk). Some computers also look in a CD or DVD drive for system files.
6. Once located, the system files load into memory (RAM) from storage (usually the hard disk) and execute. Next, the kernel of the operating system loads into memory. Then, the operating system in memory takes control of the computer.
7. The operating system loads system configuration information. In Windows XP, the *registry* consists of several files that contain the system configuration information. Windows XP constantly accesses the registry during the computer's operation for information such as installed hardware and software devices and individual user preferences for mouse speed, passwords, and other user-specific information.

   Necessary operating system files are loaded into memory. On some computers, the operating system verifies that the person attempting to use the computer is a legitimate user. Finally, the Windows XP desktop and icons are displayed on the screen. The operating system executes programs in the *Startup folder*, which contains a list of programs that open automatically when you boot the computer. Read Apply It 8-1 for more information.

WEB LINK 8-1

BIOS

Visit the Discovering Computers 2005 WEB LINK page (**scsite .com/dc2005/weblink**). Click BIOS below Chapter 8.

APPLY IT 8-1

Customizing the Startup Folder

Some people start their day by drinking a cup of coffee. Your computer, likewise, starts to run by loading the operating system kernel into memory from the hard disk. The kernel contains instructions that control components, memory, peripheral devices, and the system clock. It also automatically loads the programs found in the Startup folder, which is located on the All Programs submenu on the Start menu.

One program frequently found in the Startup folder is antivirus software, such as Norton AntiVirus or McAfee VirusScan. Most computer users desire this software to run at all times to protect against documents and e-mail messages infected with viruses. Most computers also have an e-mail program or Web browser added to the Startup folder because this software is used so frequently.

Some programs are installed automatically in the Startup folder, so it is a good idea to check the folder periodically if you have added or removed software. The programs listed in the Startup folder are shortcuts, meaning they are not actually stored in this folder. You can, consequently, delete or add a program in the Startup folder without modifying or damaging the existing program.

For more information about starting Windows XP, visit the Discovering Computers 2005 Apply It Web page (**scsite.com/dc2005/apply**). Click Apply It #1 below Chapter 8.

RECOVERY DISK A **boot drive** is the drive from which your personal computer boots (starts). In most cases, drive C (the hard disk) is the boot drive. Sometimes a hard disk becomes damaged and the computer cannot boot from the hard disk. In this case, you can boot from a special disk. A **recovery disk**, also called a **boot disk**, is a floppy disk, Zip disk, CD, or DVD that contains a few system files that will start the computer. For this reason, it is crucial you have a recovery disk available and ready for use — in case of computer failure.

When a user installs an operating system, one of the installation steps often involves creating a recovery disk. Most users, however, do not install an operating system because the manufacturer preinstalls it on their computer. Thus, you may not have a recovery disk. In this case, you should create one and keep it in a safe place. The steps in Figure 8-5 show how to create a recovery disk in Windows XP.

FAQ 8-1

When I am finished using the computer, can I simply turn it off?

No! You must use the operating system's shut-down procedure so various processes are closed in sequence and items in memory released properly. Depending on the computer, several shut-down options exist. The Turn Off command removes power from the computer. Restart does a warm boot. *Hibernate* saves all documents in memory and then turns off the computer. *Stand By* places the entire computer in a low-power state but does not turn it off. With Hibernate and Stand By, the next time you resume work on the computer, the desktop is restored to exactly how you left it.

For more information about shut-down options, visit the Discovering Computers 2005 FAQ Web page (**scsite.com/dc2005/faq**). Click Shut-Down Options below Chapter 8.

FIGURE 8-5 HOW TO CREATE A RECOVERY DISK IN WINDOWS XP

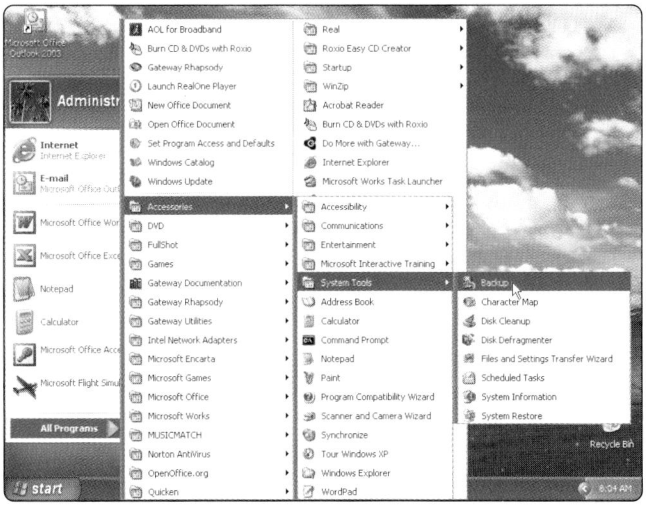

Step 1:
Click the Start button on the taskbar, point to All Programs on the Start menu, point to Accessories on the All Programs submenu, point to System Tools on the Accessories submenu, and then point to Backup.

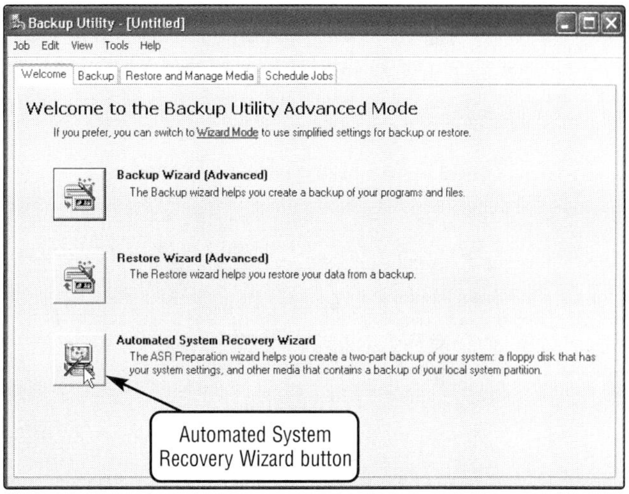

Step 2:
Click Backup on the System Tools submenu to open the Backup Utility window. (If the Backup or Restore Wizard appears, click the Advanced Mode link.) Point to the Automated System Recovery Wizard button.

Step 3:
Click the Automated System Recovery Wizard button to create the recovery disk. Follow the on-screen instructions and insert a disk into the disk drive when prompted.

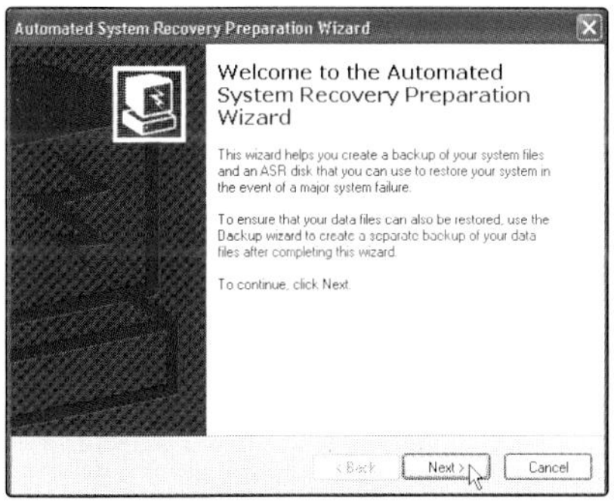

Providing a User Interface

You interact with software through its user interface. That is, a **user interface** controls how you enter data and instructions and how information is displayed on the screen. Three types of user interfaces are command-line, menu-driven, and graphical. Operating systems often use a combination of these interfaces to define how a user interacts with a computer.

COMMAND-LINE INTERFACE To configure devices, manage system resources, and troubleshoot network connections, network administrators and other advanced users work with a command-line interface. In a *command-line interface*, a user types commands or presses special keys on the keyboard (such as function keys or key combinations) to enter data and instructions (Figure 8-6a). When working with a command-line interface, the set of commands entered into the computer is called the *command language*. Command-line interfaces often are difficult to use because they require exact spelling, grammar, and punctuation. Minor errors, such as a missing period, generate an error message. Command-line interfaces, however, give a user more control to manage detailed settings. For a technical discussion about a command-line interface, read the High-Tech Talk article on page 421.

MENU-DRIVEN INTERFACE A *menu-driven interface* provides menus as a means of entering commands (Figure 8-6b). Menu-driven interfaces are easier to learn than command-line interfaces because users do not have to learn the rules of entering commands.

GRAPHICAL USER INTERFACE Most users today work with a graphical user interface. With a *graphical user interface* (*GUI*), you interact with menus and visual images such as buttons and other graphical objects to issue commands. Many current GUI operating systems incorporate features similar to those of a Web browser. The Help and Support Center window in Windows XP shown in Figure 8-6c, for example, contains links and navigation buttons such as the Back button and the Forward button.

Figure 8-6a (command-line interface)

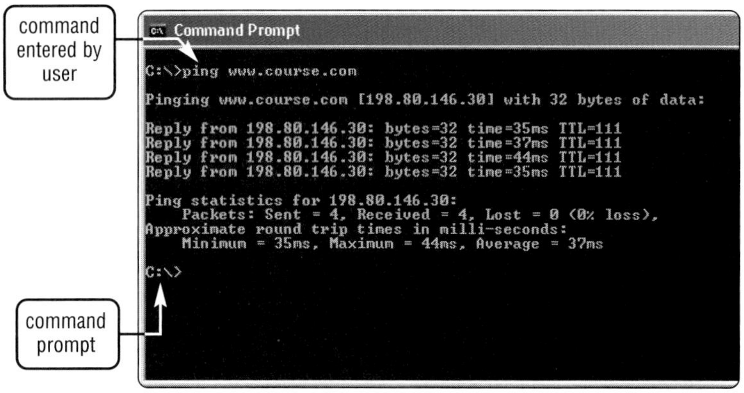

Figure 8-6b (menu-driven interface)

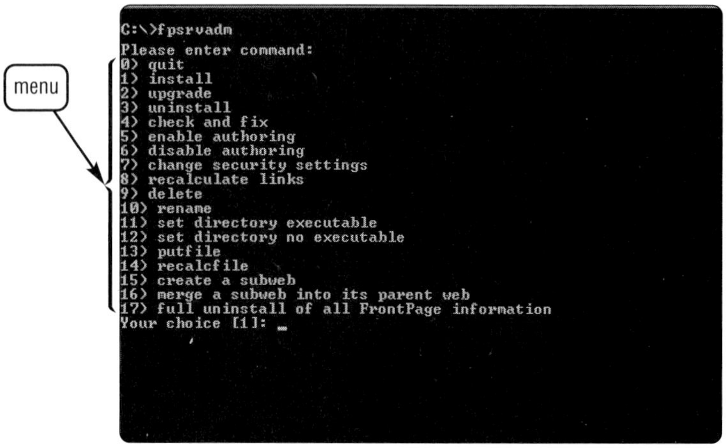

Figure 8-6c (graphical user interface)

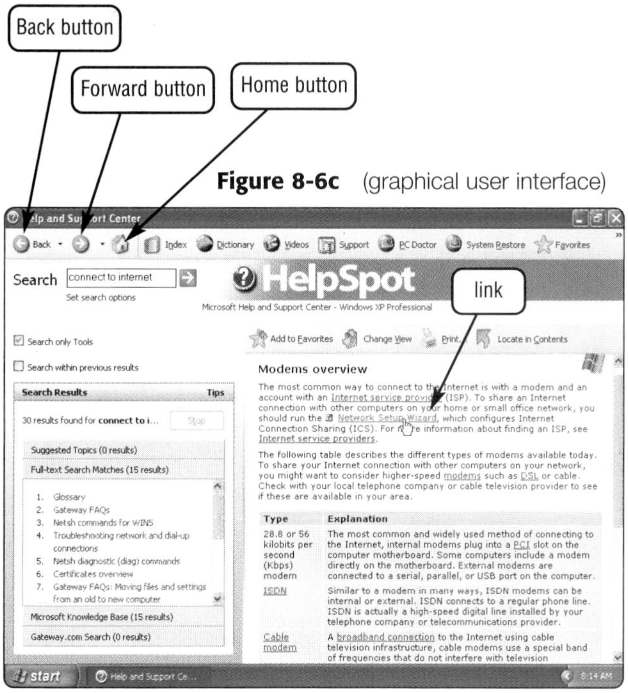

FIGURE 8-6 Examples of command-line, menu-driven, and graphical user interfaces.

Managing Programs

Some operating systems support a single user and only one running program at a time. Others support thousands of users running multiple programs. How an operating system handles programs directly affects your productivity.

A *single user/single tasking* operating system allows only one user to run one program at a time. Suppose, for example, you are creating a poster in a graphics program and then decide to check your e-mail messages. With a single tasking operating system, you must quit the graphics program before you can run the e-mail program. You then must close the e-mail program and restart the graphics program to finish the poster. Early systems were single user/single tasking. Most of today's operating systems are multitasking. PDAs and other small computing devices, however, often use a single user/single tasking operating system.

A *single user/multitasking* operating system allows a single user to work on two or more programs that reside in memory at the same time. Using the example just cited, if you are working with a single user/multitasking operating system, you do not have to quit the graphics program to run the e-mail program. Both programs can run concurrently. Users today typically run multiple programs concurrently. It is common to have an e-mail program and Web browser open at all times, while working with application programs such as word processing or graphics.

When a computer is running multiple programs concurrently, one program is in the foreground and the others are in the background. The one in the *foreground* is the active program; that is, the one you currently are using. The other programs running but not in use are in the *background*. In Figure 8-7a, the Internet Explorer program, which is showing the National Geographic Web page, is in the foreground, and three other programs are running in the background (Excel, PowerPoint, and Paint Shop Pro). The background programs can continue to execute when another program is in the foreground. For example, Excel can be updating stock quotes in a worksheet while you are browsing the Web.

Notice in Figure 8-7a that you can see the foreground program, but not the background programs. You easily can switch between foreground and background programs. To make a program active (in the foreground) in Windows XP, click its program button on the taskbar. This causes the operating system to place all other programs in the background.

In addition to application programs, an operating system manages other processes. These processes include utilities or routines that provide support to other programs or hardware. Some are memory resident. Others run as they are required. Figure 8-7b shows a list of all processes running on a Windows XP computer. The list contains the programs running, as well as other processes.

Figure 8-7a (multiple programs running)

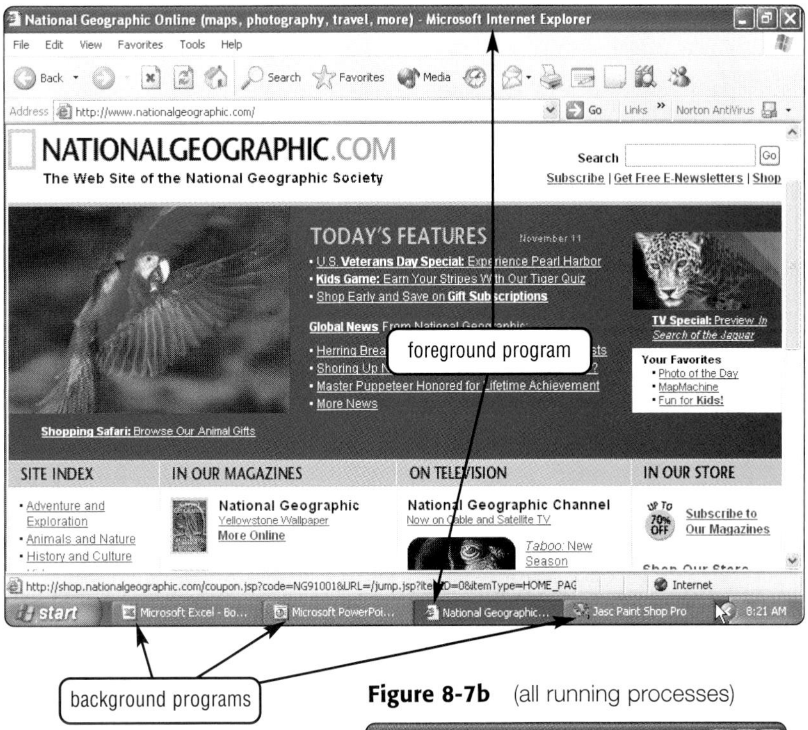

Figure 8-7b (all running processes)

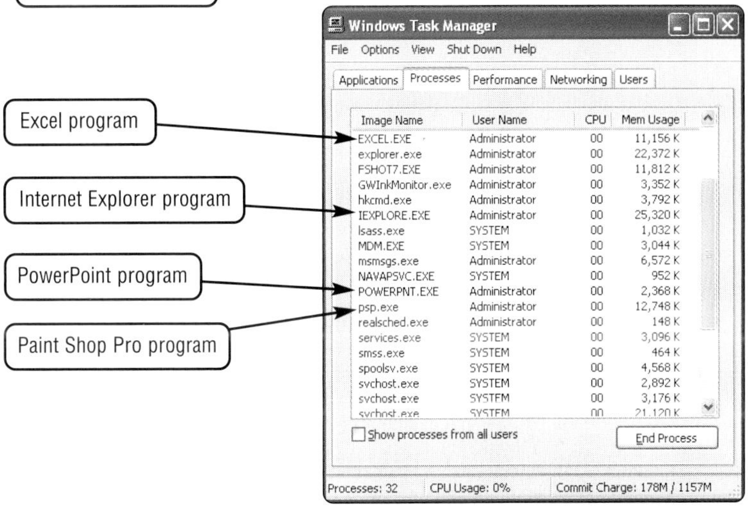

FIGURE 8-7 Windows XP manages multiple programs and processes while you use the computer.

Some operating systems use preemptive multitasking to prevent any one process from monopolizing the computer's resources. With *preemptive multitasking*, the operating system interrupts a program that is executing and passes control to another program waiting to be executed. An advantage of preemptive multitasking is the operating system regains control if one program stops operating properly.

A *multiuser* operating system enables two or more users to run programs simultaneously. Networks, midrange servers, mainframes, and supercomputers allow hundreds to thousands of users to connect at the same time, and thus are multiuser.

A *multiprocessing* operating system supports two or more processors running programs at the same time. Multiprocessing works in a manner similar to parallel processing, which was discussed in Chapter 4. Multiprocessing involves the coordinated processing of programs by more than one processor. As with parallel processing, multiprocessing increases a computer's processing speed.

A computer with separate processors also can serve as a fault-tolerant computer. A *fault-tolerant computer* continues to operate when one of its components fails, ensuring that no data is lost. Fault-tolerant computers have duplicate components such as processors, memory, and disk drives. If any one of these components fails, the computer switches to the duplicate component and continues to operate. Airline reservation systems, communications networks, automated teller machines, and other systems that must be operational at all times use fault-tolerant computers.

Managing Memory

The purpose of **memory management** is to optimize the use of random access memory (RAM). As discussed in Chapter 4, RAM consists of one or more chips on the motherboard that hold items such as data and instructions while the processor interprets and executes them. The operating system allocates, or assigns, data and instructions to an area of memory while they are being processed. Then, it carefully monitors the contents of memory. Finally, the operating system releases these items from being monitored in memory when the processor no longer requires them.

If you are working on multiple programs simultaneously, it is possible to run out of RAM. For example, assume an operating system requires 128 MB of RAM, a Web browser — 32 MB of RAM, a business software suite — 40 MB of RAM, and a photo editing program — 32 MB of RAM. With all these programs running simultaneously, the total RAM required would be 232 MB of RAM (128 + 32 + 40 + 32). If the computer has only 128 MB of RAM, the operating system may have to use virtual memory to solve the problem.

With **virtual memory**, the operating system allocates a portion of a storage medium, usually the hard disk, to function as additional RAM (Figure 8-8). As you interact with a program, part of it may be in physical RAM, while the rest of the program is on the hard disk as virtual memory. Because virtual memory is slower than RAM, users may notice the computer slowing down while it uses virtual memory.

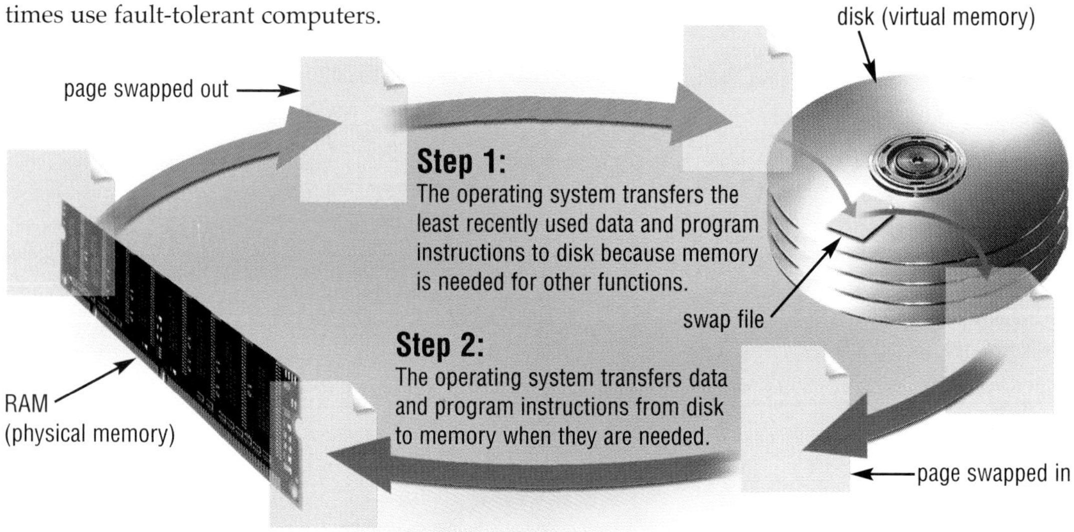

FIGURE 8-8 With virtual memory (VM), the operating system allocates a portion of a storage medium, usually the hard disk, to function as additional RAM.

The area of the hard disk used for virtual memory is called a *swap file* because it swaps (exchanges) data, information, and instructions between memory and storage. A *page* is the amount of data and program instructions that can swap at a given time. The technique of swapping items between memory and storage, called *paging*, is a time-consuming process for the computer.

When an operating system spends much of its time paging, instead of executing application software, it is said to be *thrashing*. If application software, such as a Web browser, has stopped responding and the hard disk's LED blinks repeatedly, the operating system probably is thrashing.

FAQ 8-2

How can I stop a computer from thrashing?

Try to quit the program that stopped responding. If the computer does not respond and continues to thrash, do a warm boot. When the computer reboots, check whether the available hard disk space is less than 200 MB. If it is, remove unnecessary files from the hard disk and if necessary uninstall seldom used programs. Defragment the hard disk (discussed later in this chapter). If thrashing continues to occur, you may need to install more RAM in the computer.

For more information about optimizing memory, visit the Discovering Computers 2005 FAQ Web page (**scsite.com/dc2005/faq**). Click Optimizing Memory below Chapter 8.

Scheduling Jobs

The operating system determines the order in which jobs are processed. A **job** is an operation the processor manages. Jobs include receiving data from an input device, processing instructions, sending information to an output device, and transferring items from storage to memory and from memory to storage.

A mulituser operating system does not always process jobs on a first-come, first-served basis. Sometimes, one user may have a higher priority than other users. In this case, the operating system adjusts the schedule of jobs.

Sometimes, a device already may be busy processing one job when it receives a second job. This occurs because the processor operates at a much faster rate of speed than peripheral devices. For example, if the processor sends five print jobs to a printer, the printer can print only one document at a time.

While waiting for devices to become idle, the operating system places items in buffers. A **buffer** is a segment of memory or storage in which items are placed while waiting to be transferred from an input device or to an output device.

The operating system commonly uses buffers with print jobs. This process, called **spooling**, sends print jobs to a buffer instead of sending them immediately to the printer. The buffer holds the information waiting to print while the printer prints from the buffer at its own rate of speed. By spooling print jobs to a buffer, the processor can continue interpreting and executing instructions while the printer prints. This allows users to work on the computer for other tasks while a printer is printing. Multiple print jobs line up in a **queue** (pronounced Q) within the buffer. A program, called a *print spooler*, intercepts print jobs from the operating system and places them in the queue (Figure 8-9).

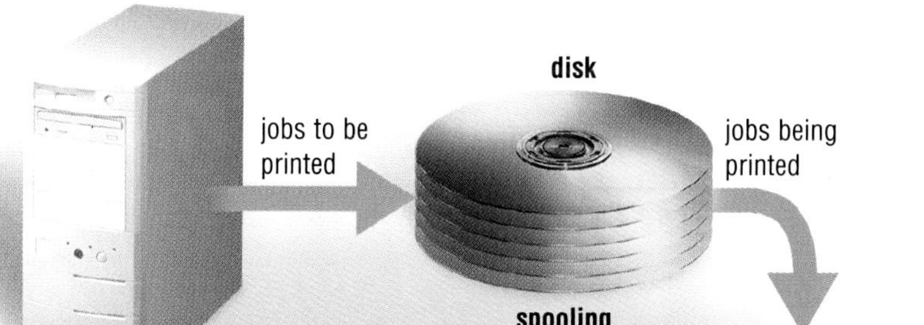

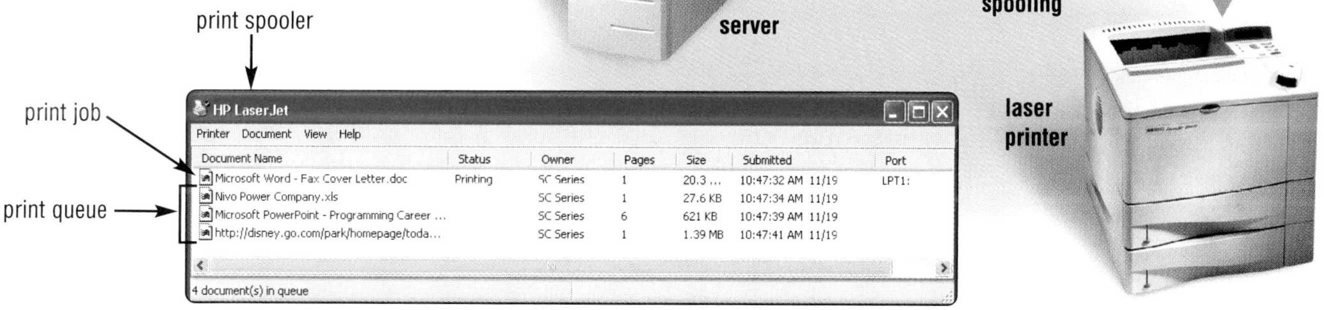

FIGURE 8-9 Spooling increases both processor and printer efficiency by placing print jobs in a buffer on disk before they are printed. This figure illustrates three jobs in the queue and one job printing.

Configuring Devices

A **driver**, short for *device driver*, is a small program that tells the operating system how to communicate with a specific device. Each device on a computer, such as the mouse, keyboard, monitor, printer, card reader/writer, and scanner, has its own specialized set of commands and thus requires its own specific driver. When you boot a computer, the operating system loads each device's driver. These devices will not function without their correct drivers.

If you attach a new device to a computer, such as a printer or scanner, its driver must be installed before you can use the device. Windows XP provides a wizard to guide users through the installation steps. Figure 8-10 shows how to install a driver for a printer. You follow the same general steps to install drivers for any type of hardware. For many devices, the computer's operating system already may include the necessary drivers. If it does not, you can install the drivers from the CD or disk provided with the purchased device.

FIGURE 8-10 HOW TO INSTALL DRIVERS FOR NEW HARDWARE IN WINDOWS XP

Step 1:
Open the Control Panel window. Point to the Printers and Other Hardware link.

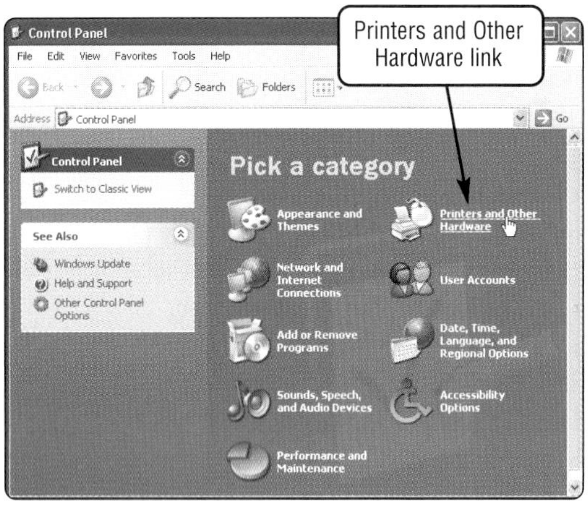

Step 2:
Click the Printers and Other Hardware link. Point to the Add a printer link.

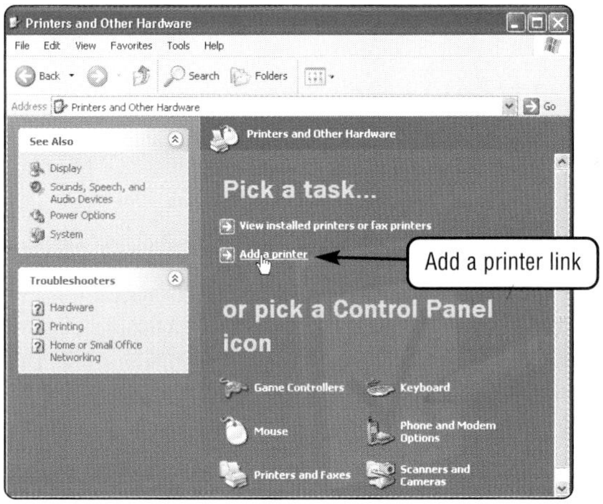

Step 3:
Click the Add a printer link. Follow the on-screen instructions.

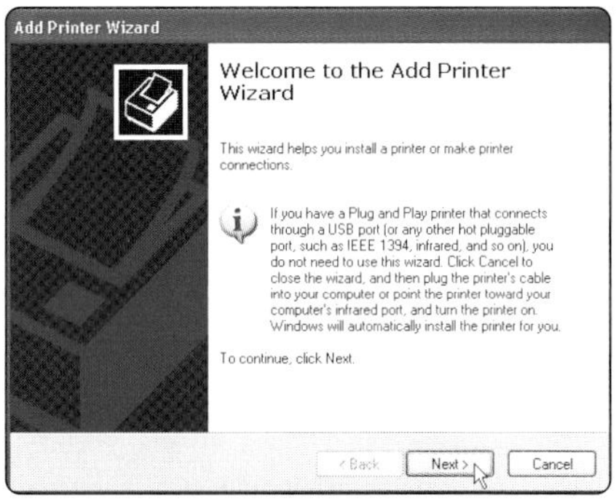

Step 4:
The Add Printer Wizard searches for Plug and Play printers on your computer. If it finds any such printers, it installs them.

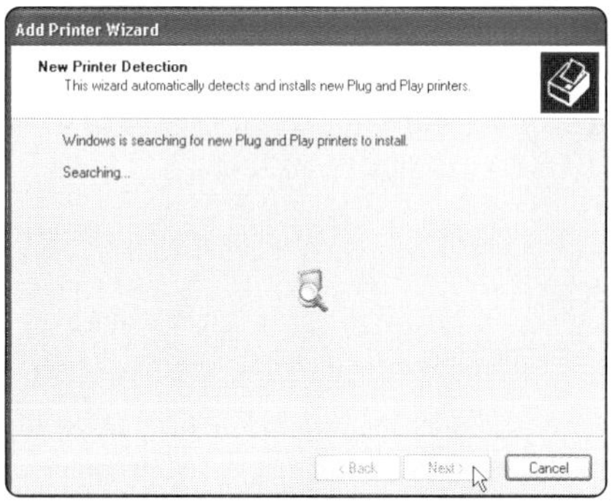

Step 5:
If the Add Printer Wizard cannot find any Plug and Play printers, you can select the type of printer you want to install. An on-screen prompt may ask you to insert the floppy disk, CD-ROM, or DVD-ROM that contains the necessary driver files to complete the installation of the printer.

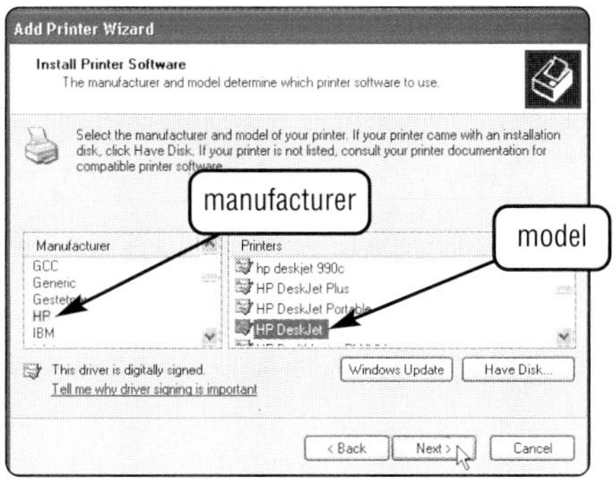

In the past, installing a new hardware device often required setting switches and other elements on the motherboard. Today, installation is easier because most devices and operating systems support Plug and Play. As discussed in Chapter 4, **Plug and Play** means the operating system automatically configures new devices as you install them. Specifically, it assists you in the device's installation by loading the necessary drivers automatically and checking for conflicts with other devices. With Plug and Play, a user plugs in a device, turns on the computer, and then uses (plays) the device without having to configure the system manually.

When installing devices in the past, users sometimes needed to tell the operating system which interrupt request line the device should use for communications. An *interrupt request line* (*IRQ*) is a communications line between a device and the processor. Most computers have 16 IRQs.

With Plug and Play, the operating system determines an appropriate IRQ to use for these communications. If the operating system uses an IRQ that already is assigned to another device, an IRQ conflict may occur and the computer may not work properly. If an IRQ conflict occurs, you will have to obtain the correct IRQ for the device. This information typically is located in the installation directions that accompany the device.

Establishing an Internet Connection

Operating systems typically provide a means to establish Internet connections. For example, Windows XP includes a New Connection Wizard that guides users through the process of setting up a connection between a computer and an Internet service provider (Figure 8-11).

FIGURE 8-11 To display the New Connection Wizard in Windows XP, click the Start button, point to All Programs, point to Accessories, point to Communications, and then click New Connection Wizard on the Communications submenu.

Some operating systems also include a Web browser and an e-mail program, enabling you to begin using the Web and communicate with others as soon as you set up the Internet connections. This feature eliminates the expense of purchasing extra software and saves the time of installing additional programs to use Internet services. Read Issue 8-1 for a related discussion.

WEB LINK 8-2

Plug and Play

Visit the Discovering Computers 2005 WEB LINK page (**scsite.com/dc2005/weblink**). Click Plug and Play below Chapter 8.

FAQ 8-3

What if I do not have the driver for a device?

When reinstalling an operating system, you may have to supply a device's driver. If you do not have the original driver disk, visit the manufacturer's Web site. Most post drivers for download at no cost, or they may suggest a similar driver that will work. If you do not have Internet access, call the manufacturer and request a new disk via the postal service.

For more information about drivers, visit the Discovering Computers 2005 FAQ Web page (**scsite.com/dc2005/faq**). Click Drivers below Chapter 8.

ISSUE 8-1

Should Manufacturers Bundle Applications?

Microsoft includes a Web browser, a paint program, a word processing program, plug-ins, and other applications and features with its Windows operating system. Apple bundles QuickTime, CD burning software, and other programs and features into Mac OS X. Manufacturers say that combining additional features and programs with their operating systems is a convenience for consumers and sometimes integral to the operating systems' performance. Yet, because other developers create programs and features similar to those included with operating systems, some consumer advocates argue that bundling applications is unfair and leads to monopolies. (Microsoft's bundling of its Web browser with its Windows operating system was the proximate cause of an antitrust action against the software giant.) Critics also insist that bundling applications with an operating system forces consumers to pay for programs they may never use. Is bundling applications with an operating system fair, or is it a monopolistic practice? Why? Who should decide what an operating system should include? The manufacturer? The government? The marketplace? Why?

For more information about bundling applications, visit the Discovering Computers 2005 Issues Web page (**scsite.com/dc2005/issues**). Click Issue #1 below Chapter 8.

Monitoring Performance

Operating systems typically contain a performance monitor. A **performance monitor** is a program that assesses and reports information about various computer resources and devices (Figure 8-12). For example, users can monitor the processor, disks, memory, and network usage. A performance monitor also can check the number of reads and writes to a disk.

The information in performance reports helps users identify a problem with resources so they can try to resolve any problems. If your computer is running extremely slow, for example, the performance monitor may determine that the computer's memory is being used to its maximum. Thus, you might consider installing additional memory in the computer.

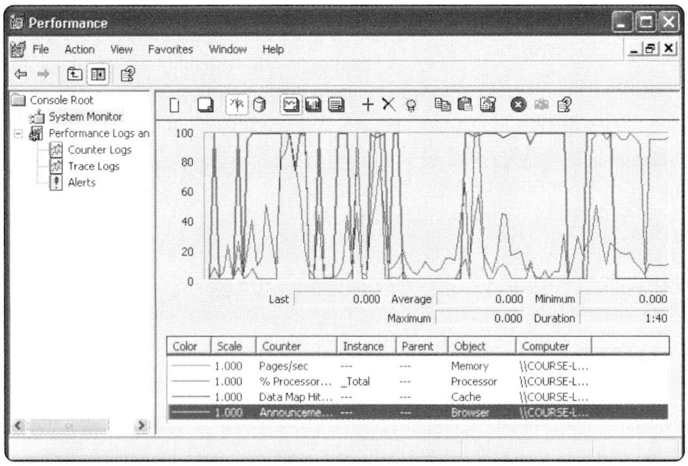

FIGURE 8-12 A performance monitor is a program that assesses and reports information about various system resources and devices. The System Monitor above is tracking the kernel usage and the amount of unused physical memory.

Providing File Management and Other Utilities

Operating systems often provide users with the capability of managing files, viewing graphics files, uninstalling programs, scanning disks, defragmenting disks, diagnosing problems, backing up files and disks, and setting up screen savers. A later section in the chapter discusses these utilities in depth.

Controlling a Network

Some operating systems are network operating systems. A **network operating system**, or *network OS*, is an operating system that organizes and coordinates how multiple users access and share resources on a network. Resources include hardware, software, data, and information. For example, a network OS allows multiple users to share a printer, Internet access, files, and programs.

Some operating systems have network features built into them. In other cases, the network OS is a set of programs separate from the operating system on the client computers that access the network. When not connected to the network, the client computers use their own operating system. When connected to the network, the network OS may assume some of the operating system functions.

The *network administrator*, the person overseeing network operations, uses the network OS to add and remove users, computers, and other devices to and from the network. The network administrator also uses the network operating system to install software and administer network security.

Administering Security

The network administrator uses the network OS to establish permissions to resources. These permissions define who can access certain resources and when they can access those resources.

For each user, the network administrator establishes a user account, which enables a user to access, or **log on** to, a computer or a network. Each user account typically consists of a user name and password (Figure 8-13). A **user name**, or **user ID**, is a unique combination of characters, such as letters of the alphabet or numbers, that identifies one specific user. Many users select a combination of their first and last names as their user name. A user named Katy Bollini might choose K Bollini as her user name.

FIGURE 8-13 Most multiuser operating systems allow each user to log on, which is the process of entering a user name and password into the computer.

A **password** is a private combination of characters associated with the user name that allows access to certain computer resources. Some operating systems allow the network administrator to assign passwords to files and commands, restricting access to only authorized users. Read Issue 8-2 for a related discussion.

ISSUE 8-2

Would You Share Your Password?

If your school uses a network, you probably must enter a user name and password to access the system. User names and passwords, however, do not guarantee network security. A recent survey by the Computer Security Institute reported that 70 percent of the organizations polled said that their network defenses had been breached. Sometimes, people outside the organization invade a network by guessing the necessary password. But in a school environment, unauthorized access often results from students sharing their passwords with nonstudents. Although students who share passwords usually believe that it is no worse than sharing a locker combination, sharing passwords with unauthorized users can drain network resources and even provide access to private information. Should sharing a password be considered a crime? Why or why not? What can be done to eliminate password sharing? One security expert suggests that password sharing could be reduced by mandating that passwords be changed every 30 to 60 days. Is this a good idea? Why?

For more information about sharing passwords, visit the Discovering Computers 2005 Issues Web page (**scsite.com/dc2005/issues**). Click Issue #2 below Chapter 8.

To prevent unauthorized users from accessing computer resources, keep your password confidential. While entering your password, most computers hide the actual password characters by displaying some other characters, such as asterisks (*) or dots. After entering a user name and password, the operating system compares the user's entry with a list of authorized user names and passwords. If the entry matches the user name and password kept on file, the operating system grants the user access. If the entry does not match, the operating system denies access to the user.

The operating system records successful and unsuccessful logon attempts in a file. This allows the network administrator to review who is using or attempting to use the computer. Network administrators also use these files to monitor computer usage.

To protect sensitive data and information further as it travels over the network, a network operating system often encrypts it. *Encryption* is the process of encoding data and information into an unreadable form. Network administrators usually set up a network to encrypt data as it travels over the network to prevent unauthorized users from reading the data. When an authorized user attempts to read the data, it automatically is decrypted, or converted back into a readable form.

QUIZ YOURSELF 8-1

To check your knowledge of types of system software and features common to most operating systems, visit the Discovering Computers 2005 Quiz Yourself Web page (**scsite.com/dc2005/quiz**). Click Objectives 1 – 4 below Chapter 8.

OPERATING SYSTEM UTILITY PROGRAMS

A **utility program**, also called a **utility**, is a type of system software that allows a user to perform maintenance-type tasks, usually related to managing a computer, its devices, or its programs. Most operating systems include several utility programs (Figure 8-14).

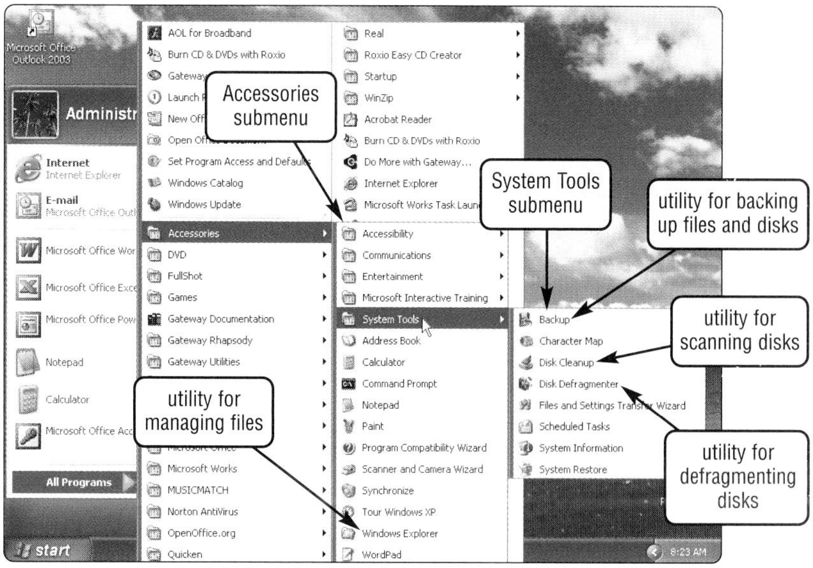

FIGURE 8-14 Many utilities available in Windows XP are accessible through the Accessories and System Tools submenus.

Users often buy stand-alone utilities, however, because they offer improvements over those included with the operating system.

Utility programs included with most operating systems provide the following functions: managing files, viewing graphics files, uninstalling programs, scanning disks, defragmenting disks, diagnosing problems, backing up files and disks, and setting up screen savers. The following paragraphs briefly discuss each of these utilities.

File Manager

A **file manager** is a utility that performs functions related to file and disk management. Windows XP includes a file manager called *Windows Explorer*. Some of the file and disk management functions that a file manager performs are formatting and copying disks; displaying a list of files on a storage medium (Figure 8-15); checking the amount of used or free space on a storage medium; organizing, copying, renaming, deleting, moving, and sorting files; and creating shortcuts. A *shortcut* is an icon on the desktop that provides a user with immediate access to a program or file.

Formatting is the process of preparing a disk for reading and writing. Most floppy and hard disk manufacturers preformat their disks. If you must format a floppy disk, do so by issuing the operating system's format command.

Various operating systems format disks differently. Thus, you may not be able to use a disk formatted in one operating system in a computer that has a different operating system. For example, you cannot use a Mac OS X floppy disk in a computer that uses Windows XP — without special hardware and software. For a technical discussion about formatting, read the High-Tech Talk article on page 377 in Chapter 7.

Image Viewer

An **image viewer** is a utility that allows users to display and copy the contents of a graphics file. With an image viewer, users can see images without having to open them in a paint or image editing program. Windows XP includes an image viewer called *Windows Picture and Fax Viewer* (Figure 8-16). To display a file in this image viewer, simply double-click the thumbnail of the image in the file manager, in this case, Windows Explorer shown in Figure 8-15.

Uninstaller

An **uninstaller** is a utility that removes a program, as well as any associated entries in the system files. In Windows XP, the uninstaller is available through the Add/Remove Programs command in the Control Panel.

When you install an application, the operating system records the information it uses to run the software in the system files. The uninstaller deletes files and folders from the hard disk, as well as removes program entries from the system files.

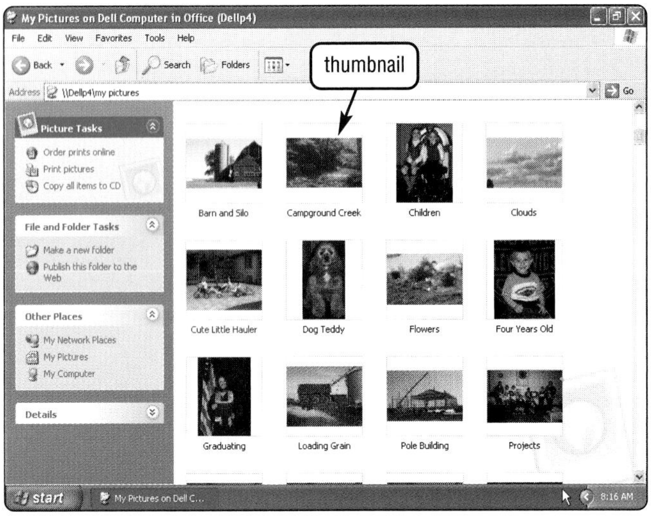

FIGURE 8-15 With Windows Explorer, which is the file manager included with Windows XP, users can display a list of graphics files on a disk. In this case, thumbnails of the files are displayed.

FIGURE 8-16 Windows Picture and Fax Viewer allows users to see the contents of a graphics file.

FAQ 8-4

Can I use the file manager to delete a program?

No! If you remove software from a computer by deleting the files and folders associated with the program without running the uninstaller, the system file entries are not updated. This may cause the operating system to display error messages when you start the computer. If the program has an uninstaller, always use it to remove software.

For more information about uninstalling programs, visit the Discovering Computers 2005 FAQ Web page (**scsite.com/dc2005/faq**). Click Uninstalling Programs below Chapter 8.

Disk Scanner

A **disk scanner** is a utility that (1) detects and corrects both physical and logical problems on a hard disk or floppy disk and (2) searches for and removes unnecessary files. A physical disk problem is a problem with the media such as a scratch on the surface of the disk. A logical disk problem is a problem with the data, such as a corrupt file. Windows XP includes two disk scanner utilities. One detects problems and the other searches for and removes unnecessary files such as temporary files (Figure 8-17).

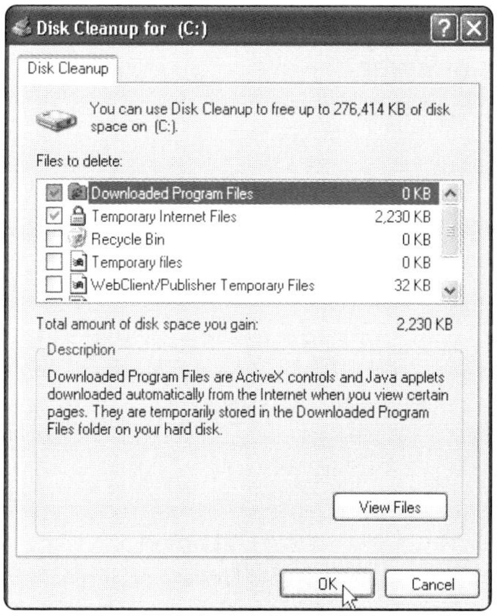

FIGURE 8-17 Disk Cleanup searches for and removes unnecessary files.

Disk Defragmenter

A **disk defragmenter** is a utility that reorganizes the files and unused space on a computer's hard disk so the operating system accesses data more quickly and programs run faster. When an operating system stores data on a disk, it places the data in the first available sector on the disk. It attempts to place data in sectors that are contiguous (next to each other), but this is not always possible. When the contents of a file are scattered across two or more noncontiguous sectors, the file is *fragmented*.

Fragmentation slows down disk access and thus the performance of the entire computer. **Defragmenting** the disk, or reorganizing it, so the files are stored in contiguous sectors, solves this problem (Figure 8-18). Windows XP includes a disk defragmenter, called Disk Defragmenter, available on the System Tools submenu. Read Apply It 8-2 for more information.

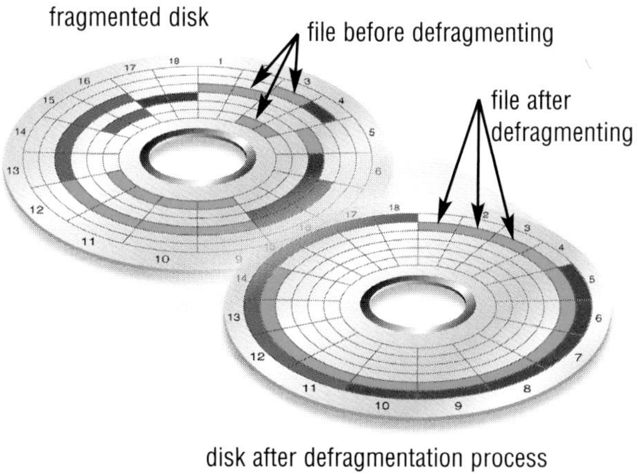

FIGURE 8-18 A fragmented disk has many files stored in noncontiguous sectors. Defragmenting reorganizes the files, so they are located in contiguous sectors, which speeds access time.

APPLY IT 8-2

Tune Up Your Computer for Optimum Performance

Your toolbox likely contains a hammer, pliers, screwdrivers, a measuring tape, and other gadgets. Having the right tool can help you save money and time while making home improvements and repairs. Your computer also has a toolbox containing a hard disk defragmenter, scanner, compressor, uninstaller, and other programs. These system tools can help your computer run quickly and smoothly.

While you might keep your toolbox in your garage or the trunk of your car, Windows XP keeps some of its tools in the System Tools subfolder of the Accessories folder. This folder is on the All Programs submenu on the Start menu. One of these tools is Disk Defragmenter, which rearranges files and unused space on your hard disk. You should run Disk Defragmenter monthly and more frequently if you add and delete files from the hard disk regularly.

You already may be familiar with the ScanDisk tool if you have turned off your computer without shutting down Windows properly. The next time you start your computer ScanDisk may check the hard disk for errors and then repair damaged areas or delete unnecessary files.

Keep your software current by visiting the Windows Update Web site regularly to download enhancements known as fixes, patches, service packs, or security rollup packages. You also can have Microsoft download the updates to your computer automatically.

For more information about system tools, visit the Discovering Computers 2005 Apply It Web page (**scsite.com/dc2005/apply**). Click Apply It #2 below Chapter 8.

Diagnostic Utility

A **diagnostic utility** compiles technical information about your computer's hardware and certain system software programs and then prepares a report outlining any identified problems. For example, Windows XP includes the diagnostic utility, *Dr. Watson*, which diagnoses problems as well as suggests courses of action (Figure 8-19). Information in the report assists technical support staff in remedying any problems.

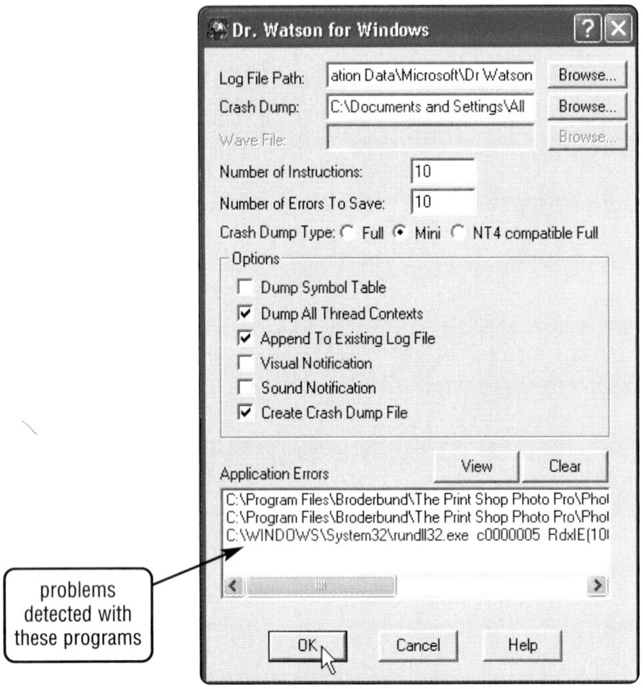

FIGURE 8-19 Dr. Watson is a diagnostic utility included with Windows.

Backup Utility

A **backup utility** allows users to copy, or *back up*, selected files or an entire hard disk onto another disk or tape. During the backup process, the backup utility monitors progress and alerts you if it needs additional disks or tapes. Many backup programs *compress*, or shrink the size of, files during the backup process. By compressing the files, the backup program requires less storage space for the backup files than for the original files.

Because they are compressed, you usually cannot use backup files in their backed up form. In the event you need to use a backup file, a **restore program** reverses the process and returns backed up files to their original form. Backup utilities include restore programs.

You should back up files and disks regularly in the event your originals are lost, damaged, or destroyed. Windows XP includes a backup utility (Figure 8-20). Instead of backing up to a local disk storage device, some users opt to back up their files to an Internet hard drive. As described in Chapter 7, an Internet hard drive is a service on the Web that provides online storage for a fee to computer users.

WEB LINK 8-3

Screen Savers

Visit the Discovering Computers 2005 WEB LINK page (**scsite.com/dc2005/weblink**). Click Screen Savers below Chapter 8.

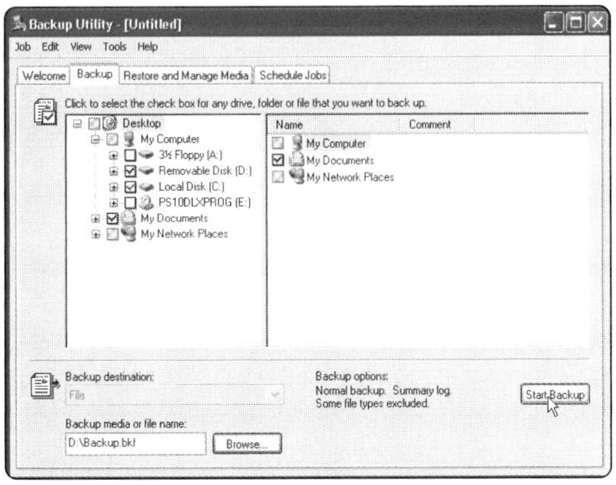

FIGURE 8-20 A backup utility allows users to copy files or an entire hard disk to another disk or tape.

Screen Saver

A **screen saver** is a utility that causes a monitor's screen to display a moving image or blank screen if no keyboard or mouse activity occurs for a specified time (Figure 8-21). When you press a key on the keyboard or move the mouse, the screen saver disappears and the screen returns to the previous state.

FIGURE 8-21 A Windows XP screen saver.

Screen savers originally were developed to prevent a problem called *ghosting*, in which images could be permanently etched on a monitor's screen. Although ghosting is not as severe of a problem with today's monitors, manufacturers continue to recommend that users install screen savers for this reason. Screen savers also are popular for security, business, and entertainment purposes. To secure a computer, users configure their screen saver to require a password to deactivate. In addition to those included with the operating system, many screen savers are available for a minimal fee in stores and on the Web.

TYPES OF OPERATING SYSTEMS

Many of the first operating systems were device dependent and proprietary. A *device-dependent* program is one that runs only on a specific type or make of computer. *Proprietary software* is privately owned and limited to a specific vendor or computer model. Historically, when manufacturers introduced a new computer or model, they often produced an improved and different proprietary operating system. Problems arose when a user wanted to switch computer models or manufacturers. The user's application software often would not work on the new computer because the programs were designed to work with a specific operating system.

Some operating systems still are device dependent. The trend today, however, is toward *device-independent* operating systems that run on computers provided by a variety of manufacturers. The advantage of device-independent operating systems is you can retain existing application software and data files even if you change computer models or vendors. This feature usually represents a sizable savings in time and money.

When you purchase a new computer, it typically has an operating system preinstalled (read Issue 8-3 for a related discussion). As new versions of the operating system are released, users upgrade their existing computers to incorporate features of the new version. An upgrade usually costs less than purchasing the entire operating system.

New versions of an operating system usually are downward compatible. That is, they recognize and work with application software written for an earlier version of the operating system (or platform). The application software, by contrast, is said to be upward compatible, meaning it will run on new versions of the operating system.

The three basic categories of operating systems that exist today are stand-alone, network, and embedded. The table in Figure 8-22 lists names of operating systems in each category. The following pages discuss the operating systems listed in the table.

CATEGORIES OF OPERATING SYSTEMS

Category	Operating System Name
Stand-alone	• DOS • Early Windows versions (Windows 3.x, Windows 95, Windows NT Workstation, Windows 98, Windows 2000 Professional, Windows Millennium Edition) • Windows XP • Mac OS X • UNIX • Linux
Network	• NetWare • Early Windows Server versions (Windows NT Server, Windows 2000 Server) • Windows Server 2003 • UNIX • Linux • Solaris
Embedded	• Windows CE .NET • Windows Mobile 2003 • Palm OS • Symbian OS

FIGURE 8-22 Examples of stand-alone, network, and embedded operating systems. Some stand-alone operating systems include the capability of configuring small home or office networks.

ISSUE 8-3

Would You Like an Operating System with That?

When Windows 98 was introduced, one retailer offered customers the chance to buy a limited number of new computers, with Windows 98 installed, for $98. The promotion worked. A buyer waited in line 11 hours for a chance to buy a discounted computer with the new operating system. When asked if he would have come out simply for Windows 98, he replied, "Not a chance." Most computers you buy come with an operating system and applications installed on the hard disk. Some buyers consider this a convenience, but others feel it forces them to accept an operating system, and other programs, they may not want. These buyers argue that merchants should sell hardware without installed software so consumers can, for example, install Linux instead of Windows if that is what they want. Should computers be sold without installed operating systems and application programs? Why or why not? Should pricing for hardware be separate from pricing for software? Why? Should computers without installed software cost more, or less, than computers with installed software? Why?

For more information about preinstalled operating systems, visit the Discovering Computers 2005 Issues Web page (**scsite.com/dc2005/issues**). Click Issue #3 below Chapter 8.

STAND-ALONE OPERATING SYSTEMS

A **stand-alone operating system** is a complete operating system that works on a desktop computer, notebook computer, or mobile computing device. Some stand-alone operating systems are called *client operating systems* because they also work in conjunction with a network operating system. Client operating systems can operate with or without a network. Other stand-alone operating systems include networking capabilities, allowing the home and small business user to set up a small network.

Examples of stand-alone operating systems are DOS, Windows XP, Mac OS X, UNIX, and Linux. The following paragraphs briefly discuss these operating systems.

DOS

The term **DOS** (*Disk Operating System*) refers to several single user operating systems developed in the early 1980s by Microsoft for personal computers. The two more widely used versions of DOS were PC-DOS and MS-DOS. The functionality of these two operating systems was essentially the same.

DOS used a command-line interface when Microsoft first developed it. Later versions included both command-line and menu-driven user interfaces. At its peak, DOS was a widely used operating system, with an estimated 70 million computers running it. DOS hardly is used today because it does not offer a graphical user interface and it cannot take full advantage of modern 32-bit personal computer processors.

Windows XP

In the mid-1980s, Microsoft developed its first version of Windows, which provided a graphical user interface (GUI). Since then, Microsoft has continually updated its Windows operating system, incorporating innovative features and functions with each new version (Figure 8-23). **Windows XP** is Microsoft's fastest, most reliable Windows operating system yet, providing quicker startup, better performance, and a new, simplified visual look (Figure 8-24).

Windows XP is available in five editions: Home Edition, Professional, Tablet PC Edition, Media Center Edition, and 64-bit Edition. The table in Figure 8-25 highlights features in all editions of Windows XP; page 422 identifies the differences. Read Looking Ahead 8-1 for a look at the next generation of the Windows operating system.

COMPARISON OF WINDOWS VERSIONS

Windows Version	Year Released	Highlights
Windows 3.x	1990	• Provided a GUI • An operating environment only — worked in combination with DOS
Windows NT 3.1	1993	• Client OS that connected to a Windows NT Advanced Server • Interface similar to Windows 3.x
Windows 95	1995	• True multitasking operating system • Improved GUI • Included support for networking, Plug and Play technology, longer file names, and e-mail
Windows NT Workstation 4.0	1996	• Client OS that connected to a Windows NT Server • Interface similar to Windows 95 • Network integration
Windows 98	1998	• Upgrade to Windows 95 • More integrated with the Internet; included *Internet Explorer* (a Web browser) • Faster system startup and shutdown, better file management, support for multimedia technologies (e.g., DVDs), and USB connectivity
Windows Millennium Edition	2000	• Upgrade to Windows 98 • Designed for the home user who wanted music playing, video editing, and networking capabilities
Windows 2000 Professional	2000	• Upgrade to Windows NT Workstation 4.0 • Complete multitasking client OS designed for business personal computers • Certified device drivers, faster performance, adaptive Start menu, image viewer, enhanced for mobile users
Windows XP	2001	• Upgrade to Windows Millennium Edition called Windows XP Home Edition • Upgrade to Windows 2000 Professional called Windows XP Professional • Windows XP Tablet PC Edition designed for Tablet PC users • Windows XP Media Center Edition designed for PCs used for home entertainment • Windows XP 64-bit Edition designed for workstations with an Itanium 2 processor • Improved interface and increased performance in all editions

FIGURE 8-23 Microsoft had many versions of Windows before Windows XP.

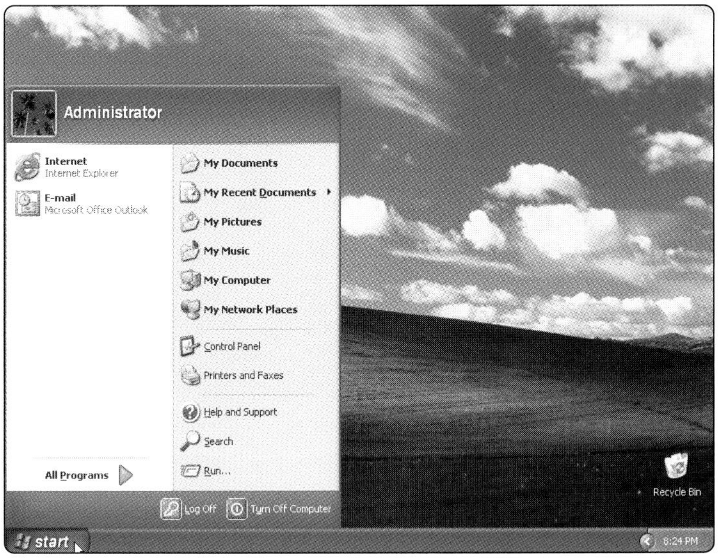

FIGURE 8-24 Windows XP, with its simplified look, is the fastest and most reliable Windows operating system to date.

WINDOWS XP FEATURES

Appearance and Performance
- New look and feel to the user interface
- Increased reliability and security
- Increased performance to run programs faster
- Redesigned Start menu and Control Panel
- Minimized clutter on the taskbar with multiple open windows organized into groups
- Crisper display of images on LCD screens with ClearType

Administration
- Improved interface for creating multiple user accounts and switching among accounts
- Enhanced system recovery from failure with System Restore, without causing loss of data
- Easy-to-install home or small office network
- Internet Connection Firewall to protect a home or small office network from hackers
- Improved wireless network support
- Improved battery-life management for notebook computers

Help and Support
- Comprehensive Help and Support system
- Remote Assistance that allows another person (with your permission) to control your computer remotely to demonstrate a process or solve a problem

Communications and the Web
- New version of Windows Messenger to send instant messages; communicate in real time using text, graphics, video, and voice to other online users; and a whiteboard available for use in video conferences
- New version of Internet Explorer with improved look
- Remote Desktop to access data and applications on your desktop computer while away from the computer using another Windows-based computer with a network or Internet connection
- Publish, store, and share text, graphics, photographs, and other items on the Web

Digital Media
- New version of Windows Media Player to listen to more than 3,000 Internet radio stations, play MP3 and Microsoft's WMA music format, copy music and data onto blank CDs, and watch DVD movies
- New version of Movie Maker
- Transfer images from a digital camera or scanner to your computer

FIGURE 8-25 Some features of Windows XP.

LOOKING AHEAD 8-1

Secure Computing – Heart of Windows Upgrade

You lock your doors, turn on porch lights after dark, and park in well-lit areas in attempts to implement safety. Microsoft, too, is exercising safety measures by developing a security initiative, Next-Generation Secure Computing Base for Windows.

Microsoft Chairman and Chief Software Architect Bill Gates promises this safety measure will be used for both hardware and software. The Next-Generation Secure Computing Base for Windows will help keep passwords secure and encrypt keystrokes and video display signals transmitted through wires. The company is collaborating with Intel and Advanced Micro Devices (AMD) to develop these security measures.

Most likely, the Next-Generation Secure Computing Base for Windows will be featured in the next version of the Windows operating system, currently code-named *Longhorn*. Overall, this new version is being developed as a consumer-friendly product with a completely object-oriented interface. When the software is released in 2006 or later, it will recognize users and tailor the systems for their specific needs by storing personal data in encrypted folders. It also will filter junk e-mail messages and prevent viruses from attacking systems. One major feature will be incorporating DRM (Digital Rights Management) technologies, which protect files from unauthorized access.

For a look at the next generation of the Windows operating system, visit the Discovering Computers 2005 Looking Ahead Web page (**scsite.com/dc2005/looking**). Click Looking Ahead #1 below Chapter 8.

WINDOWS XP HOME EDITION *Windows XP Home Edition* is an upgrade to Windows Millennium Edition. In addition to providing the capabilities of Windows Millennium Edition, Windows XP Home Edition offers features and functionality that allow users to perform the following tasks:

- Acquire, organize, and share digital pictures
- Download, store, and play back high-quality music through Windows Media Player
- Create, edit, and share videos with Windows Movie Maker
- Easily network and share multiple home computers
- Use built-in instant messaging and video conferencing with Windows Messenger
- Recover from problems with easy-to-use tools

FIGURE 8-26 With Windows XP Tablet PC Edition, users write and save handwritten notes directly on the Tablet PC.

WINDOWS XP PROFESSIONAL *Windows XP Professional* is an upgrade to Windows 2000 Professional. In addition to providing the capabilities of Windows 2000 Professional, Windows XP Professional includes all the capabilities of Windows XP Home Edition and offers the following features and functionality:

- Greater data security through encryption of files and folders
- Remote access to a computer, its data, and its files from any other computer anywhere
- Simpler administration of groups of users or computers
- Multiple language user interface
- Support for secured wireless network access

WINDOWS XP TABLET PC EDITION *Windows XP Tablet PC Edition* includes all the features of Windows XP Professional and provides the following additional features that are designed to make users more productive while working on their Tablet PCs:

- Write on screen or issue instructions to the Tablet PC using a digital pen (Figure 8-26)
- Save documents in handwritten form or convert them into typewritten text for use in other application software
- Add handwritten notes to documents created in other application software
- Enter text and instructions by speaking into the Tablet PC
- Grab-and-go: Take the Tablet PC wherever/whenever you need the convenience of a notebook computer, but the portability of a computer the size of a spiral-bound notebook

WEB LINK 8-4

Windows XP

Visit the Discovering Computers 2005 WEB LINK page (**scsite .com/dc2005/weblink**). Click Windows XP below Chapter 8.

WINDOWS XP MEDIA CENTER EDITION *Windows XP Media Center Edition* includes all the features of Windows XP Professional and is designed for Media Center PCs. A *Media Center PC* is a home entertainment desktop personal computer that includes a mid- to high-end processor, large capacity hard disk, CD and DVD drives, a remote control, and advanced graphics and audio capabilities. These computers often use a television as their display device. Windows XP Media Center Edition offers the following media features:

- Access to digital entertainment including live and recorded television programs, movies, music, radio, and photographs via a remote control device
- Up-to-date online television program guide
- Parental control for television programs
- Capability to record television programs while away from the computer
- On-screen telephone call notification alert
- Download, play, copy, and listen to music
- Listen to Internet and FM radio stations

WINDOWS XP 64-BIT EDITION *Windows XP 64-bit Edition* is designed for workstations that use an Itanium 2 processor and offers the following features and functionality:

- Supports up to 16 GB of RAM and 16 TB of virtual memory
- Supports multiprocessing
- Integrates 64-bit and 32-bit applications

Mac OS X

Since it was released with Macintosh computers in 1984, Apple's **Macintosh operating system** has set the standard for operating system ease of use and has been the model for most of the new GUIs developed for non-Macintosh systems. The latest version, **Mac OS X**, is a multitasking operating system available only for computers manufactured by Apple (Figure 8-27).

Mac OS X includes features from previous versions of the Macintosh operating system such as large photo-quality icons, built-in networking support, e-mail, online shopping, enhanced speech recognition, CD burning, and enhanced multimedia capabilities. In addition, Mac OS X includes these features:

- Built-in AOL-compatible instant messenger
- Video and voice chats
- Filter to eliminate junk e-mail messages
- Contact lists synchronized with PDA or Bluetooth-enabled smart phone
- Web search without a browser
- Latest version of QuickTime to listen to music and view videos on the Internet
- Easy networking of computers and devices
- Conversion of handwritten text into typewritten text
- Windows network connection and shared Windows documents

FIGURE 8-27 Mac OS X is the operating system used with Apple Macintosh computers.

UNIX

UNIX (pronounced YOU-nix) is a multitasking operating system developed in the early 1970s by scientists at Bell Laboratories. Bell Labs (a subsidiary of AT&T) was prohibited from actively promoting UNIX in the commercial marketplace because of federal regulations. Bell Labs instead licensed UNIX for a low fee to numerous colleges and universities, where UNIX obtained a wide following. UNIX was implemented on many different types of computers. After deregulation of the telephone companies in the 1980s, UNIX was licensed to many hardware and software companies.

Several versions of this operating system exist, each slightly different. When programmers move application software from one UNIX version to another, they sometimes have to rewrite some of the programs. Although some versions of UNIX have a command-line interface, most versions of UNIX offer a graphical user interface (Figure 8-28).

Today, a version of UNIX is available for most computers of all sizes. Power users often work with UNIX because of its flexibility and power.

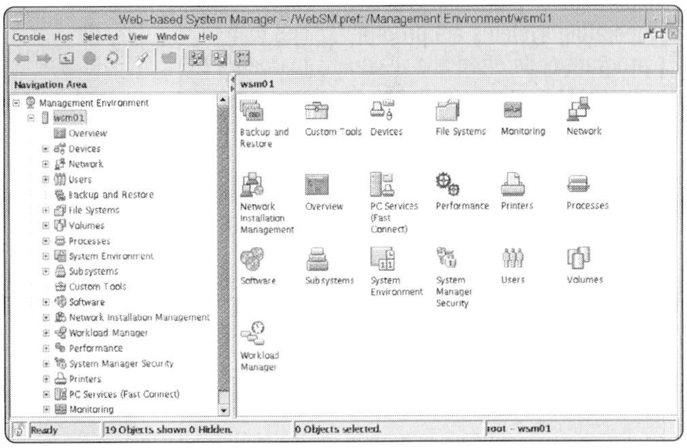

FIGURE 8-28 Some versions of UNIX have a graphical user interface.

WEB LINK 8-5

Mac OS X

Visit the Discovering Computers 2005 WEB LINK page (**scsite .com/dc2005/weblink**). Click Mac OS X below Chapter 8.

WEB LINK 8-6

UNIX

Visit the Discovering Computers 2005 WEB LINK page (**scsite .com/dc2005/weblink**). Click UNIX below Chapter 8.

Linux

Some network servers use Linux as their operating system. Thus, Linux also is a multipurpose operating system. With Linux, a network administrator can configure the network, administer security, run a Web server, and process e-mail. Clients on the network can run Linux, UNIX, or Windows. Versions of Linux include both the Netscape and Mozilla Web browsers.

Solaris

Solaris, a version of UNIX developed by Sun Microsystems, is a network operating system designed specifically for e-commerce applications. Solaris manages high-traffic accounts and incorporates security necessary for Web transactions. Client computers often use a desktop program, such as **CDE** (Common Desktop Environment) or **GNOME** desktop, that communicates with the Solaris operating system.

EMBEDDED OPERATING SYSTEMS

The operating system on most PDAs and small devices, called an **embedded operating system**, resides on a ROM chip. Popular embedded operating systems today include Windows CE .NET, Windows Mobile 2003, Palm OS, and Symbian OS. The following sections discuss these operating systems. Read Looking Ahead 8-2 for a look at the current and next generation of entertainment devices with operating systems.

WEB LINK 8-8

Windows Mobile 2003

Visit the Discovering Computers 2005 WEB LINK page (**scsite .com/dc2005/weblink**). Click Windows Mobile 2003 below Chapter 8.

Windows CE .NET

Windows CE .NET is a scaled-down Windows operating system designed for use on communications, entertainment, and mobile devices. Devices that use Windows CE .NET include Internet receivers, PDAs, smart phones, and smart displays (Figure 8-30).

Windows CE .NET is a GUI that supports color, sound, multitasking, multimedia, e-mail, Internet access, and Web browsing. Many applications, such as Word and Excel, have scaled-down versions that run with Windows CE .NET.

FIGURE 8-30 Many smart displays, which are thin desktop monitors that detach from the computer to function as portable wireless touch screens, use Windows CE .NET as their operating system to access a computer remotely that is running Windows XP Professional.

LOOKING AHEAD 8-2

Home Entertainment Systems Sound Good to Consumers

What do you get when you combine a computer with a television and stereo components? The latest in digital home entertainment systems.

Computer and consumer electronics giants like Panasonic, Sony, Hewlett-Packard, and Microsoft are developing computer-based home entertainment systems that allow users to browse the Internet, play games, and send e-mail from the comfort of a living room couch.

The key to success, according to these companies, is creating a system that works intuitively, is affordable, and yields some benefit for the user. Some systems will use the Microsoft Windows XP Media Center operating system, while others will use Linux. The operating systems will integrate a television with a built-in browser, video recorder, CD and MP3 players, radio, jukebox, digital photo viewer, and DVD player/recorder and allow users to access these components using a remote control or wireless keyboard.

Awareness in living room computing is being sparked by increasing interest in broadband Internet access, home networking, and recording and playback of television programs and music on high-density hard disk drives.

As computers invade the living room, the operating systems will serve as the core that accesses, stores, and distributes rich media content. The integrated home-entertainment systems should give users flexibility and control in their media-rich world.

For a look at the next generation of home entertainment systems, visit the Discovering Computers 2005 Looking Ahead Web page (**scsite.com/dc2005/looking**). Click Looking Ahead #2 below Chapter 8.

Devices equipped with Windows CE .NET can communicate wirelessly with computers and other devices using Bluetooth or other wireless technologies, as long as the device is equipped with the necessary communications hardware.

Windows Mobile 2003

Windows Mobile 2003 is a scaled-down operating system developed by Microsoft that works on a specific type of PDA, called a **Pocket PC** (Figure 8-31), and also on smart phones. With this operating system and a Pocket PC or smart phone, users have access to all the basic PIM (personal information manager) functions such as contact lists, schedules, tasks, calendars, and notes.

The Windows Mobile 2003 operating system, which has a Windows XP look, also provides numerous additional features that allow users to check e-mail, browse the Web, listen to music, watch a video, send and receive instant messages, record a voice message, manage finances, read an e-book, or create a word processing document or spreadsheet. Some devices with the Windows Mobile 2003 operating system also support handwriting and sometimes voice input. With the Pocket PC Phone Edition devices, users can make telephone calls and send text messages using the PDA.

FIGURE 8-31 Windows Mobile 2003 runs on Pocket PCs and many smart phones.

Palm OS

A competing operating system to Windows Mobile 2003 is *Palm OS*. Palm-powered PDAs, that use Palm OS as their operating system, include the Palm, Treo, and CLIE (Figure 8-32).

With Palm OS and a compatible PDA, users manage schedules and contacts, telephone messages, project notes, reminders, task and address lists, and important dates and appointments. Information on the PDA easily synchronizes with a personal computer using a cable or a wireless technology such as IrDA or Bluetooth. Palm OS supports handwriting recognition software, called Graffiti. Some Palm-powered PDAs allow users to connect wirelessly to the Internet; browse the Web; and send and receive e-mail messages, instant messages, and text messages.

The latest version of Palm OS includes improved security for data transmission, allows for biometric identification, and supports the use of smart cards.

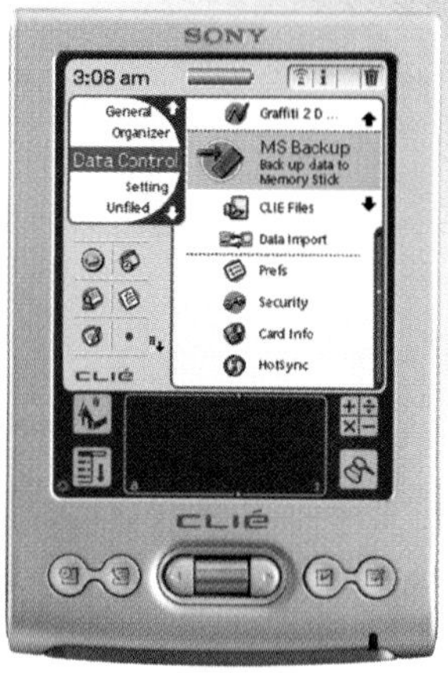

FIGURE 8-32 The Sony CLIE uses Palm OS.

WEB LINK 8-9

Palm OS

Visit the Discovering Computers 2005 WEB LINK page (**scsite .com/dc2005/weblink**). Click Palm OS below Chapter 8.

Symbian OS

Symbian OS is an open source multitasking operating system designed for smart phones (Figure 8-33). In addition to making telephone calls, users of Symbian OS can maintain contact lists; save appointments; browse the Web; and send and receive text and multimedia messages, e-mail messages, and faxes using a smart phone. Users input data by pressing keys on the keypad or keyboard, touching the screen, writing on the screen with a stylus, or speaking into the smart phone. Symbian OS allows users to communicate wirelessly using a variety of technologies including Bluetooth and IrDA.

Symbian OS has been very popular in Europe and has the support from major companies such as Motorola and Nokia. Industry analysts expect the popularity of Symbian OS in the United States to grow as increasingly more people use smart phones for data access.

FIGURE 8-33 This smart phone uses the Symbian OS.

STAND-ALONE UTILITY PROGRAMS

Although operating systems typically include some built-in utilities, many stand-alone utility programs are available for purchase. For example, you can purchase backup utilities and screen savers. These stand-alone utilities typically offer improvements over those features built-in to the operating system or provide features not included in an operating system.

Other functions provided by stand-alone utilities include protecting against viruses, securing a computer from unauthorized access, compressing files, and maintaining a personal computer. The following sections discuss each of these utilities.

Antivirus Programs

The term, computer **virus**, describes a potentially damaging computer program that affects, or infects, a computer negatively by altering the way the computer works without the user's knowledge or permission. More specifically, a computer virus is a segment of program code from some outside source that implants itself in a computer. Once the virus is in a computer, it can spread throughout and may damage your files and operating system.

Currently, more than 80,000 known virus programs exist with an estimated 6 new virus programs discovered each day. Computer viruses do not generate by chance. The programmer of a virus, known as a *virus author*, intentionally writes a virus program. Some virus authors find writing viruses a challenge. Others write virus programs to cause destruction. Writing a virus program usually requires significant programming skills.

Some viruses are harmless pranks that simply freeze a computer temporarily or display sounds or messages. The Music Bug virus, for example, instructs the computer to play a few chords of music. Other viruses destroy or corrupt data stored on the hard disk of the infected computer. If you notice any unusual changes in your computer's performance, it may be infected with a virus. Figure 8-34 outlines some common symptoms of virus infection.

WEB LINK 8-10

Antivirus Programs

Visit the Discovering Computers 2005 WEB LINK page (**scsite.com/dc2005/weblink**). Click Antivirus Programs below Chapter 8.

SIGNS OF VIRUS INFECTION

- An unusual message or image is displayed on the computer screen
- An unusual sound or music plays randomly
- The available memory is less than what should be available
- A program or file suddenly is missing
- An unknown program or file mysteriously appears
- The size of a file changes without explanation
- A file becomes corrupted
- A program or file does not work properly
- System properties change

FIGURE 8-34 Viruses attack computers in a variety of ways. This list indicates some of the more common signs of virus infection.

Viruses are just one type of malicious-logic program. A *malicious-logic program* is a program that acts without a user's knowledge and deliberately alters the computer's operations. In addition to viruses, other malicious-logic programs are worms and Trojan horses.

A **worm**, such as CodeRed, copies itself repeatedly, for example, in memory or over a network, using up system resources and possibly shutting the system down. A **Trojan horse** (named after the Greek myth) hides within or looks like a legitimate program such as a screen saver. A certain condition or action usually triggers the Trojan horse. Unlike a virus or worm, a Trojan horse does not replicate itself to other computers. For a more technical discussion about computer viruses, read the High-Tech Talk article in Chapter 3 on page 165.

To protect a computer from virus attacks, users should install an antivirus program and update it frequently. An **antivirus program** protects a computer against viruses by identifying and removing any computer viruses found in memory, on storage media, or on incoming files (Figure 8-35). Most antivirus programs also protect against worms and Trojan horses. When you purchase a new computer, it often includes antivirus software.

The two more popular antivirus programs are McAfee VirusScan and Norton AntiVirus. As an alternative to purchasing these products on CD, both McAfee and Norton offer Web-based antivirus programs. That is, during your paid subscription period, the program continuously protects the computer against viruses.

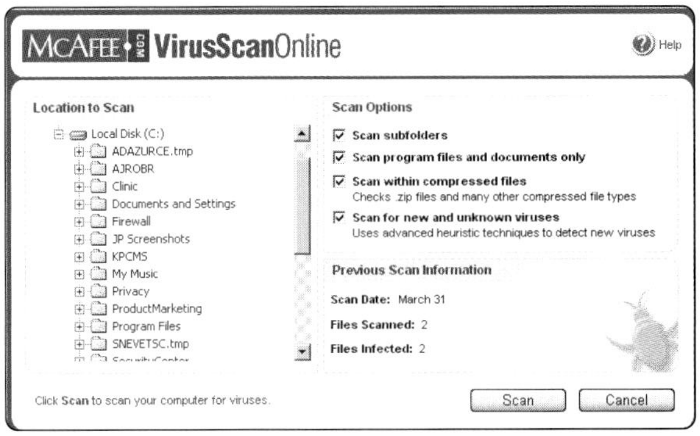

FIGURE 8-35 An antivirus program scans memory, disks, and incoming e-mail messages and attachments for viruses and attempts to remove any viruses it finds.

FAQ 8-5

Should I take any other steps to prevent virus infections on my computer?

Set up the antivirus software to scan on a regular basis. Never open an e-mail attachment unless you are expecting the attachment and it is from a trusted source. Never start a computer with a floppy disk in drive A. Set macro security in programs such as word processing and spreadsheet so you can enable or disable macros. Write-protect your recovery disk. Back up files regularly.

For more information about preventing virus infections, visit the Discovering Computers 2005 FAQ Web page (**scsite.com/dc2005/faq**). Click Preventing Virus Infections below Chapter 8.

Personal Firewalls

A **personal firewall** is a utility program that detects and protects a personal computer from unauthorized intrusions. Personal firewalls constantly monitor all transmissions to and from a computer.

When connected to the Internet, your computer is vulnerable to attacks from a hacker. A *hacker* is someone who tries to access a computer or network illegally. Users with broadband Internet connections, such as through DSL and Internet cable television, are even more susceptible than those with dial-up access because the Internet connection is always on.

Personal firewall programs often are sold as part of an Internet utility suite (Figure 8-36). In addition to including a personal firewall, Internet utility suites consist of utilities that protect against viruses, secure your data, block advertisements from Web pages, and enable parents to restrict access to certain Web sites.

WEB LINK 8-11

Personal Firewalls

Visit the Discovering Computers 2005 WEB LINK page (**scsite.com/dc2005/weblink**). Click Personal Firewalls below Chapter 8.

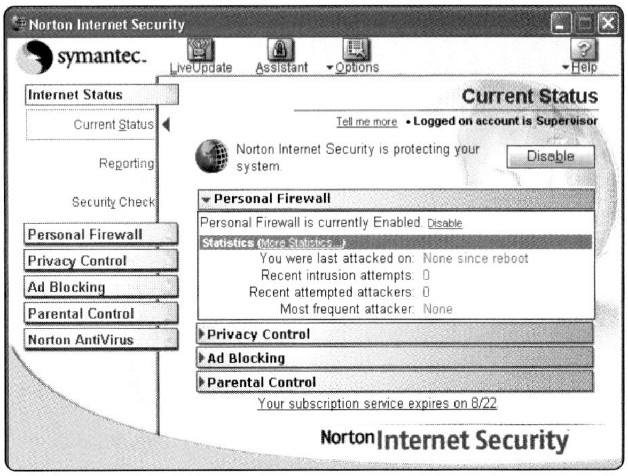

FIGURE 8-36 Internet security suites often include a variety of utilities including a personal firewall and antivirus program.

File Compression

A **file compression utility** shrinks the size of a file(s). A compressed file takes up less storage space than the original file (Figure 8-37). Compressing files frees up room on the storage media and improves system performance. Attaching a compressed file to an e-mail message, for example, reduces the time needed for file transmission. Uploading and downloading compressed files to and from the Internet reduces the file transmission time.

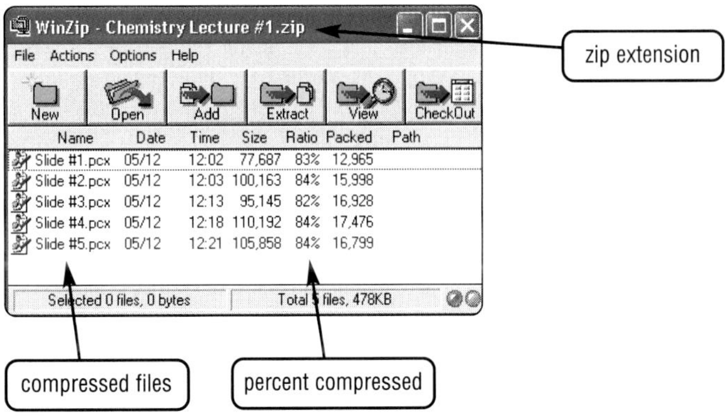

FIGURE 8-37 This file (Chemistry Lecture #1) contains five compressed files. Without being compressed, these files consume a total of 478 KB. Compressing them reduces the amount of storage by about 80 percent.

Compressed files, sometimes called **zipped files**, usually have a .zip extension. When you receive or download a compressed file, you must uncompress it. To **uncompress**, or *unzip*, a file, you restore it to its original form. Some operating systems such as Windows XP include uncompress capabilities. To compress a file, however, you need a stand-alone file compression utility. Two popular stand-alone file compression utilities are PKZIP and WinZip.

Personal Computer Maintenance

Operating systems typically include a diagnostic utility that diagnoses computer problems but does not repair them. A **personal computer maintenance utility** identifies and fixes operating system problems, detects and repairs disk problems, and includes the capability of improving a computer's performance. Additionally, some personal computer maintenance utilities continuously monitor a computer while you use it to identify and repair problems before they occur. Norton Utilities is a popular personal computer maintenance utility designed for Windows operating systems (Figure 8-38).

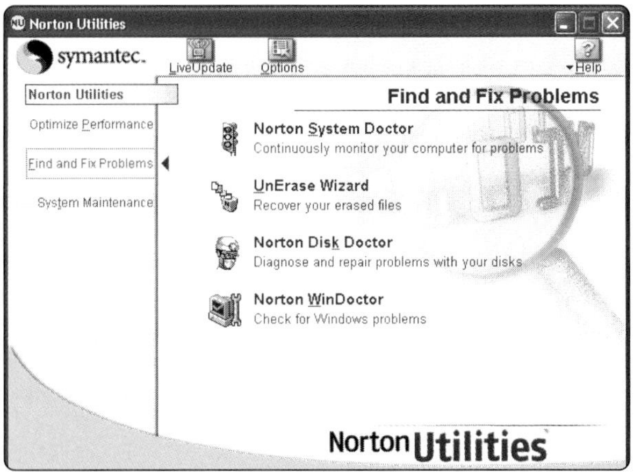

FIGURE 8-38 Norton Utilities is a popular maintenance program for users of Windows.

QUIZ YOURSELF 8-3

To check your knowledge of network operating systems, embedded operating systems, and stand-alone utility programs, visit the Discovering Computers 2005 Quiz Yourself Web page (**scsite.com/dc2005/quiz**). Click Objectives 7 – 9 below Chapter 8.

CHAPTER SUMMARY

This chapter defined an operating system and then discussed the functions common to most operating systems. Next, it introduced several utility programs commonly found in operating systems. The chapter discussed a variety of stand-alone operating systems, network operating systems, and embedded operating systems. Finally, the chapter described several stand-alone utility programs.

Systems Programmer

System software is a key component in any computer system. A *systems programmer* evaluates, installs, and maintains system software and provides technical support to the programming staff.

Systems programmers work with the programs that control computers, such as operating systems, network operating systems, and database systems. They identify current and future processing needs and then recommend the software and hardware necessary to meet those needs. In addition to selecting and installing system software, systems programmers must be able to adapt system software to the requirements of an organization, provide regular maintenance, measure system performance, determine the impact of new or updated software on the system, design and implement special software, and provide documentation. Because they are familiar with the entire system, systems programmers often help application programmers to diagnose technical problems.

Systems programmers must be thoroughly acquainted with a variety of operating systems. They must be able to think logically, pay attention to detail, work with abstract concepts, and devise solutions to complex problems. Systems programmers often work in teams and interact with programmers and nontechnical users, so communications skills are important.

Most systems programmers have a four-year B.S. degree in Computer Science or Information Technology. Depending on responsibilities and experience, salaries range from $40,000 to as much as $97,000.

To learn more about the field of Systems Programmer as a career, visit the Discovering Computers 2005 Careers Web page (**scsite.com/dc2005/careers**). Click Systems Programmer.

Windows XP: Taking Control with the Command Prompt

When Microsoft developed the Windows XP operating system, it gave it a fresh, new graphical user interface. However, you still can complete many important tasks using the command-line interface. Microsoft's first operating system, MS-DOS, was based entirely on a command-line interface. Today, Windows XP supports many of the original MS-DOS commands — and many new commands that help you complete tasks.

With Windows XP, you enter commands via a command shell. A *command shell* is a software program with a nongraphical, command-line interface that provides an environment to run text-based application software and utility programs. The Windows XP command shell is called *Command Prompt*; the file name for the Command Prompt application is cmd.exe.

To open the Command Prompt window, click the Start button and point to All Programs, point to Accessories, and then click Command Prompt. Clicking Run on the Start menu and then typing `cmd` in the Run dialog box also opens the Command Prompt window. To execute a command, type one command per line and then press the ENTER key. Many commands allow you to enter one or more *options*, or *arguments*, which are additions to a command that change or refine the command in a specified manner. To close the Command Prompt window, type `exit` and then press the ENTER key or click the Close button in the Command Prompt window.

The Command Prompt window allows you to complete a wide range of tasks, including troubleshooting network connections. The *ping command*, for example, allows you to test TCP/IP connectivity for network and Internet connections (Figure 8-6a on page 398). When you enter the ping command with an IP address, your computer sends a special packet called ICMP Echo to that address. If everything is working, a reply comes back; if not, the ping times out. You also can use *TRACERT* (*traceroute*), a command-line utility that traces a data packet's path to its destination. When you enter `tracert course.com`, for example, the tracert utility traces the path from your computer to the Course Technology Web server.

You also can use the Windows XP Command Prompt to help manage your computer. When you enter the *systeminfo command*, Command Prompt queries your computer for basic system information, including operating system configuration and hardware properties, such as RAM and disk space. If you enter the *tasklist command*, the Command Prompt window returns a list of processes running on a computer, with each process identified by a process ID (PID) (Figure 8-39). You can terminate any process by entering the *taskkill command* and the PID as the argument. For example, if you enter `taskkill /pid 5168`, the process with PID 516 ends. Network administrators can use this command to fix problems on networked computers by closing applications.

The Windows XP Command Prompt also supports commands used to manage the files and file system on your hard disk. The *chkdsk command* checks for and corrects errors on the disk. You also can defragment your hard disk by entering the *defrag command*, with an argument specifying the drive to defragment (for example, defrag c:). When you are done working, you can use the *shutdown command* to shut down or restart your local or a remote computer.

In most cases, the command-line tools perform functions similar to the GUI application. The Disk Defragmenter utility and the defrag command, for example, provide similar functionality. In others, the command-line tools provide additional functionality. For instance, the *diskpart command* starts the command-line version of the DiskPart utility and gives you access to advanced features not available in the GUI version.

The commands discussed here are just some of the wide range of commands supported by Windows XP. For more information about the Windows XP Command Prompt, visit the Discovering Computers 2005 High-Tech Talk Web page (**scsite.com/dc2005/tech**) and click Windows XP Command Prompt.

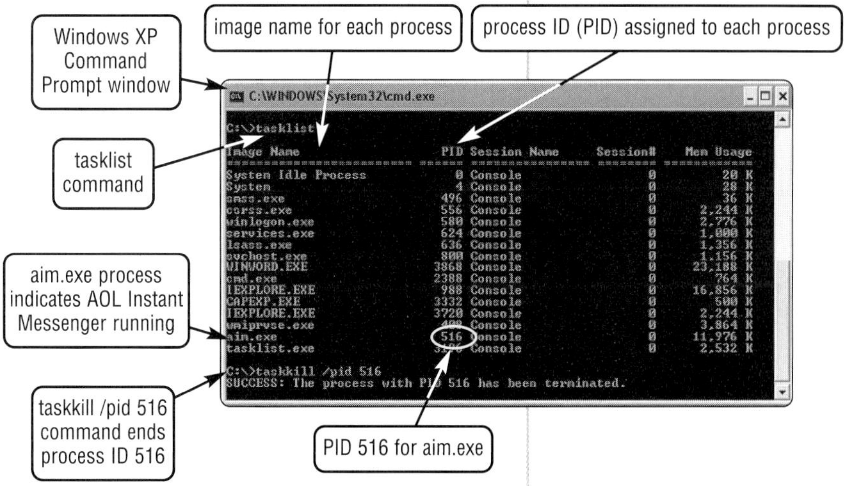

FIGURE 8-39 An example of the tasklist command.

COMPANIES ON THE CUTTING EDGE

Red Hat
Open Source Software Provider

Red Hat markets disruptive technology. According to Red Hat, disruptive technologies change the way people relate to the world. The telephone was a disruptive technology because it changed the way people communicate. The automobile was a disruptive technology because it changed the way people travel. Red Hat's disruptive technology is open source — a fundamental shift in the way software is created.

Most software is proprietary. The software code, or instructions, is known only to the companies that produce the software. Red Hat is the largest supplier of open source technology. Open source is software whose code is available to the public. Open source software allows buyers to modify, and perhaps improve, the software. Red Hat claims that the collaboration between sellers and buyers of open source software leads to rapid innovation and better software. Red Hat delivers software improvements to customers through the Red Hat Network, the company's Internet service.

Red Hat's most well-known product is Red Hat Linux. Linus Torvalds, a Finnish college student, wrote the first version of Linux in 1991 and made the operating system, together with its source code, available on the Internet. With each new version, demand for the operating system grew. In 1994, Bob Young and Marc Ewing founded Red Hat and started selling a packaged version of the operating system, called Red Hat Linux, complete with documentation and support. Today, Red Hat Linux is the most popular, and most trusted, version of Linux. In 2003, Red Hat Network registered its one millionth system. Red Hat attributes the success of Red Hat Linux to the software's reliable performance, exceptional flexibility, and low cost. Red Hat also offers a training and certification program that has become an industry standard. A recent study voted the Red Hat Certified Engineer (RHCE) program the best for overall quality.

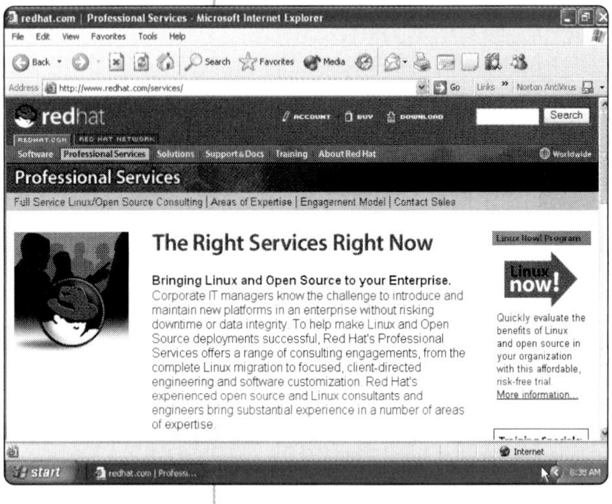

For more information about Red Hat, visit the Discovering Computers 2005 Companies Web page (**scsite.com/dc2005/companies**) and click Red Hat.

Network Associates
Security Provider

Some people take megadoses of zinc to fight a cold. Others rely on homemade chicken soup to combat viruses. But how can you protect your computer from viral attacks? The best approach is to use a combination of an antivirus program and a personal firewall, such as McAfee VirusScan and Firewall, developed by Network Associates.

Founded in 1989, *Network Associates* is a leading supplier of network security. Network Associates consists of three businesses:

- McAfee Security develops products to protect companies from security breaks and virus attacks.
- Sniffer Technologies offers products to keep networks and applications running at optimum levels.
- Magic Solutions delivers products that provide a unique, Internet-based solution for information technology resource management.

Network Associates also is the majority owner of McAfee.com, a primary source of managed online security services for consumers and small businesses. More than 80,000 strains of viruses, Trojan horses, and worms are on the rampage to infect your computer. But, the Network Associates cybersleuths are on the lookout for these malicious programs, sometimes finding as many as 6 new viruses each day. These cyberinvestigators are part of the company's 3,800 employees, making Network Associates the world's largest independent network security and management software corporation.

McAfee's VirusScan has been named the top antivirus product in independent testing performed by the University of Hamburg's Virus Test Center and by the West Coast Labs for Secure Computing. This software, along with other Network Associates e-business products, is used by more than 70 million people worldwide.

For more information about Network Associates, visit the Discovering Computers 2005 Companies Web page (**scsite.com/dc2005/companies**) and click Network Associates.

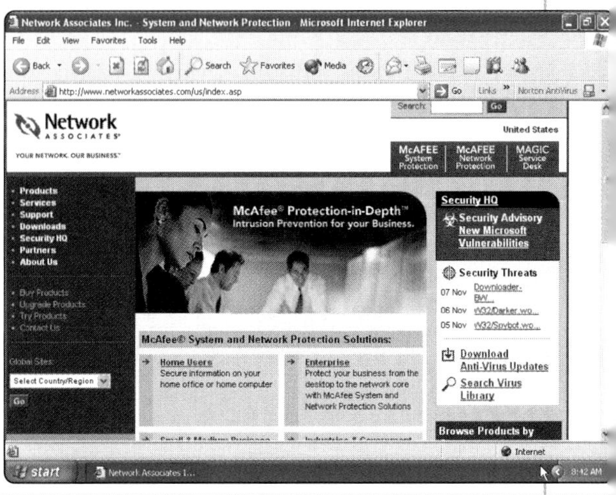

Technology Trailblazers

Linus Torvalds
Creator of Linux

Imagine creating an operating system that compares favorably with Windows and is backed by a technical support group one-million strong. Now, imagine giving that operating system away free. Unimaginable? Well, that is what happened when *Linus Torvalds* created Linux.

In 1991, Torvalds was a computer-science student in Finland. Frustrated with current operating systems, he decided to create his own. This might seem a daunting task, but the young programmer was confident. "I knew I was the best programmer in the world," Torvalds recalls. "Every 21-year-old programmer knows that. How hard can it be? It's just an operating system." He announced his project in an Internet newsgroup: "I'm doing a (free) operating system … Any suggestions are welcome, but I won't promise I'll implement them. :-)."

Torvalds soon posted the first version of the operating system. He incorporated suggestions and adopted a proposed name, Linux. As he posted new versions, the process was repeated and the number of reviewers grew. When Linux was released in 1994, the operating system had networking capability and more than 100,000 users. Torvalds eventually copyrighted Linux under a GPL (General Public License), allowing versions to be sold as long as the source code, and any alterations, remain public.

Today, Linus Torvalds works for Transmeta (a small company that develops and sells software-based microprocessors) and lives in a modest California house. He still considers himself Linux's lead technical developer. Due to Linux's popularity, however, he has to delegate some tasks and spend time answering e-mail messages and coordinating work efforts. A celebrity among programmers, Torvalds has no regrets about making the operating system available free. "A big part of personal satisfaction," Torvalds points out, "is having your work recognized by your peers."

For more information about Linus Torvalds, visit the Discovering Computers 2005 People Web page (**scsite.com/dc2005/people**) and click Linus Torvalds.

Steve Jobs
Cofounder of Apple Computer and Pixar

Before he was 35 years old, *Steve Jobs* helped build the first desktop personal computer, cofounded Apple Computer Corporation, marketed a revolutionary operating system, and became a multimillionaire. Not bad.

In 1972, Jobs graduated from high school and attended Reed College for a semester. He took classes in philosophy, embraced the contemporary counterculture, and eventually journeyed to India in search of enlightenment. When he returned, he joined Steve Wozniak's Homebrew Computer Club. "Woz[niak] was the first person I met who knew more about electronics than I did," Jobs recalls. When Wozniak designed a simple small computer, Jobs suggested they start a company and make the PC boards. The founders of Apple Computer sold their most valuable possessions — Jobs, his Volkswagen minibus and Wozniak, his scientific calculator — for capital and built a prototype. The computer, marketed in 1976 as the Apple I, was an immediate success, earning almost $775,000 from sales. The Apple II, introduced the next year, earned much more. Suddenly, Wozniak and Jobs had a very prosperous company.

As Apple grew, Jobs showed an uncompromising drive for perfection. Jobs also was a brilliant motivator, getting the best from the people around him. Employees joked about his "reality-distortion field" that allowed him to make seemingly unreasonable ideas appear reasonable. The Macintosh computer, announced in 1984, incorporated one of these ideas: a graphical interface controlled by a mouse. The Macintosh was a hit.

Jobs left Apple in 1985. He later would cofound NeXT Software and become CEO of Pixar, the computer animation studio that develops feature films. Apple eventually acquired both companies. In 1997, Jobs returned to a troubled Apple as CEO. Under his leadership, the company continues to manufacture innovative products and improve its bottom line.

For more information about Steve Jobs, visit the Discovering Computers 2005 People Web page (**scsite.com/dc2005/people**) and click Steve Jobs.

CHAPTER REVIEW

The Chapter Review section summarizes the concepts presented in this chapter.

WEB INSTRUCTIONS:

To display this page from the Web, start your browser and enter the Web address **scsite.com/dc2005/ch8/review.** Click the links for current and additional information. To listen to an audio version of this Chapter Review, click the Audio button.

1 What Are the Types of System Software?

System software consists of the programs that control or maintain the operations of a computer and its devices. Two types of system software are operating systems and utility programs. An **operating system (OS)** contains instructions that coordinate all the activities among computer hardware resources. A **utility program** performs maintenance-type tasks, usually related to managing a computer, its devices, or its programs.

2 What Is the Startup Process on a Personal Computer?

Booting is the process of starting or restarting a computer. When a user turns on a computer, the power supply sends a signal to the system unit. The processor chip finds the ROM chip(s) that contains the **BIOS**, which is firmware with the computer's startup instructions. The BIOS performs the *power-on self test (POST)* to check system components and compares the results with data in a CMOS chip. If the POST completes successfully, the BIOS searches for the *system files* and the *kernel* of the operating system, which manages memory and devices, and loads them into memory from storage. Finally, the operating system loads configuration information, requests any necessary user information, and displays the desktop on the screen.

3 What Are the Functions of an Operating System?

The operating system provides a user interface, manages programs, manages memory, schedules jobs, configures devices, establishes an Internet connection, and monitors performance. The **user interface** controls how data and instructions are entered and how information is displayed. Three types of user interfaces are a command-line interface, a *menu-driven interface*, and a *graphical user interface*. Managing programs refers to how many users, and how many programs, an operating system can support at one time. An operating system can be *single user/single tasking*, *single user/multitasking*, *multiuser*, or *multiprocessing*. **Memory management** optimizes the use of random access memory (RAM). If memory is insufficient, the operating system may use **virtual memory**, which allocates a portion of a storage medium to function as additional RAM. Scheduling jobs determines the order in which jobs are processed. A **job** is an operation the processor manages. Configuring devices involves loading each device's driver when a user boots the computer. A **driver** is a program that tells the operating system how to communicate with a specific device. Establishing an Internet connection sets up a connection between a computer and an Internet service provider. A **performance monitor** is an operating system program that assesses and reports information about computer resources and devices.

4 How Can Operating Systems Help Administrators Control a Network and Manage Security?

A network operating system, or *network OS*, is an operating system that organizes and coordinates how multiple users access and share network resources. A *network administrator* uses the network OS to add and remove users, computers, and other devices to and from the network. A network administrator also uses the network OS to administer network security. For each user, the network administrator establishes a user account that enables the user to **log on**, or access, the network by supplying the correct **user name** and **password**.

Visit **scsite.com/dc2005/quiz** or click the Quiz Yourself button. Click Objectives 1 – 4 below Chapter 8.

5 What Is the Purpose of the Utilities Included with Most Operating Systems?

Most operating systems include several utility programs. A **file manager** performs functions related to file and disk management. An **image viewer** displays and copies the contents of a graphics file. An **uninstaller** removes a program and any associated entries in the system files. A **disk scanner** detects and corrects problems on a disk and searches for and removes unnecessary files. A **disk defragmenter** reorganizes the files and unused space on a computer's hard disk. A **diagnostic utility** compiles and reports technical information about a computer's hardware and certain system software programs. A **backup utility** is used to copy, or *back up*, selected files or an entire hard disk. A **screen saver** displays a moving image or blank screen if no keyboard or mouse activity occurs for a specified time.

6 What Are Features of Several Stand-Alone Operating Systems?

A **stand-alone operating system** is a complete operating system that works on a desktop computer, notebook computer, or mobile computing device. Stand-alone operating systems include DOS, Windows XP, Mac OS X, UNIX, and Linux. **DOS** (*Disk Operating System*) refers to several single user, command-line operating systems developed for personal computers. **Windows XP** is Microsoft's fastest, most reliable Windows operating system, providing better performance and a new GUI with a simplified look. **Mac OS X** is a multitasking GUI operating system available only for Apple computers. **UNIX** is a multitasking operating system developed at Bell Laboratories. **Linux** is a popular, multitasking UNIX-type operating system that is *open source software*, which means its code is available to the public.

Visit **scsite.com/dc2005/quiz** or click the Quiz Yourself button. Click Objectives 5 – 6 below Chapter 8.

7 What Are Various Network Operating Systems?

Network operating systems include NetWare, Windows Server 2003, UNIX, Linux, and Solaris. Novell's *NetWare* is a network OS designed for client/server networks. **Windows Server 2003** is an upgrade to Windows 2000 Server and includes features of previous server versions. Linux, like UNIX, is a *multipurpose operating system* because it is both a stand-alone and network operating system. *Solaris*, a version of UNIX developed by Sun Microsystems, is a network OS designed for e-commerce applications.

8 What Devices Use Embedded Operating Systems?

Most PDAs and small devices have an **embedded operating system** that resides on a ROM chip. Popular embedded operating systems include Windows CE .NET, Pocket PC 2002, Palm OS, and Symbian OS. **Windows CE .NET** is a scaled-down Windows operating system designed for use on communications, entertainment, and mobile devices and on handheld computers. **Windows Mobile 2003** is a scaled-down operating system from Microsoft that works on a specific type of PDA, called the **Pocket PC**. *Palm OS* is an operating system used on Palm-powered PDAs. *Symbian OS* is an open source multitasking operating system designed for smart phones.

9 What Is the Purpose of Several Stand-Alone Utility Programs?

Stand-alone utility programs offer improvements over features built into the operating system or provide features not included in the operating system. An **antivirus program** protects computers against a **virus**, or potentially damaging computer program, by identifying and removing any computer viruses. A **personal firewall** detects and protects a personal computer from unauthorized intrusions. A **file compression utility** shrinks the size of a file so that it takes up less storage space. A **personal computer maintenance utility** identifies and repairs operating system problems or disk problems, and improves a computer's performance.

Visit **scsite.com/dc2005/quiz** or click the Quiz Yourself button. Click Objectives 7 – 9 below Chapter 8.

CHAPTER 8 KEY TERMS

You should know the Primary Terms and be familiar with the Secondary Terms.

QUIZZES AND LEARNING GAMES
Computer Genius
Crossword Puzzle
Interactive Labs
Practice Test
Quiz Yourself
Wheel of Terms

EXERCISES
Chapter Review
Checkpoint
Key Terms
Lab Exercises
Learn It Online
Web Research

BEYOND THE BOOK
Apply It
Career Corner
Companies
FAQ
High-Tech Talk
Issues
Looking Ahead
Trailblazers
Web Links

FEATURES
Guide to Web Sites
Making Use of the Web
Tech News
Timeline 2005

WEB INSTRUCTIONS:

To display this page from the Web, start your browser and enter the Web address **scsite.com/dc2005/ch8/terms**. Click a term to display its definition and a picture. When the picture appears, click the more info button for current and additional information about the term from the Web.

>> Primary Terms

(shown in bold-black characters in the chapter)

antivirus program (418)
backup utility (408)
BIOS (395)
boot disk (397)
boot drive (397)
booting (394)
buffer (401)
CDE (416)
cold boot (394)
defragmenting (407)
diagnostic utility (408)
disk defragmenter (407)
disk scanner (407)
DOS (410)
driver (402)
embedded operating system (416)
file compression utility (419)
file manager (406)
GNOME (416)
image viewer (406)
job (401)
Linux (414)
log on (404)
Mac OS X (413)
Macintosh operating system (413)
memory management (400)
network operating system (404)
operating system (OS) (392)
password (405)
performance monitor (404)
personal computer maintenance utility (420)
personal firewall (419)
Plug and Play (403)
Pocket PC (417)
queue (401)
recovery disk (397)
restore program (408)
screen saver (408)
spooling (401)
stand-alone operating system (410)
system software (392)
Trojan horse (418)
uncompress (420)
uninstaller (406)
UNIX (413)
user ID (404)
user interface (398)
user name (404)
utility (405)
utility program (405)
virtual memory (400)
virus (418)
warm boot (394)
Windows Mobile 2003 (417)
Windows Server 2003 (415)
Windows Server 2003 family (415)
Windows CE .NET (416)
Windows XP (410)
worm (418)
zipped files (420)

>> Secondary Terms

(shown in italic characters in the chapter)

Active Directory (415)
back up (408)
background (399)
basic input/output system (395)
client operating systems (410)
command language (398)
command-line interface (398)
compress (408)
cross-platform (393)
device driver (402)
device-dependent (409)
device-independent (409)
Disk Operating System (410)
Dr. Watson (408)
encryption (405)
fault-tolerant computer (400)
foreground (399)
formatting (406)
fragmented (407)
ghosting (409)
graphical user interface (GUI) (398)
hacker (419)
interrupt request line (IRQ) (403)
kernel (394)
malicious-logic program (418)
Media Center PC (412)
memory resident (394)
menu-driven interface (398)
multiprocessing (400)
multipurpose operating system (415)
multiuser (400)
NetWare (415)
network administrator (404)
network OS (404)
nonresident (394)
open source software (414)
page (401)
paging (401)
Palm OS (417)
platform (393)
power-on self test (POST) (396)
preemptive multitasking (400)
print spooler (401)
proprietary software (409)
registry (396)
shortcut (406)
single user/multitasking (399)
single user/single tasking (399)
Solaris (416)
Startup folder (396)
swap file (401)
Symbian OS (417)
system files (396)
thrashing (401)
unzip (420)
virus author (418)
Web services (415)
Windows Server 2003, Datacenter Edition (415)
Windows Server 2003, Enterprise Edition (415)
Windows Server 2003, Standard Edition (415)
Windows Server 2003, Web Edition (415)
Windows Explorer (406)
Windows Picture and Fax Viewer (406)
Windows Small Business Server 2003 (415)
Windows XP 64-bit Edition (412)
Windows XP Home Edition (412)
Windows XP Media Center Edition (412)
Windows XP Professional (412)
Windows XP Tablet PC Edition (412)

CHECKPOINT CHAPTER 8

Use the Checkpoint exercises to check your knowledge level of the chapter.

WEB INSTRUCTIONS:

To display this page from the Web, start your browser and enter the Web address **scsite.com/dc2005/ch8/check**. Click the links for current and additional information.

LABEL THE FIGURE

Identify each part of virtual memory.

a. disk (virtual memory)
b. page swapped in
c. swap file
d. page swapped out
e. RAM (physical memory)

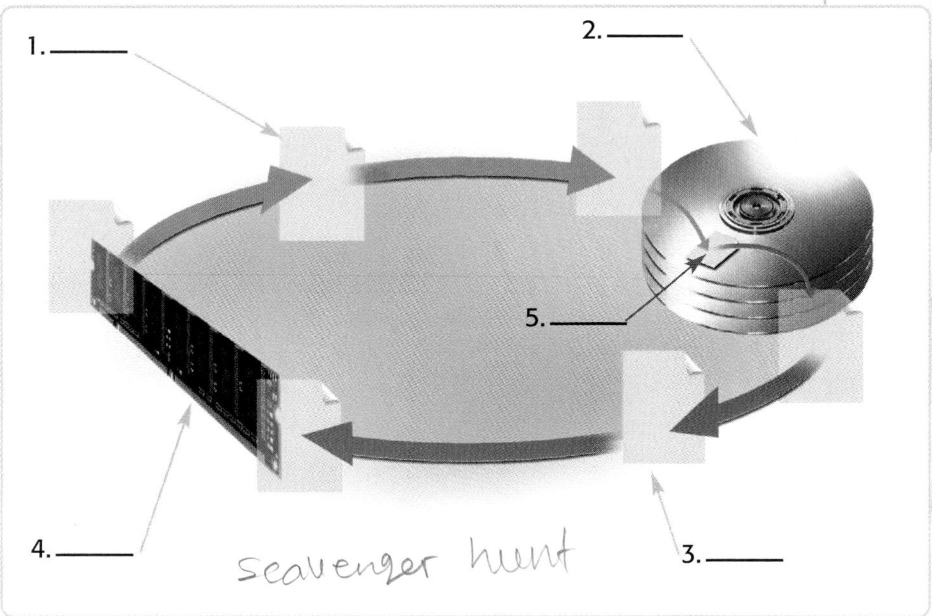

TRUE/FALSE

Mark T for True and F for False. (See page numbers in parentheses.)

__F__ 1. All sizes of computers typically use the same operating system. (393)

__T__ 2. Booting is the process of starting or restarting a computer. (394)

__T__ 3. A user interface controls how you enter data and instructions and how information is displayed on the screen. (398)

__T__ 4. By spooling print jobs to a buffer, a processor can continue interpreting and executing instructions while the printer prints, which allows users to work on the computer for other tasks. (401)

__F__ 5. A utility program is a program that assesses and reports information about various computer resources and devices. (405)

__T__ 6. A disk defragmenter is a utility that reorganizes the files and unused space on a computer's hard disk so the operating system accesses data more quickly and programs run faster. (407)

__T__ 7. Some stand-alone operating systems are called client operating systems because they also work in conjunction with a network operating system. (410)

__F__ 8. Linux is IBM's GUI multitasking client operating system that supports networking, Java, the Internet, and speech recognition. (414)

__F__ 9. Most antivirus programs do not protect against worms or Trojan horses. (418)

__T__ 10. A personal firewall is a utility program that detects and protects a personal computer from unauthorized intrusions. (419)

MULTIPLE CHOICE

Select the best answer. (See page numbers in parentheses.)

1. The _____ chip, which uses battery power, stores configuration information about the computer. (396)
   a. BIOS
   b. POST
   c. CMOS
   d. RAM
2. In Windows XP, the _____ consists of several files that contain the system configuration information. (396)
   a. shortcut
   b. page
   c. registry
   d. swap file
3. Many current _____ operating systems incorporate features similar to those of a Web browser, such as links and navigation buttons. (398)
   a. command-line interface
   b. menu-driven interface
   c. graphical user interface
   d. all of the above
4. When an operating system spends much of its time paging, instead of executing application software, it is said to be _____. (401)
   a. booting
   b. thrashing
   c. spooling
   d. formatting
5. Encryption is the process of _____. (405)
   a. encoding data and information into an unreadable form
   b. recording successful and unsuccessful logon attempts in a file
   c. establishing a user account that allows a user to log on to a network
   d. entering a user name and password
6. Defragmenting reorganizes the files on a disk so they are located in _____ access time. (407)
   a. noncontiguous sectors, which slows
   b. noncontiguous sectors, which speeds
   c. contiguous sectors, which slows
   d. contiguous sectors, which speeds
7. Windows XP includes the _____, Dr. Watson, which detects problems as well as suggests courses of action. (408)
   a. file manager
   b. backup utility
   c. image viewer
   d. diagnostic utility
8. _____ used a command-line interface when Microsoft first developed it, although later versions included menu-driven user interfaces. (410)
   a. Windows XP
   b. DOS
   c. Mac OS X
   d. UNIX
9. Apple's _____ has set the standard for operating system ease of use and has been the model for most of the new GUIs. (413)
   a. UNIX operating system
   b. Macintosh operating system
   c. Windows XP operating system
   d. Linux operating system
10. In addition to being a stand-alone operating system, _____ also is a network operating system. (415)
    a. DOS
    b. UNIX
    c. NetWare
    d. Windows XP
11. _____, developed by Sun Microsystems, manages high-traffic accounts and incorporates security necessary for Web transactions. (416)
    a. Solaris
    b. Linux
    c. Windows Server 2003
    d. Netware
12. Palm OS is an embedded operating system used with _____. (417)
    a. a specific type of PDA called a Pocket PC
    b. digital cameras, DVD players, and smart displays
    c. PDAs such as Treo and CLIE
    d. smart phones
13. A _____ is a malicious-logic program that does not replicate itself to other computers. (418)
    a. virus
    b. Trojan horse
    c. worm
    d. all of the above
14. Norton Utilities is a popular _____ designed for Windows operating systems. (420)
    a. antivirus program
    b. file compression utility
    c. personal firewall
    d. personal computer maintenance utility

CHECKPOINT CHAPTER 8

MATCHING

Match the terms with their definitions. (See page numbers in parentheses.)

_____ 1. recovery disk (397)
_____ 2. fault-tolerant computer (400)
_____ 3. page (401)
_____ 4. buffer (401)
_____ 5. interrupt request line (IRQ) (403)
_____ 6. password (405)
_____ 7. shortcut (406)
_____ 8. restore program (408)
_____ 9. proprietary software (409)
_____ 10. uncompress (420)

a. communications line between a device and the processor
b. program that tells the operating system how to communicate with a device
c. continues to operate when one of its components fails
d. private combination of characters associated with a user name
e. reverses the backup process and restores backed up files
f. contains a few system files that will start the computer
g. restore a zipped file to its original form
h. with virtual memory, the amount of data and program instructions that can be swapped at a given time
i. icon on the desktop that provides immediate access to a program or file
j. privately owned and limited to a specific vendor or computer model
k. segment of memory or storage in which items are placed while waiting to be transferred
l. contains a list of programs that open when a computer boots up

SHORT ANSWER

Write a brief answer to each of the following questions.

1. How is a cold boot different from a warm boot? ___________ How is a memory-resident part of an operating system different from a nonresident part of an operating system? ___________
2. What is a user interface? ___________ How are a command-line interface, a menu-driven interface, and a graphical user interface different? ___________
3. How is a single user/single tasking operating system different from a single user/multitasking operating system? ___________ What is preemptive multitasking? ___________
4. What are Web services? ___________ What five products are included in the Windows Server 2003 family? ___________
5. What is a malicious-logic program? ___________ How is a worm different from a Trojan horse? ___________

WORKING TOGETHER

Working with a group of your classmates, complete the following team exercises.

1. Most application programs are designed to be used with specific operating systems. When you purchase software, you should read the packaging to determine whether it is compatible with your computer's operating system. Have each member of your team visit a computer software vendor and find four application programs of interest. What operating system is required for each application? What is the earliest version of the operating system that can be used? Meet with the members of your team and compare your findings. Based on your results, what operating system would you choose? Use PowerPoint to create a group presentation and share your findings with the class.
2. Choose one Issue from the following issues in this chapter: Should Manufacturers Bundle Applications? (403), Would You Share Your Password? (405), Would You Like an Operating System with That? (409), or Is Open Source Software a Good Idea? (414). Use the Web and/or print media to research the issue. Then, present a debate for the class, with different members of your team supporting different responses to the questions that accompany the issue.
3. The Buyer's Guide on page 434 offers tips on buying a computer. Have each member of your team answer the four questions presented in the Buyer's Guide to determine the type of computer he or she needs. Then, each team member should visit one or more computer vendors and, using the guidelines and tools presented in the Buyer's Guide, find the "perfect" computer. Later, meet with the members of your team and compare your results. How are the computers similar? How are they different? Use PowerPoint to create a group presentation and share your findings with the class.

LEARN IT ONLINE

QUIZZES AND LEARNING GAMES
Computer Genius
Crossword Puzzle
Interactive Labs
Practice Test
Quiz Yourself
Wheel of Terms

EXERCISES
Chapter Review
Checkpoint
Key Terms
Lab Exercises
Learn It Online
Web Research

BEYOND THE BOOK
Apply It
Career Corner
Companies
FAQ
High-Tech Talk
Issues
Looking Ahead
Trailblazers
Web Links

FEATURES
Guide to Web Sites
Making Use of the Web
Tech News
Timeline 2005

Use the Learn It Online exercises to reinforce your understanding of the chapter concepts.

WEB INSTRUCTIONS:

To display this page from the Web, start your browser and enter the Web address **scsite.com/dc2005/ch8/learn**.

1 At the Movies – Linux Gets Personal

To view the Linux Gets Personal movie, click the number 1 button. Watch the movie and then complete the exercise by answering the question below. It looks like Microsoft Windows has some meaningful competition. The Linux operating system has shown itself to be easy to transition to from Windows, apparently more reliable in networking situations, and, at the price of free, it decidedly is less expensive. Though Linux is free, aligned companies make their money by providing customization services and selling new applications. Major companies, including IBM and HP, have formed an alliance to develop desktop office software that competes with Microsoft. Is Linux a boon to, or will it just complicate things for, computer users?

2 Student Edition Labs – Installing and Uninstalling Software

Click the number 2 button. When the Student Edition Labs menu appears, click *Installing and Uninstalling Software* to begin. A new browser window will open. Follow the on-screen instructions to complete the Lab. When finished, click the Exit button. If required, print a copy of your results to submit to your instructor.

3 Practice Test

Click the number 3 button. Answer each question. When completed, enter your name and click the Grade Test button to submit the quiz for grading. Make a note of any missed questions. If required, print a copy to submit to your instructor.

4 Web Guide

Click the number 4 button to display the Guide to Web Sites and Searching Techniques Web page. Click Reference and then click Webopedia. Search for operating system. Click one of the operating system links. Prepare a brief report about your findings and submit your assignment to your instructor.

5 Scavenger Hunt

Click the number 5 button. Print a copy of the Scavenger Hunt page; use this page to write down your answers as you search the Web. Submit your completed page to your instructor.

6 Who Wants To Be a Computer Genius?

Click the number 6 button to find out if you are a computer genius. Directions on how to play the game will be displayed. When you are ready to play, click the Play button. Submit your score to your instructor.

7 Wheel of Terms

Click the number 7 button to reinforce important terms you learned in this chapter by playing the Shelly Cashman Series version of this popular game. Directions on how to play the game will be displayed. When you are ready to play, click the Play button. Submit your score to your instructor.

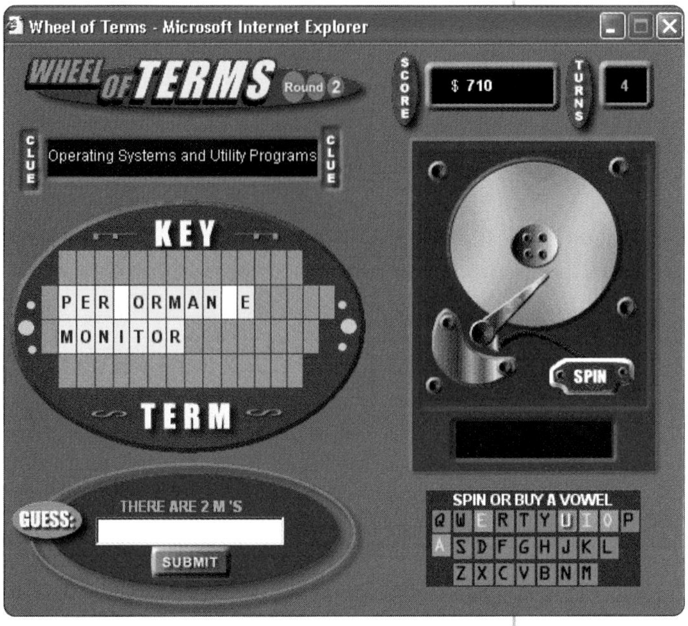

11 A Picture Is Worth a Thousand Words

Although she is not a programmer, Susan Kare's impact on the modern graphical user interface has been substantial. Kare is the person responsible for many of the icons you see in today's graphical interfaces. According to *Forbes* magazine, "When it comes to giving personality to what otherwise might be cold and uncaring office machines, Kare is the queen of look and feel." Click the number 11 button to learn more about Susan Kare and her approach to developing icons.

8 Career Corner

Click the number 8 button to display the QuintEssential Careers page. Click one of the tutorial links and complete the tutorial. Prepare a brief report describing what you learned. Submit the report to your instructor.

9 Search Sleuth

Click the number 9 button to learn search techniques that will help make you a research expert. Submit the completed assignment to your instructor.

10 Crossword Puzzle Challenge

Click the number 10 button. Complete the puzzle to reinforce skills you learned in this chapter. Directions on how to play the game will display. When you are ready to play, click the Submit button. Submit the completed puzzle to your instructor.

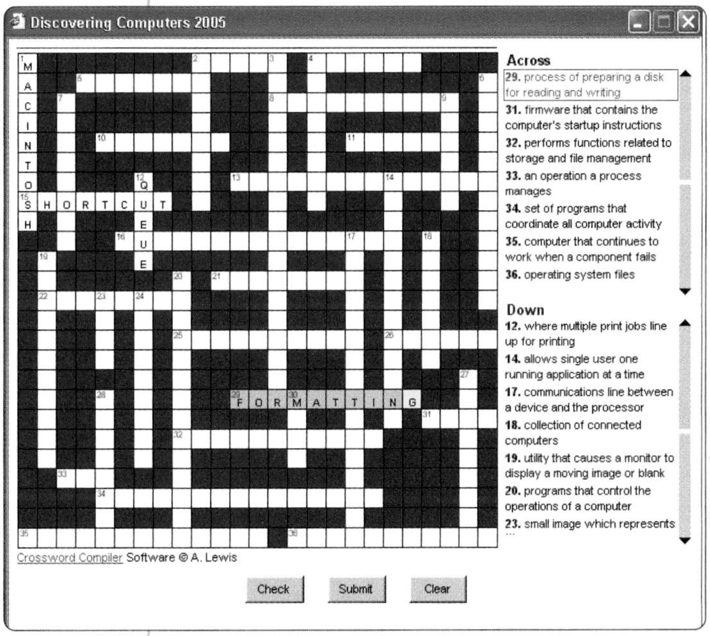

12 In the News

When Windows XP was launched in October 2001, hundreds queued up at computer outlets. It is unclear, however, whether the anticipation was caused by the new operating system or by the promotions many dealers offered. Click the number 12 button and read a news article about the impact, quality, or promotion of an operating system. What operating system was it? What was done to sell the operating system? Is the operating system recommended? Why or why not?

CHAPTER 8 LAB EXERCISES

Use the Lab Exercises to gain hands-on computer experience.

WEB INSTRUCTIONS:

To display this page from the Web, start your browser and enter the Web address **scsite.com/dc2005/ch8/lab**.

1 About Windows

This exercise uses Windows XP procedures. Click the Start button on the taskbar and then click My Computer on the Start menu. When the My Computer window is displayed, click Help on the menu bar and then click About Windows. Answer the following questions:

- What version of Windows is being used?
- To whom is Windows licensed?
- How much physical memory is available to Windows?

Click the OK button in the About Windows dialog box. Close the My Computer window.

2 Using a Screen Saver

This exercise uses Windows XP/2000/98 procedures. Right-click an empty area on the desktop and then click Properties on the shortcut menu. When the Display Properties dialog box is displayed (as shown in the figure below), click the Screen Saver tab. Click the Screen Saver box arrow and then click any new screen saver. Click the Preview button to display the actual screen saver. Move the mouse to make the screen saver disappear. Answer the following questions:

- How many screen savers are available in your Screen Saver list?
- How many minutes does your system wait before activating a screen saver?
- What other options are available?

Click the Cancel button in the Display Properties dialog box.

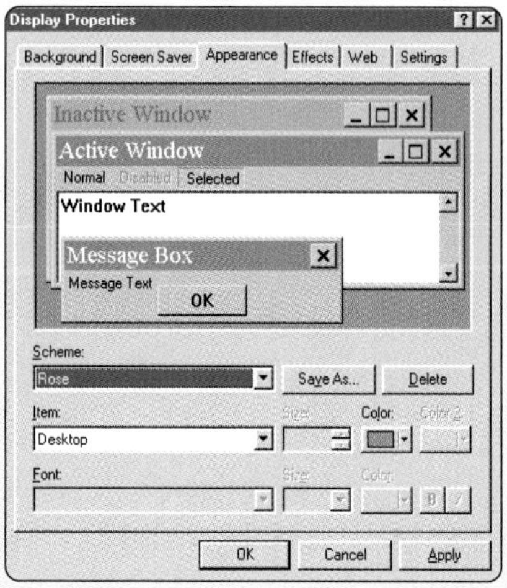

3 Changing Desktop Colors

This exercise uses Windows XP procedures. Right-click an empty area on the desktop and then click Properties on the shortcut menu. When the Display Properties dialog box is displayed, click the Appearance tab. Perform the following tasks: (1) Click the Question Mark button on the title bar and then click the Color scheme box. When the pop-up window displays, right-click it. Click Print Topic on the shortcut menu and then click the OK button in the Print dialog box. Click anywhere to remove the pop-up window. (2) Click the Color scheme box arrow and then click Silver to display the Silver color scheme. (3) Select a color scheme you like. Click the Cancel button in the Display Properties dialog box.

4 Customizing the Desktop for Multiple Users

This exercise uses Windows 2000/98 procedures. If more than one person uses a computer, how can you customize the desktop for each user? Click the Start button on the taskbar and then click Help on the Start menu. Click the Contents tab. Click the Exploring Your Computer book. Click The Windows Desktop book. Click the Customize Windows 2000/98 book. Click the Multiple Users book. Click an appropriate Help topic and read the information to answer each of the following questions:

- How can you display a list of users at startup?
- How can you add personalized settings for a new user?
- How do you log off the computer so someone else can use it?
- How can you change desktop settings for multiple users?

Click the Close button to close the Windows Help window.

WEB RESEARCH

CHAPTER 8

Use the Web Research exercises to learn more about the special features in this chapter.

WEB INSTRUCTIONS:

Use the link in each exercise or a search engine such as Google (google.com) to research the topic. Then, write a one-page, double-spaced report or create a presentation, unless otherwise directed below. Page numbers on which information can be found are in parentheses.

1. **Issue** Choose one Issue from the following issues in this chapter: Should Manufacturers Bundle Applications? (403), Would You Share Your Password? (405), Would You Like an Operating System with That? (409), or Is Open Source Software a Good Idea? (414). Use the Web to research the issue. Discuss the issue with classmates, instructors, and friends. Address the questions that accompany the issue in a report or presentation.

2. **Apply It** Choose one of the following Apply It features in this chapter: Customizing the Startup Folder (396) or Tune Up Your Computer for Optimum Performance (407). Use the Web to gather additional information about the topic. Print two Web pages that relate to the Apply It. Detail in a report or presentation what you learned.

3. **Career Corner** Read the Career Corner article in this chapter (420). Use the Web to find out more about the career. Describe the career in a report or presentation.

4. **Companies on the Cutting Edge** Choose one of the Companies on the Cutting Edge in this chapter (422). Use the Web to research the company further. Explain in a report or presentation how this company has contributed to computer technology.

5. **Technology Trailblazers** Choose one of the Technology Trailblazers in this chapter (423). Use the Web to research the person further. Explain in a report or presentation how this individual has affected the way people use, or think about, computers.

6. **Picture Yourself with a Virus-Infected Computer** Read the Picture Yourself with a Virus-Infected Computer story at the beginning of this chapter (390). Use the Web to research computer viruses further. Describe in a report or presentation the ways in which you might prevent, or respond to, a virus-infected computer.

7. **High-Tech Talk** Read the High-Tech Talk feature in this chapter (421). Use the Web to find out more about the topic. Summarize in a report or presentation what you learned.

8. **Web Links** Review the Web Link boxes found in the margins of this chapter. Visit five of the Web Link sites. Print the main Web page for each site you visit. Choose one of the Web pages and then summarize in one paragraph the content of the Web page.

9. **Looking Ahead** Choose one of the Looking Ahead articles in this chapter: Secure Computing — Heart of Windows Upgrade (411) or Home Entertainment Systems Sound Good to Consumers (416). Use the Web to find out more about the topic. Detail in a report or presentation what you learned.

10. **FAQ** Choose one FAQ found in this chapter. Use the Web to find out more about the topic. Summarize in one paragraph what you learned.

11. **Buyer's Guide** Read the Buyer's Guide Special Feature that follows this chapter (434-457). Select the area (purchasing a desktop computer, purchasing a notebook computer, purchasing a handheld computer, installing a computer, or maintaining a computer) in which you are most interested. Visit at least three of the Web addresses given to learn more about your selection. Explain what you learn in a report or presentation.

12. **Making Use of the Web** Read the Weather, Sports, News section of Making Use of the Web in Appendix A (APP 16). Complete the Weather, Sports, News Web Exercises at the end of the section (APP 17). Answer the questions posed in each exercise.

Buyer's Guide 2005

HOW TO PURCHASE, INSTALL, AND MAINTAIN A PERSONAL COMPUTER

(a) desktop computer

(b) notebook computer

(c) Tablet PC

(d) PDA

FIGURE 1

At some point, perhaps while you are taking this course, you may decide to buy a personal computer. The decision is an important one, which will require an investment of both time and money. As with many buyers, you may have little computer experience and find yourself unsure of how to proceed. You can get started by talking to your friends, coworkers, and instructors about their computers. What type of computers did they buy? Why? For what purposes do they use their computers? You also should answer the following four questions to help narrow your choices to a specific computer type, before reading the Buyer's Guide guidelines for purchasing a desktop computer, notebook computer, Tablet PC, or PDA.

1 Do you want a desktop or mobile computer?

A desktop computer (Figure 1a) is designed as a stationary device that sits on or below a desk or table in a location such as a home, office, or dormitory room. A desktop computer must be plugged into an electrical outlet to operate. A mobile computer or device, such as a notebook computer (Figure 1b), Tablet PC (Figure 1c), and PDA (Figure 1d), is smaller, more portable, and has a battery that allows you to operate it for a period without an electrical outlet.

Desktop computers are a good option if you work mostly in one place and have plenty of space in your work area. Desktop computers generally give you more performance for your money and are easier to upgrade than mobile computers.

Increasingly more desktop computer users are buying notebook computers to take advantage of their portability to work in the library, while traveling, and at home. The past disadvantages of notebook computers, such as lower processor speeds, poor-quality monitors, weight, short battery life, and significantly higher prices, have all but disappeared when compared with desktop computers.

If you are thinking of using a mobile computer to take notes in class or in business meetings, then consider a Tablet PC with handwriting and drawing capabilities. Typically, note-taking involves writing text notes and drawing charts, schematics, and other illustrations. By allowing you to write and draw directly on the screen with a digital pen, a Tablet PC eliminates the distracting sound of the notebook keyboard tapping and allows you to capture drawings. Some notebook computers can convert to Tablet PCs.

A PDA is a lightweight mobile device that easily fits in your pocket, which makes it ideal if you require a mobile computing device as you move from place to place. PDAs provide personal organizer functions, such as a calendar, appointment book, address book, and thousands of other applications. Some PDAs also function as a cellular telephone. The small size of the processor, screen, and keyboard, however, limit a PDA's capabilities when compared with a desktop or notebook computer. For this reason, most people who purchase PDAs also have a desktop or notebook computer to handle heavy-duty applications.

Drawbacks of mobile computers and devices are that they tend to have a shorter useful lifetime than desktop computers, cost more than desktop computers, and lack the high-end capabilities. Their portability makes them susceptible to vibrations, heat or cold, and accidental drops, which can cause components such as hard disks or monitors to fail. Also, because of their size and portability, they are easy to lose and are the prime targets of thieves.

2 For what purposes will you use the computer? Having a general idea of the purposes for which you want to use your computer will help you decide on the type of computer to buy. At this point in your research, it is not necessary to know the exact application software titles or version numbers you might want to use. Knowing that you plan to use the computer primarily to create word processing, spreadsheet, database, and presentation documents, however, will point you in the direction of a desktop or notebook computer. If you plan to use a mobile device to get organized, then a PDA may be your best choice. If you want the portability of a PDA, but need more computing power, then a Tablet PC may be the best alternative. You also must consider that some application software runs only on a Mac, while others run only on a PC with the Windows operating system. Still other software may run only on a PC running the UNIX or Linux operating system.

3 Should the computer be compatible with the computers at school or work? If you plan to bring work home, telecommute, or take distance education courses, then you should purchase a computer that is compatible with those at school or work.

Compatibility is primarily a software issue. If your computer runs the same operating system version, such as Microsoft Windows XP, and the same application software, such as Microsoft Office 2003, then your computer will be able to read documents created at school or work and vice versa. Incompatible hardware can become an issue if you plan to connect directly to a school or office network using a cable or wireless technology. You usually can obtain the minimum system requirements from the Information Technology department at your school or workplace.

4 Should the computer be a Mac or PC? If you ask a friend, coworker, or instructor, which is better — a Mac or a PC — you may be surprised by the strong opinion expressed in the response. No other topic in the computer industry causes more heated debate. The Mac has strengths, especially in the areas of graphics, movies, photos, and music. The PC, however, has become the industry standard with 95 percent of the market share. Figure 2 compares features of the Mac and PC in several different areas.

Area	Comparison
Cost and availability	A Mac has slightly higher prices than a PC. Mac peripherals also are more expensive. The PC offers more available models from a wide range of vendors. You can custom build, upgrade, and expand a PC for less money than a Mac.
Exterior design	The Mac has a more distinct and stylish appearance than most PCs.
Free software	Although free software for the Mac is available on the Internet, significantly more free software applications are available for the PC.
Market share	The PC dominates the personal computer market. While the Mac sells well in education, publishing, Web design, graphics, and music, the PC is the overwhelming favorite of businesses.
Operating system	Both Mac OS X and Microsoft Windows XP are stable. Users claim that Mac OS X provides a better all-around user experience than Microsoft Windows XP. The PC supports other operating systems, such as Linux and UNIX.
Program control	Both have simple and intuitive graphical user interfaces. The Mac relies more on the mouse and less on keyboard shortcuts than the PC. The mouse on the Mac has one button, whereas the mouse on a PC has a minimum of two buttons.
Software availability	The basic application software most users require, such as the Microsoft Office suite, is available for both the Mac and PC. More specialized software, however, often is only available for PCs. Many programs are released for PCs long before they are released for Macs.
Speed	The PC has faster processors than the Mac to choose from.
Viruses	Dramatically fewer viruses attack Macs. Mac viruses also generally are less infectious than PC viruses.

FIGURE 2 Comparison of Mac and PC features.

Overall, the Mac and PC have more similarities than differences, and you should consider cost, compatibility, and other factors when choosing whether to purchase a Mac or PC.

After evaluating the answers to these four questions, you should have a general idea of how you plan to use your computer and the type of computer you want to buy. Once you have decided on the type of computer you want, you can follow the guidelines presented in this Buyer's Guide to help you purchase a specific computer, along with software, peripherals, and other accessories.

Many of the guidelines presented also apply to the purchase of a mobile computer or device, such as a notebook computer, Tablet PC, and PDA. Later in this Buyer's Guide, sections on purchasing a notebook computer, PDA, or Tablet PC address additional considerations specific to those computer types.

Type of Computers	Web Site	URL
PC	CNET Shopper	shopper.cnet.com
	PC World Magazine	pcworld.com
	BYTE Magazine	byte.com
	PC Magazine	zdnet.com/reviews
	Yahoo! Computers	computers.yahoo.com
	MSN Shopping	eshop.msn.com
	Dave's Guide to Buying a Home Computer	css.msu.edu/PC-Guide/
Mac	Macworld Magazine	macworld.com
	Apple	apple.com
	Switch to Mac Campaign	apple.com/switch
For an updated list of hardware and software reviews and their Web site addresses, visit scsite.com/dc2005/ch8/buyers.		

FIGURE 3 Hardware and software reviews.

HOW TO PURCHASE A DESKTOP COMPUTER

Once you have decided that a desktop computer is most suited to your computing needs, the next step is to determine specific software, hardware, peripheral devices, and services to purchase, as well as where to buy the computer.

1 Determine the specific software you want to use on your computer. Before deciding to purchase a particular program, be sure it contains the features necessary for the tasks you want to perform. Rely on the computer users in whom you have confidence to help you decide on the software to use. The minimum requirements of the application software you select may determine the operating system (Microsoft Windows XP, Linux, UNIX, Mac OS X) you need. If you have decided to use a particular operating system that does not support application software you want to use, you may be able to purchase the similar application software from other manufacturers.

Many Web sites and trade magazines, such as those listed in Figure 3, provide reviews of software products. These Web sites frequently have articles that rate computers and software on cost, performance, and support.

Your hardware requirements depend on the minimum requirements of the application software you will run on your computer. Some application software requires more memory and disk space than others, as well as additional input, output, and storage devices. For example, suppose you want to run software that can copy one CD's or DVD's contents directly to another CD or DVD, without first copying the data to your hard disk. To support that, you should consider a desktop computer or a high-end notebook computer, because the computer will need two CD or DVD drives: one that reads from a CD or DVD, and one that reads from and writes on a CD or DVD. If you plan to run software that allows your computer to work as an entertainment system, then you will need a CD or DVD drive, quality speakers, and an upgraded sound card.

2 Look for bundled software. When you purchase a computer, it may come bundled with several programs. Some sellers even let you choose which application software you want. Remember, however, that bundled software has value only if you would have purchased the software even if it had not come with the computer. At the very least, you probably will want word processing software and a browser to access the Internet. If you need additional applications, such as a spreadsheet, a database, or presentation graphics, consider purchasing Microsoft Works, Microsoft Office, or Sun StarOffice, which include several programs at a reduced price.

3 Avoid buying the least powerful computer available. Once you know the application software you want to use, you then can consider the following important criteria about the computer's components: (1) processor speed, (2) size and types of memory (RAM) and storage, (3) types of input/output devices, (4) types of ports and adapter cards, and (5) types of communications devices. The information in Figures 4 and 5 can help you determine what system components are best for you. Figure 4 outlines considerations for specific hardware components. Figure 5 (on page 439) provides a Base Components worksheet that lists PC recommendations for each category of user discussed in this book: Home User, Small Office/Home Office User, Mobile User, Large Business User, and Power User. In the worksheet, the Home User category is divided into two groups: Application Home User and Game Home User. The Mobile User recommendations list criteria for a notebook computer, but do not include the PDA or Tablet PC options.

Computer technology changes rapidly, meaning a computer that seems powerful enough today may not serve your computing needs in a few years. In fact, studies show that many users regret not buying a more powerful computer. To avoid this, plan to buy a computer that will last you for two to three years. You can help delay obsolescence by purchasing the fastest processor, the most memory, and the largest hard disk you can afford. If you must buy a less powerful computer, be sure you can upgrade it with additional memory, components, and peripheral devices as your computer requirements grow.

CD/DVD Drives: Most computers come with a 32X to 48X speed CD-ROM drive that can read CDs. If you plan to write music, audio files, and documents on a CD or DVD, then you should consider upgrading to a CD-RW. An even better alternative is to upgrade to a DVD+R/+RW combination drive. It allows you to read DVDs and CDs and to write data on (burn) a DVD or CD. A DVD has a capacity of at least 4.7 GB versus the 650 MB capacity of a CD.

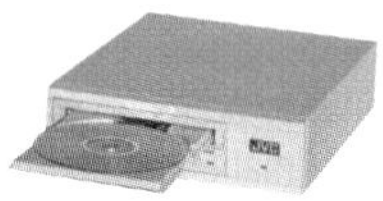

Card Reader/Writer: A card reader/writer is useful for transferring data directly to and from a removable flash memory card, such as the ones used in your camera or music player. Make sure the card reader/writer can read from and write to the flash memory cards that you use.

Digital Camera: Consider an inexpensive point-and-shoot digital camera. They are small enough to carry around, usually operate automatically in terms of lighting and focus, and contain storage cards for storing photographs. A 1.3- to 2.2-megapixel camera with an 8 MB or 16 MB storage card is fine for creating images for use on the Web or to send via e-mail.

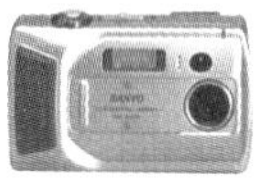

Digital Video Capture Device: A digital video capture device allows you to connect your computer to a camcorder or VCR and record, edit, manage, and then write video back to a VCR tape, a CD, or a DVD. The digital video capture device can be an external device or an adapter card. To create quality video (true 30 frames per second, full-sized TV), the digital video capture device should have a USB 2.0 or FireWire port. You will find that a standard USB port is too slow to maintain video quality. You also will need sufficient storage: an hour of data on a VCR tape takes up about 5 GB of disk storage.

Floppy Disk Drive: If you plan to use a floppy disk drive, then make sure the computer you purchase has a standard 3.5", 1.44 MB floppy disk drive. A floppy disk drive is useful for backing up and transferring files.

Hard Disk: It is recommended that you buy a computer with 40 to 60 GB if your primary interests are browsing the Web and using e-mail and Office suite-type applications; 60 to 80 GB if you also want to edit digital photographs; 80 to 100 GB if you plan to edit digital video or manipulate large audio files even occasionally; and 100 to 160 GB if you will edit digital video, movies, or photography often or store audio files and music or consider yourself to be a power user.

Joystick/Wheel: If you use your computer to play games, then you will want to purchase a joystick or a wheel. These devices, especially the more expensive ones, provide for realistic game play with force feedback, programmable buttons, and specialized levers and wheels.

Keyboard: The keyboard is one of the more important devices used to communicate with the computer. For this reason, make sure the keyboard you purchase has 101 to 105 keys, is comfortable, easy to use, and has a USB connection. A wireless keyboard should be considered, especially if you have a small desk area.

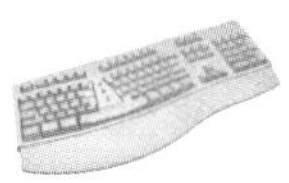

Microphone: If you plan to record audio or use speech recognition to enter text and commands, then purchase a close-talk headset with gain adjustment support.

Modem: Most computers come with a modem so that you can use your telephone line to dial out and access the Internet. Some modems also have fax capabilities. Your modem should be rated at 56 Kbps.

Monitor: The monitor is where you will view documents, read e-mail messages, and view pictures. A minimum of a 17" screen is recommended, but if you are planning to use your computer for graphic design or game playing, then you may want to purchase a 19" or 21" monitor. The LCD flat panel monitor should be considered, especially if space is an issue.

FIGURE 4 Hardware guidelines.

(continued)

HOW TO PURCHASE A TABLET PC

The Tablet PC (Figure 16) combines the mobility features of a traditional notebook computer with the simplicity of pencil and paper, because you can create and save Office-type documents by writing and drawing directly on the screen with a digital pen. Tablet PCs use the Windows XP Tablet PC Edition operating system, which expands on Windows XP Professional by including digital pen and speech capabilities. A notebook computer and a Tablet PC have many similarities. For this reason, if you are considering purchasing a Tablet PC, review the guidelines for purchasing a notebook computer, as well as the guidelines below.

FIGURE 16 The lightweight Tablet PC, with its handwriting capabilities, is the latest addition to the family of mobile computers.

1 Make sure the Tablet PC fits your mobile computing needs. The Tablet PC is not for every mobile user. If you find yourself in need of a computer in class or you are spending more time in meetings than in your office, then the Tablet PC may be the answer. Before you invest money in a Tablet PC, however, determine the programs you plan to use it for. You should not buy a Tablet PC simply because it is a new and interesting type of computer. For additional information on the Tablet PC, visit the Web sites listed in Figure 17. You may have to use the search capabilities on the home page of the companies listed to locate information about the Tablet PC.

Company	URL
Fujitsu	fujitsu.com
Hewlett-Packard	hp.com
Microsoft	microsoft.com/windowsxp/tabletpc
ViewSonic	viewsonic.com

For an updated list of companies and their Web site addresses, visit scsite.com/dc2005/ch8/buyers.

FIGURE 17 Companies involved with Tablet PCs and their Web sites.

2 Decide whether you want a convertible or pure Tablet PC. **Convertible Tablet PCs** have an attached keyboard and look like a notebook computer. You rotate the screen and lay it flat against the computer for note-taking. The **pure Tablet PCs** are slim and lightweight, weighing less than four pounds. They have the capability of easily docking at a desktop to gain access to a large monitor, keyboard, and mouse. If you spend a lot of time attending lectures or meetings, then the pure Tablet PC is ideal. Acceptable specifications for a Tablet PC are shown in Figure 18.

3 Be sure the weight and dimensions are conducive to portability. The weight and dimensions of the Tablet PC are important because you carry it around like a notepad. The Tablet PC you buy should weigh in at four pounds or less. Its dimensions should be approximately 12 inches by 9 inches by 1.5 inches.

4 Port availability, battery life, and durability are even more important with a Tablet PC than they are with a notebook computer. Make sure the Tablet PC you purchase has the ports required for the applications you plan to run. As with any mobile computer, battery life is important especially if you plan to use your Tablet PC for long periods without access to an electrical outlet. A Tablet PC must be durable because if you use it for what it was built for, then you will be handling it much like you handle a pad of paper.

Tablet PC Specifications	
Dimensions	12" x 9" x 1.5"
Weight	Less than 4 Pounds
Processor	Pentium M at 1.20 GHz
RAM	256 MB
Hard Disk	40 GB
Display	12.1" XGA TFT
Digitizer	Electromagnetic Digitizer
Battery	4-Cell (3-Hour)
USB	2
FireWire	1
Docking Station	Grab and Go with CD-ROM, Keyboard, and Mouse
Bluetooth Port	Yes
802.11b Card	Yes
Network Card	10/100 Ethernet
Modem	56 Kbps
Speakers	Internal
Microphone	Internal
Operating System	Windows XP Tablet PC Edition
Application Software	Office 2003 Small Business Edition
Antivirus Software	Yes – 12 Month Subscription
Warranty	1-Year Limited Warranty Parts and Labor

FIGURE 18 Tablet PC specifications.

FIGURE 19 A Tablet PC lets you handwrite notes and draw on the screen using a digital pen.

Mouse Unit	Digital Pen
Point	Point
Click	Tap
Double-click	Double-tap
Right-click	Tap and hold
Click and drag	Drag

FIGURE 20 Standard point-and-click of a mouse unit compared with the gestures made with a digital pen.

5 Experiment with different models of the Tablet PC to find the digital pen that works best for you. The key to making use of the Tablet PC is to be comfortable with its handwriting capabilities and on-screen keyboard. Not only is the digital pen used to write on the screen (Figure 19), but you also use it to make gestures to complete tasks, in a manner similar to the way you use a mouse. Figure 20 compares the standard point-and-click of a mouse unit with the gestures made with a digital pen. Other gestures with the digital pen replicate some of the commonly used keys on a keyboard.

6 Check out the comfort level of handwriting in different positions. You should be able to handwrite on a Tablet PC with your hand resting on the screen. You also should be able to handwrite holding the Tablet PC in one hand, as well as with it sitting in your lap.

7 Make sure the LCD display device has a resolution high enough to take advantage of Microsoft's ClearType technologies. Tablet PCs use a digitizer under a standard 10.4-inch motion-sensitive LCD display to make the digital ink on the screen look like real ink on paper. The Tablet PC also uses ClearType technology that makes the characters crisper on the screen, so your notes are easier to read and cause less fatigue to the eyes. To ensure you get the maximum benefits from the new ClearType technology, make sure the LCD display has a resolution of 800 × 600 in landscape mode and a 600 × 800 in portrait mode.

8 Test the built-in Tablet PC microphone and speakers. With many application software packages recognizing human speech, such as Microsoft Office 2003, it is important that the Tablet PC's built-in microphone operates at an acceptable level. If the microphone is not to your liking, you may want to purchase a close-talk headset with your Tablet PC. Increasingly more users are sending information as audio files, rather than relying solely on text. For this reason, you also should check the speakers on the Tablet PC to make sure they meet your standards.

9 Consider a Tablet PC with a built-in PC video camera. A PC video camera adds streaming video and still photography capabilities to your Tablet PC, while still allowing you to take notes in lecture or in meetings.

10 Review the docking capabilities of the Tablet PC. The Microsoft Windows XP Tablet PC Edition operating system supports a grab-and-go form of docking, so you can pick up and take a docked Tablet PC with you, just as you would pick up a notepad on your way to a meeting. Two basic types of docking stations are available. One type of docking station (Figure 21) changes the Tablet PC into a desktop computer. It uses the Tablet PC as a monitor. The station has a CD or DVD drive, full-sized keyboard, mouse, and other accessories. Another type of docking station lets you dock your PC to your desktop computer and use Microsoft Windows XP Dual Monitor support. **Windows XP Dual Monitor support** allows you to work on one monitor while using the Tablet PC monitor to display often-used applications, such as your calendar or address book.

FIGURE 21 A Tablet PC docked to create a desktop computer with the Tablet PC as the monitor.

11 Wireless access to the Internet and your e-mail is essential with a Tablet PC. Make sure the Tablet PC has wireless networking, so you can access the Internet and your e-mail anytime and anywhere. Your Tablet PC also should include standard network connections, such as dial-up and Ethernet connections.

12 Review available accessories to purchase with your Tablet PC. Tablet PC accessories include docking stations, mouse units, keyboards, security cables, additional memory and storage, protective handgrips, screen protectors, and various types of digital pens. You should review the available accessories when you purchase a Tablet PC.

HOW TO PURCHASE A PDA

If you need to stay organized when you are on the go, then a lightweight, palm-sized or pocket-sized mobile device, called a PDA, may be the right choice. PDAs typically are categorized by the operating system they run. Although several are available, the two primary operating systems are Palm OS (Figure 22) or a Windows-based operating system, such as Windows Mobile 2003 (Figure 23).

FIGURE 22 Sony's UX50 CLIE PDA with Palm OS. The T665c lets you take pictures with its digital camera, listen to MP3 files, display videos and images, plus keep your datebook and contact list organized.

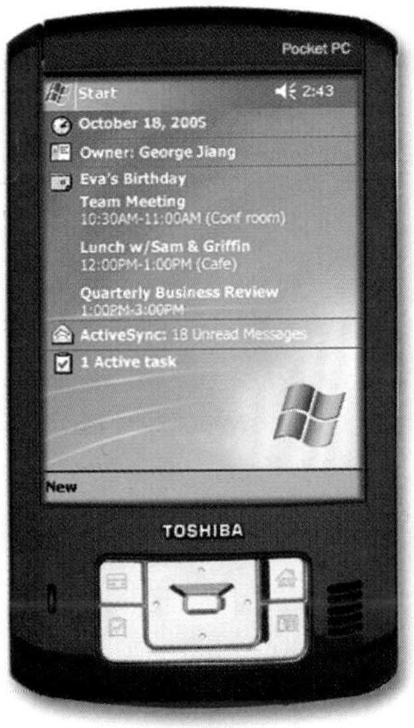

FIGURE 23 Toshiba Pocket PC e800 with Windows Mobile 2003 includes wireless connectivity. The iPaq plays MP3 music or audio programs from the Web, as well as records and plays back voice notes or meeting notes.

This section lists guidelines you will want to consider when purchasing a PDA. You also should visit the Web sites listed in Figure 24 to gather more information about the type of PDA that best suits your computing needs.

Web Site	URL
Hewlett-Packard	hp.com
CNET Shopper	shopper.cnet.com
palmOne	palmone.com
Microsoft	pocketpc.com
PDA Buyers Guide	pdabuyersguide.com
SonyStyle USA	sonystyle.com
Wireless Developer Network	wirelessdevnet.com
For an updated list of reviews and information about PDAs and their Web site addresses, visit scsite.com/dc2005/ch8/buyers.	

FIGURE 24 Reviews and information about PDAs.

1 Determine the programs you plan to run on your PDA. All PDAs can handle basic organizer-type software such as a calendar, address book, and notepad. The availability of other software depends on the operating system you choose. The depth and breadth of software for the Palm OS is significant, with more than 11,000 basic programs and over 600 wireless programs. PDAs that run Windows-based operating systems, such as Windows Mobile 2003, may have fewer programs available, but the operating system and application software are similar to those with which you are familiar, such as Word and Excel.

2 Consider how much you want to pay. The price of a PDA can range from $100 to $800, depending on its capabilities. In general, Palm OS devices are at the lower end of the cost spectrum and Windows-based devices are at the higher end. For the latest PDA prices, capabilities, and accessories, visit the Web sites listed in Figure 24.

3 Determine whether you need wireless access to the Internet and e-mail or mobile telephone capabilities with your PDA. Some PDAs offer wireless access to the Internet, instant messaging, and e-mail for a monthly network connection fee. To run the wireless, the functionality of the PDAs often is stripped down to conserve battery power. Some wireless

PDAs, such as palmOne's Treo 600, come with a mobile telephone built-in (Figure 25). These features and services allow PDA users to access real-time information from anywhere to help make decisions while on the go.

FIGURE 25 The palmOne Treo 600 running Palm OS has a full-color display and can be used as a telephone, an organizer, a digital camera, or to access e-mail and the Web.

4 Make sure your PDA has enough memory. Memory (RAM) is not a major issue with low-end PDAs with monochrome displays and basic organizer functions. Memory is a major issue, however, for high-end PDAs that have color displays and wireless features. Without enough memory, the performance level of your PDA will drop dramatically. If you plan to purchase a high-end PDA running the Palm OS operating system, the PDA should have at least 16 MB of RAM. If you plan to purchase a high-end PDA running the Windows Mobile 2003 operating system, the PDA should have at least 48 MB of RAM.

5 Practice with the touch screen, handwriting recognition, and built-in keyboard before deciding on a model. To enter data into a PDA, you use a pen-like stylus to handwrite on the screen or a keyboard. The keyboard either is mounted on the front of the PDA or it slides out. The palmOne Treo shown in Figure 25, comes with a small, built-in keyboard that works like a mobile telephone keypad. With handwriting recognition, the PDA translates the handwriting into a computerized font. You also can use the stylus as a pointing device to select items on the screen and enter data by tapping on an on-screen keyboard. By practicing data entry before buying a PDA, you can learn if one PDA may be easier for you to use than another. You also can buy third-party software to improve a PDA's handwriting recognition.

6 Decide whether you want a color display. Pocket PC devices usually come with a color display that supports as many as 65,536 colors. Palm OS devices also have a color display, but the less expensive ones have a monochrome display in 4 to 16 shades of gray. Having a color display does result in greater on-screen detail, but it also requires more memory and uses more power. Resolution also influences the quality of the display.

7 Compare battery life. Any mobile device is good only if it has the power required to run. Palm OS devices with monochrome screens typically have a much longer battery life than Pocket PC devices with color screens. To help alleviate this problem, many Palm OS and Pocket PC devices have incorporated rechargeable batteries that can be recharged by placing the PDA in a cradle or connecting it to a charger.

8 Even with PDAs, seriously consider the importance of ergonomics. Will you put the PDA in your pocket, a carrying case, wear it on your belt? How does it feel in your hand? Will you use it indoors or outdoors? Many screens are unreadable outdoors. Do you need extra ruggedness, such as would be required in construction, in a plant, or in a warehouse?

9 Check out the accessories. Determine which accessories you want for your PDA. PDA accessories include carrying cases, portable mini- and full-sized keyboards, removable storage, modems, synchronization cradles and cables, car chargers, wireless communications, global positioning system modules, digital camera modules, expansion cards, dashboard mounts, replacement styli, and more.

10 Decide whether you want additional functionality. In general, off-the-shelf Pocket PC devices have broader functionality than Palm OS devices. For example, voice-recording capability, e-book players, MP3 players, and video players are standard on most Pocket PC devices. If you are leaning towards a Palm OS device and want these additional functions, you can purchase additional software or expansion modules to add them later.

11 Determine whether synchronization of data with other PDAs or personal computers is important. Most PDAs come with a cradle that connects to the USB or serial port on your computer so you can synchronize data on your PDA with your desktop or notebook computer. Increasingly more PDAs are Bluetooth and/or 802.11b enabled, which gives them the capability of synchronizing wirelessly. Most PDAs today also have an infrared port that allows you to synchronize data with any device that has a similar infrared port, including desktop and notebook computers or other PDAs.

HOW TO INSTALL A COMPUTER

It is important that you spend time planning for the installation of your computer. Follow these steps to ensure your installation experience will be a pleasant one and that your work area is safe, healthy, and efficient.

1 **Read the installation manuals before you start to install your equipment.** Many manufacturers include separate installation manuals that contain important information with their equipment. You can save a great deal of time and frustration if you make an effort to read the manuals before starting the installation process.

2 **Do some additional research.** To locate additional instructions or advice about installing your computer, review the computer magazines or Web sites listed in Figure 26 to search for articles about installing a computer.

Web Site	URL
Getting Started/Installation	
HelpTalk Online	www.helptalk.com
Ergonomics	
HealthyComputing.com	healthycomputing.com
IBM Healthy Computing	www.pc.ibm.com/ww/healthycomputing
Apple Ergonomics	apple.com/about/ergonomics/
For an updated list of reference materials, visit scsite.com/dc2005/ch8/buyers.	

FIGURE 26 Web references on setting up and using your personal computer.

3 Set up your computer in a well-designed work area and remain aware of health issues as you work. Ergonomic studies have shown that using the correct type and configuration of chair, keyboard, monitor, and work surface will help you work comfortably and efficiently, and help protect your health. For your computer work space, experts recommend an area of at least two feet by four feet. You also should set up a document holder that keeps documents at the same height and distance as your computer screen to minimize neck and eye discomfort. Finally, use non-glare lightbulbs that illuminate your entire work area to reduce eyestrain. Figure 27 illustrates additional guidelines for setting up your work area. Figure 28 provides computer user health guidelines.

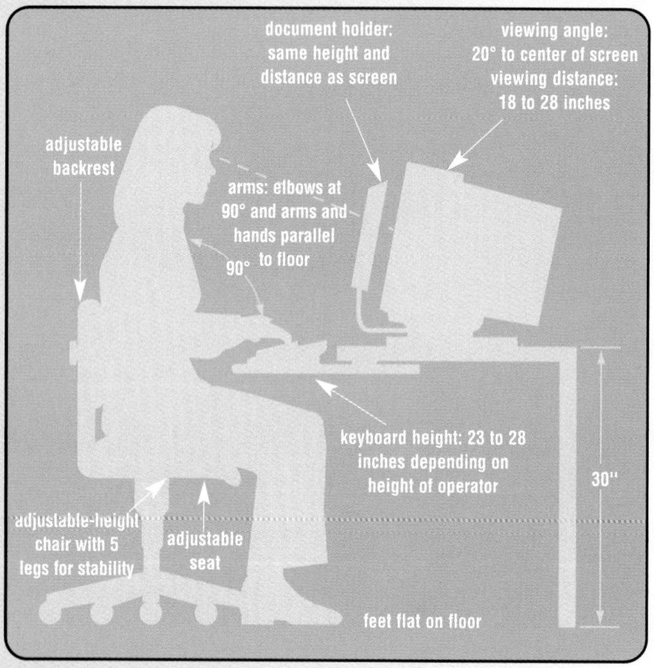

FIGURE 27 A well-designed work area should be flexible to allow adjustments to the height and build of different individuals. Good lighting and air quality also are important considerations.

1. Work in a well-designed work area, as shown in Figure 27.
2. Alternate work activities to prevent physical and mental fatigue. If possible, change the order of your work to provide some variety.
3. Take frequent breaks. Every 15 minutes, look away from the screen to give your eyes a break. At least once per hour, get out of your chair and move around. Every two hours, take at least a 15-minute break.
4. Incorporate hand, arm, and body stretching exercises into your breaks. During your lunch break, try to get outside and walk.
5. Make sure your computer monitor is designed to minimize electromagnetic radiation (EMR).
6. Try to eliminate or minimize surrounding noise that contributes to stress and tension.
7. If you frequently use the telephone and the computer at the same time, consider using a telephone headset. Cradling the telephone between your head and shoulder can cause muscle strain.
8. Be aware of symptoms of repetitive strain injuries: soreness, pain, numbness, or weakness in neck, shoulders, arms, wrists, and hands. Do not ignore early signs; seek medical advice.

FIGURE 28 Following these health guidelines can help computer users maintain their health.

4 Install your computer in a work space where you can control the temperature and humidity. You should keep the computer in an area with a constant temperature between 60°F and 80°F. High temperatures and humidity can damage electronic components. Be careful when using space heaters, for example, as the hot, dry air they generate can cause disk problems.

5 Set up your work space near an available electrical outlet and set aside a proper location for the electrical wires. Your computer and peripheral devices, such as the monitor and printer, require an electrical outlet. To maintain safety and simplify the connections, purchase a surge protector to connect the computer and peripheral devices to the electrical outlet. Place the electrical wires in a location where they are not a fire risk and you can avoid tripping on them. After you turn your computer off, turn the master switch on the surge protector to off.

6 Have a telephone outlet and telephone or cable connection near your work space so you can connect your modem and/or place calls while using your computer. To plug in your modem to dial up and access the Internet, you will need a telephone outlet or cable connection close to your computer. Having a telephone nearby also helps if you need to place business or technical support calls while you are working on your computer. Often, if you call a vendor about a hardware or software problem, the support person can talk you through a correction while you are on the telephone. To avoid data loss, however, do not place floppy disks on the telephone or near any other electrical or electronic equipment.

7 If you plan to set up a wireless network, choose an area that is free from potential signal interference. Low-level basement areas, doors, trees, and walls, for example, can affect the signals between wireless devices. The signal pattern for most wireless antennae is circular, with the strongest signal closest to the antenna. The best advice is to give the antenna ample room and determine its placement by trial and error.

8 Install bookshelves. When you set up your work space, install bookshelves above and/or to the side of your computer area to keep manuals and other reference materials handy.

9 Obtain a computer tool set. Computer tool sets include any screwdrivers and other tools you might need to work on your computer. Computer dealers, office supply stores, and mail-order companies sell these tool sets. To keep all the tools together, get a tool set that comes in a zippered carrying case.

10 Save all the paperwork that comes with your computer. Keep the documents that come with your computer in an accessible place, along with the paperwork from your other computer-related purchases. To keep different-sized documents together, consider putting them in a manila file folder, large envelope, or sealable plastic bag.

11 Record the serial numbers of all your equipment and software. Write the serial numbers of your equipment and software on the outside of the manuals packaged with these items. As noted in the next section, you also should create a single, comprehensive list that contains the serial numbers of all your equipment and software.

12 Complete and mail your equipment and software registration cards or register online. When you register your equipment and software, the vendor usually enters you in its user database. Being a registered user not only can save you time when you call with a support question, it also makes you eligible for special pricing on software upgrades.

13 **Keep the shipping containers and packing materials for all your equipment.** Shipping containers and packing materials will come in handy if you have to return your equipment for servicing or must move it to another location.

14 **Identify device connectors.** At the back or front of your computer, you will find a number of connectors for your printer, monitor, mouse, telephone line, and so forth (Figure 29). If the manufacturer has not identified them for you, use a marking pen to write the purpose of each connector on the back or front of the computer case, or photograph or draw the connectors and label them in a notebook.

15 **Keep your computer area clean.** Avoid eating and drinking around your computer. Also avoid smoking, because cigarette smoke can damage floppy disk drives and floppy disk surfaces.

16 **Check your home or renter's insurance policy.** Some renter's insurance policies have limits on the amount of computer equipment they cover. Other policies do not cover computer equipment at all if it is used for business. In this instance, you may want to obtain a separate insurance policy.

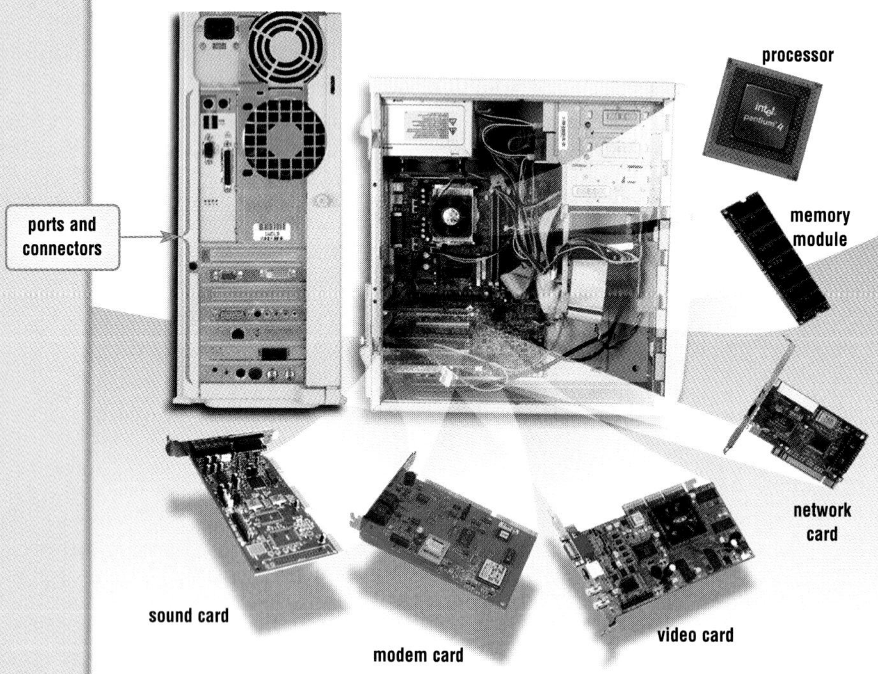

FIGURE 29 Adapter cards have a connector that is positioned in the back of the computer when the card is inserted in an expansion slot on the motherboard.

HOW TO MAINTAIN YOUR COMPUTER

Even with the most sophisticated hardware and software, you may need to do some type of maintenance to keep your computer working properly. You can simplify and minimize the maintenance by following the steps listed in this section.

1 Start a notebook or file using a simple outline that includes information about your computer. Keep a notebook that provides a single source of information about your entire computer, both hardware and software and network connectivity. Each time you make a change to your computer, such as adding or removing hardware or software or altering computer parameters, record the change in your notebook. Include the following items in your notebook:

- Vendor support numbers from your user manuals
- Serial numbers of all equipment and software
- User IDs, passwords, and nicknames for your ISP or OSP, network access, Web sites, and so on
- Vendor and date of purchase for all software and equipment
- Trouble log that provides a chronological history of equipment or software problems
- Notes on any discussions with vendor support personnel

Figure 30 provides a suggested outline for the contents of your Computer Owner's Notebook.

OUTLINE FOR COMPUTER OWNER'S NOTEBOOK

1. **List of Vendors**
   Vendor
   Product(s)
   City/State
   URL
   E-mail address
   Telephone number
   Technical support telephone number
2. **Internet and online services information**
   Service provider name
   URL
   E-mail address
   Logon telephone number
   Alternate logon telephone number
   Technical support telephone number
   User ID
   Password
3. **Serial numbers**
   Product
   Manufacturer
   Serial number
4. **Hardware purchase history**
   Date
   Product
   Manufacturer
   Vendor
   Cost
   Warranty information
5. **Software purchase history**
   Product
   Manufacturer
   Vendor
   Cost
   Date purchased
   Date installed/uninstalled
   Product keys/registration numbers
6. **Trouble log**
   Date
   Time
   Problem
   Resolution
7. **Support calls**
   Date
   Time
   Company
   Contact
   Problem
   Comments
8. **Vendor paperwork**

FIGURE 30 To keep important information about your computer on hand and organized, use an outline such as this sample outline.

2 Before you work inside your computer, turn off the power and disconnect the equipment from the power source. Working inside your computer with the power on can affect both you and the computer adversely. In addition, before you touch anything inside the computer, you should touch an unpainted metal surface, such as the power supply. Doing so will help discharge any static electricity that could damage internal components. As an added protection, for less than $10 from an electronics or computer store, buy an antistatic wristband to prevent static electricity from damaging the computer's circuitry while you replace components. Do not twist, bend, or force components into place. Gently work around existing cables.

If your operating system does not provide the tools, you can purchase a stand-alone utility program to perform basic maintenance functions.

3 Keep the area surrounding your computer dirt and dust free. Reducing the dirt and dust around your computer will reduce the need to clean the inside of your computer. If dust builds up inside the computer, remove it carefully with compressed air and a small vacuum. Do not touch the components with the vacuum.

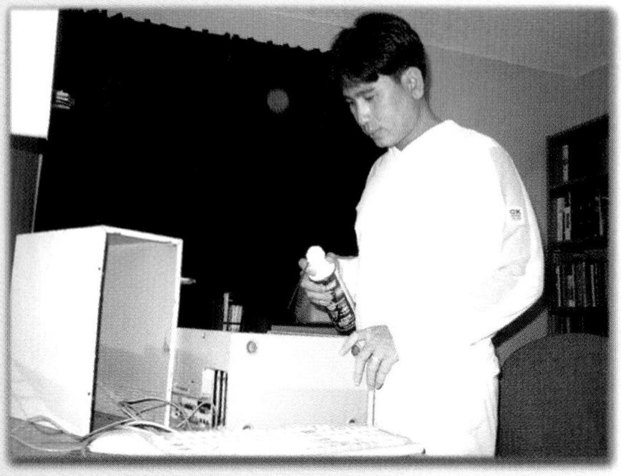

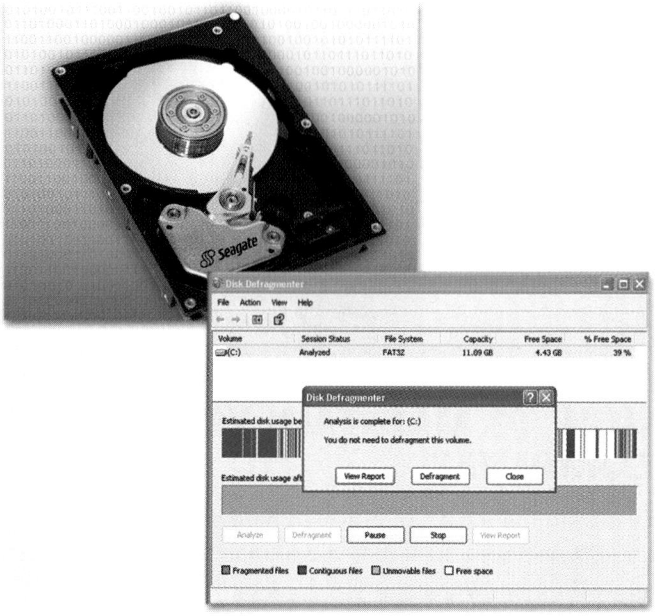

FIGURE 31 The Disk Defragmenter utility defragments the hard disk by reorganizing the files so they are in contiguous (adjacent) clusters, making disk operations faster.

4 Back up important files and data. Use a utility program included with the operating system or from a third-party to create a recovery or rescue disk to help you restart your computer if it crashes. Regularly copy important data files to disks, tape, or another computer.

5 Protect your computer from viruses. You can protect your computer from viruses by installing an antivirus program and then periodically updating the program by connecting to the manufacturer's Web site. Also, never open a file from an unknown user, particularly those received as e-mail attachments.

6 Keep your computer tuned. Most operating systems include several computer utilities that provide basic maintenance functions. In Windows, for example, these utilities are available via the System Tools submenu on the Accessories submenu. One important utility is the disk defragmenter, which allows you to reorganize files so they are in contiguous (adjacent) clusters, making disk operations faster (Figure 31). Some programs allow you to schedule maintenance tasks for times when you are not using your computer. If necessary, leave your computer on at night so it can run the required maintenance programs.

7 Learn to use diagnostic tools. Diagnostic tools help you identify and resolve problems, thereby helping to reduce your need for technical assistance. Diagnostic tools help you test components, monitor resources such as memory and processing power, undo changes made to files, and more. As with basic maintenance tools, most operating systems include diagnostic tools; you also can purchase or download many stand-alone diagnostic tools.

8 Conserve energy wherever possible. A simple way to conserve energy is to avoid animated screen savers, which use additional power and prevent your computer from going into hibernation. Fortunately, many of the recent computer, monitor, and printer models go into a very low power mode when not in use for a few minutes. If your printer does not go into a very low power mode, then keep it turned off until you need to print a document or report. Finally, shut your computer system down at night and turn off the main switch on your surge protector.

NOTES

CHAPTER 9

Communications and Networks

Picture Yourself Using a WISP

While golfing with some friends, you realize you forgot to pay bills before leaving on the trip. All you need is an Internet connection because you use online banking. You are in luck. One friend brought his notebook computer.

Later that day, your friend takes you to a coffee shop. He orders a cup of Espresso Macchiato, sits down at a table, opens up his notebook computer, connects to the Internet, slides you the computer, and then says, "Go ahead and pay your bills." How did he connect to the Internet without any cords? He explains that the coffee shop is one of many hot spots across the country that provide wireless Internet access. Did he have to buy anything special for the computer to work in a hot spot? For less than $70, he bought a PC Card that functions as a wireless network card. He also signed up for Internet access from a wireless Internet service provider, which he calls his WISP. How much does that cost? He pays $3 each time he connects to the Internet. Right now, that is the most economical plan for him. When his hot spot visits become more regular, though, he intends to switch to a monthly plan that offers unlimited nationwide Internet access.

As you read Chapter 9, you will learn about wireless communications and discover other uses of communications.

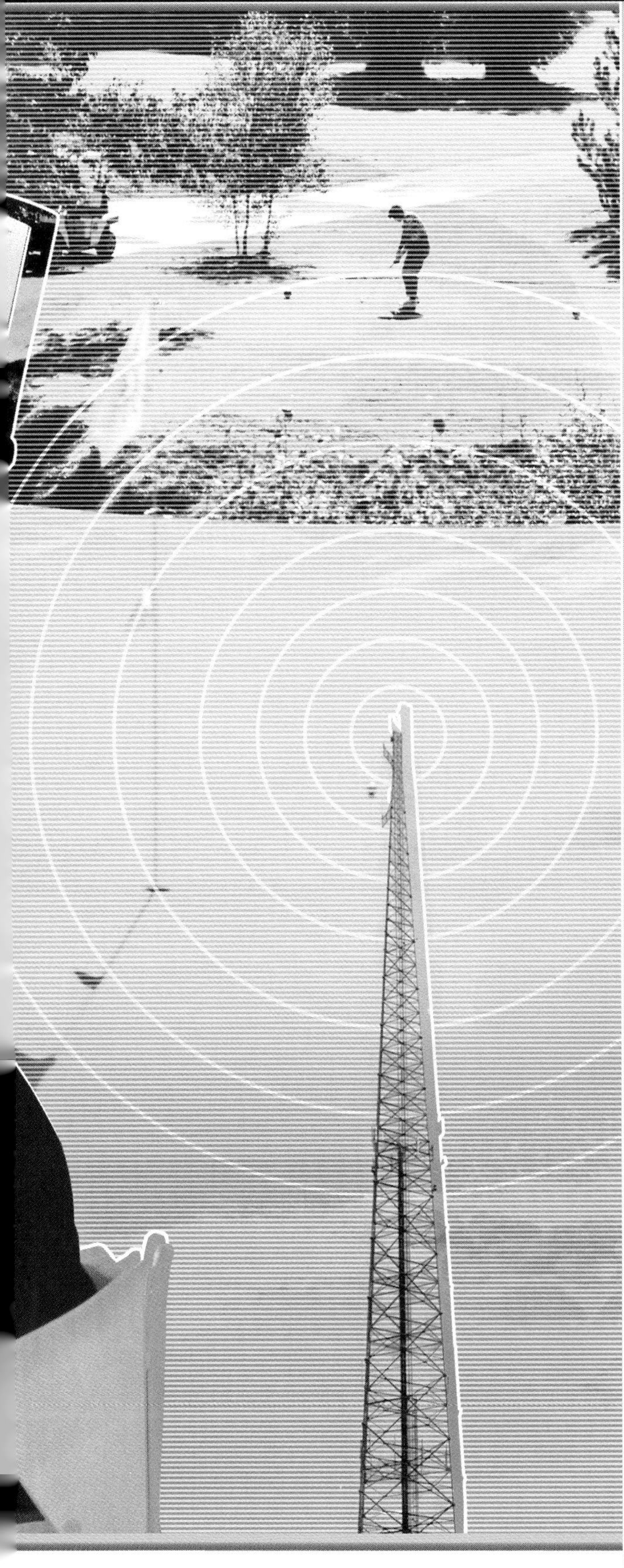

OBJECTIVES

After completing this chapter, you will be able to:

1. Discuss the components required for successful communications
2. Identify various sending and receiving devices
3. Describe uses of computer communications
4. List advantages of using a network
5. Differentiate among client/server, peer-to-peer, and P2P networks
6. Describe the various network communications technologies
7. Explain the purpose of communications software
8. Describe various types of lines for communications over the telephone network
9. Describe commonly used communications devices
10. Discuss different ways to set up a home network
11. Identify various physical and wireless transmission media

CONTENTS

COMMUNICATIONS

Computer **communications** describes a process in which two or more computers or devices transfer data, instructions, and information. Originally, only large computers had communications capabilities. Today, even the smallest computers and devices communicate directly with one another, with hundreds of computers on a company network, or with millions of other computers around the globe. The Internet provides a means for worldwide communications.

Figure 9-1 shows a sample communications system. Some communications involve cables and wires; others communicate wirelessly sending signals through the air. As illustrated in this figure, communications systems contain all types of computers and computing devices. For successful communications, you need the following:

- A **sending device** that initiates an instruction to transmit data, instructions, or information.
- A communications device that connects the sending device to a communications channel.

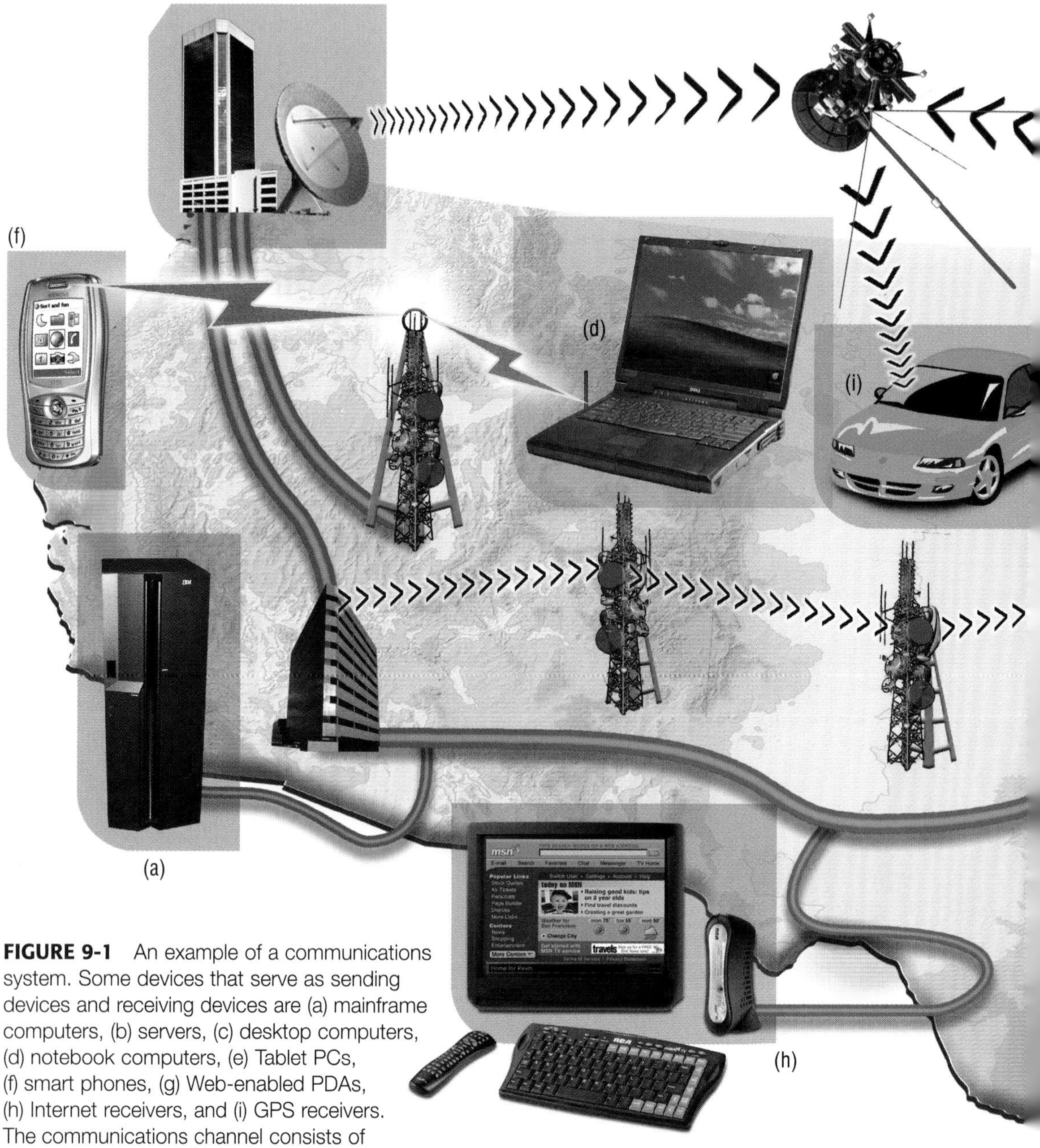

FIGURE 9-1 An example of a communications system. Some devices that serve as sending devices and receiving devices are (a) mainframe computers, (b) servers, (c) desktop computers, (d) notebook computers, (e) Tablet PCs, (f) smart phones, (g) Web-enabled PDAs, (h) Internet receivers, and (i) GPS receivers. The communications channel consists of telephone lines, cable television and other underground lines, microwave stations, and satellites.

- A **communications channel**, or transmission media on which the data, instructions, or information travel.
- A communications device that connects the communications channel to a receiving device.
- A **receiving device** that accepts the transmission of data, instructions, or information.

As shown in Figure 9-1, all types of computers and mobile devices serve as sending and receiving devices in a communications system. This includes mainframe computers, servers, desktop computers, notebook computers, Tablet PCs, PDAs, smart phones, Internet receivers, and GPS receivers. People use sending and receiving devices for many different types of communications.

Analog and Digital Communications

Data, instructions, and information travel along a communications channel in either analog or digital form, depending on the type of communications channel. Two examples of communications channels are cable television lines and telephone lines. Cable television lines use digital signals, while some telephone lines use analog signals. An *analog signal* consists of a continuous electrical wave. A *digital signal* consists of individual electrical pulses that represent bits grouped together into bytes.

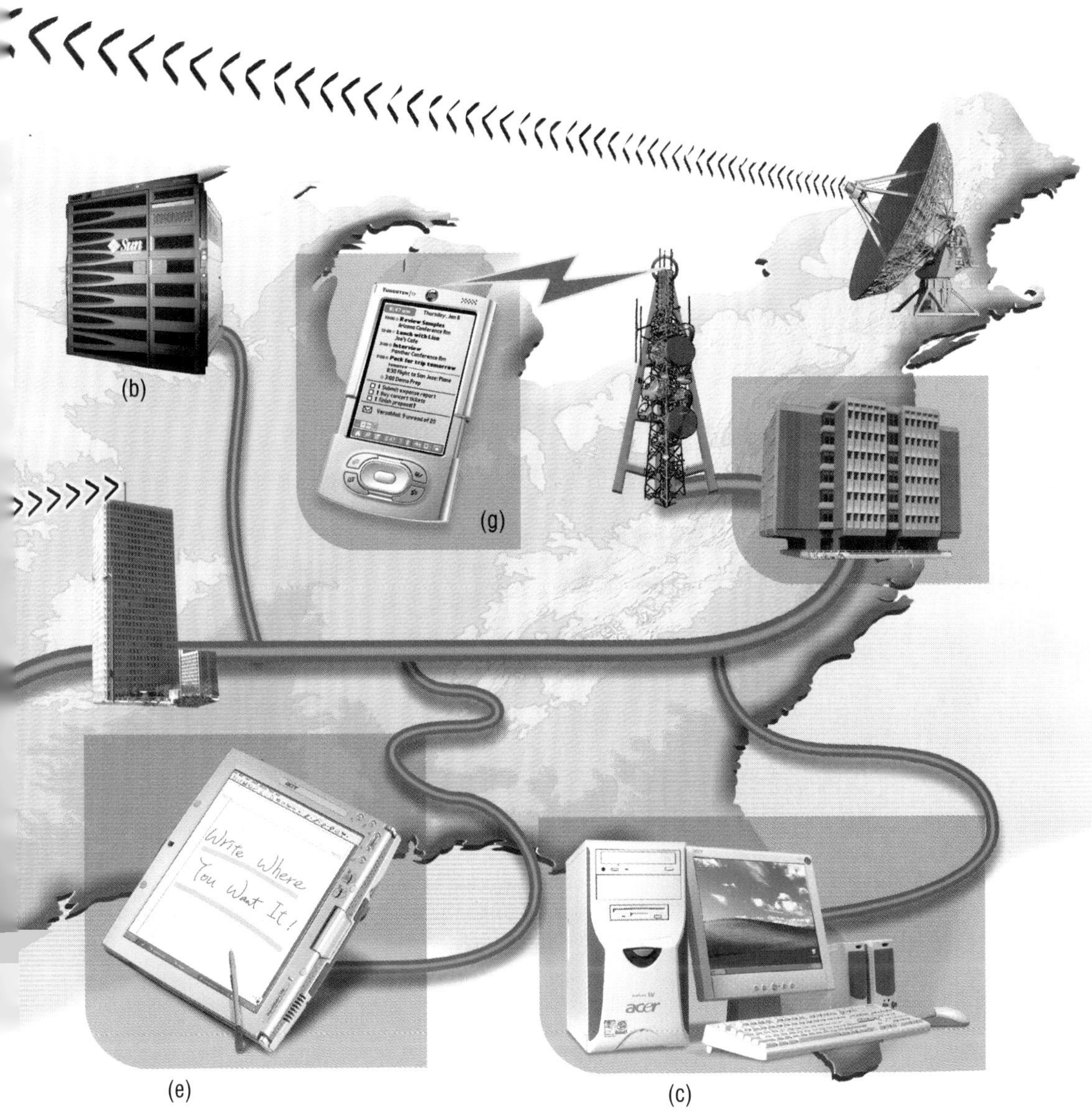

One type of communications device that connects a communications channel to a sending or receiving device such as a computer is a modem. Computers process data as digital signals. Thus, for communications channels that use digital signals, the modem transfers the digital signals between the computer and the communications channel (Figure 9-2a). If a communications channel uses analog signals, however, the modem first converts between analog and digital signals (Figure 9-2b).

This chapter presents various uses of communications, discusses different types of networks, and then presents several types of communications devices and communications channels.

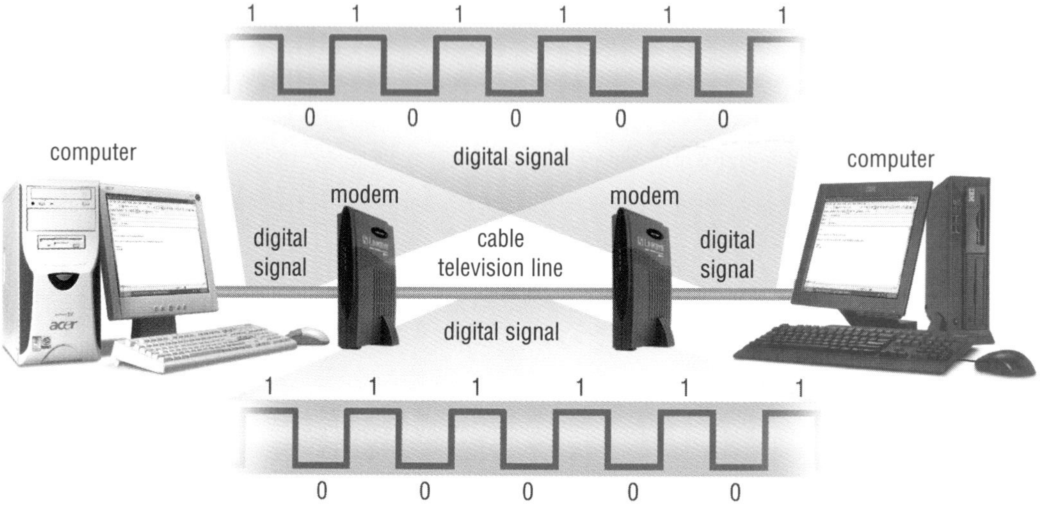

Figure 9-2a (all digital communications channel)

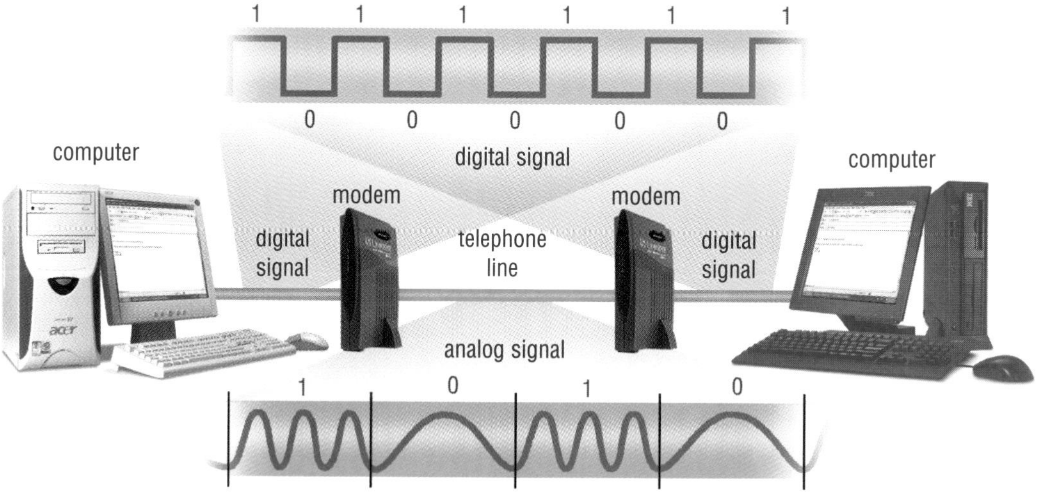

Figure 9-2b (digital to analog to digital communications channel)

FIGURE 9-2 A modem connects a communications channel, such as a cable television line or a telephone line, to a sending or receiving device such as a computer. Depending on the type of communications channel, a modem may need to convert digital signals to analog signals (and vice versa) before transferring data, instructions, and information to or from a sending or receiving device.

USES OF COMPUTER COMMUNICATIONS

Computer communications are everywhere. Many require that users subscribe to an Internet access provider. With other computer communications, an organization such as a business or school provides communications services to employees, students, or customers. The following pages discuss a variety of computer communications.

Internet, Web, E-Mail, Instant Messaging, Chat Rooms, Newsgroups, FTP, Web Folders, Video Conferencing, and Fax

Previous chapters discussed many uses of computer communications as they related to a particular topic. In the course of a day, it is likely you use, or use information generated by, one or more of these previously discussed communications technologies. The table in Figure 9-3 reviews the features of these uses of communications.

PREVIOUSLY DISCUSSED USES OF COMMUNICATIONS

Internet	Worldwide collection of networks that link millions of businesses, government agencies, educational institutions, and individuals
Web	Worldwide collection of electronic documents on the Internet that users access through a Web browser
E-Mail	Transmission of messages and files via a computer network (read Issue 9-1 for a related discussion)
Instant Messaging	Real-time Internet communications service that notifies you when one or more people are online and then allows you to exchange messages or files
Chat Rooms	Real-time typed conversations that take place on computers connected to a network (read Apply It 9-1 for more information)
Newsgroups	Online areas in which users conduct written discussions about a particular subject
FTP	Internet standard that permits users to upload and download files to and from FTP servers on the Internet
Web Folders	Shortcuts to a location on a Web server to which users publish documents and other files
Video Conferencing	Real-time meeting between two or more geographically separated people who use a network to transmit audio and video data
Fax Machine or Computer Fax/Modem	Transmits and receives documents over telephone lines

FIGURE 9-3 Uses of communications discussed in earlier chapters.

ISSUE 9-1

How Good Is Your E-Mail Writing?

E-mail may be today's most popular and influential method of communications. Millions of people around the world send and receive e-mail messages. E-mail links the geographically distanced, connects the economically separated, enables the physically challenged, and encourages the publicly timid. Because of e-mail, people are writing more than ever before — but is it *good* writing? The carefully crafted letters of an era gone by, handwritten in beautiful penmanship, have been replaced by e-mail messages stylistically equivalent to notes on the refrigerator. E-mail's immediacy often results in messages that are ill conceived, casually spelled, poorly worded, grammatically flawed, and tritely expressed (some trite phrases such as *in my humble opinion* are used so routinely they are replaced by abbreviations — IMHO). In general, has e-mail's impact on communications been positive or negative? Why? Should the quality of e-mail communications be a reason for concern? Why? Could someone's professional reputation be enhanced or hindered by the quality and effectiveness of his or her e-mail messages?

For more information about e-mail and the writing process, visit the Discovering Computers 2005 Issues Web page (**scsite.com/dc2005/issues**). Click Issue #1 below Chapter 9.

APPLY IT 9-1

Chat Room Attack!

When you feel like talking, you probably can find someone in a chat room to discuss just about any topic. Chat rooms are similar to conference calls, where everyone is online and available to talk simultaneously. Chat room members may live in your community or halfway across the world.

You can join an ongoing conversation at anytime, or you can be a lurker and just watch the chat without joining. While hosts moderate some chat sessions, others are open discussions. One of the more popular chat sites on the Web is Yahoo! Chat.

Before chatting, review the netiquette rules that govern online behavior. Foremost, be courteous and adhere to the same standards of behavior online that you follow in your everyday life.

Also become familiar with *Spk 'n Txt*, the cyber lingo used to convey messages using the fewest number of keystrokes possible. For example:

AFK – Away From Keyboard
BAK – Back At Keyboard
BBS – Be Back Soon
BRB – Be Right Back
BBIAB – Be Back In A Bit
c-ya – A quick way to say, see you
<g> – Grin
:-D – Laugh
L8R – Later
j/k – Just Kidding
TTUL – Talk To You Later
TY – Thank You
WB – Welcome Back

For more information about chat rooms and netiquette, visit the Discovering Computers 2005 Apply It Web page (**scsite.com/dc2005/apply**). Click Apply It #1 below Chapter 9.

The following pages discuss a variety of other uses of communications that have not been discussed previously. These include Internet telephony, Internet printing, Web services, collaboration, groupware, public Internet access points, cybercafés, global positioning systems, voice mail, and wireless messaging services.

Internet Telephony

Internet telephony, sometimes called *Voice over IP* (*VoIP*), enables users to talk to other users over the Internet. That is, Internet telephony uses the Internet (instead of the public switched telephone network) to connect a calling party and one or more called parties.

To place an Internet telephone call, you need Internet telephone software. As you speak into a computer microphone, the *Internet telephone software* and the computer's sound card digitize and compress your spoken words (the audio) and then transmit the digitized audio over the Internet to the called parties. Software and equipment at the receiving end reverse the process so the receiving parties can hear what you have said, just as if you were speaking on a telephone.

Internet Printing

Most newer network printers have Web addresses built into them. This feature allows users to send a print job to the printer from anywhere in the world. Instead of printing to a local printer, with *Internet printing*, users print to a Web address that is associated with a particular printer.

With the necessary software, a printer with Internet printing capability can receive print instructions from desktop computers, mobile computers, or mobile devices such as PDAs and smart phones. Many hotels use Internet printing, which enables hotel guests to print to the hotel printer — as long as they have the printer's Web address. Airlines also use Internet printing so air travelers can print while in flight and then pick up their printed documents when they arrive at an airport. Some industry experts predict that Internet printing will replace the need for faxes.

Web Services

Web services describe standardized software that enables programmers to create applications that communicate with other remote computers over the Internet or on an internal business network (Figure 9-4). Businesses are the primary users of Web services because this technology provides a means for departments to communicate with each other, suppliers, vendors, and with clients. For example, third-party vendors can use Web services to communicate with their online retailer's Web site to manage their inventory levels.

Web services do not require a specific programming language, operating system, or Web browser. Different applications from different platforms can communicate with each other by sending properly formatted *XML* (eXtensible Markup Language) to the Web services. A Windows application, for example, can communicate with a UNIX application. Web services do not have a user interface because the application's user interface interacts with the Web service.

FIGURE 9-4 An example of Web services.

Collaboration

Many software products provide a means to **collaborate**, or work online, with other users connected to a server. With Microsoft Office 2003, for example, users can conduct online meetings (Figure 9-5). An *online meeting* allows users to share documents with others in real time. That is, all participants see the document at the same time. As someone changes the document, everyone in the meeting sees the changes being made. During the online meeting, participants have the ability to open a separate window and type messages to one another. Some programs refer to this window as a chat room.

Instead of interacting in a live meeting, users often collaborate via e-mail. For example, if users want others to review a document, they can attach a routing slip to the document and send it via e-mail to everyone on the routing slip. When the first person on the routing slip receives the document, he or she may add comments to the document. As changes are made to the document, both the original text and the changes are displayed. When subsequent persons on the routing slip receive the document via e-mail, they see all the previous users' changes and can make additional changes. Once everyone on the routing slip has reviewed the document, it automatically returns to the sender.

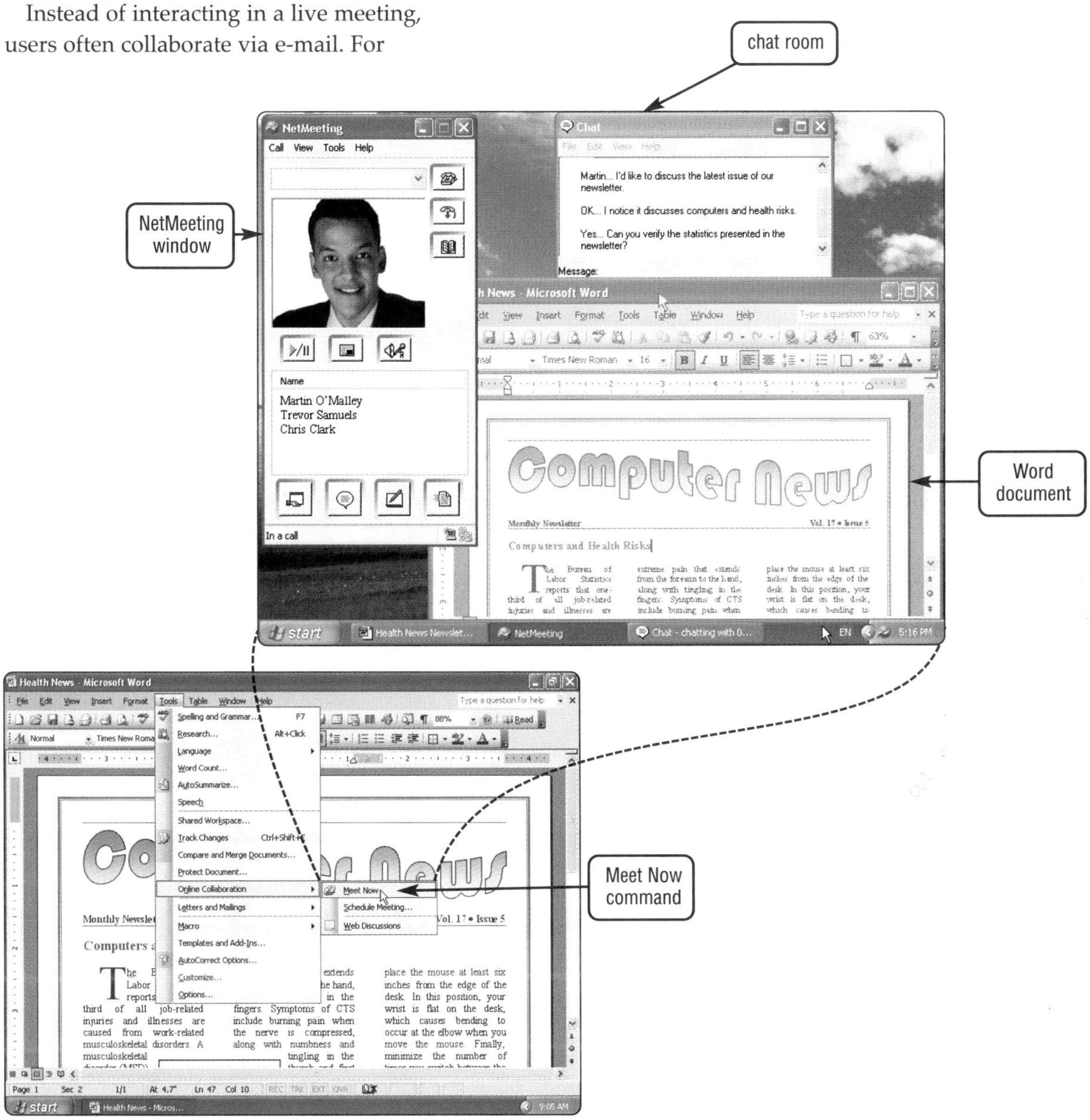

FIGURE 9-5 When you start an online meeting from a Microsoft Office 2003 program, the participants use NetMeeting to collaborate on the document.

Groupware

Groupware is a software application that helps groups of people work together on projects and share information over a network. Groupware is a component of a broad concept called *workgroup computing*, which includes network hardware and software that enables group members to communicate, manage projects, schedule meetings, and make group decisions. To assist with these activities, most groupware provides personal information manager (PIM) functions, such as an electronic appointment calendar, an address book, and a notepad. A major feature of groupware is group scheduling, in which a group calendar tracks the schedules of multiple users and helps coordinate appointments and meeting times.

Public Internet Access Points

In many public locations, people connect wirelessly to the Internet through a **public Internet access point** using their mobile computers or devices. Public Internet access points are appearing in airports, hotels, schools, shopping malls, and coffee shops. Through the public Internet access point, mobile users check e-mail, browse the Web, and access any service on the Internet — as long as their computers or devices have an appropriate network card and they are in a hot spot. A *hot spot* is an area with the capability of wireless Internet connectivity. Most hot spots range from 100 to 300 feet; some can extend to 15 miles.

Some public Internet access points provide free Internet access, while others charge a fee. Another type of access requires users to subscribe to a *wireless Internet service provider* (*WISP*), to which they pay per access fees, daily fees, or a monthly fee. Per access fees average $3, daily fees range from $5 to $20, and monthly fees range from $35 to $50 for unlimited access. Higher monthly fees provide national Internet access, while lower fees limit access to local areas.

WEB LINK 9-1

Public Internet Access Points

Visit the Discovering Computers 2005 WEB LINK page (**scsite.com/dc2005/weblink**). Click Public Internet Access Points below Chapter 9.

Cybercafés

More than 6,000 cybercafés exist in cities around the world. A **cybercafé** is a coffee house or restaurant that provides computers with Internet access to its customers (Figure 9-6). Although some provide free Internet access, most charge a per-hour or per-minute fee. Cybercafés allow the mobile user access to e-mail, the Web, and other services on the Internet when traveling without a computer.

FIGURE 9-6 People using Internet-connected computers, drinking beverages, and conversing in a cybercafé.

FAQ 9-1

What are the typical fee structures in a cybercafé?

Internet connection fees at a cybercafé usually range from $1.50 to $10.00 per hour. To print, the fees range from $0.25 per page to $3.00 per page. Printing fees vary depending on black-and-white versus color printouts and the type of paper used (e.g., plain paper, photo paper). Some cybercafés offer lower or waived rates to customers who purchase food or become a member of the café.

For more information about cybercafés, visit the Discovering Computers 2005 FAQ Web page (**scsite.com/dc2005/faq**). Click Cybercafés below Chapter 9.

Global Positioning System

A **global positioning system** (**GPS**) is a navigation system that consists of one or more earth-based receivers that accept and analyze signals sent by satellites in order to determine the receiver's geographic location (Figure 9-7). A *GPS receiver* is a handheld, mountable, or embedded device that contains an antenna, a radio receiver, and a processor. Many include a screen display that shows an individual's location on a map.

FIGURE 9-7 HOW A GPS WORKS

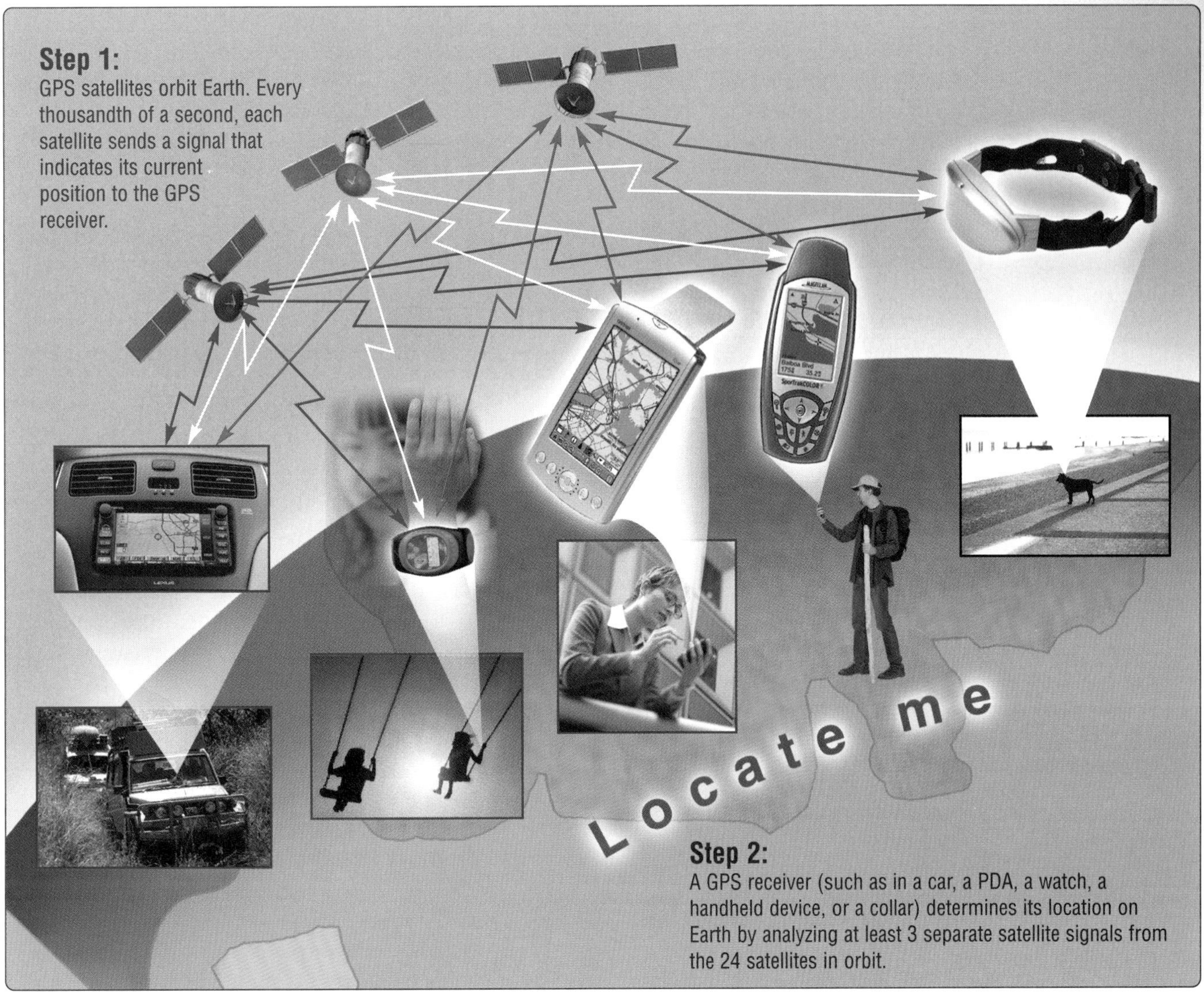

Several models of GPS receivers are available as stand-alone units. Many mobile devices such as PDAs and smart phones have GPS capability built into the device or as an add-on feature. Some users carry a handheld GPS receiver; others mount a receiver to an object such as an automobile, boat, airplane, farm and construction equipment, or computer.

The first and most used application of GPS technology is to assist people with determining where they are located. The data obtained from a GPS, however, can be applied to a variety of other uses: creating a map, ascertaining the best route between two points, locating a lost person or stolen object, or monitoring the movement of a person or object. A surveyor might use a GPS to design maps for construction projects. Many cars use GPSs to provide drivers with directions or other information, automatically call for help if the airbag is deployed, dispatch roadside assistance, unlock the driver's side door if keys are locked in the car, and track the vehicle if it is stolen. Hikers and remote campers may carry GPS receivers in case they need emergency help or directions. A rescue worker might use a GPS to locate a motorist stranded in a blizzard.

For applications that locate or track people, the GPS receiver typically works in conjunction with a cellular wireless network. When a user presses a button on the receiver or at regularly scheduled times, the GPS receiver captures data from the satellite and sends location information to a cellular wireless network. Once the cellular wireless network receives the data, its computer calculates the exact location of a person or object.

WEB LINK 9-2

GPS

Visit the Discovering Computers 2005 WEB LINK page (**scsite .com/dc2005/weblink**). Click GPS below Chapter 9.

A new use of GPS places the GPS receiver on a computer chip. One chip, called *Digital Angel*, is worn as a wristwatch or chain or woven into fabric. The chip measures and sends a person's biological information to a cellular wireless network. If the information relayed indicates a person needs medical attention, dispatchers use data from the GPS receiver to calculate the person's location and immediately send emergency medical help. Other possible uses of Digital Angel and similar products include locating a missing person or pet, tracking parolees, and protecting valuables. Read Issue 9-2 for a related discussion.

ISSUE 9-2

What Is Under Your Skin?

The FDA recently agreed to allow a group of about 50 volunteers to have a computer chip, called the *VeriChip*, implanted in their bodies. The cylindrical chip, a little larger than a grain of rice, can be scanned for medical and identification information and someday may allow people to be tracked by global positioning systems (GPSs). Developers say that, when the chip is read by a VeriChip scanner, the chip can communicate a patient's medical history, identify a lost child, or even locate the victim of a kidnapping. Similar technologies have been used with pets and farm animals for almost a decade. Yet, despite its potential benefits, the chip has its critics. Detractors fear the chip will destroy personal privacy and someday could lead to government attempts to track citizens and control individual freedoms. Is VeriChip a good idea? Why or why not? In what other ways do you think a VeriChip could be used? Would you be willing to have a VeriChip implanted in your body? Why?

For more information about VeriChip, visit the Discovering Computers 2005 Issues Web page (**scsite.com/dc2005/issues**). Click Issue #2 below Chapter 9.

Voice Mail

Voice mail, which functions much like an answering machine, allows someone to leave a voice message for one or more people. Unlike answering machines, however, a computer in the voice mail system converts an analog voice message into digital form. Once digitized, the message is stored in a voice mailbox. A *voice mailbox* is a storage location on a hard disk in the voice mail system.

A voice mail system usually provides individual voice mailboxes for many users (for example, employees in a company or students and faculty at a college). By accessing their voice mailboxes, recipients of a call listen to messages, may add comments to a message, and reply or forward a message to another voice mailbox in the voice mail system. Some voice mail systems allow users to broadcast a message, which sends the same message to a group of people or to everyone listed in the system's database. Colleges, for example, might use voice mail to notify every student of registration deadlines and weather-related school closings.

Wireless Messaging Services

Users can send and receive wireless messages to and from smart phones, cellular telephones, or PDAs using three techniques: text messaging, instant messaging, and picture messaging. In most cases, you can receive these messages at no cost but pay a per use fee to send messages to others — usually about $5 per month. The type of messaging you use depends primarily on the services offered by the wireless Internet service provider (WISP) that works with the cellular phone or PDA you select.

TEXT MESSAGING With **text messaging**, also called **SMS** (*short message service*), users type and send short text messages from a smart phone, PDA, or a personal computer to a smart phone or PDA with a compatible text messaging service. Most text messages have a limit of about 160 characters per message. Read Issue 9-3 for a related discussion.

INSTANT MESSAGING As discussed in Chapter 2, instant messaging (IM) is a real-time Internet communications service that allows you to exchange messages with one or more online users. Some WISPs partner with IM services so you can use your smart phone or PDA to send instant messages. AT&T Wireless, for example, allows communications through AOL Instant Messenger and Yahoo! Messenger. With these services, you can send instant messages to other online computer users, PDA users, or smart phone users — as long as you and the message recipient(s) have a compatible IM service.

PICTURE MESSAGING Users can send graphics, pictures, video clips, and sound files, as well as short text messages with **picture messaging**, also called *MMS* (*multimedia message service*) to another smart phone or PDA with a compatible picture messaging service (Figure 9-8). Smart phones and PDAs with picture messaging capability typically have a digital camera built into the device.

FIGURE 9-8 With picture messaging, users send each other photographs on a device such as a smart phone.

QUIZ YOURSELF 9-1

To check your knowledge of required components for communications, sending and receiving devices, and uses of computer communications, visit the Discovering Computers 2005 Quiz Yourself Web page (**scsite.com/dc2005/quiz**). Click Objectives 1 – 3 below Chapter 9.

NETWORKS

As discussed in Chapter 1, a **network** is a collection of computers and devices connected together via communications devices and transmission media. Many businesses network their computers together to facilitate communications, share hardware, share data and information, share software, and transfer funds (Figure 9-9). The next page elaborates on how businesses use networks.

ISSUE 9-3

High-Tech Crib Notes?

Several schools have banned student cell phones claiming that they disrupt classes and sometimes are used for illegal activities, such as drug sales. Now, schools may have another reason to prohibit cell phones and other wireless devices among students. Once, teachers only had to watch test-takers to make sure that no one was copying from a neighbor's paper or secretly referring to notes concealed under a desk. Recently, however, students were caught using their cellular telephones' messaging service to send each other answers to a test. Some teachers fear that more students soon may be using wireless devices to communicate covertly with classmates during a test, or even to receive messages from sources outside the classroom. To eliminate this high-tech method of passing crib notes, should cell phones, laptop computers, Tablet PCs, PDAs, and other wireless devices be banned from schools? Why or why not? Short of banning wireless devices, what, if anything, can schools do to prevent students from using them to cheat?

For more information about smart phones in the classroom, visit the Discovering Computers 2005 Issues Web page (**scsite .com/dc2005/issues**) and click Issue #3 below Chapter 9.

FIGURE 9-9 Businesses use networks to facilitate communications, share hardware, share data and information, share software, and transfer funds.

A network can be internal to an organization or span the world by connecting itself to the Internet. Networks facilitate communications among users and allow users to share resources with other users. Some examples of resources are data, information, hardware, and software.

The following paragraphs explain the advantages of using a network.

- Facilitating communications — Using a network, people communicate efficiently and easily via e-mail, instant messaging, chat rooms, video telephone calls, video conferencing, Internet telephony, groupware, and wireless messaging services. Some of these communications such as e-mail occur within a business's internal network. Other times, they occur globally over the Internet. As discussed earlier in this chapter, users have a multitude of devices available to send and receive communications. Read Issue 9-4 for a related discussion.

ISSUE 9-4

Are Cameras at Intersections Inappropriate?

Cameras that photograph real-time situations are everywhere — in parking garages, at day-care centers, in public buildings, and even at street corners. In more than 50 cities, video cameras are installed at intersections to catch speeding motorists and those who run red lights. When a violator is spotted, the cameras transmit a taped image to the local police network, and computers automatically send a citation to the vehicle's owner. Supporters of the video cameras say the systems promote safety and free police officers for other duties. Yet, critics express concerns about privacy issues. A U.S. congressman who opposes the video cameras questions how long tapes are kept, how officials can be sure a violator is the vehicle's owner, what safeguards are in place to prevent the tapes from being misused, and whether the systems violate a defendant's right to face his or her accuser. Are video cameras at intersections a good idea? Why or why not? How can the concerns of opponents of the systems be answered?

For more information about video camera communications, visit the Discovering Computers 2005 Issues Web page (**scsite.com/dc2005/issues**). Click Issue #4 below Chapter 9.

- Sharing hardware — In a networked environment, each computer on the network has access to hardware on the network. Suppose several desktop computers on a network each require the use of a laser printer. If the computers and a laser printer are connected to a network, the computer users each access the laser printer on the network, as they need it. Business and home users network their hardware to save money. That is, it may be too costly to provide each user with the same piece of hardware such as a printer.
- Sharing data and information — In a networked environment, any authorized computer user can access data and information stored on other computers on the network. A large company, for example, might have a database of customer information. Any authorized person, including a mobile user with a PDA or smart phone connected to the network, has access to the database. The capability of providing access to and storage of data and information on shared storage devices is an important feature of many networks.

  Most businesses use a standard, such as *EDI* (*electronic data interchange*), that defines how data transmits across telephone lines or other means. For example, companies use EDI to handle product catalog distribution, bids, requests for quotations, proposals, order placement, shipping notifications, invoicing, and payment processing. EDI enables businesses to operate with a minimum amount of paperwork.
- Sharing software — Users connected to a network have access to software on the network. To support multiple users' access of software, most vendors sell network versions or site licenses of their software, which usually cost less than buying individual copies of the software for each computer. A *network license* is a legal agreement that allows multiple users to access the software on a server simultaneously. The network license fee usually is based on the number of users or the number of computers attached to the network. Some organizations, instead, have a site license agreement with a software vendor. A *site license* is a legal agreement that permits users to install the software on multiple computers — usually at a volume discount.

- Transferring funds — Called *electronic funds transfer* (*EFT*), it allows users connected to a network to transfer money from one bank account to another via telephone lines or other transmission media. Both businesses and consumers use EFT. For example, consumers use an ATM to access their bank account. Businesses deposit payroll checks directly in employees' bank accounts. Consumers use credit cards to make purchases from a retail Web site. Businesses use EFT to purchase and pay for goods purchased from vendors. Both businesses and consumers pay bills online, with which they instruct a bank to use EFT to pay creditors.

Instead of using the Internet or investing in and administering an internal network, some companies hire a value-added network provider for network functions. A *value-added network* (*VAN*) is a third-party business that provides networking services such as secure data and information transfer, e-mail, and management reports. Some VANs charge an annual or monthly fee; others charge by service used.

For a technical discussion about networks, read the High-Tech Talk article on page 495.

FIGURE 9-10 An example of a local area network (LAN).

LANs, MANs, and WANs

Networks usually are classified as a local area network, metropolitan area network, or wide area network. The main differentiation among these classifications is their area of coverage, as described in the following paragraphs.

LAN A **local area network** (**LAN**) is a network that connects computers and devices in a limited geographical area such as a home, school computer laboratory, office building (Figure 9-10), or closely positioned group of buildings. Each computer or device on the network, called a *node*, often shares resources such as printers, large hard disks, and programs. Often, the nodes are connected via cables. A **wireless LAN** (**WLAN**), by contrast, is a LAN that uses no physical wires.

MAN A *metropolitan area network* (*MAN*) is a high-speed network that connects local area networks in a metropolitan area such as a city or town and handles the bulk of communications activity across that region. A MAN typically includes one or more LANs, but covers a smaller geographic area than a WAN. The state of Pennsylvania, for example, has a MAN that connects state agencies and individual users in the region around the state capital.

A MAN usually is managed by a consortium of users or by a single network provider that sells the service to the users. Local and state governments, for example, regulate some MANs. Telephone companies, cable television operators, and other organizations provide users with connections to the MAN.

WEB LINK 9-3

LANs

Visit the Discovering Computers 2005 WEB LINK page (**scsite.com/dc2005/weblink**). Click LANs below Chapter 9.

WAN A **wide area network** (**WAN**) is a network that covers a large geographic area (such as a city, country, or the world) using a communications channel that combines many types of media such as telephone lines, cables, and radio waves (Figure 9-11). A WAN can be one large network or can consist of two or more LANs connected together. The Internet is the world's largest WAN.

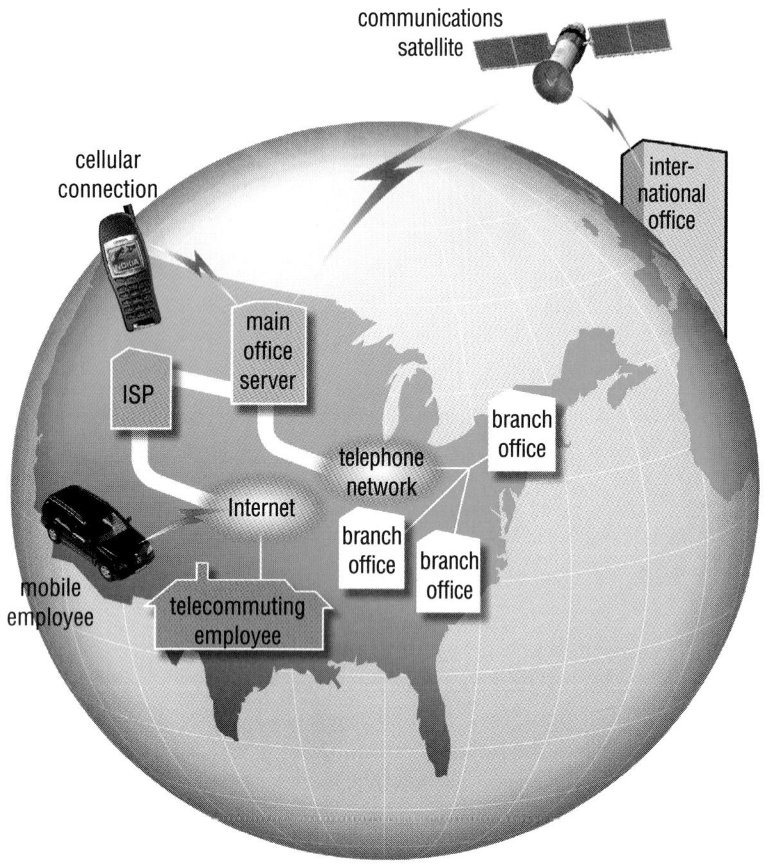

FIGURE 9-11 An example of a WAN.

Network Architectures

The design of computers, devices, and media in a network, sometimes called the *network architecture*, is categorized as either client/server or peer-to-peer. The following paragraphs discuss these network architectures.

CLIENT/SERVER On a **client/server network**, one or more computers act as a server, and the other computers on the network request services from the server (Figure 9-12). A **server**, sometimes called a *host computer*, controls access to the hardware, software, and other resources on the network and provides a centralized storage area for programs, data, and information. The **clients** are other computers on the network that rely on the server for its resources. For example, a server might store a database of customers. Clients on the network (company employees) access the customer database on the server.

Some servers, called *dedicated servers*, perform a specific task and can be placed with other dedicated servers to perform multiple tasks. For example, a *file server* stores and manages files. A *print server* manages printers and print jobs. A *database server* stores and provides access to a database. A *network server* manages network traffic (activity).

Although it can connect a smaller number of computers, a client/server network typically provides an efficient means to connect 10 or more computers. Most client/server networks require a person to serve as a network administrator because of the large size of a client/server network.

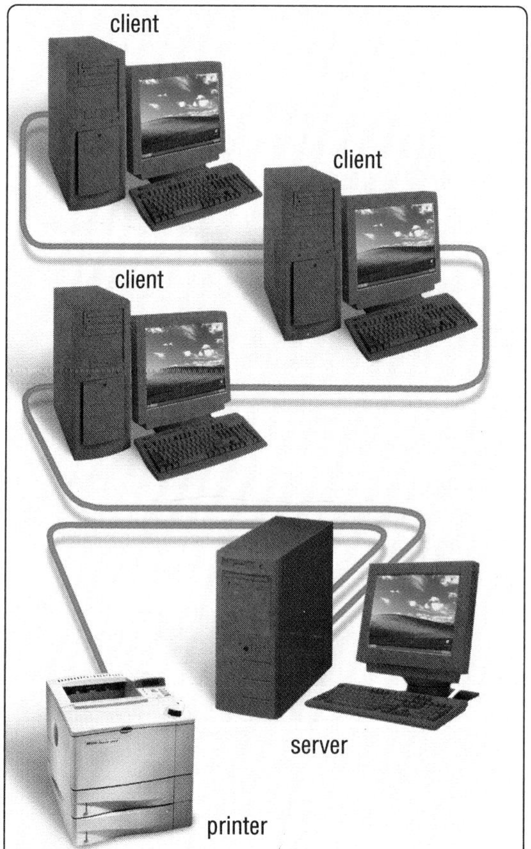

FIGURE 9-12 On a client/server network, one or more computers act as a server, and the clients access the server(s).

PEER-TO-PEER A *peer-to-peer network* is a simple, inexpensive network that typically connects less than 10 computers. Each computer, called a *peer*, has equal responsibilities and capabilities, sharing hardware (such as a printer), data, or information with other computers on the peer-to-peer network (Figure 9-13). Each computer stores files on its own storage devices. Thus, each computer on the network contains both the network operating system and application software. All computers on the network share any peripheral device(s) attached to any computer. For example, one computer may have a laser printer and a scanner, while another has an ink-jet printer and an external hard disk.

Peer-to-peer networks are ideal for very small businesses and home users. Some operating systems, such as Windows, include a peer-to-peer networking utility that allows users to set up a peer-to-peer network.

INTERNET PEER-TO-PEER Another type of peer-to-peer, called *P2P*, describes an Internet network, on which users connect directly to each other's hard disks and exchange files over the Internet (Figure 9-14). This type of peer-to-peer network sometimes is called a *file sharing network* because users with compatible software and an Internet connection copy files from someone else's hard disk to their hard disks. As more users connect to the network, each user has access to the other users' hard disks. When users log off, others no longer have access to their hard disks. To maintain an acceptable speed for communications, some implementations of P2P limit the number of users.

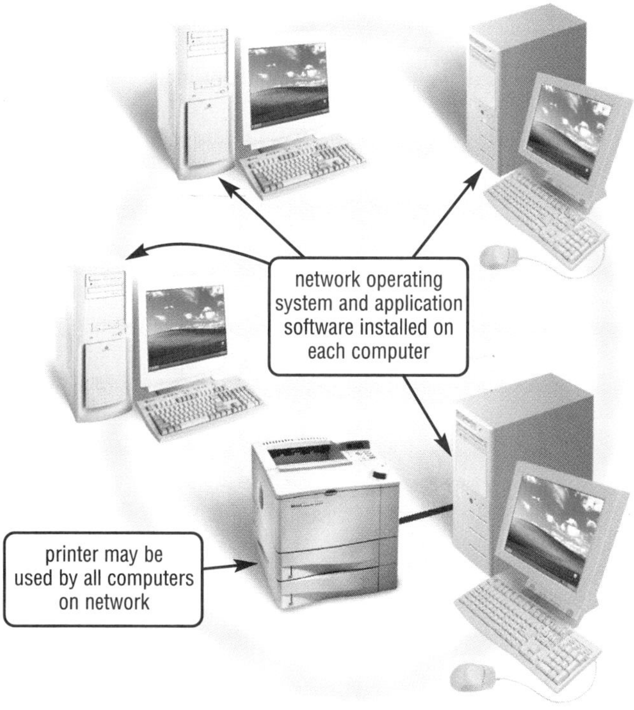

FIGURE 9-13 Each computer on a peer-to-peer network shares its hardware and software with other computers on the network.

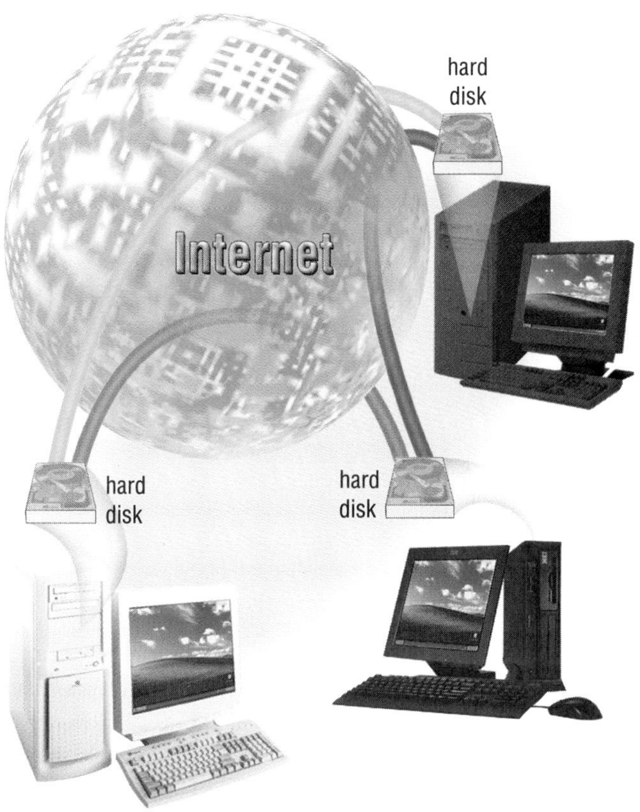

FIGURE 9-14 P2P describes an Internet network on which users connect to each other's hard disks and exchange files directly.

Examples of networking software that support P2P are Gnutella, KaZaA, and K-Lite, which allow users to swap MP3 music files via the Web. For example, when one user requests a song, the program searches all connected users' hard disks. If a match is located, the MP3 file is copied to the requesting computer. These programs initially stirred much controversy with respect to copyright infringement of music because they allowed users easily to copy MP3 music files free from one computer to another. To help reduce copyright infringement, today's music-sharing services are fee based, and music files are encrypted as they travel across the Internet.

Many businesses also see an advantage to using P2P. That is, companies and employees can exchange files using P2P, freeing the company from maintaining a network server for this purpose. Business-to-business e-commerce Web sites find that P2P easily allows buyers and sellers to share company information such as product databases.

WEB LINK 9-4

P2P

Visit the Discovering Computers 2005 WEB LINK page (**scsite .com/dc2005/weblink**). Click P2P below Chapter 9.

Network Topologies

A **network topology** refers to the layout of the computers and devices in a communications network. Three commonly used network topologies are bus, ring, and star. Networks usually use combinations of these topologies. The following pages discuss each of these topologies.

BUS NETWORK A *bus network* consists of a single central cable, to which all computers and other devices connect (Figure 9-15). The *bus* is the physical cable that connects the computers and other devices. The bus in a bus network transmits data, instructions, and information in both directions. When a sending device transmits data, the address of the receiving device is included with the transmission so the data is routed to the appropriate receiving device.

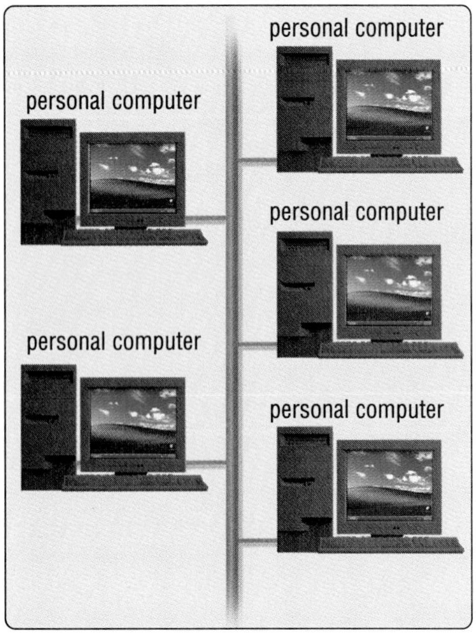

FIGURE 9-15 Devices in a bus network share a single data path.

Bus networks are popular on LANs because they are inexpensive and easy to install. One advantage of the bus network is that computers and other devices can be attached and detached at any point on the bus without disturbing the rest of the network. Another advantage is that failure of one device usually does not affect the rest of the bus network. The transmission simply bypasses the failed device. The greatest risk to a bus network is that the bus itself might become inoperable. If that happens, the network remains inoperative until the bus is back in working order.

RING NETWORK On a *ring network*, a cable forms a closed loop (ring) with all computers and devices arranged along the ring (Figure 9-16). Data transmitted on a ring network travels from device to device around the entire ring, in one direction. When a computer or device sends data, the data travels to each computer on the ring until it reaches its destination.

If a computer or device on a ring network fails, all devices before the failed device are unaffected, but those after the failed device cannot function. A ring network can span a larger distance than a bus network, but it is more difficult to install.

The ring topology primarily is used for LANs, but also is used in WANs.

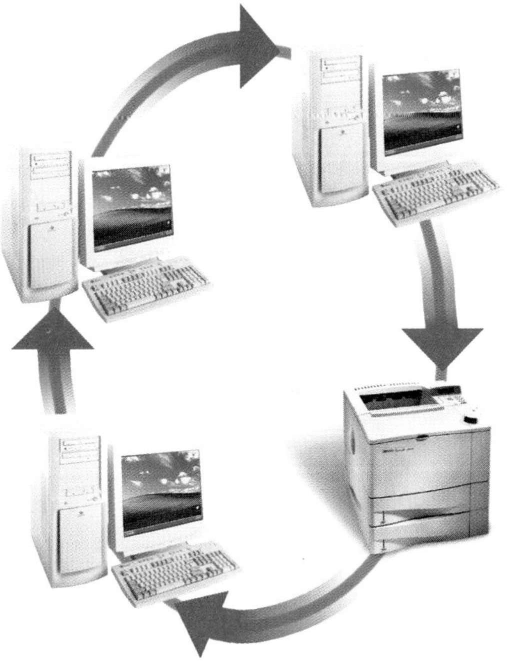

FIGURE 9-16 On a ring network, all connected devices form a continuous loop.

STAR NETWORK On a *star network*, all of the computers and devices (nodes) on the network connect to a central device, thus forming a star (Figure 9-17). The central device that provides a common connection point for nodes on the network is called the *hub*. All data that transfers from one node to another passes through the hub.

Similar to a bus network, star networks are fairly easy to install and maintain. Nodes can be added to and removed from the network with little or no disruption to the network.

On a star network, if one node fails, only that node is affected. The other nodes continue to operate normally. If the hub fails, however, the entire network is inoperable until the hub is repaired. Most large star networks, therefore, keep backup hubs available in case the primary hub fails.

FIGURE 9-17 A star network contains a single, centralized hub through which all the devices in the network communicate.

Network Communications Technologies

Today's networks connect terminals, devices, and computers from many different manufacturers across many types of networks, such as wide area, local area, and wireless. For the different devices on several types of networks to be able to communicate, the network must use a specific combination of hardware and software that has common network technology that allows them to communicate. The following sections discuss some of the more widely used network communications technologies for both wired and wireless networks including Ethernet, token ring, TCP/IP, 802.11, Bluetooth, IrDA, RFID, and WAP.

Ethernet

Ethernet is a network technology that allows nodes to contend for access to the network. If two computers on an Ethernet network attempt to send data at the same time, a collision will occur, and the computers must attempt to send their messages again.

Ethernet is based on a bus topology, but Ethernet networks can be wired in a star pattern. Today, Ethernet is the most popular LAN technology because it is relatively inexpensive and easy to install and maintain.

Ethernet networks often use cables to transmit data. At a 10 Mbps (million bits per second) data transfer rate, the original Ethernet standard is not very fast by today's standards. For small to mid-sized networks, however, Ethernet works quite well. A more recent Ethernet standard, called *Fast Ethernet*, has a data transfer rate of 100 Mbps, ten times faster than the original standard. *Gigabit Ethernet* provides an even higher speed of transmission, with transfer rates of 1 Gbps (1 billion bits per second). The *10-Gigabit Ethernet* supports transfer rates up to 10 Gbps.

WEB LINK 9-5

Ethernet

Visit the Discovering Computers 2005 WEB LINK page (**scsite .com/dc2005/weblink**). Click Ethernet below Chapter 9.

Token Ring

The second most popular LAN technology is **token ring**, which controls access to the network by requiring that devices on the network share or pass a special signal, called a token. A *token* is a special series of bits that function like a ticket. The device with the token can transmit data over the network. Only one token exists per network. This ensures that only one computer transmits data at a time. Token ring is based on a ring topology (although it can use a star topology).

Some token ring networks connect up to 72 devices. Others use a special type of wiring that allows up to 260 connections. The data transfer rate on a token ring network can be 4 Mbps, 16 Mbps, or up to 100 Mbps.

TCP/IP

Short for *Transmission Control Protocol/Internet Protocol*, **TCP/IP** is a network technology that manages the transmission of data by dividing it up into packets. Internet transmissions commonly use TCP/IP. When a computer sends data over the Internet, the data is divided into small pieces, or *packets*. Each packet contains the data, as well as the recipient (destination), the origin (sender), and the sequence information used to reassemble the data at the destination. Each packet travels along the fastest individual available path to the recipient's computer via communications devices called routers.

This technique of breaking a message into individual packets, sending the packets along the best route available, and then reassembling the data is called *packet switching*.

802.11

Developed by IEEE (pronounced I triple E), **802.11** is a family of standards for wireless LANs. Using 802.11, wireless computers or devices communicate via radio waves with other computers or devices. The table in Figure 9-18 outlines the various 802.11 standards and their data transfer rates. The term **Wi-Fi** (*wireless fidelity*) identifies any network based on the 802.11 family of standards. Wi-Fi Certified products are guaranteed to be able to communicate with each other. Windows XP and Windows Mobile 2003 include support for Wi-Fi. Because this standard uses Ethernet technology, Wi-Fi networks easily can be integrated with wired Ethernet networks.

One popular use of the Wi-Fi standard is in public Internet access points, discussed earlier in this chapter, that offer mobile users the ability to connect to the Internet with their wireless computers and devices. Many homes and small businesses also use Wi-Fi to network computers and devices together wirelessly. In open or outdoor areas free from interference, the computers or devices should be within 1,000 feet of each other. In closed areas, the wireless network range is about 300 feet. To obtain communications at the maximum distances, you may need to install extra antennas.

802.11 FAMILY OF STANDARDS

Standard	Transfer Rates
802.11	1 or 2 Mbps
802.11a	Up to 54 Mbps
802.11b	Up to 11 Mbps
802.11g	54 Mbps and higher

FIGURE 9-18 A comparison of standards in the 802.11 family.

Bluetooth

As discussed in Chapter 4, **Bluetooth** technology uses short-range radio waves to transmit data between two Bluetooth devices. The data transfers between devices at a rate of 1 Mbps. To communicate with each other, Bluetooth devices often must be within about 10 meters (about 33 feet) but can be extended to 100 meters with additional equipment.

A Bluetooth device contains a small chip that allows it to communicate with other Bluetooth devices. Examples of these devices can include desktop computers, notebook computers, handheld computers, PDAs (Figure 9-19), smart phones, headsets, microphones, digital cameras, fax machines, and printers. Windows XP has built-in Bluetooth support that allows users easily to configure Bluetooth communications.

IrDA

FAQ 9-2

Are Wi-Fi and Bluetooth competing technologies?

Not really. Bluetooth is designed for shorter-range communications between two devices, one of which usually is a mobile device (e.g., a notebook computer and a printer, a digital camera and a desktop computer, two PDAs). With Wi-Fi, by contrast, users wirelessly network many computers and devices together, which can be dispersed physically across a much wider area.

For more information about Wi-Fi and Bluetooth, visit the Discovering Computers 2005 FAQ Web page (**scsite.com/dc2005/faq**). Click Wi-Fi and Bluetooth below Chapter 9.

As discussed in Chapter 4, some computers and devices use the **IrDA** specification to transmit data wirelessly to each other via infrared (IR) light waves. The devices transfer data at rates from 115 Kbps to 4 Mbps between their IrDA ports.

Infrared requires a *line-of-sight transmission*; that is, the sending device and the receiving device must be in line with each other so that nothing obstructs the path of the infrared light wave. Because Bluetooth does not require

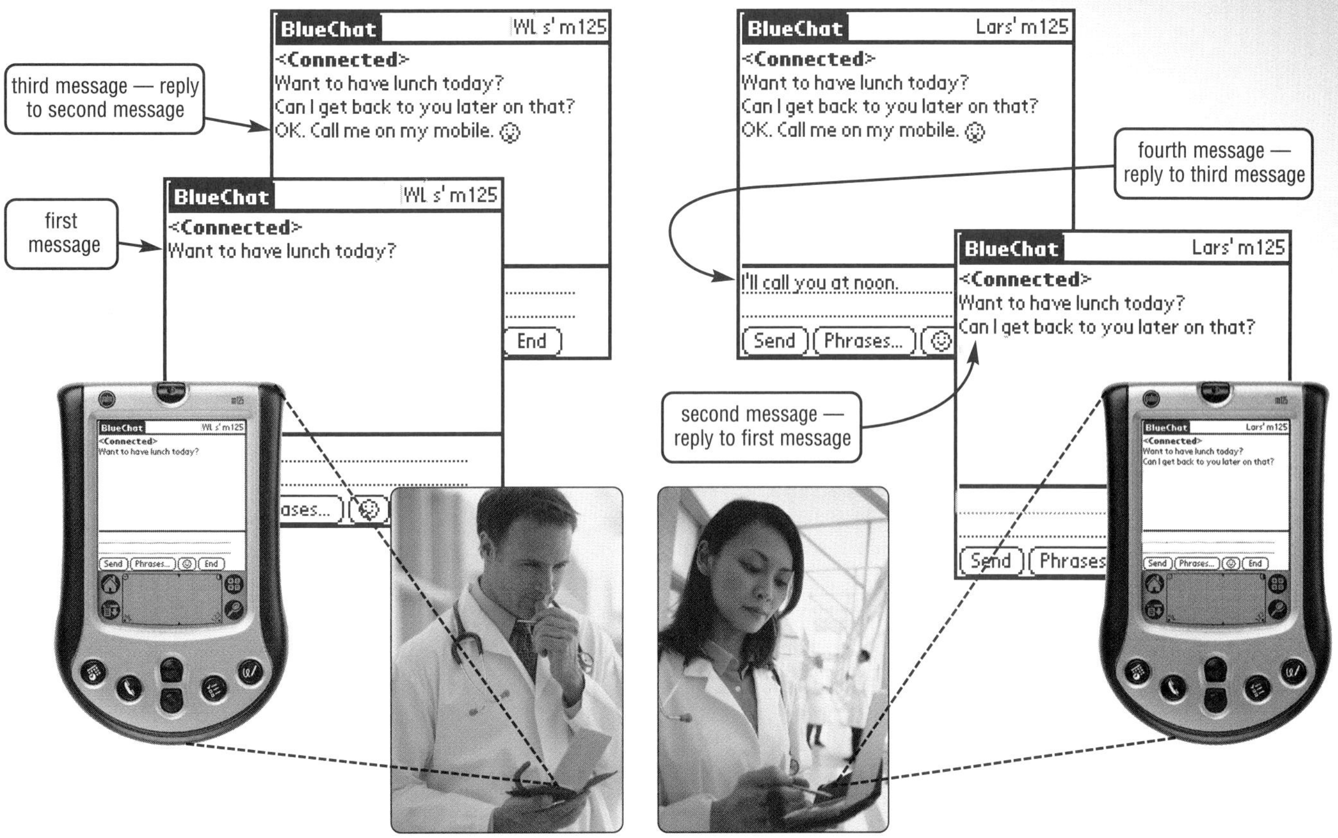

FIGURE 9-19 An example of colleagues using Bluetooth PDAs to communicate with each other in a hospital.

line-of-sight transmission, some industry experts predict that Bluetooth technology will replace infrared.

RFID

RFID (*radio frequency identification*) is a technology that uses radio signals to communicate with a tag placed in an object, an animal, or a person. The tag, called a transponder, is a computer chip that contains the information to be transmitted via radio waves. Through an antenna, a transceiver reads the radio signals and transfers the information to a computer or computing device.

Many retailers see RFID as an alternative to bar code identification because it does not require direct contact or line-of-site transmission. In this application, each product in a store would contain a tag that identifies the product. As consumers remove products from the store shelves and place them in a shopping cart, transceivers identify shelves that need restocking and automatically reorder products low in inventory. When the consumer finishes shopping, he or she pushes a full shopping cart by a transceiver that communicates with a computer to calculate the amount due, eliminating the need for checking out each item.

Other uses of RFID tags include tracking times of runners in a marathon; tracking the location of soldiers, employee wardrobes, and airline baggage; and tracking payment as vehicles pass through booths on tollway systems.

WAP

The **Wireless Application Protocol (WAP)** allows wireless mobile devices such as smart phones and PDAs to access the Internet and its services such as the Web, e-mail, chat rooms, and newsgroups. For example, to display a Web page on a smart phone, the phone must be WAP enabled and contain a microbrowser.

WAP uses a client/server network. The wireless device contains the client software, which connects to the Internet service provider's server. On WAP-enabled devices, data transfer rates range from 9.6 to 153 Kbps depending on the type of service. As the demand for wireless Internet access grows, the availability of WAP-enabled devices increases.

WEB LINK 9-6

WAP

Visit the Discovering Computers 2005 WEB LINK page (**scsite.com/dc2005/weblink**). Click WAP below Chapter 9.

Intranets

Recognizing the efficiency and power of the Internet, many organizations apply Internet and Web technologies to their own internal networks. An *intranet* (intra means within) is an internal network that uses Internet technologies. Intranets generally make company information accessible to employees and facilitate working in groups.

Simple intranet applications include electronic publishing of organizational materials such as telephone directories, event calendars, procedure manuals, employee benefits information, and job postings. Additionally, an intranet typically includes a connection to the Internet. More sophisticated uses of intranets include groupware applications such as project management, chat rooms, newsgroups, group scheduling, and video conferencing.

An intranet essentially is a small version of the Internet that exists within an organization. It uses TCP/IP technologies, has a Web server, supports multimedia Web pages coded in HTML, and is accessible via a Web browser such as Microsoft Internet Explorer or Netscape Navigator. Users update information on the intranet by creating and posting a Web page, using a method similar to that used on the Internet.

Sometimes a company uses an *extranet*, which allows customers or suppliers to access part of its intranet. Package shipping companies, for example, allow customers to access their intranet to print air bills, schedule pickups, and even track shipped packages as the packages travel to their destinations.

COMMUNICATIONS SOFTWARE

Communications software consists of programs that (1) help users establish a connection to another computer or network; (2) manage the transmission of data, instructions, and information; and (3) provide an interface for users to communicate with one another. The first two are system software and the third is application software. Chapter 3 presented a variety of examples of application software for communications: e-mail, FTP, Web browser, newsgroup/message boards, chat rooms, instant messaging, video conferencing, and video telephone calls. Read Issue 9-5 for a related discussion.

Some communications devices are preprogrammed to accomplish communications tasks. Other communications devices require separate communications software to ensure proper transmission of data. For two computers to communicate, they must have compatible communications software. Communications software usually is bundled with the operating system or purchased network devices.

Often, a computer has various types of communications software, each serving a different purpose. One type of communications software helps users establish an Internet connection using wizards, dialog boxes, and other on-screen messages (Figure 9-20).

Communications software also allows users to configure a network such as a home or office network and connect devices to an existing network (Figure 9-21). You also can use communications software to connect to an FTP server.

ISSUE 9-5

Should Libraries Use Filtering Software?

Many libraries offer computers that adults and children can use to connect to the Internet. To prevent children from using these computers to access obscene material on the Web, Congress enacted the *Children's Internet Protection Act* (*CIPA*). The act mandates that libraries must install filtering software in order to receive federal funds. A group of librarians, library users, and Web site operators challenged the act, arguing that it violates the First Amendment right of free speech. In 2003, the Supreme Court upheld the law. Supporters of the decision claim that filtering software protects children. Opponents insist, however, that filtering software restricts intellectual freedom and prevents library patrons from accessing some unobjectionable sites. To control the impact of filtering software, the American Library Association has asked each manufacturer to provide a database of blocked sites that librarians can use to determine the software that best meets their needs. Yet, manufacturers are reluctant to supply the database, fearing it may be valuable to competitors. Should libraries have to use filtering software in order to receive federal funds? Why or why not? What measures, if any, should libraries be allowed to adopt instead? Is it reasonable to ask filtering software manufacturers to reveal their databases? Why?

For more information about libraries and the Internet, visit the Discovering Computers 2005 Issues Web page (**scsite.com/dc2005/issues**) and click Issue #5 below Chapter 9.

FIGURE 9-20 HOW TO CREATE A DIAL-UP INTERNET CONNECTION

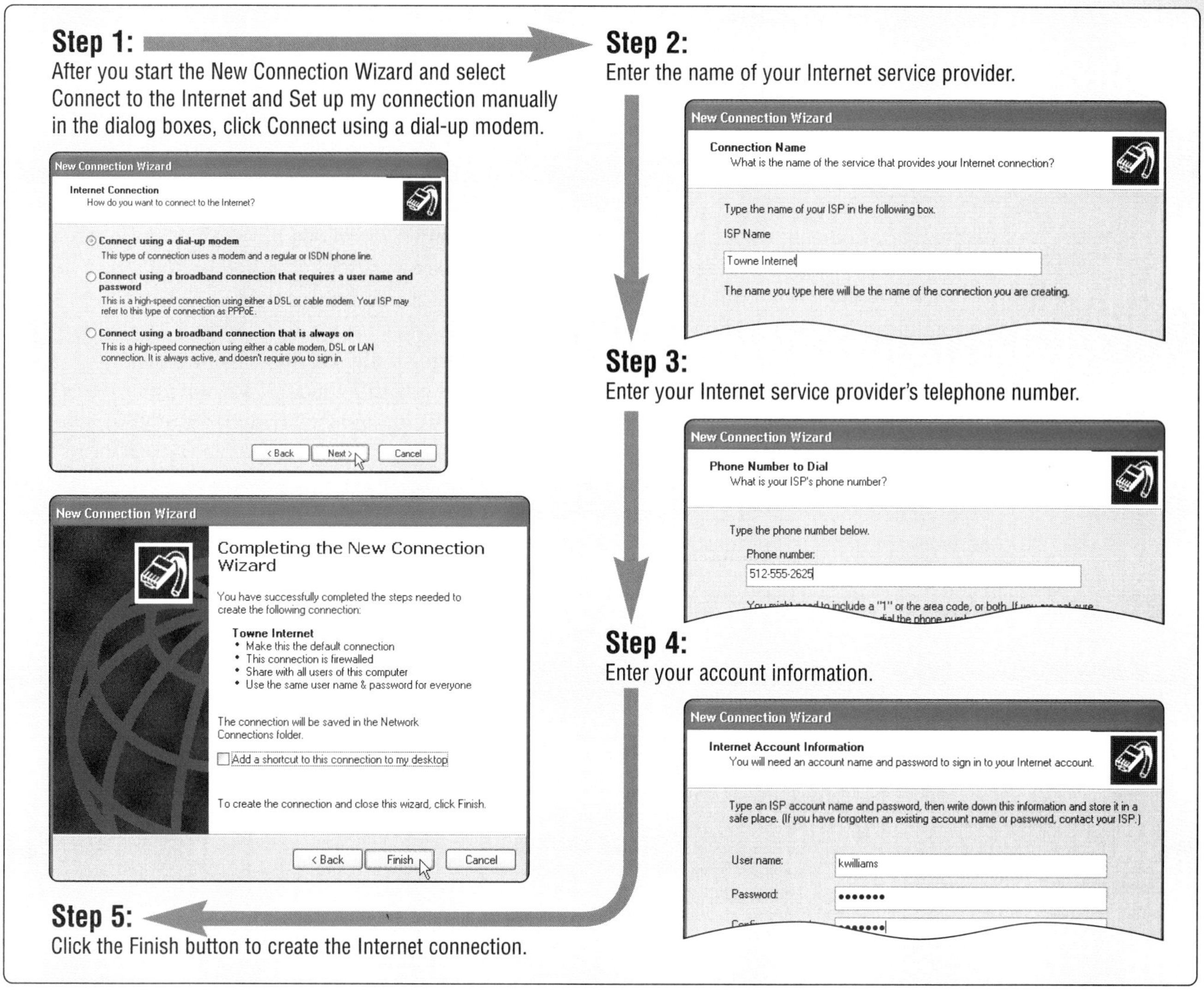

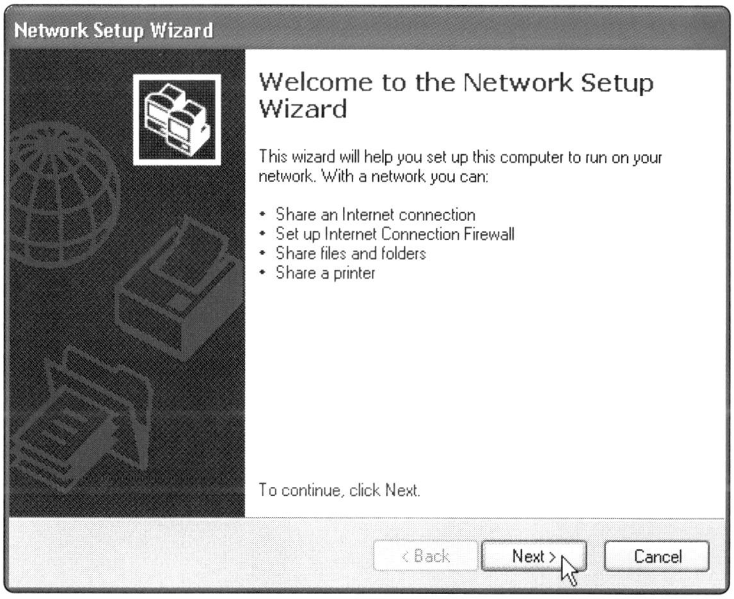

FIGURE 9-21 Windows XP includes communications software that guides a user through setting up a home network.

COMMUNICATIONS OVER THE TELEPHONE NETWORK

The *public switched telephone network* (*PSTN*) is the worldwide telephone system that handles voice-oriented telephone calls (Figure 9-22). Nearly the entire telephone network today uses digital technology, with the exception of the final link from the local telephone company to a home, which often is analog.

While initially it was built to handle voice communications, the telephone network also is an integral part of computer communications. Data, instructions, and information are transmitted over the telephone network using dial-up lines or dedicated lines. The following sections discuss dial-up lines and the various types of dedicated lines that use the telephone network for data communications.

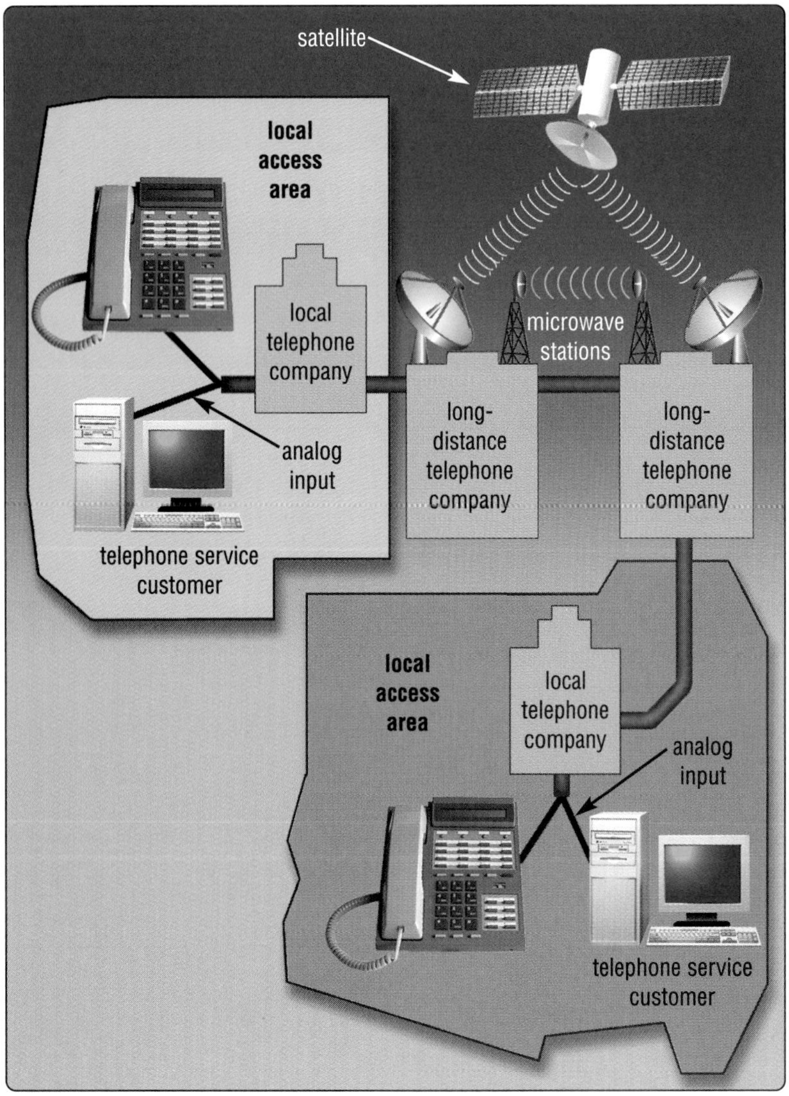

FIGURE 9-22 A sample telephone network configuration.

Dial-Up Lines

A **dial-up line** is a temporary connection that uses one or more analog telephone lines for communications. A dial-up connection is not permanent. Using a dial-up line to transmit data is similar to using the telephone to make a call. A modem at the sending end dials the telephone number of a modem at the receiving end (Figure 9-23). When the modem at the receiving end answers the call, a connection is established and data can be transmitted. When either modem hangs up, the communications end.

Using a dial-up line to connect computers costs no more than making a regular telephone call. Computers at any two locations establish an Internet or network connection using modems and the telephone network. Mobile users, for example, can use dial-up lines in hotels to connect to their main office network to read e-mail messages, access the Internet, and upload files.

FIGURE 9-23 When using a dial-up line, users enter the telephone number of their Internet access provider's computer to connect to the Internet.

Dedicated Lines

A **dedicated line** is a type of always-on connection that is established between two communications devices (unlike a dial-up line where the connection is reestablished each time it is used). The quality and consistency of the connection on a dedicated line are better than a dial-up line because dedicated lines provide a constant connection.

Businesses often use dedicated lines to connect geographically distant offices. Dedicated lines can be either analog or digital. Digital lines increasingly are connecting home and business users to networks around the globe because they transmit data and information at faster rates than analog lines.

Four popular types of digital dedicated lines are ISDN lines, DSL, T-carrier lines, and ATM. Although cable television (CATV) lines are not a type of standard telephone line, they are a very popular type of dedicated line that allows the home user to connect to the Internet. A later section in this chapter discusses the use of CATV lines to connect to the Internet.

The table in Figure 9-24 lists the approximate monthly costs of various types of lines and transfer rates (speeds), as compared with dial-up lines. The following sections discuss ISDN lines, DSL, T-carrier lines, and ATM.

SPEEDS OF VARIOUS INTERNET CONNECTIONS

Type of Line	Approximate Monthly Cost	Transfer Rates
Dial-up	Local or long-distance rates	Up to 56 Kbps
ISDN	$10 to $40	Up to 128 Kbps
DSL	$40 to $80	128 Kbps to 8.45 Mbps
Cable TV (CATV)	$30 to $50	128 Kbps to 10 Mbps
Fractional T1	$150 to $350	128 Kbps to 768 Kbps
T1	$1,000 or more	1.544 Mbps
T3	$10,000 or more	44.736 Mbps
ATM	$8,000 or more	155 Mbps to 622 Mbps, can reach 10 Gbps

FIGURE 9-24 The speeds of various lines that can be used to connect to the Internet.

ISDN Lines

For the small business and home user, an ISDN line provides faster transfer rates than dial-up telephone lines. *ISDN* (*Integrated Services Digital Network*) is a set of standards for digital transmission of data over standard copper telephone lines. With ISDN, the same telephone line that could carry only one computer signal now can carry three or more signals at once through the same line, using a technique called *multiplexing*.

ISDN requires that both ends of the connection have an ISDN modem. This type of modem is different from the type used in dial-up connections. ISDN lines also may require a special ISDN telephone for voice communications. Home and business users who choose ISDN lines benefit from faster Web page downloads and clearer video conferencing. ISDN connections also produce voice conversations that are very clear, when used with ISDN voice equipment.

DSL

DSL is another digital line alternative for the small business or home user. **DSL** (*Digital Subscriber Line*) transmits at fast speeds on existing standard copper telephone wiring. Some DSL installations include a dial tone, providing users with both voice and data communications. Others share services with an existing telephone line.

To connect to DSL, a customer must have a special network card and a DSL modem. Similar to an ISDN modem, a DSL modem is different from the modem used for dial-up connections. A disadvantage of DSL is that the user's location (and DSL modem) and the telephone company's DSL modem must be located within a certain distance from each other. Thus, for rural residents, DSL may not be an option.

WEB LINK 9-7

DSL

Visit the Discovering Computers 2005 WEB LINK page (**scsite .com/dc2005/weblink**). Click DSL below Chapter 9.

ADSL is one of the more popular types of DSLs. As shown in Figure 9-25, *ADSL* (*asymmetric digital subscriber line*) is a type of DSL that supports faster transfer rates when receiving data (the *downstream rate*) than when sending data (the *upstream rate*). ADSL is ideal for Internet access because most users download more information from the Internet than they upload. Some experts predict that DSL eventually will replace ISDN because it is much easier to install and provides much faster data transfer rates.

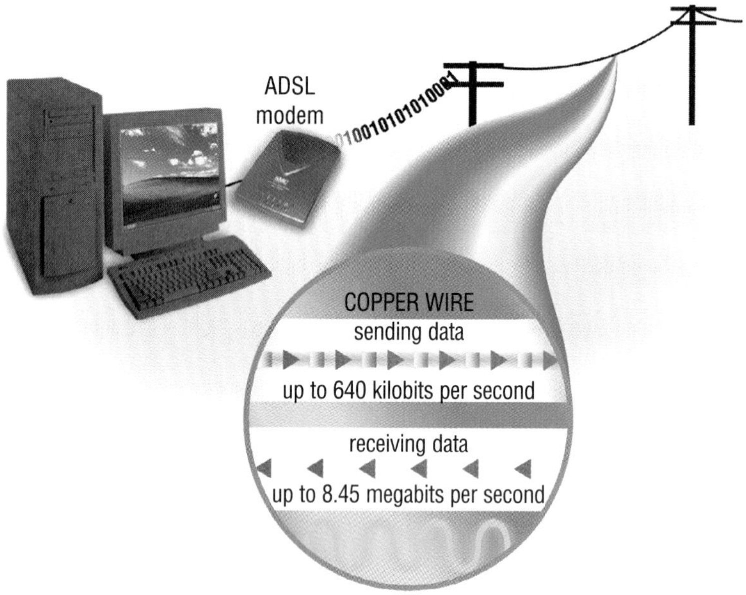

FIGURE 9-25 ADSL connections transmit data downstream (receiving) at a much faster rate than upstream (sending).

T-carrier Lines

A **T-carrier line** is any of several types of long-distance digital telephone lines that carry multiple signals over a single communications line. Whereas a standard dial-up telephone line carries only one signal, digital T-carrier lines use multiplexing so that multiple signals share the line. T-carrier lines provide very fast data transfer rates. Only medium to large companies usually can afford the investment in T-carrier lines because these lines are so expensive.

The most popular T-carrier line is the *T1 line*. Businesses often use T1 lines to connect to the Internet. Many Internet access providers use T1 lines to connect to the Internet backbone. Home and small business users purchase *fractional T1*, in which they share a connection to the T1 line with other users. Fractional T1 is slower than a dedicated T1 line, but it also is less expensive. Users who do not have other high-speed Internet access in their areas can opt for fractional T1.

A *T3 line* is equal in speed to 28 T1 lines. T3 lines are quite expensive. Main users of T3 lines include large companies, telephone companies, and Internet access providers connecting to the Internet backbone. The Internet backbone itself also uses T3 lines.

ATM

ATM (*Asynchronous Transfer Mode*) is a service that carries voice, data, video, and multimedia at very high speeds. Telephone networks, the Internet, and other networks with large amounts of traffic use ATM. Some experts predict that ATM eventually will become the Internet standard for data transmission, replacing T3 lines.

QUIZ YOURSELF 9-2

To check your knowledge of networks, communications software, and communications over the telephone network, visit the Discovering Computers 2005 Quiz Yourself Web page (**scsite.com/dc2005/quiz**). Click Objectives 4 – 8 below Chapter 9.

COMMUNICATIONS DEVICES

A **communications device** is any type of hardware capable of transmitting data, instructions, and information between a sending device and a receiving device. At the sending end, a communications device sends the data, instructions, or information from the sending device to a communications channel. At the receiving end, a communications device receives the signals from the communications channel. Sometimes, the communications device also converts the data, instructions, and information from digital to analog signals or vice versa, depending on the devices and media involved.

Some of the more common types of communications devices are dial-up modems, ISDN and DSL modems, cable modems, network cards, wireless access points, routers, and hubs. The following pages describe these devices.

Dial-Up Modems

As previously discussed, a computer's digital signals must be converted to analog signals before they are transmitted over standard telephone lines. The communications device that performs this conversion is a **modem**, sometimes called a *dial-up modem*. The word, modem, is derived from the combination of the words, *modulate*, to change into an analog signal, and *demodulate*, to convert an analog signal into a digital signal.

Both the sending and receiving ends of a standard telephone line (communications channel) must have a dial-up modem for data transmission to occur. For example, a dial-up modem connected to a sending computer converts the computer's digital signals into analog signals. The analog signals then can travel over a standard telephone line. At the receiving end, another dial-up modem converts the analog signals back into digital signals that a receiving computer can process.

A modem usually is in the form of an adapter card (Figure 9-26) that you insert into an expansion slot on a computer's motherboard. One end of a standard telephone cord attaches to a port on the modem card and the other end plugs into a telephone outlet. Devices other than computers also use modems. A stand-alone fax machine, for example, has a modem that converts a scanned digitized image into an analog signal that is sent to a recipient's fax machine.

As discussed in Chapter 4, notebook and other mobile computers often use a PC Card modem inserted into a PC Card slot on the computer. The PC Card modem attaches to a telephone outlet with a standard telephone cord. Mobile users without access to a telephone outlet also can use a special cable to attach the PC Card modem to a cellular telephone, thus enabling them to transmit data over a cellular telephone (Figure 9-27). Some mobile users have a **wireless modem** that allows access to the Web wirelessly from a notebook computer, a PDA, cellular telephones, and other mobile devices. Wireless modems typically use the same waves used by cellular telephones. Read Looking Ahead 9-1 for a look at the next generation of cellular telephone communications.

FIGURE 9-26 A modem for a desktop computer usually is in the form of an adapter card you install in the system unit.

WEB LINK 9-8

Dial-Up Modems

Visit the Discovering Computers 2005 WEB LINK page (**scsite.com/dc2005/weblink**). Click Dial-Up Modems below Chapter 9.

FIGURE 9-27 This user is accessing the Internet through her cellular telephone by connecting one end of a cable to the cellular telephone and the other end to the PC Card in the notebook computer.

LOOKING AHEAD 9-1

Molar Phone Receives Calls

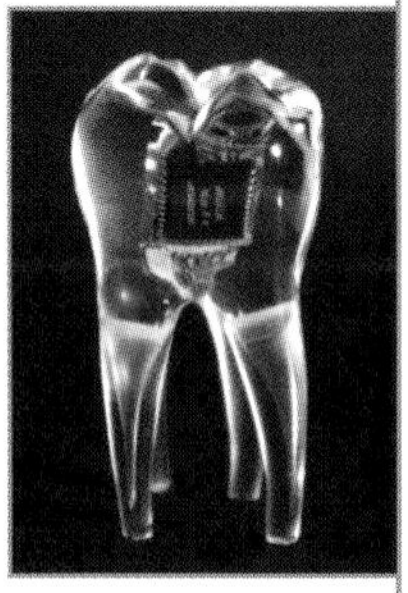

Hands-free telephone calls may grow to a new dimension if a prototype becomes fully functional.

Two graduate students at the Royal College of Art in London, England, designed the mobile telephone to fit inside a tooth, and dentists could implant the device during surgery. It works by using a radio receiver to gather signals and then having a small plate vibrate inside the tooth to send the signals from the jawbone to the inner ear.

The students' prototype, which is smaller than a grain of rice, requires a communications chip to become workable, but the students say this hardware is readily available.

Their project is part of a future product competition sponsored by the United Kingdom's National Endowment for Science, Technology and the Arts to spark interest in wearable computers. Practical applications might be having a coach transmit plays to his quarterback or a stockbroker relay current stock prices to a stock trader.

Critics are concerned about the risk of infection and the ability to turn off the device when calls are not desired.

For a look at the next generation of molar telephones, visit the Discovering Computers 2005 Looking Ahead Web page (**scsite.com/dc2005/looking**). Click Looking Ahead #1 below Chapter 9.

ISDN and DSL Modems

If you access the Internet using ISDN or DSL, you need a communications device to send and receive the digital ISDN or DSL signals. A modem used for dial-up access will not work because it converts digital signals to analog signals and vice versa. In the case of ISDN and DSL, this conversion is not necessary. Both the computer and the ISDN or DSL already use digital signals, thus no digital-to-analog conversion is required.

A *digital modem* is a modem that sends and receives data and information to and from a digital telephone line such as ISDN or DSL. An *ISDN modem* sends digital data and information from a computer to an ISDN line and receives digital data and information from an ISDN line. A **DSL modem** sends digital data and information from a computer to a DSL line and receives digital data and information from a DSL line. ISDN and DSL modems usually are external devices, in which one end connects to the telephone line and the other end connects to a port on the system unit.

FAQ 9-3

Are digital modems really modems?

According to the definition of a modem (to convert from analog to digital signals and vice versa), the use of the term modem in this context is not correct. Although the original term for these devices was terminal adapter, the industry refers to ISDN, DSL, and cable modems as digital modems.

For more information about digital modems, visit the Discovering Computers 2005 FAQ Web page (**scsite.com/dc2005/faq**). Click Digital Modems below Chapter 9.

Cable Modems

A **cable modem**, sometimes called a *broadband modem*, is a digital modem that sends and receives digital data over the cable television (CATV) network. With more than 100 million homes wired for cable television, cable modems provide a faster Internet access alternative to dial-up for the home user and have speeds similar to DSL. Cable modems currently can transmit data at speeds that are much faster than either a dial-up modem or ISDN (Figure 9-24 on page 481). Home and business users may be able to take advantage of the resources available on the Internet and other networks with high-speed cable Internet service — provided the CATV service uses digital cable capable of providing Internet service.

As shown in Figure 9-28, CATV service enters your home through a single line. To access the Internet using the CATV service, the CATV company installs a splitter inside your house. From the splitter, one part of the cable runs to your televisions and the other part connects to the cable modem. Most CATV operators provide a cable modem as part of the installation; others require that you purchase one separately. A cable modem usually is an external (separate) device, in which one end of a cable connects to a CATV wall outlet and the other end plugs into a port, such as on an Ethernet card, in the system unit. An Ethernet card is a type of network card. The next section discusses network cards.

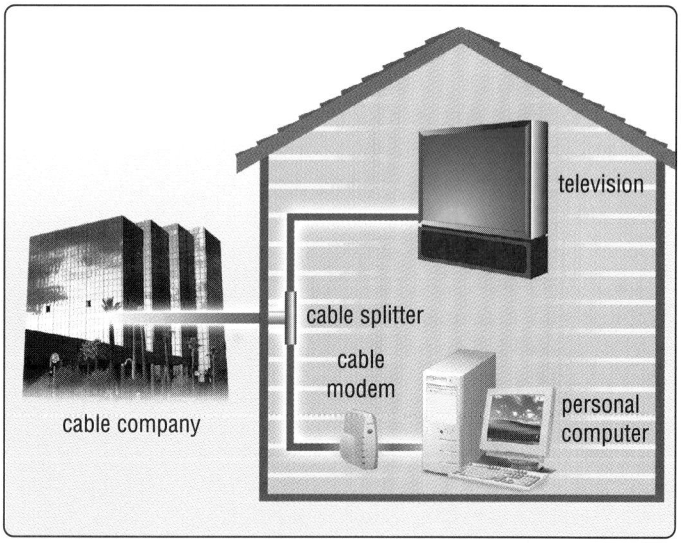

FIGURE 9-28 A typical cable modem installation.

FAQ 9-4

Which is better, DSL or cable Internet service?

Each has its own advantages. DSL uses a line that is not shared with other users in the neighborhood. With cable Internet service, by contrast, users share the node with up to 500 other cable Internet users. Simultaneous access by many users can cause the cable Internet service to slow down. Cable Internet service, however, has widespread availability.

For more information about DSL and cable Internet service, visit the Discovering Computers 2005 FAQ Web page (**scsite.com/dc2005/faq**). Click DSL and Cable Internet Service below Chapter 9.

Network Cards

A **network card**, sometimes called a *network interface card* (*NIC* pronounced nick), is an adapter card, PC Card, or compact flash card that enables a computer or device to access a network. Personal computers on a LAN typically contain a network card. The network card coordinates the transmission and receipt of data, instructions, and information to and from the computer or device containing the network card.

Network cards are available in a variety of styles (Figure 9-29). A network card for a desktop computer is an adapter card that has a port to which a cable connects. A network card for mobile computers and devices is in the form of a Type II PC Card or a compact flash card. Many of these network cards have more than one type of port, that enable different types of cables to attach to the card. For example, some cable modems and DSL modems require that one end of a cable plug into the modem and the other end into a network card.

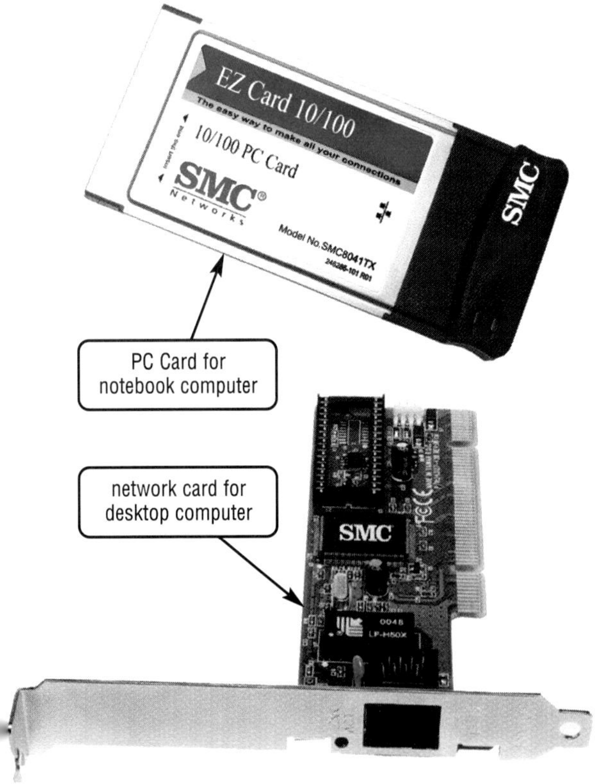

FIGURE 9-29 Network cards are available for both desktop and notebook computers.

Network cards that provide wireless data transmission also are available. These adapter cards often have an antenna. Sometimes the antenna is detachable, allowing the user to position it in a location with the best signal strength. Some network cards include support for both wired and wireless networks.

A network card works with a particular network technology, such as Ethernet or token ring. An Ethernet card is the most common type of network card. Depending on the type of wiring used, the transfer rate on an Ethernet network is 10 Mbps, 100 Mbps, or 1,000 Mbps (1 Gbps). Ethernet cards typically support one or more of these speeds. For example, some are called 10/100 because they support both 10 Mbps and 100 Mbps. Some network cards also are a combination Ethernet and dial-up modem card.

Wireless Access Points

A *wireless access point* is a communications device that allows computers and devices to transfer data wirelessly among themselves or to transfer data wirelessly to a wired network (Figure 9-30). Wireless access points have high-quality antennas for optimal signals. For the best signal, some manufacturers suggest positioning the wireless access point at the highest possible location.

FIGURE 9-30 A wireless access point allows computers to communicate wirelessly with an Ethernet network, a cable modem, or a DSL modem.

Routers

A *router* is a communications device that connects multiple computers or other routers together and transmits data to its correct destination on the network. All sizes of networks use routers. On the largest scale, routers along the Internet backbone forward data packets to their destination using the fastest available path. For smaller business and home networks, a router allows multiple computers to share a single high-speed Internet connection such as through a cable modem or DSL modem (Figure 9-31). These routers connect from 2 to 250 computers.

To prevent unauthorized users from accessing files and computers, many routers are protected by built-in firewalls. Some also have built-in antivirus protection. Routers also may serve as print servers or support wireless communications, eliminating the need for a separate wireless access point in a wireless network. If the network has a separate wireless access point, it connects to the router via a cable.

WEB LINK 9-9

Routers

Visit the Discovering Computers 2005 WEB LINK page (**scsite .com/dc2005/weblink**). Click Routers below Chapter 9.

FIGURE 9-31 Through a router, home and small business networks can share access to a high-speed Internet connection such as through a cable modem.

Connecting Networks

Today, thousands of computer networks exist, ranging from small networks operated by home users to global networks operated by numerous telecommunications firms. Interconnecting these many types of networks requires various types of communications devices. For example, as shown in Figure 9-32, a *hub* is a device that provides a central point for cables in a network. Some hubs include routers. That is, the hub receives data from many directions and then forwards it to one or more destinations.

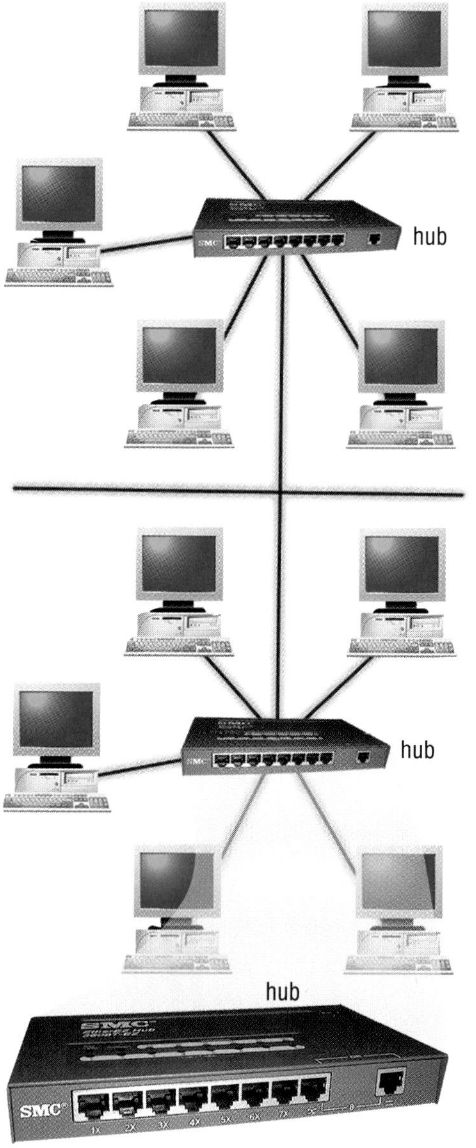

FIGURE 9-32 A hub is a central point that connects several devices in a network together.

HOME NETWORKS

An estimated 20 million homes have more than one computer. Thus, many home users are connecting multiple computers and devices together into a **home network**. Home networking saves the home user money and provides many conveniences. For example, an older computer that does not have a CD drive can access the CD drive on a newer computer. Instead of using a floppy disk to transfer files from one computer to another, a home network allows users to access files on other computers in the home. Each networked computer in the house has the following capabilities:

- Connect to the Internet at the same time
- Share a single high-speed Internet connection
- Access files and programs on the other computers in the house
- Share peripherals such as a printer, scanner, external hard disk, or DVD drive
- Play multiplayer games with players on other computers in the house

Many vendors offer home networking packages that include all the necessary hardware and software to network your home using wired or wireless techniques. Some of these packages also offer intelligent networking capabilities. An *intelligent home network* extends the basic home network to include features such as lighting control, thermostat adjustment, and a security system.

Wired Home Networks

As with other networks, a home network can use wires, be wireless, or use a combination of wired and wireless. Three types of wired home networks are Ethernet, powerline cable, and phoneline.

ETHERNET Some home users have an Ethernet network. As discussed earlier in this chapter, traditional Ethernet networks require that each computer contain a network card, which connects to a central network hub or similar device with a physical cable. This may involve running cable through walls, ceilings, and floors in the house. For the average home user, the hardware and software of an Ethernet network can be difficult to configure.

POWERLINE CABLE NETWORK A home *powerline cable network* is a network that uses the same lines that bring electricity into the house. This network requires no additional wiring. One end of a cable plugs into the computer's parallel or USB port and the other end of the cable plugs into a wall outlet. The data transmits through the existing power lines in the house.

PHONELINE NETWORK A *phoneline network* is an easy-to-install and inexpensive network that uses existing telephone lines in the home. With this network, one end of a cable connects to an adapter card or PC Card in the computer and the other end plugs into a wall telephone jack. The phoneline network does not interfere with voice and data transmissions on the telephone lines. That is, you can talk on the telephone and use the same line to connect to the Internet. One slight disadvantage is that the room with the computer must have a wall telephone jack.

Wireless Home Networks

To network computers and devices that span multiple rooms or floors in a home, it may be more convenient to use a wireless strategy. One advantage of wireless networks is that you can take a mobile computer outside, for example in the backyard, and connect to the Internet through the home network, as long as you are in the network's range. Two types of wireless home networks are HomeRF and Wi-Fi.

A *HomeRF (radio frequency) network* uses radio waves, instead of cables, to transmit data. A HomeRF network sends signals through the air over distances up to 150 feet. One end of a cable connects to a special card in the computer and the other end connects to a transmitter/receiver that has an antenna to pick up signals. A HomeRF network usually can connect up to 10 computers.

Another home network that uses radio waves is a Wi-Fi network, which sends signals over a wider distance than the HomeRF network — up to 1,500 feet in some configurations. A Wi-Fi home network is more expensive than a HomeRF network. Despite the increased costs, increasingly more home users set up Wi-Fi networks in their homes because they are fairly easy to configure. Each computer that accesses the network needs a wireless network card,

WEB LINK 9-10

Home Networks

Visit the Discovering Computers 2005 WEB LINK page (**scsite .com/dc2005/weblink**). Click Home Networks below Chapter 9.

which may communicate with a wireless access point or a combination router/wireless access point (Figure 9-33). Even in a wireless home network, one desktop computer usually connects to the router/wireless access point using a cable.

Wireless networks do have the disadvantage of interference. Walls, ceilings, and electrical devices such as cordless telephones and microwave ovens can disrupt wireless communications.

FAQ 9-5

Do I need a wireless network card to access a Wi-Fi network?

No. Some computers and devices have built-in Wi-Fi hardware. For those requiring a wireless network card, some users instead purchase a wireless USB network adapter that connects to a USB port on the computer. Wireless USB network adapters are ideal for users who have no open expansion slots in their computers or for users not comfortable working inside the system unit.

For more information about wireless network cards and adapters, visit the Discovering Computers 2005 FAQ Web page (**scsite.com/dc2005/faq**). Click Wireless Network Cards and Adapters below Chapter 9.

FIGURE 9-33 HOW TO SET UP HARDWARE FOR A WI-FI HOME NETWORK

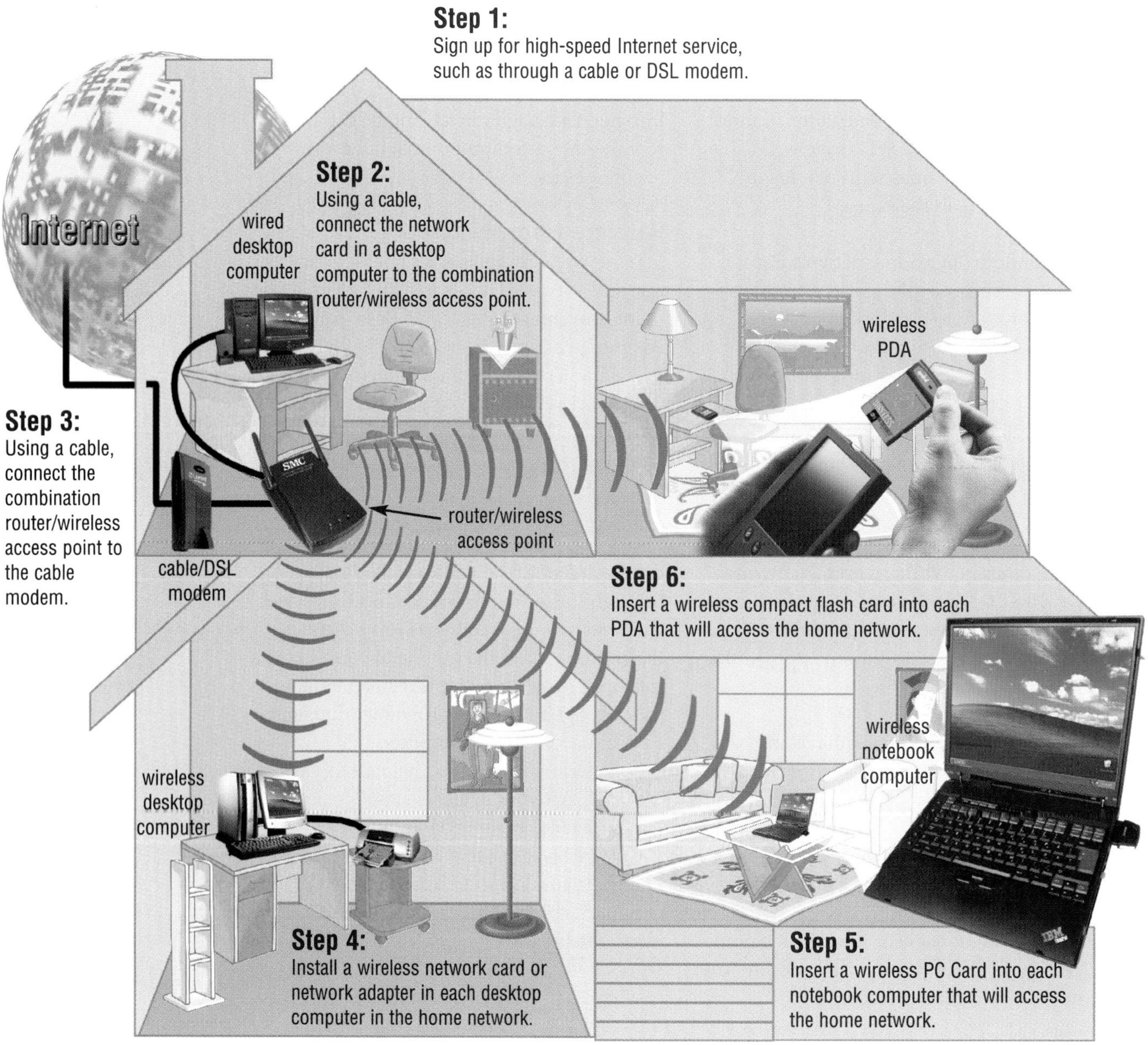

COMMUNICATIONS CHANNEL

As described at the beginning of the chapter, a communications channel is the transmission media on which data, instructions, or information travel in a communications system. The amount of data, instructions, and information that can travel over a communications channel sometimes is called the **bandwidth**. The higher the bandwidth, the more the channel transmits. For example, a cable modem has more bandwidth than a dial-up modem.

For transmission of text only, a lower bandwidth is acceptable. For transmission of music, graphics, and photographs, or work with virtual reality or 3-D games, however, you need a higher bandwidth. When the bandwidth is too low for the application, you will notice a considerable slow-down in system performance.

Latency is the time it takes a signal to travel from one location to another on a network. Several factors that can negatively affect latency include the distance between the two points, the type of transmission media, and the number of nodes through which the data must travel over the communications channel. For best performance, bandwidth should be high and latency low.

A communications channel consists of one or more transmission media. **Transmission media** consists of materials or substances capable of carrying one or more signals. When you send data from a computer, the signal that carries the data may travel over various transmission media. This is especially true when the transmission spans a long distance.

Figure 9-34 illustrates a typical communications channel — much like the one that connects a computer to the Internet — and shows the variety of transmission media used to complete the connection. The following pages discuss in depth the media shown in the figure. Although many media and devices are involved, the entire communications process could take less than one second.

FIGURE 9-34 AN EXAMPLE OF SENDING A REQUEST OVER THE INTERNET USING A COMMUNICATIONS CHANNEL

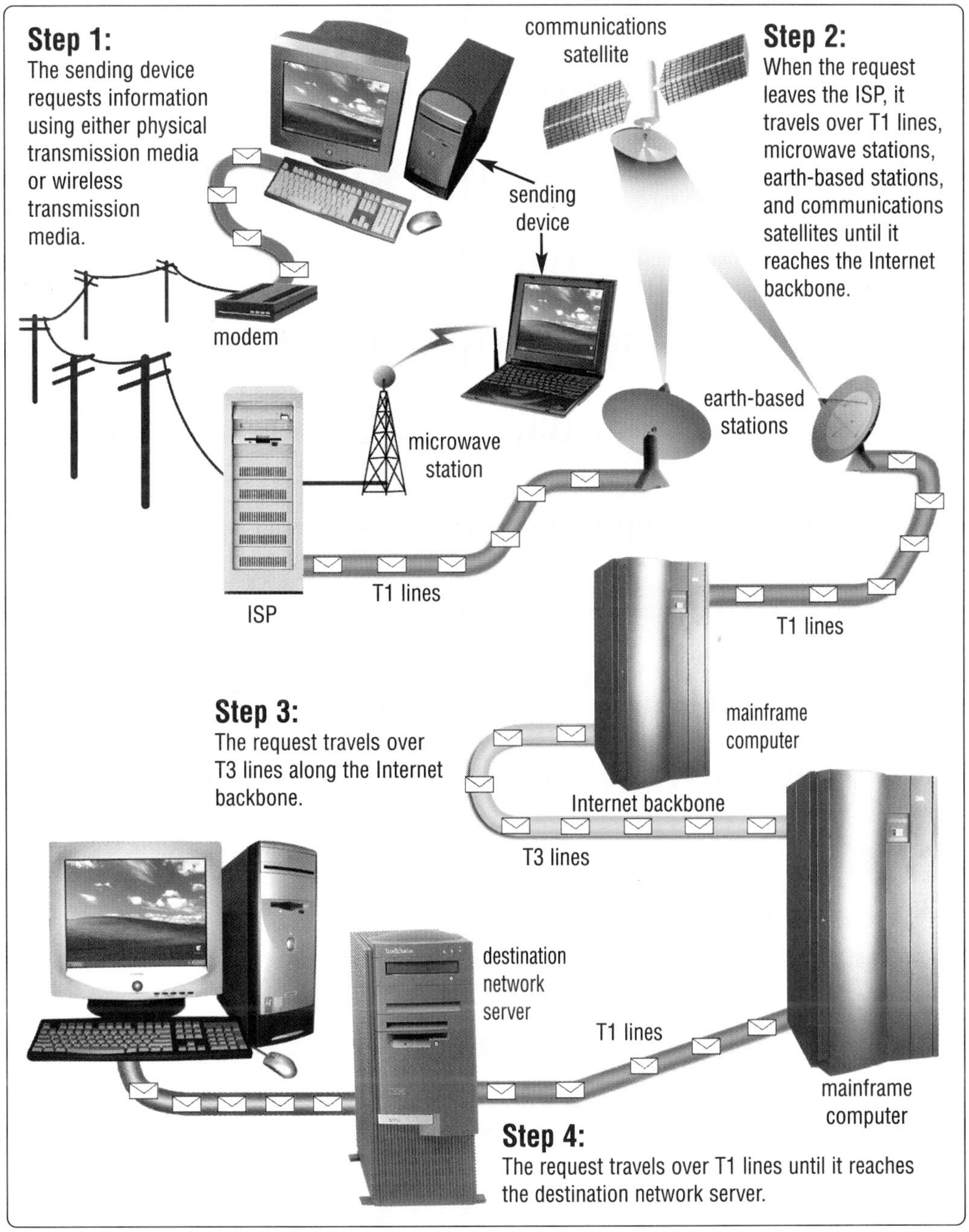

Baseband media transmit only one signal at a time. By contrast, **broadband** media transmit multiple signals simultaneously. Broadband media transmit signals at a much faster speed than baseband media. Home and business users today opt for broadband Internet access because of the much faster transfer rates. Two previously discussed services that offer broadband transmission are DSL and the cable Internet access. Satellites also offer broadband transmission.

Transmission media are one of two types: physical or wireless. *Physical transmission media* use wire, cable, and other tangible materials to send communications signals. *Wireless transmission media* send communications signals through the air or space using radio, microwave, and infrared signals. The following sections discuss these types of media.

PHYSICAL TRANSMISSION MEDIA

Physical transmission media used in communications include twisted-pair cable, coaxial cable, and fiber-optic cable. These cables typically are used within or underground between buildings. Ethernet and token ring LANs often use physical transmission media. The table in Figure 9-35 lists the transfer rates of LANs using various physical transmission media. The following sections discuss each of these types of cables.

TRANSFER RATES FOR VARIOUS TYPES OF LANS USING PHYSICAL TRANSMISSION MEDIA

Type of Cable and LAN	Maximum Transfer Rate
Twisted-Pair Cable	
• 10Base-T (Ethernet)	10 Mbps
• 100Base-T (Fast Ethernet)	100 Mbps
• 1000Base-T (Gigabit Ethernet)	1 Gbps
• Token ring	4 Mbps to 16 Mbps
Coaxial Cable	
• 10Base2 (ThinWire Ethernet)	10 Mbps
• 10Base5 (ThickWire Ethernet)	10 Mbps
Fiber-Optic Cable	
• 10Base-F (Ethernet)	10 Mbps
• 100Base-FX (Fast Ethernet)	100 Mbps
• FDDI (Fiber Distributed Data Interface) token ring	100 Mbps
• Gigabit Ethernet	1 Gbps
• 10-Gigabit Ethernet	10 Gbps

FIGURE 9-35 The speeds of various physical communications media when they are used in LANs.

Twisted-Pair Cable

One of the more widely used transmission media for network cabling and telephone systems is twisted-pair cable. **Twisted-pair cable** consists of one or more twisted-pair wires bundled together (Figure 9-36). Each *twisted-pair wire* consists of two separate insulated copper wires that are twisted together. The wires are twisted together to reduce noise. **Noise** is an electrical disturbance that can degrade communications.

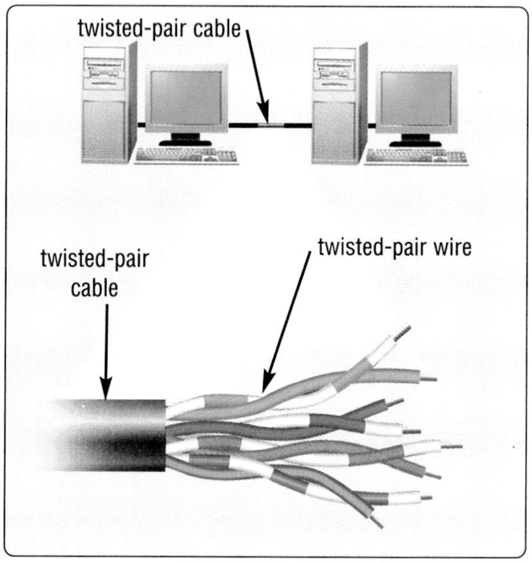

FIGURE 9-36 A twisted-pair cable consists of one or more twisted-pair wires. Each twisted-pair wire usually is color coded for identification. Telephone networks and LANs often use twisted-pair cable.

Coaxial Cable

Coaxial cable, often referred to as *coax* (pronounced KO-ax), consists of a single copper wire surrounded by at least three layers: (1) an insulating material, (2) a woven or braided metal, and (3) a plastic outer coating (Figure 9-37).

Cable television (CATV) wiring often uses coaxial cable because it can be cabled over longer distances than twisted-pair cable. Most of today's computer networks, however, do not use coaxial cable because other transmission media such as fiber-optic cable transmit signals at faster rates.

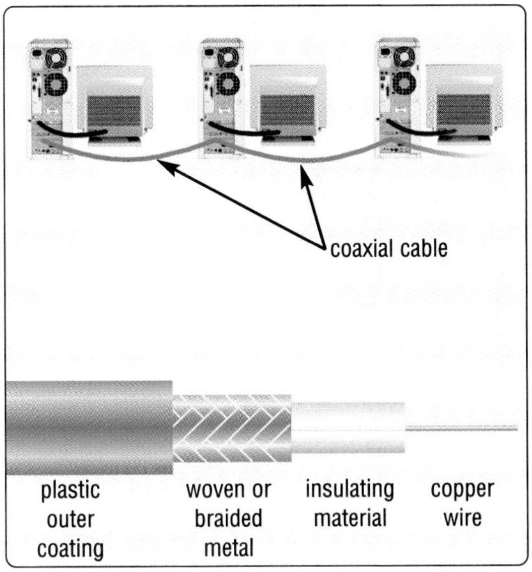

FIGURE 9-37 On a coaxial cable, data travels through a copper wire. This illustration shows computers networked together with coaxial cable.

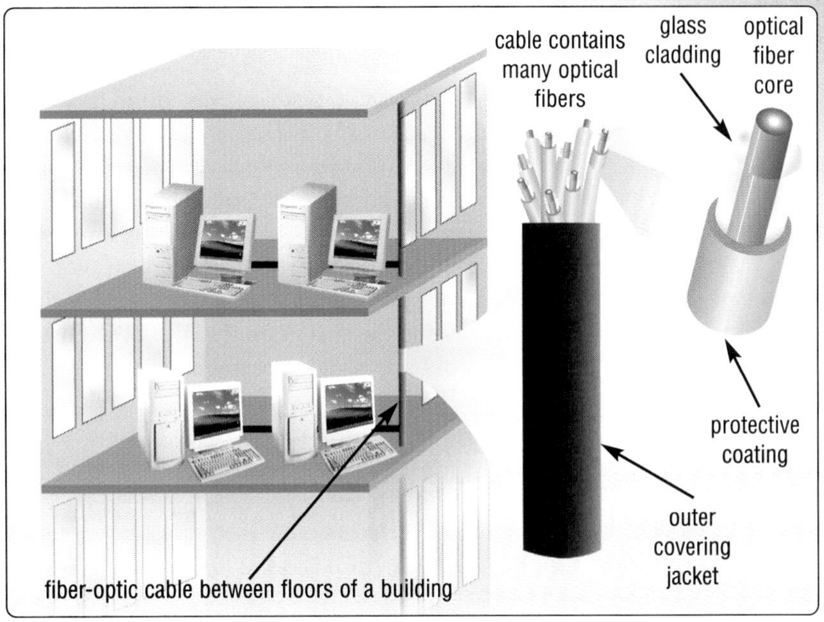

FIGURE 9-38 A fiber-optic cable consists of hair-thin strands of glass or plastic that carry data as pulses of light.

Fiber-Optic Cable

The core of a **fiber-optic cable** consists of dozens or hundreds of thin strands of glass or plastic that use light to transmit signals. Each strand, called an *optical fiber*, is as thin as a human hair. Inside the fiber-optic cable, an insulating glass cladding and a protective coating surround each optical fiber (Figure 9-38).

Fiber-optic cables have the following advantages over cables that use wire, such as twisted-pair and coaxial cables:

- Capability of carrying significantly more signals than wire cables
- Faster data transmission
- Less susceptible to noise (interference) from other devices such as a copy machine
- Better security for signals during transmission because they are less susceptible to noise
- Smaller size (much thinner and lighter weight)

Disadvantages of fiber-optic cable are it costs more than twisted-pair or coaxial cable and can be difficult to install and modify. Despite these limitations, many local and long-distance telephone companies are replacing existing telephone lines with fiber-optic cables. Businesses also are using fiber-optic cables in high-traffic networks or as the backbone in a network.

WIRELESS TRANSMISSION MEDIA

Wireless transmission media are used when it is inconvenient, impractical, or impossible to install cables. Types of wireless transmission media used in communications include infrared, broadcast radio, cellular radio, microwaves, and communications satellites. The table in Figure 9-39 lists transfer rates of various wireless transmission media. The following sections discuss these types of wireless transmission media. The special feature following this chapter illustrates a variety of wireless applications.

TRANSFER RATES FOR VARIOUS TYPES OF WIRELESS TRANSMISSION MEDIA

Transmission Medium	Maximum Transfer Rate
Infrared	115 Kbps to 4 Mbps
Broadcast radio	
• Bluetooth	1 to 2 Mbps
• HomeRF	1.6 Mbps to 10 Mbps
• 802.11b	11 Mbps
• 802.11g	54 Mbps
• 802.11a	54 Mbps to 108 Mbps
Cellular radio	
• 2G	9.6 Kbps to 19.2 Kbps
• 3G	144 Kbps to 2.4 Mbps
Microwave radio	150 Mbps
Communications satellite	1 Gbps

FIGURE 9-39 The speeds of various wireless transmission media.

Infrared

As discussed earlier in the chapter, *infrared* (*IR*) is a wireless transmission medium that sends signals using infrared light waves. Mobile computers and devices, such as a mouse, printer, and smart phones, often have an IrDA port that enables the transfer of data from one device to another using infrared light waves. If your notebook computer has an IrDA port, simply position the port in front of the IrDA port on a printer to print a document wirelessly. Many PDAs also have IrDA ports that allow users to transfer data to another PDA or a network wirelessly.

WEB LINK 9-11

Cellular Communications

Visit the Discovering Computers 2005 WEB LINK page (**scsite .com/dc2005/weblink**). Click Cellular Communications below Chapter 9.

APPLY IT 9-2

Speed Through Cashiers' Lines

Long lines at the checkout counter can be a thing of the past with *Speedpass*, a free payment service at some gas stations and supermarkets.

Speedpass uses a small transponder wand attached to a key chain or affixed to a vehicle's rear window that transmits a radio signal to a reader at the gas pump, checkout counter, or drive-through window. The radio signal contains a security code and identification information, including whether a receipt is desired and which credit or check card to process. To use Speedpass, the user simply points or waves the transponder in front of the reader.

Speedpass also sells Timex watches that function as regular watches and contain the Speedpass transponder. Users merely position their watch in front of the reader for a truly hands-free operation.

Participating Mobil and Exxon stations are located throughout the country. Other merchants are Stop & Shop Supermarkets and McDonald's restaurants, although plans call for expanding the use for video rentals and prescription drugs.

ExxonMobil developed the Speedpass system in cooperation with Texas Instruments and the Wayne Division of Dresser Industries. More than 5 million users participate in the Speedpass payment system.

For more information about Speedpass, visit the Discovering Computers 2005 Apply It Web page (**scsite.com/dc2005/apply**). Click Apply It #2 below Chapter 9.

Broadcast Radio

Broadcast radio is a wireless transmission medium that distributes radio signals through the air over long distances such as between cities, regions, and countries and short distances such as within an office or home. Read Apply It 9-2 for more information.

For radio transmissions, you need a transmitter to send the broadcast radio signal and a receiver to accept it. To receive the broadcast radio signal, the receiver has an antenna that is located in the range of the signal. Some networks use a transceiver, which both sends and receives signals from wireless devices. Broadcast radio is slower and more susceptible to noise than physical transmission media but it provides flexibility and portability.

Bluetooth, HomeRF, and Wi-Fi communications technologies discussed earlier in this chapter use broadcast radio signals. Bluetooth is an alternative to infrared communications, and HomeRF and Wi-Fi are competing technologies for home and small business networks. Public Internet access points also use Wi-Fi networks. In a Wi-Fi business network, employees have access to the network from their notebook computers while roaming from one meeting room to another.

Cellular Radio

Cellular radio is a form of broadcast radio that is used widely for mobile communications, specifically wireless modems and cellular telephones (Figure 9-40). A **cellular telephone** is a telephone device that uses high-frequency radio waves to transmit voice and digital data messages. Because only a limited number of radio frequencies exist, cellular network providers reuse frequencies so they can accommodate the large number of users.

Some mobile users connect their notebook computer or other mobile computer to a cellular telephone to access the Web, send and receive e-mail, enter a chat room, or connect to an office or school network while away from a standard telephone line, for example, from a car or a park bench.

Several categories of cellular transmissions exist, defining the development of cellular networks:

- *1G* (first generation) transmitted analog data
- *2G* (second generation) transmit digital data at speeds from 9.6 Kbps to 19.2 Kbps
- *3G* (third generation) transmit digital data at speeds from 144 Kbps to 2.4 Mbps

GSM (Global System for Mobile Communications) and *CDMA* (Code Division Multiple Access) are 2G digital cellular telephone technologies. *UMTS* (Universal Mobile Telecommunications System) and *GPRS* (General Packet Radio Service) are 3G technologies based on GSM. These 3G technologies allow users quickly to display multimedia and graphics, browse the Web, watch television or a video, have a video conference, and transfer data on a cellular device. Providers that offer 2G and 3G service include Sprint, Verizon, AT&T, Cingular, Motorola, Ericsson, and Nokia. Some providers use the term, *2.5G*, to represent services that fall between 2G and 3G.

Personal Communications Services (*PCS*) is the term used by the United States Federal Communications Commission (FCC) to identify all wireless digital communications. Devices that use PCS include cellular telephones, PDAs, pagers, and fax machines. These devices have voice mail, call forwarding, fax capability, caller ID, and wireless modems for Internet and e-mail access. Read Looking Ahead 9-2 for a look at the next generation of cellular communications.

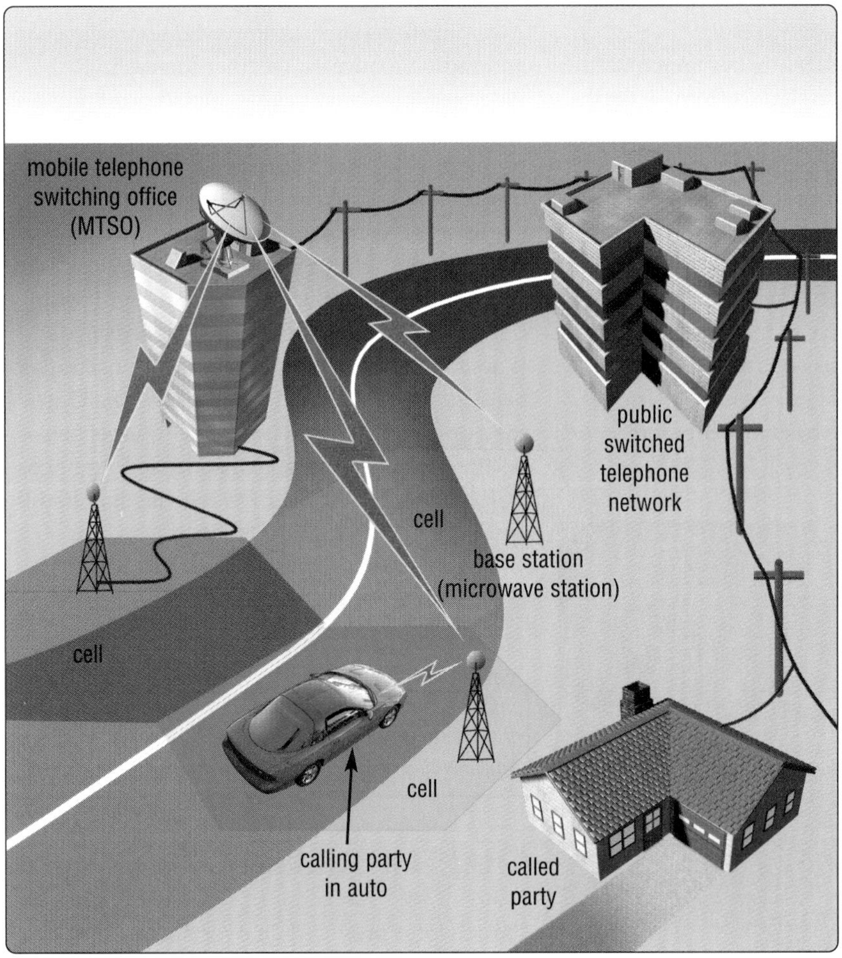

FIGURE 9-40 As a person with a cellular telephone drives from one cell to another, the radio signals transfer from the base station (microwave station) in one cell to a base station in another cell.

Microwaves

Microwaves are radio waves that provide a high-speed signal transmission. Microwave transmission, sometimes called *fixed-point wireless*, involves sending signals from one microwave station to another (Figure 9-41). Microwaves transmit data at rates up to 4,500 times faster than a dial-up modem.

A *microwave station* is an earth-based reflective dish that contains the antenna, transceivers, and other equipment necessary for microwave communications. As with infrared, microwaves use line-of-sight transmission. To avoid possible obstructions, such as buildings or mountains, microwave stations often sit on the tops of buildings, towers, or mountains.

Microwave transmission typically is used in environments where installing physical transmission media is difficult or impossible and where line-of-sight transmission is available. For example, microwave transmission is used in wide-open areas such as deserts or lakes; between buildings in a close geographic area; or to communicate with a satellite. Current users of microwave transmission include universities, hospitals, city governments, cable television providers, and telephone companies.

LOOKING AHEAD 9-2

m-Cash Provides Payment Option

The next time you are standing in front of a vending machine without coins, you may be able to push a few buttons on your cellular telephone to pay for the snacks.

Sprint PCS is one of several major developers installing *mobile cash* (*m-Cash*) software in cellular telephones. The goal is to partner with merchants and create a uniform method of purchasing goods on the mobile Web. More than 2.6 million merchants accept credit and debit cards to process payments, and Sprint hopes to convince these businesses that m-Cash is another method of buying merchandise.

Although the number of people purchasing Internet-enabled telephones has increased, the number of people who have used these telephones to access the Internet is small. A major reason for this low Web usage is lack of content developed for these devices. But consumers express interest in using this application when it becomes available. In one survey, as many as 44 percent of cellular telephone owners said they would try to use m-Cash to purchase small items, such as a soda or a transit ticket from a vending machine.

For a look at the next generation of m-Cash, visit the Discovering Computers 2005 Looking Ahead Web page (**scsite.com/dc2005/looking**). Click Looking Ahead #2 below Chapter 9.

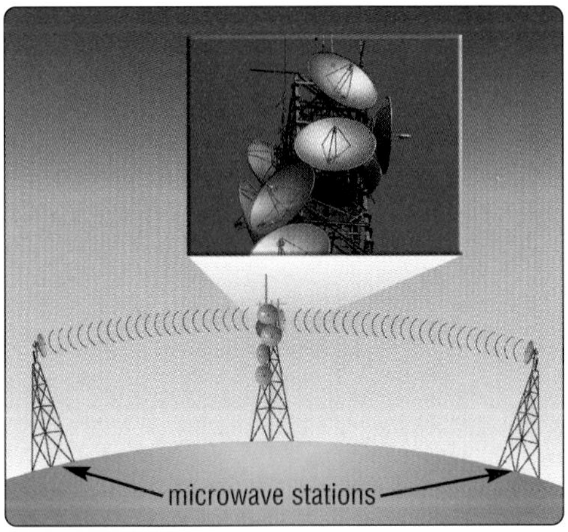

FIGURE 9-41 A microwave station is a ground-based reflective dish that contains the antenna and other equipment necessary for microwave communications.

Communications Satellite

A **communications satellite** is a space station that receives microwave signals from an earth-based station, amplifies (strengthens) the signals, and broadcasts the signals back over a wide area to any number of earth-based stations (Figure 9-42).

These earth-based stations often are microwave stations. Other devices, such as PDAs and GPS receivers, also can function as earth-based stations. Transmission from an earth-based station to a satellite is an *uplink*. Transmission from a satellite to an earth-based station is a *downlink*.

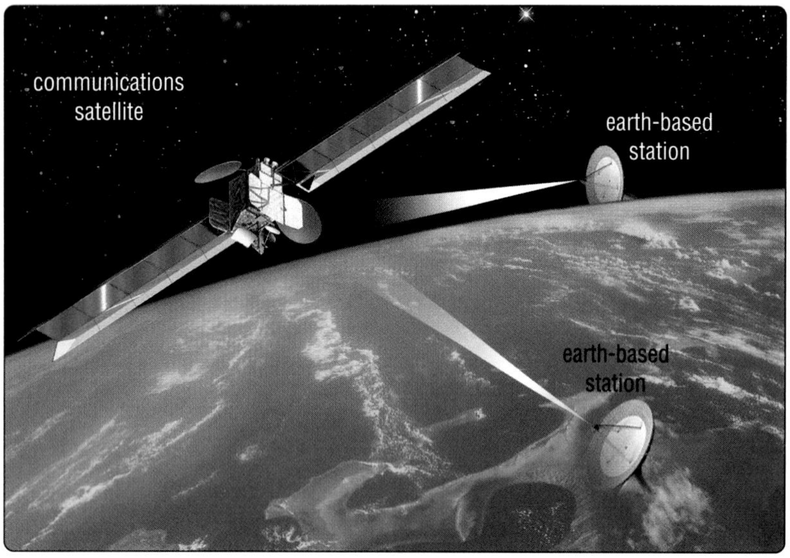

FIGURE 9-42 Communications satellites are placed about 22,300 miles above Earth's equator.

Applications such as air navigation, television and radio broadcasts, weather forecasting, video conferencing, paging, global positioning systems, and Internet connections use communications satellites. With the proper satellite dish and a satellite modem card, consumers access the Internet using satellite technology. With satellite Internet connections, however, uplink transmissions usually are slower than downlink transmissions. This difference in speeds usually is acceptable to most Internet satellite users because they download much more data than they upload. Although a satellite Internet connection is more expensive than cable Internet or DSL connections, sometimes it is the only high-speed Internet option in remote areas.

QUIZ YOURSELF 9-3

To check your knowledge of communications devices, home networks, and transmission media, visit the Discovering Computers 2005 Quiz Yourself Web page (**scsite.com/dc2005/quiz**). Click Objectives 9 – 11 below Chapter 9.

CHAPTER SUMMARY

This chapter provided an overview of communications terminology and applications. It also discussed how to join computers into a network, allowing them to communicate and share resources such as hardware, software, data, and information. It also explained various communications devices, media, and procedures as they relate to computers.

Network Administrator

Networking professionals are in high demand. A *network administrator* must have a thorough knowledge of operating system software. Network administrator generally is a multifunction position. Among other tasks, a network administrator may be responsible for ensuring that servers and workstations function properly; implementing system backups, upgrades, and security policies; identifying and resolving connectivity issues; installing and maintaining software on clients and servers; providing support for network hardware components such as terminals, servers, hubs, and routers; participating in technical group projects to provide networking-related support and keeping abreast of new developments in networking, systems, and office automation technologies; and suggesting new solutions to increase network productivity.

Because so many variables exist for network solutions, experience and training are important. Many network administrators have some type of networking certification, which is the first step in establishing a career as a networking professional. Some of the more popular of these certifications include Microsoft Certified System Engineer (MCSE) and Cisco Certified Network Associate (CCNA). Salaries for network administrators vary greatly and are based on certification, years of experience, and job responsibilities. Individuals with certifications can expect an approximate starting salary between $35,000 and $75,000.

To learn more about the field of Network Administrator as a career, visit the Discovering Computers 2005 Careers Web page (**scsite.com/dc2005/careers**). Click Network Administrator.

How Network Communications Work

Every message sent over a network — even the simplest e-mail message — must be divided into discrete packages of data and routed via transmission media such as telephone lines. While traveling from the sending computer to the receiving computer, each data package can take a different path over the network. How do these messages get to their destination, intact and accurate?

The *Open Systems Interconnection (OSI) reference model*, a communications standard developed by the International Organization for Standardization (ISO), offers an answer. The OSI reference model describes the flow of data in a network through seven layers, from the user's application to the physical transmission media.

A simple way to understand the OSI reference model is to think of it as an elevator (Figure 9-43). On the sending end, data enters at the top floor (the application layer) and travels to the bottom floor (the physical layer). Each layer communicates with the layers immediately above and below it. When a layer receives data, it performs specific functions, adds control information to the data, and passes it to the next layer. The control information contains error-checking, routing, and other information needed to ensure proper transmission along the network.

The first layer, the *application layer*, serves as the interface between the user and the network. Using application software, such as an e-mail program, a user can type a message and specify a recipient. The application then prepares the message for delivery, by converting the message data into bits and attaching a header identifying the sending and receiving computers.

The *presentation layer* translates the converted message data into a language the receiving computer can process (from ASCII to EBCDIC, for example) and also may compress or encrypt the data. Finally, the layer attaches another header specifying the language, compression, and encryption schemes.

The third layer, called the *session layer*, establishes and maintains communications sessions. A *session* is the period between establishment of a connection, transmission of the data, and termination of the connection.

The *transport layer*, also called the end-to-end layer, ensures that data arrives correctly and in proper sequence. The transport layer divides the data into segments and creates a *checksum*, a mathematical sum based on the data, and puts this information in the transport header. The checksum later is used to determine if the data was scrambled during transmission.

The *network layer* routes the message from sender to receiver. This layer splits the data segments from the transport layer into smaller groups of bits called *packets*. Next, it adds a header containing the packet sequence, the receiving computer address, and routing information. The network layer also manages network problems by re-routing packets to avoid network congestion.

The *data link layer* supervises the transmission of the message to the next network node by specifying the network technology (such as Ethernet or token ring) and grouping data accordingly. The data link layer also calculates the checksum and keeps a copy of each packet until it receives confirmation that the packet arrived undamaged at the next node.

Finally, the *physical layer* encodes the packets into a signal recognized by the medium that will carry them — such as an analog signal to be sent over a telephone line — and sends the packets along that medium to the receiving computer.

At the receiving computer, the process is reversed and the data moves back through the seven layers from the physical layer to the application layer, which identifies the recipient, converts the bits into readable data, removes some of the error-checking and control information from the data, and directs it to the appropriate application. The next time you send an e-mail to a friend, consider the network communications processes described by the OSI reference model, which ensure that your message travels safely over many networks to your friend's computer.

For more information about the OSI reference model, visit the Discovering Computers 2005 High-Tech Talk Web page (**scsite.com/dc2005/tech**) and click OSI Reference Model.

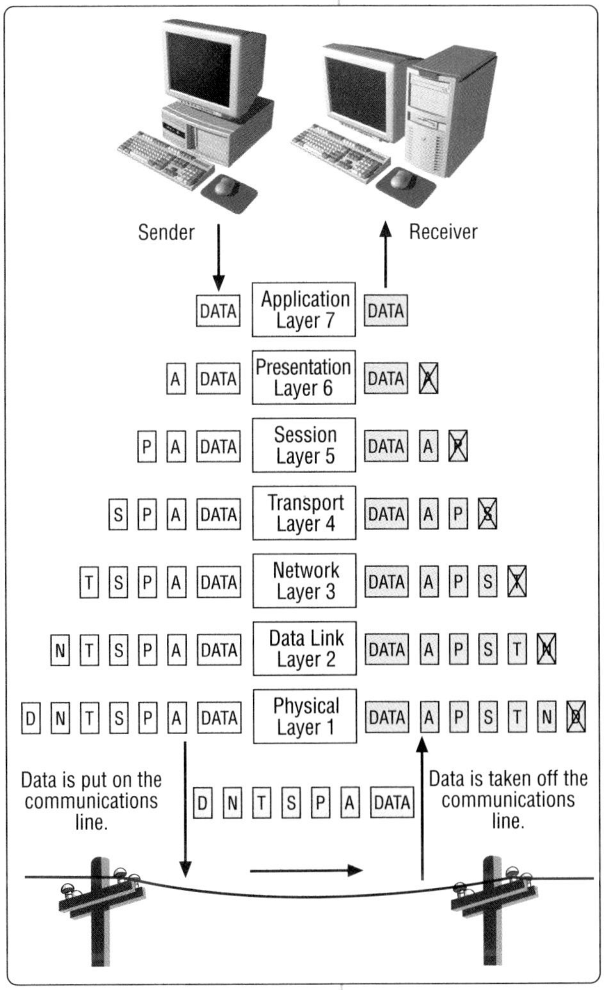

FIGURE 9-43 The seven layers of the OSI reference model.

COMPANIES ON THE CUTTING EDGE

Sun

Networking First, Last, and Always

One-half of the people on Earth never have made a telephone call, but Sun Microsystems' CEO and President Scott McNealy predicts that one day every man, woman, and child always will be connected to a network. These people could be using technology developed by *Sun*.

McNealy and three friends started their company in 1982 with the goal of building engineering workstations in the network computer model. They worked closely with the Stanford University Network (SUN), which accounts for the company name. The company had one driving vision — computers that could communicate with each other no matter who built them. Sun's first workstation included TCP/IP, the Internet communications technology. While other companies concentrated on proprietary products, Sun focused on leading companies into the network age with flexible and dependable systems and software.

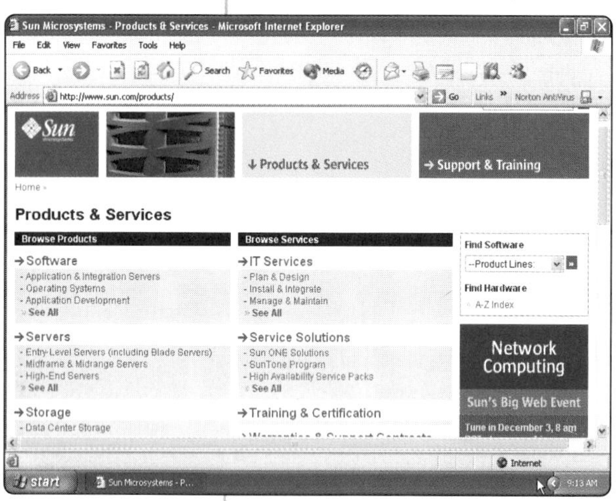

McNealy believes networking increases overall productivity, and his philosophy holds true for his own company. By 1988, Sun had reached $1 billion in revenues, making it the fastest-growing company in history. In 1995, Sun introduced Java, a universal software platform that enables developers to write applications that run on any computer. Sun later licensed Java technology to all major hardware and software companies. In 2003, Sun released StarOffice 7, a competitor to Microsoft Office 2003, that runs on Sun's Solaris operating system, Microsoft Windows, and Linux.

Today, Sun has a presence in more than 170 countries and boasts $18.25 billion in annual revenues. Building industrial-strength hardware, software, and services around its vision, The Network is The Computer, Sun's technology powers the Internet and allows companies worldwide to become involved in e-commerce.

For more information about Sun, visit the Discovering Computers 2005 Companies Web page (**scsite.com/dc2005/companies**) and click Sun.

QUALCOMM

Leader in Wireless Communications

Two of history's more important technological innovations are wireless communications and the Internet. *QUALCOMM*, a leader in wireless communications, is working to join these innovations together to improve people's lives.

In 1985, Dr. Andrew J. Viterbi and Dr. Irwin Mark Jacobs founded QUALCOMM to promote wireless communications systems and products based on CDMA. CDMA (Code Division Multiple Access) converts speech into digital information that is transmitted as a radio signal, with a unique code for each call. The technology reduces interference and increases voice quality, coverage, and security. The first CDMA networks, unveiled in 1995, provided about 10 times the capacity of analog networks. CDMA became the world's fastest-growing wireless technology, with more than 100 million users. QUALCOMM is the leading designer and supplier of CDMA chipsets, hardware, software, and tools.

The first two generations of wireless communications primarily were used for voice transmission. The popularity of the Internet has inspired a third generation of wireless communications for data transfer. In 1999, the International Telecommunication Union adopted an industry standard for third-generation (3G) wireless systems based on CDMA technology. Today, QUALCOMM is the world's largest provider of 3G technology and has shipped more than 1 million chips to the 50 leading wireless industry manufacturers.

QUALCOMM holds more than 600 patents. The company has been selected as a FORTUNE 500 company and has been cited on *FORTUNE* magazine's lists of the 100 Fastest-Growing Companies in America, 100 Best Companies to Work for in America, and America's Most Admired Companies.

For more information about QUALCOMM, visit the Discovering Computers 2005 Companies Web page (**scsite.com/dc2005/companies**) and click QUALCOMM.

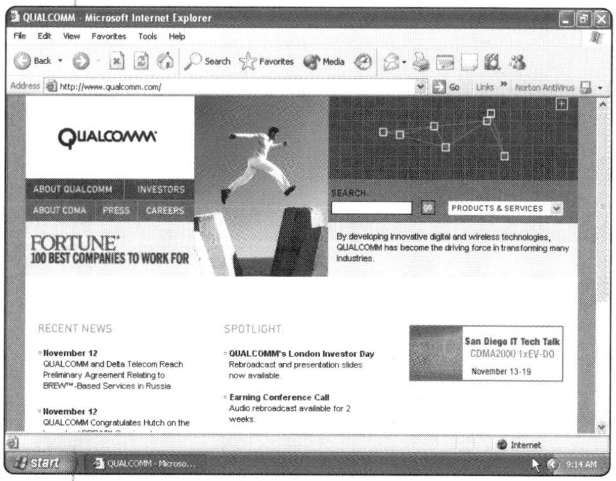

Esther Dyson

Communicator

Legend has it that *Esther Dyson* did not talk at all until she was two years old. When she did talk, however, she spoke in complete sentences. Today, Esther Dyson's sentences bring people and ideas together in creative and productive ways.

The child of an English physicist and a Swiss mathematician, Dyson entered Harvard at age 16. After graduating in 1972 with a degree in economics, Dyson worked as a fact-checker and columnist for *Forbes* magazine, a research associate at New Court Securities, and a software reporter at Oppenheimer before joining Rosen Research. In 1983, Dyson bought Rosen Research from her employer and renamed it EDventure Holdings.

EDventure Holdings is a diverse information services company that invests in information-oriented startup ventures. EDventure Holdings sponsors two of the computer industry's most important annual conferences, PC (Platforms for Communication) Forum in the United States and EDventure's High-Tech Forum in Europe. The company also publishes an influential monthly newsletter, Release 1.0, to which Dyson contributes. Dyson writes about new technologies, new markets, new business models, and new companies. She helps readers understand the fundamental ideas behind computer industry trends. She also has written a book, *Release 2.1: A Design for Living in the Digital Age*, that examines the Internet's effect on people's lives, and authors a bimonthly column, "Release 3.0," for the *New York Times* syndicate.

In addition to these achievements, Dyson served as a former chairman of the ICANN (the Internet Corporation for Assigned Names and Numbers) Board, donated time and money to a variety of organizations, and participated in major conferences around the globe. "My hope in a lot of the things that I do," she says, "is to help make people feel they have an impact on the world around them."

For more information about Esther Dyson, visit the Discovering Computers 2005 People Web page (**scsite.com/dc2005/people**) and click Esther Dyson.

Robert Metcalfe

Inventor of Ethernet

At 3Com Corporation, a plaque honors the company's cofounder, *Robert M. Metcalfe*. The plaque pictures Metcalfe, inventor of the most widely used system for networking computers, and bears a motto attributed to him: "The only difference between being visionary and being stubborn is whether you're right." In the world of computer technology, Bob Metcalfe has proven to be visionary.

Metcalfe evidenced his interest in electronics in fourth grade. With a last-minute book report due, he grabbed a college textbook on electrical engineering from his father's bookshelf. The book was incomprehensible, so Metcalfe wrote the generic book report with which most ten year olds are familiar: "I read this book and it had its high points and it had its low points, but on average it sort of averaged out." To guarantee a good grade, Metcalfe added that he planned to attend the Massachusetts Institute of Technology and major in engineering. Thirteen years later, Metcalfe graduated from MIT with a degree in electrical engineering.

Metcalfe earned a masters degree in applied mathematics and a Ph.D. in computer science from Harvard. While earning his Ph.D., Metcalfe worked at Xerox's Palo Alto Research Center (PARC). To connect the company's many computers to a laser printer, Metcalfe, together with D.R. Boggs, invented Ethernet, a LAN technology consisting of hardware and software that joins computers within a building. In 1979, Metcalfe left Xerox to found 3Com Corporation and make Ethernet the standard for computer communications. Today, Ethernet links millions of computers worldwide.

Metcalfe retired from 3Com in 1990. Now, as an *InfoWorld* magazine columnist, he is considered a technology pundit, writing articles voicing his observations, criticisms, and predictions for the computer industry to hundreds of thousands of information technology professionals.

For more information about Robert Metcalfe, visit the Discovering Computers 2005 People Web page (**scsite.com/dc2005/people**) and click Robert Metcalfe.

CHAPTER 9 CHAPTER REVIEW

The Chapter Review section summarizes the concepts presented in this chapter.

WEB INSTRUCTIONS:

To display this page from the Web, start your browser and enter the Web address **scsite.com/dc2005/ch9/review.** Click the links for current and additional information. To listen to an audio version of this Chapter Review, click the Audio button.

1 What Components Are Required for Successful Communications?

Computer **communications** describes a process in which two or more computers or devices transfer data, instructions, and information. Successful communications requires a **sending device** that initiates a transmission instruction, a communications device that connects the sending device to a communications channel, a **communications channel** on which the data travels, a communications device that connects the communications channel to a receiving device, and a **receiving device** that accepts the transmission.

2 What Are Various Sending and Receiving Devices?

All types of computers and mobile devices serve as sending and receiving devices. This includes mainframe computers, servers, desktop computers, notebook computers, Tablet PCs, PDAs, smart phones, Internet receivers, and GPS receivers.

3 How Are Computer Communications Used?

Communications technologies include the Internet, Web, e-mail, instant messaging, chat rooms, newsgroups, FTP, Web folders, video conferencing, and fax machine or computer fax/modem. People also use communications for other purposes. **Internet telephony** enables users to talk over the Internet. *Internet printing* prints to a Web address that is associated with a particular printer. *Web services* describe standardized software that enables programmers to create applications that communicate over the Internet or an internal network. Many software products provide a means to **collaborate**, or work online with other users. **Groupware** is software that helps people share information over a network. A **public Internet access point** lets people connect wirelessly to the Internet. A **cybercafé** is a coffee house or restaurant that provides computers with Internet access. A **global positioning system** (**GPS**) analyzes signals sent by satellites to determine an earth-based receiver's geographic location. **Voice mail** allows someone to leave a voice message for one or more people. Users can send and receive wireless messages to and from smart phones, cellular telephones, or PDAs using **text messaging**, **picture messaging**, and instant messaging.

Visit **scsite.com/dc2005/quiz** or click the Quiz Yourself button. Click Objectives 1 – 3 below Chapter 9.

4 What Are Advantages of Using a Network?

A **network** is a collection of computers and devices connected together via communications devices and transmission media. Advantages of using a network include facilitating communications, sharing hardware, sharing data and information, sharing software, and transferring funds.

5 How Are Client/Server, Peer-to-Peer, and P2P Networks Different?

On a **client/server network**, one or more computers acts as a **server**, which controls access to network resources and provides a centralized storage area, while the other computers on the network are **clients** that rely on the server for resources. A *peer-to-peer network* is a simple network that typically connects fewer than 10 computers, each called a *peer*, that have equal responsibilities and capabilities. A *P2P* is an Internet peer-to-peer network on which users connect directly to each other's hard disks and exchange files over the Internet.

6 What Are Various Network Communications Technologies?

Network communications technologies include Ethernet, token ring, TCP/IP, 802.11, Bluetooth, IrDA, RFID, and WAP. **Ethernet** allows nodes to contend for access to the network. **Token ring** requires devices to share or pass a special signal, called a *token*. **TCP/IP** divides data up into packets. **802.11** is a family of standards for wireless LANs. Bluetooth uses short-range radio waves to transmit data. **IrDA** transmits data wirelessly via infrared light waves. **RFID** uses radio signals for communications. The **Wireless Application Protocol** (**WAP**) allows wireless mobile devices to access the Internet.

7 What Is the Purpose of Communications Software?

Communications software helps users establish a connection to another computer or network, manages the transmission of data, and provides an interface for users to communicate with one another.

8 What Are Various Types of Lines for Communications Over the Telephone Network?

The telephone network uses dial-up lines or dedicated lines. A **dial-up line** is a temporary connection that uses one or more analog telephone lines for communications. A **dedicated line** is an always-on connection established between two communications devices. Dedicated lines include ISDN lines, DSL, T-carrier lines, and ATM. *ISDN* is a set of standards for digital transmission over standard copper telephone lines. DSL transmits at fast speeds on existing standard copper telephone wiring. A **T-carrier line** is a long-distance digital telephone line that carries multiple signals over a single communications line. **ATM** (*Asynchronous Transfer Mode*) is a service that carries voice, data, video, and multimedia at extremely high speeds.

Visit **scsite.com/dc2005/quiz** or click the Quiz Yourself button. Click Objectives 4 – 8 below Chapter 9.

9 What Are Commonly Used Communications Devices?

A **communications device** is hardware capable of transmitting data between a sending device and a receiving device. A **modem** converts a computer's digital signals to analog signals for transmission over standard telephone lines. An *ISDN modem* transmits digital data to and from an ISDN line, while a **DSL modem** transmits digital data to and from a DSL line. A **cable modem** is a digital modem that sends and receives digital data over the cable television network. A **network card** is an adapter card, PC Card, or compact flash card that enables a computer or device to access a network. A *wireless access point* allows computers and devices to transfer data wirelessly. A *router* connects multiple computers together and transmits data to its destination on the network. A *hub* provides a central point for cables in a network.

10 How Can a Home Network Be Set Up?

A **home network** connects multiple computers and devices in a home. An Ethernet network connects each computer to a hub with a physical cable. A home *powerline cable network* uses the same lines that bring electricity into the house. A *phoneline network* uses existing telephone lines in a home. A *HomeRF* (*radio frequency*) *network* and **Wi-Fi** network use radio waves, instead of cable, to transmit data.

11 What Are Various Physical and Wireless Transmission Media?

Transmission media consists of materials or substances capable of carrying one or more signals. *Physical transmission media* use tangible materials to send communications signals. **Twisted-pair cable** consists of one or more twisted-pair wires bundled together. **Coaxial cable** consists of a single copper wire surrounded by at least three layers: an insulating material, a woven or braided metal, and a plastic outer coating. **Fiber-optic cable** consists of thin strands of glass or plastic that use light to transmit signals. *Wireless transmission media* send communications signals through the air or space. *Infrared* (*IR*) sends signals using infrared light waves. Broadcast radio distributes radio signals through the air over long and short distances. **Cellular radio** is a form of broadcast radio that is used widely for mobile communications. **Microwaves** are radio waves that provide a high-speed signal transmission. A **communications satellite** is a space station that receives microwave signals from an earth-based station, amplifies the signals, and broadcasts the signals back over a wide area.

Visit **scsite.com/dc2005/quiz** or click the Quiz Yourself button. Click Objectives 9 – 11 below Chapter 9.

CHAPTER 9 KEY TERMS

QUIZZES AND LEARNING GAMES
Computer Genius
Crossword Puzzle
Interactive Labs
Practice Test
Quiz Yourself
Wheel of Terms

EXERCISES
Chapter Review
Checkpoint
Key Terms
Lab Exercises
Learn It Online
Web Research

BEYOND THE BOOK
Apply It
Career Corner
Companies
FAQ
High-Tech Talk
Issues
Looking Ahead
Trailblazers
Web Links

FEATURES
Guide to Web Sites
Making Use of the Web
Tech News
Timeline 2005

You should know the Primary Terms and be familiar with the Secondary Terms.

WEB INSTRUCTIONS:

To display this page from the Web, start your browser and enter the Web address **scsite.com/dc2005/ch9/terms**. Click a term to display its definition and a picture. When the picture appears, click the more info button for current and additional information about the term from the Web.

>> Primary Terms

(shown in bold-black characters in the chapter)

802.11 (476)
ATM (482)
bandwidth (489)
Bluetooth (476)
broadband (490)
broadcast radio (492)
cable modem (484)
cellular radio (492)
cellular telephone (492)
client/server network (472)
clients (472)
coaxial cable (490)
collaborate (465)
communications (460)
communications channel (461)
communications device (482)
communications satellite (494)
communications software (478)
cybercafé (466)
dedicated line (481)
dial-up line (480)
DSL (481)
DSL modem (484)
Ethernet (475)
fiber-optic cable (491)
global positioning system (GPS) (466)
groupware (466)
home network (487)
Internet telephony (464)
IrDA (476)
latency (489)
local area network (LAN) (471)
microwaves (493)
modem (483)
network (469)
network card (485)
network topology (474)
noise (490)
picture messaging (468)
public Internet access point (466)
receiving device (461)
RFID (477)
sending device (460)
server (472)
SMS (468)
text messaging (468)
T-carrier line (482)
TCP/IP (476)
token ring (475)
transmission media (489)
twisted-pair cable (490)
voice mail (468)
wide area network (WAN) (472)
Wi-Fi (476)
Wireless Application Protocol (WAP) (477)
wireless LAN (WLAN) (471)
wireless modem (483)

>> Secondary Terms

(shown in italic characters in the chapter)

10-Gigabit Ethernet (475)
1G (492)
2G (492)
3G (492)
ADSL (asymmetric digital subscriber line) (482)
analog signal (461)
Asynchronous Transfer Mode (482)
baseband (490)
broadband modem (484)
bus (474)
bus network (474)
CDMA (492)
coax (490)
database server (472)
dedicated servers (472)
demodulate (483)
dial-up modem (483)
Digital Angel (468)
digital modem (484)
digital signal (461)
Digital Subscriber Line (481)
downlink (494)
downstream rate (482)
EDI (Electronic Data Interchange) (470)
electronic funds transfer (EFT) (471)
extranet (478)
Fast Ethernet (475)
file server (472)
file sharing network (473)
fixed-point wireless (493)
fractional T1 (482)
Gigabit Ethernet (475)
GPRS (492)
GPS receiver (466)
GSM (492)
HomeRF (radio frequency) network (487)
host computer (472)
hot spot (466)
hub (connecting networks) *(486)*
hub (star network) *(475)*
infrared (IR) (492)
intelligent home network (487)
Internet printing (464)
Internet telephone software (464)
intranet (478)
ISDN (Integrated Services Digital Network) (481)
ISDN modem (484)
line-of-sight transmission (476)
metropolitan area network (MAN) (471)
microwave station (493)
MMS (multimedia message service) (468)
modulate (483)
multiplexing (481)
network architecture (472)
network interface card (NIC) (485)
network license (470)
network server (472)
node (471)
online meeting (465)
optical fiber (491)
P2P (473)
packet switching (476)
packets (476)
peer (473)
peer-to-peer network (473)
Personal Communications Services (PCS) (492)
phoneline network (487)
physical transmission media (490)
powerline cable network (487)
print server (472)
public switched telephone network (PSTN) (480)
radio frequency identification (477)
ring network (474)
router (486)
short message service (468)
site license (470)
star network (475)
T1 line (482)
T3 line (482)
token (475)
Transmission Control Protocol/Internet Protocol (476)
twisted-pair wire (490)
UMTS (492)
uplink (494)
upstream rate (482)
value-added network (VAN) (471)
voice mailbox (468)
Voice over IP (VoIP) (464)
Web services (464)
wireless fidelity (476)
wireless access point (485)
wireless Internet service provider (WISP) (466)
wireless transmission media (490)
workgroup computing (466)
XML (464)

Use the Checkpoint exercises to check your knowledge level of the chapter.

WEB INSTRUCTIONS:

To display this page from the Web, start your browser and enter the Web address **scsite.com/dc2005/ch9/check**. Click the links for current and additional information.

LABEL THE FIGURE

Identify each sending device and receiving device.

a. desktop computer
b. GPS receiver
c. mainframe computer
d. notebook computer
e. Web-enabled PDA
f. server
g. Internet receiver
h. smart phone
i. Tablet PC

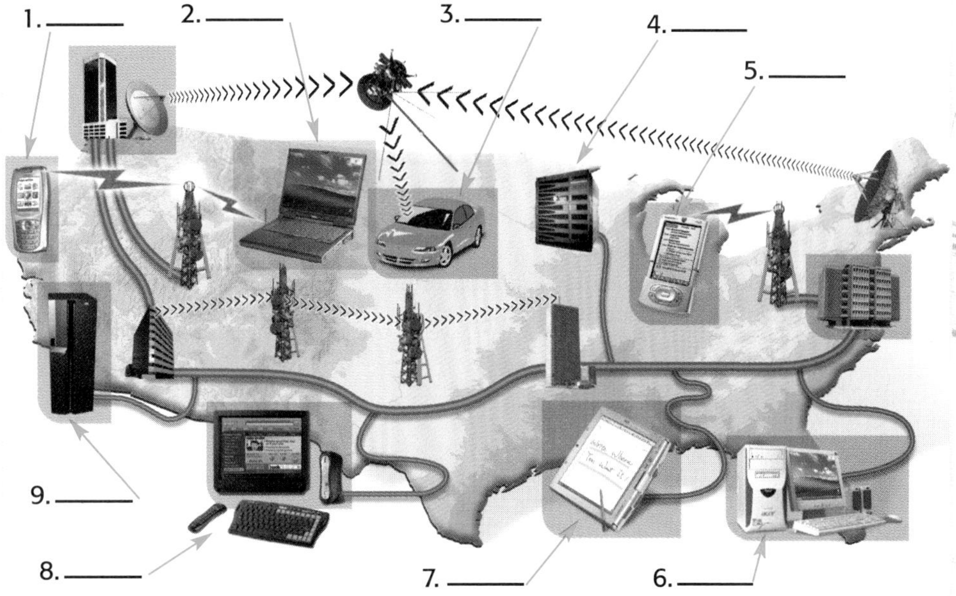

TRUE/FALSE

Mark T for True and F for False. (See page numbers in parentheses.)

T 1. Communications systems contain all types of computers and computing devices. (460)

T 2. Chat rooms are locations for real-time typed conversations that take place on computers connected to a network. (461)

T 3. Groupware is a software application that helps groups of people work together on projects and share information over a network. (466)

T 4. A network is a collection of computers and devices connected together via communications devices and transmission media. (469)

F 5. A metropolitan area network (MAN) is a network that covers a large geographic area using a communications channel that combines many types of media such as telephone lines, cables, and radio waves. (471)

F 6. On a ring network, all of the computers and devices on the network connect to a central device. (474)

F 7. An extranet is an internal network that uses Internet technologies. (478)

T 8. A dial-up line is a temporary connection that uses one or more analog telephone lines for communications. (480)

T 9. A cable modem is a digital modem that sends and receives digital data over the cable television network. (484)

F 10. Fiber-optic cable costs less than twisted-pair or coaxial cable and is easy to install and modify. (491)

T 11. Because microwaves use line-of-sight transmission, microwave stations often sit on the tops of buildings, towers, or mountains. (493)

CHAPTER 9 CHECKPOINT

MULTIPLE CHOICE

Select the best answer. (See page numbers in parentheses.)

1. One type of communications device that connects a communications channel to a sending or receiving device is a _____. (462)
   a. coax
   b. server
   c. modem
   d. peer
2. Sending and receiving devices include _____. (462)
   a. mainframe computers and servers
   b. desktop computers and notebook computers
   c. Tablet PCs, PDAs, and smart phones
   d. all of the above
3. Different applications can communicate with each other by sending XML to the _____. (464)
   a. Internet telephony
   b. Internet printing
   c. Web services
   d. global positioning systems
4. An online meeting allows users to _____. (465)
   a. share documents with others in real time
   b. leave voice messages for one or two people
   c. determine the receiver's geographic location
   d. print to a Web address that is associated with a particular printer
5. Because of its larger size, most _____ networks require a person to serve as a network administrator. (472)
   a. client/server
   b. peer-to-peer
   c. P2P
   d. all of the above
6. Today _____ is the most popular LAN technology because it is relatively inexpensive and easy to install and maintain. (475)
   a. token ring
   b. Ethernet
   c. TCP/IP
   d. Bluetooth
7. When a computer uses TCP/IP to send data over the Internet, the data is divided into small pieces, or _____. (476)
   a. tokens
   b. packets
   c. hubs
   d. nodes
8. Communications software consists of programs that do all of the following, except _____. (478)
   a. help users establish a connection to another computer or network
   b. manage the transmission of data, instructions, and information
   c. provide an interface for users to communicate with one another
   d. convert a computer's analog signals into digital signals for transmission
9. With ISDN, a telephone line can carry three or more signals at once using a technique called _____. (481)
   a. packet switching
   b. multiplexing
   c. file sharing
   d. collaborating
10. The most popular T-carrier line is the _____. (482)
    a. T1 line
    b. ATM
    c. T3 line
    d. DSL
11. Most CATV operators provide a(n) _____ as part of the installation. (484)
    a. dial-up modem
    b. ISDN modem
    c. cable modem
    d. DSL modem
12. Two types of wireless home networks are _____. (487)
    a. Ethernet and powerline
    b. phoneline and HomeRF
    c. Ethernet and Wi-Fi
    d. HomeRF and Wi-Fi
13. _____ media transmit multiple signals simultaneously. (490)
    a. Baseband
    b. Sideband
    c. Broadband
    d. Trainband
14. When compared to cables that use wire, fiber-optic cables _____. (491)
    a. are capable of carrying significantly more signals
    b. provide slower data transmission
    c. are more susceptible to noise
    d. have larger size (much thicker and greater weight)

CHECKPOINT CHAPTER 9

MATCHING Match the terms with their definitions. (See page numbers in parentheses.)

_____ 1. Internet telephony (464)
_____ 2. Internet printing (464)
_____ 3. Web services (464)
_____ 4. groupware (466)
_____ 5. cybercafé (466)
_____ 6. voice mail (468)
_____ 7. text messaging (468)
_____ 8. intranet (478)
_____ 9. extranet (478)
_____ 10. baseband (490)

a. allows users to print to a Web address associated with a particular printer
b. allows customers or suppliers to access part of a company's intranet
c. coffee house or restaurant that provides computers with Internet access
d. standardized software that enables programmers to create applications that communicate over the Internet or an internal network
e. enables users to talk to other users over the Internet
f. has billions of Web pages that contain text, graphics, audio, and video
g. internal network that uses Internet technologies
h. functions like an answering machine, allowing people to leave voice messages
i. online area in which users have written discussions about a subject
j. type of media that transmits only one signal at a time
k. allows smart phone, PDA, or personal computer users to send and receive brief text messages
l. software that helps groups of people share information

SHORT ANSWER Write a brief answer to each of the following questions.

1. What is a global positioning system (GPS)? ___________ What is Digital Angel? ___________
2. How are a local area network (LAN), a metropolitan area network (MAN), and a wide area network (WAN) different? ___________ What is a wireless LAN? ___________
3. What is a dedicated server? ___________ How are a file server, a print server, a database server, and a network server different? ___________
4. What is a network topology? ___________ How are a bus network, a ring network, and a star network different? ___________
5. What are bandwidth and latency? ___________ How do bandwidth and latency affect the performance of a communications channel? ___________

WORKING TOGETHER Working with a group of your classmates, complete the following team exercises.

1. Assume you are part of a group hired as consultants to recommend a network plan for a small company of 20 employees. Using the Internet and other available resources, develop a network plan for the company. Include the following components in your plan: (1) the type of network — peer-to-peer or client/server, (2) the suggested topology, (3) the type and number of servers, (4) the peripheral devices, and (5) the communications media. Prepare a written report and a PowerPoint presentation to share with the class.
2. Choose one Issue from the following issues in this chapter: How Good Is Your E-Mail Writing? (463), What Is Under Your Skin? (468), High-Tech Crib Notes? (469), Are Cameras at Intersections Inappropriate? (470), or Should Libraries Use Filtering Software? (478). Use the Web and/or print media to research the issue. Then, present a debate for the class, with different members of your team supporting different responses to the questions that accompany the issue.
3. Many schools and offices have a local area network connecting their computers. Have each member of your team locate a school or office that uses a network and talk to someone about how the network works. What network architecture, topology, and communications technology are used? Why? What communications software is used? Why? What are the advantages and disadvantages of having a network? Is the network connected to another network? If so, how? Meet with the members of your team to discuss the results of your interviews. Then, use PowerPoint to create a group presentation and share your findings with the class.

FIGURE 8 Ericsson introduced the first Bluetooth product — a headset that communicates with a wireless telephone, thus enabling users to talk hands-free. Wireless headsets also can connect to notebook computers and handheld computers.

FIGURE 9 Public access points, also called hot spots, allow wireless networking in public areas. For a fee, and sometimes free, notebook computer users can wander into designated places and access the Internet. In 2002, the number of hot spots worldwide jumped from 2,000 to 12,000. For example, American Airlines, United, and Delta have set up these high-speed access points at their main hubs. More than 1,000 Starbucks Coffee shops currently offer high-speed wireless Internet access in Wireless HotSpot Stores, and the company plans to provide it in all its North American stores. McDonald's has launched Internet access for customers in Chicago, New York, and San Francisco.

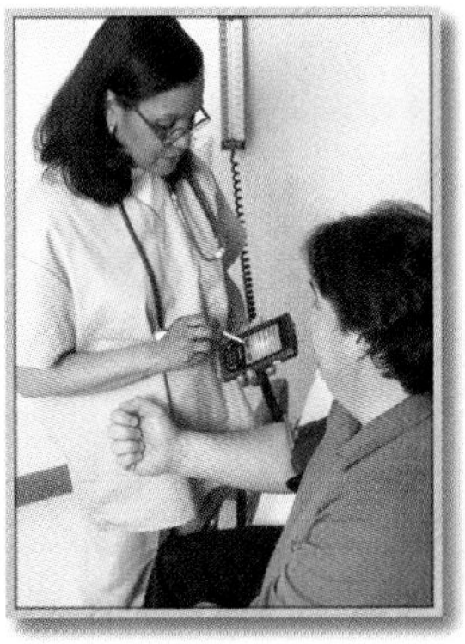

FIGURE 10 Health-care professionals, police officers, package couriers, and retail sales personnel are using hand-held computers to help them work more efficiently. Ambulance crews use PDAs to collect and transmit patient data while en route to hospitals. Doctors and nurses access patients' records and then record treatments and prescribed medications. Patrol officers conduct vehicle registration checks and record crime scene details. Delivery personnel scan package bar codes to track pickup and delivery times and record signatures. Retail managers use PDAs to monitor, transfer, and reorder product inventory.

FIGURE 11 Wireless connectivity makes it easy to synchronize files on your handheld computers and notebook computers. When you are on the road, you can connect your wireless devices to an office network and automatically transfer databases, appointments, to-do lists, and other files, just as if you were seated in front of your computer. Back in the office, you can update your notebook computer and handheld computer the instant you enter the room.

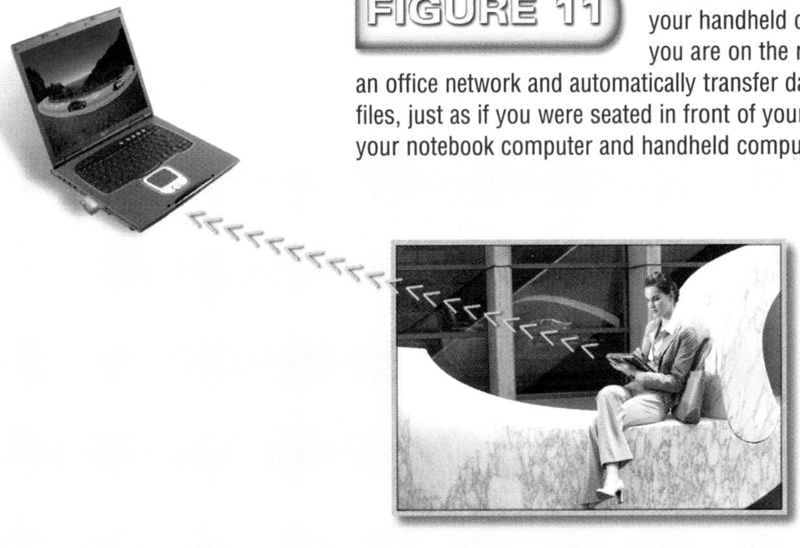

FIGURE 12 Your friend is vacationing in sunny Hawaii; you are shoveling snow in icy Chicago. You can bask in your friend's warmth with instant postcards. All your friend needs to do is capture an image with a cellular telephone or PDA equipped with a built-in digital camera and then transmit the image to your compatible cellular telephone or PDA or to your e-mail address. Your friend can add a personalized voice or text message to the photo.

FIGURE 13 Millions of hikers, boaters, pilots, drivers, and other navigators never feel lost with the aid of global positioning system (GPS) devices. These products rely on 24 satellites that circle Earth twice a day in a very precise orbit and transmit data to Earth. The GPS products then use 3 to 12 of these satellites to determine the receivers' precise geographic locations. Some GPS devices include color mapping capability that gives detail for any United States city. GPS modules also are available for handheld computers. By the middle of this decade, analysts predict that 25 million vehicles, including all new cars, will be equipped with GPS navigational devices.

FIGURE 14 Instructors now can determine just how well students are comprehending class material with the help of interactive wireless computers. They can ask a multiple-choice or true-false question and then ask students to respond using a wireless keypad resembling a remote control. Within seconds, an infrared reader captures the students' responses, and then a computer tabulates the results and tracks their scores.

Wireless Summary

Your pockets and backpack may be overflowing with small electronic devices, but the wireless revolution is making headway to combine some of these products and simplify your life. Wireless networks are growing throughout the world, driven by convenience, cost, and access. The ways you communicate at home, in the office, and at school are forever changed in the world without wires.

CHAPTER 10

Database Management

Picture Yourself Using a Web Database

Your Walt Disney World vacation has been so awesome. While strolling through the park today, you think about all the fun you have had the past few days. As you walk by a Disney character, you remember that your favorite nephew's birthday is tomorrow … but you will not be home for three days. He will be very disappointed if you miss his birthday. Wait! You can solve that problem when you return to the hotel.

Your hotel provides a service for guests that allows them to connect a notebook computer to a telephone line using the hotel's data port. Because you travel with your notebook computer, you can use this service. After establishing an Internet connection, you display the Web page of your online florist. Within about fifteen minutes, you have selected and paid for a bouquet of cookies, two birthday balloons, a baseball hat, and a basket filled with treats. You schedule the delivery for tomorrow.

Online shopping no doubt has been a timesaver for you and millions of other shoppers worldwide. When ordering online, you access a merchant's huge inventory database. These databases store thousands of products. You certainly are grateful to the people who design those product databases for the Web. Now, you can relax again and enjoy the rest of your vacation.

As you read Chapter 10, you will learn about Web databases and discover features common to most databases.

OBJECTIVES

After completing this chapter, you will be able to:

1. Identify the qualities of valuable information
2. Explain why data is important to an organization
3. Discuss the terms character, field, record, and file
4. Identify file maintenance techniques
5. Differentiate between a file processing system approach and the database approach
6. Discuss the functions common to most DBMSs
7. Describe characteristics of relational, object-oriented, and multidimensional databases
8. Explain how Web databases work
9. Discuss the responsibilities of database analysts and administrators

CONTENTS

DATA AND INFORMATION

Data is a collection of unprocessed items, which can include text, numbers, images, audio, and video. In the past, data was limited to words and numbers. Today, data is much more interesting because it includes sounds, images, and video. For example, you can talk into a computer's microphone. Images taken with a digital camera can be transferred into a computer. By attaching a video camera to a computer, it stores captured motion and sounds.

Information is processed data; that is, it is organized, meaningful, and useful. Voice communications can be sent in an e-mail message for a family member, friend, or coworker to hear. You can post photographs taken with a digital camera on a Web page for others to view. With a PC video camera, others can see you in real time during a conference call.

Computers process data into information. A membership coordinator, for example, enters several data items into a computer. The coordinator also uses a digital camera to photograph the new member. This picture, along with the other entered data, is stored in the database on a server's hard disk. A computer in a fitness center then processes this new member data and payment data and prints information on a receipt (Figure 10-1).

FIGURE 10-1 HOW A FITNESS CENTER MIGHT PROCESS DATA INTO INFORMATION

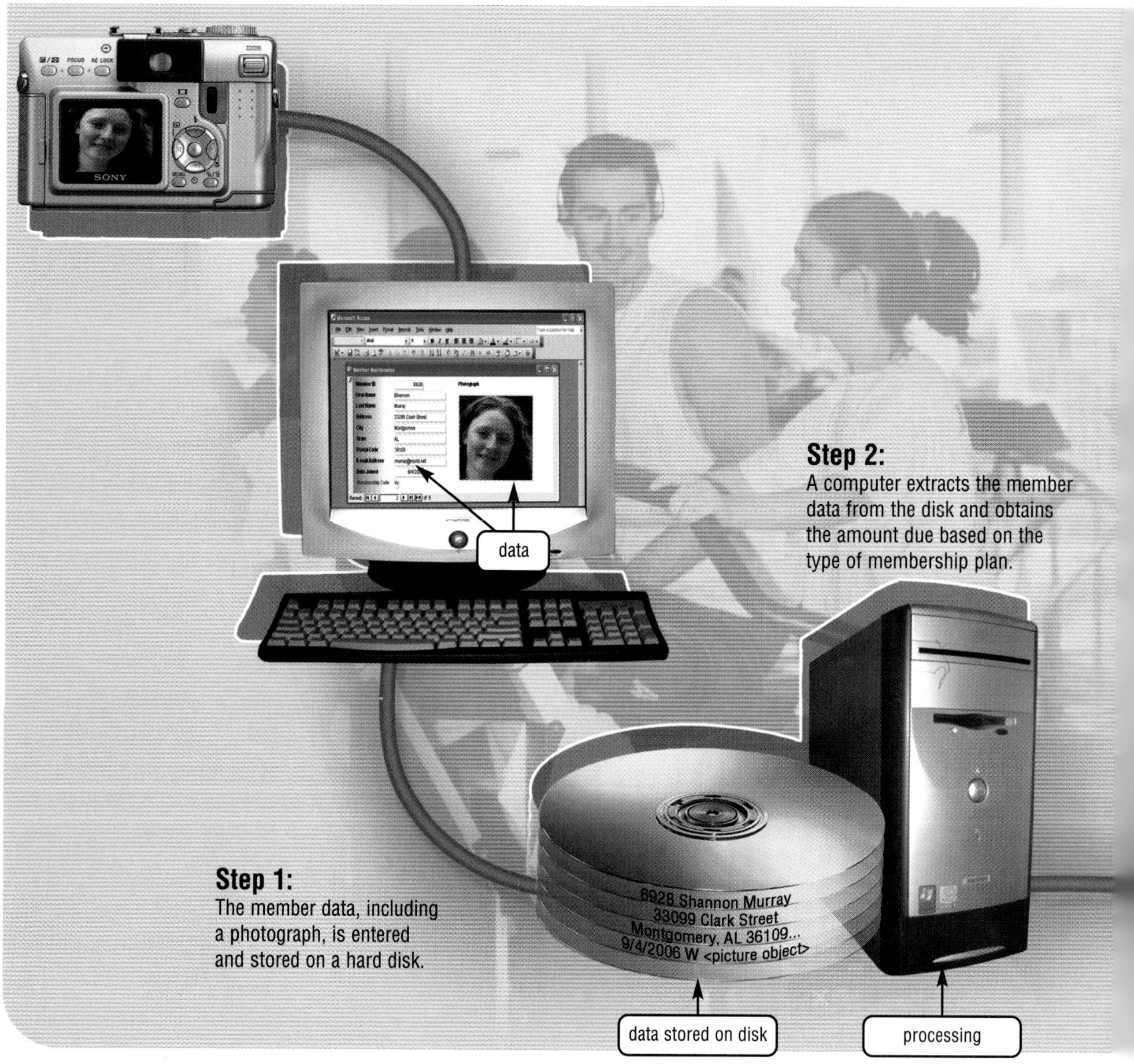

As presented in Chapter 3, a **database** is a collection of data organized in a manner that allows access, retrieval, and use of that data. A database at a fitness center, for example, contains data about members, e.g., personal data, payment data, trainer data, training schedules, etc.

With **database software**, often called a **database management system (DBMS)**, users create a computerized database; add, change, and delete data in the database; sort and retrieve data from the database; and create forms and reports from the data in the database. A fitness center might use Microsoft Access as its database software. When a new member joins the fitness center, a membership coordinator enters the member data. Then, the database software creates and prints a receipt. Database software includes these and many other powerful features, as you will discover later in this chapter.

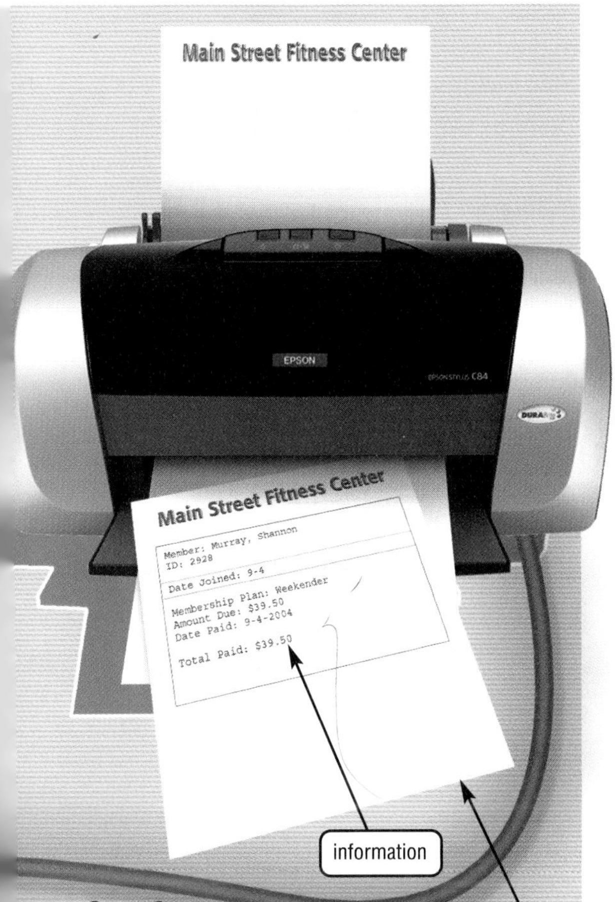

Step 3:
When the amount due of $39.50 is paid, the receipt is created and printed. (The Weekender plan is $39.50 per month.)

Data Integrity

Most companies realize that data is one of their more valuable assets — because data is used to generate information. Many business transactions take less time when employees have instant access to information. For example, if membership coordinators in a fitness center have instant access to training schedules, they can determine which fitness classes are open upon member request. When employees are more productive, customers (members, in this case) usually are more satisfied. When customers are happy, typically they become loyal to that business. Loyal customers can lead to referrals and an increase in profits.

To ensure that data is accessible on demand, a company must manage and protect its data just as it would any other resource. Thus, it is very important that the data has integrity and is kept secure. Chapter 11 presents a variety of methods to secure data. The following paragraphs discuss data integrity.

For a computer to produce correct information, the data that is input into a database must have integrity. *Data integrity* identifies the quality of the data. An erroneous member address in a member database is an example of incorrect data. When a database contains this type of error, it loses integrity. The more errors the data contains, the lower its integrity. Users will not rely on data that has little or no integrity.

Garbage in, garbage out (*GIGO*) is a computer phrase that means you cannot create correct information from data that is incorrect. If you enter incorrect data into a computer (garbage in), the computer will produce incorrect information (garbage out). Correct data does not guarantee the information is correct, but it does increase the chances.

Data integrity is very important because computers and people use information to make decisions and take actions. When you sign up for a fitness center membership and pay with a credit card, a process begins that charges an amount to your credit card. If the membership price is not correct in the fitness center's database, an incorrect amount will be billed to your credit card. This type of error causes both you and the membership coordinator extra time and effort to remedy.

Qualities of Valuable Information

The information that data generates also is an important asset. People make decisions daily using all types of information such as receipts, bank statements, pension plan summaries, stock analyses, and credit reports (read Apply It 10-1 for more information). At school, students use grade reports and degree audits to make decisions. In a business, managers make decisions based on sales trends, competitors' products and services, production processes, and even employee skills.

To assist with sound decision making, the information must have value. For it to be valuable, information should be accurate, verifiable, timely, organized, accessible, useful, and cost-effective.

- *Accurate information* is error free. Inaccurate information can lead to incorrect decisions. For example, consumers assume their credit report is accurate. If your credit report incorrectly shows past due payments, a bank may not lend you money for a car or house.
- *Verifiable information* can be proven as correct or incorrect. For example, a ticket agent at an airport usually requests some type of photo identification to verify that you are the person named on the ticket.
- *Timely information* has an age suited to its use. A decision to build additional schools in a particular district should be based on the most recent census report — not on one that is 20 years old.

Most information loses its value with time. Some information, such as information about trends, gains value as time passes and more information is obtained. Your transcript gains value as you take more classes. A transcript that shows six semesters of course grades has more meaning than one showing just two semesters.

- *Organized information* is arranged to suit the needs and requirements of the decision maker. Two different people may need the same information presented in a different manner. For example, an inventory manager may want an inventory report to list out-of-stock items first. The purchasing agent, instead, wants the report alphabetized by vendor.
- *Accessible information* is available when the decision maker needs it. Having to wait for information may delay an important decision. For example, a sales manager cannot decide which sales representative deserves the award for highest annual sales if the programmer has not finished writing the program that lists sales for each representative.
- *Useful information* has meaning to the person who receives it. Most information is important only to certain people or groups of people. Always consider the audience when collecting and reporting information. Avoid distributing useless information. For example, an announcement of an alumni association meeting is useful only to school alumni — it is not useful to students not yet graduated.
- *Cost-effective information* should give more value than it costs to produce. A company occasionally should review the information it produces to determine if it still is cost-effective to produce. Sometimes, it is not easy to place a value on information. For this reason, some companies create information only on demand, that is, as people request it, instead of on a regular basis. Many companies make information available online. Users then can access and print online information as they need it. For example, sending a printed benefits manual to each employee in a company could be quite costly. Instead, employees can access an online benefits manual, when they need to review it.

APPLY IT 10-1

Take Charge of Your Credit

The notion of giving credit where credit is due takes on a new meaning among today's consumers. The average household credit card debt is approximately $12,000, according to the Federal Reserve. As Americans apply for loans or make payments to reduce debts, their credit activity is reported to at least one of the three major credit bureaus — Equifax, Experian, or TransUnion — and stored in a database.

These agencies sell this data to credit-granting companies in the form of a report, which is used to determine if credit is granted and sometimes to verify whether job candidates have a solid history of making timely payments. It is a good idea, consequently, to check credit files at least once a year for accuracy because numerous studies have found that errors do occur. Each credit bureau's Web site has information about retrieving a credit report.

Credit history checks also can uncover credit fraud, which is increasing due to telemarketing and Internet scams. In addition, identity theft is on the rise and occurs when one person steals someone's personal information for fraudulent activities, such as applying for credit, leasing an apartment, or finding a job.

For more information about credit databases, visit the Discovering Computers 2005 Apply It Web page (**scsite.com/dc2005/apply**). Click Apply It #1 below Chapter 10.

Oct - 8

FAQ 10-1

How can I tell if information is useful?

If you stop distributing information and find that those who had received it do not notify you, then it might be that the information was not very useful. In many cases, what was useful information at one time now may in fact end up in the wastebasket or recycle bin — possibly without even being reviewed.

For more information about useful information, visit the Discovering Computers 2005 FAQ Web page (**scsite.com/dc2005/faq**). Click Useful Information below Chapter 10.

THE HIERARCHY OF DATA

Data is organized in layers. In the computer profession, data is classified in a hierarchy. Each higher level of data consists of one or more items from the lower level. For example, a member has an address, and an address consists of letters and numbers. Depending on the application and the user, different terms describe the various levels of the hierarchy.

As shown in Figure 10-2, a database contains files, a file contains records, a record contains fields, and a field is made up of one or more characters. The Fitness Center database contains four files: Member, Membership Plans, Personal Trainer, and Training Session. The Member file contains records about current members. The Membership Plans file contains records identifying a type of membership and its monthly fee. The Personal Trainer file contains records about trainers at the fitness center, and the Training Session file contains records that identify the time and date a member has a session with a trainer.

Characters

As discussed in Chapter 4, a bit is the smallest unit of data the computer can process. Eight bits grouped together in a unit comprise a byte. In the ASCII and EBCDIC coding schemes, each byte represents a single **character**, which can be a number (4), letter (R), punctuation mark (?), or other symbol (&). (Read Appendix B for more information about coding schemes.)

Fields

A **field** is a combination of one or more related characters or bytes and is the smallest unit of data a user accesses. A **field name** uniquely identifies each field. When searching for data in a database, you often specify the field name. Field names for the data in the Membership Plans file are Membership Code, Membership Name, and Monthly Fee.

FITNESS CENTER DATABASE

Membership Plans file

Membership Code	Membership Name	Monthly Fee
L	Late Shift	$20.25
M	Matinee	$25.75
P	Prime Time	$45.50
R	Round the Clock	$55.50
W	Weekender	$39.50

field names

records

fields

Characteristics of Membership Code field

Field Size	1
Format	
Input Mask	
Caption	Membership Code
Default Value	
Validation Rule	"L" Or "M" Or "P" Or "R" Or "W"
Validation Text	Please enter valid membership code.
Required	Yes
Allow Zero Length	No
Indexed	Yes (No Duplicates)

maximum characters in Membership Code field

FIGURE 10-2 A sample fitness center database with four files: Member, Membership Plans, Personal Trainer, and Training Session. The sample Membership Plans file contains five records. Each record contains three fields. The Membership Code field can contain a maximum of 1 character (byte).

A database uses a variety of characteristics, such as field size and data type, to define each field. The **field size** defines the maximum number of characters a field can contain. For example, the Membership Code field contains one character. Valid entries include L (Late Shift), M (Matinee), P (Prime Time), R (Round the Clock), and W (Weekender). Thus, as shown in Figure 10-2 on the previous page, the Membership Code field has a field size of 1.

The type of data in a field is an important consideration. Figure 10-3 identifies the data types for fields in the Membership Plans and Member files. The **data type** specifies the kind of data a field can contain and how the field is used. Common data types include:

- Text (also called *alphanumeric*) — letters, numbers, or special characters
- Numeric — numbers only
- AutoNumber — unique number automatically assigned by the DBMS to each added record
- Currency — dollar and cent amounts or numbers containing decimal values
- Date — month, day, year, and sometimes time information
- Memo — lengthy text entries
- Yes/No (also called *Boolean*) — only the values Yes or No (or True or False)
- Hyperlink — Web address that links to a document or a Web page
- Object (also called *BLOB* for binary large object) — photograph, audio, video, or a document created in other programs such as word processing or spreadsheet

In the Membership Plans file, two fields (Membership Code and Membership Name) have a text data type; the third field (Monthly Fee) has a currency data type (Figure 10-3). In the Member file, the Member ID field has an AutoNumber data type. The First Name, Last Name, Address, City, State, Postal Code, E-mail Address, and Membership Code fields have a text data type. Date Joined has a date/time data type, and Photograph has an object data type.

Membership Plans file

Membership Code	Text
Membership Name	Text
Monthly Fee	Currency

data types

Member file

Member ID	AutoNumber
First Name	Text
Last Name	Text
Address	Text
City	Text
State	Text
Postal Code	Text
E-mail Address	Text
Date Joined	Date/Time
Membership Code	Text
Photograph	Object

FIGURE 10-3 Data types of fields in the Membership Plans and Member files.

Records

A **record** is a group of related fields. For example, a member record includes a set of fields about one member. A **key field**, or **primary key**, is a field that uniquely identifies each record in a file. The data in a key field is unique to a specific record. For example, the Member ID field uniquely identifies each member because no two members can have the same Member ID.

SAMPLE MEMBER FILE

Member ID	First Name	Last Name
2295	Donna	Vandenburg
6928	Shannon	Murray
3876	Adrian	Valesquez
3928	Jonah	Weinberg
4872	Marcus	Green

records

key field

fields

FAQ 10-2

Do users enter a primary key value?

Users only enter a primary key value if the program requests one, such as a driver's license number or student identification number. Often, the database program automatically assigns a unique primary key number to each newly added record. In this case, the data type of the primary key field is AutoNumber.

For more information about primary keys, visit the Discovering Computers 2005 FAQ Web page (**scsite.com/dc2005/faq**). Click Primary Key Fields below Chapter 10.

Files

A **data file** is a collection of related records stored on a disk such as a hard disk, CD, or DVD. A fitness center's Member file might consist of hundreds of individual member records. Each member record in the file contains the same fields. Each field, however, contains different data. Figure 10-4 shows a small sample Member file that contains five member records, each with 11 fields. Typical fields about people often include First Name, Last Name, Address, City, State, Postal Code, and E-mail Address.

A database includes a group of related data files. With a DBMS, users access and set relationships in the data in data files. Read Issue 10-1 for a discussion related to a use of databases.

ISSUE 10-1

Should Americans Have a National Identification Card?

Calls for a national identification card in the United States have sparked heated debate, although such cards are the norm in most of the world. A *national ID card* could do more than simply assert the cardholder's identity. Some card proponents have called for embedding a biometric identifier, such as a fingerprint or facial scan, into the cards as an added security measure. Larry Ellison, Oracle CEO, proposes tying the cards to a combination of national databases related to personal information. Law enforcement officials contend that national ID cards would provide tamper-resistant proof of identification and improve national security. Civil liberties groups fear that the cards would facilitate information sharing among government agencies, increase police power, and lead to unjustified suspicion when someone fails to produce a card. Should the United States require a national identification card? Why or why not? If a national ID card is used, should it have biometric identifiers or be tied to a national database? Why?

For more information about national identification cards, visit the Discovering Computers 2005 Issues Web page (**scsite.com/dc2005/issues**). Click Issue #1 below Chapter 10.

FAQ 10-3

Do any programs besides databases use data files?

Yes. When you create form letters using a word processing program, the data for the form letters is stored in a data file. The names and addresses that an e-mail program accesses are stored in a data file. The materials list for a CAD (computer-aided design) program is kept in a data file.

For more information about data files, visit the Discovering Computers 2005 FAQ Web page (**scsite.com/dc2005/faq**). Click Data Files below Chapter 10.

Address	City	State	Postal Code	E-mail Address	Date Joined	Membership Code	Photograph
1029 Wolf Avenue	Montgomery	AL	36109		2/10/2005	R	
33099 Clark Street	Montgomery	AL	36109	murray@world.net	9/4/2006	W	
15 Duluth Street	Prattville	AL	36068	valesquez@prattville.net	4/22/2005	P	
P.O. Box 45	Clanton	AL	35046		10/8/2005	P	
22 Fifth Avenue	Auburn	AL	36830	rng@earth.com	11/6/2005	L	

fields

FIGURE 10-4 A sample data file, stored on a hard disk, that contains five records, each with 11 fields.

MAINTAINING DATA

File maintenance refers to the procedures that keep data current. File maintenance procedures include adding records to, changing records in, and deleting records from a file.

Adding Records

Users add new records to a file when they obtain new data. If a new member wants to join the fitness center, a membership coordinator adds a new record to the fitness center's Member file. The process required to add this record to the file might include the following steps:

1. A membership coordinator displays a Member Maintenance form that gives him or her access to the Member file. The coordinator then clicks the New Record button, which begins the process of adding a record to the Member file.
2. The coordinator fills in the fields of the member record with data (except for the Member ID, which automatically is assigned by the program). In this example, the data entered is kept to a minimum.
3. The coordinator takes a picture of the member using a digital camera. The program stores this picture in the Member file and prints it on a membership ID card.
4. The membership coordinator verifies the data on the screen and then presses a key on the keyboard or clicks a button on the screen to add the new member record to the Member file. The system software that manages the disk determines where to write the record on the disk. In some cases, it writes the new record at the end of the file. In other cases, such as illustrated in Figure 10-5, it writes the new record for Shannon Murray between existing records in the file.

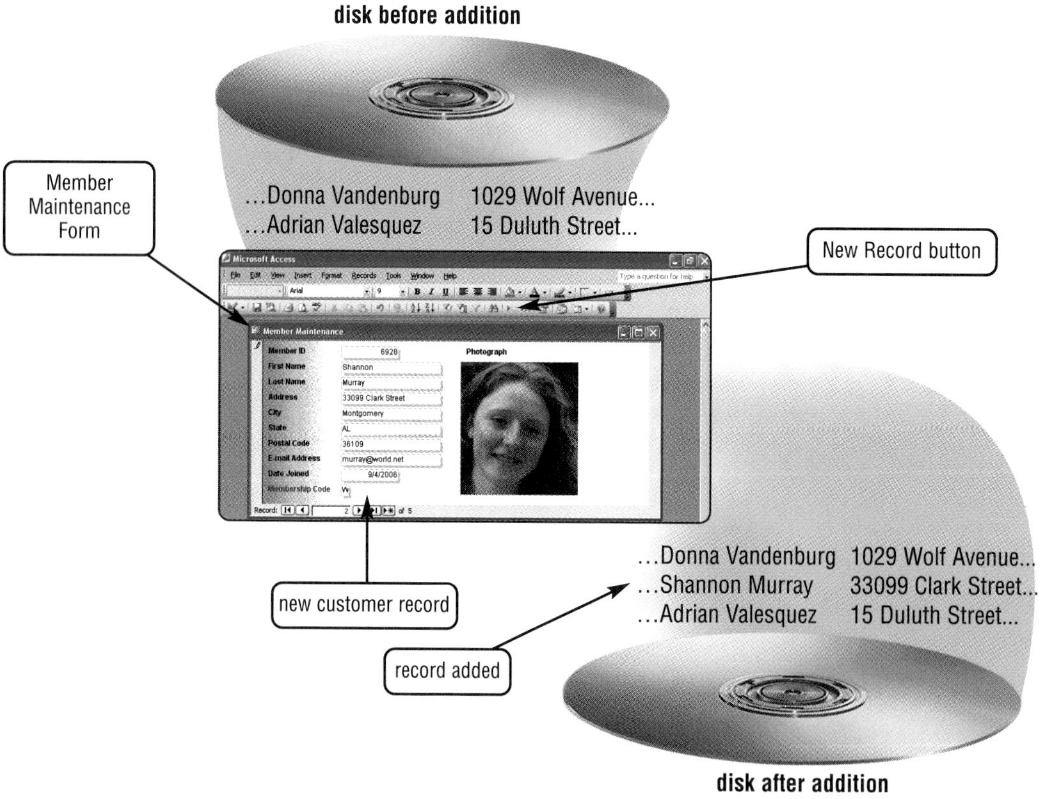

FIGURE 10-5 Using the Member Maintenance form, a membership coordinator adds a new member record for Shannon Murray. After the coordinator takes the photograph with the digital camera and confirms the data is correct, he or she adds the record to the database file.

Changing Records

Generally, users change a record in a file for two reasons: (1) to correct inaccurate data or (2) to update old data with new data.

As an example of the first type of change, assume that a membership coordinator enters a member's e-mail address as gm@earth.com, instead of mg@earth.com. The member notices the error when he reviews his membership agreement at home. The next time he visits the fitness center, he requests that the membership coordinator correct his e-mail address.

A more common reason to change a record is to update old data with new data. Suppose, for example, that Shannon Murray moves from 33099 Clark Street to 15 Southgate Road. The process to change the address and update Shannon Murray's record might include the following steps:

1. The membership coordinator displays the Member Maintenance form.
2. Assuming Shannon Murray is present, the coordinator inserts Shannon's membership ID card in a card reader to display her member record on the screen. If Shannon did not have her ID card or was not present, the coordinator could enter Shannon's Member ID — if Shannon knew it. Otherwise, the coordinator could enter Murray in the Last Name field, which would retrieve all members with that same last name. The coordinator then would scroll through all of the retrieved records to determine which one is Shannon's.
3. The program displays data about Shannon Murray so that the coordinator can confirm the correct member record is displayed.
4. The coordinator enters the new street address, 15 Southgate Road.
5. The membership coordinator verifies the data on the screen and then clicks the Save button to change the record in the Member file. The program changes the record on the disk (Figure 10-6).

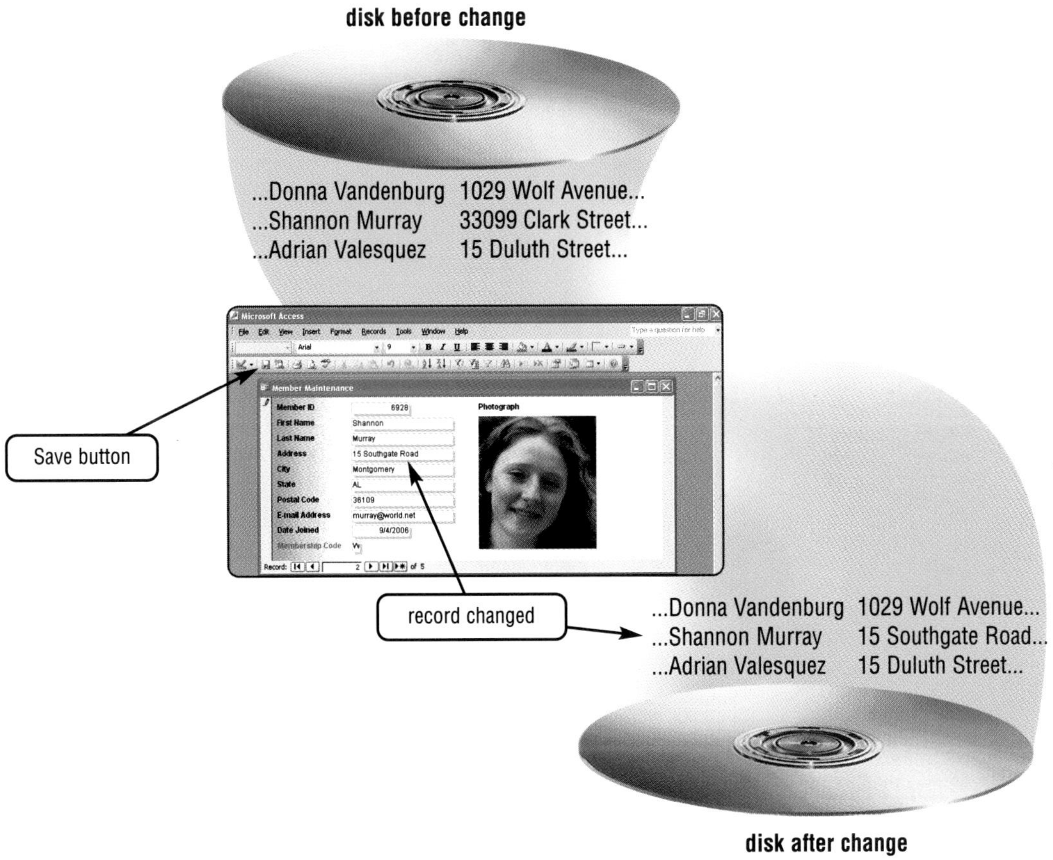

FIGURE 10-6 The membership coordinator inserts the membership ID card in a card reader to display the member's record. After confirming that the correct member record is displayed, the coordinator changes the member's address.

Deleting Records

When a record no longer is needed, a user deletes it from a file. Assume a member named Marcus Green is moving out of state. The process required to delete a record from a file includes the following steps:

1. The membership coordinator displays the Member Maintenance form.
2. The coordinator displays Marcus Green's member record on the screen.
3. The coordinator confirms the correct member record is displayed. Then, the coordinator clicks the Delete Record button to delete the record from the Member file and then clicks the Save button to save the modified file.

Programs use a variety of techniques to manage deleted records. Sometimes, the program removes the record from the file immediately. Other times, the record is flagged, or marked, so the program will not process it again. In this case, the program places an asterisk (*) or some other character at the beginning of the record (Figure 10-7).

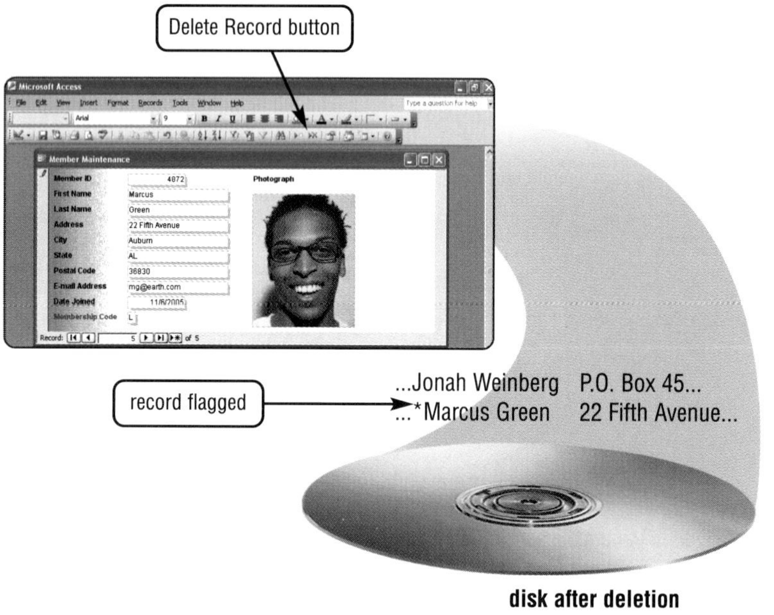

FIGURE 10-7 The membership coordinator displays the member's record on the screen. After the coordinator verifies that the correct member record is displayed, he or she deletes the record. The program flags the member record on disk by placing an asterisk in the first position of the record.

Programs that maintain inactive data for an extended period commonly flag records. For example, a fitness center might flag canceled memberships. When a program flags a deleted record, the record remains physically on the disk. The record, however, is deleted logically because the program will not process it. Programs will ignore flagged records unless an instruction is issued to process them.

From time to time, users should run a utility program that removes flagged records and reorganizes current records. For example, the fitness center may remove from disk any accounts that have been canceled for more than one year. Deleting unneeded records reduces the size of files and frees up storage space.

Validating Data

Validation is the process of comparing data with a set of rules or values to find out if the data is correct. Many programs perform a *validity check* that analyzes entered data to help ensure that it is correct. For instance, when a membership coordinator adds or changes data in a member record, the DBMS tests the entered data.

With a monthly fee, you would expect to see numbers before and after a decimal point. For example, a valid monthly fee is 25.50. An entry of XR.WP clearly is not correct. If the entered data fails a validity check, the computer should display an error message that instructs the user to enter the data again. Validity checks, also called *validation rules*, reduce data entry errors. Validating data enhances its integrity before the program writes the data on disk. Validation reduces the possibility of GIGO (garbage in, garbage out).

Various types of validity checks include alphabetic checks, numeric checks, range checks, consistency checks, and completeness checks. Check digits also validate data accuracy. The following paragraphs describe the purpose of these validity checks. The table in Figure 10-8 illustrates several of these validity checks and shows valid data that passes the check and invalid data that fails the check.

SAMPLE VALID AND INVALID DATA

Validity Check	Field Being Checked	Valid Data	Invalid Data
Alphabetic Check	First Name	Adrian	Ad33n
Numeric Check	Postal Code	36109	3rto9
Range Check	Monthly Fee	$39.50	$95.25
Consistency Check	Date Joined Training Date	10/20/2005 10/27/2005	10/20/2005 10/13/2005
Completeness Check	Last Name	Valesquez	

FIGURE 10-8 In this table of sample valid and invalid data, the first column lists commonly used validity checks. The second column lists the name of the field that contains data being checked. The third column shows valid data that passes the validity checks. The fourth column shows invalid data that fails the validity checks.

ALPHABETIC/NUMERIC CHECK An *alphabetic check* ensures that users enter only alphabetic data into a field. A *numeric check* ensures that users enter only numeric data into a field. For example, data in a First Name field should contain only characters from the alphabet. Data in a postal code field should contain numbers (with the exception of the special characters such as a hyphen).

RANGE CHECK A *range check* determines whether a number is within a specified range. Assume the lowest monthly fee at a fitness center is $20.25 and the highest is $55.50. A range check on the Monthly Fee field ensures it is a value between $20.25 and $55.50.

CONSISTENCY CHECK A *consistency check* tests the data in two or more associated fields to ensure that the relationship is logical. For example, the value in a Training Date field cannot occur earlier in time than the value in the Date Joined field.

COMPLETENESS CHECK A *completeness check* verifies that a required field contains data. For example, in many programs, you cannot leave the Last Name field blank. The completeness check ensures that data exists in the Last Name field.

CHECK DIGIT A *check digit* is a number(s) or character(s) that is appended to or inserted into a primary key value. A check digit often confirms the accuracy of a primary key value. Bank account, credit card, and other identification numbers often include one or more check digits.

A program determines the check digit by applying a formula to the numbers in the primary key value. An oversimplified illustration of a check digit formula is to add the numbers in the primary key. For example, if the primary key is 1367, this formula would add these numbers (1 + 3 + 6 + 7) for a sum of 17. Next, the formula would add the numbers in the result (1 + 7) to generate a check digit of 8. The primary key then is 13678. This example began with the original primary key value, 1367, then the check digit, 8, was appended.

When a data entry clerk enters the primary key of 13678, for example, to look up an existing member's record, the program determines whether the check digit is valid. The program applies the check digit formula to the first four digits of the primary key. If the calculated check digit matches the entered check digit (8, in this example), the program assumes the entered primary key is valid. If the clerk enters an incorrect primary key, such as 13778, the check digit entered (8) will not match the computed check digit (9). In this case, the program displays an error message that instructs the user to enter the primary key value again.

WEB LINK 10-1

Check Digits

Visit the Discovering Computers 2005 WEB LINK page (**scsite .com/dc2005/weblink**). Click Check Digits below Chapter 10.

QUIZ YOURSELF 10-1

To check your knowledge of qualities of valuable information, the hierarchy of data, and file maintenance techniques, visit the Discovering Computers 2005 Quiz Yourself Web page (**scsite.com/dc2005/ quiz**). Click Objectives 1 – 4 below Chapter 10.

FILE PROCESSING VERSUS DATABASES

Almost all application programs use either the file processing approach or the database approach to store and manage data. The following pages discuss these two approaches.

File Processing Systems

In the past, many organizations used file processing systems to store and manage data. In a typical **file processing system**, each department or area within an organization has its own set of files. These files often are designed specifically for their particular applications. The records in one file may not relate to the records in any other file.

Companies have used file processing systems for many years. A lot of these systems, however, have two major weaknesses: they have redundant data and they isolate data.

- Data Redundancy — Each department or area in a company has its own files in a file processing system. Thus, the same fields are stored in multiple files. If a file processing system is used at the fitness center, for example, the files at the membership counter and the files in the training office store the same members' names and addresses.

  Duplicating data in this manner wastes resources such as storage space and people's time. Storing the same data in more than one file requires a larger storage capacity. When new members are added or member data is changed, file maintenance tasks consume additional time because people must update multiple files that contain the same data.

  Data redundancy also can increase the chance of errors. If a member changes his or her address, for example, the fitness center must update the address wherever it appears. In this example, the Address field is in the files at the membership counter and also in the training office files. The Address field also may be stored in other areas of the fitness center. If the Address field is not changed in all the files where it is stored, then discrepancies among the files exist.
- Isolated Data — Often it is difficult to access data stored in separate files in different departments. Assume that the member e-mail addresses exist only in the membership coordinator's files, and member training schedules are only in the training office files. To send an e-mail message informing a member that a training session has been rescheduled, data is needed from both the membership coordinator's files and the training office files. Sharing data from multiple, separate files to generate such a list in a file processing system often is a complicated procedure and usually requires the experience of a computer programmer.

The Database Approach

When a company uses the **database approach**, many programs and users share the data in the database. A fitness center's database most likely contains data about members, membership plans, training sessions, and personal trainers. As shown in Figure 10-9, various areas within the fitness center share and interact with the data in this database.

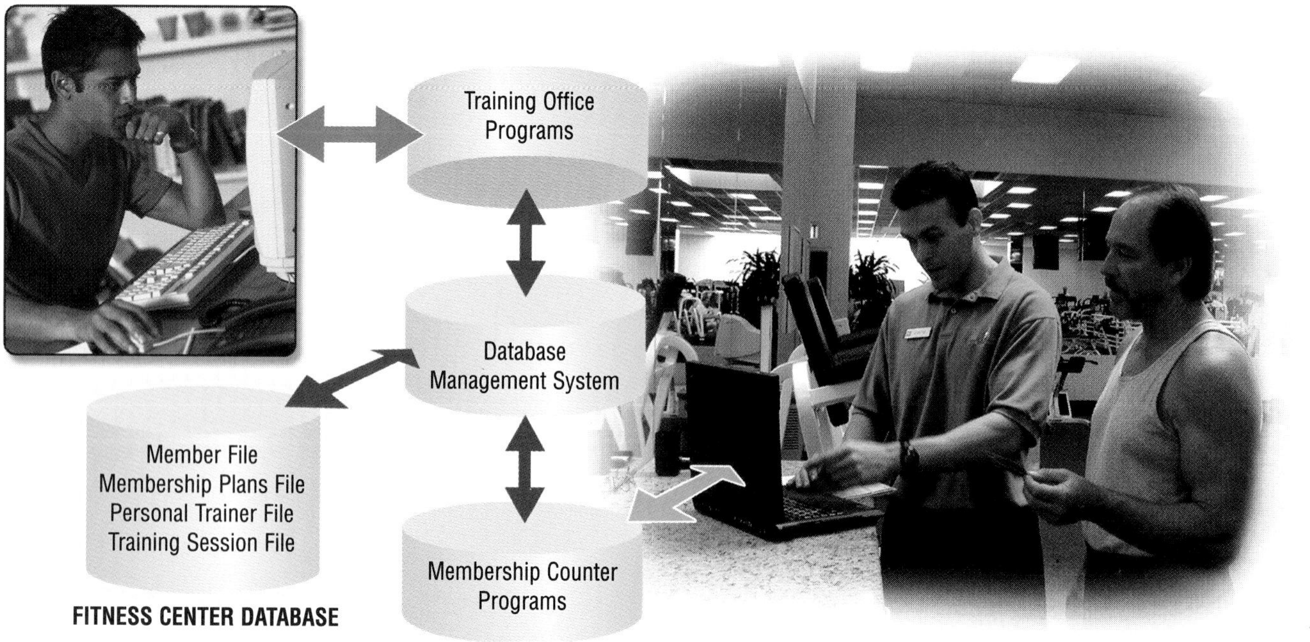

FIGURE 10-9 In a fitness center that uses a database, the training office computer and membership counter computer access data in a single database through the DBMS.

The database does secure its data, however, so only authorized users can access certain data items. Read Issue 10-2 for a related discussion.

Users can access the data in the database via application software called a DBMS. While a user is working with the database, the DBMS resides in the memory of the computer. Instead of working directly with the DBMS, some users interact with a front end. A *front end* is a program that generally has a more user-friendly interface than the DBMS. For example, a membership coordinator interacts with the Membership program. This front-end program interacts with the DBMS, which in turn, interacts with the database. Many programs today have a Web page as their front end. An application that supports a front-end program sometimes is called the *back end*. In this case, the DBMS is the back end.

The database approach addresses many of the weaknesses associated with file processing systems. The following paragraphs present some strengths of the database approach.

- Reduced Data Redundancy — Most data items are stored in only one file, which greatly reduces duplicate data. For example, a fitness center database would record a member's name and address only once. When member data is entered or changed, one employee makes the change once. Figure 10-10 demonstrates the differences between how a database application and a file processing application might store data.
- Improved Data Integrity — When users modify data in the database, they make changes to one file instead of multiple files. Thus, the database approach increases the data's integrity by reducing the possibility of introducing inconsistencies.
- Shared Data — The data in a database environment belongs to and is shared, usually over a network, by the entire organization. This data is independent, or separate from, the programs that access the data. Companies that use databases typically have security settings to define who can access, add, change, and delete the data in a database.
- Easier Access — The database approach allows nontechnical users to access and maintain data, providing they have necessary privileges. Many computer users also can develop smaller databases themselves, without professional assistance.
- Reduced Development Time — It often is easier and faster to develop programs that use the database approach. Many DBMSs include several tools to assist in developing programs, which further reduces the development time. The next section discusses these tools and other DBMS features.

Databases have many advantages as well as some disadvantages. A database can be more complex than a file processing system. People with special training usually develop larger databases and their associated applications. Databases also require more memory, storage, and processing power than file processing systems.

ISSUE 10-2

Should Criminal Databases Be Shared?

California was the first state to employ a controversial database. Based on Megan's Law — the statute named for a seven-year-old girl who was violated and killed by a paroled felon — the database listed the names and addresses of people convicted of crimes against children. Today, many states employ similar databases. In some communities, when a paroled offender moves in, the police inform the local school system, which in turn sends parents a notification that includes a history, address, and picture of the wrongdoer. Touted as a valuable tool in crime prevention, some feel that publishing this information makes it impossible for an offender to lead a normal life and can result in vigilantism — one paroled lawbreaker's car was firebombed only days after his name was released. Should a database of people paroled or released for crimes against children be made public? Why or why not? Who should have access to the database? Why? Should such a database also include accused, but not convicted, offenders? Why or why not?

For more information about sharing criminal databases, visit the Discovering Computers 2005 Issues Web page (**scsite.com/dc2005/issues**). Click Issue #2 below Chapter 10.

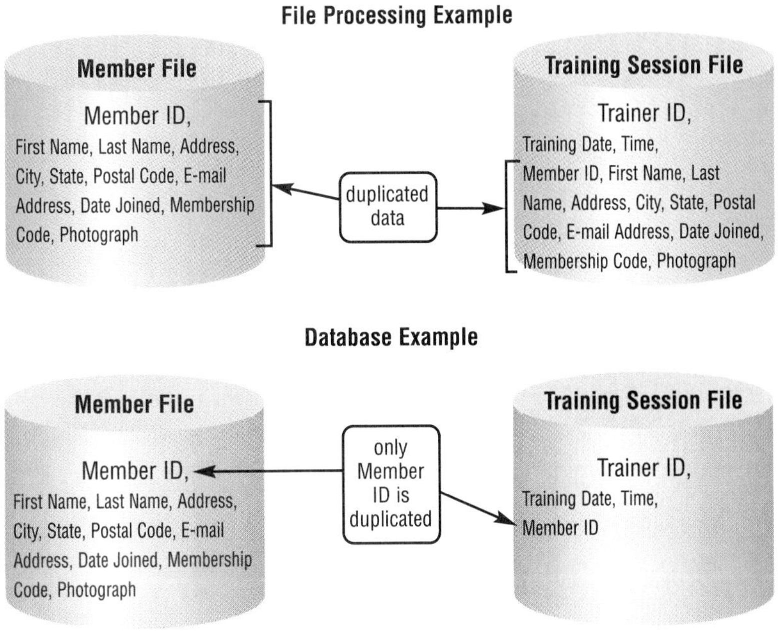

FIGURE 10-10 In the file processing environment, both files contain all member data fields. In a database environment, only the Member file contains these fields. Other files, however, such as the Training Session file, contain the Member ID, which links to the Member file when member data is needed.

Data in a database is more vulnerable than data in file processing systems. A database stores most data in a single file. Many users and programs share and depend on this data. If the database is not operating properly or is damaged or destroyed, users may not be able to perform their jobs. In some cases, certain programs may stop working. To protect their valuable database resource, individuals and companies should establish and follow security procedures. Chapter 11 discusses a variety of security methods.

Despite these limitations, many business and home users work with databases because of their tremendous advantages. Although the hardware and software costs to set up a database may seem expensive, long-term benefits exceed the initial costs.

FAQ 10-4

Can a database eliminate redundant data completely?

No, a database reduces redundant data — it does not eliminate it. Files in a database link together based on values in key fields. For example, the Member ID field will exist in any file that requires access to member data. Thus, the Member ID is duplicated (exists in many files) in the database.

For more information about database relationships, visit the Discovering Computers 2005 FAQ Web page (**scsite.com/dc2005/faq**). Click Database Relationships below Chapter 10.

WEB LINK 10-2

Database Management System

Visit the Discovering Computers 2005 WEB LINK page (**scsite.com/dc2005/weblink**). Click Database Management System below Chapter 10.

WEB LINK 10-3

Data Dictionary

Visit the Discovering Computers 2005 WEB LINK page (**scsite.com/dc2005/weblink**). Click Data Dictionary below Chapter 10.

DATABASE MANAGEMENT SYSTEMS

As previously discussed, a database management system (DBMS), or database program, is software that allows you to create, access, and manage a database. DBMSs are available for many sizes and types of computers (Figure 10-11). Whether designed for a small or large computer, most DBMSs perform common functions. The following pages discuss functions common to most DBMSs.

Data Dictionary

A **data dictionary**, sometimes called a *repository*, contains data about each file in the database and each field within those files. For each file, it stores details such as the file name, description, the file's relationship to other files, and the number of records in the file. For each field, it stores details such as the field name, description, field type, field size, default value, validation rules, and the field's relationship to other fields. Figure 10-12 shows how a data dictionary might list data for a Member file.

Because the data dictionary contains details about data, some call it *metadata* (meta means more comprehensive). Sometimes, a data dictionary also contains data about programs and users. It might keep track of who accessed data and when they accessed it. The data dictionary is a crucial backbone to a DBMS. Thus, only skilled professionals should update the contents of a data dictionary.

A DBMS uses the data dictionary to perform validation checks. When users enter data, the data dictionary verifies that the entered data matches the field's data type. For example, the data dictionary allows only numbers to be entered in a Postal Code field. The data dictionary also can limit the type of data that can be input, often allowing a user to select from a list. For example, the data dictionary ensures that the State field contains a valid two-letter state code, such as AL, by presenting a list of valid state codes to the user. By validating data, the data dictionary helps to maintain the integrity of the data.

A data dictionary allows users to specify a default value for a field. A *default value* is a value that the DBMS initially displays in a field. If most members who join the fitness center live in Alabama, then the DBMS initially could display AL in the State field. The user does not have to type in a default value. Displaying a default value reduces the possibility of errors. A user typically can override a default value if it does not apply for a certain record. For example, you can change the value from AL to TN if the member lives in Tennessee.

POPULAR DATABASE MANAGEMENT SYSTEMS

Database	Manufacturer	Computer Type
Access	Microsoft Corporation	Personal computer, server, PDA
Adabas	Software AG	Midrange server, mainframe
D^3	Raining Data	Personal computer, midrange server
DB2	IBM Corporation	Personal computer, midrange server, mainframe
Essbase	Hyperion Solutions Corporation	Personal computer, server
FastObjects	FastObjects Inc.	Personal computer, midrange server
GemFire	GemStone Systems, Inc.	Midrange server
Informix	IBM Corporation	Personal computer, midrange server, mainframe
Ingres	Computer Associates International, Inc.	Personal computer, midrange server, mainframe
InterBase	Borland Software Corporation	Personal computer, server
JDataStore	Borland Software Corporation	Personal computer, server
KE Texpress	KE Software, Inc.	Personal computer, server
MySQL	MySQL AB	Personal computer, midrange server
ObjectStore	Progress Software Corporation	Personal computer, midrange server
Oracle	Oracle Corporation	Personal computer, midrange server, mainframe, PDA
SQL Server	Microsoft Corporation	Server
Sybase	Sybase Inc.	Personal computer, midrange server, PDA
Versant	Versant Corporation	Personal computer, midrange server
Visual FoxPro	Microsoft Corporation	Personal computer, server

FIGURE 10-11 Many database management systems run on multiple types of computers.

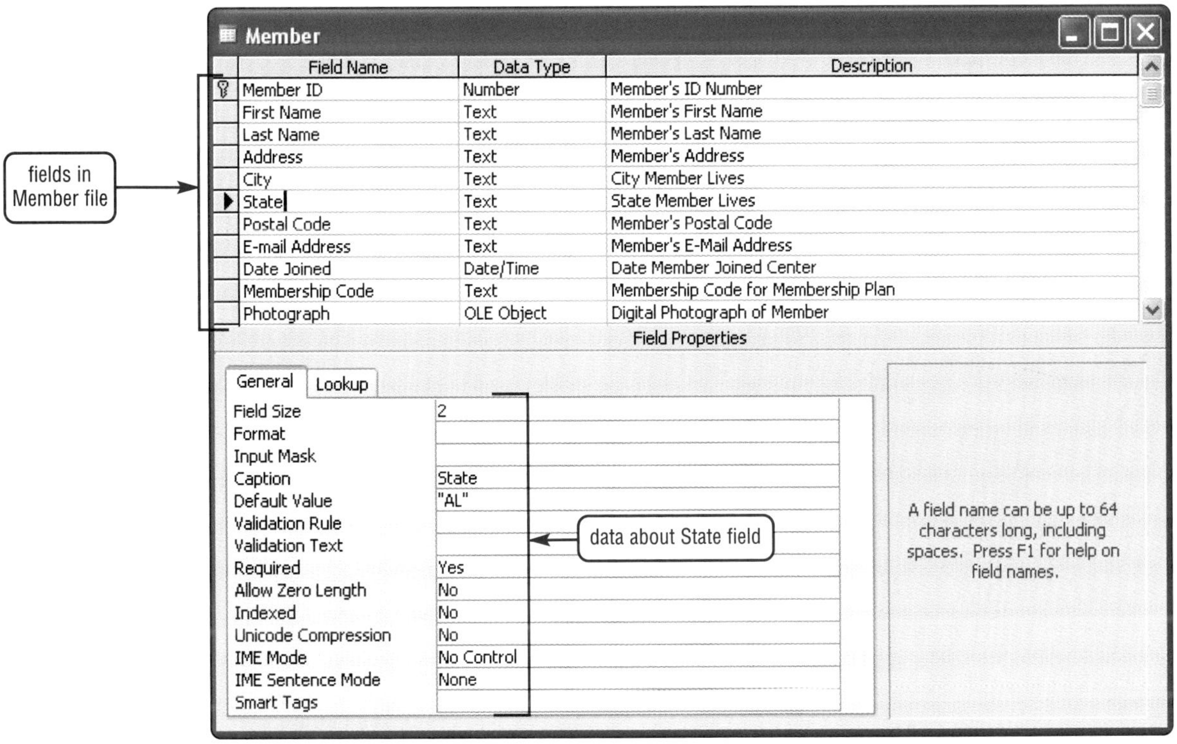

FIGURE 10-12 A sample data dictionary entry shows the fields in the Member file and the properties of the State field.

File Retrieval and Maintenance

A DBMS provides several tools that allow users and programs to retrieve and maintain data in the database. As discussed earlier in this chapter, file maintenance involves adding new records, changing data in existing records, and removing unwanted records from the database.

To retrieve or select data in a database, you query it. A **query** is a request for specific data from the database. Users can instruct the DBMS to display, print, or store the results of a query. The capability of querying a database is one of the more powerful database features.

To meet the needs of a wide variety of database users, from trained experts to nontechnical staff, a DBMS offers several methods to retrieve and maintain its data. The four more commonly used are query languages, query by example, forms, and report generators. The following paragraphs describe each of these methods.

QUERY LANGUAGE A **query language** consists of simple, English-like statements that allow users to specify the data to display, print, or store. Each query language has its own grammar and vocabulary. A person without a programming background usually can learn a query language in a short time.

Although a query language can be used to maintain (add, change, and delete) data, most users only retrieve (query) data with a query language. To simplify the query process, many DBMSs provide wizards to guide users through the steps of creating a query. Figure 10-13 shows how to use the Simple Query Wizard in Microsoft Office Access 2003 to display the First Name, Last Name, and E-mail Address fields from the Member file. For a list of all the fields in the Member file, see Figure 10-4 on pages 520 and 521. Read Looking Ahead 10-1 for a look at the next generation of query languages.

FIGURE 10-13 HOW TO USE THE SIMPLE QUERY WIZARD

Step 1:
Select the fields from the Available Fields list that you want to be displayed in the resulting query.

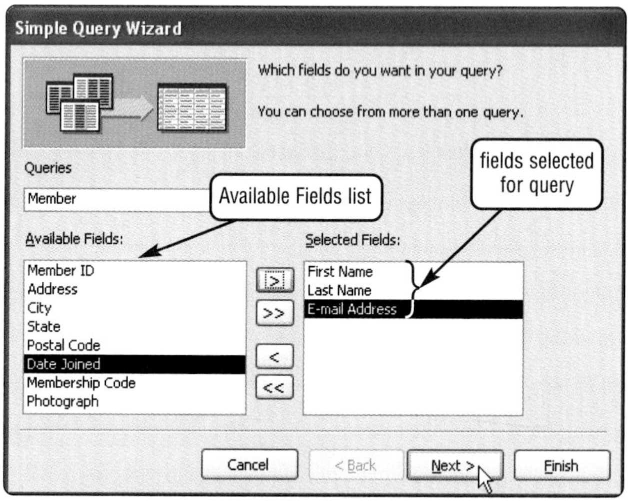

Step 2:
Assign a name to the query, so you can open it later.

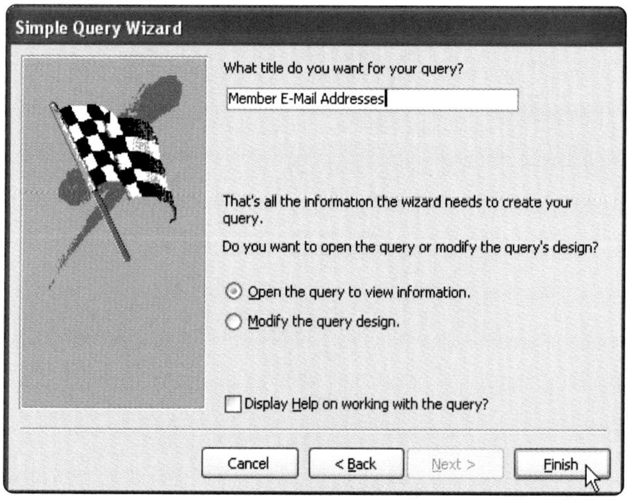

Step 3:
View the query results on the screen.

First Name	Last Name	E-mail Address
Donna	Vandenburg	
Shannon	Murray	murray@world.net
Adrian	Valesquez	valesquez@prattville.net
Jonah	Weinberg	
Marcus	Green	mg@earth.com

LOOKING AHEAD 10-1

Having a Voice in Future Databases

Successfully retrieving data from a database often depends upon the accuracy of the query. Whether query language, query by example, forms, or report generators are used, each database management system has a unique method of accessing the data.

DBMS developers are working to simplify the query process by using voice commands transmitted via the telephone. This technology will be practical for individuals who cannot use or are not located near a keyboard, such as employees who are visually impaired or are working in the field and communicating using a wireless device. They will be able to make verbal queries to access such written material as sports scores and stock prices on Web sites in speech form and can receive verbal notification of events and appointment times.

This verbal technology uses *VoiceXML* (*eXtensible Markup Language*). Software developers are finding XML technology useful in creating Internet databases, such as video catalogs, photographs, and Web pages. Traditional databases were developed to handle data that fits neatly into columns and rows, so they do not function well when records contain audio, video, and complex data.

For a look at the next generation of querying databases, visit the Discovering Computers 2005 Looking Ahead Web page (**scsite.com/dc2005/looking**). Click Looking Ahead #1 below Chapter 10.

QUERY BY EXAMPLE Instead of learning the grammar and vocabulary associated with a query language, you can use a **query by example** (**QBE**) to request data from the database. Most DBMSs include a QBE feature. QBEs have a graphical user interface that assists users with retrieving data. Figure 10-14 shows a sample QBE screen for a query that searches for and lists members on the Prime Time plan; that is, their Membership Code field value is equal to "P". Later in the chapter, specific query languages are presented in more depth.

FORM A **form**, sometimes called a *data entry form*, is a window on the screen that provides areas for entering or changing data in a database. You use forms (Figure 10-5 on page 522) to retrieve and maintain the data in a database.

To reduce data entry errors, well-designed forms should validate data as it is entered. When designing a form using a DBMS, you can make the form attractive and easy to use by incorporating color, shading, lines, boxes, and graphics; varying the fonts and font styles; and using other formatting features.

Figure 10-14a (query by example screen)

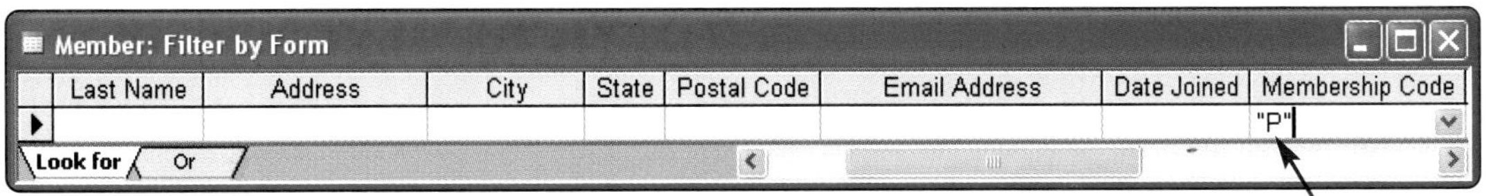

Figure 10-14b (query results)

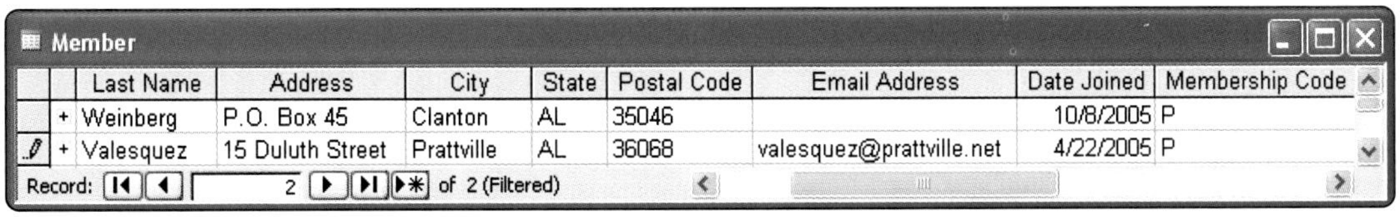

Last Name	Address	City	State	Postal Code	Email Address	Date Joined	Membership Code
Weinberg	P.O. Box 45	Clanton	AL	35046		10/8/2005	P
Valesquez	15 Duluth Street	Prattville	AL	36068	valesquez@prattville.net	4/22/2005	P

FIGURE 10-14 Access has many QBE capabilities. One QBE technique is Filter by Form, which uses a form to show available fields. The database program retrieves records that match criteria you enter in the form fields. This example searches for members whose Membership Code is equal to P.

A form that sends entered data across a network or the Internet is called an *e-form*, short for *electronic form* (Figure 10-15). E-forms generally use a means to secure the data while it is transported across the network. Often, the data in the e-form automatically enters into, or updates existing data in, a database on the network or the Internet. Thus, many DBMSs include the capability of creating e-forms.

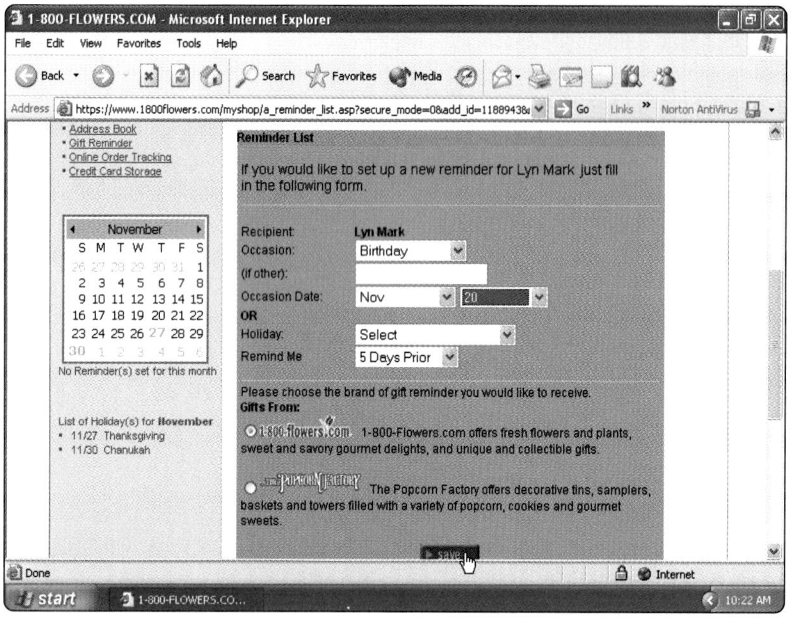

FIGURE 10-15 This e-form sends your personal reminder information to an online database at 1-800-FLOWERS.COM.

REPORT GENERATOR A **report generator**, also called a *report writer*, allows users to design a report on the screen, retrieve data into the report design, and then display or print the report (Figure 10-16). Unlike a form, you use a report generator only to retrieve data. Report generators usually allow you to format page numbers and dates; titles and column headings; subtotals and totals; and fonts, font sizes, color, and shading.

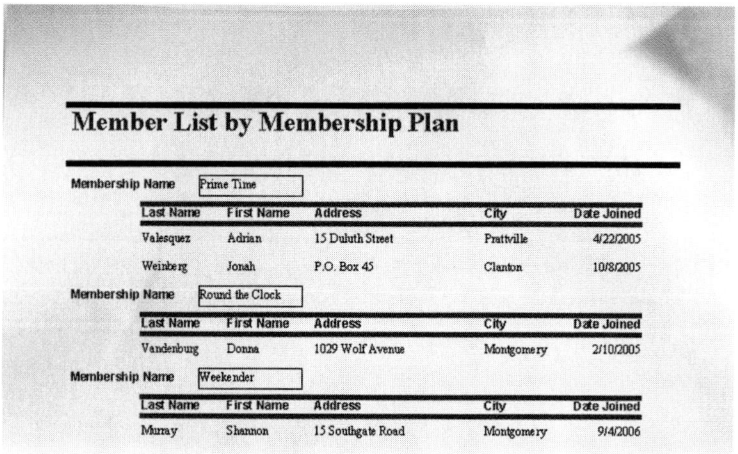
Member List by Membership Plan

Membership Name: Prime Time

Last Name	First Name	Address	City	Date Joined
Valesquez	Adrian	15 Duluth Street	Prattville	4/22/2005
Weinberg	Jonah	P.O. Box 45	Clanton	10/8/2005

Membership Name: Round the Clock

Last Name	First Name	Address	City	Date Joined
Vandenburg	Donna	1029 Wolf Avenue	Montgomery	2/10/2005

Membership Name: Weekender

Last Name	First Name	Address	City	Date Joined
Murray	Shannon	15 Southgate Road	Montgomery	9/4/2006

FIGURE 10-16 This report, created in Access, displays member information by the type of membership in which members are enrolled.

Data Security

Sometimes, users accidentally delete the data from a database; others misuse the data intentionally (read Issue 10-3 for a related discussion). Thus, a DBMS provides means to ensure that only authorized users access data at permitted times. In addition, most DBMSs allow different levels of access privileges to be identified for each field in the database. These *access privileges* define the actions that a specific user or group of users can perform.

ISSUE 10-3

Is Unauthorized Access a Crime?

An associate dean in Princeton University's admissions office allegedly accessed the supposedly secure Web site on which Yale University posted its acceptances. The Web site allowed the Princeton dean to check the acceptance status of a number of students, some of whom were from well-known families. The dean did not use the information he learned — Princeton already had made its acceptances — and the students checked on did not appear upset ("This really doesn't matter to me," one said). A member of an association for admissions officers said the incident seemed little more than simple curiosity. Yale administrators asked the FBI to determine, however, if a crime had been committed. Is it a crime to access confidential information without authorization? Why? Does it depend on the information? Does it depend on whether the information is altered? Does it depend on how the information is used? Would it be a crime for a student to access a school database of instructors' salaries? Why or why not?

For more information about stealing information, visit the Discovering Computers 2005 Issues Web page (**scsite.com/dc2005/issues**). Click Issue #3 below Chapter 10.

Access privileges for data involve establishing who can enter new data, change existing data, delete unwanted data, and view data. In the member file, a personal trainer might have *read-only privileges* for member e-mail addresses. That is, the trainer could view the e-mail address, but cannot change it. A manager, by contrast, would have *full-update privileges* to member data, meaning he or she can view and change the data. Finally, a member would have no access privileges to the data. Members neither can view nor change any data in the database. Read Issue 10-4 for a related discussion. Chapter 11 discusses access privileges and other security techniques in more depth.

ISSUE 10-4

What Access Privileges Should Be Used?

The proverb, "Do not put all your eggs in one basket," cautions against the risk of placing all of your resources in a single venture. But in *Pudd'nhead Wilson*, Mark Twain offers different advice: "...the wise man saith, 'Put all your eggs in the one basket and — WATCH THAT BASKET'". Because a database is a comprehensive basket of data, watching that basket is an important security consideration. Most database management systems specify various access privileges. When a database is created, access policies are determined. Individuals may be granted no access privileges, read-only privileges (data can be read but not changed), limited-access privileges (only certain data can be read and/or changed), or full-update privileges (all data can be read and changed). Consider a student file. In addition to a name, address, and grades, this file may contain data about ethnicity, gender, finances, family, health, activities, discipline, and so on. Using this file as an example, what access privileges should be granted to the student, other students, faculty, administrators, financial aid officers, potential employers, and other outside groups? Explain your answers.

For more information about access privileges, visit the Discovering Computers 2005 Issues Web page (**scsite.com/dc2005/issues**). Click Issue #4 below Chapter 10.

Backup and Recovery

Occasionally a database is damaged or destroyed because of hardware failure, a problem with the software, human error, or a catastrophe such as fire or flood. A DBMS provides a variety of techniques to restore the database to a usable form in case it is damaged or destroyed.

- A **backup**, or copy, of the entire database should be made on a regular basis. Some DBMSs have their own built-in backup utilities. Others require users to purchase a separate backup utility, or use one included with the operating system.
- More complex DBMSs maintain a **log**, which is a listing of activities that change the contents of the database. If a member coordinator modifies a member's address, for example, the change appears in the log. The DBMS places the following in the log: (1) a copy of the member record prior to the change, called the *before image* (Figure 10-17a); (2) the actual change of address data (Figure 10-17b); and (3) a copy of the member record after the change, called the *after image* (Figure 10-17c). The log also might store who made the change, when it was made, and from which computer it was made.

Figure 10-17a (before image)

Figure 10-17b (change)

Figure 10-17c (after image)

FIGURE 10-17 When the contents of a record are changed, the DBMS places three items in the log: the before image of the record; the actual change; and the after image of the record.

- A DBMS that creates a log usually provides a recovery utility. A **recovery utility** uses the logs and/or backups to restore a database when it becomes damaged or destroyed. The recovery utility restores the database using rollback and rollforward techniques. In a *rollforward*, also called *forward recovery*, the DBMS uses the log to reenter changes made to the database since the last save or backup. In a *rollback*, also called *backward recovery*, the DBMS uses the log to undo any changes made to the database during a certain period, such as an hour. The rollback restores the database to its condition prior to the failure. Then, users reenter any transactions entered after the failure.

Depending on the type of failure, the DBMS determines which type of recovery technique to use. For example, if the database is destroyed by a lightning strike, the DBMS would rollforward from the last backup. Assume, however, that a power failure happens at 3:15 p.m. and shuts down all computers, but does not destroy any data. Because some users may have been in the middle of entering transactions, the DBMS needs to undo any partial transactions. Thus, it would rollback the database to 3:00 p.m. and send a message to all users that they need to re-enter any transactions made after that time.

WEB LINK 10-4

Backup and Recovery

Visit the Discovering Computers 2005 WEB LINK page (**scsite.com/dc2005/weblink**). Click Backup and Recovery below Chapter 10.

QUIZ YOURSELF 10-2

To check your knowledge of file processing systems versus databases and functions of a DBMS, visit the Discovering Computers 2005 Quiz Yourself Web page (**scsite.com/dc2005/quiz**). Click Objectives 5 – 6 below Chapter 10.

RELATIONAL, OBJECT-ORIENTED, AND MULTIDIMENSIONAL DATABASES

Every database and DBMS is based on a specific data model. A **data model** consists of rules and standards that define how the database organizes data. A data model defines how users view the organization of the data. It does not define how the operating system actually arranges the data on the disk.

Three popular data models in use today are relational, object-oriented, and multidimensional. A database typically is based on one data model. For example, when using a relational database, users work with the relational data model. Some databases are called *object-relational databases* because they combine features of the relational and object-oriented data models.

The table in Figure 10-18 lists some popular DBMSs and the data model on which they are based. The following sections discuss the features of relational, object-oriented, and multidimensional databases.

DATA MODELS FOR POPULAR DBMSs

Data Model	Popular DBMSs
Relational	Access Adabas Informix Ingres InterBase MySQL SQL Server Sybase Visual FoxPro
Object-oriented	FastFire GemStone KE Texpress ObjectStore Versant
Object-relational	DB2 JDataStore Oracle Polyhedra PostgreSQL
Multidimensional	D^3 Essbase Oracle Express

FIGURE 10-18 Four popular data models are relational, object-oriented, object-relational, and multidimensional. Most DBMSs are based on one of these models.

Relational Databases

Today, a relational database is a widely used type of database. A **relational database** is a database that stores data in tables that consist of rows and columns. Each row has a primary key and each column has a unique name.

As discussed earlier in this chapter, a file processing environment uses the terms file, record, and field to represent data. A relational database uses terms different from a file processing system. A developer of a relational database refers to a file as a *relation*, a record as a *tuple*, and a field as an *attribute*.

A user of a relational database, by contrast, refers to a file as a **table**, a record as a **row**, and a field as a **column**. Figure 10-19 summarizes this varied terminology.

DATA TERMINOLOGY

File Processing Environment	Relational Database Developer	Relational Database User
File	Relation	Table
Record	Tuple	Row
Field	Attribute	Column

FIGURE 10-19 In this data terminology table, the first column identifies the terms used in a file processing environment. The second column presents the terms used by developers of a relational database. The third column indicates terms to which the users of a relational database refer.

In addition to storing data, a relational database also stores data relationships. A **relationship** is a connection within the data. In a relational database, you can set up a relationship between tables at any time. The tables must have a common column (field). For example, you would relate the Member table and the Membership Plans table using the Membership Code column. Figure 10-20 illustrates these relational database concepts. In a relational database, the only data redundancy (duplication) exists in the common columns (fields). The database uses these common columns for relationships.

Applications best suited for relational databases are those whose data can be organized into a two-dimensional table. Many businesses use relational databases for payroll, accounts receivable, accounts payable, general ledger, inventory, order entry, invoicing, and other business-related functions.

A developer of relational databases uses normalization to organize the data. *Normalization* is a process designed to ensure the data within the relations (tables) contains the least amount of duplication. For a technical discussion about normalization, read the High-Tech Talk article on page 543.

WEB LINK 10-5

Relational Databases

Visit the Discovering Computers 2005 WEB LINK page (**scsite.com/dc2005/weblink**). Click Relational Databases below Chapter 10.

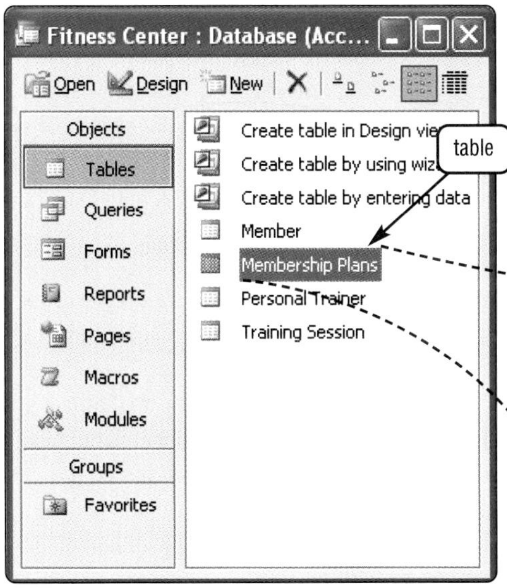

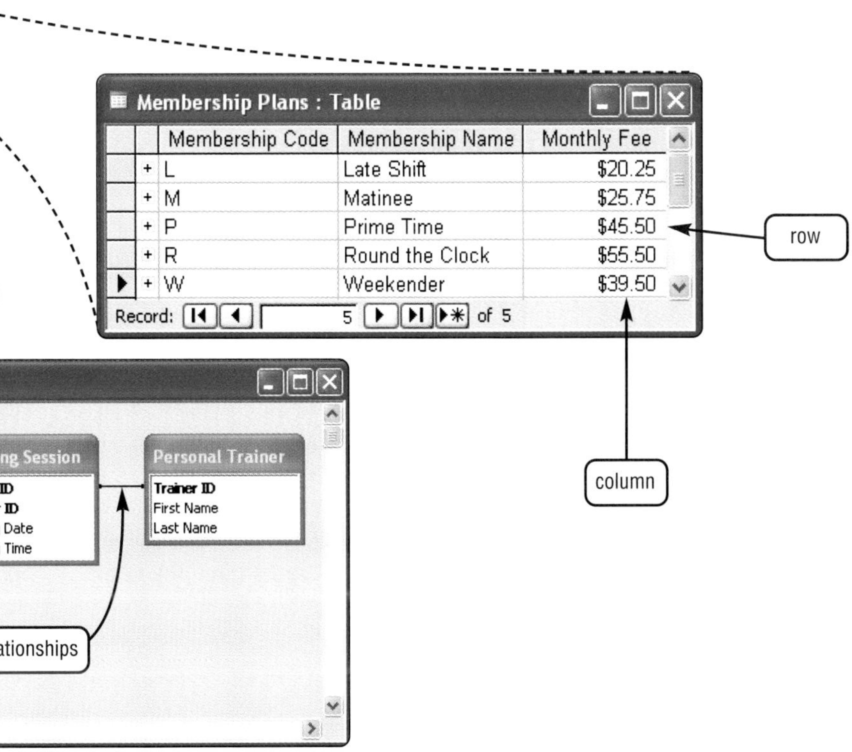

FIGURE 10-20 The Member table is linked to the Membership Plans table through the Membership Code field. The Member table is linked to the Training Session table through the Member ID field. The Training Session table is linked to the Personal Trainer table through the Trainer ID field.

SQL **Structured Query Language** (**SQL**) is a query language that allows users to manage, update, and retrieve data. SQL has special keywords and rules that users include in SQL statements. For example, the SQL statement in Figure 10-21a shows how to write the join operation that creates the results shown in Figure 10-21b. The statement displays the First Name, Last Name, and Monthly Fee fields in alphabetical order by last name for all records in the Member table.

Most relational database products for midrange servers and mainframes include SQL. Many personal computer databases also include SQL.

WEB LINK 10-6

SQL

Visit the Discovering Computers 2005 WEB LINK page (**scsite .com/dc2005/weblink**). Click SQL below Chapter 10.

Figure 10-21a (SQL statement)

```
SELECT FIRST NAME, LAST NAME, MONTHLY FEE
FROM MEMBER, MEMBERSHIP PLANS
WHERE MEMBER.MEMBER ID = MEMBERSHIP PLANS.MEMBER ID
ORDER BY LAST NAME
```

Figure 10-21b (SQL statement results)

First Name	Last Name	Monthly Fee
Marcus	Green	20.25
Shannon	Murray	39.50
Adrian	Valesquez	45.50
Donna	Vandenburg	55.50
Jonah	Weinberg	45.50

FIGURE 10-21 A sample SQL statement and its results.

Object-Oriented Databases

An **object-oriented database** (**OODB**) stores data in objects. An **object** is an item that contains data, as well as the actions that read or process the data. A Member object, for example, might contain data about a member such as Member ID, First Name, Last Name, Address, and so on. It also could contain instructions about how to print the member record or the formula required to calculate a member's balance due. A record in a relational database, by contrast, would contain only data about a member.

WEB LINK 10-7

Object-Oriented Databases

Visit the Discovering Computers 2005 WEB LINK page (**scsite .com/dc2005/weblink**). Click Object-Oriented Databases below Chapter 10.

Object-oriented databases have several advantages compared with relational databases: they can store more types of data, access this data faster, and allow programmers to reuse objects. An object-oriented database stores unstructured data more efficiently than a relational database. Unstructured data includes photographs, video clips, audio clips, and documents. When users query an object-oriented database, the results often display more quickly than the same query of a relational database. If an object already exists, programmers can reuse it instead of recreating a new object — saving on program development time.

Examples of applications appropriate for an object-oriented database include the following:

- A *multimedia database* stores images, audio clips, and/or video clips. For example, a geographic information system (GIS) database stores maps. A voice mail system database stores audio messages. A television news station database stores audio and video clips.
- A *groupware database* stores documents such as schedules, calendars, manuals, memos, and reports. Users perform queries to search the document contents. For example, you can search people's schedules for available meeting times.
- A *computer-aided design* (*CAD*) *database* stores data about engineering, architectural, and scientific designs. Data in the database includes a list of components of the item being designed, the relationship among the components, and previous versions of the design drafts.
- A *hypertext database* contains text links to other types of documents. A *hypermedia database* contains text, graphics, video, and sound. The Web contains a variety of hypertext and hypermedia databases. You can search these databases for items such as documents, graphics, audio and video clips (Figure 10-22), and links to Web pages.
- A *Web database* links to an e-form on a Web page. The Web browser sends and receives data between the form and the database. A later section in this chapter discusses Web databases in more depth.

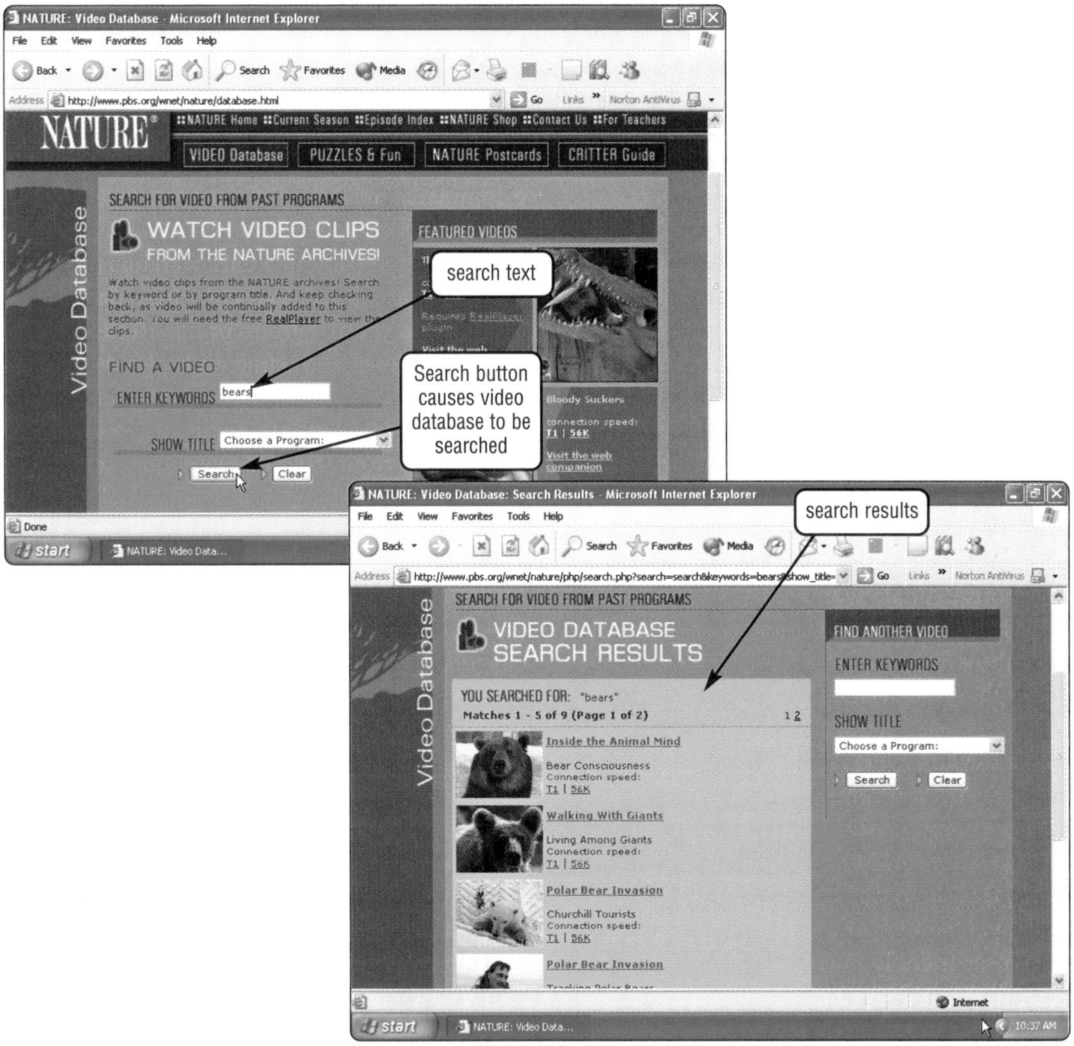

FIGURE 10-22 This hypermedia database stores video clips from various PBS shows about nature.

OBJECT QUERY LANGUAGE Object-oriented and object-relational databases often use a query language called *object query language* (*OQL*) to manipulate and retrieve data. OQL is similar to SQL. OQL and SQL use many of the same rules, grammar, and keywords. Because OQL is a relatively new query language, not all object databases support it.

Multidimensional Databases

A **multidimensional database** stores data in dimensions. Whereas a relational database is a two-dimensional table, a multidimensional database can store more than two dimensions of data. These multiple dimensions, sometimes known as a hypercube, allow users to access and analyze any view of the database data.

A Webmaster at a retailing business may want information about product sales and customer sales for each region spanning a given time. A manager at the same business may want information about product sales by department for each sales representative spanning a given time.

A multidimensional database can consolidate this type of data from multiple dimensions at very high rates of speed. The number of dimensions in a multidimensional database varies. A retailing business might have four dimensions: products, customers, regions, and time. A multidimensional database for a hospital procedure could have six dimensions: time, procedure type, patient, hospital, physician, and diagnosis. A multidimensional database for an insurance policy may include five dimensions: time, policy type, agent, customer, and coverage. Nearly every multidimensional database has a dimension of time. The content of other dimensions varies depending on the subject.

WEB LINK 10-8

Multidimensional Databases

Visit the Discovering Computers 2005 WEB LINK page (**scsite.com/dc2005/weblink**). Click Multidimensional Databases below Chapter 10.

The key advantage of the multidimensional database is that it can consolidate data much faster than a relational database. A relational database typically does not process and summarize large numbers of records efficiently. With a multidimensional database, users obtain summarized results very quickly. For example, a query that takes minutes or hours to execute in a relational database will take only seconds to execute in a multidimensional database.

No standard query language exists for multidimensional databases. Each database uses its own language. Most are similar to SQL.

DATA WAREHOUSES One application that uses multidimensional databases is a data warehouse. A **data warehouse** is a huge database that stores and manages the data required to analyze historical and current transactions. Through a data warehouse, managers and other users access transactions and summaries of transactions quickly and efficiently. Some major credit card companies monitor and manage customers' credit card transactions using a data warehouse. Additionally, consumers can access their own transactions in the data warehouse via the Web. A data warehouse typically has a user-friendly interface, so users easily can interact with its data.

The databases in a data warehouse usually are quite large. Often, the database is distributed. The data in a *distributed database* exists in many separate locations throughout a network or the Internet. The data is accessible through a single server. The data's location is transparent to the user, who usually is unaware that the data is stored in multiple servers.

WEB LINK 10-9

Data Warehouses

Visit the Discovering Computers 2005 WEB LINK page (**scsite.com/dc2005/weblink**). Click Data Warehouses below Chapter 10.

Data warehouses often use a process called *data mining* to find patterns and relationships among data. A state government could mine through data to check if the number of births has a relationship to income level. Many e-commerce sites use data mining to determine customer preferences. For more information about e-commerce, read the E-Commerce feature that follows this chapter.

A smaller version of a data warehouse is the data mart. A *data mart* contains a database that helps a specific group or department make decisions. Marketing and sales departments may have their own separate data marts. Individual groups or departments often extract data from the data warehouse to create their data marts.

WEB DATABASES

One of the more profound features of the Web is the vast amount of information it provides. The Web offers information about jobs, travel destinations, television programming, movies and videos (Figure 10-23), local and national weather, sporting events, legislative information, and movies. You can shop for just about any product or service, buy or sell stocks, search for a job, and make airline reservations. Much of this and other information on the Web exists in databases. Read Apply It 10-2 for more information.

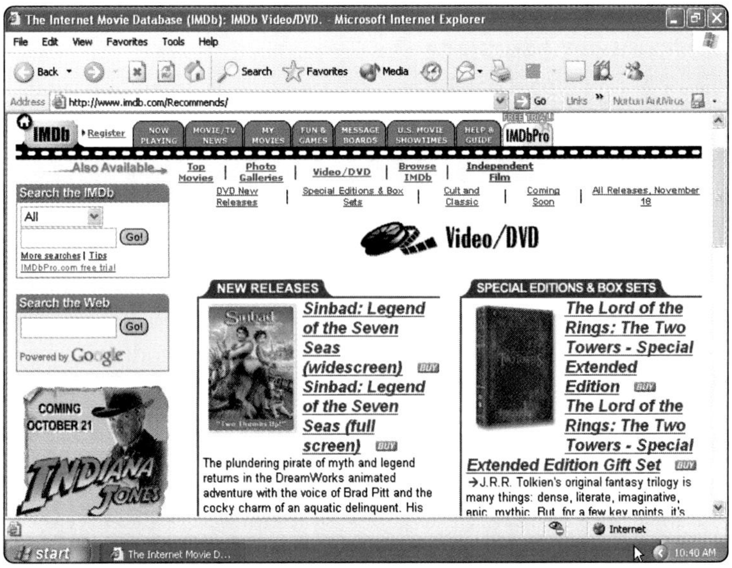

FIGURE 10-23 Through The Internet Movie Database (IMDb) Web site, users access a huge database loaded with content about current and classic movies.

To access data in a Web database, you fill in a form on a Web page. The Web page is the front end to the database. Many search engines such as Yahoo! use databases to store Web site descriptions. Thus, the search engine's home page is the front end to the database. To access the database, you enter search text into the search engine.

A Web database usually resides on a database server. A *database server* is a computer that stores and provides access to a database. One type of program that manages the sending and receiving of data between the front end and the database server is a *CGI (Common Gateway Interface) script*. CGI scripts run automatically — as soon as you click the button to send or receive information. Writing a CGI script requires computer programming skills. The steps in Figure 10-24 illustrate how a search engine might interact with a Web database.

FIGURE 10-24 HOW A SEARCH ENGINE MIGHT INTERACT WITH A WEB DATABASE

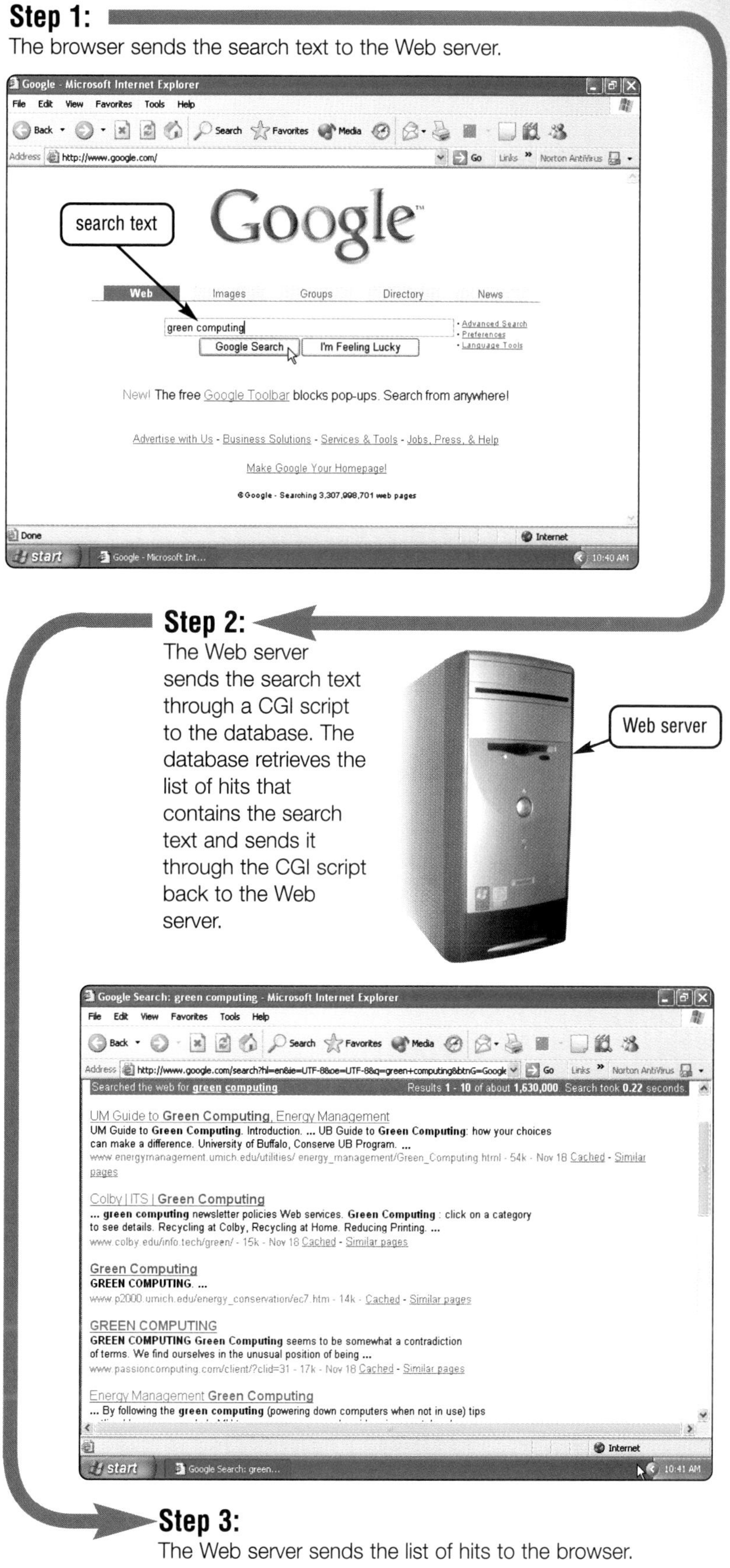

APPLY IT 10-2

Facts at Your Fingertips

What film won an Oscar for Best Picture this past year? How can you find a schoolmate you have not seen since high school graduation? The answers to these questions and many more are obtainable readily by searching databases at a variety of Web sites.

The Internet Movie Database (IMDb) has details of more than 375,000 film titles that can be downloaded for personal use. The Classmates online database contains profiles of more than 37 million members organized by particular schools, companies, and military organizations. Subscribers can search the database of 200,000 schools and 33,000 military organizations and then send e-mail messages to fellow members.

Other searchable online databases provide an abundance of information. The Internal Revenue Service Web site has tax forms, instructions, and publications for the past 10 years available for reading and downloading. Its planned Customer Account Data Engine database management system will allow taxpayers to check the status of their refunds online. Project Gutenberg has the full text of thousands of classic books published before 1923 on its Web site. The Social Security Administration's online services include applying for Social Security retirement, disability, and spouse's benefits, replacing a Social Security card, and using financial calculators to estimate future benefits.

For more information about Web databases, visit the Discovering Computers 2005 Apply It Web page (**scsite.com/dc2005/apply**). Click Apply It #2 below Chapter 10.

In addition to accessing information, users provide information to Web databases. Many Web sites request users to enter personal information, such as name, address, telephone number, and preferences, into an e-form. The database then stores this personal information for future use. A company, for example, may send e-mail messages to certain groups of customers. If you are a frequent flyer, you may receive travel information. Read Issue 10-5 for a related discussion.

For smaller databases, many personal computer database programs provide a variety of Web publishing tools. Microsoft FrontPage, for example, has a Database Results Wizard that requires no computer programming. The wizard publishes a Web page that links to your existing database such as a Microsoft Access or Oracle database.

ISSUE 10-5

When Should Web Bugs Be Exterminated?

Some Web pages have an Internet monitoring technology, popularly known as *Web bugs*, that counts visitors and gathers basic statistical information about a visitor's location and Web browser. Online advertising agencies or Internet service providers frequently place Web bugs as part of a promotion, sometimes without the knowledge of the Web page's sponsor. When the collected information is stored in a Web database and shared among several sites, the technology can track a visitor's rambles around the Web. If a visitor completes a registration, that information also can be distributed to other sites in the Web bug family. Web bugs help advertisers reach their markets and refine their messages, but opponents say the technology is little more than electronic stalking. Should Web bugs be banned or is it the right of Web page owners and advertisers to collect information about visitors? Why? Should Web page authors, and/or Web page visitors, be made aware of Web bugs? Why or why not?

For more information about Web bugs, visit the Discovering Computers 2005 Issues Web page (**scsite.com/dc2005/issues**). Click Issue #5 below Chapter 10.

DATABASE ADMINISTRATION

Managing a company's database requires a great deal of coordination. The role of coordinating the use of the database belongs to the database analysts and administrators. To carry out their responsibilities, these IT (information technology) professionals follow database design guidelines and need cooperation from all database users.

Database Design Guidelines

A carefully designed database makes it easier for a user to query the database, modify the data, and create reports. The guidelines shown in Figure 10-25 apply to databases of all sizes.

Database Design Guidelines

1. Determine the purpose of the database.
2. Design the tables.
   - Design tables on paper first.
   - Each table should contain data about one subject. The Member table, for example, contains data about members.
3. Design the fields for each table.
   - Be sure every field has a unique primary key.
   - Use separate fields for logically distinct items. For example, a name should be stored in six fields: Title (Mr., Mrs., Dr., etc.), First Name, Middle Name, Last Name, Suffix (Jr., Sr., etc.), and Nickname.
   - Do not create fields for information that can be derived from entries in other fields. For example, do not include a field for Age. Instead, store the birthdate and compute the age.
   - Allow enough space for each field.
   - Set default values for frequently entered data.
4. Determine the relationships among the tables.

FIGURE 10-25 Guidelines for developing a database.

Role of the Database Analysts and Administrators

The database analysts and administrators are responsible for managing and coordinating all database activities. The **database analyst (DA)**, or *data modeler*, focuses on the meaning and usage of data. The DA decides on the proper placement of fields, defines the relationships among data, and identifies users' access privileges. The **database administrator (DBA)** requires a more technical inside view of the data. The DBA creates and maintains the data dictionary, manages security of the database, monitors the performance of the database, and checks backup and recovery procedures.

In small companies, one person often is both the DA and DBA. In larger companies, the responsibilities of the DA and DBA are split among two or more people.

FAQ 10-5

Does DBA have two meanings?

Yes, DBA stands for either database administration or database administrator. The first, database administration, is the act of managing a database. The second, database administrator, is the person who manages the database.

For more information about DBA, visit the Discovering Computers 2005 FAQ Web page (**scsite.com/dc2005/faq**). Click DBA below Chapter 10.

Role of the Employee as a User

Employees should learn how to use the data in the database effectively. The amount of information available often amazes first-time database users. Instant access to this information helps employees perform their jobs more effectively. For example, assume a car backed into your parked car. You call your insurance agent to find out where to repair your car. The agent instantly reads to you a list of authorized car repair shops in your area. Today, employees access databases from their office desktop computers, notebook computers, or even PDAs (Figure 10-26).

Employees also must take an active role in identifying new data for the database. For example, maybe the insurance agent does not have access to the list of car repair shops on the computer. Instead, the agent looks them up in the telephone book. The agent's job would be much easier if this information was available on the computer.

WEB LINK 10-10

Database Administrators

Visit the Discovering Computers 2005 WEB LINK page (**scsite.com/dc2005/weblink**). Click Database Administrators below Chapter 10.

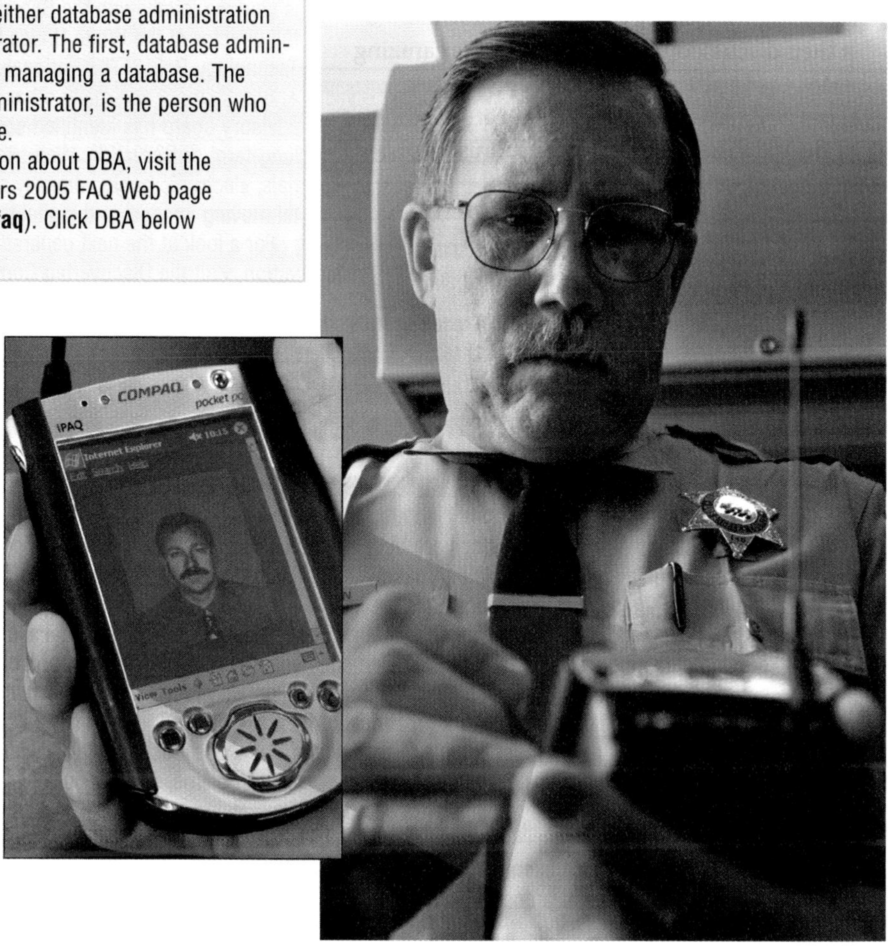

FIGURE 10-26 This police officer wirelessly accesses a database of mug shots and displays images on his PDA.

CHAPTER 10 CHAPTER REVIEW

The Chapter Review section summarizes the concepts presented in this chapter.

WEB INSTRUCTIONS:

To display this page from the Web, start your browser and enter the Web address **scsite.com/dc2005/ch10/review.** Click the links for current and additional information. To listen to an audio version of this Chapter Review, click the Audio button.

1 What Are the Qualities of Valuable Information?

Data is a collection of unprocessed items, which can include text, images, audio, and video. Computers process data into information. **Information** is processed data; that is, it is organized, meaningful, and useful. For information to be valuable, it should be accurate, verifiable, timely, organized, accessible, useful, and cost-effective.

2 Why Is Data Important to an Organization?

A **database** is a collection of data organized in a manner that allows access, retrieval, and use of that data. Because data is used to generate information, many companies realize that data is one of their more valuable assets. *Data integrity* identifies the quality of data. Data integrity is important because computers and people use information to make decisions and take actions. For a computer to produce correct information, the data that is input into a database must have integrity.

3 What Is Meant by Character, Field, Record, and File?

Data is classified in a hierarchy, with each level of data consisting of one or more items from the lower level. A bit is the smallest unit of data a computer can process. Eight bits grouped together in a unit form a byte, and each byte represents a single character. A **field** is a combination of one or more related characters and is the smallest unit of data a user accesses. A **record** is a group of related fields. A **data file** is a collection of related records stored on a disk such as a hard disk, CD, or DVD.

4 How Are Files Maintained?

File maintenance refers to the procedures that keep data current. File maintenance procedures include adding records when new data is obtained, changing records to correct inaccurate data or to update old data with new data, and deleting records when they no longer are needed. **Validation** is the process of comparing data with a set of rules or values to find out if the data is correct. Many programs perform a *validity check* that analyzes entered data to help ensure that it is correct. Types of validity checks include an *alphabetic check*, a *numeric check*, a *range check*, a *consistency check*, a *completeness check*, and a *check digit*.

Visit **scsite.com/dc2005/quiz** or click the Quiz Yourself button. Click Objectives 1 – 4 below Chapter 10.

5 How Is a File Processing System Approach Different from the Database Approach?

In a file processing system, each department or area within an organization has its own set of data files. Two major weaknesses of file processing systems are redundant data (duplicated data) and isolated data. With a **database approach**, many programs and users share the data in a database. The database approach reduces data redundancy, improves data integrity, shares data, permits easier access, and reduces development time. A database, however, can be more complex than a file processing system, requiring special training and more computer memory, storage, and processing power. Data in a database also is more vulnerable than data in file processing systems.

6 What Functions Are Common to Most DBMSs?

With **database software**, often called a **database management system** (**DBMS**), users can create and manipulate a computerized database. Most DBMSs perform common functions. A **data dictionary** contains data about each file in the database and each field within those files. A DBMS offers several methods to maintain and retrieve data, such as query languages, query by example, forms, and report generators. A **query language** consists of simple, English-like statements that allow users to specify the data to display, print, or store. Query by example (QBE) has a graphical user interface that assists users with retrieving data. A **form** is a window on the screen that provides areas for entering or changing data. A **report generator** allows users to design a report on the screen, retrieve data into the report design, and then display or print the report. To supply security, most DBMSs can identify different levels of *access privileges* that define the actions a specific user or group of users can perform for each field in a database. If a database is damaged or destroyed, a DBMS provides techniques to return the database to a usable form. A **backup** is a copy of the database. A **log** is a listing of activities that change the contents of the database. A **recovery utility** uses the backups and/or logs to restore the database.

Visit **scsite.com/dc2005/quiz** or click the Quiz Yourself button. Click Objectives 5 – 6 below Chapter 10.

7 What Are Characteristics of Relational, Object-Oriented, and Multidimensional Databases?

A **data model** consists of rules and standards that define how the database organizes data. Three popular data models are relational, object-oriented, and multidimensional. A **relational database** stores data in tables that consist of rows and columns. A relational database developer refers to a file as a *relation*, a record as a *tuple*, and a field as an *attribute*. A relational database user refers to a file as a **table**, a record as a **row**, and a field as a **column**. A **relationship** is a connection within the data in a relational database. **Structured Query Language** (**SQL**) allows users to manage, update, and retrieve data. An object-oriented database (OODB) stores data in objects. An **object** is an item that contains data, as well as the actions that read or process the data. Applications appropriate for an object-oriented database include a *multimedia database*, a *groupware database*, a *computer-aided design* (*CAD*) *database*, a *hypertext database*, a *hypermedia database*, and a *Web database*. Object-oriented databases often use an *object query language* (*OQL*) to manipulate and retrieve data. A multidimensional database stores data in dimensions. These multiple dimensions, sometimes known as a *hypercube*, allow users to access and analyze any view of the database data. One application that uses multidimensional databases is a **data warehouse**, which is a huge database system that stores and manages the data required to analyze historical and current transactions. No standard query language exists for multidimensional databases.

8 How Do Web Databases Work?

A *Web database* links to an e-form on a Web page, which is the *front end* to the database. To access data in a Web database, you fill in the form. A Web database usually resides on a *database server*, which is a computer that stores and provides access to a database. One type of program that manages the sending and receiving of data between the front end and the database is a *CGI* (*Common Gateway Interface*) *script*.

9 What Are the Responsibilities of Database Analysts and Administrators?

A **database analyst** (**DA**), or *data modeler*, focuses on the meaning and usage of data. The DA decides on the placement of fields, defines data relationships, and identifies access privileges. A **database administrator** (**DBA**) requires a more technical view of the data. The DBA creates and maintains the data dictionary, manages database security, monitors database performance, and checks backup and recovery procedures.

Visit **scsite.com/dc2005/quiz** or click the Quiz Yourself button. Click Objectives 7 – 9 below Chapter 10.

CHAPTER 10 KEY TERMS

QUIZZES AND LEARNING GAMES
Computer Genius
Crossword Puzzle
Interactive Labs
Practice Test
Quiz Yourself
Wheel of Terms

EXERCISES
Chapter Review
Checkpoint
Key Terms
Lab Exercises
Learn It Online
Web Research

BEYOND THE BOOK
Apply It
Career Corner
Companies
FAQ
High-Tech Talk
Issues
Looking Ahead
Trailblazers
Web Links

FEATURES
Guide to Web Sites
Making Use of the Web
Tech News
Timeline 2005

You should know the Primary Terms and be familiar with the Secondary Terms.

WEB INSTRUCTIONS:

To display this page from the Web, start your browser and enter the Web address **scsite.com/dc2005/ch10/terms**. Click a term to display its definition and a picture. When the picture appears, click the more info button for current and additional information about the term from the Web.

>> Primary Terms

(shown in bold-black characters in the chapter)

backup (533)
character (519)
column (535)
data (516)
data dictionary (528)
data file (521)
data model (534)
data type (520)
data warehouse (538)
database (517)
database administrator (DBA) (541)
database analyst (DA) (541)
database approach (526)
database management system (DBMS) (517)
database software (517)
field (519)
field name (519)
field size (520)
file maintenance (522)
file processing system (526)
form (531)
information (516)
key field (520)
log (533)
multidimensional database (537)
object (536)
object-oriented database (OODB) (536)
primary key (520)
query (530)
query by example (QBE) (531)
query language (530)
record (520)
recovery utility (534)
relational database (534)
relationship (535)
report generator (532)
row (535)
Structured Query Language (SQL) (536)
table (535)
validation (524)

>> Secondary Terms

(shown in italic characters in the chapter)

access privileges (532)
accessible information (518)
accurate information (518)
after image (533)
alphabetic check (525)
alphanumeric (520)
attribute (534)
back end (527)
backward recovery (534)
before image (533)
BLOB (520)
Boolean (520)
CGI (Common Gateway Interface) script (539)
check digit (525)
completeness check (525)
computer-aided design (CAD) database (536)
consistency check (525)
cost-effective information (518)
data entry form (531)
data integrity (517)
data mart (538)
data mining (538)
data modeler (541)
database server (539)
default value (528)
distributed database (538)
e-form (532)
electronic form (532)
forward recovery (534)
front end (527)
full-update privileges (533)
garbage in, garbage out (GIGO) (517)
groupware database (536)
hypercube (537)
hypermedia database (536)
hypertext database (536)
metadata (528)
multimedia database (536)
normalization (535)
numeric check (525)
object query language (OQL) (537)
object-relational databases (534)
organized information (518)
range check (525)
read-only privileges (533)
relation (534)
report writer (532)
repository (528)
rollback (534)
rollforward (534)
timely information (518)
tuple (534)
useful information (518)
validation rules (524)
validity check (524)
verifiable information (518)
Web database (536)

CHECKPOINT CHAPTER 10

Use the Checkpoint exercises to check your knowledge level of the chapter.

WEB INSTRUCTIONS:

To display this page from the Web, start your browser and enter the Web address **scsite.com/dc2005/ch10/check**. Click the links for current and additional information.

LABEL THE FIGURE

Identify each component of a relational database.

a. column
b. relationships
c. row
d. table

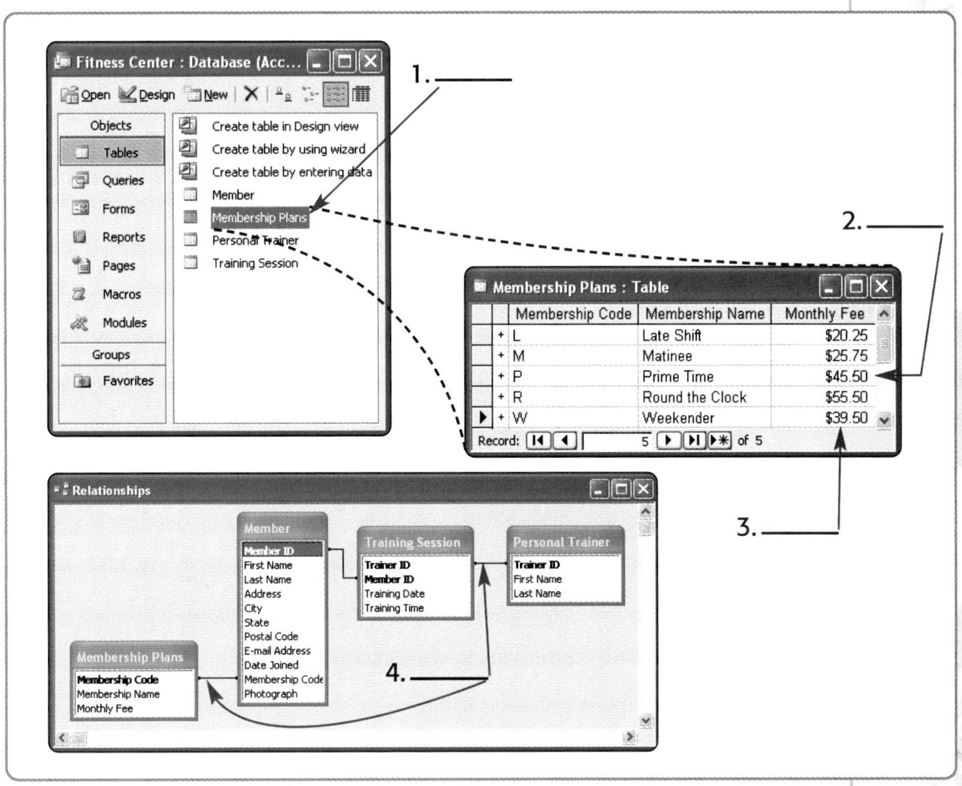

TRUE/FALSE

Mark T for True and F for False. (See page numbers in parentheses.)

_T_ 1. In addition to words and numbers, today data includes sounds, images, and video. (516)

_T_ 2. Garbage in, garbage out (GIGO) is a computer phrase that means you cannot create correct information from data that is incorrect. (517)

_F_ 3. The data in a key field is the same for every record in a file. (520)

_T_ 4. Validation is the process of comparing data with a set of rules or values to find out if the data is correct. (524)

_F_ 5. A range check tests the data in two or more associated fields to ensure that the relationship is logical. (525)

_T_ 6. A repository contains data about each file in the database and each field within those files. (528)

_T_ 7. To retrieve or select data in a database, you query it. (530)

_T_ 8. A data model consists of rules and standards that define how the database organizes data. (534)

_F_ 9. A multidimensional database is a database that stores data in tables that consist of rows and columns. (537)

_F_ 10. A database administrator requires a less technical inside view of data than a database analyst. (541)

CHAPTER 10 CHECKPOINT

MULTIPLE CHOICE

Select the best answer. (See page numbers in parentheses.)

1. Data _____ identifies the quality of data. (517)
   a. security
   b. modeling
   c. integrity
   d. mining
2. _____ information can be proven as correct or incorrect. (518)
   a. Timely
   b. Organized
   c. Cost-effective
   d. Verifiable
3. Accessible information _____. (518)
   a. is error free
   b. has an age suited to its use
   c. is available when the decision maker needs it
   d. has meaning to the person who receives it
4. The _____ data type is used for lengthy text entries. (520)
   a. memo
   b. numeric
   c. hyperlink
   d. data
5. A _____ is a collection of related records. (521)
   a. key field
   b. data file
   c. primary key
   d. data character
6. Users delete a record from a file when _____. (524)
   a. they obtain new data
   b. the record no longer is needed
   c. they correct inaccurate data
   d. all of the above
7. A completeness check _____. (525)
   a. ensures that users enter only alphabetic data into a field
   b. determines whether a number is within a specified range
   c. ensures that users enter only numeric data into a field
   d. verifies that a required field contains data
8. All of the following are strengths of the database approach, except _____. (527)
   a. less complexity
   b. improved data integrity
   c. easier access
   d. reduced development time
9. Because the _____ contains details about data, some call it metadata (meta means more comprehensive). (528)
   a. data mart
   b. data warehouse
   c. data modeler
   d. data dictionary
10. _____ has a graphical user interface that assists users with retrieving data. (531)
    a. A query language
    b. A form
    c. A report generator
    d. Query by example (QBE)
11. A _____ stores documents such as schedules, calendars, manuals, memos, and reports. (536)
    a. multimedia database
    b. groupware database
    c. computer-aided design (CAD) database
    d. hypertext database
12. The data in a(n) _____ exists in many separate locations throughout a network or the Internet. (538)
    a. hypermedia database
    b. distributed database
    c. relational database
    d. object-oriented database
13. To access data in a Web Database, users fill in a form on a Web page, which is the _____ to the database. (539)
    a. front end
    b. before image
    c. book end
    d. after image
14. The database analyst (DA) _____. (541)
    a. decides on the proper placement of fields
    b. creates and maintains the data dictionary
    c. monitors the performance of the database
    d. checks backup and recovery procedures

CHECKPOINT CHAPTER 10

MATCHING

Match the terms with their definitions. (See page numbers in parentheses.)

_____ 1. field name (519)
_____ 2. field size (520)
_____ 3. data type (520)
_____ 4. key field (520)
_____ 5. front end (527)
_____ 6. default value (528)
_____ 7. query (530)
_____ 8. normalization (535)
_____ 9. object-relational databases (534)
_____ 10. data mining (538)

a. collection of related records stored on a disk
b. combine features of the relational and object-oriented data models
c. defines the maximum number of characters a field can contain
d. used by data warehouses to find patterns and relationships in data
e. value that a DBMS initially displays in a field
f. item that contains data and the actions that read or process the data
g. process that ensures data within relations (tables) contains the least amount of duplication
h. specifies the kind of data a field can contain and how the field is used
i. uniquely identifies each field
j. uniquely identifies each record in a file
k. program that has a more user-friendly interface than the DBMS
l. request for specific data from a database

SHORT ANSWER

Write a brief answer to each of the following questions.

1. How is a field different from a record? __________ What is a data file? __________
2. What is file maintenance? __________ When are records added, changed, or deleted in a file? __________
3. Why is data redundancy a weakness of file processing systems? __________ How does the database approach reduce data redundancy? __________
4. What are access privileges? __________ How are read-only privileges different from full-update privileges? __________
5. In a log, how is a before image different from an after image? __________ How is rollforward different from rollback? __________

WORKING TOGETHER

Working with a group of your classmates, complete the following team exercises.

1. Law enforcement agencies are extensive users of databases. Have each member of your team visit a local police department to learn about the role computerized databases play in law enforcement. What databases are used by the department? What information do they contain? How are the databases used? How are they searched? How often are they updated? In what ways does a database contribute to law enforcement? What are the advantages and disadvantages of using a computerized database? Meet with the members of your team to discuss the results of your interviews. Then, use PowerPoint to create a group presentation and share your findings with the class.
2. Choose one Issue from the following issues in this chapter: Should Americans Have a National Identification Card? (521), Should Criminal Databases Be Shared? (527), Is Unauthorized Access a Crime? (532), What Access Privileges Should Be Used? (533), or When Should Web Bugs Be Exterminated? (540). Use the Web and/or print media to research the issue. Then, present a debate for the class, with different members of your team supporting different responses to the questions that accompany the issue.
3. Most libraries use databases to keep track of their collections. Have each member of your team visit a library that uses a database. Interview a librarian to find out more about the database. How many items are represented? What information does the database contain? How is the database searched? How frequently is it updated? Meet with the members of your team to discuss the results of your interviews. Use PowerPoint to create a group presentation and share your findings with the class.

QUIZZES AND LEARNING GAMES
Computer Genius
Crossword Puzzle
Interactive Labs
Practice Test
Quiz Yourself
Wheel of Terms

EXERCISES
Chapter Review
Checkpoint
Key Terms
Lab Exercises
Learn It Online
Web Research

BEYOND THE BOOK
Apply It
Career Corner
Companies
FAQ
High-Tech Talk
Issues
Looking Ahead
Trailblazers
Web Links

FEATURES
Guide to Web Sites
Making Use of the Web
Tech News
Timeline 2005

Use the Learn It Online exercises to reinforce your understanding of the chapter concepts.

WEB INSTRUCTIONS:

To display this page from the Web, start your browser and enter the Web address **scsite.com/dc2005/ch10/learn**.

1 At the Movies – Britain ID Cards Debate

To view the Britain ID Cards Debate movie, click the number 1 button. Watch the movie and then complete the exercise by answering the questions below. Tony Blair, prime minister of Britain, has proposed citizens of Great Britain obtain an entitlement card. This identification card would store specific information about each citizen, proving the citizen is the person he or she claims to be. Prime Minister Blair believes the card could reduce the threat of terrorism, illegal immigration, identity theft, and benefits fraud. What type of data would need to be stored on such a card? How important would data security be for these cards? If entitlement cards are issued only to those who request them, as Prime Minister Blair proposes, do you think the cards will effectively reduce terrorism, illegal immigration, identity theft, and benefits fraud? Why or why not?

2 Student Edition Labs – Advanced Databases

Click the number 2 button. When the Student Edition Labs menu appears, click *Advanced Databases* to begin. A new browser window will open. Follow the on-screen instructions to complete the Lab. When finished, click the Exit button. If required, print a copy of your results to submit to your instructor.

3 Student Edition Labs – Advanced Spreadsheets

Click the number 3 button. When the Student Edition Labs menu appears, click *Advanced Spreadsheets* to begin. A new browser window will open. Follow the on-screen instructions to complete the Lab. When finished, click the Exit button. If required, print a copy of your results to submit to your instructor.

4 Shopping Online

Online shopping is an increasingly prevalent Internet activity. Buying on the Web is especially popular during the Christmas season. Studies indicate that U.S. online holiday sales represent about one-third of all online sales for the entire year. Web sites that offer products for sale must provide database search capability as well as online order entry. Click the number 4 button and complete this exercise to learn more about database queries and order entry in a large online music store.

5 Practice Test

Click the number 5 button. Answer each question. When completed, enter your name and click the Grade Test button to submit the quiz for grading. Make a note of any missed questions. If required, print a copy to submit to your instructor.

6 Web Guide

Click the number 6 button to display the Guide to Web Sites and Searching Techniques Web page. Click Reference and then click Webopedia. Search for data dictionary. Click one of the data dictionary links. Use your word processing program to prepare a brief report about your findings and submit your assignment to your instructor.

7 Scavenger Hunt

Click the number 7 button. Print a copy of the Scavenger Hunt page; use this page to write down your answers as you search the Web. Submit your completed page to your instructor.

8 Who Wants To Be a Computer Genius?

Click the number 8 button to find out if you are a computer genius. Directions on how to play the game will be displayed. When you are ready to play, click the PLAY button. Submit your score to your instructor.

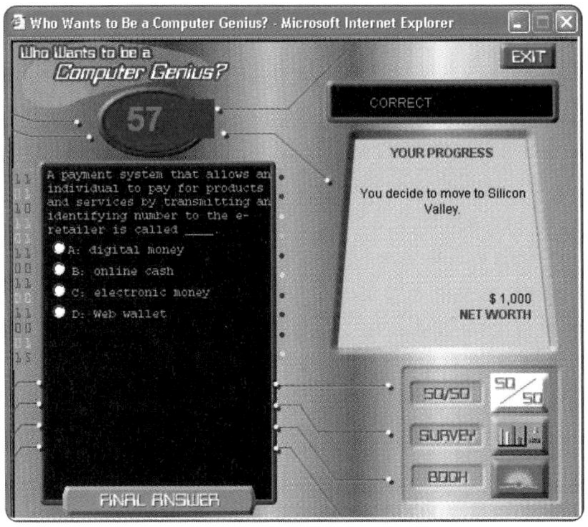

9 Wheel of Terms

Click the number 9 button to reinforce important terms you learned in this chapter by playing the Shelly Cashman Series version of this popular game. Directions on how to play the game will be displayed. When you are ready to play, click the PLAY button. Submit your score to your instructor.

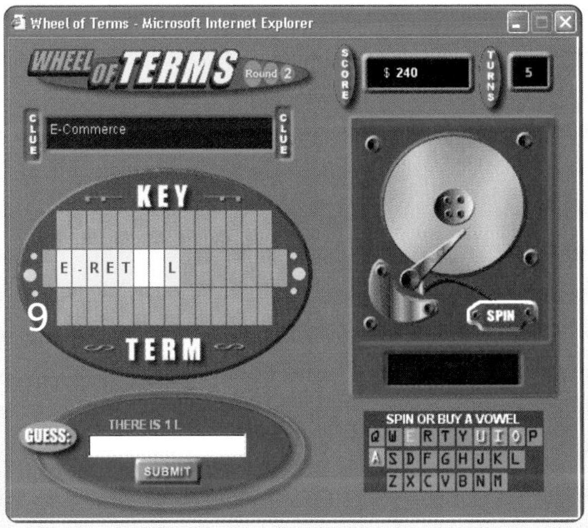

10 Career Corner

Click the number 10 button to display the JobStarCalifornia page. Click one of the Facts and Information links and then review the information. Write a brief report describing what you learned. Submit the report to your instructor.

11 Search Sleuth

Click the number 11 button to learn search techniques that will help make you a research expert. Submit the completed assignment to your instructor.

12 Crossword Puzzle Challenge

Click the number 12 button. Complete the puzzle to reinforce skills you learned in this chapter. Directions on how to play the game will be displayed. When you are ready to play, click the Submit button. Submit the completed puzzle to your instructor.

13 Newsgroup FAQ

Redundancy in data wastes storage space. Redundant questions demand valuable employee time. FAQ (frequently asked questions) help reduce the need for experienced newsgroup participants from having to read and answer the same questions more than once. Click the number 13 button for a listing of newsgroups with FAQs. Click a newsgroup folder link in which you are interested. Continue clicking folder links until you see a file link called faq.html. Click the faq.html link to see the newsgroup's FAQ. Read the frequently asked questions. What question (or answer) is most surprising to you? Why?

14 In the News

To spare harried dispatchers, police officers used to request suspect information only when it was urgent. Now, IBM's eNetwork Law Enforcement Express lets officers directly access real-time databases of stolen cars, mug shots, and warrants. With a few taps on a notebook computer keyboard, police officers can search a database to see if a suspect in custody has a past criminal record. They also can find out if a suspect stopped for speeding is wanted for any more serious infractions. Click the number 14 button and read a news article about a database that is being used in a new way. Who is using the database? How is it being used? How will the database benefit the user?

CHAPTER 10 LAB EXERCISES

Use the Lab Exercises to gain hands-on computer experience.

WEB INSTRUCTIONS:

To display this page from the Web, start your browser and enter the Web address **scsite.com/dc2005/ch10/lab**.

1 Managing Files and Folders

This exercise uses Windows XP procedures. Click the Start button on the taskbar and then click Help and Support on the Start menu. In the Search text box, type files and then click the Start searching button. Click an appropriate Help topic to answer the following questions:

- How do you create a new folder?
- How do you move a file or folder?
- How do you delete a file or folder?
- How do you save a file?

Click the Close button to close the Help and Support Center window.

2 Creating Folders

This exercise uses Windows XP/2000/98 procedures. Click the Start button on the taskbar. Right-click My Computer on the Start menu (right-click the My Computer icon on the desktop in Windows 2000/98). Click Explore on the shortcut menu to open the My Computer window (Exploring – My Computer window in Windows 2000/98). If necessary, maximize the window. Click View on the menu bar and then click Tiles (Large Icons in Windows 2000/98). Insert the Discover Data Disk into drive A. See the inside back cover of this book for instructions for downloading the Data Disk or see your instructor for information on accessing the files required in this book. If necessary, drag the vertical scroll box to the top of the scroll bar in the Folders pane. Click 3½ Floppy (A:) in the Folders pane to display the contents of drive A in the right pane. Click File on the menu bar, point to New, and then click Folder on the New submenu. Type `Lab Exercises` in the New Folder text box and then press the ENTER key. Click View on the menu bar, point to Arrange Icons by (Arrange Icons in Windows 2000/98), and then click Name on the Arrange Icons by submenu (by Name on the Arrange Icons submenu in Windows 2000/98). In the Folders pane, click the plus sign next to 3½ Floppy (A:) to display the Lab Exercises folder in the Folders pane. Click the Lab Exercises folder in the Folders pane to display its contents in the right pane. What is in the Lab Exercises folder? Click the Close button to close the Explorer window.

3 Moving and Deleting Files

This exercise uses Windows XP/2000/98 procedures. To complete this exercise, you first must complete exercise 2 in Chapter 3 Lab Exercises on page 176, exercise 2 in Chapter 7 Lab Exercises on page 388, and exercise 2 on this page. Click the Start button on the taskbar. Right-click the My Computer icon on the Start menu (right-click the My Computer icon on the desktop in Windows 2000/98). Click Explore on the shortcut menu to open the My Computer window (Exploring – My Computer window in Windows 2000/98). If necessary, maximize the window. Insert your floppy disk into drive A. If necessary, click View on the menu bar and then click Tiles (Large Icons in Windows 2000/98). Click 3½ Floppy (A:) in the Folders pane to display the contents of drive A in the right pane. Click the plus sign next to the 3½ Floppy (A:) icon in the Folders pane to display the subfolder in the 3½ Floppy (A:) drive. To move the file you created in Chapter 3 (lab3-2) into the In The Lab folder, perform the following steps:

- Click the lab3-2 icon to select the file.
- Right-drag the lab3-2 icon to the Lab Exercises folder in the right pane.
- When the Lab Exercises folder is highlighted, release the right mouse button.
- Click Move Here on the shortcut menu.
- Double-click the Lab Exercises folder.

What is in the Lab Exercises Folder?

To delete file lab7-2, perform the following steps:

- Click the minus sign next to the 3½ Floppy (A:) icon in the Folders pane to display the disk contents in the right pane.
- Right-click the lab7-2 icon.
- Click Delete on the shortcut menu.
- Click the Yes button in the Confirm File Delete dialog box.

What displays in the window? Close the Exploring window.

WEB RESEARCH

Use the Web Research exercises to learn more about the special features in this chapter.

WEB INSTRUCTIONS:

Use the link in each exercise or a search engine such as Google (google.com) to research the topic. Then, write a one-page, double-spaced report or create a presentation, unless otherwise directed below. Page numbers on which information can be found are in parentheses.

1 **Issue** Choose one Issue from the following issues in this chapter: Should Americans Have a National Identification Card? (521), Should Criminal Databases Be Shared? (527), Is Unauthorized Access a Crime? (532), What Access Privileges Should Be Used? (533), or When Should Web Bugs Be Exterminated? (540). Use the Web to research the issue. Discuss the issue with classmates, instructors, and friends. Address the questions that accompany the issue in a report or presentation.

2 **Apply It** Choose one of the following Apply It features in this chapter: Take Charge of Your Credit (518) or Facts at Your Fingertips (539). Use the Web to gather additional information about the topic. Print two Web pages that relate to the Apply It. Detail in a report or presentation what you learned.

3 **Career Corner** Read the Career Corner article in this chapter (542). Use the Web to find out more about the career. Describe the career in a report or presentation.

4 **Companies on the Cutting Edge** Choose one of the Companies on the Cutting Edge in this chapter (544). Use the Web to research the company further. Explain in a report or presentation how this company has contributed to computer technology.

5 **Technology Trailblazers** Choose one of the Technology Trailblazers in this chapter (545). Use the Web to research the person further. Explain in a report or presentation how this individual has affected the way people use, or think about, computers.

6 **Picture Yourself Using a Web Database** Read the Picture Yourself Using a Web Database story at the beginning of this chapter (514). Use the Web to research Web databases further. Describe in a report or presentation the ways in which you might use a Web database.

7 **High-Tech Talk** Read the High-Tech Talk feature in this chapter (543). Use the Web to find out more about the topic. Summarize in a report or presentation what you learned.

8 **Web Links** Review the Web Link boxes found in the margins of this chapter. Visit five of the Web Link sites. Print the main Web page for each site you visit. Choose one of the Web pages and then summarize in one paragraph the content of the Web page.

9 **Looking Ahead** Choose one of the Looking Ahead articles in this chapter: Having a Voice in Future Databases (531) or Storing Digital Files for Future Generations (542). Use the Web to find out more about the topic. Detail in a report or presentation what you learned.

10 **FAQ** Choose one FAQ found in this chapter. Use the Web to find out more about the topic. Summarize in one paragraph what you learned.

11 **E-Commerce** Read the E-Commerce Special Feature that follows this chapter (556-565). Select an aspect of e-commerce of particular interest. Use the Web to learn more about your selection. Describe in a report or presentation how your selection affects e-commerce.

12 **Making Use of the Web** Read the Science section of Making Use of the Web in Appendix A (APP 20). Complete the Science Web Exercises at the end of the section (APP 21). Answer the questions posed in each exercise.

BECOMING AN E-COMMERCE MERCHANT

With such a tremendous business potential on the Web, many people and companies are venturing into this worldwide horizon. Depending on the nature of the existing business, the approach used to establish an online presence varies. Some merchants start an e-retail store without having a physical presence. Others establish an electronic storefront as an extension of an existing bricks-and-mortar business. Some expand an informational Web site into a full-featured e-commerce Web site.

Regardless of the scope or size of business, all e-commerce must address some common concerns. To provide for e-commerce, a company or individual must decide how to do the following: (1) build an electronic storefront; (2) manage payments; (3) manage product delivery; (4) manage customer service requests; (5) design a Web site that attracts customers and keeps them returning; (6) manage the Web site; and (7) promote the Web site (Figure 12).

E-COMMERCE REVENUE STREAMS

E-commerce businesses generate revenues in many ways. A revenue stream is the method a business uses to generate income. Some of the more common e-commerce revenue streams are listed in Figure 11.

REVENUE STREAM	DESCRIPTION
Advertisements	Web sites, especially major portals, generate revenue by selling advertising space on Web pages
Application Service Providers (ASPs)	Customer pays rental fee before accessing the software on the Web and using it
Electronic Software Distribution (ESD)	Delivers goods electronically, such as software, music, movies, books, and photographs
Host Web Sites	Customer leases hardware, software, and the communications equipment required for a Web server
Informational Web Sites	Visitors subscribe to the service; as you would subscribe to a magazine
Online Storage Services	Provides data storage to customers
Sales of Goods	Generates revenue from sales of goods to consumers or other businesses; goods shipped to buyers via postal or parcel service
Service Providers	Offers Internet access for a monthly fee
Web Services	E-commerce company purchases "behind the scenes" programs that interact with programs that a company uses to interact with its customers

FIGURE 11 E-commerce revenue streams.

FIGURE 12 You must make several decisions before developing an e-commerce Web site.

Building Your Own Electronic Storefront

If you have goods you want to sell on the Web, you can start by building your own electronic storefront on one of many Web hosting sites. Many ISPs, online service providers (OSPs), content portals such as Yahoo!, and online malls provide Web hosting services. Most also offer Web site development services that assist you throughout the process of creating an electronic storefront (Figure 13). These types of services allow small businesses and individuals to participate in the e-commerce arena with a minimum investment. A hosting service charges a monthly fee, or may take a percentage of the sales income.

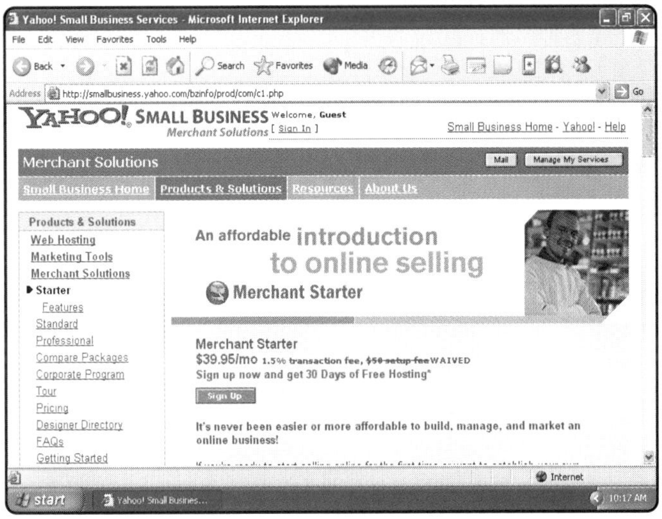

FIGURE 13 Through Yahoo! Store at store.yahoo.com, you can build an electronic storefront in minutes using your Web browser.

LEARNING MORE ABOUT E-COMMERCE

Many sources for news and information about e-commerce are available online. Using the popular Web portals such as Google, Yahoo!, AltaVista, and others, you will find links to thousands of other e-commerce sites. Figure 14 lists several areas of interest and gives their Web addresses.

WEB SITE	URL
Online Magazines	
eMarketer	emarketer.com
InternetWeek.com	internetwk.com
E-Commerce Guide.com	ecommerce.internet.com
New York Times: E-Commerce	nytimes.com/library/tech/00/03/biztech/technology/
TelecomWeb E-Business	telecomweb.com/ebusiness
The Industry Standard	thestandard.com
Wilson Internet Web Marketing & E-Commerce	wilsonweb.com
Online Guides	
About Electronic Commerce	ecommerce.about.com/mbody.htm
eCommerce Guidebook	online-commerce.com
Ecommerce Webopedia	e-comm.webopedia.com
Beginners Guide to Ecommerce	nightcats.com/sales/free.html
Hosting Services	
Candidinfo.com	web-hosting.candidinfo.com
Hosting.com	adgrafix.com
NTT/VERIO	verio.com
SBC Ameritech	ameritech-hosting.net
Yahoo! Small Business	smallbusiness.yahoo.com/webhosting/
Government and Nonprofit	
BBBOnLine	bbbonline.org
Data Interchange Standards Association (DISA)	disa.org
FTC Consumer Protection	www.ftc.gov/bcp/menu-internet.htm
InterNIC	www.internic.net
U.S. Department of Commerce Home Page	ecommerce.gov

For an updated list, visit scsite.com/dc2005/ch10/e-commerce

FIGURE 14 Online sources for information about e-commerce.

CHAPTER 11

Computers and Society, Security, Privacy, and Ethics

Picture Your Personal Information Going Public

While enjoying your favorite soup for lunch, you read an offer for a card game CD-ROM on the back of the can. All you have to do to receive it is send two soup-can UPC labels and $1 for processing and handling. You immediately pull off the order form and fill in your name, home address, e-mail address, and telephone number. Card games are your favorite pastime!

Three weeks later the software arrives. While installing the software, you register the product online. The next day, the manufacturer sends you an e-mail message with a list of other entertainment software in which you might be interested. As time passes, increasingly more e-mail messages from vendors of game and entertainment software show up in your inbox. In addition, you begin to receive brochures in the U.S. mail from various related sources. Then, you receive a call from one of the vendors. How did all these companies obtain your name, telephone number, and other personal information?

With school starting soon, you decide to buy your semester books from the campus online bookstore. While placing your order, the advertisement banner on the bookstore's Web page reads, Click here for a 50 percent discount on entertainment software. Has your personal information been shared with the vendor of this entertainment software?

As you read Chapter 11, you will learn ways to safeguard personal information and discover techniques to secure your computer.

OBJECTIVES

After completing this chapter, you will be able to:

1. Describe the types of computer security risks
2. Identify ways to safeguard against computer viruses, worms, and Trojan horses
3. Discuss techniques to prevent unauthorized computer access and use
4. Identify safeguards against hardware theft and vandalism
5. Explain the ways software manufacturers protect against software piracy
6. Define encryption and explain why it is necessary
7. Discuss the types of devices available that protect from system failure
8. Explain the options available for backing up computer resources
9. Identify safeguards that protect against Internet security risks
10. Recognize issues related to information accuracy, rights, and conduct
11. Discuss issues surrounding information privacy
12. Discuss ways to prevent health-related disorders and injuries due to computer use

CONTENTS

COMPUTER SECURITY RISKS

Today, people rely on computers to create, store, and manage critical information. Thus, it is important that the computers and the data they store are accessible and available when needed. It also is crucial that users take measures to protect their computers and data from loss, damage, and misuse. For example, businesses must ensure that information such as credit records, employee and customer data, and purchase information is secure and confidential. Home users must ensure that their credit card number is secure when they use it to purchase goods and services from Web-based businesses.

A **computer security risk** is any event or action that could cause a loss of or damage to computer hardware, software, data, information, or processing capability. Some breaches to computer security are accidental. Others are planned. An intentional breach of computer security often involves a deliberate act that is against the law. Any illegal act involving a computer generally is referred to as a **computer crime**. The term **cybercrime** refers

FIGURE 11-1 Computer users are exposed to several types of computer security risks.

to online or Internet-based illegal acts. Today, cybercrime is one of the FBI's top-ten priorities.

The more common computer security risks include computer viruses, worms, and Trojan horses; unauthorized access and use; hardware theft; software theft; information theft; and system failure (Figure 11-1). The following pages describe these computer security risks and also discuss protective measures, or *safeguards,* users might take to minimize or prevent their consequences.

COMPUTER VIRUSES, WORMS, AND TROJAN HORSES

Nearly every computer user is susceptible to the first type of computer security risk — a computer virus, worm, and/or Trojan horse.

- A computer **virus** is a potentially damaging computer program that affects, or infects, a computer negatively by altering the way the computer works without the user's knowledge or permission. Once the virus infects the computer, it can spread throughout and may damage files and system software, including the operating system.
- A **worm** is a program that copies itself repeatedly, for example, in memory or on a network, using up resources and possibly shutting down the computer or network.
- A **Trojan horse** (named after the Greek myth) is a program that hides within or looks like a legitimate program. A certain condition or action usually triggers the Trojan horse. Unlike a virus or worm, a Trojan horse does not replicate itself to other computers.

Computer viruses, worms, and Trojan horses are classified as *malicious-logic programs,* which are programs that act without a user's knowledge and deliberately alter the computer's operations. Although these programs often are one of the three types (virus, worm, Trojan horse), some have characteristics of two or all three types. For examples, Blaster and Sobig are worms; Melissa is a virus, worm, and Trojan horse.

Unscrupulous programmers write malicious-logic programs and then test the programs to ensure they can deliver their payload. The *payload* is the destructive event or prank the program is intended to deliver. A computer infected by a virus, worm, or Trojan horse often has one or more of the following symptoms:

- Screen displays unusual message or image
- Music or unusual sound plays randomly
- Available memory is less than expected
- Existing programs and files disappear
- Files become corrupted
- Programs or files do not work properly
- Unknown programs or files mysteriously appear
- System properties change

Computer viruses, worms, and Trojan horses deliver their payload on a computer in three basic ways: when a user (1) opens an infected file, (2) runs an infected program, or (3) boots the computer with an infected disk in a disk drive. Today, the most common way computers become infected with viruses, worms, and Trojan horses is through users opening infected e-mail attachments. Figure 11-2 shows how a virus can spread from one computer to another through an infected e-mail attachment.

Malicious-logic programs have become a serious problem in recent years. Currently, more than 80,000 known viruses, worms, and Trojan horse programs exist with an estimated 6 new programs discovered each day. Many Web sites maintain lists of all known malicious-logic programs. For a technical discussion about viruses, worms, and Trojan horses, read the High-Tech Talk article on page 603 in Chapter 3.

Safeguards against Computer Viruses, Worms, and Trojan Horses

Methods that guarantee a computer or network is safe from computer viruses, worms, and Trojan horses simply do not exist. Users can take several precautions, however, to protect their home and work computers from these malicious infections. The following paragraphs discuss these precautionary measures.

Do not start a computer with a floppy disk in drive A — unless you are certain the disk is an uninfected boot disk. All floppy disks contain a boot sector. During the startup process, the computer attempts to execute the boot sector on a disk in drive A. Even if the attempt is unsuccessful, any virus on the floppy disk's boot sector can infect the computer's hard disk.

FIGURE 11-2 HOW A VIRUS CAN SPREAD THROUGH AN E-MAIL MESSAGE

Never open an e-mail attachment unless you are expecting the attachment and it is from a trusted source. A **trusted source** is a company or person you believe will not send a virus-infected file knowingly. If the e-mail is from an unknown source or untrusted source, delete the e-mail message immediately — without opening or executing any attachments.

Many e-mail programs allow users to preview an e-mail message before or without opening it. Some viruses and worms can deliver their payload when a user simply previews the message. Thus, users should turn off message preview in their e-mail programs.

Some viruses are hidden in *macros*, which are instructions saved in an application such as a word processing or spreadsheet program. In applications that allow users to write macros, set the macro security level to medium. With a medium security level, the application software warns users that a document they are attempting to open contains a macro (Figure 11-3). From this warning, a user chooses to disable or enable the macro. If the document is from a trusted source, the user can enable the macro. Otherwise, it should be disabled.

Figure 11-3a (dialog box to set macro security)

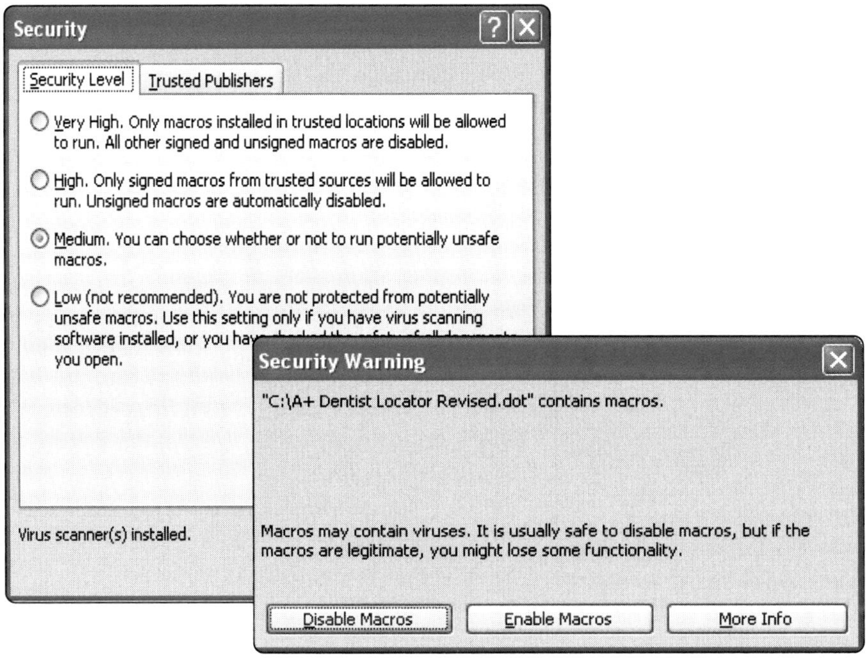

Figure 11-3b (warning is displayed because security is set to medium)

FIGURE 11-3 Many application programs, such as Microsoft Office Word 2003, allow users to set security levels for macros. To display the dialog box shown in Figure 11-3a in Word, click Tools on the menu bar, point to Macro, and then click Security.

Users should install an antivirus program and update it frequently. As discussed in Chapter 8, an **antivirus program** protects a computer against viruses by identifying and removing any computer viruses found in memory, on storage media, or on incoming files. Most antivirus programs also protect against worms and Trojan horses. When you purchase a new computer, it often includes antivirus software. The table in Figure 11-4 lists popular antivirus programs.

POPULAR ANTIVIRUS PROGRAMS

AVG Anti-Virus
Command Antivirus
eTrust Antivirus
F-Secure Anti-Virus
McAfee VirusScan
Norton AntiVirus
RAV AntiVirus
Trend Micro PC-cillin

FIGURE 11-4 Popular antivirus software.

An antivirus program scans for programs that attempt to modify the boot program, the operating system, and other programs that normally are read from but not modified. In addition, many antivirus programs automatically scan files downloaded from the Web, e-mail attachments, opened files, and all types of removable media inserted into the computer such as floppy disks and Zip disks.

One technique that antivirus programs use to identify a virus is to look for virus signatures. A **virus signature**, also called a **virus definition**, is a known specific pattern of virus code. Computer users should update their antivirus program's signature files regularly. Updating signature files brings in any new virus definitions that have been added since the last update (Figure 11-5). This extremely important activity allows the antivirus software to protect against viruses written since the antivirus program was released. Most antivirus programs contain an autoupdate feature that regularly prompts users to download the virus signature. The vendor usually provides this service to registered users at no cost for a specified time.

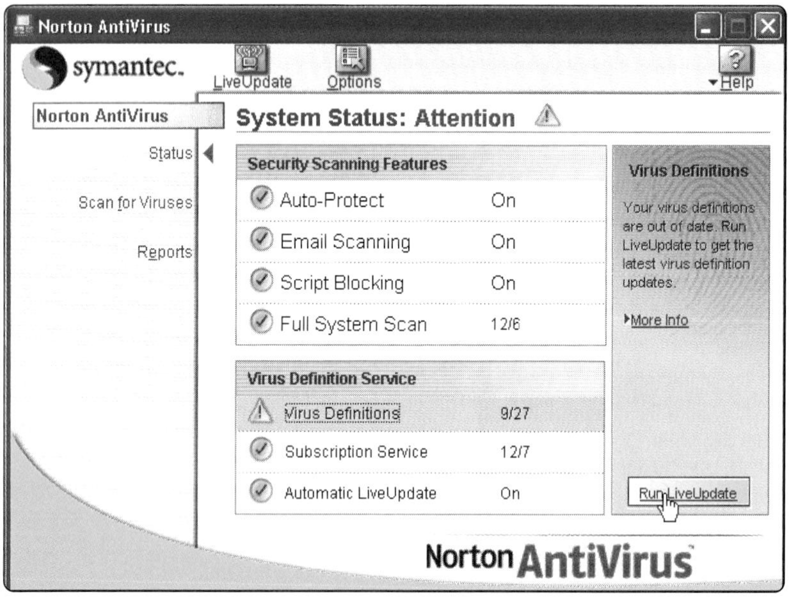

FIGURE 11-5 Many vendors of antivirus programs allow registered users to update signature files automatically from the Web at no cost for a specified time.

Another technique that antivirus programs use to detect viruses is to inoculate existing program files. To **inoculate** a program file, the antivirus program records information such as the file size and file creation date in a separate inoculation file. The antivirus program then uses this information to detect if a virus tampers with the data describing the inoculated program file.

If an antivirus program identifies an infected file, it attempts to remove its virus, worm, or Trojan horse. If the antivirus program cannot remove the infection, it often quarantines the infected file. A **quarantine** is a separate area of a hard disk that holds the infected file until the infection can be removed. This step ensures other files will not become infected. Users also can quarantine suspicious files themselves.

In addition to detecting, inoculating, and removing viruses, worms, and Trojan horses, most antivirus programs have utilities that create a recovery disk. The **recovery disk**, also called a **rescue disk**, is a removable disk that contains an uninfected copy of key operating system commands and startup information that enables the computer to restart correctly. Floppy disks and Zip disks often serve as recovery disks. Once you have restarted the computer using a write-protected recovery disk, the antivirus program can attempt to repair damaged files. If it cannot repair the damaged files, you may have to restore them with uninfected backup copies of the files.

In extreme cases, you may need to reformat the hard disk to remove a virus. Having uninfected, or clean, backups of all files is important. A later section in this chapter covers backup and restore procedures in detail.

In addition to an antivirus program, users often install a personal firewall program to protect a computer and its data from unauthorized intrusions. A section later in this chapter discusses firewalls.

Finally, stay informed about new virus alerts and virus hoaxes. A **virus hoax** is an e-mail message that warns users of a nonexistent virus, worm, or Trojan horse. Often, these virus hoaxes are in the form of a chain letter that requests the user to send a copy of the e-mail message to as many people as possible. Instead of forwarding the message, visit a Web site that publishes a list of virus alerts and virus hoaxes.

The list in Figure 11-6 summarizes important tips for protecting your computer from virus, worm, and Trojan horse infection.

TIPS FOR PREVENTING VIRUS, WORM, AND TROJAN HORSE INFECTIONS

1. Never start a computer with a floppy disk in drive A, unless it is an uninfected boot disk. Turn off message preview.
2. Never open an e-mail attachment unless you are expecting it and it is from a trusted source. Turn off message preview.
3. Set the macro security in programs so you can enable or disable macros. Only enable macros if the document is from a trusted source and you are expecting it.
4. Install an antivirus program on all of your computers. Obtain updates to the antivirus signature files on a regular basis.
5. Check all downloaded programs for viruses, worms, or Trojan horses. These malicious-logic programs often are placed in seemingly innocent programs, so they will affect a large number of users.
6. If the antivirus program flags an e-mail attachment as infected, delete the attachment immediately.
7. Before using any floppy disk or Zip disk, use the antivirus scan program to check the disk for infection. Incorporate this procedure even for shrink-wrapped software from major developers. Some commercial software has been infected and distributed to unsuspecting users this way.
8. Create a recovery disk and write-protect it.
9. Install a personal firewall program.

FIGURE 11-6 With the growing number of new viruses, worms, and Trojan horses, it is crucial that users take steps to protect their computers. Experts recommend the precautions listed here.

FAQ 11-1

Should I inform others if my computer gets a virus, worm, or Trojan horse?

If you share data with other users, such as via e-mail attachments, instant message attachments, floppy disks, or Zip disks, then you should inform these users of your virus, worm, or Trojan horse infection. This courteous gesture allows fellow users to check their computers for the same type of infection. Be careful not to spread the virus inadvertently.

For more information about viruses, worms, and Trojan horses, visit the Discovering Computers 2005 FAQ Web page (**scsite.com/dc2005/faq**). Click Viruses, Worms, and Trojan Horses below Chapter 11.

WEB LINK 11-1

Virus Hoaxes

Visit the Discovering Computers 2005 WEB LINK page (**scsite .com/dc2005/weblink**). Click Virus Hoaxes below Chapter 11.

UNAUTHORIZED ACCESS AND USE

Another type of computer security risk is unauthorized access and use. **Unauthorized access** is the use of a computer or network without permission. In a recent survey, 85 percent of the organizations polled indicated their company's network had been breached by a cracker or hacker, with losses exceeding $350 million.

A **cracker** is someone who tries to access a computer or network illegally. The term **hacker**, although originally a complimentary word for a computer enthusiast, now has a derogatory connotation with the same definition as cracker. Some hackers break into a computer for the challenge. Other hackers use or steal computer resources or corrupt a computer's data.

Hackers typically break into a computer by connecting to it and then logging in as a legitimate user. Some intruders do no damage; they merely access data, information, or programs on the computer before logging off. Other intruders indicate some evidence of their presence either by leaving a message or by deliberately altering data.

Unauthorized use is the use of a computer or its data for unapproved or possibly illegal activities. Unauthorized use includes a variety of activities: an employee using an organization's computer to send personal e-mail messages, an employee using the organization's word processing software to track his or her child's soccer league scores, or someone gaining access to a bank computer and performing an unauthorized transfer. For the home user, most unauthorized use occurs on computers that have always on Internet connections, such as through Internet cable or DSL.

FAQ 11-2

What punishments do hackers receive?

Depending on the severity of the crime, offenders can be sentenced to serve time in jail, pay fines, or perform community service work. One hacker who used the Internet to obtain credit card information illegally and defraud many companies and consumers was sentenced to 27 months in jail with 3 years of probation following release from jail, and to pay fines of about $116,000.

For more information about hacker crimes and sentences, visit the Discovering Computers 2005 FAQ Web page (**scsite.com/dc2005/faq**). Click Hacker Crimes and Sentences below Chapter 11.

Safeguards against Unauthorized Access and Use

Companies take several measures to help prevent unauthorized access and use. At a minimum, they should have a written *acceptable use policy* (*AUP*) that outlines the computer activities for which the computer and network may and may not be used. A company's AUP should specify the acceptable use of computers by employees for personal reasons. Some companies prohibit such use entirely. Others allow personal use on the employee's own time such as a lunch hour. Whatever the policy, a company should document and explain it to employees.

Other measures that safeguard against unauthorized access and use include firewalls, intrusion detection software, access controls, and audit trails. The following paragraphs discuss each of these measures.

Firewalls

A **firewall** is a security system consisting of hardware and/or software that prevents unauthorized access to data, information, and storage media on a network (Figure 11-7). Companies use firewalls to deny network access to outsiders and to restrict employees' access to sensitive data such as payroll or personnel records.

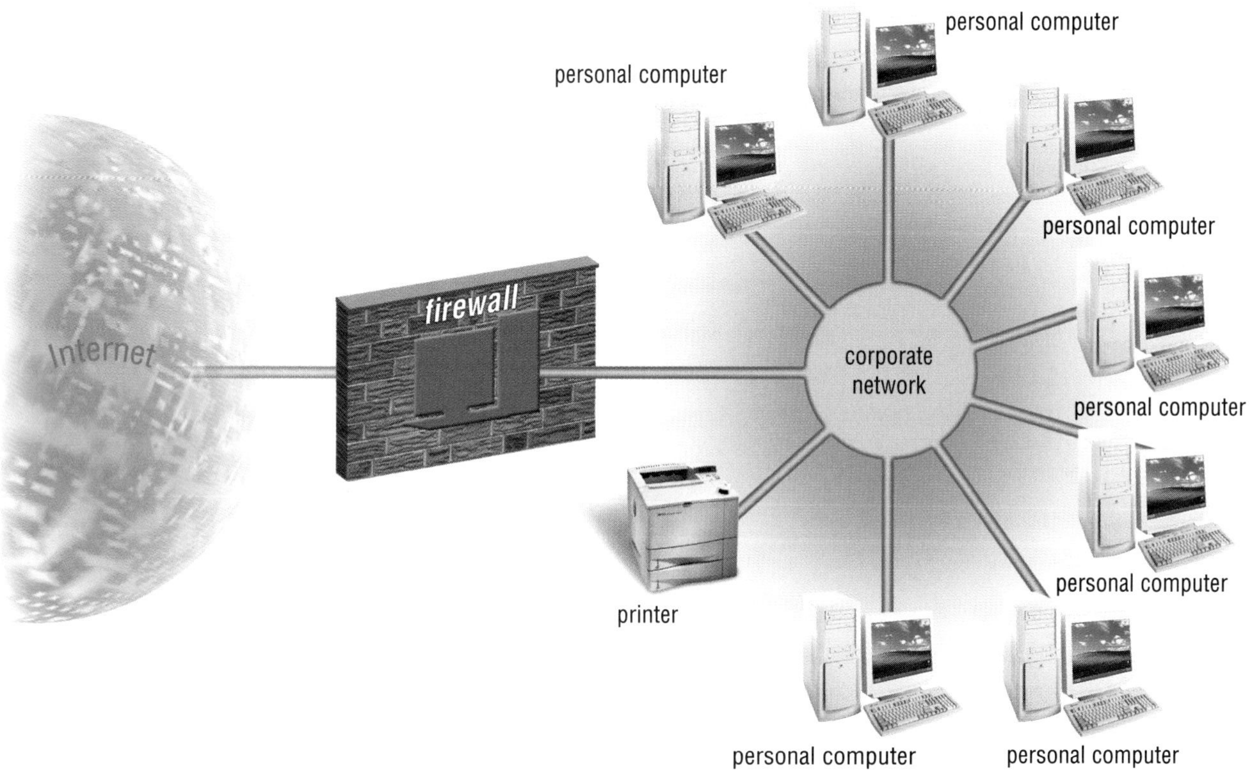

FIGURE 11-7 A firewall restricts unauthorized intruders from accessing data, information, and programs on a network.

Large companies often route all their communications through a proxy server, which is a component of the firewall. A *proxy server* is a server outside the company's network that controls which communications pass into the company's network. That is, the proxy server carefully screens all incoming and outgoing messages. Proxy servers use a variety of screening techniques. Some check the domain name or IP address of the message for legitimacy. Others require that the messages have digital signatures. A section later in this chapter discusses digital signatures.

All networked and online computer users should have a firewall. Businesses can implement a firewall solution themselves or outsource their needs to a company specializing in providing firewall protection. Home and small office/home office users should install personal firewalls.

As discussed in Chapter 8, a **personal firewall** is a utility program that detects and protects a personal computer and its data from unauthorized intrusions. Personal firewalls constantly monitor all transmissions to and from the computer and inform you of any attempted intrusion. Some operating systems, such as Windows XP, include personal firewalls. For added protection, many users purchase stand-alone personal firewall software, usually for less than $50. The table in Figure 11-8 lists popular personal firewall programs.

PERSONAL FIREWALL SOFTWARE

BlackICE PC Protection
McAfee Personal Firewall Plus
Norton Personal Firewall
Sygate Personal Firewall
Tiny Personal Firewall
ZoneAlarm

FIGURE 11-8 Popular personal firewall products.

To protect your personal computer further from unauthorized intrusions, you should disable file and printer sharing on your Internet connection (Figure 11-9). This security measure attempts to ensure that others cannot access your files or your printer. To display the dialog box shown in Figure 11-9 in Windows XP, click the Start button on the taskbar, point to All Programs, point to Accessories, point to Communications, and then click Network Connections. Right-click the appropriate network connection in the list, click Properties on the shortcut menu, and then click the Networking tab.

To determine if your computer is vulnerable to a hacker attack, you could use an online security service. An **online security service** is a Web site that evaluates your computer to check for Web and e-mail vulnerabilities. The service then provides recommendations of how to deal with the vulnerabilities.

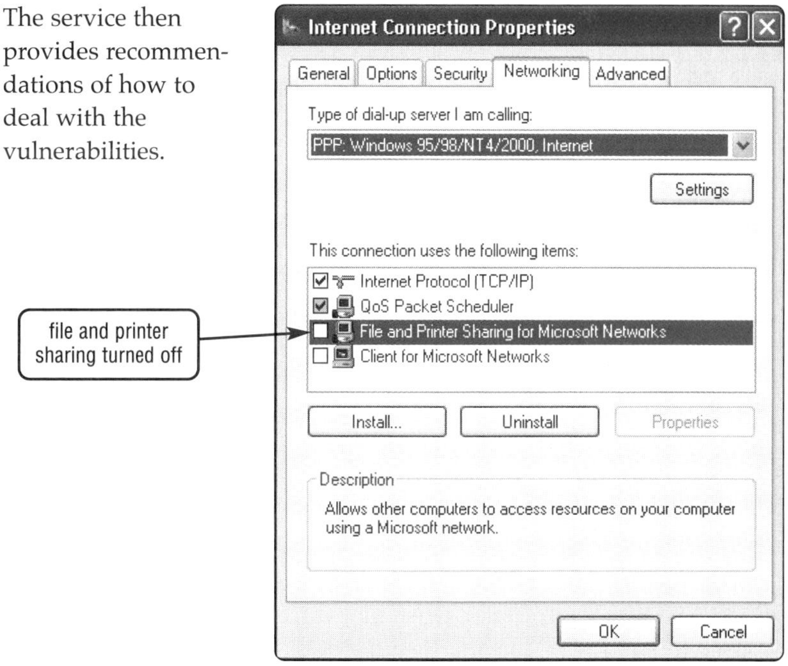

FIGURE 11-9 To protect files on your local hard disk from hackers, turn off file and print sharing on your Internet connection.

FAQ 11-3

Why would a hacker want to access my home computer?

One reason hackers access home computers is to search for personal information, for example, resumes, wills, credit card numbers, bank account numbers, and Social Security numbers. Armed with this information, a hacker can make a fraudulent purchase or obtain a loan using your name. To help prevent this type of *identify theft*, install a personal firewall.

For more information about personal firewalls, visit the Discovering Computers 2005 FAQ Web page (**scsite.com/dc2005/faq**). Click Personal Firewalls below Chapter 11.

Intrusion Detection Software

To provide extra protection against hackers, large companies sometimes use intrusion detection software to identify possible security breaches. *Intrusion detection software* automatically analyzes all network traffic, assesses system vulnerabilities, identifies any unauthorized access (intrusions), and notifies network administrators of suspicious behavior patterns or system breaches.

To utilize intrusion detection software requires the expertise of a network administrator because the programs are complex and difficult to use and interpret. These programs also are quite expensive. This software, however, when combined with a firewall, provides an added layer of protection to companies with highly sensitive data such as credit card databases.

In addition to intrusion detection software, some companies have honeypots. A *honeypot* is a program designed to entice an intruder to hack into the computer. These computers, which appear real to the intruder, actually are separated safely from the company network. Honeypots allow the company to learn how hackers are exploiting its network. They also enable the company to attempt to catch hackers who have been doing damage elsewhere on the company's network.

WEB LINK 11-2

Intrusion Detection Software

Visit the Discovering Computers 2005 WEB LINK page (**scsite .com/dc2005/weblink**). Click Intrusion Detection Software below Chapter 11.

Access Controls and Audit Trails

Many companies use access controls to minimize the chance that a hacker may intentionally access or an employee may accidentally access confidential information on a computer. An *access control* is a security measure that defines who can access a computer, when they can access it, and what actions they can take while accessing the computer. In addition, the computer should maintain an **audit trail**, or *log*, that records in a file both successful and unsuccessful access attempts. An unsuccessful access attempt could result from a user mistyping his or her password, or it could result from a hacker trying thousands of passwords.

Companies should investigate unsuccessful access attempts immediately to ensure they are not intentional breaches of security. They also should review successful access for irregularities, such as use of the computer after normal working hours or from remote computers. In addition, a company regularly should review users' access privilege levels to determine whether they still are appropriate.

Many systems implement access controls using a two-phase process called identification and authentication. *Identification* verifies that an individual is a valid user. *Authentication* verifies that the individual is the person he or she claims to be. Four methods of identification and authentication exist: user names and passwords, possessed objects, biometric devices, and callback systems. The technique(s) a company uses should correspond to the degree of risk associated with the unauthorized access. The following paragraphs discuss each of these methods.

USER NAMES AND PASSWORDS A **user name**, or *user ID* (identification), is a unique combination of characters, such as letters of the alphabet or numbers, that identifies one specific user. A **password** is a private combination of characters associated with the user name that allows access to certain computer resources.

As discussed in Chapter 8, most multiuser (networked) operating systems require that users correctly enter a user name and a password before they can access the data, information, and programs stored on a computer or network. Many other systems that maintain financial, personal, and other confidential information also require a user name and password as part of their logon procedure (Figure 11-10).

Some systems assign a user name or user ID to each user. For example, a school may use the student identification number as a user ID. With other systems, users select their own user name or user ID. Many users select a combination of their first and last names. For example, a user named Michelle Reeves might choose mreeves as her user name.

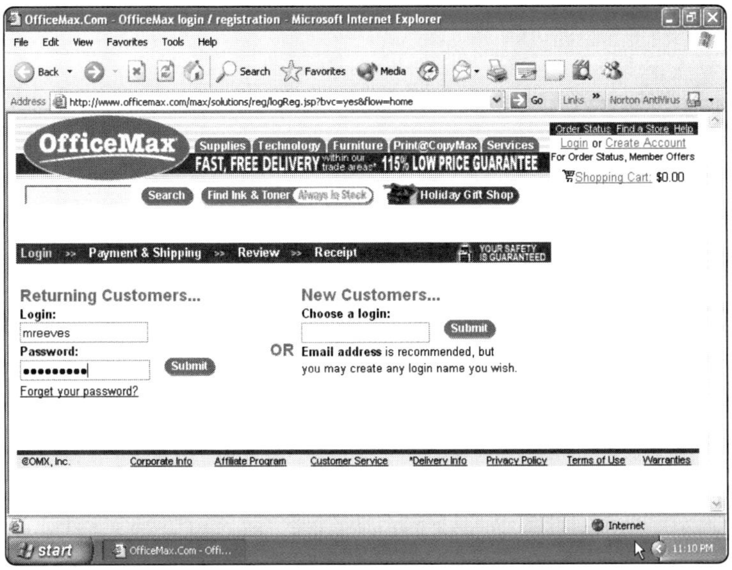

FIGURE 11-10 Many Web sites that maintain personal and confidential data require a user to enter a user name and password.

Most systems require that users select their own passwords. Users typically choose an easy-to-remember word or series of characters for passwords. If your password is too obvious, however, such as your initials or birthday, others can guess it easily. Easy passwords make it simple for hackers to break into the system. Hackers use computer automated tools to assist them with guessing passwords. Thus, you should select a password carefully. Longer passwords provide greater security than shorter ones. Each character added to a password significantly increases the number of possible combinations and the length of time it might take for someone or for a hacker's computer to guess the password (Figure 11-11). Generally, the more creative you are when selecting a password, the more difficult it is to figure out.

Most programs have general guidelines users must follow when creating their passwords. One system, for instance, may require a password be at least six characters long and contain at least one number. Following these guidelines, the password 0831 is invalid (it is too short), but STING0831 is valid. This password also is easy for the user to remember because *The Sting* is the user's favorite movie and August 31 is the user's anniversary (08/31). Although easy for the user to remember, this password is difficult for a hacker to guess easily.

PASSWORD PROTECTION

		AVERAGE TIME TO DISCOVER	
Number of Characters	**Possible Combinations**	**Human**	**Computer**
1	36	3 minutes	.000018 second
2	1,300	2 hours	.00065 second
3	47,000	3 days	.02 second
4	1,700,000	3 months	1 second
5	60,000,000	10 years	30 seconds
10	3,700,000,000,000,000	580 million years	59 years

- *Possible characters include the letters A–Z and numbers 0–9*
- *Human discovery assumes 1 try every 10 seconds*
- *Computer discovery assumes 1 million tries per second*
- *Average time assumes the password would be discovered in approximately half the time it would take to try all possible combinations*

FIGURE 11-11 This table shows the effect of increasing the length of a password that consists of letters and numbers. The longer the password, the more effort required to discover it. Long passwords, however, are more difficult for users to remember.

To provide even more protection, some systems ask users to enter one of several pieces of personal information. The question is chosen randomly from information on file. Such items can include a spouse's first name, a birth date, a place of birth, or a mother's maiden name. As with a password, if the user's response does not match the information on file, the system denies access. Read Apply It 11-1 for more information.

APPLY IT 11-1

Protecting Your Password

Your mother's maiden name often has much value to financial institutions, as it can be the password to access your accounts. This name, however, can be the key that thieves use to open the door to your private information. While passwords are beneficial to secure online banking accounts, access the network at school, and log on to your employer's computer, they also can be detrimental when they fall into the wrong hands.

The fundamental rule in choosing a password is to use one that no one could guess. The most common passwords are a spouse's, child's, or pet's name; the word, password; or the user's last name. The best passwords are something that only you would know. They should have a combination of letters and numbers, be at least eight characters (if supported by the software), and be something you can type without looking at the keyboard.

Once you select a password, change it frequently. Do not disclose it to anyone or write it on a slip of paper kept near the computer, especially under the keyboard. E-mail and telemarketing scams often ask unsuspecting users to disclose this password, so be wary if you did not initiate the inquiry or telephone call.

For more information about passwords, visit the Discovering Computers 2005 Apply It Web page (**scsite.com/dc2005/apply**). Click Apply It #1 below Chapter 11.

POSSESSED OBJECTS A *possessed object* is any item that you must carry to gain access to a computer or computer facility. Examples of possessed objects are badges, cards, smart cards, and keys. The card you use in an automated teller machine (ATM) is a possessed object that allows access to your bank account (Figure 11-12).

FIGURE 11-12 The card you use in an automated teller machine (ATM) is a possessed object that allows access to your bank account.

Possessed objects often are used in combination with personal identification numbers. A **personal identification number (PIN)** is a numeric password, either assigned by a company or selected by a user. PINs provide an additional level of security. An ATM card typically requires a four-digit PIN. Most debit cards and some credit cards now even use PINs. If someone steals these cards, the thief must enter the user's PIN to access the account. PINs are passwords. Select them carefully and protect them as you do any other password.

BIOMETRIC DEVICES As discussed in Chapter 5, a **biometric device** authenticates a person's identity by translating a personal characteristic, such as a fingerprint, into a digital code that is then compared with a digital code stored in the computer verifying a physical or behavioral characteristic. If the digital code in the computer does not match the personal characteristic code, the computer denies access to the individual.

Biometric devices grant access to programs, computers, or rooms using computer analysis of some biometric identifier. Examples of biometric devices and systems include fingerprint scanners (Figure 11-13), hand geometry systems, face recognition systems, voice verification systems, signature verification systems, and iris recognition systems.

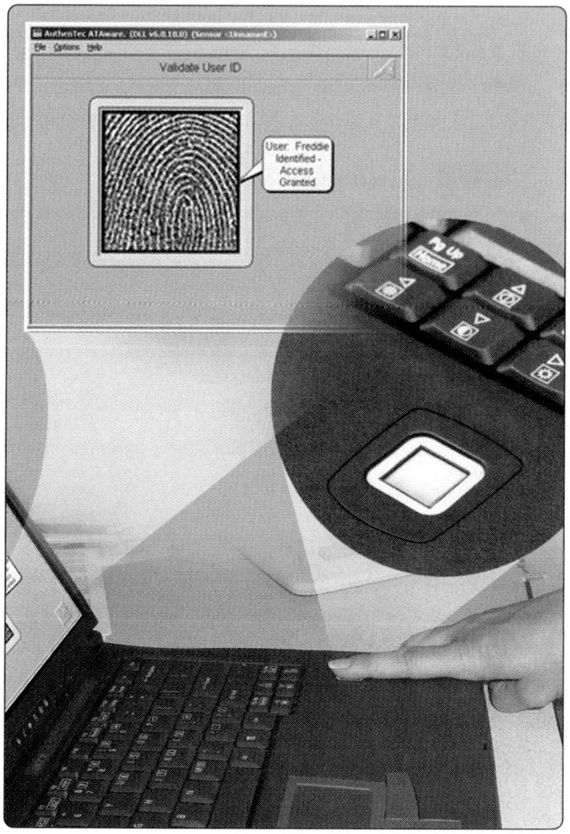

FIGURE 11-13 Many people believe fingerprint scanners will become the authentication device for notebook computers.

Biometric devices are gaining popularity as a security precaution because they are a virtually foolproof method of identification and authentication. Users can forget their user names and passwords. Possessed objects can be lost, copied, duplicated, or stolen. Personal characteristics, by contrast, are unique and cannot be forgotten or misplaced.

Biometric devices do have some disadvantages. If you cut your finger, a fingerprint scanner might reject you as a legitimate user. Hand geometry readers can transmit germs. If you are nervous, a signature might not match the one on file. If you have a sore throat, a voice recognition system might reject you. Many people are uncomfortable with the thought of using an iris scanner.

CALLBACK SYSTEM With a *callback system*, a user connects to a computer only after the computer calls that user back at a previously established telephone number. Some networks utilize callback systems as an access control method to authenticate remote or mobile users.

To initiate the callback system, you call a computer and enter a user name and password. If these entries are valid, the computer instructs you to hang up and then calls you back. A callback system provides an added layer of security. Even if a person steals or guesses a user name and password, that person also must be at the authorized telephone number to access the computer.

Callback systems work best for users who regularly work at the same remote location such as from home or a branch office. Mobile users who need to access a computer from different locations and telephone numbers can use a callback system, but they have to change the callback number stored by the callback system each time they move to a different location.

HARDWARE THEFT AND VANDALISM

Hardware theft and vandalism are another type of computer security risk. **Hardware theft** is the act of stealing computer equipment. **Hardware vandalism** is the act of defacing or destroying computer equipment. Hardware vandalism takes many forms, from someone cutting a computer cable to individuals breaking into a business or school computer lab and aimlessly smashing computers.

Hardware theft and vandalism do not really pose a threat to the home computer user. Companies and schools and other organizations that house many computers, however, are at risk to hardware theft and vandalism. Mobile users also are susceptible to hardware theft. Increasingly, businesses and schools provide or loan out notebook computers to employees and students.

It is estimated that more than one-half million notebook computers are stolen each year. The size and weight of these computers make them easy to steal. Thieves often target notebook computers of company executives, so they can use the stolen computer to access confidential company information illegally.

Safeguards against Hardware Theft and Vandalism

To help reduce the chances of theft, companies and schools use a variety of security measures. Physical access controls, such as locked doors and windows, usually are adequate to protect the equipment. Many businesses, schools, and some homeowners install alarm systems for additional security. School computer labs and other areas with a large number of semifrequent users often attach additional physical security devices such as cables that lock the equipment to a desk (Figure 11-14), cabinet, or floor. Small locking devices also exist that require a key to access a hard disk, CD or DVD drive, or floppy disk drive.

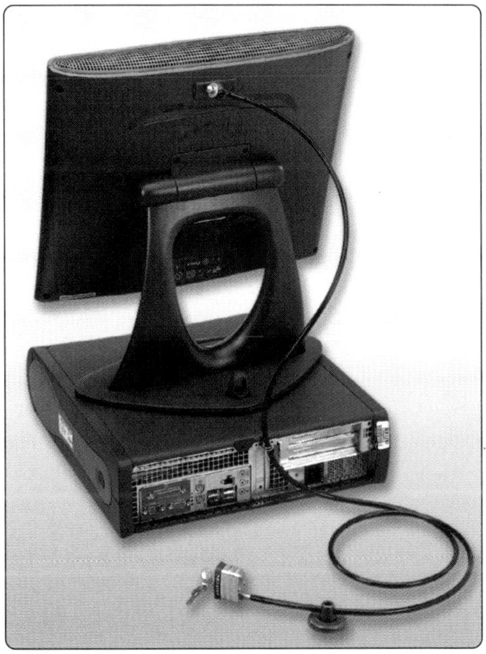

FIGURE 11-14 Using cables to lock computers can help prevent the theft of computer equipment.

Mobile computer users must take special care to protect their equipment. The best preventive measures are common sense and a constant awareness of the risk. For example, never leave a notebook computer or PDA unattended in a public place such as an airport or a restaurant or out in the open such as on the seat of a car.

Some users attach a physical device such as a cable to lock a mobile computer temporarily to a stationary object. For example, a hotel guest could lock a notebook computer to a desk or table in a hotel room when he or she leaves the room. Other mobile users install a mini-security system in the notebook computer. Some of these security systems shut down the computer and sound an alarm if the computer moves outside a specified distance. Others can track the location of the stolen notebook computer.

Some notebook computers use passwords, possessed objects, and biometrics as methods of security. When you boot up these computers, you must enter a password, slide a card in a card reader, or press your finger on a fingerprint scanner before the hard disk unlocks. This type of security does not prevent theft, but it renders the computer useless if it is stolen. As a precaution against theft, you should back up the files stored on your notebook computer regularly.

For PDAs, you also can password-protect the device. This allows only authorized users to access its data. You usually can instruct the password screen to display your name and telephone number, so a Good Samaritan can return it to you if lost. Several models allow you to encrypt data in the device. A later section in this chapter discusses encryption.

QUIZ YOURSELF 11-1

To check your knowledge of the types of computer security risks; safeguards against viruses, worms, and Trojan horses; preventing unauthorized computer access and use; and safeguards against hardware theft and vandalism, visit the Discovering Computers 2005 Quiz Yourself Web page (**scsite.com/dc2005/quiz**). Click Objectives 1 – 4 below Chapter 11.

SOFTWARE THEFT

Another type of computer security risk is software theft. As with hardware theft and vandalism, software theft can take many forms. **Software theft** occurs when someone steals software media, intentionally erases programs, or illegally copies a program.

The first type of software theft involves someone physically stealing the media that contain the software. For example, an unscrupulous library patron might steal the Microsoft Encarta Encyclopedia CD-ROM. Another type of software theft can occur when a programmer is terminated from, or stops working for, a company. Although the programs are company property, some dishonest programmers intentionally remove the programs they have written from company computers.

Software also can be stolen from software manufacturers. This type of theft, called piracy, is by far the most common form of software theft. Software **piracy** is the unauthorized and illegal duplication of copyrighted software.

Safeguards against Software Theft

To protect software media from being stolen, owners should keep original software boxes and media in a secure location, out of sight of prying eyes. When some companies terminate a programmer or if the programmer quits, they escort the employee off the premises immediately. These companies believe that allowing terminated employees to remain on the premises gives them time to sabotage files and other network procedures.

To protect themselves from software piracy, software manufacturers issue users license agreements. A **license agreement** is the right to use the software. That is, you do not own the software. The license agreement provides specific conditions for use of the software, which a user must accept before using the software (Figure 11-15). These terms usually are displayed when you install the software. In the case of software on the Web, the terms are displayed on a page at the manufacturer's Web site. Use of the software constitutes acceptance of the terms on the user's part.

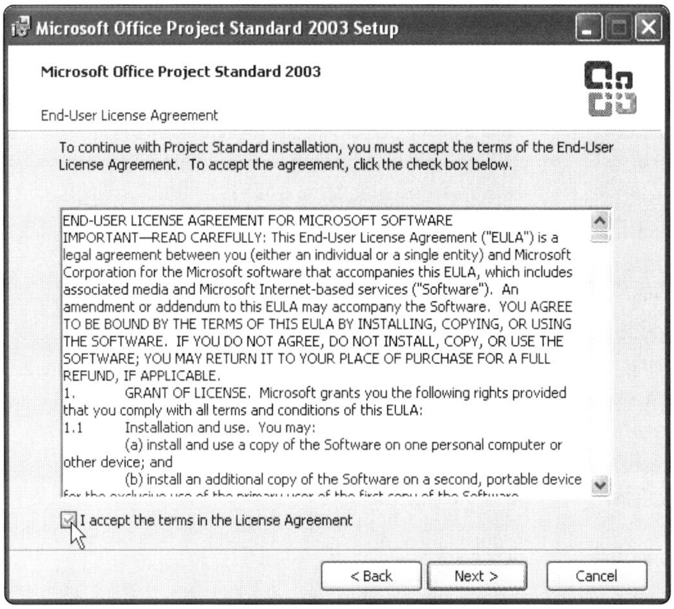

FIGURE 11-15 A user must accept the terms in the license agreement before using the software.

The most common type of license included with software purchased by individual users is a *single-user license agreement*, also called an *end-user license agreement* (*EULA*). A single-user license agreement typically includes many of the following conditions that specify a user's responsibility upon acceptance of the agreement.

Users are permitted to:

- Install the software on only one computer. (Some license agreements allow users to install the software on one desktop computer and one notebook computer.)
- Make one copy of the software as a backup.
- Give or sell the software to another individual, but only if the software is removed from the user's computer first.

Users are not permitted to:

- Install the software on a network, such as a school computer lab.
- Give copies to friends and colleagues, while continuing to use the software.
- Export the software.
- Rent or lease the software.

Unless otherwise specified by a license agreement, you do not have the right to copy, loan, borrow, rent, or in any way distribute software. Doing so is a violation of copyright law. It also is a federal crime. Despite this, some experts estimate for every authorized copy of software in use, at least one unauthorized copy exists.

Software piracy continues for several reasons. In some countries, legal protection for software does not exist. In other countries, laws rarely are enforced. In addition, many buyers believe they have the right to copy the software for which they pay hundreds, even thousands, of dollars. Finally, software piracy is a fairly simple crime to commit. Read Issue 11-1 for a related discussion.

Software piracy, however, is a serious offense. For one, it introduces a number of risks into the software market. It increases the chance of spreading viruses, reduces your ability to receive technical support, and drives up the price of software for all users. Further, software companies take illegal copying seriously. In some cases, offenders have been prosecuted to the fullest extent of the law with penalties including fines up to $250,000 and five years in jail.

To promote a better understanding of software piracy problems and, if necessary, to take legal action, a number of major worldwide software companies formed the *Business Software Alliance* (*BSA*). The BSA operates a Web site and antipiracy hotlines in the United States and more than 60 other countries.

WEB LINK 11-3

Software Piracy

Visit the Discovering Computers 2005 WEB LINK page (**scsite .com/dc2005/weblink**). Click Software Piracy below Chapter 11.

WEB LINK 11-4

Business Software Alliance

Visit the Discovering Computers 2005 WEB LINK page (**scsite .com/dc2005/weblink**). Click Business Software Alliance below Chapter 11.

ISSUE 11-1

Is That Software Legal?

Web sites post hundreds of software applications that are sold in stores. The programs can be downloaded by anyone with access to the Internet. Software on the Web may be sold, or it may be traded so that no money changes hands. According to the Business Software Alliance (BSA), approximately 840,000 Internet sites sell pirated software. An investigation found that more than 90 percent of the software at Internet auction sites was exchanged in violation of the end-user license agreement. One expert estimates that software publishers lose more than $100 billion through the illegal buying and trading of software on the Internet. Swapping $2,500 in software is punishable by as much as 3 years in jail, but who should be indicted for illegal software exchanges on the Web? The creator of the Web site? The people who download software? Both? What, if any, responsibility should Internet auction sites have for the software they offer? Why?

For more information about illegal software on the Web, visit the Discovering Computers 2005 Issues Web page (**scsite.com/dc2005/issues**). Click Issue #1 below Chapter 11.

In an attempt to prevent software piracy, Microsoft has incorporated an activation process into many of its consumer products. During the **product activation**, which is conducted either online or by telephone, users provide the software product's 25-character identification number to receive an installation identification number unique to the computer on which the software is installed.

Many organizations and businesses also have strict written policies governing the installation and use of software and enforce their rules by checking networked or online computers periodically to ensure that all software is licensed properly. If you are not completely familiar with your school or employer's policies governing installation of software, check with the information technology department or your school's technology coordinator.

INFORMATION THEFT

Information theft is yet another type of computer security risk. As discussed in Chapter 10, information is a valuable asset to a company. **Information theft** occurs when someone steals personal or confidential information. If stolen, the loss of information can cause as much damage as (if not more than) hardware or software theft. According to a major survey, information theft is one of the "Top Ten Security Threats Facing Corporate America."

Both business and home users can fall victim to information theft. An unethical company executive may steal or buy stolen information to learn about a competitor. A corrupt individual may steal credit card numbers to make fraudulent purchases. Information theft often is linked to other types of computer crime. For example, an individual first might gain unauthorized access to a computer and then steal credit card numbers stored in a firm's accounting department. Read Issue 11-2 for a discussion about a different form of information theft.

ISSUE 11-2

How Should Schools Deal with Internet Plagiarism?

A high school teacher in Kansas failed 28 students for plagiarizing material from the Internet. When parents complained, the school board passed the students and the teacher resigned. Plagiarism is not new, but the Internet has made it easier than ever. One study reported that 74 percent of high school students have cheated or plagiarized. A second study showed that more than 35 percent of college students had copied material from Internet sources. Students who plagiarize blame peer pressure, classroom competition, and the anarchistic attitude that pervades the Internet. Some educators feel plagiarizing is unfair to students who do not cheat, and that students caught should be punished. Yet, others believe it is not their job to investigate the integrity of a student's work and possibly ruin an academic career. How should educators deal with plagiarism? Why? Should a school's response to plagiarism depend on such factors as the material copied, the assignment for which it was copied, or the reason it was copied? Why or why not?

For more information about Web plagiarism, visit the Discovering Computers 2005 Issues Web page (**scsite.com/dc2005/issues**). Click Issue #2 below Chapter 11.

Safeguards against Information Theft

Most companies attempt to prevent information theft by implementing the user identification and authentication controls discussed earlier in this chapter. These controls are best suited for protecting information on computers located on a company's premises. Information transmitted over networks offers a higher degree of risk because unscrupulous users can intercept it during transmission.

One way to protect sensitive data and information is to encrypt it. **Encryption** is a process of converting readable data into unreadable characters to prevent unauthorized access. You treat encrypted data just like any other data. That is, you can store it or send it in an e-mail message. To read the data, the recipient must **decrypt**, or decipher, it into a readable form.

In the encryption process, the unencrypted, readable data is called *plaintext*. The encrypted (scrambled) data is called *ciphertext*. To encrypt the data, the originator of the data converts the plaintext into ciphertext using a password or an encryption key. In its simplest form, an *encryption key* is a programmed formula that the recipient of the data uses to decrypt ciphertext.

Many data encryption methods exist. Figure 11-16 shows examples of some simple encryption methods. Figure 11-17 shows the contents of a sample encrypted file. An encryption key (formula) often uses more than one of these methods, such as a combination of transposition and substitution. For a more technical discussion about encryption, read the High-Tech Talk article on page 603.

Most organizations use available software for encryption. Others develop their own encryption programs.

Many mobile users today access their company networks through a virtual private network. When a mobile user connects to a main office using a standard Internet connection, a *virtual private network* (*VPN*) provides the mobile user with a secure connection to the company network server, as if the user has a private line. VPNs help ensure that data is safe from being intercepted by unauthorized people by encrypting data as it transmits from a notebook computer, Tablet PC, PDA, or other mobile device.

WEB LINK 11-5

Encryption

Visit the Discovering Computers 2005 WEB LINK page (**scsite .com/dc2005/weblink**). Click Encryption below Chapter 11.

SAMPLE ENCRYPTION METHODS

Name	Method	Plaintext	Ciphertext	Explanation
Transposition	Switch the order of characters	PASSWORD	APSSOWDR	Adjacent characters swapped
Substitution	Replace characters with other characters	ACCESS	DRROYY	Each letter replaced with another
Expansion	Insert characters between existing characters	VIRUS	XVXIXRXUXS	Letter X inserted before each character
Compaction	Remove characters and store elsewhere	IDENTIFICATION	IDNTFIATON	Every third letter removed (E, I, C, I)

FIGURE 11-16 This table shows four simple methods of encryption, which is the process of translating plaintext into ciphertext. Most encryption programs use a combination of these four methods.

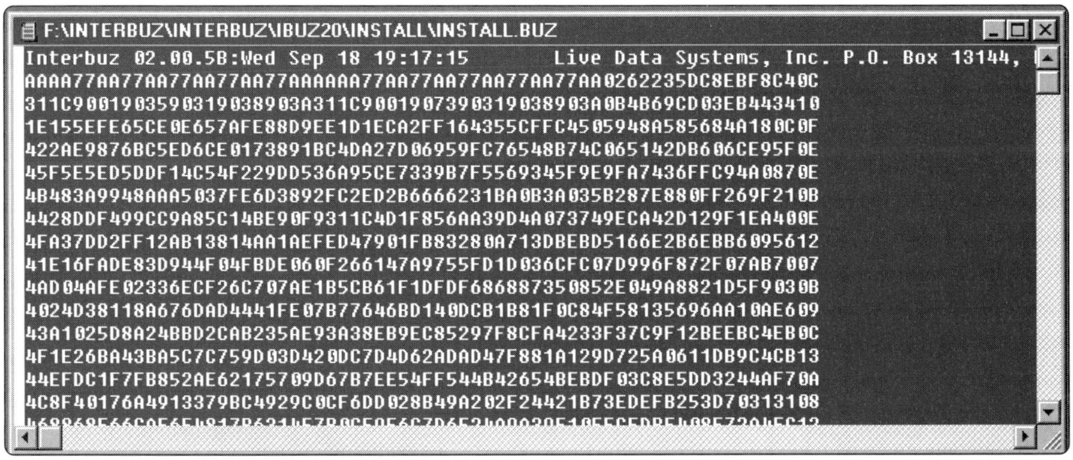

FIGURE 11-17 A sample encrypted file.

SYSTEM FAILURE

System failure is yet another type of computer security risk. A *system failure* is the prolonged malfunction of a computer. System failure also can cause loss of hardware, software, data, or information. A variety of causes can lead to system failure. These include aging hardware; natural disasters such as fires, floods, or hurricanes; random events such as electrical power problems; and even errors in computer programs (read Issue 11-3 for a related discussion).

One of the more common causes of system failure is an electrical power variation. Electrical power variations can cause loss of data or loss of equipment. If the computer equipment is networked, a single power disturbance can damage multiple systems. Electrical disturbances include noise, undervoltages, and overvoltages.

Noise is any unwanted signal, usually varying quickly, that is mixed with the normal voltage entering the computer. Noise is caused by external devices such as fluorescent lighting, radios, and televisions, as well as by components within the computer itself. Noise generally is not a risk to hardware, software, or data. Computer power supplies, however, do filter out noise.

An **undervoltage** occurs when the electrical supply drops. In North America, a wall plug usually supplies electricity at approximately 120 volts. Any significant drop below 120 volts is an undervoltage. A *brownout* is a prolonged undervoltage. A *blackout* is a complete power failure. Undervoltages can cause data loss but generally do not cause equipment damage.

ISSUE 11-3

Who Should Pay for Software Bugs?

Xerox, a major supplier of office equipment and supplies, traced three major network outages to installation of the prerelease version of a new operating system. Not surprisingly, Xerox subsequently banned the software throughout the company. A major research firm estimates that bugs (errors) and defects in operating systems and application programs cost companies $85 billion a year in lost revenue due to system downtime. When the possible impact on network security and customer loyalty is taken into account, the consequences are even more serious. Many failures and security compromises are a result of bugs in application software or the underlying operating system. Should software providers be held accountable for financial damages due to bugs? Why or why not? When someone is hurt in an automobile accident because of a car's faulty design or a flawed part, the automobile manufacturer can be sued for criminal negligence. In a similar way, should software providers be liable for defects in their products? Why?

For more information about software bugs, visit the Discovering Computers 2005 Issues Web page (**scsite.com/dc2005/issues**). Click Issue #3 below Chapter 11.

An **overvoltage**, or **power surge**, occurs when the incoming electrical power increases significantly above the normal 120 volts. A momentary overvoltage, called a *spike*, occurs when the increase in power lasts for less than one millisecond (one thousandth of a second). Uncontrollable disturbances such as lightning bolts cause spikes. Overvoltages can cause immediate and permanent damage to hardware.

Safeguards against System Failure

To protect against overvoltages, use a surge protector. A **surge protector**, also called a *surge suppressor*, uses special electrical components to smooth out minor noise, provide a stable current flow, and keep an overvoltage from reaching the computer and other electronic equipment (Figure 11-18). Sometimes resembling a power strip, the computer and other devices plug into the surge protector, which plugs into the power source. The surge protector absorbs small overvoltages — generally without damage to the computer and equipment. To protect the computer and other equipment from large overvoltages, such as those caused by a lightning strike, some surge protectors completely stop working when an overvoltage reaches a certain level.

FIGURE 11-18 Circuits inside a surge protector safeguard against overvoltages and undervoltages.

No surge protectors are 100 percent effective. Large power surges can bypass the protector. Repeated small overvoltages can weaken a surge protector permanently. Some experts recommend replacing a surge protector every two to three years. Typically, the amount of protection offered by a surge protector is proportional to its cost. That is, the more expensive, the more protection the protector offers.

The surge protector you purchase should meet the safety specification for surge suppression products. This specification, which is called the *Underwriters Laboratories (UL) 1449 standard*, allows no more than 500 maximum volts to pass through the line. The response time of the surge protector should be less than one nanosecond. The surge protector also should have a Joule rating of at least 200. A *Joule* is the unit of energy a surge protection device can absorb before it can be damaged. The higher the Joule rating, the better the protection.

If your computer connects to a network or the Internet, also be sure to have protection for your modem, telephone lines, DSL lines, Internet cable lines, and network lines. Many surge protectors include plug-ins for telephone lines and other cables. If yours does not, you can purchase separate devices to protect these lines.

For additional electrical protection, some applications connect an uninterruptible power supply to the computer. An **uninterruptible power supply (UPS)** is a device that contains surge protection circuits and one or more batteries that can provide power during a temporary or permanent loss of power (Figure 11-19). A UPS connects between your computer and a power source. UPS software can shut down computers cleanly if power is removed for a pre-specified number of minutes.

FIGURE 11-19 If power fails, an uninterruptible power supply (UPS) uses batteries to provide electricity for a limited amount of time.

Two types of UPS devices are standby and online. A *standby UPS*, sometimes called an *offline UPS*, switches to battery power when a problem occurs in the power line. The amount of time a standby UPS allows a user to continue working depends on the electrical requirements of the computer and the size of the batteries in the UPS. A UPS for a personal computer should provide from 10 to 30 minutes of use in the event of a total power loss. This should be enough time to save current work and shut down the computer properly. An *online UPS* always runs off the battery, which provides continuous protection. An online UPS is much more expensive than a standby UPS.

Some companies use duplicate components or computers to protect against system failure. A *fault-tolerant computer* has duplicate components so it can continue to operate when one of its main components fail. Companies that must have their computers operational at all times may have two separate duplicate computers running simultaneously. Airline reservation systems, communications networks, and automated teller machines are examples of systems that duplicate components or computers to ensure that no data is lost in the event of a system failure.

FAQ 11-4

Should I use a surge protector on all my electronics?

It is a good idea to use a surge protector on high-end, expensive electronic equipment such as entertainment systems, DVD players, fax machines, and copy machines. A lightning strike or other substantial power surge could cause damage to any of this equipment.

For more information about surge protectors, visit the Discovering Computers 2005 FAQ Web page (**scsite.com/dc2005/faq**). Click Surge Protectors below Chapter 11.

WEB LINK 11-6

Uninterruptible Power Supply

Visit the Discovering Computers 2005 WEB LINK page (**scsite .com/dc2005/weblink**). Click Uninterruptible Power Supply below Chapter 11.

BACKING UP — THE ULTIMATE SAFEGUARD

To prevent against data loss caused by a system failure, computer users should back up files regularly. A **backup** is a duplicate of a file, program, or disk that can be used if the original is lost, damaged, or destroyed. Thus, to **back up** a file means to make a copy of it. In the case of a system failure or the discovery of corrupted files, you **restore** the files by copying the backed up files to their original location on the computer.

You can use just about any media to store backups. Be sure to use high-quality media. Losing data is expensive. High-quality media are worth the investment. A good choice for a home user might be Zip disks, CD-RWs, or DVD+RWs.

Keep backup copies in a fireproof and heatproof safe or vault, or offsite. *Offsite* means in a location separate from the computer site. Home and business users keep backup copies offsite so that a single disaster, such as a fire, does not destroy both the original and the backup copy of the data. An offsite location can be a safe deposit box at a bank or a briefcase. A growing trend is to use an Internet hard drive as an offsite location. As discussed in Chapter 7, an Internet hard drive, or online storage, is a service on the Web that provides storage to computer users.

Most backup programs for the home user provide for a full backup and a selective backup. A *full backup* copies all of the files in the computer. Because programs can reinstall from their installation CD or DVD, many users opt to do selective backups. With a *selective backup*, users choose which folders and files to include in a backup.

Some users implement a *three-generation backup* policy to preserve three copies of important files. The *grandparent* is the oldest copy of the file. The *parent* is the second oldest copy of the file. The *child* is the most recent copy of the file.

Backup programs are available from many sources. Most operating systems include a backup program. Backup devices, such as tape and removable disk drives, also include backup programs. Numerous stand-alone backup utilities exist. Many of these can be downloaded from the Web at no cost. As discussed in Chapter 8, some vendors offer utility suites that combine several utility programs into a single package or make them available on the Web. These suites typically include a backup utility.

Some companies choose to use an online backup service to handle their backup needs. An *online backup service* is a Web site that automatically backs up files to its online location. These sites usually charge a monthly or annual fee. If the system crashes, the online backup service typically sends the company one or more CD-ROMs that contains all its backed up data. Users with high-speed Internet connections opt for online backup services. For slower connections, these services are not practical.

INTERNET SECURITY RISKS

Information transmitted over networks has a higher degree of security risk than information kept on a company's premises. In a business, the network administrators usually take measures to protect a network from security risks. Many of the techniques include safeguards discussed thus far such as firewalls, intrusion detection systems, encryption, user names, passwords, biometrics, callback systems, and backups.

On the Internet, where no central administrator is present, the security risk is greater. Every computer along the path of your data can see what you send and receive (read Looking Ahead 11-1 for a look at the next generation of Internet security risks). Fortunately, most Web browsers and many Web sites also use techniques to keep data secure and private.

Additional risks associated with large networks and the Internet include denial of service attacks, unsecured business transactions, and unsecured e-mail messages. The following pages address these risks and suggest measures businesses and individuals can take to protect their computers while on the Internet.

LOOKING AHEAD 11-1

Cyberterrorism Attack Threatens Networks

Organized threats to attack corporate and government networks are a reality, according to some security professionals. The extensive damage might destroy the nation's air traffic control system, electricity-generating companies, or telecommunications infrastructure. Such action most likely would require a team of individuals with computer networking expertise, millions of dollars, and several years of planning.

Only slightly more than one-half of United States corporations, however, are protected to fight these attacks, according to the Internet Security Alliance. One method of fighting cyberterrorism might be by using *brain fingerprinting*, also known as computerized knowledge assessment. In this security system, individuals are attached to sensors while they are shown a series of words, pictures, or video images, such as a crime scene or anthrax handling procedures. If they are familiar with an image, their brains create a particular brainwave pattern that cannot be faked or controlled; if they are unfamiliar with an image, they produce a different brainwave pattern.

In less than 10 minutes, people can be tested without human intervention. Their brainwave patterns can be recorded and stored, and a risk profile can be created. Some security experts advocate requiring testing for people applying for U.S. visas. Privacy experts, on the other hand, believe government agencies might misuse the screening procedures and that terrorists might be able to fool the system.

For a look at the next generation of cyberterrorism, visit the Discovering Computers 2005 Looking Ahead Web page (**scsite.com/dc2005/looking**). Click Looking Ahead #1 below Chapter 11.

Denial of Service Attacks

A **denial of service attack**, or **DoS attack**, is an assault on a computer whose purpose is to disrupt access to the Web. Malicious hackers carry out a DoS attack in a variety of ways. For example, they may use an unsuspecting computer to send an influx of confusing data messages or useless traffic to a computer network. The victim computer network eventually jams, blocking legitimate visitors from accessing the network.

A more devastating type of DoS attack is the *DDoS (distributed DoS) attack*, in which multiple unsuspecting computers are used to attack multiple computer networks. DDoS attacks have been able to stop operations temporarily at several Web sites, including powerhouses such as Yahoo!, Amazon.com, eBay, and CNN.com.

The computer that a hacker uses to execute the DoS or DDoS attack, known as a *zombie*, is completely unaware that it is being used to attack other systems. Many of the latest antivirus and firewall programs include provisions to protect from DoS and DDoS attacks.

Companies and individuals requiring assistance or information about DDoS attacks and other Internet security breaches can contact or visit the Web site for the *Computer Emergency Response Team Coordination Center*, or *CERT/CC*, which is a federally funded research and development center.

WEB LINK 11-7

Computer Emergency Response Team Coordination Center

Visit the Discovering Computers 2005 WEB LINK page (**scsite.com/dc2005/weblink**). Click Computer Emergency Response Team Coordination Center below Chapter 11.

Securing Internet Transactions

To attempt to provide secure data transmission, many Web browsers use encryption. For example, recent versions of Netscape Navigator and Microsoft Internet Explorer use encryption. Some browsers offer a protection level known as *40-bit encryption*. Many also offer *128-bit encryption*, which is an even higher level of protection because it has a longer encryption key. Applications requiring more security, such as banks, brokerage firms, or online retailers that use credit card or other financial information, require 128-bit encryption.

A Web site that uses encryption techniques to secure its data is known as a **secure site**. Secure sites use digital certificates along with a security protocol. Two popular security protocols are Secure Sockets Layer and Secure HTTP. Credit card transactions sometimes use the Secure Electronics Transactions Specification. The following paragraphs discuss each of these encryption techniques.

DIGITAL CERTIFICATES A **digital certificate** is a notice that guarantees a user or a Web site is legitimate. E-commerce applications commonly use digital certificates.

A *certificate authority* (*CA*) is an authorized person or company that issues and verifies digital certificates. Users apply for a digital certificate from a CA (Figure 11-20). A digital certificate typically contains information such as the user's name, the issuing CA's name and signature, and the serial number of the certificate. The information in a digital certificate is encrypted.

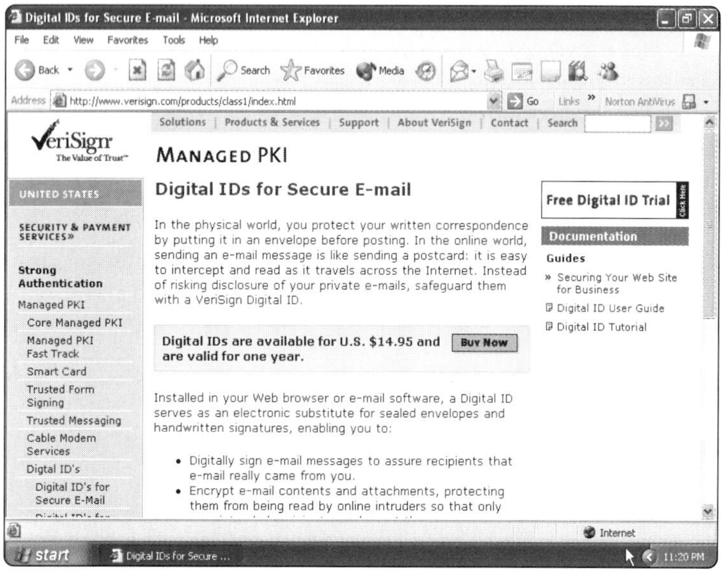

FIGURE 11-20 VeriSign is a certificate authority that issues and verifies digital certificates.

SECURE SOCKETS LAYER *Secure Sockets Layer* (*SSL*) provides encryption of all data that passes between a client and an Internet server. SSL requires the client have a digital certificate. Once the server has a digital certificate, the Web browser communicates securely with the client. Web addresses of pages that use SSL typically begin with https, instead of http (Figure 11-21). SSL is available in both 40-bit and 128-bit encryption.

SECURE HTTP *Secure HTTP* (*S-HTTP*) allows users to choose an encryption scheme for data that passes between a client and a server. With S-HTTP, the client and server both must have digital certificates. S-HTTP is more difficult to use than SSL, but it is more secure. Applications that must verify the authenticity of a client, such as for online banking, use S-HTTP.

SECURE ELECTRONICS TRANSACTIONS The *Secure Electronics Transactions* (*SET*) *Specification* uses encryption to secure financial transactions on the Internet, such as payment by credit card. To make purchases through a Web site that uses SET, the users typically download a *wallet program*, which stores their credit card information on their computer, and then select the wallet as the method of payment. The SET Specification is quite complex, making it slow on some computers.

Securing E-Mail Messages

When users send an e-mail message over the Internet, they never know who might intercept it, who might read it, or to whom it might be forwarded. If a message contains personal or confidential information, users should protect the message. An unprotected e-mail message sent over the Internet is similar to sending a postcard through the United States mail. Two ways you can protect an e-mail message are to encrypt it and to sign it digitally.

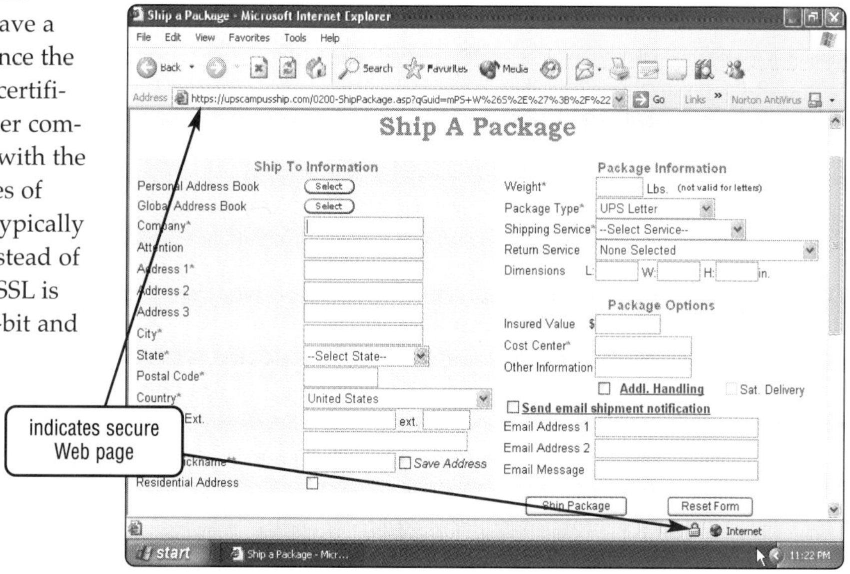

FIGURE 11-21 Web addresses of secure Web pages often begin with https instead of http.

One of the more popular e-mail encryption programs is called *Pretty Good Privacy* (*PGP*). PGP is freeware for personal, noncommercial users. Home users can download PGP from the Web at no cost.

A **digital signature** is an encrypted code that a person, Web site, or company attaches to an electronic message to verify the identity of the message sender. The code usually consists of the user's name and a hash of all or part of the message. A *hash* is a mathematical formula that generates a code from the contents of the message. Thus, the hash differs for each message. Receivers of the message decrypt the digital signature. The recipient then generates a new hash of the received message and compares it with one in the digital signature to ensure they match.

Digital signatures often are used to ensure that an impostor is not participating in an Internet transaction. That is, digital signatures help to prevent e-mail forgery. A digital signature also can verify that the content of a message has not changed.

QUIZ YOURSELF 11-2

To check your knowledge of software piracy, encryption, protection against system failure, backing up, and Internet security risks, visit the Discovering Computers 2005 Quiz Yourself Web page (**scsite.com/dc2005/quiz**). Click Objectives 5 – 9 below Chapter 11.

ETHICS AND SOCIETY

As with any powerful technology, computers can be used for both good and bad intentions. The standards that determine whether an action is good or bad are known as ethics.

Computer ethics are the moral guidelines that govern the use of computers and information systems. Six frequently discussed areas of computer ethics are unauthorized use of computers and networks, software theft (piracy), information accuracy, intellectual property rights, codes of conduct, and information privacy. The questionnaire in Figure 11-22 raises issues in each of these areas.

Previous sections in this chapter discussed unauthorized use of computers and networks, and software theft (piracy). The following pages discuss issues related to information accuracy, intellectual property rights, codes of conduct, and information privacy.

WEB LINK 11-8

PGP

Visit the Discovering Computers 2005 WEB LINK page (**scsite.com/dc2005/weblink**). Click PGP below Chapter 11.

	Ethical	Unethical
1. A company requires employees to wear badges that track their whereabouts while at work.	☐	☐
2. A supervisor reads an employee's e-mail.	☐	☐
3. An employee uses his computer at work to send e-mail messages to a friend.	☐	☐
4. An employee sends an e-mail message to several coworkers and blind copies his supervisor.	☐	☐
5. An employee forwards an e-mail message to a third party without permission from the sender.	☐	☐
6. An employee uses her computer at work to complete a homework assignment for school.	☐	☐
7. The vice president of your Student Government Association (SGA) downloads a photograph from the Web and uses it in a flier recruiting SGA members.	☐	☐
8. A student copies text from the Web and uses it in a research paper for his English Composition class.	☐	☐
9. An employee sends political campaign material to individuals on her employer's mailing list.	☐	☐
10. As an employee in the registration office, you have access to student grades. You look up grades for your friends, so they do not have to wait for delivery of grade reports from the postal service.	☐	☐
11. An employee makes a copy of software and installs it on her home computer. No one uses her home computer while she is at work, and she uses her home computer only to finish projects from work.	☐	☐
12. An employee who has been laid off installs a computer virus on his employer's computer.	☐	☐
13. A person designing a Web page finds one on the Web similar to his requirements, copies it, modifies it, and publishes it as his own Web page.	☐	☐
14. A student researches using only the Web to write a report.	☐	☐
15. In a society in which all transactions occur online (a cashless society), the government tracks every transaction you make and automatically deducts taxes from your bank account.	☐	☐
16. Someone copies a well-known novel to the Web and encourages others to read it.	☐	☐

FIGURE 11-22 Indicate whether you think the situation described is ethical or unethical. Discuss your answers with your classmates.

Information Accuracy

Society needs to be aware of issues associated with the accuracy of computer input. Inaccurate input can result in erroneous information and incorrect decisions based on that information.

Information accuracy today is even more of a concern because many users access information maintained by other people or companies, such as on the Internet. Do not assume that because the information is on the Web that it is correct. As Chapter 2 discussed, users should evaluate the value of a Web page before relying on its content.

Be aware that the company providing access to the information may not be the creator of the information. For example, airline flight schedules are available through several Web sites. The question that arises is who is responsible for the accuracy of this information? Does the responsibility rest solely with the original creator of the information, or does the service that passes along the information also have some responsibility to verify its accuracy? Legally, these questions have not been resolved.

In addition to concerns about the accuracy of computer input, some individuals and organizations raise questions about the ethics of using computers to alter output, primarily graphical output such as retouched photographs. Using graphics equipment and software, users easily can digitize photographs and then add, change, or remove images (Figure 11-23).

One group that completely opposes any manipulation of an image is the National Press Photographers Association. It believes that allowing even the slightest alteration eventually could lead deliberately to misrepresentative photographs. Others believe that digital photograph retouching is acceptable as long as the significant content or meaning of the photograph does not change. Digital retouching is an area in which legal precedents so far have not been established.

Intellectual Property Rights

Intellectual property (IP) refers to unique and original works such as ideas, inventions, writings, art, processes, company and product names, and logos. **Intellectual property rights** are the rights to which creators are entitled for their work. Certain issues arise surrounding IP today because many of these works are available digitally.

A **copyright** gives authors and artists exclusive rights to duplicate, publish, and sell their materials. A copyright protects any tangible form of expression.

FIGURE 11-23 A digitally altered photograph shows sports legend Michael Jordan (born in 1963) meeting the famous scientist Albert Einstein (who died in 1955).

A common infringement of copyright is piracy. People pirate (illegally copy) software, movies, and music. Many areas are not clear-cut with respect to the law, because copyright law gives the public fair use to copyrighted material. The issues surround the phrase, fair use, which allows use for educational and critical purposes. This vague definition is subject to widespread interpretation and raises many questions:

- Should individuals be able to download contents of your Web site, modify it, and then put it on the Web again as their own?
- Should a faculty member have the right to print material from the Web and distribute it to all members of the class for teaching purposes only?
- Should someone be able to scan photographs or pages from a book, publish them to the Web, and allow others to download them?
- Should someone be able to put the lyrics of a song on the Web?
- Should students be able to post term papers they have written on the Web, making it tempting for other students to download and submit them as their own work?

These and many other issues are being debated strongly by members of society.

Codes of Conduct

Recognizing that individuals need specific standards for the ethical use of computers, a number of computer-related organizations have established IT (information technology) codes of conduct (Figure 11-24). An IT **code of conduct** is a written guideline that helps determine whether a specific computer action is ethical or unethical.

INFORMATION PRIVACY

Information privacy refers to the right of individuals and companies to deny or restrict the collection and use of information about them. In the past, information privacy was easier to maintain because information was kept in separate locations. Each retail store had its own credit files. Each government agency maintained separate records. Doctors had their own patient files.

Today, huge databases store this data online. Much of the data is personal and confidential and should be accessible only to authorized users. Many individuals and organizations, however, question whether this data really is private. That is, some companies and individuals collect and use this information without your authorization. Web sites often collect data about you, so they can customize advertisements and send you personalized e-mail messages. Some employers monitor your computer usage and e-mail messages.

WEB LINK 11-9

Intellectual Property Rights

Visit the Discovering Computers 2005 WEB LINK page (**scsite.com/dc2005/weblink**). Click Intellectual Property Rights below Chapter 11.

IT CODE OF CONDUCT

1. Computers may not be used to harm other people.
2. Employees may not interfere with others' computer work.
3. Employees may not meddle in others' computer files.
4. Computers may not be used to steal.
5. Computers may not be used to bear false witness.
6. Employees may not copy or use software illegally.
7. Employees may not use others' computer resources without authorization.
8. Employees may not use others' intellectual property as their own.
9. Employees shall consider the social impact of programs and systems they design.
10. Employees always should use computers in a way that demonstrates consideration and respect for fellow humans.

FIGURE 11-24 Sample IT code of conduct employers may distribute to employees.

Figure 11-25 lists many techniques you can take to make your personal data more private. Read Apply It 11-2 for more information. The following sections address techniques companies and employers use to collect your personal data.

HOW TO SAFEGUARD PERSONAL INFORMATION

1. Fill in only necessary information on rebate, warranty, and registration forms.
2. Do not preprint your telephone number or Social Security number on personal checks.
3. Have an unlisted or unpublished telephone number.
4. If Caller ID is available in your area, find out how to block your number from displaying on the receiver's system.
5. Do not write your telephone number on charge or credit receipts.
6. Ask merchants not to write credit card numbers, telephone numbers, Social Security numbers, and driver's license numbers on the back of your personal checks.
7. Purchase goods with cash, rather than credit or checks.
8. Avoid shopping club and buyer cards.
9. If merchants ask personal questions, find out why they want to know before releasing the information.
10. Inform merchants that you do not want them to distribute your personal information.
11. Request, in writing, to be removed from mailing lists.
12. Obtain your credit report once a year from each of the three major credit reporting agencies (Equifax, Experian, and TransUnion) and correct any errors.
13. Request a free copy of your medical records once a year from the Medical Information Bureau.
14. Limit the amount of information you provide to Web sites. Fill in only required information.
15. Install a cookie manager to filter cookies.
16. Clear your history file when you are finished browsing.
17. Set up a free e-mail account. Use this e-mail address for merchant forms.
18. Turn off file and printer sharing on your Internet connection.
19. Install a personal firewall.
20. Sign-up for e-mail filtering through your Internet service provider or use an antispam program such as Brightmail.
21. Do not reply to spam for any reason.
22. Surf the Web anonymously with a program such as Freedom WebSecure or through an anonymous Web site such as Anonymizer.com.

FIGURE 11-25 Techniques to keep personal data private.

APPLY IT 11-2

Mind Your Own Identity

Technology has made shopping, banking, and communicating easy and quick for consumers. It also has made stealing information easy and quick for thieves. As many as 10 million personal identities are pirated each year, according to some consumer advocates.

Each time you rent a car, write a check at the mall, charge tickets for a concert using your cellular telephone, and apply for a credit card, you release personal information that could be useful to thieves. You can minimize this risk of identity theft in several ways.

First, protect your credit. Consumer advocates recommend ordering and carefully reviewing a credit report yearly from each of the three credit reporting bureaus: Equifax, Experian, and TransUnion. In addition, be certain you receive all your credit card bills, for identity thieves often change billing addresses.

Other simple measures can include carrying only a few credit cards in your wallet and leaving your Social Security card at home. If your wallet is stolen, cancel all credit cards. Shred or tear bank statements, credit card receipts, and credit card solicitations you receive in the mail. Do not disclose your Social Security number unless absolutely necessary; businesses often can substitute other types of identifiers.

For more information about minimizing identity theft, visit the Discovering Computers 2005 Apply It Web page (**scsite.com/dc2005/apply**). Click Apply It #2 below Chapter 11.

Electronic Profiles

When you fill out a form such as a magazine subscription, product warranty registration card, or contest entry form, the merchant that receives the form usually enters it into a database. Likewise, every time you click an advertisement on the Web or register software online, your information and preferences enter a database. Merchants then sell the contents of their databases to national marketing firms and Internet advertising firms. By combining this data with information from public sources such as driver's licenses and vehicle registrations, these firms create an electronic profile of individuals.

The marketing and advertising firms pride themselves on being able to collect accurate, in-depth information about people. The information in these electronic profiles include personal details such as your age, address, telephone number, spending habits, marital status, number of dependents, ages of dependents, and so on.

These firms then sell your electronic profile to any company that requests it. A car dealership, for example, may want to send an advertisement piece or e-mail message to all sports car owners in its vicinity. Thus, the dealership may request a list of all sports car owners living in the southeastern United States. Read Issue 11-4 for a related discussion.

Direct marketing supporters say that using information in this way lowers overall selling costs, which lowers product prices. Critics contend that the information in an electronic profile reveals more about an individual than anyone has a right to know. They claim that companies should inform people if they plan to provide personal information to others. Further, people should have the right to deny such use. Many companies today allow people to specify whether they want their personal information distributed (Figure 11-26).

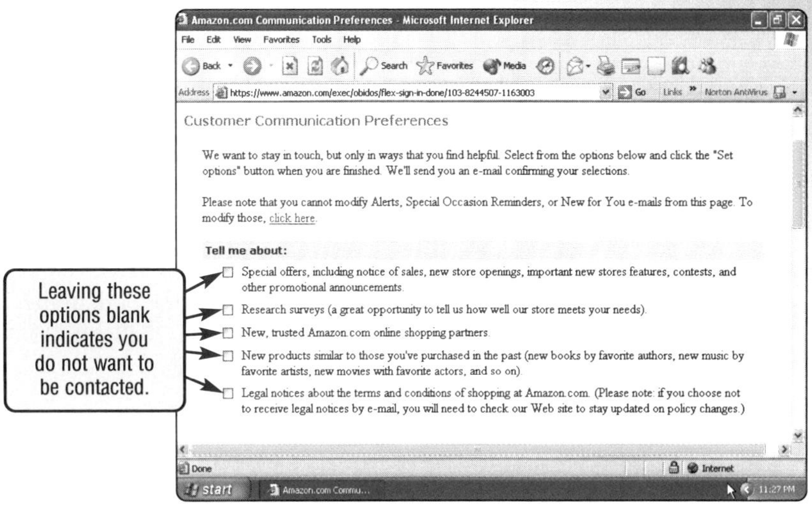

FIGURE 11-26 Many companies today allow people to specify whether they want their personal information distributed.

ISSUE 11-4

What Information Should Be Available?

After public protest, the Canadian government dismantled a comprehensive database comprised of records from several departments, reputed to contain 2,000 pieces of information about every citizen. Information privacy is a hotly contested issue. Some companies collect information from a number of resources to build individual profiles. The files can be used for target advertising or sold to government for law enforcement purposes. Members of the U.S. Congress have debated allowing agencies such as the FBI or IRS access to any database. Using information about automotive magazine subscribers, the IRS identified owners of luxury cars who reported little income for possible audit. Should the government be allowed to access private databases or compile information from multiple department databases? Why? One privacy advocate suggests that any information collected by the government should be available to the general public. If releasing the data would endanger privacy rights, the government should have to justify its collection. Is this a good guiding rule? Why or why not?

For more information about database profiles, visit the Discovering Computers 2005 Issues Web page (**scsite.com/dc2005/issues**). Click Issue #4 below Chapter 11.

Cookies

E-commerce and other Web applications often rely on cookies to identify users and customize Web pages. A **cookie** is a small text file that a Web server stores on your computer. Cookie files typically contain data about you, such as your user name or viewing preferences.

Web sites use cookies for a variety of purposes.

- Most Web sites that allow for personalization use cookies to track user preferences. On such sites, users may be asked to fill in a form requesting personal information, such as their name, postal code, or site preferences. A news Web site, for example, might allow users to customize their viewing preferences to display certain stock quotes. The Web site stores their preferences in a cookie on the users' hard disks.
- Some Web sites use cookies to store users' passwords, so they do not need to enter it every time they log in to the Web site.
- Online shopping sites generally use a *session cookie* to keep track of items in a user's shopping cart. This way, users can start an order during one Web session and finish it on another day in another session. Session cookies usually expire after a certain time, such as a week or a month.
- Some Web sites use cookies to track how regularly users visit a site and the Web pages they visit while at the site.

- Web sites may use cookies to target advertisements. These sites store a user's interests and browsing habits in the cookie.

Many commercial Web sites send a cookie to your browser, and then your computer's hard disk stores the cookie. The next time you visit the Web site, your browser retrieves the cookie from your hard disk and sends the data in the cookie to the Web site. Figure 11-27 illustrates how Web sites work with cookies.

WEB LINK 11-10

Cookies

Visit the Discovering Computers 2005 WEB LINK page (**scsite .com/dc2005/weblink**). Click Cookies below Chapter 11.

FIGURE 11-27 HOW COOKIES WORK

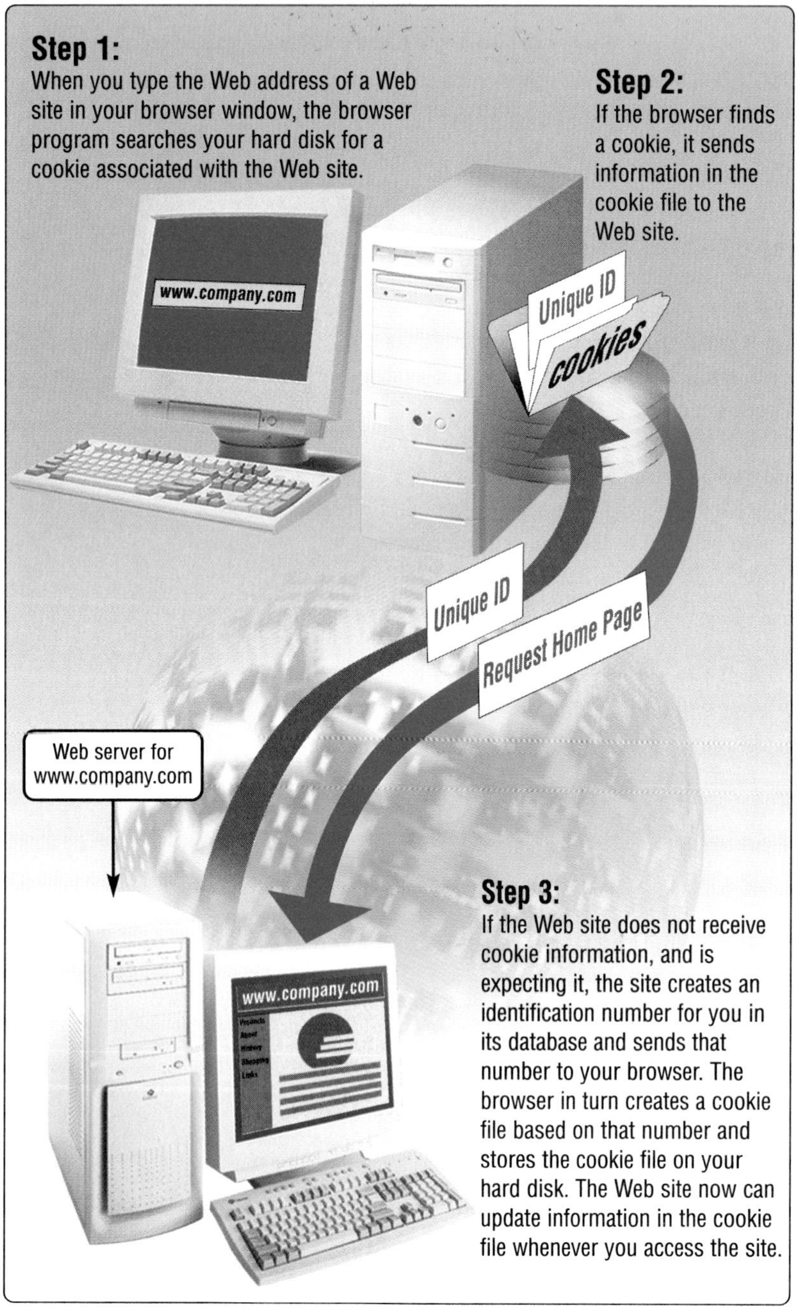

Some Web sites do sell or trade information stored in your cookie to advertisers — a practice many believe to be unethical. If you do not want your personal information distributed, you should limit the amount of information you provide to a Web site.

You can set your browser to accept cookies automatically, prompt you if you want to accept a cookie, or disable cookie use altogether. Keep in mind if you disable cookie use, you may not be able to use many of the e-commerce Web sites. As an alternative, you can purchase a software program that selectively blocks cookies. Figure 11-28 outlines these and other types of cookie managers.

COOKIE MANAGERS

Program Name	Function
AdSubtract	Blocks advertising and cookies
BPS Popup & Cookie Shield	Accepts or rejects cookies, blocks offensive Web sites and advertisements, disables pop-up windows
Cookie Cruncher	Views, edits, and deletes cookies
Cookie Crusher	Accepts or rejects cookies by Web site — tells you the purpose of cookie (tracking, shopping cart, etc.)
Guidescope	Allows you to block or allow cookies and advertising based on their domain names
IEClean, NSClean	Deletes cookies; also can delete cache, history files, and other browsing files
WebWasher	Blocks advertising banners and associated cookies
Window Washer	Deletes cache, history, and cookie files

FIGURE 11-28 Popular cookie manager programs.

FAQ 11-5

Can a Web site read data in all the cookie files on my computer's hard disk?

No, a Web site can read data only from its own cookie file stored on your hard disk. It cannot access or view any other data on your hard disk — including another cookie file.

For more information about cookies, visit the Discovering Computers 2005 FAQ Web page (**scsite.com/dc2005/faq**). Click Cookies below Chapter 11.

Spyware

Spyware is a program placed on a computer without the user's knowledge that secretly collects information about the user. Spyware can enter a computer as a virus or as a result of a user installing a new program. The spyware program communicates information it collects to some outside source while you are online.

Some vendors or employers use spyware to collect information about program usage or employees. Internet advertising firms often use spyware, which in this case is called *adware*, to collect information about users' Web browsing habits. (Cookies are not considered spyware because you know they exist.)

One type of spyware, called a *Web bug*, is hidden on Web pages or in e-mail messages in the form of graphical images. Web businesses use Web bugs to monitor online habits of Web site visitors. Often, Web bugs link to a cookie stored on the hard disk.

If you download software from the Web, pay careful attention to the license agreement and registration information requested during installation. The software provider, in principle, should notify you that your information may be communicated to advertisers. To remove spyware, you need to purchase a special program that can detect and delete it.

Spam

Spam is an unsolicited e-mail message or newsgroup posting sent to many recipients or newsgroups at once. Spam is Internet junk mail (Figure 11-29). The content of spam ranges from selling a product or service, to promoting a business opportunity, to advertising offensive material. One study indicates the average user receives more than 1,000 spam e-mail messages each year. Read Issue 11-5 for a related discussion.

Users can reduce the amount of spam they receive with a number of techniques. Some e-mail programs also have built-in settings that allow users to delete spam automatically. Users also can sign up for e-mail filtering from their Internet service provider. **E-mail filtering** is a service that blocks e-mail messages from designated sources. These services typically collect the spam in a central location that users can view at anytime. An alternative to e-mail filtering is to purchase an **anti-spam program** that attempts to remove spam before it reaches your inbox. The disadvantage of e-mail filters and anti-spam programs is that sometimes they remove valid e-mail messages.

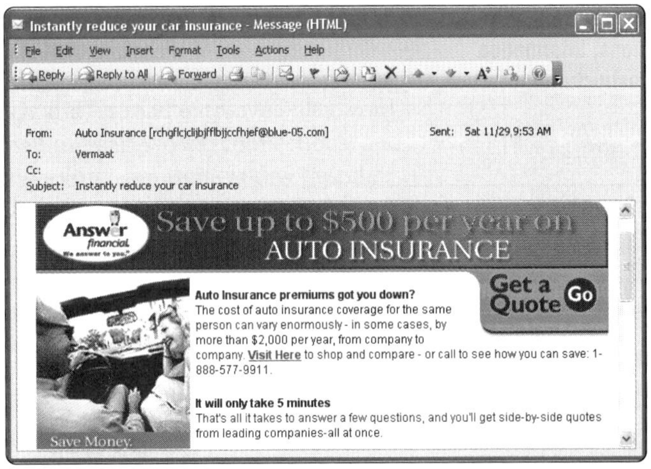

FIGURE 11-29 Spam is Internet junk mail.

ISSUE 11-5

Should We Can Spam?

Every day, e-mail users receive dozens of unsolicited messages offering a variety of goods, services, and opinions. These unwanted messages are called spam — based on a Monty Python skit in which a restaurant customer, repeatedly urged to order canned meat, finally shouts in frustration, "I don't want any Spam!" Most e-mail users do not want any spam either. The president recently signed a bill mandating that all spam include an identifying label in the message's subject line and give recipients a way to avoid future mass-mailings. An additional provision authorizes the establishment of a do-not-spam list similar to the do-not-call list of telephone numbers that telemarketers are not to call. Proponents of the bill argue that not only is spam annoying, but every year dealing with spam costs companies up to $750 per employee in lost productivity. Opponents of the bill insist that spam works, and restrictions on spam violate the constitutional right to free speech. Should spam be regulated? Why? If spam is regulated, then how? Should anti-spam legislation be limited to unsolicited commercial messages, or should it also include unsolicited political or personal messages? Why?

For more information about spam, visit the Discovering Computers 2005 Issues Web page (**scsite.com/dc2005/issues**) and click Issue #5 below Chapter 11.

CHAPTER 11 CHAPTER REVIEW

The Chapter Review section summarizes the concepts presented in this chapter.

WEB INSTRUCTIONS:

To display this page from the Web, start your browser and enter the Web address **scsite.com/dc2005/ch11/review.** Click the links for current and additional information. To listen to an audio version of this Chapter Review, click the Audio button.

1 What Are Types of Computer Security Risks?

A **computer security risk** is any event or action that could cause a loss of or damage to computer hardware, software, data, information, or processing capability. Common computer security risks include computer **viruses**, worms, and Trojan horses; unauthorized access and use; hardware theft; software theft; information theft; and system failure.

2 How Can Users Safeguard against Computer Viruses, Worms, and Trojan Horses?

A computer virus is a potentially damaging program that affects, or infects, a computer negatively by altering the way the computer works. A worm is a program that copies itself repeatedly, using up resources and possibly shutting down the computer or network. A Trojan horse is a program that hides within or looks like a legitimate program. Users can take precautions to guard against these malicious-logic programs. Do not start a computer with a floppy disk in drive A (unless the disk is an uninfected boot disk). Never open an e-mail attachment unless it is from a trusted source. Disable macros in documents that are not from a trusted source. Install an **antivirus program** and a personal firewall. Stay informed about any new virus alert or virus hoax.

3 What Are Techniques to Prevent Unauthorized Access and Use?

Unauthorized access is the use of a computer or network without permission. **Unauthorized use** is the use of a computer or its data for unapproved or illegal activities. A written *acceptable use policy* (*AUP*) outlines the activities for which the computer and network may and may not be used. A **firewall** consists of hardware and/or software that prevents unauthorized access to data, information, and storage media. *Intrusion detection software* analyzes network traffic, assesses vulnerability, identifies unauthorized access, and notifies network administrators of suspicious behavior patterns or system breaches. An *access control* defines who can access a computer, when they can access it, and what actions they can take. Access controls include a **user name** and **password**, a *possessed object*, a **biometric device**, and a *callback system*. An **audit trail** records in a file both successful and unsuccessful access attempts.

4 What Are Safeguards against Hardware Theft and Vandalism?

Hardware theft is the act of stealing computer equipment. **Hardware vandalism** is the act of defacing or destroying computer equipment. The best preventive measures against hardware theft and vandalism are common sense and a constant awareness of the risk. Physical devices and practical security measures, passwords, possessed objects, and biometrics can reduce the risk of theft or render a computer useless if it is stolen.

Visit **scsite.com/dc2005/quiz** or click the Quiz Yourself button. Click Objectives 1 – 4 below Chapter 11.

5 How Do Software Manufacturers Protect against Software Piracy?

Software **piracy** is the unauthorized and illegal duplication of copyrighted software. To protect themselves from software piracy, manufacturers issue a **license agreement** that provides specific conditions for use of the software. **Product activation** is a process during which users provide the product's identification number to receive an installation identification number unique to their computer.

6 What Is Encryption and Why Is It Necessary?

Information theft occurs when someone steals personal or confidential information. **Encryption** prevents information theft by converting readable data into unreadable characters. To read the data, a recipient must **decrypt**, or decipher, it into a readable form.

7 What Types of Devices Are Available to Protect against System Failure?

A *system failure* is the prolonged malfunction of a computer. A common cause of system failure is an electrical disturbance such as **noise**, an **overvoltage**, or an **undervoltage**. A **surge protector** uses special electrical components to smooth out minor noise, provide a stable current flow, and keep an overvoltage from reaching the computer. An **uninterruptible power supply (UPS)** contains surge protection circuits and one or more batteries that can provide power during an undervoltage.

8 What Are Options for Backing Up Computer Resources?

A **backup** is a duplicate of a file, program, or disk that can be used to **restore** the file if the original is lost, damaged, or destroyed. Most operating systems and backup devices include a backup program, and numerous stand-alone backup utilities exist. An *online backup service* is a Web site that automatically backs up files to its online location.

9 What Are Safeguards that Protect against Internet Security Risks?

Internet security risks include denial of service attacks, unsecured business transactions, and unsecured e-mail messages. A **denial of service attack**, or **DoS attack**, is an assault on a computer whose purpose is to disrupt access to the Web. Many of the latest antivirus and firewall programs protect against DoS attacks. To secure business transactions, a **secure site** uses a **digital certificate** to guarantee the Web site is legitimate and a security protocol such as *Secure Sockets Layer* (*SSL*), *Secure HTTP (S-HTTP)*, or *Secure Electronics Transactions* (*SET*) *Specification* to encrypt data that passes between a client and the server. To secure e-mail, senders can encrypt it with a program such as *Pretty Good Privacy* (*PGP*) and attach a **digital signature** that verifies their identity.

Visit **scsite.com/dc2005/quiz** or click the Quiz Yourself button. Click Objectives 5 – 9 below Chapter 11.

10 What Are Issues Related to Information Accuracy, Rights, and Conduct?

Computer ethics govern the use of computers and information systems. Issues in computer ethics include the responsibility for information accuracy and the **intellectual property rights** to which creators are entitled for works that are available digitally. An IT (information technology) **code of conduct** helps determine whether a specific computer action is ethical or unethical.

11 What Are Issues Surrounding Information Privacy?

Information privacy is the right of individuals and companies to restrict the collection and use of information about them. Issues surrounding information privacy include electronic profiles, cookies, spyware, and employee monitoring. An electronic profile combines data about an individual's Web use with data from public sources, which then is sold. A **cookie** is a file that a Web server stores on a computer to collect data about the user. *Spyware* is a program placed on a computer that secretly collects information about the user. **Spam** is an unsolicited e-mail message or newsgroup posting sent to many recipients. **Employee monitoring** uses computers to observe, record, and review an employee's computer use.

12 How Can Health-Related Disorders and Injuries Due to Computer Use Be Prevented?

A **repetitive strain injury** (**RSI**) is an injury or disorder of the muscles, nerves, tendons, ligaments, and joints. Computer-related RSIs include *tendonitis* and *carpal tunnel syndrome* (*CTS*). Another health-related condition is eyestrain associated with **computer vision syndrome** (*CVS*). To prevent health-related disorders, take frequent breaks, use precautionary exercises and techniques, and use *ergonomics* when planning the workplace. **Computer addiction** occurs when the computer consumes someone's entire social life. Computer addiction is a treatable illness through therapy and support groups.

Visit **scsite.com/dc2005/quiz** or click the Quiz Yourself button. Click Objectives 10 – 12 below Chapter 11.

CHAPTER 11 KEY TERMS

QUIZZES AND LEARNING GAMES
Computer Genius
Crossword Puzzle
Interactive Labs
Practice Test
Quiz Yourself
Wheel of Terms
EXERCISES
Chapter Review
Checkpoint
Key Terms
Lab Exercises
Learn It Online
Web Research
BEYOND THE BOOK
Apply It
Career Corner
Companies
FAQ
High-Tech Talk
Issues
Looking Ahead
Trailblazers
Web Links
FEATURES
Guide to Web Sites
Making Use of the Web
Tech News
Timeline 2005

You should know the Primary Terms and be familiar with the Secondary Terms.

WEB INSTRUCTIONS:

To display this page from the Web, start your browser and enter the Web address **scsite.com/dc2005/ch11/terms**. Click a term to display its definition and a picture. When the picture appears, click the more info button for current and additional information about the term from the Web.

>> Primary Terms

(shown in bold-black characters in the chapter)

anti-spam program (595)
antivirus program (571)
audit trail (576)
back up (586)
backup (586)
biometric device (578)
code of conduct (591)
computer addiction (601)
computer crime (568)
computer ethics (589)
Computer Fraud and Abuse Acts (597)
computer security risk (568)
computer vision syndrome (599)
content filtering (597)
cookie (593)
copyright (590)
cracker (573)
cybercrime (568)
decrypt (582)
denial of service attack (587)
digital certificate (587)
digital signature (589)
DoS attack (587)
Electronic Communications Privacy Act (597)
e-mail filtering (595)
employee monitoring (597)
encryption (582)
Fair Credit Reporting Act (597)
firewall (574)
green computing (601)
hacker (573)
hardware theft (579)
hardware vandalism (579)
information privacy (591)
information theft (582)
inoculate (572)
intellectual property rights (590)
license agreement (580)
noise (584)
online security service (575)
overvoltage (584)
password (576)
personal firewall (575)
personal identification number (PIN) (578)
piracy (580)
power surge (584)
product activation (582)
quarantine (572)
recovery disk (572)
repetitive strain injury (RSI) (598)
rescue disk (572)
restore (586)
secure site (587)
software theft (580)
spam (595)
surge protector (584)
Trojan horse (569)
trusted source (571)
unauthorized access (573)
unauthorized use (574)
undervoltage (584)
uninterruptible power supply (UPS) (585)
user name (576)
virus (569)
virus definition (572)
virus hoax (572)
virus signature (572)
Web filtering software (598)
worm (569)

>> Secondary Terms

(shown in italic characters in the chapter)

128-bit encryption (587)
40-bit encryption (587)
acceptable use policy (AUP) (574)
access control (576)
adware (595)
authentication (576)
blackout (584)
brownout (584)
Business Software Alliance (BSA) (581)
callback system (579)
carpal tunnel syndrome (CTS) (598)
CERT/CC (587)
certificate authority (CA) (588)
child (586)
ciphertext (582)
Computer Emergency Response Team Coordination Center (587)
Computer Matching and Privacy Protection Act (597)
CVS (599)
DDoS (distributed DoS) attack (587)
ECPA (597)
encryption key (583)
end-user license agreement (EULA) (581)
ergonomics (600)
fault-tolerant computer (585)
full backup (586)
grandparent (586)
hash (589)
honeypot (576)
identification (576)
intellectual property (IP) (590)
Internet addiction disorder (IAD) (601)
Internet Content Rating Association (ICRA) (598)
intrusion detection software (576)
Joule (585)
log (576)
macros (571)
malicious-logic programs (569)
MPR II standard (600)
musculoskeletal disorder (MSD) (598)
offline UPS (585)
offsite (586)
online backup service (586)
online UPS (585)
parent (586)
payload (569)
plaintext (582)
possessed object (578)
Pretty Good Privacy (PGP) (589)
proxy server (575)
safeguards (569)
Secure Electronics Transactions (SET) Specification (588)
Secure HTTP (S-HTTP) (588)
Secure Sockets Layer (SSL) (588)
selective backup (586)
session cookie (593)
single-user license agreement (581)
spike (584)
spyware (595)
standby UPS (585)
surge suppressor (584)
system failure (584)
tendonitis (598)
three-generation backup (586)
Underwriters Laboratories (UL) 1449 standard (585)
user ID (576)
virtual private network (VPN) (583)
wallet program (588)
Web bug (595)
zombie (587)

CHECKPOINT CHAPTER 11

Use the Checkpoint exercises to check your knowledge level of the chapter.

WEB INSTRUCTIONS:

To display this page from the Web, start your browser and enter the Web address **scsite.com/dc2005/ch11/check**. Click the links for current and additional information.

LABEL THE FIGURE

Identify types of computer security risks.

a. Computer viruses, worms, and Trojan horses
b. Hardware theft
c. Information theft
d. Software theft
e. System failure
f. Unauthorized access and use

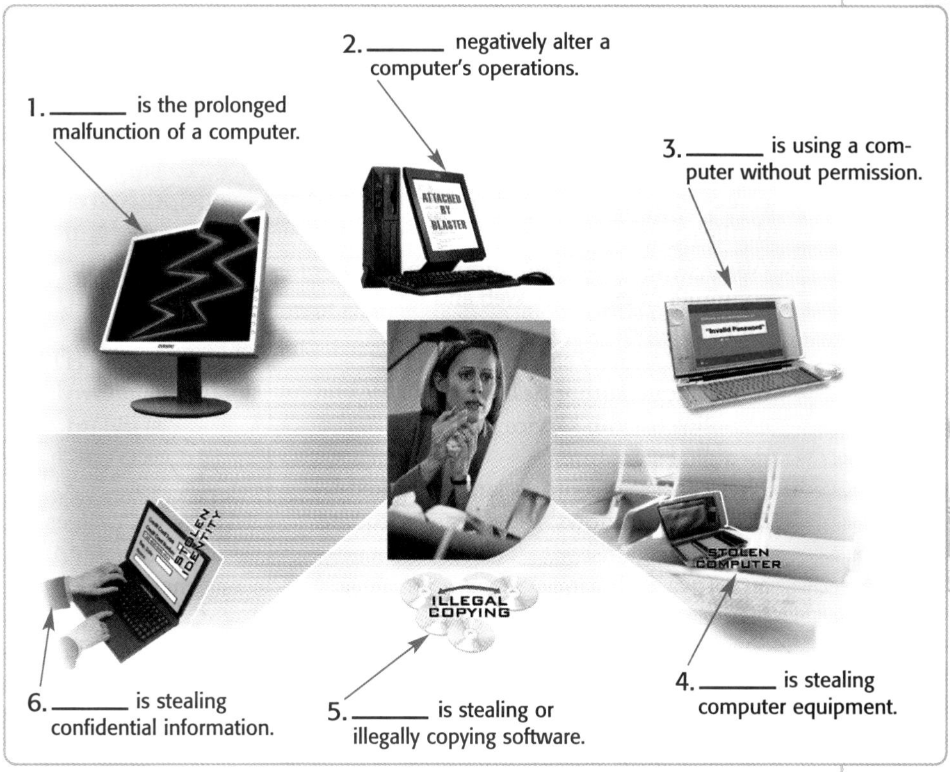

TRUE/FALSE

Mark T for True and F for False. (See page numbers in parentheses.)

____ 1. All breaches to computer security are planned. (568)
____ 2. A worm is a program that hides within or looks like a legitimate program. (569)
____ 3. A recovery disk is a removable disk that contains an uninfected copy of key operating system commands and startup information that enables the computer to restart correctly. (572)
____ 4. A cracker is someone who tries to access a computer or network illegally. (573)
____ 5. A honeypot is a program designed to entice an intruder to hack into the computer. (576)
____ 6. Software piracy reduces the chance of spreading viruses, increases your ability to receive technical support, and drives down the price of software. (581)
____ 7. Noise generally is not a risk to hardware, software, or data. (584)
____ 8. A digital certificate is a notice that guarantees a user or a Web site is legitimate. (587)
____ 9. A digital signature is a mathematical formula that generates a code from the contents of the message. (589)
____ 10. A cookie is a small text file that a Web server stores on your computer. (593)
____ 11. Web filtering software is a program that allows access to specified Web sites. (598)
____ 12. Internet addiction disorder (IAD) describes the condition attributed to users who are dependent on or abusing the Internet. (601)

CHAPTER 11 LEARN IT ONLINE

QUIZZES AND LEARNING GAMES
Computer Genius
Crossword Puzzle
Interactive Labs
Practice Test
Quiz Yourself
Wheel of Terms

EXERCISES
Chapter Review
Checkpoint
Key Terms
Lab Exercises
Learn It Online
Web Research

BEYOND THE BOOK
Apply It
Career Corner
Companies
FAQ
High-Tech Talk
Issues
Looking Ahead
Trailblazers
Web Links

FEATURES
Guide to Web Sites
Making Use of the Web
Tech News
Timeline 2005

Use the Learn It Online exercises to reinforce your understanding of the chapter concepts.

WEB INSTRUCTIONS:

To display this page from the Web, start your browser and enter the Web address **scsite.com/dc2005/ch11/learn**.

1 At the Movies – SPAM Wars

To view the SPAM Wars movie, click the number 1 button. Watch the movie, and then complete the exercise by answering the questions below. Today's technology makes it easy for companies desiring to send Internet junk mail to do so. Senate Bill 630 would make it more difficult. The bill requires e-mailers to identify themselves, provide an honest reason for their e-mail message, and an honest return address. It allows consumers to opt out of receiving such mail and places hefty fines on senders who violate these rules. But finding a way to balance First Amendment rights of the sender with the rights of the consumer is complicated. The average e-mail user receives 1,000 spam e-mail messages each year. Do you think spam mail is unethical? How is it different from junk mail received via the post office? What information in your electronic profile might be of interest to a direct marketer, and how might the marketer obtain it?

2 Student Edition Labs – Protecting Your Privacy Online

Click the number 2 button. When the Student Edition Labs menu appears, click *Protecting Your Privacy Online* to begin. A new browser window will open. Follow the on-screen instructions to complete the Lab. When finished, click the Exit button. If required, print a copy of your results to submit to your instructor.

3 Student Edition Labs – Keeping Your Computer Virus Free

Click the number 3 button. When the Student Edition Labs menu appears, click *Keeping Your Computer Virus Free* to begin. A new browser window will open. Follow the on-screen instructions to complete the Lab. When finished, click the Exit button. If required, print a copy of your results to submit to your instructor.

4 Digital Cameras

The Creative Web Cam is a digital camera that not only takes photographs but, when folded in half and placed on a display device, can serve as a Web cam. Other digital camera innovations include a digital camera that downloads pictures simply by placing it in a cradle attached to a computer; a digital camera that boasts a 4x optical zoom; and a digital camera that packs auto focus, auto flash, and auto exposure into a package smaller than most conventional cameras. Click the number 4 button to learn more about digital cameras and complete this exercise.

5 Practice Test

Click the number 5 button. Answer each question. When completed, enter your name and click the Grade Test button to submit the quiz for grading. Make a note of any missed questions. If required, print a copy to submit to your instructor.

6 Web Guide

Click the number 6 button to display the Guide to Web Sites and Searching Techniques Web page. Click Shopping and then click Consumer World. Scroll down the page and locate an article of interest. Prepare a brief report about your findings and submit your assignment to your instructor.

7 Scavenger Hunt

Click the number 7 button. Print a copy of the Scavenger Hunt page; use this page to write down your answers as you search the Web. Submit your completed page to your instructor.

8 Who Wants To Be a Computer Genius?

Click the number 8 button to find out if you are a computer genius. Directions on how to play the game will be displayed. When you are ready to play, click the PLAY button. Submit your score to your instructor.

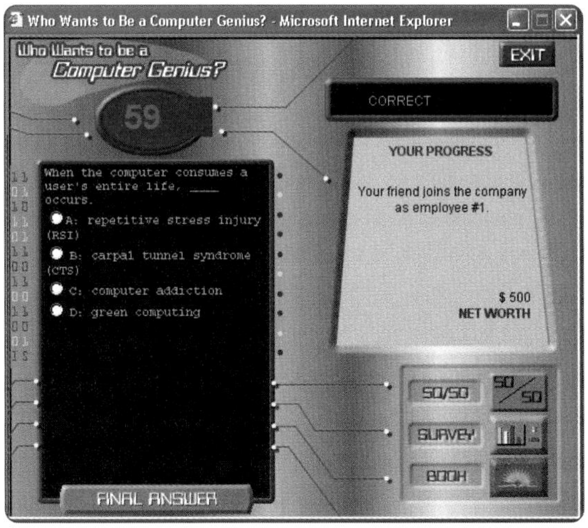

9 Wheel of Terms

Click the number 9 button to reinforce important terms you learned in this chapter by playing the Shelly Cashman Series version of this popular game. Directions on how to play the game will be displayed. When you are ready to play, click the PLAY button. Submit your score to your instructor.

10 Career Corner

Click the number 10 button to display the careermag.com page. Scroll down the page and then click a link of interest. Review the information contained within your selection. Write a brief report about what you learned. Submit the report to your instructor.

11 Search Sleuth

Click the number 11 button to learn search techniques that will help make you a research expert. Submit the completed assignment to your instructor.

12 Crossword Puzzle Challenge

Click the number 12 button. Complete the puzzle to reinforce skills you learned in this chapter. Directions on how to play the game will be displayed. When you are ready to play, click the Submit button. Submit the completed puzzle to your instructor.

13 Graphics and Animation

Graphics and animation add visual interest to games, educational applications, and Web pages. Graphics were introduced to the Web by the IMG tag, in NCSA's (National Center for Supercomputing Applications) Mosaic for X, written by Marc Andreessen and Eric Bina. Today's high-end software animation programs are used to produce quality graphics and sophisticated animations. Video games and Web pages come to life with realistic scenery and characters. Click the number 13 button to complete this exercise to visit a Web page with hundreds of free animations and graphics you can download to use on your Web pages.

14 In the News

Why own the latest video game when you can rent it from the comfort of your personal computer? Yummy Interactive has agreements with leading video-game publishers — ARUSH Entertainment, Ripcord Games, and The 3DO Company — that will allow broadband users to download files from the Yummy Interactive Web site to play stand-alone or multiplayer games. The Yummy Web site sends users all they need to get started playing the games, and as more bytes are needed, they are sent from the server to the users. Click the number 14 button and read a news article about online games and edutainment applications. What applications have been developed? Do you think the applications will be successful? Why or why not? Do you think online games will replace the traditional, local CD-ROM game?

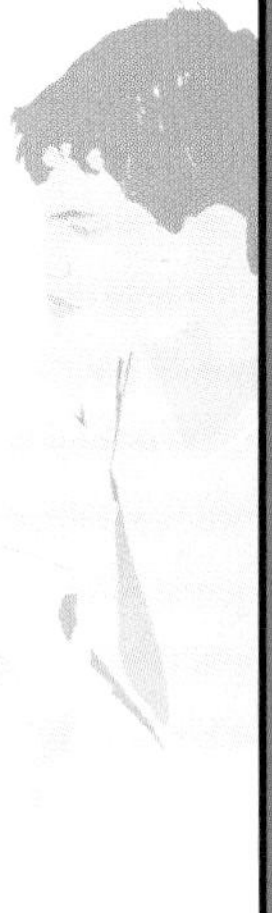

LAB EXERCISES

Use the Lab Exercises to gain hands-on computer experience.

WEB INSTRUCTIONS:

To display this page from the Web, start your browser and enter the Web address **scsite.com/dc2005/ch11/lab**.

1 Playing Audio Compact Disks

This exercise uses Windows XP procedures. Click the Start button on the taskbar, point to All Programs on the Start menu, and then point to Accessories on the All Programs submenu. Point to Entertainment on the Accessories submenu, and then click CD Player on the Entertainment submenu. When the CD Player is displayed, click the Options button and then click CD Player Help on the Options menu. When the CD Player window opens, read the Help information and answer the following questions:

- How do you play a CD?
- How do you stop a CD?
- How do you eject a CD from the drive?

Close the CD Player window. If your computer has a CD-ROM drive and a sound card, insert a CD into the CD-ROM drive and then play it. Close the CD Player.

2 Understanding Multimedia Properties

This exercise uses Windows XP procedures. Click the Start button on the taskbar, and then click Control Panel on the Start menu. In Categories View, click the Sounds, Speech, and Audio Devices icon in the Control Panel window. Click the Sounds and Audio Devices icon in the Sounds, Speech, and Audio Devices window. If necessary, click the Audio tab in the Sounds and Audio Devices Properties dialog box and then answer the following question:

- What is the Sound playback Default device?

Click the Volume tab and then answer the following question:

- Will the volume control icon display on the taskbar of your computer?

Click the Hardware tab. Write down the name(s) of the audio device(s) installed on your computer. Close the Sounds and Audio Devices Properties dialog box and the Sounds, Speech, and Audio Devices window.

3 Dragging and Dropping Windows Objects

This exercise uses Windows XP procedures. To complete this exercise, you first must complete Lab Exercises 2 in Chapter 7 on page 388. Dragging and dropping objects in Windows causes different events to happen. For example, if you drag a program icon from one folder to another or to the desktop, Windows assumes you want to create a shortcut. If you drag a file from one folder to another or to the desktop, Windows assumes you want to move it. Or, if you drag an object from one drive to another, Windows assumes you want to copy it. You can specify the kind of drag-and-drop operation you want to perform by holding down the right mouse button and dragging the object (right-dragging). Insert the Data Disk into drive A. Right-click the Start button on the taskbar and then click Explore on the shortcut menu. Click the 3½ Floppy (A:) icon in the Folders pane of the Start Menu window. If necessary, click the Restore Down button on the title bar of the 3½ Floppy (A:) window, so the desktop displays behind the window. Right-drag the file name lab7-2 in the right pane to the desktop. Release the right mouse button. What are the three commands on the shortcut menu that allow you to perform drag-and-drop operations? What is a shortcut? Click Cancel on the shortcut menu. Close the 3½ Floppy (A:) window.

4 System Sounds

This exercise uses Windows 2000/98 procedures. Double-click the My Computer icon on the desktop. Double-click the Control Panel icon in the My Computer window. Double-click the Sounds icon in the Control Panel window. In the Sounds Properties dialog box, some of the items in the Events list have an associated sound. To hear the sound for an event, click the event in the Events list and then click the right arrow button in the Sound area.

- What events have the same sound?
- Do any events listed have no sound?

Close the Sounds Properties dialog box and the Control Panel window.

WEB RESEARCH CHAPTER 11

Use the Web Research exercises to learn more about the special features in this chapter.

WEB INSTRUCTIONS:

Use the link in each exercise or a search engine such as Google (google.com) to research the topic. Then, write a one-page, double-spaced report or create a presentation, unless otherwise directed below. Page numbers on which information can be found are in parentheses.

1 **Issue** Choose one Issue from the following issues in this chapter: Is That Software Legal? (581), How Should Schools Deal with Internet Plagiarism? (582), Who Should Pay for Software Bugs? (584), or What Information Should Be Available? (593), or Should We Can Spam? (595). Use the Web to research the issue. Discuss the issue with classmates, instructors, and friends. Address the questions that accompany the issue in a report or presentation.

2 **Apply It** Choose one of the following Apply It features in this chapter: Protecting Your Password (578) or Mind Your Own Identity (592). Use the Web to gather additional information about the topic. Print two Web pages that relate to the Apply It. Detail in a report or presentation what you learned.

3 **Career Corner** Read the Career Corner article in this chapter (602). Use the Web to find out more about the career. Describe the career in a report or presentation.

4 **Companies on the Cutting Edge** Choose one of the Companies on the Cutting Edge in this chapter (604). Use the Web to research the company further. Explain in a report or presentation how this company has contributed to computer technology.

5 **Technology Trailblazers** Choose one of the Technology Trailblazers in this chapter (605). Use the Web to research the person further. Explain in a report or presentation how this individual has affected the way people use, or think about, computers.

6 **Picture Your Personal Information Going Public** Read the Picture Your Personal Information Going Public story at the beginning of this chapter (566). Use the Web to research further how personal information is shared. Describe in a report or presentation the ways in which you might safeguard personal information.

7 **High-Tech Talk** Read the High-Tech Talk feature in this chapter (603). Use the Web to find out more about the topic. Summarize in a report or presentation what you learned.

8 **Web Links** Review the Web Link boxes found in the margins of this chapter. Visit five of the Web Link sites. Print the main Web page for each site you visit. Choose one of the Web pages and then summarize in one paragraph the content of the Web page.

9 **Looking Ahead** Choose one of the Looking Ahead articles in this chapter: Cyberterrorism Attack Threatens Networks (587) or Electronic Sensors Track Shoppers (602). Use the Web to find out more about the topic. Detail in a report or presentation what you learned.

10 **FAQ** Choose one FAQ found in this chapter. Use the Web to find out more about the topic. Summarize in one paragraph what you learned.

11 **Making Use of the Web** Read the Environment section of Making Use of the Web in Appendix A (APP 22). Complete the Environment Web Exercises at the end of the section (APP 23). Answer the questions posed in each exercise.

CHAPTER 12

Information System Development

Picture Yourself on a System Development Team

Just as you sit down to dinner, the telephone rings. It never fails. You decide to let the answering machine take the call. As you begin to eat, the caller begins to leave his message. He identifies himself as the marketing manager where you do your banking. You panic. Did you forget to deposit your last paycheck? Have you lost your checkbook or ATM card? Has someone illegally accessed your online bank account and transferred money from your account to theirs? You decide to take the call. Dinner can wait this time.

His reason for calling amazes you. The bank is going to redesign its entire Web site. For this system development project, it is forming a customer advisory board. The board will work with the bank's computer professionals. Advisory board members will participate in all aspects of the project: make design suggestions, review work in progress, and test the new Web site.

The marketing manager asks if you would be willing to be on the customer advisory board. It will require your attention for about two hours per week during the next six months. As a thank you for your time, your online banking will be free for the next three years. Are you interested?

As you read Chapter 12, you will learn about system development and discover several tools used by a systems analyst.

OBJECTIVES

After completing this chapter, you will be able to:

1. List the phases in the system development cycle
2. Identify the guidelines for system development
3. Discuss the importance of project management, feasibility assessment, data and information gathering techniques, and documentation
4. Explain the activities performed in the planning phase
5. Discuss the purpose of the activities performed in the analysis phase
6. Describe the various tools used in process modeling
7. Describe the various tools used in object modeling
8. Explain the activities performed in the design phase
9. Recognize program development as part of the system development cycle
10. Discuss the activities performed in the implementation phase
11. Understand how IT professionals support an information system

CONTENTS

WHAT IS THE SYSTEM DEVELOPMENT CYCLE?

A **system** is a set of components that interact to achieve a common goal. Your body, for example, contains many systems. The digestive system consists of organs that allow your body to process food. The immune system includes the elements that protect your body from disease. The respiratory system has many parts that work together, so you can breathe.

You use, observe, and interact with systems during daily activities. You drive a highway system to reach a destination. Your home maintains a comfortable temperature with its heating and cooling systems. You use the decimal number system to calculate an amount due. You see the planets in the solar system.

Businesses also use many types of systems. A billing system allows a company to send invoices and receive payments from customers. Through a payroll system, employees receive paychecks. A manufacturing system produces the goods that customers order. An inventory system keeps track of the items in a warehouse. Very often, these systems also are information systems.

An **information system** (**IS**) is hardware, software, data, people, and procedures that work together to produce quality information. You play an important role in many information systems. You provide data to some information systems. For example, many systems display forms that ask you to enter personal information such as your name, address, telephone number, and interests. With other information systems, you use their information. When you receive a deposit slip from the bank, you verify the deposit amount is correct.

An information system supports daily, short-term, and long-range activities of users. Some examples of users include store clerks, sales representatives, accountants, supervisors, managers, executives, and customers. As time passes, the kinds and types of information that users need often change. A sales manager may want the weekly summary report grouped by district instead of by product. When information requirements change, the information system must meet the new requirements. In some cases, the developers modify the current information system. In other cases, they develop an entirely new information system.

As a computer user in a business, you someday may participate in the modification of an existing system or the development of a new system. Thus, it is important that you understand the system development process. The **system development cycle** is a set of activities developers use to build an information system. System developers also use a system development cycle to maintain and monitor ongoing activities.

Some activities in the system development cycle may be performed concurrently. Others are performed sequentially. Depending on the type and complexity of the information system, the length of each activity varies from one system to the next. In some cases, a developer skips an activity entirely.

Phases in the System Development Cycle

To organize the process, system development cycles often group many activities into larger categories called **phases**. Most system development cycles contain five phases:

1. Planning
2. Analysis
3. Design
4. Implementation
5. Support

As shown in Figure 12-1, each phase in the system development cycle consists of a series of activities, and the phases form a loop. That is, information system development is an ongoing process. The loop forms when the support phase points to the planning phase. This connection occurs when the information system requires changing. A variety of situations can lead to a change in the information system. A report might generate an incorrect total. Users

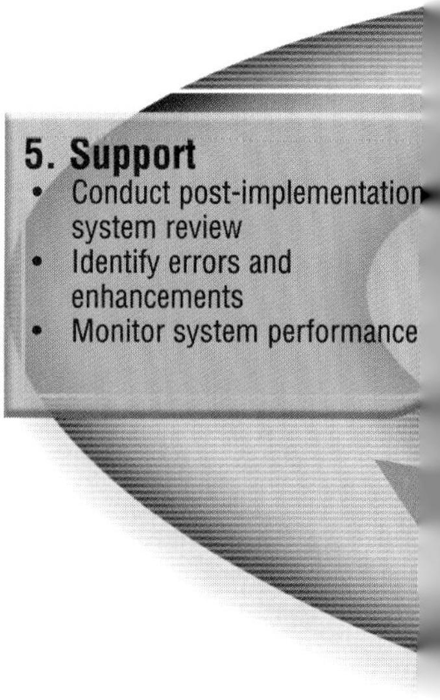

may want information in a different format. A vendor may release a new version of software. Hardware might become obsolete. When change occurs, the planning phase for a new or modified system begins and the system development cycle process starts again.

Developers follow established guidelines during the entire system development cycle process. These developers also interact with a variety of IT professionals and others during the system development cycle. Although the system development cycle contains a set of five phases, several ongoing activities take place during the entire process. The following sections discuss each of these issues.

Guidelines for System Development

System development should follow three general guidelines: arrange activities into phases, involve the users, and develop standards.

1. The system development cycle should group activities or tasks into phases. Many system development cycles contain the five major phases shown in Figure 12-1. Others have more or fewer phases. Regardless, all system development cycles have similar activities. Figure 12-1 shows the Develop programs activity in the Implementation phase. Some system development cycles have another phase called Construction or Development, which includes the Develop programs activity. Other differences among system development cycles are the terminology they use, the order of their activities, and the level of detail within each phase.
2. System developers must involve users throughout the entire system development process. **Users** include anyone for whom the system is being built. Customers, data entry clerks, accountants, sales managers, and owners all are examples of users. You are a user of many information systems. You, as a user, might interact with an information system at your bank, library, grocery store, fitness center, work, and school. System developers must remember they ultimately deliver the system to the user. If the system is to be successful, the user must be included in all stages of development. Users are more apt to accept a new system if they contribute to its design.
3. The development process should have standards clearly defined. **Standards** are sets of rules and procedures a company expects employees to accept and follow. Having standards helps people working on the same project produce consistent results.

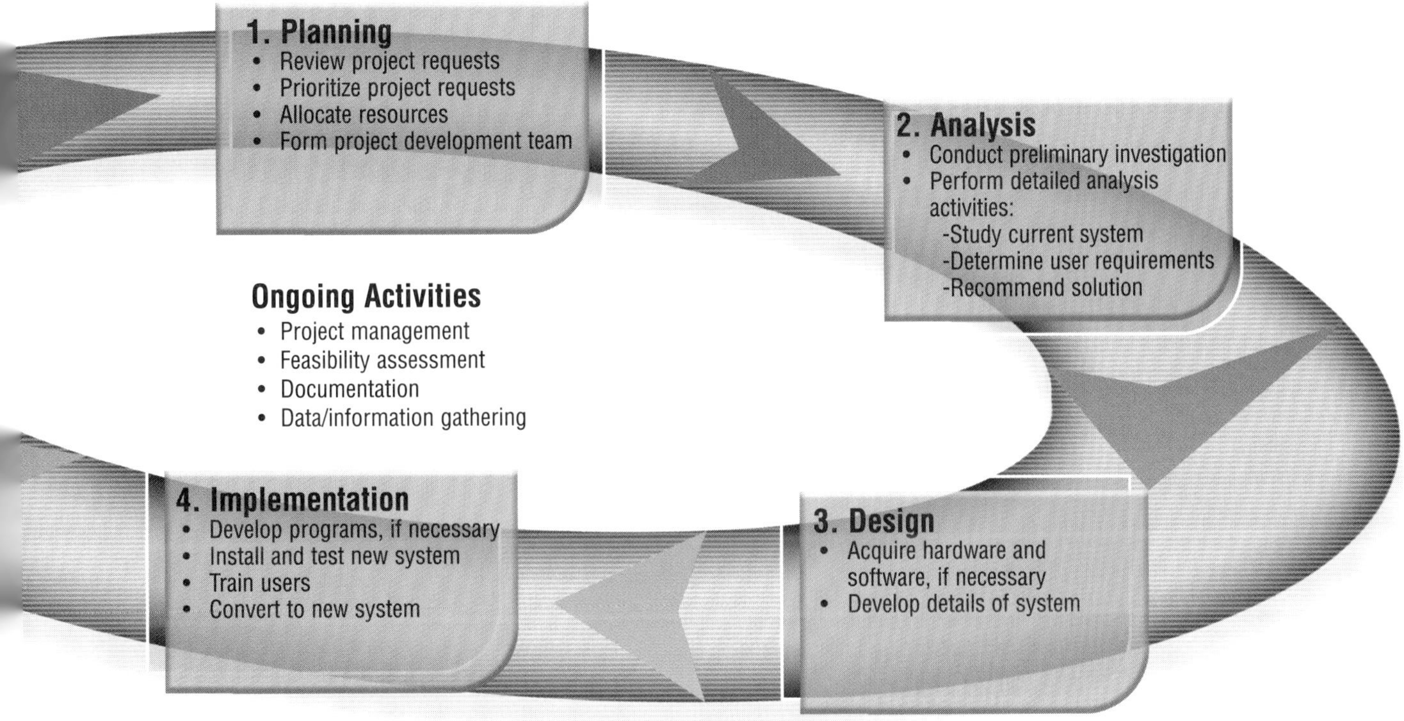

FIGURE 12-1 The system development cycle consists of five phases that form a loop. Several ongoing activities also take place throughout the entire system development cycle.

For example, one developer might refer to a product number in a database as a product ID. Others may call it a product identification number, product code, and so on. A system created in this way would be so confusing that it never could function correctly. If the system development cycle has defined standards, then everyone involved uses the same terms, such as product number. Many system development cycles implement standards by using a data dictionary.

Who Participates in the System Development Cycle?

System development should involve representatives from each department in which the proposed system will be used. This includes both nontechnical users and IT professionals. During the course of the system development cycle, the systems analyst meets and works with a variety of people (Figure 12-2). A **systems analyst** is responsible for designing and developing an information system. The systems analyst is the users' primary contact person.

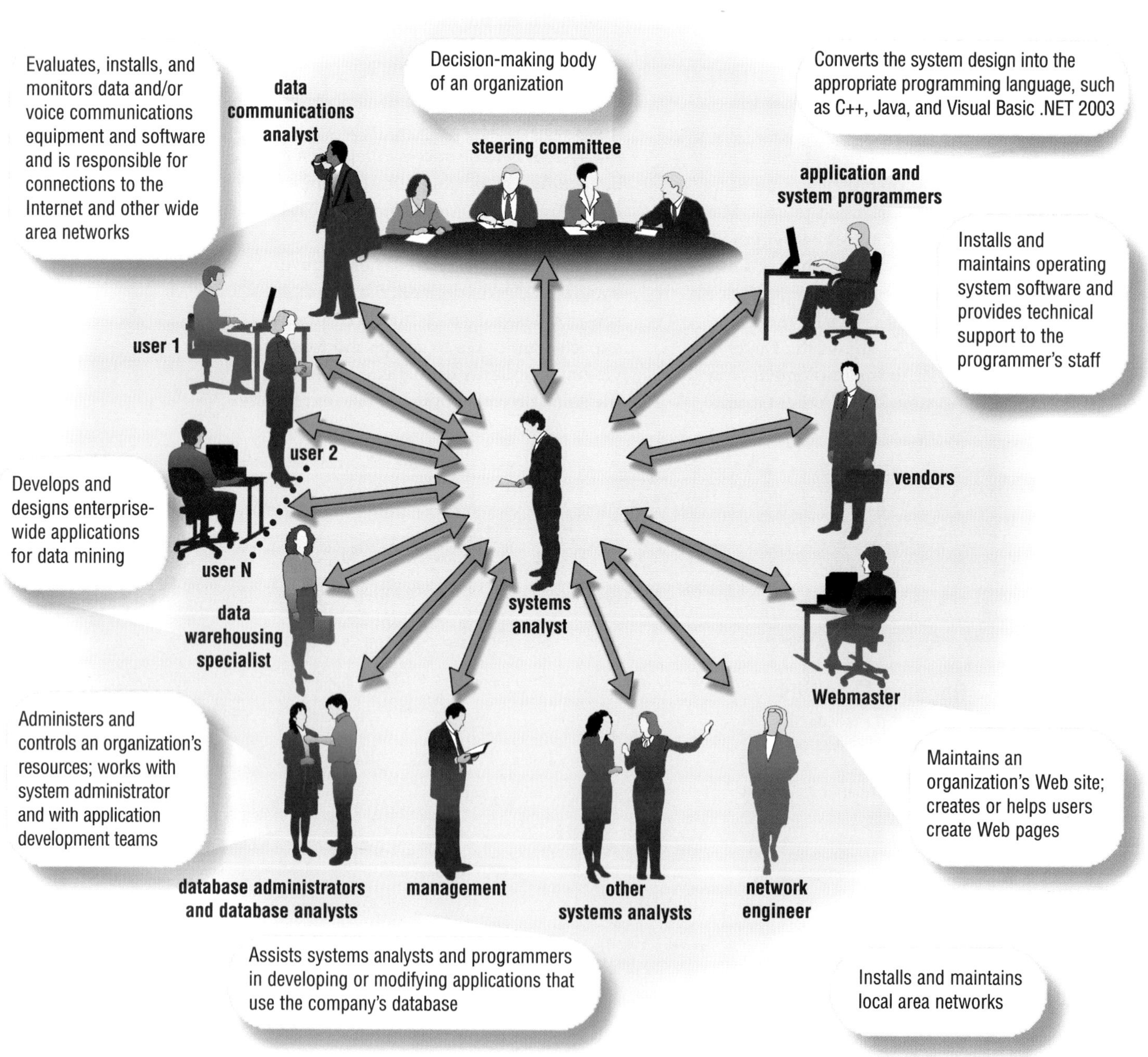

FIGURE 12-2 A systems analyst meets with a variety of people during a system development project.

Depending on the size of the organization or company, the tasks performed by the systems analyst may vary. Smaller companies may have one systems analyst or even one person who assumes the roles of both systems analyst and programmer. Larger companies often have multiple systems analysts.

The systems analysts are the liaison between the users and the IT professionals. They convert user requests into technical specifications. Thus, systems analysts must have superior technical skills. They also must be familiar with business operations, be able to solve problems, have the ability to introduce and support change, and possess excellent communications and interpersonal skills. Systems analysts prepare many reports, drawings, and diagrams. They discuss various aspects of the development project with users, management, other analysts, database analysts, database administrators, network administrators, the Webmaster, programmers, vendors, and the steering committee. The **steering committee** is a decision-making body in a company.

For each system development project, a company usually forms a **project team** to work on the project from beginning to end. The project team consists of users, the systems analyst, and other IT professionals. One member of the team is the **project leader**, who manages and controls the budget and schedule of the project. The systems analyst may or may not be selected as the project leader of the project.

Project Management

Project management is the process of planning, scheduling, and then controlling the activities during the system development cycle. The goal of project management is to deliver an acceptable system to the user in an agreed-upon time frame, while maintaining costs.

To plan and schedule a project effectively, the project leader identifies the following elements for the project:

- Goal, objectives, and expectations of the project, collectively called the *scope*
- Required activities
- Time estimates for each activity
- Cost estimates for each activity
- Order of activities
- Activities that can take place at the same time

When these items are identified, the project leader usually records them in a *project plan*. A popular tool used to plan and schedule the time relationships among project activities is a Gantt chart (Figure 12-3). A *Gantt chart*, developed by Henry L. Gantt, is a bar chart that uses horizontal bars to show project phases or activities. The left side, or vertical axis, displays the list of required activities. A horizontal axis across the top or bottom of the chart represents time.

After a project begins, the project leader monitors and controls the project. Some activities take less time than originally planned. Others take longer. The project leader may realize that an activity is taking excessive time or that scope creep has occurred. *Scope creep* occurs when one activity has led to another that was not originally planned; thus, the scope of the project now has grown.

Project leaders should have good *change management skills* so they can recognize when a change in the project has occurred, take actions to react to the change, and plan for opportunities because of the change. For example, the project leader may recognize the team will not be able to meet the original deadline of the project due to scope creep. Thus, the project leader may extend the deadline or may change or reduce the scope of the system development. If the latter occurs, the users will receive a less comprehensive system at the original deadline. In either case, the project leader revises the first project plan and presents the new plan to users for approval. It is crucial that everyone is aware of and agrees on any changes made to the project plan.

WEB LINK 12-1

Project Management

Visit the Discovering Computers 2005 WEB LINK page (**scsite .com/dc2005/weblink**). Click Project Management below Chapter 12.

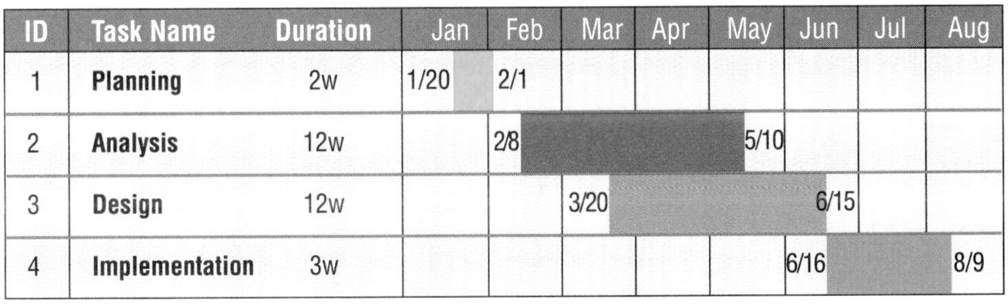

FIGURE 12-3 A Gantt chart is an effective way to show the time relationships of a project's activities.

One aspect of managing projects is to ensure that everyone submits deliverables on time and according to plan. A *deliverable* is any tangible item such as a chart, diagram, report, or program file. Project leaders can use **project management software** such as Microsoft Office Project 2003 to assist them in planning, scheduling, and controlling development projects (Figure 12-4). Read Looking Ahead 12-1 for a look at the next generation of project management.

Figure 12-4a (Gantt chart)

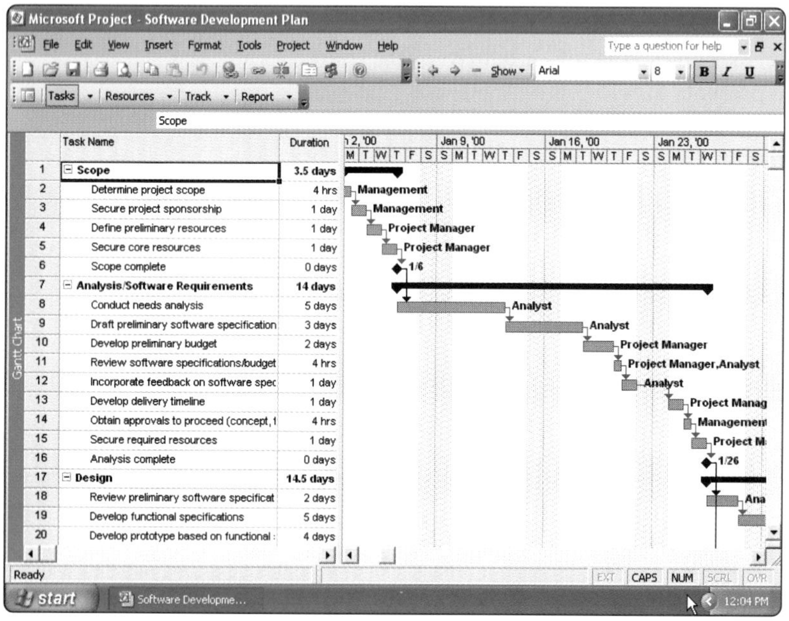

Figure 12-4b (calendar of events)

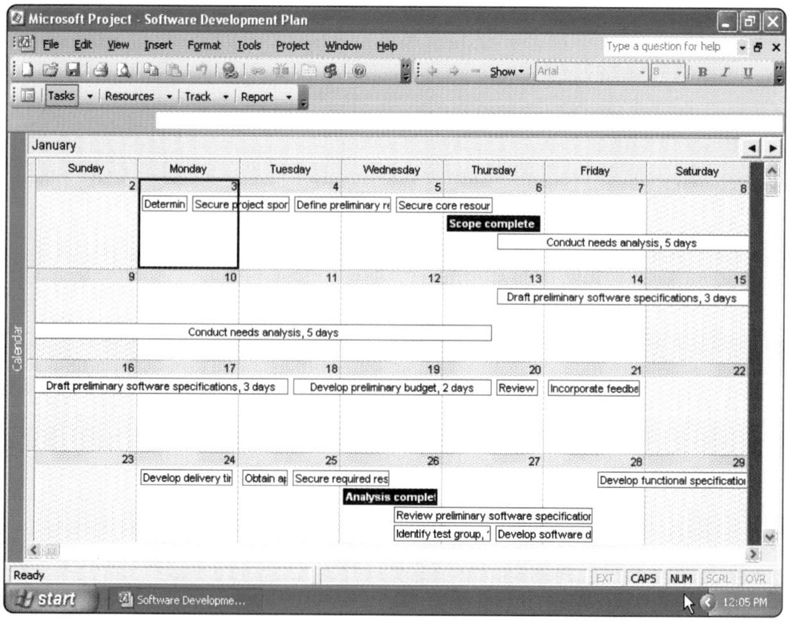

FIGURE 12-4 Microsoft Office Project 2003 is a popular project management program. A Gantt chart and calendar for a software development project are illustrated in this figure.

Feasibility Assessment

Feasibility is a measure of how suitable the development of a system will be to the company. A project that is feasible at one point of the system development cycle might become infeasible at a later point. Thus, systems analysts frequently reevaluate feasibility during the system development cycle.

A systems analyst typically uses four tests to evaluate feasibility of a project: operational feasibility, schedule feasibility, technical feasibility, and economic feasibility.

LOOKING AHEAD 12-1

Extreme Project Management Leads to Success

More than one-half of all information technology projects exceed their budgets by more than 189 percent, according to an estimate by the Gartner Group. In addition, 30 percent of these projects never are completed satisfactorily. With these startling statistics and challenging economic conditions, project managers need skills to plan and execute their projects successfully and within budgets.

One method of organizing and executing these plans is called *extreme project management.* Like extreme sports, it requires proficient participants who are committed totally to achieving success. This nonstandard approach is used rarely in United States corporations, but it is growing in popularity when businesses must execute projects under severe budgetary and time constraints.

Extreme project management principles require project managers to take entire control of the planning process and not delegate responsibilities. They must take whatever action is necessary for the project's success, including convincing employees to complete their assigned tasks on time and correctly. They also must communicate the plan by giving specific instructions to employees, coordinating workflow schedules in writing, following up with the next activity, and giving constructive, timely feedback.

Project managers who use this style report successful outcomes because their employees sense that their involvement is crucial for the project's completion.

For a look at the next generation of extreme project management, visit the Discovering Computers 2005 Looking Ahead Web page (**scsite.com/dc2005/looking**). Click Looking Ahead #1 below Chapter 12.

- *Operational feasibility* measures how well the proposed information system will work. Will the users like the new system? Will they use it? Will it meet their requirements? Will it cause any changes in their work environment?
- *Schedule feasibility* measures whether the established deadlines for the project are reasonable. If a deadline is not reasonable, the project leader might make a new schedule. If a deadline cannot be extended, then the scope of the project might be reduced to meet the mandatory deadline.
- *Technical feasibility* measures whether the company has or can obtain the hardware, software, and people needed to deliver and then support the proposed information system. For most system projects, the technology exists. Hardware, software, and people typically are available to support an information system. The challenge is obtaining funds to pay for these resources. Economic feasibility addresses funding.
- *Economic feasibility*, also called *cost/benefit feasibility*, measures whether the lifetime benefits of the proposed information system will be greater than its lifetime costs. A systems analyst uses many financial techniques, such as return on investment (ROI) and payback analysis, to perform the cost/benefit analysis.

FAQ 12-1

Does the systems analyst also perform the financial analysis?

Although some systems analysts perform a financial analysis, many are not familiar with financial assessment techniques. Instead, they ask a financial analyst to assist them with the financial requirements of the economic feasibility.

For more information about financial indicators, visit the Discovering Computers 2005 FAQ Web page (**scsite.com/dc2005/faq**). Click Financial Indicators below Chapter 12.

Documentation

During the entire system development cycle, project team members produce much documentation. **Documentation** is the collection and summarization of data and information. It includes reports, diagrams, programs, or any other deliverables generated during the system development cycle.

A *project notebook* contains all documentation for a single project. The project notebook might be a simple three-ring binder. Many companies, however, have analysis and design software that systems analysts use to create an automated project notebook.

Users and IT professionals refer to existing documentation when working with and modifying current systems. It is important that all documentation be well written, thorough, and understandable. Maintaining up-to-date documentation should be an ongoing part of the system development cycle. Too often, project team members put off documentation until the end because it is time-consuming. They mistakenly regard it as an unimportant or unproductive part of the system development cycle.

Data and Information Gathering Techniques

During the system development cycle, members of the project team gather data and information. They need accurate and timely data and information for many reasons. They must keep a project on schedule, evaluate feasibility, and be sure the system meets requirements. Systems analysts and other IT professionals use several techniques to gather data and information. They review documentation, observe, send questionnaires, interview, conduct joint-application design sessions, and research. The following paragraphs discuss these techniques.

- Review Documentation — By reviewing documentation such as a company's organization chart, memos, and meeting minutes, system developers learn about the history of a project. Documentation also provides information about the company such as its operations, weaknesses, and strengths.
- Observe — Observing people helps system developers understand exactly how they perform a task. Likewise, observing a machine allows you to see how it works. Read Issue 12-1 for a related discussion.

ISSUE 12-1

Does Observation Improve Productivity?

During the data and information gathering stage of the system development cycle, employees are involved actively in the process. They complete questionnaires, participate in interviews, and are observed while performing their jobs. Many researchers suggest that during observation, employees may not exhibit everyday behavior and may perform above and beyond their normal workday activities. They base this premise on the *Hawthorne Effect*, which is the result of a study performed in the 1920s in the Hawthorne plant of the Western Electric Company in Hawthorne, Illinois. The study discovered that productivity improved during observation, whether the conditions were made better or worse. Researchers concluded that productivity seemed to improve whenever the workers knew they were being observed. What is your opinion of the Hawthorne Effect? Do you agree with the research? If someone is observing you at work or if you are receiving increased attention, does this cause you to alter your behavior? Why or why not?

For more information about the system development cycle and the Hawthorne Effect, visit the Discovering Computers 2005 Issues Web page (**scsite.com/dc2005/issues**). Click Issue #1 below Chapter 12.

- Questionnaire — To obtain data and information from a large number of people, system developers send questionnaires.
- Interview — The interview is the most important data and information gathering technique for the system developer. It allows the system developer to clarify responses and probe for feedback face to face. Read Apply It 12-1 for more information.
- JAD Session — An alternative to the one-on-one interview is a joint-application design session. A *joint-application design (JAD) session* is a lengthy, structured, group meeting in which users and IT professionals work together to design or develop an application (Figure 12-5). The goal of this type of JAD session is to obtain group agreement on an issue. For example, the participants may try to identify problems associated with an existing system.
- Research — Newspapers, computer magazines, reference books, trade shows, and the Web are excellent sources of information. These sources can provide the system developer with information such as the latest hardware and software products and explanations of new processes and procedures.

APPLY IT 12-1

Interviewing for Success

Part of the success of a system development cycle is the quality of client interviews. If selected as an interviewee, you can do your part to enhance the process.

Begin by gathering documentation that might help the interviewer understand your business's structure and needs. These papers include organization charts, an annual report, budgets, and short- and long-term goals.

When the interview begins, the interviewer should establish rapport to make you feel at ease and set the tone. He or she should inform you of the length of the interview, the information being sought, and how he or she will use your answers to help design a system. Keep these goals in mind as you respond to the questions so that your answers stay on track.

Expect two types of questions: close-ended and open-ended. The close-ended questions generally are easy to answer, such as the number of years a system has been in place. The open-ended questions, by contrast, require more explanation. For example, an open-ended question may be, Describe three problems with your current system.

To make a lasting impression, be cooperative, ask questions if you need clarification of what information is needed, and give honest answers.

For more information about interviews, visit the Discovering Computers 2005 Apply It Web page (**scsite.com/dc2005/apply**). Click Apply It #1 below Chapter 12.

FIGURE 12-5 During a JAD session, the systems analyst is the ***moderator***, or leader, of the discussion. Another member, called the ***scribe***, records facts and action items assigned during the session.

WHAT INITIATES THE SYSTEM DEVELOPMENT CYCLE?

A user may request a new or modified information system for a variety of reasons. The most obvious reason is to correct a problem. The computed GPA on a grade report may be incorrect. Another reason is to improve the information system. For example, if a school wants to allow students to register for classes online, it would have to modify the existing registration system to include this new feature.

Sometimes situations outside your control cause an information system to require modification. Corporate management or some other governing body may mandate a change. For example, a nationwide insurance company might require all offices to use the same calendar software. Competition also can lead to change. After one pharmacy offers online shopping, others follow for fear of losing customers. In recent years, another source of change has resulted from one company merging with or acquiring another company.

A user may request a new or modified information system verbally in a telephone conversation or written as an e-mail message (Figure 12-6a). In larger companies, users write a formal request for a new or modified information system, which is called a *request for system services* or *project request* (Figure 12-6b). This document becomes the first item in the project notebook. It also triggers the first phase of the system development cycle: planning.

Figure 12-6a (informal project request)

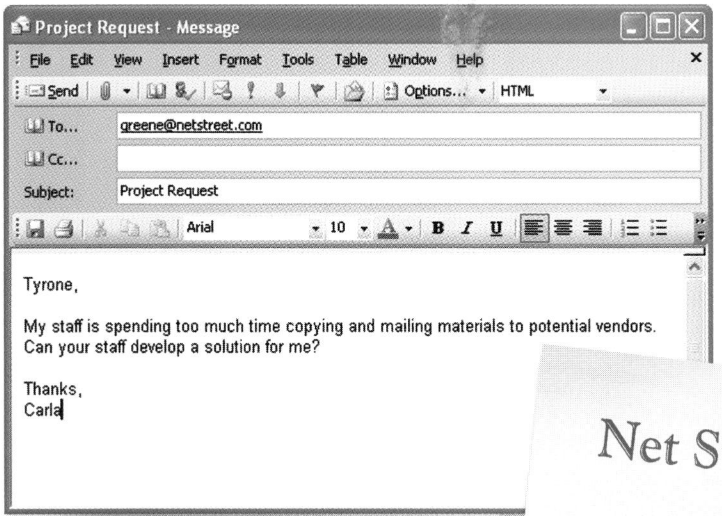

Tyrone,

My staff is spending too much time copying and mailing materials to potential vendors. Can your staff develop a solution for me?

Thanks,
Carla

Figure 12-6b (formal project request)

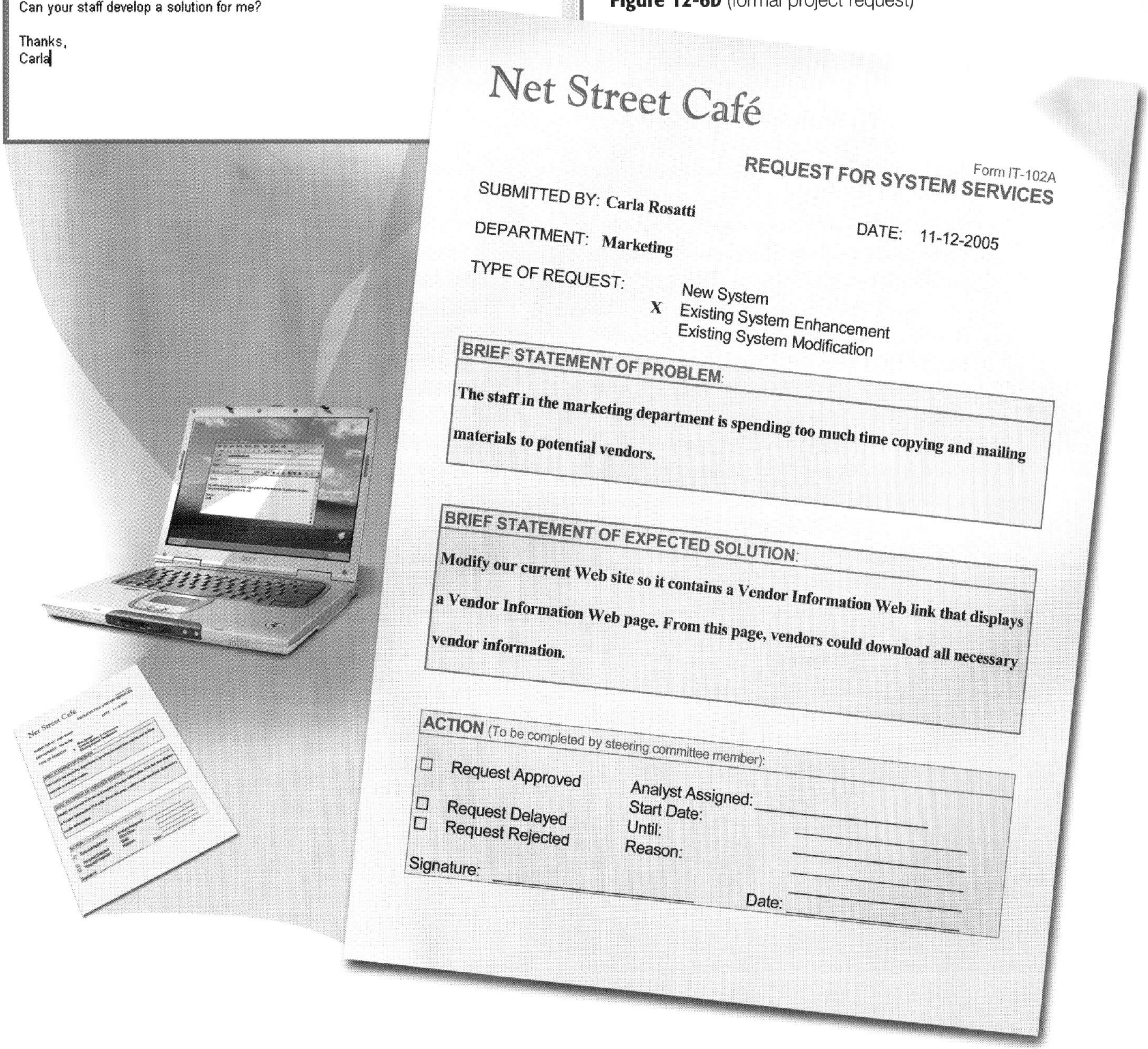

Net Street Café

Form IT-102A

REQUEST FOR SYSTEM SERVICES

SUBMITTED BY: **Carla Rosatti**

DATE: 11-12-2005

DEPARTMENT: **Marketing**

TYPE OF REQUEST:
New System
X Existing System Enhancement
Existing System Modification

BRIEF STATEMENT OF PROBLEM:

The staff in the marketing department is spending too much time copying and mailing materials to potential vendors.

BRIEF STATEMENT OF EXPECTED SOLUTION:

Modify our current Web site so it contains a Vendor Information Web link that displays a Vendor Information Web page. From this page, vendors could download all necessary vendor information.

ACTION (To be completed by steering committee member):

☐ Request Approved — Analyst Assigned: ______ Start Date: ______

☐ Request Delayed — Until: ______

☐ Request Rejected — Reason: ______

Signature: ______ Date: ______

FIGURE 12-6 Sometimes users informally communicate a project request verbally or as an e-mail message. In larger companies, requests often are documented on a form such as this Request for System Services.

Net Street Café — A Case Study

This chapter includes a case study to help you understand real-world system development applications. The case study appears shaded in yellow immediately after the discussion of each phase in the system development cycle. The case is based on a fictitious company. The following paragraphs present a background about Net Street Café, a cybercafé.

Net Street Café is a worldwide chain of cybercafés. With locations in 40 cities around the world, Net Street Café is one of the more technologically advanced cybercafés on the planet.

At these cafés, you can do the following: connect to the Web while drinking your favorite specialty beverage and eating a snack; chat with or send e-mail to coworkers, friends, and family; and play online games or read an online book.

If customers have questions while using the computer, any staff member can provide assistance. Each café also offers training courses for beginning computer users.

Through high-speed T1 lines, customers have fast Internet access. Monitors are 19 inches. Each café has a minimum of 25 computers, along with a color printer, a laser printer, a digital camera, and a scanner. All computers have popular programs such as Microsoft Office 2003 and Adobe Photoshop. The café also is a hot spot, which means customers can use their own mobile computer or mobile device to connect wirelessly to the Internet. For each beverage or snack purchased, customers receive 30 minutes of free computer and/or Web access. If they would like additional time, the fee is $5.00 per hour.

Since Net Street Café started operations in 1995, business has been thriving. The cafés serve thousands of customers around the world. The Web site (Figure 12-7) has hundreds of hits a day. John Simmons, chief information officer (CIO) for Net Street Café, offers one suggestion for the company's financial success. "We do not pay for the computers and equipment in our cafés. Instead, we allow computer vendors to use our café as a storefront for their products. This provides customers with the opportunity to try out the hardware and software before making a purchase. When customers are ready to purchase computers, we direct them to the vendor's online storefront for discount pricing."

To showcase their hardware and software in the cafés, computer vendors request information from Carla Rosatti, the marketing manager. The number of these requests is rising quickly. The cost of copying and mailing this material is becoming excessive. For this reason, Carla would like this vendor information made available on the Web. Vendors could download information sheets, press releases, photographs, and other information from the Web site. Placing this information on the Web would save Carla and her staff a great deal of time and money.

Carla realizes this task will require substantial company resources. She believes a systems study is necessary. She sends an e-mail message to the vice president of information systems (Figure 12-6a on the previous page). He agrees and tells her to fill out a Request for System Services form (Figure 12-6b on the previous page) and submit it to George Chambers, chair of the steering committee at Net Street Café.

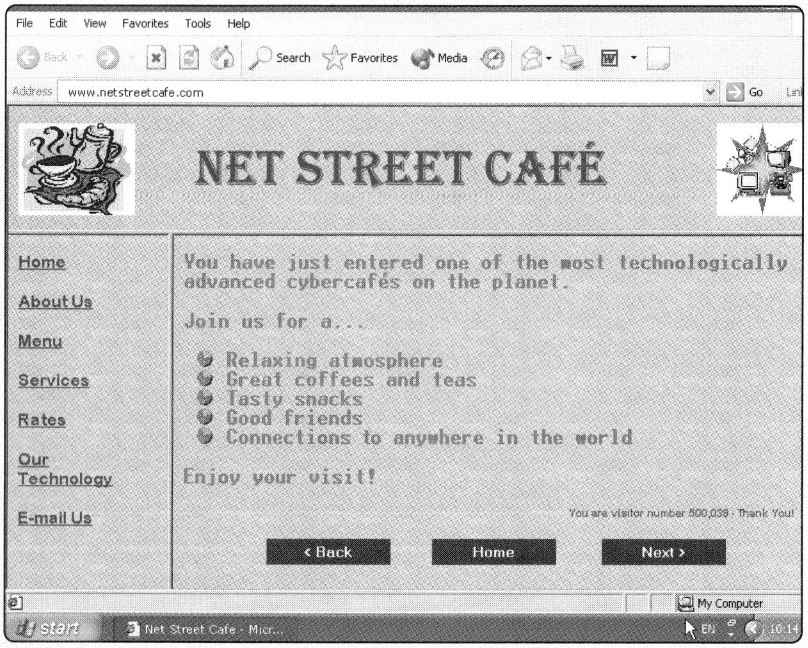

FIGURE 12-7 To help you understand real-world applications of the system development cycle better, this chapter presents a case study about Net Street Café. At this cybercafé, you can connect to the Web while eating a snack and drinking your favorite specialty coffee, tea, or other beverage.

PLANNING PHASE

The **planning phase** for a project begins when the steering committee receives a project request. As mentioned earlier in this chapter, the steering committee is a decision-making body for a company. This committee usually consists of five to nine people. It typically includes a mix of vice presidents, managers, nonmanagement users, and IT personnel.

During the planning phase, four major activities are performed: (1) review and approve the project requests; (2) prioritize the project requests; (3) allocate resources such as money, people, and equipment to approved projects; and (4) form a project development team for each approved project. Read Issue 12-2 for a discussion related to team formation.

ISSUE 12-2

Should Companies Use Distributed Development?

Distributed development is an increasingly popular trend, especially in the software industry. *Distributed development* is the creation of products or applications by developers in separate geographic locations, taking advantage of global talent pools and supply chains. Companies generate a basic design and then send it to more cost-effective sites for development. The wide adoption of distributed development is attributed to the evolution of the Internet, the shortage of human resources, the availability of global markets, and the ability to reduce labor costs. Distributed developers around the world work from their own homes and communicate using e-mail, Internet telephony, video conferencing, and online meetings. These tools allow the dispersed developers to stay in touch with administrators and have up-to-date knowledge of project advancement. Managers can supervise development, providing companies the benefits of subcontracting without the risk of unpleasant surprise. But, is distributive development fair to a company's home labor force? Why or why not? What other problems might be associated with distributed development? How can these problems be addressed?

For more information about distributed development, visit the Discovering Computers 2005 Issues Web page (**scsite.com/dc2005/issues**). Click Issue #2 below Chapter 12.

The projects that receive the highest priority are those mandated by management or some other governing body. These requests are given immediate attention. The steering committee evaluates the remaining project requests based on their value to the company. The steering committee approves some projects and rejects others. Of the approved projects, it is likely that only a few will begin their system development cycle immediately. Others will have to wait for additional funds or resources to become available.

Planning at Net Street Café

After receiving the project request (Figure 12-6b on page 627) from Carla, George Chambers distributes it to all members of the steering committee. They will discuss the request at their next meeting. The steering committee members of Net Street Café are George Chambers, controller and chair of the steering committee; Levona Shor, vice president of operations; Jesse Martinez, Webmaster; Mae Ling, training specialist; Sadie Lapinski, senior systems analyst; and Tyrone Greene, vice president of information systems. George also invites Carla Rosatti to the next steering committee meeting. Because she originated the project request, Carla will have the knowledge to answer questions.

During the meeting, the committee decides the project request identifies an improvement to the system, instead of a problem. They feel the nature of the improvement (to make vendor information available on the Web) could lead to considerable savings for the company. It also will provide quicker service to potential vendors.

The steering committee approves the request. George points out that the company has enough funds in its budget to begin the project immediately. Thus, Tyrone assembles a system development project team. He assigns Sadie Lapinski, senior systems analyst, as the project leader. Sadie and her team immediately begin the next phase: analysis.

QUIZ YOURSELF 12-1

To check your knowledge of the names of the system development cycle phases, guidelines for system development, ongoing system development cycle activities, and the planning phase, visit the Discovering Computers 2005 Quiz Yourself Web page (**scsite.com/dc2005/quiz**). Click Objectives 1 – 4 below Chapter 12.

ANALYSIS PHASE

The **analysis phase** consists of two major activities: (1) conduct a preliminary investigation and (2) perform detailed analysis. Detailed analysis has three activities: (1) study how the current system works; (2) determine the users' wants, needs, and requirements; and (3) recommend a solution.

The Preliminary Investigation

The main purpose of the **preliminary investigation**, sometimes called the *feasibility study,* is to determine the exact nature of the problem or improvement and decide whether it is worth pursuing. Should the company continue to assign resources to this project? To answer this question, the systems analyst conducts a very general study of the project. Then, the systems analyst presents his or her findings in a report. Figure 12-8 shows a sample feasibility report, also sometimes known as the feasibility study.

In this phase, the systems analyst defines the problem or improvement accurately. The actual problem may be different from the one suggested in the project request. For example, suppose vendors complain that the marketing department takes too long to send customer names and addresses. An investigation might reveal the marketing department is not the problem. The problem exists because some cafés wait three weeks before sending customer names and addresses to the marketing department. Thus, the preliminary investigation determines the real problem, which is the marketing department does not have instant access to the customer names and addresses.

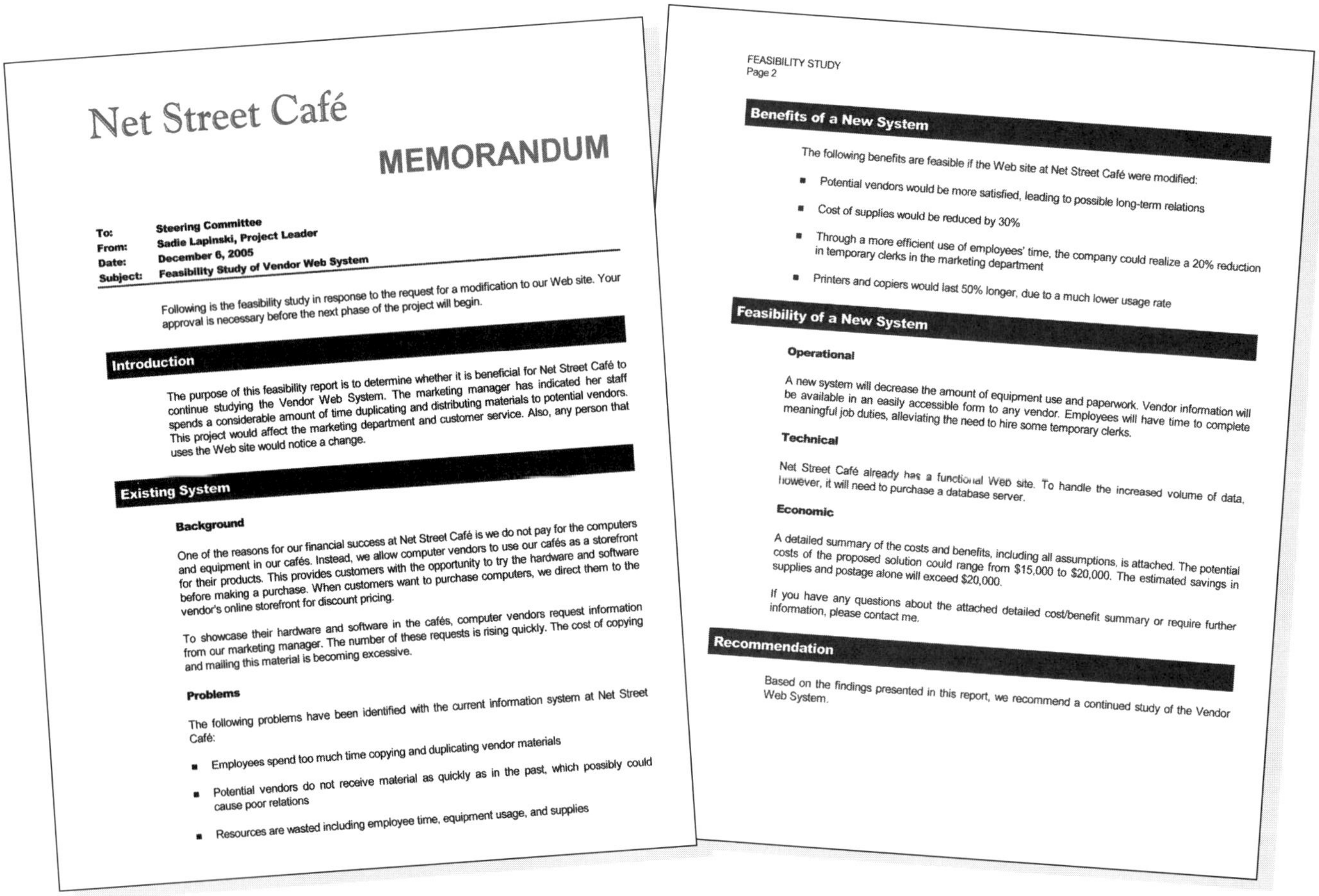

Net Street Café

MEMORANDUM

To: Steering Committee
From: Sadie Lapinski, Project Leader
Date: December 6, 2005
Subject: Feasibility Study of Vendor Web System

Following is the feasibility study in response to the request for a modification to our Web site. Your approval is necessary before the next phase of the project will begin.

Introduction

The purpose of this feasibility report is to determine whether it is beneficial for Net Street Café to continue studying the Vendor Web System. The marketing manager has indicated her staff spends a considerable amount of time duplicating and distributing materials to potential vendors. This project would affect the marketing department and customer service. Also, any person that uses the Web site would notice a change.

Existing System

Background

One of the reasons for our financial success at Net Street Café is we do not pay for the computers and equipment in our cafés. Instead, we allow computer vendors to use our cafés as a storefront for their products. This provides customers with the opportunity to try the hardware and software before making a purchase. When customers want to purchase computers, we direct them to the vendor's online storefront for discount pricing.

To showcase their hardware and software in the cafés, computer vendors request information from our marketing manager. The number of these requests is rising quickly. The cost of copying and mailing this material is becoming excessive.

Problems

The following problems have been identified with the current information system at Net Street Café:

- Employees spend too much time copying and duplicating vendor materials
- Potential vendors do not receive material as quickly as in the past, which possibly could cause poor relations
- Resources are wasted including employee time, equipment usage, and supplies

FEASIBILITY STUDY
Page 2

Benefits of a New System

The following benefits are feasible if the Web site at Net Street Café were modified:

- Potential vendors would be more satisfied, leading to possible long-term relations
- Cost of supplies would be reduced by 30%
- Through a more efficient use of employees' time, the company could realize a 20% reduction in temporary clerks in the marketing department
- Printers and copiers would last 50% longer, due to a much lower usage rate

Feasibility of a New System

Operational

A new system will decrease the amount of equipment use and paperwork. Vendor information will be available in an easily accessible form to any vendor. Employees will have time to complete meaningful job duties, alleviating the need to hire some temporary clerks.

Technical

Net Street Café already has a functional Web site. To handle the increased volume of data, however, it will need to purchase a database server.

Economic

A detailed summary of the costs and benefits, including all assumptions, is attached. The potential costs of the proposed solution could range from $15,000 to $20,000. The estimated savings in supplies and postage alone will exceed $20,000.

If you have any questions about the attached detailed cost/benefit summary or require further information, please contact me.

Recommendation

Based on the findings presented in this report, we recommend a continued study of the Vendor Web System.

FIGURE 12-8 A feasibility report presents the results of the preliminary investigation. The report must be prepared professionally and be well organized to be effective.

The first activity in the preliminary investigation is to interview the user who submitted the project request. In the case of the cybercafé, the marketing manager submitted the request. Depending on the nature of the request, project team members may interview other users too. A request, for example, might involve data or a process that affects more than one department. In the case of the cybercafé, members of the team might interview the controller for costs of copying and mailing materials. They also might interview one or two vendors.

In addition to interviewing, members of the project team may use other data gathering techniques such as reviewing existing documentation. The time spent on this phase of the system development cycle is quite short when compared with the remainder of the project. Often, the preliminary investigation takes just a few days.

Upon completion of the preliminary investigation, the systems analyst writes the feasibility report. This report presents the team's findings to the steering committee. The feasibility report contains these major sections: introduction, existing system, benefits of a new system, feasibility of a new system, and the recommendation.

The introduction states the purpose of the report, the problem or improvement, and the scope of the project. The existing system section describes the background of the request and the problems or limitations of the current system. The next section identifies the benefits the company will realize from the proposed solution. The feasibility section assesses operational, technical, and economic feasibility of the proposed solution. The last section recommends whether the company should continue the project.

In some cases, the project team may recommend not to continue the project. In other words, the team considers the project infeasible. If the steering committee agrees, the project ends at this point. If the project team recommends continuing and the steering committee approves this recommendation, however, then detailed analysis begins.

Preliminary Investigation at Net Street Café

Sadie Lapinski, senior systems analyst and project leader, meets with Carla Rosatti to discuss the project request. During the interview, Sadie looks at the material that Carla's staff sends to a potential vendor. She asks Carla how many vendor requests she receives in a month. Then Sadie interviews the controller, George Chambers, to obtain some general cost and benefit figures for the feasibility report. She also calls a vendor. She wants to know if the material Carla's department sends is helpful.

Next, Sadie prepares the feasibility report (Figure 12-8). After the project team members review it, Sadie submits it to the steering committee. The report recommends continuing into the detailed analysis phase for this project. The steering committee agrees. Sadie and her team begin detailed analysis.

Detailed Analysis

Detailed analysis involves three major activities: (1) study how the current system works; (2) determine the users' wants, needs, and requirements; and (3) recommend a solution. Detailed analysis sometimes is called *logical design* because the systems analysts develop the proposed solution without regard to any specific hardware or software. That is, they make no attempt to identify the procedures that should be automated and those that should be manual.

During these activities, systems analysts use all of the data and information gathering techniques. They review documentation, observe employees and machines, send questionnaires, interview employees, conduct JAD sessions, and do research. An important benefit from these activities is that they build valuable relationships among the systems analysts and users.

While studying the current system and identifying user requirements, the systems analyst collects a lot of data and information. A major task for the systems analyst is to document these findings in a way that can be understood by everyone. Both users and IT professionals refer to this documentation.

Most systems analysts use either a process modeling or object modeling approach to analysis and design. The following sections discuss these approaches.

FAQ 12-2

Why is it necessary for the systems analyst to build relationships with users?

Systems analysts have much more credibility with users if the analysts understand user concerns. If users are involved, they are more likely to accept and use the new system — called *user buy-in*. The reason some systems are a failure is because some developers create or modify systems with little or no user participation.

For more information about systems analysts, visit the Discovering Computers 2005 FAQ Web page (**scsite.com/dc2005/faq**). Click Systems Analyst below Chapter 12.

WEB LINK 12-2

Process Modeling

Visit the Discovering Computers 2005 WEB LINK page (**scsite.com/dc2005/weblink**). Click Process Modeling below Chapter 12.

Process Modeling

Process modeling, sometimes called *structured analysis and design*, is an analysis and design technique that describes processes that transform inputs into outputs. Tools that a systems analyst uses for process modeling include entity-relationship diagrams, data flow diagrams, and the project dictionary. The following pages discuss these tools.

ENTITY-RELATIONSHIP DIAGRAMS An **entity-relationship diagram** (*ERD*) is a tool that graphically shows the connections among entities in a system. An *entity* is an object in the system that has data. For example, a cybercafé might have customer, order, menu item, computer, and vendor entities.

On the ERD, entity names usually are nouns. You write the entity name in all capital letters. Each relationship describes a connection between two entities. In the ERD shown in Figure 12-9, a vendor supplies one or more computers to the cafés. A computer is supplied by a single vendor. A customer may or may not sit down and use one of these computers during a visit to the café. A customer may or may not place an order. Some customers place multiple orders. Each order contains one or more items from the menu.

It is important that the systems analyst has an accurate understanding of the system. The systems analyst reviews the ERD with the user. After users approve the ERD, the systems analyst identifies data items associated with an entity. For example, the VENDOR entity might have these data items: Vendor Number, Vendor Name, Vendor Contact Name, Address, City, State, Postal Code, Telephone Number, and E-mail Address.

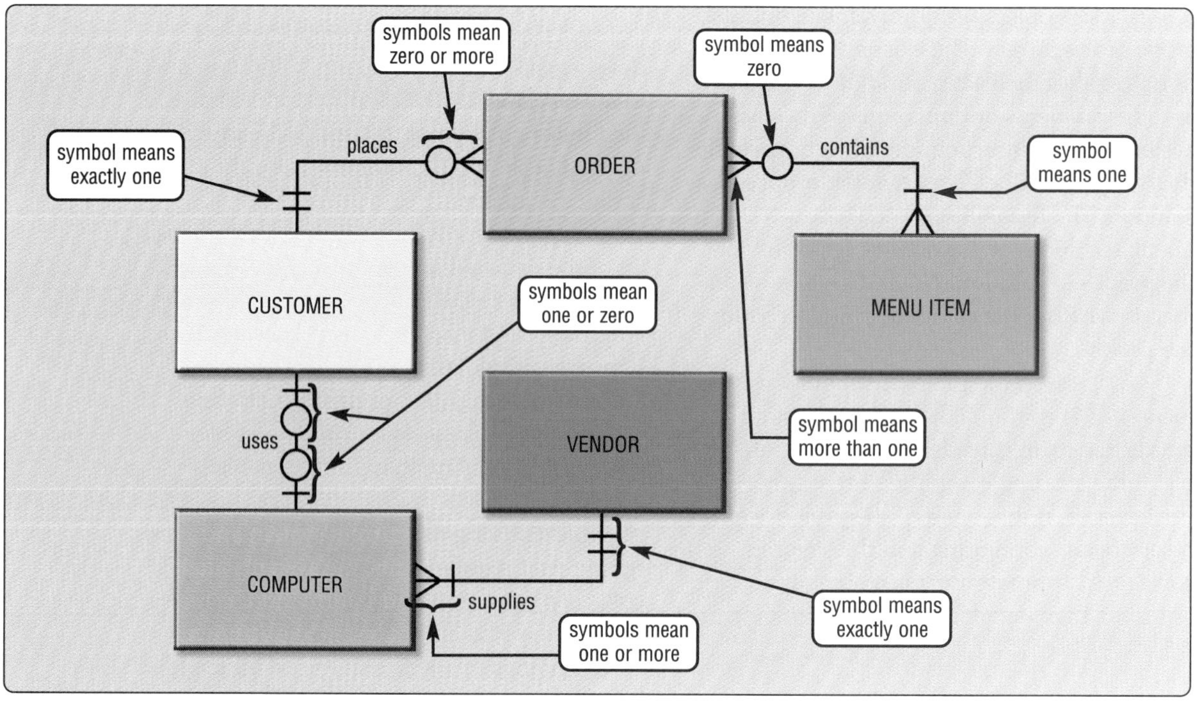

FIGURE 12-9 This ERD shows the relationships among entities in the Vendor Web System at Net Street Café. A vendor supplies one or more computers to the cafés. A computer is supplied by a single vendor. A customer may or may not sit down and use one of these computers during a visit to the café. A customer may or may not place an order. Some customers place multiple orders. Each order contains one or more items from the menu.

DATA FLOW DIAGRAMS A **data flow diagram** (*DFD*) is a tool that graphically shows the flow of data in a system. The key elements of a DFD are the data flows, the processes, the data stores, and the sources (Figure 12-10). A line with an arrow indicates a data flow. A *data flow* shows the input or output of data or information into or out from a process. A *process*, which is drawn as a circle, transforms an input data flow into an output data flow. A rectangle with no sides is a data store. A *data store* is a holding place for data and information. Examples of data stores are filing cabinets, checkbook registers, or electronic files in a computer. The squares on the DFD are sources. A *source* identifies an entity outside the scope of the system. Sources send data into the system or receive information from the system.

Like ERDs, systems analysts often use DFDs to review processes with users. Systems analysts prepare DFDs on a level-by-level basis. The top level DFD, known as a *context diagram*, identifies only the major process. The context diagram shows the system being studied. Lower-level DFDs add detail and definition to the higher levels, similar to zooming in on a computer screen. The lower-level DFDs then contain subprocesses. For example, Figure 12-10 shows a context diagram that contains the Vendor Web System process. This process might be split into three subprocesses: (1) gathering and organizing vendor information, (2) converting vendor information into electronic format, and (3) uploading the files to the Web page.

PROJECT DICTIONARY The **project dictionary**, sometimes called the *repository*, contains all the documentation and deliverables of a project. The project dictionary helps everyone keep track of the huge amount of details in a system. The dictionary explains every item found on these diagrams. Each process, data store, data flow, and source on every DFD has an entry in the project dictionary. Every entity on the ERD has an entry in the project dictionary. The dictionary also contains an entry for each data item associated with the entities. Some systems can be represented with 25 or more DFDs and have hundreds of data items.

The number of entries added to the dictionary at this point can be enormous. As you might imagine, this activity requires a huge amount of time.

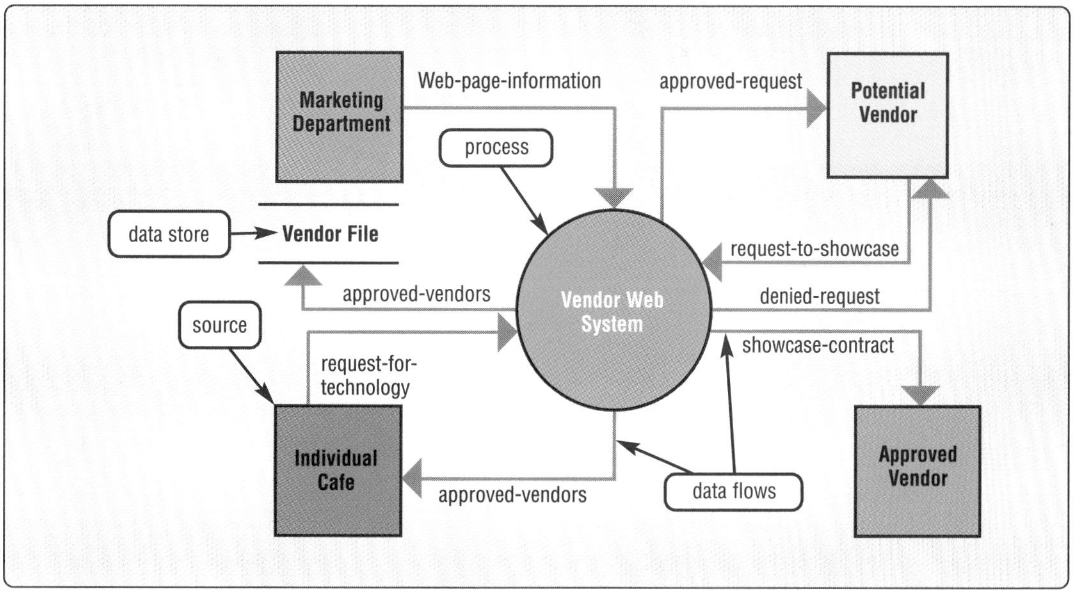

FIGURE 12-10 This data flow diagram, called the context diagram, has one process — the Vendor Web System being studied at Net Street Café. The Vendor File is a data store. Sources both send and receive data and information to and from the system. For example, a café sends a request for technology (hardware and/or software) into the Vendor Web System, which then sends out a list of approved vendors for that technology. The list of approved vendors is stored in the Vendor File.

The systems analyst uses a variety of techniques to enter these items in the project dictionary. Some of these include structured English, decision tables and decision trees, and the data dictionary.

- *Structured English* is a style of writing that describes the steps in a process. Many systems analysts use structured English to explain the details of a process. Figure 12-11 shows an example of structured English that describes the process of uploading vendor information.
- Sometimes, a process consists of many conditions or rules. In this case, the systems analyst may use a decision table or decision tree instead of structured English. A **decision table** is a table that lists a variety of conditions and the actions that correspond to each condition. A *decision tree* also shows conditions and actions, but it shows them graphically. Figures 12-12 and 12-13 show a decision table and decision tree for the same process: determining whether a vendor is approved.
- Each data item has an entry in the data dictionary section of the project dictionary (Figure 12-14). The **data dictionary** stores the data item's name, description, and other details about each data item. The systems analyst creates the data dictionary during detailed analysis. In later phases of the system development cycle, the systems analyst refers to and updates the data dictionary.

UPLOADING VENDOR INFORMATION

For each item containing vendor information, perform the following steps:

    If the item is not a computer file then

        Use the scanner to convert it into a file format.

    Copy the file into the Vendor Information folder on the hard disk.

Zip all new files in the Vendor Information folder into a single file.

Save the zipped file in a Web folder.

E-mail the Webmaster with the name of the zipped file.

FIGURE 12-11 Structured English is a technique used to describe a process in the project dictionary. This structured English example describes the process of uploading vendor information to a Web page. The indented text is part of the loop.

		RULES							
		1	2	3	4	5	6	7	8
CONDITIONS	Background check results (S = Satisfactory, U = Unsatisfactory)	S	S	S	S	U	U	U	U
	References furnished?	Y	Y	N	N	Y	Y	N	N
	Passed credit check?	Y	N	Y	N	Y	N	Y	N
ACTIONS	Vendor approved	X							
	Vendor not approved		X			X	X	X	X
	Waiting for additional information			X	X				

FIGURE 12-12 This decision table describes the policy for determining whether vendors are approved to showcase their products at Net Street Café. Vendors are approved if they meet all conditions in Rule #1. For example, vendors are approved if their background check results are satisfactory, they have furnished all of their references, and have passed a credit check.

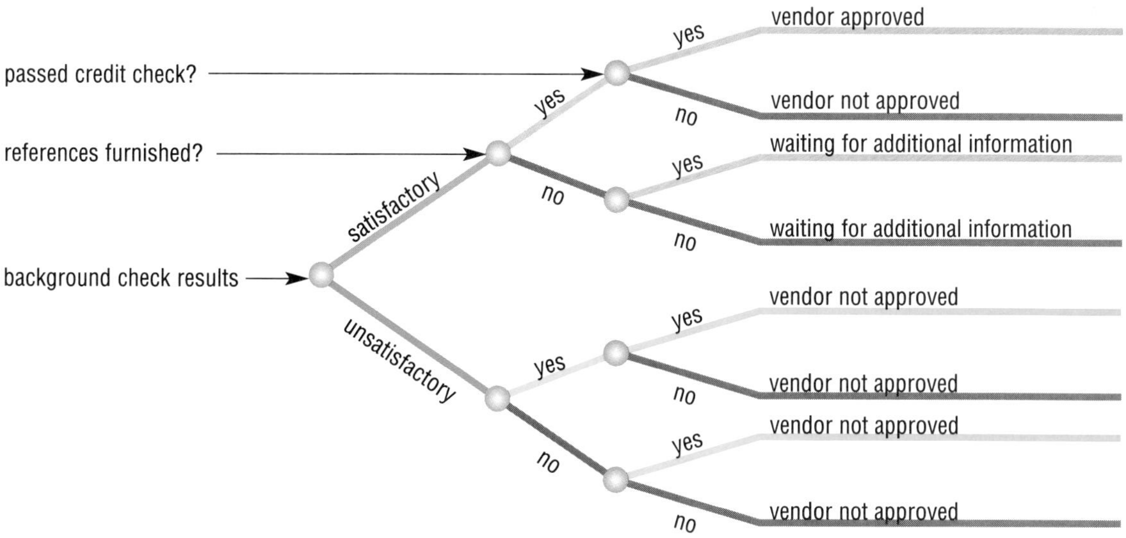

FIGURE 12-13 Some systems analysts prefer decision trees instead of decision tables because decision trees are graphical. The decision tree in this figure shows the same conditions as the decision table in Figure 12-12.

Date: 12/19/2005 *Project:* NET STREET CAFE *Page:* 11
Time: 10:36:28 AM

Detailed Listing -- Alphabetically
All Entries -- Data Flow Diagrams

Vendor-ID Data Element
Vendor File::Vendor-ID
Description:
A unique identification number assigned to each vendor.
Alias:
Vendor Code
Values & Meanings:
Required element
Cannot be blank
May not be duplicated
Data element attributes
Storage Type: Char
Length: 4
Display Format: AAAA
Null Type: NotNull
Location:
File --> Vendor File
Date Last Altered: 12/19 *Date Created:* 12/19

FIGURE 12-14 The data dictionary records details about each of the data items that make up the data flows and entities in the system. This is a dictionary entry for the VendorID data element.

Object Modeling

Object modeling, sometimes called *object-oriented (OO) analysis and design*, combines the data with the processes that act on that data into a single unit, called an object. An **object** is an item that can contain both data and the procedures that read or manipulate that data. For example, a Customer object might contain data about a customer (Customer ID, First Name, Last Name, Address, and so on) and instructions about how to print a customer's record or the formula required to compute a customer's amount due. Each data element is called an *attribute* or *property*. The procedure in the object, called an *operation* or *method*, contains activities that read or manipulate the data. For example, a cybercafé would create a new customer object (method) for each new customer.

WEB LINK 12-3

Object Modeling

Visit the Discovering Computers 2005 WEB LINK page (**scsite.com/dc2005/weblink**). Click Object Modeling below Chapter 12.

Object modeling can use the same tools as those used in process modeling. Many developers, however, choose to use tools defined in the UML. Although used in all types of business modeling, the **UML** (*Unified Modeling Language*) has been adopted as a standard notation for object modeling and development. The UML is a graphical tool that enables analysts to document a system. It consists of many interrelated diagrams. Each diagram conveys a view of the system.

Instead of developing their own object diagrams and steps in an object-oriented system development cycle, most companies use an existing methodology to guide them through the steps in the system development cycle. A popular methodology on the market today that uses the UML is the *Rational Unified Process* (*RUP*) by Grady Booch, Ivar Jacobsen, and James Rumbaugh.

Two of the more common tools in the UML are the use case diagram and class diagram. The following paragraphs describe these diagrams.

USE CASE DIAGRAM A **use case diagram** graphically shows how actors interact with the information system. An *actor* is a user or other entity such as application software. The function that the actor can perform is called the *use case*. Thus, a use case diagram shows actors and their use cases (Figure 12-15). The actor is drawn as a stick figure that connects to each use case with an arrow.

Because these diagrams are easy to understand, analysts find that the use case diagram is an ideal tool for communicating system requirements with users.

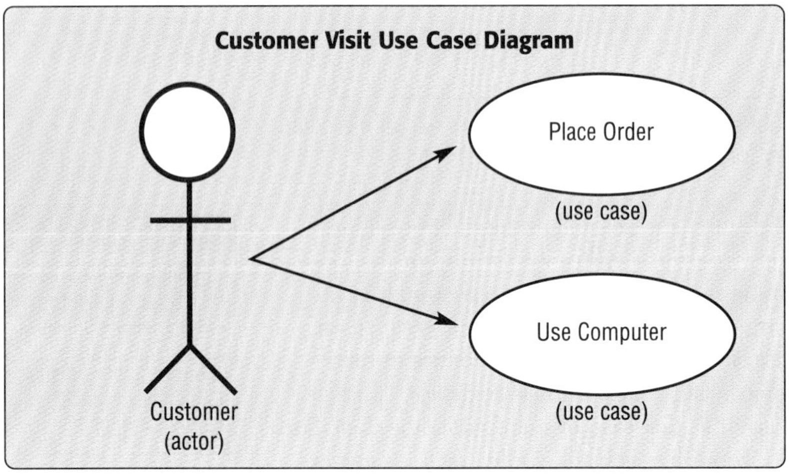

FIGURE 12-15 This use case diagram shows that the customer needs the system for two use cases: place an order and use a computer.

CLASS DIAGRAM A **class diagram** graphically shows classes and subclasses in a system (Figure 12-16). On a class diagram, objects are grouped into classes. Each class can have one or more lower levels called *subclasses*. Each subclass inherits the operations and attributes of the objects in its superclass. Every object in a class shares operations and attributes that are part of its higher-level class. This concept of lower levels inheriting methods and attributes of higher levels is called *inheritance*. For example, Food Order and Drink Order are subclasses of the higher-level class, called Order. All orders have an Order Number and Order Date (which would be attributes in the Order object), but only drink orders have a Size attribute (with values of small, medium, or large).

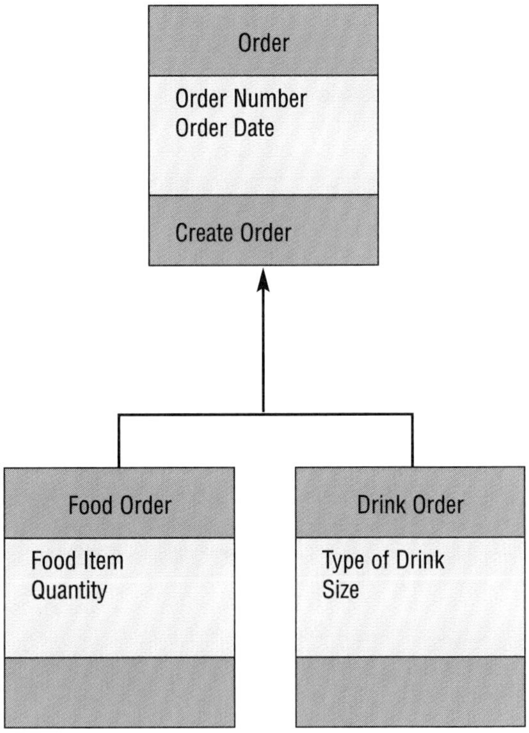

FIGURE 12-16 In this class diagram, the Order class has two subclasses: Food Order and Drink Order. The subclasses inherit the attributes (Order Number and Order Date) and the method (Create Order) of the Order class and also contain some unique attributes of their own.

The System Proposal

At this point, the systems analyst has studied the current system and determined all user requirements. The next step is to communicate possible solutions for the project in a system proposal. The purpose of the *system proposal* is to assess the feasibility of each alternative solution and then recommend the most feasible solution for the project. The systems analyst reevaluates feasibility at this point in the system development cycle, especially economic feasibility. The systems analyst presents the system proposal to the steering committee. If the steering committee approves a solution, the project enters the design phase.

When the steering committee discusses the system proposal and decides which alternative to pursue, it often is deciding whether to buy packaged software from an outside source, build its own custom software, or hire an outside firm to handle some or all of its IT needs.

PACKAGED SOFTWARE **Packaged software** is mass-produced, copyrighted, prewritten software available for purchase. Packaged software is available for different types of computers. Chapter 3 presented many types of application software available for personal computers. These include word processing, spreadsheet, note taking, database, desktop publishing, paint/image editing, Web page authoring, personal finance, legal, tax preparation, educational/reference, e-mail, and Web browser software. Read Looking Ahead 12-2 for a look at the future of purchasing software.

Vendors offer two types of packaged software: horizontal and vertical. *Horizontal market software* meets the needs of many different types of companies. The programs discussed in Chapter 3 were horizontal. If a company has a unique way of accomplishing activities, then it also may require vertical market software. *Vertical market software* specifically is designed for a particular business or industry. Examples of companies that use vertical market software include banks, schools, hospitals, real estate offices, libraries, and insurance companies. Each of these industries has unique information processing requirements.

Horizontal market software tends to be widely available because a large number of companies use it. Thus, it typically is less expensive than vertical market software. You can search for names and vendors of vertical and horizontal market software on the Web simply by entering your requirement as the search criteria. Other sources for vendor names include computer magazines, trade shows, and trade publications. A *trade publication* is a magazine written for a specific business or industry. Companies and individuals that have written software for these industries often advertise in trade publications.

WEB LINK 12-4

Vertical Market Software

Visit the Discovering Computers 2005 WEB LINK page (**scsite .com/dc2005/weblink**). Click Vertical Market Software below Chapter 12.

LOOKING AHEAD 12-2

Buying Software May Not Be the Best Buy

You may rent your apartment, lease your car, and subscribe to the local newspaper, and soon you may subscribe to your software. Several software manufacturers are considering nontraditional methods of distributing their products, including subscription and rental schemes.

Almost all personal and small business programs are sold and distributed on a CD-ROM or DVD-ROM for installation on one desktop computer. In the corporate world, however, some software and hardware are rented with a mandatory annual fee for upgrades, technical support, and maintenance.

The Internet has created a whole new venue for distributing software. In one method, programs can be downloaded and installed easily on a user's computer. Application service providers (ASPs), by contrast, install the programs on their computers and then allow subscribers to access this software via the Internet. These vendors will customize the software for each subscriber and also store and back up data files.

Another method of software distribution is via annual subscriptions. Microsoft has proposed this technique as one solution to curbing software piracy, especially for Office; industry experts estimate that one of every three copies of Office installed on computers today is illegal.

Microsoft also has begun using subscriptions with its SPOT devices. *SPOT*, which stands for *Smart Personal Objects Technology*, uses software to make everyday objects, such as watches, alarm clocks, pens, wallets, refrigerator magnets, and key chains, more personal and useful for the consumer. For example, in addition to the most up-to-date time, a user is able to view sports scores, traffic reports, schedule updates, and other services right on a SPOT watch. To receive software for a SPOT device, users subscribe to a service from Microsoft. Services transmit to a SPOT device through a radio network.

For a look at the next generation of buying software, visit the Discovering Computers 2005 Looking Ahead Web page (**scsite.com/dc2005/looking**). Click Looking Ahead #2 below Chapter 12.

CUSTOM SOFTWARE Instead of buying packaged software, some companies opt to write their own applications using programming languages such as C++, Java, and Visual Basic .NET 2003. Application software developed by the user or at the user's request is called **custom software**. With so many programs available, why would a company choose to write its own application software? Sometimes a company cannot find a program that meets all its needs because its software requirements are so unique.

The main advantage of custom software is that it matches the company's requirements exactly. The disadvantages usually are that it is more expensive and takes longer to design and implement than packaged software.

OUTSOURCING Companies can develop software in-house using their own IT personnel or *outsource* it, which means having an outside source develop it for them. By outsourcing, companies can focus on their core business while allowing others with more expertise to conduct some aspect of their facilities management. Some companies outsource just the software development aspect of their IT operation. Others outsource more or all of their IT operation. They do this to remain competitive in this age of constantly changing technology. Read Issue 12-3 for a related discussion.

Depending on a company's needs, outside firms can handle as much or as little of the IT requirements as desired. They can provide hardware and software. Others provide a variety of services such as Web design and development, Web hosting, sales, marketing, billing, customer service, and legal assistance. For example, an *Internet solutions provider* is a company that provides Web hosting services that include managing shopping carts, inventory, and credit card processing (Figure 12-17).

ISSUE 12-3

Should a Company Outsource IT Needs?

Instead of maintaining their own IT department and hiring their own staff, many companies are turning to outside providers, in a process called outsourcing, to satisfy their IT requirements. Once an innovative management idea, outsourcing IT services has become an effective management tool. Most FORTUNE 500 companies have outsourced, or have considered outsourcing, at least part of their IT needs. For certain companies, outsourcing some IT work has moved from temporary technique to permanent practice. IT departments are under constant pressure to produce. Outsourcing some IT services can reduce the pressure on a company's internal IT department by alleviating part of the workload, or increase the pressure by demanding continued cooperation between the internal and external IT providers. Should a company outsource none, some, or all of its IT needs? Why? How might considerations such as the nature of the company, the availability of IT personnel, and the type of IT work required affect a company's decision? What other factors might sway a company one way or another? Why?

For more information about outsourcing IT needs, visit the Discovering Computers 2005 Issues Web page (**scsite.com/dc2005/issues**). Click Issue #3 below Chapter 12.

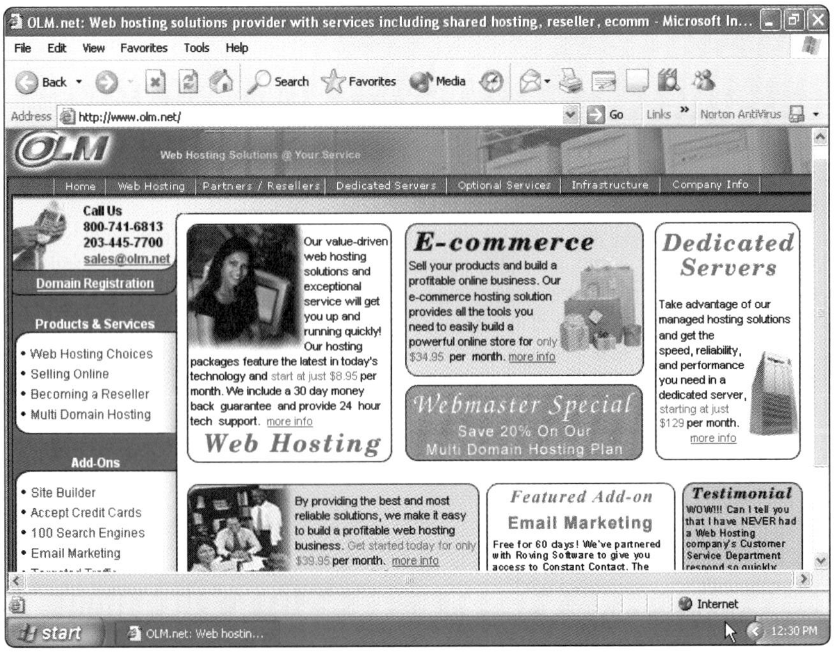

FIGURE 12-17 A Web site of an Internet solutions provider.

WEB LINK 12-5

Outsourcing

Visit the Discovering Computers 2005 WEB LINK page (**scsite.com/dc2005/weblink**). Click Outsourcing below Chapter 12.

Detailed Analysis at Net Street Café

Sadie and her team begin performing the activities in the detailed analysis phase of the Vendor Web System. As part of the study and requirements activities, they use several of the data and information gathering techniques available to them. They interview employees throughout the company and meet with some vendors. They observe the marketing staff copy and mail vendor information. Because the team is using structured analysis and design techniques, they prepare many process modeling deliverables to record their findings: an entity-relationship diagram (Figure 12-9 on page 632), a data flow diagram (Figure 12-10 on page 633), a process specification using structured English (Figure 12-11 on page 634), a process specification using a decision table (Figure 12-12 on page 634), and a data dictionary entry for a VendorID data item (Figure 12-14 on page 635). These documents all become part of the project notebook. Members of the project team refer to these documents during the remainder of the system development cycle.

After two months of studying the existing system and obtaining user requirements, Sadie discusses her findings with her supervisor, Tyrone Greene. Sadie recommends that a link to Vendor Information be added to their current Web site. When a vendor clicks this link, a Vendor Information page will be displayed. This Web page should contain all information that the marketing department usually sends to a vendor.

Based on Sadie's findings, Tyrone writes a system proposal for the steering committee to review. Jesse Martinez, Webmaster at Net Street Café, developed the current Web site. Thus, Tyrone recommends that Jesse's staff modify the Web site in-house. Tyrone also recommends Net Street Café invest in a larger database server to handle the additional vendor information.

The steering committee agrees with Tyrone's proposal. Sadie and her team begin the design phase of the project.

QUIZ YOURSELF 12-2

To check your knowledge of the analysis phase, process modeling, and object modeling, visit the Discovering Computers 2005 Quiz Yourself Web page (**scsite.com/dc2005/quiz**). Click Objectives 5 – 7 below Chapter 12.

DESIGN PHASE

The **design phase** consists of two major activities: (1) if necessary, acquire hardware and software and (2) develop all of the details of the new or modified information system. The systems analyst often performs these two activities at the same time instead of sequentially.

Acquiring Necessary Hardware and Software

When the steering committee approves a solution, the systems analyst begins the activity of obtaining additional hardware or software. The systems analyst may skip this activity if the approved solution does not require new hardware or software. If this activity is required, the selection of appropriate products is crucial for the success of the information system. The activity consists of four major tasks: (1) identify technical specifications, (2) solicit vendor proposals, (3) test and evaluate vendor proposals, and (4) make a decision.

Identifying Technical Specifications

The first step in acquiring the necessary hardware and software is to identify all the hardware and software requirements of the new or modified system. To do this, the systems analysts use a variety of research techniques. They talk with other systems analysts, visit vendors' stores, and surf the Web. Many trade journals, newspapers, and magazines provide some or all of their printed content as e-zines. An **e-zine** (pronounced ee-zeen), or *electronic magazine*, is a publication available on the Web. By using the Web, the systems analyst can locate information more quickly and easily than in the past.

After the systems analyst defines the technical requirements, the next step is to summarize these requirements for potential vendors. The systems analyst can use three basic types of documents for this purpose: an RFQ, an RFD, or an RFI. A *request for quotation* (*RFQ*) identifies the product(s) you want. With an RFQ, the vendor quotes a price for the listed product(s).

With a *request for proposal* (*RFP*), the vendor selects the product(s) that meets specified requirements and then quotes the price(s). Software exists that assist with the creation of a professional RFP. Just as the depth of an information system varies, so does the length of an RFQ or RFP. Some can be as short as a couple of pages. Others consist of more than one hundred pages. Instead of an RFQ or RFP, some companies prefer to use a request for information. A *request for information* (*RFI*) is a less formal method that uses a standard form to request information about a product or service.

WEB LINK 12-6

Request for Proposals

Visit the Discovering Computers 2005 WEB LINK page (**scsite.com/dc2005/weblink**). Click Request for Proposals below Chapter 12.

Soliciting Vendor Proposals

Systems analysts send the RFQ, RFP, or RFI to potential hardware and software vendors. They have a variety of ways to locate vendors. Many vendors publish their product catalogs on the Internet. These online catalogs provide up-to-date and easy access to products, prices, technical specifications, and ordering information. For those products that do not have vendors on the Internet, the systems analyst could visit local computer stores or contact computer manufacturers and software vendors.

Another source for hardware and software products is a value-added reseller. A *value-added reseller* (*VAR*) is a company that purchases products from manufacturers and then resells these products to the public — offering additional services with the product. Examples of additional services include user support, equipment maintenance, training, installation, and warranties.

To be an authorized VAR, most manufacturers have requirements the VAR must meet. Various terms that identify a VAR's relationship with a manufacturer are strategic partner, business partner, authorized reseller, or solutions provider. Some VARs offer one product or service. Others provide complete systems, also known as a *turnkey solution* (Figure 12-18). The advantage of a full-service VAR is you deal with only one company for an entire system.

Instead of dealing with vendors, some companies hire a computer consultant. A *computer consultant* is a professional who is hired based on expertise in a specialized area of computers, including service and advice. Consultants often specialize in configuring hardware and software for businesses of all sizes.

FAQ 12-3

Where do I find a computer consultant?

For a reliable consultant reference, look through a consultant reference guide on the Internet; attend a user meeting; contact a professional organization in your industry, a hardware vendor, or a local university; browse the Web; peruse a local newspaper; or get a personal referral.

For more information about computer consultants, visit the Discovering Computers 2005 FAQ Web page (**scsite.com/dc2005/faq**). Click Computer Consultants below Chapter 12.

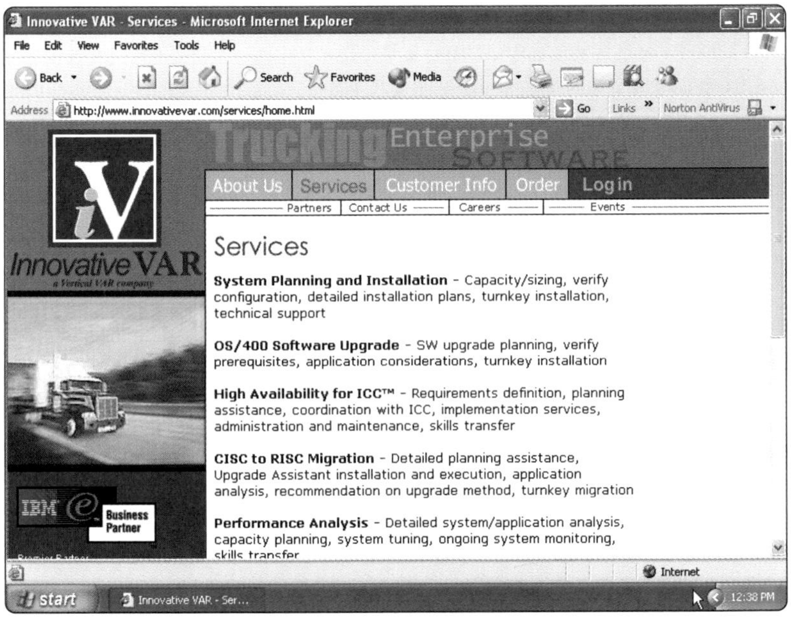

FIGURE 12-18 Many VARs advertise their services on the Internet.

Testing and Evaluating Vendor Proposals

After sending RFQs and RFPs to potential vendors, the systems analyst will receive completed quotations and proposals. Evaluating the proposals and then selecting the best one is often a difficult task. Many systems analysts use a scoring system to rate each proposal. It is important to be as objective as possible while rating each proposal.

Systems analysts use many techniques to test the various software products from vendors. They obtain a list of user references from the software vendors. They also talk to current users of the software for their opinions. Some vendors will give a demonstration of the product(s) specified. Other vendors provide demonstration copies or trial versions, allowing the companies to test the software themselves. Demonstration copies usually are free and have limited functionality. Trial versions are free or have minimal fees and provide full functionality for a set time (Figure 12-19). In some cases, the demonstration copies and trial versions are available to download from the Web.

Sometimes it is important to know whether the software can handle a certain volume of transactions efficiently. In this case, the systems analyst conducts a benchmark test. A *benchmark test* measures the performance of hardware or software. For example, a benchmark test could measure the time it takes a payroll program to print 50 paychecks. Comparing the time it takes various accounting programs to print the same 50 paychecks is one way of measuring each program's performance. Some computer magazines conduct benchmark tests while evaluating hardware and software and then publish these results for consumers to review. For a technical discussion about benchmark tests, read the High-Tech Talk article on page 649 at the end of this chapter.

Making a Decision

Having rated the proposals, the systems analyst presents a recommendation to the steering committee. The recommendation could be to award a contract to a vendor or to not make any purchases at this time.

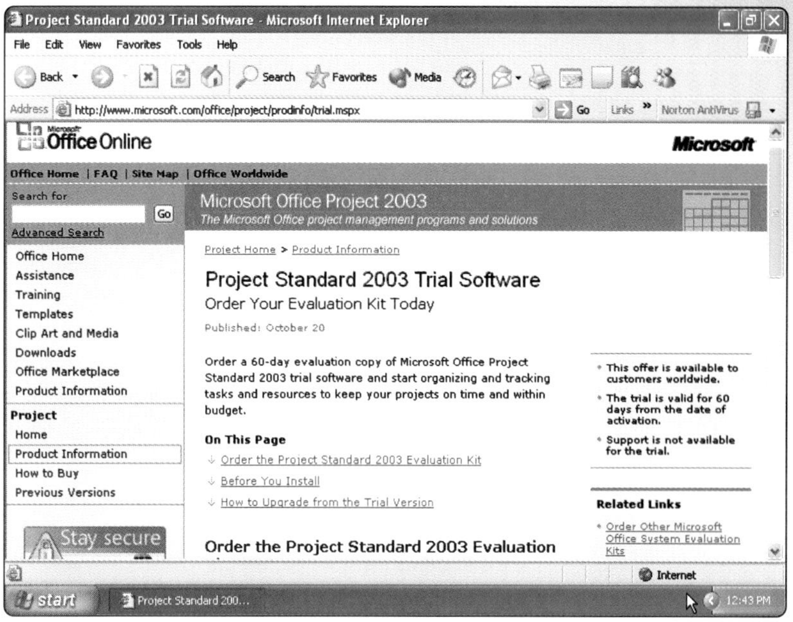

FIGURE 12-19 This trial version of Microsoft Office Project 2003 costs only $7.95 and expires 60 days after installation.

Hardware Acquisition at Net Street Café

Sadie and her team compile a requirements list for the database server. They prepare an RFP and submit it to twelve vendors: eight through the Internet and four local computer stores. Ten vendors reply within the three-week deadline.

Of the ten replies, the development team selects two to evaluate. They eliminate the other eight because these vendors did not offer adequate warranties for the database server. The project team members ask for benchmark test results for each server. In addition, they contact two current users of this database server for their opinions about its performance. After evaluating these two servers, the team selects the best one.

Sadie summarizes her team's findings in a report to the steering committee. The committee gives Sadie authorization to award a contract to the proposed vendor. As a courtesy and to maintain good working relationships, Sadie sends a letter to all twelve vendors informing them of the committee's decision.

WEB LINK 12-7

Benchmark Tests

Visit the Discovering Computers 2005 WEB LINK page (**scsite.com/dc2005/weblink**). Click Benchmark Tests below Chapter 12.

Detailed Design

When the systems analyst identifies the data and process requirements, the next step is to develop detailed design specifications for the components in the proposed solution. A detailed design sometimes is called a *physical design* because it specifies hardware and software for automated procedures. The activities to be performed include developing designs for the databases, inputs, outputs, and programs.

The length and complexity of these activities vary depending on previous decisions. For example, the systems analyst may skip many of these activities when purchasing packaged software. If the company is developing custom software, however, these activities can be quite time-consuming.

DATABASE DESIGN During database design, the systems analyst builds upon the data dictionary developed during the analysis phase. The dictionary should represent accurately the data requirements of the company. The systems analyst works closely with the database analysts and database administrators to identify those data elements that currently exist within the company and those that are new.

With relational database systems, the systems analyst defines the structure of each table in the system, as well as relationships among the tables. The systems analyst also addresses user access privileges. This means that the systems analyst defines which data elements each user can access, when they can access the data elements, what actions they can perform on the data elements, and under what circumstances they can access the elements. The systems analyst also considers the volume of database activity. For example, large, frequently accessed tables may be organized in a manner so that the database processes requests in an acceptable time frame.

INPUT AND OUTPUT DESIGN Because users will work with the inputs and outputs of the system, it is crucial to involve users during input and output design. During this activity, the systems analyst carefully designs every menu, screen, and report specified in the requirements. The outputs often are designed first because they help define the requirements for the inputs. Thus, it is very important that outputs are identified correctly and that users agree to them.

The systems analyst typically develops two types of designs for each input and output: a mockup and a layout chart. A *mockup* is a sample of the input or output that contains actual data (Figure 12-20). The systems analyst shows mockups to users for their approval. After users approve the mockup, the systems analyst develops a layout chart for the programmer. A *layout chart* is more technical and contains programming-like notations for the data items (Figure 12-21).

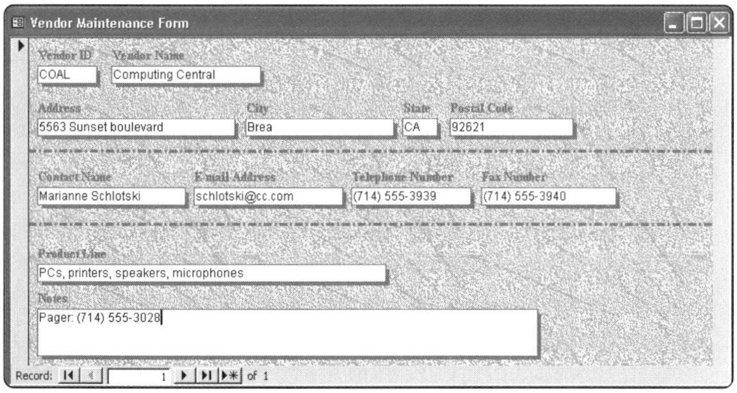

FIGURE 12-20 Users must give their approval on all inputs and outputs. This input screen is a mockup (containing actual data) for users to review.

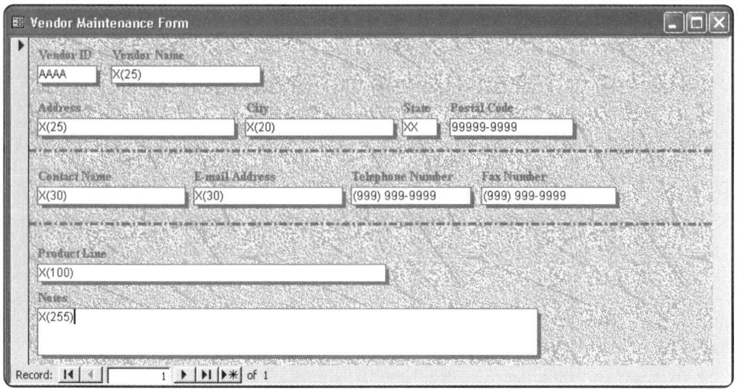

FIGURE 12-21 Once users approve a mockup, the layout chart (with technical specifications) is given to the programmer. This layout chart is for the mockup in Figure 12-20.

Other issues that must be addressed during input and output design include the types of media to use (paper, video, audio); formats (graphical or narrative); and data entry validation techniques, which include making sure the inputted data is correct (for example, a state code has to be one of the fifty valid two-letter state abbreviations).

PROGRAM DESIGN During program design, the systems analyst identifies the processing requirements, or the *logic*, for each program in the system. To do this, a systems analyst uses structured design or object-oriented design techniques. The next chapter discusses these design techniques in depth.

Next, the systems analyst prepares the *program specification package*, which communicates program requirements clearly to the programmer. This package identifies the relationship among each program in a process, as well as the input, output, processing, and database specifications.

Prototyping

Many systems analysts today use prototypes during detailed design. A **prototype** is a working model of the proposed system. The systems analyst actually builds a functional form of the solution during design. The main advantage of a prototype is users can work with the system before it is completed — to make sure it meets their needs.

The Vendor Maintenance Form shown in Figure 12-20 could be an example of a screen in a prototype of the Vendor Web System. As soon as users approve a prototype, system developers can implement a solution more quickly than without a prototype.

Some systems analysts use prototyping during the design phase. Others begin earlier in the system development cycle — during analysis or even planning. Beginning a prototype too early, however, might lead to problems. When the development team sees a working model so early in the system development cycle, they tend to skip critical analysis and design steps and may overlook key features in the proposed solution.

A common problem with prototypes is they have inadequate documentation, or worse, none at all. Another drawback is that users tend to embrace the prototype as a final system, which may not be the result of an extensive analysis. Prototyping can be an effective tool if the development team and the users discipline themselves to follow all activities within the system development cycle. Prototyping should not eliminate or replace activities — just improve the quality of these activities.

CASE Tools

Many systems analysts use computer software to assist in the system development cycle. *Computer-aided software engineering* (*CASE*) products are software tools designed to support one or more activities of the system development cycle. The purpose of these products is to increase the efficiency and productivity of the project development team. CASE tools typically include diagrams to support both process and object modeling.

Some CASE tools exist separately. One program might be a dictionary and another allows you to create drawings. The most effective tools, however, are integrated (Figure 12-22).

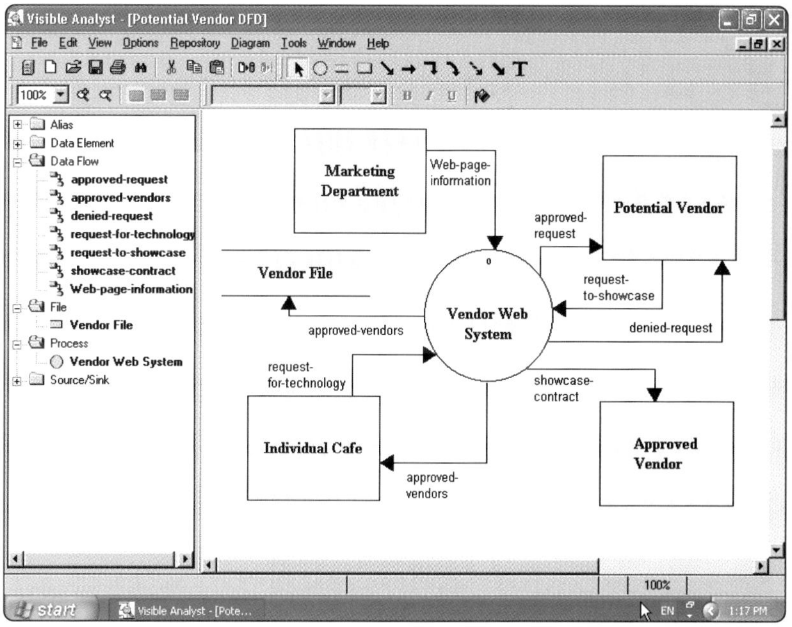

FIGURE 12-22 Integrated computer-aided software engineering (I-CASE) programs assist analysts in the development of an information system. Visible Analyst by Visible Systems Corporation enables analysts to create diagrams, as well as build the project dictionary. Figures 12-9 on page 632, 12-10 on page 633, and 12-14 on page 635 were created using Visible Analyst.

Integrated case products, sometimes called I-CASE or a CASE workbench, include the following capabilities:

- Project Repository — Stores diagrams, specifications, descriptions, programs, and any other deliverable generated during the system development cycle.
- Graphics — Enables the drawing of diagrams, such as DFDs and ERDs.
- Prototyping — Creates models of the proposed system.
- Quality Assurance — Analyzes deliverables, such as graphs and the data dictionary, for accuracy.
- Code Generators — Create actual computer programs from design specifications.
- Housekeeping — Establishes user accounts and provides backup and recovery functions.

WEB LINK 12-8

Case Tools

Visit the Discovering Computers 2005 WEB LINK page (**scsite.com/dc2005/weblink**). Click Case Tools below Chapter 12.

CASE tools support a variety of system development cycles. Depending on the one the company uses, the systems analyst can customize the CASE tools so all deliverables such as DFDs and ERDs use consistent terms.

Quality Review Techniques

Several people should review the detailed design specifications before they are given to the programming team. The review process should include users, the senior systems analyst, and members of the project team.

One popular review technique is a structured walkthrough. A *structured walkthrough* is a step-by-step review of any system development cycle deliverable. The systems analyst walks through items such as reports, diagrams, mockups, layout charts, and dictionary entries. The purpose of a walkthrough is to identify errors in the item being reviewed. If any errors are identified, the IT personnel correct them. Developers use structured walkthroughs throughout the entire system development cycle to review a variety of deliverables.

Once again, the systems analyst reevaluates feasibility to determine if it still is beneficial to proceed with the proposed solution. If the steering committee decides the project still is feasible, which usually is the case, the project enters the implementation phase.

FAQ 12-4

Why reassess feasibility at this late stage in system development?

It does not happen often, but companies cancel some projects at the end of the Design phase because they become infeasible. Although much time and money may have been spent, it is less costly to cancel the project than to proceed with an inadequate or incorrect solution.

For more information about feasibility, visit the Discovering Computers 2005 FAQ Web page (**scsite.com/dc2005/faq**). Click Feasibility below Chapter 12.

Detailed Design at Net Street Café

As approved by the steering committee, Sadie and her team begin designing the Vendor Web System. After studying current vendor information and interviewing more users and vendors, the team designs changes to the company's database, Web site, and the associated programs. They prepare several documents including a mockup (Figure 12-20 on page 642) and a layout chart (Figure 12-21 on page 642).

After completing the detailed design, Sadie meets with several users and IT personnel to walk through the deliverables. They locate two errors. She corrects the errors and then presents the design to the steering committee. The committee agrees with the design solution and consents to implement it.

IMPLEMENTATION PHASE

With the design phase complete, the project enters the implementation phase. The purpose of the **implementation phase** is to construct, or build, the new or modified system and then deliver it to the users. System developers perform four major activities in this phase: (1) develop programs, (2) install and test the new system, (3) train users, and (4) convert to the new system. The following sections discuss each of these activities.

Develop Programs

If the company purchases packaged software, the development team skips this activity. For custom software, however, programs are developed either by an outside firm or in-house. Programmers write programs from the program specification package created during the analysis phase. Just as the system development cycle follows an organized set of activities, so does program development. These program development activities are known as the *program development cycle*.

The program development cycle follows these six steps: (1) analyze the requirements, (2) design the solution, (3) validate the design, (4) implement the design, (5) test the solution, and (6) document the solution. Chapter 13 explains the program development cycle in depth. The important concept to understand now is that the program development cycle is a part of the implementation phase, which is part of the system development cycle.

Install and Test the New System

If the company acquires new hardware or software, someone must install and test it. It is imperative that the hardware and software be tested thoroughly. Obviously, the system developers should test individual programs. They also should be sure that all the programs work together in the system. It is better to find errors early in the process, so errors can be corrected before placing the system into production. System developers do not want errors in the system after it is delivered to the users.

System developers perform various tests. A *unit test* verifies that each individual program works by itself. A *systems test* verifies that all programs in an application work together properly. An *integration test* verifies that an application works with other applications. An *acceptance test* is performed by end-users and checks the new system to ensure that it works with actual data.

Train Users

For a system to be effective, users must be trained properly on its functionality. **Training** involves showing users exactly how they will use the new hardware and software in the system. This training could be one-on-one sessions or classroom-style lectures (Figure 12-23). Whichever technique is used, it should include hands-on sessions with realistic sample data. Users should practice on the actual system during training. Users also should receive user manuals for reference. It is the systems analyst's responsibility to create user manuals, both printed and electronic. Read Issue 12-4 for a related discussion.

FIGURE 12-23 Organizations must ensure that users are trained properly on the new system. One training method uses hands-on classes to learn the new system.

ISSUE 12-4

Who Should Pay for Training?

According to Mark Twain in *Pudd'n'head Wilson*, "Training is everything… cauliflower is nothing but cabbage with a college education." When companies implement or upgrade an information system, employees must be trained to use the new system. Training leads to greater efficiency, fewer errors, and improved employee confidence. The importance of training is clear, but the responsibility for and timing of training are not. Training can be expensive. Training costs might include the trainer's fee, instructional materials, and the time employees spend away from their work. Some employers believe that employees should train on their own time and bear their own training costs. It also can be difficult to determine when training should start. Training early in implementation prepares employees to use a new system as soon as it is fully operational. But, early in implementation, a new system may be error prone or incomplete, making training frustrating and worthless. Is the employer or the employee responsible for training on a new system? Why? When should training begin? Why?

For more information about training users, visit the Discovering Computers 2005 Issues Web page (**scsite.com/dc2005/issues**). Click Issue #4 below Chapter 12.

Convert to the New System

The final implementation activity is to change from the old system to the new system. This change can take place using one or more of the following conversion strategies: direct, parallel, phased, or pilot (Figure 12-24).

With *direct conversion*, the user stops using the old system and begins using the new system on a certain date. The advantage of this strategy is that it requires no transition costs and is a quick implementation technique. Some systems analysts call this technique an *abrupt cutover*. The disadvantage is that it is extremely risky and can disrupt operations seriously if the new system does not work correctly the first time.

Parallel conversion consists of running the old system alongside the new system for a specified time. Results from both systems are compared. If the results are the same, the company either terminates the old system abruptly or phases it out. The advantage of this strategy is that you can fix any problems in the new system before you terminate the old system. The disadvantage is that it is costly to operate two systems at the same time.

Larger systems that have multiple sites often use a phased conversion. With a *phased conversion*, each location converts at a separate time. For example, an accounting system might convert its accounts receivable, accounts payable, general ledger, and payroll sites in separate phases. Each site can use a direct or parallel conversion.

With a *pilot conversion*, only one location in the company uses the new system — so it can be tested. After the pilot site approves the new system, other sites convert using one of the other conversion strategies. Read Issue 12-5 for a related discussion.

At the beginning of the conversion, existing data must be made ready for the new system. Converting existing manual and computer files so the new system can use them is known as *data conversion*.

WEB LINK 12-9

Conversion Strategies

Visit the Discovering Computers 2005 WEB LINK page (**scsite.com/dc2005/weblink**). Click Conversion Strategies below Chapter 12.

ISSUE 12-5

What Type of Conversion Is Best?

Any organization using a computer eventually will need to update. The first step most organizations take is to research and compare existing systems. Once a suitable system is chosen, the next step is implementation. This means converting from the old system to the new system. Suppose that the educational institution you attend plans to convert to a new registration system. The administration is vacillating between direct conversion and parallel conversion. Direct conversion is less expensive, but risky. If the new system does not work correctly, student registration could be a disaster. In contrast, parallel conversion is safe, but costly and time-consuming. Registration surely will be a success, but the school's operating budget will suffer. If you were responsible for the decision, which method would you choose? Why? Should another alternative, such as phased conversion or pilot conversion, be considered? Why or why not?

For more information about system conversion, visit the Discovering Computers 2005 Issues Web page (**scsite.com/dc2005/issues**). Click Issue #5 below Chapter 12.

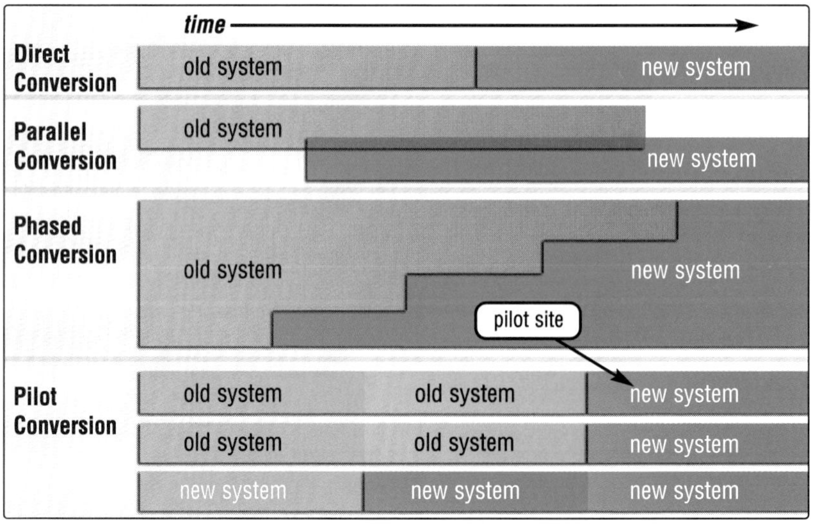

FIGURE 12-24 Converting from the old system to the new system usually follows one of these strategies.

Implementation at Net Street Café

Upon receiving the program specification package, Sadie forms an implementation team of Jesse Martinez, Webmaster; Andrea Travnik, programmer; and Kelly Sarkis, data modeler. The team works together to implement the Vendor Web System.

Sadie works closely with the team to answer questions about the design and to check the progress of their work. When the team completes its work, they ask Sadie to test it. She does and it works great!

Sadie arranges a training class for the employees of the marketing and customer service departments. During the training session, she shows them how to use the new Vendor Information page on the company's Web site. Sadie gives each attendee a printed user guide and indicates that she will e-mail them the electronic file. She wants to prepare everyone thoroughly for the new Web pages once they are posted. Sadie also sends a letter to all existing vendors informing them when this new service will be available and how to use it.

SUPPORT PHASE

The purpose of the **support phase** is to provide ongoing assistance for an information system and its users after the system is implemented. The support phase consists of four major activities: (1) conduct a post-implementation system review, (2) identify errors, (3) identify enhancements, and (4) monitor system performance.

One of the first activities the company performs in the support phase is to meet with users. The purpose of this meeting, called the *post-implementation system review*, is to find out if the information system is performing according to the users' expectations. If it is not, the systems analyst must determine what must be done to satisfy the users — back to the planning phase.

Sometimes users identify errors in the system when the program does not produce correct results. Problems with design (logic) or programming (syntax) are the cause of these errors. Often these errors are minor. For example, the total of a column might be incorrect on a daily order summary. Other times, however, the error requires more serious investigation — back to the planning phase.

In some cases, users would like the system to do more. Maybe they have additional requirements. *System enhancement* involves modifying or expanding an existing information system — back to the planning phase. Read Apply It 12-2 for information about the IRS's system enhancement.

APPLY IT 12-2

IRS Develops Modernization Plan

On April 15, many United States taxpayers file their income taxes frantically. The Internal Revenue Service is in the process of easing this pressure as part of its Prime Systems Integration Services Contract program.

The IRS announced its massive computer system overhaul plan in 1998. The project was expected to last up to 15 years at a cost of $3 billion. During the first six months, the IRS set aside $10.6 million for preliminary planning. In the initial phase of the project, the IRS identified and then prioritized the services required to meet taxpayers' needs.

During 1999 and 2000, the IRS installed a new voice recognition telephone and communications system to route the more than 150 million telephone calls received from taxpayers yearly.

Designing and implementing the IRS's new Customer Account Data Engine are currently underway. The database management system will replace a 40-year-old system. The new system will create a centralized database for taxpayers' records and be updated daily. More tax returns are being filed electronically, and the software will check the returns automatically for missing forms and computation errors. The five-phase project is anticipated to be completed by 2006.

For more information about the IRS modernization plan, visit the Discovering Computers 2005 Apply It Web page (**scsite.com/dc2005/apply**). Click Apply It #2 below Chapter 12.

During the support phase, the systems analyst monitors performance of the new or modified information system. The purpose of *performance monitoring* is to determine whether the system is inefficient at any point. If so, is the inefficiency causing a problem? Is the time it takes to download vendor information reasonable? If not, the systems analyst must investigate solutions to make the download time more acceptable — back to the planning phase.

Support at Net Street Café

During the post-implementation system review, Sadie learns that the new Web page is receiving many hits. Vendors are using it and they like it. Customer service regularly receives e-mail messages from vendors that appreciate the new service. Carla says her staff is working efficiently on their primary tasks without the interruption and additional workload of making copies and sending out vendor data, now that the system has been automated.

Six months after the Vendor Web System has been in operation, Carla would like to add more information to the Vendor Information page. She sends an e-mail message to Sadie requesting the change. Sadie asks her to fill out a Request for System Services and puts her on the agenda of the next steering committee meeting. Back to the planning phase again!

QUIZ YOURSELF 12-3

To check your knowledge of the design phase, program development, the implementation phase, and the support phase, visit the Discovering Computers 2005 Quiz Yourself Web page (**scsite.com/dc2005/quiz**). Click Objectives 8 – 11 below Chapter 12.

CHAPTER SUMMARY

This chapter discussed the phases in the system development cycle. The guidelines for system development also were presented. Activities that occur during the entire system development cycle including project management, feasibility assessment, data and information gathering, and documentation also were addressed. Throughout the chapter, a case study about Net Street Café illustrated and reinforced activities performed during each phase of the system development cycle.

Systems Analyst

One of the more in-demand IT (information technology) positions is that of *systems analyst*. The primary focus of this type of work is to design and develop new hardware and software systems and to incorporate new technologies.

Typically, systems analysts are more involved in design issues than in day-to-day coding. Systems analyst is a somewhat arbitrary title, however, as companies have varying definitions for the role. Systems analysts work closely with users to identify operating procedures and clarify system objectives. They must be familiar with concepts and practices within a specific field. A successful systems analyst is willing to embrace new technologies and is open to continued learning. Good communications skills are important. Systems analysts may be expected to write program documentation and operating manuals. Some emerging paradigms for the systems analyst include e-commerce, enterprise-wide networking, and intranet technologies. Given the technology available today, telecommuting is common for computer professionals, including the systems analyst. Many analysts work as consultants.

The minimum educational requirement is a bachelor's degree, but many people opt for a master's degree. Salaries are excellent in this fast-growing occupation in the IT field. They range from $40,000 to $80,000 and up. Graduates can expect to earn up to $50,000 per year.

To learn more about the field of Systems Analyst as a career, visit the Discovering Computers 2005 Careers Web page (**scsite.com/dc2005/careers**). Click Systems Analyst.

Benchmarking: Testing Performance through Calculations

A benchmark is a surveyor's reference mark. It is a post established at a known elevation and then used as the basis for measuring other elevations. In computer technology, a benchmark is a set of conditions used to measure a product or system. Benchmark testing involves running a set of standard tests to compare the performance of two or more systems.

Suppose you are a network administrator and need to buy new servers to support your company's e-commerce Web site. To start, you can access published benchmark results from organizations such as SPEC and TPC. Both SPEC (Standard Performance Evaluation Corporation) and TPC (Transaction Processing Performance Counsel) are nonprofit groups that define and maintain benchmarks for the computer industry. TPC, for example, tests using its TPC Benchmark W (*TPC-W*), which measures how servers perform while supporting an e-commerce Web site. Reading published benchmark test results from these groups can help you determine how one vendor's system might perform relative to another.

To understand benchmark results fully, you should understand the design and measurements (or *metrics*) used for the test. The TPC-W benchmark, for example, uses two primary metrics: WIPS and $/WIPS. *WIPS* is the number of Web Interactions Per Second that can be sustained by the *system under test*, or *SUT* (in this case, multiple servers). The *$/WIPS* is the *system cost per WIPS*, which is the total cost of the SUT divided by WIPS.

To calculate WIPS, TPC-W uses several algorithms, or formulas (Figure 12-25). One calculation is *Web Interaction Response Time* (*WIRT*), which is the time it takes to complete a Web interaction. A Web interaction might start when a user clicks a link to request a Web page and ends when the browser receives all of the data from the requested page. WIRT is calculated using the algorithm shown in Figure 12-25. Using this algorithm, if a Web interaction starts at 1:00:00 and the last byte of data is sent at 1:00:07, the WIRT is 7 seconds.

WIRT is used to calculate the number of Web interactions successfully completed during the length of the benchmark test, or *measurement interval*. During the measurement interval, the browser repeatedly cycles through requesting and then receiving a requested page, measuring the time to receive it (WIRT), and then requesting the next page. To be considered a successful Web interaction, each type of Web interaction must have a WIRT less than the TPC-specified constraint. For example, a home page Web interaction must have a WIRT of less than 3 seconds or it is not used when calculating WIPS.

The total number of successful Web interactions completed in a measurement interval is used to calculate WIPS. WIPS is calculated using the algorithm shown in Figure 12-25. Using this algorithm, if 14,009,400 Web interactions are completed successfully during a 30-minute test period, the WIPS rating for the system is 14,009,400 / 1,800 or 7,783 WIPs. The higher the WIPs rating, the more requests the Web server can handle per second.

Web Interaction Response Time (WIRT)

Defined by the algorithm, **WIRT** = **T2** - **T1**, where
T1 = time when the first byte of request is sent to the Web server; and
T2 = time after the last byte of a requested page is received by the browser

Web Interaction Per Second (WIPS)

Defined by the algorithm, **WI**/(**MI**), where:
WI = total number of Web interactions completed successfully; and
MI = length of the measurement interval in seconds

System Cost per WIPS ($/WIPS)

Defined by the algorithm, **System Cost/WIPS**, where:
System Cost = entire price of the SUT, including all new hardware, software, and 3-year maintenance charges; and
WIPS = Web interactions successfully completed

Total Number of Connections Supported by a Web Server

Defined by the algorithm, **2** * (**Number of Browsers** / **Web Servers**), where:
2 represents the 2 connections per user (one nonsecure, one secure)
Number of Browsers is the number of users browsing the Web site; and
Web Servers is the number of Web servers supporting the Web site

FIGURE 12-25 Some benchmark algorithms.

The $/WIPS rating is determined by dividing the price of the SUT by the WIPS value (Figure 12-25). Using this algorithm, if a system rated as 7,783 WIPS costs $190,036, the $/WIPS rating is $190,036 / 7,783 or 24.42.

The TPC-W benchmark also measures the total number of connections a Web server can handle. Using the algorithm shown in Figure 12-25, if a Web site supports 35,000 browsers using 10 Web servers, each Web server is supporting 2 * (35,000 / 10) = 7,000 connections.

Data points such as WIPS, $/WIPS, and number of connections are the result of a benchmarking process. These data points provide the detailed information required to make informed purchasing decisions. For example, the WIPS and $/WIPS ratings in a benchmark report can help you better understand how the servers will perform in the real-world environment of your e-commerce Web site.

The TPC-W benchmark is just one of numerous industry benchmarks used to test different aspects of systems' performance. For more information about benchmarking, visit the Discovering Computers 2005 High-Tech Talk Web page (**scsite.com/dc2005/tech**) and click Benchmarking.

COMPANIES ON THE CUTTING EDGE

Computer Associates

Enterprise Software

The information technology (IT) department has always used information to help people perform efficiently and effectively. The structure of the IT department continues to evolve, however, with the growth of the information industry. In today's e-commerce climate, an IT department colors every part of a company's business, from planning and production to sales and supply. The impact of IT problems can be catastrophic, destroying a company's profits, reputation, and market assessment.

Computer Associates develops and supports the IT software that companies need to participate successfully in e-commerce.

Charles B. Wang founded Computer Associates in 1976 with three associates, no venture capital, and one product — a sort/merge utility called CA-SORT. Three decades later, Computer Associates offers products that address all aspects of e-commerce management in six focus areas:

1. Enterprise management products to manage networks for optimal performance.
2. Security products to defend against potential information attacks.
3. Storage products to combine storage functions across a network.
4. Application life cycle management products to shorten development cycle times.
5. Data management and application development products to join applications, databases, and business partner systems.
6. Portal and business intelligence products to present information in a personalized environment.

All Computer Associates products are integrated, are platform-independent, and can be used in a variety of environments. Computer Associates was the first global enterprise software company to meet the demanding standards of ISO 9001:2000 quality certification. More than 99 percent of FORTUNE 500 companies rely on Computer Associates technology.

For more information about Computer Associates, visit the Discovering Computers 2005 Companies Web page (**scsite.com/dc2005/companies**) and click Computer Associates.

PeopleSoft

Fans Share Data Efficiently

The Rolling Stones have a fan club with members worldwide. So do Harry Potter and the Loch Ness Monster. But a fan club for software? That is the case with *PeopleSoft* users. PeopleSoft Fan Club members eagerly exchange ideas and tips, list job openings, and read daily news about their favorite software.

Dave Duffield and Ken Morris cofounded PeopleSoft in 1987 with a human resources application built on a client-server platform instead of the conventional mainframe. In the 1990s, the company shifted from a client-server platform to Internet architecture, allowing organizations to improve both internal and external connections. PeopleSoft's applications run on the Internet through a Web browser with real-time access to a variety of customer data. The company's 5,100 customers use the software to help them network and collaborate effectively with employees, clients, and suppliers. In 2002, the company renamed its human resources application division Human Capital Management to indicate its emphasis on applications that boost employee productivity and performance. Today, PeopleSoft offers applications that create compensation and motivation programs for sales staff, develop training programs and track employee participation and success in training courses, and evaluate and provide feedback on employee achievement. PeopleSoft has grown to a global presence in more than 140 countries. In 2003, PeopleSoft's purchase of J.D. Edwards helped the corporation expand its products and serve a larger portion of the enterprise software market. Oracle then made a hostile tender offer of PeopleSoft, and PeopleSoft responded by promising its customers that they would receive refunds ranging from two- to five-times their licensing fees if Oracle won its takeover bid.

For more information about PeopleSoft, visit the Discovering Computers 2005 Companies Web page (**scsite.com/dc2005/companies**) and click PeopleSoft.

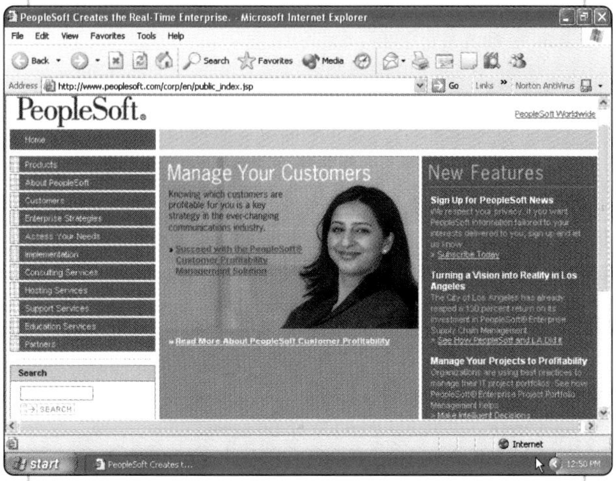

TECHNOLOGY TRAILBLAZERS

Ed Yourdon

Analysis and Design Developer

Ed Yourdon is a self-proclaimed alligator trainer, daredevil parachutist, and Himalayan mountain climber. He is recognized in the Computer Hall of Fame and as one of the ten Most Influential Men and Women of Software by *CrossTalk, The Journal of Defense Software Engineering.* Yourdon was the lead developer of structured analysis and design methods in the 1970s, and was a codeveloper of the Yourdon/Whitehead method of object-oriented analysis and design and the popular Coad/Yourdon OO methodology in the early 1990s.

Yourdon earned a B.S. in Applied Mathematics from MIT and did graduate work at MIT and the Polytechnic Institute of New York. In 1964, he began his work with computers at Digital Equipment Corporation (DEC) as an undergraduate student hired to write the FORTRAN math library for a small programmable controller. In 1974, Yourdon founded his own consulting firm, YOURDON Inc., to provide consulting and educational services in modern software engineering technology and project management techniques. As CEO, Yourdon supervised an operation that trained more than 250,000 people around the world in analysis and design methodologies that ensured delivery of high-quality systems, on time and under budget.

YOURDON Inc. was sold in 1986, but Yourdon continues his work as consultant, lecturer, and author. He has written more than 26 computer books and 550 technical articles and is the publisher of *American Programmer*. In 2003, he completed the second edition of his 1997 work, *Death March*, which guides software developers through project completion. As cofounder and fellow of the Cutter Consortium, he helps companies build and implement successful information technology strategies. Subscribers to his weekly e-zine, *The YOURDON Report*, can read about the latest business trends and products in the software field. His Web site contains resources for students, software professionals and managers, and book lovers.

For more information about Ed Yourdon, visit the Discovering Computers 2005 People Web page (**scsite.com/dc2005/people**) and click Ed Yourdon.

Tom DeMarco

Software Development Expert

Do you know why software is so expensive? *Tom DeMarco* knows. As author of *Why Does Software Cost So Much? And Other Puzzles of the Information Age,* he explores the successes and the absurdities of the software development process.

DeMarco has examined productive business principles for project management and the process of system development in more than 100 books, articles, and papers. His work centers on software specification and design, software metrics, people-aware project management, and risk management. DeMarco urges software developers to identify and take risks in his newest nonfiction book, *Waltzing with Bears: Managing Risk on Software Projects*. In *The Deadline: A Novel About Project Management*, DeMarco tells the story of a software manager who bets his life on a delivery date. The entertaining fictional account reveals both successful and unsuccessful system development practices. In *Slack, Getting Past Burnout, Busywork, and the Myth of Total Efficiency*, DeMarco emphasizes the importance of giving people time to think. "When companies can't invent," he writes, "it's usually because their people are too ... busy." Good managers motivate employees and design organizations to work efficiently, but they do not pressure employees to produce under extreme deadlines. In contrast, poor managers exert pressure because they know of no other solution.

Tom DeMarco earned a B.S. from Cornell University, an M.S. from Columbia University and a diploma from the University of Paris at the Sorbonne. He is a principal for The Atlantic Systems Guild, Inc., which is a software think tank exploring issues facing the computer industry. DeMarco lectures and consults throughout the world on managing projects and facilitating change. He has written two fiction works: *Lieutenant America and Miss Apple Pie* and *Dark Harbor House*.

For more information about Tom DeMarco, visit the Discovering Computers 2005 People Web page (**scsite.com/dc2005/people**) and click Tom DeMarco.

CHAPTER 12 CHAPTER REVIEW

QUIZZES AND LEARNING GAMES
Computer Genius
Crossword Puzzle
Interactive Labs
Practice Test
Quiz Yourself
Wheel of Terms
EXERCISES
Chapter Review
Checkpoint
Key Terms
Lab Exercises
Learn It Online
Web Research
BEYOND THE BOOK
Apply It
Career Corner
Companies
FAQ
High-Tech Talk
Issues
Looking Ahead
Trailblazers
Web Links
FEATURES
Guide to Web Sites
Making Use of the Web
Tech News
Timeline 2005

The Chapter Review section summarizes the concepts presented in this chapter.

WEB INSTRUCTIONS:

To display this page from the Web, start your browser and enter the Web address **scsite.com/dc2005/ch12/review.** Click the links for current and additional information. To listen to an audio version of this Chapter Review, click the Audio button.

1 What Are the System Development Cycle Phases?

An **information system** (**IS**) is hardware, software, data, people, and procedures that work together to produce quality information. The system development cycle is a set of activities developers use to build an information system. Most system development cycles contain five **phases**: planning, analysis, design, implementation, and support.

2 What Are Guidelines for System Development?

System development should follow three general guidelines: (1) arrange tasks into phases, (2) involve the **users**, who include anyone for whom a system is being built, and (3) develop standards, which are sets of rules and procedures a company expects employees to accept and follow. A **systems analyst** is responsible for designing and developing an information system.

3 Why Are Project Management, Feasibility Assessment, Data and Information Gathering Techniques, and Documentation Important?

Project management is the process of planning, scheduling, and then controlling the activities during the system development cycle. To manage a project, the **project leader** identifies the *scope* of the project, required activities, time estimates, cost estimates, the order of activities, and activities that can take place simultaneously. The project leader records this information in a *project plan*. **Feasibility** is a measure of how suitable the development of a system will be to the company. A systems analyst typically uses four tests to evaluate feasibility of a project: *operational feasibility*, *schedule feasibility*, *technical feasibility*, and *economic feasibility*. To gather data and information, systems analysts and other IT professionals review data, observe, send questionnaires, interview, participate in a *joint-application design* (*JAD*) *session*, and perform research. **Documentation** is the collection and summarization of data and information. A *project notebook* contains all documentation for a single project.

4 What Activities Are Performed in the Planning Phase?

The **planning phase** for a project begins when the decision-making body of the company, called the **steering committee**, receives a project request. During the planning phase, four major activities are performed: (1) review and approve the project requests, (2) prioritize the project requests, (3) allocate resources to approved projects, and (4) form a project development team for each approved project.

Visit **scsite.com/dc2005/quiz** or click the Quiz Yourself button. Click Objectives 1 – 4 below Chapter 12.

5 What Is the Purpose of Activities Performed in the Analysis Phase?

The **analysis phase** consists of two major tasks: (1) conduct a **preliminary investigation** to determine the exact nature of the problem or improvement and decide whether it is worth pursuing, and (2) perform detailed analysis. Detailed analysis involves three major activities: (1) study how the current system works, (2) determine the users' wants, needs, and requirements, and (3) recommend a solution. Most systems analysts use either a process modeling or object modeling approach to analysis and design.

6 What Are Tools Used in Process Modeling?

Process modeling is an analysis and design technique that describes processes that transform inputs into outputs. Tools used for process modeling include entity-relationship diagrams, data flow diagrams, and the project dictionary. An **entity-relationship diagram** (*ERD*) graphically shows the connections among entities in a system.

An *entity* is an object in the system that has data. A **data flow diagram** (*DFD*) graphically shows the flow of data in a system. Key elements of a DFD are a *data flow*, which shows the input or output of data or information, a *process*, which transforms an input data flow into an output data flow, a *data store*, which is a holding place for data and information, and a *source*, which identifies an entity outside the scope of the system. The project dictionary contains all the documentation and deliverables of a project. Techniques used to enter items in the project dictionary include *structured English*, a **decision table** and/or a *decision tree*, and a **data dictionary**.

7 What Are Tools Used in Object Modeling?

Object modeling combines the data with processes that act on the data into a single unit, called an **object**. Object modeling can use the same tools as those used in process modeling, but the UML (*Unified Modeling Language*) has been adopted as a standard notation for object modeling and development. Two common tools in the UML are the use case diagram and the class diagram. A **use case diagram** graphically shows how actors interact with the information system. An *actor* is a user or other entity, and the *use case* is the function that the actor can perform. A **class diagram** graphically shows classes and one or more lower levels, called *subclasses*, in a system. Lower levels (subclasses) contain attributes of higher levels (classes) in a concept called *inheritance*.

Visit **scsite.com/dc2005/quiz** or click the Quiz Yourself button. Click Objectives 5 – 7 below Chapter 12.

8 What Activities Are Performed in the Design Phase?

The **design phase** consists of two major activities: (1) if necessary, acquire hardware and software and (2) develop all of the details of the new or modified information system. Acquiring necessary hardware and software involves identifying technical specifications, soliciting vendor proposals, testing and evaluating vendor proposals, and making a decision. Detailed design includes developing designs for the databases, inputs, outputs, and programs. During detailed design, many systems analysts use a **prototype**, which is a working model of the proposed system. *Computer-aided software engineering (CASE)* products are software tools designed to support one or more activities of the system development cycle. A popular technique used to review detailed design is a *structured walkthrough*, which is a step-by-step review of any system development cycle tangible item, or *deliverable*.

9 Why Is Program Development Part of the System Development Cycle?

During the design phase, a company can purchase packaged software, which is mass produced, copyrighted, prewritten software. If suitable packaged software is not available, however, a company may opt for **custom software**, which is application software developed at the user's request to match the user's requirements exactly. Programmers write custom software from the program specification package created during the analysis phase, following an organized set of activities known as the *program development cycle*.

10 What Activities Are Performed in the Implementation Phase?

The purpose of the **implementation phase** is to construct, or build, the new or modified system and then deliver it to the users. System developers perform four major activities in this phase: (1) develop programs, (2) install and test the new system, (3) train users, and (4) convert to the new system.

11 How Do IT Professionals Support an Information System?

The purpose of the **support phase** is to provide ongoing assistance for an information system and its users after the system is implemented. The support phase consists of four major activities: (1) conduct a *post-implementation system review* to find out if the system is performing according to the users' expectation, (2) identify errors, (3) identify any *system enhancement*, and (4) monitor system performance.

Visit **scsite.com/dc2005/quiz** or click the Quiz Yourself button. Click Objectives 8 – 11 below Chapter 12.

CHAPTER 12 KEY TERMS

QUIZZES AND LEARNING GAMES
Computer Genius
Crossword Puzzle
Interactive Labs
Practice Test
Quiz Yourself
Wheel of Terms

EXERCISES
Chapter Review
Checkpoint
Key Terms
Lab Exercises
Learn It Online
Web Research

BEYOND THE BOOK
Apply It
Career Corner
Companies
FAQ
High-Tech Talk
Issues
Looking Ahead
Trailblazers
Web Links

FEATURES
Guide to Web Sites
Making Use of the Web
Tech News
Timeline 2005

You should know the Primary Terms and be familiar with the Secondary Terms.

WEB INSTRUCTIONS:

To display this page from the Web, start your browser and enter the Web address **scsite.com/dc2005/ch12/terms**. Click a term to display its definition and a picture. When the picture appears, click the more info button for current and additional information about the term from the Web.

>> Primary Terms

(shown in bold-black characters in the chapter)

analysis phase (630)
class diagram (636)
custom software (638)
data dictionary (634)
data flow diagram (633)
decision table (634)
design phase (639)
documentation (625)
entity-relationship diagram (632)
e-zine (639)
feasibility (624)
implementation phase (644)
information system (IS) (620)
object (635)
object modeling (635)
packaged software (637)
phases (620)
planning phase (629)
preliminary investigation (630)
process modeling (632)
project dictionary (633)
project leader (623)
project management (623)
project management software (624)
project team (623)
prototype (643)
standards (621)
steering committee (623)
support phase (647)
system (620)
system development cycle (620)
systems analyst (622)
training (645)
UML (636)
use case diagram (636)
users (621)

>> Secondary Terms

(shown in italic characters in the chapter)

abrupt cutover (646)
acceptance test (645)
actor (636)
attribute (635)
benchmark test (641)
change management skills (623)
computer consultant (640)
computer-aided software engineering (CASE) (643)
context diagram (633)
cost/benefit feasibility (625)
data conversion (646)
data flow (633)
data store (633)
decision tree (634)
deliverable (624)
detailed analysis (631)
DFD (633)
direct conversion (646)
economic feasibility (625)
electronic magazine (639)
entity (632)
ERD (632)
feasibility study (630)
Gantt chart (623)
horizontal market software (637)
inheritance (636)
integration test (645)
Internet solutions provider (638)
joint-application design (JAD) session (626)
layout chart (642)
logic (643)
logical design (631)
method (635)
mockup (642)
object-oriented (OO) analysis and design (635)
operation (635)
operational feasibility (625)
outsource (638)
parallel conversion (646)
performance monitoring (648)
phased conversion (646)
physical design (642)
pilot conversion (646)
post-implementation system review (647)
process (633)
program development cycle (645)
program specification package (643)
project notebook (625)
project plan (623)
project request (626)
property (635)
Rational Unified Process (RUP) (636)
repository (633)
request for information (RFI) (640)
request for proposal (RFP) (640)
request for quotation (RFQ) (640)
request for system services (626)
schedule feasibility (625)
scope (623)
scope creep (623)
source (633)
structured analysis and design (632)
structured English (634)
structured walkthrough (644)
subclasses (636)
system enhancement (647)
system proposal (637)
systems test (645)
technical feasibility (625)
trade publication (637)
turnkey solution (640)
Unified Modeling Language (636)
unit test (645)
use case (636)
value-added reseller (VAR) (640)
vertical market software (637)

CHECKPOINT CHAPTER 12

Use the Checkpoint exercises to check your knowledge level of the chapter.

WEB INSTRUCTIONS:

To display this page from the Web, start your browser and enter the Web address **scsite.com/dc2005/ch12/check**. Click the links for current and additional information.

LABEL THE FIGURE

Identify each element in the data flow diagram (DFD).

a. data flows
b. data store
c. process
d. source

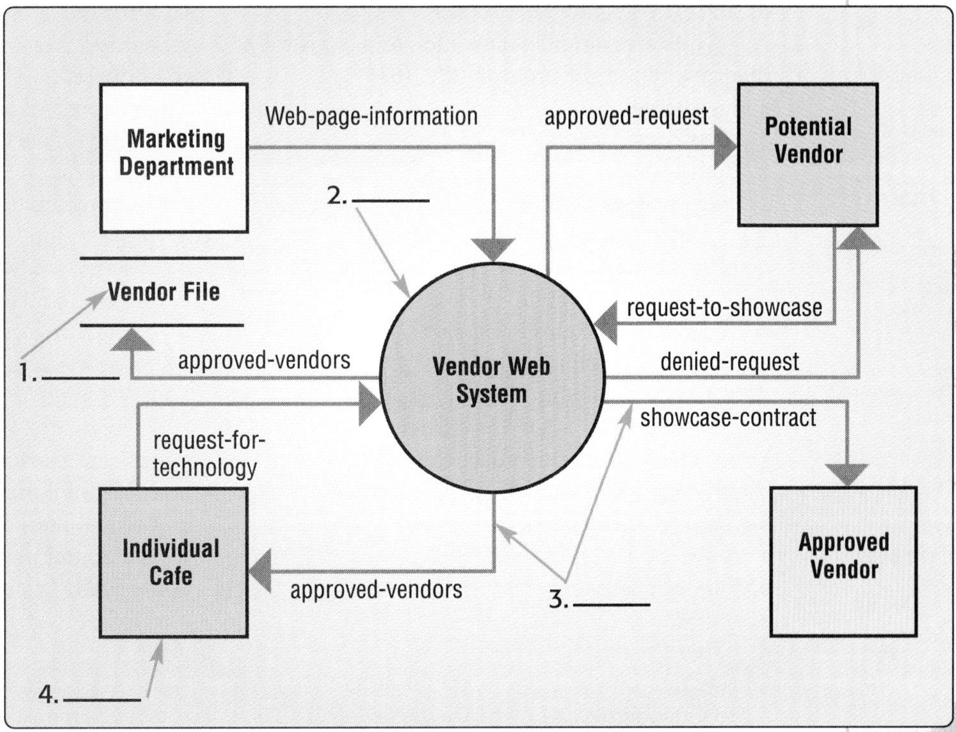

TRUE/FALSE

Mark T for True and F for False. (See page numbers in parentheses.)

_____ 1. An information system supports daily, short-term, and long-range activities of users. (620)

_____ 2. A systems analyst is responsible only for maintaining and troubleshooting an existing information system. (622)

_____ 3. Operational feasibility measures whether a company has the hardware, software, and people needed to support a proposed information system. (625)

_____ 4. The main purpose of the preliminary investigation is to determine the exact nature of the problem or improvement and decide whether it is worth pursuing. (630)

_____ 5. In detailed analysis, the systems analysts develop the proposed solution with a specific hardware or software in mind. (631)

_____ 6. A data store contains all the documentation and deliverables of a project. (633)

_____ 7. An attribute is an item that can contain both data and the procedures that read or manipulate the data. (635)

_____ 8. Companies can develop software in-house or outsource it, which means having an outside source develop it for them. (638)

_____ 9. A prototype is a working model of the proposed system. (643)

_____ 10. The purpose of the implementation phase is to construct the new or modified system and then deliver it to the users. (644)

_____ 11. During the support phase, a systems analyst monitors performance of a new or modified information system. (648)

QUIZZES AND LEARNING GAMES
Computer Genius
Crossword Puzzle
Interactive Labs
Practice Test
Quiz Yourself
Wheel of Terms

EXERCISES
Chapter Review
Checkpoint
Key Terms
Lab Exercises
Learn It Online
Web Research

BEYOND THE BOOK
Apply It
Career Corner
Companies
FAQ
High-Tech Talk
Issues
Looking Ahead
Trailblazers
Web Links

FEATURES
Guide to Web Sites
Making Use of the Web
Tech News
Timeline 2005

MULTIPLE CHOICE

Select the best answer. (See page numbers in parentheses.)

1. The steering committee _____. (623)
   a. works on a project from beginning to end
   b. is a decision-making body in a company
   c. tests and evaluates vendor proposals
   d. all of the above
2. A _____ is any tangible item such as a chart, diagram, report, or program file. (624)
   a. receivable
   b. repository
   c. deliverable
   d. conservatory
3. _____ measures whether the established deadlines for a project are reasonable. (625)
   a. Operational feasibility
   b. Technical feasibility
   c. Economic feasibility
   d. Schedule feasibility
4. A _____ session is a lengthy, structured, group meeting in which users and IT professionals work together to design or develop an application. (626)
   a. request for proposal (RFP)
   b. joint-application design (JAD)
   c. request for quotation (RFQ)
   d. data-flow design (DFD)
5. During the planning phase, the projects that receive the highest priority are those _____. (629)
   a. mandated by management or some other governing body
   b. suggested by the greatest number of users
   c. thought to be of highest value to the company
   d. proposed by the information technology (IT) department
6. Detailed analysis sometimes is called _____ because the systems analysts develop a proposed system without regard to specific hardware or software. (631)
   a. unit testing
   b. physical design
   c. systems testing
   d. logical design
7. The top-level DFD (data flow diagram), known as a _____, identifies only the major process. (633)
   a. project dictionary
   b. data flow
   c. context diagram
   d. data store
8. In object modeling, the procedure in an object, called a(n) _____ or method, contains activities that read or manipulate the data. (635)
   a. operation
   b. attribute
   c. entity
   d. property
9. The purpose of the _____ is to assess the feasibility of each alternative solution and then recommend the most feasible solution for the project. (637)
   a. project plan
   b. system review
   c. project request
   d. system proposal
10. Word processing, spreadsheet, database, and Web page authoring are examples of _____ software. (637)
    a. vertical market, custom
    b. horizontal market, custom
    c. vertical market, packaged
    d. horizontal market, packaged
11. Some VARs (value-added resellers) provide a complete system, also known as a(n) _____. (640)
    a. turnkey solution
    b. scope creep
    c. project plan
    d. abrupt cutover
12. During _____, the systems analyst identifies the processing requirements, or the logic, for each program in the system. (643)
    a. input design
    b. program design
    c. output design
    d. database design
13. With a direct conversion _____. (646)
    a. the old system runs alongside the new system for a specified time
    b. only one location in the company uses the new system — so it can be tested
    c. users stop using the old system and begin using the new system on a certain date
    d. each location in the company converts at a separate time
14. The purpose of _____ is to determine whether a system is inefficient at any point. (648)
    a. system enhancement
    b. structured walkthrough
    c. performance monitoring
    d. program development

CHECKPOINT

MATCHING

Match the terms with their definitions. (See page numbers in parentheses.)

_____ 1. project team (623)
_____ 2. Gantt chart (623)
_____ 3. request for system services (626)
_____ 4 project dictionary (633)
_____ 5. data dictionary (634)
_____ 6. trade publication (637)
_____ 7. value-added reseller (VAR) (640)
_____ 8. benchmark test (641)

a. stores a name, description, and other details for each data item
b. contains all the documentation and deliverables of a project
c. shows how actors interact with an information system
d. becomes the first item in the project notebook and triggers the planning phase
e. purchases products and then resells them along with additional services
f. users and IT professionals who work on a project from beginning to end
g. specific business or industry magazine
h. working model of a proposed system
i. measures the performance of hardware or software
j. bar chart that shows project phases or activities

SHORT ANSWER

Write a brief answer to each of the following questions.

1. What is a scope creep? ___________ Why should a project leader have good change-management skills? ___________
2. What is feasibility? ___________ How are operational feasibility, schedule feasibility, technical feasibility, and economic feasibility different? ___________
3. How is a decision table similar to, and different from, a decision tree? ___________ What is structured English? ___________
4. How is horizontal market software different from vertical market software? ___________ What is the advantage and disadvantage of custom software? ___________
5. How is a request for quotation (RFQ) different from a request for proposal (RFP)? ___________ What is a request for information? ___________

WORKING TOGETHER

Working with a group of your classmates, complete the following team exercises.

1. A recent development in information systems is communication and data sharing among different organizations. Some companies use electronic data interchange to facilitate the exchange of data. Have each member of your team investigate interorganizational information systems. How are these systems used? How are these systems managed? What are their benefits? What are their drawbacks? Meet with the members of your team and prepare a PowerPoint presentation to share your findings with the class.
2. Choose one Issue from the following issues in this chapter: Does Observation Improve Productivity? (625), Should Companies Use Distributed Development? (629), Should a Company Outsource IT Needs? (638), Who Should Pay for Training? (645), or What Type of Conversion Is Best? (646). Use the Web and/or print media to research the issue. Then, present a debate for the class, with different members of your team supporting different responses to the questions that accompany the issue.
3. A survey found that 40 percent of information technology (IT) professionals reported decreased job satisfaction, and 60 percent felt they were not working to their full potential. Many believed management failed to appreciate their efforts. Have each member of your team interview an IT professional. How satisfied are they with their work? Why? Are their efforts appreciated? What, if anything, could be done to improve the morale of IT professionals? Meet with members of your team and prepare a PowerPoint presentation to share your findings with the class.

CHAPTER 12 LEARN IT ONLINE

QUIZZES AND LEARNING GAMES
Computer Genius
Crossword Puzzle
Interactive Labs
Practice Test
Quiz Yourself
Wheel of Terms
EXERCISES
Chapter Review
Checkpoint
Key Terms
Lab Exercises
Learn It Online
Web Research
BEYOND THE BOOK
Apply It
Career Corner
Companies
FAQ
High-Tech Talk
Issues
Looking Ahead
Trailblazers
Web Links
FEATURES
Guide to Web Sites
Making Use of the Web
Tech News
Timeline 2005

Use the Learn It Online exercises to reinforce your understanding of the chapter concepts.

WEB INSTRUCTIONS:

To display this page from the Web, start your browser and enter the Web address **scsite.com/dc2005/ch12/learn**.

1 At the Movies – BizTech & Productivity

To view the BizTech & Productivity movie, click the number 1 button. Watch the movie and then complete the exercise by answering the question below. For decades, business productivity climbed at a comfortable, steady rate. Then, in the 1990s, expanding implementation of computer applications, the proliferation of personal computers, and dramatic increases in the level of Internet usage caused the percentage of productivity gain to more than double by the year 2000. What new technologies or Internet-like medium do you foresee keeping these high-gain rates going?

2 Student Edition Labs – Project Management

Click the number 2 button. When the Student Edition Labs menu appears, click *Project Management* to begin. A new browser window will open. Follow the on-screen instructions to complete the Lab. When finished, click the Exit button. If required, print a copy of your results to submit to your instructor.

3 Student Edition Labs – Web Design Principles

Click the number 3 button. When the Student Edition Labs menu appears, click *Web Design Principles* to begin. A new browser window will open. Follow the on-screen instructions to complete the Lab. When finished, click the Exit button. If required, print a copy of your results to submit to your instructor.

4 Customizing Your E-Mail Program

To complete this exercise, you first must complete Learn It Online 12 in Chapter 3 on page 175. Many e-mail programs can be customized. To customize your e-mail program, click the number 4 button to display your e-mail service. Enter your Sign-In Name and Password and then click the Sign in button. When the Home screen is displayed, click the Options tab. On the Options sheet, click the Block Sender link in the Mail Handling column. Follow the directions on the Options Block Sender sheet to block senders of mail you do not want to receive. Click the OK button. On the Options sheet, click the Signature link in the Additional Options column. Follow the directions on the Options Signature sheet to create a signature that will be added to outgoing messages. Click the OK button. Click the Inbox tab. Read any new mail. When you have read all of your messages, click the Sign Out button to exit.

5 System Development Cycle

People deal with problems in a variety of ways. An anthropologist studying workers in Silicon Valley tells the story of an engineer who kept a list of dilemmas with possible answers. When the list grew too long, the engineer's solution simply was to combine the problems into a shorter list. The core of the system development cycle is based on a standard, more effective approach to problem solving. To learn about different approaches, click the number 5 button and complete this exercise.

6 Practice Test

Click the number 6 button. Answer each question. When completed, enter your name and click the Grade Test button to submit the quiz for grading. Make a note of any missed questions. If required, print a copy to submit to your instructor.

7 Web Guide

Click the number 7 button to display the Guide to Web Sites and Searching Techniques Web page. Click Reference and then click Webopedia. Search for CASE. Click one of the CASE links. Use your word processing program to prepare a brief report about your findings and submit your assignment to your instructor.

8 Scavenger Hunt

Click the number 8 button. Print a copy of the Scavenger Hunt page; use this page to write down your answers as you search the Web. Submit your completed page to your instructor.

9 Who Wants To Be a Computer Genius?

Click the number 9 button to find out if you are a computer genius. Directions on how to play the game will be displayed. When you are ready to play, click the PLAY button. Submit your score to your instructor.

10 Wheel of Terms

Click the number 10 button to reinforce important terms you learned in this chapter by playing the Shelly Cashman Series version of this popular game. Directions on how to play the game will be displayed. When you are ready to play, click the PLAY button. Submit your score to your instructor.

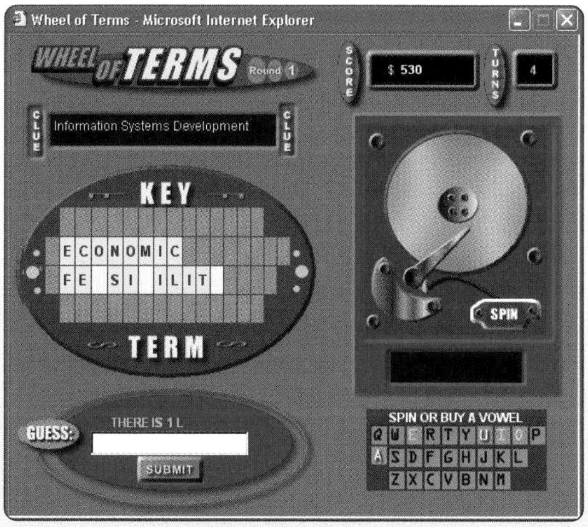

11 Career Corner

Click the number 11 button to display the TechSoup.org page. Click one of the Career Resource List links and then review the information. Write a brief report describing what you learned. Submit the report to your instructor.

12 Search Sleuth

Click the number 12 button to learn search techniques that will help make you a research expert. Submit the completed assignment to your instructor.

13 Crossword Puzzle Challenge

Click the number 13 button. Complete the puzzle to reinforce skills you learned in this chapter. Directions on how to play the game will be displayed. When you are ready to play, click the PLAY button. Submit the completed puzzle to your instructor.

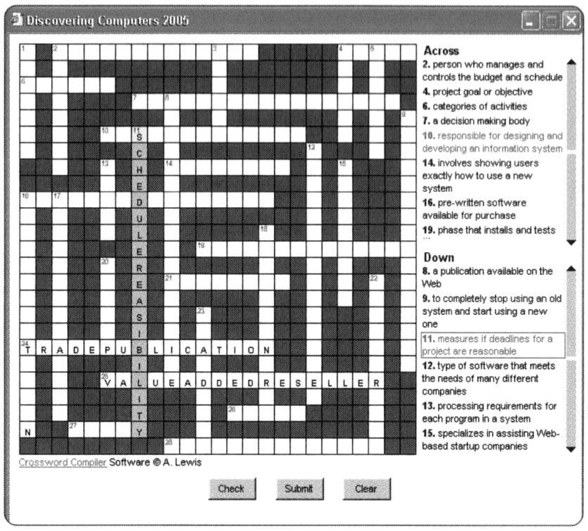

14 Computer-Aided Software Engineering (CASE)

A difficult task in the design phase is to organize all of the information needed by an organization and document the flow of data within the organization. One estimate indicates that the amount of material amassed in this phase is greater than the quantity of information an average person in the seventeenth century would acquire in a lifetime. To learn more about one of the many CASE products available for managing information and tracking data, click the number 14 button and complete this exercise.

15 In the News

When teams from around the world gathered in Japan and Korea for the World Cup soccer championship, more than 180 groups of researchers met at a Japanese stadium for another event — the annual Robot Football World Cup. Click the number 15 button and read a news article about an innovative development or use of a computer information system. Who developed or used the system? In what way is the development or use of the system original?

CHAPTER 12 LAB EXERCISES

Use the Lab Exercises to gain hands-on computer experience.

WEB INSTRUCTIONS:

To display this page from the Web, start your browser and enter the Web address **scsite.com/dc2005/ch12/lab**.

1 Traffic Sign Tutorial

This exercise uses Windows XP/2000/98 procedures. Insert the Data Disk into drive A. See the inside back cover of this book for instructions for downloading the Data Disk or see your instructor for information on accessing the files required in this book. Click the Start button on the taskbar and then click Run on the Start menu. In the Open text box, type `a:traffic.exe` and then click the OK button to display the Traffic Sign Tutorial window. This program was written in Visual Basic. Drag the signs to their correct containers. Click Options on the menu bar and then click Clear to reset the tutorial. Click Options on the menu bar and then click Show. Click Options on the menu bar and then click Clear. Click Options on the menu bar and then click Quiz. Answer the quiz questions. Close the Traffic Sign Tutorial.

2 Dr. Watson

This exercise uses Windows XP procedures. Dr. Watson is a Windows diagnostic tool used to identify faults in a system. To find out more about Dr. Watson, click the Start button on the taskbar and then click Help and Support on the Start menu. Click the Index button on the Help and Support Center toolbar. Type `dr watson` in the Type in the keyword to find text box. Click an appropriate Help topic in the Index pane, click the Display button, and answer the following questions:

- How is Dr. Watson used to diagnose system faults?
- How can you open Dr. Watson from the Start menu?

Click the Close button to close the Help and Support Center window.

3 Creating a Drawing

This exercise uses Windows XP/2000/98 procedures. Click the Start button on the taskbar, point to All Programs (Programs in Windows 2000/98) on the Start menu, point to Accessories on the All Programs submenu (Programs submenu in Windows 2000/98), and then click Paint on the Accessories submenu. If necessary, maximize the Paint window and drag the lower-right corner of the image area to the right to increase its size. Change the background color to orange by clicking the color orange in the color box at the bottom of the Paint window, clicking the Fill With Color tool (row 2, column 2) in the tool box on the left edge of the window, and then clicking the image area. Change the foreground color to red by clicking the color red in the color box. Use the Rectangle tool (row 7, column 1) and the Line tool (row 6, column 1) in the tool box to draw the box (shown in the figure below). Use the Fill With Color tool (row 2, column 2) in the tool box and color box to color the box. If you make a mistake, click Edit on the menu bar and then click Undo to erase your last draw. Click File on the menu bar and then click Save. With a floppy disk in drive A, type `a:\lab12-3` in the File name text box. Click the Save button. Click Print on the File menu and then click the Print button. Click the OK button. Close the Paint window.

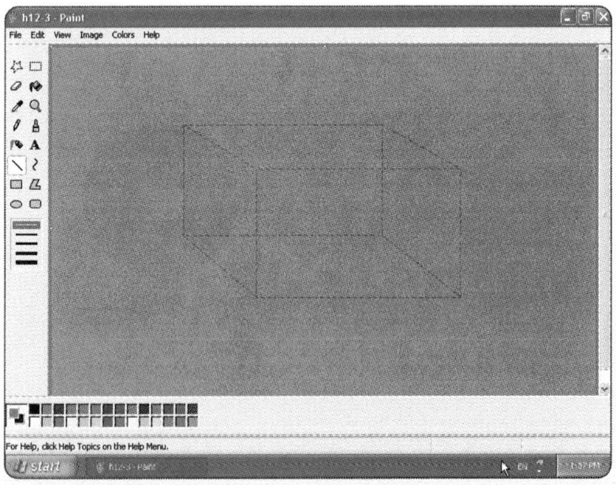

4 Capturing Screen Images

This exercise uses Windows XP/2000/98 procedures. Click the Start button on the taskbar, point to All Programs (Programs in Windows 2000/98) on the Start menu, and then point to Accessories on the All Programs submenu (Programs submenu in Windows 2000/98). Press the PRINT SCREEN key on your keyboard. Click WordPad on the Accessories submenu. In WordPad, type your name and then type `Below is a Windows Screen Shot:`. Press the ENTER key twice. Click Edit on the menu bar and then click Paste. Use the scroll bar to scroll through the document. Click the Print button on the toolbar to print the file. Do not save the file unless your instructor tells you to do so. Close WordPad.

WEB RESEARCH

Use the Web Research exercises to learn more about the special features in this chapter.

WEB INSTRUCTIONS:

Use the link in each exercise or a search engine such as Google (google.com) to research the topic. Then, write a one-page, double-spaced report or create a presentation, unless otherwise directed below. Page numbers on which information can be found are in parentheses.

1 **Issue** Choose one Issue from the following issues in this chapter: Does Observation Improve Productivity? (625), Should Companies Use Distributed Development? (629), Should a Company Outsource IT Needs? (638), Who Should Pay for Training? (645), or What Type of Conversion Is Best? (646). Use the Web to research the issue. Discuss the issue with classmates, instructors, and friends. Address the questions that accompany the issue in a report or presentation.

2 **Apply It** Choose one of the following Apply It features in this chapter: Interviewing for Success (626) or IRS Develops Modernization Plan (647). Use the Web to gather additional information about the topic. Print two Web pages that relate to the Apply It. Detail in a report or presentation what you learned.

3 **Career Corner** Read the Career Corner article in this chapter (648). Use the Web to find out more about the career. Describe the career in a report or presentation.

4 **Companies on the Cutting Edge** Choose one of the Companies on the Cutting Edge in this chapter (650). Use the Web to research the company further. Explain in a report or presentation how this company has contributed to computer technology.

5 **Technology Trailblazers** Choose one of the Technology Trailblazers in this chapter (651). Use the Web to research the person further. Explain in a report or presentation how this individual has affected the way people use, or think about, computers.

6 **Picture Yourself on a System Development Team** Read the Picture Yourself on a System Development Team story at the beginning of this chapter (618). Use the Web to research system development further. Describe in a report or presentation the ways in which you might be a part of system development.

7 **High-Tech Talk** Read the High-Tech Talk feature in this chapter (649). Use the Web to find out more about the topic. Summarize in a report or presentation what you learned.

8 **Web Links** Review the Web Link boxes found in the margins of this chapter. Visit five of the Web Link sites. Print the main Web page for each site you visit. Choose one of the Web pages and then summarize in one paragraph the content of the Web page.

9 **Looking Ahead** Choose one of the Looking Ahead articles in this chapter: Extreme Project Management Leads to Success (624) or Buying Software May Not Be the Best Buy (637). Use the Web to find out more about the topic. Detail in a report or presentation what you learned.

10 **FAQ** Choose one FAQ found in this chapter. Use the Web to find out more about the topic. Summarize in one paragraph what you learned.

11 **Making Use of the Web** Read the Health section of Making Use of the Web in Appendix A (APP 24). Complete the Health Web Exercises at the end of the section (APP 25). Answer the questions posed in each exercise.

CHAPTER 13

Programming Languages and Program Development

Picture Yourself Learning How to Program

As you walk into the computer lab room to finish typing your research paper for American History, you see a group of friends huddled around a computer. Wondering what is so interesting, you decide to look over one of their shoulders. They are playing tic-tac-toe. As the game ends, one exclaims, "It worked!"

You ask them why they are so excited about a game of tic-tac-toe. They explain that they had to write a computer program as their final semester team project in their Introduction to Computer Programming class. The program had to be interactive. The teacher offered ideas such as a calculator, a simple game, or a loan calculator. Their team decided to write a program for the tic-tac-toe game.

After working on it for three weeks, they finished the game program this morning and are making sure it runs properly by playing the game. One student asks if you would like to try it. As the Xs and Os appear in the grid, you think this is great stuff. You wonder whether it was difficult. You ask them if they think you could do it. "Of course you could," they say. You decide to take the same computer programming class next semester, as a math elective.

As you read Chapter 13, you will learn about a variety of programming languages and discover the steps in program development.

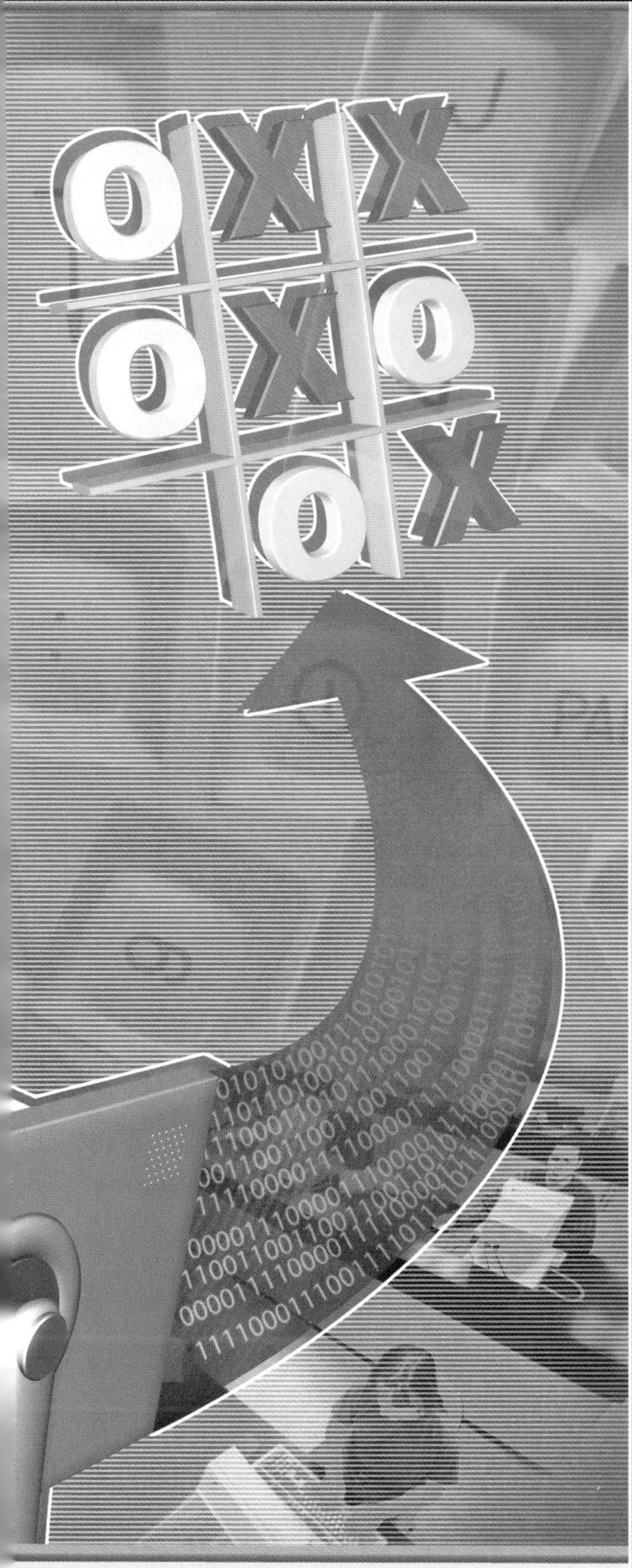

OBJECTIVES

After completing this chapter, you will be able to:

1. Differentiate between machine and assembly languages
2. Identify and discuss the purpose of procedural programming languages
3. Discuss the advantages and uses of visual programming languages
4. Identify and discuss the characteristics of object-oriented programming languages
5. Identify the uses of various nonprocedural languages and tools
6. Describe various ways to develop Web pages, including HTML, scripting languages, DHTML, XML, WML, and Web page authoring software
7. Identify the uses of popular multimedia authoring programs
8. List the six steps in the program development cycle
9. Differentiate between structured design and object-oriented design
10. Explain the basic control structures used in designing solutions to programming problems

CONTENTS

COMPUTER PROGRAMS AND PROGRAMMING LANGUAGES

Although you may never write a computer program, information you request may require a programmer to write or modify a program. Thus, you should understand how programmers develop programs to meet information requirements. A **computer program** is a series of instructions that directs a computer to perform tasks. A computer **programmer** writes and modifies computer programs.

To write a program's instructions, programmers often use a programming language. A **programming language** is a set of words, symbols, and codes that enables a programmer to communicate instructions to a computer. Just as humans speak a variety of languages (English, Spanish, French, and so on), programmers use a variety of programming languages and tools to write, or *code*, a program (Figure 13-1).

Several hundred programming languages exist today. Each language has its own rules for writing the instructions. Languages often are designed for specific purposes, such as scientific applications, business solutions, or Web page development.

Two types of languages are low-level and high-level. A *low-level language* is a programming language that is machine dependent. A *machine-dependent language* runs on only one

FIGURE 13-1 Programmers must decide which programming languages and tools to use when they write programs.

particular type of computer. These programs are not easily portable to other types of computers. Each language instruction in a low-level language usually equates to a single machine instruction. With a *high-level language*, by contrast, each language instruction typically equates to multiple machine instructions. High-level languages often are machine independent. A *machine-independent language* can run on many different types of computers and operating systems.

The following pages discuss low-level languages, as well as several types of high-level languages including procedural languages, visual programming languages, object-oriented programming languages, nonprocedural languages and tools, Web page programming languages, and multimedia programming languages.

LOW-LEVEL LANGUAGES

Two types of low-level languages are machine languages and assembly languages. **Machine language**, known as the first generation of programming languages, is the only language the computer directly recognizes (Figure 13-2). Machine language instructions use a series of binary digits (1s and 0s) or a combination of numbers and letters that represents binary digits. The binary digits correspond to the on and off electrical states of a computer. As you might imagine, coding in machine language is tedious and time-consuming.

					00090
000090	50E0	30B2			010B4
000094	1B44				
000096	1B77				
000098	1B55				
00009A	F273	30D6	2C81	010D8	00C83
0000A0	4F50	30D6			010D8
0000A4	F275	30D6	2C7B	010D8	00C7D
0000AA	4F70	30D6			010D8
0000AE	5070	304A			0104C
0000B2	1C47				
0000B4	5050	304E			01050
0000B8	58E0	30B2			010B4
0000BC	07FE				
					000BE
0000BE	50E0	30B6			010B8
0000C2	95F1	2C85		00C87	
0000C6	4770	20D2		000D4	
0000CA	1B55				
0000CC	5A50	35A6			015A8
0000D0	47F0	2100		00102	
0000D4	95F2	2C85		00C87	
0000D8	4770	20E4		000E6	
0000DC	1B55				
0000DE	5A50	35AA			015AC
0000E2	47F0	2100		00102	
000102	1B77				
000104	5870	304E			01050
000108	1C47				
00010A	4E50	30D6			010D8
00010E	F075	30D6	003E	010D8	0003E
000114	4F50	30D6			010D8
000118	5050	3052			01054
00011C	58E0	30B6			010B8
000120	07FE				
					00122
000122	50E0	30BA			010BC
000126	1B55				
000128	5A50	304E			01050
00012C	5B50	3052			01054
000130	5050	305A			0105C
000134	58E0	30BA			010BC
000138	07FE				

FIGURE 13-2 A sample machine language program, coded using the hexadecimal number system. For information about hexadecimal, read Appendix B at the back of this book.

With an **assembly language**, the second generation of programming languages, a programmer writes instructions using symbolic instruction codes (Figure 13-3). *Symbolic instruction codes* are meaningful abbreviations and codes. With an assembly language, a programmer writes codes such as A for addition, C for compare, L for load, and M for multiply.

Assembly languages also use symbolic addresses. A *symbolic address* is a meaningful name that identifies a storage location. For example, a programmer can use the name RATE to refer to the storage location that contains a pay rate.

```
*         THIS MODULE CALCULATES THE REGULAR TIME PAY
CALCSTPY  EQU    *
          ST     14,SAVERTPY
          SR     4,4
          SR     7,7
          SR     5,5
          PACK   DOUBLE,RTHRSIN
          CVB    4,DOUBLE
          PACK   DOUBLE,RATEIN
          CVB    7,DOUBLE
          ST     7,RATE
          MR     4,7
          ST     5,RTPAY
          L      14,SAVERTPY
          BR     14
*         THIS MODULE CALCULATES THE OVERTIME PAY
CALCOTPY  EQU    *
          ST     14,SAVEOTPY
TEST1     CLI    CODEIN,C'O'
          BH     TEST2
          SR     5,5
          A      5,=F'0'
          ST     5,OTPAY
          B      AROUND
TEST2     SR     4,4
          SR     7,7
          SR     5,5
          PACK   DOUBLE,OTHRSIN
          CVB    4,DOUBLE
          PACK   DOUBLE,RATEIN
          CVB    7,RATE
          MR     4,7
          MR     4,=F'1.5'
          ST     5,OTPAY
AROUND    L      14,SAVEOTPY
          BR     14
*         THIS MODULE CALCULATES THE GROSS PAY
CALCGPAY  EQU    *
          ST     14,SAVEGPAY
          SR     5,5
          A      5,RTPAY
          A      5,OTPAY
          ST     5,GRPAY
          L      14,SAVEGPAY
          BR     14
```

FIGURE 13-3 An excerpt from an assembly language payroll program. The code shows the computations for regular time pay, overtime pay, and gross pay and the decision to evaluate the overtime hours.

Despite these advantages, assembly languages can be difficult to learn. In addition, programmers must convert an assembly language program into machine language before the computer can *execute*, or run, the program. That is, the computer cannot execute the assembly source program. A **source program** is the program that contains the language instructions, or code, to be converted to machine language. To convert the assembly language source program into machine language, programmers use a program called an *assembler*.

One assembly language instruction usually equates to one machine language instruction. In some cases, however, the assembly language includes macros. This type of *macro* generates many machine language instructions for a single assembly language instruction. Macros save the programmer time during program development.

PROCEDURAL LANGUAGES

The disadvantages of machine and assembly (low-level) languages led to the development of procedural languages in the late 1950s and 1960s. In a **procedural language**, the programmer writes instructions that tell the computer what to accomplish and how to do it.

With a procedural language, often called a **third-generation language** (**3GL**), a programmer uses a series of English-like words to write instructions. For example, ADD stands for addition or PRINT means to print. Many 3GLs also use arithmetic operators such as * for multiplication and + for addition. These English-like words and arithmetic symbols simplify the program development process for the programmer.

As with an assembly language program, the 3GL code (instructions) is called the source program. Programmers must convert this source program into machine language before the computer can execute the program. This translation process often is very complex, because one 3GL source program instruction translates into many machine language instructions. For 3GLs, programmers typically use either a compiler or an interpreter to perform the translation.

A *compiler* is a separate program that converts the entire source program into machine language before executing it. The machine language version that results from compiling the 3GL is called the *object code* or *object program*. The compiler stores the object code on disk for execution later.

While it is compiling the source program into object code, the compiler checks the source program for errors. It also makes sure the program properly defines the data it will use in calculations or comparisons. The compiler then produces a program listing that contains the source code and a list of any errors. This listing helps the programmer make necessary changes to the source code and correct errors in the program. Figure 13-4 shows the process of compiling a source program.

A compiler translates an entire program before executing it. An interpreter, by contrast, translates and executes one program code statement at a time. An *interpreter* reads a code statement, converts it to one or more machine language instructions, and then executes those machine language instructions. It does this all before moving to the next code statement in the program. Each time the source program runs, the interpreter translates and executes it, statement by statement. An interpreter does not produce an object program. Figure 13-5 shows the process of interpreting a program.

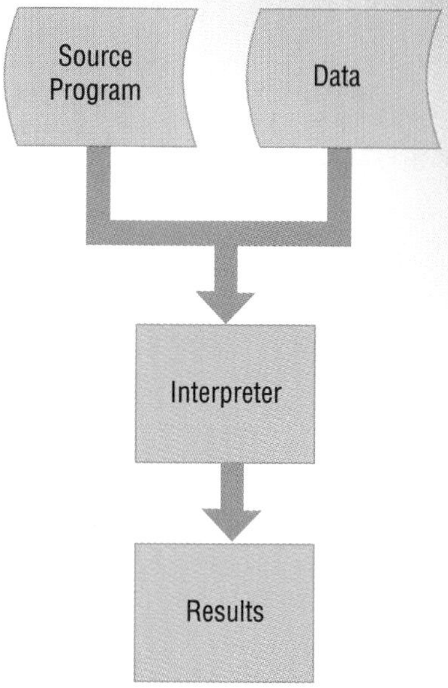

FIGURE 13-5 With an interpreter, one line of the source program at a time is converted into machine language and then immediately executed by the computer. If the interpreter encounters an error while converting a line of code, an error message immediately is displayed on the screen and the program stops.

```
*    COMPUTE REGULAR TIME PAY
     MULTIPLY REGULAR-TIME-HOURS BY HOURLY-PAY-RATE
         GIVING REGULAR-TIME-PAY.

*    COMPUTE OVERTIME PAY
     IF OVERTIME-HOURS > 0
         COMPUTE OVERTIME-PAY = OVERTIME-HOURS * 1.5 * HOURLY-PAY-RATE
     ELSE
         MOVE 0 TO OVERTIME-PAY.

*    COMPUTE GROSS PAY
     ADD REGULAR-TIME-PAY TO OVERTIME-PAY
         GIVING GROSS-PAY.

*    PRINT GROSS PAY
     MOVE GROSS-PAY TO GROSS-PAY-OUT.
     WRITE REPORT-LINE-OUT FROM DETAIL-LINE
         AFTER ADVANCING 2 LINES.
```

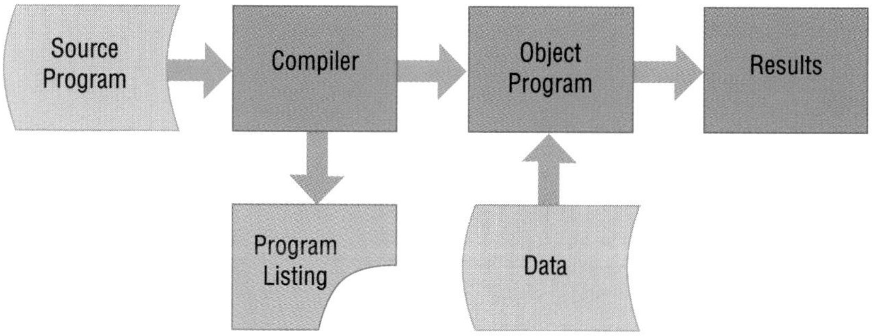

FIGURE 13-4 A compiler converts the entire source program into a machine language object program. If the compiler encounters any errors, it records them in a program-listing file, which the programmer may print when the entire compilation is complete. When a user wants to run the program, the object program is loaded into the memory of the computer and the program instructions begin executing.

One advantage of an interpreter is that when it finds errors, it displays feedback immediately. The programmer can correct any errors before the interpreter translates the next line of code. The disadvantage is that interpreted programs do not run as fast as compiled programs. This is because an interpreter must translate the source program to machine language each time the program executes. Once a program is compiled, by contrast, users simply execute the object code to run the program.

Many programming languages include both an interpreter and a compiler. In this case, the programmer can use the interpreter during program development. When the program is complete and error free, the programmer can compile the program so it runs faster when it is placed into production for users to execute.

Hundreds of procedural languages exist. Only a few, however, are used widely enough for the industry to recognize them as standards. These include BASIC, COBOL, and C. To illustrate the similarities and differences among these programming languages, the figures on the following pages show program code in these languages. The code solves a simple payroll problem — computing the gross pay for an employee.

The process used to compute gross pay can vary from one system to another. The examples on the following pages use a simple *algorithm*, or set of steps, to help you easily compare one programming language with another.

BASIC

John Kemeny and Thomas Kurtz developed a programming language called **BASIC** (*Beginner's All-purpose Symbolic Instruction Code*) in the mid-1960s at Dartmouth College. Kemeny and Kurtz designed BASIC for use as a simple, interactive problem-solving language (Figure 13-6).

BASIC originally was intended as the language to be used in a student's first programming course because it is so easy to learn and use. Today, BASIC is used on both personal computers and midrange servers to develop some business applications. Many versions of BASIC exist, including QBasic, QuickBASIC, and MS-BASIC.

COBOL

COBOL (*COmmon Business-Oriented Language*) evolved out of a joint effort between the United States government, businesses, and major universities in the early 1960s. Naval officer *Grace Hopper*, a pioneer in computer programming, was a prime developer of COBOL.

COBOL is a programming language designed for business applications. Although COBOL programs often are lengthy, their English-like statements make the code easy to read, write, and maintain (Figure 13-7). COBOL especially is useful for processing transactions, such as payroll and billing, on mainframe computers. COBOL programs also run on other types of computers. The most popular personal computer COBOL program is *Micro Focus Net Express*, which enables programmers to create and migrate COBOL programs to the Web.

```
REM COMPUTE REGULAR TIME PAY
Regular.Time.Pay = Regular.Time.Hours * Hourly.Pay.Rate

REM COMPUTE OVERTIME PAY
If Overtime.Hours > 0 THEN
    Overtime.Pay = Overtime.Hours * 1.5 * Hourly.Pay.Rate
ELSE
    Overtime.Pay = 0
END IF

REM COMPUTE GROSS PAY
Gross.Pay = Regular.Time.Pay + Overtime.Pay
REM PRINT GROSS PAY
PRINT USING "The gross pay is $##,###.##"; Gross.Pay
```

FIGURE 13-6 This figure illustrates an excerpt from a BASIC payroll program. The code shows the computations for regular time pay, overtime pay, and gross pay; the decision to evaluate the overtime hours; and the output of the gross pay.

```
*    COMPUTE REGULAR TIME PAY
     MULTIPLY REGULAR-TIME-HOURS BY HOURLY-PAY-RATE
         GIVING REGULAR-TIME-PAY.

*    COMPUTE OVERTIME PAY
     IF OVERTIME-HOURS > 0
         COMPUTE OVERTIME-PAY = OVERTIME-HOURS * 1.5 * HOURLY-PAY-RATE
     ELSE
         MOVE 0 TO OVERTIME-PAY.

*    COMPUTE GROSS PAY
     ADD REGULAR-TIME-PAY TO OVERTIME-PAY
         GIVING GROSS-PAY.

*    PRINT GROSS PAY
     MOVE GROSS-PAY TO GROSS-PAY-OUT.
     WRITE REPORT-LINE-OUT FROM DETAIL-LINE
         AFTER ADVANCING 2 LINES.
```

FIGURE 13-7 An excerpt from a COBOL payroll program. The code shows the computations for regular time pay, overtime pay, and gross pay; the decision to evaluate the overtime hours; and the output of the gross pay. Notice how much wordier this program is compared with the BASIC program in Figure 13-6. It is more readable, however, than the BASIC program.

WEB LINK 13-1

COBOL

Visit the Discovering Computers 2005 WEB LINK page (**scsite.com/dc2005/weblink**). Click COBOL below Chapter 13.

C

The **C** programming language, developed in the early 1970s by Dennis Ritchie at Bell Laboratories, originally was designed for writing system software. Today, many software programs are written in C (Figure 13-8). This includes operating systems and application software such as word processing and spreadsheet programs.

C is a powerful language that requires professional programming skills. Many programmers use C for business and scientific problems. C runs on almost any type of computer with any operating system, but it is used most often with the UNIX operating system. In fact, most of the UNIX operating system is written in C.

```
/* Compute Regular Time Pay                        */
rt_pay = rt_hrs * pay_rate;

/* Compute Overtime Pay                            */
if (ot_hrs > 0)
    ot_pay = ot_hrs * 1.5 * pay_rate;
else
    ot_pay = 0;

/* Compute Gross Pay                               */
gross = rt_pay + ot_pay;

/* Print Gross Pay                                 */
printf("The gross pay is %d\n", gross);
```

FIGURE 13-8 An excerpt from a C payroll program. The code shows the computations for regular time pay, overtime pay, and gross pay; the decision to evaluate the overtime hours; and the output of the gross pay.

OBJECT-ORIENTED PROGRAMMING LANGUAGES

Programmers use an **object-oriented programming (OOP) language** to implement an object-oriented design. Recall from Chapter 12 that an *object* is an item that can contain both data and the procedures that read or manipulate that data. An object represents a real person, place, event, or transaction.

A major benefit of OOP is the ability to reuse and modify existing objects. For example, once a developer creates an Employee object, it is available for use by any other existing or future program. Thus, programmers repeatedly reuse existing objects. Programs developed using the object-oriented approach have several advantages. The objects can be reused in many systems, are designed for repeated use, and become stable over time. In addition, programmers create applications faster because they design programs using existing objects.

In addition to being able to work with objects, an OOP language is event driven. An *event* is an action to which the program responds. Examples of events include pressing a key on the keyboard, typing a value into a text box, moving the mouse, clicking a button, or speaking an instruction. An *event-driven program* checks for and responds to events. Some programming languages such as Visual Basic are event driven, but are not complete OOP languages. Other programming languages, such as C++ and Java, are complete object-oriented languages. The following sections discuss these languages.

C++

Developed in the 1980s by Bjarne Sroustrup at Bell Laboratories, **C++** (pronounced SEE-plus-plus) is an object-oriented programming language that is an extension of the C programming language. C++ includes all the elements of the C language plus it has additional features for working with objects, classes, events, and other object-oriented concepts (Figure 13-9). Programmers commonly use C++ to develop database and Web applications. Much application software, such as word processing and spreadsheet programs, also is written in C++. Although C++ is an outgrowth of the C programming language, a programmer does not need C programming experience to be a successful C++ programmer.

WEB LINK 13-2

C++

Visit the Discovering Computers 2005 WEB LINK page (**scsite .com/dc2005/weblink**). Click C++ below Chapter 13.

Java

Java is an object-oriented programming language developed by Sun Microsystems. Figure 13-10 shows a portion of a Java program and the window that the program displays.

The Java language is very similar to C++. One difference is that Java uses a *just-in-time (JIT) compiler* to convert its source code into machine code — as it is needed. A Java interpreter executes the resulting machine code, called *bytecode*, because the operating system cannot execute it. Java-enabled Web browsers contain Java bytecode interpreters.

J2EE (*Java 2 Platform Enterprise Edition*) is a set of technologies by Sun Microsystems that allows programmers to develop and deploy Web services for a company. The goal of J2EE is to simplify and reduce program development time by developing standard, reusable objects.

```
// portion of a C++ program that allows users to create a new zip code from a
// string or a number and expand zip codes, as appropriate, to a 10-digit number

ZipC::ZipC( const unsigned long zipnum )
{
  ostringstream strInt;
  strInt << zipnum;
  code = strInt.str();
}

const string ZipC::getCode()
{
  return code;
}

void ZipC::setCode(const string newCode)
{
  code = newCode;
}

void ZipC::expand( const string suffix )
{

  if(code.length() == 5 &&          // small size?
     suffix.length() == 4)          // length ok?
  {
     code += "-";
     code.append(suffix);
  }
}
```

FIGURE 13-9 Sample C++ program.

```
public void actionPerformed(ActionEvent e)
   {
      foundKey = false;

      //Search for the key pressed
      for (int i = 0; i < keysArray.length && !foundKey; i++)
         if(e.getSource() == keysArray[i])    //key match found
         {
            foundKey = true;
            switch(i)
            {
               case 0: case 1: case 2: case 3: case 4:  //number buttons
               case 5: case 6: case 7: case 8: case 9:  //0 - 9
               case 15:                                 //decimal point button
                  if(clearText)
                  {
                     lcdField.setText("");
                     clearText = false;
                  }
                  lcdField.setText(lcdField.getText() + keysArray[i].getLabel());
                  break;
```

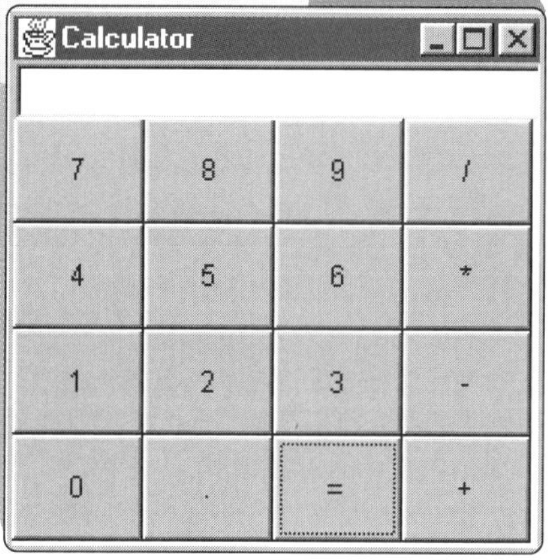

FIGURE 13-10 A portion of a Java program and the window the program displays.

> **WEB LINK 13-3**
>
> **Java**
>
> Visit the Discovering Computers 2005 WEB LINK page (**scsite.com/dc2005/weblink**). Click Java below Chapter 13.

> **FAQ 13-1**
>
> **What is a Java applet?**
>
> A *Java applet* is a small Java program that runs inside another program such as a Web browser. Both Internet Explorer and Netscape Navigator can run Java applets. Programmers write Java applets to add multimedia and interactivity to Web pages such as rotating images, fireworks, interactive animations, games, shopping carts, and surveys.
>
> For more information about Java applets, visit the Discovering Computers 2005 FAQ Web page (**scsite.com/dc2005/faq**). Click Java Applets below Chapter 13.

Visual Programming Languages

A **visual programming language**, sometimes called a *fifth-generation language*, is a language that provides a visual or graphical interface for creating source code. The graphical interface, called a *visual programming environment* (*VPE*), allows developers to drag and drop objects to build programs. The visual programming language may use a compiler or a JIT compiler to convert the source code to machine language.

Visual programming languages often are used in a RAD environment. **RAD** (*rapid application development*) is a method of developing software, in which a programmer writes and implements a program in segments instead of waiting until the entire program is completed. Users begin working with sections of the program as they are completed. An important concept in RAD is the use of prebuilt components. For example, programmers do not have to write code for buttons and text boxes on Windows forms because they already exist in the programming language or tools provided with the language. The next pages discuss these languages.

> **WEB LINK 13-4**
>
> **RAD**
>
> Visit the Discovering Computers 2005 WEB LINK page (**scsite.com/dc2005/weblink**). Click RAD below Chapter 13.

WEB LINK 13-5

Visual Studio .NET 2003

Visit the Discovering Computers 2005 WEB LINK page (**scsite.com/dc2005/weblink**). Click Visual Studio .NET 2003 below Chapter 13.

Visual Studio .NET 2003

Visual Studio .NET 2003 is the latest suite of visual programming languages and RAD tools from Microsoft that assists programmers in developing programs for Windows or any operating system that supports Microsoft's .NET architecture. As discussed in Chapter 9, *.NET* (pronounced dot net) is a set of technologies that allows almost any type of program to run on the Internet or an internal business network. The following paragraphs discuss the programming languages in the Visual Studio .NET 2003 suite.

- **Visual Basic .NET 2003** (sometimes referred to as *VB .NET*) is a visual programming language that allows programmers easily to build complex task oriented object-based programs. Visual Basic .NET 2003 is based on the Visual Basic programming language, which was developed by Microsoft Corporation in the early 1990s. This language is very similar to BASIC and easy to learn and use. Thus, Visual Basic .NET 2003 is ideal for beginning programmers.

  The first step in building a Visual Basic .NET 2003 program is to design the graphical user interface using Visual Basic .NET 2003 objects (Steps 1 and 2 in Figure 13-11). Visual Basic .NET 2003 objects include items such as command buttons, text boxes, and labels. Next, the programmer writes instructions to define any actions that should occur in response to specific events (Step 3 in Figure 13-11). Finally, the programmer generates and tests the final program (Step 4 in Figure 13-11).

FIGURE 13-11 CREATING A VISUAL BASIC .NET 2003 PROGRAM

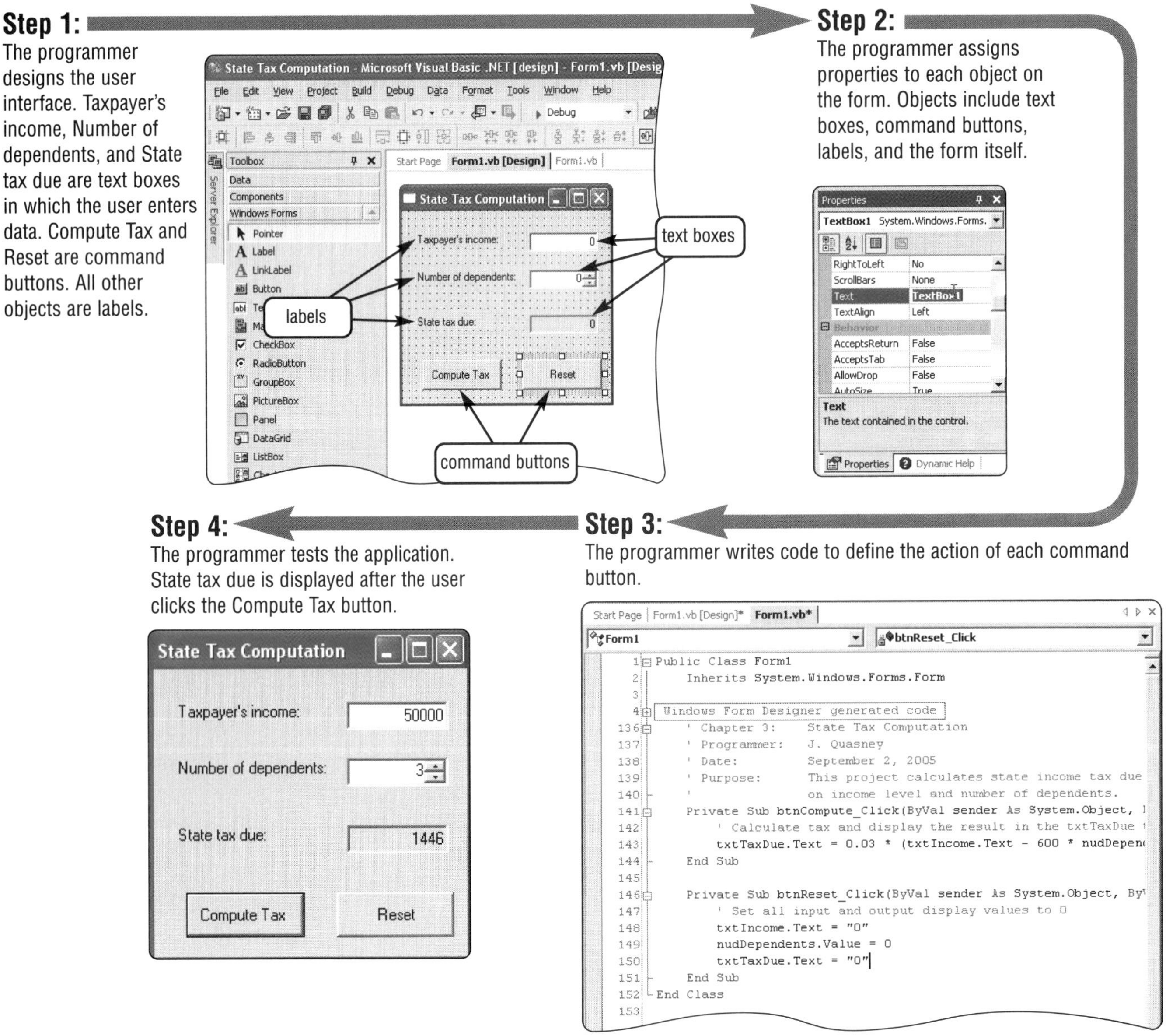

An event in Visual Basic .NET 2003 might be the result of an action that a user initiates. For example, when a user clicks a button in a Visual Basic .NET 2003 program, the program executes the Click event. Programmers define Visual Basic .NET 2003 events by writing instructions with its built-in programming language.

- **Visual C++ .NET 2003** is a visual programming language based on C++. Not only is Visual C++ .NET 2003 a powerful object-oriented programming language, it enables programmers to write Windows and .NET applications quickly and efficiently. With Visual C++ .NET 2003, however, programmers can develop applications for nearly every platform. Features that make Visual C++ .NET 2003 so powerful include reusable templates, direct access to machine level memory locations, an optimizing compiler, and advanced error reporting.
- **Visual C# .NET 2003** (pronounced SEE-sharp) is a visual programming language that combines programming elements of C++ with an easier development environment. The purpose of Visual C# .NET 2003 is to take the complexity out of Visual C++ .NET 2003 and still provide an object-oriented programming language. Programmers familiar with the C/C++ programming language family often migrate to the easier-to-use Visual C# .NET.
- **Visual J# .NET 2003** (pronounced JAY-sharp) is a visual programming language that allows Java program development in the .NET environment. Programmers familiar with Java or Visual J++ easily can migrate their skills to Visual J# .NET 2003. Colleges today often teach Visual J# .NET 2003 in their introductory computer programming course because it is much easier to learn than the Visual C family of languages.

Delphi

Borland's **Delphi** is a powerful visual programming tool that is ideal for large-scale enterprise and Web application development. Programmers use Delphi to develop programs quickly for Windows, Linux, and .NET platforms.

Delphi also provides visual modeling tools based on the UML (Figure 13-12). Recall from Chapter 12 that the UML (Unified Modeling Language) has been adopted as a standard notation for object modeling and development. With Delphi, programmers easily link the UML designs to the working solutions.

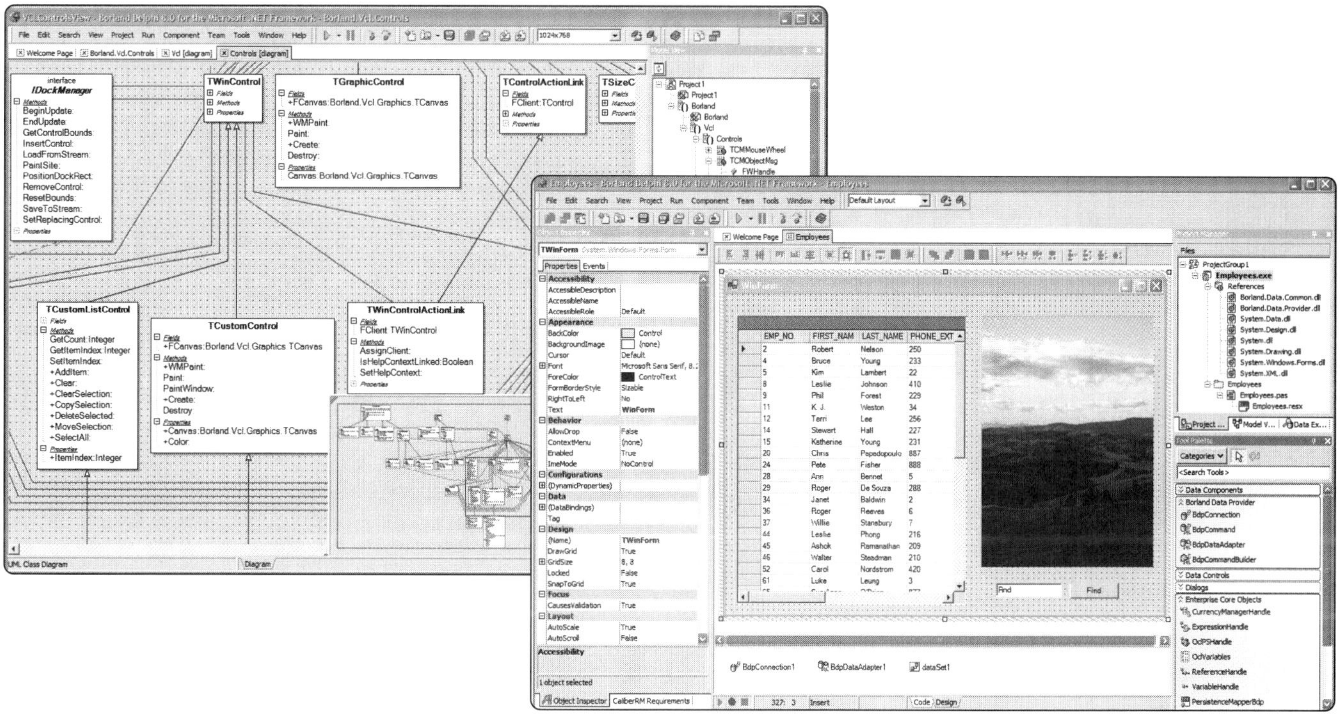

FIGURE 13-12 Delphi is a visual programming tool that allows programmers to migrate their UML designs easily into working solutions.

PowerBuilder

PowerBuilder, developed by Sybase, is another powerful visual programming tool best suited for Web-based and large-scale enterprise object-oriented applications. Programmers also use PowerBuilder to develop small- and medium-scale client/server applications. A widely used RAD tool, PowerBuilder includes a consistent interface, wizards, and many other features that enable developers to develop applications quickly (Figure 13-13).

In terms of complexity, PowerBuilder is comparable to Delphi.

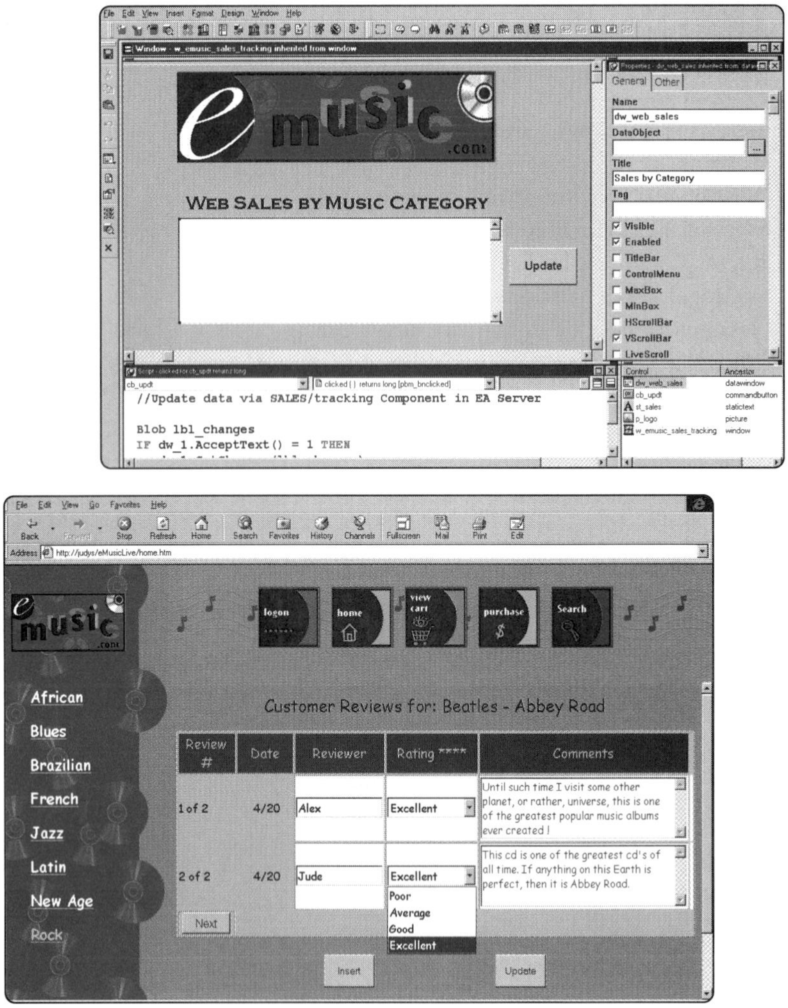

FIGURE 13-13 PowerBuilder is a visual programming tool ideal for developing large-scale and Web-based applications.

QUIZ YOURSELF 13-1

To check your knowledge of the machine languages, assembly languages, procedural languages, visual programming languages, and object-oriented programming languages, visit the Discovering Computers 2005 Quiz Yourself Web page (**scsite.com/dc2005/quiz**). Click Objectives 1 – 4 below Chapter 13.

NONPROCEDURAL LANGUAGES AND PROGRAM DEVELOPMENT TOOLS

With a **nonprocedural language**, the programmer writes English-like instructions or interacts with a visual environment to retrieve data from files or a database. Nonprocedural languages typically are easier to use than procedural languages. Thus, nontechnical users can create solutions to information requirements using a nonprocedural language.

Program development tools are user-friendly programs designed to assist both programmers and users in creating programs. In many cases, the program automatically generates the procedural instructions necessary to communicate with the computer. Consequently, programmers spend much less time and effort coding programs with a nonprocedural language. Because these tools tend to be user-friendly, they enable users with very little programming background to develop programs.

The following sections discuss a variety of these languages and tools.

RPG

In the early 1960s, IBM introduced **RPG** (*Report Program Generator*) to assist businesses in generating reports (Figure 13-14). Today, businesses also use RPG to access and update data in databases. Some versions of RPG are similar to 3GLs, while others provide a visual environment for programmers to design reports that extract data from the database.

Many users of RPG (and other report generators) claim it paved the way for 4GLs (which are discussed in the next section). RPG primarily is used for application development on IBM midrange computers, such as the AS/400. A version is available for the personal computer.

```
C* COMPUTE REGULAR TIME PAY
C          RTHRS     MULT RATE                  RTPAY      72
C*
C* COMPUTE OVERTIME PAY
C          OTHRS     IFGT 0
C          RATE      MULT 1.5                   OTRATE     72
C          OTRATE    MULT OTHRS                 OTPAY      72
                     ELSE
C                    INZ                        OTPAY      72
C
C* COMPUTE GROSS PAY
C          RTPAY     ADD  OTPAY                 GRPAY      72
C
C* PRINT GROSS PAY
C                    EXCPTDETAIL
C
C*
O* OUTPUT SPECIFICATIONS
OQPRINT   E          DETAIL
O                                   23 'THE GROSS PAY IS $'
O                    GRPAY   J       34
```

FIGURE 13-14 This figure shows an excerpt from an RPG payroll program. The code shows the computations for regular time pay, overtime pay, and gross pay; the decision to evaluate the overtime hours; and the output of the gross pay.

4GLs

A **4GL** (*fourth-generation language*) is a nonprocedural language that enables users and programmers to access data in a database. One popular 4GL is SQL. As discussed in Chapter 10, **SQL** is a query language that allows users to manage, update, and retrieve data in a relational DBMS (Figure 13-15). These powerful languages allow database administrators to define a database and its structure. They also enable users to maintain and access the data in the database.

Application Generators

An **application generator** is a program that creates source code or machine code from a specification of the required functionality. When using an application generator, the developer (a programmer or user) works with menu-driven tools and graphical user interfaces to define the desired specifications. Programmers who use application generators can be more productive in a shorter time frame. In addition, users who are unfamiliar with programming concepts can build applications with an application generator. Application generators most often are bundled with or are included as part of a DBMS.

An application generator typically consists of a report writer, form, and menu generator. As discussed in Chapter 10, a *report writer* allows a developer to design a report on the screen, retrieve data into the report design, and then display or print the report. A *form* is a window on the screen that provides areas for entering or changing data in a database.

SQL

```
SELECT LAST_NAME, FIRST_NAME, GROSS_PAY
FROM EMPLOYEE
WHERE OVERTIME_HOURS > 0
ORDER BY LAST_NAME;
```

results

```
LAST_NAME     FIRST_NAME     GROSS_PAY

Antiqua       Martin            780.00
Charles       Leslie            715.00
Guillan       Anita             847.50
.
.
.
```

FIGURE 13-15 SQL is a fourth-generation language that can be used to query database tables. This query produces an alphabetical list of those employees who receive overtime pay; that is, their overtime hours are greater than 0.

Figure 13-16 shows a sample form design and the resulting form it generates. A *menu generator* enables the developer to create a menu for the application options. If you create three reports and two forms for an application, for example, the menu would contain at least six options: one for each report, one for each form, and one to exit, or quit, the application.

Figure 13-16a (form design)

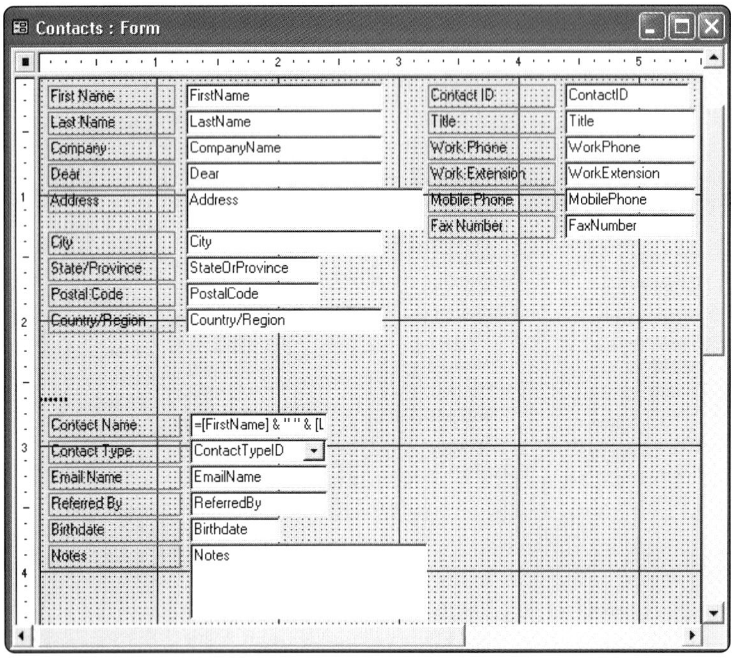

Figure 13-16b (resulting form)

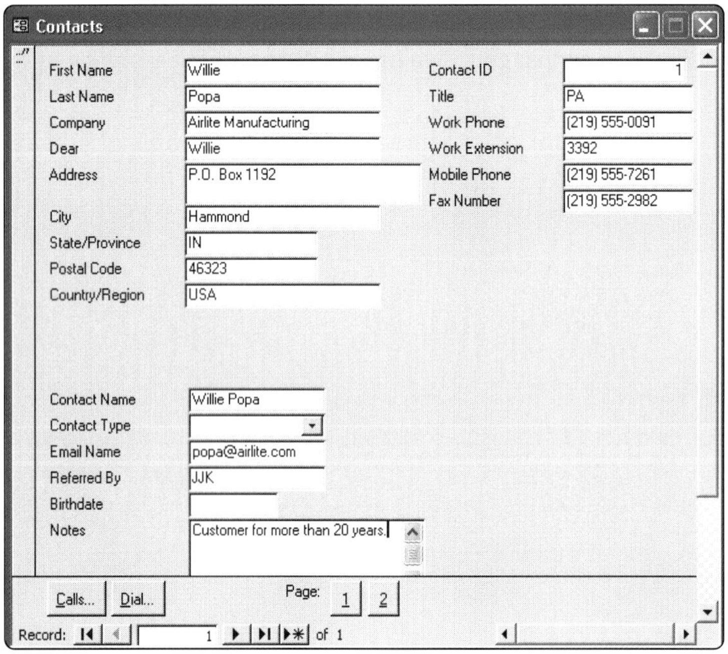

FIGURE 13-16 A form design and the resulting form created with Microsoft Office Access 2003.

Macros

A **macro** is a series of statements that instructs an application how to complete a task. Macros allow users to automate routine, repetitive, or difficult tasks in application software such as word processing, spreadsheet, or database programs. That is, users can create simple programs within the software by writing macros. You usually create a macro in one of two ways: (1) record the macro or (2) write the macro.

If you want to automate a routine or repetitive task such as formatting or editing, you would record a macro. A *macro recorder* is similar to a movie camera because both record all actions until turned off.

To record a macro, start the macro recorder in the software. Then, perform the steps to be part of the macro, such as clicks of the mouse or keystrokes. Once the macro is recorded, you can run it anytime you want to perform that same sequence of actions. For example, if you always print three copies of certain documents, you could record the actions required to print three copies. To print three copies, you would run the macro called PrintThreeCopies.

When you become familiar with programming techniques, you can write your own macros instead of recording them. Many programs use *Visual Basic for Applications* (*VBA*) or a similar language as their macro programming language. The macro in Figure 13-17a shows an Excel VBA macro that automates the data entry process to determine the interest and principal for a car loan. Figure 13-17b shows the dialog box generated from the macro that prompts the user to enter the purchase price of the vehicle. Read Issue 13-1 for a related discussion.

Figure 13-17a (VBA macro)

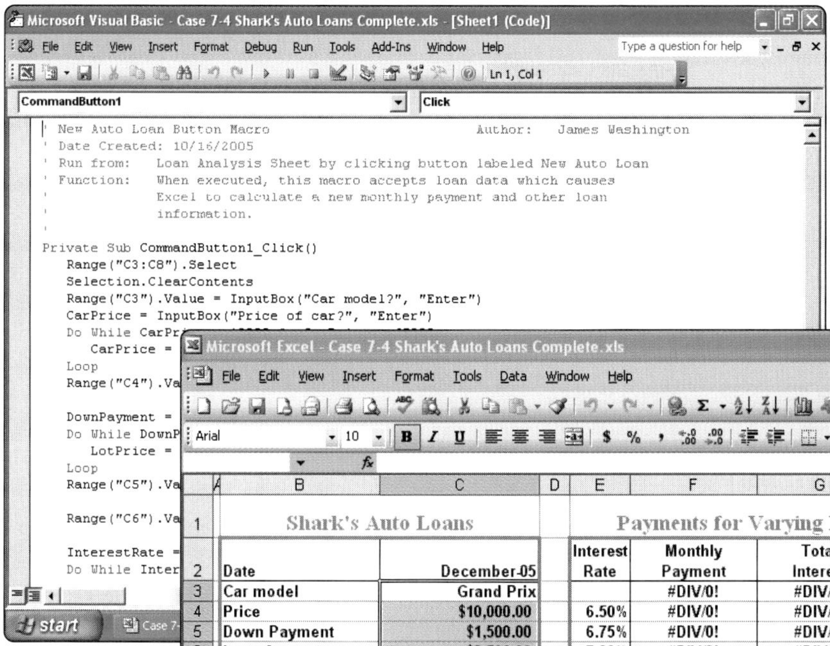

Figure 13-17b (macro dialog box in Excel window)

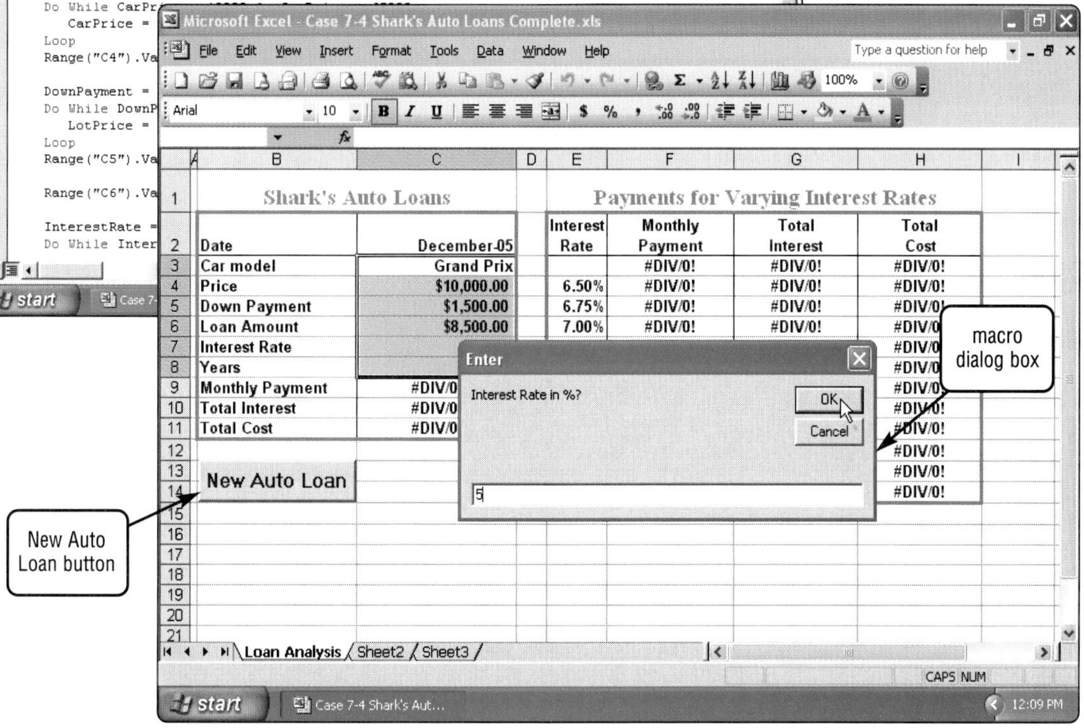

FIGURE 13-17 The top screen shows a VBA macro used to automate an auto loan computation. After a macro is written, the user clicks the New Auto Loan button to launch the macro. The bottom screen shows the macro guiding the user through the data entry process.

WEB LINK 13-6

Macros

Visit the Discovering Computers 2005 WEB LINK page (**scsite.com/dc2005/weblink**). Click Macros below Chapter 13.

ISSUE 13-1

Should Students Learn Computer Programming?

When computers were introduced in schools, instructors taught programming routinely. As time passed, however, the emphasis turned towards learning to use application software and the Internet. Some educators feel programming still should be an integral part of computer education. They point out that application software often includes a programming language, such as Visual Basic for Applications (VBA), with which users can customize the software. People who have knowledge of programming can recognize more readily the kinds of problems that computers are likely to be able to solve. Some teachers even claim that programming improves logical reasoning and critical thinking skills. Yet, other instructors feel that program development is irrelevant for most students and an unnecessary impediment to achieving computer literacy. How important is it to learn programming? Why? Should programming in some form be a part of computer education? Why or why not? Who should be taught computer programming?

For more information about programming, visit the Discovering Computers 2005 Issues Web page (**scsite.com/dc2005/issues**). Click Issue #1 below Chapter 13.

FAQ 13-2

How do I record a macro?

In Microsoft Office 2003 programs, click Tools on the menu bar, point to Macro, click Record New Macro, and then click the OK button. As you click the mouse and make choices on menus and in dialog boxes, the macro recorder records every move you make. To stop recording the macro, click the Stop Recording button on the Stop Recording toolbar.

For more information about macros, visit the Discovering Computers 2005 FAQ Web page (**scsite.com/dc2005/faq**). Click Macros below Chapter 13.

WEB PAGE DEVELOPMENT

The designers of Web pages, known as *Web page authors,* use a variety of techniques to develop Web pages. The following sections discuss these techniques.

HTML

HTML (*Hypertext Markup Language*) is a special formatting language that programmers use to format documents for display on the Web. You view a Web page written with HTML in a Web browser such as Microsoft Internet Explorer or Netscape Navigator. Figure 13-18a shows part of the HTML code used to create the Web page shown in Figure 13-18b.

Figure 13-18a (portion of HTML program)

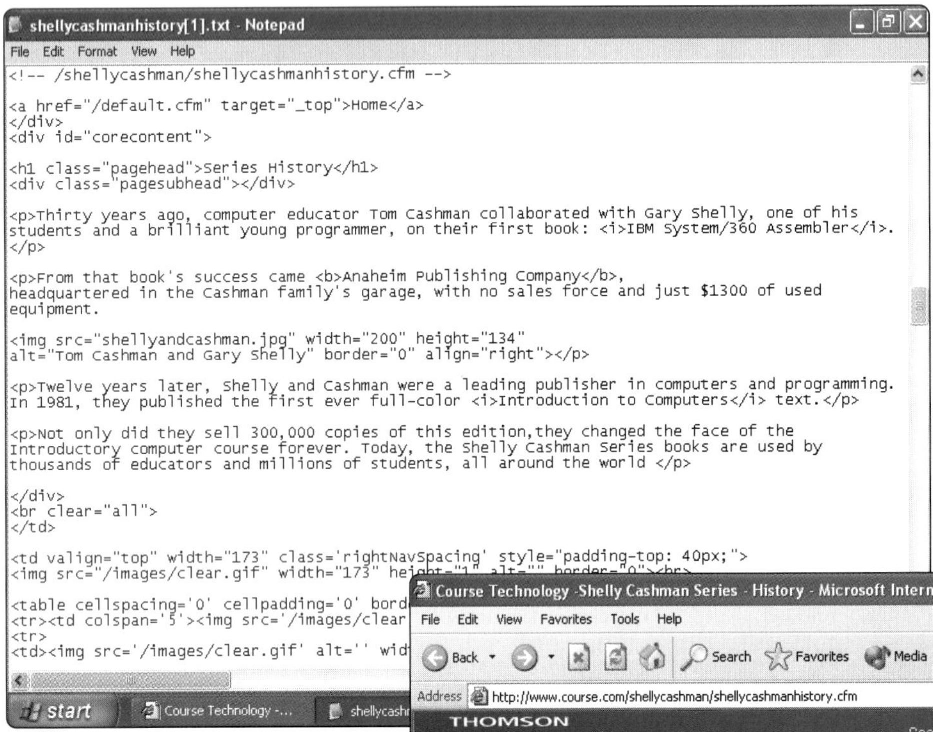

```
<!-- /shellycashman/shellycashmanhistory.cfm -->

<a href="/default.cfm" target="_top">Home</a>
</div>
<div id="corecontent">

<h1 class="pagehead">Series History</h1>
<div class="pagesubhead"></div>

<p>Thirty years ago, computer educator Tom Cashman collaborated with Gary Shelly, one of his
students and a brilliant young programmer, on their first book: <i>IBM System/360 Assembler</i>.
</p>

<p>From that book's success came <b>Anaheim Publishing Company</b>,
headquartered in the Cashman family's garage, with no sales force and just $1300 of used
equipment.

<img src="shellyandcashman.jpg" width="200" height="134"
alt="Tom Cashman and Gary Shelly" border="0" align="right"></p>

<p>Twelve years later, Shelly and Cashman were a leading publisher in computers and programming.
In 1981, they published the first ever full-color <i>Introduction to Computers</i> text.</p>

<p>Not only did they sell 300,000 copies of this edition,they changed the face of the
Introductory computer course forever. Today, the Shelly Cashman Series books are used by
thousands of educators and millions of students, all around the world </p>

</div>
<br clear="all">
</td>

<td valign="top" width="173" class='rightNavSpacing' style="padding-top: 40px;">
<img src="/images/clear.gif" width="173" he

<table cellspacing='0' cellpadding='0' bord
<tr><td colspan='5'><img src='/images/clear
<tr>
<td><img src='/images/clear.gif' alt='' wid
```

Figure 13-18b (portion of resulting Web page)

FIGURE 13-18 HTML (Hypertext Markup Language) is used to create Web pages. The portion of the HTML code in the top figure generates a portion of a Web page shown in the bottom figure.

HTML is not actually a programming language. It is, however, a language that has specific rules for defining the placement and format of text, graphics, video, and audio on a Web page. HTML uses *tags*, which are codes that specify links to other documents and indicate how a Web page is displayed when viewed on the Web.

A Web page, thus, is a file that contains both text and HTML tags. Examples of tags are <B> to bold text, <P> to indicate a new paragraph, and <HR> to display a horizontal rule across the page.

You can write HTML code using any text editor such as Notepad. The HTML code also can be entered into any standard word processing program, such as Word. You must save the code, however, as an ASCII file, instead of as a formatted word processing document.

FAQ 13-3

What is an ASCII file?

An *ASCII file* is a file that does not contain any formatting. That is, ASCII files do not contain graphics, italics, bold, underlining, styles, bullets, shading, color, or any other type of graphical format. Word processing programs typically have an option to save a file as text only, which means ASCII.

For more information about ASCII files, visit the Discovering Computers 2005 FAQ Web page (**scsite.com/dc2005/faq**). Click ASCII Files below Chapter 13.

Scripts, Applets, Servlets, and ActiveX Controls

HTML tells a browser how to display text and images, set up lists and option buttons, and establish links on a Web page. By adding dynamic content and interactive elements such as scrolling messages, animated graphics, forms, pop-up windows, and interaction, Web pages become much more interesting. To add these elements, Web page developers write small programs called scripts, applets, servlets, and ActiveX controls. These programs run inside of another program. This is different from programs discussed thus far, which are executed by the operating system. In this case, the Web browser executes these short programs.

As discussed in Chapter 9, your computer is the client computer when it is connected to the Web. A **script** is an interpreted program that runs on the client. That is, a script runs on your computer, instead of running on a Web server. An **applet** also usually runs on the client, but it is compiled. Thus, an applet usually runs faster than a script. Scripts and applets shift the computational work from the Web server to the client. A **servlet** is an applet that runs on the server.

Similar to an applet, an **ActiveX control** is a small program that runs on the client computer, instead of the server. ActiveX controls use ActiveX technology. **ActiveX** is a set of object-oriented technologies by Microsoft that allows components on a network to communicate with one another. To run an ActiveX control, the Web browser must support ActiveX technology. If it does not, you will need a plug-in program to run ActiveX controls.

One reason for using scripts, applets, servlets, and ActiveX controls is to add special multimedia effects to Web pages. Examples include animated graphics, scrolling messages, calendars, and advertisements. Another reason to use these programs is to include interactive capabilities on Web pages. Cookies, shopping carts, games, counters, image maps, and processing forms are types of scripts, applets, servlets, and ActiveX controls that allow you to transfer information to and from a Web server.

A **counter** tracks the number of visitors to a Web site. An **image map** is a graphical image that points to a URL. Web pages use image maps in place of, or in addition to, text links. When you click a certain part of the graphical image, the Web browser sends the coordinates of the clicked location to the Web server, which in turn locates the corresponding Web address and sends the Web page to your computer.

A **processing form** collects data from visitors to a Web site, who fill in blank fields and then click a button that sends the information. When a user clicks that button on the processing form, that action executes the script or applet. It transmits the data to the server, processes it, and then, if appropriate, sends information back to your Web browser via the server.

WEB LINK 13-7

HTML

Visit the Discovering Computers 2005 WEB LINK page (**scsite.com/dc2005/weblink**). Click HTML below Chapter 13.

To send and receive information between your computer and a Web server, the script, applet, or servlet uses the CGI. The *CGI* (*common gateway interface*) is the communications standard that defines how a Web server communicates with outside sources. Many times, the outside source is a database. The program that manages the sending and receiving across the CGI is a *CGI script*. The steps in Figure 13-19 show how a CGI script works.

A CGI script can be in the form of a script, applet, servlet, or ActiveX control. You can download CGI scripts from the Web and purchase them. If one does not exist that meets your needs, you can write your own CGI script using a scripting language. The next section discusses scripting languages.

FIGURE 13-19 HOW A CGI SCRIPT WORKS

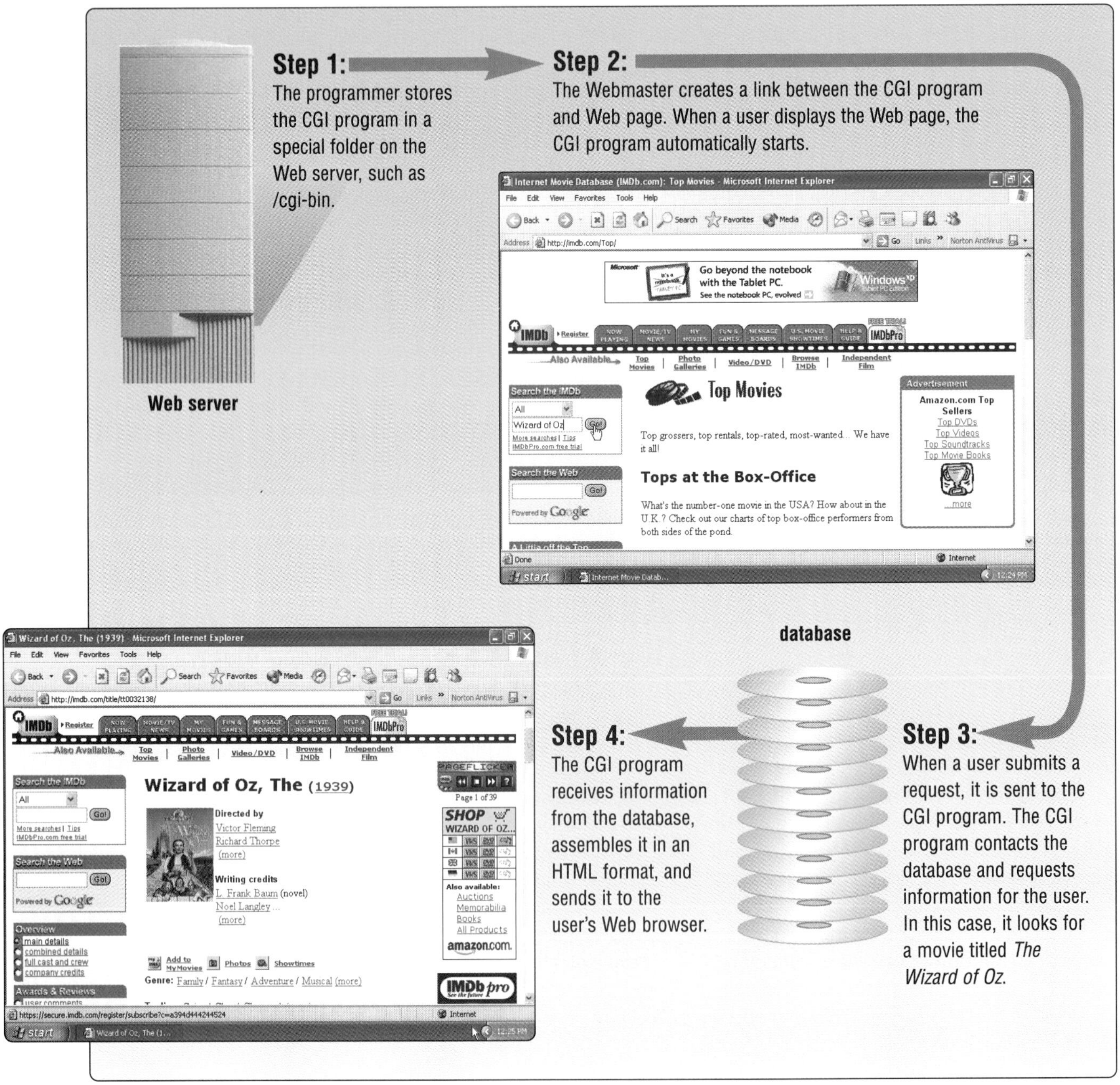

Scripting Languages

Programmers write scripts, applets, servlets, or ActiveX controls using a variety of languages. These include some of the languages previously discussed, such as C, C++, Java, and Visual Basic .NET 2003. Some programmers use scripting languages. A *scripting language* is an interpreted language that typically is easy to learn and use. Popular scripting languages include JavaScript, VBScript, and Perl.

- **JavaScript** is an interpreted language that allows a programmer to add dynamic content and interactive elements to a Web page (Figure 13-20). These elements include alert messages, scrolling text, animations, drop-down menus, data input forms, pop-up windows, and interactive quizzes. Web page developers insert JavaScript code directly into an HTML document. Although it shares many of the features of the full Java language, JavaScript is a much simpler language.

  JavaScript is the result of a joint venture between Sun Microsystems and Netscape Communications Corporation. Today, many software companies endorse JavaScript. The program is an *open language*, which means anyone can use it without purchasing a license. JavaScript thus allows the programmer to improve the appearance of Web pages without spending a large amount of money.

  To run a JavaScript program, your Web browser must support it. Netscape supports JavaScript. Internet Explorer supports a subset of JavaScript, called *JScript*.
- **VBScript** (*Visual Basic, Scripting Edition*) is a subset of the Visual Basic language that allows programmers to add intelligence and interactivity to Web pages. As with JavaScript, Web page developers embed VBScript code directly into an HTML document. Programmers already familiar with Visual Basic choose VBScript as their scripting language, so they do not have to learn a new scripting language. The latest version of Internet Explorer includes VBScript.
- **Perl** (*Practical Extraction and Report Language*) originally was developed by Larry Wall at NASA's Jet Propulsion Laboratory as a procedural language similar to C and C++. The latest release of Perl, however, is an interpreted scripting language. Because Perl has powerful text processing capabilities, it has become a popular language for writing scripts.

WEB LINK 13-8

Scripting Languages

Visit the Discovering Computers 2005 WEB LINK page (**scsite .com/dc2005/weblink**). Click Scripting Languages below Chapter 13.

Figure 13-20a (pop-up window)

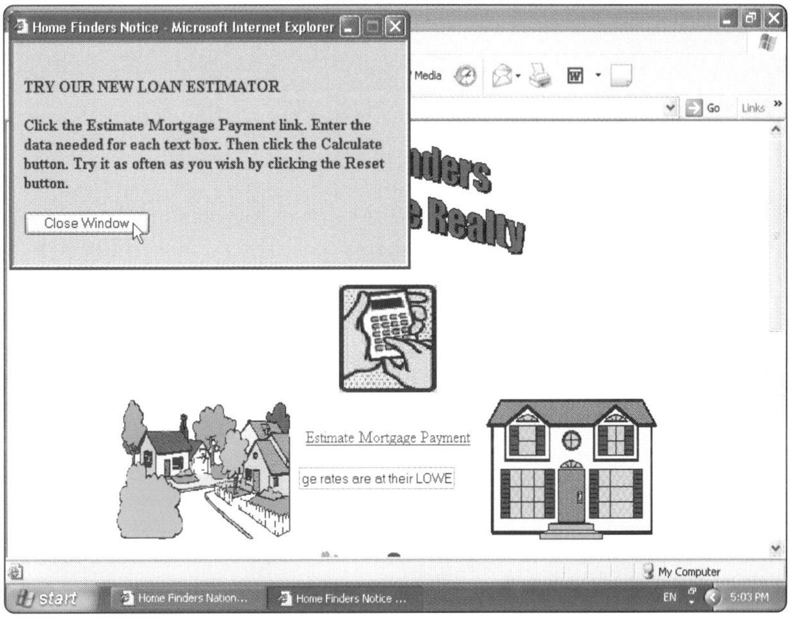

Figure 13-20b (JavaScript code)

notice - Notepad

File Edit Format View Help

```
<HTML>
<HEAD>
<TITLE>Home Finders Notice</TITLE>
</HEAD>

<BODY bgColor="B0C4DE">

<P><BR>
<FONT COLOR="8b0000"><B>TRY OUR NEW LOAN ESTIMATOR</P>
<P>Click the Estimate Mortgage Payment link. Enter the
data needed for each text box. Then click the Calculate
button. Try it as often as you wish by clicking the
Reset button.</B> </P>

<FORM>
<P><INPUT Type="Button" Value="Close Window" onclick="window.close()"> </P>
</FORM>
</FONT>
</BODY>
</HTML>
```

FIGURE 13-20 Shown here is a pop-up window that is displayed on a Web page and its associated JavaScript code.

Dynamic HTML

Dynamic HTML (**DHTML**) is a newer type of HTML that allows developers to include more graphical interest and interactivity in a Web page, without the Web page accessing the Web server. That is, the client's computer automatically updates and changes its own content. These Web pages display much faster than Web pages created with HTML.

Typically, Web pages created with DHTML are more animated and responsive to user interaction. After these pages are downloaded, the pages seem to come to life. Colors change, font sizes grow, objects appear and disappear as a user moves the mouse (Figure 13-21), and animations dance around the screen.

Dynamic HTML works by using the document object model, style sheets, and scripting languages. The *document object model* (*DOM*) defines every item on a Web page as an object. Fonts, graphics, headlines, tables, and every other page element are objects. With DOM, developers can change properties, such as color or size, of any or all of these objects on the Web page.

A *style sheet* contains descriptions of a document's characteristics. Many word processing documents use style sheets to define formats of characters and paragraphs. *Cascading style sheets* (*CSS*) contain the formats for how a particular object should be displayed in a Web browser. For example, the CSS specify items such as background colors and images and link colors, fonts, and font sizes. A single HTML document can contain multiple cascading style sheets, thus, the name cascading. As a user moves the mouse or clicks an item, a new style sheet can be applied to change the appearance of the screen.

After a developer has defined and formatted objects on a Web page, a scripting language such as JavaScript manipulates them. A script can move, display, hide, or change the appearance of an object as the mouse moves over the object.

XHTML, XML, and WML

XHTML (*Extensible HTML*) is a markup language that enables Web sites to be displayed more easily on microbrowsers in PDAs and cellular telephones. XHTML includes features of HTML and XML. **XML** (*eXtensible Markup Language*) is an increasingly popular

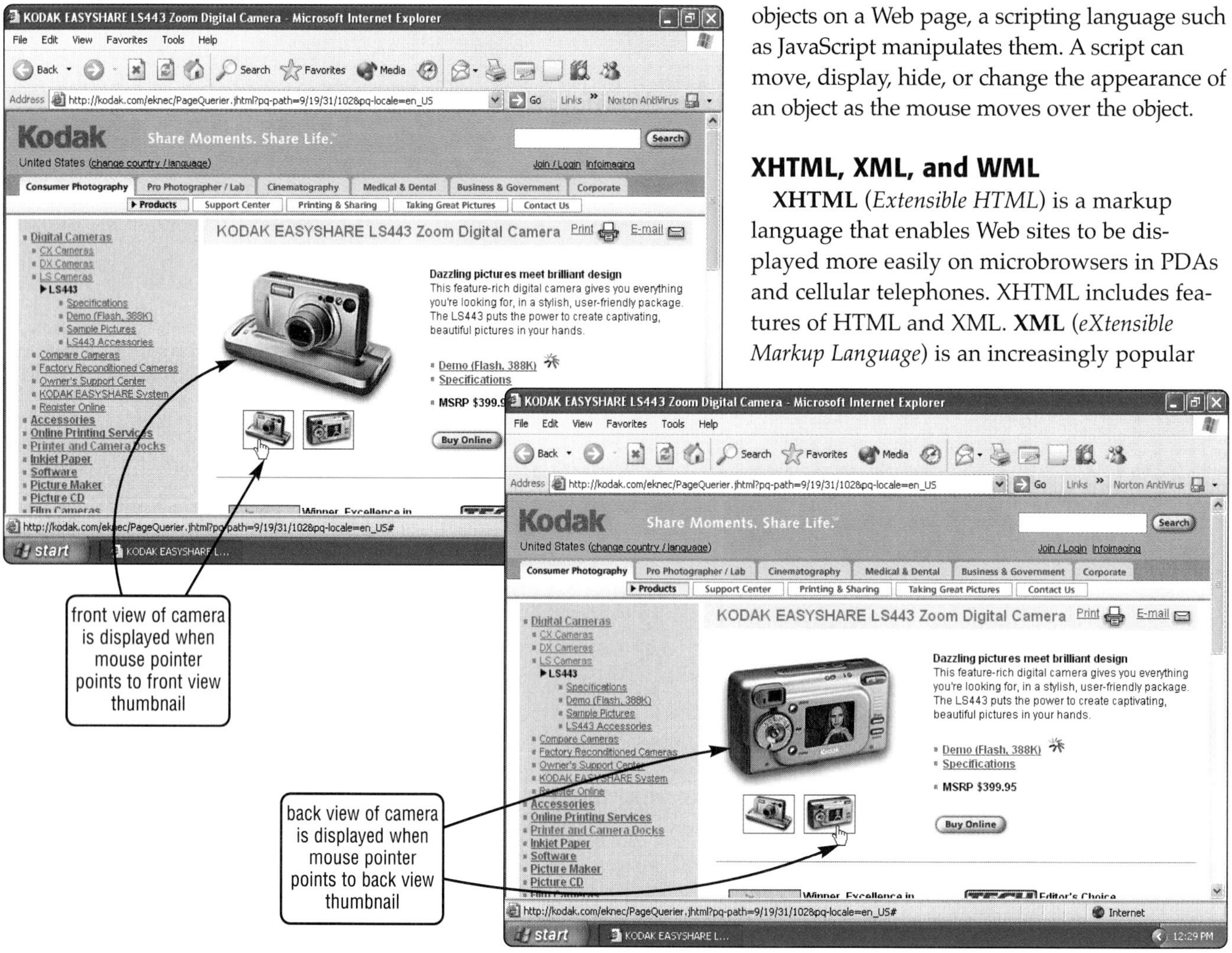

FIGURE 13-21 Web pages at Kodak's Web site use DHTML. When you point to the front view thumbnail, a larger image of the front of the digital camera is displayed. When you point to the back view thumbnail, a larger image of the back of the digital camera is displayed.

format for sharing data that allows Web page developers to create customized tags, as well as use predefined tags. With XML, a server sends an entire record to the client, enabling the client to do much of the processing without going back to the server. In XML, developers also can define a link that points to multiple Web sites instead of a single site.

XML separates the Web page content from its format, allowing the Web browser to display the contents of a Web page in a form appropriate for the display device. For example, a PDA, a notebook computer, and a desktop computer all could display the same XML page. A Web page written with only HTML probably would require multiple versions to run on each of these types of computers. For a technical discussion about XML, read the High-Tech Talk article on page 699.

One application of XML is the RSS specification. *RSS*, which stands for either Rich Site Summary or RDF (Resource Description Framework) Site Summary, describes a method that online publishers can use to distribute their syndicated content on the Web. The online publisher creates an RSS document that is made available to Web sites for publication. News Web sites often use RSS to publish headlines and stories. Most Web browsers can read RSS documents.

Wireless devices use a subset of XML called WML. **WML** (*wireless markup language*) allows Web page developers to design pages specifically for microbrowsers. Many Web-enabled PDAs, cellular telephones, and pagers use WML as their markup language. WML uses the *wireless application protocol* (*WAP*), which is a standard that specifies how wireless devices communicate with the Web.

Web Page Authoring Software

As discussed in Chapter 3, you do not need to learn HTML to develop a Web page. Many developers use **Web page authoring software** to create sophisticated Web pages that include graphical images, video, audio, animation, and other special effects.

Web page authoring software generates HTML tags from your Web page design. With the Web page authoring software, you can view or modify the HTML associated with a Web page. Sometimes, you may add an HTML tag that the Web page authoring software does not provide. Learning HTML basics will enable you to fine-tune Web page formats created with authoring software. Read Issue 13-2 for a related discussion.

Three popular Web page authoring programs are Dreamweaver MX, Flash MX, and FrontPage 2003.

- **Dreamweaver MX**, developed by Macromedia, is a Web page authoring program that allows Web site designers and developers to create, maintain, and manage professional Web sites. Some features of Dreamweaver MX include its visual environment, use of cascading style sheets, capability of manipulating code, built-in graphics editor (called Fireworks), and XML support.
- **Flash MX**, also by Macromedia, is a Web page authoring program that enables Web site developers to combine interactive content with text, graphics, audio, and video. For example, marketing and WBT (Web-based training) sites often use Flash MX. Features of Flash MX include its animation and interactive tools, professional video capabilities, easy deployment to mobile devices such as PDAs, and XML support.
- **FrontPage 2003**, developed by Microsoft, is a Web page authoring program that provides nontechnical and professional users with the ability to create and manage Web sites easily. FrontPage 2003 is part of the Microsoft Office System. Features of FrontPage 2003 include its easy-to-use graphics tools, HTML code generator, scripting tools, and XML support.

WEB LINK 13-9

XML

Visit the Discovering Computers 2005 WEB LINK page (**scsite.com/dc2005/weblink**). Click XML below Chapter 13.

ISSUE 13-2

Should You Know HTML?

Most Web pages are written in HTML (Hypertext Markup Language) with tags that indicate how the pages are displayed in a browser window. You can see the HTML code for a Web page by clicking View on the browser menu bar and then clicking Source or Source Code on the View menu. Today, high-end Web page authoring software such as Dreamweaver and FrontPage allows people to develop Web pages without any knowledge of HTML. With these programs, you use templates, menus, panels, and toolbars to generate HTML tags from a Web page design. If necessary, you can use HTML to enhance the Web page and debug problems. Some people believe knowledge of HTML is essential to create an effective Web page, but others feel that creativity and familiarity with Web page authoring software are more important. If you were hiring a Web page developer for a company, would you insist on knowledge of HTML? Why or why not? Should HTML be a required course for students majoring in Web page design? Why?

For more information about HTML, visit the Discovering Computers 2005 Issues Web page (**scsite.com/dc2005/issues**). Click Issue #2 below Chapter 13.

MULTIMEDIA PROGRAM DEVELOPMENT

Multimedia authoring software allows developers to combine text, graphics, animation, audio, and video into an interactive presentation. Many developers use multimedia authoring software for computer-based training (CBT) and Web-based training (WBT). Most of today's popular authoring software share similar features and are capable of creating similar applications. Popular software includes ToolBook, Authorware, and Director.

- **ToolBook**, from Click2learn, Inc., has a graphical user interface and uses an object-oriented approach, so developers can design multimedia applications using basic objects. These objects include buttons, fields, graphics, backgrounds, and pages.

  In ToolBook, developers can convert a multimedia application into HTML and Java, so it can be distributed over the Internet. Figure 13-22 shows a sample application developed in ToolBook that uses DHTML. Many businesses and colleges use ToolBook to create content for distance learning courses.

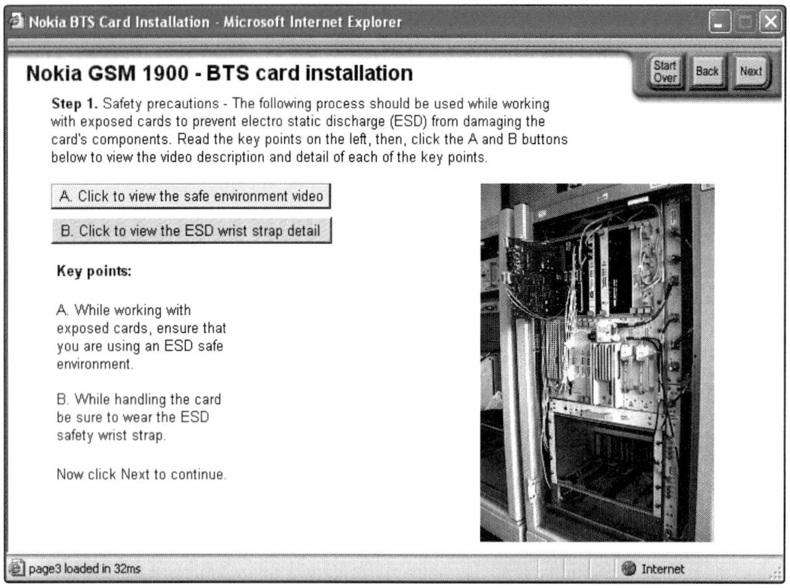

FIGURE 13-22 A sample ToolBook application.

- **Authorware**, from Macromedia, is a multimedia authoring program that provides the tools developers need to build interactive multimedia training and educational programs. Authorware offers a powerful authoring environment for the development of interactive multimedia magazines, catalogs, reference titles for CD-ROMs and DVD-ROMs, and applications for kiosks. Authorware also offers tools for bundling the content, student tracking, and course management components of a WBT or other distance learning course. Users view Authorware applications distributed over the Web using the Shockwave plug-in.
- **Director**, also from Macromedia, is a popular multimedia authoring program with powerful features that allow developers to create highly interactive multimedia applications.

  Director includes Lingo, which is a built-in object-oriented scripting language. Director's powerful features make it well suited for developing electronic presentations, CD-ROMs or DVD-ROMs for education and entertainment, and simulations. Web-based applications can include streaming audio and video, interactivity, and multiuser functionality. As with Authorware, users view applications developed in Director on the Web using the Shockwave plug-in.

OTHER PROGRAMMING LANGUAGES

In addition to the programming languages discussed on the previous pages, programmers sometimes use other languages (Figure 13-23). Some of the languages listed in Figure 13-23, although once popular, find little use today. Read Issue 13-3 for a discussion about programmers. Read Looking Ahead 13-1 for a look at the next generation of programming.

Ada	Derived from Pascal, developed by the U.S. Department of Defense, named after Augusta Ada Lovelace Byron, who is thought to be the first female computer programmer
ALGOL	ALGOrithmic Language, the first structured procedural language
APL	A Programming Language, a scientific language designed to manipulate tables of numbers
Forth	Similar to C, used for small computerized devices
FORTRAN	FORmula TRANslator, one of the first high-level programming languages used for scientific applications
HyperTalk	An object-oriented programming language developed by Apple to manipulate cards that can contain text, graphics, and sound
LISP	LISt Processing, a language used for artificial intelligence applications
Logo	An educational tool used to teach programming and problem-solving to children
Modula-2	A successor to Pascal used for developing systems software
Pascal	Developed to teach students structured programming concepts, named in honor of Blaise Pascal, a French mathematician who developed one of the earliest calculating machines
PILOT	Programmed Inquiry Learning Or Teaching, used to write computer-aided instruction programs
PL/I	Programming Language One, a business and scientific language that combines many features of FORTRAN and COBOL
Prolog	PROgramming LOGic, used for development of artificial intelligence applications
Smalltalk	Object-oriented programming language

FIGURE 13-23 Other programming languages.

ISSUE 13-3

Who Will Be Future Programmers?

Despite a growing need for programmers and other workers in computer-related fields, a recent survey suggests that the demand may not be satisfied. A survey of California students found that although almost all had access to computers, only about 32 percent were interested in high-tech careers. Many of those who rejected high-tech work said that the careers seemed unexciting or intimidating. The survey responses also indicated a significant gender gap. While 42 percent of males considered working in high-tech fields, only 23 percent of females expressed a similar interest. Students often change their minds about what they want to do. But, because they seldom change their minds about what they do not want to do, the survey's findings could foretell future shortages in the high-tech workforce. What, if anything, can and should be done to increase interest in computer-related careers? Why are females less interested in technology careers than males? What can be done to increase interest among females?

For more information about high-tech careers, visit the Discovering Computers 2005 Issues Web page (**scsite.com/dc2005/issues**). Click Issue #3 below Chapter 13.

LOOKING AHEAD 13-1

Seeing Clearly with Vision Systems

Narrow-minded people often are described as having tunnel vision because they have difficulty accepting views from a variety of sources. Another form of tunnel vision is retinitis pigmentosa (RP), which is a physical condition that occurs when the light-sensing cells in the eyes' retinas have difficulty accepting light signals, sometimes causing complete blindness.

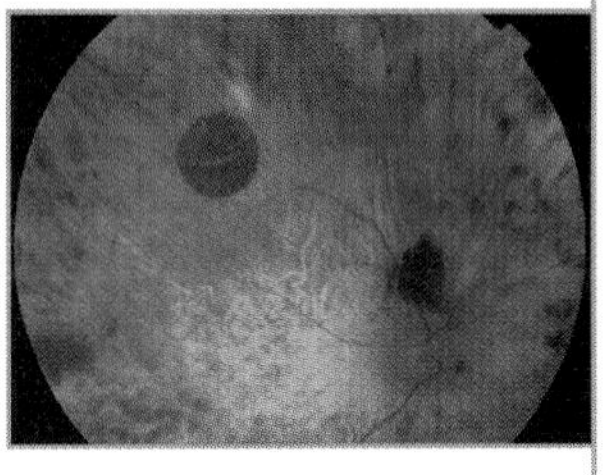

A second form of retinal disease is age-related macular degeneration (AMD), which often affects the elderly and also decreases the cells' ability to function properly. At least 30 million people worldwide suffer from RP or AMD. An artificial retina, however, may help them see.

This tiny chip contains approximately 5,000 solar cells and is implanted under the damaged retina. Each solar cell is programmed to convert light to electrical impulses. These signals are sent via the optic nerve to the brain, and, in turn, the brain stimulates the damaged cells to send signals once again.

While this chip is programmed to help people see more clearly, machine vision systems are being developed for industrial and medical applications. These systems accept light through video cameras and then convert the wavelengths to digital signals. The data can be used to analyze medical images, identify signatures, and inspect currency.

For a look at the next generation of vision systems, visit the Discovering Computers 2005 Looking Ahead Web page (**scsite.com/dc2005/looking**). Click Looking Ahead #1 below Chapter 13.

QUIZ YOURSELF 13-2

To check your knowledge of nonprocedural languages, Web page program development, and multimedia authoring programs, visit the Discovering Computers 2005 Quiz Yourself Web page (**scsite.com/dc2005/quiz**). Click Objectives 5 – 7 below Chapter 13.

THE PROGRAM DEVELOPMENT CYCLE

The **program development cycle** is a series of steps programmers use to build computer programs. As Chapter 12 discussed, the system development cycle guides information technology (IT) professionals through the development of an information system. Likewise, the program development cycle guides computer programmers through the development of a program. The program development cycle consists of six steps (Figure 13-24):

1. Analyze Requirements
2. Design Solution
3. Validate Design
4. Implement Design
5. Test Solution
6. Document Solution

As shown in Figure 13-24, the steps in the program development cycle form a loop. Program development is an ongoing process within system development. Each time someone identifies errors in or improvements to a program and requests program modifications, the Analyze Requirements step begins again. When programmers correct errors or add enhancements to an existing program, they are said to be **maintaining** the program.

What Initiates the Program Development Cycle?

As discussed in Chapter 12, the system development cycle consists of five phases: planning, analysis, design, implementation, and support. During the analysis phase, the development team recommends how to handle software needs. Choices include purchasing packaged software, building custom software in-house, or outsourcing some or all of the IT operation.

If the company opts for in-house development, the design and implementation phases of the system development cycle become quite extensive. In the design phase, the analyst creates a detailed set of requirements for the programmers. Once the programmers receive the requirements, the implementation phase

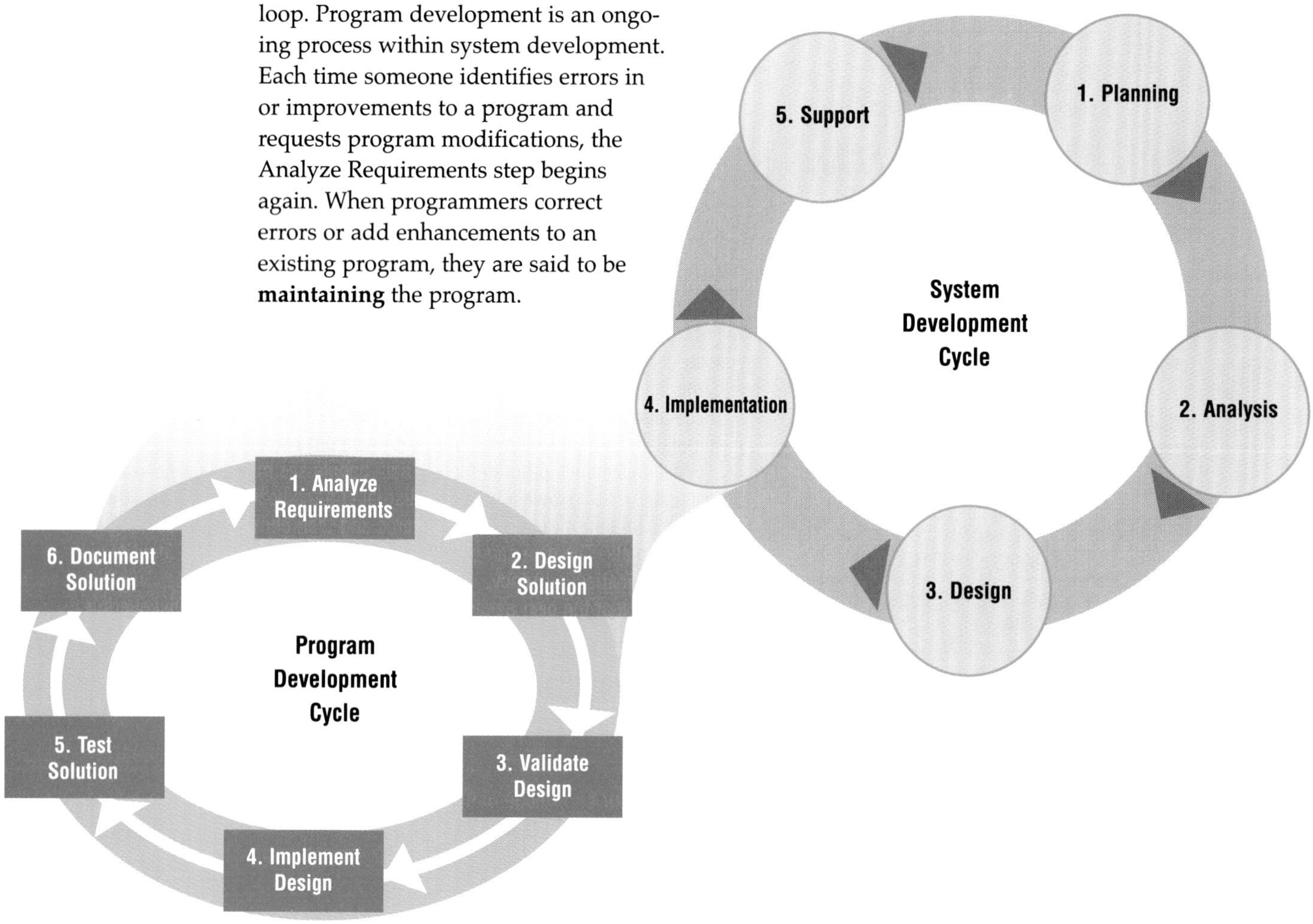

FIGURE 13-24 The program development cycle consists of six steps that form a loop. The program development cycle is part of the implementation phase of the system development cycle.

begins. At this time, the programmer analyzes the requirements of the problem to be solved. The program development cycle thus begins at the start of the implementation phase in the system development cycle.

The scope of the requirements largely determines how many programmers work on the program development. If the scope is large, a **programming team** that consists of a group of programmers may develop the programs. If the specifications are simple, a single programmer might complete all the development tasks. Whether a single programmer or a programming team, all the programmers involved must interact with users and members of the development team throughout the program development cycle.

By following the steps in the program development cycle, programmers create programs that are correct (produce accurate information) and maintainable (easy to modify). The following sections address each of the steps in the program development cycle.

STEP 1 – ANALYZE REQUIREMENTS

The first step in the program development cycle is to analyze the requirements of the problem the program(s) should solve, so the programmer can begin to develop an appropriate solution. In most cases, the solution requires more than one program. This analysis step consists of three major tasks: (1) review the requirements, (2) meet with the systems analyst and users, and (3) identify input, output, processing, and data components.

First, the programmer reviews the requirements. The requirements may be in the form of deliverables such as charts, diagrams, and reports. These deliverables document various aspects of the users' requirements. For example, screen and report layout charts show input and output requirements. Structured English, decision tables, and decision trees convey processing requirements. The data dictionary identifies the data requirements. By thoroughly reviewing these deliverables, the programmer understands the nature of the requirements.

During this step, the programmer also meets with the systems analyst and the users. This enables the programmer to understand the purpose of the requirements from the users' perspective. Recall from Chapter 12 that a guideline of system development is to involve users throughout the entire system development cycle.

After reviewing the requirements and meeting with the systems analyst and users, the programmers may decide to recommend a change to some aspect of the requirements. In this case, they discuss the change with the systems analyst and the users. A programmer should not make any change without the systems analyst's and users' approval. Sometimes the analyst or programmer decides to defer some requirements until a later step in the program development cycle.

After design specifications are established, the programmer defines the input, processing, and output (IPO) requirements for each program. Many programmers use an IPO chart for this task (Figure 13-25). An *IPO chart* identifies a program's inputs, its outputs, and the processing steps required to transform the inputs into the outputs. Programmers review the contents of the IPO chart with the systems analyst and the users. This allows programmers to be sure they completely understand the purpose of the program. Read Apply It 13-1 for information about how one user analyzed a program.

APPLY IT 13-1

Virtual Reality Chess Match Ends in Draw

When world champion chess player Garry Kasparov tied his computer opponent, *X3D Fritz*, in the final match, he said that people are learning while the machines are improving. The four-game match in 2003 was the first official virtual reality world chess championship sanctioned by the International Computer Games Association and the U.S. Chess Federation.

Kasparov wore 3-D glasses while he played the game developed by X3D Technologies. The chessboard was suspended in the air, and Kasparov moved the chess pieces by voice activation and used a joystick to rotate the board. He earned $175,000 for the draw; he would have received $200,000 for a win and $150,000 for a loss.

Kasparov is no stranger to computerized chess; this tournament was a highly anticipated sequel to his IBM *Deep Blue* contest in New York in 1997. Deep Blue won that tournament, partly because the computer had 256 processors designed specifically to play chess and could calculate up to 200 million moves each second. The X3D Fritz can compute 5 million chess positions per second. The human brain is capable of computing three moves per second.

When the final match ended, the X3D Fritz congratulated Kasparov with these words: "With your brainpower, you challenged my Intel Quad Processor, Xeon 2.8 MHz chip with four gigs of RAM. Not an easy task."

For more information about computer chess tournaments, visit the Discovering Computers 2005 Apply It Web page (**scsite.com/dc2005/apply**). Click Apply It #1 below Chapter 13.

IPO CHART

Input	Processing	Output
Regular Time Hours Worked Overtime Hours Worked Hourly Pay Rate	Read regular time hours worked, overtime hours worked, hourly pay rate. Calculate regular time pay. If employee worked overtime, calculate overtime pay. Calculate gross pay. Print gross pay.	Gross Pay

FIGURE 13-25 An IPO (Input Process Output) chart is a tool that assists the programmer in analyzing a program.

STEP 2 – DESIGN SOLUTION

The next step is to design the solution that will meet the users' requirements. Designing the solution involves devising a solution algorithm to satisfy the requirements. A *solution algorithm*, also called *program logic*, is a graphical or written description of the step-by-step procedures to solve the problem. Determining the logic for a program often is a programmer's most challenging task. It requires that the programmer understand programming concepts, as well as use creativity in problem solving. Thus, defining the solution algorithm is both a skill and an art. Read Issue 13-4 for a related discussion about programmers.

Recall from Chapter 12 that a system can be designed using process modeling (structured analysis and design) or object modeling (object-oriented analysis and design). The approach used during the system development cycle determines the techniques a programmer uses in designing a solution.

ISSUE 13-4

Could You Be a Computer Programmer?

Computer programmers have an unenviable image. They frequently are pictured as boring technocrats lucky enough to be in the right place at the right time. Often, people jokingly characterize programmers as socially awkward introverts with thick glasses and plastic pocket protectors (a perception implied in the title of Robert X. Cringely's book, *Accidental Empires: How the Boys of Silicon Valley Make Their Millions, Battle Foreign Competition, and Still Can't Get a Date*). In reality, programmers are like other highly talented white-collar workers. Computer programming demands patience and persistence, ingenuity and imagination, an eye for detail, and the ability to work under pressure. Successful programmers have described their jobs as a combination of engineer, inventor, entrepreneur, and artist. What is meant by this? What other occupations, if any, demand similar abilities? Is computer programming a science, a skill, a craft, or an art? Why? Would you make a good computer programmer? Why or why not?

For more information about computer programmers, visit the Discovering Computers 2005 Issues Web page (**scsite.com/dc2005/issues**). Click Issue #4 below Chapter 13.

Structured Design

In **structured design**, sometimes called *top-down design*, the programmer typically begins with a general design and moves toward a more detailed design. That is, the programmer begins with the big picture and then zooms in on the details. This approach breaks down the original set of requirements into smaller, more manageable sections.

The first step in top-down design is to identify the major function of a program, sometimes called the *main routine*. Next, the programmer decomposes (breaks down) the main routine into smaller sections, called *subroutines*. Then, the programmer analyzes each subroutine to determine if it can be decomposed further. The programmer continues decomposing subroutines until each one performs a single function. A section of a program that performs a single function is a *module*. Each subroutine also is a module. The main routine often is called the *main module*.

Programmers use a **hierarchy chart**, also called a *structure chart*, to show program modules graphically (Figure 13-26). A hierarchy chart contains rectangles and lines. The rectangles are the modules. The main module is at the top of the chart. All other modules are placed below the main module. Modules connect by lines to indicate their relationships. In Figure 13-26, for example, the Initialization, Process, and Wrap-Up modules are subordinate to the MAIN module.

Programs developed using the top-down approach benefit from the simplicity of their design. They usually are reliable and easy to read and maintain.

Structured design, however, does not provide a way to keep the data and the program (or procedure) together. Each program has to define how it will use the data. This can result in redundant programming code that must change every time the structure of the data changes. To eliminate this problem, some IT professionals use the object-oriented approach for program development.

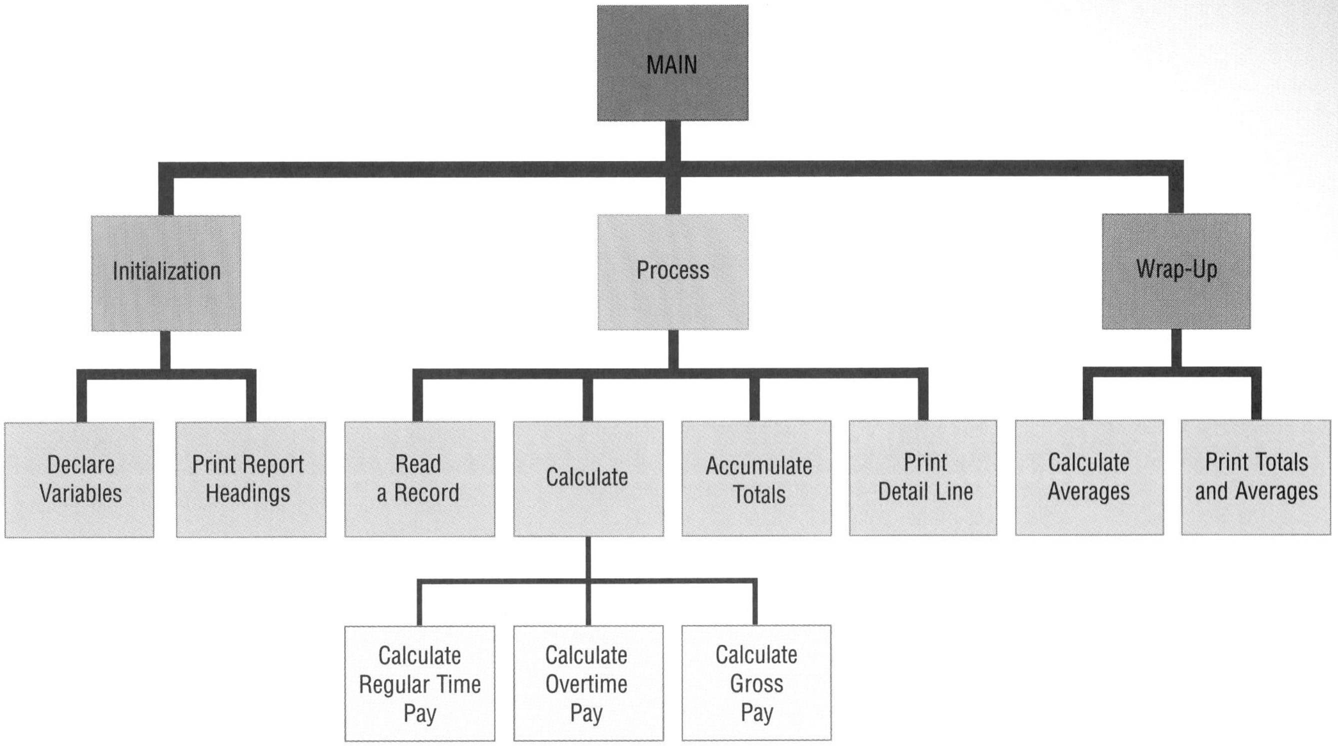

FIGURE 13-26 The hierarchy chart is a tool the programmer uses during structured design. On the hierarchy chart, program modules are drawn as rectangles. All modules are subordinate to the main module.

Object-Oriented Design

With **object-oriented (OO) design**, the programmer packages the data and the program (or procedure) into a single unit, an object. When the structure of an object changes, any program that accesses the object automatically accesses the change.

The concept of packaging data and procedures into a single object is called *encapsulation*. That is, an object encapsulates (hides) the details of the object. Think of an object as a box, and you cannot see inside the box. The box sends and receives messages. It also contains code and data. For example, when users want to print a document, they click the Print button (the object). They probably do not know how the Print button actually communicates with the hardware to print the document. Thus, the details of the print object are encapsulated (hidden) from the user. Programmers, however, need to know how the object works, so they can send messages to it and use it effectively.

As described in Chapter 12, objects are grouped into classes. To represent classes and their hierarchical relationships graphically, programmers use a class diagram. Figure 13-27 shows a high-level class diagram. In this diagram, a construction site needs many jobs performed, a job is completed by several workers, and each worker receives one paycheck for work performed. The 1 below the Construction Site class indicates that each Construction Site class must have at least one Job class associated with it. The 1..* above the Job class indicates that each Job class must be associated with at least one Construction Site class above it.

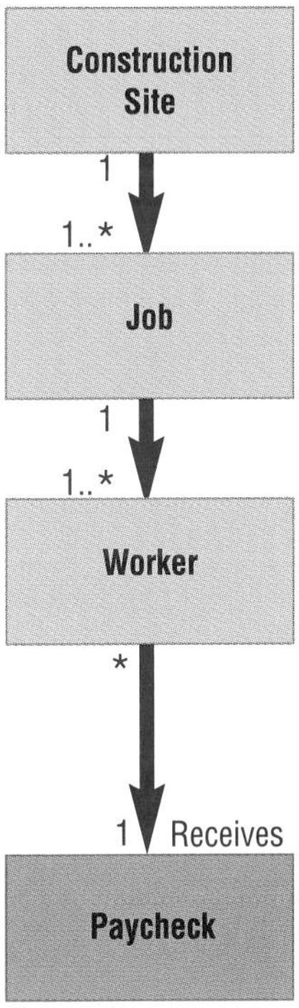

FIGURE 13-27 A class diagram is a hierarchical tool the programmer uses during object-oriented design.

With the high-level class diagram complete, the programmer develops a detailed class diagram that provides a visual representation of each object, its attributes, and its methods. Then, the programmer translates the methods into program instructions.

WEB LINK 13-10

Object-Oriented Design

Visit the Discovering Computers 2005 WEB LINK page (**scsite.com/dc2005/weblink**). Click Object-Oriented Design below Chapter 13.

FAQ 13-4

How can objects written in different programming languages communicate with each other?

They follow a specification that states how objects in separate programs on a network communicate with each other. Thus, the programs do not need to know the details of the program in which the object is created. Two popular specifications are *CORBA* and *COM+*.

For more information about CORBA and COM+, visit the Discovering Computers 2005 FAQ Web page (**scsite.com/dc2005/faq**). Click CORBA and COM+ below Chapter 13.

Control Structures

Whether using structured design or object-oriented design, programmers typically use control structures to describe the tasks a program is to perform. A **control structure**, also known as a *construct*, depicts the logical order of program instructions. Three basic control structures are sequence, selection, and repetition.

SEQUENCE CONTROL STRUCTURE A *sequence control structure* shows one or more actions following each other in order (Figure 13-28). Actions include inputs, processes, and outputs. Examples of actions are reading a record, calculating averages or totals, and printing totals.

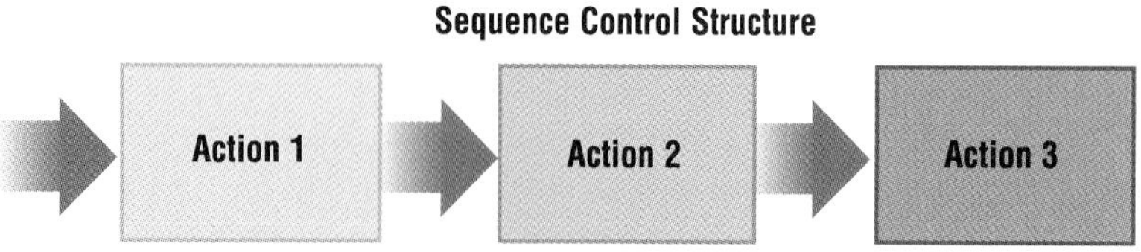

FIGURE 13-28 The sequence control structure shows one or more actions followed by another.

SELECTION CONTROL STRUCTURE A *selection control structure* tells the program which action to take, based on a certain condition. Two common types of selection control structures are the if-then-else and the case.

When a program evaluates the condition in an *if-then-else control structure*, it yields one of two possibilities: true or false. Figure 13-29 shows the condition as a diamond symbol. If the result of the condition is true, then the program performs one action. If the result is false, the program performs a different (or possibly no) action. For example, the selection control structure can determine if an employee should receive overtime pay. A possible condition might be the following: Is Overtime Hours greater than 0? If the response is yes (true), then the action would calculate overtime pay. If the response is no (false), then the action would set overtime pay equal to 0.

With the *case control structure*, a condition can yield one of three or more possibilities (Figure 13-30). The size of a beverage, for example, might be one of these options: small, medium, large, or extra large. A case control structure would determine the price of the beverage based on the size purchased.

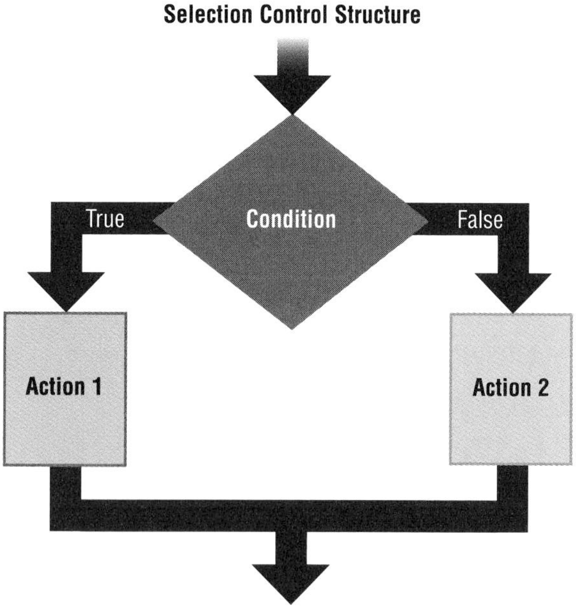

FIGURE 13-29 The if-then-else control structure directs the program toward one course of action or another based on the evaluation of a condition.

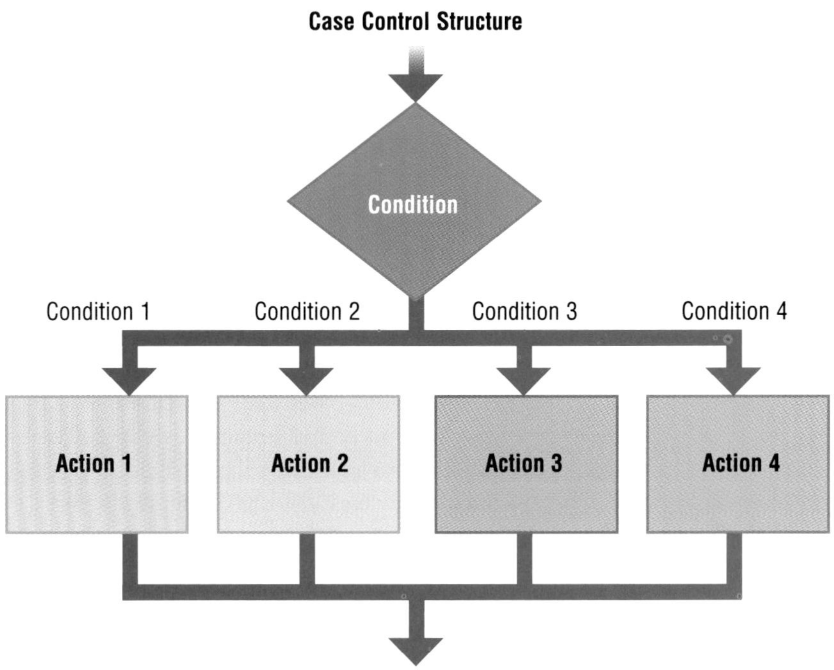

FIGURE 13-30 The case control structure allows for more than two alternatives when a condition is evaluated.

REPETITION CONTROL STRUCTURE The *repetition control structure* enables a program to perform one or more actions repeatedly as long as a certain condition is met. Many programmers refer to this construct as a *loop*. Two forms of the repetition control structure are the do-while and do-until.

A *do-while control structure* repeats one or more times as long as a condition is true (Figure 13-31). This control structure tests a condition at the beginning of the loop. If the result of the condition is true, the program executes the action(s) inside the loop. Then, the program loops back and tests the condition again. If the result of the condition still is true, the program executes the action(s) inside the loop again. This looping process continues until the condition being tested becomes false. At that time, the program stops looping and moves to another set of actions.

The do-while control structure normally is used when occurrence of an event is not quantifiable or predictable. For example, programmers frequently use the do-while control structure to process all records in a file. A payroll program using a do-while control structure loops once for each employee. This program stops looping when it processes the last employee's record.

The *do-until control structure* is similar to the do-while but has two major differences: where it tests the condition and when it stops looping. First, the do-until control structure tests the condition at the end of the loop (Figure 13-32). The action(s) in a do-until control structure thus always will execute at least once. The loop in a do-while control structure, by contrast, might not execute at all. That is, if the condition immediately is false, the action or actions in the do-while loop never execute. Second, a do-until control structure continues looping until the condition is true — and then stops. This is different from the do-while control structure, which continues to loop while the condition is true.

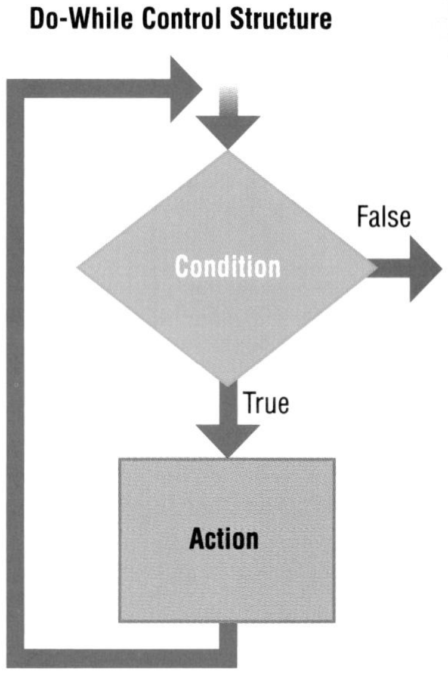

FIGURE 13-31 The do-while control structure tests the condition at the beginning of the loop. It exits the loop when the result of the condition is false.

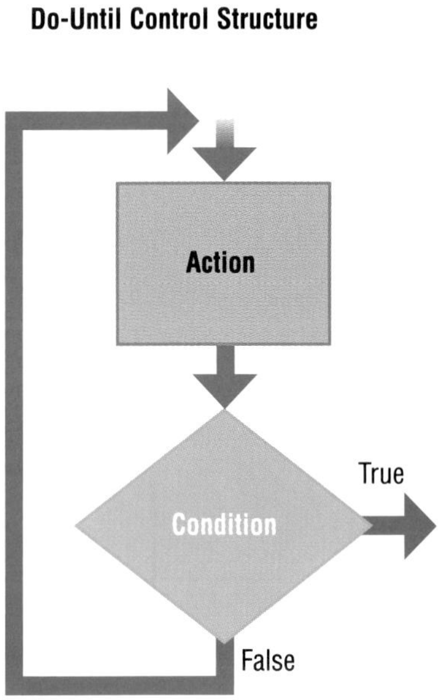

FIGURE 13-32 The do-until control structure tests the condition at the end of the loop. It exits the loop when the result of the condition is true.

Design Tools

To help document a solution algorithm, programmers use *design tools*. Two design tools are program flowcharts and pseudocode.

- A *program flowchart*, or simply **flowchart**, graphically shows the logic in a solution algorithm. The American National Standards Institute (ANSI) published a set of standards for program flowcharts in the early 1960s. These standards, still used today, specify symbols for various operations in a program's logic (Figure 13-33).

  Programmers connect most symbols on a program flowchart with solid lines. These lines show the direction of the program. Dotted lines on a flowchart connect comment symbols. A *comment symbol*, also called an *annotation symbol*, explains or clarifies logic in the solution algorithm. Figure 13-34 shows the program flowchart for three modules of the program shown in the hierarchy chart in Figure 13-26 on page 689.

  In the past, programmers used a template to trace the symbols for a flowchart on a piece of paper. Today, programmers use commercial **flowcharting software** to develop flowcharts. This software makes it easy to modify and update flowcharts. Two popular flowcharting programs are SmartDraw and Visio 2003 (Figure 13-36).

ANSI FLOWCHART SYMBOLS

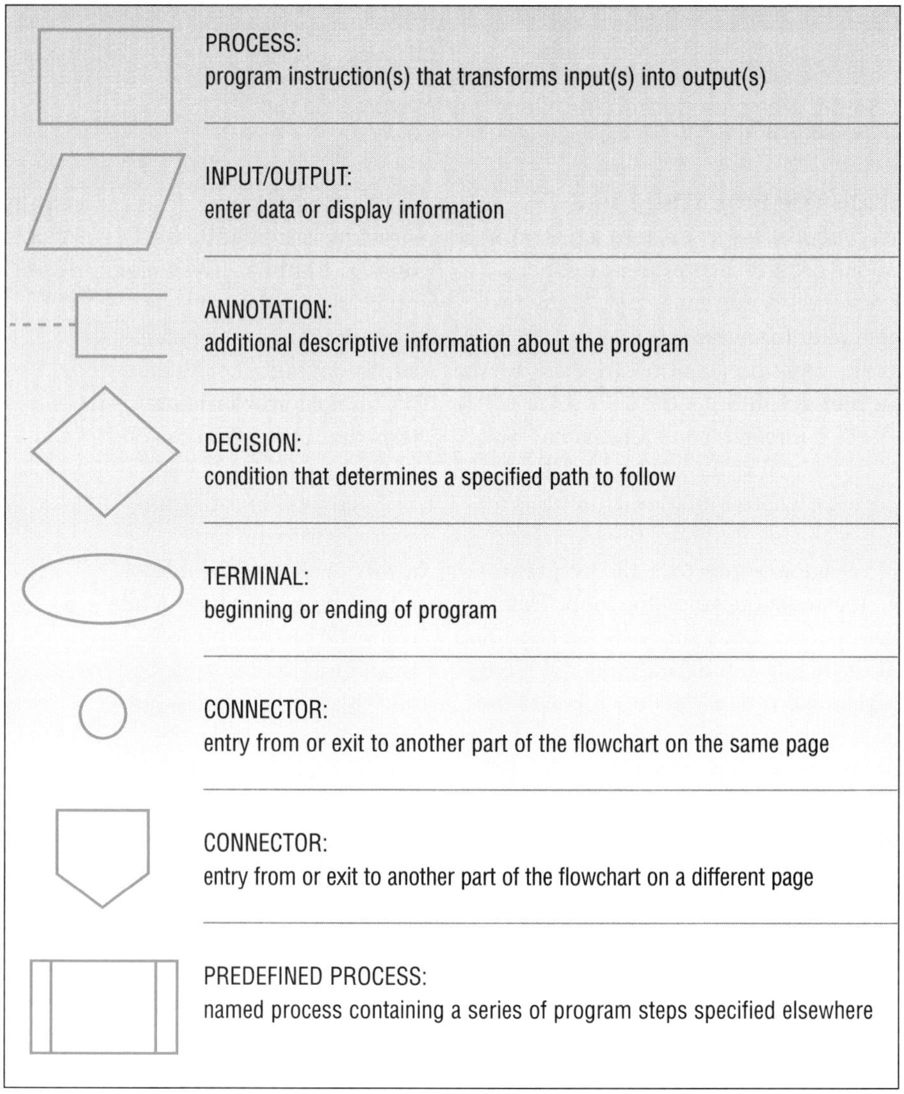

FIGURE 13-33 Standard symbols used to create program flowcharts.

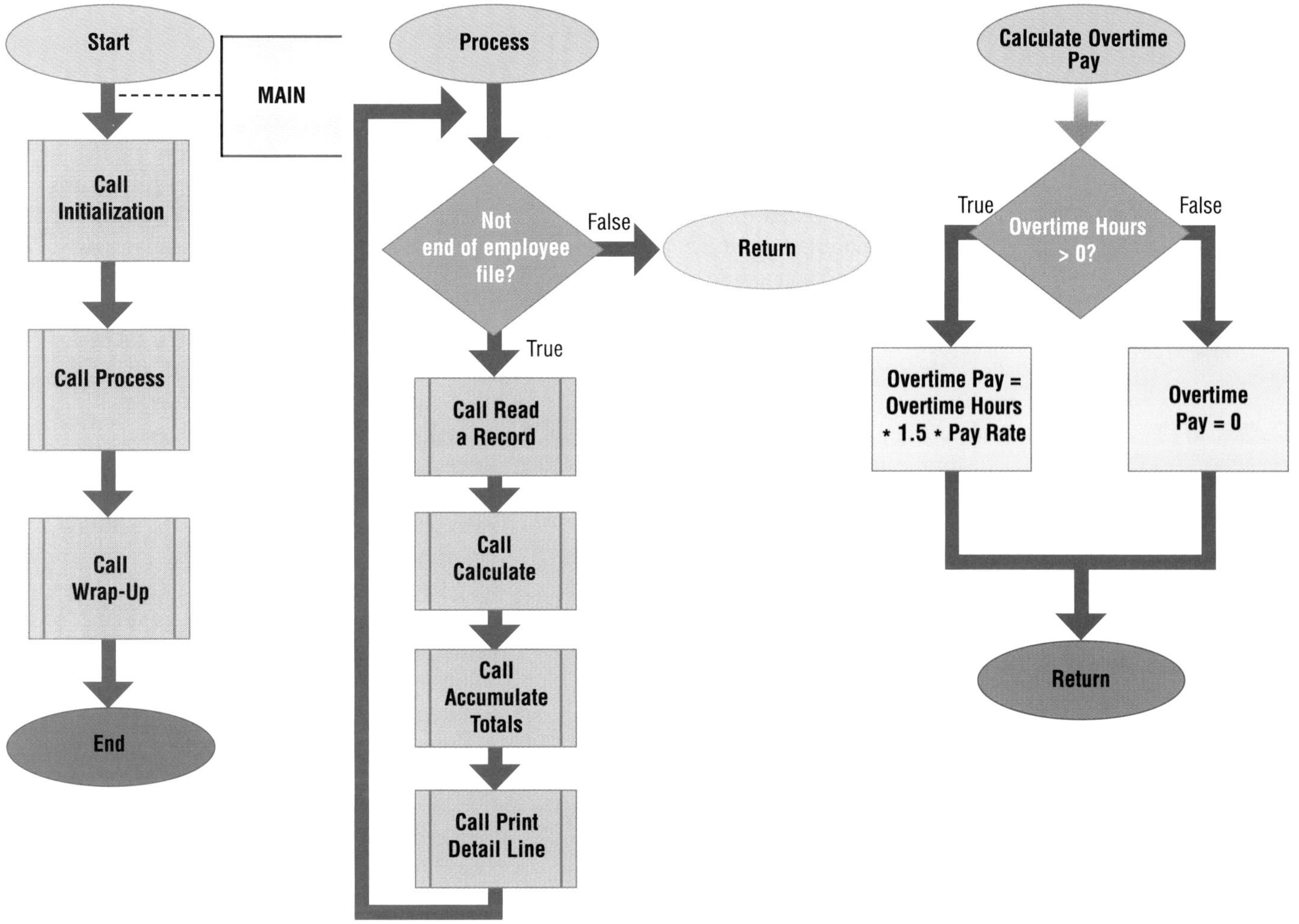

FIGURE 13-34 This figure shows a program flowchart for three of the modules on the hierarchy chart in Figure 13-26 on page 689: MAIN, Process, and Calculate Overtime Pay. Notice the main module is terminated with the word, End; whereas, the subordinate modules end with the word, Return, because they return to a higher-level module.

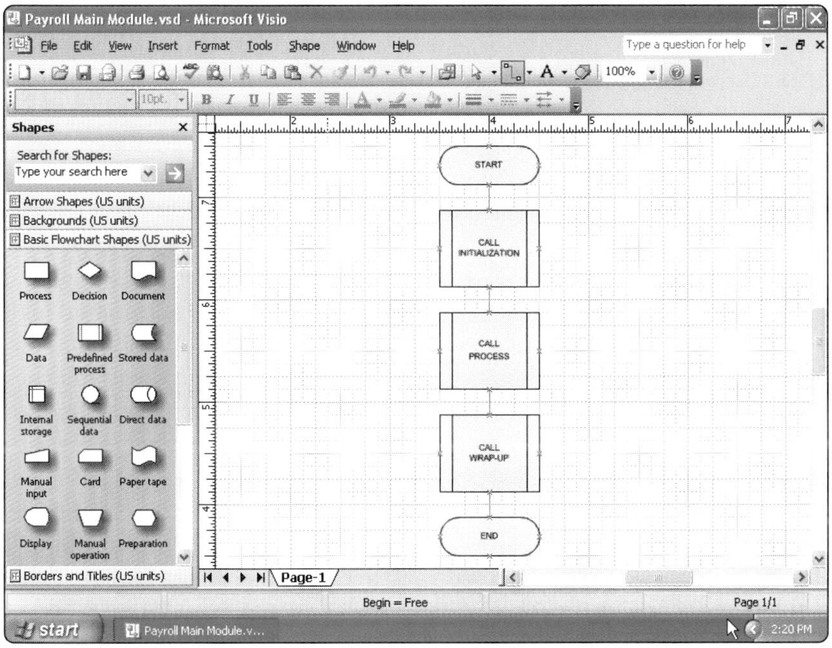

FIGURE 13-35 Visio 2003 is a popular flowcharting program.

WEB LINK 13-11

Flowcharting Software

Visit the Discovering Computers 2005 WEB LINK page (**scsite .com/dc2005/weblink**). Click Flowcharting Software below Chapter 13.

- *Pseudocode* uses a condensed form of English to convey program logic. Some programmers prefer to explain the logic of a solution algorithm with words (pseudocode), instead of a graphical flowcharting technique. Pseudocode also uses indentation to identify the control structures. The beginning and ending of the module start at the left margin. The actions within the module are indented. The actions within a selection or repetition control structure are indented again. This allows the programmer to identify clearly the beginning and ending of the control structure. Figure 13-36 shows the pseudocode for the same three program modules as in Figure 13-34 on the previous page.

```
MAIN MODULE:

    CALL Initialization
    CALL Process
    CALL Wrap-Up

END

PROCESS MODULE:

    DO WHILE Not EOF
        CALL Read a Record
        CALL Calculate
        CALL Accumulate Totals
        CALL Print Detail Line
    ENDDO

RETURN

CALCULATE OVERTIME PAY MODULE:

    IF Overtime Hours > 0 THEN
        Overtime Pay = Overtime Hours * 1.5 * Pay Rate
    ELSE
        Overtime Pay = 0
    ENDIF

RETURN
```

FIGURE 13-36 Pseudocode is yet another alternative method of showing program logic. This figure shows the same three modules (MAIN, Process, and Calculate Overtime Pay) as illustrated in Figure 13-35 on the previous page with program flowcharts.

STEP 3 – VALIDATE DESIGN

Once programmers develop the solution algorithm using a program flowchart or pseudocode, they should *validate*, or check, the program design for accuracy. During this step, the programmer checks the logic for correctness and attempts to uncover logic errors. A **logic error** is a flaw in the design that causes inaccurate results. Two techniques for reviewing a solution algorithm are a desk check and a structured walkthrough.

When programmers do a *desk check*, they use test data to step through its logic. **Test data** is sample data that mimics real data the program will process once it is in production. Users should assist in the development of test data. The programmer who developed the solution algorithm usually performs the desk check, but another programmer also can perform this task. Desk checking involves five steps.

1. Develop various sets of test data (inputs).
2. Determine the expected result (output) for each set of data, without using the solution algorithm.
3. Step through the solution algorithm using one set of test data and write down the actual result obtained (output) using the solution algorithm.
4. Compare the expected result from Step 2 to the actual result from Step 3.
5. Repeat Steps 3 and 4 for each set of test data.

If the expected result and actual result do not match for any set of data, the program has a logic error. When this occurs, the programmer must review the logic of the solution algorithm to determine the reason for the error and then correct it.

A more formal technique for checking the solution algorithm is a structured walkthrough. As discussed in Chapter 12, a systems analyst often uses a structured walkthrough to review deliverables during the system development cycle. Likewise, programmers use walkthroughs of solution algorithms during the program development cycle. In this case, the programmer explains the logic of the algorithm while members of the programming team step through the program logic. The purpose of this *structured walkthrough* is to identify errors in the program logic and check for possible improvements in program design.

Usually, a programmer easily can correct errors or improvements identified at this point. After program design is complete and the programmer begins implementing the design, errors are more difficult to fix. Thus, detecting errors and making improvements early in the program development cycle reduces the overall time and cost of program development.

STEP 4 – IMPLEMENT DESIGN

Implementation of the design includes writing the code that translates the design into a program and, if necessary, creating the user interface. **Coding** a program involves translating the solution algorithm into a programming language (usually on paper) and then typing the programming language code into the computer. Of all tasks, programmers usually find coding the most tedious.

As previously mentioned, many different programming languages exist. Each of these has a particular syntax. A language's **syntax** is the set of grammar and rules that specifies how to write instructions for a solution algorithm. For example, a programmer writes an instruction to add three numbers differently in each language, according to its syntax.

As programmers enter a program into a computer, they should take time to document the program code thoroughly. Thus far, the programmer has created external program documentation in the form of flowcharts or pseudocode. A program also has its own documentation, called *comments*.

Programs should include both global and internal comments (Figure 13-37). *Global comments* explain the program's purpose and identify the program name, its author, and the date written. Generally, global comments are at the top of the program. Internal comments, by contrast, appear throughout the body of the program. *Internal comments* explain the purpose of the code statements within the program. Programs that include global and internal comments are much easier to maintain.

global comments

internal comments

```
' Chapter 2:     Take-home pay calculator
' Programmer:    J. Quasney
' Date:          September 2, 2005
' Purpose:       This application calculates a worker's take-
'                home pay per paycheck. The inputs are salary,
'                percentage of salary contributed to a retirement
'                account, and a selection of a health plan.
Private Sub CalculateTakeHomePay()
    Dim dblSocial, dblFed, dblState, dblMedicare, dblWeeklyPay As Double
    Dim dblRetirement, dblInsurance, dblTakeHomePay As Double

    ' Calculate gross paycheck amount
    dblWeeklyPay = Convert.ToDouble(nudSalary.Value) / 26.0

    ' Calculate individual deductions from gross paycheck amount
    dblSocial = dblWeeklyPay * 0.062
    dblFed = dblWeeklyPay * 0.18
    dblState = dblWeeklyPay * 0.025
    dblMedicare = dblWeeklyPay * 0.0145

    ' Calculate retirement contribution from user input
    dblRetirement = dblWeeklyPay * (tbRetirement.Value / 100)

    ' Determine insurance cost based on user input
    If rbInsuranceNone.Checked = True Then
        dblInsurance = 0
    Else
        If rbInsuranceIndividual.Checked = True Then
            dblInsurance = 20.0
        Else
            dblInsurance = 30.0
        End If
    End If

    ' Subtract all deductions from gross paycheck amount and
    ' display the result
    dblTakeHomePay = dblWeeklyPay - dblSocial - dblFed - dblMedicare - dblState - dblInsurance - dblRetirement
    txtTakeHomePay.Text = Format(dblTakeHomePay, "Currency")
End Sub

Private Sub nudSalary_ValueChanged(ByVal sender As System.Object, ByVal e As System.EventArgs) Handles nudSalary.ValueChanged
    CalculateTakeHomePay()
End Sub

Private Sub tbRetirement_Scroll(ByVal sender As System.Object, ByVal e As System.EventArgs) Handles tbRetirement.Scroll
    CalculateTakeHomePay()
End Sub

Private Sub rbInsuranceNone_CheckedChanged(ByVal sender As System.Object, ByVal e As System.EventArgs) Handles rbInsuranceNone.CheckedChanged
    CalculateTakeHomePay()
End Sub

Private Sub rbInsuranceIndividual_CheckedChanged(ByVal sender As System.Object, ByVal e As System.EventArgs) Handles rbInsuranceIndividual.CheckedChanged
    CalculateTakeHomePay()
End Sub

Private Sub rbInsuranceFamily_CheckedChanged(ByVal sender As System.Object, ByVal e As
```

FIGURE 13-37 Thorough documentation leads to maintainable programs. A program should contain global comments (at the top of the program) and internal comments (throughout the body of the program). In this Visual Basic .NET 2003 program, the first character of the comment is an apostrophe.

Extreme Programming

As an alternative to coding in this step of the program development cycle, some companies use extreme programming to develop programs. *Extreme programming* (*XP*) is a new strategy that proposes that programmers should immediately begin coding and testing solutions as soon as requirements are defined. The code continually is tested and refined until it works. This strategy essentially eliminates the design solution and validate design steps of the traditional program development cycle. Extreme programming also suggests that programmers work in pairs, with each communicating code to the other and

WEB LINK 13-12

Extreme Programming

Visit the Discovering Computers 2005 WEB LINK page (**scsite.com/dc2005/weblink**). Click Extreme Programming below Chapter 13.

generating ideas for proper solutions. Proponents of extreme programming claim it reduces the time required for the program development cycle. Read Looking Ahead 13-2 for a look at the next generation of programming.

LOOKING AHEAD 13-2

Genetic Programming Solves Complex Problems

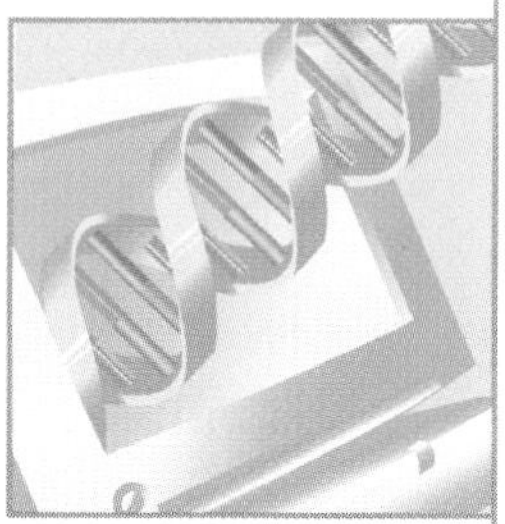

Water sprinkling systems are a convenient method of keeping flower beds and front lawns healthy and colorful. Just set the timer to start and stop the water flow at particular times each day. This simplicity, however, has its limitations. For example, what if rain is predicted? Water pressure is low? A watering ban is in effect due to drought conditions? These factors make the simple watering schedule more complex.

Many routine tasks, likewise, are not as simple as they appear, such as using a robot to pick items in a warehouse and crossbreeding corn to resist disease. To handle these issues, researchers can use *genetic programming* to help them derive the optimal solution. This approach helps solve a problem when a variety of fluctuating variables complicate the issue.

Genetic programming borrows theories used in biological evolution studies, especially survival of the fittest. In this manner, one possible solution is compared with another, and the better one then is compared with a third solution. In addition, two programs sometimes are crossbred to design a new program containing the best features of the two original programs. The program design that best solves the problem eventually is developed.

For a look at the next generation of genetic programming, visit the Discovering Computers 2005 Looking Ahead Web page (**scsite.com/dc2005/looking**). Click Looking Ahead #2 below Chapter 13.

STEP 5 – TEST SOLUTION

Once a programmer codes and enters the program, the next step is to test it. Thorough testing is very important. After developers place the program into production, many users rely on the program and its output to support their daily activities and decisions.

The goal of program testing is to ensure the program runs correctly and is error free. Errors uncovered during this step usually are one of two types: (1) syntax errors or (2) logic errors.

A **syntax error** occurs when the code violates the syntax, or grammar, of the programming language. Misspelling a command, leaving out required punctuation, or typing command words out of order all will cause syntax errors. Programmers usually discover syntax errors the first time they attempt to compile or interpret the program code on the computer. When a syntax error is located, a message either is displayed on the screen immediately or is written to a log file. Either way, the programmer must review and correct all syntax errors. The procedure for testing for logic errors at this step is much like the desk checking techniques used in the Validate Design step.

The test data should include both valid (correct) and invalid (incorrect) input data. When valid test data is input, the program should produce the correct result. If the expected result and actual result do not match, the program has a logic error. In this case, the programmer must review the logic of the program code to determine the cause of the logic error and then correct it.

Another purpose of using test data is to try to cause a **run-time error**, which is an error that occurs while the program is running. If the pay rate for employees cannot exceed $55.00 per hour, then the test data should use some valid pay rates, such as $25.00 and $10.50, as well as some invalid ones, such as $-32.00 and $72.50. When inputting an invalid pay rate, the program should display an error message and allow the user to reenter the pay rate. If the program accepts an invalid pay rate, then it contains a logic error. In addition, the program should handle data exception errors such as division by zero.

The process of locating and correcting syntax and logic errors in a program is known as **debugging** the program. The program errors themselves are the **bugs**. Thus, removing the errors is de*bug*ging. The term bug originated when the failure of one of the first computers supposedly was traced to an actual bug. A moth lodged in the computer's electronic components was the cause of the failure (Figure 13-38). Read Issue 13-5 for a related discussion.

Most programming languages include a debug utility. A *debug utility*, or *debugger*, assists programmers with identifying syntax errors and finding logic errors. With a debugger, a programmer examines program values (such as the result of a calculation) while the program runs in slow motion.

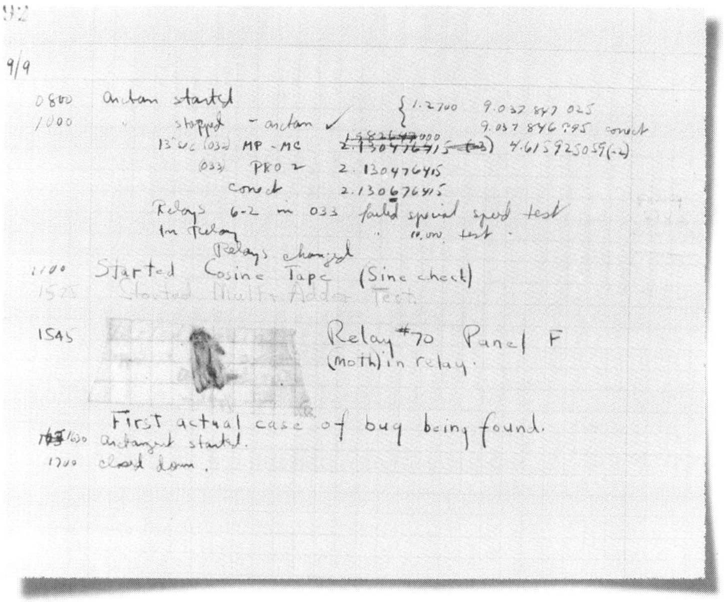

FIGURE 13-38 The temporary failure of one of the first computers was traced to a dead moth (shown taped to the log book) caught in the electrical components. Some say this event is the origin of the term bug, which means computer error.

A bug that had the potential to cause serious financial losses for computers around the world was the millennium bug. The *millennium bug*, or *Y2K bug*, took effect when the computer date rolled over to January 1, 2000. At this time, non-Y2K compliant computers read the date as 01/01/00. Computer programs that used just the last two digits of a year could not distinguish 01/01/1900 from 01/01/2000. Thus, these programs had the potential to make incorrect date calculations, for example, finding if someone were older than age 65.

Some software companies distribute a beta of their software to users. A **beta** is a program that has most or all of its features and functionality implemented. Users test the beta program and send in bug reports to the software company. This enables the software manufacturer to fix any errors before the software is released to the public for sale. Read Apply It 13-2 for more information.

If a programmer designs a program properly during the Design Solution step, then testing in this step should not require much time. When a programmer does not test the solution algorithm thoroughly during design, many logic errors may exist and testing can take longer. As a general rule, the more time and effort programmers spend analyzing and designing the solution algorithm, the less time spent debugging the program.

ISSUE 13-5

Who Is Responsible for Bugs?

The consequences of bugs, or mistakes, in computer programs can be staggering. An error in the code controlling a Canadian nuclear facility caused more than 3,000 gallons of radioactive water to be spilled. A bug in long-distance switching software cost AT&T more than $60 million. A flaw in a popular operating system frustrated users when their computers locked up and displayed the dreaded "Blue Screen of Death." Experts estimate that one in every 5,000 lines of code contains a mistake. Given that many programs contain hundreds of thousands, even millions, of code lines, bugs are not surprising. Most software licenses absolve the software creator of any responsibility for the end user getting the wrong information from a buggy program. Who should be responsible for buggy software? Why? When you buy some software today and have trouble installing it and have problems, you often get charged for technical support. Should manufacturers be required to provide free technical support for a specified time? Why or why not?

For more information about computer bugs, visit the Discovering Computers 2005 Issues Web page (**scsite.com/dc2005/issues**). Click Issue #5 below Chapter 13.

APPLY IT 13-2

Beta Testing Offers Benefits

The best things in life are free, according to an adage. That may include the software a participant acquires as a member of a beta testing program.

Beta testers test software while it is being developed with the goal of bridging the gap between the programmers and potential customers. They obtain the software free and generally receive no compensation. Their responsibilities are to install and use the software, discover syntax, run-time, and logic errors, recommend enhancements, and then report these problems and suggestions.

Some beta testers agree to test all versions of a program within a specific period of time, such as one year, and others agree to test one specific version of a program until it has been released to the public. Participants are selected in many ways. Often they are current users of software that is being upgraded. Others apply by responding to announcements on a software company's Web site.

Because the software is not at the end of its program development cycle, the beta testers can expect some problems. They need to keep detailed records of what functions caused errors, how the interface can be enhanced, and what documentation can be clarified.

For more information about beta testing, visit the Discovering Computers 2005 Apply It Web page (**scsite.com/dc2005/apply**). Click Apply It #2 below Chapter 13.

STEP 6 – DOCUMENT SOLUTION

In documenting the solution, the programmer performs two activities: (1) review the program code and (2) review all the documentation.

First, programmers review the program for any dead code and remove it. *Dead code* is any program instructions that a program never executes. When programmers write a program, they often write a section of code at a time. Sometimes, they decide not to use the code, but leave it in the program anyway. This dead (unused) code serves no purpose and should not exist.

Next, programmers should run the program one final time to verify it still works. After reviewing the program code, the programmer gives the program and all of its documentation to the systems analyst. The documentation includes all charts, solution algorithms in the form of program flowcharts or pseudocode, test data, and program code listings that contain global and internal comments.

The programmer should be sure all documentation is complete and accurate. This becomes especially valuable if the program requires changes in the future. One year later, a different programmer might have to update these programs. Proper documentation greatly reduces the amount of time a new programmer spends learning about existing programs.

QUIZ YOURSELF 13-3

To check your knowledge of the program development cycle, structured versus object-oriented design, and basic control structures, visit the Discovering Computers 2005 Quiz Yourself Web page (**scsite.com/dc2005/quiz**). Click Objectives 8 – 10 below Chapter 13.

CHAPTER SUMMARY

This chapter explained various programming languages used to write and develop computer programs. It also presented a variety of Web development and multimedia development tools. Finally, the chapter discussed each step in the program development cycle and presented the tools used to make this process efficient.

Programmer

If you are the curious, creative type, enjoy solving puzzles, and gain satisfaction in making things work, then consider a career in programming. A programmer designs, writes, and tests the code that tells computers what to do. Most programmers specialize in one of three fields: system programming, application programming, or Web development programming.

Some jobs may require that the programmer develop an entire program, while other jobs require program maintenance. Likewise, programmers can work for a small company in which they are responsible for the entire system development cycle, or for a larger company in which they are part of a team and individual duties are specialized. Projects can range from computer games to essential business applications. Programmers enjoy the achievements of working with computers to accomplish objectives as well as developing efficient instructions that tell computers how to perform specific tasks.

Some programmers believe that computer programming is an art. Nevertheless, academic credentials are essential for success in this career. A bachelor's degree in Computer Science or Information Technology usually is required. The key to success is familiarity with programming languages and a good foundation in programming logic. Surveys indicate that average salaries for entry level programmers are about $40,000 and can exceed $75,000 for senior programmers.

To learn more about the field of programmer as a career, visit the Discovering Computers 2005 Careers Web page (**scsite.com/dc2005/careers**). Click Programmer.

Extending the Web Using XML

Imagine that your marine supply company provides vendor information to clients around the world. Your clients must access the information not only from their notebook computers, but also on their wireless PDAs and cellular telephones. You use the same database for direct mailings to vendors.

As discussed in this chapter, XML (eXtensible Markup Language) is a format for structuring data that allows Web developers to create one version of a Web page that then can be displayed in a form appropriate for the display device. Using HTML, a developer must create three separate Web sites, with special coding for each device — HTML for the notebook computer, WML for the cellular telephone, and Web clipping (small pieces of information) for a PDA. With XML, a developer can create just one version of the Web site and the content can be formatted to display appropriately on various devices.

How does XML differ from HTML? HTML was designed to display data and to focus on how data looks. XML, by contrast, was designed to describe data and to focus on what data is. The XML specification describes how to organize structured data into documents.

As with HTML, XML uses tags to mark various parts of a document. XML, however, uses tags to describe the structure of the data, not the display. The XML document shown in Figure 13-39, for example, uses tags to structure a list of vendors. Tags are set in pairs, with a start tag (<city>) and an end tag (</city>). A pair of tags, along with all of the text and other tags they enclose, is called an *element*. The XML document in Figure 13-39 contains eight different elements, including a <vendor> element that encloses the tags and data for each vendor and a <vendorlist> element that encloses all tags and data and constitutes the entire document.

In this example, the XML elements are nested to structure the vendor address data. Different XML documents can use different element names in different hierarchical arrangements. Although in principle every XML document can have a unique structure, XML supports the notion of a *DTD* (*document type definition*), a document that specifies a particular arrangement of elements that should be used within an XML document. For example, a DTD might specify that a vendor database consists of a vendor list element containing one or more vendor elements, and that each vendor element contains a name, address, city, state, Zip code, and Web address, in exactly that order. Using a DTD ensures that XML documents adhere to some basic guidelines for structure, to make it easier to share data with other organizations using the same DTD.

After the XML document is structured, you can apply different styles to the content so that it is usable in various formats. Remember that the XML document describes only the content, not the display or rendering of that content. By applying a different style sheet to the same document, an XML document can be rendered in different formats.

XML works with *XSL* (*Extensible Stylesheet Language*), a language for creating a stylesheet that describes how to present the data described in the XML document in a Web page. For example, using XSL, you could tell a Web browser to display any data in the element <name> as left-aligned bold text.

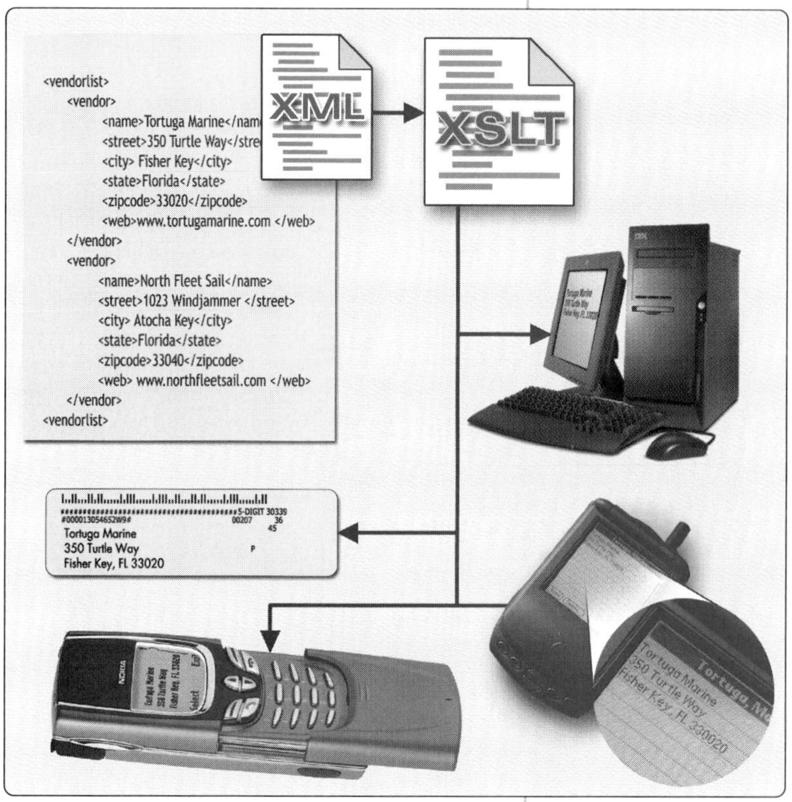

FIGURE 13-39 A sample XML document converted by an XSLT document for display on various devices.

XSLT (*Extensible Style Language Transformations*) is an extension of XSL, which is used to create stylesheets that describe how to transform XML documents into other types of documents. When a device requests a page from a Web site built with XML, a CGI script can detect what device has requested the page from the server. The server then uses the format described in the XSLT document to transform the XML into the proper format — whether a WAP document for a cellular telephone microbrowser, a Web clipping document for a PDA, an HTML Web page for a browser on a client's notebook computer, or mailing label data for a mailing label program.

For more information about XML, visit the Discovering Computers 2005 High-Tech Talk Web page (**scsite.com/dc2005/tech**) and click XML.

COMPANIES ON THE CUTTING EDGE

Macromedia

Multimedia Dominates Web Sites

Do you want to demo a new Ford Thunderbird without leaving your house? Check the features on a Timex Helix sport watch on your notebook computer? Create fun and educational science projects with your PDA? You can, with the help of Macromedia's lineup of splashy products, including Dreamweaver MX, for building and managing Web sites, Flash Player that allows viewing of vivid content and applications on the Web, and Shockwave that permits viewing of media and 3-D Web content.

In 1984, Marc Canter founded a company called MacroMind in a Chicago suburb. The company's goal was to supply artists with tools to create high-quality audio, video, and animation. (Among its innovations was Videoworks, which later was called Director, Macromedia's popular multimedia authoring program.) In 1992, MacroMind merged with Paracomp and Authorware to form Macromedia. Today, *Macromedia* provides software that people use to create powerful experiences on the Internet and across a range of platforms and devices. Its award-winning products help designers and developers offer more pleasing Web encounters and facilitate more effective e-business. More than 1 million professional Web developers use Macromedia software worldwide to author, produce, deliver, and analyze Web content that is rich in motion, sound, and graphics. They make the most of the high-quality, interactive user interfaces, which have been translated in eight languages. Dreamweaver is the leading platform in 70 percent of the market. More than 1.4 million copies of Flash Player are downloaded from the Macromedia Web site daily, making it the most widely Web-distributed software in history. Nearly 20 million users have registered their copies of Shockwave, with an average of 70,000 new users each day.

Macromedia is headquartered in San Francisco and has 1,100 employees in offices around the world. Its software tools, which are available on the Internet, are installed by 98 percent of Web users and a wide network of industry partners.

For more information about Macromedia, visit the Discovering Computers 2005 Companies Web page (**scsite.com/dc2005/companies**) and click Macromedia.

Borland

Application Development Pioneer

Researchers at St. Jude Children's Research Hospital in Memphis, TN, continually execute clinical trials in attempts to find cures for children with catastrophic illnesses. Each trial requires establishing a database to collect data on each patient to study the effects of new combinations of therapies and drugs. The software development group needs to perform each step in the program development cycle to build a computer program that analyzes, designs, and tests the research.

St. Jude's software developers occasionally needed as much as a year to create these computer programs, so they sought alternate means to help them accelerate the development cycle. They turned to Borland for help. Since 1983, *Borland* has helped companies develop, deploy, and integrate software applications. Borland's software tools helped St. Jude reduce its database creation times tenfold; programming that previously took four months to complete now is finished in less than 20 hours.

Borland's technology was among the first to help companies develop applications for the personal computer environment. Starting with Turbo Pascal more than 20 years ago, Borland now has program development tools that support Linux and object-oriented programming languages, such as Java, C++, and Microsoft Visual Studio .NET.

Borland and Microsoft have entered into a $100 million partnership that allows Borland to license key Microsoft technology. The relationship between these two companies, however, has not always been so amicable. In 1997, Borland sued Microsoft for hiring many of Borland's key employees. The two corporations settled in 1999 when Microsoft invested $25 million in Borland.

For more information about Borland, visit the Discovering Computers 2005 Companies Web page (**scsite.com/dc2005/companies**) and click Borland.

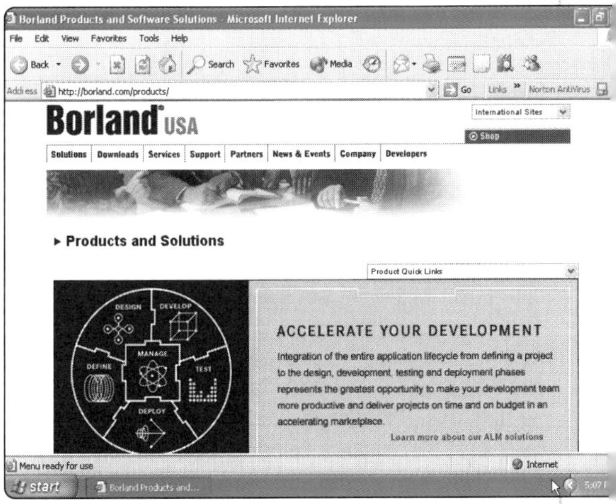

TECHNOLOGY TRAILBLAZERS

Dennis Ritchie
Creator of C

Without Dennis Ritchie, programmers might not be using C++ today. Many of today's Internet applications and commercial programs are written using C++, a useful object-oriented language. C++ is an expansion of C, which *Dennis Ritchie* developed at Bell Labs in the early 1970s.

Ritchie joined Bell Labs after doing undergraduate and graduate work in physics at Harvard University. Ritchie claims his undergraduate work convinced him that he was not smart enough to be a physicist, but he enjoyed working with computers. At that time, system programmers were using the UNIX operating system on meager Digital Equipment Corporation PDP-11 computers with 24 KB of memory and a programming language called B, which was developed by Ken Thompson. Ritchie added data types and original syntax to B, producing a new language called C. Ritchie and Thompson rewrote the UNIX operating system in C to make it more portable, so it could be installed easily on computers other than the PDP-11 without extensive software rewrites. C became extremely popular outside of Bell Labs after 1980 and turned into a standard programming language in the microcomputer/workstation market.

Ritchie has received numerous awards and recognitions. In 1998, he was elected into the National Academy of Engineering. *PC Magazine* recognized Ritchie with its Lifetime Achievement Award for Technical Excellence, and, in 1999, President Bill Clinton awarded Ritchie and Thompson the National Medal of Technology, the country's highest prize for achievement in technology.

Besides being a powerful force behind Bell Labs' Computer Sciences Research Center, Ritchie also drove a tractor-trailer for the Roush Racing Valvoline/Cummings NASCAR team, and served as a mechanic on Mark Martin's racecar and a front tire carrier during pit stops.

For more information about Dennis Ritchie, visit the Discovering Computers 2005 People Web page (**scsite.com/dc2005/people**) and click Dennis Ritchie.

James Gosling
Java Engineer and Architect

When people think of programming languages for the Internet, they think of HTML and Java. When people think of Java, they should think of *James Gosling*, who designed and implemented one of the more popular programming languages for the Web.

Gosling earned his B.S. at the University of Calgary and his Ph.D. in computer science at Carnegie-Mellon University. After graduating, Gosling joined Sun Microsystems where he built a multiprocessor version of UNIX, developed compilers to convert program code into machine language, engineered a window manager called NeWS, and wrote a UNIX text editor called Emacs.

In an interview with Bill Venners of JavaWorld, Gosling said that innovation is "not like a lightbulb going off. It's more like there's something irritating you and you fix it until it goes away." He should know. In 1990, Gosling led the Green Project, which set out to produce software for the consumer electronics industry that would allow appliances to communicate. The programming language chosen originally for the project, however, proved incapable of meeting the networking and security requirements. To remedy this irritation, Gosling developed a programming language called Oak, named after a tree outside his window. The name Oak was similar to the name of another programming language, so Gosling's new language was renamed Java. "It was really the first and only language designed around networking," Gosling recalls. Java's release was timed perfectly. The powerful, portable language that Gosling described as a "really fancy wrench" proved to be a perfect tool for building applications on the expanding Internet.

Today, Gosling is a vice president and Sun Fellow at Sun Microsystems, where he continues his work with Java. "It used to be that all developers were colored by their programming tools," Gosling says, "but Java developers can work everywhere."

For more information about James Gosling, visit the Discovering Computers 2005 People Web page (**scsite.com/dc2005/people**) and click James Gosling.

CHAPTER 13 CHAPTER REVIEW

The Chapter Review section summarizes the concepts presented in this chapter.

WEB INSTRUCTIONS:

To display this page from the Web, start your browser and enter the Web address **scsite.com/dc2005/ch13/review.** Click the links for current and additional information. To listen to an audio version of this Chapter Review, click the Audio button.

1 How Are Machine Languages Different from Assembly Languages?

A computer program is a series of instructions that directs a computer to perform tasks. A **programming language** is a set of words, symbols, and codes that enables a *programmer* to write the instructions in a computer program. Two low-level programming languages are machine language and assembly language. A **machine language** uses a series of binary digits, or combinations of numbers and letters that represent binary digits, and is the only language a computer directly understands. With an **assembly language**, a programmer writes instructions using *symbolic instruction codes*, which are meaningful abbreviations and codes.

2 What Is the Purpose of Procedural Programming Languages?

In a **procedural language**, or **third-generation language** (**3GL**), a programmer writes instructions that tell a computer what to accomplish and how to do it. Programmers use English-like words to write instructions, which simplifies the program development process. A *compiler* or an *interpreter* translates the 3GL **source program** into machine language *object code* that a computer can execute. Standard procedural languages include **BASIC** (a simple, interactive problem-solving language), COBOL (a language designed for business applications), and **C** (a powerful language that requires professional programming skills).

3 What Are the Advantages and Uses of Visual Programming?

A **visual programming language**, sometimes called a *fifth-generation language*, provides a visual or graphical interface, called a *visual programming environment* (*VPE*), for creating source code. Visual programming languages often are used in a RAD environment. **RAD** (*rapid application development*) allows programmers to implement a program in segments and use prebuilt components, thus simplifying program development. Visual programming languages include **Visual Basic .NET 2003, Visual C++ .NET 2003, Visual C# .NET 2003, Visual J# .NET 2003, Delphi**, and PowerBuilder.

4 What Are the Characteristics of Object-Oriented Programming Languages?

Programmers use an **object-oriented programming** (**OOP**) **language** to implement object-oriented design. An *object* is an item that can contain both data and the procedures that read or manipulate the data. A major benefit of OOP is the ability to reuse and modify existing objects, allowing programmers to create applications faster. OOP languages include C++, which is an object-oriented extension of the C programming language, and **Java**, which is similar to C++ but uses a *just-in-time* (*JIT*) *compiler* to convert its source code into machine code.

Visit **scsite.com/dc2005/quiz** or click the Quiz Yourself button. Click Objectives 1 – 4 below Chapter 13.

5 How Are Nonprocedural Languages and Tools Used?

Nonprocedural languages and program development tools allow people with little programming background to develop programs. With a **nonprocedural language**, programmers write English-like instructions that retrieve data from files or a database. **Program development tools** are user-friendly programs that assist in creating programs. **RPG** (*Report Program Generator*) is a nonprocedural language that helps businesses generate reports. A **4GL** (*fourth-generation language*) is a nonprocedural language that enables users to access data in a database. An **application generator** creates source code or machine code from a specification of the required functionality. A macro is a series of statements that instructs an application how to complete a task.

6 What Are Web Page Program Development Techniques such as HTML, Scripting Languages, DHTML, XML, WML, and Web Page Authoring Software?

Web page authors use a variety of techniques to design and develop Web pages. **HTML** (*Hypertext Markup Language*) is a special formatting language that programmers use to format documents for display on the Web. A *scripting language* is an easy-to-use, interpreted language that programmers use to add dynamic content and interactive elements to Web pages. DHTML (Dynamic HTML) is a newer type of HTML that allows developers to include more graphical interest and interactivity in a Web page. **XML** (*eXtensible Markup Language*) is a popular format for sharing data that allows Web page developers to create customized tags, as well as predefined tags. **WML** is a subset of XML used to design Web pages for microbrowsers. Developers use **Web page authoring software** to create sophisticated Web pages that include graphical images, video, audio, animation, and other special effects.

7 How Are Popular Multimedia Authoring Programs Used?

Multimedia authoring software allows developers to combine text, graphics, animation, audio, and video into an interactive presentation. Popular authoring software includes ToolBook, Authorware, and Director. ToolBook has a graphical user interface and uses an object-oriented approach. **Authorware** provides the tools developers need to build interactive multimedia training and educational programs. **Director** has powerful features that allow developers to create highly interactive multimedia applications.

Visit **scsite.com/dc2005/quiz** or click the Quiz Yourself button. Click Objectives 5 – 7 below Chapter 13.

8 What Are the Six Steps in the Program Development Cycle?

The program development cycle is a series of steps programmers use to build computer programs. The program development cycle consists of six steps: (1) analyze requirements, (2) design solution, (3) validate design, (4) implement design, (5) test solution, and (6) document solution.

9 How Is Structured Design Different from Object-Oriented Design?

In **structured design**, a programmer typically begins with a general design and moves toward a more detailed design. A programmer starts with the program's major function, called the *main routine*, and breaks it down into smaller sections, called *subroutines*. Structured design results in programs that are reliable and easy to read and maintain, but it does not provide a way to keep the data and the program together and can result in redundant programming code. With **object-oriented** (**OO**) **design**, the programmer packages the data and the program (or procedure) into a single unit, an object. Objects are grouped into classes. A detailed class diagram represents each object, its attributes (data) and its methods (procedures). The programmer translates the methods into program instructions.

10 What Are the Basic Control Structures Used in Designing Solutions to Programming Problems?

A **control structure** depicts the logical order of program instructions. A *sequence control structure* shows one or more actions following each other. A *selection control structure* tells the program which action to take, based on certain conditions. Two types of selection control structures are the *if-then-else control structure*, which yields one of two possibilities (true or false), and the *case control structure*, which can yield one of three or more possibilities. The *repetition control structure* enables a program to perform one or more actions repeatedly as long as a certain condition is met. Two forms of the repetition control structure are the *do-while control structure*, which tests a condition at the beginning of the loop and continues looping as long as a condition is true, and the *do-until control structure*, which tests a condition at the end of the loop and continues looping until the condition is true.

Visit **scsite.com/dc2005/quiz** or click the Quiz Yourself button. Click Objectives 8 – 10 below Chapter 13.

CHAPTER 13 KEY TERMS

QUIZZES AND LEARNING GAMES
Computer Genius
Crossword Puzzle
Interactive Labs
Practice Test
Quiz Yourself
Wheel of Terms

EXERCISES
Chapter Review
Checkpoint
Key Terms
Lab Exercises
Learn It Online
Web Research

BEYOND THE BOOK
Apply It
Career Corner
Companies
FAQ
High-Tech Talk
Issues
Looking Ahead
Trailblazers
Web Links

FEATURES
Guide to Web Sites
Making Use of the Web
Tech News
Timeline 2005

You should know the Primary Terms and be familiar with the Secondary Terms.

WEB INSTRUCTIONS:

To display this page from the Web, start your browser and enter the Web address **scsite.com/dc2005/ch13/terms**. Click a term to display its definition and a picture. When the picture appears, click the more info button for current and additional information about the term from the Web.

>> Primary Terms

(shown in bold-black characters in the chapter)

4GL (675)
ActiveX (679)
ActiveX control (679)
Ada (685)
ALGOL (685)
APL (685)
applet (679)
application generator (675)
assembly language (666)
Authorware (684)
BASIC (668)
beta (697)
bugs (696)
C (669)
C++ (670)
COBOL (668)
coding (695)
computer program (664)
control structure (690)
counter (679)
debugging (696)
Delphi (673)
Director (684)
Dreamweaver MX (683)
dynamic HTML (DHTML) (682)
Flash MX (683)
flowchart (692)
flowcharting software (692)
Forth (685)
FORTRAN (685)
FrontPage 2003 (683)
hierarchy chart (688)
HTML (678)
HyperTalk (685)
image map (679)
implementation (695)
Java (670)
JavaScript (681)
LISP (685)
logic error (694)
Logo (685)
machine language (665)
macro (application program) (676)
maintaining (686)
Modula-2 (685)
multimedia authoring software (684)
nonprocedural language (674)
object-oriented (OO) design (689)
object-oriented programming (OOP) language (669)
Pascal (685)
Perl (681)
PILOT (685)
PL/I (685)
PowerBuilder (674)
procedural language (666)
processing form (679)
program development cycle (686)
program development tools (674)
programmer (664)
programming language (664)
programming team (687)
Prolog (685)
RAD (671)
RPG (674)
run-time error (696)
script (679)
servlet (679)
Smalltalk (685)
source program (666)
SQL (675)
structured design (688)
syntax (695)
syntax error (696)
test data (694)
third-generation language (3GL) (666)
ToolBook (684)
VBScript (681)
Visual Basic .NET 2003 (672)
Visual C++ .NET 2003 (673)
Visual C# .NET 2003 (673)
Visual J# .NET 2003 (673)
visual programming language (671)
Visual Studio .NET 2003 (672)
Web page authoring software (683)
WML (683)
XHTML (682)
XML (682)

>> Secondary Terms

(shown in italic characters in the chapter)

algorithm (668)
annotation symbol (692)
assembler (666)
Beginners All-purpose Symbolic Instruction Code (668)
bytecode (670)
cascading style sheets (CSS) (682)
case control structure (690)
CGI (common gateway interface) (680)
CGI script (680)
code (664)
comment symbol (692)
comments (695)
COmmon Business-Oriented Language (668)
compiler (667)
construct (690)
dead code (698)
debug utility (696)
debugger (696)
design tools (692)
desk check (694)
document object model (DOM) (682)
do-until control structure (691)
do-while control structure (691)
encapsulation (689)
event (670)
event-driven program (670)
execute (666)
Extensible HTML (682)
eXtensible Markup Language (682)
extreme programming (XP) (695)
fifth-generation language (671)
form (675)
fourth-generation language (675)
global comments (695)
high-level language (665)
Hopper, Grace (668)
Hypertext Markup Language (678)
if-then-else control structure (690)
internal comments (695)
interpreter (667)
IPO chart (687)
J2EE (Java 2 Platform Enterprise Edition) (670)
JScript (681)
just-in-time (JIT) compiler (670)
loop (691)
low-level language (664)
machine-dependent language (664)
machine-independent language (665)
macro (assembly language) (666)
macro recorder (676)
main module (688)
main routine (688)
menu generator (676)
Micro Focus Net Express (668)
millennium bug (697)
module (688)
.NET (672)
object (669)
object code (667)
object program (667)
open language (681)
Practical Extraction and Report Language (681)
program flowchart (692)
program logic (688)
pseudocode (694)
rapid application development (671)
repetition control structure (691)
Report Program Generator (674)
report writer (675)
RSS (683)
scripting language (681)
selection control structure (690)
sequence control structure (690)
solution algorithm (688)
structure chart (688)
structured walkthrough (694)
style sheet (682)
subroutines (688)
symbolic address (666)
symbolic instruction codes (666)
tags (679)
top-down design (688)
validate (694)
VB .NET (672)
Visual Basic for Applications (VBA) (676)
Visual Basic, Scripting Edition (681)
visual programming environment (VPE) (671)
Web page authors (678)
wireless application protocol (WAP) (683)
wireless markup language (683)
Y2K bug (697)

CHECKPOINT CHAPTER 13

Use the Checkpoint exercises to check your knowledge level of the chapter.

WEB INSTRUCTIONS:

To display this page from the Web, start your browser and enter the Web address **scsite.com/dc2005/ch13/check**. Click the links for current and additional information.

LABEL THE FIGURE

Identify the steps in the program development cycle.

a. analyze requirements
b. design solution
c. document solution
d. implement design
e. test solution
f. validate design

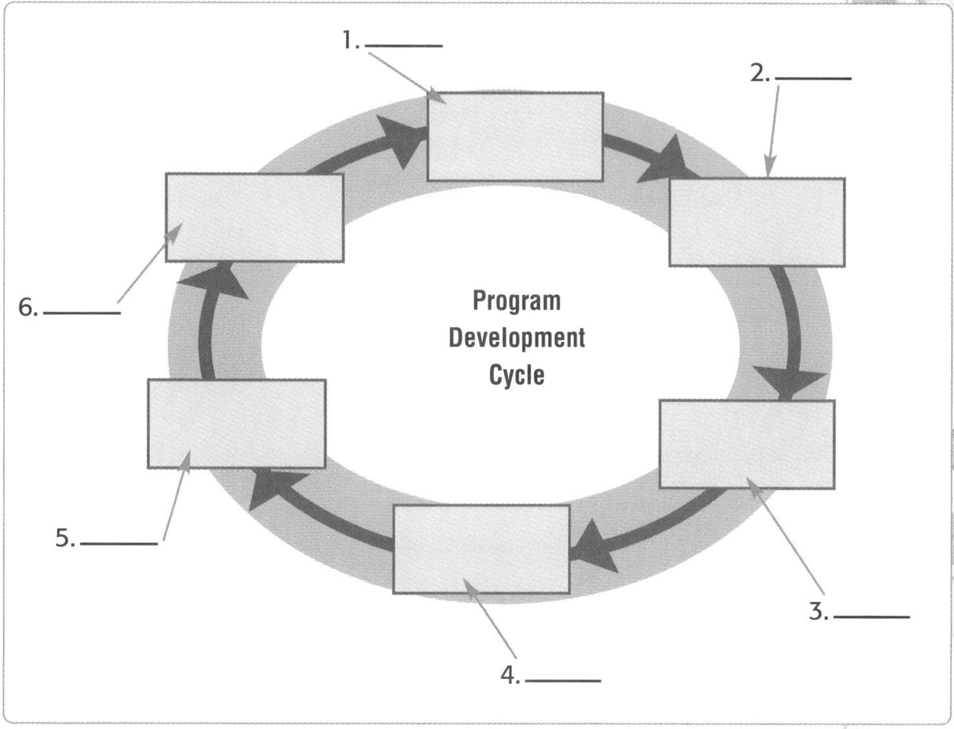

TRUE/FALSE

Mark T for True and F for False. (See page numbers in parentheses.)

_____ 1. Just as humans speak a variety of languages, programmers use a variety of programming languages and tools to write, or code, a program. (664)

_____ 2. Programmers must convert an assembly language program into machine language before the computer can execute, or run, the program. (666)

_____ 3. A compiler is a separate program that converts the entire source program into machine language before executing it. (667)

_____ 4. A disadvantage of OOP is the inability to reuse and modify existing objects. (669)

_____ 5. With a nonprocedural language, the programmer writes English-like instructions that retrieve data from files or a database. (674)

_____ 6. An application generator enables the developer to create a menu for the application options. (676)

_____ 7. A script is an interpreted program that runs on your computer instead of running on a Web server. (679)

_____ 8. The document object model (DOM) contains descriptions of a document's characteristics. (682)

_____ 9. A sequence control structure tells the program which action to take based on a certain condition. (690)

_____ 10. Users test beta programs and send in bug reports to the software company, which enables manufacturers to fix any errors before the software is released for sale. (697)

CHAPTER 13 CHECKPOINT

MULTIPLE CHOICE

Select the best answer. (See page numbers in parentheses.)

1. To convert an assembly language source program into machine language, programmers use a program called a(n) _____. (666)
   a. debugger
   b. interpreter
   c. compiler
   d. assembler
2. Widely used procedural languages include all of the following, except _____. (668)
   a. RPG
   b. BASIC
   c. C
   d. COBOL
3. The most popular personal computer _____ program is Micro Focus Net Express, which enables programmers to create and migrate programs to the Web. (668)
   a. COBOL
   b. Logo
   c. BASIC
   d. Pascal
4. An OOP language is _____, which means an OOP language program checks for and responds to events such as pressing a key or typing a value. (670)
   a. event based
   b. interpreted
   c. event driven
   d. compiled
5. _____ is a visual programming language that allows Java program development in the .NET environment. (672)
   a. Visual C# .NET 2003
   b. Visual J# .NET 2003
   c. Visual C++ .NET 2003
   d. Visual Basic .NET 2003
6. _____ is a popular fourth-generation query language that allows users to manage, update, and retrieve data in a relational DBMS. (675)
   a. RPG
   b. Ada
   c. XML
   d. SQL
7. ____ is not actually a programming language, but it has specific rules for defining the placement and format of text, graphics, and video on a Web page. (679)
   a. VBA (Visual Basic for Applications)
   b. HTML (Hypertext Markup Language)
   c. RPG (Report Program Generator)
   d. LISP (LISt Processing)
8. Examples of _____ are <B> to bold text and <P> to indicate a new paragraph. (679)
   a. bugs
   b. macros
   c. tags
   d. objects
9. A(n) _____ is a graphical image that points to a URL. (679)
   a. processing form
   b. report writer
   c. image map
   d. flowchart
10. _____ is a popular multimedia authoring program that includes Lingo, which is a built-in object-oriented language. (684)
    a. ToolBook
    b. Authorware
    c. Director
    d. All of the above
11. Many programmers use a(n) _____ to identify a program's inputs, its outputs, and the processing steps required to transform the inputs into the outputs. (687)
    a. IPO chart
    b. case diagram
    c. program flowchart
    d. hierarchy chart
12. In structured design, a section of a program that performs a single function is a(n) _____. (688)
    a. object
    b. module
    c. servlet
    d. beta
13. A _____ control structure tells a program what action to take, based on a certain condition. (690)
    a. repetition
    b. sequence
    c. loop
    d. selection
14. When programmers review program code, they remove any _____, which is any program instructions that a program never executes. (698)
    a. source code
    b. test code
    c. object code
    d. dead code

CHECKPOINT CHAPTER 13

MATCHING

Match the terms with their definitions. (See page numbers in parentheses.)

_____ 1. BASIC (668)
_____ 2. COBOL (668)
_____ 3. C++ (670)
_____ 4. Java (670)
_____ 5. Visual Basic .NET 2003 (672)
_____ 6. PowerBuilder (674)
_____ 7. JavaScript (681)
_____ 8. VBScript (681)
_____ 9. Perl (681)
_____ 10. XHTML (682)

a. interpreted language used to add dynamic content and interactive elements to Web pages
b. object-oriented language that uses a just-in-time compiler
c. visual programming tool for Web-based enterprises
d. simple, interactive, problem-solving procedural language
e. procedural language designed for business applications
f. used to add intelligence and interactivity to Web pages
g. powerful procedural language that requires professional programming skills
h. once a procedural language, but the latest release is an interpreted scripting language
i. nonprocedural language that assists in report generation
j. visual programming language used for object-based programs
k. markup language that enables Web sites to display more easily on microbrowsers
l. object-oriented extension of the C programming language

SHORT ANSWER

Write a brief answer to each of the following questions.

1. How is a compiler different from an interpreter? ___________ What is the advantage, and disadvantage, of an interpreter? ___________
2. What is a macro? ___________ How are macros created? ________
3. What is a script, an applet, a servlet, and an ActiveX control? ___________ Why are they used? ___________
4. What are program flowcharts and pseudocode? ___________ How is a desk check different from a structured walkthrough? ___________
5. What is debugging? ___________ How is a logic error different from a syntax error? ___________

WORKING TOGETHER

Working with a group of your classmates, complete the following team exercises.

1. To address the problem of out-of-date hardware and software, a new wave of Web sites delivers software and services online. Microsoft Office Online, for example, provides a choice for Office customers who prefer the benefits of centrally managed software. Have each member of your team investigate the possibilities of online software. Then, create a PowerPoint presentation addressing the advantages and disadvantages of obtaining software online. In particular, focus your presentation on software errors and the possible impact of those errors. Share your presentation with your class.
2. Choose one Issue from the following issues in this chapter: Should Students Learn Computer Programming? (677), Should You Know HTML? (683), Who Will Be Future Programmers? (685), Could You Be a Computer Programmer? (688), or Who Is Responsible for Bugs? (697). Use the Web and/or print media to research the issue. Then, present a debate for the class, with different members of your team supporting different responses to the questions that accompany the issue.
3. Choosing a programming language is an important decision. A poor choice can result in a program that is difficult, incompatible, or unproductive. Have each member of your team interview someone in the IT department of a local organization about recently developed software. What application was developed? What programming language was used? Why? What factors were important in selecting the programming language? Were other factors considered (such as the expertise of available programmers)? In hindsight, was the best language chosen? Why or why not? Meet with your team to discuss the results of your interviews. Then, create a PowerPoint presentation to share your findings with the class.

LEARN IT ONLINE

QUIZZES AND LEARNING GAMES
Computer Genius
Crossword Puzzle
Interactive Labs
Practice Test
Quiz Yourself
Wheel of Terms

EXERCISES
Chapter Review
Checkpoint
Key Terms
Lab Exercises
Learn It Online
Web Research

BEYOND THE BOOK
Apply It
Career Corner
Companies
FAQ
High-Tech Talk
Issues
Looking Ahead
Trailblazers
Web Links

FEATURES
Guide to Web Sites
Making Use of the Web
Tech News
Timeline 2005

Use the Learn It Online exercises to reinforce your understanding of the chapter concepts.

WEB INSTRUCTIONS:

To display this page from the Web, start your browser and enter the Web address **scsite.com/dc2005/ch13/learn**.

1 At the Movies – JavaOne Conference

To view the JavaOne Conference movie, click the number 1 button. Watch the movie and then complete the exercise by answering the questions below. Java is a programming language used to write software. Since its inception in 1995, it has gained a major presence on the Internet and has drawn a near-cult following. More than a third of global billion-dollar companies use Java somewhere in their enterprises. IBM, Hewlett-Packard, Nokia, and Sony are just a few of the companies that have jumped onto the Java bandwagon. The JavaOne Conference currently is the world's largest software developer conference. The video states that Java is open-source software. What does this mean? Is Java a visual or object-oriented programming language? How do you account for Java's popularity?

2 Student Edition Labs – Visual Programming

Click the number 2 button. When the Student Edition Labs menu appears, click *Visual Programming* to begin. A new browser window will open. Follow the on-screen instructions to complete the Lab. When finished, click the Exit button. If required, print a copy of your results to submit to your instructor.

3 Student Edition Labs – Creating Web Pages

Click the number 3 button. When the Student Edition Labs menu appears, click *Creating Web Pages* to begin. A new browser window will open. Follow the on-screen instructions to complete the Lab. When finished, click the Exit button. If required, print a copy of your results to submit to your instructor.

4 Image Maps

One common use of a script is to create an image map — a Web page picture that points to a URL and is used in place of, or in addition to, plain text hyperlinks (shown in the figure below). When you click a part of the picture, the Web browser locates the corresponding URL and sends the Web page to your computer. To work with image maps on Web pages, click the number 4 button and complete this exercise.

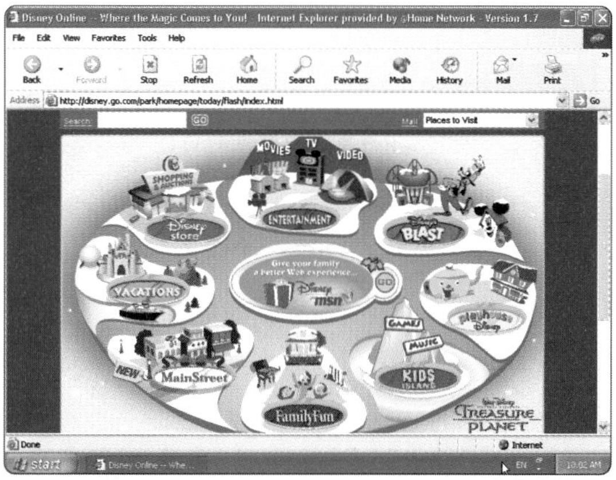

5 Practice Test

Click the number 5 button. Answer each question. When completed, enter your name and click the Grade Test button to submit the quiz for grading. Make a note of any missed questions. If required, print a copy to submit to your instructor.

6 Web Guide

Click the number 6 button to display the Guide to Web Sites and Searching Techniques Web page. Click Reference and then click Ask Jeeves. Search for Java programming. Click one of the Java programming links. Use your word processing program to prepare a brief report about your findings and submit your assignment to your instructor.

7 Scavenger Hunt

Click the number 7 button. Print a copy of the Scavenger Hunt page; use this page to write down your answers as you search the Web. Submit your completed page to your instructor.

8 Who Wants To Be a Computer Genius?

Click the number 8 button to find out if you are a computer genius. Directions on how to play the game will be displayed. When you are ready to play, click the Play button. Submit your score to your instructor.

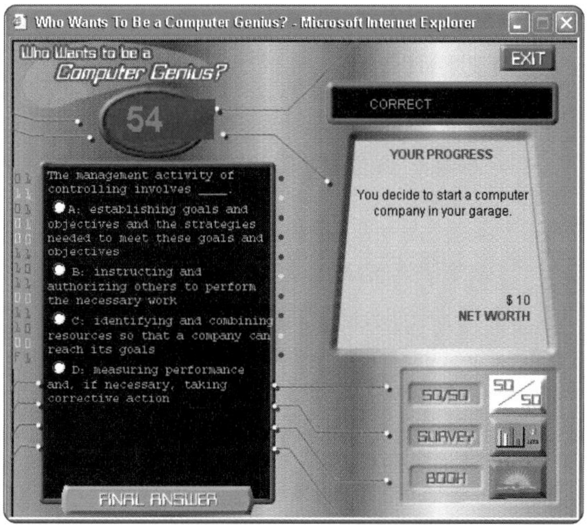

9 Wheel of Terms

Click the number 9 button to reinforce important terms you learned in this chapter by playing the Shelly Cashman Series version of this popular game. Directions on how to play the game will be displayed. When you are ready to play, click the Play button. Submit your score to your instructor.

10 Career Corner

Click the number 10 button to display the IBM page. Click a link of interest to you and then review the information. Write a brief report describing what you learned. Submit the report to your instructor.

11 Search Sleuth

Click the number 11 button to learn search techniques that will help make you a research expert. Submit the completed assignment to your instructor.

12 Crossword Puzzle Challenge

Click the number 12 button. Complete the puzzle to reinforce skills you learned in this chapter. Directions on how to play the game will be displayed. When you are ready to play, click the Submit button. Submit the completed puzzle to your instructor.

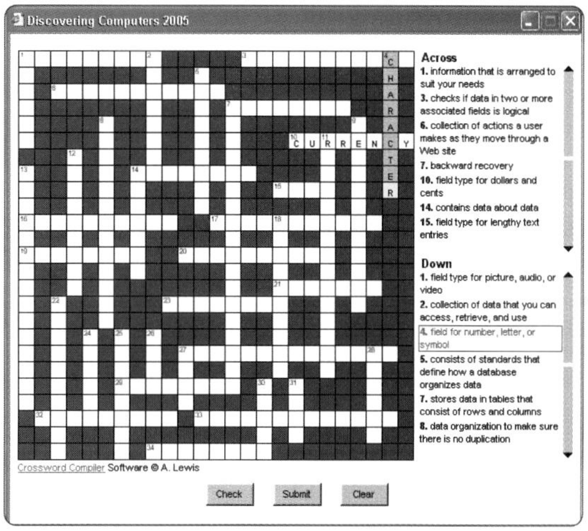

13 Application Generators

When using an application generator, a developer works with menu-driven tools that have easy-to-use graphical interfaces. To use an application generator to produce Web pages, click the number 13 button and complete this exercise.

14 In the News

Programming is not just for programmers anymore. Yaroze is a Japanese expression meaning, let us work together. Net Yaroze is a project that lets members and educational institutions work together with Sony to create their own games for Sony's PlayStation. Increasingly, entertainment and productivity applications are offering tools, such as macros, that allow users to program their own innovations. Click the number 14 button and read a news article about programming. Who is doing the programming? How is the programming different?

CHAPTER 13 LAB EXERCISES

QUIZZES AND LEARNING GAMES
Computer Genius
Crossword Puzzle
Interactive Labs
Practice Test
Quiz Yourself
Wheel of Terms
EXERCISES
Chapter Review
Checkpoint
Key Terms
Lab Exercises
Learn It Online
Web Research
BEYOND THE BOOK
Apply It
Career Corner
Companies
FAQ
High-Tech Talk
Issues
Looking Ahead
Trailblazers
Web Links
FEATURES
Guide to Web Sites
Making Use of the Web
Tech News
Timeline 2005

Use the Lab Exercises to gain hands-on computer experience.

WEB INSTRUCTIONS:

To display this page from the Web, start your browser and enter the Web address **scsite.com/dc2005/ch13/lab**.

1 Searching for Executable Files

This exercise uses Windows XP procedures. In Windows, application files have an .exe extension, meaning that they are executable. To find the executable program files on your computer, click the Start button on the taskbar, and then click Search on the Start menu. In the Search Results window, if necessary, click View on the menu bar, and then click Details. Click the All files and folders link on the left. Type `*.exe` in the All or part of the file name text box. Select Local Hard Drives (C:) in the Look in list. Click the Search button. Sort the files alphabetically by name by clicking the Name column heading. Scroll through the list of files and find the file name, Notepad.exe. In what folder is Notepad.exe located? How large is the file? Close the Search Results window.

2 Movie Box Office Simulation

This exercise uses Windows XP/2000/98 procedures. Insert the Data Disk into drive A. See the inside back cover of this book for instructions for downloading the Data Disk or see your instructor for information on accessing the files required in this book. Click the Start button on the taskbar and then click Run on the Start menu. In the Open text box, type `a:movie.exe` and then click the OK button. This program was written in Visual Basic. The first customer purchases three tickets to a matinee performance of *The Abyss*. Notice the amount due and then click the Enter button. Enter the following transactions and then write down the amount due for each transaction: (1) `The Client, no matinee, 3 tickets`; (2) `Forrest Gump, matinee, 1 ticket`; (3) `Beverly Hills Cop, matinee, 2 tickets`. Close the Movie Box Office program.

3 Adjusting Keyboard Speed

This exercise uses Windows XP procedures. Windows allows users to adjust the keyboard to their own specifications. To customize the keyboard, click the Start button on the taskbar and then click Control Panel on the Start menu. In Category View, click the Printers and Other Hardware icon. Click the Keyboard icon in the Printers and Other Hardware window. When the Keyboard Properties dialog box is displayed, if necessary, click the Speed tab. Use the Question Mark button on the title bar to answer the following questions: What is repeat delay? What is repeat rate? Click the Cancel button in the Keyboard Properties dialog box. Close the Printers and Other Hardware window.

4 Loan Payment Calculator

This exercise uses Windows XP/2000/98 procedures. Insert the Data Disk into drive A. Click the Start button on the taskbar, and then click Run on the Start menu to display the Run dialog box. In the Open text box, type `a:loancalc.exe` and then click the OK button to open the Loan Payment Calculator window. This program was written in Visual Basic. Type `12500` in the LOAN AMOUNT text box. Click the YEARS right scroll arrow or drag the scroll box until YEARS equals 15. Click the APR right scroll arrow or drag the scroll box until APR equals 8.5. Click the Calculate button. Write down the monthly payment and sum of payments. Click the Clear button. What are the monthly payment and sum of payments for each of these loan amounts, years, and APRs? (1) 28000, 5, 7.25; (2) 98750, 30, 9; (3) 6000, 3, 8.75; and (4) 62500, 15, 9.25. Close the Loan Payment Calculator.

WEB RESEARCH

Use the Web Research exercises to learn more about the special features in this chapter.

WEB INSTRUCTIONS:

Use the link in each exercise or a search engine such as Google (google.com) to research the topic. Then, write a one-page, double-spaced report or create a presentation, unless otherwise directed below. Page numbers on which information can be found are in parentheses.

1 **Issue** Choose one Issue from the following issues in this chapter: Should Students Learn Computer Programming? (677), Should You Know HTML? (683), Who Will Be Future Programmers? (685), Could You Be a Computer Programmer? (688), or Who Is Responsible for Bugs? (697). Use the Web to research the issue. Discuss the issue with classmates, instructors, and friends. Address the questions that accompany the issue in a report or presentation.

2 **Apply It** Choose one of the following Apply It features in this chapter: Virtual Reality Chess Match Ends in a Draw (687) or Beta Testing Offers Benefits (697). Use the Web to gather additional information about the topic. Print two Web pages that relate to the Apply It. Detail in a report or presentation what you learned.

3 **Career Corner** Read the Career Corner article in this chapter (698). Use the Web to find out more about the career. Describe the career in a report or presentation.

4 **Companies on the Cutting Edge** Choose one of the Companies on the Cutting Edge in this chapter (700). Use the Web to research the company further. Explain in a report or presentation how this company has contributed to computer technology.

5 **Technology Trailblazers** Choose one of the Technology Trailblazers in this chapter (701). Use the Web to research the person further. Explain in a report or presentation how this individual has affected the way people use, or think about, computers.

6 **Picture Yourself Learning How to Program** Read the Picture Yourself Learning How to Program story at the beginning of this chapter (662). Use the Web to research programming further. Describe in a report or presentation the ways in which you might use programming.

7 **High-Tech Talk** Read the High-Tech Talk feature in this chapter (699). Use the Web to find out more about the topic. Summarize in a report or presentation what you learned.

8 **Web Links** Review the Web Link boxes found in the margins of this chapter. Visit five of the Web Link sites. Print the main Web page for each site you visit. Choose one of the Web pages and then summarize in one paragraph the content of the Web page.

9 **Looking Ahead** Choose one of the Looking Ahead articles in this chapter: Seeing Clearly with Vision Systems (685) or Genetic Programming Solves Complex Problems (696). Use the Web to find out more about the topic. Detail in a report or presentation what you learned.

10 **FAQ** Choose one FAQ found in this chapter. Use the Web to find out more about the topic. Summarize in one paragraph what you learned.

11 **Making Use of the Web** Read the Research section of Making Use of the Web in Appendix A (APP 26). Complete the Research Web Exercises at the end of the section (APP 27). Answer the questions posed in each exercise.

CHAPTER 14

Enterprise Computing

Picture Yourself Interacting with Customer Service

With your holiday party just around the corner, you still are waiting anxiously for a replacement part for your oven that you can install yourself. The part did not arrive today, as you expected. After you call the company's customer support telephone number, an automated message suggests you visit the company's Web site for customer support issues. You wonder how much of your day will be spent dealing with the enormous, multinational corporation.

After typing your e-mail address on the customer support Web site, you enter a chat session with a live customer support person. She checks the order and informs you it was delayed at the shipping dock. She apologizes and tells you that the shipping dock can ship the part overnight. She also checked with the store where you purchased the oven, and informs you that you can drive there right now to pick up the part. Additionally, she has instructed the store manager to give you a free DVD from your favorite movie director if you stop by. As you type a note thanking her, you are shocked at how quickly all this happened. How did she know about your replacement part just from your e-mail address? How did she communicate so quickly with the shipping dock and the store where you shop? And how does she know what movies you like?

As you read Chapter 14, you will learn about enterprise computing and how large organizations manage data and information.

OBJECTIVES

After completing this chapter, you will be able to:

1. Discuss the special information requirements of an enterprise-sized corporation
2. Identify information systems used in the functional units of an enterprise
3. List general purpose and integrated information systems used throughout an enterprise
4. List types of technologies used throughout an enterprise
5. Explain how e-retailing works
6. Identify e-commerce market sectors
7. Discuss the computer hardware needs and solutions for an enterprise
8. Determine why computer backup is important and how it is accomplished
9. Discuss the steps in a disaster recovery plan
10. Discuss the importance of computer security in an enterprise

CONTENTS

WHAT IS ENTERPRISE COMPUTING?

A large organization, commonly referred to as an **enterprise**, requires special computing solutions because of its size and large geographical extent. The term, enterprise, commonly describes a business or venture of any size. In this chapter, the term enterprise refers to large multinational corporations, universities, hospitals, research laboratories, and government organizations. **Enterprise computing** involves the use of computers in networks, such as LANs and WANs, or series of interconnected networks that encompass a variety of different operating systems, protocols, and network architectures.

Enterprises produce and gather enormous volumes of information regarding customer, supplier, and employee activity. The information flows among a variety of entities both inside and outside of the enterprise, and users consume the information during a variety of activities (Figure 14-1). Customers, suppliers, and employees interact with the enterprise in a variety of ways, and computers track each interaction. Each sale of a product, purchase of a piece of equipment, or paycheck generates activity involving information systems.

Large computers connected by vast networks allow the enterprise to manage and distribute information quickly and efficiently. Procedures safeguard information when disaster strikes. Security policies ensure that people, computers, and networks access only the information they require.

For example, when a customer purchases goods or services on a Web site, many activities occur behind the scenes at a company.

FIGURE 14-1 An enterprise manages large amounts of information over an extensive geographic area and disparate groups of people.

A customer views an advertisement on a Web site created by the company's marketing department. The customer purchases a product at a Web site. The customer makes a credit card payment that is processed by a financial system connected to the company's bank. The company's accounting system records the payment and transaction. The distribution center receives a message telling it to ship the product. The marketing department notes the advertising that was successful in generating the sale to the customer, and informs the sales department that this customer may be interested in purchasing complementary products.

When the customer calls to check the status of an order, a computer routes the telephone call to the proper customer service representative who checks the status of the order in a database shared with the distribution department. Finally, the activity generated by the purchase finds its way onto management reports, and managers make decisions based on the information collected in the purchase process. For example, a manager may make a decision to order more parts for inventory because a product is selling particularly well.

As just illustrated, information is combined and analyzed by the management and decisions are made based on the information. The divisions and departments within the enterprise use specialized hardware and software to perform their tasks. These same units may share hardware and software with each other to become more effective. Some large organizations employ enterprise-wide networks that help manage all aspects of a company and are used by many or all of the divisions and departments.

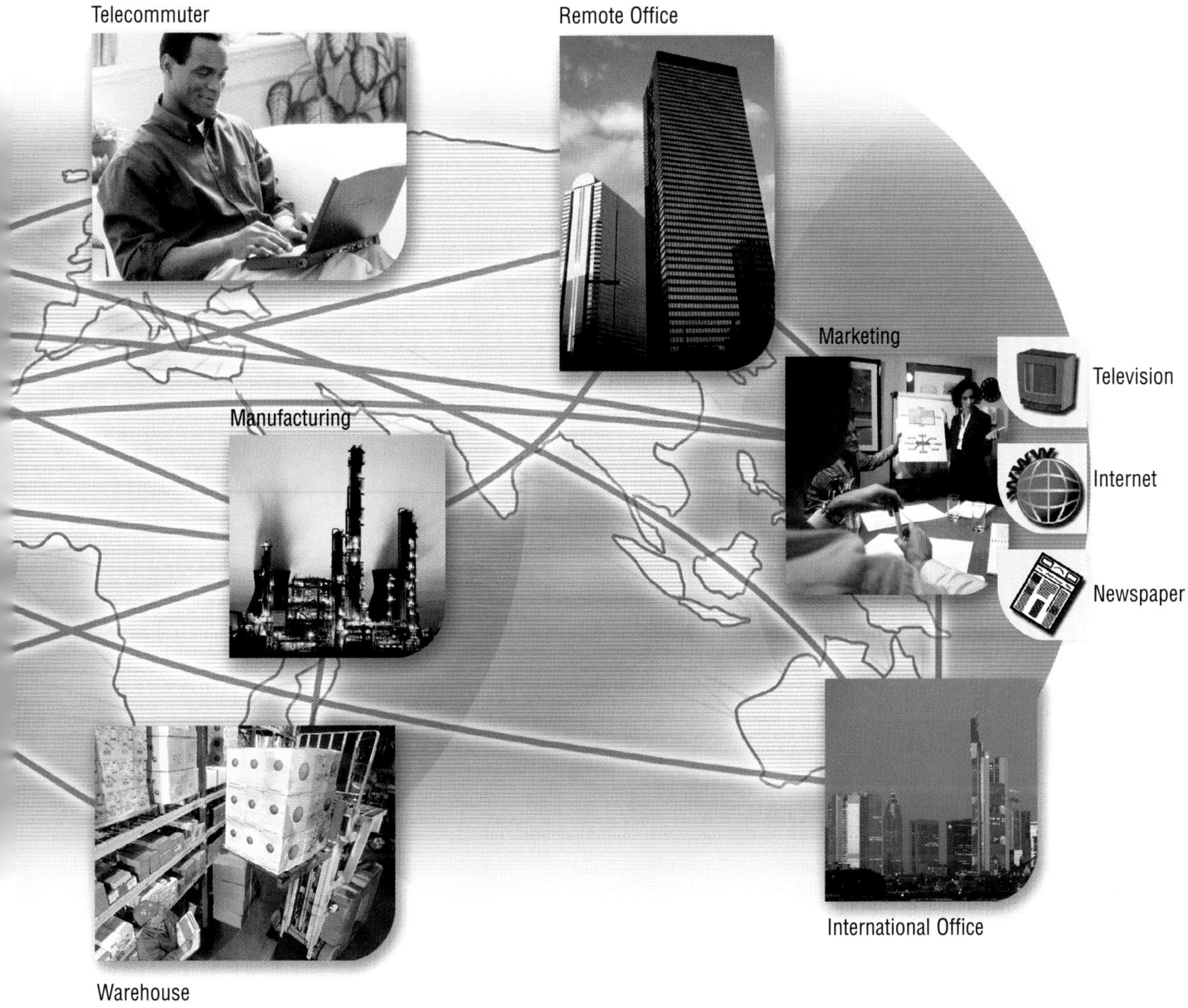

Organizational Structure of an Enterprise

Most traditional enterprises are organized in a hierarchical manner. Figure 14-2 shows an example of an organization chart of a large manufacturing company. Managers at the first two levels at the top of the chart, including the Chief Executive Officer (CEO), mainly concern themselves with strategic decisions and long-term planning.

The activities relating to running the business are called *supporting activities.* Supporting activities usually are separated from those involving what the business does, which are the *core activities. Operations* refer to the core activities of a business, and involve the creation, selling, and support of the products and services that the company produces. In Figure 14-2, the Chief Operations Officer (COO) manages the core activities. The supporting activities include financial departments and information technology (IT) departments. In Figure 14-2, the Chief Financial Officer (CFO) and the Chief Information Officer (CIO) lead these supporting roles.

Each enterprise includes its own special needs and the organizational structure of every enterprise varies. Companies may include all or some of the managers and departments shown in Figure 14-2. Companies also may include additional departments or combine some of those shown.

A *decentralized* approach to information technology exists when departments and divisions

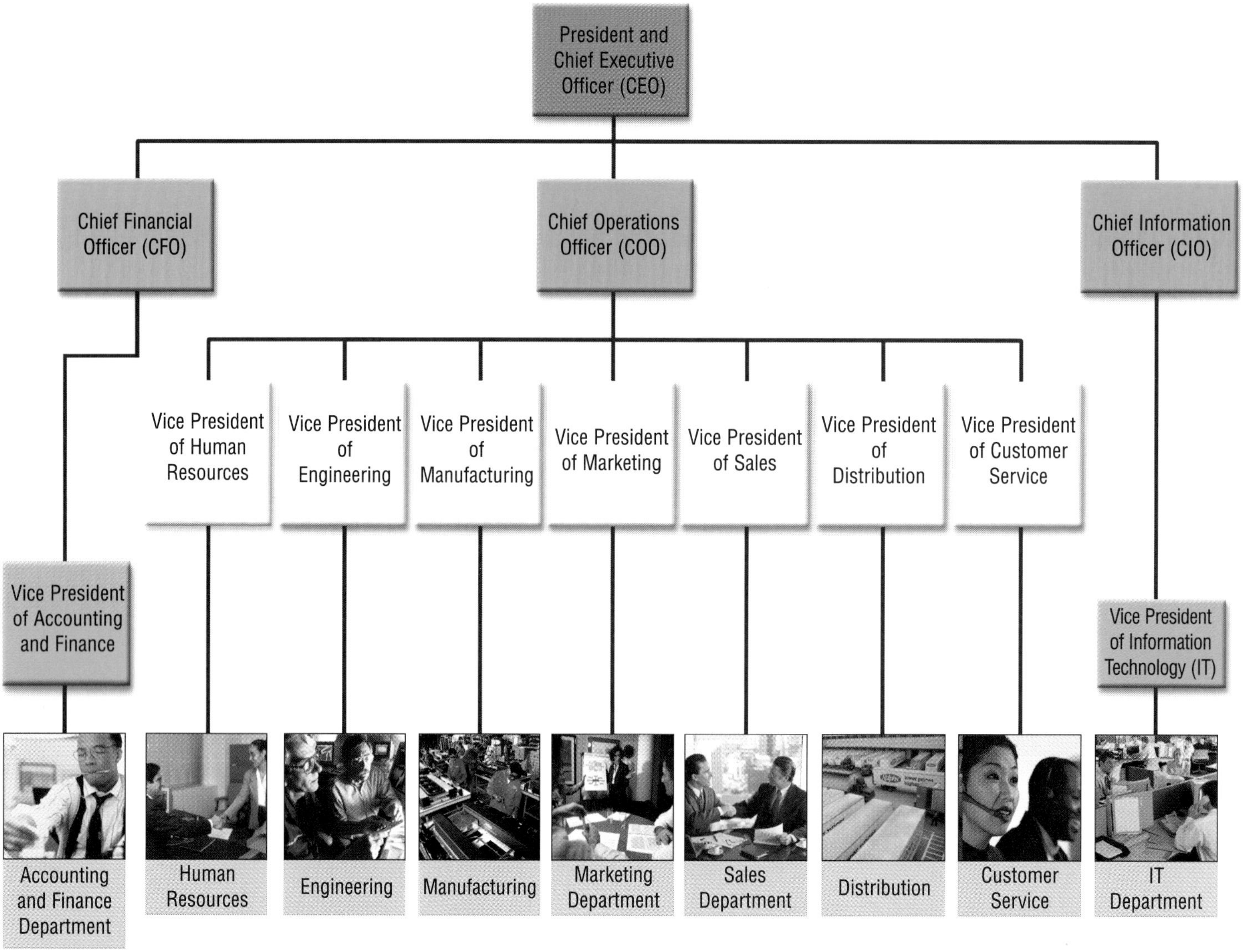

FIGURE 14-2 A typical organization chart for an enterprise illustrates the hierarchy within the enterprise.

maintain their own information systems. Some companies maintain central computers, supported by a central IT department, referred to as a *centralized* approach to information technology. Companies decide whether to support a centralized or decentralized approach based on a number of factors, including cost, efficiency, and the interdependence of departments. A centralized approach to information systems usually reduces costs of maintenance and increases manageability. A decentralized approach allows for greater flexibility, allowing each functional unit or department to customize information systems to their particular needs. Both centralized and decentralized approaches focus on the sharing of information with other departments and divisions.

Levels of Users

In an enterprise, users typically fall into one of four categories: executive management, middle management, operational management, and nonmanagement employees (Figure 14-3). The types of information that users require often depends on their employee level in the company. The following paragraphs discuss the four categories of users and their information requirements.

EXECUTIVE MANAGEMENT **Executive management**, which includes the highest management positions in a company, focuses on the long-range direction of the company. These managers primarily are responsible for *strategic decisions* that center on the company's overall goals and objectives. Executive management oversees middle management.

MIDDLE MANAGEMENT **Middle management** is responsible for implementing the strategic decisions of executive management. Middle managers make *tactical decisions*, which are short-range decisions that apply specific programs and plans necessary to meet the stated objectives. Middle management oversees operational management.

OPERATIONAL MANAGEMENT **Operational management** supervises the production, clerical, and other nonmanagement employees of a company. In performing their duties, operational managers make numerous operational decisions. An *operational decision* involves day-to-day activities within the company. These decisions should be consistent with and support the tactical decisions made by middle management.

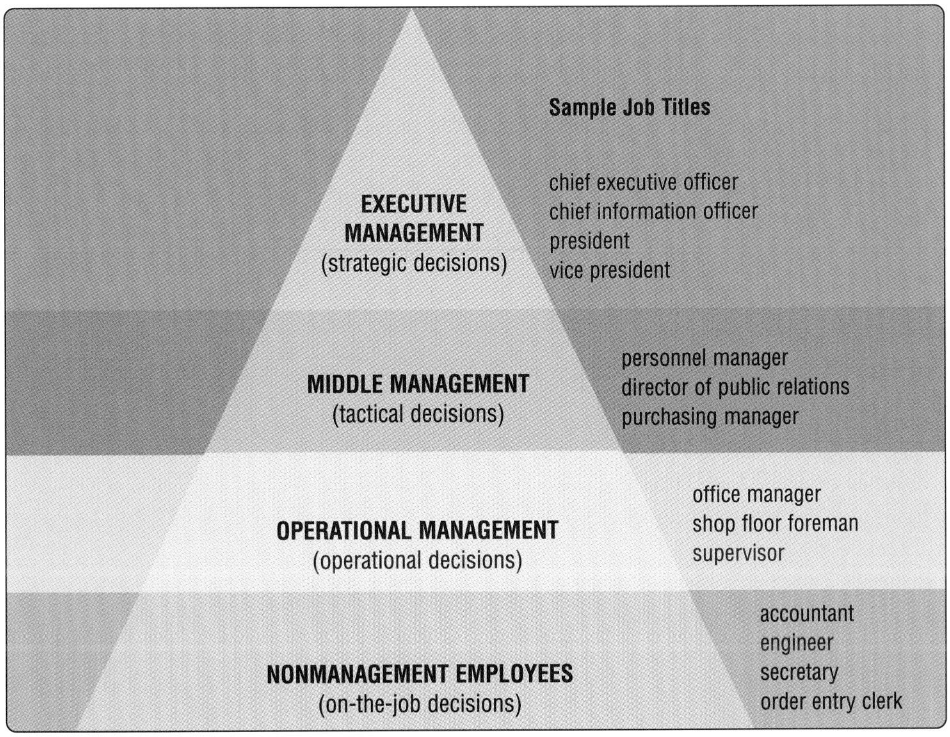

FIGURE 14-3 This pyramid illustrates the levels of users, sample job titles of each level of user, and the types of decisions these users make.

NONMANAGEMENT EMPLOYEES

Nonmanagement employees include production, clerical, and other personnel. Nonmanagement employees frequently need information to perform their jobs. Today, these employees have more information available to them than in the past. They have access to the information necessary to make decisions that previously were made by managers — a trend called *empowering* users.

How Managers Use Information

Enterprise information is the information gathered in the ongoing operations of an enterprise-sized organization. Enterprise information begins with the day-to-day transactions that occur within a company, such as sales receipts or payroll checks. The company gathers and stores the information. Over time, employees collect, combine, and analyze the information. Ultimately, the role of information gathered in this way is to allow managers to make better decisions.

All employees, including managers, in a company need accurate information to perform their jobs effectively. **Managers** are responsible for coordinating and controlling an organization's resources. Resources include people, money, materials, and information. Managers coordinate these resources by performing four activities: planning, organizing, leading, and controlling (read Issue 14-1 for a related discussion).

- *Planning* involves establishing goals and objectives. It also includes deciding on the strategies needed to meet these goals and objectives.
- *Organizing* includes identifying and combining resources so that the company can reach its goals and objectives. Organizing also involves setting up the management structure of a company, such as the departments and reporting relationships.
- *Leading*, sometimes referred to as directing, involves instructing and authorizing others to perform the necessary work.
- *Controlling* involves measuring performance and, if necessary, taking corrective action.

ISSUE 14-1

Would You Work in a Monitored Office?

Once, the main concern of an office loafer was the snitch at the next desk. Now, a lazy worker has more to worry about. Employers can use a number of products to monitor employee activity. Software can track Internet use, scrutinize keyboard activity, and even observe general office behavior. One privacy group estimates that more than one-third of today's office employees are subject to some form of electronic surveillance. New software uses a digital video camera with real-time image recognition to watch and record all office activity. Advocates argue that employee monitoring conserves office resources and makes workers more productive. Opponents maintain, however, that constant inspection results in uncomfortable, unimaginative, and less productive employees. Besides, they insist, such observation is an invasion of privacy. Should employers use computers to monitor some, or all, office activity? Why or why not? How does employee monitoring affect worker productivity? Why? Would you want to work in an area where all your actions were monitored constantly? Why or why not?

For more information about employee monitoring, visit the Discovering Computers 2005 Issues Web page (**scsite.com/dc2005/issues**). Click Issue #1 below Chapter 14.

Figure 14-4 shows how these four management activities usually occur in an order that forms an endless cycle. During the controlling activity, managers measure actual performance against a previously established plan. Following this measurement, they may revise the plan. Revised plans may result in additional organizational and leadership activities. Managers then measure performance against the revised plan, and the cycle repeats itself. The four tasks are linked. A change in one task usually affects one or more of the other tasks.

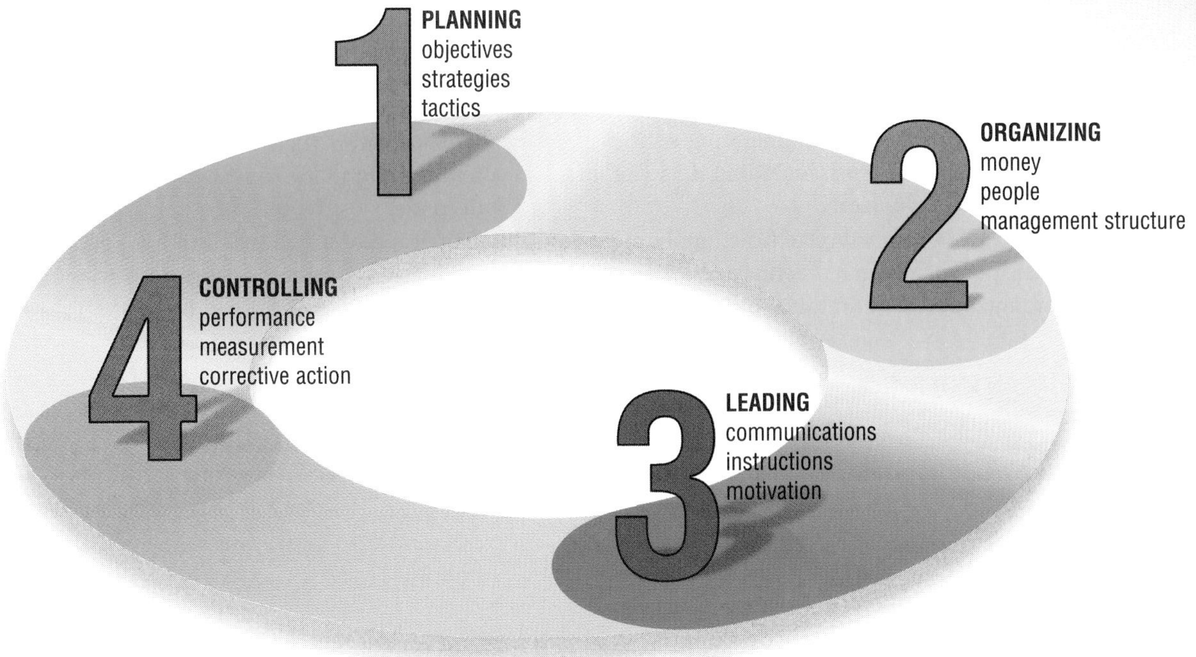

FIGURE 14-4 The four management activities include planning, organizing, leading, and controlling. The activities usually are performed in a continuous sequence.

INFORMATION SYSTEMS IN THE ENTERPRISE

An **information system** is a set of hardware, software, data, people, and procedures that works together to produce information (Figure 14-5). A *procedure* is an instruction, or set of instructions, a user follows to accomplish an activity. An information system supports daily, short-term, and long-range activities of users in a company.

Information systems can be used in a variety of ways in an enterprise. Some information systems are used exclusively by only one type of department, or unit, within the enterprise. General purpose information systems include categories of information systems that can be used by almost any department within the enterprise. Integrated information systems are used by multiple departments and facilitate information sharing and communication within the enterprise. The following sections discuss each of these three uses of information systems.

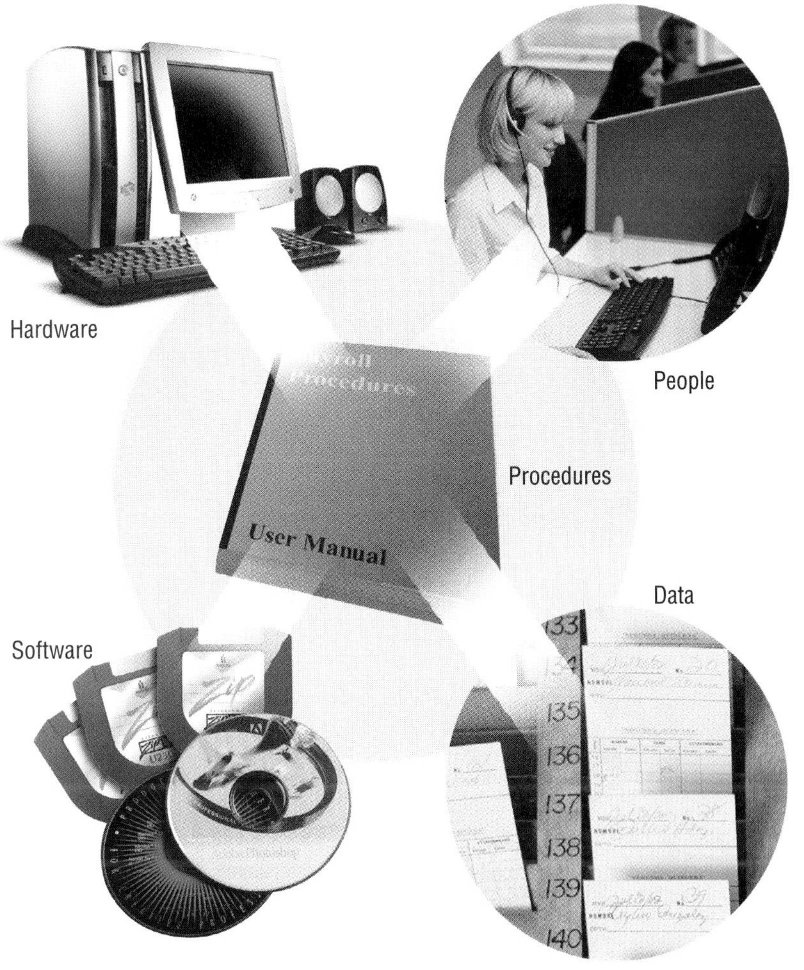

FIGURE 14-5 An information system typically contains five components: hardware, software, data, people, and procedures.

WEB LINK 14-1

Employee Relationship Management

Visit the Discovering Computers 2005 WEB LINK page (**scsite.com/dc2005/weblink**). Click Employee Relationship Management below Chapter 14.

Information Systems within Functional Units

A typical enterprise consists of hundreds or thousands of individual operating entities, called *functional units*, including departments, centers, and divisions.

Figure 14-6 lists typical functional units and their purpose within an enterprise. Often, organizations within the enterprise may have similar responsibilities within the divisions to which they belong. For example, a large automobile company may organize its divisions based on the model of car that the business unit produces.

Each division includes a group of engineers that designs the automobiles. Each of the engineering groups may have similar or different information systems based on its needs or the culture of the company. Some companies allow for independence within their divisions, while others attempt to standardize systems across the enterprise.

Each type of functional unit has specialized requirements for their information systems. These units can be grouped by the functions they perform. The types of functional units within a typical manufacturing enterprise are human resources, accounting and finance, engineering, manufacturing, marketing, sales, distribution, customer service, and information technology. The sections that follow discuss the types of information systems and software used within the units.

HUMAN RESOURCES **Human Resources Information Systems (HRIS)** manage one or more human resources functions (Figure 14-7). An HRIS and its associated software help a company such as Wal-Mart maintain records on its 1.3 million employees.

FUNCTIONAL UNITS WITHIN AN ENTERPRISE

Functional Unit	Description
Human Resources (HR)	Responsible for recruiting and promoting employees, maintaining employee records, evaluating employees, training employees, and managing employee benefits and compensation.
Accounting and Finance	Responsible for managing the business's money. Accounting department tracks every financial transaction that occurs within the company. Finance department manages the business's money as efficiently as possible.
Engineering or Product Development	Responsible for developing ideas into a product that can be used by customers. Ensures that the product can be manufactured effectively and designs the methods for manufacturing the product.
Manufacturing	Responsible for converting raw materials into physical products.
Marketing	Responsible for researching the market in which a business operates to determine the products and features that the business should develop. Determines the demographics to target with sales efforts and informs the target market about the company's products through advertising and education.
Sales	Responsible for selling the company's products and services.
Distribution	Responsible for delivery of products to customers.
Customer Service	Responsible for maintaining a relationship with a customer both before and after a sale has been made.
Information Technology	Responsible for designing, purchasing, implementing, testing, and maintaining information systems for the rest of the organization. Sometimes called the information services (IS) department.

FIGURE 14-6 An enterprise is composed of several functional units.

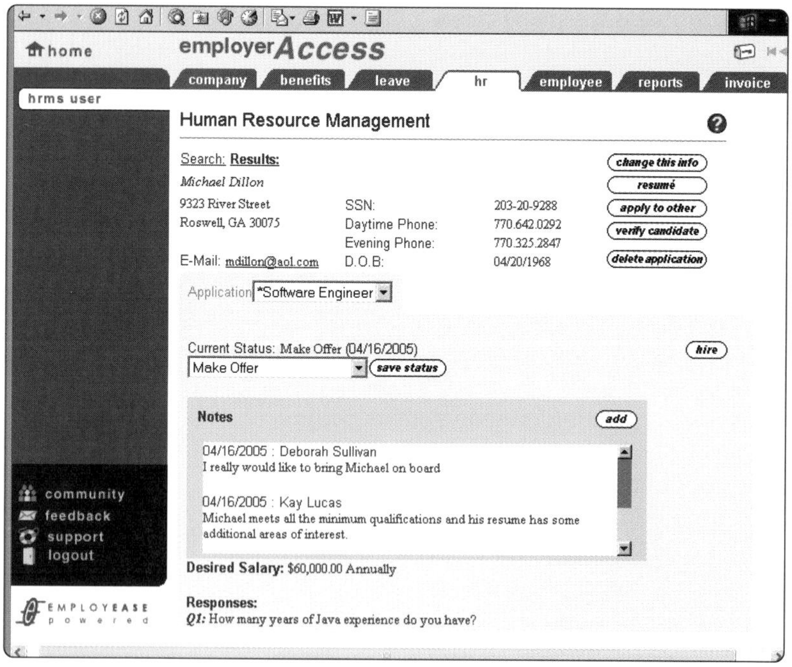

FIGURE 14-7 A human resources information system (HRIS) allows human resources personnel to manage employee information such as benefits, personal information, performance evaluations, training, and vacation time.

An *employee relationship management* (*ERM*) *system* automates and manages much of the communications between employees and the business. An ERM system facilitates communication with employees. For example, an employee may interact with ERM software to gather information regarding the employee's retirement account. Most ERM software applications include a Web interface for the employees and the human resources personnel, allowing both to interact with the system when they are in the office or at home.

ACCOUNTING AND FINANCE Figure 14-8 illustrates the separate functions of accounting and financial systems used by accounting and finance departments. Accounting software manages everyday transactions, such as sales and payments to suppliers. Financial software helps managers budget, forecast, and analyze. Both types of software include comprehensive and flexible reporting tools to assist managers in making decisions, provide historical documentation, and meet regulatory requirements.

ENGINEERING OR PRODUCT DEVELOPMENT Professional workers, such as engineers, require specialized software and systems to perform their tasks. **Computer-aided design (CAD)** uses a computer and special software to aid in engineering, drafting, and design (Figure 14-9). Using CAD offers several advantages over traditional manual drafting methods. CAD software, for example, allows a designer to modify a design more easily than before, as well as dynamically change the size of some or all of the subject and view the design from different angles.

WEB LINK 14-2

CAD

Visit the Discovering Computers 2005 WEB LINK page (**scsite.com/dc2005/weblink**). Click CAD below Chapter 14.

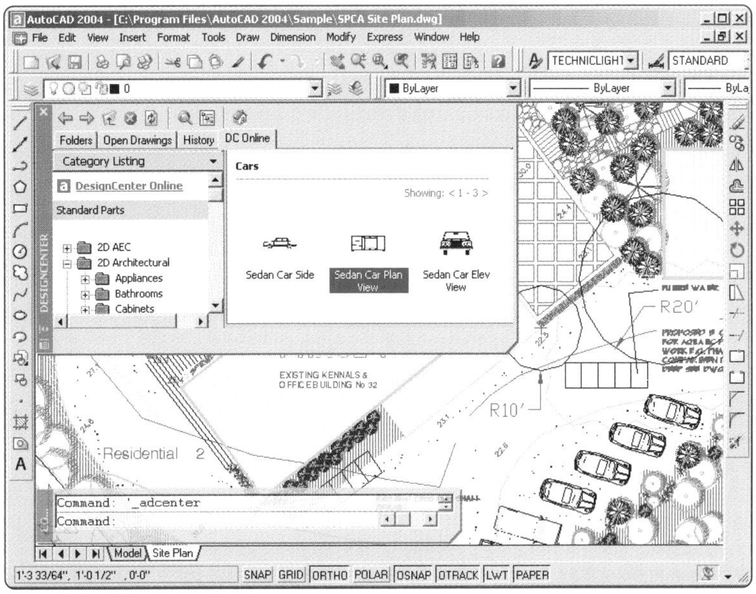

FIGURE 14-9 Computer-aided design (CAD) is an efficient way to develop plans for new products.

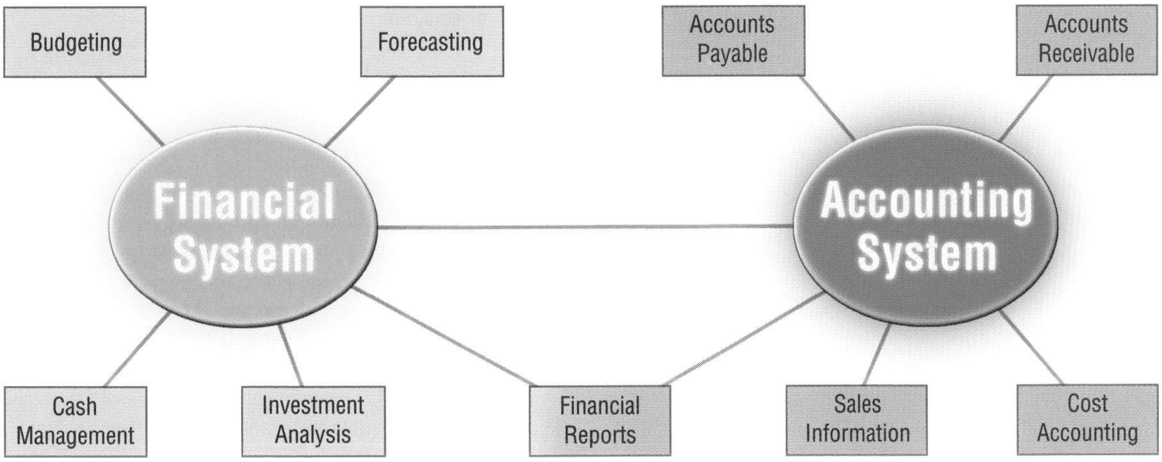

FIGURE 14-8 Accounting and financial systems perform different tasks, but share information and produce financial reports that help management make decisions.

Computer-aided engineering (**CAE**) uses computers to test product designs. Using CAE, engineers can test the design of a car or bridge before it is built. These sophisticated programs simulate the effects of wind, temperature, weight, and stress on product shapes and materials. CAE also allows engineers to create a computer prototype for use in testing under a variety of conditions, such as hurricanes and earthquakes.

MANUFACTURING Manufacturing information systems and software not only assist in the actual assembly process, but also assist in scheduling and managing the inventory of parts and products. **Computer-aided manufacturing** (**CAM**) is the use of computers to control production equipment. CAM production equipment includes software-controlled drilling, lathe, welding, and milling machines.

WEB LINK 14-3

MRP II

Visit the Discovering Computers 2005 WEB LINK page (**scsite.com/dc2005/weblink**). Click MRP II below Chapter 14.

Computer-integrated manufacturing (**CIM**) uses computers to integrate the many different operations of the manufacturing process, using such technologies as CAD, CAE, and CAM. Using CIM (Figure 14-10), for example, a factory can link individual processes so that production is balanced, efficient, driven by customer demand, and results in high-quality products.

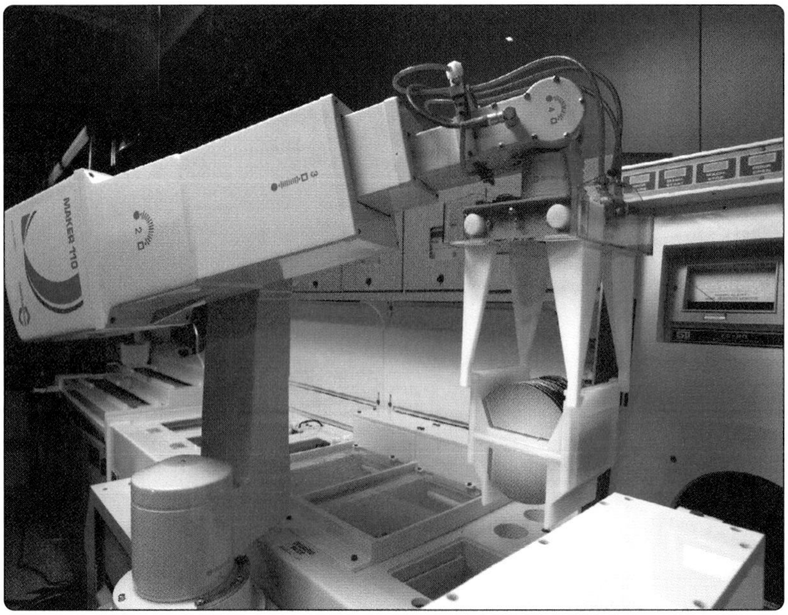

FIGURE 14-10 Computer-integrated manufacturing (CIM) speeds the manufacturing process and reduces product defects.

Formal manufacturing methods help guide enterprises in their manufacturing processes. **Material Requirements Planning** (**MRP**) is an approach to information management in a manufacturing environment that uses software to help monitor and control processes related to production. MRP focuses on issues related to inventory of parts and forecasting future demand so that materials needed for manufacturing can be on hand when they are needed.

Manufacturing Resource Planning II (**MRP II**) is an extension of MRP and also includes software that helps in scheduling, tracking production in real time, and monitoring product quality. Companies use MRP and MRP II systems to facilitate an MRP or MRP II approach to their manufacturing. Read Apply It 14-1 for more information on how parts and equipment can be tracked by a company.

APPLY IT 14-1

Smart Chips Gather Useful Data

Managers often are swamped with reports on everything from production quotas to inventory supplies. One technological innovation that may help them manage their workload is a smart chip.

IBM is one company at the forefront of this technology. Its Global Services department is developing new smart chip applications for e-business. For example, IBM has teamed with Shell Oil Company to develop eShell applications that embed these chips on cards, inventory, or equipment and then gather data that can monitor and manage gas pumps; car wash systems; and heating, ventilation, and air conditioning systems at its stores.

Other smart chip applications will be developed throughout the business community during the next few years. ePurses will be used for cashless purchasing with prepaid funds. In manufacturing, equipment performance will be managed remotely, and inventory status will be monitored. Iris scans and thumbprints will be encrypted for security services.

Smart chip developers also are addressing concerns about security and authentication, especially when the data is transmitted wirelessly from the manufacturing site or business to the manager's office. As smart chip interest increases and the cost of the chip decreases, however, security measures will intensify. Supervisors, therefore, will breathe easier as their workloads become more manageable and their data becomes more secure.

For more information about smart chips, visit the Discovering Computers 2005 Apply It Web page (**scsite.com/dc2005/apply**). Click Apply It #1 below Chapter 14.

MARKETING A **marketing information system** serves as a central repository for the tasks of the marketing functional unit (Figure 14-11). One type of marketing information system is a *market research system*, which stores and analyzes data gathered from demographics and surveys. Many companies gather information via the Web and store information about individuals' Web browsing habits and interests. Market research software assists in target marketing by allowing marketing personnel to query databases based on criteria such as income, gender, previous purchases, and favorite recreational activities. The relationship between marketing and the Internet is discussed later in this chapter.

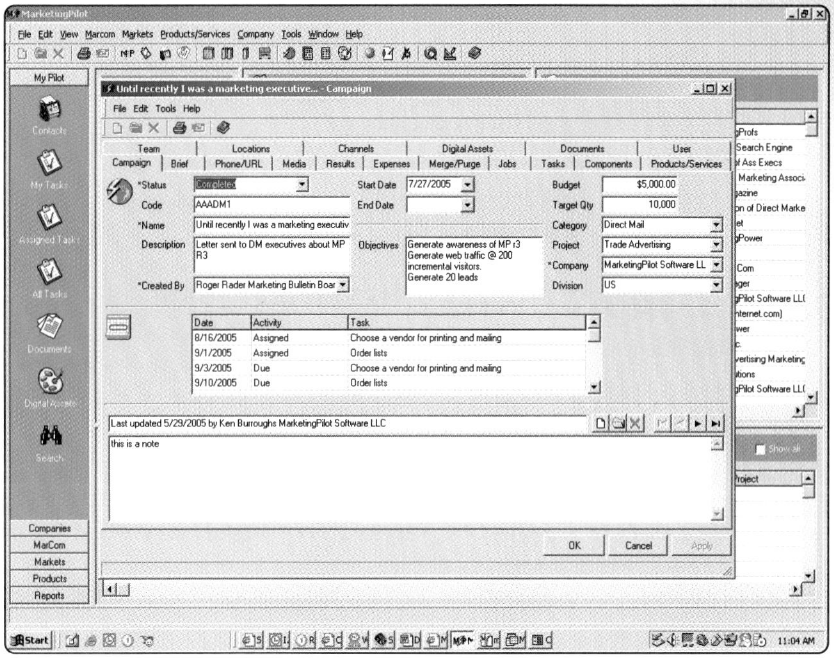

FIGURE 14-11 Marketing information systems allow marketing departments to create marketing campaigns and track their effectiveness.

SALES **Sales force automation** (**SFA**) software equips traveling salespeople with the electronic tools they need to be more productive. SFA software help salespeople manage customer contacts, schedule customer meetings, log customer interactions, manage product information, and take orders from customers.

SFA software (Figure 14-12) often runs on PDAs or notebook computers. The PDA or notebook computer may connect wirelessly to the central office, allowing the salesperson to access up-to-date corporate information in real time no matter where he or she is.

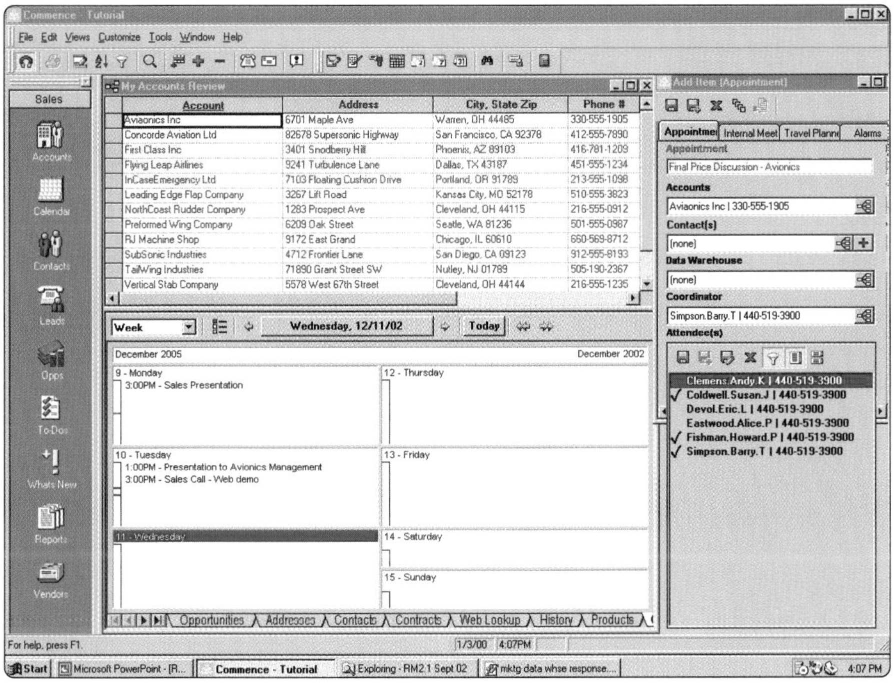

FIGURE 14-12 Sales force automation (SFA) software allows the mobile sales force to manage customer and prospective customer relationships more effectively.

WEB LINK 14-4

Sales Force Automation

Visit the Discovering Computers 2005 WEB LINK page (**scsite.com/dc2005/weblink**). Click Sales Force Automation below Chapter 14.

Alternatively, some SFA programs allow the salesperson to upload information to the central office at the end of the day or end of the week. The programs also allow salespeople to download updated product and pricing information. Read Issue 14-2 for a related discussion.

DISTRIBUTION **Distribution systems** provide forecasting for inventory control, manage and track shipping of products, and provide information and analysis on inventory in warehouses. Some distribution systems rely on GPS and other navigation technologies to track shipping in real time. Distribution systems strive to maximize the value of each shipment made by the company while keeping costs to a minimum.

CUSTOMER SERVICE **Customer interaction management** (**CIM**) software (Figure 14-13) manages the day-to-day interactions with customers, such as telephone calls, e-mail interactions, Web interactions, and instant messaging sessions (read Apply It 14-2 for more information). A CIM program routes customer telephone calls to the most appropriate support person depending on the identity of the customer or responses the customer gives to prompts.

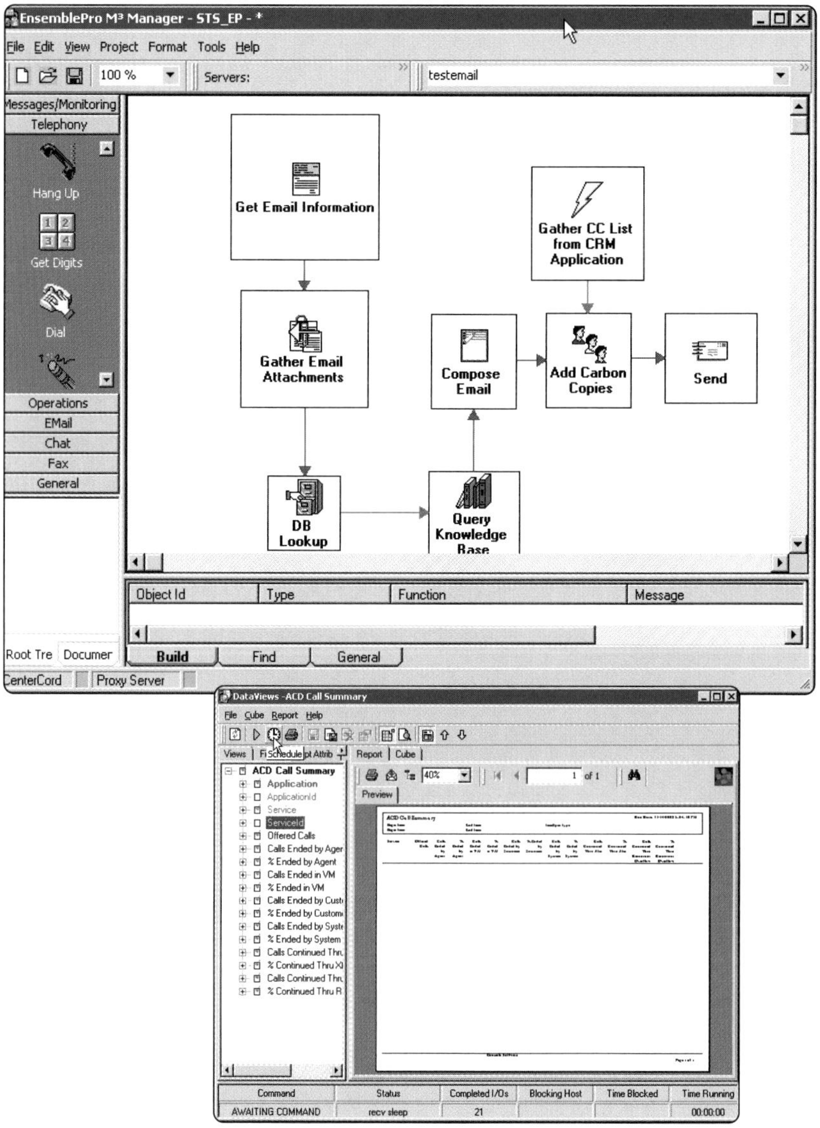

FIGURE 14-13 A customer interaction management (CIM) system manages and reports on daily interactions with customers, such as telephone support calls or customer support requests via e-mail.

ISSUE 14-2

Can You Take It with You?

In the past, salespeople who left a company often took with them a list of clients. When a salesperson joins a new firm, he or she could use the list to reestablish contacts with past customers. Some questioned the morality of this practice, but most agreed the salesperson had little more than a list of names. With sales force automation (SFA) software, however, a former salesperson can unearth a treasure chest of client information. SFA stores information about clients, products, and transactions on a central office computer that salespeople can access remotely using notebook computers or PDAs. A departing salesperson could download customer information to a personal notebook computer or PDA before leaving the company, or later use any computer to access the information on the central office computer, and then draw on the information obtained to steal customers. Many companies prohibit this practice in employee contracts. Yet, some insist that companies have no right to control ex-employees. Should salespeople be prohibited contractually from taking, or accessing, customer information if they leave the company? Why? Should the practice be made illegal? How else might companies respond to this problem?

For more information about SFA, visit the Discovering Computers 2005 Issues Web page (**scsite.com/dc2005/issues**). Click Issue #2 below Chapter 14.

CIM software also assists support personnel in providing the best solutions for customers. The CIM program may provide a customer support representative with a choice of several e-mail messages to send to a customer in response to the problem. The representative chooses the best response and requests that the CIM software send the e-mail message. Information gathered in a CIM program during interactions, such as reasons for the interaction and the resolution of the interaction, may be collected and made available through other information systems throughout the company.

FAQ 14-1

When should I supply personal information to a company?

Companies gather personal information about consumers for a variety of reasons. Unless you are sure you want the company to communicate with you in some way, few reasons exist to supply personal information to a company. Ask the company why it needs the information and use your judgment. Most companies can supply you with a privacy policy upon request.

For more information about sharing personal information, visit the Discovering Computers 2005 FAQ Web page (**scsite.com/dc2005/faq**). Click Sharing Personal Information below Chapter 14.

APPLY IT 14-2

Instant Messaging Finds Business Home

You have found the perfect shirt while shopping online. The Web site indicates it is available in your size and desired color. But what material is it made of? Can you wash it, or must you have it dry-cleaned? No information about the fabric is available anywhere on the Web page. It would be convenient and helpful to obtain this simple information instantly without having to call a customer service center or send an e-mail message.

Businesses have recognized this problem and are developing instant messaging (IM) applications for customer support. They realize that nearly one-half of North American online consumers use instant messaging at least once a week and that 90 percent of this group uses IM daily, according to Forrester Research.

IM has many benefits. By keeping customers online, they are more likely to make a purchase. In addition, a written transcript of the IM dialog can be archived and analyzed to enhance quality control. The IM agents can handle multiple inquiries simultaneously, and they can have scripted answers to copy and paste for commonly asked questions.

Many companies are phasing in IM gradually to ensure they have adequately trained staff and can handle message volume during peak times.

For more information about instant messaging in business contexts, visit the Discovering Computers 2005 Apply It Web page (**scsite.com/dc2005/apply**). Click Apply It #2 below Chapter 14.

INFORMATION TECHNOLOGY The IT department makes technology decisions for the enterprise, such as a decision whether to build or buy new computers and information systems or when a computer or information system has outlived its useful life. The overall technology strategy often is referred to as the *information architecture* of the company. Many companies elevate the importance of IT by including a *chief information officer* (*CIO*) executive position that reports to the CEO.

The IT department uses software to maintain hardware and software applications. For example, *Web site management programs* allow the IT department to track Web site usage and statistics. *Security software* enables the IT department to limit access to sensitive information.

General Purpose Information Systems

Some information systems in an enterprise cross the boundaries of functional units and are used by one or more functional units in an enterprise. These general purpose, or *enterprise-wide systems,* become necessary in an enterprise for two reasons. First, functional units within an enterprise have a significant need to share data among the units. Second, enterprise-wide systems can collect and combine data more quickly and provide executive management access to a more up-to-date and accurate view of what is happening in the organization. Advances in computing speed, storage capacity, security, and networking have made enterprise-wide systems more attractive to companies in recent years.

General purpose information systems generally fall into one of five categories: office information systems, transaction processing systems, management information systems, decision support systems, and expert systems. The following sections present each type of these general purpose information systems.

OFFICE INFORMATION SYSTEMS An **office information system** (**OIS** pronounced oh-eye-ess) is an information system that enables employees to perform tasks using computers and other electronic devices, instead of manually. An OIS increases employee productivity and assists with communications among employees. Some people describe an OIS as *office automation*.

Just about every type of business or organization uses some form of OIS. For example, a school might post its class schedules on the Internet. When the school updates the schedule, students receive an e-mail notification. In a manual system, the school would photocopy the schedule and mail it to each student's house.

An OIS supports many administrative activities. With an OIS, users create and distribute graphics and documents, send messages, schedule appointments, browse the Web, and publish Web pages. All levels of users utilize and benefit from the features of an OIS.

An OIS uses many common software products to support its activities. Typical software in an OIS includes word processing, spreadsheet, database, presentation graphics, e-mail, Web browser, Web page authoring, personal information management, and groupware. To send text, graphics, audio, and video to others, an OIS uses communications technology such as voice mail, fax, video conferencing, and EDI.

In an OIS, computers have modems, video cameras, speakers, and microphones. Employees in an OIS often use other types of hardware such as scanners, fax machines, digital cameras, and Web-enabled cellular telephones and PDAs.

TRANSACTION PROCESSING SYSTEMS A **transaction processing system** (**TPS**) is an information system that captures and processes data from day-to-day business activities. When you make a purchase with a credit card at a store, you are interacting with a TPS (Figure 14-14). A *transaction* is an individual business activity. Examples of transactions are deposits, payments, orders, and reservations. In a company, clerical staff typically uses computers and special software to perform the following activities associated with a TPS:

1. Recording a transaction such as a student's registration, a customer's order, an employee's time card, or a car owner's payment.
2. Confirming an action or causing a response, such as printing a student's schedule, sending a thank-you note to a customer, printing an employee's paycheck, or issuing a receipt to a car owner.
3. Maintaining data, which involves adding new data, changing existing data, or removing unwanted data.

Transaction processing systems were among the first computerized systems that processed business data. Many people initially referred to the functions of a TPS as *data processing*. The first TPSs computerized an existing manual system. The intent of these TPSs was to process faster, reduce clerical costs, and improve customer service.

The first TPSs mostly used batch processing. With *batch processing*, the computer collects data over time and processes all transactions later, as a group. As computers became more powerful, system developers created online transaction processing information systems. With *online transaction processing* (*OLTP*), the computer processes each transaction as it is entered.

FIGURE 14-14 When you make a purchase with a credit card, you are using a transaction processing system.

For example, when you register for classes, your school probably uses OLTP. The registration clerk enters your desired schedule. The computer immediately prints your statement of classes. The invoices often print using batch processing. That is, the computer later prints and mails all student invoices.

Today, most transaction processing systems use OLTP. For some routine processing tasks, they also use batch processing. Many enterprise-sized organizations use batch processing to calculate paychecks and print invoices.

MANAGEMENT INFORMATION SYSTEMS

A **management information system** (**MIS** pronounced em-eye-ess) is an information system that generates accurate, timely, and organized information, so managers and other users can make decisions, solve problems, supervise activities, and track progress. Management information systems evolved from transaction processing systems. Managers realized the computer and its software had more potential than just supporting a TPS. Its capability of quickly computing and comparing data could produce meaningful information for managers.

MISs often are integrated with transaction processing systems. To process a sales order, the TPS records the sale, updates the customer's account balance, and reduces the inventory count. Using this information, the related MIS produces reports that recap daily sales activities, summarize weekly and monthly sales activities, list customers with past due account balances, chart slow- or fast-selling products, and highlight inventory items that need reordering. An MIS focuses on creating information that managers and other users need to perform their jobs.

An MIS creates three basic types of reports: detailed, summary, and exception (Figure 14-15). A *detailed report* usually lists just transactions. For example, a Detailed Order Report lists orders taken during a given period. A *summary report* consolidates data usually with totals, tables, or graphs, so managers can review it quickly and easily.

An *exception report* identifies data outside of a normal condition. These out-of-the-ordinary conditions, called the *exception criteria*, define the normal activity or status range. For example, an Inventory Exception Report notifies the purchasing department of items it needs to reorder.

Exception reports save managers time. Instead of searching through a detailed report, managers simply review the exception report. These reports help managers focus on situations that require immediate decisions or actions. Most information systems support all three types of reports shown in Figure 14-15.

Figure 14-15a (detailed report)

DETAILED ORDER REPORT for May 21, 2005

Part Number	Part Description	Customer	Quantity Purchased
1788	Stapler	Starlight Foods	15
		Wilson Automotive	40
		Victor Lighting	13
2372	Postage scale	Regal Camera	1
		Wilson Automotive	4
3029	Letter opener	AAA Rentals	25
		Starlight Foods	10
8942	Bulletin board	Wilson Automotive	8

Figure 14-15b (summary report)

SUMMARY REPORT for May 21, 2005
by Part Number

Part Number	Part Description	Total Quantity Sold	Vendor
1788	Stapler	68	Geo Supplies
2372	Postage scale	5	Marham Industries
3029	Letter opener	35	Geo Supplies
8942	Bulletin board	8	Geo Supplies

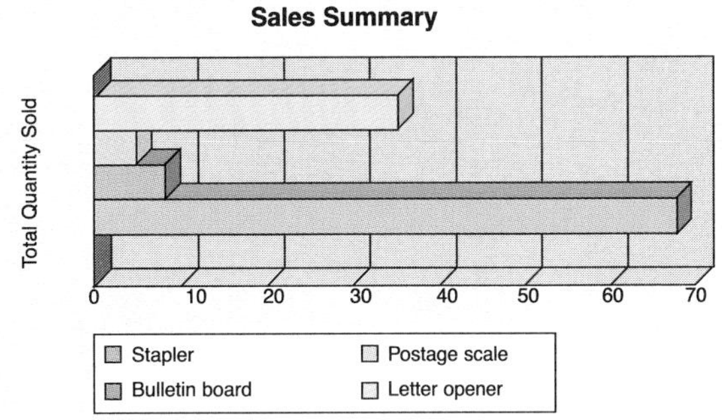

Figure 14-15c (exception report)

INVENTORY EXCEPTION REPORT for May 21, 2005

Part Number	Part Description	Total Quantity on Hand	Reorder Point
8942	Bulletin board	228	240
3029	Letter opener	558	560

FIGURE 14-15 Three basic types of reports generated in an MIS are detailed, summary, and exception.

DECISION SUPPORT SYSTEMS A **decision support system** (**DSS**) helps users analyze data and make decisions. Often, a TPS or MIS does not generate the type of report a manager needs to make a decision. Different managers need various types of information. A marketing manager might need to know how much he or she has spent on Internet advertising in the past three months, whereas an office manager might need to know how many pads of paper were used.

A variety of DSSs exist. Some are company specific and designed solely for managers. Others are available to everyone on the Web. Programs that analyze data, such as those in a DSS, sometimes are called *online analytical processing* (*OLAP*) programs. Because they summarize information, these programs process many records at a time often using multidimensional databases. This is different from OLTP programs, which process individual records at one time and typically use relational databases.

A DSS uses data from internal and external sources. *Internal sources* of data might include sales orders, MRP and MRP II results, inventory records, or financial data from accounting and financial analyses. Data from *external sources* could include interest rates, population trends, costs of new housing construction, or raw material pricing.

Some DSSs include their own query languages, statistical analyses, spreadsheets, and graphics that help users retrieve data and analyze the results. Some also allow managers to create a model of the factors affecting a decision. A product manager might need to decide on a price for a new product. A simple model for finding the best price would include factors for the expected sales volume at various price levels. The model allows the user to ask what-if questions and view the expected results.

A special type of DSS, called an *executive information system* (*EIS*), supports the strategic information needs of executive management. An EIS presents information as charts and tables that show trends, ratios, and statistics (Figure 14-16). An EIS typically uses external data sources such as the Dow Jones Interactive or the Internet. These external data sources provide current information about interest rates, commodity prices, and other leading economic indicators.

FAQ 14-2

Are other alternatives available to a complete DSS?

Instead of buying a DSS, many people use their application software to perform DSS functions. With Microsoft Office Excel 2003, for example, you can model data and create what-if scenarios.

For more information about Web services, visit the Discovering Computers 2005 FAQ Web page (**scsite.com/dc2005/faq**). Click Web Services below Chapter 14.

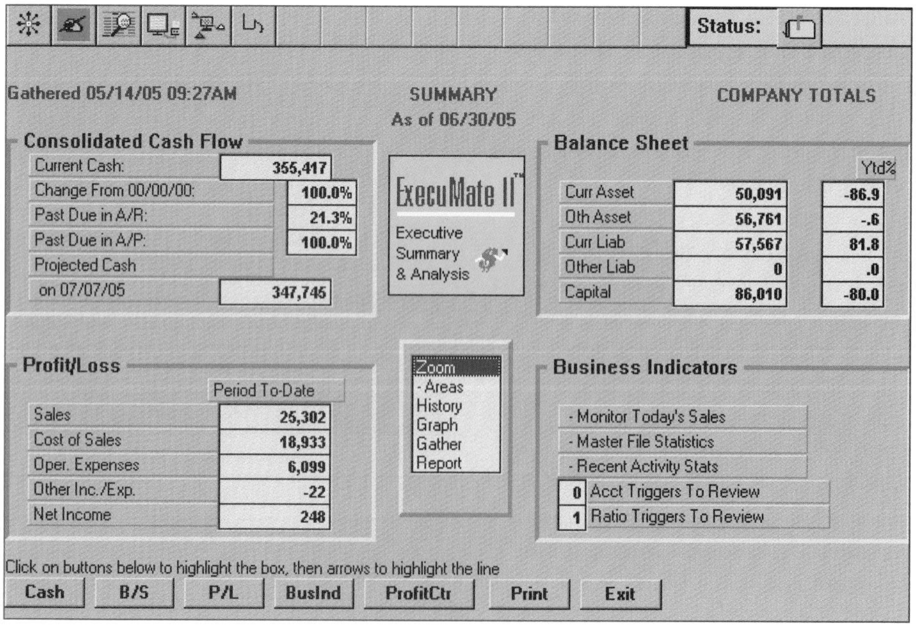

FIGURE 14-16 This executive information system (EIS) presents information to senior management in the form of graphics and reports.

EXPERT SYSTEMS An **expert system** is an information system that captures and stores the knowledge of human experts and then imitates human reasoning and decision making. Figure 14-17 shows how one expert system assists with a customer support request.

Expert systems consist of two main components: a knowledge base and inference rules. A *knowledge base* is the combined subject knowledge and experiences of the human experts. The *inference rules* are a set of logical judgments that are applied to the knowledge base each time a user describes a situation to the expert system.

FIGURE 14-17 A SAMPLE EXPERT SYSTEM

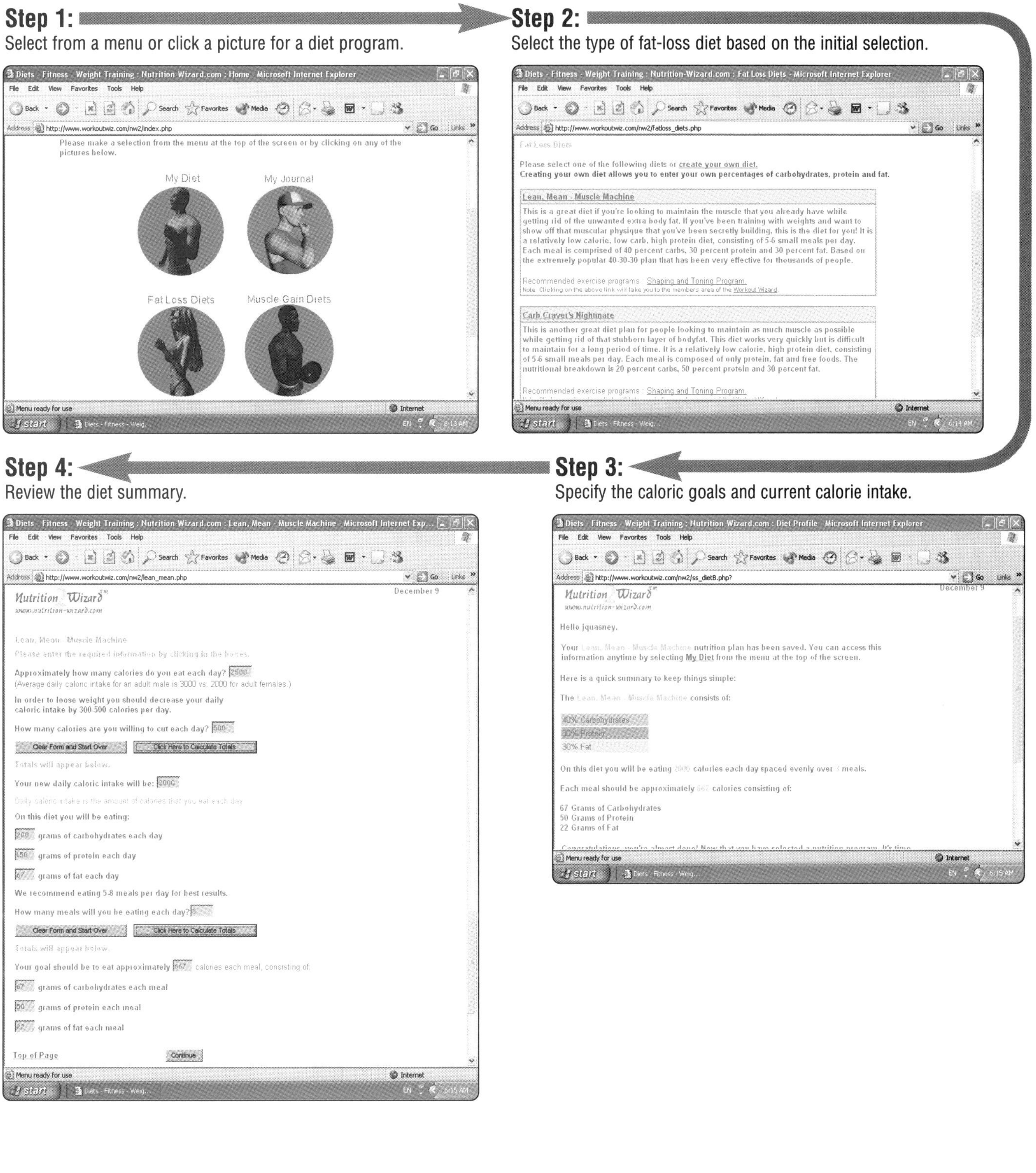

Expert systems help all levels of users make decisions. Nonmanagement employees use them to help with job-related decisions. Expert systems also successfully have resolved such diverse problems as diagnosing illnesses, searching for oil, and making soup.

Expert systems are one aspect of an exciting branch of computer science called artificial intelligence. **Artificial intelligence** (**AI**) is the application of human intelligence to computers. AI technology senses a person's actions and, based on logical assumptions and prior experience, takes the appropriate action to complete the task. AI has a variety of capabilities, including speech recognition, logical reasoning, and creative responses.

Enterprises employ expert systems in a variety of roles, such as answering customer questions, training new employees, and analyzing data.

The knowledge and experience of a professional worker is an important asset to any business. *Knowledge workers*, such as accountants, engineers, and other professionals, include individuals whose jobs center on the collection, processing, and application of information. **Knowledge management** (**KM**) is the process by which an enterprise collects, archives, indexes, and retrieves its knowledge, or resources. The knowledge worker performs the tasks to develop or use the knowledge. Organizations implement **knowledge management software** (**KMS**) to assist in the task of knowledge management. Knowledge management software captures the expertise of knowledge workers, so their knowledge is not lost when they leave the company.

Integrated Information Systems

It often is difficult to classify an information system as belonging to only one of the five general types of information systems. Much of today's application software, such as ERP and MRP II software, supports transaction processing and creates MIS reports. Other applications provide transaction processing, management information, and decision support. Read Looking Ahead 14-1 for a look at how cellular telephones can integrate with information systems.

LOOKING AHEAD 14-1

Cellular Telephones Allow Remote Monitoring

Emergency room personnel connect individuals suffering from heart attacks to computers that monitor every heartbeat. During their hospital stay, telemetry systems transmit heartbeats to nursing stations. Soon, cellular telephones will measure outpatients' heartbeats and then transmit this data to medical centers worldwide.

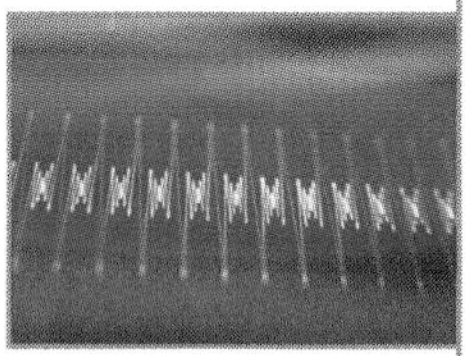

Patients will have heart monitors strapped to their chests, and the monitors will be plugged into their cellular telephones. The sensors in cellular telephones will collect data 40 times per second and then transmit these vital signs every five seconds. The data can be viewed on a Web site, Web-enabled cellular telephone or pager, or fax machine. If irregularities are present, the system rings cardiologists' cellular telephones to notify them of possible serious conditions.

Heart patients are not the only individuals who will benefit from this technology. Athletes can transmit their vital signs to their personal trainers to enhance performance. Environmentalists can install monitoring systems at weather stations and bodies of water to warn of impending floods and avalanches. The sensors can measure air temperature, precipitation, relative humidity, soil moisture, and snow depth and then transmit the data via cellular telephones and two-way radios to wireless networks and the World Wide Web.

For a look at the next generation of cellular telephones, visit the Discovering Computers 2005 Looking Ahead Web page (**scsite.com/dc2005/looking**). Click Looking Ahead #1 below Chapter 14.

ENTERPRISE RESOURCE PLANNING

Enterprise resource planning (**ERP**) provides centralized, integrated software applications to help manage and coordinate the ongoing activities of the functional units of an enterprise, including manufacturing and distribution, accounting, finance, sales, product planning, and human resources. Figure 14-18 shows how ERP fits into the operations of an enterprise. Companies such as SAP and PeopleSoft provide the fundamental framework for building these software-based systems.

The ERP system installed at each company must be customized to match the business requirements of the enterprise. At a large company, an ERP system may take four to six years to implement and cost hundreds of millions of dollars. The company hopes to regain the investment through the advantages offered by ERP.

Advantages of ERP include complete integration of information systems across departments, better project management, and better customer service. Complete integration means information is rapidly shared and management receives a more complete and timely view of the organization through the information. Better and faster reporting of the state of the enterprise leads managers to better decisions. ERP also helps to better manage the global nature of many enterprises. The reliance on one information system, rather than up to several hundred systems, allows the IT department to focus on one type of technology and simplifies relationships with IT vendors.

WEB LINK 14-5

Enterprise Resource Planning

Visit the Discovering Computers 2005 WEB LINK page (**scsite .com/dc2005/weblink**). Click Enterprise Resource Planning below Chapter 14.

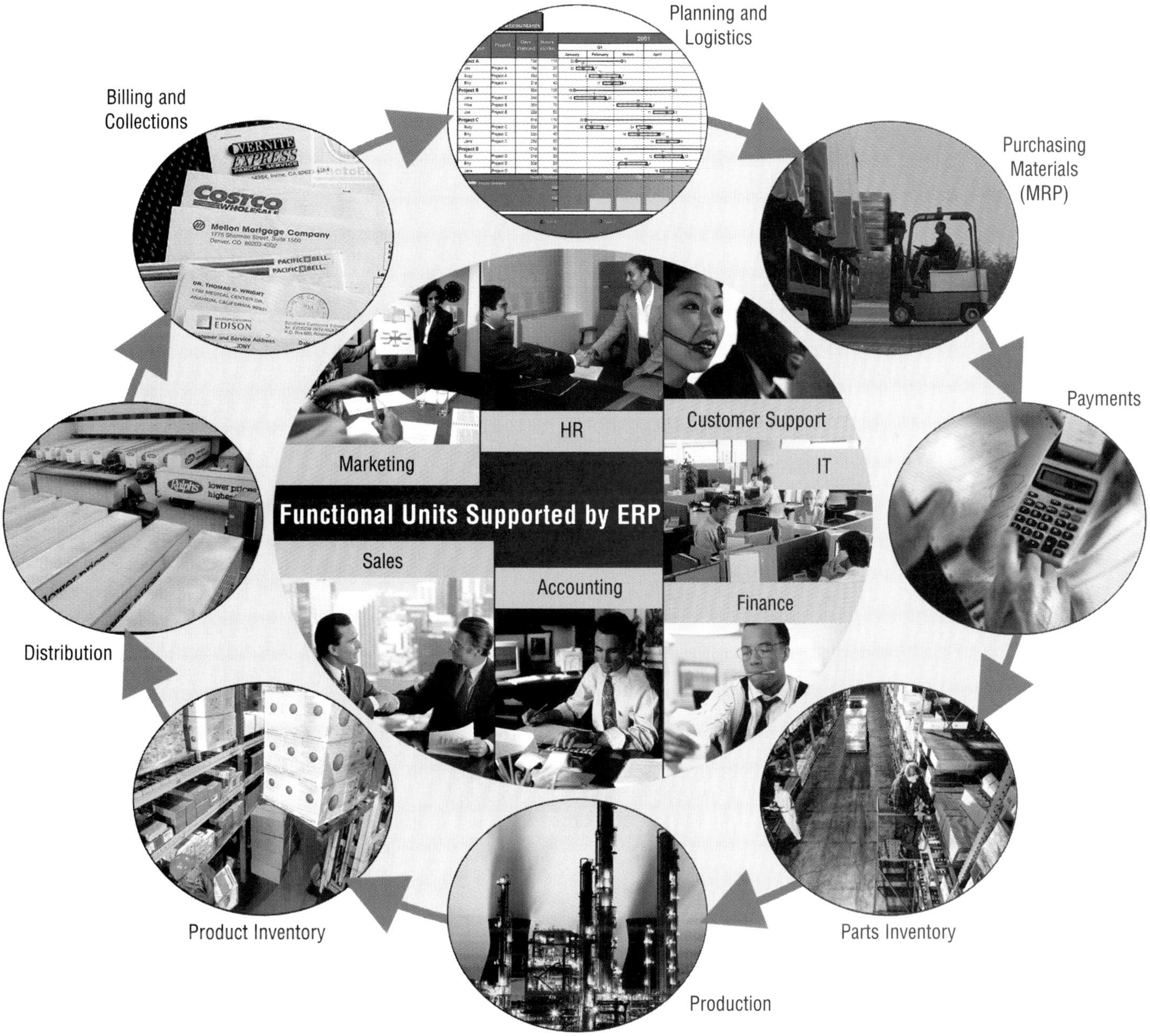

FIGURE 14-18 Enterprise resource planning (ERP) encompasses all of the major information systems needed throughout a business.

CUSTOMER RELATIONSHIP MANAGEMENT **Customer relationship management (CRM)** systems manage information about customers, interactions with customers, past purchases, and interests. CRM mainly is used across sales, marketing, and customer service departments. CRM software tracks leads and inquiries from customers, stores a history of all correspondence and sales to a customer, and allows for tracking of outstanding issues with customers. Enterprise resource planning systems often serve as a basis for CRM.

Marketing departments use CRM software to learn about current customers and design new products based on customer experiences. The sales department utilizes CRM software to track the sales process from initial contact through the final purchase. The customer support organization tracks ongoing correspondence with the customer and the CRM system may be linked to a customer interaction management system. All of the functional units have access to each other's information, allowing for a more consistent, knowledgeable approach to managing interactions with the customer. Read Issue 14-3 for a related discussion.

ISSUE 14-3

Should ISPs Share Customer Information?

It is illegal under state and federal law for video rental stores to tell which movies their customers have rented. A proposed law would make ISPs (Internet service providers) subject to a similar constraint. Under the law, ISPs would have to notify customers whenever they disclose information about accounts, such as e-mail addresses or Web pages visited, and explain why the information is being shared. ISP contracts would have to inform customers how they could prevent such information sharing. Major ISPs oppose the law, claiming that any state regulations would be unwieldy for companies that operate on a national, and even international, level. Supporters of the law claim that sharing customer information violates customer privacy. Some argue that the law should go further, making it illegal to disclose any customer information, even to law enforcement agencies. Should ISPs have to inform customers when they disclose personal information, such as the Web sites that a customer visits? Why? Should any such disclosure be illegal, or restricted to law enforcement agencies? Why or why not?

For more information about Internet privacy, visit the Discovering Computers 2005 Issues Web page (**scsite.com/dc2005/issues**). Click Issue #3 below Chapter 14.

CONTENT MANAGEMENT SYSTEMS A **content management system (CMS)** is a combination of databases, software, and procedures that organizes and allows access to various forms of documents and other files, including images and multimedia content. A CMS includes information about the files and data, called *metadata*. For example, the metadata for a company's employee manual may include the author's name, revision number, a brief summary, and last revision date. The CMS also provides security controls for the content, such as who is allowed to add, view, and modify content and on which content the user is allowed to perform those operations.

Users add content to a CMS using a graphical user interface or Web page. Based on the user's actions, the CMS processes content, categorizes the content, *indexes* the content so that it can later be searched, and stores the content. Users then have access to the content stored in the CMS through other applications, such as an enterprise portal (Figure 14-19). An enterprise portal gathers information from the CMS, other information sources from within the enterprise, and information external to the enterprise, such as news services.

Publishing entities, such as news services, use content management systems to keep Web sites up-to-date. As news or information is published, it is categorized and updated on the appropriate sections of the Web site. For example, a sports writer may submit a story to the CMS and add metadata that indicates that the story is a headline story. The CMS categorizes the story so that it is displayed as the first item with a large headline on the sports section of the Web site. The CMS indexes the information in the story so that users who search the Web site based on keywords in the story will find a link to the story.

Many content management systems serve to enhance the effectiveness of groupware and collaboration software. Groupware, such as Lotus Notes from IBM, can be integrated with content management systems.

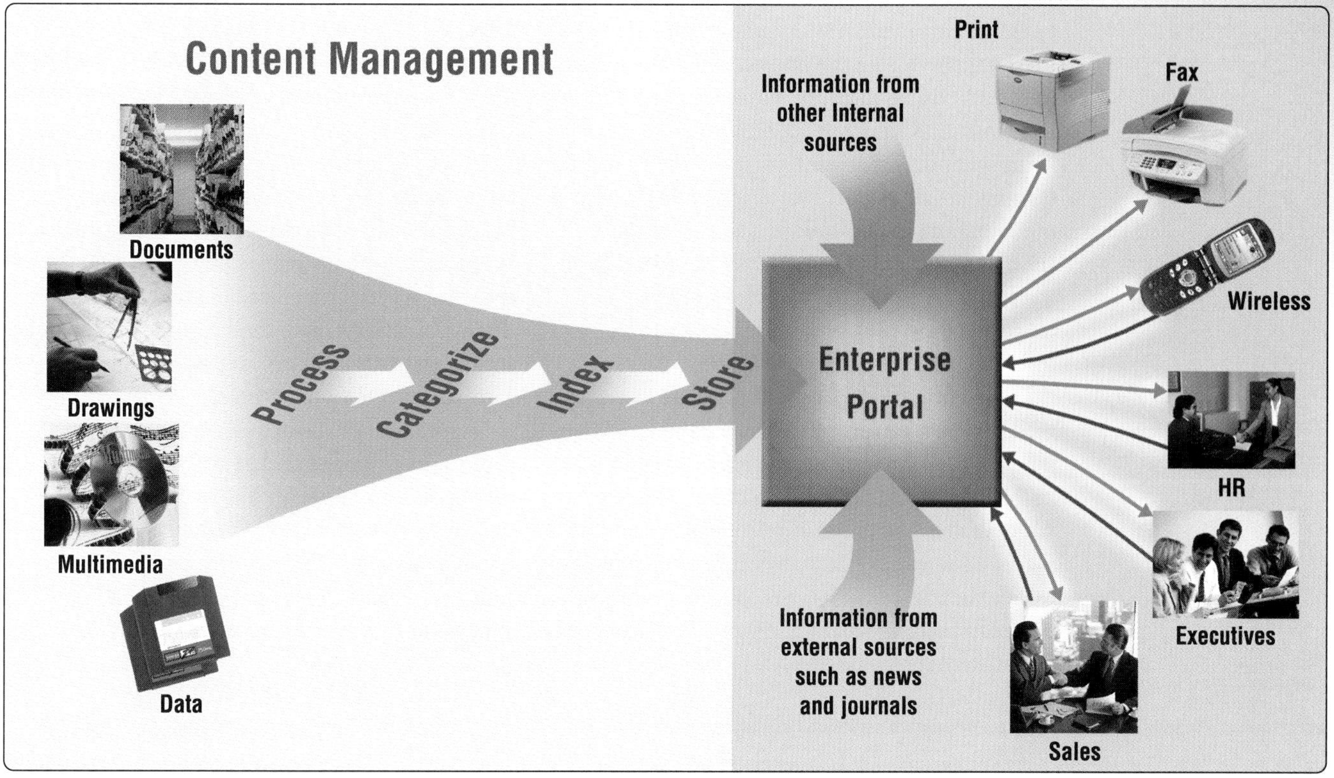

FIGURE 14-19 A content management system (CMS) helps a company classify and manage volumes of documents and media for future retrieval and use.

> **QUIZ YOURSELF 14-1**
>
> To check your knowledge of enterprise information requirements and information systems used throughout an enterprise, visit the Discovering Computers 2005 Quiz Yourself Web page (**scsite.com/dc2005/quiz**). Click Objectives 1 – 3 below Chapter 14.

ENTERPRISE-WIDE TECHNOLOGIES

Several technologies adopted by enterprises allow companies flexibility and the ability to move swiftly in a business environment. By using standard and accepted technologies, the company does not need to reengineer solutions to typical problems. Commonly used technologies provide the organization with a starting point to solve problems present in many large organizations.

Some of the common technologies used in enterprises include portals, electronic data interchange, data warehouses, extranets, Web services, workflow, and virtual private networks. The following sections discuss each of these technologies.

Portals

A **portal** is a collection of links, content, and services presented on a Web page and designed to guide users to information they likely are to find interesting for their particular job function. A service may include a portion of a Web page that allows the user to check package shipment status for an overnight delivery service or the ability to check airline flight schedules or flight status. Portals combine information from several business sources, both inside and outside the enterprise (Figure 14-20). A portal often includes searching capabilities or a link to a search engine, such as Google. Users typically can customize the portal Web site to meet their needs. The customization of users' portal pages to meet their needs is called *personalization*.

Users within a department or those working together on a project often have similar views of the portal. An executive may have access to daily financial summaries on the portal Web page, while a customer service representative views updates to product problems. Information from external sources included on a portal Web page can include weather, news, reference tools, and instant messaging.

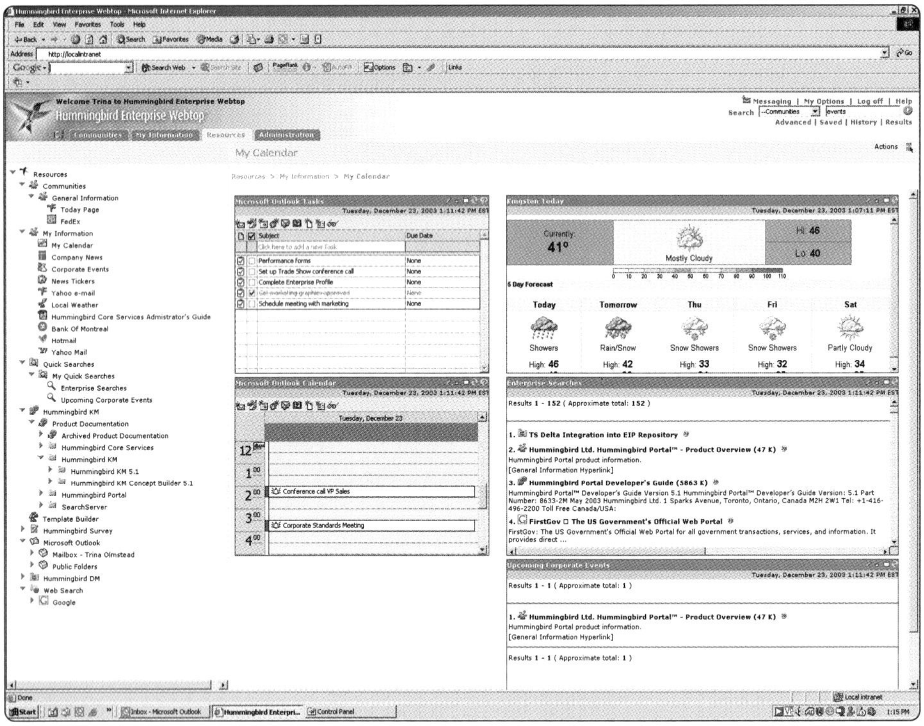

FIGURE 14-20 Portals allow users quick access to a multitude of information sources that they access on a regular basis.

EDI

EDI (**electronic data interchange**) is a set of standards that controls the transfer of business data and information among computers both within and among enterprises. One of the first steps in the development of e-commerce was electronic data interchange, which originally was created to eliminate paperwork and increase response time in business interactions. Today, businesses use these standards to communicate with industry partners over the Internet and telephone lines.

Despite the introduction of newer technologies, EDI continues to thrive in many businesses. Companies can set up their own EDI networks or subscribe to a third party EDI service provider. Errors in processing are reduced because EDI validates information that is communicated by both parties.

Data Warehouses

A **data warehouse** is a huge database that stores and manages the data required to analyze historical and current transactions. Software applications, such as ERP and MRP II programs, store and access data in a data warehouse.

Most data warehouses include one or more databases and one or more information systems storing data in the data warehouse. The data in the databases consists of transaction data required for decision-making. This data may come from internal or external sources (Figure 14-21). Some data warehouses use Web farming for their external data. *Web farming* is the process of collecting data from the Internet as a source for the data warehouse. With Web resources, the company must convert the data to a form suitable for the data warehouse.

Another growing external source of information is a click stream. A *click stream* is a

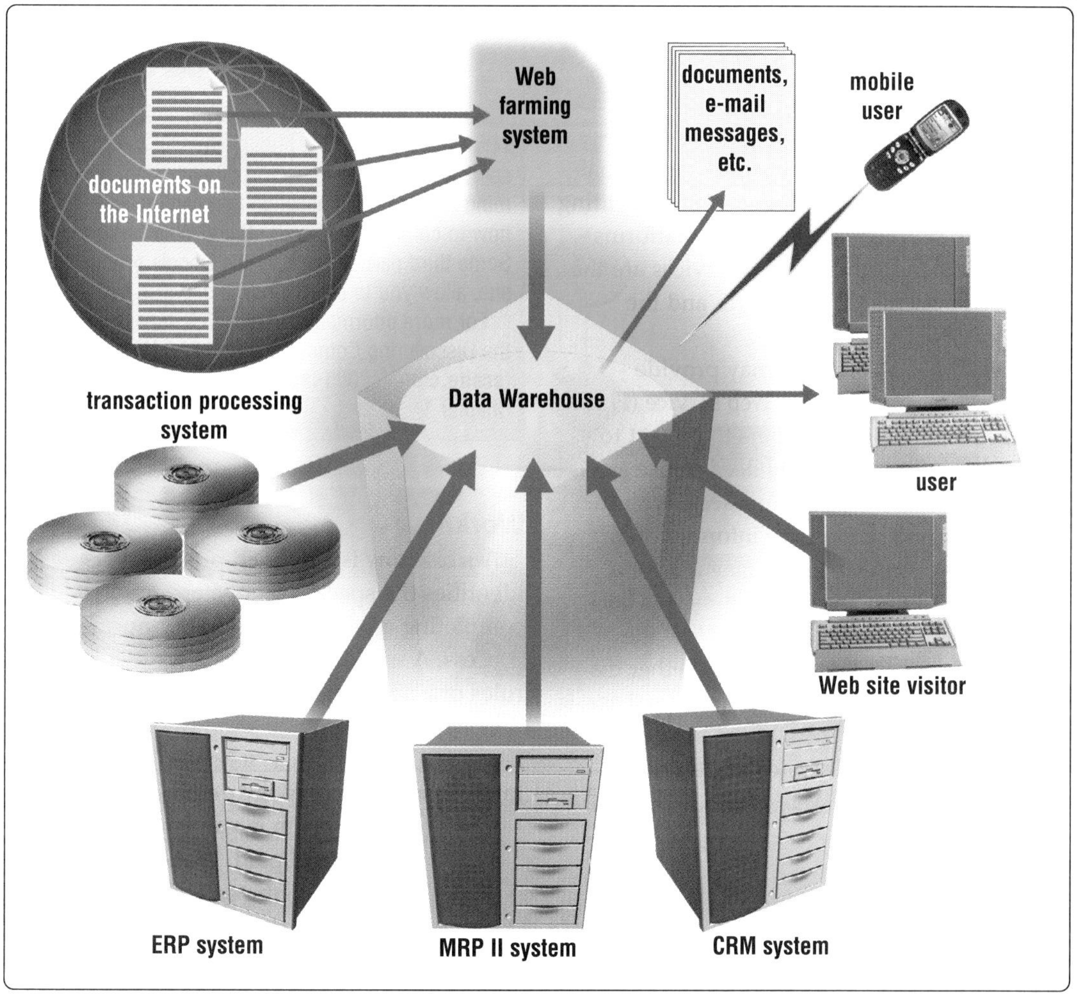

FIGURE 14-21 A data warehouse can receive from a variety of sources, including company transactions, the Internet, and Web site visitor click streams.

WEB LINK 14-6

Data Warehouse

Visit the Discovering Compute rs 2005 WEB LINK page (**scsite .com/dc2005/weblink**). Click Data Warehouse below Chapter 14.

collection of every action that users make as they move through a Web site. By analyzing visitors' click streams, companies identify consumer preferences and determine which Web pages are most attractive to visitors.

The data in a data warehouse is accurate as of a moment in time. It contains snapshots of current and historical transactions. Thus, you usually do not change the content of existing data in a data warehouse. As time passes, you simply add new data. The data warehouse also contains summarizations of this data.

Extranets

An **extranet** is the portion of a company's network that allows customers or suppliers of a company to access parts of an enterprise's intranet. An extranet provides a secure, physical connection to the company's network. Customers may use the extranet to place and monitor orders electronically or to make payments. Suppliers may check inventory levels of the parts they supply to the company and receive orders and payments from the company. Extranets improve efficiency by replacing the postal service, faxes, or telephone calls as the communications medium of choice. Recently, extranets have replaced or supplemented existing EDI (electronic data interchange) systems.

Web Services

Web services include a relatively new set of software technologies that allows businesses to create products and B2B (business-to-business) interactions over the Internet. Web services represent an evolutionary step when compared with EDI. They send and receive requests for information from an enterprise's Web site using the XML markup language. Recall that XML is discussed in Chapter 12. Web services are made available either internally or externally.

RAID

For applications that depend on reliable data access, users must have the data available when they attempt to access it. Some manufacturers provide a type of hard disk system that connects several smaller disks into a single unit that acts like a single large hard disk. A group of two or more integrated hard disks is called a **RAID** (**redundant array of independent disks**). Although quite expensive for large computers, RAID is more reliable than traditional hard disks (Figure 14-28). Thus, networks and Internet servers often use RAID.

A RAID system duplicates data, instructions, and information to improve data reliability. RAID systems implement this duplication in different ways, depending on the storage design, or level, being used. (These levels are not hierarchical. That is, higher levels are not necessarily better than lower levels.) The simplest RAID storage design is *level 1*, called *mirroring*, which writes data on two disks at the same time to duplicate the data (Figure 14-29a). A level 1 configuration enhances storage reliability because, if a drive should fail, a duplicate of the requested item is available elsewhere within the array of disks.

Other RAID levels use a technique called *striping*, which splits data, instructions, and information across multiple disks in the array (Figure 14-29b). Striping improves disk access times, but does not offer data duplication. For this reason, some RAID levels combine both mirroring and striping.

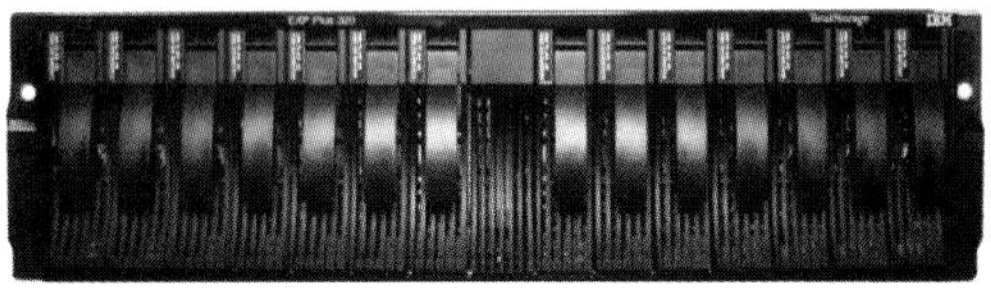

FIGURE 14-28 A group of two or more integrated hard disks, called a RAID (redundant array of independent disks), often is used with network servers. Shown here is a rack-mounted RAID chassis including the hard disks.

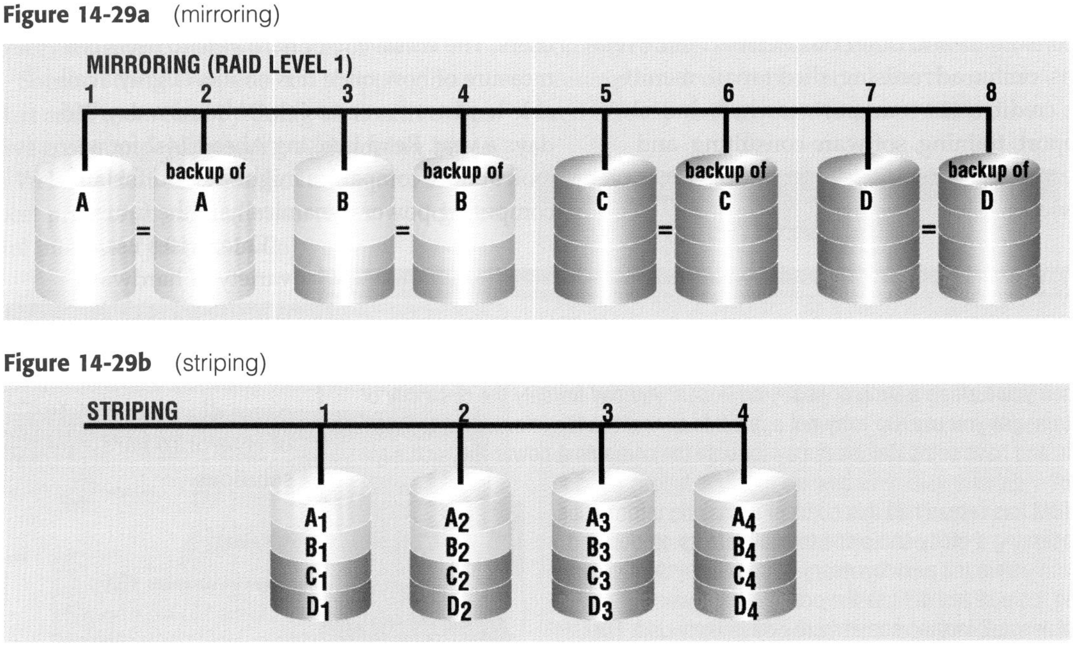

FIGURE 14-29 In RAID level 1, called mirroring, a backup disk exists for each disk. Other RAID levels use striping; that is, portions of each disk are placed on multiple disks.

FAQ 14-5

Can I use RAID in my personal computer?

Yes. RAID is becoming more common in personal computers. Using RAID level 1 in a personal computer is relatively inexpensive. You only need a second hard disk and an inexpensive RAID controller to implement your own RAID system. Using RAID at home protects your data from hard disk glitches and crashes, and gives you peace of mind.

For more information about RAID, visit the Discovering Computers 2005 FAQ Web page (**scsite.com/dc2005/faq**). Click RAID below Chapter 14.

Network Attached Storage and Storage Area Networks

Network attached storage (NAS) is a server that is placed on a network with the sole purpose of providing storage to users and information systems attached to the network (Figure 14-30a). A NAS server often is called a *storage appliance* because it is a piece of equipment with only one function — to provide additional storage. Administrators quickly add storage to an existing network simply by attaching a new NAS server to the network.

A **storage area network (SAN)** is a high-speed network with the sole purpose of providing storage to other servers to which it is attached (Figure 14-30b). A SAN is a network that includes only storage devices. High-speed fiber-optic cable connects other networks and servers to the SAN, so the networks and servers have fast access to large storage capacities. A SAN connects to networks and other servers up to seven miles away using high-speed network connections.

Figure 14-30a (network-attached storage on a LAN)

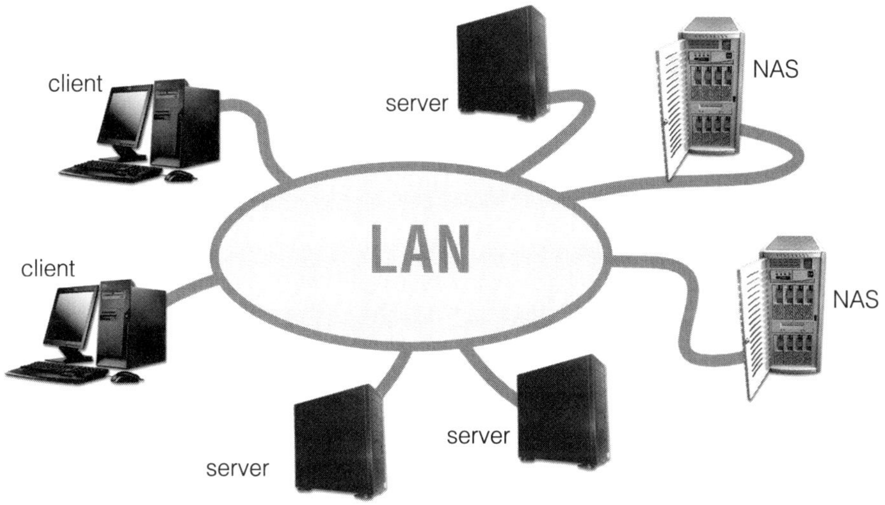

Figure 14-30b (a SAN provides centralized storage for servers and networks)

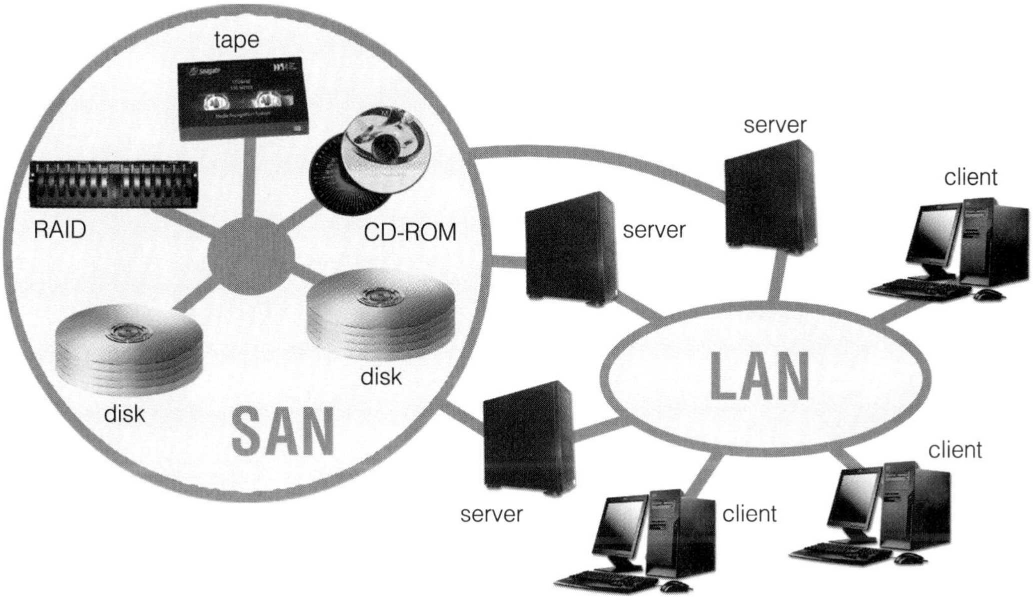

FIGURE 14-30 Network-attached storage (NAS) and a storage area network (SAN) connect to existing servers and networks in different ways.

Both NAS and SAN solutions offer easier management of storage, fast access to storage, sharing of storage, and isolation of storage from other servers. Isolation of storage from other servers lets other servers concentrate on performing a specific task, rather than consuming resources involved in the tasks related to storage. NAS and SAN systems connect to existing networks and servers in different manners as shown in Figure 14-31. Both storage solutions include disk, tape, DVD-ROM, and CD-ROM types of storage.

Enterprises sometimes choose to implement both NAS and SAN solutions. A NAS server is suited better for adding additional storage to an existing network, such as a department's file server. A company typically implements a SAN solution as central storage for an entire enterprise or a large information system, such as an ERP (enterprise resource planning) system.

WEB LINK 14-9

NAS and SAN

Visit the Discovering Computers 2005 WEB LINK page (**scsite .com/dc2005/weblink**). Click NAS and SAN below Chapter 14.

Enterprise Storage Systems

Many companies use networks. Data, information, and instructions stored on the network must be easily accessible to all authorized users. The data, information, and instructions also must be secure, so unauthorized users cannot access the network. An **enterprise storage system** is a strategy that focuses on the availability, protection, organization, and backup of storage in a company.

The goal of an enterprise storage system is to consolidate storage so operations run as efficiently as possible. Most enterprise storage systems manage extraordinary amounts of data. For example, a large bank recently installed a 185-terabyte (185,000,000,000,000 bytes) storage system to store financial information.

To implement an enterprise storage system, a company uses a combination of techniques. As shown in Figure 14-31, an enterprise storage system may use servers, RAID, a tape library, CD-ROM and DVD-ROM jukeboxes, Internet backup, NAS devices, and/or a storage area network. The following list explains these storage techniques.

- A server stores data, information, and instructions needed by users on the network.
- RAID ensures that data is not lost if one drive fails.
- A *tape library* is a high-capacity tape system that works with multiple tape cartridges for storing backups.
- A **CD-ROM server**, or **DVD-ROM server**, also called a *CD-ROM jukebox*, or *DVD-ROM jukebox*, holds hundreds of CD-ROMs or DVD-ROMs that can contain programs and data.

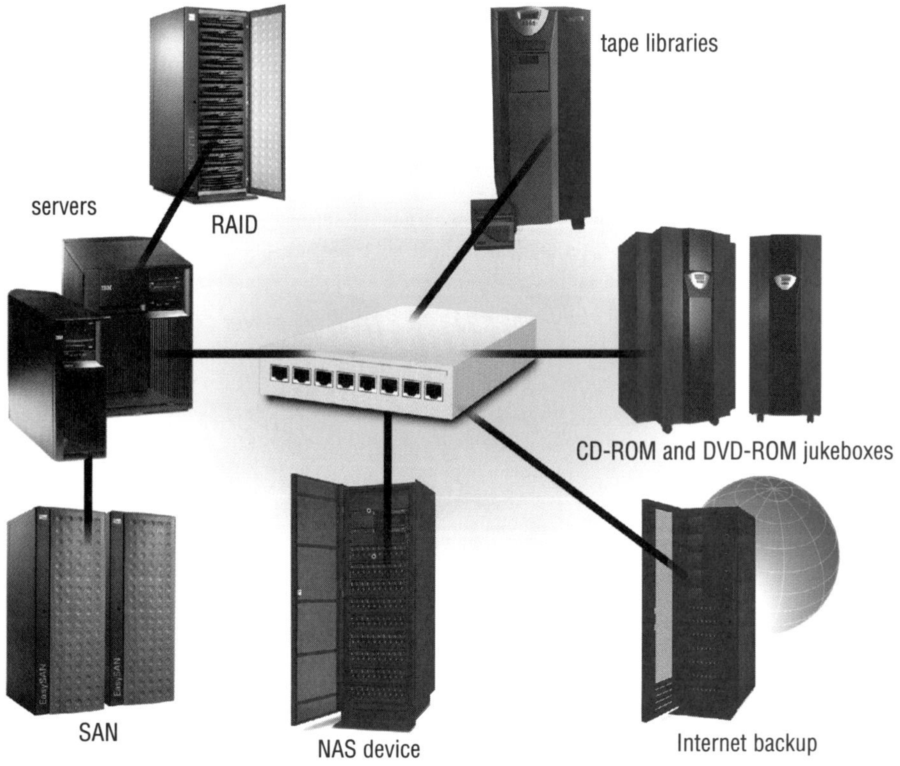

FIGURE 14-31 An enterprise storage system uses many types of storage.

- Companies using *Internet backup* store data, information, and instructions on the Web.
- A network-attached storage (NAS) device is an easy way to add additional hard disk space to the network.
- A storage area network (SAN) is a high-speed network that connects storage devices.

Some companies manage an enterprise storage system in-house. Other enterprises elect to offload all (or at least the backup) storage management to an outside organization or online Web service. This practice is known as *outsourcing*. Some vendors focus on providing enterprise storage systems to clients. A data warehouse might seek this type of outside service.

Blade Servers

Blade servers, sometimes called *ultradense servers*, pack a complete computer server, such as a Web server or network server, on a single card, or *blade*, rather than a system unit. Each blade server includes a processor, memory, hard disk, network card, and ports on the card. The individual blades insert into a *blade server chassis* that can hold many blades. Using blade servers allow an organization to fit 16 or more blades in the physical space occupied by a single server. Figure 14-32 shows a blade and a chassis that holds many blades.

Besides the savings in space offered by blade servers, blade servers require less maintenance, use less energy, generate less heat, and easily are replaced or upgraded. The hardware industry, however, disagrees on a standard for blade servers. A blade server made by one manufacturer is incompatible with the blade server chassis of another manufacturer.

High-Availability Systems

High-availability systems continue running and performing tasks for at least 99 percent of the time. Some users demand that high-availability systems be available for 99.9 percent or 99.99 percent of the time. *Uptime* is a measurement of availability. A system that has uptime of 99.99 percent is nonfunctional for less than one hour per year. That one hour, called *downtime*, includes any time that the computer crashes, needs repairs, or requires installation of replacement or upgrade parts.

Critical business systems demand high levels of availability. Telecommunications companies, such as local telephone companies, rely on high-availability systems to deliver telephone service. Emergency 911 communications centers require almost 100 percent uptime for their hardware and software applications as mandated by law. Centralized accounting or financial systems must be available to gather sales and other accounting information from locations scattered around the globe.

High-availability systems often include a feature called hot-swapping. *Hot-swapping* allows components, such as a RAID hard disk or power supplies, to be replaced while the rest of the system continues to perform its tasks. A high-availability system also may include redundant components. **Redundant components**, such as redundant power supplies, allow for a functioning component to take over automatically the tasks of a similar component that fails. When a component fails, the system administrator is notified, but the computer continues to perform its tasks because a redundant component has taken its place automatically in the system.

FIGURE 14-32 A blade server contains several small servers, each on its own blade within the server.

Scalability

As an enterprise grows, its information systems either must grow with it or must be replaced. **Scalability** is a measure of how well a computer hardware system, software application, or information system can grow to meet increasing performance demands. A system that is designed, built, or purchased when the company is small may be inadequate when the company doubles in size. Read Looking Ahead 14-3 for a look at the next generation of grid computing, which allows computer hardware systems to scale in unique ways.

A company may find that its Web site is becoming overwhelmed by customers and prospective customers. If the Web site is scalable, then the Web administrator can add more Web servers to handle the additional visitors to the Web site. Similarly, an enterprise's storage needs usually grow daily, meaning that storage systems should be scalable to store the ever-growing data generated by users.

Adding additional hardware often is the easiest method to grow, or scale, an information system. Because of software constraints, however, information systems may grow to a point at which adding more hardware does not achieve the return on investment required to justify the cost of the hardware. Often, at some point, a system no longer scales and must be replaced with a new system.

Interoperability

Enterprises typically build and buy a diverse set of information systems. An information system often must share information, or have **interoperability**, with other information systems within the enterprise. Information systems that more easily share information with other information systems are said to be *open*. Information systems that are more difficult to interoperate with other information systems are said to be *closed*, or *proprietary*. Recent open systems employ XML and Web services to allow a greater level of interoperability.

Enterprises own diverse hardware, software, and information systems for a variety of reasons. The enterprise may want to diversify its technology to reduce the risk of relying on just one type of technology. When a company relies on one type of technology, it risks that the technology may be limited in its ability to grow or change with the company, that the technology may become obsolete, and that the technology may become more expensive relative to competing technologies. Enterprises also grow through acquisitions of other companies, and the systems of the acquired companies must be integrated into the enterprise's existing systems.

LOOKING AHEAD 14-3

Grid Computing Increases Processing Power

The synergy of teamwork generally results in increased productivity and accuracy. Information technology researchers have harnessed the advantages of teamwork by pooling computers and storage systems to form supercomputers. Using grid computing, multiple personal computers are hooked up across the Internet, so the systems can tackle computing problems collectively.

Research universities and large-scale technology companies, such as IBM, Sun Microsystems, Compaq Computer, and Hewlett-Packard, have used grid computing to interpret signals from radio telescopes and to discover how proteins contain genetic information.

The next phase of grid computing will be business oriented. IBM is teaming with the U.S. Department of Energy to build a grid composed of more than 3,000 processors and a storage system with 1.3 petabytes (1,300,000 GB or 1,300,000,000,000,000 bytes) of space. Various communities will benefit from grid computing. In the entertainment field, online video gamers will benefit from the Butterfly Grid. In this system, IBM will supply the servers and physical space to help run multiplayer games, such as EverQuest and Ultima Online. In the science community, the National Science Foundation's TeraGrid will have the capacity to perform 13.6 trillion calculations per second and will help researchers investigate climate modeling and life science problems.

For a look at the next generation of grid computing, visit the Discovering Computers 2005 Looking Ahead Web page (**scsite.com/dc2005/looking**). Click Looking Ahead #3 below Chapter 14.

QUIZ YOURSELF 14-2

To check your knowledge of technologies used throughout an enterprise, e-retailing, e-commerce, and enterprise hardware, visit the Discovering Computers 2005 Quiz Yourself Web page (**scsite.com/dc2005/quiz**). Click Objectives 4 – 7 below Chapter 14.

BACKUP PROCEDURES AND SECURITY

Business and home users can perform four types of backup: full, differential, incremental, or selective. A *full backup*, sometimes called an *archival backup*, copies all of the files in the computer. A full backup provides the best protection against data loss because it copies all program and data files. Performing a full backup can be time-consuming. Users often combine full backups with differential and incremental backups. A *differential backup* copies only the files that have changed since the last full backup. An *incremental backup* copies only the files that have changed since the last full or last incremental backup. A *selective backup*, sometimes called a *partial backup*, allows the user to choose specific files to back up, regardless of whether or not the files have changed since the last incremental backup.

The main differences between a differential backup and an incremental backup is the number of backup files and the time required for backup. With a differential backup, you always have two backups: the full backup and the differential backup that contains all changes since the last full backup.

With incremental backups, you have the full backup and one or more incremental backups. The first incremental backup contains changes since the last full backup. Each subsequent incremental backup contains changes only since the previous incremental backup. For files that contain many changes and are comprised of a large portion of the total data, incremental backup usually is fastest. If files contain only a few changes, differential backups may be appropriate. For the greatest flexibility or if backup space is limited, a selective backup allows you to choose specific files that you would like to back up. Figure 14-33 outlines the advantages and disadvantages of each type of backup.

Backup procedures specify a regular plan of copying and storing important data and program files. Generally, users should perform a full backup at regular intervals, such as at the end of each week and at the end of the month. Between full backups, you can perform differential or incremental backups. Figure 14-34 illustrates a sample approach a company might follow for backing up its computer for one month. This combination of full and incremental backups provides an efficient way to protect data. Whatever backup procedures a company adopts, they should be stated clearly, documented in writing, and followed consistently.

September 2005

MONDAY	TUESDAY	WEDNESDAY	THURSDAY	FRIDAY	SAT/SUN
29 DAILY INCREMENTAL	30 DAILY INCREMENTAL	31 END OF MONTH FULL BACKUP	1 DAILY INCREMENTAL	2 WEEKLY FULL BACKUP	3/4
5 DAILY INCREMENTAL	6 DAILY INCREMENTAL	7 DAILY INCREMENTAL	8 DAILY INCREMENTAL	9 WEEKLY FULL BACKUP	10/11
12 DAILY INCREMENTAL	13 DAILY INCREMENTAL	14 DAILY INCREMENTAL	15 DAILY INCREMENTAL	16 WEEKLY FULL BACKUP	17/18
19 DAILY INCREMENTAL	20 DAILY INCREMENTAL	21 DAILY INCREMENTAL	22 DAILY INCREMENTAL	23 WEEKLY FULL BACKUP	24/25
26 DAILY INCREMENTAL	27 DAILY INCREMENTAL	28 DAILY INCREMENTAL	29 DAILY INCREMENTAL	30 END OF MONTH FULL BACKUP	1/2

FIGURE 14-34 This calendar shows a backup method strategy for a month. End-of-month backups usually are kept for at least one year.

VARIOUS BACKUP METHODS

TYPE OF BACKUP	ADVANTAGES	DISADVANTAGES
Full	Fastest recovery method. All files are saved.	Longest backup time.
Differential	Fast backup method. Requires minimal storage space to back up.	Recovery is time-consuming because the last full backup plus the differential backup are needed.
Incremental	Fastest backup method. Requires minimal storage space to back up. Only most recent changes saved.	Recovery is most time-consuming because the last full backup and all incremental backups since the last full backup are needed.
Selective	Fast backup method. Provides great flexibility.	Difficult to manage individual file backups. Least manageable of all the backup methods.

FIGURE 14-33 The advantages and disadvantages of various backup methods.

Disaster Recovery Plan

A **disaster recovery plan** is a written plan describing the steps a company would take to restore computer operations in the event of a disaster. Every company and each department or division within an enterprise usually has its own disaster recovery plans. A disaster recovery plan contains four major components: the emergency plan, the backup plan, the recovery plan, and the test plan.

THE EMERGENCY PLAN An *emergency plan* specifies the steps to be taken immediately after a disaster strikes. The emergency plan usually is organized by type of disaster, such as fire, flood, or earthquake. Depending on the nature and extent of the disaster, the procedures that are followed in an emergency will differ. All emergency plans should contain the following information:

1. Names and telephone numbers of people and organizations to notify (e.g., management, fire department, police department)
2. Procedures to follow with the computer equipment (e.g., equipment shutdown, power shutoff, file removal)
3. Employee evacuation procedures
4. Return procedures; that is, who can reenter the facility and what actions they are to perform

THE BACKUP PLAN Once the procedures in the emergency plan have been executed, the next step is to follow the backup plan. The *backup plan* specifies how a company uses backup files and equipment to resume information processing. The backup plan should specify the location of an alternate computer facility in the event the company's normal location is destroyed or unusable.

When operations are so important that a company cannot afford to lose the operations to a disaster, the company often maintains a *hot site*, which is a separate facility that mirrors the systems and operations of the critical site. The hot site always operates concurrently with the main site, so that if either site becomes unavailable, the other site continues to meet the company's needs. A *cold site* is a site that mirrors the critical site, but does not become operational until the critical site becomes unavailable. When using a cold site, some time elapses between the disaster and when the cold site becomes functional.

The backup plan identifies these items:

1. The location of backup data, supplies, and equipment
2. The personnel responsible for gathering backup resources and transporting them to the alternate computer facility
3. A schedule indicating the order in which, and approximate time by which, each application should be up and running

For a backup plan to be successful, the company must back up all critical resources. Also, additional people, including possibly nonemployees, must be trained in the backup and recovery procedures because company personnel could be injured in a disaster.

The location of the alternate computer facility is important. It should be close enough to be convenient, yet not too close that a single disaster, such as an earthquake, could destroy both the main and alternate computer facilities. Some companies preinstall all the necessary hardware, software, and communications devices at the alternate computer facility. These facilities immediately are ready in the event of a disaster. In other cases, the alternate computer facility is simply an empty facility that can accommodate the necessary computer resources, if needed. One more alternative is to enter into a *reciprocal backup relationship* with another firm, where one firm provides space and sometimes equipment to the other in case of a disaster.

FAQ 14-6

Should I have a backup plan?

Yes! Even home computers need a backup plan. You probably know someone who lost valuable personal information due to a hard disk crash or other problem. Most modern operating systems include backup software. You should familiarize yourself with the software, develop a plan, and test both backing up and recovering data.

For more information about personal backup software, visit the Discovering Computers 2005 FAQ Web page (**scsite.com/dc2005/faq**). Click Backup Software below Chapter 14.

THE RECOVERY PLAN The *recovery plan* specifies the actions to be taken to restore full information processing operations. As with the emergency plan, the recovery plan differs for each type of disaster. To prepare for disaster recovery, a company should establish planning committees, with each one responsible for different forms of recovery. For example, one committee is in charge of hardware replacement. Another is responsible for software replacement.

THE TEST PLAN To provide assurance that the disaster plan is complete, it should be tested. A disaster recovery *test plan* contains information for simulating various levels of disasters and recording an organization's ability to recover. In a simulation, all personnel follow the steps in the disaster recovery plan. Any needed recovery actions that are not specified in the plan should be added. Although simulations can be scheduled, the best test of the plan is to simulate a disaster without advance notice.

Security in the Enterprise

Large organizations must deal with complex computer security issues. Web sites and hardware must be secure from threats both inside and outside the enterprise. Users should be allowed access only to the data and information for which they are authorized, which typically is limited to the amount necessary to do their job.

In recent years, the role of *chief security officer* (*CSO*) has been added to the executive ranks at many companies. Besides being trusted with the physical security of a company's property and people, the person in charge of security often is trusted with securing computing resources.

The goals of enterprise-wide information security include maintaining confidentiality or limited access to information, ensuring integrity and reliability of systems, ensuring uninterrupted availability of systems, ensuring compliance with laws, and cooperation with law enforcement agencies.

Developing a Computer Security Plan

A company should incorporate the individual risks and safeguards previously mentioned and the disaster recovery into an overall computer security plan. A **computer security plan** summarizes in writing all of the safeguards that are in place to protect a company's information assets. A computer security plan should do the following:

1. Identify all information assets of an organization, including hardware, software, documentation, procedures, people, data, facilities, and supplies.
2. Identify all security risks that may cause an information asset loss. Rank risks from most likely to occur to least likely to occur. Place an estimated value on each risk, including the value of lost business. For example, what is the estimated loss if customers cannot place orders for one hour, one day, or one week?
3. For each risk, identify the safeguards that exist to detect, prevent, and recover from a loss.

The company should evaluate the computer security plan annually or more frequently for major changes in information assets, such as the addition of a new computer or the implementation of a new application. In developing the plan, keep in mind that some degree of risk is unavoidable. The more secure a system is, the more difficult it is for everyone to use. The goal of a computer security plan is to match an appropriate level of safeguards against the identified risks. Fortunately, most organizations will never experience a major information system disaster.

WEB LINK 14-10

Disaster Recovery

Visit the Discovering Computers 2005 WEB LINK page (**scsite.com/dc2005/weblink**). Click Disaster Recovery below Chapter 14.

Companies and individuals that need help with computer security plans can contact the *International Computer Security Association (ICSA) Labs* via the telephone or on the Web for assistance (Figure 14-35).

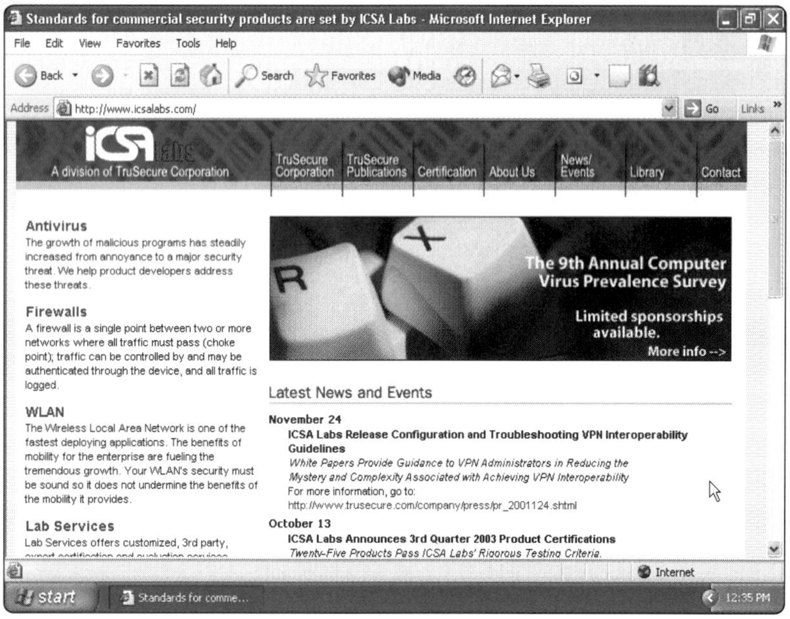

FIGURE 14-35 The ISCA Labs division of TruSecure Corporation sets performance standards for security products and is available to assist companies and individuals that need computer security plans.

QUIZ YOURSELF 14-3

To check your knowledge of enterprise backup procedures, a disaster recovery plan, and security, visit the Discovering Computers 2005 Quiz Yourself Web page (**scsite.com/dc2005/quiz**). Click Objectives 8 – 10 below Chapter 14.

CHAPTER SUMMARY

This chapter reviewed the special computing requirements present in an enterprise-sized organization. Various types of users within an organization require different types of information systems. Large information systems become more valuable when they communicate with each other and offer users a great deal of flexibility in interacting with the information system and other users. The chapter discussed e-retailing and the types of businesses that use e-commerce.

Enterprises manage complex hardware, including SANs, RAID, and blade servers. Requirements for this enterprise hardware often include high-availability, scalability, and interoperability. The chapter also discussed the backup procedures and security needs present in a large organization.

CIO

CIO (chief information officer) is the highest-ranking position in an information technology (IT) department. The CIO manages all of a company's information systems and computer resources. In large organizations, the CIO typically is a vice president and reports directly to the organization's CEO.

Depending on the organization, a CIO can be called an MIS (management information systems) manager, an IS (information systems) manager, or an IT (information technology) manager. Regardless of the title, the CIO determines an organization's information needs and provides the systems to meet those needs. The CIO sets an IT department's goals, policies, and procedures. In addition, the CIO evaluates technology, hires and supervises staff, oversees the network, directs user services, develops backup and disaster recovery plans, and manages the department budget. Perhaps most important, the CIO provides leadership, creating a vision for an IT department and helping the department deliver that vision.

Some CIOs work as consultants, providing corporate IT departments with short-term or long-term guidance. Most CIOs rise through the ranks of an organization's IT department. Generally, CIOs have a bachelor's degree or higher in computer science and at least ten years' experience in an IT department. Today, many CIOs also have an MBA. Pay reflects the importance of the CIO, with starting salaries approaching $150,000.

To learn more about the field of CIO as a career, visit the Discovering Computers 2005 Careers Web page (**scsite.com/dc2005/careers**). Click CIO.

HIGH-TECH TALK

Neural Networks: Learning from Experience

A *neural network* is a type of artificial intelligence system that attempts to emulate the way the human brain works. Neural networks are named after *neurons*, which are the billons of cells in the human brain that perform intelligent operations. Each neuron is like a small computer with basic capabilities. When billions of neurons are connected together, however, these cells are the intellectual capacity in the human brain, the most intelligent system known.

Neural networks are modeled on the human brain. A neural network uses an interconnected system of hundreds or thousands of specially designed circuits, also called *artificial neurons*. Like the brain's neurons, these circuits are connected together. Neural networks also are called *artificial neural networks* (*ANNs*) to differentiate the network of artificial neurons from the network of biological neurons in the human brain.

A neural network uses these circuits to create connections between inputs and outputs. The most common neural network model is the *multilayer perceptron* (*MLP*), which consists of at least three layers of circuits: a layer of input circuits, which is connected to one or more layers of hidden circuits, which are connected to a layer of output circuits (Figure 14-36). The knowledge of a neural network is housed in the hidden layers, which store the information that defines relationships between inputs and outputs.

Just as people do, neural networks learn from experience. Some neural networks are trained using a process called backpropagation, as shown in Figure 14-36. During *backpropagation*, the input data, which is the information used to make a decision, repeatedly is presented to the neural network via the input layer. The neural network then generates an output, which is the resulting decision, prediction, or response, based on the weighted connections between the inputs and outputs, as stored in the hidden layers.

The output of the neural network then is compared with the desired output and the error is calculated based on historical or known data. This error then is fed back, or backpropagated, to the hidden layer to adjust the weights of the connection. During each repetition, the neural network learns to associate the weight of the relationship between certain inputs and outputs. It then adjusts the weights of the connections between the inputs and outputs accordingly. The hidden layers thus store a neural network's knowledge as weighted connections between inputs and outputs, which are known as *synaptic weights*. As training continues, the extent of the error decreases with each iteration, until the neural network reaches a fully trained state where it reliably produces the desired output. The neural network then is ready to produce outputs when the desired output is unknown.

Unlike humans, once trained fully, a neural network recognizes and classifies patterns in huge quantities of complex data, at high speeds that humans cannot duplicate. Uses of neural networks include a wide range of applications, such as sorting mail at the U.S. Postal Service, determining the number of jurors to call at county courthouses, and identifying police officers with a potential for misconduct. Scientists use neural networks to predict rainfall and forecast air quality. Manufacturers benefit from neural networks that allow them to test the quality of plastics and welding and determine which type of concrete to use on a highway. In health care, neural networks help predict heart attacks and cancer risk, while helping to improve treatment.

For more information about neural networks, visit the Discovering Computers 2005 High-Tech Talk Web page (**scsite.com/dc2005/tech**) and click Neural Networks.

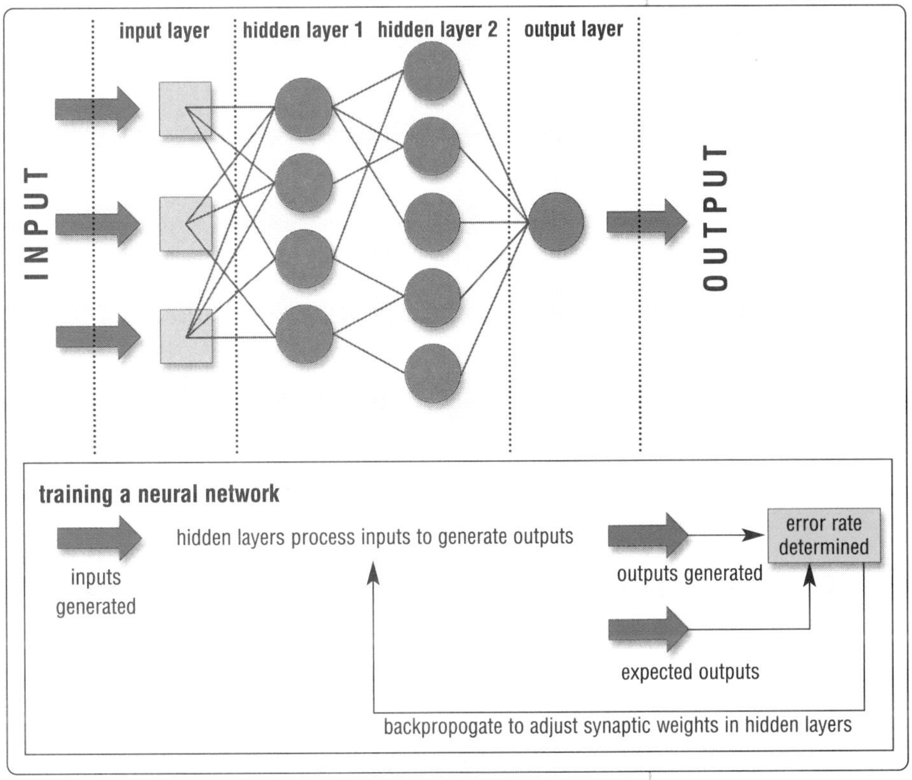

FIGURE 14-36 How a neural network works.

COMPANIES ON THE CUTTING EDGE

SAP

E-Business Solutions

About 30 years ago, a client asked whether IBM could develop a fully integrated software product that would support all facets of a company's operations. Unsure if the concept was feasible at that time, the computer giant was reluctant to start the project. Five of IBM's system engineers were more confident, however, and in 1972 the quintet founded their own company in Walldorf, Germany, with just such a product in mind. Today that company, called *SAP*, is one of the world's leading developers of enterprise software.

SAP is short for Systeme, Anwendugen, und Produkte in der Datenverarbeitung. The acronym works in English translation just as well: Systems, Applications, and Products in data processing. From its inception, the company's founders thought globally. Working on borrowed computers, the engineers developed their software to run on a multinational, multilingual level. SAP combined multiple applications linked to a single database, letting companies route an order from the moment it was placed until the day it was delivered. In 1979, the company released the R/2 Enterprise System for mainframes, which allowed companies to organize all of their data into a single database and then choose only the modules they wanted. In 1992, SAP launched R/3, a quicker, more adaptable, less labor-intensive version of R2 that coincided neatly with the trend toward corporate downsizing. In 1999, SAP introduced mySAP.com, a product the company describes as the definitive e-business platform. mySAP.com helps business partners, employees, and customers work together by supporting software and hardware from almost every major vendor.

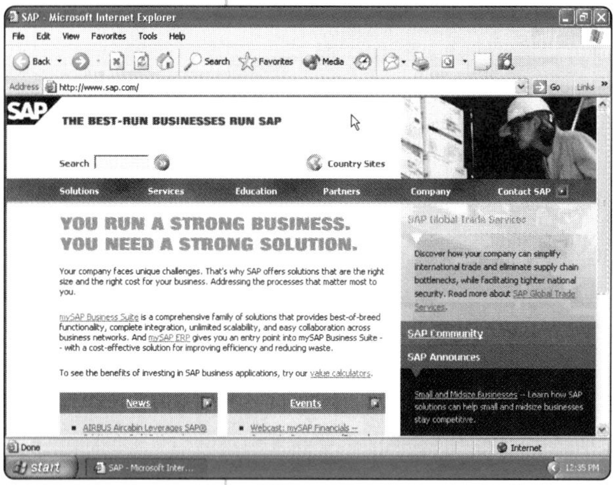

With such innovative products, it is no wonder that SAP continues to grow. From five engineers in 1972, the company now employs more than 28,900 people in over 50 countries and supports more than 12 million users.

For more information about SAP, visit the Discovering Computers 2005 Companies Web page (**scsite.com/dc2005/companies**) and click SAP.

IBM

Big Blue

In 1911, the Computing Scale Company of America, the Tabulating Machine Company, and the International Time Recording Company merged and incorporated to form the Computing – Tabulating – Recording Company (C-T-R). The company sold a variety of business-related gadgets, including a machine that used punched cards to catalogue data. Nine years after the merger, the company changed its name to the International Business Machines (IBM) Corporation. Today, *IBM* is a leader in the computer industry with a reputation for pioneering products.

IBM has a history of computer innovation. In 1944, it's first electronic computer, the huge Mark I, performed long computations automatically (although far more slowly than today's pocket calculators). In 1957, IBM introduced the first computer disk storage system and FORTRAN, a scientific programming language. In 1964, IBM's System/360 was the first family of computers with interchangeable software and peripherals. In 1969, IBM unbundled components (hardware, software, and services), selling each separately and giving birth to the software and service industries. In 1981, the IBM personal computer revolutionized the computer industry by offering 16 KB of memory, a floppy disk drive, an optional color monitor, and prices starting at $1,565. In 1992, IBM's ThinkPad notebook computer combined two inventive input devices: a butterfly-like keyboard and a pointing stick positioned between the keys. The ThinkPad collected more than 300 awards for its creative design.

In a survey of the world's 100 most powerful supercomputers, 55 of IBM's products top the list in computing power with a total of 188 teraflops (trillions of calculations per second) of power. When its Blue Gene/L supercomputer is completed for the Lawrence Livermore National Laboratory in 2005, that machine is expected to be six times faster than today's fastest computers.

For more information about IBM, visit the Discovering Computers 2005 Companies Web page (**scsite.com/dc2005/companies**) and click IBM.

TECHNOLOGY TRAILBLAZERS

Tom Siebel

Siebel Systems CEO

According to a friend, Tom Siebel can sell anything to anyone. In just one year at Oracle, Siebel sold 280 percent of his sales quota and was named the company's top salesperson.

Today, *Tom Siebel* is CEO of Siebel Systems, Inc., a company that focuses on software to support sales forces.

Siebel attended the University of Illinois at Urbana-Champaign where he earned a B.A. in history, an M.B.A., and an M.S. in computer science. In 1984, he joined Oracle, a leading marketer of database software. Within a year, Siebel smashed existing sales goals. In 1989, Siebel became head of Oracle's direct marketing division. There, he developed a new sales and marketing information system to assist in recording customer data. The system, Siebel thought, could form the basis for a "pretty good company." Siebel left Oracle in 1990. He worked as CEO for a small multimedia software company and later engineered the company's merger with Sybase, another large database software firm. In 1993, with his earnings from the merger, Siebel founded his pretty good company – Siebel Systems, Incorporated.

Siebel Systems sells customer relationship management (CRM) software, which tracks sales transactions from beginning to end, cutting costs and improving customer satisfaction. The company opened in a ramshackle building with second-hand office furniture, and a lot of the original employees worked for stock options instead of salary. Today, Siebel Systems is a leader in CRM sales, and many of the employees who worked for stock options are millionaires. Business Week recognized Siebel Systems as the world's second leading information technology company and Tom Siebel as one of the world's top 25 managers. A few years ago, Siebel Systems expanded into employee relationship management (ERM) software, which has been called the next decade's hottest enterprise software application.

For more information about Tom Siebel, visit the Discovering Computers 2005 People Web page (**scsite.com/dc2005/people**) and click Tom Siebel.

Jim Clark

Corporate Visionary

Jim Clark is hard to describe. Entrepreneur? Innovator? Searcher? Prophet? Clark is all of these, and more. This multibillionaire is responsible for several companies that have changed the ways people use computers. When *Jim Clark* has an idea, smart people listen.

James H. Clark's early life was inauspicious. The child of a poor family in a small Texas town, Clark was a troublemaker in high school — smuggling a skunk into a dance, setting off a stink bomb on a bus, and swearing at a teacher who scolded him. Suspended from school, Clark joined the Navy. When he returned, he earned his high school equivalency, went on to college, and eventually obtained a doctorate in computer science.

Clark became a professor at Stanford University, where he developed a computer chip that processed 3-D images in real time. The chip formed the basis of Clark's first company, Silicon Graphics, a very successful company in California's Silicon Valley. Clark's high-powered chip was used to create everything from suspension bridges to Hollywood movies. Looking for more, Clark contacted Marc Andreessen, creator of the Web browser, Mosaic. Together, they launched Netscape Communications Corporation, the source of one of the world's more successful Web browsers, Netscape Navigator. After a motorcycle accident, Clark created his next company, Healtheon, which marketed software to link doctors, patients, and health insurance providers. Since then, Clark has started two other computer-related companies: MyCFO, a Web-based financial advisory firm, and Shutterfly, an online digital photo printing service. Clark is an avid sailor and has captained several vessels including the *Hyperion*, a 155-foot sailboat controlled by 25 high-powered Silicon Graphics workstations.

Jim Clark may be hard to describe, but one thing is clear. Clark does not merely lead the way in computer science; he is a pioneer of innovation in the field.

For more information about Jim Clark, visit the Discovering Computers 2005 People Web page (**scsite.com/dc2005/people**) and click Jim Clark.

CHAPTER 14 CHAPTER REVIEW

The Chapter Review section summarizes the concepts presented in this chapter.

WEB INSTRUCTIONS:

To display this page from the Web, start your browser and enter the Web address **scsite.com/dc2005/ch14/review.** Click the links for current and additional information. To listen to an audio version of this Chapter Review, click the Audio button.

1 What Are the Special Information Requirements of an Enterprise-Sized Corporation?

A large organization, or **enterprise**, requires special computing solutions because of its size and geographical extent. Enterprise computing uses computers in networks or series of interconnected networks to satisfy the information needs of an enterprise. The types of information employees require depend on their level in the company. **Executive management** needs information to make *strategic decisions* that center on a company's overall goals and objectives. **Middle management** needs information to make *tactical decisions* that apply specific programs and plans to meet stated objectives. **Operational management** needs information to make an *operational decision* that involves day-to-day activities. **Nonmanagement employees** also need information to perform their jobs and make on-the-job decisions.

2 What Information Systems Are Used in the Functional Units of an Enterprise?

An **information system** is a set of hardware, software, data, people, and procedures that works together to produce information. In an enterprise, the individual operating entities, called *functional units*, have specialized requirements for their information systems. **Human Resources Information Systems** (**HRIS**) manage one or more human resources functions. Accounting and financial systems manage everyday transactions and help budget. **Computer-aided design** (**CAD**) assists engineers in product design, and **computer-aided engineering** (**CAE**) tests product designs. **Computer-aided manufacturing** (**CAM**) controls production equipment, and **computer-integrated manufacturing** (**CIM**) integrates operations in the manufacturing process. A **marketing information system** serves as a central repository for marketing tasks. Sales force automation (SFA) software equips salespeople with the tools they need. **Distribution systems** control inventory and manage shipping. **Customer interaction management** (**CIM**) software manages interactions with customers. The information technology (IT) department makes technology decisions for an enterprise and maintains hardware and software applications.

3 What Are Information Systems Used Throughout an Enterprise?

Some general purpose information systems, called *enterprise-wide systems*, are used throughout an enterprise. An **office information system** (**OIS**) enables employees to perform tasks using computers and other electronic devices. A transaction processing system (TPS) captures and processes data from day-to-day business activities. A **management information system** (**MIS**) generates accurate, timely, and organized information, so users can make decisions, solve problems, and track progress. A **decision support system** (**DSS**) helps users analyze data and make decisions. An **expert system** stores the knowledge of human experts and then imitates human reasoning and decision making. **Enterprise resource planning** (**ERP**) provides applications to help manage and coordinate ongoing activities. **Customer relationship management** (**CRM**) systems manage information about customers. A **content management system** (**CMS**) organizes and allows access to various forms of documents and files.

Visit **scsite.com/dc2005/quiz** or click the Quiz Yourself button. Click Objectives 1 – 3 below Chapter 14.

4 What Are Types of Technologies Used Throughout an Enterprise?

Technologies used throughout an enterprise include portals, electronic data interchange, data warehouses, extranets, Web services, workflow, and virtual private networks. A **portal** is a collection of links, content, and services on a Web page designed to guide users to information related to their jobs. **EDI** (**electronic data interchange**) controls the transfer of data and information among computers. A **data warehouse** stores and manages the data required to analyze transactions. An **extranet** allows customers or suppliers to access part of an enterprise's intranet. **Web services** allow businesses to create products and B2B interactions. A **workflow application** assists in the management and tracking of the activities in a business process. A virtual private network (VPN) provides users with a secure connection to a company's network server.

5 How Does E-Retailing Work?

E-retail occurs when retailers use the Web to sell their products and services. A customer visits an e-retailer's electronic storefront, adds items to a shopping cart, proceeds to a checkout, and enters personal and financial data through a secure Web connection. For payment, the e-retailer can bill the customer, set up a *merchant account*, or accept *e-money*. The e-retailer sends the customer a confirmation notice, processes the order, and forwards it to a fulfillment center where it is packaged and shipped.

6 What Are E-Commerce Market Sectors?

In addition to e-retail, several other market sectors take advantage of the Web. In finance, **online banking** allows users to pay bills from their computers, and online investing lets users invest without using a broker. Entertainment and media on the Web include music, videos, news, sporting events, and 3-D multiplayer games. Travel-related services on the Web include directions; airline, hotel or car reservations; and a **shopping bot** that searches for the best price on a product or service. Many Web sites provide medical, nutrition, or fitness information.

7 What Are the Computer Hardware Needs and Solutions for an Enterprise?

Enterprise hardware allows large organizations to manage and share information and data using devices geared for maximum availability and efficiency. Enterprises use a variety of hardware types to meet their needs. A **RAID** (**redundant array of independent disks**) is a group of integrated disks that duplicates data and information to improve data reliability. **Network attached storage** (**NAS**) is a server that provides storage for users and information systems. A **storage area network** (**SAN**) provides storage to other servers. An **enterprise storage system** uses a combination of techniques to consolidate storage so operations run efficiently. Blade servers pack a complete computer server on a single card. **High-availability systems** continue running and performing tasks for at least 99 percent of the time.

Visit **scsite.com/dc2005/quiz** or click the Quiz Yourself button. Click Objectives 4 – 7 below Chapter 14.

8 Why Is Computer Backup Important and How Is It Accomplished?

A backup duplicates a file or program to protect an enterprise if the original is lost or damaged. A *full backup* copies all of the files in a computer. A *differential backup* copies only files that have changed since the last full backup. An *incremental backup* copies only files that have changed since the last full or incremental backup. A *selective backup* allows users to back up specific files. *Backup procedures* specify a regular plan of copying and storing data and program files.

9 What Are the Steps in a Disaster Recovery Plan?

A **disaster recovery plan** describes the steps a company would take to restore computer operations in the event of a disaster. A disaster recovery plan contains four components. The *emergency plan* specifies the steps to be taken immediately after a disaster strikes. The *backup plan* stipulates how a company uses backup files and equipment to resume information processing. The *recovery plan* identifies the actions to be taken to restore full information processing operations. The *test plan* contains information for simulating disasters and recording an organization's ability to recover.

10 Why Is Computer Security Important to an Enterprise?

The goals of enterprise-wide information security are to maintain confidentiality, ensure integrity and reliability of systems, guarantee availability of systems, assure compliance with laws, and cooperate with law enforcement agencies. A computer security plan summarizes the safeguards that are in place to protect a company's information assets.

Visit **scsite.com/dc2005/quiz** or click the Quiz Yourself button. Click Objectives 8 – 10 below Chapter 14.

CHAPTER 14 KEY TERMS

QUIZZES AND LEARNING GAMES
Computer Genius
Crossword Puzzle
Interactive Labs
Practice Test
Quiz Yourself
Wheel of Terms

EXERCISES
Chapter Review
Checkpoint
Key Terms
Lab Exercises
Learn It Online
Web Research

BEYOND THE BOOK
Apply It
Career Corner
Companies
FAQ
High-Tech Talk
Issues
Looking Ahead
Trailblazers
Web Links

FEATURES
Guide to Web Sites
Making Use of the Web
Tech News
Timeline 2005

You should know the Primary Terms and be familiar with the Secondary Terms.

WEB INSTRUCTIONS:

To display this page from the Web, start your browser and enter the Web address **scsite.com/dc2005/ch14/terms**. Click a term to display its definition and a picture. When the picture displays, click the more info button for current and additional information about the term from the Web.

>> Primary Terms

(shown in bold-black characters in the chapter)

artificial intelligence (AI) (730)
blade servers (745)
CD-ROM server (744)
computer-aided design (CAD) (721)
computer-aided engineering (CAE) (722)
computer-aided manufacturing (CAM) (722)
computer-integrated manufacturing (CIM) (722)
computer security plan (749)
content management system (CMS) (732)
customer interaction management (CIM) (724)
customer relationship management (CRM) (732)
data warehouse (734)
decision support system (DSS) (728)
disaster recovery plan (748)
distribution systems (724)
DVD-ROM server (744)
EDI (electronic data interchange) (734)
enterprise (714)
enterprise computing (714)
enterprise hardware (741)
enterprise information (718)
enterprise resource planning (ERP) (730)
enterprise storage system (744)
e-retail (738)
executive management (717)
expert system (729)
extranet (735)
high-availability systems (745)
Human Resources Information Systems (HRIS) (720)
information system (719)
interoperability (746)
knowledge management (KM) (730)
knowledge management software (KMS) (730)
management information system (MIS) (727)
managers (718)
Manufacturing Resource Planning II (MRP II) (722)
marketing information system (723)
Material Requirements Planning (MRP) (722)
middle management (717)
network attached storage (NAS) (743)
nonmanagement employees (718)
office information system (OIS) (726)
online banking (739)
online trading (739)
operational management (717)
portal (733)
RAID (redundant array of independent disks) (742)
redundant components (745)
sales force automation (SFA) (723)
scalability (746)
shopping bot (740)
storage area network (SAN) (743)
transaction processing system (TPS) (726)
virtual private network (VPN) (737)
Web services (735)
workflow (736)
workflow application (736)

>> Secondary Terms

(shown in italic characters in the chapter)

archival backup (747)
availability (741)
backup plan (748)
backup procedures (747)
batch processing (726)
blade (745)
blade server chassis (745)
CD-ROM jukebox (744)
centralized (717)
chief information officer (CIO) (725)
chief security officer (CSO) (749)
click stream (734)
closed (746)
cold site (748)
controlling (718)
core activities (716)
cyber cash (738)
data processing (726)
decentralized (716)
detailed report (727)
differential backup (747)
digital cash (738)
downtime (745)
DVD-ROM jukebox (744)
electronic money (738)
emergency plan (748)
e-money (738)
employee relationship management (ERM) system (721)
empowering (718)
enterprise-wide systems (725)
e-tail (738)
exception criteria (727)
exception report (727)
executive information system (EIS) (728)
external sources (728)
full backup (747)
functional units (720)
hot site (748)
hot-swapping (745)
incremental backup (747)
indexes (732)
inference rules (729)
information architecture (725)
internal sources (728)
International Computer Security Association (ICSA) Labs (750)
Internet backup (745)
knowledge base (729)
knowledge workers (730)
leading (718)
level 1 (742)
market research system (723)
merchant account (738)
metadata (732)
mirroring (742)
office automation (726)
online analytical processing (OLAP) (728)
online transaction processing (OLTP) (726)
open (746)
operational decision (717)
operations (716)
organizing (718)
outsourcing (745)
partial backup (747)
personalization (734)
planning (718)
procedure (719)
proprietary (746)
reciprocal backup relationship (748)
recovery plan (749)
redundancy (741)
security software (725)
selective backup (747)
storage appliance (743)
strategic decisions (717)
striping (742)
summary report (727)
supporting activities (716)
tactical decisions (717)
tape library (744)
test plan (749)
transaction (726)
ultradense servers (745)
uptime (745)
VPN tunnel (737)
Web farming (734)
Web site management programs (725)

CHECKPOINT CHAPTER 14

Use the Checkpoint exercises to check your knowledge level of the chapter.

WEB INSTRUCTIONS:

To display this page from the Web, start your browser and enter the Web address **scsite.com/dc2005/ch14/check**. Click the links for current and additional information.

LABEL THE FIGURE

Identify the types of storage used in an enterprise storage system.

a. CD-ROM and DVD-ROM jukeboxes
b. Internet backup
c. NAS device
d. RAID
e. SAN
f. servers
g. tape libraries

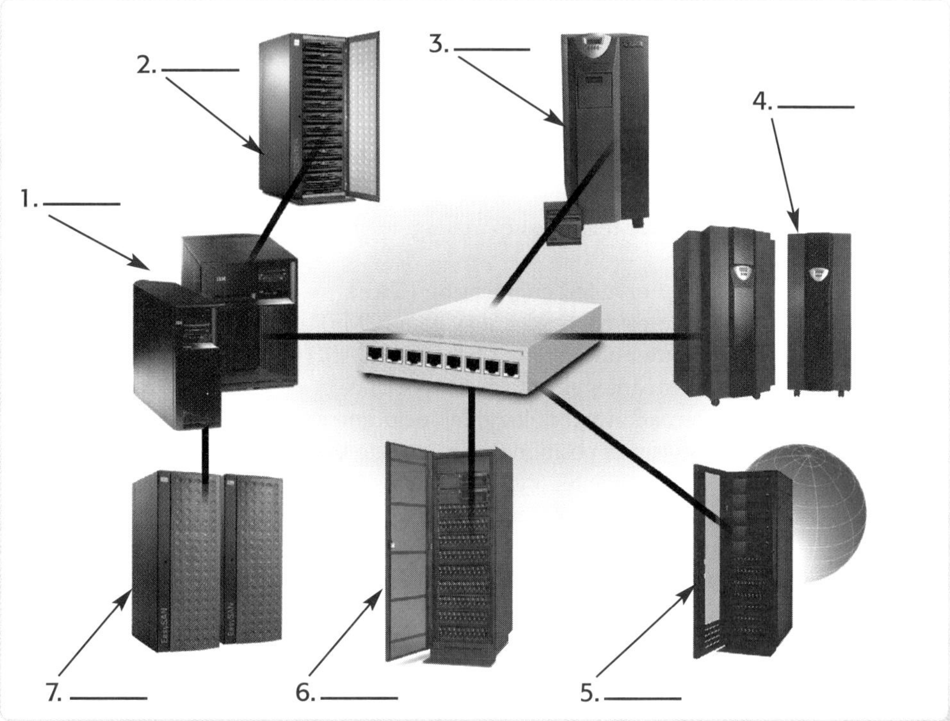

TRUE/FALSE

Mark T for True and F for False. (See page numbers in parentheses.)

_____ 1. Enterprises produce and gather enormous volumes of information. (714)

_____ 2. The activities relating to running the business are called supporting activities. (716)

_____ 3. Operational management is responsible for implementing the strategic decisions of executive management. (717)

_____ 4. An information system is a set of hardware, software, data, people, and procedures that works together to produce information. (719)

_____ 5. Manufacturing Resource Planning II includes software that helps in scheduling and tracking production in real time, and monitoring product quality. (722)

_____ 6. An MIS summary report usually lists only transactions. (727)

_____ 7. Artificial intelligence is the application of human intelligence to computers. (730)

_____ 8. A workflow application is a program that assists in the management and tracking of all the activities in a business from start to finish. (736)

_____ 9. Network attached storage is a high-speed network with the sole purpose of providing storage to other servers to which it is attached. (743)

_____ 10. Information systems that have interoperability and easily share information with other information systems are said to be closed, or proprietary. (746)

MULTIPLE CHOICE

Select the best answer. (See page numbers in parentheses.)

1. A centralized approach to information systems usually _____ manageability. (717)
   a. reduces costs of maintenance and increases
   b. reduces costs of maintenance and reduces
   c. increases costs of maintenance and increases
   d. increases costs of maintenance and reduces
2. _____ is the use of computers to control production equipment. (722)
   a. Computer relationship management (CRM)
   b. Computer-aided engineering (CAE)
   c. Computer management system (CMS)
   d. Computer-aided manufacturing (CAM)
3. Many companies elevate the importance of IT (information technology) by including a _____ executive position that reports to the CEO. (725)
   a. chief operations officer (COO)
   b. chief financial officer (CFO)
   c. chief security officer (CSO)
   d. chief information officer (CIO)
4. An exception report _____. (727)
   a. lists all transactions during a given period
   b. consolidates data with totals, tables, or graphs
   c. identifies data outside a normal condition
   d. all of the above
5. An advantage of ERP is _____. (731)
   a. complete integration of information systems across departments
   b. better project management
   c. better customer service
   d. all of the above
6. A _____ is a collection of every action that users make as they move through a Web site. (734)
   a. cold site
   b. click stream
   c. workflow
   d. hot site
7. The secure connection created between a user's computer and a company's network is called a(n) _____. (737)
   a. VPN tunnel
   b. blade server
   c. EDI portal
   d. data warehouse
8. If an e-retailer wants to accept credit card payments from customers, it sets up a _____ with a credit card company. (738)
   a. merchant account
   b. shopping bot
   c. distribution system
   d. knowledge base
9. A shopping bot is a Web site that _____. (740)
   a. allows users to pay bills from their computers
   b. guides users to information about their jobs
   c. searches the Internet for the best price on a product or service
   d. allows businesses to create products and B2B interactions
10. The _____ of hardware to users is a measure of how often it is online. (741)
    a. redundancy
    b. scalability
    c. availability
    d. interoperability
11. Companies using _____ store data, information, and instructions on the Web. (745)
    a. RAID
    b. Internet backup
    c. a CD-ROM server
    d. a tape library
12. A(n) _____ allows a user to choose specific files to back up, regardless of whether or not the files have changed. (747)
    a. full backup
    b. selective backup
    c. incremental backup
    d. differential backup
13. A(n) _____ contains information for simulating various levels of disaster and recording an organization's ability to recover from the simulation. (749)
    a. emergency plan
    b. test plan
    c. backup plan
    d. recovery plan
14. Besides being trusted with the physical security of a company's property and people, the _____ often is trusted with securing computing resources. (749)
    a. chief operations officer (COO)
    b. chief financial officer (CFO)
    c. chief security officer (CSO)
    d. chief information officer (CIO)

CHECKPOINT CHAPTER 14

MATCHING

Match the terms with their definitions. (See page numbers in parentheses.)

_____ 1. supporting activities (716)
_____ 2. core activities (716)
_____ 3. MRP (722)
_____ 4. enterprise-wide systems (725)
_____ 5. personalization (734)
_____ 6. Web farming (734)
_____ 7. workflow (736)
_____ 8. tape library (744)
_____ 9. CD-ROM server (744)
_____ 10. redundant components (745)

a. activities relating to running a business
b. instructing and authorizing others to perform necessary work
c. holds hundreds of CD-ROMs that can contain programs and data
d. customization of a portal page to meet a user's needs
e. process of collecting data from the Internet as a source for a data warehouse
f. monitors and controls processes related to production
g. process that identifies the specific set of steps involved in completing a project
h. business activities that involve what the business does
i. high-capacity system that uses multiple tape cartridges for storing backups
j. allow for a functioning system component to take over if a similar component fails
k. allow business to create products and B2B interactions
l. used by one or more functional units in an enterprise

SHORT ANSWER

Write a brief answer to each of the following questions.

1. What are managers? ___________ What four activities do managers perform to coordinate resources? ___________
2. What is a management information system (MIS)? ___________ How are a detailed report, a summary report, and an exception report different? ___________
3. In an expert system, how is the knowledge base different from the inference rules? ___________ What is artificial intelligence (AI)? ___________
4. What is RAID? ___________ How is mirroring different from striping? ___________
5. What are scalability and interoperability? ___________ How is an open information system different from a closed system? ___________

WORKING TOGETHER

Working with a group of your classmates, complete the following team exercises.

1. Intelligent machines have intrigued humans since ancient times. Today, computers and artificial intelligence (AI) capture our imagination. Categories within this topic include expert systems, neural networks, artificial life, fuzzy logic, natural language processing, and robotics. Together with your team, select one of these categories and explore it using printed material and the Web. Then, create a PowerPoint presentation to share with the class how the category of artificial intelligence is used today and might be used in the future.
2. Choose one Issue from the following issues in this chapter: Would You Work in a Monitored Office? (718), Can You Take It with You? (724), Should ISPs Share Customer Information? (732), Would You Buy Online? (738), or Is It Serious, Doc? (740). Use the Web and/or print media to research the issue. Then, present a debate for the class, with different members of your team supporting different responses to the questions that accompany the issue.
3. The type of information system employed and the purpose for which it is used depend on an individual's place in an organization. Have each member of your team interview a manager and a nonmanagement employee at a local company. What type of information systems do they use? Why? How do the information systems influence their work? How were their jobs different before the information systems were introduced? Meet with the members of your team to discuss your findings. Then, create a PowerPoint presentation and share with the class how different managers and nonmanagement employees use information systems.

CHAPTER 14 LEARN IT ONLINE

QUIZZES AND LEARNING GAMES
Computer Genius
Crossword Puzzle
Interactive Labs
Practice Test
Quiz Yourself
Wheel of Terms

EXERCISES
Chapter Review
Checkpoint
Key Terms
Lab Exercises
Learn It Online
Web Research

BEYOND THE BOOK
Apply It
Career Corner
Companies
FAQ
High-Tech Talk
Issues
Looking Ahead
Trailblazers
Web Links

FEATURES
Guide to Web Sites
Making Use of the Web
Tech News
Timeline 2005

Use the Learn It Online exercises to reinforce your understanding of the chapter concepts.

WEB INSTRUCTIONS:

To display this page from the Web, start your browser and enter the Web address **scsite.com/dc2005/ch14/learn**.

1 At the Movies – Technosaurs

To view the Technosaurs movie, click the number 1 button. Watch the movie and then complete the exercise by answering the questions below. Just as rapid, massive climate changes are said to have rendered dinosaurs extinct, dizzying changes in computer technology challenge today's companies to evolve, adapt, or ... die off. Traditional brokerages are losing billions of dollars to online trading. Travel Web sites on the Internet are siphoning billions of dollars from bricks-and-mortar travel agencies. Changes in communications hardware and software for sales and service functions threaten companies as well. What are some of the new technologies that radically can improve the competitiveness of a company's sales force? What are some of the new software programs to manage customer relationships better?

2 Student Edition Labs – E-Commerce

Click the number 2 button. When the Student Edition Labs menu appears, click *E-Commerce* to begin. A new browser window will open. Follow the on-screen instructions to complete the Lab. When finished, click the Exit button. If required, print a copy of your results to submit to your instructor.

3 Student Edition Labs – Backing Up Your Computer

Click the number 3 button. When the Student Edition Labs menu appears, click *Backing Up Your Computer* to begin. A new browser window will open. Follow the on-screen instructions to complete the Lab. When finished, click the Exit button. If required, print a copy of your results to submit to your instructor.

4 Online Banking

Online banking is a standard offering in the United States. Online banking effectively transforms your personal computer into a bank teller. Using an online banking service, you can complete nearly all transactions, with the exception of a cash withdrawal, that you would take care of during a trip to the bank. Access to more detailed financial information allows you to track better where your money is going, as well as plan where you want it to go in the future. To determine if online banking is for you, click the number 4 button and read Online Banking: The Basics.

5 E-Government

Will e-government revolutionize the way U.S. citizens interact with government? The increased use of Internet-based solutions to facilitate business-to-business and business-to-consumer interactions has major implications for federal, state, and local governments. The ideal concept of e-government would be to provide services and information to citizens electronically, 24 hours a day, 7 days a week. Many government agencies have some of these services in place. Click the number 5 button to find out more about what governmental agencies are doing. Download and review one of the PowerPoint presentations. Write a summary about your discoveries.

6 Practice Test

Click the number 6 button. Answer each question. When completed, enter your name and click the Grade Test button to submit the quiz for grading. Make a note of any missed questions. If required, print a copy to submit to your instructor.

7 Web Guide

Click the number 7 button to display the Guide to Web Sites and Searching Techniques Web page. Click Reference and then click About.com. Search for electronic commerce. Click one of the electronic commerce links. Use your word processing program to prepare a brief report about your findings and submit your assignment to your instructor.

8 Scavenger Hunt

Click the number 8 button. Print a copy of the Scavenger Hunt page; use this page to write down your answers as you search the Web. Submit your completed page to your instructor.

9 Who Wants To Be a Computer Genius?

Click the number 9 button to find out if you are a computer genius. Directions on how to play the game will be displayed. When you are ready to play, click the Play button. Submit your score to your instructor.

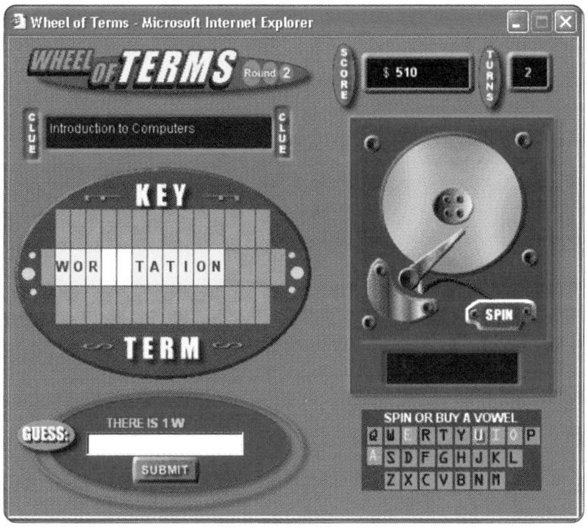

10 Wheel of Terms

Click the number 10 button to reinforce important terms you learned in this chapter by playing the Shelly Cashman Series version of this popular game. Directions on how to play the game will be displayed. When you are ready to play, click the Play button. Submit your score to your instructor.

11 Career Corner

Click the number 11 button to display the BrainBuzz page. In the Job Search text box, type Web developer. Select your state and click the Go button. Scroll through the results until you find a link in which you are interested. Write a brief report on what you discovered by clicking this link. Submit the report to your instructor.

12 Search Sleuth

Click the number 12 button to learn search techniques that will help make you a research expert. Submit the completed assignment to your instructor.

13 Crossword Puzzle Challenge

Click the number 13 button. Complete the puzzle to reinforce skills you learned in this chapter. Directions on how to play the game will be displayed. When you are ready to play, click the Submit button. Submit the completed puzzle to your instructor.

14 Online Sales

A recent Forrester Research report predicts that by the year 2007, U.S. online retail sales will total $218 billion, or 8% of U.S. retail sales. The report further projects large increases in Web-researched offline sales and factors that determine which items are purchased offline versus online. Click the number 14 button to access a list of some of the more successful online e-retailers. Click one of the company links. Which company did you select? What products does it have available? Is the Web site easy to navigate? Does it have a product you would purchase online?

15 In the News

The Internet is predicted to be a driving force in both the new and used vehicle market over the next five years. A survey released by the National Automobile Dealers Association indicates that e-commerce is starting to pay off for car dealers that have a well-established Internet presence. As more dealerships recognize the Web's power as a sales tool, online sales are expected to continue to increase. Click the number 15 button and read a news article about a recent e-commerce success story. What is the product or company? How has it been successful? Is this success expected to continue?

CHAPTER 14 LAB EXERCISES

Previous | Next

Use the Lab Exercises to gain hands-on computer experience.

WEB INSTRUCTIONS:

To display this page from the Web, start your browser and enter the Web address **scsite.com/dc2005/ch14/lab**.

1 Changing Views in Windows XP

This exercise uses Windows XP procedures. Windows XP provides five ways of viewing folders and files. Right-click the Start button on the taskbar and then click Explore on the shortcut menu. When the Start Menu window is displayed, click View on the menu bar and then click Thumbnails. Notice how Windows XP displays the folder/file names in the right pane in Thumbnails view. Click View on the menu bar and then click Tiles. Notice again how Windows XP displays the folder/file names in the right pane. Repeat the above procedure to display the Icons, List, and Details views. Answer the following questions:

- Which view option displays the type of file?
- Which view option displays the date the file or folder was modified?
- What is the difference between the List view and the Icon view?
- Which view is easiest to read?

Close the Start Menu window.

2 Using Windows Update

This exercise uses Windows XP procedures. You must be connected to the Internet to complete this exercise. Click the Start button on the taskbar and then click Help and Support on the Start menu. When the Help and Support Center window is displayed, click the Index button on the toolbar. Type `support` in the Type keyword to find text box. Select the Web sites for Windows information and support topic and then click the Display button. Click the plus sign next to Online product support in the right pane and then click the Online product support link. When the Windows XP Support Center window is displayed, if necessary, maximize the window. Click the Frequently Asked Questions link in the Highlights & Top Issues area. Answer the following questions by clicking the appropriate links.

- How do you connect more than one computer to the Internet?
- How do you copy music to and from an audio CD in Windows XP?
- How do you determine if your programs are compatible with Windows XP?

Close each open window.

3 Create a Desktop Shortcut to the Printer

This exercise uses Windows 2000/98 procedures. To create a desktop shortcut to a printer, click the Start button on the taskbar, point to Settings, and then click Printers. Right-click the icon of your default printer and then click Create Shortcut. When Windows indicates that the shortcut has to go on the desktop, click the OK or Yes button to place the shortcut on the desktop. After you create a shortcut to a printer, you can print documents by dragging them to the printer shortcut on the desktop. The program used to print the document will open briefly and then close. Close the Printers window. Right-click the printer desktop shortcut icon, click Shortcut Properties, and then click the General tab. What information is contained in this dialog box? Click the Shortcut tab. What are the two settings that can be modified? Close the Properties dialog box. Right-click the printer desktop shortcut icon and then click Confirm File Delete on the shortcut menu. If necessary, click the Yes button in the Delete dialog box.

4 Determine the Brand and Model of Sound Cards or Audio Devices in Your Computer

This exercise uses Windows XP procedures. To determine the brand and model of the sound cards or audio devices installed in your computer, click the Start button on the Windows taskbar and then click Control Panel. In Category View, click the Performance and Maintenance icon in the Control Panel window. Click the System icon in the Performance and Maintenance window to display the System Properties dialog box. Click the Hardware tab and then click the Device Manager button. Double-click Sound, video and game controllers to expand the structure. What sound devices are listed? What video devices are listed? What game controller devices are listed? What media control devices are listed? Close the Device Manager window and then close the System Properties dialog box. Close the Performance and Maintenance window.

WEB RESEARCH

Use the Web Research exercises to learn more about the special features in this chapter.

WEB INSTRUCTIONS:

Use the link in each exercise or a search engine such as Google (google.com) to research the topic. Then, write a one-page, double-spaced report or create a presentation, unless otherwise directed below. Page numbers on which information can be found are in parentheses.

1 **Issue** Choose one Issue from the following issues in this chapter: Would You Work in a Monitored Office? (718), Can You Take It with You? (724), Should ISPs Share Customer Information? (732), Would You Buy Online? (738), or Is It Serious, Doc? (740). Use the Web to research the issue. Discuss the issue with classmates, instructors, and friends. Address the questions that accompany the issue in a report or presentation.

2 **Apply It** Choose one of the following Apply It features in this chapter: Smart Chips Gather Useful Data (722) or Instant Messaging Finds Business Home (725). Use the Web to gather additional information about the topic. Print two Web pages that relate to the Apply It. Detail in a report or presentation what you learned.

3 **Career Corner** Read the Career Corner article in this chapter (750). Use the Web to find out more about the career. Describe the career in a report or presentation.

4 **Companies on the Cutting Edge** Choose one of the Companies on the Cutting Edge in this chapter (752). Use the Web to research the company further. Explain in a report or presentation how this company has contributed to computer technology.

5 **Technology Trailblazers** Choose one of the Technology Trailblazers in this chapter (753). Use the Web to research the person further. Explain in a report or presentation how this individual has affected the way people use, or think about, computers.

6 **Picture Yourself Interacting with Customer Service** Read the Picture Yourself Interacting with Customer Service story at the beginning of this chapter (712). Use the Web to research enterprise computing further. Describe in a report or presentation the ways in which you might interact with an enterprise.

7 **High-Tech Talk** Read the High-Tech Talk feature in this chapter (751). Use the Web to find out more about the topic. Summarize in a report or presentation what you learned.

8 **Web Links** Review the Web Link boxes found in the margins of this chapter. Visit five of the Web Link sites. Print the main Web page for each site you visit. Choose one of the Web pages and then summarize in one paragraph the content of the Web page.

9 **Looking Ahead** Choose one of the Looking Ahead articles in this chapter: Cellular Telephones Allow Remote Monitoring (730), On-Demand Computing Uses Utility Model (741), or Grid Computing Increases Processing Power (746). Use the Web to find out more about the topic. Detail in a report or presentation what you learned.

10 **FAQ** Choose one FAQ found in this chapter. Use the Web to find out more about the topic. Summarize in one paragraph what you learned.

11 **Making Use of the Web** Read the Careers section of Making Use of the Web in Appendix A (APP 28). Complete the Careers Web Exercises at the end of the section (APP 29). Answer the questions posed in each exercise.

CHAPTER 15

Computer Careers and Certification

Picture Yourself Career Planning

College life has been much more than you anticipated… more demanding, more challenging, more rewarding, and more fun! It took a few weeks to coordinate all your classes and activities, but now with the semester under way, you are settling into the school atmosphere. Classes are intense, but all the hard work and efforts are paying off. Your grades so far have been good. Best of all, you have made many new friends. In fact, you just joined a few of them in the student lounge.

The group's conversation centers on registration, which starts tomorrow. You, and most of your friends, are in the General Studies program. The dilemma now is selecting a major. That decision will determine which classes you take next semester. You have not made an appointment with an advisor yet because you still are contemplating your course options.

One friend mentions that some departments offer one-credit courses that explore careers in a field of study. He is interested in computers, so he plans to sign up for the Computing Careers course next semester. You like working with computers. Immediately, you add the Computing Careers course to your schedule.

As you read Chapter 15, you will learn about careers in the computer industry and discover types of information technology certifications.

OBJECTIVES

After completing this chapter, you will be able to:

1. Describe career opportunities available in various segments of the computer industry
2. Discuss functions of jobs available in an IT department
3. Differentiate among various college computer-related courses of study
4. Identify ways to stay current with changing technology after graduation
5. List the benefits of certification for employers, employees, and vendors
6. Identify ways to prepare for certification
7. List the general areas of IT certification
8. Name some specific IT certifications in each certification area

CONTENTS

THE COMPUTER INDUSTRY

In today's technology-rich world, a high demand for computer professionals exists. The U.S. Department of Labor's Bureau of Labor Statistics (BLS) reports that of the 10 fastest growing occupations, 8 are in computer-related fields. These include software engineers, computer support specialists, network administrators, data communications analysts, desktop publishers, database administrators, and systems analysts.

The Information Technology Association of America (ITAA) estimates that the current computer workforce is about 10 million workers with an expected net increase of about 86,000 new computer-related jobs available annually. One of every three jobs in the United States is a computer-related job with a computer firm or with a firm that requires the skills of a computer professional.

While the use of computers and the demand for computer specialists continue to grow, the number of students majoring in computer-related fields is much less than what the industry needs. According to the United States Department of Education, less than 10 percent of college students are graduating with degrees in computer-related fields. Clearly, a demand exists for students majoring in computers (Figure 15-1).

As presented in the Career Corner feature at the end of each chapter of this book, the computer industry offers many rewarding careers. These computer-related careers often require a unique combination of hands-on skills, creative problem solving, and an understanding of business needs. This chapter discusses a variety of careers in the computer industry, how to prepare for these types of jobs, and available certifications.

FIGURE 15-1 Many computer career opportunities are available to computer specialists.

CAREERS IN THE COMPUTER INDUSTRY

With billions of dollars in annual revenue, the computer industry is one of the larger worldwide industries. This emphasis on computers has created thousands of new high-tech jobs, even in noncomputer-related companies. Job opportunities in the computer industry generally fall into these areas:

- General business and government organizations
- Computer equipment industry
- Computer software industry
- Computer service and repair industry
- Computer sales
- Computer education and training industry
- Computer consulting industry

The following pages discuss the function of each of these areas, as well as career opportunities and specific jobs available. In the fast-paced world of technology, job titles are not standardized. Some companies are reducing their number of job titles or combining job titles into one position such as programmer/analyst. Other companies create a new job title each time they hire someone.

Computer Careers in General Business and Government Organizations

Businesses and government offices of all sizes use computers. Without computers, very few could operate in today's economy. Nearly every organization uses computers for basic document preparation. Employees of all types, from the office workers to the shop foreman, use business software such as word processing to prepare daily documents (read Apply It 15-1 for more information). Other employees in the organization use computers for specialized activities such as the management of company finances.

Most organizations have networks to help ensure smooth communications among employees, vendors, and customers. As discussed in Chapter 14, larger businesses use computers to answer and route telephone calls, process orders, update inventory, and manage accounts receivable, accounts payable, billing, and payroll activities. Some firms use computers to order raw materials automatically, control manufacturing, and ship finished goods.

APPLY IT 15-1

Application Software Skills Essential for Career

Can you think of a business that does not use a computer? Today, almost every career field — from accounting to zoology — requires computers for its everyday business operations.

Potential employees should be comfortable using a computer and familiar with Microsoft Office applications. For example, some companies test applicants' abilities to customize Windows; edit and format a Word document from a rough draft; enter and graph data and use functions in an Excel worksheet; and create, query, and maintain an Access database.

Business employees also should be able to navigate the Internet and send and receive e-mail. Employers often assess applicants' keyboarding skills, especially for customer service, order taking, and information processing positions, by measuring their speed and accuracy in using data entry forms.

If you enjoy sharing your computer knowledge with others, a career as a help desk specialist may prove rewarding. This field is one of the more in-demand careers. According to the Information Technology Association of America, 25 percent of the new computer-related positions are for help desk specialists.

For more information about computer usage in careers, visit the Discovering Computers 2005 Apply It Web page (**scsite.com/dc2005/apply**). Click Apply It #1 below Chapter 15.

Government offices use computers and the Web to provide the public with a means to access their facilities. For example, people in the United States use computers to file taxes, apply for permits and licenses, pay parking tickets, buy stamps, report crimes, apply for financial aid, and renew vehicle registrations and driver's licenses.

To manage their computers and operations, businesses and government offices have a variety of computer-related job opportunities. Most medium and large businesses and governmental agencies have an **information technology (IT) department** that employs people in computer-related jobs (Figure 15-2). Employees in the **IT department** are responsible for keeping all the computer operations and networks in business and government running smoothly. They also determine when and if the company requires new hardware or software. A later section in this chapter discusses the specific jobs available in an IT department. Read Looking Ahead 15-1 for a look at the future of IT careers.

FIGURE 15-2 In larger businesses and government offices, the IT department includes professionals who set up and manage the computer equipment and software to ensure that it produces quality information for users.

LOOKING AHEAD 15-1

When Can You Start?

The information technology (IT) field is a $2.5 trillion global industry, according to some estimates, and employs more than 10 million people. As companies retool in response to the economic downturn in 2001, they are hiring candidates who offer the widest range of expertise, including an understanding of technology's impact in today's world.

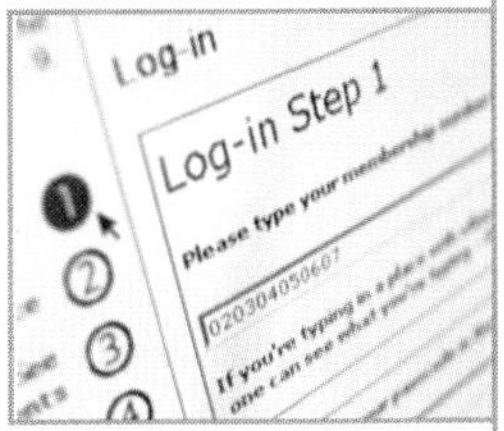

The top skill, according to the Information Technology Association of America (ITAA), is experience, particularly in C++, Oracle, SQL, Java, and Windows NT. Certification has increased as an important means of assessing entry-level candidates. A bachelor's degree is essential for people pursuing positions as a database developer, programmer and software engineer, enterprise system integrator, and technical writer.

The ITAA urges U.S. workers to remain competitive for jobs in today's global market. The best method of preparing for a career in the IT field is through education at an early age, particularly in elementary and high school. Educators need to create a mindset that jobs in the field are rewarding and challenging and should motivate students to pursue undergraduate and graduate degrees in the field. The organization adds that keeping abreast of IT trends is a lifelong process, so companies are encouraged to continue to retrain workers throughout their tenure.

For a look at the future of IT careers, visit the Discovering Computers 2005 Looking Ahead Web page (**scsite.com/dc2005/looking**). Click Looking Ahead #1 below Chapter 15.

The Computer Equipment Industry

The **computer equipment industry** consists of manufacturers and distributors of computers and computer-related hardware such as disk and tape drives, monitors, printers, and communications and networking devices. In addition to the companies that make end-user equipment, thousands of companies build components that most users never see. These companies manufacture chips, motherboards, power supplies, and the hundreds of other parts used inside a computer.

Careers in this industry involve the design, manufacture, and production of computer equipment. Jobs include designing and fabricating computer chips, testing internal components (Figure 15-3), assembling computers, and packing computers and peripherals. In larger companies several levels exist for each job, including management careers.

Computer equipment manufacturers include such companies as AMD, Apple Computer, Cisco Systems, Dell Computer, Gateway, Hewlett-Packard, IBM, Intel, Logitech, Lucent Technologies, Motorola, Nokia, QUALCOMM, Sun Microsystems, and 3Com. Many of these firms are huge organizations with thousands of employees worldwide. IBM, for example, is one of the larger computer companies with more than 315,000 employees and annual sales of more than $81 billion.

The computer equipment industry also is well known for the many startup companies that appear each year. These new companies take advantage of rapid changes in equipment technology, such as wireless communications, networking, multimedia, and fiber optics, to create new products and new job opportunities. Often these companies offer stock options to influence college graduates to join their firms instead of the larger, more established companies.

FIGURE 15-3 Computer-related manufacturing jobs are found throughout the computer equipment industry.

The Computer Software Industry

The **computer software industry** consists of companies that develop, manufacture, and support a wide range of software. Some software companies specialize in a particular type of software such as business software or utility programs. Other software companies, especially larger firms such as Microsoft, produce and sell a variety of programs.

Career opportunities in the software industry involve designing and programming all kinds of software, including operating systems and utility programs; business, graphics, multimedia, home, personal, educational, and entertainment software; network software; software development tools; and Internet and Web page authoring software.

Job titles for careers related to the development of software include project developer, programmer, software engineer, and computer scientist. Some work with application software; others work with system software. A **project developer** analyzes software requirements, designs software solutions, and oversees the software development process. A **programmer** writes and tests computer programs (read Issue 15-1 for a related discussion). A **software engineer** designs and develops software. A **computer scientist** researches, invents, and develops innovative solutions to complex software requirements or problems.

WEB LINK 15-1

Computer Scientists

Visit the Discovering Computers 2005 WEB LINK page (**scsite .com/dc2005/weblink**). Click Computer Scientists below Chapter 15.

ISSUE 15-1

Should Programmers Be Licensed?

In most states, physicians and attorneys must be licensed in order to practice. Pharmacists, therapists, public accountants, architects, surveyors, engineers, contractors, and veterinarians are among other occupations that are licensed in some states. Licensing ensures that individuals evidence certain competencies to obtain their certification and demonstrate specific practical and ethical standards to maintain their certification. Licensing requirements vary by state and by occupation. For a medical clinic to obtain licensing in New York State, for example, it must meet rigorous benchmarks for equipment, procedures, cleanliness, and staff training both during initial examination and at subsequent periodic inspections. By regulating occupations that have a direct effect on health or well-being, licensing protects the public interest. Computer programmers work on programs that have a huge influence on people's lives. Should programmers be licensed? Why or why not? If programmers were licensed, what competencies should they have to demonstrate to earn their certification? What standards should they practice to maintain their certification?

For more information about licensing programmers, visit the Discovering Computers 2005 Issues Web page (**scsite.com/dc2005/issues**). Click Issue #1 below Chapter 15.

The software industry is huge, with annual sales exceeding $200 billion. Leading software companies include Adobe Systems, BMC Software, Broderbund, Computer Associates, IBM, Intuit, Macromedia, Microsoft, Network Associates, Novell, Oracle, RealNetworks, Red Hat, Sybase, and Symantec. The largest software company, Microsoft, has nearly 55,000 employees and annual sales of more than $32 billion.

Computer Careers in the Service and Repair Industry

The **computer service and repair industry** provides preventive maintenance, component installation, and repair services to customers. Typical job titles for workers in this field include service technician, computer repairperson, repair technician, and computer technician.

A **computer technician** installs, maintains, and repairs hardware (Figure 15-4); installs, upgrades, and configures software; and troubleshoots hardware problems. Being a computer technician is a challenging job for people who like to troubleshoot and solve problems and have a strong background in electronics.

In the early days of computers, computer technicians often made repairs at the site of the computer equipment. Today, however, computer technicians first replace a malfunctioning component, such as a hard disk, and then take the faulty part back for repair at an office or special repair facility.

Many computer equipment manufacturers include diagnostic software with their computer equipment that assists computer technicians in identifying problems.

FIGURE 15-4 Computer technicians require a knowledge of electronics.

Some computers even use a modem to call a computer automatically at a repair technician's office and leave a message that a malfunction has been detected. Today's technology also allows computer technicians to diagnose and repair software problems from a remote location. That is, the technician accesses the user's hard disk from a different location.

Computer Careers in Sales

Computer sales representatives must have a general understanding of computers and a specific knowledge of the product they are selling. Strong people skills are important, including a strong listening ability and good oral communications skills. Computer sales representatives generally determine a buyer's needs and match it to the correct hardware and software. Thus, they also need a good understanding of the products available, and they need to know how to explain computers without using jargon.

Some sales representatives work directly for computer equipment and software manufacturers such as Apple Computer, Dell, Hewlett-Packard, IBM, and Palm. Others work for resellers, including retailers that sell personal computer products, such as Best Buy, Circuit City, CompUSA, and OfficeMax (Figure 15-5).

FIGURE 15-5 Computer retailers need salespeople who understand the products they sell and have good people skills.

Computer sales representative for a retail store often is a suitable entry-level job for students majoring in computers. Computer manufacturers, software vendors, and retail stores usually pay sales representatives based on the amount of product they sell. More experienced corporate sales representatives can be among an organization's more highly paid employees.

The Computer Education and Training Industry

The increased sophistication and complexity of today's computer products have opened extensive opportunities in computer-related education and training. Schools, colleges, universities, and private companies all need qualified educators. In fact, the high demand has led to a shortage of qualified instructors at the college level as instructors increasingly move into careers in private industry with the promise of higher pay. This shortage probably will not end in the near future because the supply of educators with Ph.D. degrees is not keeping pace with the demand.

Corporate trainers teach employees how to use software, design and develop systems, program, and perform other computer-related activities (Figure 15-6). Many companies have their own training departments. Corporations usually do not require as much educational background from trainers as educational institutions do from instructors.

FIGURE 15-6 Corporate trainers lead continuing education classes and introduce new software.

Consulting in the Computer Industry

After building experience in one or more computer-related areas, some people decide to become computer consultants. A **computer consultant** is a professional who draws upon his or her expertise in a specialized area of computers, including service and advice. Many companies hire a computer consultant to fill in for an employee on an extended leave of absence. Large enterprises often hire teams of consultants to offer advice on technology-related concerns.

Computer consultants not only must have strong technical skills in their specialized area, but also they must have the people skills necessary to communicate their suggestions effectively to their clients. Qualified consultants are in high demand for tasks such as computer selection, system design, communications, network design and installation, and Web development.

Read Issue 15-2 for a discussion related to outsourcing consultants and other IT professionals.

WEB LINK 15-2

Computer Consultants

Visit the Discovering Computers 2005 WEB LINK page (**scsite.com/dc2005/weblink**). Click Computer Consultants below Chapter 15.

QUIZ YOURSELF 15-1

To check your knowledge of careers available in various areas of the computer industry, visit the Discovering Computers 2005 Quiz Yourself Web page (**scsite.com/dc2005/quiz**). Click Objective 1 below Chapter 15.

ISSUE 15-2

Should Companies Send IT Jobs Abroad?

To cut costs, some U.S. companies are replacing their American workers with workers in foreign countries. Many of these displaced workers are IT professionals, such as programmers and technical support specialists. In an age of high-speed computer communications, companies believe that IT workers in countries such as India and Russia can be just as effective as, and far less expensive than, their American counterparts. Executives say that outsourcing IT jobs to foreign countries increases corporate profits and benefits shareholders. Disgruntled employees maintain that substituting low-cost foreign workers for American job-holders is unpatriotic, morally wrong, and often frustrating because of language barriers. Should companies replace American workers with workers in foreign countries? Why or why not? What can be done to counter the trend to outsource IT work overseas? Should laws be enacted to protect American jobs? Or should American workers simply accept that, to compete in today's global marketplace, they must be willing to do more for less? Why?

For more information about outsourcing IT jobs, visit the Discovering Computers 2005 Issues Web page (**scsite.com/dc2005/issues**) and click Issue #2 below Chapter 15.

WEB LINK 15-3

Computer Career Salaries

Visit the Discovering Computers 2005 WEB LINK page (**scsite .com/dc2005/weblink**). Click Computer Career Salaries below Chapter 15.

WORKING IN AN IT DEPARTMENT

The employees in an IT department work together as a team to meet the information requirements of their organization. An IT department provides career opportunities for people with a variety of skills and talents. Several jobs in an IT department have been discussed previously, including database administrators (Chapter 10), systems analysts (Chapter 12), and programmers (Chapter 13).

In addition to these, many other careers exist. Usually, these jobs fall into five main areas:

1. *Management* — directs the planning, research, development, evaluation, and integration of technology.
2. *System development and programming* — analyzes, designs, develops, and implements new information technology and maintains and improves existing systems.

INFORMATION TECHNOLOGY JOBS

Area	Job Title	Function	Usual Education Required	Annual Salary Range
Management	**E-commerce administrator**	Supervises the development and execution of Internet or e-commerce systems; works with the company's marketing and customer service divisions	Bachelor's degree in Management Information Technology	$59,000 to $125,000
	Network administrator	Installs, configures, and maintains LANs, WANs, intranets, and Internet systems; identifies and resolves connectivity issues	Bachelor's degree in Computer Information Systems or Electrical Engineering Technology	$51,000 to $70,000
	Project leader	Coordinates projects; performs systems analysis and programming tasks	Bachelor's degree in Management Information Technology	$62,000 to $98,000
	Project manager	Oversees all assigned projects; allocates resources, selects teams, conducts performance appraisals	Bachelor's degree in Management Information Technology	$81,000 to $110,000
System development and programming	**Vice president of IT/chief information officer (CIO)**	Directs the company's information service and communications functions	Bachelor's degree in Management Information Technology	$122,000 to $254,000
	Application programmer	Converts the system design into the appropriate computer language, such as Visual Basic .NET 2003, Java, and C++	Associate's or Bachelor's degree in Computer Information Systems	$30,000 to $93,000
	Database analyst	Uses data modeling techniques and tools to analyze, tune, and specify data usage within an application area	Bachelor's degree in Computer Science or Computer Information Systems	$40,000 to $105,000
	Software engineer	Specifies, designs, implements, tests, and documents high-quality software in a variety of fields, including robotics, operating systems, animation, and applications	Bachelor's degree in Computer Science or Software Engineering	$47,000 to $106,000
	Systems analyst	Works closely with users to analyze their requirements, designs and develops new information systems, and incorporates new technologies	Bachelor's degree in Computer Information Systems	$41,000 to $105,000
	Systems programmer	Installs and maintains operating system software and provides technical support to the programming staff	Bachelor's degree in Computer Science or Computer Information Systems	$40,000 to $106,000
	Technical writer	Works with the analyst, programmer, and user to create system documentation and user materials	Associate's or bachelor's degree in Computer Information Systems or in English	$37,000 to $84,000
	Web developer	Analyzes, designs, implements, and supports Web applications; works with HTML, JavaScript, and multimedia	Bachelor's degree in Computer Information Systems	$54,000 to $82,000
	Web programmer	Analyzes, designs, implements, and supports Web-related applications	Associate's degree in Computer Information Systems	$48,000 to $84,000

FIGURE 15-7 Some of the careers available in each of the five main areas of a typical IT department. **(continued)**

3. *Technical services* — evaluates and integrates new technologies, administers the organization's data resources, and supports the centralized computer operating system or servers.
4. *Operations* — operates the centralized computer equipment and administers the network including both data and voice communications.
5. *End-user computing* — assists end users in working with existing systems and in using software and query languages to obtain the information necessary to perform their jobs.

The table in Figure 15-7 shows some of the jobs in each of these areas of a typical IT department along with job functions, usual educational requirements, and national salary ranges.

(continued)

Area	Job Title	Function	Usual Education Required	Annual Salary Range
Technical services	**Database administrator**	Creates and maintains the data dictionary, manages security of the database, monitors the performance of the database, and checks backup and recovery procedures	Bachelor's degree in Computer Information Systems	$67,000 to $98,000
	Desktop publisher	Produces documents such as newsletters, brochures, and books by combining text and graphics	Certificate	$37,000 to $43,000
	Graphic designer/ illustrator	Creates visual impressions of products and advertisements in the fields of graphics, theater, and fashion	Certificate	$36,000 to $49,000
	Network security specialist	Configures routers and firewalls; specifies Web protocols and enterprise technologies	Bachelor's degree in Computer Science or Computer Information Systems	$55,000 to $100,000
	Quality assurance specialist	Reviews programs and documentation to ensure they meet the organization's standards	Bachelor's degree in Computer Information Systems	$47,000 to $73,000
	Web administrator	Oversees Web site performance; maintains links between company's Web server and Internet access provider	Bachelor's degree in Computer Information Systems	$83,000 to $143,000
	Web graphic designer	Develops graphical content using Photoshop, Flash, and other multimedia tools	Bachelor's degree in Computer Information Systems	$48,000 to $72,000
	Webmaster	Maintains an organization's Web site; creates or helps users create Web pages	Bachelor's degree in Computer Information Systems	$51,000 to $82,000
Operations	**Computer operator**	Performs equipment-related activities such as monitoring performance, running jobs, backup, and restore	Associate's degree in Computer Information Systems	$26,000 to $48,000
	Data communications analyst	Evaluates, installs, and monitors data and/or voice communications equipment and software; maintains connections to the Internet and other WANs	Bachelor's degree in Computer Information Systems or Electrical Engineering Technology	$38,000 to $74,000
End-user computing	**Computer technician**	Installs, maintains, and repairs hardware; installs, upgrades, and configures software; and troubleshoots hardware problems	Associate's degree in Computer Information Systems or Electrical Engineering	$32,000 to $63,000
	Help desk specialist	Solves procedural and software questions in person and over the telephone for hardware, software, or networking	Associate's degree in Computer Information Systems	$35,000 to $49,000

WEB LINK 15-5

Trade Schools

Visit the Discovering Computers 2005 WEB LINK page (**scsite.com/dc2005/weblink**). Click Trade Schools below Chapter 15.

- **Computer engineering** (CE) programs teach students how to design and develop the electronic components found in computers and peripheral devices. Students usually are required to take mathematics, physics, and basic engineering courses during the program (Figure 15-11). As with CS, computer engineers work independently or with teams of other engineers.

Entry-level jobs for graduating CE students include software engineer, network security specialist, computer technician, and computer consultant.

As in most other industries, individuals with advanced degrees in specific fields have a better chance of success. Thus, to round out their education, many graduates with a computer degree change direction and obtain a master's degree in business, education, or other field of study.

POSSIBLE COURSES FOR THE FIRST TWO YEARS OF A CE PROGRAM

Computer Courses:
- Introduction to Computers
- Object-Oriented Programming
- Data and File Structures
- Networks
- Systems Programming
- Computer Operating Systems
- Two semesters of one of the following programming languages: C++, Java

Math and Physics Courses:
- Calculus – 2 semesters
- Linear Algebra
- Differential Equations
- Physics – 2 semesters
- Statistics

Engineering Courses:
- Digital Fundamentals
- Circuits and Machines
- Microcontroller Fundamentals
- Digital Design
- Electronic Devices

FIGURE 15-11 Types of courses that may be required for students majoring in computer engineering.

FAQ 15-1

What programming languages should I learn so that I am marketable?

According to a recent study by the Information Technology Association of America (ITAA), the hottest programming language is C++. Other programming languages currently in high demand include SQL, Java, XML, Visual Basic .NET 2003, HTML, and C#.

For more information about computer hiring trends, visit the Discovering Computers 2005 FAQ Web page (**scsite.com/dc2005/faq**). Click Computer Hiring Trends below Chapter 15.

Attending a Trade School

An alternative to enrolling in a college or university is to attend a trade school. **Trade schools** offer programs primarily in the areas of programming, Web development, graphic design, hardware maintenance, networking, and security. One advantage of attending a trade school is time. Trade schools develop specific skills instead of requiring a broad range of courses in the sciences and humanities. Thus, students often complete trade school programs in a shorter time than college and university programs.

As with any post-secondary school, when deciding on a trade school, you should compare curricula, laboratory facilities, instructors, and the types of jobs the school's graduates have obtained.

Searching for Computer-Related Jobs

Many companies list their job openings, internship opportunities, and career opportunities on their Web sites (Figure 15-12). Most computer-related careers offer excellent opportunities but usually require initial and continuing formal education. If you are serious about interviewing with a company, you often can obtain a wealth of information about the firm, its employment opportunities, and its educational requirements by visiting the company's Web site. Some companies even allow job seekers to submit their resumes online. Read Apply It 15-2 for more information.

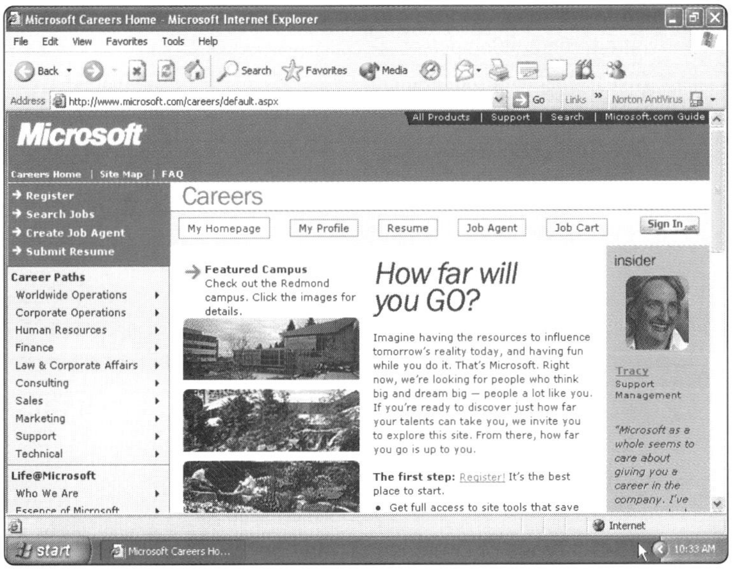

FIGURE 15-12 Many companies' Web sites provide information about their career opportunities.

Some Web sites specialize in helping people find jobs. Figure 15-13 shows some of the more widely used job-search Web sites. In addition to searching millions of job postings, these Web sites offer a variety of services including resume writing tips, resume posting, interviewing advice, and current salary information. The Web sites provide services free to job seekers – it is the employers who typically pay the fees.

APPLY IT 15-2

Online Resume Helps Job Hunting Experience

Creating an *online resume* may be the key to opening doors in the job-hunting world. When you publish your resume on a Web site, the Internet provides a convenient method of introducing you to potential employers around the world. Some hiring managers prefer viewing these electronic documents instead of reading printed resumes because they can search for keywords that match desired skills and academic degrees.

One method of developing this document is by using resume building software, such as Web Resume Writer. Another method is by using the resume database feature found on several online career recruitment Web sites. Most of these Web sites, such as Monster.com, provide e-forms onto which you can publish your information. As an alternative, you can use Word's wizards to perform such tasks as creating resumes.

When creating an online resume, the first step is to decide which skills are most valuable to a potential employer. Your resume is not an autobiography, so you need to select your main credentials and place them in a prominent location on the form. Most employers decide whether to interview the candidate within 15 seconds.

Employment experts give the following formatting advice: use a plain font, such as Times New Roman or Courier; avoid columns and borders; do not use bold or italic font styles; and use nouns, such as manager and graduate, to describe experience and credentials. Most importantly, be honest in representing your schooling, certifications, and experience.

For more information about online resumes, visit the Discovering Computers 2005 Apply It Web page (**scsite.com/dc2005/apply**). Click Apply It #2 below Chapter 15.

FIGURE 15-13 Information about computer-related jobs is available on many Web sites.

FAQ 15-2

Is it worth the time to post my resume on a job-search Web site?

Yes, major organizations have indicated they search these Web sites for candidates to fill job openings. With all the competition out there, be sure your resume stands apart from the rest. Spend time tailoring the online resume, so it contains the automated keywords recognized by search tools that employers use to screen candidates.

For more information about job-search Web sites, visit the Discovering Computers 2005 FAQ Web page (**scsite.com/dc2005/faq**). Click Job-Search Web Sites below Chapter 15.

Planning for Career Development

The computer-related industry is one of the more fluid parts of today's marketplace. Someone who is an expert today may realize that as technology changes, his or her career path also must change and grow. As a computer professional, you must find methods to keep up to date on industry trends and technologies, to develop new skills, and to increase recognition among peers within your company. Three primary ways to achieve these objectives are through professional organizations, professional growth and continuing education activities, and certification. Numerous computer publications also can help an individual keep up with changes in the computer industry.

Professional Organizations

Computer professionals with common interests and a desire to extend their proficiency have formed computer-related professional organizations to share their knowledge. Two organizations that are influential in the computer industry are the Association for Computing Machinery and the Association of Information Technology Professionals.

The **Association for Computing Machinery** (**ACM**) is a scientific and educational organization dedicated to advancing knowledge and proficiency of information technology. The ACM consists of more than 75,000 professional and student members in more than 100 countries. The focus of the ACM is computer science and computer science education. A large number of college and university computer educators are members of the ACM.

The **Association of Information Technology Professionals** (**AITP**), formerly called the *Data Processing Management Association* (*DPMA*), is a professional association with nearly 9,000 members consisting of programmers, systems analysts, and information processing managers.

Both ACM and AITP offer the following features and benefits:

- Chapters throughout the United States, for both professionals and students
- Monthly meetings
- Workshops, seminars, and conventions
- Publications, including magazines, journals, and books that help computing professionals negotiate industry and career challenges
- *Special Interest Groups* (*SIGs*) that bring together members with shared interests, needs, knowledge, and experience
- Programs to help with continuing education needs

Attending professional meetings as a guest or student member provides an excellent opportunity for students to learn about the information processing industry and to meet and talk with professionals in the field. Figure 15-14 lists several professional computer organizations. Often, student chapters of professional organizations exist on college campuses. The student chapters provide students with the ability to develop leadership skills. They also provide students with an excellent opportunity to become acquainted with professionals who speak at their chapter meetings.

PROFESSIONAL COMPUTER ORGANIZATIONS

Association for Computing Machinery (ACM)
Association for Information Systems (AIS)
Association of Information Technology Professionals (AITP) (formerly DPMA)
IEEE Computer Society
Independent Computer Consultants Association (ICCA)
Information Systems Security Association (ISSA)
Institute of Electrical and Electronics Engineers (IEEE)
National Association of Programmers (NAP)

FIGURE 15-14 Professional organizations help employees, employers, managers, and students remain current with trends in information technology.

In addition to professional organizations, many user groups exist for a wide range of computers, operating systems, application software, and more. A *user group* is a collection of people with common computer equipment or software interests that meets regularly to share information. Most metropolitan areas have one or more local computer user groups that meet monthly to discuss mutual interests about computers (Figure 15-15). For anyone employed or simply interested in the computer industry, these groups can be an effective and rewarding way to learn about and continue career development.

FAQ 15-3

How much does it cost to join a professional organization such as ACM or AITP?

An annual professional membership into ACM is $99. ACM has a student membership plan for high school and undergraduate students that ranges in cost from $18 to $60, depending on the membership package selected. AITP dues range from $100 to $200 per year, depending on the chapter. Students can join for $35.

For more information about ACM and AITP, visit the Discovering Computers 2005 FAQ Web page (**scsite.com/dc2005/faq**). Click ACM and AITP below Chapter 15.

EXAMPLES OF USER GROUPS

Apple Computer User Groups Association (ACUGA)
Association of Personal Computer User Groups
C/C++ Users Group
International Oracle User Group
Java Users Group
Linux Users Groups WorldWide (LUGWW)
Macromedia User Groups
.NET User Group
UNIX User Group

FIGURE 15-15 User groups provide computer users with a means of sharing ideas and information.

Professional Growth and Continuing Education

Staying aware of new products and services in the computer industry is a challenging task because technology changes so rapidly. One way to stay informed is to participate in professional growth and continuing education activities. This broad category includes events such as workshops, seminars, conferences, conventions, and trade shows. These events provide both general and specific information about equipment, software, services, and issues affecting the computer industry.

Workshops and seminars usually last one or two days. Conferences, conventions, and trade shows often run for a week. One of the larger technology trade shows in the world is **COMDEX**, which brings together hundreds of vendors and more than 50,000 attendees (Figure 15-16).

Many companies also offer training on their products in the form of books, video-based training, computer-based training (CBT), Web-based training (WBT), and instructor-led training in a classroom.

WEB LINK 15-6

COMDEX

Visit the Discovering Computers 2005 WEB LINK page (**scsite.com/dc2005/weblink**). Click COMDEX below Chapter 15.

FIGURE 15-16 COMDEX, held each November in Las Vegas, Nevada, is one of the larger technology trade shows in the world. Hundreds of vendors display their newest products and services to more than 50,000 attendees.

Computer Publications

Another way to stay informed about happenings in the computer industry is to read one or more computer industry publications regularly (Figure 15-17) or visit Web news sites (Figure 15-18).

FIGURE 15-17 Numerous computer industry publications are available.

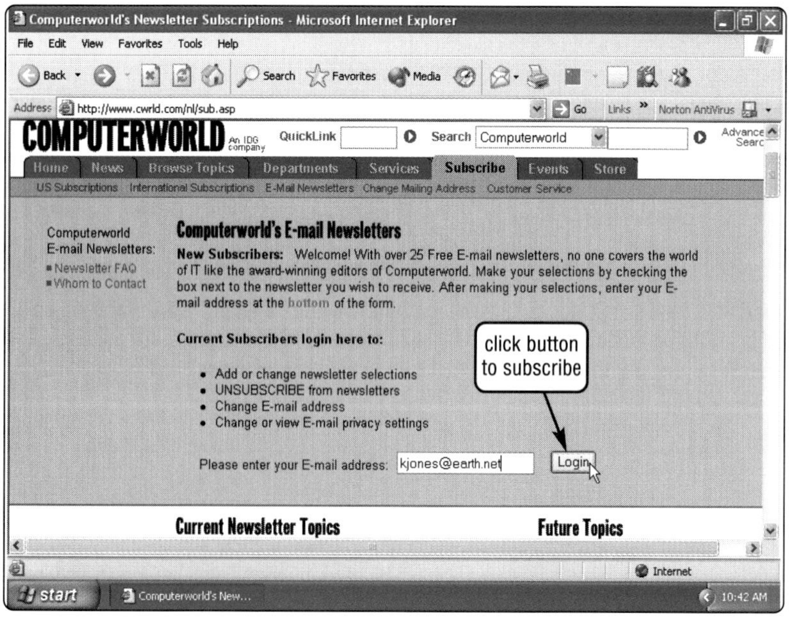

FIGURE 15-18 News Web sites often have a free subscription feature that delivers current technology news to your inbox regularly.

Hundreds of publications are available from which to choose. Some magazines, such as *COMPUTERWORLD, InfoWorld,* and *PC Magazine,* are similar to newspapers and cover a wide range of issues. Other periodicals are oriented toward a particular topic such as communications, personal computers, or a specific equipment manufacturer. You can find many of the more popular publications in public or school libraries. Most of them also have Web sites to visit for news about the latest developments in the computer industry.

QUIZ YOURSELF 15-2

To check your knowledge of jobs available in an IT department, college computer programs, and methods of staying current with IT technology, visit the Discovering Computers 2005 Quiz Yourself Web page (**scsite.com/dc2005/quiz**). Click Objectives 2 – 4 below Chapter 15.

CERTIFICATION

Certification is a process of verifying the technical knowledge of an individual who has demonstrated competence in a particular area. Now more than ever, technology innovations are spawning major opportunities in new occupations within the IT industry. Certification continues to ensure quality and workmanship standards and is one way companies can help ensure their workforce remains up to date with respect to computers and technology.

Computer certification demonstrates the mastery of a skill set and knowledge base in a specific IT area. Certifications are available in many areas including application software, operating systems, programming, hardware, networking, Internet, and database systems. The last section of this chapter discusses specific certifications in each of these areas.

Computing professionals typically obtain a certification by taking and passing an examination. Preparation for a certification exam requires experience or special classes, many of which are offered by community colleges and adult education centers. After certification requirements are met, proficiency in an area is acknowledged with a certificate (Figure 15-19).

FIGURE 15-19 Many certifications are available in the information technology industry.

> **ISSUE 15-3**
>
> **How Valuable Is Certification?**
>
> Certification has become an important commercial enterprise. Certification sponsors establish their own certification requirements. Some certifications are rigorous, requiring extensive training and success on a number of tests. Other certifications are little more than rubber stamps of approval. Some certifications are more respected and in higher demand. If more certifications are conferred than the market can support, a sponsor may make the certification more difficult to earn to increase its value. Organizations such as the Association of Internet Professionals (AIP) have established systems of accreditation to provide quality control and create standards, but no single organization oversees certifications. How important is it to investigate a certification to determine its worth? When should a sponsor adjust difficulty of a certification? Why? Should a single organization oversee certification? Why or why not? As an employer, would you be more impressed by a job candidate's certifications or college degrees? Why?
>
> For more information about certification, visit the Discovering Computers 2005 Issues Web page (**scsite.com/dc2005/issues**). Click Issue #3 below Chapter 15.

Many vendors such as Microsoft and Novell offer technical certification programs for their products. These vendors, called *sponsoring organizations*, develop and administer the examinations to determine whether a person is qualified for certification. These sponsors of IT certifications include computer equipment and software vendors, independent training companies, and professional organizations. Read Issue 15-3 for a related discussion.

Both IT professionals and users should be familiar with IT certifications. The following sections discuss certification benefits, choosing a certification, preparing for a certification, and certification examinations.

Certification Benefits

IT certification can enhance employees' careers and provide them with a better standing as industry professionals. As shown in Figure 15-20, a salary survey conducted by Microsoft reported that 69 percent of the respondents had a salary increase due to certification, with 17 percent of these workers reporting significant raises of more than 25 percent.

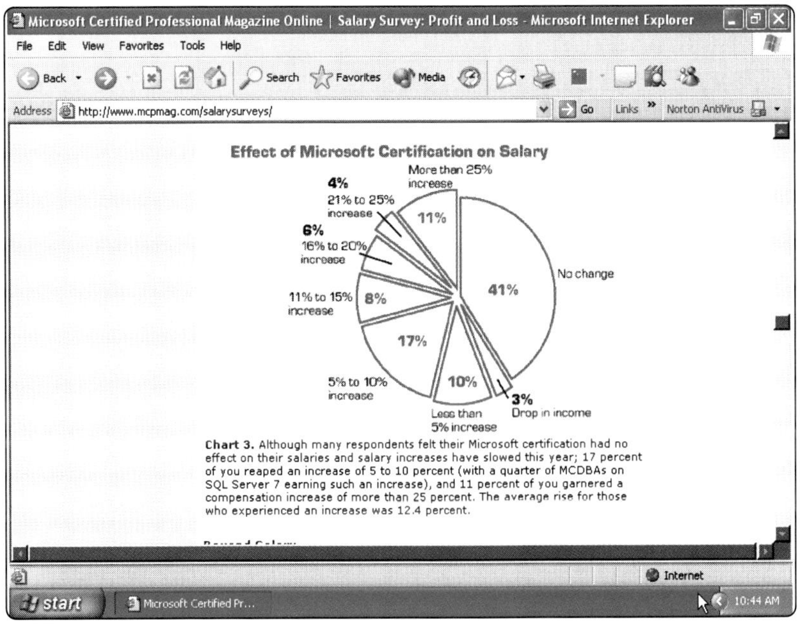

FIGURE 15-20 Microsoft's Eighth Annual Salary Survey of Microsoft Certified Professionals shows that certification can increase salary.

Many job listings ask for specific skills represented by certifications, and the number of companies requiring these skills is expected to grow in the future. Figure 15-21 describes three benefits employees or potential employees derive from certification.

Vendor-sponsored certifications offer many special benefits as incentives. As shown in Figure 15-22, vendors often provide special privileges to certified professionals, such as access to technical and product information. This may include access to secure online electronic resources, special technical support, automatic notification of updates, and access to beta products.

In addition, vendors may offer advanced training opportunities to certification holders. Free vendor magazine subscriptions and discounts on product-support publications and tools sometimes are available. Some vendors even have authorized clothing lines with T-shirts embellished with the certification logo. Although nothing guarantees job security, certification helps to give the IT professional reassurance. Read Issue 15-4 for a related discussion.

BENEFITS OF CERTIFICATION

Benefit	Description
Career	Certification accomplishments are one of the first listings an employer notices on a resume. Certification provides a benchmark, or a means, to measure a person's skills. It can set an individual apart from other potential candidates who may be vying for a similar advancement or position. Often, a professional studies and takes training to move into another area of the computer industry. Even for those not currently looking for a career change, certification can serve as insurance.
Professional	Certification is a personal achievement that adds credibility among peers and employers. To identify certified individuals, sponsors award certificates of accomplishment. Certification also authorizes the person to use the product's official logo or symbol on items, such as business cards and Web pages. These emblems represent a person's skills and knowledge in a concise form. As an additional bonus, some certification training can be used for college credit.
Salary	Numerous salary surveys have shown that certification is one of the top factors influencing raises. Companies often pay a bonus as an incentive for certification. Individuals with more than one area of expertise can command even higher salaries.

FIGURE 15-21 Employees benefit from computer certification.

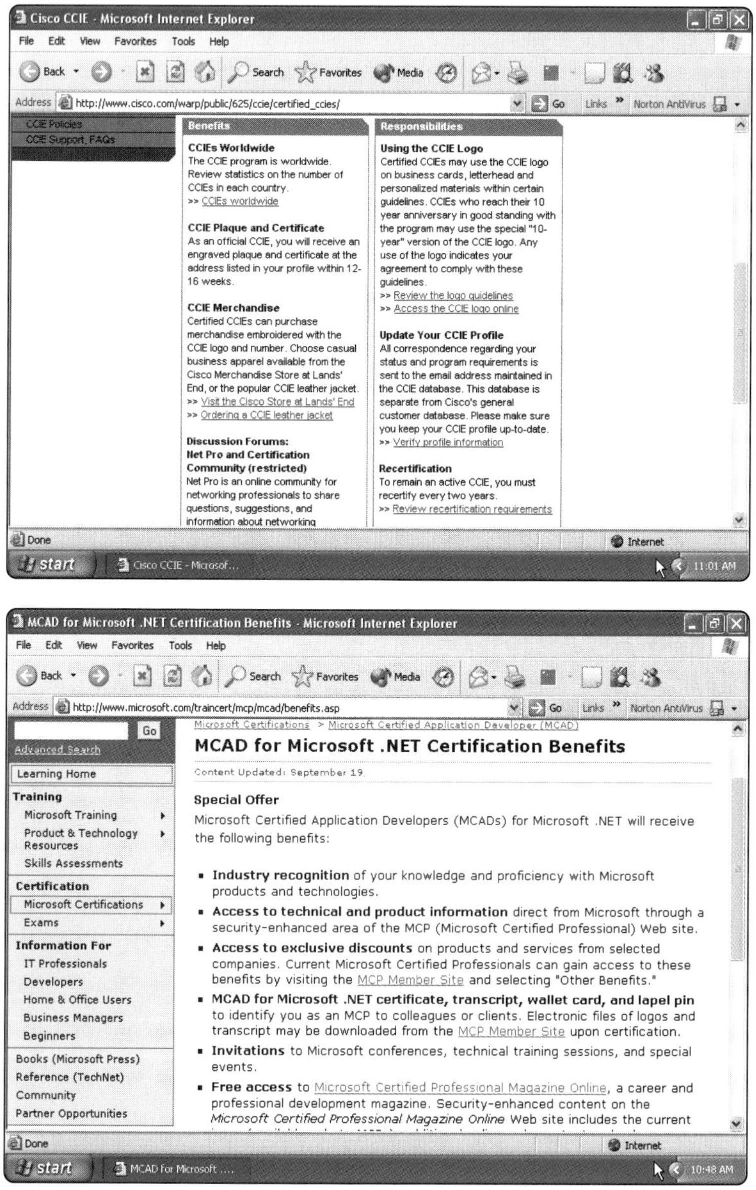

FIGURE 15-22 Certification sponsors often offer a variety of benefits to certificate holders.

ISSUE 15-4

Are Vendor-Specific Certifications Worthwhile?

Vendor-specific certifications are sponsored by the producers of specific computer products. Some people feel that vendor-specific certifications are shameless promotions. They argue that the certification training programs simply enhance vendor name recognition and profits. Certification, they insist, should be based on general products or practices – such as using spreadsheet software instead of using a specific spreadsheet program. Like a diploma, the certification should be permanent. These more generic certifications would prove that an individual has the background necessary to master a specific computer program or skill. Supporters of vendor-specific certifications believe every computer product has unique features that would not be covered in a general course. Because products change, certification also should be renewed periodically. Should certification be general or tied to a specific product or practice? Why? Should certification be permanent? For example, should certification in a specific product remain valid regardless of how subsequent versions of the product have changed or the amount of time that has elapsed? Why?

For more information about vendor-specific certifications, visit the Discovering Computers 2005 Issues Web page (**scsite.com/dc2005/issues**). Click Issue #4 below Chapter 15.

Professional organizations that offer certifications, such as the *Institute for Certification of Computer Professionals* (*ICCP*), define standards designed to raise the competence level for the computer industry. With respect to certifications, organizations send IT professionals a clear message. Certifications offer many benefits. Figure 15-23 summarizes the benefits of certifications to customers, employers, and industry.

Choosing a Certification

Certifications are not the same with respect to training and options. Selecting a certification is a personal process that requires careful thought and research. If you are considering obtaining a certification, reflect on your career goals and interests. Consider your career path during the long term. Then, assess your background knowledge and experience. Finally, research certifications to find those that best match your needs. Figure 15-24 describes factors to consider.

WEB LINK 15-7

Institute for Certification of Computer Professionals

Visit the Discovering Computers 2005 WEB LINK page (**scsite .com/dc2005/weblink**). Click Institute for Certification of Computer Professionals below Chapter 15.

BENEFICIARIES OF CERTIFICATION

Beneficiary	Description
Customers	Customers receive better service from employees with certification(s). They gain confidence in a company when its IT professionals have earned a certification. Multiple certifications show that the professional can deal with many aspects of a problem, using several areas of expertise. As an added benefit, certification implies motivation to expend extra effort to go beyond basic job requirements, which often benefits the customer.
Employers	An industry-sponsored study indicates that certified workers are more productive and knowledgeable than noncertified employees. Certified help desk specialists are able to handle more support calls. Companies with certified personnel experience less network downtime. As an added bonus, users are more satisfied with the company's work, and the professional employees within the company have higher morale and job contentment. Certification is an incentive for employees to upgrade their skills continuously.
Industry	Certification is a form of industry self-regulation. It sets computer professionals' competence standards and raises the level of expertise and knowledge in the IT industry as a whole. This, in turn, enhances the reputation of the professionals within the industry. As more people become certified, the industry professionals are perceived as reliable and capable support for the computers on which society has come to rely.

FIGURE 15-23 Certification benefits extend beyond the certified individual.

FACTORS TO CONSIDER IN SELECTING A CERTIFICATION

- Consider the expenses and the time involved to obtain the certification
- Examine employment projections
- Look at job listings to see what certifications are sought
- Read evaluations of certifications
- Talk to people in the industry
- Think about complementary combinations of certifications to meet your goals

FIGURE 15-24 Considerations when selecting a certification.

If you are new to the computer field, it is best to start with a general, entry-level certification. You may want to choose a certification that has immediate benefits for your current job. If you are more experienced, consider building on your existing experience with a certification that helps you reach career goals.

A certification represents a major commitment in time and money. Thoughtful research and planning can serve to guide your career to your chosen destination.

Preparing for Certification

Most certification programs do not require academic coursework. Test results alone determine certification. Very few professionals, however, have the experience and skill set to take a certification exam without preparation. Most people prefer to follow a study program to prepare for the test. Even with experience, study serves as a review and may help to fill gaps in knowledge.

Training options are available to suit every learning style. You can study on your own using a variety of educational materials. Or, you can take online training classes. A third option is to select an instructor-led class to guide you through the training process. In addition, the Internet contains many resources. Most people prefer to use a combination of these options, which are described in the table in Figure 15-25.

WEB LINK 15-8

Instructor-Led Certification Classes

Visit the Discovering Computers 2005 WEB LINK page (**scsite.com/dc2005/weblink**). Click Instructor-Led Certification Classes below Chapter 15.

FAQ 15-4

Are study guides and practice tests available for certification exams?

Some sponsors make practice tests available. If your sponsoring company does not, try visiting a certification Web community such as CramSession. Certification Web communities often provide the public with news, resources, information, study guides, chat rooms, newsgroups, and other resources for IT certification exams — at no cost.

For more information about certification Web communities, visit the Discovering Computers 2005 FAQ Web page (**scsite.com/dc2005/faq**). Click Certification Web Communities below Chapter 15.

CERTIFICATION STUDY PROGRAMS AND WEB RESOURCES

Method	Description
Self-Study	Flexible self-study programs help professionals prepare for certification at their own pace and supplement other training methods. Self-study requires high motivation and discipline, but many people like the convenience of setting their own pace while studying at home or in the office. Self-study is the least expensive option. Hundreds of books, workbooks, videotapes, and computer-based training programs on CD-ROM or DVD-ROM are available.
Online Training Classes	Many online training classes are available on the Internet and by many companies that have set up intranets to provide online training within their organizations. Online training allows students to set their own pace in an interactive environment and combines the technological advantages of computer-based training with the connectivity of the Internet. Some programs allow students to take certification examinations online. Online programs can cost approximately one-third the price of the traditional instructor-led programs.
Instructor-Led Training	Estimates show that 80 percent of all certification preparation is classroom-based. Instructor-led training is available in a variety of forms, including seminars, which traditionally are held for several days within the span of one week; boot camps, which immerse students in intensive coursework for up to two weeks; and academic-style classes, which span a period of several weeks or months. Some sponsors operate their own training sessions and also authorize independent training centers.
Web Resources	The certification sponsor's Web site generally contains descriptions of the available certifications, with frequently asked questions (FAQs) and links to authorized training and testing centers. Many Web sites include detailed course objectives, training guides, and sample test questions. Some sponsors have online resources to help you plan and track your training program. Most sell books and other training resources. Many Web sites offer practice test sessions, chat rooms, and discussion groups. Individuals often set up Web sites to offer their own views and tips on the testing process.

FIGURE 15-25 Study programs help professionals prepare for certification examinations.

Certification Examinations

Authorized testing companies, such as Prometric (Figure 15-26), Pearson VUE, and Brainbench, provide most certification exams. Many colleges also are authorized testing facilities. Certification sponsors often have a link to the testing company's Web site from their own Web page.

At the sponsor's Web site, you can use the test center locator to find a list of testing centers near you. The list includes addresses and telephone numbers. Most testing centers allow you to pay for the test either online or by telephone with a credit card. Fees for each test range from $50 to more than $1,500, depending on the type of test. Typically, the more technical tests have higher fees. On the day of the test, you must present two forms of identification, one of which must be a photo identification.

At the testing centers, examinations are taken using computers, which process the results as you take a test. You will know immediately whether you pass the examination. Some tests are in a multiple-choice format; others are skill based.

Some tests use a technique known as *computerized adaptive testing* (*CAT*), where the tests analyze a person's responses while taking the test. The number and order of the test questions are modified to correspond to each individual's progress and demonstrated ability. Occasionally, a certification requires a hands-on lab test. The certification sponsor typically administers these tests. These examinations are much more expensive than the traditional tests. In addition, the number of testing facilities is limited. Read Issue 15-5 for a related discussion.

If you do not pass an exam, you must pay the fee again to retake the test. In some cases, you can retake the test immediately. Most people, however, opt to review before trying to take the test again. Some training centers offer a guarantee for their program. They provide discounts, or even free sessions, for individuals who have completed their program, yet do not pass a test. Most sponsors allow candidates a set time, such as a year, in which to complete the test.

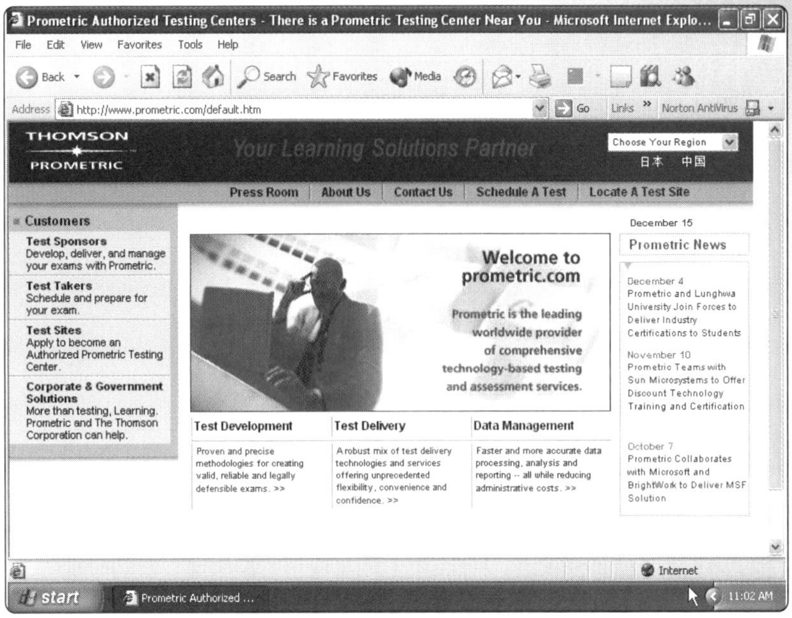

FIGURE 15-26 Prometric is a testing center for information technology certifications.

ISSUE 15-5

How Good Are Certification Tests?

Critics say that certification tests cannot truly measure a person's ability to work effectively with computers. Most certification tests consist of multiple-choice questions, and detractors feel the tests fail to reflect real-world situations. They argue that because certification candidates often concentrate solely on the test, using Web sites that post sample questions and offer advice garnered from former test-takers, they never acquire a comprehensive knowledge of the field. Some maintain that the entire concept of certification tests is flawed, focusing on facts needed for short-term success instead of on the reasoning required for long-term skill development. Some certification sponsors address these issues by using simulations and problem solving in examinations. Can the ability to work with computers be measured successfully with a test? Why or why not? To prevent focusing on particular questions, should sponsors randomize their tests, require test takers to sign nondisclosure statements, or include simulations and problem solving? Why? When hiring an employee, how much emphasis should be given on certification versus experience versus a degree? Why?

For more information about certification tests, visit the Discovering Computers 2005 Issues Web page (**scsite.com/dc2005/issues**). Click Issue #5 below Chapter 15.

FAQ 15-5

Do computer certifications expire?

Most certifications expire after a set time because product-based skills remain current for about only 18 months. Sponsors specify training or examinations to maintain the certification. In addition, if a vendor issues a product update, certificate holders must retrain almost immediately.

For more information about computer certifications, visit the Discovering Computers 2005 FAQ Web page (**scsite.com/dc2005/faq**). Click Computer Certifications below Chapter 15.

WEB LINK 15-9

Microsoft Office Specialist

Visit the Discovering Computers 2005 WEB LINK page (**scsite.com/dc2005/weblink**). Click Microsoft Office Specialist below Chapter 15.

A GUIDE TO CERTIFICATION

The IT industry has grown by phenomenal proportions, and certification has grown as quickly. Today, more than 200 certifications are available. Each month, more certifications are announced. Some certifications have a broad focus. Others require an in-depth knowledge of a single computing aspect. Often, a sponsor establishes a series of related certifications to show levels of expertise within a single area.

Certifications usually are classified based on the computer industry area to which they most closely relate: application software, operating systems, programming, hardware, networking, Internet, and database systems. Some certifications are related to more than one category. For example, a certification in networking also may indicate knowledge of hardware and operating systems.

This section describes the major certifications and certification sponsors in each industry area. Some certifications have components that fall into multiple categories. In this case, they are placed in the area for which they are known best.

Application Software Certifications

Although numerous types of application software exist, several programs have achieved national recognition for use as business and graphics tools. Figure 15-27 identifies popular application software certifications, sometimes called *end-user certifications*, and their sponsors. Most sponsors of application software certifications have a partner training program and encourage computer-training centers to be authorized training representatives.

As with most other certifications, vendor-authorized testing facilities take registrations and administer the certification test. An end-user certification is very helpful to anyone who works in the computer industry. People who work in the following areas can benefit from application software certifications:

- Computer sales representatives
- Computer teachers
- Corporate trainers
- Desktop publishers
- Draftspeople
- Graphic designers
- Help desk specialists
- Office managers/workers

Operating System Certifications

Several options for different knowledge levels are available to those seeking operating system certifications. These certifications focus on particular skills — the user, the operator, the system administrator, and the system engineer. Since the inception of the Internet, networking has grown in importance, spawning new certifications that include operating system and networking components. The table in Figure 15-28 lists a few of the certifications available in the operating systems area.

If you are interested in an occupation as an operating system administrator or engineer, you also may benefit from certifications in networking, hardware, and the Internet. These additional certifications are linked closely to the operating system and serve to broaden your expertise in that area. People in the following jobs may be interested in a certification in operating systems:

- Computer consultants
- Hardware technicians
- Help desk specialists
- Network security specialists
- System administrators

APPLICATION SOFTWARE CERTIFICATIONS

Certification	Description	Sponsor
Microsoft Office Specialist (Office Specialist)	Tests a user's basic (specialist) and advanced (expert) skills of Microsoft Office programs	Microsoft
Microsoft Certified Desktop Support Technician (MCDST)	Tests a user's skills solving problems associated with applications that run on Windows XP and the operating system itself	Microsoft
Adobe Certified Expert (ACE)	Tests a user's expertise on Adobe software	Adobe Systems
IBM Certified Professional for Lotus Software	Tests knowledge of Lotus programs	IBM
Macromedia Certified Professional	Tests user's expertise in a variety of Macromedia software including Flash MX and Dreamweaver MX	Macromedia

FIGURE 15-27 Application software certifications are available to anyone who works in the computer industry.

OPERATING SYSTEM CERTIFICATIONS

Certification	Description	Sponsor
Microsoft Certified Professional (MCP)	Tests technical expertise in one of several areas including managing and troubleshooting Windows operating systems, designing and deploying Web sites, developing .NET applications, or administering a database server	Microsoft
Red Hat Certified Engineer (RHCE)	Tests technical expertise of setting up and administering network services and security administration of the Linux operating system	Red Hat
Red Hat Certified Technician (RHCT)	Tests basic knowledge of setting up and managing a Linux operating system	Red Hat
Sun Certified System Administrator	Tests knowledge of administering the Solaris operating system	Sun
IBM Certified Specialist	Tests knowledge of AIX or UNIX operating system and network security	IBM

FIGURE 15-28 Operating system certifications test the knowledge level of a specific operating system.

Programming Certifications

Various certifications are available in the programming area. These certifications are valuable in two ways: (1) a programming certification usually is supported with training programs that prepare applicants for the certification test, and (2) they enable programmers to add to their knowledge and skill base. The preparation classes for certifications provide an opportunity for professionals to share ideas.

If you are interested in writing application software, you also may benefit from certifications in networking and Web design. These certifications are tied closely to programming and broaden employment opportunities. Read Issue 15-6 for a related discussion.

The table shown in Figure 15-29 identifies a few of the certifications available in the programming area. People in the following jobs may be interested in a certification in programming:

- Java programmers
- Oracle database managers
- Programming consultants
- SQL programmers
- Web page designers
- XML programmers

ISSUE 15-6

Should Programming Require a College Degree?

Typical programmers can earn up to $100,000, with substantial hiring bonuses and annual pay increases. Many star programmers do not have degrees, but have achieved certification in many areas of expertise. Some companies will not tap this talent pool due to lack of academic accreditation. Yet, other companies not only hire these star programmers, they attempt to lure them right out of high school with attractive training programs that lead to lucrative jobs. The market for programmers has fluctuated wildly, and today's need is no guarantee of tomorrow's employment. Some argue that students tempted into technological training right out of high school will not have a background general enough for other pursuits if their interest fades or the market withers. Should companies actively recruit high-school students with high level technology skills or should they encourage students to attend college? Why? What can be done to address long-term concerns? Are companies that demand college degrees being unfair to gifted programmers who learn on their own or through certification training?

For more information about programming certifications, visit the Discovering Computers 2005 Issues Web page (**scsite.com/dc2005/issues**). Click Issue #6 below Chapter 15.

PROGRAMMING CERTIFICATIONS

Certification	Description	Sponsor
Certified Software Development Professional (CSDP)	Tests knowledge of software development process and tools	IEEE Computer Society
IBM Certified Solution Developer	Tests knowledge of developing XML applications and Web services	IBM
Microsoft Certified Application Developer (MCAD)	Tests knowledge of developing Web or Windows-based applications using programs in the Visual Studio .NET suite and XML Web services components	Microsoft
Microsoft Certified Solution Developer (MCSD)	Tests knowledge of developing Web and Windows-based applications using programs in the Visual Studio .NET suite and XML Web services components; more extensive testing than MCAD	Microsoft
Sun Certified Enterprise Architect	Tests knowledge of creating and maintaining J2EE applications	Sun
Sun Certified Java Developer	Tests advanced knowledge of Java programming language	Sun
Sun Certified Programmer	Tests basic knowledge of Java programming language	Sun

FIGURE 15-29 Various certifications are available in programming.

Hardware Certifications

The IT industry recognizes that knowledge of the hardware and the controlling software is necessary to set up, maintain, and repair a computer. Hardware certifications vary in scope from a narrow focus with an emphasis on the repair of a specific device to an integrated hardware solution that addresses a company's current and future computing needs. Obtaining an advanced certification in hardware implies that you have achieved a standard of competence in assessing a company's hardware needs, and you can implement solutions to help the company achieve its computing goals.

If hardware is your specialty, you also may benefit from networking and operating system software certifications. These certifications are tied closely to advanced hardware knowledge. The table in Figure 15-30 represents a few available hardware certifications. People in the following careers may be interested in hardware certification:

- Cable installation technicians
- Computer consultants
- Computer repair technicians
- Corporate trainers
- Help desk specialists
- System engineers and administrators

WEB LINK 15-10

A+ Certification

Visit the Discovering Computers 2005 WEB LINK page (**scsite .com/dc2005/weblink**). Click A+ Certification below Chapter 15.

Networking Certifications

Professionals with the expertise to design, administer, and maintain a network are rewarded for their skills. Networking certification holders earn salary levels from 5 to 30 percent more than those without certification.

Network expertise is acquired through years of experience and training because so many variables exist for a total network solution. Obtaining an advanced certification in networking implies that you have achieved a standard of competence, enabling you to address the complex issues that arise when planning, installing, managing, and troubleshooting a network.

The table shown in Figure 15-31 identifies a few of the certifications available in the networking area. People in the following careers may be interested in network certification:

- Hardware service technicians
- Network consultants
- Network managers
- Network engineers
- System administrators

HARDWARE CERTIFICATIONS

Certification	Description	Sponsor
A+	Tests entry-level knowledge of personal computer setup, configuration, maintenance, troubleshooting; basic networking skills; and system software	Computing Technology Industry Association (CompTIA)
IBM eServer Certified Specialist	Tests knowledge of IBM eServer line	IBM
NACSE Network Technician (NNT)	Tests basic knowledge of personal computers, operating systems, networks, and cabling	National Association of Communication System Engineers (NACSE)

FIGURE 15-30 Hardware certifications may test general knowledge of hardware or test knowledge of a specific type of hardware.

NETWORKING CERTIFICATIONS

Certification	Description	Sponsor
Certified Novell Administrator (CNA)	Tests knowledge of Novell's networking products including NetWare, intraNetWare, and GroupWise	Novell
Certified Novell Engineer (CNE)	Tests in-depth knowledge of designing, configuring, implementing, administering, and troubleshooting the Novell network system	Novell
Cisco Certified Network Professional (CCNP)	Tests advanced knowledge of installing, configuring, and operating LANs and WANs	Cisco
Network+	Tests competency in several network areas including transmission media and topologies, protocols, and standards	Computing Technology Industry Association (CompTIA)
Sun Certified Network Administrator	Tests knowledge of administering Sun networks	Sun

WEB LINK 15-11

Certified Novell Administrator

Visit the Discovering Computers 2005 WEB LINK page (**scsite .com/dc2005/weblink**). Click Certified Novell Administrator below Chapter 15.

FIGURE 15-31 Networking certifications usually test knowledge of a company-specific network.

Internet Certifications

Many Internet certification tracks that prepare individuals for certification programs are available. Some of these certifications are hardware based. They cover technology often used by an Internet access provider or a large company developing an intranet.

Internet certifications are demanding and require technical expertise in networking hardware and configuration before enrollment in the training program. Web management and Web programming certifications also are among the tracks. Web development certifications are demanding. Success in the field requires special resources, including an aptitude for programming, marketing and graphical design skills, a customer service-oriented attitude, and good communications skills.

If you are interested in working in an Internet-related occupation, you can benefit from certifications in hardware, networking, operating systems, and programming. These certifications are tied closely to the Internet and broaden and hasten your opportunities to acquire internetworking and Internet knowledge.

The table shown in Figure 15-32 identifies a few of the certifications available in the Internet area. People in the following careers may be interested in Internet certification:

- Internet and intranet managers
- Internet service provider staff
- Network administrators
- Webmasters
- Web page designers
- Web programmers

INTERNET CERTIFICATIONS

Certification	Description	Sponsor
Certified Internet Webmaster (CIW)	Tests knowledge of Web development, administration, and security	ProsoftTraining
Cisco Certified Internetwork Expert (CCIE)	Tests expert level knowledge in areas of internetwork communications, security, routing, and switching	Cisco
Certified Web Professional (CWP)	Tests advanced knowledge in areas of Web site design and development, and server administration and security	International Webmasters Association

FIGURE 15-32 Internet certifications are demanding and require technical expertise in networking hardware.

Database System Certifications

Supporting a large database management system requires a professional staff. The various tasks the staff performs are a core around which the database management certifications are based. If you are interested in working with a database management system, you also may benefit from certifications in hardware, Internet, networking, and programming.

The table shown in Figure 15-33 identifies a few of the certifications available in the database area. People in the following careers may be interested in database certification:

- Database administrators
- Database analysts
- Database application developers
- Database designers

DATABASE CERTIFICATIONS

Certification	Description	Sponsor
IBM Certified Solutions Expert - DB2	Tests advanced skills of administration of the DB2 database management system	IBM
IBM Certified Solutions Expert - Informix	Tests advanced skills of administration of the Informix database management system	IBM
Microsoft Certified Database Administrator (MCDBA)	Tests skills required to implement and administer an SQL Server database management system	Microsoft
Oracle Certified Professional	Tests knowledge of developing and deploying large-scale Oracle database management systems	Oracle
Sybase Certified Professional	Tests skills in developing and administering Sybase database management systems	Sybase

FIGURE 15-33 Database certifications usually test knowledge of a specific database management system.

WEB LINK 15-12

Cisco Certified Internetwork Expert

Visit the Discovering Computers 2005 WEB LINK page (**scsite.com/dc2005/weblink**). Click Cisco Certified Internetwork Expert below Chapter 15.

QUIZ YOURSELF 15-3

To check your knowledge of benefits of certification, preparing for certification, areas of certification, and specific certifications, visit the Discovering Computers 2005 Quiz Yourself Web page (**scsite.com/dc2005/quiz**). Click Objectives 5 – 8 below Chapter 15.

CHAPTER SUMMARY

This chapter discussed the strong demand for computer and IT professionals. It presented a variety of available computer-related careers. For additional discussion about 15 of the more popular careers, read the Career Corner features at the end of each chapter in this book. The table in Figure 15-34 lists the page number on which each career is presented.

This chapter also focused on educational courses of study, trade schools, job searches, career development planning, professional organizations, and professional growth. Information about certification preparation, examinations, and resources also was presented. Finally, specific certifications were discussed.

CAREER CORNER FEATURES

Chapter Number	Chapter Title	Job Title	Page Number
1	Introduction to Computers	Personal Computer Salesperson	38
2	The Internet and World Wide Web	Web Developer	102
3	Application Software	Help Desk Specialist	164
4	The Components of the System Unit	Computer Engineer	214
5	Input	Data Entry Clerk	264
6	Output	Graphic Designer/Illustrator	320
7	Storage	Computer Technician	376
8	Operating Systems and Utility Programs	Systems Programmer	420
9	Communications and Networks	Network Administrator	494
10	Database Management	Database Administrator	543
11	Computers and Society, Security, Privacy, and Ethics	Network Security Specialist	602
12	Information System Development	Systems Analyst	648
13	Programming Languages and Program Development	Programmer	698
14	Enterprise Computing	CIO	750
15	Computer Careers and Certification	Computer Science/IT Instructor	790

FIGURE 15-34 Each chapter in this book ends with a Career Corner feature. The table lists the job title and page number for each career corner.

Computer Science/IT Instructor

Computer science/IT instructors are in demand. From K-12, to higher education, to business and corporate training, skilled teachers are encouraged and enticed with many benefits and rewards.

Instructors in K-12 usually teach computer literacy or specific computer applications. Teaching in K-12 requires at least a bachelor's degree with some computer-related courses. Instructors in higher education teach basic computer courses in addition to specialized classes such as computer engineering, Internet development, networking, programming, or systems analysis and design. Generally, these instructors have at least a master's degree with 18 graduate hours in the subject area. To teach software and/or hardware design usually requires a master's degree and/or a Ph.D. in software engineering or electrical engineering.

Corporate trainers teach employees systems development, programming, and other computer-related courses. Corporate trainers lead continuing education classes and introduce new software. Many companies have their own training departments. Qualifications for the corporate world are less stringent than those for educational institutions. Often, companies hire instructors with trainer certifications, such as the Microsoft Certified Trainer (MCT) and Cisco Certified Trainer.

Salaries range widely. In a traditional educational setting, salaries vary from about $30,000 to $70,000, depending on the area of expertise, years of experience, and location. In the corporate world, salaries are considerably higher, ranging up to $90,000 or more.

To learn more about the field of Computer Science/IT Instructor as a career, visit the Discovering Computers 2005 Careers Web page (**scsite.com/dc2005/careers**). Click Computer Science/IT Instructor.

HIGH-TECH TALK

Magnetic Motion Capture: Making the Game

That lifelike quarterback in your favorite computer game most likely got his moves thanks to motion capture. As computer gamers demand increasingly realistic action and animation in games, *motion capture technology* is allowing programmers to develop computer games populated by animated characters with natural, highly realistic human movements.

Several technologies are available for motion capture, including optical, inertial, and AC and DC magnetic. DC magnetic motion capture generally provides more accurate capture than the other technologies, because the sensors do not need line of sight and are not affected greatly if other metals, such as steel or aluminum, are located near the sensors.

How does motion capture work? In a DC *magnetic motion capture system*, a transmitter is located at the center of a measured space that encloses an electromagnetic field. To start the process of motion capture, a performer must secure magnetic sensors to various points on his or her body. A simple way to attach the sensors is to have performers wear a motion capture body suit with sensor holders where sensors are mounted (Figure 15-35). Performers also can wear peripherals, such as data gloves, which capture subtle movements such as hand gestures.

The sensors on the suit and peripherals use the electromagnetic field to measure their spatial relationship to the transmitter in the center of the measured space. In developing a football computer game, for example, you could attach up to 20 sensors to key points on several athlete-performers. As the performers complete the motion of a touchdown pass, the motion capture system tracks the position and orientation of each magnetic sensor more than 100 times per second to identify the location of the performers' bodies in space. This rapid tracking records every bodily motion and provides highly accurate capture of such actions as a batter's home run swing, a gymnast's handspring, or a golfer's putt.

Input from these sensors is transmitted to a recording device via cables (a *tethered system*) or via wireless connections (an *untethered system*). In an untethered or wireless system, input from the sensors travels over sensor cables to a battery-powered electronic unit mounted in a small, lightweight backpack worn by the performer. The body suit and peripherals have channeled tubes and closures that secure and guide the sensor cables into the electronic unit. A wireless system thus allows performers to complete complex motions without tangling cables.

The motion data captured by the sensors then is sent over a wireless connection to a base station for final processing. This data then instantly can be mapped to the corresponding features of a computer-generated animated character, to give it the exact movements of the live performers. Because many motion capture systems can track up to 90 sensors, a developer can create four or five animated characters and then track and map movements to multiple characters as several performers interact with each other. This makes magnetic motion capture technology ideal for creating highly realistic multiplayer sports games.

The entertainment industry rapidly has embraced this dynamic technology. Magnetic motion capture was used to create complex, multiple-character interactions for the television show "Donkey Kong", to give the Pillsbury Doughboy lifelike movement, and to add life to characters in Keebler and Monopoly commercials. Game programmers such as Sony, SEGA, and Microsoft are using magnetic motion capture to give animated characters hundreds of body motions.

That realistic motion makes characters more believable and keeps players interested in the game. Motion capture also gives games star quality. By using motion capture to capture the movements and expressions of a leading athlete, a game programmer captures both the athletic and personal qualities of these stars and then gives the game player a chance to coach these stars. Motion capture provides an excitement and realism that engages players and viewers – and that makes motion capture captivating to programmers.

For more information about motion capture, visit the Discovering Computers 2005 High-Tech Talk Web page (**scsite.com/dc2005/tech**) and click Motion Capture.

FIGURE 15-35 A motion capture body suit.

COMPANIES ON THE CUTTING EDGE

Monster

Career Opportunities Online

Monster is the world's largest job-search Web site. Monster posts approximately 800,000 job listings, including more than 90 of the FORTUNE 100 and approximately 490 of the FORTUNE 500 companies. Monster Worldwide is the parent company of Monster and of TMP Worldwide Advertising & Communications, an online recruitment firm. According to CEO Jeff Taylor, the purpose of Monster is connecting people, giving employees and employers the best opportunity to find each other.

Taylor founded The Monster Board, an online bulletin board for his recruitment agency, in 1994. Five years later, The Monster Board merged with Online Career Center to form Monster.com, a global online career network. The name was memorable and created a theme for the company Web site. "Looking for a job on an electronic database is inherently boring," Taylor says. "Wrapping a theme around it made my site fun."

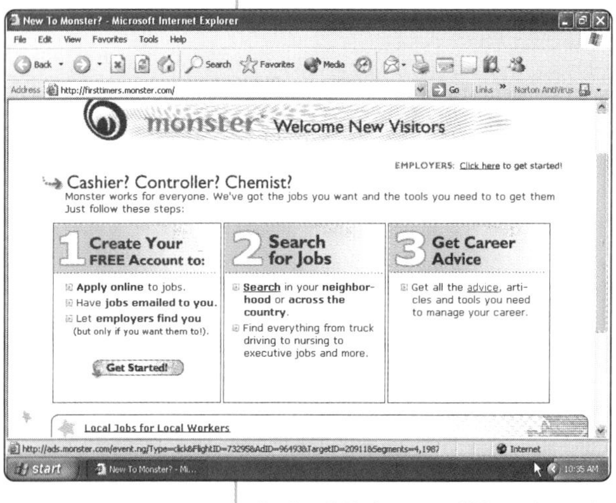

Monster is more than fun. For job seekers, the company provides a variety of individualized interactive tools, such as personal career management, multiple resume postings, career networks, chat and message boards, continuing education resources, senior executive strategies, and job-search advice. Prospective employees also search posted job opportunities by location, category, or keyword; sort search results by date or relevance; see search results in brief or detailed view; or even use a job search agent to find jobs automatically based on specified criteria.

For employers, Monster offers efficient and cost-effective recruitment solutions. Employers post jobs, search and screen more than 25 million resumes, recruit in real time, and obtain online hiring advice. Costs, which vary based on geographic scope and time frame, are less than recruitment agencies or comparable newspaper classified ads. Prices range from $400 for companies with local, short-term, infrequent hiring needs to more than $10,000 for companies with national, long-term, ongoing hiring requirements.

For more information about Monster, visit the Discovering Computers 2005 Companies Web page (**scsite.com/dc2005/companies**) and click Monster.

Cisco

Networking the Internet

The two great equalizers in life are education and the Internet, according to Cisco Systems CEO and president John Chambers. Universal learning opportunities, such as Web-based training and distance education, potentially can unite people and create a borderless society. These prospects are possible, in part, due to Cisco Systems's critical equipment that allows many individuals to connect to the Internet simultaneously.

A group of computer scientists from Stanford University founded Cisco in 1984. From the beginning, the company focused on communicating over networks. In the mid-1990s, Cisco predicted that the Internet would alter the way people work, live, play, and learn. Today, Cisco's Internet Protocol-based (IP) networking equipment is the basis of the Internet and most networks. As the world leader in networking equipment, the company strives to empower the Internet generation by connecting people and networks regardless of differences in locations, time, or types of computers. *Cisco* offers the broadest line of networking equipment for transporting data within a building, across a campus, or around the globe.

Customers are part of three target markets: enterprises with large networking needs, such as corporations and government agencies; service providers that provide information services; and small and medium businesses.

The company began shipping products in 1986 and has grown into a market leader in more than 115 countries. It has one of the world's larger e-commerce sites and uses the Web in all areas of its operations. Annual revenues exceed $18.9 billion. Headquartered in San Jose, California, Cisco employs more than 34,000 people worldwide. The company ranked 24th in *FORTUNE* magazine's annual list of Best Companies to Work For and second in the magazine's list of America's Most Admired Companies.

For more information about Cisco, visit the Discovering Computers 2005 Companies Web page (**scsite.com/dc2005/companies**) and click Cisco.

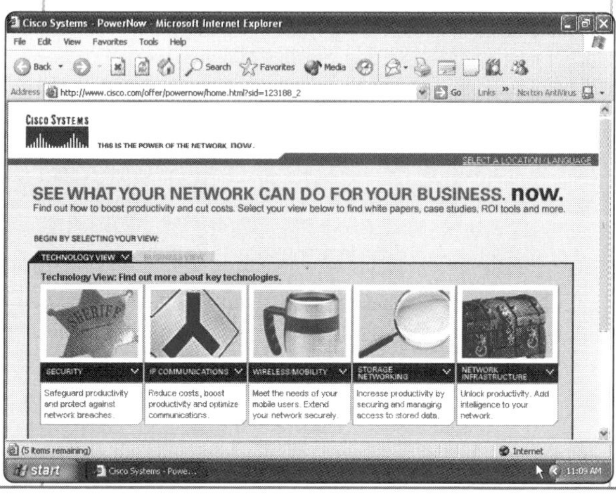

TECHNOLOGY TRAILBLAZERS

Steve Ballmer

Microsoft CEO

If Bill Gates is Microsoft's brain, *Steve Ballmer* is the company's heart. For more than 20 years, Ballmer has brought his passion and leadership to the world's leading software company. Employees still tell tales of the gentle giant leaping onto the stage at a sales convention, shouting "I love this company! I love this company!" and bringing his audience to their feet in an enthusiastic ovation. In 2000, Steve Ballmer was named CEO of Microsoft Corporation, assuming full management responsibility for the company.

Ballmer attended Harvard University where he managed the football team, worked on the school paper, and formed a lasting friendship with a dorm-mate who shared his love of science and mathematics – Bill Gates. The two studied together and competed academically. Gates dropped out of Harvard to start Microsoft. Ballmer graduated magna cum laude, worked at Proctor & Gamble for two years, then enrolled in Stanford Business School. There, Gates found Ballmer and recruited him to be Microsoft's first business manager. Ballmer made an immediate impression on the company, increasing hiring, negotiating the purchase of DOS (Microsoft's first operating system), and managing the development of Windows, which today is the world's most popular operating system.

Ballmer is known for his energy, enthusiasm, charm, determination, and sense of humor. He is a likable guy according to his coworkers, and a fellow executive insists that no one is more loved inside of Microsoft. Above all, Ballmer is renowned for his dedication to the company, devotion to the needs of customers, and a passion for the company's products and services.

In 2003, Ballmer began efforts to increase Microsoft's partnerships with Chinese governments and businesses, with a focus on education, by donating $10 million during the next five years to promote information technology in elementary schools.

For more information about Steve Ballmer, visit the Discovering Computers 2005 People Web page (**scsite.com/dc2005/people**) and click Steve Ballmer.

Steve Wozniak

Cofounder of Apple Computer

Steve Wozniak always was interested in electronics. Growing up, much of his time was devoted to designing and building sophisticated machines. All of the work was self-done, with Wozniak just piecing parts together. He told his father, an engineer, that someday he would own a computer. His father chided him saying that they cost as much as a house, but Wozniak's response was that he would live in an apartment.

After dropping out of the University of California at Berkeley, Wozniak began working at Hewlett-Packard. There he met Steve Jobs, who was a summer employee. On his own time, Wozniak built a "blue box" that, with a toy whistle from Cap'n Crunch cereal boxes, could generate tones capable of making long-distance telephone calls. Jobs helped Wozniak sell the device.

Jobs joined Wozniak's Homebrew Computer Club, which focused on small computers. At that time, small computers were built from kits and programmed with a confusing array of switches. Wozniak envisioned a small computer laid out like a typewriter with a video screen. The concept of an easy-to-use computer would be a Wozniak benchmark. In 1976, the two creative visionaries developed their first personal computer, the Apple I, and it was an instant success. It led to the Apple II in 1979, which was the first mass-marketed personal computer, and eventually to the Macintosh in 1984.

Wozniak was named to the National Inventors Hall of Fame in Akron, Ohio, for his $666 Apple II. Although Wozniak left Apple in 1985 to spend time with his family, work with community projects, and teach, he still serves as an adviser to the corporation.

Today he leads a very private life in Los Gatos, California, where he attends to his charitable activities. He also helps the local school district keep at the forefront of technology and trains the staff and students.

One of Wozniak's latest products in his Wheels of Zeus Inc. startup corporation is wOzNet, wireless monitoring technology that tracks the location of pets, people, or valuable property, such as cars. Motorola will help develop the simple and inexpensive system, which will use radio signals and global positioning satellite data to monitor up to hundreds of inexpensive tags, so that parents would know when their children have arrived home from school or when their car has left a parking space.

For more information about Steve Wozniak, visit the Discovering Computers 2005 People Web page (**scsite.com/dc2005/people**) and click Steve Wozniak.

CHAPTER 15 CHAPTER REVIEW

◄ Previous | Next ►

QUIZZES AND LEARNING GAMES
Computer Genius
Crossword Puzzle
Interactive Labs
Practice Test
Quiz Yourself
Wheel of Terms
EXERCISES
Chapter Review
Checkpoint
Key Terms
Lab Exercises
Learn It Online
Web Research
BEYOND THE BOOK
Apply It
Career Corner
Companies
FAQ
High-Tech Talk
Issues
Looking Ahead
Trailblazers
Web Links
FEATURES
Guide to Web Sites
Making Use of the Web
Tech News
Timeline 2005

The Chapter Review section summarizes the concepts presented in this chapter.

WEB INSTRUCTIONS:

To display this page from the Web, start your browser and enter the Web address **scsite.com/dc2005/ch15/review.** Click the links for current and additional information. To listen to an audio version of this Chapter Review, click the Audio button.

1 What Career Opportunities Are Available in the Computer Industry?

Career opportunities in the computer industry fall into several areas. In most medium and large businesses and government offices, staff in an **information technology (IT) department** is responsible for keeping all computer operations and networks running smoothly. Workers in the **computer equipment industry** manufacture and distribute computers and computer-related hardware. Employees in the **computer software industry** develop, manufacture, and support a wide range of software. People in the **computer service and repair industry** provide preventive maintenance, component installation, and repair services to computers. **Computer sales representatives** determine a buyer's needs and match them to the correct hardware and software. Computer educators and **corporate trainers** teach students and employees how to use software, design and develop systems, program, and perform other computer-related activities. A **computer consultant** is a professional who draws upon his or her expertise in a specialized area of computers, including service and advice.

Visit **scsite.com/dc2005/quiz** or click the Quiz Yourself button. Click Objective 1 below Chapter 15.

2 What Are the Functions of Jobs in an IT Department?

Jobs in an IT department fall into five main areas. *Management* directs the planning, research, development, evaluation, and integration of technology. *System development and programming* analyzes, designs, develops, and implements new information technology and maintains and improves existing systems. *Technical services* evaluates and integrates new technologies, administrates the organization's data resources, and supports the centralized computer operating system or services. *Operations* operates the centralized computer equipment and administers the network including both data and voice communications. *End-user computing* assists end users in working with existing systems and in using software and query languages to obtain the information necessary to perform their jobs.

3 How Are the Various College Computer-Related Courses of Study Different?

Three broad disciplines in higher education produce the majority of entry-level employees in the computer industry. **Computer information systems** (**CIS**), sometimes called *computer technology*, programs emphasize the practical aspects of computing. Degree recipients understand how to design and implement information systems. **Computer science** (**CS**), also called **software engineering**, programs stress the theoretical side of programming. Degree recipients recognize the fundamental nature of hardware and software. **Computer engineering (CE)** programs teach students how to develop the electronic components found in computers and peripheral devices. Degree recipients comprehend the fundamental nature of hardware.

4 How Can People Stay Current with Changing Technology?

Three primary ways to stay current with computer technology are professional organizations, professional growth and continuing education activities, and certification. Professional organizations are formed by computer professionals with common interests and a desire to extend their proficiency. The **Association for Computing Machinery** (**ACM**) is a scientific and educational organization dedicated to advancing knowledge and proficiency of information technology. The **Association of Information Technology Professionals** (**AITP**) is a professional association of programmers, systems analysts, and managers. Professional growth and continuing education include events such as workshops, seminars, conferences, conventions, and trade shows. **COMDEX** is one of the larger technology trade shows, bringing together hundreds of vendors and more than 50,000 attendees. Certification demonstrates mastery of a skill set and knowledge base in a specific IT area. Computer industry publications, such as *COMPUTERWORLD*, *InfoWorld*, and *PC Magazine*, also help to keep people informed about happenings in the computer industry.

Visit **scsite.com/dc2005/quiz** or click the Quiz Yourself button. Click Objectives 2 – 4 below Chapter 15.

5 What Are the Benefits of Certification for Employers, Employees, and Vendors?

Certification is a process of verifying the technical knowledge of an individual who has demonstrated competence in a particular area. For employers, certification ensures quality workmanship standards and can help keep their workforce up to date with respect to computers and technology. For employees, certification can enhance careers and provide better standing as industry professionals. For vendors, certification is a form of industry self-regulation that improves the reputation of the professionals within the industry.

6 How Can People Prepare for Certification?

Certification training options are available to suit every learning style. Self-study programs help professionals prepare for certification at their own pace and supplement other training methods. Online training classes, which are available on the Internet and on many company intranets, allow students to set their own pace in an interactive environment. Instructor-led training classes are available in a variety of forms, including seminars, boot camps, and academic-style classes. Web resources include the certification sponsor's Web site and individual Web sites. The certification sponsor's Web site can contain descriptions of certifications, frequently asked questions, links to training and testing centers, online resources, training materials, practice tests, chat rooms, and discussion groups. Individuals also set up Web sites to offer their own views and tips.

7 What Are the General Areas of IT Certification?

Certifications usually are classified based on the computer industry area to which they most closely relate: application software, operating systems, programming, hardware, networking, Internet, and database systems.

8 What Are Some Specific IT Certifications in Each Certification Area?

Application software certifications, sometimes called *end-user certifications,* include *Microsoft Office Specialist (Office Specialist), Microsoft Certified Desktop Support Technician, Adobe Certified Expert (ACE), IBM Certified Professional for Lotus Software,* and *Macromedia Certified Professional*. Operating system certifications include *Microsoft Certified Professional (MCP), Red Hat Certified Engineer (RHCE), Red Hat Certified Technician (RHCT), Sun Certified System Administrator,* and *IBM Certified Specialist*. Programming certifications include *Sun Certified Enterprise Architect, Sun Certified Java Developer, Sun Certified Programmer, IBM Certified Solution Developer, Microsoft Certified Application Developer (MCAD), Certified Software Development Professional (CSDP),* and *Microsoft Certified Solution Developer (MCSD)*. Hardware certifications include *A+, IBM eServer Certified Specialist,* and *NACSE Network Technician (NNT)*. Networking certifications include *Certified Novell Administrator (CNA), Certified Novell Engineer (CNE), Cisco Certified Network Professional (CCNP), Network+,* and *Sun Certified Network Administrator*. Internet certifications include *Certified Internet Webmaster (CIW), Cisco Certified Internetwork Expert (CCIE),* and *Certified Web Professional (CWP)*. Database certifications include *IBM Certified Solutions Expert – DB2, IBM Certified Solutions Expert – Informix, Microsoft Certified Database Administrator (MCDBA), Oracle Certified Professional,* and *Sybase Certified Professional*.

Visit **scsite.com/dc2005/quiz** or click the Quiz Yourself button. Click Objectives 5 – 8 below Chapter 15.

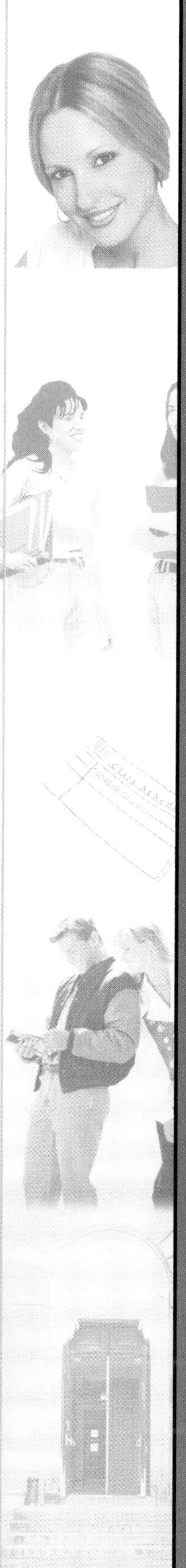

CHAPTER 15 KEY TERMS

You should know the Primary Terms and be familiar with the Secondary Terms.

WEB INSTRUCTIONS:

To display this page from the Web, start your browser and enter the Web address **scsite.com/dc2005/ch15/terms**. Click a term to display its definition and a picture. When the picture appears, click the more info button for current and additional information about the term from the Web.

>> Primary Terms

(shown in bold-black characters in the chapter)

application programmer (772)
Association for Computing Machinery (ACM) (778)
Association of Information Technology Professionals (AITP) (778)
certification (780)
COMDEX (779)
computer consultant (771)
computer engineering (CE) (776)
computer equipment industry (768)
computer information systems (CIS) (775)
computer operator (773)
computer sales representatives (770)
computer science (CS) (775)
computer scientist (769)
computer service and repair industry (770)
computer software industry (769)
computer technician (770, 773)
corporate trainers (771)
data communications analyst (773)
database administrator (773)
database analyst (772)
desktop publisher (773)
e-commerce administrator (772)
graphic designer/illustrator (773)
Help desk specialist (773)
information technology (IT) department (768)
IT department (768)
network administrator (772)
network security specialist (773)
programmer (769)
project developer (769)
project leader (772)
project manager (772)
quality assurance specialist (773)
software engineer (769, 772)
software engineering (775)
systems analyst (772)
systems programmer (772)
technical writer (772)
trade schools (776)
vice president of IT/chief information officer (CIO) (772)
Web administrator (773)
Web developer (772)
Web graphic designer (773)
Web programmer (772)
Webmaster (773)

>> Secondary Terms

(shown in italic characters in the chapter)

A+ (788)
Adobe Certified Expert (ACE) (786)
articulation agreement (775)
Certified Internet Webmaster (CIW) (789)
Certified Novell Administrator (CNA) (788)
Certified Novell Engineer (CNE) (788)
Certified Software Development Professional (CSDP) (787)
Certified Web Professional (CWP) (789)
Cisco Certified Internetwork Expert (CCIE) (789)
Cisco Certified Network Professional (CCNP) (788)
computer technology (775)
computerized adaptive testing (CAT) (785)
COMPUTERWORLD (780)
Data Processing Management Association (DPMA) (778)
end-user certifications (786)
end-user computing (773)
IBM Certified Professional for Lotus Software (786)
IBM Certified Solution Developer (787)
IBM Certified Solutions Expert – DB2 (789)
IBM Certified Solutions Expert – Informix (789)
IBM Certified Specialist (787)
IBM eServer Certified Specialist (788)
InfoWorld (780)
Institute for Certification of Computer Professionals (ICCP) (783)
Macromedia Certified Professional (786)
management (772)
Microsoft Certified Application Developer (MCAD) (787)
Microsoft Certified Database Administrator (MCDBA) (789)
Microsoft Certified Desktop Support Technician (MCDST) (786)
Microsoft Certified Professional (MCP) (787)
Microsoft Certified Solution Developer (MCSD) (787)
Microsoft Office Specialist (Office Specialist) (786)
NACSE Network Technician (NNT) (788)
Network+ (788)
operations (773)
Oracle Certified Professional (789)
PC Magazine (780)
Red Hat Certified Engineer (RHCE) (787)
Red Hat Certified Technician (RHCT) (787)
Special Interest Groups (SIGs) (778)
sponsoring organizations (781)
Sun Certified Enterprise Architect (787)
Sun Certified Java Developer (787)
Sun Certified Network Administrator (788)
Sun Certified Programmer (787)
Sun Certified System Administrator (787)
Sybase Certified Professional (789)
system development and programming (772)
technical services (773)
user group (779)

CHECKPOINT CHAPTER 15

Use the Checkpoint exercises to check your knowledge level of the chapter.

WEB INSTRUCTIONS:

To display this page from the Web, start your browser and enter the Web address **scsite.com/dc2005/ch15/check**. Click the links for current and additional information.

LABEL THE FIGURE

Identify each computer discipline.

a. Computer Engineering
b. Computer Information Systems
c. Computer Science/Software Engineering

1. ______	2. ______	3. ______
Practical and application oriented	Theory oriented	Design oriented
Business and management oriented	Mathematics and science oriented	Mathematics and science oriented
Understand how to design and implement information systems	Understand the fundamental nature of hardware and software	Understand the fundamental nature of hardware
Degrees include A.A., A.A.S., A.S., B.A., B.S., M.S., Ph.D.	Degrees include B.S., M.S., Ph.D.	Degrees include B.S., M.S., Ph.D.

TRUE/FALSE

Mark T for True and F for False. (See page numbers in parentheses.)

_____ 1. As the use of computers and the demand for computer specialists continues to decline, the number of students majoring in computer-related fields is much more than what the industry needs. (766)

_____ 2. An IT department is responsible for keeping all the computer operations and networks in business and government running smoothly. (768)

_____ 3. Computer sales representative for a retail store often is a suitable entry-level job for students majoring in computers. (771)

_____ 4. A computer consultant is a professional who draws upon his or her expertise in a specialized area of computers. (771)

_____ 5. In general, CS programming courses are less rigorous than CIS programming courses. (775)

_____ 6. Trade schools offer programs primarily in the areas of programming, Web development, graphic design, hardware maintenance, networking, and security. (776)

_____ 7. The Association of Information Technology Professionals (AITP) is a scientific and educational organization dedicated to advancing knowledge and proficiency of information technology. (778)

_____ 8. Vendors, called sponsoring organizations, develop and administer examinations to determine whether a person is qualified for certification. (781)

_____ 9. All certification programs require academic coursework. (784)

_____ 10. The preparation classes for programming certifications provide an opportunity for professionals to share ideas. (787)

CHAPTER 15 CHECKPOINT

QUIZZES AND LEARNING GAMES
Computer Genius
Crossword Puzzle
Interactive Labs
Practice Test
Quiz Yourself
Wheel of Terms

EXERCISES
Chapter Review
Checkpoint
Key Terms
Lab Exercises
Learn It Online
Web Research

BEYOND THE BOOK
Apply It
Career Corner
Companies
FAQ
High-Tech Talk
Issues
Looking Ahead
Trailblazers
Web Links

FEATURES
Guide to Web Sites
Making Use of the Web
Tech News
Timeline 2005

MULTIPLE CHOICE

Select the best answer. (See page numbers in parentheses.)

1. A _____ installs, maintains, and repairs hardware. (770)
   a. computer technician
   b. project developer
   c. computer scientist
   d. computer consultant
2. Many companies hire a _____ to fill in for an employee on an extended leave of absence. (771)
   a. computer technician
   b. project developer
   c. computer scientist
   d. computer consultant
3. A technical writer _____. (772)
   a. reviews programs and documentation to ensure they meet an organization's standards
   b. combines text and graphics to produce newsletters, brochures, and books
   c. works with the analyst, programmer, and user to create system documentation
   d. creates and maintains the data dictionary and checks backup and recovery procedures
4. _____ is a job title in the technical services area of an IT department. (773)
   a. E-commerce administrator
   b. Systems programmer
   c. Webmaster
   d. Computer operator
5. _____ is a business and management oriented computer discipline. (774)
   a. Computer information systems (CIS)
   b. Computer science (CS)
   c. Computer engineering (CE)
   d. All of the above
6. A(n) _____ ensures that if a student transfers to a college or university, he or she will receive credit for most of the courses taken at the community college level. (775)
   a. technical service
   b. articulation agreement
   c. tethered system
   d. user group
7. Both the Association for Computing Machinery (ACM) and the Association of Information Technology Professionals (AITP) offer _____. (778)
   a. chapters throughout the United States
   b. workshops, seminars, and conventions
   c. Special Interest Groups (SIGs)
   d. all of the above
8. One of the larger technology trade shows in the world is _____. (779)
   a. AITP
   b. COMDEX
   c. MCDBA
   d. CCNP
9. Sponsors of IT certifications include all of the following except _____. (781)
   a. computer equipment and software vendors
   b. independent training companies
   c. professional organizations
   d. user groups and trade schools
10. _____ is/are the least expensive option for certification training. (784)
    a. Self-study
    b. Online training classes
    c. Instructor-led training
    d. Web resources
11. _____ is/are available in a variety of forms, including seminars, boot camps, and academic-style classes. (784)
    a. Self-study
    b. Online training classes
    c. Instructor-led training
    d. Web resources
12. Certifications usually are classified based on the _____. (786)
    a. location and availability of the certification program
    b. computer industry area to which they most closely relate
    c. amount of time and money required to obtain certification
    d. difficulty of the certification requirements
13. _____ certifications include Microsoft Office Specialist (Office Specialist), Adobe Certified Expert (ACE), and IBM Certified Professional for Lotus Software. (786)
    a. Programming
    b. Application software
    c. Internet
    d. Operating system
14. Hardware certifications include _____. (788)
    a. IBM eServer Certified Specialist
    b. Sun Certified Enterprise Architect
    c. Red Hat Certified Engineer
    d. all of the above

CHECKPOINT CHAPTER 15

MATCHING Match the terms with their definitions. (See page numbers in parentheses.)

_____ 1. network administrator (772)
_____ 2. project manager (772)
_____ 3. chief information officer (CIO) (772)
_____ 4. systems analyst (772)
_____ 5. Web developer (772)
_____ 6. database administrator (773)
_____ 7. network security specialist (773)
_____ 8. Web administrator (773)
_____ 9. data communications analyst (773)
_____ 10. help desk specialist (773)

a. installs, configures, and maintains LANs, WANs, intranets, and Internet systems
b. solves procedural and software questions in person and over the telephone
c. oversees Web site performance and maintains links
d. directs information service and communications functions
e. manages database security and monitors database performance
f. analyzes, designs, implements, and supports Web-related applications
g. supervises the execution of Internet or e-commerce systems
h. oversees projects, allocates resources, selects teams, and appraises performance
i. evaluates, installs, and monitors communications equipment and software
j. combines text and graphics to produce documents such as brochures and books
k. configures routers and firewalls and specifies Web protocols
l. analyzes user requirements and designs and develops new information systems

SHORT ANSWER Write a brief answer to each of the following questions.

1. How is a project developer different from a programmer? __________ How is a software engineer different from a computer scientist? __________
2. What is a trade school? __________ What is an advantage of attending a trade school? __________
3. What do student chapters of professional organizations offer students? __________ What is a user group? __________
4. What is the Institute for Certification of Computer Professionals? __________ What should be considered when choosing a certification? __________
5. How are tests taken at certification testing centers? __________ What is CAT?__________

WORKING TOGETHER Working with a group of your classmates, complete the following team exercises.

1. Study options for obtaining certifications include self-study, online courses, and instructor-led courses. Have each member of your team find a Web site for each study option. Select a common certification track. Compare the training program and meet to discuss your findings. Then, prepare a report and a PowerPoint presentation to share your findings with the class.
2. Choose one Issue from the following issues in this chapter: Should Programmers Be Licensed? (769), Should Companies Send IT Jobs Abroad? (771), How Valuable Is Certification? (781), Are Vendor-Specific Certifications Worthwhile? (783), How Good Are Certification Tests? (785), or Should Programming Require a College Degree? (787). Use the Web and/or print media to research the issue. Then, present a debate for the class, with different members of your team supporting different responses to the questions that accompany the issue.
3. Jobs in the computer industry can be found almost everywhere. How does a region attract high-tech corporations? Have each member of your team visit a high-tech company in your area to learn why the company chose its location. Was it tax incentives? Corporate climate? Employee availability? Cost of living? Quality of life? Some other factor? Meet to discuss your findings. Then, create a PowerPoint presentation showing what a region can do to become a hotbed of high-tech corporations.

CHAPTER 15 LEARN IT ONLINE

QUIZZES AND LEARNING GAMES
Computer Genius
Crossword Puzzle
Interactive Labs
Practice Test
Quiz Yourself
Wheel of Terms

EXERCISES
Chapter Review
Checkpoint
Key Terms
Lab Exercises
Learn It Online
Web Research

BEYOND THE BOOK
Apply It
Career Corner
Companies
FAQ
High-Tech Talk
Issues
Looking Ahead
Trailblazers
Web Links

FEATURES
Guide to Web Sites
Making Use of the Web
Tech News
Timeline 2005

Use the Learn It Online exercises to reinforce your understanding of the chapter concepts.

WEB INSTRUCTIONS:

To display this page from the Web, start your browser and enter the Web address **scsite.com/dc2005/ch15/learn**.

1 At the Movies – Internet Economy

To view the Internet Economy movie, click the number 1 button. Watch the movie and then complete the exercise by answering the questions below. Skyrocketing growth of the Internet has created a massive shortfall of qualified employees. College graduates with degrees in engineering or computer science, however, can expect at least a dozen job offers upon graduation. Internet employment has lured job seekers with the dream of latching onto a winner and becoming quick millionaires before hitting age 30. At the same time, chaos and uncertainty prevail in the industry as thousands of companies go under. If you are looking for an Internet-related job, what are the things to look for in a company? Where do you look for Internet-related jobs? What skills are required?

2 Interviewing for an IT Career

Being prepared for an interview is vital in making a good impression and one of the more important steps to getting a job. To begin your preparation, compose a list of common questions that you may be asked. Most employers will ask about experience, qualifications, and future plans. Next, prepare a list of questions that you can ask your potential employer. Some common questions are about benefits, types of training programs, and available career paths. Then practice, practice, practice. One way to practice in a safe environment is through a virtual interview. Click the number 2 button and complete the virtual interview. Was the interview helpful? What questions were the most difficult?

3 Microsoft Office Specialist Certification

One of the more popular application certification programs is the Microsoft Office Specialist (Office Specialist) certification. The certification program recognizes individuals who have achieved a certain level of mastery with Microsoft Office products and provides a framework for measuring end-user proficiency with the Microsoft Office applications. Attaining Microsoft Office Specialist certification proves you have met an industry-recognized standard for measuring an individual's mastery of Office applications, demonstrates proficiency in a given Office application to employers, and provides a competitive edge in the job marketplace. Click the number 3 button for a list of frequently asked questions (FAQs) about the Office Specialist program. Read the questions. What types of certifications are available? What kind of preparation is necessary for certification? Does your educational institution offer Office Specialist courses?

4 Practice Test

Click the number 4 button. Answer each question. When completed, enter your name and click the Grade Test button to submit the quiz for grading. Make a note of any missed questions. If required, print a copy to submit to your instructor.

5 Web Guide

Click the number 5 button to display the Guide to Web Sites and Searching Techniques Web page. Click Reference and then click Webopedia. Search for e-commerce. Click one of the e-commerce links of interest to you. Use your word processing program to prepare a brief report about your findings and submit your assignment to your instructor.

6 Scavenger Hunt

Click the number 6 button. Print a copy of the Scavenger Hunt page; use this page to write down your answers as you search the Web. Submit your completed page to your instructor.

7 Who Wants To Be a Computer Genius?

Click the number 7 button to find out if you are a computer genius. Directions on how to play the game will be displayed. When you are ready to play, click the Play button. Submit your score to your instructor.

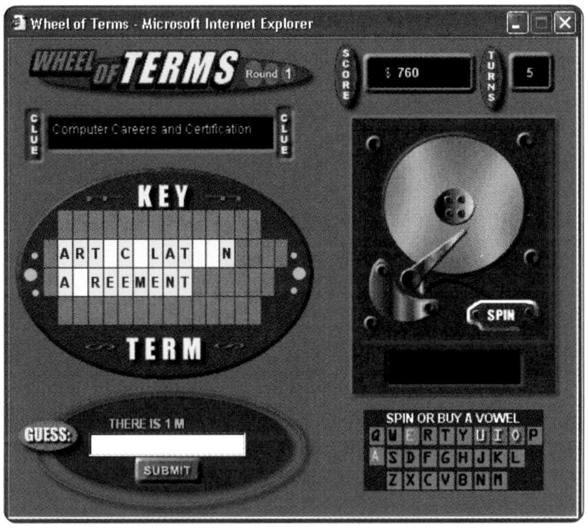

8 Wheel of Terms

Click the number 8 button to reinforce important terms you learned in this chapter by playing the Shelly Cashman Series version of this popular game. Directions on how to play the game will be displayed. When you are ready to play, click the Play button. Submit your score to your instructor.

9 Career Corner

Click the number 9 button to display the CareerBuilder Web site. Click the advanced search link and search keywords for an IT job. Scroll through the results until you find a job in which you are interested. Write a brief report on the job you selected and what you discovered. Submit the report to your instructor.

10 Search Sleuth

Click the number 10 button to learn search techniques that will help make you a research expert. Submit the completed assignment to your instructor.

11 Crossword Puzzle Challenge

Click the number 11 button. Complete the puzzle to reinforce skills you learned in this chapter. Directions on how to play the game will be displayed. When you are ready to play, click the Submit button. Submit the completed puzzle to your instructor.

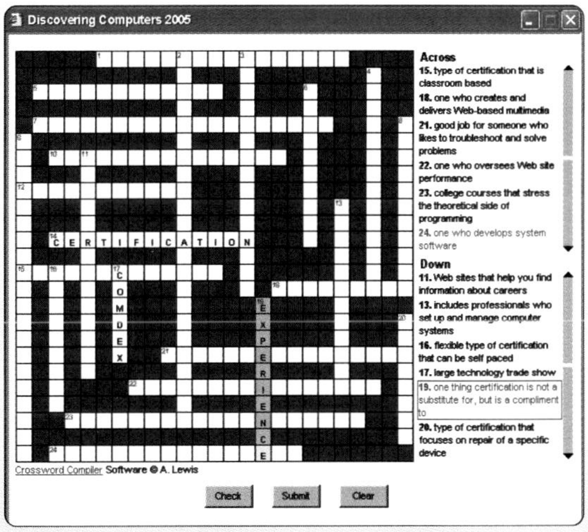

12 In the News

As the IT professionals shortage continues, several certification sponsors have started offering certification training and testing to high school students. The students choose computers as a major and take courses in certification programs such as A+ and MCSE. Many states have magnet schools where most of the curriculum is focused on technology. Click the number 12 button and read a news article about a recent high school certification story. Could this trend cause a potential problem with students not attending college?

CHAPTER 15 LAB EXERCISES

QUIZZES AND LEARNING GAMES
Computer Genius
Crossword Puzzle
Interactive Labs
Practice Test
Quiz Yourself
Wheel of Terms
EXERCISES
Chapter Review
Checkpoint
Key Terms
Lab Exercises
Learn It Online
Web Research
BEYOND THE BOOK
Apply It
Career Corner
Companies
FAQ
High-Tech Talk
Issues
Looking Ahead
Trailblazers
Web Links
FEATURES
Guide to Web Sites
Making Use of the Web
Tech News
Timeline 2005

Use the Lab Exercises to gain hands-on computer experience.

WEB INSTRUCTIONS:

To display this page from the Web, start your browser and enter the Web address **scsite.com/dc2005/ch15/lab**.

1 Using the Character Map Utility

This exercise uses Windows XP procedures. Word processing programs have their own process for accessing special characters. The Character Map Utility lets you retrieve characters for use in other programs. Click the Start button, point to All Programs on the Start menu, point to Accessories on the All Programs submenu, point to System Tools on the Accessories submenu, and then click Character Map on the System Tools submenu. When the Character Map window is displayed, click a character of your choice, and then click the Select button. Click a second character and then click the Select button again. Click the Copy button. Click the Close button in the Character Map window. Click the Start button, point to All Programs on the Start menu, point to Accessories on the All Programs submenu, and then click WordPad on the Accessories submenu. Click Format on the menu bar and then click Font. Scroll down the Font list in the Font dialog box. Click Symbol as the new font. Click the OK button. Click Edit on the menu bar and then click Paste to paste your characters into the WordPad window. Press the ENTER key and then type your name. Click File on the menu bar and then click Print. Close the WordPad program. Do not save the file unless your instructor tells you to do so.

2 Adding a Scrap to the Desktop

This exercise uses Windows XP/2000/98 procedures. To keep the contents of the Clipboard on your desktop for later reference, you can create a scrap. The two ways to create a scrap are drag and drop and copy and paste. You can recognize a scrap by its icon — a document file with a torn edge along the bottom. Click the Start button, point to All Programs (Programs in Windows 2000 and 98) on the Start menu, point to Accessories on the All Programs submenu (Programs submenu in Windows 2000 and 98), and then click WordPad on the Accessories submenu. When the WordPad window is displayed, if necessary, click the Restore Down button (Restore button in Windows 2000 and 98) on the title bar, so the desktop displays behind the window. Type your name and address. To use drag and drop, select the text in the WordPad window and then drag it to the desktop to create a scrap. To use copy and paste, select the text in the WordPad window, click Edit on the menu bar and then click Copy. Right-click the desktop and then click Paste on the shortcut menu to create a scrap. To use the scrap in a document, drag it into the document. Or, right-click the scrap, click Copy on the shortcut menu, and then paste it into your document. Close WordPad. Do not save the file. Delete the scraps on the desktop by dragging them to the Recycle Bin.

3 Toggle Keys

This exercise uses Windows XP procedures. Microsoft's Accessibility Options allow you to sound a beep when the CAPS LOCK and other keys are engaged. Click the Start button on the taskbar and then click Control Panel on the Start menu. In Category View, click the Accessibility Options icon to display the Accessibility Options window. Click the Accessibility Options icon to display the Accessibility Options dialog box. If necessary, click the Keyboard tab and then click Use ToggleKeys. Click the Apply button and then click the OK button. Press the CAPS LOCK key to hear the sound. Press the NUM LOCK and SCROLL LOCK keys to hear the sound. To return these toggle keys to their original settings, in the Accessibility Options window, click the Accessibility Options icon and deselect the Use ToggleKeys check box. Click the Apply button and then click the OK button. Close the Accessibility Options window.

4 Disk Maintenance

This exercise uses Windows 2000/98 procedures. Hard disk backup, error checking, and defragmentation should be done on a regular basis. If you are unsure when these operations were performed last, quick and easy access to this information is available. Right-click the Start button and then click Explore. In the Exploring - (C:) window, right-click the (C:) icon and then click Properties on the shortcut menu. When the (C:) Properties dialog box is displayed, click the Tools tab. How many days have elapsed since the drive was checked for errors? How many days have elapsed since the files were backed up? How many days have elapsed since the disk was defragmented? Close the (C:) Properties dialog box and the Exploring - (C:) window.

WEB RESEARCH CHAPTER 15

Use the Web Research exercises to learn more about the special features in this chapter.

WEB INSTRUCTIONS:

Use the link in each exercise or a search engine such as Google (google.com) to research the topic. Then, write a one-page, double-spaced report or create a presentation, unless otherwise directed below. Page numbers on which information can be found are in parentheses.

1 **Issue** Choose one Issue from the following issues in this chapter: Should Programmers Be Licensed? (769), Should Companies Send IT Jobs Abroad? (771), How Valuable Is Certification? (781), Are Vendor-Specific Certifications Worthwhile? (783), How Good Are Certification Tests? (785), or Should Programming Require a College Degree? (787). Use the Web to research the issue. Discuss the issue with classmates, instructors, and friends. Address the questions that accompany the issue in a report or presentation.

2 **Apply It** Choose one of the following Apply It features in this chapter: Application Software Skills Essential for Career (767) or Online Resume Helps Job Hunting Experience (777). Use the Web to gather additional information about the topic. Print two Web pages that relate to the Apply It. Detail in a report or presentation what you learned.

3 **Career Corner** Read the Career Corner article in this chapter (790). Use the Web to find out more about the career. Describe the career in a report or presentation.

4 **Companies on the Cutting Edge** Choose one of the Companies on the Cutting Edge in this chapter (792). Use the Web to research the company further. Explain in a report or presentation how this company has contributed to computer technology.

5 **Technology Trailblazers** Choose one of the Technology Trailblazers in this chapter (793). Use the Web to research the person further. Explain in a report or presentation how this individual has affected the way people use, or think about, computers.

6 **Picture Yourself Career Planning** Read the Picture Yourself Career Planning story at the beginning of this chapter (764). Use the Web to research career planning further. Describe in a report or presentation the ways in which you might plan for a career in the computer industry.

7 **High-Tech Talk** Read the High-Tech Talk feature in this chapter (791). Use the Web to find out more about the topic. Summarize in a report or presentation what you learned.

8 **Web Links** Review the Web Link boxes found in the margins of this chapter. Visit five of the Web Link sites. Print the main Web page for each site you visit. Choose one of the Web pages and then summarize in one paragraph the content of the Web page.

9 **Looking Ahead** Choose one of the Looking Ahead articles in this chapter: When Can You Start? (768) or Starting Your Computer-Related Business (774). Use the Web to find out more about the topic. Detail in a report or presentation what you learned.

10 **FAQ** Choose one FAQ found in this chapter. Use the Web to find out more about the topic. Summarize in one paragraph what you learned.

11 **Trends** Read the Trends Special Feature that follows this chapter (804–816). Select a trend in which you are interested. Use the Web to learn more about your selection. Describe in a report or presentation how the trend will impact information technology and influence the direction of the computer field.

12 **Making Use of the Web** Read the Arts and Literature section of Making Use of the Web in Appendix A (APP 30). Complete the Arts and Literature Web Exercises at the end of the section (APP 31). Answer the questions posed in each exercise.

TRENDS 2005
A Look to the Future

FIGURE 1 In the future, computers will have an even more important role in all aspects of your life by providing vast information resources, fast communications, and powerful support for activities in homes, schools, and businesses.

The digital revolution has affected all aspects of people's lives (Figure 1). Computers have become a mainstay in our daily activities and have influenced all individuals, families, organizations, and schools, as discussed throughout this book. In the twentieth century, the automobile, telephone, and television revolutionized travel and communications. In this century, computers will continue to shape business transactions and interactions with people in all parts of the world. Computers will undertake new functions and become an even more pervasive and critical part of home, school, and work. This feature explores several computer technology trends that are affecting the direction of the computer field and then looks at the influence these technologies will have on information technology in business.

TRENDS IN COMPUTER TECHNOLOGY

During the next several years, the greatest advances in computer technology will occur in areas such as hardware, software, communications and networks, mobile and wireless connectivity, and robotics.

Hardware

Manufacturers intensely are developing and producing new devices, including Tablet PCs, microdisplays, and headsets, that will pervade all aspects of people's lives, especially learning and playing. This hardware will contain faster and smaller chips, which could be implanted in your body. Atomic Quantum computers and optical computers could process data at record-breaking speeds. Fluorescent multi-player discs and digital books will revolutionize the ways information is stored and accessed.

UBIQUITOUS COMPUTING Computers are not yet everywhere, but as they get smaller, faster, and less expensive, they are being utilized in everything from toothbrushes and curling irons to cars and spaceships. Ralph Merkle, a research scientist at Xerox's Palo Alto Research Center, envisions a "not-so-distant future, maybe by 2020, definitely by 2050, [in which] we will have devices with the computational power of roughly a billion Pentium computers." Every device known to man, including the human body, will use some type of computer.

NANOPARTICLES The data storage industry is making headway in reducing the size of components to 1/10,000 the width of human hair. Researchers at Purdue University have developed a way to create tiny, bracelet-like magnetic rings from cobalt particles that can store magnetic information at room temperature. These nanorings, shown below, assemble spontaneously by themselves.

NEXT-GENERATION CHIP The 21st Century Nanotechnology Research and Development Act of 2003 authorizes nearly $3.7 billion to support the growing field of nanotechnology, which is the science of building molecular devices one atom at a time. The precise positioning of these atoms increases computing power, which enhances the intelligence needed to solve some of the most complex problems worldwide. Engineers are using extreme ultra-violet lithography (UVL) to turn their circuit designs into silicon chips. This technology uses ultrasmooth mirrors, rather than optical projection, to draw circuits that are 100 times more powerful than today's chips, which contain 42 million transistors that are 0.13 of a micron wide. By 2005, chip manufacturers plan to introduce multi-chip processors that will contain 1 billion transistors that are just 0.03 of a micron wide. Intel's 64-bit Itanium processor family also will improve processing speed (Figure 2).

FIGURE 2 Fluent Inc. engineers use computers powered by Intel's Itanium processor to study fluid dynamics. Among their studies are the aerodynamics of the original 1903 Wright Flyer aircraft. One simulation examined the surface pressures experienced by the pilot on the wing of the aircraft.

MICRODISPLAYS AND HEADSETS You will be seeing technology in a whole new way with visual devices that resemble glasses and sunglasses (Figure 3). One model replicates a 52-inch television screen or Sony PlayStation 2 on an LCD screen. IBM has developed glasses that translate Japanese signs to English. Headsets plug into computers, digital cameras, and DVD players and allow a display measuring one-tenth of an inch to look like a full-sized theater screen. Microdisplays the size of postage stamps fill your field of vision and appear as large as a regular monitor when magnified (Figure 4).

FIGURE 3 Headmount displays provide a viewing area resolution similar to that of a desktop monitor. The handheld optical pointing device allows Internet and Windows navigation, and the integrated MP3 player provides access to music and videos.

FIGURE 4
Microdisplays give you the visual equivalent of a 19-inch monitor and allow you to view Web pages, e-mail, maps, and calendars.

HUMAN COMPUTER INTEGRATION Some researchers believe the processor eventually will become an integral part of the most complex device known — the human body. Physical therapists, athletic trainers, and footware designers will use the data collected by sensors integrated into smart sneakers. Computers already are used inside the human body. Cochlear implants, for example, help some deaf people hear by stimulating the ear and the nerves that send information to the brain (Figure 5). Solar-powered microchips surgically implanted behind the retina convert light into electrical impulses and help the blind to see. The chips have an added benefit: doctors are discovering that cells are regenerating near the implant site. Another innovation is a body-scanning machine that will evaluate a patient's pain. This device will be helpful especially for patients who cannot communicate. The next step in human computer integration will involve implanting chips in the body to help it perform basic functions. A processor, for example, could help regulate the release of hormones in the same way that a processor regulates the fuel mixture in modern automobiles.

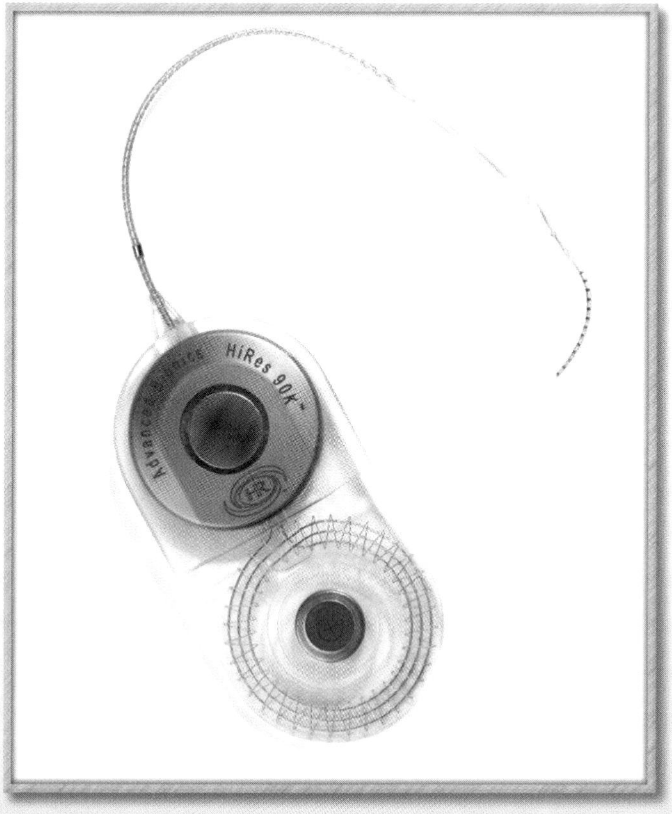

FIGURE 5 Children with hearing loss may benefit from bionic ear implants. These tiny, flexible, soft implants digitize sounds and then send signals through electrodes to the hearing nerve.

Canadian futurist Frank Ogden has conceived an even more futuristic use of embedded processors called CyberSight that interface with a person's optic nerve and transmit information over a wireless link. The CyberSight system, for example, could transmit the floor plans of a building to a firefighter and display in the vision of the firefighter allowing him or her to determine the best way to enter a burning building.

Your body and a 60-watt lightbulb radiate the same amount of heat, and engineers are developing apparatus that harnesses this energy to power such devices as MP3 players.

ATOMIC QUANTUM COMPUTERS By the middle of this century, the computer on your desk could very well be filled with liquid instead of transistors and chips. It probably will be called a QC for Quantum computer, rather than a personal computer. In theory, the speed of Quantum computers could be up to a billion times faster than today's fastest Pentium 4 computers. At that speed, a Quantum computer could search the entire Internet instantaneously or break any security code in a second. Quantum computers use quantum mechanics, rather than digital technology. In a Quantum computer, bits are replaced by atoms.

OPTICAL COMPUTERS Transmitting data using optical technology has become commonplace in CD-ROM drives, laser printers, photocopiers, and scanners and in fiber-optic digital communications. Some engineers believe this technology will extend to computers using visible light or infrared beams to perform digital computations, increasing the speed of operations tenfold. Likewise, it should decrease the optical computers' physical size because the light beams can pass through each other without interacting.

FLUORESCENT MULTILAYER DISC AND HOLOGRAPHIC VIDEO STORAGE High-definition television, digital cinema, and digital cameras may benefit from two new forms of storage. The first generation of the Fluorescent Multilayer Disc (FMD) stores 140 GB of data, which is almost 30 times more than a DVD-ROM disc can hold; upcoming generations promise to increase capacity to 1 terabyte (1 trillion bytes). The five-inch clear optical medium has as many as 100 layers, and data is recorded on fluorescent materials found on each of these layers. Holographic video storage devices record images as holograms on the entire thickness of a DVD-like disc. Capacity is expected to reach 1.3 terabytes. The holographic disc is expected to have a storage life of 50 years, which is 30 years longer than that of a CD or DVD.

GETTING UNDER YOUR SKIN Stop worrying about losing your wallet or key fobs with credit card information. A chip implanted in the flesh of your arm could hold all the identification you need to pay for merchandise or obtain cash from an automatic teller. This radio frequency identification (RFID) chip is smaller than a grain of sand (Figure 6) and transmits a signal with one of 18 thousand trillion unique ID codes. Privacy experts warn that thieves may try to steal the chips or intercept and then rebroadcast the radio signal.

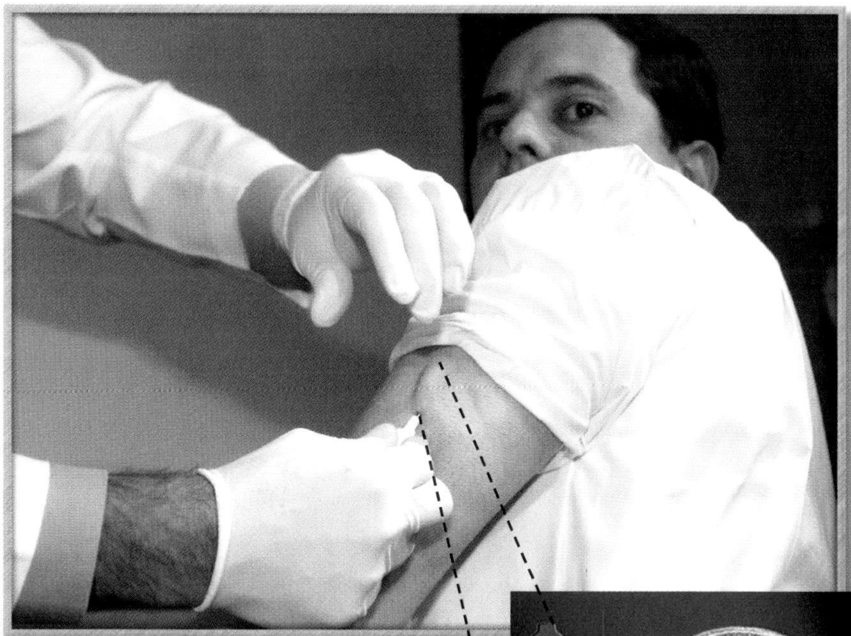

FIGURE 6 The RFID VeriChip, manufactured by Applied Digital Solutions, is implanted in the skin and transmits information identifying a particular person. The chip could be used to obtain cash from an automatic teller or pay for groceries.

FUEL AND SOLAR CELLS Methanol fuels Indianapolis-type race cars because of its low cost, high performance, and fire safety, and it soon may fuel your cellular telephone and notebook computer. Researchers are developing replaceable fuel cells powered by methanol that may replace the lithium ion batteries found in today's mobile devices. They eventually will power a device for 10 hours. An even less expensive source of energy is the sun, and computers are refining powerful solar-powered cells, so they possibly can be used to supply energy for space exploration and to countries throughout the world.

MAKE A FASHION STATEMENT Wearable computers are among the hottest fashion trends. The Accenture Technology Labs Personal Awareness Assistant (PAA) is a small device resembling a watch and is used to record notes and images. It could be handy if you forget someone's name. If you have met this person previously and stored his name in your PAA, you could retrieve this name by scrolling through the database. Microsoft's SPOT watch (Figure 7) allows wearers to receive instant personal messages discreetly with a slight vibration or visual display alert. It uses MSN Direct, a specialized wireless service. This watch also delivers news, weather, sports, stocks, and appointment reminders.

FIGURE 7 The Microsoft SPOT watch has downloadable watch faces to complement your personal style and mood. The MSN Direct network provides information tailored to your interests and location.

EDUCATION The use of personal computers in educational and laboratory settings is another rapidly growing area. The Internet and the World Wide Web are affecting education, as distance education allows students to take classes or Webinars — online seminars — whenever they have time from home or workplace computers. Such courses are ideal for workers seeking advanced training but lacking the time to pursue on-campus studies or for undergraduates living far from campus.

HOME IMPROVEMENTS Developers are creating the home of the future today. As residential projects are being developed, contractors are laying the infrastructure for powerful networks with telephone, cable, coaxial, Category 5 Ethernet, and fiber-optic cables. This structured wiring travels through the walls in every room, and routers and switches are hidden in closets. These wires eventually will link computers throughout the house.

ENTERTAINMENT For the younger members of the family, playing games using entertainment software always has had a large appeal. Many adults, however, find that entertainment software also provides them with hours of enjoyment. Popular types of entertainment software include arcade games, board games, and simulations.

Entertainment software also consists of a variety of interactive adventure games, which range from rescuing a princess from a castle's dungeon to solving a murder mystery. You can play many of these games in groups using a network or on the World Wide Web, or you can play simply with the computer as your opponent.

Virtual reality (VR) is the use of computers to simulate a real or imagined environment that appears as a three-dimensional (3-D) space. VR allows you to explore and manipulate controls to experience the 3-D space completely (Figure 8). One futurist suggests that VR someday will allow moviegoers to pretend they are one of the movie characters. In such an environment, the virtual reality technology would link the moviegoer's sensory system (sight, smell, hearing, taste, and touch) to the character's sensory system.

FIGURE 8 Design engineers at the U.S. Army Tank Automotive Research, Development & Engineering Center use a Cave Automatic Virtual Environment from Fakespace Systems Inc. to collaborate with end-users and to develop and test advanced vehicle and weapon designs.

Software

A second major area of technology innovation involves the instructions that tell computers what tasks to perform. Software trends include improved user interfaces, enhanced Internet content, forensic animation, MP4 video compression, intelligent agents, speech recognition, and remote control of home appliances.

USER INTERFACE Most computers use a graphical user interface (GUI), which developers have dubbed the WIMP (windows, icons, menus, and pointer) interface. To use the WIMP interface, you must learn a new mode of communications that includes pointing, clicking, dragging, and so on. Next-generation operating systems will be more natural and human-centric, meaning they will allow you to interface with a computer using many of the methods you now use to communicate with humans. Such methods will include natural language, hand gestures, facial expressions, and of course, spoken words.

THE INTERNET AND THE WEB In this decade, the Internet and the Web promise many exciting developments. The Internet is the fastest growing segment of the computer industry and is a major reason why consumers are buying personal computers and handheld devices at a record pace. Today, more than one-half of U.S. homes have access to the Internet. At present, individuals primarily use the Internet to access information and communicate using e-mail. In the future, individuals increasingly will rely on two other Internet-based applications — telephony and videoconferencing.

FORENSIC ANIMATION Forensic animation is gaining increased acceptance in courtrooms nationwide (Figure 9). This animation uses full-motion computer graphics to recreate an event such as an automobile accident, the collapse of a building, an assault, or the workings of a mechanical device from a variety of vantage points. For example, a collision between a small car and a truck might portray the moments before, during, and after the collision as seen by the driver of the car and by the driver of the truck, and also as it would appear from several external locations. Forensic experts, police officers, engineers, and eyewitnesses compile the data and supply it to the animators, who create a series of fixed video images that are assembled to create a cartoon-movie-like rendition of the event. Scenes are generated using various computer programs working in combination.

FIGURE 9 Courtrooms will be wired with state-of-the-art electronic equipment designed to make attorneys' presentations effective and efficient for everyone in the room. Forensic animation, live video feeds, virtual reality, three-dimensional graphics, and PowerPoint presentations will help the litigators present evidence.

MP4 VIDEO COMPRESSION Video files can be compressed to 10 percent of their original size with MP4 technology, which filters out images the eye cannot perceive. Using today's standards, a full-length compressed video would take two hours to download, but as broadband Internet access and data transfer rates increase, the download time should become more manageable. Entertainment companies are considering sending movie trailers and video messages on wireless handheld devices.

INTELLIGENT AGENTS For more than 40 years, artificial intelligence (AI) experts promoted the advantages of smart software — that is, software with built-in intelligence. In recent years, as this concept has become reality, the term, intelligent agent, has evolved to describe any software program that independently asks questions, pays attention to work patterns, and carries out tasks on behalf of a user (Figure 10).

FIGURE 10 An air traffic controller manages simulated aircraft traffic at the Los Angeles International Airport from the NASA FutureFlight Central tower. Personnel from various federal agencies worked together to simulate and then evaluate a new center taxiway at the airport as part of the airport's modernization plan. The data indicated that a center taxiway would be viable for improving the movement of aircraft on the runways and taxiways.

Some intelligent agents are embedded and work within a single program. Other intelligent agents, sometimes called network agents, perform tasks on multiple remote computers with different platforms before bringing the results back to the user. Intelligent agents already are a part of several productivity software packages. Some e-mail software, for example, includes intelligent agents that allow individuals and businesses to filter incoming messages and request immediate notification of messages about specific subjects or from specific individuals. The Intellisense technology built into Microsoft Office also is based on an intelligent agent.

BLOGGING UP A STORM Web logging, or blogging, is a public online journal. A blogger creates a Web site, updates it periodically, and encourages others to add comments. Microsoft is encouraging blogging communities among college students by sponsoring The Spoke. Sites such as blogger.com, which is owned by Google, help people develop their blogs in a few minutes. Specific blogger communities exist to discuss professional basketball, pediatrics, and traveling.

A similar form of online communication is social networking. Friendster, Tickle (Figure 11), and Tribe Networks are among the more popular Web sites for entertainment and business. A person joins the network and meets others with similar interests, such as finding information about working at a particular corporation or applying to a specific college. Another person on the network reads the query and either answers the questions or suggests contacting another person who may know the answers. That person introduces another person to the social network, and the process continues ad infinitum.

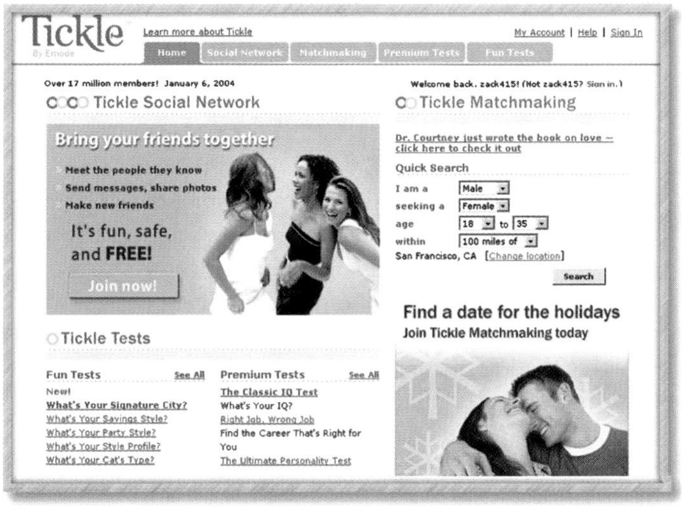

FIGURE 11 Tickle is an online social networking community that enables thousands of people to meet virtually. Some social networks exist to promote business relationships, such as to help salesmen learn about a specific corporation before visiting the site.

MORE THAN COOKING IN THE KITCHEN In many homes, the office serves as the hub of computer-related work. With kitchens increasing in size and serving as an entertainment center and family-gathering area, more than cooking will be done in the kitchen of the future. Internet-enabled refrigerators (Figure 12) download e-mail, show television programs, and control cameras positioned in rooms, such as the nursery. Combination refrigerator/oven units will keep foods cold until a set time is reached or after receiving a signal from a cellular telephone, PDA, or computer. Then the oven heats and begins baking dinner. Nearly 40 percent of homeowners have expressed interest in connecting their kitchen appliances wirelessly to the Internet and then controlling security systems, lighting, and heating and cooling systems.

FIGURE 12 Internet-enabled refrigerators connect to broadband or cable television. They check the expiration dates on items stored on the shelves and alert users when these products should be discarded. Family members can leave video messages and photos using the built-in video or digital cameras and also watch television or listen to MP3 files.

Smart appliances using the Sun Microsystems Java and Jini technologies can perform time-consuming chores. For example, your refrigerator or pantry will be linked through a home control system to the grocery store and order groceries without your intervention. Dishwashers will communicate with their manufacturers to report malfunctions or maintenance problems and then be repaired remotely. Coffeemakers will download new functions as they become available. In the adjacent family room, media center computers will feature the latest version of Windows XP Media Center Edition (Figure 13), which will support an FM radio tuner, online games, on-demand movies, a TV tuner, and paid music downloads.

FIGURE 13 More than 40 computer manufacturers will feature the Windows XP Media Center Edition. Initially designed for small studio apartments, the software will be expanded to feature on-demand programming to meet the entertainment needs of an entire family.

Communications and Networks

The methods of transmitting and sharing data are changing dramatically. Updates include Microsoft's .NET strategy, personal area networks, home wireless networks, wired broadband, wireless communications, the Bluetooth standard, mobile Internet access, global positioning systems, electronic paper and ink, and multiple-function telephones.

.NET AND SOFTWARE SUBSCRIPTIONS Microsoft's .NET strategy is a new environment for developing and running software applications. .NET will provide instant access to data and services in the context of your current task. Microsoft plans to shift the focus of software from the desktop to Web-based services and to extend Windows XP elements to the Internet.

PERSONAL AREA NETWORKS A handshake may mean more than a goodwill gesture. Two people wearing small transmitters and receivers could communicate by exchanging digital data using the electrical conductivity of their bodies. Their handshake will complete the electric circuit needed to transfer this data.

HOME WIRELESS NETWORKS Most technology companies are taking sides and backing one of two competing wireless standards for the home, but others are backing both. Apple Computer, Dell Inc., Sony, 3Com, and 70 other companies are supporting the Wi-Fi (wireless fidelity), or 802.11B, standard, while Intel, Motorola, Hewlett-Packard, and 80 other corporations are backing the alternate HomeRF standard. IBM and other companies are backing both, reluctant to be caught with obsolete equipment. The battle for dominance likely is to continue as new Net appliances and wireless devices emerge, data transfer rates increase, and prices drop.

SUPERBROADBAND During the next few years, home and business computer users can expect access to the Internet thousands of times faster than with today's cable and telephone dial-up services. The key to speeding up Internet access is to increase the bandwidth of the communications channel between the user and the access provider. Bandwidth is the measure of the amount of data a communications channel can transmit over a given period, and computer scientists are experimenting with superbroadband optical networks.

Mobile and Wireless Connectivity

As the personal-computing market matures, consumers are looking for new ways to access the Internet and to communicate. Cordless products are in high demand, and these devices with Bluetooth technology should flood the market in the next few years. Third-generation communications service will increase Internet services. Other advances will be made in global positioning systems, electronic paper and ink, and multiple-function telephones.

WIRELESS DEVICES Recent advances in digital wireless technology have focused on cellular telephones and PDAs. As these forms of communication saturate the marketplace, attention is turning toward developing cordless computers (Figures 14 and 15). Aircraft maintenance workers at FedEx use wearable computers to complete and repair logs, research databases, and view video-based training. Utility workers and maintenance personnel working in the field can give voice-activated commands to their wearable computers and receive information ranging from a tutorial about an assigned task to the location of their next repair job.

FIGURE 14 Workers who maintain aircraft and vehicles can improve their productivity when they are equipped with a Maintenance Repair and Repair Support System (MARRS) vest, which permits a voice-controlled wireless Internet-connection.

FIGURE 15 Wireless Internet connections will boost sales of handheld computers, particularly with expansion port add-ons such as keyboards, GPS modules, and bar code scanners.

BLUETOOTH Bluetooth technology allows cellular telephones, pagers, PDAs, and other wireless products to detect each other and communicate across short distances, usually a maximum of 30 feet. According to IDC, a leading market research firm, by 2006 the Bluetooth semiconductor market will become a $2.6 billion industry, up from $76.6 million in 2001. The Bluetooth Special Interest Group (SIG) developers from the computing, networking, and telecommunications fields jointly are planning a wide range of applications, such as those that allow shoppers with Bluetooth-enabled cellular telephones to receive coupons as they walk past displays. Saab Automotive was the first car manufacturer to use Bluetooth technology in its vehicles by supporting hands-free telephone use via a Bluetooth headset and wireless networking using a PDA or notebook computer. Future refinements will include having this Bluetooth system convert e-mail or other files to speech from the driver's notebook computer.

MOBILE INTERNET ACCESS Japan's pioneer mobile-Internet company, NTT DoCoMo, Inc., plans to lead the world's new phase of broadband services, Wideband Code Division Multiple Access (W-CDMA). This third-generation (3G) mobile communications service has the data-transmission capacity to download songs and short video clips. Each day, more than 50,000 new Japanese consumers subscribe to DoCoMo's mobile Internet service, i-mode (Figure 16), which provides access to thousands of official i-mode and independent news services, information, and entertainment, as well as such specialized services as airline reservations, online shopping and banking, and the ability to exchange digital images. In contrast, American consumers have been reluctant to subscribe to mobile services that offer shopping, weather updates, and e-mail. A significant United States audience exists, however, as more than 10 million people use a PDA or cellular telephone to access the Internet. DoCoMo has invested $9.8 billion in AT&T's wireless unit, representing a venture to close the gap between wireless technologies in the two countries.

FIGURE 16 NTT DoCoMo's i-mode mobile Internet service is immensely popular among Japanese consumers.

GLOBAL POSITIONING SYSTEMS The U.S. Department of Defense developed the Global Positioning System (GPS) for national security, but today this technology is being used for civilian applications when position awareness is necessary. Cellular telephones equipped with the Enhanced 911 feature will provide information to help emergency personnel detect the precise location from which a call was placed, usually within 300 feet. Reading maps will become easier if PDAs, notebook computers, and cellular telephones are equipped with GPS chips used in conjunction with mapping software. Some location systems, such as Apple Computer cofounder Steve Wozniak's wOzNet, send and receive GPS data to provide monitoring information to track children, elderly parents, and Alzheimer's patients. Other microchip identification systems include a tiny biosensor implanted under the skin to identify livestock and pets (Figure 17).

FIGURE 17 Location and alert systems provide tracking information that can be used to monitor the location of animals.

FIGURE 18 Electronic paper and ink products can be used for commercial displays. The messages can be changed by remote control.

ELECTRONIC PAPER/ELECTRONIC INK Engineers are developing electronic paper and ink products (Figure 18) that combine the strengths of digital technology with the qualities of paper, including its light weight and high contrast. Several companies are developing this rewriteable medium. Some use microscopic liquid particles or beads that are white on one side and black or red on the other and are suspended in a transparent plastic cavity. This display screen currently is as thick as a mouse pad, but eventually it will become as thin as four sheets of paper. The particles or beads respond to electronic impulses and move depending on the images requested. The next generation of e-paper will add organic light-emitting diodes (OLEDs) to the plastic sheets to display full color and full-motion video.

MULTIPLE-FUNCTION TELEPHONES AND PDAs PDAs and cellular telephones will share features and be capable of communicating with each other (Figure 19). The target group for these newest products is young users who are between the ages of 10 and 24. Nearly every digital wireless telephone sold will feature FM radios and two-way text messaging. Other cellular telephones will combine video and a handheld computer, so you can download the latest movies and information about products and places by pointing at a device in the store and clicking. FM radios will be added to all reasonably priced cellular telephones.

More people worldwide will be accessing the Internet via these cellular telephones and PDAs rather than by personal computers. Fourth-generation (4G) wireless standards are predicted to be in place by 2010, and they will offer even faster mobile Internet access.

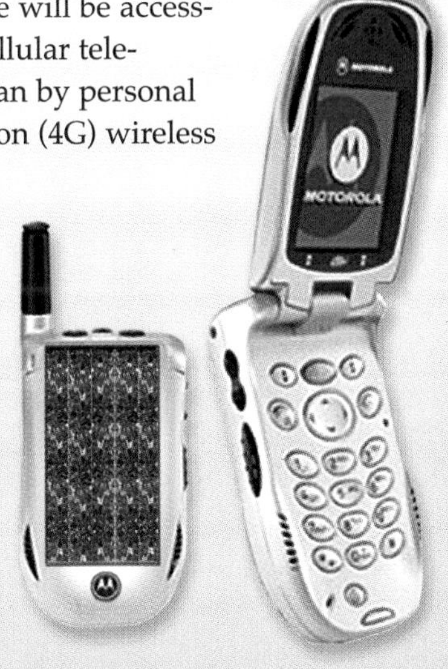

FIGURE 19 Solar battery cells will power PDAs packed with standard voice and e-mail features, cameras, and wireless keyboards.

Robotics

Computers capable of performing human tasks will be seen everywhere from hospitals to your home. Medical breakthroughs achieved in hospitals include brain pacemaker implants and distance surgery. Homes are becoming lively and clean with the advent of robots for entertainment and vacuuming.

BRAIN PACEMAKER Scientists working with monkeys and studying how brain cells interact are perfecting a type of pacemaker to implant in the brain and send brain waves directly to a robot or device (Figure 20). One practical use is for reading the brain waves of people with seizure disorders, anticipating a seizure, and delivering drugs or electrical impulses that can stop or prevent a seizure.

FIGURE 20 Research involving monkeys is helping researchers record brain cell activity. When the monkeys perform a learned task, their neurons generate brain waves that are transmitted to computers via wires implanted in the monkeys' brains. The computer decodes and sends the data to a robot that replicates the monkey's movements.

DISTANCE SURGERY The next generation of health care will promote the use of robots to perform surgeries (Figure 21). The robots' precise skills and small sizes — less than one-fifth the size of traditional instruments — make surgeries less invasive and recovery times less prolonged. Surgeons view three-dimensional images of internal organs on large monitors and can control the robots' actions through voice commands.

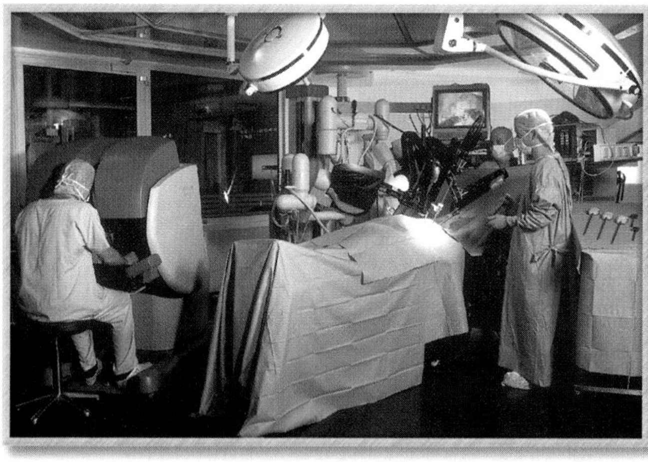

FIGURE 21 Robot-aided surgeries help surgeons remove brain tumors. Information regarding the precise location of the tumor is displayed on the monitor and fed into the robot's computer. Robotic surgeries result in minimal damage to the surrounding brain tissue.

Operating rooms will undergo another dramatic change when surgeons practice telemedicine. Through the use of videoconferencing and satellites, doctors can perform surgery when they are in locations other than the operating room.

AIBO Now you can have mankind's best friend without the mess and expensive veterinarian bills. Sony Corporation's AIBO (Artificial Intelligence Robot), which coincidentally is the Japanese word for companion, is a breed of entertainment robot with voice recognition technology, emotions, instincts, the ability to learn 50 verbal commands, and senses for touch, hearing, sight, and balance (Figure 22). AIBO is part of Sony's development efforts to create robots that coexist with people and create unlimited opportunities for humans to interact with computers.

FIGURE 22 Each AIBO develops an individual personality based on its interaction with its environment.

HOME AND BUSINESS MONITORING Check your home and office from remote locations using the Spy-Cye (Figure 23). Program the robot to dial into the Internet at scheduled times, and then log onto the web-bots.com Web site at those times to see the Spy-Cye move to specific locations.

FIGURE 23 See and hear the events at your house or work environment with the Spy-Cye personal robot. As you move your mouse pointer, the Spy-Cye responds by navigating in the same direction. The robot will operate for two hours before needing recharging.

THE FUTURE OF INFORMATION SYSTEMS IN BUSINESS

Although millions of homes now include one or more computers, businesses by far are the largest users of computers. Around the world, organizations install and use millions of computers of all types – mainframes, personal computers, and more – for applications such as inventory control, billing, and accounting. These computers often are part of a large information system that includes data, people, procedures, hardware, and software.

Existing business information systems will undergo profound changes as a result of the computer trends just described. As computers become increasingly ubiquitous and technologies converge, businesses will rely on computers for communications – and users at all levels will need to be computer literate. These new technologies will enhance security measures, provide computers for all employees, improve communications and health care in hospitals, and shape t-commerce (embedded television advertising) and e-business.

AUTHENTICATION/SECURITY Public surveillance by businesses, government, and institutions is a growing industry, spurred by smaller and less expensive technology. According to the Security Industry Association, nearly $2 billion has been spent on computer controlled closed-circuit television networks such as those being used in more than 60 U.S. cities to curb vandalism, prevent crime, and record incidents.

Surveillance is being taken to a higher level with software that converts images of faces to a series of 14 reference points, such as the eyebrows' bone structure and the distance between the eyes. This data is stored in databases and compared at rates of 45 million records per minute with people who pass by security cameras at countries' border crossings and who apply for new driver's licenses.

Upcoming software can be trained to recognize threatening behavior, such as when someone points a gun, and then alert the police. Applications also could help maintain security at automatic teller machines, where cardholders' facial images could be stored in a database and compared with a person using the machine. Computers also will use video cameras to record and identify individuals through facial expressions (Figure 24) and fingerprint recognition (Figure 25). Industry experts project that surveillance cameras could become so prevalent that everyone could watch everyone at anytime.

FIGURE 24 Enhanced security measures at many corporations include face recognition systems to verify employees' identities.

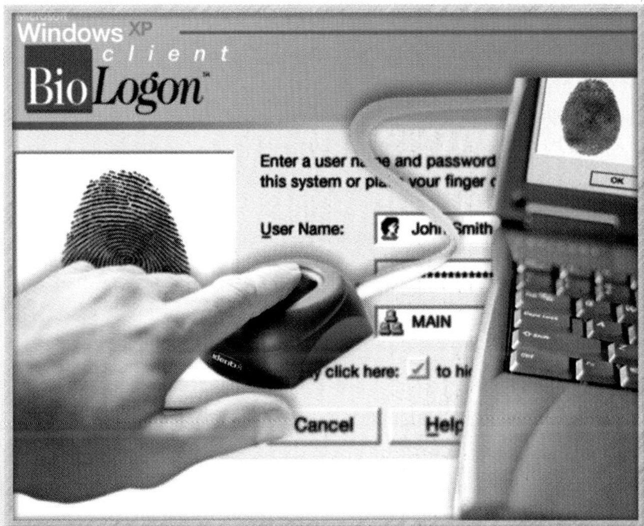

FIGURE 25 A fingerprint reader captures the curves and indentations of a fingerprint.

WIRING THE ENTIRE WORKFORCE For many years, computer use centered around white-collar professionals sitting at desks using wired computers. Indeed, of all employees, nearly 70 percent use some type of computer during the workday. With the influx of wireless products, manufacturers are striving to wire the other 30 percent of workers holding mobile positions, such as mechanics, inspectors, messengers, and warehouse workers, so they can send and retrieve detailed information while keeping their hands free for other tasks. The Palm OS and Windows Mobile 2003 platforms are opening opportunities for the blue-collar world, as are hardware and software advances in speech recognition, wireless headsets, and wearable computers equipped with processing power equal to that of desktop computers.

HEALTH-CARE INDUSTRY The medical industry has been recognized, in general, as being one of the last fields to integrate the Internet and high-tech solutions. Recent cuts in insurance reimbursements and federal Medicare spending have decreased revenues, resulting in budget-cutting measures. Many health-care facilities, however, are integrating online medical-records systems, electronic medical charts, and medical literature searches. Wireless products will help improve patient care and communications; for example, some emergency room personnel use PDAs to access patients' medical records.

T-COMMERCE Television advertising is taking a new turn with the advent of t-commerce. Instead of buying commercial time, advertisers embed their ads in actual television programs. Viewers use their remote controls to interact with the television programs and advertisements by replying to free offers, buying items, receiving sports scores, and participating in games. The Wink service is featured on CNN, The Weather Channel, ESPN, and "The Tonight Show with Jay Leno." This form of advertisement can be termed merchantainment — a combination of merchandising and entertainment.

WORKING SMART Microsoft has developed the Center for Information Work (Figure 26) with the goal of helping Information Workers become more productive through software. Customers can visit the facility to experiment with technological prototypes. The Center includes RingCam, a video conferencing device that captures a 360-degree view of a room from the center of a conference table during meetings, using software to digitally isolate whoever is currently speaking. Innovative LCD, plasma, and flat-panel monitors also are on display, showcasing how upcoming applications may use these new hardware configurations to make workers more productive.

FIGURE 26 The semicircular display at Microsoft's Centers for Information Work is a seamless curved surface that allows employees to multitask using peripheral vision, such as opening e-mail messages while editing word processing documents and analyzing data.

FEATURE SUMMARY

The computer industry has become a pervasive part of people's lives, and businesses have developed innovative products and strategies to remain competitive. They are facing critical issues about how and when companies, educators, and consumers will use many of the products featured in their professional and personal lives. As they develop products and marketing plans, 5.6 million new software engineers, Web programmers, optical networking specialists, programmers, and systems analysts will be needed by 2006. Their decisions will affect global society and direct the digital revolution.

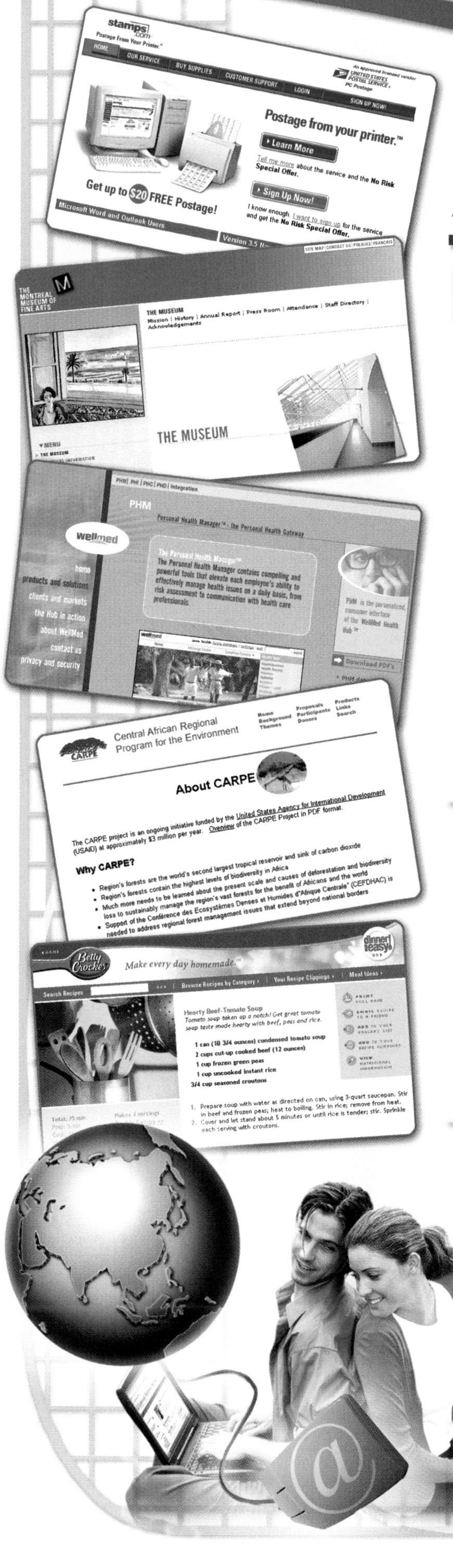

APPENDIX A

Making Use of the Web

A wealth of information is available on the World Wide Web. The riches are yours if you know where to find this material. Locating useful Web sites may be profitable for your educational and professional careers, as the resources may help you research class assignments and make your life more fulfilling and manageable.

Because the World Wide Web does not have an organizational structure to assist you in locating reliable material, you need additional resources to guide you in searching. To help you find useful Web sites, this appendix describes specific information about a variety of Web pages, and it includes tables of Web addresses, so you can get started. The material is organized in several categories.

CATEGORIES

FUN AND ENTERTAINMENT	LEARNING
TRAVEL	SCIENCE
FINANCE	ENVIRONMENT
RESOURCES	HEALTH
AUCTIONS	RESEARCH
GOVERNMENT	CAREERS
SHOPPING	ARTS AND LITERATURE
WEATHER, SPORTS, AND NEWS	

Web Exercises at the end of each category will reinforce the material and help you discover Web sites that may add a treasure of wealth to your life.

Fun and Entertainment

THAT'S ENTERTAINMENT

Surf's Up for Fun Web Sites

Girls just want to have fun, according to singer Cyndi Lauper. The Internet abounds with fun sites for both gals and guys, with everything from the Rock and Roll Hall of Fame and Museum to the Rock of Gibraltar.

Do you want to see the surfers riding the waves in Hawaii? Or, how about wild animals at a game preserve in Africa, pandas at the San Diego Zoo, and landmarks in Yosemite Valley (Figure A-1)? Travel to the South Pole and hear the frigid wind blow, to Yellowstone Park to see the Old Faithful geyser, and to Loch Ness for a possible glimpse of the famous monster. Web cams take armchair travelers across the world for views of natural attractions, historical monuments, colleges, and cities. Some of the world's Web cams are listed in Figure A-2.

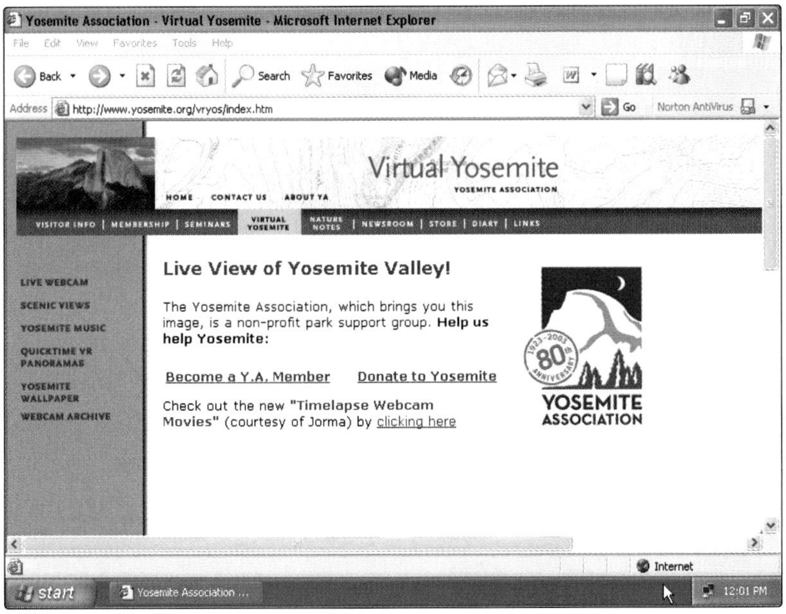

FIGURE A-1 Web cams provide a glimpse of locations throughout the world, including landmarks in Yosemite Valley.

FUN AND ENTERTAINMENT WEB SITES	URL
Web Cams	
AfriCam Virtual Game Reserve	africam.com
Discovery Channel Cams	dsc.discovery.com/cams/cams.html
Iowa State Insect Zoo Live Camera	zoocam.ent.iastate.edu
Panda Cam San Diego Zoo	sandiegozoo.org/pandas/pandacam/index.html
The Automated Astrophysical Site-Testing Observatory (AASTD) (South Pole)	www.phys.unsw.edu.au/southpolediaries/webcam.html
Weather and Webcams from OnlineWeather.com and CamVista	onlineweather.com/v4/webcams/index.html
Wild Birds Unlimited Bird FeederCam	wbu.com/feedercam_home.htm
World Map of Live Webcams	members.ozemail.com.au/~worldmap/World.html
World Surf Cameras	surfrock.com.br/surfcam.htm
WorldLIVE	worldlive.cz/en/webcams
Entertainment	
AMG All Music Guide	allmusic.com
E! Online	eonline.com
Entertainment Tonight	etonline.com
Entertainment Weekly's EW.com	ew.com/ew
Old Time Radio (OTR) - Radio Days: A Soundbite History	otr.com
Rock and Roll Hall of Fame and Museum	rockhall.com
Spinner	spinner.com
The Internet Movie Database (IMDb)	imdb.com
World Radio Network (WRN)	wrn.org

For an updated list of fun and entertainment Web sites, visit scsite.com/dc2005/web.

FIGURE A-2 When you visit Web sites offering fun and entertainment resources, you can be both amused and informed.

If you need an update on your favorite reality-based television program or a preview of the upcoming Halle Berry movie, the Web can satisfy your entertainment thirst. E! Online (Figure A-3) and Entertainment Tonight provide the latest features on television and movie stars. The Internet Movie Database contains credits and reviews of more than 378,000 titles.

If your passion is music and radio, the AMG All Music Guide provides backgrounds on new releases and top artists. See and hear the musicians inducted into the Rock and Roll Hall of Fame and Museum (Figure A-4). The World Radio Network features international public radio programs, such as the *Radio Sweden* and *United Nations Radio*.

For more information about fun and entertainment Web sites, visit the Discovering Computers 2005 Making Use of the Web page (scsite.com/dc2005/web) and click Fun and Entertainment.

FIGURE A-3 The entertainment Web sites feature celebrity news and profiles.

FIGURE A-4 Visitors exploring the Rock and Roll Hall of Fame and Museum Web site will find history, exhibitions, programs, and the names and particulars of the latest inductees.

Fun *and* Entertainment

WEB EXERCISES

1. Visit the World Map of Live Webcams site listed in Figure A-2. View two of the Web cams closest to your hometown, and describe the scenes. Then, visit the Discovery Channel Cams Web site and view two of the animal cams in the Featured Cams. What do you observe? Visit another Web site listed in Figure A-2 and describe the view. What are the benefits of having Web cams at these locations throughout the world?

2. What are your favorite movies? Use The Internet Movie Database Web site listed in Figure A-2 to search for information about two of these films, and write a brief description of the biographies of the major stars and director for each movie. Then, visit one of the entertainment Web sites and describe three of the featured stories. At the Rock and Roll Hall of Fame and Museum Web site, view the information on Elvis and one of your favorite musicians. Write a paragraph describing the information available about these rock stars.

Travel

GET PACKING!

Explore the World without Leaving Home

Balmy beaches. Majestic mountains. Exotic destinations. Just dreaming of experiencing these locales can lift your spirits. Researchers conclude that vacations are healthy for your mind and body because they help eliminate stress, offer opportunities to spend quality time with family and friends, and provide exercise. Whether you are ready to arrange your next travel adventure or just want to explore destination possibilities, the Internet provides ample resources to set your plans in motion.

Some good starting places are all-encompassing Web sites such as Travelocity.com, which is owned by Sabre, the electronic booking service travel agents use, Expedia Travel (Figure A-5), and Cheap Tickets (Figure A-6). These general travel Web sites have tools to help you find the lowest prices and details on flights, car rentals, cruises, and hotels, and they include such features as airplane seating maps, local weather, popular restaurants, and photos. Each of the major airlines and cruise lines also has a Web site where you can check prices, purchase tickets and tour packages, and sign up for weekly e-mail alerts about specials and new services.

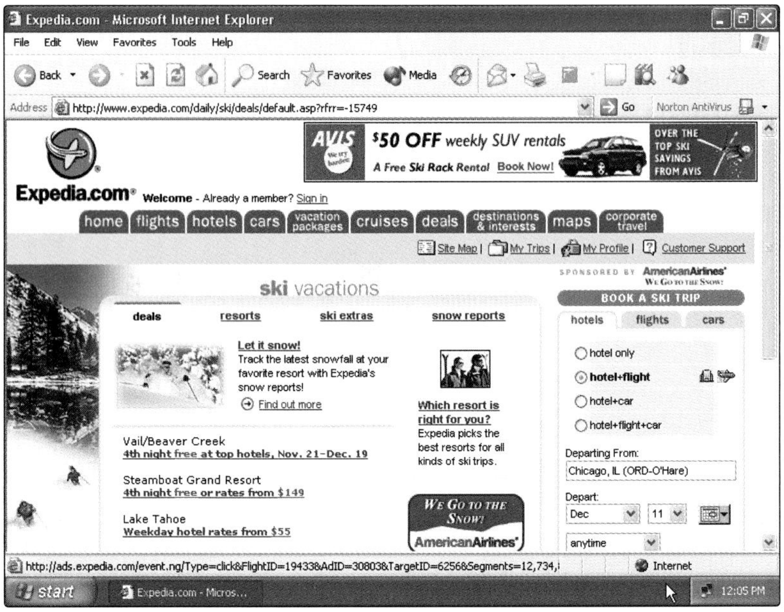

FIGURE A-5 Book flights, cruises, and ski trips with all-encompassing travel resources.

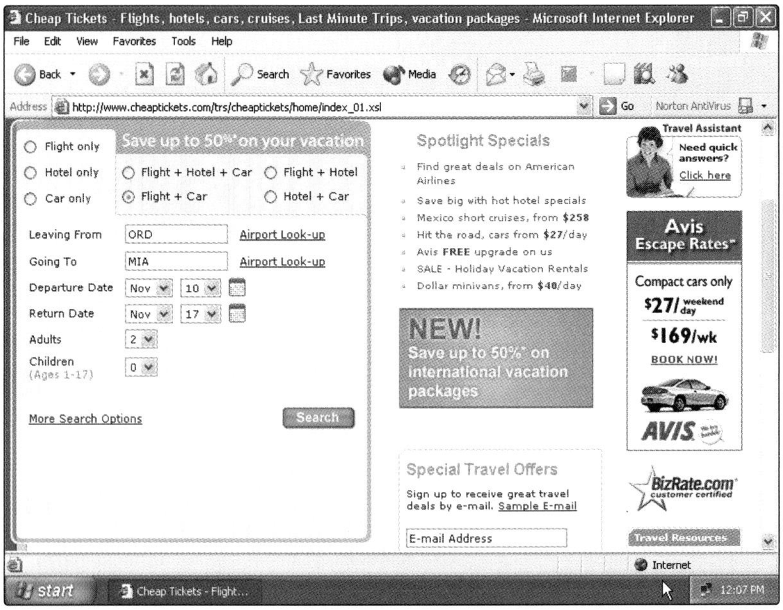

FIGURE A-6 General travel Web sites allow users to check fares to their favorite cities.

FIGURE A-7 Cartography Web sites such as MapQuest provide directions, traffic reports, maps, and more.

To discover exactly where your destination is on this planet, cartography Web sites, including MapQuest (Figure A-7), Maps.com, and Rand McNally, allow you to pinpoint your destination. These Web pages generally are divided into geographical areas, such as North America and Europe. When you choose an area, you see a subject-based index that lists helpful tools such as route planners, subway maps, entertainment, and ski trails.

For more information about travel Web sites, visit the Discovering Computers 2005 Making Use of the Web page (scsite.com/dc2005/web) and click Travel.

TRAVEL WEB SITES	URL
General Travel	
Cheap Tickets	cheaptickets.com
Expedia.com	expedia.com
Orbitz	orbitz.com
Travelocity.com	travelocity.com
Yahoo! Travel	travel.yahoo.com
Cartography	
MapQuest	mapquest.com
Maps.com	maps.com
Rand McNally	randmcnally.com
Travel and City Guides	
All the Largest Cities of the World	greatestcities.com
Frommers.com	frommers.com
U.S.-Parks.com - US National Parks Adventure Travel Guide	us-parks.com

For an updated list of travel Web sites, visit scsite.com/dc2005/web.

FIGURE A-8 These travel resources Web sites offer travel information to exciting destinations throughout the world.

Travel

WEB EXERCISES

1. Visit one of the cartography Web sites listed in Figure A-8 and print directions from your campus to one of these destinations: the White House in Washington, D.C.; Elvis's home in Memphis, Tennessee; Walt Disney World in Orlando, Florida; or the Grand Old Opry in Nashville, Tennessee. How many miles is it to your destination? What is the estimated driving time? Then, visit one of the general travel Web sites listed in the table and plan a flight from the nearest major airport to one of the four destinations for the week after finals and a return trip one week later. What is the lowest economy coach fare for this round-trip flight? What airline, flight numbers, and departure and arrival times did you select? Finally, explore car rental rates for a subcompact car for this one-week vacation. What rental agency and rate did you choose?
2. Visit one of the travel and city guide Web sites listed in Figure A-8, and choose a destination for a getaway this coming weekend. Write a one-page paper giving details about this location, such as popular hotels and lodging, expected weather, population, local colleges and universities, parks and recreation, ancient and modern history, and tours. Print a map of this place. Why did you select this destination? How would you travel there and back? What is the breakdown of expected costs for this weekend, including travel expenditures, meals, lodging, and tickets to events and activities? What URLs did you use to complete this exercise?

Finance

KA-CHING, KA-CHING

Cashing In on Financial Advice

"Money makes the world go 'round," according to Liza Minnelli and her friends in the 1972 hit musical, *Cabaret*. If that musical were written today, the lyrics would be updated to "Money makes the World Wide Web go 'round," based on the volume of financial Web sites available to Internet users.

When Doug Lebda became thoroughly disgusted with all the red tape he encountered trying to apply for a home mortgage, he took matters into his own hands. He started LendingTree®, a Web site that helps consumers conveniently obtain mortgages, loans, and credit cards, as shown in Figure A-9. This Web site and a growing number of other Internet companies work with hundreds of national lenders to match consumers' needs with the marketplaces' lenders. One of the leading online banks is Wells Fargo (listed in Figure A-10), with a Web site that features online banking, tax help, personal finance, and small business and commercial services.

If you do not have a personal banker or a financial planner, consider a Web adviser to guide your investment decisions. Three highly recognized financial Web sites are MSN Money, Yahoo! Finance, and The Motley Fool (Figure A-11) for commentary and education on investing strategies, financial news, and taxes.

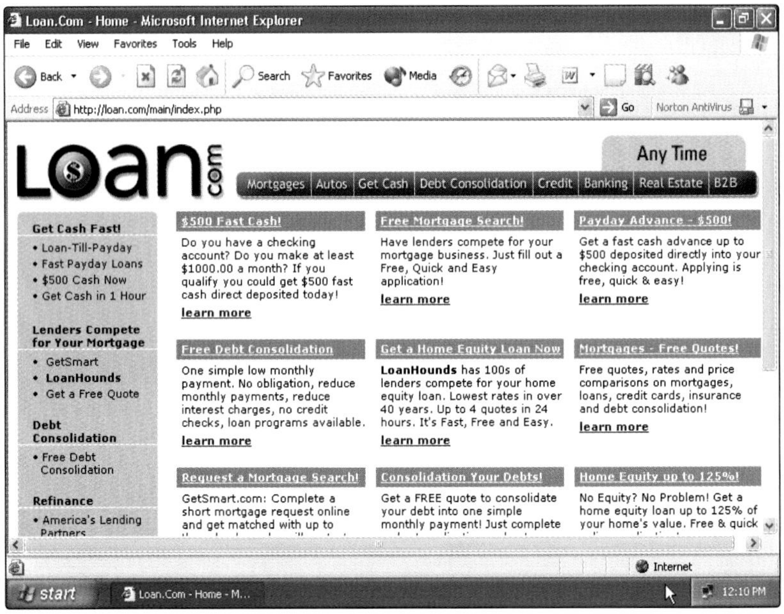

FIGURE A-9 Online lending Web sites can help consumers seeking assistance with financial matters, including obtaining loans or comparing mortgage rates.

FINANCE WEB SITES	URL
Advice and Education	
Bankrate.com	bankrate.com
LendingTree	lendingtree.com
Loan.com	loan.com
MSN Money	money.msn.com
The Motley Fool	fool.com
Wells Fargo	wellsfargo.com
Yahoo! Finance	finance.yahoo.com
Stock market	
E*TRADE Financial	us.etrade.com
Financial Engines	financialengines.com
FreeEDGAR®	www.freeedgar.com
Harris*direct*	harrisdirect.com
Merrill Lynch Direct	mldirect.ml.com
MeVC	mevc.com
Morningstar.com	morningstar.com
The Vanguard Group	vanguard.com
Taxes	
H&R Block	hrblock.com
Internal Revenue Service - The Digital Daily	www.irs.gov
For an updated list of finance Web sites, visit scsite.com/dc2005/web.	

FIGURE A-10 Financial resources Web sites offer general information, stock market analyses, and tax advice, as well as guidance and tips.

FIGURE A-11 The Motley Fool Web site contains strategies and news stories related to personal financing and investing.

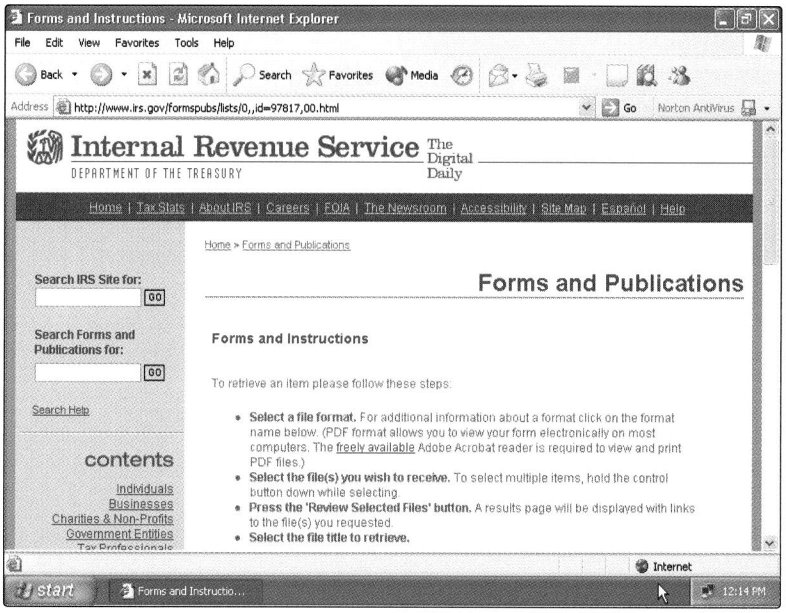

FIGURE A-12 Income tax forms, employment opportunities, and filing procedures and regulations are posted on the Internal Revenue Service The Digital Daily Web page.

You likely have heard stories of people who have made — and lost — their fortunes in the stock market. If you are ready to ride the ups and downs of the NASDAQ and the Dow, an abundance of Web sites can help you pick companies that fit your interests and financial needs. For example, FreeEDGAR allows you to read company filings with the SEC. Morningstar.com gives you research reports and the latest market news to help you reach your financial goals.

When April 15 rolls around, many taxpayers mutter the words, Internal Revenue Service. But the IRS can be a friend, too, when you visit Internal Revenue Service The Digital Daily (Figure A-12). Claiming to be the fastest, easiest tax publication on the planet, this Web page contains procedures for filing tax appeals, and contains IRS forms, publications, and legal regulations. H&R Block also offers tax information on its Taxes Web page.

For more information about financial Web sites, visit the Discovering Computers 2005 Making Use of the Web page (scsite.com/dc2005/web) and click Finance.

Finance

WEB EXERCISES

1. Visit three advice and education Web sites listed in Figure A-10 and read their top business world reports. Write a paragraph about each, summarizing these stories. Which stocks or mutual funds do these Web sites predict as being sound investments today? What are the current market indexes for the DJIA (Dow Jones Industrial Average), S&P 500, and NASDAQ, and how do these figures compare with the previous day's numbers?

2. Using two of the stock market Web sites listed in Figure A-10, search for information about Microsoft, Adobe Systems, and one other software vendor discussed in Chapter 3. Write a paragraph about each of these stocks describing the revenues, net incomes, total assets for the previous year, current stock price per share, highest and lowest prices of each stock during the past year, and other relevant investment information.

Resources

LOOK IT UP

Web Resources Ease Computer Concerns

Have you heard of a dead pixel or a mouse potato? If you do not know a JDK from an OSS, then an online computer technology dictionary may be the tool you need. From dictionaries and encyclopedias to online technical support, the Web is filled with a plethora of resources, including those listed in Figure A-13, to answer your computer questions and resolve specialized problems.

Chapter 4 describes the components of the system unit, including the different processors, various types of memory, and other devices associated with it, as well as the components of notebook and handheld computers. With the continual developments in technology and communications, new products reach the marketplace daily.

A way to keep up with the latest developments is to look to online dictionaries that add to their collections of computer and product terms on a regular basis and include thousands of descriptions and designations. An example is the whatis?com Web site listed in the table in Figure A-13 and shown in Figure A-14. The whatis?com Web site contains more than 4,000 cyberterms, with daily updates to the words and definitions. This Web site and many other reference Web pages feature a word of the day that identifies a new product or industry standard as well as highlight recently added or revised terms.

RESOURCES WEB SITES	URL
Dictionaries and Encyclopedias	
CDT's Guide to Online Privacy	cdt.org/privacy/guide/terms
ComputerUser High-Tech Dictionary	computeruser.com/resources/dictionary
TechWeb: The Business Technology Network	techweb.com/encyclopedia
Webopedia: Online Computer Dictionary for Computer and Internet Terms	webopedia.com
whatis?com	whatis.com
Computer Shopping Guides	
A Computer Guide: Reviews on Software and Hardware	acomputerguide.com
Online Computer Buying Guide™	grohol.com/computers
Viewz Desktop Computer Buying Guide	viewz.com/shoppingguide/compbuy.shtml
The CPU Scorecard	cpuscorecard.com
ZDNet Shopper	zdnetshopper.cnet.com
Upgrading Guides	
CNET Shopper.com	shopper.cnet.com
eHow™	ehow.com
Focus on Mac Support	macsupport.about.com
PCWorld.com	pcworld.com/howto
Upgrade Source™	upgradesource.com
Online Technical Support	
Dux Computer Digest	duxcw.com
MSN Tech & Gadgets	computingcentral.msn.com
PC911	pcnineoneone.com
PC Pitstop	pcpitstop.com
Technical and Consumer Information	
CNET.com	cnet.com
CompInfo - The Computer Information Center	www.compinfo-center.com
NewsHub	newshub.com/tech
Wired News	wirednews.com
ZDNet	zdnet.com

For an updated list of resources Web sites, visit scsite.com/dc2005/web.

FIGURE A-13 A variety of Web resources can provide information about buying, repairing, and upgrading computers.

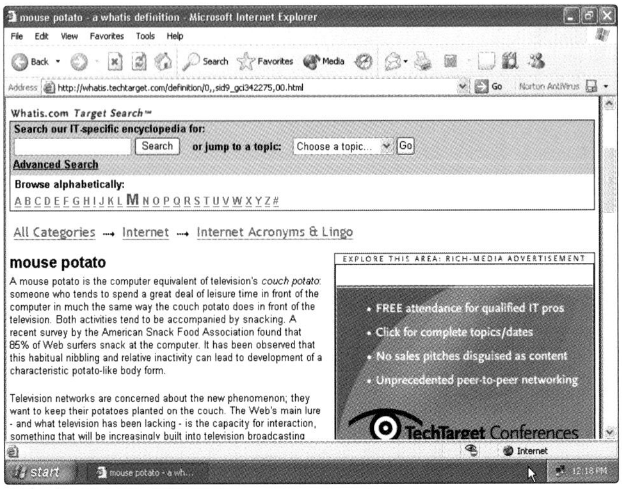

FIGURE A-14 Thousands of technology terms are defined at the whatis?com Web site.

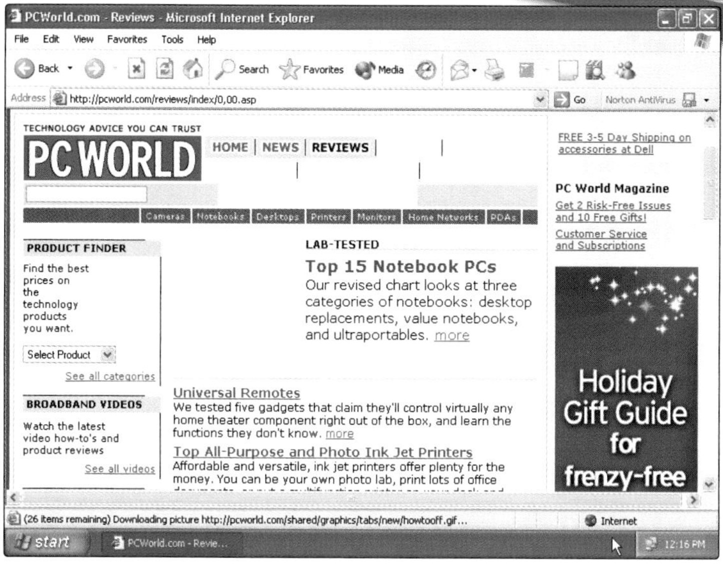

FIGURE A-15 Buying and upgrading a computer is simplified with helpful Web sites such as PCWorld.com.

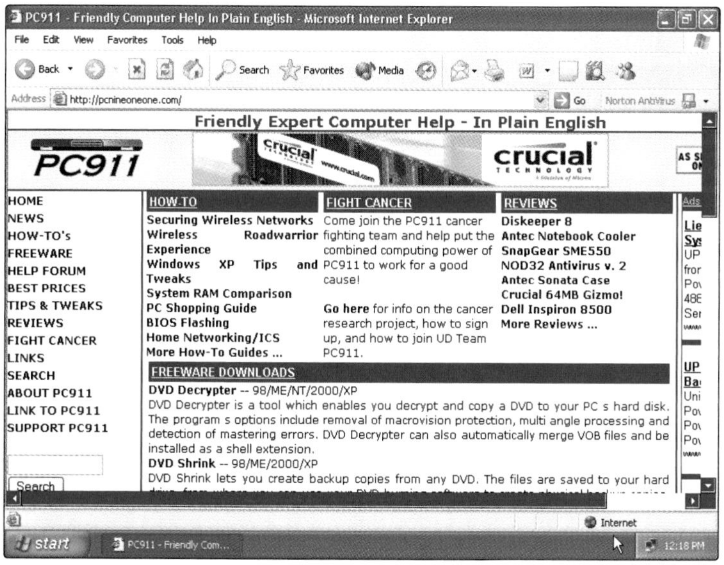

FIGURE A-16 Articles at the PC911 Web site provide useful technological information.

Shopping for a new computer can be a daunting experience, but many online guides can help you select the components that best fit your needs and budget. Most of these Web sites, including PCWorld.com (Figure A-15), feature the latest desktop and notebook computer prices, hardware and software reviews, bargains, and links to popular manufacturers' sale Web pages. If you want to upgrade your present computer, several online guides, such as CNET Shopper.com and Upgrade Source, give current prices for these components and list the more popular products.

If you are not confident in your ability to solve a problem alone, turn to online technical support. Such Web sites, including PC911 (Figure A-16), often provide streaming how-to video lessons, tutorials, and real-time chats with experienced technicians.

The Web offers a variety of technical and consumer information. Hardware and software reviews, price comparisons, shareware, technical questions and answers, and breaking technology news are found on comprehensive portals such as CNET and ZDNet.

For more information on Web resources sites, visit the Discovering Computers 2005 Making Use of the Web page (scsite.com/dc2005/web) and click Resources.

Resources

Web Exercises

1. Visit the dictionaries and encyclopedias Web sites listed in Figure A-13. Search these resources for five terms. Create a table with two columns: one for the cyberterm and one for the Web definition. Then, create a second table listing five recently added or updated words and their definitions on these Web sites. Next, visit two of the listed computer shopping guides Web sites to choose the components you would buy if you were building a customized desktop computer and notebook computer. Create a table for both computers, listing the computer manufacturer, processor model name or number and manufacturer, clock speed, RAM, cache, number of expansion slots, and number of bays.

2. Visit three upgrading guides Web sites listed in Figure A-13. Write a paragraph describing available advice for buying a motherboard. Describe the strengths and weaknesses of these Web sites, focusing on such criteria as clarity of instructions, thoroughness, and ease of navigation. Would you use these Web sites as a resource to troubleshoot computer problems? Then, view two technical and consumer information Web sites listed in the table and write a paragraph about each one, describing the top two news stories of the day.

Auctions

GOING ONCE, GOING TWICE

Rare, Common Items Flood Web Sites

Getting a few personal golfing tips from Tiger Woods might be the key to a lower scorecard. An undisclosed winner of an eBay auction and three friends paid $425,000 to play a round of golf with Woods at his home course in Florida. The proceeds of the auction went to the charitable Tiger Woods Foundation, which initializes and supports community-based programs for disadvantaged children.

The golfing experience is among the high-profile items offered on online auction Web sites. George Lucas donated *Star Wars* props and memorabilia, including a light saber used in *The Phantom Menace* and a Darth Vader helmet, for eBay's Auction for America, which benefited families of the September 11 terrorist attacks. PepsiCo donated a replica of Jeff Gordon's NASCAR racecar.

eBay (Figure A-17) is one of thousands of Internet auction Web sites and is the world's largest personal online trading community. The company's assortment of auctioned items has ranged from the usual to the unusual. Among the unusual was the opportunity to become the 43rd president of the United States. Bidding opened at one penny and soared to $100 million in four hours before eBay officials canceled the offer.

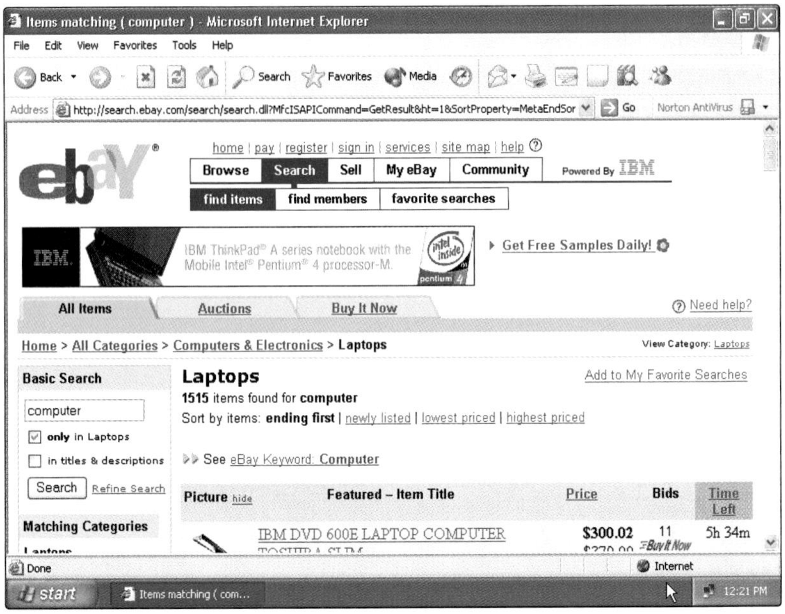

FIGURE A-17 eBay is one of the world's more popular auction Web sites.

FIGURE A-18 Rare and valuable art, jewelry, and furniture are featured on Sotheby's Web pages.

Traditional auction powerhouses, such as Christie's in London and Sotheby's (Figure A-18) on Manhattan's Upper East Side, are known for their big-ticket items: selected pieces of Elton John's clothing sold for $615,000, a bottle of Italian red wine for $13,000, and a Tyrannosaurus rex fossil for $8.4 million.

If those prices are a bit out of your league, you can turn to a wealth of other auction Web sites to find just the items you need, and maybe some you really do not need, for as little as $1. Some of these auction Web sites are listed in Figure A-19. Categories include antiques and collectibles such as the fountain pen shown in Figure A-20, automotive, computers, electronics, music, sports, sports cards and memorabilia, and toys.

For more information about auction Web sites, visit the Discovering Computers 2005 Making Use of the Web page (scsite.com/dc2005/web) and click Auctions.

AUCTION WEB SITES	URL
Christie's	christies.com
CNET Auctions	auctions.cnet.com
eBay®	ebay.com
Dargate Auction Galleries	dargate.com
musichotbid	musichotbid.com
Penbid.com	penbid.com
Sotheby's	sothebys.com
uBid™	ubid.com
Yahoo! Auctions	auctions.yahoo.com

For an updated list of auction Web sites, visit scsite.com/dc2005/web.

FIGURE A-19 These auction Web sites feature a wide variety of items.

FIGURE A-20 Rare and unusual pens are featured on the Penbid auction Web site.

Auctions

WEB EXERCISES

1. Visit the Christie's and Sothebys.com Web sites and read about the items that have been sold recently. Find two unusual objects and write a paragraph about each one summarizing your discoveries. What were the opening and final bids on these objects? Then, review two of the upcoming auctions. When are the auctions' dates? What items are available? What are some of the opening bids? What are the advantages and disadvantages of bidding online?

2. Using one of the auction Web sites listed in Figure A-19, search for two objects pertaining to your hobbies. For example, if you are a baseball fan, you can search for a complete set of Topps cards. If you are a car buff, search for your dream car. Describe these two items. How many people have bid on these items? Who are the sellers? What are the opening and current bids?

Government

STAMP OF APPROVAL

Making a Federal Case for Useful Information

When it is time to buy stamps to mail your correspondence, you no longer need to wait in long lines at your local post office. Instead, log on to the Internet and download a stamp right to your personal computer.

The U.S. Postal Service has authorized several corporations to sell stamps online. Users can download software from a company's Web site, charge the postage fee to a credit card, and then print the postage on a label printer or directly onto envelopes and labels. Some of these Web sites, such as Stamps.com, shown in Figure A-21, charge a small percentage of each order as a convenience fee.

Although citizens may not be enthusiastic about paying income taxes, April 15 can be more tolerable knowing that some of their hard-earned dollars are spent subsidizing useful government Web sites.

You can recognize these Web sites on the Internet by their .gov top-level domain abbreviation. For example, The Library of Congress Web site is lcweb.loc.gov. As the oldest federal cultural institution in the United States and the largest library in the world, the mission of The Library of Congress is to serve the research needs of the U.S. Congress. Patrons can visit one of 22 reading rooms on Capitol Hill and access more than 120 million items written in 470 languages. The Library of Congress Web site, shown in Figure A-22, has forms

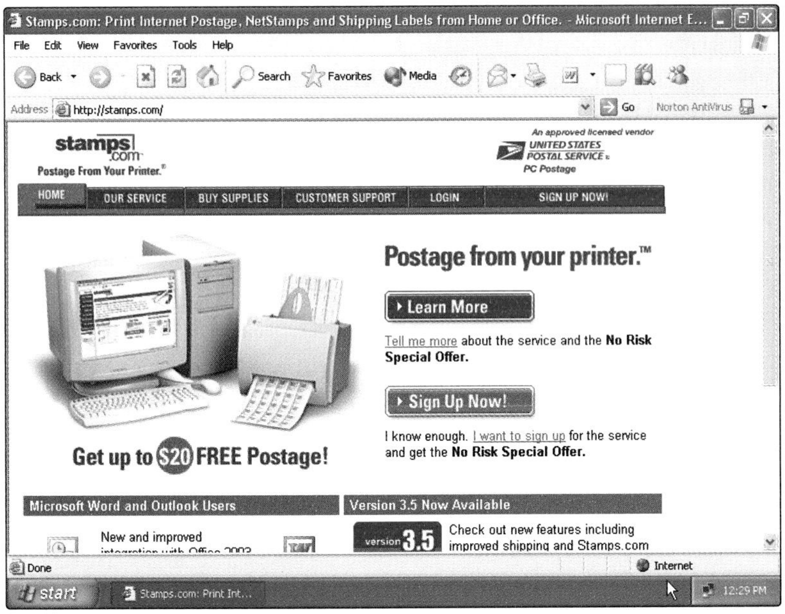

FIGURE A-21 Purchasing stamps on the Internet eliminates making a trip to the post office and waiting in long lines.

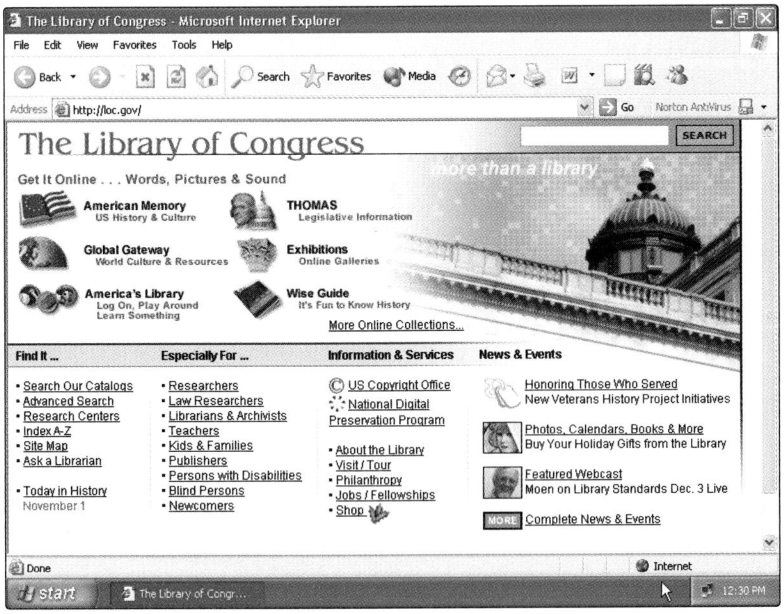

FIGURE A-22 The Library of Congress Web site contains more than 119 million items written in 470 languages.

and information from the Copyright Office, an online gallery, and links to a variety of topics, including the National Agricultural Library and the United States National Library of Medicine. These and other government resources Web sites are listed in Figure A-23.

Government and military Web sites offer a wide range of information. The Time Service Department Web site will provide you with the correct time. If you are looking for a federal document, FedWorld lists thousands of documents distributed by the government on its Web site. For access to the names of your congressional representatives, the president's cabinet members, and the Supreme Court justices, or to read portions of a federal statute or the U.S. Constitution, visit the extensive Hieros Gamos Web site, which is a governmental and legal portal with links to the legislative, judicial, and executive branches of government.

For more information about government resources Web sites, visit the Discovering Computers 2005 Making Use of the Web page (scsite.com/dc2005/web) and click Government.

GOVERNMENT WEB SITES	URL
Postage	
Pitney Bowes	pb.com
Neopost Online	simplypostage.com
Stamps.com	stamps.com
Government	
FedWorld	www.fedworld.gov
Hieros Gamos - Law and Legal Research Center	hg.org
NARA - United States National Archives and Records Administration	archives.gov
National Agricultural Library	www.nal.usda.gov
The Library of Congress	lcweb.loc.gov
THOMAS Legislative Information	thomas.loc.gov
Time Service Department	tycho.usno.navy.mil
United States Department of Education	ed.gov
United States Department of the Treasury	treas.gov
United States Government Printing Office	www.access.gpo.gov
United States National Library of Medicine	www.nlm.nih.gov
United States Patent and Trademark Office	www.uspto.gov
USAJOBS	www.usajobs.opm.gov
White House	whitehouse.gov

For an updated list of government Web sites, visit scsite.com/dc2005/web.

FIGURE A-23 These Web sites offer information about buying U.S.-approved postage online and researching federal agencies.

Government

WEB EXERCISES

1. View the three postage Web sites listed in Figure A-23. Compare and contrast the available services on each one. Consider postage cost, necessary equipment, shipping services, security techniques, and tracking capability. Explain why you would or would not like to use this service.
2. Visit the Hieros Gamos Web site listed in Figure A-23. What are the names, addresses, and telephone numbers of your two state senators and your local congressional representative? On what committees do they serve? Who is the chief justice of the Supreme Court, and what has been this justice's opinion on two recently decided cases? Who are the members of the president's cabinet? Then, visit two other Web sites listed in Figure A-23. Write a paragraph about each Web site describing its content and features.

Shopping

CYBERMALL MANIA

Let Your Mouse Do Your Shopping

From groceries to clothing to computers, you can buy just about everything you need with just a few clicks of your mouse. Electronic retailers (e-tailers), especially those listed in Figure A-24, are cashing in on cybershoppers' purchases. Books, computer software and hardware, and music are the hottest commodities. Online sales in the United States exceed $65 billion yearly. E-shoppers can browse for a variety of goods at these popular Web sites.

Holiday sales account for a large portion of Internet purchases with nearly nine million households doing some of their holiday shopping online. During the holiday season, some Web sites such as BestBuy.com (Figure A-25) receive thousands of hits per day. Macy's, Bloomingdale's, and other e-tailers ship more than 300,000 boxes daily out of warehouses the size of 20 football fields and stocked with five million items.

The two categories of Internet shopping Web sites are those with physical counterparts, such as Eddie Bauer (Figure A-26), Wal-Mart, and Tower Records, and those with only a Web presence, such as Amazon.com (Figure A-27).

Some e-shoppers, however, are finding online shopping even more frustrating than finding a convenient parking space at the neighborhood mall on Saturday afternoon.

SHOPPING WEB SITES	URL
Apparel	
Eddie Bauer Since 1920	eddiebauer.com
J.Crew	jcrew.com
Lands' End	landsend.com
Books and Music	
Amazon.com	amazon.com
Barnes & Noble.com	bn.com
Tower Records	towerrecords.com
Computers and Electronics	
Crutchfield.com	crutchfield.com
BestBuy.com	bestbuy.com
buy.com	buy.com
Miscellaneous	
1-800-flowers.com	1800flowers.com
drugstore.com	drugstore.com
The Sharper Image	sharperimage.com
Walmart.com	walmart.com

For an updated list of shopping Web sites, visit scsite.com/dc2005/web.

FIGURE A-24 Popular shopping Web sites.

FIGURE A-25 Shopping for popular computer equipment online eliminates waiting in lines in stores.

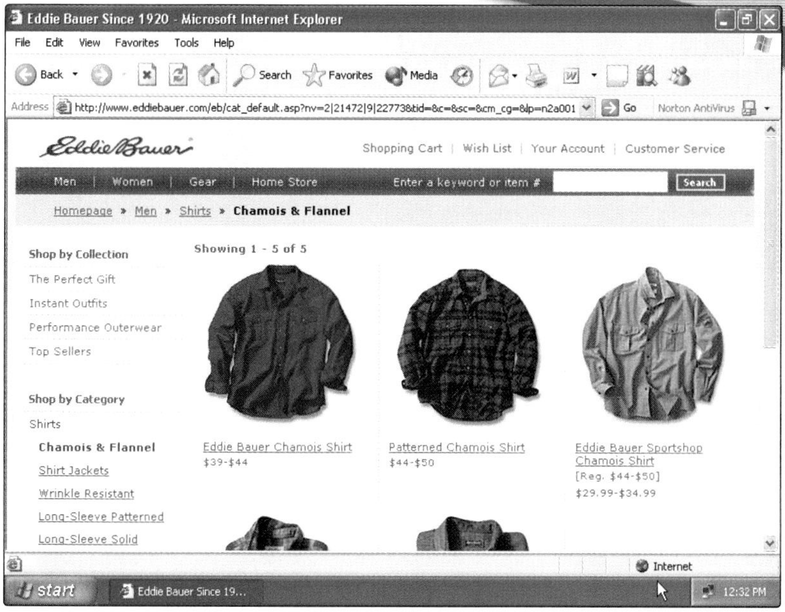

FIGURE A-26 Stores such as Eddie Bauer have both a physical and an Internet presence.

FIGURE A-27 Amazon.com is a business with only an Internet presence.

Delayed shipments, out-of-stock merchandise, poor customer service, and difficult return policies have left some savvy shoppers with a poor impression of their Internet experience. As e-tailers rush to set up an Internet site, they sometimes overlook important considerations, such as customer service telephone numbers and e-mail addresses, adequate staff to answer queries quickly and courteously, and sufficient in-stock merchandise.

Paying for the merchandise online causes concern for many e-shoppers. Although online merchants promise secure transactions, some users are wary of cyberthieves. One way of calming their fears may be through the use of e-money, which is a payment system that allows consumers to purchase goods and services anonymously. Several computer companies, Web merchants, and credit card companies are collaborating to develop a standard method of transferring money securely and quickly from electronic wallets, which verify a user's identity.

For more information about shopping Web sites, visit the Discovering Computers 2005 Making Use of the Web page (scsite.com/dc2005/web) and click Shopping.

Shopping

WEB EXERCISES

1. Visit two of the three apparel Web sites listed in the table in Figure A-24 and select a specific pair of jeans and a shirt from each one. Create a table with these headings: e-tailer, style, fabric, features, price, tax, and shipping fee. Enter details about your selections in the table. Then, visit two of the books and music Web sites and search for a CD you would consider purchasing. Create another table with the names of the Web site, artist, and CD, as well as the price, tax, and shipping fee.

2. Visit two of the computers and electronics and two of the miscellaneous Web sites listed in Figure A-24. Write a paragraph describing the features these Web sites offer compared with the same offerings from stores. In another paragraph, describe any disadvantages of shopping at these Web sites instead of actually seeing the merchandise. Then, describe their policies for returning unwanted merchandise and for handling complaints.

Weather, Sports, and News

WHAT'S NEWS?

Weather, Sports, and News Web Sites Score Big Hits

Rain or sun? Hot or cold? Do you toss a coin to determine tomorrow's forecast? Or, do you study weather maps displayed on television and Internet sites? The world seems neatly divided into these two camps, with Web sites such as The Weather Channel (Figure A-28) receiving more than 10 million hits each day. Weather is the leading online news item, with at least 10,000 Web sites devoted to this field. A few of the more popular Web sites are listed in Figure A-29. A multitude of weather, sports, and news Web sites resides on the Internet.

Baseball may be the national pastime, but sports aficionados yearn for major league football, basketball, and hockey along with everything from auto racing to cricket. Although television has four major networks and two live, 24-hour all-sports channels, these media outlets do not provide enough action to quench the thirst of fans across the globe. The Internet fills this void with such Web sites as CBS SportsLine.com (Figure A-30), with more than one million pages of multimedia sports news, entertainment, and merchandise, and Sports.com, which covers rugby, cricket, Formula One racing, tennis, and golf. CBS SportsLine.com creates the official Major League Football and the PGA Tour Web sites and provides content for America Online and Netscape.

Olympics fans are hungry for sports action, results, and athlete profiles. The biggest event ever delivered on the Internet was the 2000 Olympic Games in Sydney, Australia. The official Olympic

FIGURE A-28 Local, national, and international weather conditions and details about breaking weather stories are available on The Weather Channel Web pages. Various sections provide information about the effects and interactions of weather that influence a variety of activities and conditions, such as Recreation.

WEATHER, SPORTS, AND NEWS WEB SITES	URL
Weather	
Infoplease Weather	infoplease.com/weather.html
Intellicast.com	intellicast.com
STORMFAX®	stormfax.com
The Weather Channel	weather.com
WX.com	wx.com
Sports	
CBS SportsLine.com	cbs.sportsline.com
ESPN.com	espn.com
NCAA Online	ncaa.org
OFFICIAL WEBSITE OF THE OLYMPIC MOVEMENT	www.olympic.org
SIRC - A World of Sport Information	sirc.ca
Sporting News Radio	radio.sportingnews.com
Sports.com	sports.com
News	
MSNBC	msnbc.com
NYPOST.COM	nypost.com
onlinenewspapers.com	onlinenewspapers.com
Privacy.org	privacy.org
SiliconValley.com	siliconvalley.com
Starting Page Best News Sites	startingpage.com/html/news.html
USATODAY.com	usatoday.com
washingtonpost.com	washingtonpost.com

For an updated list of weather, sports, and news Web sites, visit scsite.com/dc2005/web.

FIGURE A-29 Numerous weather, sports, and news Web sites reside on the Internet.

Games Web site received more than 6.5 billion hits during the 17-day event. That number is greater than the number of Internet visitors at the 2002 Salt Lake Winter Olympic Games Web site. The IBM-run Web site also permitted fans to send e-mail to the 10,500 competitors.

The Internet has emerged as a major source for news, with one-third of Americans going online at least once a week and 15 percent going online daily for reports of major news events. These viewers, who tend to be under the age of 50 and college graduates, are attracted to the Internet's flashy headline format, immediacy, and in-depth reports.

Users are attracted to Web news sites that have a corresponding print or television presence. MSNBC, CNN, ABC News, USA TODAY, FOX News, The Washington Post, and The New York Times are among the more popular Internet news destinations. The technology content in the SiliconValley.com Web site (Figure A-31) and crime, justice, and safety news in APBnews.com appeal to users.

For more information about weather, sports, and news Web sites, visit the Discovering Computers 2005 Making Use of the Web page (scsite.com/dc2005/web) and click Weather, Sports, and News.

FIGURE A-30 Sports fans can catch the latest scores and player profiles on sports Web sites.

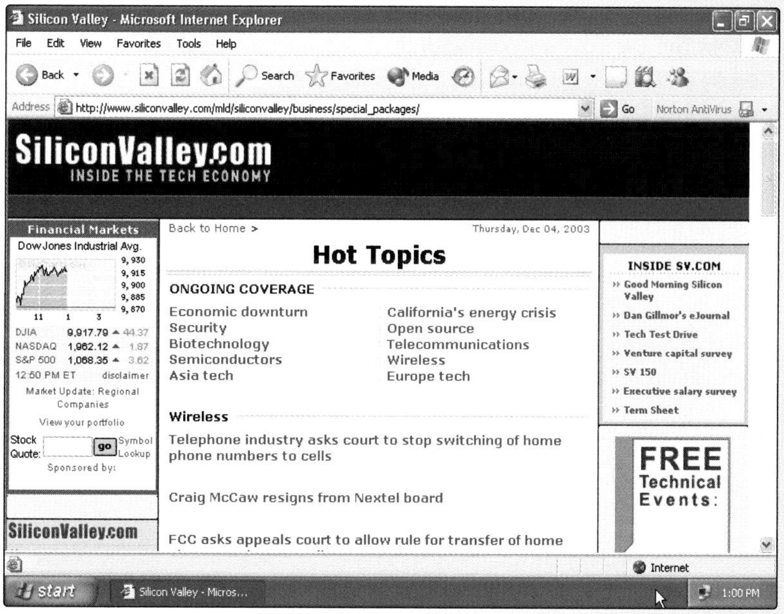

FIGURE A-31 The SiliconValley.com Web site posts feature stories with details on the ever-changing world of technology.

Weather, Sports, and News

WEB EXERCISES

1. Visit two of the weather Web sites listed in the table in Figure A-29. Do they contain the same local and five-day forecasts for your city? What similarities and differences do they have in coverage of a national weather story? Next, visit two of the sports Web sites in the table and write a paragraph describing the content these Web sites provide concerning your favorite sport.

2. Visit the OnlineNewspapers.com and Starting Page Best News Sites Web sites listed in Figure A-29 and select two newspapers from each site. Write a paragraph describing the top national news story featured in each of these four Web pages. Then, write another paragraph describing the top international news story displayed at each Web site. In the third paragraph, discuss which of the four Web sites is the most interesting in terms of story selection, photographs, and Web page design.

Learning

YEARN TO LEARN

Discover New Worlds Online

"To try and fail is at least to learn. To fail to try is to suffer the loss of what might have been." Benjamin Franklin's words bring home the point that despite setbacks encountered along the way, learning nurtures the creative spirit and helps people grow.

While you may believe your education ends when you finally graduate from college, learning is a lifelong process. Although much of this learning may occur on the job and through personal experiences, the Internet can fuel much of your desire and need to expand your mind. Many Web sites use streaming media and graphic-intense applications, so the high-speed Internet connections such as cable modems and DSL, are ideal for these online learning tools.

Learning to enhance your culinary skills can be a rewarding endeavor. No matter if you are a gourmet chef or a weekend cook, you will be cooking in style with the help of online resources. At the Betty Crocker Web site (Figure A-32), you can learn how to prepare nutritious meals and bake for special occasions, almost as if Betty Crocker herself were guiding you along. If you find your kitchen familiar territory, the photographs from recipecenter.com can add flair and finesse to your style.

If you would rather sit in front of the computer than stand in front of the stove, you can learn to search the Internet skillfully and delve into its treasures by visiting several Web sites, including Learn the Net (Figure A-33) and NetLearn. These learning Web sites offer tutorials

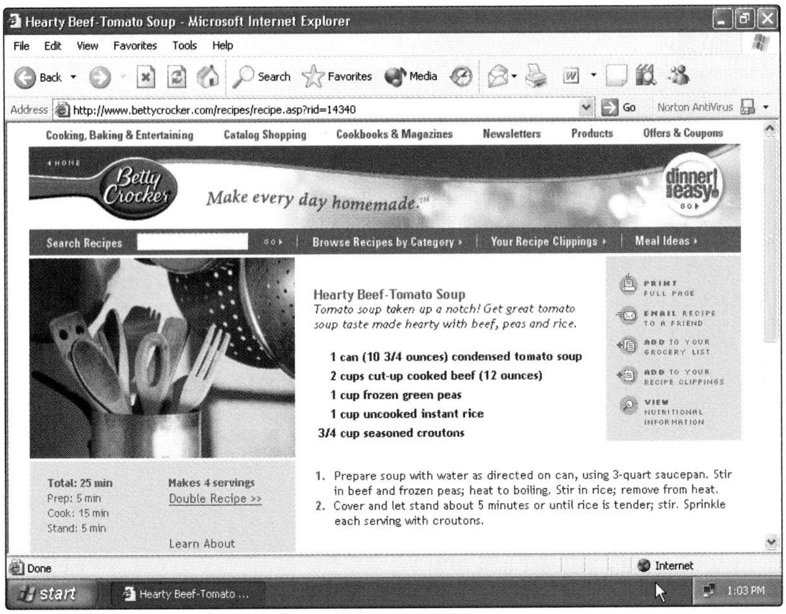

FIGURE A-32 From soups to soufflés, cooking and baking will be a piece of cake with tips from the Betty Crocker and other culinary Web sites.

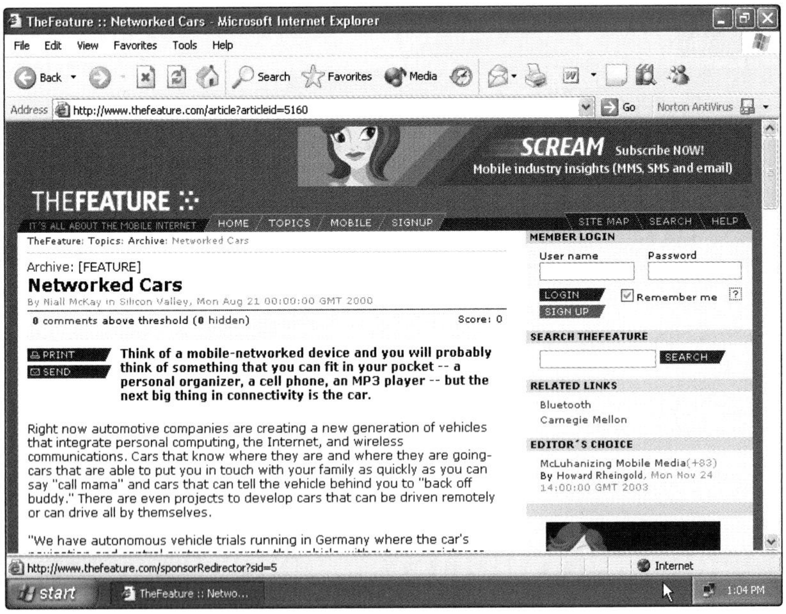

FIGURE A-33 Web sites such as Learn the Net make navigating the Web a more rewarding experience.

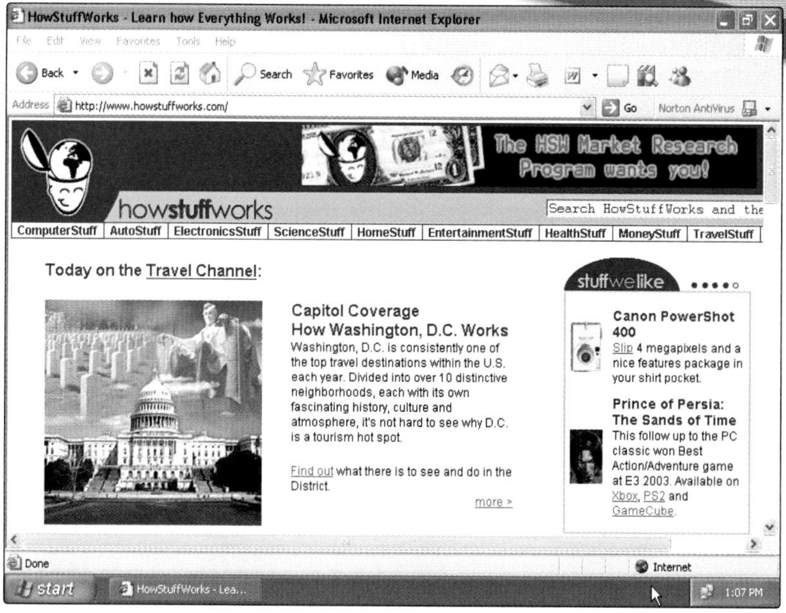

FIGURE A-34 The Internet has something for everyone with numerous Web sites that help you find information quickly and easily about how technology works, the principles of flight, or educational adventures.

on building your own Web sites, the latest news about the Internet, and resources for visually impaired users.

Have you ever wondered how to fly an airplane? Take a look at the ScienceMaster site. You might be interested in finding out about how your car's catalytic converter reduces pollution or how the Electoral College functions. Marshall Brain's HowStuffWorks Web site (Figure A-34) is filled with articles and animations.

The table in Figure A-35 lists some innovative and informative learning Web sites. Have a seat in this virtual classroom, and do not be afraid to fail along the way.

For more information about learning Web sites, visit the Discovering Computers 2005 Making Use of the Web page (scsite.com/dc2005/web) and click Learning.

LEARNING WEB SITES	URL
Cooking	
Betty Crocker	bettycrocker.com
recipecenter.com	recipecenter.com
Internet	
Learn the Net	learnthenet.com
NetLearn	www.rgu.ac.uk/~sim/research/netlearn/callist.htm
Wiredguide™	www.wiredguide.com/
Technology and Science	
HowStuffWorks	howstuffworks.com
ScienceMaster	sciencemaster.com
General Learning	
Bartleby.com: Great Books Online	bartleby.com
Blue Web'n	www.kn.pacbell.com/wired/bluewebn
MSN Learning & Research	encarta.msn.com

For an updated list of learning Web sites, visit scsite.com/dc2005/web.

FIGURE A-35 These Web sites contain a variety of topics that can help you learn about all aspects of life.

Learning

WEB EXERCISES

1. Visit one of the cooking Web sites listed in Figure A-35 and find two recipes or cooking tips that you can use when preparing your next meal. Write a paragraph about each one, summarizing your discoveries. What are the advantages and disadvantages of accessing these Web sites on the new Web appliances that might someday be in your kitchen?

2. Using one of the technology and science Web sites and one of the other Web sites listed in Figure A-35, search for information about communications and networks. Write a paragraph about your findings. Then, review the material in the two general learning Web sites listed in Figure A-35, and write a paragraph describing the content on each Web site that is pertinent to your major.

Science

E = MC²

Rocket Science on the Web

For some people, space exploration is a hobby. Building and launching model rockets allow these scientists to participate in exploring the great frontier of space. For others, space exploration is their life. For National Aeronautics and Space Administration (NASA) engineers and scientists, rockets are their full-time job. These employees launch rockets at NASA's Cape Canaveral facility in Florida and direct them from the Johnson Space Center in Houston, Texas.

The NASA Liftoff Web site, shown in Figure A-36, contains information about rockets, the space shuttle, the International Space Station, space transportation, and communications. Other science resources explore space-related questions about astronomy, physics, the earth sciences, microgravity, and robotics. Information about training to become an astronaut and current astronaut biographies and photographs also are available.

Rockets and space are not the only areas to explore in the world of science. Where can you find the latest pictures taken with the *Hubble Space Telescope*? Do you know which cities experienced an earthquake today? Have you ever wondered what a 3-D model of the amino acid glutamine looks like? You can find the answer to these questions and many others through the Librarians' Index to the Internet (lii.org) shown in Figure A-37.

This index can take you to the National Hurricane Center so you can track a hurricane or fly through

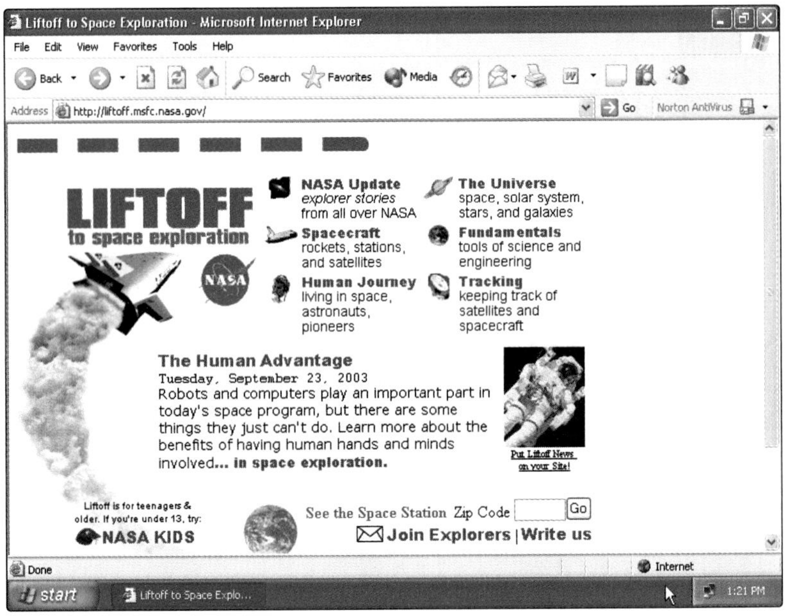

FIGURE A-36 The NASA Liftoff Web site takes space exploration to new heights.

FIGURE A-37 Numerous science resources are organized clearly in the Librarians' Index to the Internet.

the eye of a hurricane with the Hurricane Hunters. It also provides a link to the National Earthquake Information Center where you can learn the locations and the intensities of earthquakes that have occurred in the past few days.

The Yuckiest Site on the Internet Web site (Figure A-38) from Discovery Communications entertains as it teaches, especially when children are involved. Combined with Discovery Kids TV, the Web site features fun and games, crafts, recipes, and other activities that capture kids' imaginations as they learn science through adventure and experiments.

The Web offers a wide variety of science resources designed for all ages. Professional scientists, students, hobbyists, and children can find information with a few clicks of the mouse. The Web sites listed in Figure A-39 include up-to-date science resources, discuss the latest research, and can provide answers to technical questions, helping students or anyone who has a thirst for scientific knowledge.

For more information about science Web sites, visit the Discovering Computers 2005 Making Use of the Web page (scsite.com/dc2005/web) and click Science.

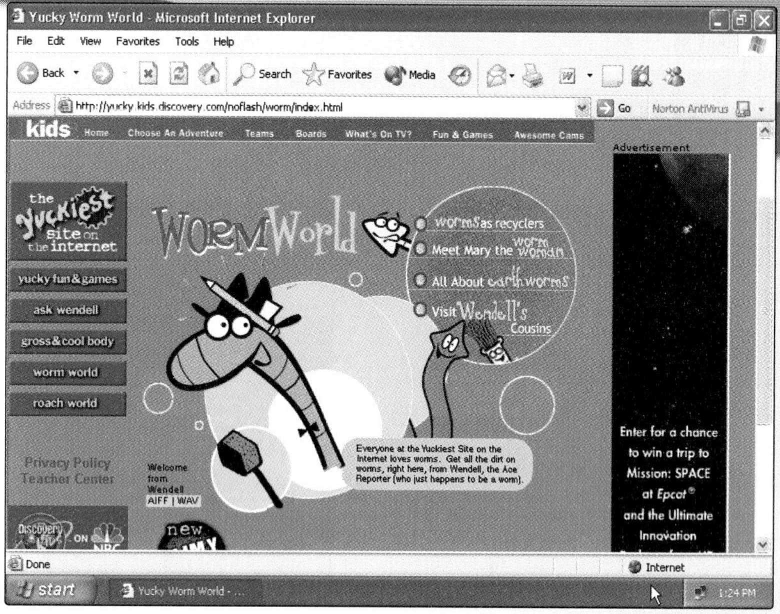

FIGURE A-38 The Yuckiest Site on the Internet Web site makes learning science fun for children.

SCIENCE WEB SITES	URL
Periodicals	
Astronomy.com	astronomy.com
Archaeology Magazine	archaeology.org
NewScientist.com	newscientist.com
OceanLink	oceanlink.island.net
Science Magazine	sciencemag.org
SCIENTIFIC AMERICAN.com	sciam.com
Resources	
National Science Foundation (NSF)	nsf.gov
Science.gov: FirstGov for Science	science.gov
SOFWeb	www.sofweb.vic.edu.au
Science Community	
American Scientist, The Magazine of Sigma Xi, The Research Society	amsci.org
Federation of American Scientists	fas.org
Liftoff to Space Exploration	liftoff.msfc.nasa.gov
Sigma Xi, The Scientific Research Society	sigmaxi.org

For an updated list of science Web sites, visit scsite.com/dc2005/web.

FIGURE A-39 Resources available on the Internet offer a wide range of subjects for enthusiasts who want to delve into familiar and unknown territories in the world of science.

Science

WEB EXERCISES

1. Visit the Liftoff to Space Exploration Web site listed in the table in Figure A-39. View the links about spacecraft, the universe, or tracking satellites and spacecraft, and then write a summary of your findings.
2. Visit the Librarians' Index to the Internet shown in Figure A-37. Click the Science, Computers, & Technology link and then click the Inventions topic. View the Web site for the Greatest Engineering Achievements of the Twentieth Century. Pick two achievements, read their history, and write a paragraph summarizing each of these accomplishments. Then, view two of the science Web sites listed in Figure A-39 and write a paragraph about each of these Web sites describing the information each contains.

Environment

THE FATE OF THE ENVIRONMENT

Protecting the Planet's Ecosystem

The figures are startling: Each year Americans consume 1.4 trillion sheets of paper, an increase of 76 percent since the 1980s. In the past 50 years, people have consumed as many natural resources as every human who has ever lived. According to The Center for a New American Dream (Figure A-40), the U.S. Postal Service's letter carriers deliver an average of 17.8 tons of junk mail each year, which is the weight of four male elephants.

From the rain forests of Africa to the marine life in the Pacific Ocean, the fragile ecosystem is under extreme stress. Many environmental groups have developed Internet sites in attempts to educate worldwide populations and to increase resource conservation.

The U.S. federal government has a number of Web sites devoted to specific environmental concerns. For example, the Acid Rain Data and Reports Web site, developed by the U.S. Geological Survey, monitors the chemicals found in acid rain and conducts research to analyze the effects of these atmospheric deposits on aquatic and terrestrial ecosystems. Figure A-41 shows the home page for the Central African Regional Program for the Environment (CARPE). This continuing project of The United States Agency for International Development (USAID) protects the Congo Basin's tropical forests from population growth, deforestation,

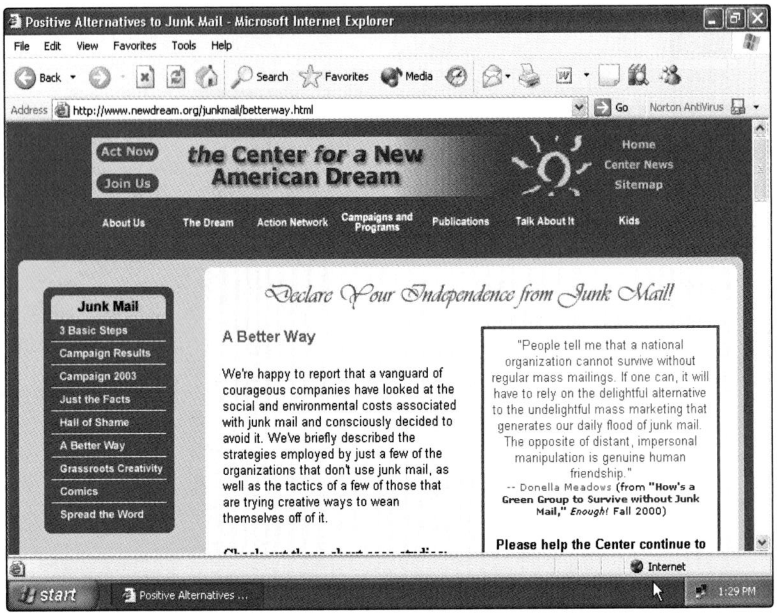

FIGURE A-40 The Center for a New American Dream Web site provides an area where you can declare your independence from junk mail and get your address removed from bulk mail lists.

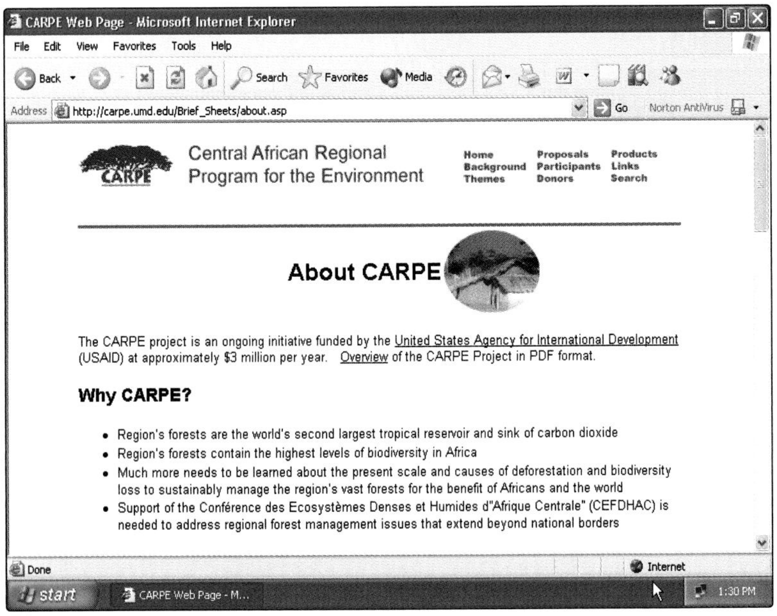

FIGURE A-41 The Congo Basin's ecological, economic, and political issues are discussed in the CARPE Web site.

and other economic and political problems. In another Web site, the U.S. Environmental Protection Agency (EPA) provides pollution data, including ozone levels and air pollutants, for specific areas. Its AirData Web site, shown in Figure A-42, displays air pollution emissions and monitoring data from the entire United States and is the world's most extensive collection of air pollution data.

On an international scale, the Environmental Sites on the Internet Web page developed by the Royal Institute of Technology in Stockholm, Sweden, has been rated as one of the better ecological Web sites. Its comprehensive listing of environmental concerns range from aquatic ecology to wetlands. This Web site is among the environment Web sites listed in Figure A-43.

For more information about environment Web sites, visit the Discovering Computers 2005 Making Use of the Web page (scsite.com/dc2005/ web) and click Environment.

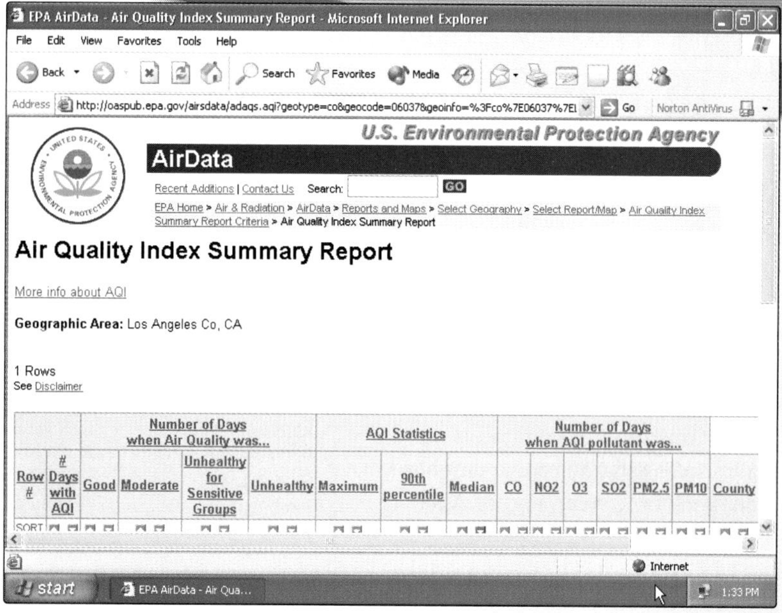

FIGURE A-42 A visit to the EPA AirData Web site, with its extensive database, can assist you in checking your community's ozone and air pollutant levels.

ENVIRONMENT WEB SITES	URL
Central African Regional Program for the Environment (CARPE)	carpe.umd.edu
Earthjustice	www.earthjustice.org
EarthTrends: The Environmental Information Portal	earthtrends.wri.org
Environmental Defense	edf.org
Environmental Sites on the Internet	www.lib.kth.se/~lg/envsite.htm
EPA AirData - Access to Air Pollution Data	epa.gov/air/data
Green Solitaire.org	greensolitaire.bizland.com
GreenNet	www.gn.apc.org
The Center for a New American Dream	newdream.org
The Virtual Library of Ecology & Biodiversity	conbio.org/vl
USGS Acid rain data and reports	btdqs.usgs.gov/acidrain
UWM Environmental Health, Safety & Risk Management	www.uwm.edu/Dept/EHSRM/ EHSLINKS

For an updated list of environment Web sites, visit scsite.com/dc2005/web.

FIGURE A-43 Environment Web sites provide vast resources for ecological data and action groups.

Environment

WEB EXERCISES

1. The Center for a New American Dream Web site encourages consumers to reduce the amount of junk mail sent to their homes. Using the table in Figure A-43, visit the Web site and write a paragraph stating how many trees are leveled each year to provide paper for these mailings, how many garbage trucks are needed to haul this waste, and other statistics. Read the letters that you can use to eliminate your name from bulk mail lists. To whom would you mail these letters? How long does it take to stop these unsolicited letters?

2. Visit the EPA AirData Web site. What is the highest ozone level recorded in your state this past year? Where are the nearest air pollution monitoring Web sites, and what are their levels? Where are the nearest sources of air pollution? Read two reports about two different topics, such as acid rain and air quality, and summarize their findings. Include information on who sponsored the research, who conducted the studies, when the data was collected, and the impact of this pollution on the atmosphere, water, forests, and human health. Whom would you contact for further information regarding the data and studies?

Health

NO PAIN, ALL GAIN

Store Personal Health Records Online

Ouch! You stepped on a rusty nail with your bare foot and made your way to the local hospital's emergency room. The admitting nurse asks when you had your last tetanus shot. You give her a sheepish grin and shrug your shoulders.

You might have been able to eliminate the pain and expense of an immunization if you had tracked your shots using an online database management system. Figure A-44 lists a few of the more than 25 Internet health services and portals available online to store your personal health history, including prescriptions, lab test results, doctor visits, allergies, and immunizations. Web sites such as WellMed (Figure A-45) are free to consumers; revenue is generated in many ways, including charging insurance companies, physicians, and employers that offer this service.

HEALTH WEB SITES	URL
AboutMyHealth	aboutmyhealth.com
Aetnasm IntelliHealth	intellihealth.com
GlobalMedic	globalmedic.com
PersonalMD	personalmd.com
WebMD®	my.webmd.com/my_health_record
WellMed	wellmed.com

For an updated list of health Web sites, visit scsite.com/dc2005/web.

FIGURE A-44 These Internet-based health database management systems Web sites allow you to organize your medical information and store it in an online database.

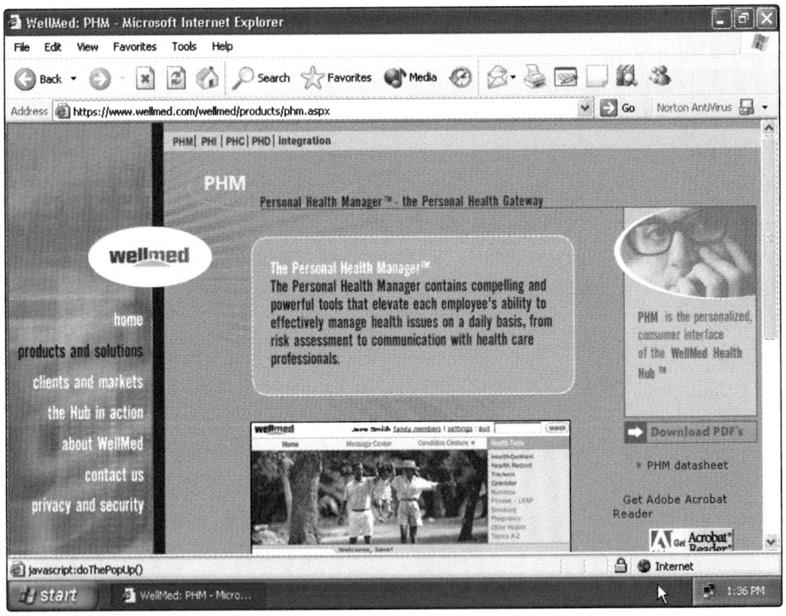

FIGURE A-45 You can store health records for you and your family in the WellMed database.

In minutes, you can register with a health Web site by choosing a user name and password. Then you create a record to enter your medical history. You also can store data for your emergency contacts, primary care physicians, specialists, blood type, cholesterol levels, blood pressure, and insurance plan.

Similar to the records stored in a company or school database, you can access, retrieve, add, change, delete, and use these online records in a variety of ways. You can decide what data to include. You also can determine who can access this medical data under specific circumstances. No matter where you are in the world, you and medical personnel can obtain records such as the health record shown in Figure A-46 via the Internet or fax machine. Some Web sites offer an audit log that displays the names of people who have accessed your record and when this action occurred.

Some Web sites issue a wallet-sized emergency medical card with instructions for paramedics and other emergency medical personnel about how they can access your vital data (Figure A-47). Other Web sites can import data directly from pharmacies, hospitals, and physicians' offices.

More than 70 million consumers use the Internet yearly to search for health information, so using the Web to store personal medical data is a natural extension of the Internet's capabilities. Health-care reformers strongly support comprehensive online databases. They explain that using the Internet as a health-history database helps eliminate administrative inefficiencies by automatically transferring data among patients, doctors, and insurance providers. The net results are improved health care overall.

For more information about online health database management systems and for an updated list of health Web sites, visit the Discovering Computers 2005 Making Use of the Web page (scsite.com/dc2005/web) and click Health.

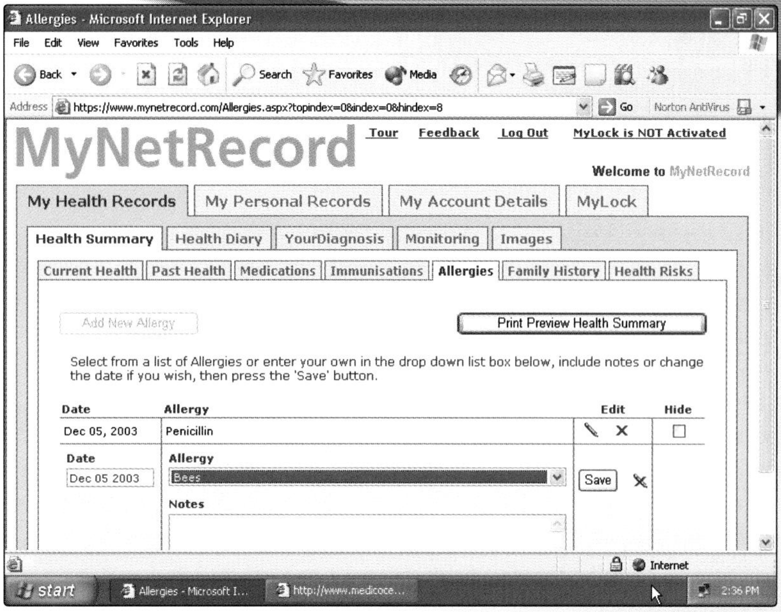

FIGURE A-46 The MyNetRecord database allows you to create, store, and access secure online health information whenever the need arises.

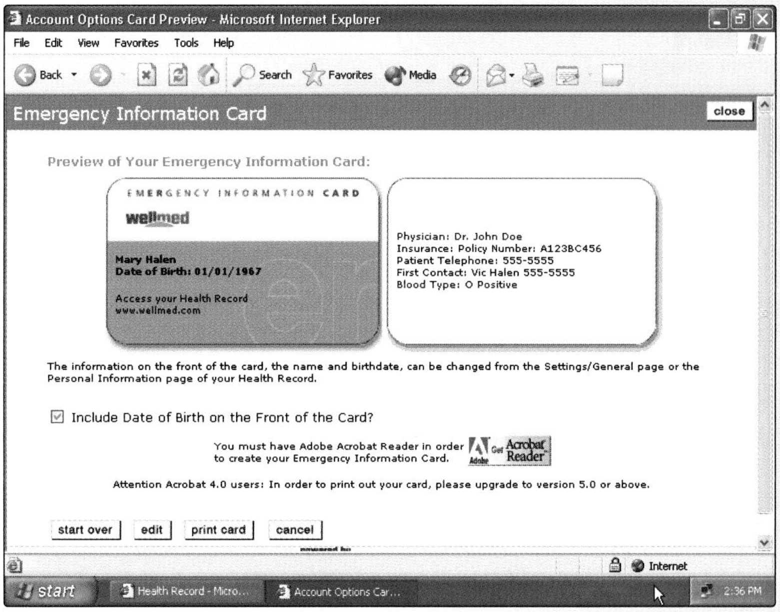

FIGURE A-47 The Emergency Information Card alerts health-care providers that your medical records are stored online.

Health

WEB EXERCISES

1. Access one of the health Web sites listed in Figure A-44. Register yourself or a family member, and then enter the full health history. Create an emergency medical card if the Web site provides the card option. Print this record and emergency card.
2. Visit three of the health Web sites listed in Figure A-44. Describe the features of each. Which of the three is the most user-friendly? Why? Describe the privacy policies of these three Web sites. Print your analysis of these Web sites.

Research

SEARCH AND YE SHALL FIND

Info on the Web

Just about everyone these days wants to know how to find information using the Internet. From students doing research, to teachers, to the general Web surfer, people are using search engines on the Web to get their answers.

Unlike the days when you used the Dewey Decimal Classification or the Library of Congress system to locate reference materials easily, you will not find Internet documents organized in any systematic manner. And no helpful, patient reference librarian is working behind a desk to assist you in your quest for information. Instead, you are on your own when you navigate the tangled Web. But you have some tools: search engines and subject directories.

Yahoo!, AltaVista, GO.com, Northern Light, Excite, FAST Search, and Google are some of the more popular search engines. They crawl through a Web page, and with the help of programs such as spiders and robots, they record each word in their enormous databases. When you enter a key term, search text, or query in their search boxes, the search engines scan the databases and list the Web sites that contain the specified search text. As shown in Figure A-48, the Yahoo! News search results for the phrase, DVD-ROM, lists 323 stories.

The key to effective searching on the Web is composing search queries that narrow the search results and place the most relevant Web sites at the top of the list. Think of major terms that describe the issue or item you are researching and use Boolean operators — and, or, and not — to help retrieve appropriate Web sites.

The GO.com search in Figure A-49 locates Web sites describing the Beatles platinum albums and eliminates Web sites describing platinum jewelry or Beatles memorabilia.

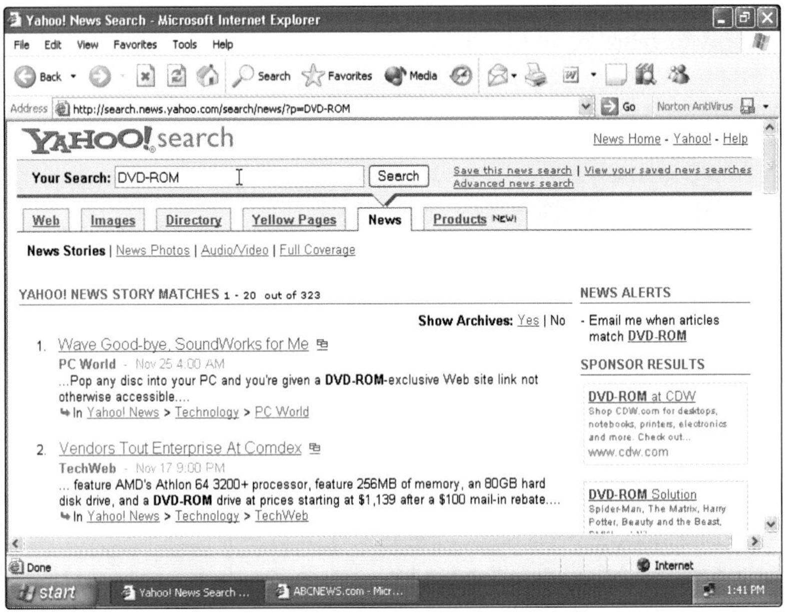

FIGURE A-48 Search the Yahoo! News Web site for information about computer products and technology issues.

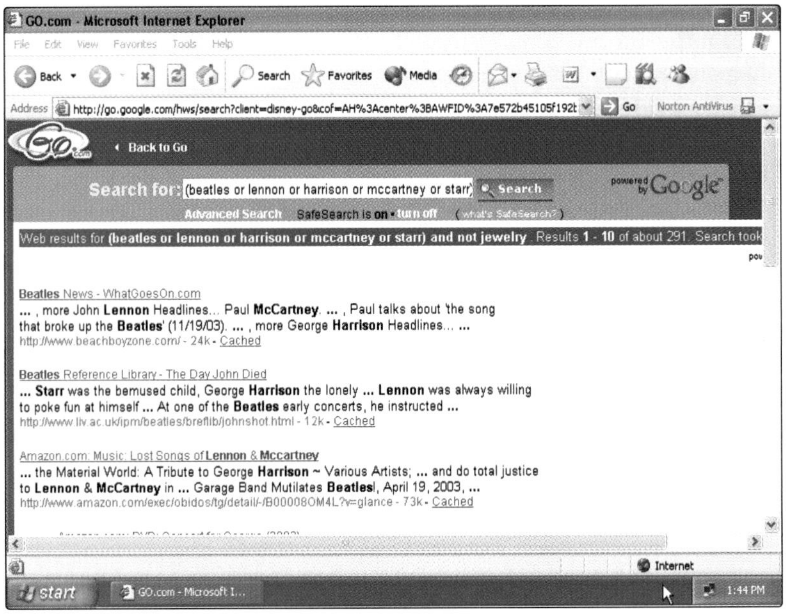

FIGURE A-49 The GO.com Web site features a search engine to locate information such as Beatles platinum albums.

Using the search terms beatles, or lennon, or harrison, or mccartney, or starr along with platinum and not jewelry helps narrow the list of results.

Even when using these searching techniques, one search engine can explore only 20 percent of the 5.5 billion Web pages. All the search engines combined can rummage through less than half of these Web sites.

Another search tool is a subject directory, which is a collection of related Web sites. Yahoo! and LookSmart have two of the more comprehensive subject directories on the Web. Their organized lists often are called trees because a few main categories, such as Entertainment, Computing, Lifestyle, and Work, branch out to more specific subtopics. Figure A-50 shows LookSmart's tree for buying or selling a used car. The list begins with the Buy or Sell a Used Car main category and branches to Auction Lots, Brokers & Services, Classifieds by State, Online Auctions, and finally Vintage Classifieds. A listing of search engines and subject directories is included in the table in Figure A-51.

For more information about searching on the Web and for an updated list of research Web sites, visit the Discovering Computers 2005 Making Use of the Web page (scsite.com/dc2005/web) and click Research.

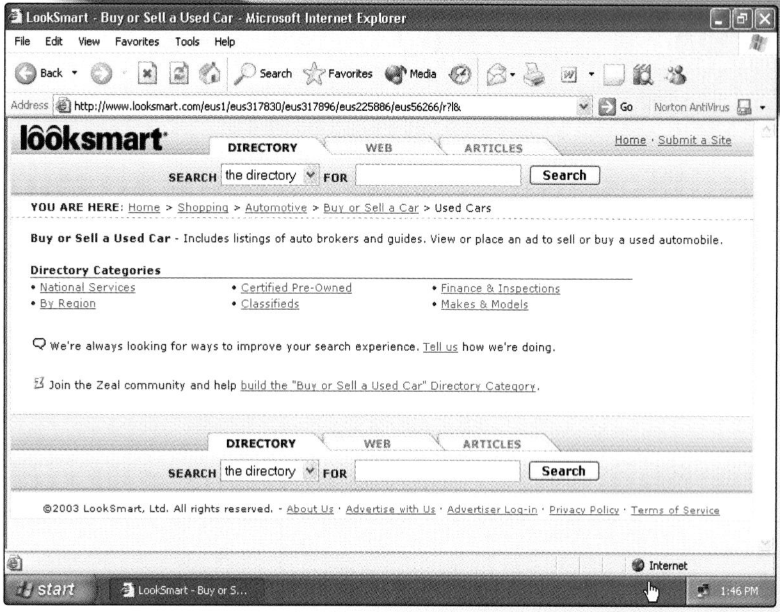

FIGURE A-50 Webrarians index millions of Web pages into more than 200,000 categories.

RESEARCH WEB SITES	URL
Search Engines	
AltaVista	altavista.com
Excite	excite.com
Fast Search & Transfer (FAST)	fastsearch.com
GO.com	go.com
Google	google.com
Northern Light®	northernlight.com
Yahoo!	yahoo.com
Subject Directories	
About	about.com
Librarians' Index to the Internet	lii.org
LookSmart	looksmart.com
The Internet Public Library	ipl.org
The WWW Virtual Library	vlib.org
Yahoo!	yahoo.com

For an updated list of research Web sites, visit scsite.com/dc2005/web.

FIGURE A-51 Web users can find information by using search engines and subject directories.

Research

WEB EXERCISES

1. Use two of the search engines listed in Figure A-51 to find three Web sites that review the latest digital cameras from Sony and Kodak. Make a table listing the search engines, Web site names, and the cameras' model numbers, suggested retail price, megapixels, memory, and features.
2. If money were no object, virtually everyone would have an exquisite car. On the other hand, drivers need a practical vehicle to drive around town daily. Use one of the subject directories listed in Figure A-51 to research your dream car and another directory to research your practical car. Write a paragraph about each car describing the particular subject directory tree you used, the MSRP of the car, standard and optional equipment, engine size, miles per gallon, and safety features.

Careers

IN SEARCH OF THE PERFECT JOB

Web Helps Career Hunt

If you choose a job you love, you never will have to work a day in your life, according to Confucius. Does that sound good? All you need to do is find that perfect job, but that is no easy feat.

While your teachers give you valuable training to prepare you for a career, they rarely teach you how to begin that career. On-campus interviews are a start, but you can broaden your horizons by searching the Internet for career information and job openings.

First, examine some of the job search Web sites. These resources list thousands of openings in hundreds of fields, companies, and locations. For example, the Monster Web site, shown in Figure A-52, allows you to choose a broad job area, such as programmer, narrow your search to specific fields within that area, and then search for specific salary ranges, locations, and job functions. Other job search Web sites are listed in Figure A-53.

Next, prepare your resume. Some Web sites have forms that allow you to type pertinent information into the blank form. Other Web sites want you to submit, or post, a document. If so, write your resume using nouns to describe your skills and experience, such as team player, Spanish, and Microsoft Word. Be sure to check spelling and scan the document for viruses.

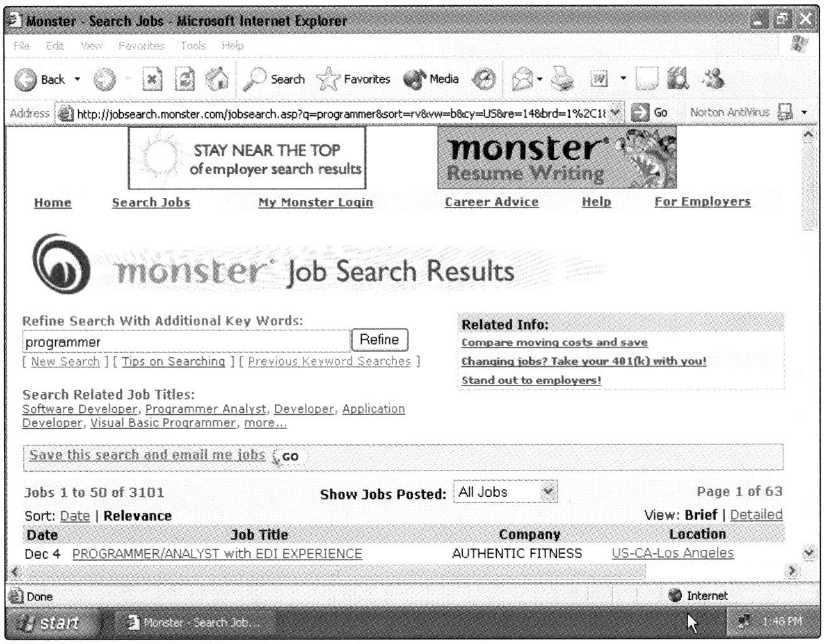

FIGURE A-52 Monster's global online network connects companies with career-minded individuals.

CAREERS WEB SITES	URL
Job Search	
BestJobsUSA.com	ultimatecareerfair.com
CareerBuilder	careerbuilder.com
CareerExchange.com	careerexchange.com
CareerNet	careernet.com
College Grad Job Hunter	collegegrad.com
EmploymentGuide.com	employmentguide.com
HotJobs.com	hotjobs.com
JobBankUSA.com	jobbankusa.com
JobOptions	joboptions.com
JobsOnline™	jobsonline.com
JobWeb.com	www.jobweb.com
Monster	monster.com
MonsterTRAK	www.jobtrak.com
USAJOBS	usajobs.opm.gov
VolunteerMatch	volunteermatch.com
Company/Industry Information	
AmericanCompanies.com	www.americancompanies.com
Career ResourceCenter.com	www.resourcecenter.com
FASTCOMPANY	fastcompany.com
FORTUNE	fortune.com
Hoover's Online	hoovers.com
Occupational Outlook Handbook	stats.bls.gov/oco

For an updated list of careers Web sites, visit scsite.com/dc2005/web.

FIGURE A-53 Careers Web sites provide a variety of job openings and information about major companies worldwide.

When you write your cover letter, use words the company incorporated in its job posting. Many companies use computer software applications, not humans, to find interviewees. The software searches for particular buzzwords, called keywords, in the files and then lists the documents that contain the most matches.

When a company contacts you for an interview, learn as much about it and the industry as possible before the interview. Many of the Web sites listed in Figure A-53 include detailed company profiles and links to their corporate Web sites. For instance, company information about Microsoft Corporation is displayed in the Hoover's Online Web site, as shown in Figure A-54. Also, look at Web sites for professional organizations and discussion groups for further insights.

For more information about using the Web for career information and for an updated list of career Web sites, visit the Discovering Computers 2005 Making Use of the Web page (scsite.com/dc2005/web) and click Careers.

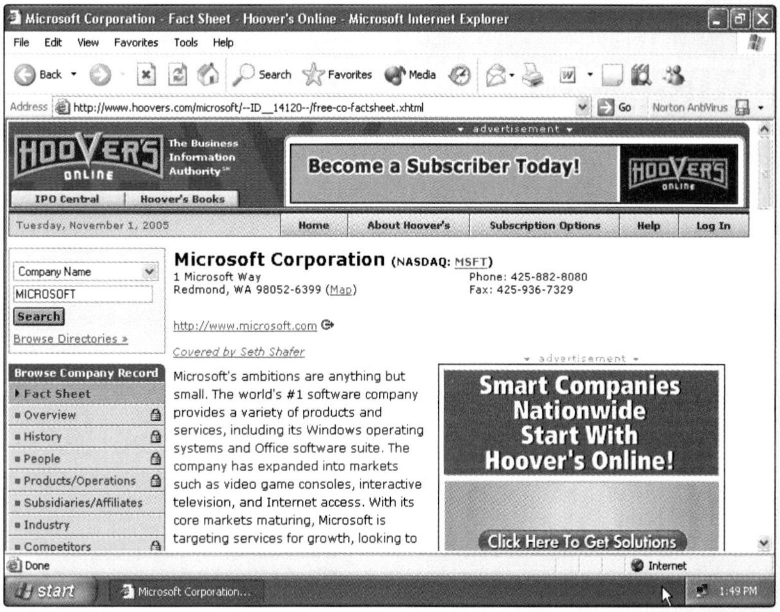

FIGURE A-54 Company and industry information form the core of Hoover's Online Web site.

Careers

WEB EXERCISES

1. Use two of the job search Web sites listed in Figure A-53 to find three companies with job openings in your field. Make a table listing the Web site name, position available, description, salary, location, desired education, and desired experience.

2. It is a good idea to acquire information before graduation about the industry in which you would like to work. Are you interested in the automotive manufacturing industry, the restaurant service industry, or the financial industry? Use two of the company/industry information Web sites listed in Figure A-53 to research a particular career related to your major. Write a paragraph naming the Web sites and the specific information you found, such as the nature of the work, recommended training and qualifications, employment outlook, and earnings. Then, use two other Web sites to profile three companies with positions available in this field. Write a paragraph about each of these companies, describing the headquarters' location, sales and earnings for the previous year, total number of employees, working conditions, perks, and competitors.

Arts and Literature

FIND SOME CULTURE

Get Ready to Read, Paint, and Dance

Brush up your Shakespeare. Start quoting him now. Brush up your Shakespeare. And the women you will wow. This refrain to one of the songs in Broadway's hit musical, Cole Porter's *Kiss Me Kate*, emphasizes the value of knowing the Bard of Avon's words. You can expand your knowledge of Shakespeare and other literary greats with a little help from the Internet.

For example, Shakespeare.com provides in-depth reviews and news of the world's most famous playwright and his works. The Bartleby.com Web site features biographies, definitions, quotations, dictionaries, and indexes. At the Fantastic Fiction Bibliographies Web site, you can peruse an online bibliography database of science fiction authors and book titles. The Electronic Literature Directory allows you to search for genres, titles, authors, and publishers.

The full text of hundreds of books is available online from the Bibliomania (Figure A-55) and Project Gutenberg Web sites. If you are not keen on reading all of Dostoevsky's *Crime and Punishment* or Homer's *Iliad* on your desktop computer monitor, you can download these works to your e-book or PDA.

When you are ready to absorb more culture, you can turn to various art Web sites on the Internet. Many museums have images of their collections online. Among them are the Getty Museum in Los Angeles, the Montreal Museum of Fine Arts (Figure A-56), the

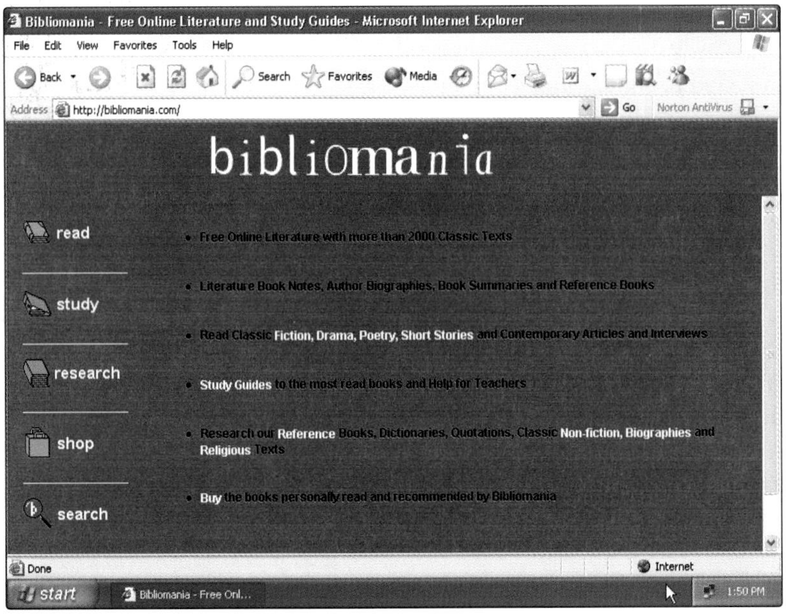

FIGURE A-55 Classic fiction, short stories, drama, poetry, and dictionaries are available for viewing or downloading from Bibliomania and other Web sites.

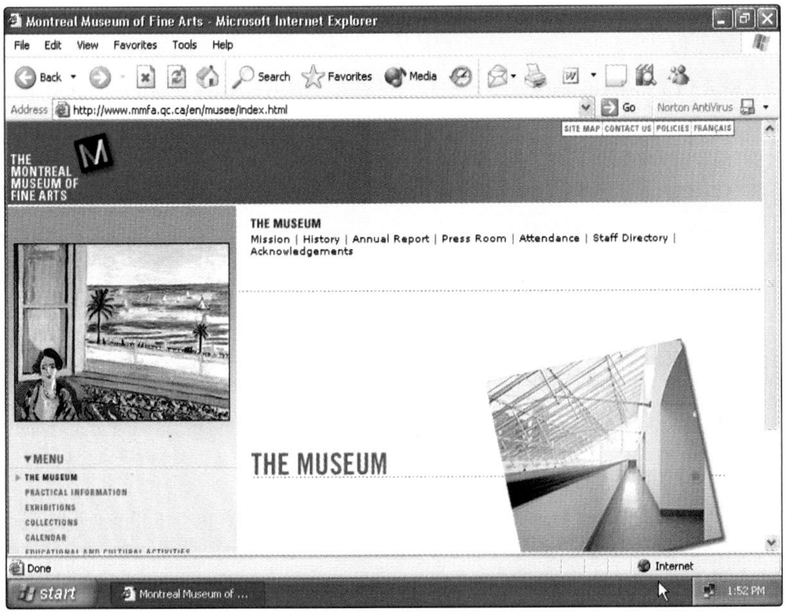

FIGURE A-56 Permanent, temporary, and virtual exhibitions, educational activities, a boutique, and a bookstore are featured on the Montreal Museum of Fine Arts Web site.

Children's Museum of Indianapolis, and the Louvre Museum in Paris (Figure A-57). Comprehensive glimpses of galleries, museums, and other cultural meccas throughout the world as well as paintings and sculptures are found on such Web sites as Art News – absolutearts.com and the GalleryGuide.org.

Access Place Arts and The New York Times Web sites focus on the arts and humanities and provide fascinating glimpses into the worlds of dance, music, performance, cinema, and other topics pertaining to creative expression.

So brush up your knowledge of Shakespeare, grab a canvas, and put on your dancing shoes. The visual arts and literature Web sites on the Internet (Figure A-58) are about to sweep you off your cyberfeet.

For more information about arts and literature Web sites, visit the Discovering Computers 2005 Making Use of the Web page (scsite.com/dc2005/web) and click Arts and Literature.

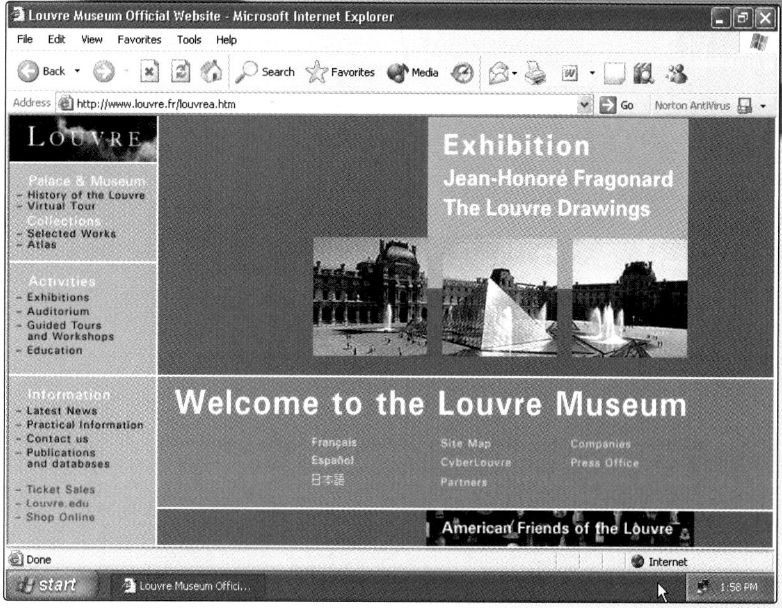

FIGURE A-57 Established in 1793 by the French Republic, the Louvre Museum is one of the earlier European museums. You can view its collections online.

ARTS AND LITERATURE WEB SITES	URL
Arts	
Access Place Arts	accessplace.com/arts.htm
Art News - absolutearts.com	absolutearts.com
GalleryGuide.org	galleryguide.org
Louvre Museum	www.louvre.fr
Montreal Museum of Fine Arts	www.mmfa.qc.ca
The Children's Museum of Indianapolis	childrensmuseum.org
The Getty	getty.edu
The New York Times: Arts	nytimes.com/pages/arts/index.html
Virtual Library museums pages (VLmp)	vlmp.museophile.com
Literature	
Bartleby.com	bartleby.com
Bibliomania	bibliomania.com
Electronic Literature Directory	directory.wordcircuits.com
Fantastic Fiction Bibliographies	fantasticfiction.co.uk
Project Gutenberg	promo.net/pg
shakespeare.com	shakespeare.com
The Modern Library eBook List	randomhouse.com/modernlibrary/ebookslist.html

For an updated list of arts and literature Web sites, visit scsite.com/dc2005/web.

FIGURE A-58 Discover culture throughout the world by visiting these arts and literature Web sites.

Arts *and* Literature

WEB EXERCISES

1. Visit The Modern Library eBook List Web site listed in Figure A-58 and view one book in the 20TH CENTURY NOVELS, 19TH CENTURY NOVELS, BRITISH LITERATURE, and HISTORY sections. Create a table with columns for the book name, author, cost, online store, local store, and description. Then, read the excerpt from each of the four books and write a paragraph describing which of these four books is the most interesting to you. What are the advantages and disadvantages of reading classic literature electronically?
2. Using the arts Web sites listed in Figure A-58, search for three temporary exhibitions in galleries throughout the world. Describe the venues, the artists, and the works. What permanent collections are found in these museums? Some people shop for gifts in the museums' stores. View and describe three items for sale.

APPENDIX B

Coding Schemes and Number Systems

CODING SCHEMES

As discussed in Chapter 4, a computer uses a coding scheme to represent characters. This appendix presents the ASCII, EBCDIC, and Unicode coding schemes and discusses parity.

ASCII and EBCDIC

Two widely used codes that represent characters in a computer are the ASCII and EBCDIC codes. The **American Standard Code for Information Interchange**, called ASCII (pronounced ASK-ee), is the most widely used coding system to represent data. Many personal computers and midrange servers use ASCII. The **Extended Binary Coded Decimal Interchange Code**, or EBCDIC (pronounced EB-see-dik), is used primarily on mainframe computers. Figure B-1 summarizes these codes. Notice how the combination of bits (0s and 1s) is unique for each character.

When the ASCII or EBCDIC code is used, each character that is represented is stored in one byte of memory. Other binary formats exist, however, that the computer sometimes uses to represent numeric data. For example, a computer may store, or pack, two numeric characters in one byte of memory. The computer uses these binary formats to increase storage and processing efficiency.

Unicode

The 256 characters and symbols that are represented by ASCII and EBCDIC codes are sufficient for English and western European languages but are not large enough for Asian and other languages that use different alphabets. Further compounding the problem is that many of these languages use symbols, called **ideograms**, to represent multiple words and ideas. One solution to this situation is Unicode. **Unicode** is a 16-bit code that has the capacity of representing more than 65,000 characters and symbols.

ASCII	SYMBOL	EBCDIC
00110000	0	11110000
00110001	1	11110001
00110010	2	11110010
00110011	3	11110011
00110100	4	11110100
00110101	5	11110101
00110110	6	11110110
00110111	7	11110111
00111000	8	11111000
00111001	9	11111001
01000001	A	11000001
01000010	B	11000010
01000011	C	11000011
01000100	D	11000100
01000101	E	11000101
01000110	F	11000110
01000111	G	11000111
01001000	H	11001000
01001001	I	11001001
01001010	J	11010001
01001011	K	11010010
01001100	L	11010011
01001101	M	11010100
01001110	N	11010101
01001111	O	11010110
01010000	P	11010111
01010001	Q	11011000
01010010	R	11011001
01010011	S	11100010
01010100	T	11100011
01010101	U	11100100
01010110	V	11100101
01010111	W	11100110
01011000	X	11100111
01011001	Y	11101000
01011010	Z	11101001
00100001	!	01011010
00100010	"	01111111
00100011	#	01111011
00100100	$	01011011
00100101	%	01101100
00100110	&	01010000
00101000	(	01001101
00101001	)	01011101
00101010	*	01011100
00101011	+	01001110

FIGURE B-1

Unicode represents all the world's current languages using more than 34,000 characters and symbols (Figure B-2). A code for a symbol in Figure B-2 is obtained by appending the symbol's corresponding digit in the left-most column to the symbol's corresponding three-digit code in the column heading. For example, the Unicode for the letter C in row 2 is 0421. In Unicode, 30,000 codes are reserved for future use, such as ancient languages, and 6,000 codes are reserved for private use. Existing ASCII coded data is fully compatible with Unicode because the first 256 codes are the same. Unicode currently is implemented in several operating systems, including Windows XP.

	041	042	043	044	045	046	047
0	А	Р	а	р		Ѡ	Ѱ
1	Б	С	б	с	ё	ѡ	ѱ
2	В	Т	в	т	ђ	Ѣ	Ѳ
3	Г	У	г	у	ѓ	ѣ	ѳ
4	Д	Ф	д	ф	є	Ѥ	Ѵ
5	Е	Х	е	х	ѕ	ѥ	ѵ
6	Ж	Ц	ж	ц	і	Ѧ	Ѷ
7	З	Ч	з	ч	ї	ѧ	ѷ
8	И	Ш	и	ш	ј	Ѩ	Ѹ
9	Й	Щ	й	щ	љ	ѩ	ѹ
A	К	Ъ	к	ъ	њ	Ѫ	Ѻ
B	Л	Ы	л	ы	ћ	ѫ	ѻ
C	М	Ь	м	ь	ќ	Ѭ	Ѽ
D	Н	Э	н	э		ѭ	ѽ
E	О	Ю	о	ю	ў	Ѯ	Ѿ
F	П	Я	п	я	џ	ѯ	ѿ

FIGURE B-2

Parity

Regardless of whether ASCII, EBCDIC, or other binary methods are used to represent characters in memory, it is important that the characters be stored accurately. For each byte of memory, most computers have at least one extra bit, called a **parity bit**, that is used by the computer for error checking. A parity bit can detect if one of the bits in a byte has been changed inadvertently. While such errors are extremely rare (most computers never have a parity error during their lifetime), they can occur because of voltage fluctuations, static electricity, or a memory failure.

Computers are either odd- or even-parity machines. In computers with odd-parity, the total number of on bits in the byte (including the parity bit) must be an odd number (Figure B-3). In computers with even parity, the total number of on bits must be an even number. The computer checks parity each time it uses a memory location. When the computer moves data from one location to another in memory, it compares the parity bits of both the sending and receiving locations to see if they are the same. If the system detects a difference or if the wrong number of bits is on (e.g., an odd number in a system with even parity), an error message is displayed. Many computers use multiple parity bits that enable them to detect and correct a single-bit error and detect multiple-bit errors.

NUMBER SYSTEMS

This section describes the number systems that are used with computers. Whereas thorough knowledge of this subject is required for technical computer personnel, a general understanding of number systems and how they relate to computers is all most users need.

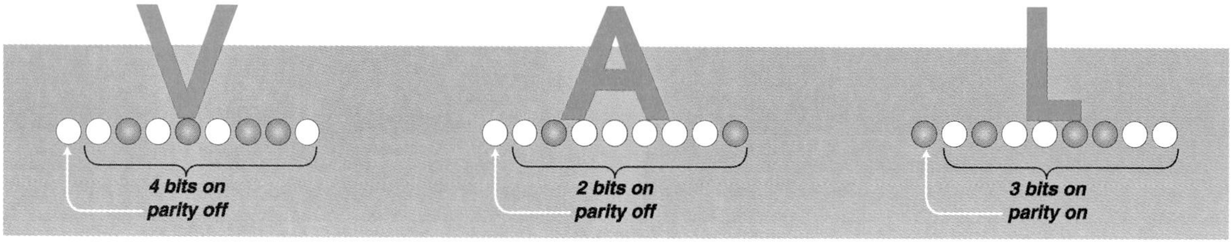

FIGURE B-3

The binary (base 2) number system is used to represent the electronic status of the bits in memory. It also is used for other purposes such as addressing the memory locations. Another number system that commonly is used with computers is **hexadecimal** (base 16). The computer uses the hexadecimal system to communicate with a programmer when a problem with a program exists, because it would be difficult for the programmer to understand the 0s and 1s of binary code. Figure B-4 shows how the decimal values 0 through 15 are represented in binary and hexadecimal.

The mathematical principles that apply to the binary and hexadecimal number systems are the same as those that apply to the decimal number system. To help you better understand these principles, this section starts with the familiar decimal system, then progresses to the binary and hexadecimal number systems.

DECIMAL	BINARY	HEXADECIMAL
0	0000	0
1	0001	1
2	0010	2
3	0011	3
4	0100	4
5	0101	5
6	0110	6
7	0111	7
8	1000	8
9	1001	9
10	1010	A
11	1011	B
12	1100	C
13	1101	D
14	1110	E
15	1111	F

FIGURE B-4

The Decimal Number System

The decimal number system is a base 10 number system (deci means ten). The base of a number system indicates how many symbols are used in it. The decimal number system uses 10 symbols: 0 through 9. Each of the symbols in the number system has a value associated with it. For example, 3 represents a quantity of three and 5 represents a quantity of five.

The decimal number system also is a positional number system. This means that in a number such as 143, each position in the number has a value associated with it. When you look at the decimal number 143, the 3 is in the ones, or units, position and represents three ones or (3 x 1); the 4 is in the tens position and represents four tens or (4 x 10); and the 1 is in the hundreds position and represents one hundred or (1 x 100). The number 143 is the sum of the values in each position of the number (100 + 40 + 3 = 143). The chart in Figure B-5 shows how you can calculate the positional values (hundreds, tens, and units) for a number system. Starting on the right and working to the left, the base of the number system, in this case 10, is raised to consecutive powers (10^0, 10^1, 10^2). These calculations are a mathematical way of determining the place values in a number system.

When you use number systems other than decimal, the same principles apply. The base of the number system indicates the number of symbols that are used, and each position in a number system has a value associated with it. By raising the base of the number system to consecutive powers beginning with zero, you can calculate the positional value.

power of 10	10^2	10^1	10^0
positional value	100	10	1
number	1	4	3

$$1 \quad 4 \quad 3 =$$

$$(1 \times 10^2) + (4 \times 10^1) + (3 \times 10^0) =$$

$$(1 \times 100) + (4 \times 10) + (3 \times 1) =$$

$$100 + 40 + 3 = 143$$

FIGURE B-5

The Binary Number System

As previously discussed, binary is a base 2 number system (bi means two), and the symbols it uses are 0 and 1. Just as each position in a decimal number has a place value associated with it, so does each position in a binary number. In binary, the place values, moving from right to left, are successive powers of two (2^0, 2^1, 2^2, 2^3) or (1, 2, 4, 8). To construct a binary number, you place ones in the positions where the corresponding values add up to the quantity you want to represent; you place zeros in the other positions. For example, in a four-digit binary number, the binary place values are (from right to left) 1, 2, 4, and 8. The binary number 1001 has ones in the positions for the values 1 and 8 and zeros in the positions for 2 and 4. Therefore, the quantity represented by binary 1001 is 9 (8 + 0 + 0 + 1) (Figure B-6).

The Hexadecimal Number System

The hexadecimal number system uses 16 symbols to represent values (hex means six, deci means ten). These include the symbols 0 through 9 and A through F (Figure B-4 on the previous page). The mathematical principles previously discussed also apply to hexadecimal (Figure B-7).

The primary reason why the hexadecimal number system is used with computers is because it can represent binary values in a more compact and readable form and because the conversion between the binary and the hexadecimal number systems is very efficient.

An eight-digit binary number (a byte) can be represented by a two-digit hexadecimal number. For example, in the ASCII code, the character M is represented as 01001101. This value can be represented in hexadecimal as 4D. One way to convert this binary number (4D) to a hexadecimal number is to divide the binary number (from right to left) into groups of four digits; calculate the value of each group; and then change any two-digit values (10 through 15) into the symbols A through F that are used in hexadecimal (Figure B-8).

power of 2	2^3	2^2	2^1	2^0
positional value	8	4	2	1
binary	1	0	0	1

$$1 \quad 0 \quad 0 \quad 1 =$$
$$(1 \times 2^3) + (0 \times 2^2) + (0 \times 2^1) + (1 \times 2^0) =$$
$$(1 \times 8) + (0 \times 4) + (0 \times 2) + (1 \times 1) =$$
$$8 + 0 + 0 + 1 = 9$$

FIGURE B-6

power of 16	16^1	16^0
positional value	16	1
hexadecimal	A	5

$$A \quad 5 =$$
$$(10 \times 16^1) + (5 \times 16^0) =$$
$$(10 \times 16) + (5 \times 1) =$$
$$160 + 5 = 165$$

FIGURE B-7

positional value	8421	8421
binary	0100	1101
decimal	4	13
hexadecimal	4	D

FIGURE B-8

APPENDIX C

Computer Acronyms

Acronym	Description	Page
$/WIPS	system cost per Web Interactions Per Second	649
0NF	zero normal form	543
1NF	first normal form	543
2NF	second normal form	543
3GL	third-generation language	666
3NF	third normal form	543
4GL	fourth-generation language	675
AC	alternating current	211
ACE	Adobe Certified Expert	786
ACM	Association for Computing Machinery	778
ADA	Americans with Disabilities Act	263
ADC	analog-to-digital converter	39, 242
ADSL	asymmetric digital subscriber line	482
AES	advanced encryption standard	603
AGP	Accelerated Graphics Port	210
AI	artificial intelligence	730
AITP	Association of Information Technology Professionals	778
ALGOL	ALGOrithmic Language	685
ALU	arithmetic logic unit	184
AMD	Advanced Micro Devices	216
ANNs	artificial neural networks	751
ANSI	American National Standards Institute	692
AOL	America Online	72, 82, 104
APL	A Programming Language	685
ARPA	Advanced Research Projects Agency	68
ARPANET	Advanced Research Projects Agency network	69
ASCII	American Standard Code for Information Interchange	192, 519
ASCII file	American Standard Code for Information Interchange file	679
ASP	application service provider	162, 637
ATM	Asynchronous Transfer Mode	482
ATM	automated teller machine	259
AUP	acceptable use policy	574
B2B	business-to-business	91, 735-36
B2C	business-to-consumer	90
BASIC	Beginner's All-purpose Symbolic Instruction Code	668
BIOS	basic input/output system	395-96
Bit	binary digit	191, 193
BLOB	binary large object	520
BMP	bit map	84, 85
BSA	Business Software Alliance	581
C2C	consumer-to-consumer	91
CA	certificate authority	588
CAD	computer-aided design	151, 721
CAD database	computer-aided design database	536
CAD software	computer-aided design software	151, 320
CAE	computer-aided engineering	722
CAI	computer-aided instruction	158, 779
Caller ID	caller identification	592
CAM	computer-aided manufacturing	38, 722
CASE	computer-aided software engineering	643-44
CASE workbench	computer-aided software engineering workbench	644

Acronym	Description	Page
CAT	computerized adaptive testing	785
CATV	cable television	484
CBT	computer-based training	158, 779
CCD	charge-coupled device	248
CCIE	Cisco Certified Internetwork Expert	789
CCNP	Cisco Certified Network Professional	788
CD	compact disc	8, 9, 361-67
CD recorder	compact disc recorder	366
CD-E	erasable compact disc	366
CDMA	Code Division Multiple Access	492
CD-R	compact disc-recordable	366
CD-R drive	compact disc-recordable drive	366
CD-ROM	compact disc read-only memory	363-64
CD-ROM drive	compact disc read-only memory drive	363
CD-ROM jukebox	compact disc read-only memory jukebox	744
CD-ROM server	compact disc read-only memory server	744
CD-RW	compact disc-rewritable	366, 586
CD-RW drive	compact disc-rewritable drive	366
CD-RW/DVD	compact disc-rewritable drive/digital video disc	368
CE	computer engineering	776
CERT/CC	Computer Emergency Response Team Coordination Center	587
CF	CompactFlash	372
CGI	Common Gateway Interface	680, 699
CGI script	Common Gateway Interface script	680, 699
CIM	computer-integrated manufacturing	724
CIO	chief information officer	725, 750, 772
CIS	computer information systems	775
CIW	Certified Internet Webmaster	789
CMOS	complementary metal-oxide semiconductor	200
CMOS chip	complementary metal-oxide semiconductor chip	396
CMS	content management system	732
CNA	Certified Novell Administrator	788
CNE	Certified Novell Engineer	788
Coax	coaxial cable	490
COBOL	COmmon Business-Oriented Language	668
COM port	communications port	205
COM+	Component Object Model extension	690
COMDEX	Computer Dealer Expo	779
COO	Chief Operations Officer	716
CORBA	Common Object Request Broker Architecture	690
CPU	central processing unit	8, 183
CRM	customer relationship management	31, 732
CRT	cathode-ray tube	294
CRT monitor	cathode-ray tube monitor	294-98
CS	computer science	775
CSDP	Certified Software Development Professional	787
CSO	chief security officer	749
CSS	cascading style sheets	682
CTS	carpal tunnel syndrome	598
CVS	computer vision syndrome	599
CWP	Certified Web Professional	789

Acronym	Description	Page
DA	database analyst	541, 772
DAC	digital-to-analog converter	39, 321
DBA	database administrator	541, 773
DBMS	database management system	517
DC	direct current	211
DDoS attack	distributed denial of service attack	587
DDR SDRAM	double data rate synchronous dynamic random access memory	196
DDWG	Digital Display Working Group	301
DFD	data flow diagram	633
DHCP	Dynamic Host Configuration Protocol	103
DHTML	Dynamic Hypertext Markup Language	682
DIAD	Delivery Information Acquisition Device	21
DIMM	dual inline memory module	196
DIP	dual inline package	183
DL	distance learning	162
DLP projector	digital light processing projector	316
DNA	Windows Distributed interNet Applications	415
DNS	domain name system	74
DNS server	domain name system server	74, 103
DOM	document object model	682
DOS	Disk Operating System	410
DoS attack	denial of service attack	587
Dpi	dots per inch	250, 306
DPMA	Data Processing Management Association	778
DRAM	dynamic random access memory	196
DRM	Digital Rights Management	411
DSL	Digital Subscriber Line	71, 481-82
DSL modem	Digital Subscriber Line modem	484
DSP	digital signal processor	39, 248
DSS	decision support system	728
DTD	document type definition	699
DTP	desktop publishing	151
DTP software	desktop publishing software	151
DTV	digital television	302
DV camera	digital video camera	250
DVD	digital versatile disc or digital video disc	8, 361-62
DVD drive	digital versatile disc or digital video disc drive	9, 14, 210
DVD writer	digital versatile disc or digital video disc writer	369
DVD-R	digital versatile disc or digital video disc recordable	369
DVD+RAM	digital versatile disc or digital video disc + random access memory	369
DVD-ROM	digital versatile disc or digital video disc read-only memory	9, 368
DVD-ROM drive	digital versatile disc or digital video disc read-only memory drive	368
DVD-ROM jukebox	digital versatile disc or digital video disc read-only memory jukebox	744
DVD-ROM server	digital versatile disc or digital video disc read-only memory server	744
DVD+RW	digital versatile disc or digital video disc + rewriteable	369
DVD+RW drive	digital versatile disc or digital video disc + rewriteable drive	369

Acronym	Description	Page
DVD-video format	digital versatile disc or digital video disc-video format	368
DVI	Digital Video Interface	301
DVI port	Digital Video Interface port	301
Dynamic IP address	dynamic Internet protocol address	108
EBCDIC	Extended Binary Coded Decimal Interchange	192, 519
E-book	electronic book	300
E-commerce	electronic commerce	29, 31, 90-91
E-commerce administrator	electronic commerce administrator	772
ECPA	Electronic Communications Privacy Act	597
EDI	electronic data interchange	470, 734
EEPROM	electrically erasable programmable read-only memory	198
E-filing	electronic filing	156
E-form	electronic form	532, 536
EFT	electronic funds transfer	471
EIDE	Enhanced Integrated Drive Electronics	360
EIS	executive information system	728
E-mail	electronic mail	13, 68, 90-91
E-mail address	electronic mail address	93
E-mail filtering	electronic mail filtering	595
E-mail program	electronic mail program	92, 160
E-money	electronic money	374, 738
EMR	electromagnetic radiation	296
Enterprise ASP	enterprise application service provider	162
EP	Enterprise Portal	544
EP solutions	Enterprise Portal solutions	544
ePurses	electronic Purses	722
Erasable CD	compact disc-erasable	366
ERD	entity-relationship diagram	632
E-retail	electronic retail	738
ERM system	employee relationship management system	721
ERP	enterprise resource planning	730
E-tags	electronic tags	602
E-tail	electronic retail	738
EULA	end-user license agreement	581
Extensible HTML	Extensible Hypertext Markup Language	682
E-zine	electronic magazine	639
FAQ	frequently asked questions	100, 163
Fax	facsimile	315-16
Fax machine	facsimile machine	315-16
Fax modem	facsimile modem	315
FC-PGA	flip chip-PGA	183
FORTRAN	FORmula TRANslator	685
FTP	File Transfer Protocol	95
FTP server	File Transfer Protocol server	95, 478
GB	gigabyte	194
GHz	gigahertz	186
GIF	Graphics Interchange Format	85, 86
GIGO	garbage in, garbage out	10, 517
GPRS	General Packet Radio Service	492

Acronym	Description	Page
GPS	global positioning system	466, 513, 724
GPS receiver	global positioning system receiver	466-68, 513
GPU	graphics processing unit	298
GSM	Global System for Mobile Communications	492
GUI	graphical user interface	14, 135, 398, 413, 414
HD	high density	352
HDTV	high-definition television	302
HomeRF network	home radio frequency network	487, 510
HPA	high-performance addressing	301
HRIS	Human Resources Information Systems	720
HTML	Hypertext Markup Language	678-79
http	Hypertext Transfer Protocol	77
Hz	hertz	186
I-4	International Information Integrity Institute	605
IAD	Internet addiction disorder	601
IBM	International Business Machines	752
IC	integrated circuit	182, 217
ICANN	Internet Corporation for Assigned Names and Numbers	74
I-CASE	integrated computer-aided software engineering	644
ICCP	Institute for Certification of Computer Professionals	783
ICRA	Internet Content Rating Association	598
ICSA Labs	International Computer Security Association Labs	750
IDE controllers	Integrated Device Electronics controllers	360
IM	instant messaging	98
IMDb	Internet Movie Database	538, 539
Interactive TV	interactive television	302
IP	intellectual property	590
IP address	Internet Protocol address	74, 103
IPng	Internet protocol Next Generation	103
IPO chart	input, processing, output chart	687
IPv6	Internet Protocol version 6	103
IR	infrared	265, 492
IrDA	Infrared Data Association	207, 477
IrDA port	Infrared Data Association port	477
IRQ	interrupt request	403
IRS	Internal Revenue Service	647
IS	information system	24, 620, 719-32
ISA bus	Industry Standard Architecture bus	210
ISDN	Integrated Services Digital Network	71, 481
ISDN modem	Integrated Services Digital Network modem	484
ISP	Internet service provider	72
IT	information technology	716-717
IT department	information technology department	31, 768
IT instructor	information technology instructor	786, 790
ITAA	Information Technology Association of America	768
J2EE	Java 2 Platform Enterprise Edition	464, 670, 736
JAD session	joint-application design session	626
JIT compiler	just-in-time compiler	670, 671
JPEG	Joint Photographic Experts Group	84, 337
K	kilobyte	194
KB	kilobyte	194

Acronym	Description	Page
KBps	kilobytes per second	351, 364
KM	knowledge management	730
KMS	knowledge management software	730
L1 cache	Level 1 cache	198
L2 cache	Level 2 cache	198
L3 cache	Level 3 cache	198
LAN	local area network	471, 474, 475
LCD	liquid crystal display	300, 447
LCD monitor	liquid crystal display monitor	299-302
LCD projector	liquid crystal display projector	316
LISP	LISt Processing	685
Local/regional ASP	local/regional application service provider	162
LQ	letter-quality	305
Mac OS	Macintosh Operating System	19
Mac OS X	Macintosh Operating System X	133, 135, 413
MAN	metropolitan area network	471
MB	megabyte	194
MBps	megabytes per second	351, 360
MCAD	Microsoft Certified Application Developer	787
M-Cash	mobile cash	493
MCDBA	Microsoft Certified Database Administrator	789
MCDST	Microsoft Certified Desktop Support Technician	786
M-commerce	mobile commerce	90
MCP	Microsoft Certified Professional	787
MCSD	Microsoft Certified Solution Developer	787
MHz	megahertz	200
MICR	magnetic-ink character recognition	257
MICR reader	magnetic-ink character recognition reader	257
MIDI	Musical Instrument Digital Interface	207, 243
MIDI port	Musical Instrument Digital Interface port	207
Mini-DVD media	mini-digital video disc media	369
MIPS	millions of instructions per second	186
MIS	management information system	727
MIS manager	management information systems manager	750
MLP	multilayer perception	751
MMS	multimedia message service	468
Modem	modulate/demodulate	9, 462, 483-84
MP	million pixels	249
MPEG	Moving Pictures Experts Group	88
MPEG-4	Moving Pictures Experts Group 4	88
MRAM	magnetoresistive random access memory	196
MRP	Material Requirements Planning	722
MRP II	Manufacturing Resource Planning II	722
MSD	musculoskeletal disorder	598
MS-DOS	Microsoft Disk Operating System	410, 421
MSN	Microsoft Network, The	72, 82
MSN Hotmail	Microsoft Network Hotmail	93
Multiread CD drive	multiread compact disc drive	366
NACSE NNT	National Association of Communication Systems Engineers Network Technician	788
NAS	network attached storage	743-44, 745

Acronym	Description	Page
National ID card	national identification card	521
National ISP	national Internet service provider	72
Netiquette	Internet etiquette	100, 463
Network OS	network operating system	404, 415-16
NIC	network interface card	485
NLQ	near letter quality	304
Ns	nanosecond	200
NSF	National Science Foundation	69, 70
NTSC	National Television Standards Committee	69
NTSC converter	National Television Standards Committee converter	69
OCR	optical character recognition	254
OCR devices	optical character recognition devices	254
OCR software	optical character recognition software	254
Offline UPS	offline uninterruptible power supply	585
OIS	office information system	726
OLAP	online analytical processing	545, 728
OLED	organic light emitting diode	301
OLTP	online transaction processing	726
OMR	optical mark recognition	255
Online UPS	online uninterruptible power supply	585
OO analysis and design	object-oriented analysis and design	635
OO design	object-oriented design	689-90
OODB	object-oriented database	536
OOP language	object-oriented programming language	669
OQL	object query language	537
OS	operating system	15-16, 392-417
OSI reference model	Open Systems Interconnection reference model	495
OSP	online service provider	72
P2P	peer-to-peer	473-74
Palm OS	Palm operating system	417
PC	personal computer	18-19
PC Card	personal computer card	202, 370-73
PC camera	personal computer camera	250
PC Card bus	personal computer card bus	210
PC Card modem	personal computer card modem	483
PC Card slot	personal computer card slot	202
PC video camera	personal computer video camera	250-51
PC-compatible	personal computer compatible	19
PCD file format	photo compact disc file format	365
PC-DOS	personal computer Disk Operating System	410
PCI bus	Peripheral Component Interconnect bus	210
PCL	Printer Control Language	309
PCMCIA	Personal Computer Memory Card International Association	202
PCMCIA cards	Personal Computer Memory Card International Association cards	202, 371

Acronym	Description	Page
PCS	Personal Communications Services	492
PC-to-TV port	personal computer-to-television port	444
PDA	personal digital assistant	21
PDL	page description language	309
Perl	Practical Extraction and Report Language	681
Personal DTP software	personal desktop publishing software	157
PGA	pin grid array	183
PGP	Pretty Good Privacy	589
PhotoCD	photo compact disc	365
Picture CD	picture compact disc	365
PILOT	Programmed Inquiry Learning Or Teaching	685
PIM	personal information manager	148
PIN	personal identification number	259, 578
Pixel	picture element	249, 294
PL/I	Programming Language One	685
PNG format	Portable Network Graphics format	85
POP	point of presence	71
POP	Post Office Protocol	93
POP3	Post Office Protocol 3	93
POS	point of sale	258
POS terminal	point of sale terminal	258
POST	power-on self test	396
ppi	pixels (picture elements) per inch	249
Prolog	PROgramming LOGic	685
PROM chip	programmable read-only memory chip	198
PSTN	public switched telephone network	480
Pure Tablet PCs	Pure Tablet personal computers	446
QBE	query by example	531
RAD	rapid application development	671
RAID	redundant array of independent disks	742
RAM	random access memory	194, 195-97
RAM chips	random access memory chips	396
Rambus DRAM	Rambus dynamic random access memory	196
RDF site summary	Resource Description Framework Site Summary	683
RDRAM	Rambus dynamic random access memory	196
Regional ISP	regional Internet service provider	72
RF	radio frequency	265
RFI	request for information	640
RFID	radio frequency identification	31, 477
RFP	request for proposal	640
RFQ	request for quotation	640
RHCE	Red Hat Certified Engineer	787
RHCT	Red Hat Certified Technician	787
RHD	removable hard disk	359
RIMM	Rambus inline memory module	196
ROM	read-only memory	198
ROM chips	read-only memory chips	395
RPG	Report Program Generator	674

Acronym	Description	Page
Rpm	revolutions per minute	357
RSA encryption	Rivest-Shamir-Adleman encryption	603
RSI	repetitive strain injury	598
RSS specification	Rich Site Summary specification	683
RUP	Rational Unified Process	636
SAN	storage area network	743
SCSI	small computer system interface	207
SCSI controller	small computer system interface controller	360
SCSI port	small computer system interface port	207
SD	Secure Digital	372
SDRAM	synchronous dynamic random access memory	196
Secure HTTP	secure hypertext transfer protocol	587, 588
SET Specification	Secure Electronics Transactions Specification	588
SFA	sales force automation	723
S-HTTP	secure hypertext transfer protocol	588
SIGs	Special Interest Groups	778
SIMM	single inline memory module	196
SMS	short message service	246, 468
SMTP	simple mail transfer protocol	93
SOHO	small office/home office	28
Specialist ASP	specialist application service provider	162
SPOT	Smart Personal Objects Technology	637
SQL	Structured Query Language	536, 675
SQL programmers	Structured Query Language programmers	787
SRAM	static random access memory	196
SSL	Secure Sockets Layer	588
Standby UPS	standby uninterruptible power supply	585
Static IP addresses	static Internet protocol addresses	103
SUT	system under test	649
SVGA	super video graphics array	298
Symbian OS	Symbian operating system	417
Synchronous DRAM	synchronous dynamic random access memory	196
System cost per WIPS	system cost per Web Interactions Per Second	649
TCP/IP	Transmission Control Protocol/Internet Protocol	476
TFT display	thin-film transistor display	301
TIFF	Tagged Image File Format	85, 337
TPC-W	Transaction Processing Performance Council Workload	649
TPS	transaction processing system	726
TRACERT	traceroute	421
UL 1449 standard	Underwriters Laboratories 1449 standard	585
UML	Unified Modeling Language	636
UMTS	Universal Mobile Telecommunications System	492
UPC	Universal Product Code	256
UPS	uninterruptible power supply	585
URL	Uniform Resource Locator	76
USB	universal serial bus	210
USB 2.0	universal serial bus 2.0	206
USB flash drive	universal serial bus flash drive	9, 349, 373
USB hub	universal serial bus hub	206
USB port	universal serial bus port	204, 206
USB transfer rate	universal serial bus transfer rate	360
User ID	user identification	404, 576
VAN	value-added network	471
VAR	value-added reseller	640
VB .NET 2003	Visual Basic .NET 2003	672-73
VBA	Visual Basic for Applications	676
VBScript	Visual Basic, Scripting Edition	681
VCD	video CD	345
Vertical market ASP	vertical market application service provider	162
VESA	Video Electronics Standards Association	298
VESA local bus	Video Electronics Standards Association local bus	210
VoiceXML	Voice eXtensible Markup Language	531
VoIP	voice over Internet protocol	464
Volume business ASP	volume business application service provider	162
VPE	visual programming environment	671
VPN	virtual private network	583, 737
VPN tunnel	virtual private network tunnel	737
VR	virtual reality	88
VR world	virtual reality world	88
W3C	World Wide Web Consortium	70, 105
WAN	wide area network	472
WAP	Wireless Application Protocol	477, 683
WBT	Web-based training	162, 779
Wi-Fi	wireless fidelity	476
Windows DNA	Windows Distributed interNet Applications	415
WIPS	Web Interactions Per Second	649
Wireless LAN	wireless local area network	471
Wireless LAN Access Point	wireless local area network Access Point	438
WIRT	Web Interaction Response Time	649
WISP	wireless Internet service provider	466
WLAN	wireless local area network	471
WML	wireless markup language	683
WWW	World Wide Web	75
WYSIWYG	what you see is what you get	135
XHTML	eXtensible Hypertext Markup Language	682
XML	eXtensible Markup Language	464, 682-83, 699, 735
XP	extreme programming	695-96
XSL	Extensible Stylesheet Language	699
XSLT	Extensible Style Language Transformations	699
Y2K bug	year 2000 bug	697
ZIF	zero-insertion force	189

INDEX

PHOTO CREDITS

Cover: keyboard, mouse, CD, and satellite © 2002 Dynamic Graphics; monitor and man with PDA, © 2002-2004 ArtToday, Inc.; flash drive and memory cardholder, Courtesy of SanDisk®. ***Chapter 1:*** *PY2* tablet PC, Courtesy of Microsoft Corporation; *PY3* black Corvette, © Ride & Drive Features; *PY4* man looking at camera, © PhotoDisc/Getty Images; *PY5* Pocket PC, Courtesy of ViewSonic® Corporation. All rights reserved.; *Figure 1-1a* couple at computer, © Darama/CORBIS; *Figure 1-1b* boy with PDA, David Roth/Getty Images; *Figure 1-1c* teen at laptop, Gen Nishino/Getty Images; *Figure 1-1d* couple with tablet PC, Courtesy of Microsoft Corporation; *Figure 1-1e* man with PDA, © Kaz Chiba/Getty Images; *Figure 1-2* receipt, © Eyewire/Getty Images; *Figure 1-3a* cable modem, Courtesy of Linksys; *Figure 1-3b* computer, speakers, camera, Courtesy of Sony Electronics Inc., Courtesy of Logitech Inc.; *Figure 1-3c* inkjet printer, Courtesy of EPSON America Inc.; *Figure 1-3d* card reader/writer, Courtesy of SanDisk Corporation; *Figure 1-3e* digital camera, Courtesy of Logitech Inc.; *Figure 1-3f* USB flash drive, Courtesy of TrekStor USA; *Figure 1-3g* microphone, Courtesy of Telex Communications Inc.; *Figure 1-3h* flatbed scanner, Courtesy of EPSON America Inc.; *Figure 1-4* 3.5 floppy, © PhotoDisc/Getty Images; *Figure 1-5* USB flash drive, © 2004 DiskOnKey. All rights reserved.; *Figure 1-6* hard disk, Courtesy of Seagate Technology; *Figure 1-7* DVD-ROM drive, © Scott Goodwin Photography; *Figure 1-15* man looking at software, © Scott Goodwin Photography; *Looking Ahead 1-1* wearable computer, Courtesy of Xybernaut Corporation; *Looking Ahead 1-1* mechanic, Courtesy of Xybernaut Corporation; *Figure 1-18* personal computer, Courtesy of International Business Machines Corporation; *Figure 1-19* iMac 17", Courtesy of Apple Computer; *Figure 1-20* laptop, Courtesy of Dell Computer Corporation; *Figure 1-21* tablet PC, Courtesy of ViewSonic® Corporation. All rights reserved.; *Figure 1-22* UPS DIAD, Courtesy of United Parcel Service of America, Inc.; *Figure 1-23a* PDA, Courtesy of Handspring, Inc.; *Figure 1-23b* PDA, Courtesy of Toshiba America Inc.; *Figure 1-24* smart phone, Courtesy of © Siemens AG, Munich/Berlin; *Figure 1-25* midrange server, Courtesy of Sun Microsystems, Inc.; *Figure 1-26* mainframe computer, Courtesy of IBM Corporation; *Figure 1-27* supercomputer, Courtesy of International Business Machines Corporation; *Figure 1-28, Step 3* printer, © Eyewire/Getty Images; *Figure 1-29a* woman eating salad, © Gary Buss/Getty Images; *Figure 1-29b* man videoconferencing, © Ulf Wallin/Getty Images; *Figure 1-29c* mobile user, Courtesy of Nokia. Copyright © 2002 Nokia. All rights reserved. Nokia and Nokia Connecting People are registered trademarks of Nokia Corporation.; *Figure 1-29d* workers in cubicles, © Charles Gupton/CORBIS; *Figure 1-29e* man at workstation, © L. Lefkowitz /Getty Images; *Figure 1-30* woman eating salad, © Gary Buss/Getty Images; *Figure 1-31* father using PC video, © Jose Luis Pelaez, Inc./CORBIS; *Figure 1-32* wireless internet keyboard, Courtesy of RCA; *Figure 1-33* man videoconferencing, © Ulf Wallin/Getty Images; *Figure 1-35a* PDA, Courtesy of Microsoft Corporation; *Figure 1-35b* young woman and laptop, Courtesy of Nokia Networks; *Figure 1-35c* smart phone, Courtesy of Motorola; *Figure 1-35d* young woman and cell phone, © Darren Robb/Getty Images; *Figure 1-36* notebook, © Britt Erlanson/Getty Images; *Figure 1-37* workers in cubicles, © Charles Gupton/ CORBIS; *Figure 1-39* woman at kiosk, Courtesy of NCR Corporation; *Figure 1-40* woman working at home, ©LWA- JDC/CORBIS; *Figure 1-41* man at workstation, © L. Lefkowitz /Getty Images; *Looking Ahead 1-2* robot pet, © AFP/CORBIS; *Figure 1-42* students in computer lab, © Digital Vision/Getty Images; *Figure 1-45* technician looking at cat scan, © Lester Lefkowitz/CORBIS; *Figure 1-46, Step 1* capsule, © AP/Wide World Photos; *Figure 1-46, Step 3* doctor, © Allan H. Shoemake/Getty Images; *Figure 1-48* Saab, Courtesy of Saab Cars USA; *Figure 1-48* OnStar call button, Courtesy of OnStar; *Figure 1-48* customer service rep, © CORBIS; *Figure 1-49* robotic welding, © Luis Castaneda/Getty Images; *Technology Trailblazer* Bill Gates, © Reuters New Media Inc./CORBIS; *Technology Trailblazer* Carly Fiorina, © Reuters New Media Inc./CORBIS. ***Special Feature ~ Timeline:*** *1937* Clifford Berry, Courtesy of Iowa State University; *1937* Atanasoff-Berry-Computer (ABC), Courtesy of Iowa State University; *1937* Dr. John V. Atanasoff, Courtesy of Iowa State University; *1943* Alan Turing, Courtesy of The Computer History Museum; *1943* Colossus computer, Courtesy of The Computer History Museum; *1945* Dr. John von Neumann, Courtesy of the Archives of the Institute for Advanced Study; *1945* Dr. von Neumann with computer, Courtesy of the Archives of the Institute for Advanced Study; *1946* The ENIAC (Electronic Numerical Integrator and Computer), Courtesy of the Collections of the University of Pennsylvania Archives; *1947* transfer resistance device (transistor), © IBM Corporate Archives; *1947* transistor, © IBM Corporate Archives; *1951* Univac I (UNIVersal Automatic Computer), Courtesy Unisys Corporation; *1952* Dr. Grace Hopper, Courtesy of Hagley Museum and Library; *1953* IBM model 650, Courtesy of © IBM Corporate Archives; *1957* Fortran (FORmula TRANslation), Courtesy of © IBM Corporate Archives; *1957* IBM 305 RAMAC system, Courtesy of © IBM Corporate Archives; *1957* magnetic disks, Courtesy of the Department of the Navy; *1958* Jack Kilby, Courtesy of Texas Instruments; *1958,* integrated circuit, Courtesy of Texas Instruments; *1958* integrated circuit, Courtesy of Texas Instruments; *1959* IBM 1602 CADET, Courtesy of © IBM Corporate Archives; *1960* Dr. Grace Hopper, Courtesy of Hagley Museum and Library; *1964* computer chip, Courtesy of © IBM Corporate Archives; *1964* typewriter, Courtesy © IBM Corporate Archives; *1964* IBM System/360, Courtesy of © IBM Corporate Archives; *1965* Dr. John Kenney of Dartmouth, Courtesy of Dartmouth College; *1965* first mini-computer (PDP-8), Courtesy of Digital Equipment Corporation; *1970* LSI (large-scale integration) chip, Courtesy of © IBM Corporate Archives; *1971* Dr. Ted Hoff, Courtesy of Intel Corporation; *1971* Intel 4004, Courtesy of Intel Corporation; *1975* Bob Metcalfe, Courtesy of InfoWorld; *1975* Altair photo, Courtesy of The Computer History Museum; *1976* first Apple Computer, Courtesy of Apple Computer Corporation; *1976* Steve Wozniak and Steve Jobs, © Bettmann/CORBIS; *1979,* Bob Frankston and Dan Bricklin, Courtesy of The Computer History Museum; *1980* Alan Shugart, Courtesy of © IBM Corporate Archives; *1980* Bill Gates, Courtesy of Microsoft® Corporation; *1981* IBM PC, Courtesy of © IBM Corporate Archives; *1982* Hayes 300 bps smart modem, Courtesy of Zoom Telephonics, Inc.; *1983* Lotus 1-2-3, Courtesy of © IBM Corporate Archives; *1983* magazine cover, © 2001 Time Inc. Reprinted by permission.; *1984* laser-jet printer, Courtesy of Hewlett-Packard Company; *1984* IBM's PC AT using Intel 80286, Courtesy of © IBM Corporate Archives; *1984* Macintosh computer, Courtesy of Apple Computer Corporation; *1987* Personal computer using Intel 80386, Courtesy of © IBM Corporate Archives; *1989* Intel 486 transistor microprocessor, Courtesy of Intel Corporation; *1989* Tim Berners-Lee, © 1997-*1998* W3C (MIT, INRIA, Keio); *1992* Windows 3.1, Courtesy of Microsoft® Corporation; *1993* Intel Pentium processor chip, Courtesy of Intel Corporation; *1993* Marc Andreessen, © Jim Clark/Getty Images; *1993* Mosaic and Netscape logo, Courtesy of Netscape Communications Corporation; *1994* Netscape Navigator 1.0, Courtesy of Netscape Communications Corporation; *1995* Windows 95 box shot, Courtesy of Microsoft® Corporation; *1995* Java logo, Courtesy of Sun Microsystems, Inc.; *1996* Microsoft Windows NT 4.0 Server box shot, Courtesy of Microsoft® Corporation; *1996* summer Olympics, © Reuters/Rick T. Wilking/ Archive Photos; *1996* Webtv, Courtesy of Microsoft® Corporation; *1997* Intel Pentium II, Courtesy of Intel Corporation; *1997* Terminator DVD, Courtesy of Motion Picture & Television Archives; *1997* DVD player, Courtesy of Denon Electronics; *1997* Gary Kasparov, I. Uiomonen/CORBIS Sygma; *1998* Windows 98 box shot, Courtesy of Microsoft® Corporation; *1998* iMac, Courtesy of Apple Computer Corporation; *1999* Microsoft Office 2000 box shot, Courtesy of Microsoft® Corporation; *2000* Microsoft Windows Me box shot, Courtesy of Microsoft® Corporation; *2000* Microsoft's Windows 2000 Professional box shot, Courtesy of Microsoft® Corporation; *2000* Intel Pentium 4 chip, Courtesy of Intel Corporation; *2001* Windows XP, box shot, Courtesy of Microsoft® Corporation; *2001* Office XP Standard box shot, Courtesy of Microsoft® Corporation; *2002* DVD drive, © Scott Goodwin Photography; *2002* digital video camera, video editing software, Courtesy of Sharp Electronics; *2002* Handspring TREO, Courtesy of Handspring, Inc.; *2002* Pentium 4, Courtesy of Intel Corporation; *2002* e-book, Courtesy of RCA/Thomson Consumer Electronics; *2002* judge with gavel, © PhotoDisc/Getty Images; *2003 t*ablet PC, Courtesy of ViewSonic® Corporation All rights reserved.; *2003* Palm VIIx, Courtesy of palmOne, Inc. palmOne, Zire, and Tungsten are among the trademarks owned by or exclusively licensed to palmOne, Inc.; *2003* computer with bugs, © Artville/Getty Images; *2003* wireless devices, Courtesy of Fujitsu Siemens Computers; *2003* wireless device, © PhotoDisc/Getty Images; *2003* downloading graphic, © PhotoDisc/Getty Images; *2003* recording industry Association of America (RIAA), © REUTERS/Mannie Garcia; *2003* Microsoft Office 2003 box shot, Courtesy of Microsoft® Corporation; *2004* monitor, Courtesy of Sony Electronics Inc.; *2004* monitor, Courtesy of ViewSonic® Corporation All rights reserved.; *2004* USB flash drive, © Transcend Information Inc. All rights reserved.; *2004* USB flash drive, Courtesy of Sandisk Corporation; *2004* RFID tags, Courtesy of © Siemens AG, Munich/Berlin; *2004* photo, © Photos.com. ***Chapter 2:*** *Figure 2-2f* PDA with wireless connection, Courtesy of Symbol Technologies, Inc.; *Figure 2-7a* PDA, Courtesy of palmOne, Inc., palmOne, Zire, and Tungsten are among the trademarks owned by or exclusively licensed to palmOne, Inc.; *Figure 2-7c* smart phone, Courtesy of Nokia; *Figure 2-7d* microbrowser screen for Smartphone, Courtesy of AT&T Wireless; *Looking Ahead 2-1* woman with notebook, © PhotoDisc/Getty Images; *Figure 2-23* woman with credit card, © Ron Chapple/Getty Images; *Figure 2-25* man at computer, © PhotoDisc/Getty Images; *Figure 2-26* desktop computer, Courtesy of IBM Corporation; *Looking Ahead 2-2* in-car navigation, © NOGUES Ala/Corbis Sygma; *Figure 2-18* PC, Courtesy of IBM Corporation; *Figure 2-30* man at computer, © PhotoDisc/Getty Images; *Figure 2-33, Step 1* woman, © Walter Hodges/CORBIS; *Figure 2-33, Step 2* woman's hand, © Walter Hodges/CORBIS; *Figure 2-33, Step 3,4,5* woman, © AJA Productions/Getty Images; *Career Corner,* web developer, © Andreas Pollock/Getty Images; *Technology Trailblazer* Tim Berners-Lee, © Sam Ogden/Photo Researchers, Inc.; *Technology Trailblazer* Anita Brown, Courtesy of Anita Brown. ***Chapter 3:*** *Figure 3-3* printer, © Eyewire/Getty Images; *Figure 3-9* woman with headset, © PhotoDisc/Getty Images; *Figure 3-17* One-Note software, Courtesy of Microsoft® Corporation; *Figure 3-18a* PDA in cradle, Courtesy of Dell Computer Corporation; *Figure 3-18b* PDA in cradle, Courtesy of Sony Electronics Inc.; *Looking Ahead 3-1* "downloading" graphic, © PhotoDisc/Getty Images; *Figure 3-22* engineers, © Greg Pease/Getty Images; *Figure 3-23* screen shot of DTP software, Courtesy of Quark, Inc.; *Figure 3-24* screen shot of image editing software, Courtesy of Ulead Systems, Inc.; *Figure 3-25* screen shot of video editing software, Courtesy of Ulead Systems, Inc.; *Figure 3-28* woman with checkbook, © PhotoDisc/Getty Images; *Figure 3-29* legal software, Courtesy of Cosmi Corporation; *Figure 3-30* tax software, Courtesy of Intuit; *Figure 3-32* paint/image editing programs, Courtesy of Adobe; *Figure 3-34,* 3D Home Landscape Designer Deluxe 5 box shot, Courtesy of © 2003 Riverdeep Interactive Learning Limited; *Figure 3-35* soldier, © AFP/CORBIS; *Looking Ahead 3-2* plagiarism, © PhotoDisc/Getty Images; *Figure 3-43* man in software book aisle, © Scott Goodwin Photography; *Career Corner* woman with headset, Eyewire © 2002 Eyewire Collection; *High Tech Talk* computer bugs, Artville © Copyright 1999-2003 Getty Images, Inc. All rights reserved.; *Technology Trailblazer* Dan Bricklin, © Louis Fabian Bachrach/Daniel Bricklin; *Technology Trailblazer* Masayoshi Son, © Reuters New Media Inc./CORBIS; *Upper left hand page folio* woman with headphone, © PhotoDisc/Getty Images; *Upper right hand page folio* finger on keyboard, © PhotoDisc/Getty Images. ***Chapter 4:*** *Figure 4-1a* desktop computer, Courtesy of IBM Corporation; *Figure 4-1b* Apple iMac – 17", Courtesy of Apple Computer Corporation; *Figure 4-1c* tablet PC, Courtesy of Microsoft® Corporation; *Figure 4-1d* laptop computer, Courtesy of Gateway, Inc.; *Figure 4-1e* PDA, Courtesy of Microsoft® Corporation; *Figure 4-1e* PDA screen, Courtesy of Microsoft® Corporation; *Figure 4-2a* open computer © Scott Goodwin Photography; *Figure 4-2b* Intel P4 chip, Courtesy of Intel Corporation; *Figure 4-2c* memory card, Courtesy of Kingston Technology Company, Inc.; *Figure 4-2d* sound card, Courtesy of Creative Labs, Inc.; *Figure 4-2e* video card, Courtesy of Matrox Graphics, Inc.; *Figure 4-2f* modem card, Courtesy of Creative Labs, Inc.; *Figure 4-2g* network card, Courtesy of 3Com Corporation; *Figure 4-3* motherboard, © Scott Goodwin Photography; *Figure 4-4a* finger, © James A. Sugar/CORBIS; *Figure 4-4c* Lab tech holding Intel Pentium 4 PGA, Courtesy of Intel Corporation; *Figure 4-4b* memory chips, © PhotoDisc/Getty Images; *Figure 4-4d* Intel Pentium 4 pin grid array (PGA), Courtesy of Intel Corporation; *Figure 4-6* man with computer, © PhotoDisc/Getty Images; *Figure 4-9a* Itanium chip, Courtesy of Intel Corporation; *Figure 4-9b* Xeon chip, Courtesy of Intel Corporation; *Figure 4-9c* Pentium 4 processor, Courtesy of Intel Corporation; *Figure 4-9d* Celeron, Courtesy of Intel Corporation; *Figure 4-10, Step 1* Zero-force insertion socket, © Scott Goodwin Photography; *Figure 4-10, Step 2* Zero-force insertion socket, © Scott Goodwin Photography; *Figure 4-10, Step 3* Zero-force insertion socket, © Scott Goodwin Photography; *Figure 4-11* heat sink, Courtesy of HLS Systems, Inc.; *Figure 4-16, Step 2* open system unit, © Scott Goodwin Photography; *Figure 4-17a* passenger train, Courtesy of Amtrak; *Figure 4-17b* train seats, © PhotoDisc/Getty Images; *Figure 4-19a* hard disk drive, Courtesy of Seagate Technology; *Figure 4-19b* memory module, Courtesy of Kingston Technology Company, Inc.; *Figure 4-20a* memory module inserted into motherboard, © Scott Goodwin Photography; *Figure 4-20b* memory module, Courtesy of Kingston Technology Company, Inc.; *Figure 4-21* Norton utilities box shot, Courtesy of Symantec Corp.; *Figure 4-24* mp3 player, Courtesy of RCA/Thomson Consumer Electronics; *Looking Ahead 4-1* Ovonic memory, © 2000 IEEE; *Figure 4-26a* one eye open, © Scott Goodwin Photography; *Figure 4-26b* one eye closed, © Scott Goodwin Photography; *Figure 4-28* adaptor card, © Scott Goodwin Photography; *Figure 4-29* PC card, © Scott Goodwin Photography; *Figure 4-30a* compact Flash card 4.0GB, Courtesy of Sandisk Corporation; *Figure 4-30b* memory stick 256 MB, Courtesy of Sandisk Corporation; *Figure 4-30c* SD card 1.0GB, Courtesy of Sandisk Corporation; *Figure 4-30d* Smart media card 128 MB, Courtesy of Sandisk Corporation; *Figure 4-30e* 512 MB xD-Picture Card, Courtesy of Sandisk Corporation; *Figure 4-37* smart phone with IrDA, Courtesy of Nokia; *Figure 4-31a* ports on back of system unit, © Scott Goodwin Photography; *Figure 4-31b* ports on front of system unit, Courtesy of Symantec Corp.; *Figure 4-32* back of system unit with ports plugged, © Scott Goodwin Photography; *Figure 4-38* Intel pentium 4 processor, Courtesy of Intel Corporation; *Figure 4-39* memory card, Courtesy of Kingston Technology Company, Inc.; *Figure 4-39* Intel chipset, Courtesy of Intel Corporation; *Figure 4-40* DVD, CD drive, ZIP drive bays, Courtesy of Symantec Corp.; *Figure 4-41a* notebook computer, © Scott Goodwin Photography; *Figure 4-41b* PDA with flash memory card, Courtesy of palmOne, Inc. palmOne, Zire, and Tungsten are among the trademarks owned by or exclusively licensed to palmOne, Inc.; *Figure 4-42a* motherboard of a notebook computer, © Scott Goodwin Photography; *Figure 4-42b* motherboard of a PDA, © Scott Goodwin Photography; *Figure 4-43* back ports of notebook computer, © Scott Goodwin Photography; *Figure 4-44* tablet PC, Courtesy of Microsoft® Corporation; *Figure 4-45a* woman eating salad, © Gary Buss/Getty Images; *Figure 4-45b* man videoconferencing, © Ulf Wallin/Getty Images; *Figure 4-45c* young woman working on laptop, Courtesy of Nokia; *Figure 4-45d* workers in cubicles, © Charles Gupton/CORBIS; *Figure 4-45e* man at workstation, © L. Lefkowitz/Getty Images; *Looking Ahead 4-2* rat robots, © 2001 Time Inc. Reprinted by permission.; *Career Corner* Computer Engineer, Courtesy of Intel Corporation; *Technology Trailblazer 1* Jack Kilby, © AFP/CORBIS; *Technology Trailblazer 2* Gordon Moore, © Borensztein, Leon/TimePix; *Upper left hand corner* image, © PhotoDisc/Getty Images; *Upper right hand corner,* motherboard, © Scott Goodwin Photography. ***Chapter 5:*** *Opener 1* Veo PDA camera, Courtesy of Veo Inc.; *Opener 2* socket PDA scan, Courtesy of Socket Communications, Inc.; *Opener 3* Belkin foldable keyboard, Courtesy of Belkin Corporation; *Opener 4* PDA writing tablet, Courtesy of Seiko Instruments USA Inc.; *Opener 5* PDA, Courtesy of Toshiba; *Figure 5-1a* hands typing on keyboard, © PhotoDisc/Getty Images; *Figure 5-1b* wireless mouse, © PhotoDisc/Getty Images; *Figure 5-1c* hand on touch screen, Courtesy of 3M Touch Systems; *Figure 5-1d* tablet PC, Courtesy of Microsoft® Corporation; *Figure 5-1e* person with headset talking into computer, © Bruce Ayres/Getty Images; *Figure 5-1f-1* digital camera, © 2002 Photodex Corporation; *Figure 5-1f-2* digital camera, Courtesy of Casio, Inc.; *Figure 5-1g* video conference, © Jose Luis Pelaez, Inc./CORBIS; *Figure 5-1h* flatbed scanner, Courtesy of Epson America, Inc.; *Figure 5-3* keyboard, Courtesy of Logitech; *Figure 5-6* wireless keyboard and receiver, Courtesy of Fujitsu Siemens Computers; *Figure 5-7* ergonomic keyboard, Courtesy of Microsoft® Corporation; *Figure 5-9* corded mouse with optical sensor, Courtesy of Microsoft® Corporation; *Figure 5-12a* trackball, © Scott Goodwin Photography; *Figure 5-12b* trackball, © Scott Goodwin Photography; *Figure 5-13* touchpad on laptop computer, © Bruce Avery/SuperStock; *Figure 5-14* pointing stick, © PhotoDisc/Getty Images; *Figure 5-15a* joystick, Courtesy of Logitech, Inc.; *Figure 5-15b* wheel, Courtesy of Logitech, Inc.; *Figure 5-15c* pedal, Courtesy of Logitech, Inc.; *Figure 5-16* light pen, © Greg Pease/Getty Images; *Figure 5-17* touch screen on a kiosk, Charles Brown/Bloomberg News /Landov; *Figure 5-18a* pen on a graphics tablet, Courtesy of Wacom Technology Corp.; *Figure 5-18b* cursor on a digitizer, Courtesy of GTCO CalComp; *Figure 5-19a* pen on touch screen monitor, Courtesy of Wacom Technology Corp.; *Figure 5-19b* tablet PC, updated, Courtesy of Microsoft® Corporation; *Figure 5-19c* PDA, © PhotoDisc/Getty Images; *Looking Ahead 5-1* wireless pens, VPen Courtesy of OTM Technologies Ltd; *Figure 5-21* electronic piano keyboard, © Durand Patrick/Corbis Sygma; *Figure 5-22a* pen/stylus combination for PDA, Courtesy of Toshiba America Information Systems, Inc.; *Figure 5-22b* digital camera for PDA, Courtesy of LifeView, Inc.; *Figure 5-22c* keyboard for PDA, Courtesy of Belkin Corporation; *Figure 5-22d* mini-keyboard for PDA, Courtesy of Targus Inc.; *Figure 5-22e* PDA in cradle, Courtesy of Toshiba America Information Systems, Inc.; *Figure 5-22f* scanner for PDA, Courtesy of Socket Communications, Inc.; *Figure 5-22g* Ink-link Courtesy of Seiko Instruments USA Inc.; *Figure 5-22h* l PDA, Courtesy of Toshiba America Information Systems, Inc.; *Figure 5-23a* portable keyboard, Courtesy of palmOne, Inc. palmOne, Zire, and Tungsten are among the trademarks owned by or exclusively licensed to palmOne, Inc.; *Figure 5-24a* tablet PC in docking station, Courtesy of ViewSonic® Corporation All rights reserved.; *Figure 5-25* smartphone, © Siemens AG, Munich/Berlin; *Figure 5-29* video editing software, © Gary Buss/Getty Images; *Figure 5-30* video telephone call, © Adrian Weinbrecht/Getty Images; *Figure 5-31* corporate meeting with videoconference, © Jon Feingersh/CORBIS; *Figure 5-32a* flatbed scanner, Courtesy of Epson America, Inc.; *Figure 5-32b* pen scanner, Courtesy of C Technologies AB; *Figure 5-32c* sheet fed scanner, Courtesy of Visioneer, Inc.; *Figure 5-32d* Howtek HiResolve 8000 Drum Scanner, Courtesy of Howtek, Inc.; *Figure 5-35* bill with OCR characters, Courtesy of Symantec Corp.; *Figure 5-36a* grocery store bar code reader, © David Frazier/Getty Images; *Figure 5-36b* bar code reader, Courtesy of Symbol Technologies, Inc.; *Figure 5-40* PDA/bar code reader (wireless), Courtesy of Symbol Technologies, Inc.; *Figure 5-41* self-service checkout, Courtesy of NCR Corporation; *Figure 5-42* bank card in ATM, © Tony Freeman/PhotoEdit. All rights reserved.; *Figure 5-43* smart display, Courtesy of Microsoft® Corporation; *Figure 5-44* keyboard with fingerprint recognition, Courtesy of Fujitsu Siemens Computers; *Figure 5-45* hand recognition, Courtesy of IR Recognition Systems; *Figure 5-46* iris recognition, Courtesy of Iridian Technologies, Inc.; *Figure 5-47a* Smartcard reader, Courtesy of Fujitsu Siemens Computers; *Figure 5-47b* microprocessor on smart card, Courtesy of Fujitsu Siemens Computers; *Figure 5-48a* woman eating salad, © Gary Buss/Getty Images; *Figure 5-48b* man videoconferencing with headset, © Ulf Wallin/Getty Images; *Figure 5-48c* woman working on laptop, Courtesy of Nokia; *Figure 5-48d* workers in cubicles, © Charles Gupton/CORBIS; *Figure 5-48e* man at workstation, L. Lefkowitz /Getty Images; *Figure 5-49* keyguard, Courtesy of www.keytools.com; *Figure 5-51* receiver/camera on desktop pc, Courtesy of NaturalPoint; *Career Corner* data entry clerk, Courtesy Superstock; *Technology Trailblazer 1* Douglas Engelbart, © AP/Wide World Photos; *Technology Trailblazer 2* Don Wetzel, © John Harrington Photography; *Looking Ahead 5-2* brain implants, © International Stock; *Checkpoint* keyboard, Courtesy of Logitech; *Learn Online* tablet PC in docking station, Courtesy of ViewSonic® Corporation All rights reserved.; *Upper left hand corner* touch-screen, Courtesy of 3M Touch Systems; *Upper right hand corner* finger on notebook touch-pad, © Bruce Avery/SuperStock. ***Special Feature ~ PDA:*** *Figure 1a* Palm Tungsten, © Copyright 2004 palmOne, Inc. palmOne, Zire, and Tungsten are among the trademarks owned by or exclusively licensed to palmOne, Inc.; *Figure 1b, Opener 1* PDA, Courtesy of Fujitsu Siemens Computers; *Figure 1c, Opener 2* PDA, © PhotoDisc/Getty Images; *Figure 2a* PDA, Courtesy of Fujitsu Siemens Computers; *Figure 2b* PDA, © Copyright 2004 palmOne, Inc. palmOne, Zire, and Tungsten are among the trademarks owned by or exclusively licensed to palmOne, Inc.; *Figure 4* PDA, Courtesy of Fujitsu Siemens Computers; *Figure 6* Group of executives, © Ryan McVay/Getty Images; *Figure 8* PDA in a medical setting, Courtesy of Symbol Technologies, Inc.; *Figure 10* Garmin iQue 3600, Courtesy of Garmin Ltd.; *Figure 11* PDA for Education, © PhotoDisc/Getty Images; *Figure 12* Sony Clie, Courtesy of Sony Electronics Inc.; *Figure 14* PDA user, © PhotoDisc/Getty Images. ***Chapter 6:*** *Opener 1* card reader, Courtesy of Sandisk Corporation; *Opener 2* photo printer, Courtesy of Epson America, Inc.; *Figure 6-1a-1* PDA, Courtesy of Microsoft® Corporation; *Figure 6-1a-2,* screen shot of text for PDA, Courtesy of Microsoft® Corporation; *Figure 6-1a-3,* Laser printer, Courtesy of Genicom; *Figure 6-1a-4* LCD monitor, Courtesy of Sony Electronics Inc.; *Figure 6-1b-1* screen shot on tablet PC, Courtesy of Microsoft® Corporation; *Figure 6-1b-2* tablet PC, Courtesy of Microsoft® Corporation; *Figure 6-1b-3* photo printer, Courtesy of Epson America, Inc.; *Figure 6-1c-1* speakers, Courtesy of Altec Lansing® Technologies, Inc.; *Figure 6-1c-2,* PDA with mp3, © Copyright 2004 palmOne, Inc. palmOne, Zire, and Tungsten are among the trademarks owned by or exclusively licensed to palmOne, Inc.; *Figure 6-1d-1,* smart phone with video on screen, © Siemens AG, Munich/Berlin; *Figure 6-2* 19" CRT desktop flat screen monitor, Courtesy of ViewSonic® Corporation All rights reserved.; *Figure 6-4* Energy Star ® label, Courtesy of Environmental Protection Agency; *Figure 6-6, Step 1* Intel Pentium 4 processor, Courtesy of Intel Corporation; *Figure 6-9* LCD monitor, Courtesy of Sony Electronics Inc.; *Figure 6-10,* flat panel monitors, Courtesy of ViewSonic® Corporation All rights reserved.; *Figure 6-11a* notebook, Courtesy of Dell Computer Corporation; *Figure 6-11b* tablet PC, Courtesy of ViewSonic® Corporation All rights reserved.; *Figure 6-11c* PDA with color screen, © Copyright 2004 palmOne, Inc. palmOne, Zire, and Tungsten are among the trademarks owned by or exclusively licensed to palmOne, Inc.; *Figure 6-11d* smart phone with color screen, Courtesy of

Panasonic Consumer Electronics Company; *Figure 6-13* graphics card with DVI port, Courtesy of ATI Technologies, Inc.; *Figure 6-14* gas plasma display, Courtesy of ViewSonic® Corporation All rights reserved.; *Looking Ahead 6-1* electronic paper, Courtesy of Palo Alto Research Center (PARC); *Figure 6-17* dot matrix printer, Courtesy of Oki Data Americas, Inc.; *Figure 6-18* line printer, Courtesy of IBM Corporation; *Figure 6-19* Epson, Courtesy of Epson America, Inc.; *Figure 6-22, Step 1* digital camera, Courtesy of SanDisk; *Figure 6-23* laser printer, Courtesy of Lexmark International, Inc.; *Figure 6-25b* dye sublimation printer, Courtesy of Sony Electronics Inc.; *Figure 6-26a* mobile printer, Courtesy of Canon U.S.A, Inc.; *Figure 6-27* label printer, Courtesy of Seiko Instruments USA Inc.; *Figure 6-28* large-format printer, Courtesy of MacDermid ColorSpan Inc.; *Figure 6-29a-1* Bluetooth printer adapter, Courtesy of 3Com Corporation; *Figure 6-29a-2* inkjet printer, Courtesy of Epson America, Inc.; *Figure 6-29b-1* Palm PDA with bluetooth card, © Copyright 2004 palmOne, Inc. palmOne, Zire, and Tungsten are among the trademarks owned by or exclusively licensed to palmOne, Inc.; *Figure 6-29b-2* Palm Bluetooth card, © Copyright 2004 palmOne, Inc. palmOne, Zire, and Tungsten are among the trademarks owned by or exclusively licensed to palmOne, Inc.; *Figure 6-29b-3* : Bluetooth card in laptop, © Copyright Socket Communications, Inc. All rights reserved.; *Figure 6-29b-4* Bluetooth card, © Copyright Socket Communications, Inc. All rights reserved.; *Figure 6-30*, personal computer, Courtesy of Fujitsu Siemens Computers; *Figure 6-31* headsets, Copyright ©Bill Aron/PhotoEdit. All rights reserved.; *Figure 6-33* stand-alone fax machine, ©LWA-Stephen Welstead/ CORBIS; *Figure 6-35* color printer, Courtesy of Panasonic; *Figure 6-36a* DLP projector, Courtesy of InFocus®; *Figure 6-36b* DLP projector, Courtesy of InFocus®; *Looking Ahead 6-2* digital movies picture-desk.com, © PhotoDisc/Getty Images; *Figure 6-37a* Sidewinder Force Feedback Wheel, Courtesy of Microsoft® Corporation; *Figure 6-37b* Sidewinder Force Feedback 2, Courtesy of Microsoft® Corporation; *Figure 6-38a* woman eating salad, © Gary Buss/Getty Images; *Figure 6-38b* man videoconferencing with headset, © Ulf Wallin/Getty Images; *Figure 6-38c* woman working on laptop, Courtesy of Nokia; *Figure 6-38d* workers in cubicles, © Charles Gupton/CORBIS; *Figure 6-38e* man at workstation, © L. Lefkowitz/Getty Images; *Figure 6-40a* Braille printer, Courtesy of Freedom Scientific Inc.; *Career Corner* Graphic Illustrator ©David Young-Wolff/PhotoEdit. All rights reserved.; *Technology Trailblazer 1* Heidi Van Arnem, Courtesy of Copyright © 1999-2003 iCan! Inc. All rights reserved. Heidi Van Armen, founder of iCan! Inc. and iCan.com, an online community for people with disabilities, their families and friends.; *Technology Trailblazer 2* Donna Dubinsky, Courtesy of Handspring, Inc.; *CheckPoint* video card, Courtesy of ATI Technologies, Inc.; *Upper right hand folio* girl with headphones, © Charles Gupton/CORBIS. ***Special Feature ~ Digital Imaging:*** *Opener* couple with a camcorder, © George Shelley/CORBIS; *Figure 1a* digital camera, Courtesy of Sony Electronics Inc.; *Figure 1b* digital video camera, Courtesy of Sony Electronics Inc.; *Figure 1c* plasma TV, Courtesy of Sony Electronics Inc.; *Figure 1d* PC, Courtesy of Sony Electronics Inc.; *Figure 1e* DVD-RW drive, Courtesy of Sony Electronics Inc.; *Figure 1f* VCR, Sony HI-FI VHS SLV-N900, Courtesy of JVC Company of America; *Figure 1g* photo-quality printer, Courtesy of Sony Electronics Inc.; *Figure 1h* video camera, © Thinkstock/Getty Images; *Figure 2a* shoot camera, Courtesy of Canon U.S.A, Inc.; *Figure 2b* shoot camera, Courtesy of Sony Electronics Inc.; *Figure 2c* professional camera, Courtesy of Olympus America Inc.; *Figure 5a* 4GB Hitachi Microdrive card, Courtesy of Hitachi Global Storage Technologies; *Figure 5b* compact Flash 4GB from SanDisk, Courtesy of Sandisk Corporation; *Figure 5c* Memory Stick, PRO DUO Media from Sony 512MB, Courtesy of Sony Electronics Inc.; *Figure 6* card reader, Courtesy of SanDisk Corporation; *Figure 7a* screenshot of photo edit software, Courtesy of Ulead Systems, Inc.; *Figure 8a* digital picture kiosk, Courtesy of Sony Electronics Inc.; *Figure 8b* picture phone, © Siemens AG, Munich/Berlin; *Figure 10a* video camera, Courtesy of Canon U.S.A, Inc.; *Figure 10b* video camera, Courtesy of Sony Electronics Inc.; *Figure 10c* webcasting and monitoring Courtesy of Logitech; *Figure 11* camera, Courtesy of Sony Electronics Inc.; *Figure 12a* PC, Courtesy of Sony Electronics Inc.; *Figure 12c* Analog camera, Courtesy of Sony Electronics Inc.; *Figure 12d* JVC HM-DH30000 VCR, Courtesy of JVC Company of America; *Figure 12e* PC, Courtesy of Sony Electronics Inc.; *Figure 16a* screen-shot from Canopus, Courtesy of Canopus Corporation; *Figure 17* video editing software, Courtesy of Ulead Systems, Inc.; *Figure 18* screen shot of video editing software, Courtesy of Canopus Corporation; *Figure 19a* screen shot from Sonic.com, Courtesy of Sonic Solutions; *Last images in film strip*, photo, © PhotoDisc/Getty Images. ***Chapter 7:*** *Figure 7-1a* floppy disk, © PhotoDisc/Getty Images; *Figure 7-1b* internal 750MB Atapi zip disk, Courtesy of Iomega Corporation Copyright © 2003 Iomega Corporation All Rights Reserved. Zip is a registered trademark in the United States and/or other countries. Iomega, the stylized "i" logo and product images are property of Iomega Corporation in the United States and/or other countries.; *Figure 7-1c* C193 internal hard disk, Courtesy of IBM Corporation; *Figure 7-1d* external hard disk, Courtesy of SimpleTech, Inc.; *Figure 7-1e* removable hard disk for PC, Courtesy of Kanguru Solutions; *Figure 7-1g* DLT tape cassette, Courtesy of Imation Corp.; *Figure 7-1h* PC card, Courtesy of Kingston Technology Company, Inc.; *Figure 7-1i* media card in a digital camera, Courtesy of Sony Electronics Inc.; *Figure 7-1j* USB flash drive, Courtesy of Kingston Technology Company, Inc.; *Figure 7-6a* floppy disk, © PhotoDisc/Getty Images; *Figure 7-6b* external floppy disk drive, Courtesy of IBM Corporation; *Figure 7-11* external 750MB zip disk, Courtesy of Iomega Corporation Copyright © 2003 Iomega Corporation All Rights Reserved. Zip is a registered trademark in the United States and/or other countries. Iomega, the stylized "i" logo and product images are property of Iomega Corporation in the United States and/or other countries.; *Figure 7-12a* external 750MB Zip disk, Courtesy of IBM Corporation; *Figure 7-12b* open vertical system unit, © Scott Goodwin Photography; *Figure 7-13* hard disk, © Biondo Productions/Getty Images; *Figure 7-14* internal hard disk, Courtesy of IBM Corporation; *Figure 7-17a* Intel Celeron processor, Courtesy of Intel Corporation; *Figure 7-17c* internal hard disk, Courtesy of IBM Corporation; *Figure 7-18a* external hard disk, Courtesy of Iomega Corporation Copyright © 2003 Iomega Corporation All Rights Reserved. Zip is a registered trademark in the United States and/or other countries. Iomega, the stylized "i" logo and product images are property of Iomega Corporation in the United States and/or other countries.; *Figure 7-18b* removable hard disk, Courtesy of Kanguru Solutions; *Figure 7-25c* Kodak picture kiosk, ©Michael Newman/PhotoEdit. All rights reserved.; *Figure 7-27c* DVD-ROM drive, Courtesy of IBM Corporation, Inc.; *Looking Ahead 7-1* holographic storage, Courtesy of InPhase; *Figure 7-29* tape cartridge and tape drive, Courtesy of Seagate Removable Storage Solutions LLC; *Figure 7-31* PC card in a handheld computer, Courtesy of Nokia. Copyright © 2002 Nokia. All rights reserved. Copyright © 2002 Nokia. All rights reserved. Nokia and Nokia Connecting People are registered trademarks of Nokia Corporation.; *Looking Ahead 7-2* punch card, Courtesy of IBM Research; *Figure 7-33a* miniature storage media, Courtesy of palmOne, Inc. palmOne, Zire, and Tungsten are among the trademarks owned by or exclusively licensed to palmOne, Inc.; *Figure 7-33b* miniature storage media, Courtesy of Fujitsu Siemens Computers; *Figure 7-33c* miniature storage media, Courtesy of Sandisk Corporation; *Figure 7-34a* CompactFlash card, Courtesy of LexarMedia; *Figure 7-34c* SecureDigital card, Courtesy of Sandisk Corporation; *Figure 7-34d* 512MB xD-Picture Card, Courtesy of Sandisk Corporation; *Figure 7-34e* memory stick, Courtesy of LexarMedia; *Figure 7-34f* Microdrive, Courtesy of Hitachi Global Storage Technologies; *Figure 7-35* flash card reader/writer, Courtesy of Sandisk Corporation; *Figure 7-36* USB flash drive, Courtesy of IBM Corporation; *Figure 7-37* smart card, Courtesy of Fujitsu Siemens Computers; *Figure 7-40a* woman eating salad, © Gary Buss/Getty Images; *Figure 7-40b* videoconferencing, © Ulf Wallin/Getty Images; *Figure 7-40c* woman working on laptop, Courtesy of Nokia; *Figure 7-40d* workers in cubicles, © Charles Gupton/CORBIS; *Figure 7-40e* man at workstation, © L. Lefkowitz /Getty Images; *Career Corner* Computer Technician, © Royalty-Free/CORBIS; *Technology Trailblazer 1* Al Shugart, © AP/Wide World Photos; *Technology Trailblazer 2* Mark Dean, © AP/Wide World Photos; *Upper left hand corner* hard disk drive, Courtesy of IBM Corporation; *CheckPoint* internal hard drive, Courtesy of IBM Corporation; *CheckPoint* external hard disk, Courtesy of SimpleTech, Inc.; *CheckPoint* removable hard disk, Courtesy of Kanguru Solutions; *CheckPoint* tape, Courtesy of Imation Corp. ***Chapter 8:*** *Opener* LCD monitor, Courtesy of Sony Electronics Inc.; *Opener* McAfee VirusScan box, Courtesy of McAfee. McAfee is a business unit of Network Associates, Inc. Copyright © 2003 , Networks Associates Technology, Inc. All Rights Reserved.; *Figure 8-1b* memory module, Courtesy of Kingston Technology Company, Inc.; *Figure 8-1c* laser printer, Courtesy of IBM Corporation; *Figure 8-1d* C334 keyboard and monitor, Courtesy of NEC Solutions (America), Inc.; *Figure 8-1d-2* speakers, Courtesy of Altec Lansing® Technologies, Inc.; *Figure 8-4* flat screen monitor, Courtesy of ViewSonic® Corporation All rights reserved.; *Figure 8-26* tablet PC, Courtesy of Microsoft® Corporation; *Looking Ahead 8-1* Greek image "The Last Night of Troy," © Araldo de Luca/CORBIS; *Figure 8-27*, screen shot of Mac OS X, Courtesy of Apple Computer Corporation; *Figure 8-30* smart display with screen, Courtesy of Microsoft® Corporation; *Looking Ahead 8-2* computer-based home entertainment system, © Touhig Sion/CORBIS SYGMA; *Figure 8-31* pocket PC with Windows Mobile 2003 on screen, Courtesy of Microsoft® Corporation; *Figure 8-32* PDA with Palm OS, Courtesy of Sony Electronics Inc.; *Figure 8-33* phone with Symbian OS, Courtesy of Nokia; *Career Corner* systems programmer, © PhotoDisc/Getty Images; *Technology Trailblazer 1* Linus Torvalds, © Reuters NewMedia Inc./CORBIS; *Technology Trailblazer 2* Steve Jobs, © AP/Wide World Photos; *Upper left hand corner* Windows XP Tablet PC, Courtesy of Microsoft® Corporation; ***Special Feature ~ Buyer's Guide:*** *Figure 1a* desktop computer, Courtesy of IBM Corporation; *Figure 1b* notebook, Courtesy of Dell Computer Corporation; *Figure 1c* tablet PC, Courtesy of Microsoft® Corporation; *Figure 1d* PDA/bar code reader, Courtesy of palmOne, Inc. palmOne, Zire, and Tungsten are among the trademarks owned by or exclusively licensed to palmOne, Inc.; *Figure 12* tablet PC, Courtesy of Acer Inc.; *Figure 13* carrying case, Courtesy of Toshiba America; *Figure 14* electrical adapters for travel abroad, Courtesy of Toshiba America; *Figure 15* executives in a meeting, © Jon Feingersh/CORBIS; *Figure 16* tablet PC, Courtesy of Acer Inc.; *Figure 18* tablet PC, Courtesy of Microsoft® Corporation; *Figure 21* tablet PC docked, Courtesy of Fujitsu Siemens Computers; *Figure 22* Sony UX50 Clie, Courtesy of Sony Electronics Inc.; *Figure 23* Toshiba Pocket PC e800, Courtesy of Toshiba America Information Systems, Inc.; *Figure 25* palmOne Treo 600, Courtesy of palmOne, Inc. palmOne, Zire, and Tungsten are among the trademarks owned by or exclusively licensed to palmOne, Inc.; *Figure 26* How to Install a Computer, © Jiang Jin/SuperStock; *Figure 29a* PC opened, © Scott Goodwin Photography; *Figure 29b-3* processor, Courtesy of Intel Corporation; *Figure 29c* memory module, Courtesy of Kingston Technology Company, Inc.; *Figure 29d, e* network card, Courtesy of SMC; *Figure 31a*, How to Maintain Your Computer, ©E. Dygas/Getty Images; *Figure 31b* hard disk drive, Courtesy of Seagate Technology. ***Chapter 9:*** *Figure 9-1a* mainframe computer, Courtesy of IBM Corporation; *Figure 9-1b* mid-range server, Courtesy of Sun Microsystems, Inc.; *Figure 9-1d* notebook computer, Courtesy of Dell Computer Corporation; *Figure 9-1e* tablet PC product shot, Courtesy of Acer Inc.; *Figure 9-1f* smart phone, © Siemens AG, Munich/Berlin; *Figure 9-1g* PDA product shot, Courtesy of palmOne, Inc. palmOne, Zire, and Tungsten are among the trademarks owned by or exclusively licensed to palmOne, Inc.; *Figure 9-1h* Internet applicance, Courtesy of Microsoft© Corporation; *Figure 9-2a,b* Modem, Courtesy of Linksys;

Figure 9-2c computer angled right, Courtesy of IBM Corporation; *Figure 9-2d* computer angled left, Courtesy of Acer Inc.; *Figure 9-4a* smart phone, Courtesy of Microsoft® Corporation; *Figure 9-4b* PDA, Courtesy of Microsoft® Corporation; *Figure 9-4c* working at computer, © Leland Bobbé/CORBIS; *Figure 9-6* Cybercafe, © PhotoDisc/Getty Images; *Figure 9-7b-1* GPS locator watch, © AP/Wide World Photos; *Figure 9-7b-2* child on a swing, © Harald Sund/Getty Images; *Figure 9-7c-1* GPS device attached, Courtesy of Garmin Ltd.; *Figure 9-7c-2* GPS device in city, © Paul Barton/CORBIS; *Figure 9-7d-1* handheld GPS device, Magellan™ SporTrak™ handheld GPS receiver. Used by permission. Thales Navigation Inc. 2003; *Figure 9-7d-2* person hiking, © PhotoDisc/Getty Images; *Figure 9-7e-1* dog © Dante Burn-Forti/Getty Images; *Figure 9-7e-2* pet collar with GPS, Courtesy of GPS Tracks, Inc.; *Figure 9-8* smart phone with picture, Courtesy of palmOne, Inc. palmOne, Zire, and Tungsten are among the trademarks owned by or exclusively licensed to palmOne, Inc.; *Figure 9-11* Nokia cell phone, Courtesy of Nokia; *Figure 9-17* hub, Courtesy of SMC Networks Inc.; *Figure 9-19a* Palm with Bluetooth capabilities, Courtesy of palmOne, Inc. palmOne, Zire, and Tungsten are among the trademarks owned by or exclusively licensed to palmOne, Inc.; *Figure 9-19a* PDA, © Jim Craigmyle/CORBIS; *Figure 9-19b* PDA, © Jim Craigmyle/CORBIS; *Figure 9-25* external DSL modem, © SMC Networks; *Figure 9-26* modem card, Courtesy of Creative Labs, Inc.; *Figure 9-27* Internet connection via cellular telephone, © PhotoDisc/Getty Images; *Looking Ahead 9-1* Molar phone receives calls, Courtesy of NESTA (the National Endowment for Science, Technology and the Arts); *Figure 9-29a* network PC card for notebook computer, Courtesy of SMC Networks Inc.; *Figure 9-29b* Internal network card, Courtesy of SMC Networks Inc.; *Figure 9-30* wireless access point, Courtesy of SMC Networks Inc.; *Figure 9-31a* cable modem, Courtesy of Dlink; *Figure 9-31b* router, Courtesy of Dlink; *Figure 9-31c* laptop computer, Courtesy of Dell Computer Corporation; *Figure 9-32* hub, Courtesy of SMC Networks Inc.; *Figure 9-33a* PDA with network card, Courtesy of Symbol Technologies, Inc.; *Figure 9-33b* notebook with network card, Courtesy of Nokia; *Figure 9-33b* cable/DSL modem, Courtesy of Linksys; *Figure 9-33c* router/wireless access point, Courtesy of SMC Networks Inc.; *Figure 9-33e* wireless computer, Courtesy of Gateway, Inc; *Figure 9-34b* mainframe computer, Courtesy of Gateway, Inc; *Looking Ahead 9-2* M-Cash, © Ghislain & Marie David de Lossy/Getty Images; *Figure 9-41* Microwave ground station, © Jim Zuckerman/CORBIS; *Career Corner* network administrator, © LWA-Sharie Kennedy/CORBIS; *Technology Trailblazer 1* Esther Dyson, © Reuters NewMedia Inc./CORBIS; *Technology Trailblazer 2* Robert Metcalfe, Courtesy of Polaris Ventures; *Upper left hand corner* hiker, © PhotoDisc/Getty Images; *Upper right hand corner,* microwave ground station, © Jim Zuckerman/CORBIS. ***Special Feature ~ Wireless:*** *Figure 1, Intro 1* smart phone, Courtesy of Microsoft® Corporation; *Figure 1, Intro 2* Blackberry 7280, Courtesy of Research In Motion (RIM); *Figure 1, Intro 3b* PDA with phone, Courtesy of Microsoft® Corporation; *Figure 1, Intro 4,* tablet PC, Courtesy of ViewSonic® Corporation All rights reserved.; *Figure 1, Intro 5a* notebook with wireless card, Courtesy of Acer Inc.; *Figure 1, Intro 5b* Wireless card and notebook, Courtesy of Fujitsu Siemens Computers; *Figure 2a* notebook with wireless card, Courtesy of Acer Inc.; *Figure 2c* Blackberry 7280, Courtesy of Research In Motion (RIM); *Figure 3* laptop, Courtesy of Fujitsu Siemens Computers; *Figure 3b* handheld computer, Courtesy of Fujitsu Siek with wireless card, © Royalty-Free/CORBIS; *Figure 4d* plasma TV, © 2003 Getty Images; *Figure 4e* laptop in kitchen, © LWA-JDC/CORBIS; *Figure 5a-1* Construction worker talking on cell phone, © Royalty-Free/CORBIS; *Figure 5a-2* Construction supervisor talking on cell phone, © Ralf Gerard/Getty Images; *Figure 5b* Student using cordless phone, Copyright © Myrleen Ferguson Cate/PhotoEdit. All rights reserved.; *Figure 5c-1* two-way radio © AP/Wide World Photos; *Figure 5c-2* two-way radio, Copyright ©David Young-Wolff/PhotoEdit. All rights reserved.; *Figure 6* Microsoft Wrist Net, Courtesy of Fossil, Inc.; *Figure 7* Blackberry 7280, Courtesy of Research In Motion (RIM); *Figure 8* Bluetooth headset, Courtesy of Bluetooth Special Interest Group; *Figure 9* Starbucks, © AP/Wide World Photos; *Figure 10* Medical personnel using PDA, Courtesy of Symbol Technologies, Inc.; *Figure 11a-1* notebook with wireless card, Courtesy of Acer Inc.; *Figure 11a-2* wireless card, Courtesy of D-Link; *Figure 11b* woman using tablet PC, Coutesy of Acer Inc.; *Figure 12a* smart phone, © David Stoecklein/CORBIS; *Figure 12b* viewing picture on home computer, Copyright ©David Young-Wolff/PhotoEdit. All rights reserved.; *Figure 12c* camera phone, Courtesy of Nokia; *Figure 13* GPS device, © Ian Logan/Getty Images; *Figure 14* wireless keypad, Courtesy of eInstruction Corporation; *Figure 14b* keypad, Courtesy of eInstruction Corporation. ***Chapter 10:*** *Opener* fingerprint ID, Courtesy of Identix Incorporated; *Opener* laptop computer in hotel room, © Jon Riley/Getty Images; *Figure 10-01a* digital camera, Courtesy of Sony Electronics Inc.; *Figure 10-1b* photo, © Carl & Ann Purcell/CORBIS; *Figure 10-1c* photo, ©Spencer Grant/PhotoEdit. All rights reserved.; *Figure 10-5* photo, © Carl & Ann Purcell/CORBIS; *Figure 10-6* photo, © Carl & Ann Purcell/CORBIS; *Figure 10-7* photo, © Royalty-Free/CORBIS; *Figure 10-9* Fitness trainer on computer, © AJA Productions/Getty Images; *Looking Ahead 10-1* Having a Voice in Future Databases, © Digital Vision/Getty Images; *Figure 10-17a* photo, © Carl & Ann Purcell/ CORBIS; *Figure 10-17c* photo, © Carl & Ann Purcell/CORBIS; *Figure 10-26a* policeman using PDA, John Lok/Los Angeles Times; *Figure 10-26b* PDA, John Lok/Los Angeles Times; *Looking Ahead 10-2* Storing Digital Files for Future Generations, Courtesy of Library of Congress; *Career Corner Box* Database Administrator, © Steve Chenn/CORBIS; *Technology Trailblazer 1* E.F. Codd, Courtesy of The National Academy of Engineering (NAE); *Technology Trailblazer 2* Larry Ellison © AP/Wide World Photos. ***Chapter 11:*** *Figure 11-1b* empty laptop case, © 2003 Thinkstock/Getty Images; *Figure 11-1c* empty seats in an airport, © Randy Faris/CORBIS; *Figure 11-1d* woman at computer, © Royalty-Free/CORBIS; *Figure 11-1e,* desktop computer, Courtesy of IBM Corporation; *Figure 11-1f* LCD monitor, Courtesy of Sony Electronics Inc.; *Figure 11-2, Step 1* © PhotoDisc/Getty Images; *Figure 11-2, Step 1* Courtesy of IBM Corporation; *Figure 11-2, Step 2* © PhotoDisc/Getty Images; *Figure 11, Step 2* © PhotoDisc/Getty Images; *Figure 11-2, Step 3* © PhotoDisc/Getty Images; *Figure 11-2, Step 3* © PhotoDisc/Getty Images; *Figure 11-2, Step 4* © PhotoDisc/Getty Images; *Figure 11-2, Step 4* Courtesy of IBM Corporation; *Figure 11-12* card inserted into ATM machine, © PhotoDisc/Getty Images; *Figure 11-13a* fingerprint scanner, Courtesy of AuthenTec, Inc.; *Figure 11-13b* fingerprint scanner software, Courtesy of AuthenTec, Inc.; *Figure 11-13c* fingerprint scanner, Courtesy of AuthenTec, Inc.; *Figure 11-14* cables locking desktop computer, Courtesy of Secure-It, Inc.; *Figure 11-18* surge protector, Courtesy of American Power Conversion Corp.; *Figure 11-19* Uninterruptible Power Supply (UPS), Courtesy of American Power Conversion Corp.; *Figure 11-34* good posture at computer, © PhotoDisc/Getty Images; *Looking Ahead 11-1* Cyberterrorism Attack Threatens Networks, © PhotoDisc/Getty Images; *Looking Ahead 11-2* Electronic Sensors Track Shoppers, © PhotoDisc/Getty Images; *Technology Trailblazer 1* Donn Parker, © Roger Ressmeyer/CORBIS; *Technology Trailblazer 2* Clifford Stoll, © STEVE LISS/TIMEPIX; *Career Corner Box* Network Security Specialist, © Paul Edmondson/CORBIS. ***Chapter 12.*** *Looking Ahead 12-1* Object-Oriented Programs May Reap Benefits, © PhotoDisc/Getty Images; *Figure 12-5* a meeting, © 2003 Getty Images; *Figure 12-6* laptop computer, Courtesy of Acer Inc.; *Figure 12-23,* training class, Copyright © Jeff Greenberg/PhotoEdit. All rights reserved.; *Looking Ahead 12-2* Buying Software May Not be Best Buy, © 2002 Artville/Getty Images; *Career Corner Box* Systems Analyst, © Jon Riley/Getty Images; *Technology Trailblazer 1* : Ed Yourdon, Courtesy of Ed Yourdon; *Technology Trailblazer 2* Tom DeMarco, © James Robertson/Courtesy of Tom DeMarco. ***Chapter 13:*** *Figure 13-1* programmers working on computer, Copyright © Myrleen Ferguson Cate/PhotoEdit. All rights reserved.; *Figure 13-12a and Figure 13-12b* screen shots of Borland's Delphi visual programming tools, Courtesy of Borland Software Corporation Copyright ©1983-2003. All rights reserved, reprinted by permission. Borland Software Corporation, 100 Enterprise Way, Scotts Valley, CA, 95066-3249 USA. www.borland.com.; *Figure 13-13a* "Powerbuilder" screen shot, Courtesy of Sybase Inc.; *Figure 13-13b* "Powerbuilder" screen shot, Courtesy of Sybase Inc.; *Looking Ahead 13-1* Seeing Clearly with Vision Systems, Courtesy of Optobionics Corporation; *Looking Ahead 13-2* Genetic Programming Solves Complex Problems, © 2002 Artville/Getty Images; *Figure 13-38* first computer, Courtesy of The Computer Museum History Center; *Figure 13-39* Nokia phone, Courtesy of Nokia; *Career Corner* programmer, © Larry Bray/Getty Images; *High Tech Talk* Nokia phone, Courtesy of Nokia; *Technology Trailblazer 1* Dennis Ritchie, Courtesy of Bell Labs/Lucent Technologies; *Technology Trailblazer 2* James Gosling, Courtesy of Sun Microsystems. ***Chapter 14:*** *Figure 14-1a* mobile sales, Copyright ©Michael Newman/PhotoEdit. All rights reserved.; *Figure 14-1b* accounting, © Chuck Savage/CORBIS; *Figure 14-1c* telecommuter, © Jose Luis Pelaez, Inc./CORBIS; *Figure 14-1d* remote office, © John Dakers/Life File/Getty Images; *Figure 14-1e* customer service, © Royalty-Free/CORBIS; *Figure 14-1f* corporate headquarters, © Alan Schein Photography/CORBIS; *Figure 14-1g* manufacturing, © Premium Stock/CORBIS; *Figure 14-1h* marketing, © 2003 Getty Images; *Figure 14-1i* customers in a retail setting, Copyright © Michael Newman/PhotoEdit. All rights reserved.; *Figure 14-1j* distribution, Copyright © Michael Newman/PhotoEdit. All rights reserved.; *Figure 14-1k* warehouse, © Lester Lefkowitz/CORBIS; *Figure 14-1l* international office, © Keute/Getty Images; *Figure 14-2a* accounting, © Chuck Savage/CORBIS; *Figure 14-2b* human resources, Copyright © Robert Brenner/PhotoEdit. All rights reserved.; *Figure 14-2c* engineering, © Inc. Ted Kawalerski Photography/Getty Images; *Figure 14-2d* manufacturing, © Peter Vadnai/CORBIS; *Figure 14-2e* marketing, © 2003 Getty Images; *Figure 14-2f* sales department, © 2003 Getty Images; *Figure 14-2g* distribution, Copyright © Michael Newman/PhotoEdit. All rights reserved.; *Figure 14-2h,* customer service, © Royalty-Free/CORBIS; *Figure 14-2i* IT department, © Paul Thomas/Getty Images; *Figure 14-5a* desktop computer, Courtesy of Gateway, Inc; *Figure 14-5b* worker in office setting, © 2003 Getty Images; *Figure 14-5c* time card, © Julius/CORBIS; *Figure 14-7* HRIS software, Courtesy of Employease, Inc.; *Figure 14-9* AutoCad screen shot, Courtesy of Autodesk, Inc.; *Figure 14-10* robots at work, © Charles O'Rear/ CORBIS; *Figure 14-11* Management Information Systems (MIS), Courtesy of Marketing Pilot Software; *Figure 14-12* Sales Force Automation Software (SFA), Courtesy of Commence® Corporation; *Figure 14-13a* EnsemblePro software screen shot, Courtesy of Concerto Software, Inc.; *Looking Ahead 14-1* data gathering cell phones, © PhotoDisc/Getty Images; *Figure 14-13b* EnsemblePro software screen shot, Courtesy of Concerto Software, Inc.; *Figure 14-14* retail setting, Copyright © David Young-Wolff/Photo Edit. All rights reserved.; *Figure 14-17* sample expert system, Courtesy of Powerful Training Systems; *Figure 14-18b* purchasing materials, © Jean Louis Batt/Getty Images; *Figure 14-18a* Planning & Logistics, Courtesy of Kidasa Software, www.kidasa.com; *Figure 14-18c* payments, © V.C.L./Getty Images; *Figure 14-18d* parts inventory, © Yellow Dog Productions/Getty Images; *Figure 14-18e* production, © Premium Stock/CORBIS; *Figure 14-18f* product Inventory, © Antonio Mo/Getty Images; *Figure 14-18g* distribution, Copyright © Michael Newman/Photo Edit. All rights reserved.; *Figure 14-18h* billing and collections, Copyright ©Tony Freeman/Photo Edit. All rights reserved.; *Figure 14-18i* marketing, © PhotoDisc/Getty Images; *Figure 14-18j* human resources, Copyright ©Robert Brenner/Photo Edit. All rights reserved.; *Figure 14-18k* customer service, © Royalty-Free/CORBIS; *Figure 14-18l* sales setting, © 2003 Getty Images; *Figure 14-18m* accounting, © Gary D. Landsman/CORBIS; *Figure 14-18n* accounting, © Chuck Savage/CORBIS; *Figure 14-18o* IT department, © PhotoDisc/Getty Images; *Figure 14-19a* documents, ©

Karen Moskowitz/Getty Images; *Figure 14-19b* drawings, © Howard Grey/Getty Images; *Figure 14-19c* multimedia, © Felix Clouzot/Getty Images; *Figure 14-19d* data, Courtesy of Iomega Corporation Copyright © 2003 Iomega Corporation All Rights Reserved. Zip is a registered trademark in the United States and/or other countries. Iomega, the stylized "i" logo and product images are property of Iomega Corporation in the United States and/or other countries.; *Figure 14-19e* print, Courtesy of IBM Corporation; *Figure 14-19f* fax, Courtesy of Panasonic; *Figure 14-19g* wireless, Courtesy of Nokia; *Figure 14-19h* human resources, Copyright © Robert Brenner/Photo Edit. All rights reserved.; *Figure 14-19i* executives, © Tim Brown/Getty Images; *Figure 14-19j* sales department, © 2003 Getty Images; *Figure 14-20* portals, Courtesy of Hummingbird Ltd.; *Figure 14-22a* inventory, © PhotoDisc/Getty Images; *Figure 14-22b* User at computer, Copyright ©Gary Conner/Photo Edit. All rights reserved.; *Figure 14-23* DralaSoft (www.dralasot.com), Copyright © 2002-03 Dralasoft, Inc. All rights reserved.; *Figure 14-24a* home office, © PhotoDisc/Getty Images; *Figure 14-24b* main office, © Chris Sanders/Getty Images; *Figure 14-24c* mobile worker, © Tom & Dee Ann McCarthy/CORBIS; *Figure 14-24d* business partner, © 2002 EyeWire Collection; *Figure 14-24e* remote office, © Doug Armand/Getty Images; *Looking Ahead 14-2* on-demand computing uses utility model, © PhotoDisc/Getty Images; *Figure 14-28* RAID, Courtesy of IBM Corporation; *Figure 14-30b-1* raid disk, Courtesy of Digi-Data Corporation; *Figure 14-30b-2* tape, Courtesy of Seagate Removable Storage Solutions LLC; *Figure 14-31a* RAID, Courtesy of Fujitsu Siemens Computers; *Figure 14-31b* tape libraries, Courtesy of Plasmon USA; *Figure 14-31c* CD-ROM jukeboxes, Courtesy of Plasmon USA; *Figure 14-31d* Internet back-up device, Courtesy of IBM Corporation; *Figure 14-31e* IBM NAS300G2, Courtesy of IBM Corporation; *Figure 14-31f* SAN, Courtesy of Fujitsu Siemens Computers; *Figure 14-32* blade server, Courtesy of IBM Corporation; *Looking Ahead 14-3* Grid Computing, © PhotoDisc/Getty Images; *Career Corner* CIO, © Jim Cummins/Getty Images; *Technology Trailblazer 1* Tom Siebel, © AP/Wide World Photos; *Technology Trailblazer 2* Jim Clark, © AP/Wide World Photos. ***Chapter 15:*** *Opener1* group of students, © PhotoDisc/Getty Images; *Opener2* computer class, © EyeWire Collection/Getty Images; *Opener3* students reading paper © PhotoDisc/Getty Images; *Figure 15-01* photo, © Walter Hodges/CORBIS; *Figure 15-2* people working at computers, © DPA/Landov; *Looking Ahead 15-1* Semantic web, © PhotoDisc/Getty Images; *Figure 15-03* production of computer equipment, Copyright © Mark Richards/Photo Edit. All rights reserved.; *Figure 15-4* computer technician, Copyright © Michael Newman/Photo Edit. All rights reserved.; *Figure 15-05* computer sales representative, © Najlah Feanny/Corbis; *Figure 15-6* computer training, © 2003 Getty Images; *Looking Ahead 15-2* Starting your Computer-related business, © Larry Williams/CORBIS; *Figure 15-16,* Comdex 2003, Las Vegas, © AP/Wide World Photos; *Career Corner* Computer Science/IT Instructor, © Steve McAlister Productions/Getty Images; *High-Tech Talk* motion capture suit, Courtesy of The DAVE School; *Technology Trailblazer 1* Steve Ballmer, Koichi Kamoshida/Getty Images; *Technology Trailblazer 2* Steve Wozniak, Peter DaSilva/Corbis Sygma. ***Special Feature ~ Trends:*** *Figure 1* group shot, © Jose Luis Pelaez, Inc./CORBIS; *Figure 2a* "nanorings" from Purdue University research, © Graphic/VCH Publishers; *Figure 2b* CFD analysis of the Wright Flyer propeller blade, Courtesy of Fluent Inc.; *Figure 3a* headmount display, Courtesy of 5DT, Inc.; *Figure 3b* Optical pointing device, Courtesy of Logitech; *Figure 3c* MP3 player, Courtesy of Creative Labs, Inc.; *Figure 4* microdisplay, Courtesy of Interactive Imaging Systems, Inc.; *Figure 5* bionic ear, Courtesy of Advanced Bionics Corporation; *Figure 6a* RFID VeriChip, © AP/Wide World Photos; *Figure 6b* RFID VeriChip, © AP/Wide World Photos; *Figure 7* wrist net photo, Courtesy of Fossil, Inc.; *Figure 8* astronaut using virtual reality, Courtesy of TARDEC/Fakespace Systems Inc.; *Figure 9* courtroom with computers, Courtesy of Courtroom 21 Project/Courtroom Information Project, William & Mary School of Law; *Figure 10* virtual environment, Courtesy of National Aeronautics and Space Administration (NASA); *Figure 11b* logo, Courtesy of Tickle Inc.; *Figure 11c* Tickle.com screen shot, Courtesy of Tickle Inc.; *Figure 12,* internet-enabled refrigerator, Courtesy of LG Electronics, U.S.A., Inc.; *Figure 13* Windows XP Media Center Edition logo, Courtesy of Microsoft® Corporation; *Figure 14* Bell Canada utility worker, © Fabrizio Bensch/Reuters/Landov; *Figure 15* handheld device, Courtesy of Nokia; *Figure 16* DoCoMo user, © Haruyoshi Yamaguchi/Reuters/Landov; *Figure 17* implanted GPS device, © PhotoDisc/Getty Images; *Figure 18* electronic paper and ink product, Courtesy of Gyricon, LLC; *Figure 19* electronic device powered by solar batteries, Courtesy of Sunpower Systems, Inc.; *Figure 20* monkey with a researcher, © Dan Lamont/CORBIS; *Figure 21* robot used in surgery, Courtesy of Intuitive Surgical, Inc.; *Figure 22* Sony AIBO, Courtesy of Sony Electronics Inc.; *Figure 23* Spy-Cye personal robot, Courtesy of Probotics, Inc.; *Figure 24* Face recognition on an ATM, Courtesy of Viisage Inc.; *Figure 25a* fingerprint reader, Courtesy of Identix Incorporated; *Figure 25b* fingerprint software, Courtesy of Identix Incorporated; *Figure 26* Microsoft Center for Information Work, Courtesy of Microsoft® Corporation.